MANAGEMENT

About the Authors

John A. Pearce II, **Ph.D.**, holds the Eakin Endowed Chair in Strategic Management in the School of Business Administration at George Mason University; he is Chairman of the school's Management Department. Professor Pearce has published more than 100 journal articles, invited book chapters, and professional papers in many publications, including the *Academy of Management Journal* and the *Strategic Management Journal*. He has served on the editorial boards of four journals, and he is currently the Consulting Editor in Strategic Management for the *Journal of Management*. Professor Pearce is also the coauthor or coeditor of 17 texts, proceedings, and supplements.

Elected to more than a dozen offices in national and regional professional associations, Professor Pearce is also the 1989 President-elect of the Southern Management Association. An active consultant and management trainer, Professor Pearce specializes in helping executive teams to develop and activate their firms' strategic plans.

Richard B. Robinson, Jr., **Ph.D.**, is Professor of Strategy and Entrepreneurship in the College of Business Administration at the University of South Carolina. Professor Robinson has published more than 100 journal articles, invited chapters, and professional papers in many publications, including the *Academy of Management Journal* and the *Strategic Management Journal*. He is also coauthor or coeditor of 16 texts, proceedings, and supplements. Professor Robinson is the recipient of several awards in recognition of his work in strategic management and entrepreneurship, including awards from New York University Center for Entrepreneurial Studies, the Heizer Capital Corporation, the Academy of Management, among others. He has also held offices in the Academy of Management, the Southern Management Association, and the International Council on Small Business. Professor Robinson is an active consultant in strategic management of growth-oriented ventures.

MANAGEMENT

John A. Pearce II

George Mason University

Richard B. Robinson, Jr.

University of South Carolina

McGraw-Hill Publishing Company
New York St. Louis San Francisco Auckland Bogotá Caracas
Hamburg Lisbon London Madrid Mexico Milan Montreal
New Delhi Oklahoma City Paris San Juan São Paulo Singapore
Sydney Tokyo Toronto

First Edition
98765432
MANAGEMENT

Library of Congress Cataloging-in-Publication Data

Pearce, John A.
  Management / John A. Pearce, II, Richard B. Robinson, Jr.
    p.   cm.
  Includes index.
  ISBN 0-07-556981-7
  1. Management   I. Robinson, Richard B. (Richard Braden), 1947–   . II. Title.
HD31.P43 1989
658—dc19   88-39738
                                                                           CIP

Cover art:
Alexander Calder. *Constellation With Quadrilateral.* 1943. Wood and wire. $15 \times 18 \times 7\frac{3}{4}$ inches. Collection of Whitney Museum of American Art. 50th Anniversary Gift of the Howard and Jean Lipman Foundation, Inc. 80.28.1. (Photography by Jerry L. Thompson, N.Y.).

Cover design: Jack Ehn

Preface

Design of the Book

In preparing to write this text, we surveyed more than a thousand practicing managers, professors, and students. We asked them to help us design a book that they believed could make an important contribution to the education of future managers. Their responses became our priorities.

The *managers* said that we should focus our conceptual materials on only those theories that had been shown to have an impact on improving organizational performance. This is precisely what we have tried to do. In selecting the many worthwhile models presented in the following chapters, we have been careful to choose those that have been demonstrated to work. Company successes are described and critiques are included to help you recognize the limitations as well as the strengths of each of the approaches.

Professors advised us to make sure that the book conveyed a consensus of informed views about what management practices work best and why. What we have done as a result of their recommendations is to present the prevailing views of practicing managers and research scholars. There are up-to-date references, examples, and other supporting evidence for every major contention in this book. We thus have demonstrated that the views expressed are generally held to be accurate by managers and researchers.

The professors also asked that we provide a number of different ways to help students learn the material in the chapters. They asked that we provide the proven pedagogical features they have come to expect. And they challenged us to create innovative yet substantive learning methods to enhance their management education efforts. We are excited about both the traditional and the innovative features we have developed in this book. The next section describes these features in some detail.

Finally, the *students* we surveyed stressed the need to include only information that would make them knowledgeable and skillful managers. They asked for meaningful and professional materials that are easy to read, yet worthwhile to learn. Complaining that too many texts are like "overcrowded flea markets of random facts," they asked for a well-integrated book. We hope they will be pleased with this book. It contains no cartoons, no simplistic stories, no unrealistic examples, no gazing into crystal balls, and no pretense of offering foolproof formulas for instant managerial success. Instead, it provides the best available information on how students can enhance their potentials to become successful managers in the 1990s and beyond. The findings, experiences, and recommendations of some of the world's best managers and management scholars have been assembled and condensed into this book's twenty-two chapters. And we have tried to present them in a manner that makes them stimulating and rewarding to learn.

Special Features of the Book

Challenged by the excellent ideas and opinions we received from managers, professors, and students, we invested considerable time in the development of special features for this book that we were confident would meet their needs. Following are the major requests and the features we designed to accommodate them.

HELP STUDENTS APPLY MANAGEMENT CONCEPTS

We worked hard to provide the readable, thorough coverage of management concepts and theories that this book provides. And we have gone further. Each chapter contains three or more Guidelines to Management Practice, a special feature we have pioneered to help students apply concepts to practical management situations. Each Guideline highlights what is really entailed in acting on the ideas and recommendations presented in the chapter. They offer guidance that is practical, action-oriented, and insightful for future managers.

GET STUDENTS EXPERIENTIALLY INVOLVED IN THEIR MANAGEMENT EDUCATION

We pioneered a concept called the Cohesion Case for strategic management education. We have created a similar pedagogical feature for this book—the Cohesion Incidents, which let students apply chapter concepts to realistic business situations. Two incidents appear at the end of each chapter, tying together various management concepts. Each recounts the experiences of two managers: Charles Richards holds a B.S. in management and is employed in a service industry; Leslie Phillips is an M.B.A. working for a manufacturing company. The strikingly different problems they encounter—and the ways they go about solving them—make for thought-provoking reading that students will find intriguing and informative.

Another experiential feature in each chapter is the Management Development Exercise. These exercises allow students to assess their level of mastery of chapter material, often in a manner similar to the ways practicing managers must evaluate themselves.

DEVELOP AN APPRECIATION FOR INTERNATIONAL MANAGEMENT AND ENTREPRENEURSHIP

The American Assembly of Collegiate Schools of Business (AACSB) is a strong advocate of the internationalization of the management curricula. We have positioned this text at the forefront of this trend in two ways. First, a special Insights for International Managers section appears in each chapter to expose students to international aspects of key chapter topics. Second, Chapter 22 provides comprehensive, state-of-the-art coverage of international management issues.

Entrepreneurship and innovation have also become central themes for improving the global competitiveness of companies as well as whole economies. Chapter 21 provides contemporary coverage of entrepreneurship, self-employment, and corporate intrapreneurship that is both interesting and practical.

GIVE THOROUGH, PRACTICAL EXAMPLES

Each chapter begins with an opening case that gives students an opportunity to observe the major consequences that the overall topic of the chapter has had in a particular business setting. This case is referred to throughout the chapter to point out to students how specific aspects of the chapter topics were of importance in the opening case example.

The conceptual material in each chapter is supported by numerous brief examples and by special In Practice boxes that provide more detailed examples of how the experiences of specific organizations illustrate the key points in each chapter.

DEVELOP A TEXT SUPPORTED BY A SOLID RESEARCH BASE

The research and theory-building successes of hundreds of management scholars have been synthesized and integrated into this text. We have tried to avoid the tedious research details. Rather, our challenge was to screen thousands of technical manuscripts for our readers. We report in this book only summary conclusions of the best validated and most useful findings from the foremost books, journals, and magazine articles published on management topics.

The book's extensive, up-to-date referencing and footnoting are evidence that each chapter is carefully developed around accepted, widely practiced, and well-supported conceptual materials on managerial action.

PROVIDE BASIC LEARNING TOOLS

Learning Objectives are presented at the beginning of each chapter to help focus the student's attention on important material that should be mastered. The learning objectives are reviewed at the end of each chapter. These reviews emphasize material that is important for present and prospective managers to have learned.

Questions for Discussion are provided at the end of each chapter for instructors to use to extend discussions of the chapter topics. And reference Notes are provided to make it easy to further investigate many of the main points made, and the studies cited, in each chapter.

PROVIDE PRACTICAL, EASY-TO-USE ANCILLARIES

An extensive package of supplements, carefully developed to meet a variety of instructor and student needs, is available to be used with the text.

- **Text Bank**   The Test Bank includes approximately 2,000 quality multiple-choice, true/false, and essay test items covering all the major topics in each chapter. The *Test Bank* was prepared by Hrach Bedrosian of New York University.

- **Testing Services and Software**   Through its Customized Testing Service, Random House will supply instructors with custom-made tests consisting of items selected from the printed *Test Bank*. Tests can be ordered either by phone (toll-free) or mail. The *Test Bank* is also available in an exclusive microcomputer format, RH TEST. This powerful program includes a variety of test-making functions including scrambling, editing, selection of questions by type, and random selections.

In addition, the following student software to accompany *Management* is available: THRESHOLD (computer simulation); PC CASE (computerized cases).

- **Instructor's Manual**   The *Instructor's Manual* offers essential chapter support materials including detailed chapter outlines, key-term definitions, lecture outline overhead masters, answers to discussion questions and Cohesion Incident questions, and solutions to the Management Development Exericses. In addition, the manual features an array of lecture enrichment materials such as supplementary cases and exercises, film and video listings, and a transparency script featuring descriptions of each acetate transparency. The *Instructor's Manual* was prepared by Patricia A. Wells of Oregon State University.

- **Acetate Transparency Program**   The transparency program includes 150 color acetates that will add visual excitement to the classroom and bring important management concepts to life. Each transparency is keyed to the lecture outlines in the *Instructor's Manual.*

- **Study Guide**   A valuable learning tool, the *Study Guide* features a variety of chapter review materials and self-tests to help students to master the concepts presented in the text. The *Study Guide* was prepared by Thomas Sharkey of the University of Toledo.

- **Other Ancillary Materials**   For information concerning free videos, the Random House/Penn State Media Resource Library, the Random House Business Library, and the Random House Audio Library, please contact your local Random House Representative.

Content of the Book

This text emphasizes the functional or process approach to the study of management. Its twenty-two chapters are therefore grouped into sections that are structured around the four management functions.

Section I of the book sets the stage for the functional approach through the discussion of topics that are so pervasive as to influence almost every aspect of managerial behavior. Chapters 1 through 5 describe and explain the nature of management, the evolution of management thought, the alternative approaches to managerial decision making, the dynamics of environmental forces, and the effects of social responsibility and business ethics on management practice.

Section II addresses the planning function in organizations. Each of the four chapters in this section focuses on one of the major managerial issues in planning: setting objectives, strategic management, planning and implementation, and managerial planning techniques.

Section III looks at managers' responsibilities for the organizing function. Its four chapters cover the fundamentals of organizing, organizational design and structure, development and change, and human resource management, staffing, and labor relations.

Section IV covers the managerial function of directing. The major topics in this section are motivating subordinates, leadership, managing groups, and interpersonal and organizational communications.

Section V covers the controlling function of management. Individual chapters examine various approaches to performance monitoring, production and operations management, and information management.

The final section of the text, Section VI, addresses two special perspectives on management: entrepreneurship and innovation, and international management. These chapters have been written to allow the instructor to assign them at any point in the course.

Taken as a whole, these twenty-two chapters provide a framework for analyzing and understanding the nature of managerial work and success. They also provide information that students can use to enhance their performance of the managerial functions in our complex, global, and highly competitive society.

ACKNOWLEDGEMENTS

The valuable ideas, recommendations, and support of many outstanding scholars and teachers have added quality to this book. For their reviews of various stages of the manuscript, we thank Raymond Alie, *Western Michigan University;* Hrach Bedrosian, *New York University;* Allen Bluedorn, *University of Missouri—Columbia;* Sam Chapman, *Diablo Valley College;* Kenneth N. Ehrensal, *St. Francis College;*

David S. Fearon, *Central Connecticut State University;* Bruce Fortado, *University of North Florida;* Edson Hammer, *University of Tennessee, Chattanooga;* Ronald A. Klocke, *Mankato State University;* G. H. Manoochehri, *California State University—Fullerton;* James McElroy, *Iowa State University;* Nikki Paahana, *DeVry Institute of Technology;* Monique A. Pelletier, *San Francisco State University;* Thomas Petit, *University of North Carolina at Greensboro;* E. Leroy Plumlee, *Western Washington University;* Richard Randall, *Nassau Community College;* Mark Sandberg, *Rider College;* Theresa C. Scott, *Community College of Philadelphia;* Michelle L. Slagle, *University of South Alabama;* Leo Spier, *San Francisco State University;* Mary S. Thibodeaux, *North Texas State University;* and Patricia A. Wells, *Oregon State University.* Our special thanks are due to James B. Dilworth, *University of Alabama at Birmingham,* for his insightful comments on Chapter 19 and to John F. Steiner, *California State University—Los Angeles,* for his assistance on Chapter 5.

We also extend our thanks to Phil Anderson, *College of St. Thomas;* Allen Bluedorn, *University of Missouri—Columbia;* G. H. Manoochehri, *California State University—Fullerton;* and Janet Stern Solomon, *Towson State University* for their participation in our focus group.

We wish to thank as well Martha L. Knight of St. Andrews Presbyterian College and Mark McLean of the University of South Carolina at Lancaster for their work in helping us to develop, class-test, and refine many of the Cohesion Incidents. They made important contributions to a major pedagogical strength of this book.

Because we are affiliated with two separate universities, we have two sets of co-workers to thank.

The growth and dynamic environment at George Mason University have contributed directly to the development of this edition. Valuable critiques and helpful recommendations have been made by management colleagues Bill Bolce, Debra Cohen, Jon English, Carolyn Erdener, Ellen Fagenson, Larry Fink, Freda Hartman, Eileen Hogan, Janice Jackson, Ken Kovach, Steve Patrick, Keith Robbins, and Shaker Zahra. For his gracious support and personal encouragement, we also wish to thank Coleman Raphael, Dean of George Mason University's School of Business Administration. For her excellent administrative, editorial, and secretarial assistance, we most sincerely appreciate the work of Sondra Patrick.

We are especially grateful to LeRoy Eakin, Jr., and his family for their generous endowment of the Eakin Endowed Chair in Strategic Management at George Mason University that Jack Pearce holds. The provisions of the Chair have enabled him to continue his dual involvements with this book and with strategic management research.

The stimulating environment at the University of South Carolina has contributed to the development of this book as well. Thoughtful discussions with management colleagues Carl Clamp, Angelo De Nisi, Jim Estes, Shirley Keiper, John Logan, Bruce Meglino, Liz Ravlin, Bill Sandberg, and David Sweiger provided many useful ideas. Input from USC colleagues Kay Keels, John Weitzel (now at the University of Cincinnati), and Tim Fry was particularly helpful in developing specific parts of the book. The continued interest and support of James F. Kane, Dean of the College of Business Administration; James G. Hilton, Associate Dean; and Joe Ullman, Program Director of Management, is gratefully acknowledged. Likewise, Sandy Murrah's skilled word-processing support was an integral part of this project.

We wish also to express our most heartfelt appreciation to our excellent partners-in-publishing at Random House, Inc. We were drawn to this outstanding organization by the professionalism and competitive insights of acquisitions editor Susan Badger. Not only did she campaign for our cause, she helped to refine our ideas in the formation stages of the project.

We are most especially grateful to June Smith, executive director. She dedicated an extraordinary amount of her time and energies to the sheparding of the enormous diversity of reviewing, editing, and marketing activities that were required in the development of the book and its numerous support materials.

Our work was greatly enhanced by the truly superb editorial talents of Mary Shuford, the senior project editor on this book.

The direction and coordination needed in the creation of our ancillary materials was expertly provided by our senior development editor, Dan Alpert.

The insights and professionalism of Liz Israel, our project's marketing manager, provided the critical final link in the editorial chain. Under her direction, the enormous talents of the Random House marketing staff could be focused on accurately presenting the qualities of our project to the marketplace.

We also want to thank the Random House organization that, through the administrative leadership of general manager Siebert Adams, provided the encouragement and resources to make this book the flagship of the Random House Management Series.

Finally, we want to express our gratitude to the Random House sales force. They also worked with us to understand the needs of professors and students, and to make this a book that contributes to the clarification of key principles of management thought and practice.

In using this text, we hope that both students and instructors will share our enthusiasm for the rich subject of management and for the learning approach that we have taken. We value your recommendations and thoughts about our materials. Please write to John A. Pearce II, at the School of Business Administration, George Mason University, Fairfax, Virginia 22030, or Richard B. Robinson, Jr., at the College of Business Administration, University of South Carolina, Columbia, South Carolina 29208.

John A. Pearce II
Richard B. Robinson, Jr.

We dedicate this project with love and appreciation to our wives and children:

Susie, David, and Mark Pearce
Joby, Kate, and John Robinson

Contents in Brief

Contents

Special Features:
Guidelines for
Management Practice
140, 143, 155

Insights for International
Managers 5: If You Must
Grease Palms, Do It
Right   150

Cohesion Incident 5-1:
Play Ball!   158

Cohesion Incident 5-2:
Crisis and
Responsibility   159

Management
Development Exercise 5:
Management Ethics
Questionnaire   161

SECTION II: *Planning*

Special Features:
Guidelines for
Management Practice
169, 178, 182, 186

Insights for International
Managers 6: Setting
Objectives in Different
Countries   176

Cohesion Incident 6-1:
What is the "Objective"
of Happy Hour?   195

Cohesion Incident 6-2:
Management by Whose
Objectives?   196

Management
Development Exercise 6:
Setting Management
Objectives   198

SECTION III: *Organizing*

SECTION V: *Controlling*

CHAPTER 18   *Principles of Control*

SECTION VI: *Special Perspectives on Management*

CHAPTER 21   *Entrepreneurship and Innovation*

CHAPTER 22   *International Management*

Perspectives on Management

In our complex, dynamic, and global society, the practice of management has become extremely diverse and complicated. To set the stage for studying the four basic functions that every managerial position involves, it is important to look at several critical topics that influence almost every aspect of the theory and practice of management.

In Chapter 1 the successful practice of management is shown to involve both art and science. Because managerial responsibilities differ depending on various organizational factors, managerial competence is measured by the relative mastery of seven different skills. But, most important, this chapter introduces the four basic management functions—planning, organizing, directing, and controlling—that are the universal keys to management success.

Because historical precedents underlie the modern approaches to management practice, Chapter 2 introduces the classical, behavioral, and managerial science schools of management thought.

Decision making is a key component of management practice. In Chapter 3, the decision-making process is examined; programmed and nonprogrammed decisions are compared; various approaches to decision making are explored; and methods for enhancing the rationality of decision making are examined.

Three levels of environmental forces—remote, industry, and operating—affect managerial behavior and success. The components and potential impacts of each of these environmental levels are discussed in Chapter 4.

The basic philosophies and some arguments for and against in inclusion of social responsibility and ethics in managerial decision making are presented in Chapter 5. Also included in this discussion are guidelines to understanding the distinctions among required, expected, and desired ethical behaviors; the nature of social audits; and the utilitarian, moral rights, and social justice approaches to management ethics.

1

Management and the Manager

Learning Objectives

Your study of this chapter will enable you to do the following:

1. Define the term *management* and evaluate management's claim to recognition as a profession, as an art, and as a science.
2. Explain three different ways of classifying managers.
3. Describe the management functions approach and the management skills approach to the study of management.
4. Cite what conclusions can be reached from the studies that have been conducted of what managers do.
5. Explain the difference between efficiency and effectiveness.

Patricia M. Carrigan of General Motors Corporation

Says Patricia M. Carrigan, fifty-seven, a one-time teacher and now the highly successful plant manager of the General Motors Corporation automobile factory in Bay City, Michigan, "In the academic world we tended to have the view that industry was cold and heartless and not too concerned with people. And this was an area where I always felt I could make a difference. . . . Industry in general used to expect [workers] to park their brains at the front door and use only their brawn. We have now learned that management is not smart enough to beat the competition by itself."

The seventy-year-old Bay City plant, which belongs to the GM Chevrolet-Pontiac-Canada (CPC) Group, makes parts. In this setting Carrigan has begun an experiment that, if successful, could save thousands of jobs across the country. Workers in several units of the plant have taken on many duties normally reserved for supervisors. So far the hourly employees have been supervising their own production, charting efficiency, gauging quality, signing material requisitions, and even scheduling their own vacations. Carrigan says, "It's a step toward building the factory of the future. We have to get people excited about using their talents or we'll all end up going down the tube together. In essence we're saying to them: Find ways to eliminate your present jobs through improved efficiency and cost reduction to ensure future employment."

Jim Volk, a group leader, says, "Before this program started, hourly employees would never think of making an independent decision. It just wasn't done. Now we take the initiative and get things done without standing around waiting for orders."

Carrigan operates on the principle that people are more important than things. When she arrived in Bay City, she decided that communications—up and down—could be improved. Acting on the conviction that "there's no substitute for personal contact," she embarked on a tour of the entire plant, which makes transmission valves and channel plates, carburetors, spindles, oil pumps, and camshafts. She was surprised to discover that some supervisors had never made a plant tour. She familiarized herself with the parts and with the machines that make them, and—although it took her several days to do it—she looked every one of her 2,300 workers in the eye and shook their hands. "People want to be recognized as people," she says.

She noticed that almost all plant management personnel worked in their offices behind closed doors. Without saying anything or issuing any new policy statements, she made a conspicuous point of keeping her own office door wide open. Then she watched to see who followed suit.

Her premise, which raised eyebrows at GM at the time, is that for a plant to succeed, crucial management decisions must originate at the lowest possible level—perhaps even on the shop floor. "People are very comfortable coming up to me; it's the atmosphere I tend to create," she says.

Carrigan worked during the mid-1960s as director of research and evaluation for the Ann Arbor public school system; she then joined the Bendix Corporation as corporate director of human resources. She was hired by GM in 1976 for an employee-relations job where she worked on "people problems." Her management grooming began when she was assigned as executive-in-training at the huge Wil-

Patricia Carrigan's career path led her from research-oriented academic to prominent practicing manager. (Courtesy of General Motors)

low Run plant at Ypsilanti, west of Detroit, in 1977. In two years she was appointed general superintendent of production at the plant. In 1981 she took over the job of plant comptroller.

In 1982 GM plunged Carrigan into its troubled Lakewood assembly plant in Atlanta, Georgia, where a work force of 3,100 made Chevettes. A few months after she arrived the plant was shut down due to lack of demand for its product. To address a history of difficult labor relations in the plant, she introduced, for managers and laborers alike, a reeducation plan emphasizing a philosophy of cooperation. Through her leadership, the plant reopened in 1984 with very tough standards of quality and cost control.

"You know, in some ways I wish I'd started with GM a long time ago because there are so many exciting things happening. But twenty years ago the industry wasn't ready for democracy in the workplace, for a woman with ideas like mine. No way."[1]

Introduction

What Is Management?

Management is the process of optimizing human, material, and financial contributions for the achievement of organizational goals. In order to help you understand this definition, we need to explain its component parts. In this context, *process* encompasses a systematic series of actions taken by managers. *Optimize* means that managers should work for the best possible long-term results. And, *goals* are the results that are sought by the major stakeholders of an organization.

Our definition of management is quite different from those found in the early books written to teach the principles of management. One such definition, of management as "the art of getting work done through others," has the undeniable appeal of simplicity. It is, however, inadequate and inappropriate for managers faced with increasing complexity in the management of organizations. General Motors' Carrigan is clearly more than just a "people person"; she expresses equal concern for production methods and cost minimization. Fortunately, research in the academic and business communities provides us with a clear view of advances in management. We have drawn on the best of these studies, as well as on the advice of practicing managers. As you will see, management is aptly described as a field of endeavor that combines art and science and that exhibits growing professionalism. The intent of this book is to prepare you to become a manager capable of meeting the demands of all three of these facets of management.

Before beginning our examination of the various dimensions of management, it is important to emphasize that few factors impact the performance of managers more profoundly than their involvement in international operations. Whenever organizational activities encompass managers from multiple cultures, products or services from multiple countries, or customers of varied nationalities, the formula for managerial success becomes more complex. The impacts of international activities are so critical in our nearly global multinational business environment that they must be given special attention in our study of managerial functions. Therefore, in addition to a full chapter in International Management (Chapter 22), we have included a series of "Insights for International Managers" throughout the

---

Insights for International Managers 1

WHY ARE WE INNOCENTS ABROAD?

Fewer than 8 percent of U.S. colleges and universities require knowledge of a foreign language for entrance. Fewer than 5 percent of America's prospective teachers take any courses in international subjects as part of their professional training. Some years ago a UNESCO study in nine countries placed American students next-to-last in their comprehension of foreign cultures. Only a few years ago, 40 percent of high school seniors in a national poll thought Israel was an Arab nation.

America's labor and management pool is critically deficient in skills required for competence today. Only 3.4 percent of MBAs major in international business, and worse, 61 percent of business schools offer no international courses. Curricula have not been internationalized to provide American graduates with the knowledge today's manager needs to maintain a competitive edge in the international arena. Nor are multinational organizations bringing managers up through the international divisions. Nearly two-thirds of the presidents and chairmen of the largest international firms are guiding those companies without having had any experience in the international divisions or overseas.

Meanwhile, other nationalities tend to be better informed about Americans. Mitsubishi has 800 employees in New York simply for the purpose of gathering information about American rivals and markets.

Source: From L. Copeland and L. Griggs, *Going International* (New York: Random House, 1985), p. xxii.

---

text. These Insights will provide you with some ideas and the techniques for dealing with the unique complications of being a manager in the highly competitive international environment. The first of the "Insights for International Managers" addresses the question "Why Are We Innocents Abroad?"

MANAGEMENT AS A PROFESSION

We will begin our study of management by considering whether the field of management can, indeed, be considered a full-fledged profession. Researcher Edgar H. Schein argues that management is a profession, and he supports his belief by maintaining that management exhibits the three essential qualities of a profession.[2]

The first of the criteria Schein applies is the existence of a set of general principles to guide decision making. Management certainly has such principles, although it must be conceded that these principles are not universally applicable. For example, almost all experienced managers believe that they should "promote from within," which means that they should give first consideration to current employees before looking at outside applicants. However, almost every manager can name situations when to get an outstanding person for a job, he or she violated this principle. Nevertheless, as you will see, principles of management do abound.

Second, in a profession, Schein contends, status is achieved through accomplishment, not through favoritism or political advantage. On this dimension, it seems to us that management is less clearly a profession. Because management positions differ so greatly in their demands and because so many styles of management can prove to be successful in varied situations, it is almost impossible to predetermine with precision which individuals will or will not succeed as managers. This lack of clear-cut criteria sometimes allows selection of managers to be based on factors not directly related to their expected job performance—such as, for example, friendships with members of the selection team. However, managers are chosen for the most part because of their own job competence. Managers who hire subordinate managers know that their own futures depend in large measure on the collective successes of their subordinates, so they usually select the best candidates for managerial positions.

Finally, professionals are guided by a stated code of ethics. Unfortunately, and good intentions notwithstanding, no such formal code exists for managers. Although individual management organizations sometimes have such codes, the overall standards of managerial behavior are governed largely by individual ethics. Thus, although research shows that managers view themselves and other managers as highly ethical, the absence of an explicit code weakens management's claim to professional status.[3]

A clear answer to the question of whether management is a profession is hard to reach. It certainly exhibits some professional qualities, and a code of ethical behavior for managers continues to be developed. As you pursue a career in management, you will certainly contribute, through your behavior and continued interest in the theory and philosophy of management, to its recognition as a profession.

MANAGEMENT AS AN ART

Another aspect to consider in trying to understand how to characterize management today is that of management as an art; here we need not be so equivocal. In that art requires a personal aptitude or skill, managers who must make organizational decisions about how best to position their resources in certain future markets are surely involved in an artistic process.[4] Much of what a manager knows about how to manage a particular individual or group of individuals is learned from first-hand experience with them in the work setting or with other individuals in similar situations. Understanding subordinates in order to create an appropriately motivating environment in which they are likely to achieve organizational goals is certainly an art.

MANAGEMENT AS A SCIENCE

The final aspect of management we will consider is that of a science. Science involves the systemic development and testing of theories based on observation of behavior; such study leads to the creation of a general body of knowledge.[5] The refinement of case, field, and laboratory research projects over the last sixty years has made the study of management much more scientific.[6] The study of management must progress still further before we will be able to prescribe appropriate behavior in all situations. However, by virtue of the advances already achieved in our ability to suggest specific courses of action, management can be regarded as a rapidly developing science.

In characterizing management as an endeavor that partakes of both art and science and aspires to professional status, we have spoken almost as though "management" were a single activity. Actually, managers do many different jobs, and there are several ways to classify their activities.

Ways of Classifying Managers

The study of management and managers is complicated by the vast number of labels that business people use to distinguish one type of manager from another. In this section you will have a chance to learn about the significance of management categories. You will learn about systems classifying managers according to their level in the organizational hierarchy, their performance in line or staff positions, and their role as functional or general managers.

Levels of Management

The hierarchical relationship of managerial and nonmanagerial employees in an organization, whereby those in a superior position are placed above those in a subordinate position, is best represented by a pyramid similar to the one shown in Figure 1-1. The largest number of employees in an organization are typically nonsupervisory; they are commonly called nonmanagerial employees. Above them, at the lowest level of managerial responsibility, are first-line managers; the titles they may have include supervisor, foreman, project manager, coordinator, operating manager, and office manager. The principal tasks of first-line managers involve the coordination of the work of nonmanagerial employees and the direct management of other resources, including machinery and materials. At this level, most managers are reasonably skilled both at overseeing and at doing. They are able to supervise *and* to fill in when needed, as a trainer or as a worker, to maintain the smooth operation of the system.

Immediately above the first-line managers in the organizational hierarchy are **middle-level managers** such as Patricia Carrigan of GM. These managers are typically defined in terms of their reporting relationships in the organization. Specifically, first-line managers report to them and they, in turn, report to the executive officers of the firm. Large firms often have several levels of middle managers. The organizational chart is the best place to look to find out how many middle-level

Representative Titles

Chairman of the Board, Board of Directors, President, Chief Executive (Administrative, Operating) Officer, Group Vice-President

Divisional Manager, Plant Manager, Functional Area Vice-President, Sales Manager, Unit Manager, Comptroller

Supervisor, Department Head, Area Coordinator, Foreman

Salespeople, Skilled, Semiskilled and Unskilled Workers, Secretarial and Clerical Employees, Craftspeople

FIGURE 1-1
Management Levels in an Organizational Hierarchy

managers the firm employs and also to determine the nature of these managers' relationships to one another.

Middle-level managers are most often the principal internal managers of the business; that is, they typically spend about 75 percent of their time managing the day-to-day operations of the business. For example, in a manufacturing firm, very little of their time is spent with clients, customers, and other outside groups. Instead, they focus their attention on coordinating the work of groups headed by various first-line managers.

Top managers are the executives at the highest levels of the organizational pyramid. They are responsible for the overall coordination of the firm and for directing the major activities of the company's various divisions or units. Their time is divided between performing major companywide planning, organizing, directing, and controlling activities and attending to the demands imposed on the firm by various external groups, such as customers.

Organization charts are used to depict the formal relationships among people or groups of people in an organization. They are intended to show the managerial relationships among all levels of organizational employees. Figure 1-2 is an actual organization chart. The top managers are the board of directors and the company president. The firm's middle-level managers include the vice presidents of production, staff services, and marketing. At the first line of management are the director of research and development, the shift foremen, the controller, the head

FIGURE 1-2
Example of an
Organization Chart

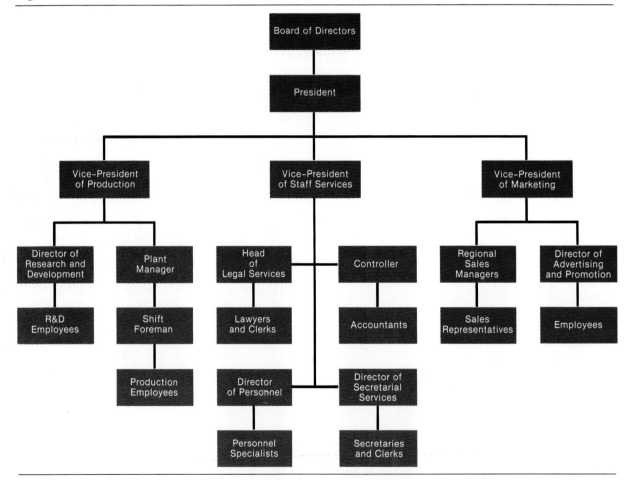

Guidelines for Management Practice

Throughout this book, usually at the end of a major section, you will find "Guidelines for Management Practice." These boxes will provide you with some practical insights into ways in which the chapter material can prepare you for a successful career in management.

In dealing with managers from another company, you might find it advantageous for a number of reasons to know where they appear on their firm's organization chart.

1. Such knowledge can help you assess their authority to make decisions.

2. An organization chart will indicate the number of managers above them who could approve or veto

any tentative decisions that you and they have reached.

3. Their position on the chart will provide information about the level of expertise that they might reasonably be expected to possess on various functional or general management issues.

Such charts may not be readily available in many companies; however, they sometimes appear in company brochures or annual reports, and they can help you overcome a fairly recent problem in business—title inflation. For example, at the now-bankrupt People Express, all employees were given managerlike titles. However, a quick look at its organization chart reveals the weak power position of a flight service manager, otherwise known as a flight attendant.

---

of legal services, the director of personnel, the director of secretarial services, the regional sales managers, and the director of advertising and promotion. What about the plant manager? The plant manager is a second level of middle-level manager; the organization chart reflects his or her position under the vice president of production and above the shift foremen. Figure 1-3 offers one company's view of ten reasons why firms should develop organization charts. The figure is part of a 1988 advertising campaign mounted by software manufacturer Banner Blue, Inc.

Line and Staff Managers

In addition to classifying managers according to the level in the organizaton at which they serve, it is also common to classify them as either line or staff. **Line managers** are those who are directly responsible for functions or activities central to creating the main product line or service that the organization markets. **Staff managers** are those who, in various ways, support the work of line operations. Typical staff functions include the provision of accounting, financial, legal, and scientific expertise to those directly involved in production activities. For example, line managers who supervise the parts assembly operations of manufacturing firms are often able to increase their groups' productivity by having training specialists from the personnel department (directed by staff managers) conduct programs for their operators on machine safety.

In the organization chart shown in Figure 1-2, the line managers are all board members, the president, the vice presidents of production and marketing, and all the managers who report to them. The staff managers in this example are the vice president of staff services and the four managers who report to that vice president.

Functional and General Managers

A third useful way to classify managers is in terms of the scope of the activities they manage. A manager who is responsible for just one type of organizational

10 Reasons why you should use organization charts

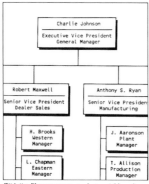

With Org Plus you create org charts quickly and professionally. Use any IBM PC or compatible.

How can using an org chart make you a better manager?

The clarity of a picture

1. Your organization chart communicates structure that is difficult to describe in words. It is concise, clear, and requires minimal explanation.

2. Organization charts are more accurate than the grapevine, more easily understood than a memo, and they reduce the need for verbal explanation.

Accurate, timely communication of change

3. You can quickly update your organization chart. Use the chart for timely explanation of organizational changes and stop inaccurate rumors spread by word-of-mouth.

4. Quickly and professionally identify key contacts for outsiders like customers, suppliers, even top recruits. An organization chart tells them who to call for an immediate response to their questions.

5. Organization charts can highlight information that usually requires hours of searching personnel files. Use them for succession planning, tracking affirmative action objectives, and monitoring employee turnover.

Reduce wasted time and minimize confusion

6. Organization charts establish the ground rules. This eliminates confusion about responsibilities, and when appropriate, formalizes communication lines.

7. You can stay ahead of the game by producing alternative organization charts before you reorganize. An impractical span of control or improper balance of resources becomes obvious at a glance.

Now an organization chart can manage numbers too

8. Keep track of numerical information such as salaries, commissions, budgets, office space, and project hours with a mini-spreadsheet for each employee. Org Plus™ does the arithmetic so it is easy to compare results by individual, department, or level. Even perform "what if" analysis on your organization.

A tool proven by "Excellent" companies

9. Over 90% of the companies cited for excellence in the book *In Search of Excellence* use organization charts. And they have purchased Org Plus to do the job. Align yourself with leaders like 3M, IBM, and Marriott.

Now they are quick and easy to produce

10. Just enter the names, titles, and comments. Then Org Plus does the hard work. It automatically draws and spaces the boxes, centers the text, and precisely lays out the connecting lines.

Using your IBM PC and printer, you'll have final results you can use in any situation, no matter how formal.

For the cost of producing one chart by hand you can use Org Plus. 30 day money back guarantee if you are not satisfied for any reason.

Order today, call 415-794-6850

Org Plus for *quick* and *easy* organization charts

$79.95 plus $3.00 shipping, $82.95 total. CA residents add $5.60 sales tax.

Org Plus works on an IBM PC/XT/AT, the Personal System/2 Family or 100% compatible computer with a minimum of 320Kb of RAM. DOS version 2.0 or higher and a printer or HP plotter are required. Compatible with Sideways™. Org Plus is not copy protected. A 120 page User's Guide and telephone support are included. IBM is a registered trademark of International Business Machines Corp. Sideways is a trademark of Funk Software. © 1987 Banner Blue Software Incorporated. Main offices at Fountain Square.

FIGURE 1-3
Reasons to Use Organization Charts

activity (such as accounting, finance, personnel, production, or marketing) is known as a **functional manager**. Typically, his or her subordinates are engaged in similar activities. For example, most of an accounting manager's subordinates are involved in accounting activities, such as recordkeeping, handling customer accounts, and auditing.

A manager who is responsible for all of the activities of a corporation or one or more of its complex subunits is referred to as a **general manager**. The president of a corporation, a company's division manager, plant manager Patricia Carrigan, and the manager of a local restaurant or dry cleaner are all general managers. In Figure 1-2, the only general managers shown are the board of directors and the president. All the other managers listed are functional managers.

"In Practice 1-1" illustrates the role that managers at several different levels play in the recruitment of management trainees in one company.

In Practice 1-1

MANAGING 1776 ENTERPRISES

1776 Enterprises, a small but growing restaurant company based in San Antonio, Texas, requires management applicants to undergo a grueling and time-consuming process in order to get hired. Those who survive the rigorous screening, however, are treated so well they rarely want to leave.

Management applicants who are invited for an interview meet the director of human resources, Andrew Guy. After a thirty-minute interview, he sends them out to any six of the company's seven restaurants to interview the managers there. "By talking to the managers, they get a good perspective of the company from the people actually in the restaurants; they hear the good and bad," Guy says. When management applicants want to meet with Guy again, he initiates a second interview. This time Guy spends a great deal of time talking to the applicants about their experience, what they learned in their conversations with the other managers, and explaining the company in detail. "By seeing how much they learned from the managers, I can tell how inquisitive they are, and how motivated. Their performance reflects how they would carry out a project for us in the future," Guy explains.

Guy then contacts the six restaurant managers and gets their honest opinions of the man or woman they may eventually have to train. If all goes in the applicant's favor, the director of operations and then the president interview the applicant. Finally, Guy and the other two executives discuss the applicant. Only applicants who get a unanimous vote in their favor are offered a job.

Overall training takes as long as twelve weeks. The bulk of the training occurs in the restaurants, but it is supplemented by classroom education. The company's philosophy is "Teach correct principles and let people govern themselves." In order to prepare trainees to run a restaurant on their own, 1776 Enterprises teaches them to perform each restaurant task by actually doing it—from dishwashing and janitorial work to cooking and bookkeeping.

Following management training, an individual becomes a manager of one of three departments (customer service, food service, or marketing) and then works up to general manager.

Source: Adapted from R. Gindin, "Human Resources: The People Commitment," *Restaurant Business*, January 20, 1984, pp. 81–132, by permission of Bill Communications, Inc.

Approaches to the Study of Managers

Because there are so many different kinds of managers (e.g., first-line, middle-level, and top managers; line and staff managers; functional and general managers), and because the organizations in which managers perform are so varied (e.g., manufacturing, service, retail, wholesale) on so many dimensions (e.g., size, age, geographical dispersion, customer base), it is difficult to generalize about what managers do. Fortunately, there are two meaningful approaches that we can take to gain an understanding of what all managerial positions have in common: the *management functions approach* and the *management skills approach.*

The Management Functions Approach

There have been numerous attempts to categorize the managerial functions. In fact, not long ago texts listed seven functions (and students had to devise complex acronyms to memorize them). More recently, however, there has been a growing consensus that four major functions appropriately represent management responsibilities. These functions are as follows:

1. **Planning** involves determining the direction of a business by establishing objectives and by designing and implementing the strategies necessary to achieve those objectives.

2. **Organizing** involves determining the specific activities and resources that will be needed to put the business plan into effect, as well as making decisions about how work authority, assignments, and responsibilities should be allocated and coordinated.

3. **Directing** involves communicating to others what their responsibilities are in achieving the company plan, as well as providing an organizational environment in which employees can become motivated to perform well.

4. **Controlling** involves guiding, monitoring, and adjusting work activities in order to help ensure that organizational performance stays in line with the firm's needs and expectations.

Figure 1-4 presents what is generally accepted as the relative importance of each of the four management functions for each of the three broad levels of management. Top managers spend the greatest amount of their time, and exert the greatest influence, in the planning function. Their unique perspective on the organization overall, coupled with their working knowledge of the firm's external environment, makes top managers the ideal candidates to spearhead the planning efforts of the company.

Middle-level managers, as their titles suggest, are involved to a moderate extent in most of the management functions. The exception to this is their considerable responsibility for control activities at their level. Middle-level managers, then, need not shoulder the major responsibility for any function at the organizational level, but they are expected to exhibit some competence in all managerial tasks. This places difficult demands on middle-level managers, for they must be at least moderately talented in every major managerial function in order to be successful in their jobs.

First-line managers find their principal responsibilities in the leadership function because of the relatively large numbers of subordinates with whom they come into direct contact (Figure 1-4). Their organizing and controlling responsibilities are medium in importance, and their involvement in the organization's planning function is low. This low level of planning involvement is appropriate, given the narrow organizational perspective of most first-line managers and their relative inexperience in the varied and complex activities that make up the planning function. It is important to note at this point that the planning activities we refer to here are those that are intended to affect the long-term prospects of the firm. This "strategic planning" differs from short-range planning, which has a time horizon of one year or less, involves a narrower scope of operations, and entails the commitment of smaller amounts of resources. The influence of lower-level managers in such short-term planning is considerable. It will be discussed in Section II of this book.

The Managerial Skills Approach

Just as managers at all three levels spend some of their time performing each of the four management functions, the success of managers at all three levels depends in part on the managerial *skills* that they possess. As shown in Figure 1-5, these skills can be grouped under seven different categories.[7]

1. **Conceptual skills** involve a manager's ability to adopt the perspective of the organization as a whole—to see the so-called big picture. At a minimum, managers must be able to understand how their responsibilities dovetail with those

FIGURE 1-4
Relative Importance of the Management Functions

Management Level	Typical Titles	Management Functions			
		Planning	Organizing	Directing	Controlling
Top	President Chief Executive Officer Chairman of the Board Vice President Group Vice President	High	Medium	Low	Medium
Middle	Comptroller Department Head Manager Unit Manager	Medium	Medium	Medium	High
First-Line	Supervisor Foreman Project Manager Coordinator	Low	Medium	High	Medium

Management Level	Skills						
	Conceptual	Decision-Making	Analytical	Administrative	Communication	Human	Technical
Top	High	High	High	Medium	Medium	Medium	Low
Middle	Medium	Medium	Medium	Medium	Medium	Medium	Medium
First–Line	Low	Low	Medium	Medium	Medium	High	High

FIGURE 1-5
Use of Skills by
Managers

of other managers to produce desired organizational results. And they must be able to plan accordingly. Top managers endowed with a high level of this skill are able to plan the "megagoals" and overarching strategies for the organization as a whole.

2. **Decision-making skills** involve a manager's ability to choose an appropriate course of action from two or more alternatives (see Chapter 3). Refined decision-making skills are critical for successful managers because it is their responsibility for making decisions affecting the whole organization that most dramatically distinguishes managers from nonmanagers. Their subordinates actually perform the tasks directly required for production, but the managers must decide what goals are to be achieved, what strategy is to be implemented, what resources are to be acquired and how they are to be allocated, and what controls are to be applied. In short, managers are responsible for most of the major decisions that are required to accomplish any organizational activity. As is apparent in Figure 1-5, the higher a manager is positioned in an organization, the more likely that manager is to be responsible for high levels of organizational decision making.

3. **Analytical skills** involve the ability to properly use scientific and quantitative approaches, techniques, and tools to solve management problems. Managers' abilities to systematically diagnose problems and then to identify alternative solutions before selecting and implementing a corrective plan of action are the primary indication of the level of their analytical skills. Because the complexity of problems they must solve typically increases as managers are promoted, analytical skills also increase in importance as managers advance in their careers.

4. **Administrative skills** involve the ability of managers to execute organizational rules, regulations, policies, and procedures; to operate effectively within budgetary constraints; and to coordinate the flows of information and paperwork within their group and among it and other groups.

5. **Communication skills** involve the ability managers must have to transmit their ideas and preferences to others in both oral and written forms. These skills are critical determinants of the manager's success. Some studies suggest that top and middle-level managers spend about 80 percent of their time communicating with others![8] Thus managers' skills in communicating effectively in meetings, through letters and memoranda, and over the telephone are consistently important throughout their careers.

6. **Human relations skills** involve the ability of managers to deal effectively with others both inside and outside the firm who affect the business's success. These skills are widely acknowledged as a key to a company's future—and to that of the manager. Many studies have shown that managers spend approximately half of their working day in interaction with others. The success of these interactions clearly influences how much support the manager will receive in designing and executing the organization's plans.

7. **Technical skills** involve the specific competence to perform a task. The extent to which a manager needs to possess a high level of technical skill is usually directly related to the manager's level in the organizational hierarchy (Figure 1-2). The lower in the organization the manager works, the closer that manager is to hands-on production, and hence the greater his or her need for a high degree of technical skill.

You can assess your current managerial skills—especially your ability to understand and correctly predict employee behavior—by doing "Management Development Exercise 1," at the end of this chapter. Your score will not predict your own future managerial success, but your study of the exercise questions may provide you with some valuable insights into the "people-related" issues that managers face.

What Do Managers Do?

Theoretical notions about what functions managers perform and what skills they need may or may not describe their actual behaviors on the job. Thus, though the management skills approach and the management functions approach help us to understand what managers do, they provide little or no insight into how they do it. A number of studies of the way practicing managers allocate their time have been undertaken to help prospective managers visualize how they will spend their workdays in this field. Three of these studies stand out as exceptionally noteworthy, principally because of the care that was taken in collecting the information and because of the insights that analysis of the results yielded.

The Jobs of Managers

In a study that involved 452 managers from thirteen companies, researchers Thomas A. Mahoney, Thomas H. Jerdee, and Stephen J. Carroll identified eight different "jobs" that were performed by managers at all three levels.[9] As shown in Figure 1-6, the three levels differed principally in the amounts of time that managers at each level devoted to planning, to supervising subordinates' performance, and to performing tasks that required a generalist's perspective. Although these were the top three categories of jobs at all three management levels, top managers spent far more time as planners and generalists than did lower-level managers,

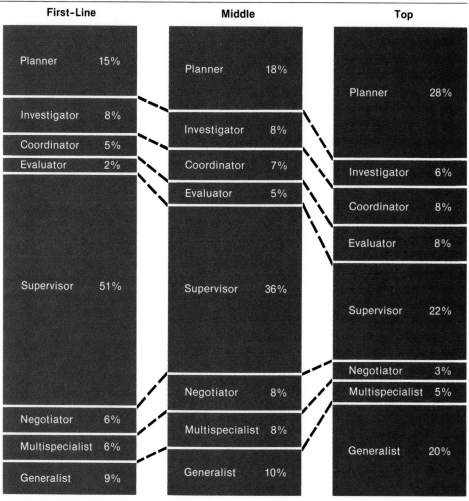

	First-Line	Middle	Top
Planner	15%	18%	28%
Investigator	8%	8%	6%
Coordinator	5%	7%	8%
Evaluator	2%	5%	8%
Supervisor	51%	36%	22%
Negotiator	6%	8%	3%
Multispecialist	6%	8%	5%
Generalist	9%	10%	20%

FIGURE 1-6
Responsibilities of
Managers by Level

Note: Totals may not add up because of rounding.

Source: T. A. Mahoney, T. H. Jerdee, and S. J. Carroll, "The Job(s) of Management," *Industrial Relations*, February 1965, p. 103. Reprinted by permission of the Institute of Industrial Management.

and first-line managers were involved in direct supervisory activities more than half of each working day.

Duties of First-Line and Middle-Level Managers

Research by Charles McDonald provides especially useful insights into the duties of first-line and middle-level managers.[10] McDonald's study of managers' actual duties showed that *first-line* supervisors perform all the functions and apply all the skills that we have spoken of in this chapter. As Figure 1-7 shows, first-line managers spent 15 percent of the workday controlling work activities, 12 percent solving problems, and 11 percent planning work activities. Note especially that if all the activities rank-ordered as items 4 through 8 are construed as forms of communication, then these managers spent 48 percent of the workday communicating.

The controlling and planning functions were also among the most time-consuming aspects of *middle-level* managers' jobs (see Figure 1-8). Their time was also committed to developing subordinates (14 percent), managing time (10 percent), and attending meetings (8 percent). Every management job and every firm differs somewhat, of course, but this study should give you some idea as to how you will spend your workdays as a manager.

Duties of Top Managers

In a study of what top managers actually "do" in the performance of their jobs, management expert and professor Henry Mintzberg found that these managers play three interdependent roles: interpersonal roles, informational roles, and decisional roles.[11] These roles represent sets of behaviors that are typical of people holding top managerial positions. Thus, although they differ in their interpretations of *how* their roles should be executed, every top manager performs these roles in one manner or another.

The way in which top managers decide to perform their roles is principally determined by their personal skills and characteristics and by the hierarchical position, formal authority, and status that they have in the organization. By **interpersonal roles**, Mintzberg meant the activities that top managers perform principally because of their formal position in the firm, and he identified the interpersonal roles as those of figurehead, leader, and liaison. For example, managers serve as figureheads when they fulfill the largely ceremonial and symbolic responsibilities expected of the people who occupy their positions in the organization. In presenting service awards and retirement gifts, for example, top managers play

Rank Order	Duty	Percent of Manager's Time	Frequency of Performance
1	Controlling (work activities)	15	Every day
2	Solving problems	12	Every day
3	Planning (work activities)	11	Every day
4	Communicating informally and orally	11	Every day
5	Communicating with superiors	11	Every day
6	Providing performance feedback to subordinates	10	Every day
7	Coaching subordinates	10	Every day
8	Writing letters and memos	6	Every day
9	Creating and maintaining a motivating atmosphere	5	Every day
10	Managing time	3	Every day
11	Attending meetings	3	Twice monthly
12	Reading and other self-development activities	1	Weekly
13	Career counseling with a subordinate	1	Bimonthly
14	Representing the company	1	Monthly

FIGURE 1-7
Duties of First-Line Managers

Source: Adapted from C. McDonald, *Performance Based Supervisory Development.* © 1982, HRD Press, 22 Amherst Road, Amherst, Mass., 01002.

FIGURE 1-8
Duties of Middle-Level
Managers

Rank Order	Duty	Percent of Manager's Time	Frequency of Performance
1	Controlling	21	Every day
2	Developing subordinates	14	Every day
3	Planning	14	Every day
4	Managing time	10	Every day
5	Attending meetings	8	Every day
6	Making decisions	5	Every day
7	Reading and other self-development activities	5	Every day
8	Providing performance feedback to subordinates	4	Every day
9	Writing letters and memos	4	Every day
10	Creating a motivating atmosphere	3	Every day
11	Communicating upward	3	Every day
12	Performing community-relations activities	3	Bimonthly
13	Communicating downward	3	Every day
14	Communicating with peers	3	Every day

Source: Adapted from C. McDonald, *Performance Based Supervisory Development.* © 1982, HRD Press, 22 Amherst Road, Amherst, Mass., 01002.

the *figurehead* role. As creators of a rewarding and motivating environment, top managers perform their role of *leader*.[12] When top managers work to create a more productive relationship between members of their group and members of other groups, they are performing the *liaison* role.

Informational roles pertain to the activities of top managers whereby they become the informational nerve centers of their group—focal points for receiving and sending (both inside and outside the organization) information that is vital to productivity.[13] Largely as a consequence of their formal authority and status, and their resulting interpersonal roles, managers act in the informational roles of monitor, disseminator, and spokesperson. As *monitors,* top managers use the information gathered through their activities as liaisons, together with the information that flows to them in their hierarchical positions, to assess opportunities and threats in the firm's internal and external environments. They watch for important changes in traditional patterns of customer behavior, for instance, or for unexpected variations in worker performance or economic indicators. In their *disseminator* role, top managers transmit to others in their communication channels the information that they have gathered and evaluated. They do so both in order to gain personal influence and to effect the decisions of others. In their *spokesperson* role, top managers represent their groups in interactions with others outside of the group—responding to questions asked by the press, for example, or testifying before hearings of a regulatory agency.

The nature of managerial roles develops in a sequential manner. The formal authority and status of top managers, in combination with the influence gained through their interpersonal and informational roles, culminate in four **decisional roles** that reflect the top manager's most important responsibility—decision making. In their role as *entrepreneurs,* top managers continually strive to make decisions that improve the operation of their units in new, creative, and growth-oriented ways. As *disturbance handlers,* they maintain a proper level of stability in their groups' performance. Top managers must occasionally give priority to acting quickly and decisively to retain or reestablish control over the operations under their authority. In the *resource allocator* role, top managers exercise the decision-making power of their position in the firm to decide who in their groups will receive desired (but often scarce) human, financial, physical, and informational resources. Finally, in the *negotiator* role, top managers bargain with individuals and groups within their units, with the organization as a whole, and even with outsiders for opportunities that will enable their units to prosper.

Although Mintzberg's study dealt only with top managers, the roles that he identified are widely seen as describing with equal accuracy the roles of managers at all levels. While the importance of particular roles varies with the managerial position, mastery of all of the roles is important to every manager.

People Who Make Demands on the CEO's Time

The Mintzberg study also provided interesting information on the amount of time that chief executive officers (CEOs) spend with different categories of people.[14] CEOs were found to spend 48 percent of their time with subordinates (an amount that we believe has steadily declined since Mintzberg's findings were reported in the mid-1970s). The "second most contacted" category of other people consisted of clients, suppliers, and associates (20 percent of the CEOs' time). Given the ever-increasing demands on executive officers to be active in liaison and monitor roles involving their firms' external environments, this second category has certainly increased steadily in importance to CEOs. Other people who successfully make demands on executives' time are peers (16 percent), independents (8 percent), and members of the board of directors (7 percent).

Guidelines for Management Practice

Mintzberg's three managerial roles have some important implications for practicing managers.

1. The fact that the three major roles can be broken down into ten different, though interrelated, roles should alert us to *the multidimensional nature of a manager's job.* Appreciating the number and variety of these roles helps us understand why managers' jobs are so complex, why managers are seen as "wearing so many hats," and why so many aspiring managers fail when they are finally promoted to the managerial ranks.

2. If the manager or the manager's team fails to perform all of these roles satisfactorily, the team will not be able to function properly. Because few managers are capable of being equally proficient at all ten roles, to ensure the manager's individual success and that of the group, *teams should be developed* to support managers in their performance of all roles.

3. Because of the time it takes for managers to perform all ten roles, even with the active support of a carefully developed team, *managers must manage their time effectively.*

Management of Scarce Resources

It is an axiom of management that the resources any business needs to become successful are in short supply. There is always so great a demand for these scarce resources that the competitive marketplace rarely, if ever, allows a firm to obtain all of its production inputs easily or cheaply. The resources needed by businesses fall into three categories. **Human resources** are the people needed to operate the business and to perform those tasks that require human talent, skills, and abilities. These resources include knowledge and experience related to managerial processes, technology, and the competitive business environment. **Physical resources** include the existence, condition, and location of facilities; plants and equipment; machinery; and the raw materials that the business needs to produce goods or deliver services. Finally, **financial resources** are the money that the firm has available in the short term and the long term to pay for the materials or services that it seeks from others, including the raw materials it buys from suppliers and the labor it pays its employees to provide.

Efficiency in Resource Utilization

The enduring success of a firm is largely determined by the efficiency and effectiveness of its operations. **Efficiency**, as used in the management context, is expressed as the quantity of inputs that the firm uses in order to produce one unit of its output. Therefore, when a company is able to increase the number of the units that it produces or the number of customers that it serves, while keeping the quantity of its inputs the same, the company has improved its efficiency. Alternatively, when the number of units produced remains the same in quality and quantity, while the amount of resources needed as raw materials is reduced, again the firm has become more efficient.

Effectiveness in Achieving Goals

Effectiveness refers to the successful achievement of organizational goals. Thus effectiveness has been described as a measure of whether managers are "doing the right things," whereas efficiency gauges the extent to which managers are "doing things right."[15] A company is effective when it achieves its objectives. When it fails to achieve its objectives because they were poorly chosen, the plan for achieving them was poorly designed or executed, or the hostility of the competitive environment was greater than the company had anticipated, the firm is ineffective.

As indicated in Figure 1-9, the long-term success of a firm depends on its ability to be both efficient and effective. Clearly, the firm that is able to achieve its sales objective but has a marketing cost that totally erodes its profit margin (effective but not efficient) is no more successful than the firm that has achieved low production costs per unit but has only inflexible equipment that cannot be adapted to satisfy varied customer demands (efficient but not effective). The figure shows each of the four possible combinations of efficiency and effectiveness and provides a concrete example of how each of the combinations has affected the operations of a well-known organization.

The discussion of efficiency and effectiveness may seem so straightforward that you wonder why it is worth studying these topics. The reason is that almost all operations of all businesses are both somewhat efficient and somewhat effective. The key to competitive business success is for the firm to be even slightly more

		Ineffective (company goals are not being achieved)	Effective (company goals are being achieved)
Uses of Resources	Efficient (resources contribute maximally to performance)	Resources are not wasted, but goals are not achieved. [Example: The "New Coke" was a product that tasted exactly as intended and could provide an attractive profit margin. However, because it failed to achieve market acceptance, Coke's goals were unmet.]	Goals are achieved through the proper use of resources. [Example: Chrysler, Inc., first divested itself of many of its diverse conglomerate investments in the early 1980s and then refocused its streamlined operations to achieve sustained profits throughout the late 1980s.]
	Inefficient (resources contribute minimally to performance)	Resources are underutilized and goals are unmet. [Example: A failure by Merrill Lynch, Inc., to properly use its extensive broker system to market traditional banking services contributed to a steep financial decline in the firm's profitability following the deregulation of U.S. banks.]	Excessive amounts of resources are used in accomplishing goals. [Example: In 1986 NASA was found to have wasted $3.5 billion through improper purchase practices.]

Goal Accomplishment

FIGURE 1-9
Combinations of
Efficiency and
Effectiveness

efficient and effective than others are or than it has been before. How profitable are the Fortune 500 businesses? Do they earn 40 percent profit rates after taxes? 25 percent? No. Repeatedly, the average figure is in the 5 percent range. Thus even a very small improvement in cost cutting (efficiency) or in increasing market share (effectiveness) can significantly enhance a firm's profitability and other measures of its overall success.

Excellence in Modern Management

Two recent books have helped renew Americans' confidence in the ability of American executives to achieve management excellence, even in the face of stiff foreign competition. The first of these books was *In Search of Excellence* by Thomas Peters and Robert Waterman, Jr., published in 1982. A follow-up book by Peters and Nancy Austin, entitled *A Passion for Excellence,* appeared in 1985. The studies of many successful businesses discussed in these books have helped managers correct weaknesses that once characterized many American firms, including too great a concern for short-term profits, too much reliance on quantitative techniques, and a tendency to emphasize traditional processes over direct assessments of customer needs. On the other hand, the studies concluded that American businesses are overall the best-managed firms in the world and that they have recently been made better by the competitive challenge from overseas.[16]

Forty-three of the companies studied were labeled "excellent." These companies, which included Bechtel, Boeing, Eastman Kodak, IBM, McDonald's, and

Procter & Gamble, all shared characteristics that Peters and Waterman believe were key reasons for the firms' success in remaining both increasingly productive and internationally competitive. These characteristics were as follows:

1. *A bias for action, for getting on with it.* Even though excellent companies may be analytical in their approach to decision making, they are not paralyzed by that fact (as many other companies seem to be). In many of these companies the standard operating procedure is "Do it, fix it, try it." Says a Digital Equipment Corporation senior executive, for example, "When we've got a big problem here, we grab ten senior guys and stick them in a room for a week. They come up with an answer *and* implement it." Moreover, the companies are experimenters supreme. Instead of allowing 250 engineers and marketers to work on a new product line in isolation for fifteen months, they form bands of 5 to 25 and test ideas out on a customer, often with inexpensive prototypes, within a matter of weeks. What is striking is the host of practical devices the excellent companies employ, to maintain corporate fleetness of foot and counter the stultification that almost inevitably comes with size.

2. *Close to the customer.* Excellent companies learn from the people they serve. They provide unparalleled quality, service, and reliability—things that work and last. They succeed in differentiating—*à la* Frito-Lay (potato chips), Maytag (washers), or Tupperware—the most commodity-like products. IBM's marketing vice president, Francis G. (Buck) Rogers, says, "It's a shame that, in so many companies, whenever you get good service, it's an exception." Not so at the excellent companies. Everyone gets into the act. Many of the innovative companies got their best product ideas from their customers. That comes from listening, intently and regularly.

3. *Autonomy and entrepreneurship.* The innovative companies foster many leaders and many innovators throughout the organization. They are a hive of what we've come to call champions; 3M has been described as "so intent on innovation that its essential atmosphere seems not like that of a large corporation but rather a loose network of laboratories and cubbyholes populated by feverish inventors and dauntless entrepreneurs who let their imaginations fly in all directions." They don't try to hold everybody on so short a rein that he can't be creative. They encourage practical risk taking and support good tries. They follow Fletcher Byrom's [chairman and chief executive of Koppers] ninth commandment: "Make sure you generate a reasonable number of mistakes."

4. *Productivity through people.* Excellent companies treat the rank and file as the root source of quality and productivity gain. They do not foster we/they labor attitudes or regard capital investment as the fundamental source of efficiency improvement. As [former chairman] Thomas A. Watson, Jr., said of his company, "IBM's philosophy is largely contained in three simple beliefs. I want to begin with what I think is most important: *our respect for the individual.* This is a simple concept, but in IBM it occupies a major portion of management time." Texas Instruments' chairman Mark Shepherd talks about it in terms of every worker being "seen as a source of ideas, not just acting as a pair of hands"; each of his more than 9,000 People Improvement Program, or PIP, teams (TI's quality circles) does contribute to the company's sparkling productivity record.

5. *Hands-on, value driven.* Thomas Watson, Jr., says that "the basic philosophy of

The invention of Post-its by 3M researchers Dr. Spencer Silver (left) and Dr. Arthur Fry (right) is the result of an atmosphere that encourages innovation. (Courtesy of 3M)

an organization has far more to do with its achievements than do technological or economic resources, organizational structure, innovation, and timing." Watson and HP's [Hewlett-Packard] William Hewlett are legendary for walking the plant floors. McDonald's Ray Kroc regularly visited stores and assessed them on the factors the company holds dear, Q.S.C.&V. (Quality, Service, Cleanliness, and Value).

6. *Stick to the knitting.* Robert W. Johnson, former Johnson & Johnson chairman, put it this way: "Never acquire a business you don't know how to run." Or, as Edward G. Harness, past chief executive at Procter & Gamble, said, "This company has never left its base. We seek to be anything but a conglomerate." While there were a few exceptions, the odds for excellent performance seem strongly to favor those companies that stay reasonably close to businesses they know.

7. *Simple form, lean staff.* As big as most of the companies we have looked at are, none when we looked at it was formally run with a matrix organization structure, and some which had tried that form had abandoned it. The underlying structural forms and systems in the excellent companies are elegantly simple. Top-level staffs are lean; it is not uncommon to find a corporate staff of fewer than 100 people running multibillion dollar enterprises.

8. *Simultaneous loose-tight properties.* The excellent companies are both centralized and decentralized. For the most part, as we have said, they have pushed autonomy down to the shop floor or product development teams. On the other hand, they are fanatic centralists around the few core values they hold dear. 3M is marked by barely organized chaos surrounding its product champions. Yet one analyst argues, "The brainwashed members of an extremist political sect are no more conformist in their central beliefs." At Digital the chaos is so rampant that one executive noted, "Damn few people know who they work for." Yet Digital's fetish for reliability is more rigidly adhered to than any outsider could imagine.[17]

A careful look at these eight attributes of excellent companies makes it clear that the pursuit of excellence begins as a management task. All of the attributes mentioned by Peters and Waterman are characteristics of management activities, skills, and functions. In fact, Peters and Waterman have been criticized for their failure to consider *other* probable contributors to corporate excellence, including technological advantages, national policies, and cultural norms.[18] Certainly, they identified some philosophical orientations that are especially helpful in managing a company in today's competitive environment, but their most significant contribution was to reinforce the vital importance of mastering the four basic management functions and of acquiring the seven fundamental management skills.

Review of the Learning Objectives

Having studied the chapter, you should be able to respond to the learning objectives with extensions of the following brief answers.

1. **Define the term *management* and evaluate management's claim to recognition as a profession, as an art, and as a science.**

   Management is the process of optimizing the contributions of human, material, and financial resources for the achievement of organizational goals. Management is a field of endeavor that exhibits an ever-increasing degree of professionalism, but is also part art and part science.

2. **Explain three different ways of classifying managers.**

   Managers can be classified in terms of level of management (first-line, middle-level, and top), line or staff assignments, and functional or general scope of responsibilities.

3. **Describe the management functions approach and the management skills approach to the study of management.**

   The management functions approach argues that all management activities and responsibilities fall under one or more of four broad functions: planning, organizing, directing, and controlling. The view of the management skills approach is that success as a manager depends on the mastery of seven different managerial skills: conceptual, decision-making, analytical, administrative, communication, human, and technical skills. Both approaches take the position that the degree to which a function or skill is critical to managerial success is largely dependent on the manager's position in the organizational hierarchy.

4. **Cite what conclusions can be reached from the studies that have been conducted of what managers do.**

Because all of the major studies reviewed in this chapter used different terminology to label the management behaviors that were observed, simple conclusions are hard to reach. However, it is possible to observe that managers perform all of the functions using all of the skills that we have studied in this chapter. The higher a manager's position in the organization, however, the more likely she or he is to emphasize planning activities and to adopt an external and environmental orientation rather than one focused on daily operations and supervision.

5. **Explain the difference between efficiency and effectiveness.**

Effectiveness is a measure of goal attainment, whereas efficiency is a measure of how well resources are utilized—input required per unit of output. Effectiveness reflects what was done; efficiency gauges how inexpensively it was done.

Key Terms and Concepts

Having completed your study of Chapter 1 on "Management and the Manager" you should have mastered the following terms and concepts:

management	staff manager	controlling	communication skill	decisional roles
first-line manager	functional manager	conceptual skill	human relations	human resources
middle-level	general manager	decision-making	skill	physical resources
manager	planning	skill	technical skill	financial resources
top manager	organizing	analytical skill	interpersonal roles	efficiency
organization chart	directing	administrative skill	informational roles	effectiveness
line manager				

Questions for Discussion

1. What does the opening case suggest to you about the meaning of the term *management* and about the activities that management involves?

2. This chapter maintains that defining management as "the art of getting work done through others" is inadequate and inappropriate. Explain why you agree or disagree.

3. Why is it important to understand whether management is an art and whether it is a science? How soon do you think management will achieve full status as a profession? What developments do you believe would hasten that process?

4. Describe a managerial position that does *not* require a manager to perform all four of the management functions.

5. Describe a managerial position that does *not* require a manager to demonstrate all seven of the management skills enumerated in this chapter.

6. Illustrate each of the ten managerial roles by describing how it was performed by a manager in an organization with which you have personally been associated. How seriously would the organization have been damaged if any one of these roles had not been handled well?

7. Using recent news reports from business journals, supply four appropriate new examples for Figure 1-9.

8. Explain the eight characteristics of Peters and Waterman's excellent companies in terms of the management functions and of the skills that managers must possess.

9. Peters and Waterman's conclusions have come under attack, in part because of the sharp performance downturns that befell several of their excellent companies within a year or two after their book was written. Was the book wrong? Or could these companies have performed so poorly even if they were excellently managed? Explain.

Notes

1. Adapted from H. W. McCann, "Patricia M. Carrigan: The Psychology of Management," *American Way* 19, no. 21 (October 15, 1986): 70–73. Reprinted by permission of *American Way*, in-flight magazine of American Airlines, copyright 1986 by American Airlines.
2. E. Schein, "Organizational Socialization and the Profession of Management," *Industrial Management Review*, Winter 1968, pp. 1–16.
3. J. Pearce, II, "Newcomers' Need for a Code of Business Ethics," *Collegiate Forum*, Fall 1978, pp. 11–12.
4. R. Rowan, "Those Business Hunches Are More Than Blind Faith," *Fortune*, April 23, 1979, p. 111; and H. Boettinger, "Is Management Really Art?" *Harvard Business Review*, January–February 1975, pp. 54–64.
5. L. Gulick, "Management Is a Science," *Academy of Management Journal*, March 1965, pp. 7–13.
6. R. Gribbins and S. Hunt, "Is Management a Science?" *Academy of Management Review*, January 1978, pp. 139–144.
7. This is a composite list developed in part from the work of R. Katz, "Skills of an Effective Administrator," *Harvard Business Review*, October–November 1974, pp. 90–102; and L. Megginson, *Personnel Management: A Human Resource Approach*, 4th ed. (Homewood, Ill.: Irwin, 1981), pp. 233–235.
8. H. Mintzberg, *The Nature of Managerial Work* (New York: Harper & Row, 1973); H. Mintzberg, "The Manager's Job," *Harvard Business Review*, July–August 1975, pp. 49–61; and E. Lawler, L. Porter, and A. Tannenbaum, "Managers' Attitudes Toward Interaction Episodes," *Journal of Applied Psychology* 47, no. 3 (1962): 432–439.
9. T. Mahoney, T. Jerdee, and S. Carroll, "The Job(s) of Management," *Industrial Relations*, February 1965, pp. 97–110.
10. C. McDonald, *Performance Based Supervisory Development* (Amherst, Mass.: Human Resource Development Press, 1982).
11. H. Mintzberg, *The Nature of Managerial Work* (Englewood Cliffs, N.J.: Prentice-Hall, 1980).
12. C. Pavett and A. Lau, "Managerial Work: The Influence of Hierarchial Level and Function Specialty," *Academy of Management Journal*, March 1983, pp. 170–177.
13. P. Gronn, "Talk as Work: The Accomplishment of School Administration," *Administrative Science Quarterly*, March 1983, pp. 1–21.
14. H. Mintzberg, "The Manager's Job," pp. 49–61.
15. P. Drucker, *Managing for Results* (New York: Harper & Row, 1964).
16. T. Peters and R. Waterman, Jr., *In Search of Excellence* (New York: Warner Books, 1982); T. Peters and N. Austin, *A Passion for Excellence* (New York: Random House, 1985).
17. T. Peters and R. Waterman, *In Search of Excellence*, pp. 13–16.
18. D. Carroll, "A Disappointing Search for Excellence," *Harvard Business Review*, November–December 1983, pp. 78–79.

Management Development Exercise 1
Understanding Employee Behavior

A consistent finding in the continuing study of the keys to management success is the need for managers to be insightful predictors of employee behavior. The following self-test will give you an early indication of your intuitive grasp of what motivates people to work conscientiously.

Instructions:

Read each pair of statements below and divide 10 points between the statements according to the strength of your belief in the truth of the one that seems more accurate to you.

1. A. Employees want to see their leaders succeed.   _____
   B. Employees like to see their leaders fail.   _____

                                                                         10

2. A. It is better to set your standards at a level that a majority of your people
      can reach.   _____

B. It is better to set your standards high so that only a few people will be able to reach them.

_____

10

3. A. A little success makes us want to do better.

B. A little success causes us to slow down and rest on our laurels.

_____

_____

10

4. A. Telling employees good news about their performance encourages a higher level of performance.

B. Telling employees bad news about their performance is more likely to encourage a higher level of performance.

_____

_____

10

5. A. Three well-defined objectives will motivate people more effectively than ten well-defined objectives.

B. Ten well-defined objectives will motivate people more effectively than three well-defined objectives.

_____

_____

10

6. A. Policies and regulations have a weak influence on human behavior.

B. Policies and regulations have a strong influence on human behavior.

_____

_____

10

7. A. Actions precede attitudes.

B. Attitudes precede actions.

_____

_____

10

8. A. People perform better when they are allowed to exercise some control over their work.

B. When allowed to exercise control over their work, people do not perform as well.

_____

_____

10

When you have completed this exercise, your instructor will tell you how to calculate and interpret your score.

Source: From "Understanding Human Behavior," _Applied Management Newsletter_ 7, no. 1 (December 1983): 1–4. Applied Management Newsletter, 1617 Murray, Wichita, Kansas 67212.

2

The Evolution of Management Thought

Learning Objectives

Your study of this chapter will enable you to do the following:

1. Describe three major schools in the evolution of management thought.
2. Define the key attribute of the classical school in terms of its assumptions about human motivation.
3. Explain the role that time studies have played in scientific management.
4. Discuss the ways in which the administrative approach differs from the scientific approach to management.
5. Explain the significance of the Hawthorne experiments.
6. Cite the four key features of the management science school.
7. Describe the systems approach and the contingency approach, and explain how they are related to the early schools of management thought.

Harold F. Smiddy of General Electric

Few men of his generation made a greater impact on the work of an industrial manager than Harold F. Smiddy. Although Harold Smiddy was a scholar and philosopher, he was first and foremost a manager. His individual concept of management is legendary at the General Electric Company. He is best characterized by his peers and co-workers for his sincerity, dedication, unlimited drive, comprehension, vision, and especially his ability to develop the potentials of others. He spent countless hours with many young managers and provided those who were willing to pay the demanding price for success with an opportunity. Smiddy never failed to sense the need to give a challenging idea or an inspiration to anyone who sought his counsel.

As vice president of General Electric's Management Consultation Services, he led a team of carefully selected and highly regarded managers, who had combined hundreds of years of successful contributions to General Electric's previous growth, in decentralizing that corporation's many worldwide businesses. To expedite the conclusion of this enormous undertaking this relatively small task force, representing backgrounds from every function of the company, developed a written philosophy for use by all managers in the company. It was from this structure that the original "Eight Key Result Areas" concept was developed and which led to a related project on company measurements. A few of the many spinoffs from this task force were management by objectives, the establishment of a school for General Electric managers that would be at the same level of competency as the best managerial schools in the academic world, the development of the concept of operations research and the structuring of its function within the operating departments of the General Electric Company, and, perhaps above all, the identification of the need for persuasive leadership by all managers resulting in a written philosophy of management development for the company.

Although Smiddy was usually concerned with research, he was most conscious of the need to form the theory into practice, as evidenced by the following verbal urgings:

- "The best testing ground for lab work is at the customer level."

- "I never met a researcher who was willing to let a study go; he will always find a reason to keep on researching."

- "There comes a time when the research should be tested in operational practice."

- "If you can't be practical, I can't use you."

General Electric's long-time corporate headquarters building at 570 Lexington Avenue in New York was the "Ivory Tower" in which Harold Smiddy did his pioneering work in the field of industrial management. (Courtesy of General Electric)

Smiddy's perfectionist ideals, at times, caused some to conclude wrongly that he was being unreasonably intolerant. All of what Smiddy could tolerate is really not known, of course. Yet, he was severely critical of anyone who made a mistake. He expected order and neatness in those who worked with him. This included office space, personal appearance and any material from his organization. One of Smiddy's longtime former colleagues once drew up the following list of things Harold Smiddy couldn't tolerate. The list was checked by another colleague who responded that it may not be entirely correct, but it is close enough; it included:

1. Don't make a mistake. "I can tolerate a mistake, but you won't be working for me long enough to make another."

2. Colors that he didn't like. Smiddy liked only a soft shade of green for his offices, but only a Rembrandt could consistently produce that color the same way twice.

3. Pictures that hung more than ½ a thousandth of an inch too high, too low, or not level by that amount.

4. Employees who were not around when he wanted them. Smiddy worked all the time.

5. Anyone who was lazy. Many highly intelligent people worked for only a short time with Smiddy because they did not put out that extra bit of energy.

6. People who worked normal hours. Smiddy was work-oriented and expected everyone else to be. There were no 9:00 A.M. to 5:00 P.M. employees who worked in his component and that included secretaries, analysts, accountants, and a future president of the company.

7. Delegating the blame. Smiddy believed in the doctrine of completed work. He always gave people all the tools needed to do a job and full authority to make decisions commensurate with the responsibility, but he accepted no excuse

for anything short of the best you were capable of giving. If it was not *your* very best effort then he didn't want the report.

8. Poor or inferior typing. Smiddy believed that the fault was in the manager or consultant, not the secretary or typist if a report had signs of erasures, sloppy margins, etc. He believed that the appearance of the report had to be attractive, to have good margins on both sides, no strikeovers or erasures (all typewriters had to have sharp clear letters). He once told me that "many people can write clear logical reports, but the man who packages best will go the farthest in business."

9. Decision-making committees. He was responsible for General Electric's president Ralph Cordiner's decision to discontinue them.

10. Assistant and assistants to.

11. Coordinate, coordinators, liaison. These were fighting words, deleted from General Electric's definition of the work of a manager.

12. Control. Smiddy made certain that it never be used to mean "measure."

Introduction

What Is Management Thought?

The term *management thought* refers to the theories and principles that guide the management of people in organizations. Just as the theory of relativity helps physicists understand the atom, predict its behavior, and control atomic reactions, theories of management guide managers in understanding and effectively supervising the people who work for them. Early management theorists were practicing managers who attempted to develop management principles based on their own experiences. Later management theorists were scholarly writers who built their theories on ideas borrowed from such sciences and disciplines as engineering, sociology, anthropology, psychology, economics, and philosophy. Today, many theorists are attempting to integrate the various historical approaches to management thought into a comprehensive body of management theory and practice. Instead of being discarded, those early management ideas that have stood the test of time are integrated into new approaches. After studying this chapter, you will understand how many of Harold Smiddy's ideas discussed in the opening case reflect both the strengths and shortcomings of early management thought.

Management theories are explanations of why a particular practice is effective or ineffective. They are necessary for the prediction and control of human behavior in the workplace. Without theories to guide their practice, managers might not understand the reasons behind their successes and failures. And without such understanding, managers would be less likely to ensure the achievement of future goals. Managers who are well versed in the theories that underlie their views of management, for instance, are unlikely to perpetuate notions such as those discussed in the opening case without first reflecting carefully to determine whether they are worth the money and time to be invested.

Management theory is a relatively new phenomenon in the history of business. Although it is taken for granted today, it was a radical idea in 1886, when Henry R. Towne, co-founder and president of Yale & Towne Manufacturing Company, proposed such a field of study in a paper presented to the American Society of Mechanical Engineers. Asserting that management was a field of study equal in importance to engineering, Towne observed that the management of work was a disorganized and largely intuitive enterprise. Managers, said Towne, had no associations through which they could share their experiences and no scientific discipline within which to codify that experience into principles or theories. As co-founder of the Chamber of Commerce, Towne had considerable influence in the business community. His paper, which he called "The Engineer as Economist," is often cited as the origin of the search for a modern science of management.[2]

Henry R. Towne
(Culver Pictures)

The time was ripe for Towne's thesis. The Industrial Revolution of the eighteenth and nineteenth centuries had underscored the need for an organized approach to management. The development of new technology had, for the first time in history, concentrated large numbers of workers in factories to mass-produce goods for wide distribution. The advent of mechanization had shifted the emphasis from craftsmanship to large-scale manufacturing.

This new complexity of business resulted in both economic and social changes. More goods, more services, and more people in the factories naturally spelled new, multifaceted organizational problems. These changes required a more sophisticated approach to the management of people, giving rise to the development of the modern professional manager. A society that encouraged business and profit simply had a greater need for capable, trained managers.

In this chapter we will trace the development of the field of management. You will study the progress of the practice of management from an impersonal, mechanistic, machine-oriented way of using resources, through an oversensitivity to personal preferences of workers, to a balanced perspective that views the alignment of employee and organizational needs as the critical element of managerial success.

Schools of Management Theory

There are three schools of management theory: the classical school, the behavioral school, and the management science school. These schools all emerged in different historical periods, yet all three have been blended into current management practice.

The Classical School

The **classical school** represented the first major systematic approach to management thought. It was distinguished by its emphasis on finding ways to get the work of each employee done faster. According to this view, expounded by Adam Smith, people tend to choose a course of action that maximizes their personal economic gain,[3] so financial incentives predominated in the classical school. Researchers joined with practitioners in recognizing the emotional side of human behavior and in assuming it could be controlled through the logical structuring of jobs and work schedules.

The classical school can be broken down into two historical philosophies of management, the scientific management approach and the administrative management approach.

THE SCIENTIFIC MANAGEMENT APPROACH

Scientific management was the first approach to emerge in the history of management theory. Its most fundamental feature was a concern with efficiency: the most productive use of human and material resources. This form of management developed in response to a pressing need in the United States to increase productivity in the early twentieth century, when there was a shortage of skilled labor.

Frederick W. Taylor
(The Bettmann Archive)

Frederick W. Taylor (1856–1915) is generally considered "the father of scientific management." Taylor's ideas grew out of his experience with three companies: Midvale Steel, Simonds Rolling Machine, and Bethlehem Steel. At Midvale Steel, in an attempt to maximize production, Taylor conducted a **time study** of workers, breaking down into their individual movements the actions that steel workers performed on the job and timing each of those movements. The results were then analyzed to make possible the design of more efficient methods of production. In addition, Taylor developed a piece-rate system for paying workers that enabled workers to earn more money the more work they completed. Taylor instituted this innovation in order to allay the fears of workers who thought they would be paid less or be laid off if they completed their work too quickly.[4]

Taylor continued his management innovations as a consultant, first at Simonds Rolling Machine, then at Bethlehem Steel. At Simonds he extended his time study work, isolating and analyzing the individual movements of the most productive workers engaged in making bicycle ball bearings. Other workers were then trained in what had emerged as the most effective ways of doing this often-tedious job. By introducing his "more pay for more production" system at Simonds and by including rest periods for workers, Taylor was able to achieve his first objective for management: "To unite high wages with low labor costs."

As a consultant at Bethlehem Steel in 1898, Taylor studied and attempted to improve the efficiency of a yard crew. Workers unloaded raw material from incoming railcars and loaded finished materials onto outgoing cars. Taylor calculated that each man was capable of loading 47.5 tons per day instead of the standard 12.5 tons. He worked out a system whereby each man who met that standard would be paid $1.85 a day (up from the usual daily rate of $1.15). The system led to dramatic increases in productivity. For a detailed account by Taylor of one aspect of his work, see "In Practice 2-1."

Taylor's philosophy, as described in his books *Shop Management* and *The Principles of Scientific Management*, was built on five basic principles:[6]

1. *The scientific selection of the worker.* Efficiency demanded the matching of each job with a worker who had whatever particular abilities that job called for. Tests of aptitude would be administered to see whether each person was right for the job he did. For example, Taylor developed a speed-of-reaction test for quality control inspectors.

2. *The scientific training of the worker.* Intuition and guesswork were of little use in designing a worker's job. Scientific techniques of measurement, such as time-and-motion studies, would be developed to train the worker to perform at maximum efficiency.

3. *Job specialization.* Production was broken down into its component parts, and all workers became specialists in their jobs.

In Practice 2-1

THE FAMOUS TAYLOR PIG-IRON STORY

No early contributor to the development of management theory is as famous as Frederick W. Taylor, and perhaps no single incident is as famous as Taylor's study of the pig-iron handler "Schmidt." "Schmidt" was the pseudonym for 27-year-old Henry Knolle, who weighed 135 pounds and stood 5 feet 7 inches tall. Taylor's account of his first conversation with "Schmidt" follows.

. . . Finally we selected one from among the four as the most likely man to start with. He was a little Pennsylvania Dutchman who had been observed to trot back home for a mile or so after his work in the evening, about as fresh as he was when he came trotting down to work in the morning. We found that upon wages of $1.15 a day he had succeeded in buying a small plot of ground, and that he was engaged in putting up the walls of a house for himself in the morning before starting work and at night after leaving. He also had the reputation of being exceedingly "close," that is, of placing a very high value on the dollar. As one man whom we talked to about him said, "A penny looks about the size of a cartwheel to him." This man we will call Schmidt.

The task before us, then, narrowed itself down to getting Schmidt to handle 47 tons of pig iron per day and making him glad to do it. This was done as follows. Schmidt was called out from among the gang of pig-iron handlers and talked to somewhat in this way:

"Schmidt, are you a high-priced man?"

"Vell, I don't know vat you mean."

"Oh, yes you do. What I want to know is whether you are a high-priced man or not."

"Vell, I don't know vat you mean."

"Oh, come now, you answer my questions. What I want to find out is whether you are a high-priced man or one of these cheap fellows here. What I want to find out is whether you want to earn $1.85 a day or whether you are satisfied with $1.15 just the same as all those cheap fellows are getting."

"Did I vant $1.85 a day? Vas dot a high-priced man? Vell, you, I vas a high-priced man."

"Oh, you're aggravating me. Of course you want $1.85 a day—everyone wants it! You know perfectly well that has very little to do with your being a high-priced man. For goodness sake answer my questions, and don't waste any more of my time. Now come over here. You see that pile of pig iron?"

"Yes."

"You see that car?"

"Yes."

"Well if you are a high-priced man, you will load that pig iron on that car tomorrow for $1.85. Now do wake up and answer my question. Tell me whether you are a high-priced man or not."

"Vell—did I got $1.85 for loading dot pig iron on dot car tomorrow?"

"Yes, of course you do, and you get $1.85 for loading a pile like that every day right through the year. That is what a high-priced man does and you know it as well as I do."

"Vell, dot's all right. I could load dot pig iron on the car tomorrow for $1.85, and I get it every day don't I?"

"Certainly you do—certainly you do."

"Vell, den, I vas a high-priced man."

"Now, hold on, hold on. You know just as well as I do that a high-priced man has to do exactly as he's told from morning till night. You have seen this man here before, haven't you?"

"No, I never saw him."

"Well, if you are a high-priced man, you will do exactly as this man tells you tomorrow, from morning till night. When he tells you to pick up a pig and walk, you pick it up and walk, and when he tells you to sit down and rest, you sit down and rest. You do that right straight through the day. And what's more no back talk. Now a high-priced man does just what he's told to do, and no back talk. Do you understand that? When this man tells you to walk, you walk; when he tells you to sit down you sit down, and you don't talk back to him. Now you come on to work here tomorrow morning and I'll know before night whether you are really a high-priced man or not."

Without a doubt the most notable (and unsavory) aspect of Taylor's account of his experiments with the pig-iron handler Schmidt is that the events described were fabrications.[5] Apparently Taylor believed that by retelling a story that would be perceived as factual, he could influence more managers to consider the advantages the scientific management approach offered. Had Taylor's lie been exposed in the formative days of management thought, his otherwise largely positive contributions would have been discredited, and the growth of management theory might have been severely stunted.

Source: Excerpt from *Scientific Management* by Frederick W. Taylor. Copyright 1911 by Frederick W. Taylor. Renewed 1939 by Louise M. S. Taylor.

4. *The importance of wage incentives.* Workers were to be paid for what they did and would receive bonuses if they exceeded a set standard of production.

5. *A fair division of responsibility between workers and management.* The most efficient use of personnel and resources required friendly cooperation between labor and management.

Several of Taylor's ideas have filtered down through the years.[7] That they have influenced contemporary management ideas is clearly shown in Figure 2-1.

Unlike some of the key elements of Harold Smiddy's philosophy discussed in the opening case, Taylor's fundamental notions about a professional approach to the task of managing have endured. Respect for the needs and contributions of workers, combined with a belief in the responsibility of managers to plan, lead, organize, and control the operations of the organization for the benefit of all stakeholders, has been a cornerstone of American industry since Taylor first articulated his view nearly eighty years ago.

Critique of Taylor It is important to remember that despite the relative success of Taylor's procedures, he was a controversial figure in his time. One by-product of

FIGURE 2-1
Taylor's Influence in
Contemporary
Management

	Valid?	Now Accepted?	Manifested in (Outgrowths):
Philosophy			
Scientific decsion making	Yes	Yes	Management science, operations research, cost accounting, etc.
Management/labor cooperation	Yes	Partly	Greater management/labor cooperation (but conflict not eliminated)
Techniques			
Time-and-motion study	Yes	Yes	Widespread use, standard times
Standardization	Yes	Yes	Standardized procedures in many spheres, human engineering
Task	Yes	Yes	Goal setting, MBO, feedback
Bonus	Yes	Increasingly	Proliferation of reward system, Scanlon Plan, Improshare, need to consider money in job enrichment/OD studies
Individualized work	Partly	Partly	Recognition of dangers of groups, groupthink, social loafing, contextual theories of group decision making (but group jobs sometimes more efficient)
Management training	Yes	Yes	Management responsibility for employee training
Scientific selection	Yes	Yes	Development of fields of industrial psychology and personnel management
Shorter hours, rest pauses	Yes	Yes	Forty-hour (or shorter) workweek, common use of rest pauses

Source: E. A. Locke, "The Ideas of Frederick W. Taylor: An Evaluation," *Academy of Management Review* 7, no. 1 (January 1982): 22. Reprinted by permission of the Academy of Management.

his success in improving worker efficiency was the reduction in the size of the necessary work force, which led eventually to reductions in the overall work force. At Simonds Rolling Machine, for example, Taylor's efficient methods enabled the work formerly done by 120 inspectors to be done by 35. Although Taylor declared his support for the union movement and argued that, historically, increased efficiency had led to *increased* employment, there was a strong backlash against his methods.

The perceived threat of layoffs made the unions suspicious of Taylor's methods. In 1912, protests against methods developed by Taylor led to a strike at the Watertown Arsenal in Massachusetts, a plant that had started to use scientific management. Hostility toward Taylor's methods became so great that he was called on to defend his programs before the U.S. Congress.

Taylor was a brave and responsible innovator, but many of his imitators used short-cut versions of his methods, reinforcing doubts about Taylor's scientific approach. Moreover, Taylor himself was occasionally blunt to the point of rudeness in expounding on his scientific approach. (He once said, for example, that a pig-iron handler should ideally be "so stupid and dull that he resembles an ox.") Ironically, such statements may have inspired a constructive reaction: a greater concern for the subjective human factor in job performance. And Taylor himself was not insensitive to this issue, though it was then outside the scope of his own scientific methods. In fact, he urged scientific study "of the motives which influence men." [8]

Later schools of thought argued that scientific management, as developed by Frederick W. Taylor and his contemporaries, relied on an oversimplified model of human behavior. For example, the theories of human motivation that prevailed in Taylor's time were largely based on the faulty notion that workers are motivated solely by the need to satisfy financial and physical needs.[9]

Other Perspectives on Scientific Management Among other pioneers in scientific management was the husband-and-wife team of Frank B. Gilbreth (1868–1925) and Lillian M. Gilbreth (1878–1972). The Gilbreths worked together on studies of worker fatigue and motion and on ways to improve the welfare of the individual worker.[10]

Lillian M. Gilbreth and Frank B. Gilbreth (The Bettmann Archive)

Frank Gilbreth, who had worked as a bricklayer, began to study and record on motion picture film the discrete movements a bricklayer made as he went about his job. According to the Gilbreth theory, motion and fatigue were directly related. When an unnecessary motion was eliminated from the job, a certain amount of fatigue was also eliminated. This not only made the worker more efficient but also contributed to the welfare of the worker.

The Gilbreths were scientific in their approach because they were dedicated to the elimination of unnecessary, and therefore unproductive, actions in the workplace. Rigorously analyzing the component parts of a job, they searched for the single most efficient way to perform a particular piece of work. For example, in studying the work of bricklayers, Frank Gilbreth reduced from sixteen to eight the number of basic motions that the job required.[11]

In addition to doing extensive research on time-and-motion problems, the Gilbreths also directed their attention toward the organization of the workplace as a whole. For example, they devised a promotion plan for workers that included three parts: (1) The worker did his job. (2) The worker trained his successor. (3) The worker learned new skills to ready himself for promotion to a higher job.

When Frank Gilbreth died in 1925, Lillian Gilbreth continued their work. In addition, she took the Gilbreth management science in a somewhat new direction. As the first woman to write a Ph.D. thesis in psychology in the United States, Lillian Gilbreth showed a great appreciation of the human factor in the workplace. Her work foreshadowed what is today known as human resource management, and she focused especially on the scientific selection, training, and placing of employees. In many ways ahead of her time, Lillian Gilbreth urged an end to discrimination in the hiring and retention of workers over forty.[12] She also called for research designed to compare the job performances of workers of different ages.

Critique of the Gilbreths The Gilbreths were contemporaries of Frederick W. Taylor and, for a time, disciples of his scientific management approach. However, it is important to note the differences between the methods of the Gilbreths and of Taylor. By temperament, Taylor was almost belligerently scientific, sometimes betraying insensitivity to the subjective human factor in industry. The Gilbreths were idealists who wanted to reward workers who performed well. They were interested in developing the individual employees to their full potential. Whereas Taylor laid the groundwork for scientific management, the Gilbreths helped create a bridge between strict scientific management (time studies, motion studies, and production quotas) and the scientific management of personnel, with emphasis on the *personnel*.

THE ADMINISTRATIVE MANAGEMENT APPROACH

If scientific management focused primarily on the efficiency of production, **administrative management** focused on the broader aspects of managing large groups of people. Administrative management grew out of the need to control and shape the behavior of employees in large, complex organizations.

Henri Fayol (Comité National de l'Organisation Française)

Henri Fayol is recognized as the first person to systematize the administrative approach to management. He believed that management could be taught if its underlying principles were identified. Whereas scientific management had been concerned primarily with tasks performed by workers, Fayol focused his attention on the organization as a whole.[13]

Fayol concentrated on the managerial function, which he felt had been the most neglected aspect of business. He broke the managerial function down into other basic steps, including planning, organizing, commanding, coordinating, and controlling. Furthermore, he developed fourteen management principles that have been widely circulated as guides for modern management thought. The following discussion of these principles is intended to help you understand Fayol's views.

1. *Division of labor.* The more people specialize, the better they are at their jobs. The division of labor increases production by simplifying the tasks required of each worker. The modern assembly line is clearly an example; it permits mass production to flourish. Consequently, the production process should be broken into small, manageable parts.

2. *Authority.* Authority is "the right to give orders and the power to exact obedience." There needs to be a balance between authority and responsibility. A manager's authority must be directly tied to his competence as a manager and to his knowledge of the operations under his supervision. Managers do not derive authority from holding a title but from giving evidence of their ability and experience.

3. *Discipline.* The essence of discipline is respect for the organization's rules and regulations. Discipline requires effective leadership at all levels. It also requires managerial fairness and managers' willingness to penalize employees promptly for breaking the rules. These rules must be clearly stated. Discipline helps workers develop obedience, energy, respect, and perseverance.

4. *Unity of command.* Under this principle, the worker reports to one supervisor. To avoid confusion, a chain of command must be maintained. For example, a worker in the Parts Supply Department should be required to report only to the supervisor directly in charge of that department. The worker should not take orders from a supervisor in the Production Department even though that parts supply worker's tasks directly affect the operation of the Production Department. If the production supervisor has a complaint about the work of the employee in parts supply, he should take that problem to the parts supply supervisor.

5. *Unity of direction.* Operations with the same goal should proceed with one unified plan under the direction of a single authority. For example, the company should not employ two personnel directors, each with different hiring policies and procedures for interviewing applicants.

6. *Subordination of individual interest to the common goal.* The interests of any worker, group of workers, or all workers must not take precedence over the interests of the organization as a whole. For example, various companies (including White Westinghouse) have had great difficulty in scheduling work because of a company policy of allowing workers to take unscheduled days off from work in order to transact personal business. Though such a liberal policy is great for the individual worker, the group's performance suffers appreciably when unscheduled days off are taken.

7. *Remuneration.* Employees should be paid according to a plan designed to reward good performance. Workers who increase their output should receive more pay, in the form of either a bonus or an increase in wages.

8. *Centralization.* Managers must maintain final responsibility but should delegate certain authority to subordinates. Consider a group of workers on an assembly line. These workers answer to a foreman, who in turn answers to the manager. Managers must accept ultimate responsibility but should apportion some supervisory tasks to their subordinates.

9. *Scalar chain.* There should be a clear chain of command from the top to the bottom of the organization. Workers and managers should follow this chain of command in matters of routine supervision or in the solution of special problems that arise in the workplace. This helps to ensure the orderly flow of information and supplements the principle of unity of command.

10. *Order.* The orderly supervision of workers and the efficient use of materials should be a top priority. Managers recognize the importance of scheduling work properly and making timetables for its completion. Workers and materials must be in the right place, at the right time.

11. *Equity.* Employees must be treated equally and fairly. This fairness helps inspire worker diligence and loyalty. Established rules are important, but problems should be evaluated in terms of overall fairness and sympathy with the worker.

12. *Stability of tenure of personnel.* Organizations should work toward achieving long-term commitments from their employees and managers. Earning this commitment should be a specific management goal. When turnover is minimized—especially at the management level—the organization is more likely to be successful.

13. *Initiative.* Workers should be permitted to develop and implement their own plans of action to solve problems in the workplace. This helps them to realize their own capacities to the fullest and to feel like an active part of the organization. One way to foster such initiative is to schedule periodic meetings in which managers and workers discuss job-related problems.

14. *Esprit de corps.* All these principles help bring workers and management together through awareness of the interests they share. Harmony is best maintained by having a clear chain of command and by using oral rather than written communications.

Critique of Fayol Fayol's major contribution was the basic principle that management is not an inborn talent but a skill that can be taught. He believed that management could be taught once its underlying principles were understood and that managers could be developed through training. His was the first comprehensive theory of management; he created a system of ideas that could be applied to all areas of management. And he was one of the first management theorists to set down ground rules for large organizations. As a pioneering management theorist, Fayol also contributed to the concept of management instruction in colleges and universities.

It is interesting to compare Fayol's comprehensive approach to Taylor's scientific approach. For example, among his fourteen principles, Fayol insisted on the unity of command and was critical of Taylor's idea of the functional foreman, which required the worker to answer to more than one supervisor, depending on what task he or she was performing at the time.

Weber's Perspective on Administrative Management At roughly the same time that Taylor and Fayol were writing in the United States, a German sociologist named Max Weber (1864–1920) was formulating his ideas on the ideal management approach for large organizations. Weber (pronounced *vay ber*) developed a set of rational ideas about the structure of the organization that define what has come to be known as **bureaucracy**. The cornerstone of his theory was a set of seven basic characteristics of an ideal formalized organization:[14]

Max Weber (Culver Pictures)

1. A division of labor in which authority and responsibility are clearly defined for each member and legitimized as official duties

2. Offices or positions organized in a hierarchy of authority resulting in a chain of command or the scalar principle

3. All organizational members selected on the basis of technical qualifications through formal examinations or by virtue of training or education

4. Officials appointed, not elected (with the exception, in some cases, of the chief of the whole unit—for example, an elected public official)

5. Administrative officials who work for fixed salaries and are "career" officials

6. Administrative officials who are not owners of the unit being administered

7. Administrators who are subject to strict rules, discipline, and controls regarding the conduct of their official duties (these rules and controls would be impersonal and would be uniformly applied in all cases)

As these characteristics suggest, Weber wanted to clarify the need for specialization, hierarchy, and rules in large organizations. His purpose was to depersonalize many management functions in the hope that the resulting uniformity might prompt fair and equitable treatment for all workers. Weber also felt that his "rational, dependable, and predictable system" would ensure the satisfactory performance of many routine organizational tasks.

If you would like to test your appreciation for a bureaucratic approach in modern organizations, complete "Management Development Exercise 2."

The Behavioral School

The administrative approach shifted the emphasis of management thought from production techniques to the organization as a whole. Building on the classical approach, several important authors endorsed this "people-oriented" trend. These theorists helped pave the way for a human relations approach and ultimately for the **behavioral school** of management theory, a school that was in many ways a reaction to the impersonal nature of the classical approaches.

The behavioral approach responded to the need to develop a more realistic picture of worker motivation and behavior. In some cases, the increases in productivity made possible by the application of classical principles were accompanied by a decrease in harmony among workers and by conflicts between workers and managers. Where the classical approach had focused on the particular job being done by the workers, the behavioral approach focused on the workers doing the job.

EARLY CONTRIBUTORS

The transition from a focus on the task to a more sympathetic focus on the worker is reflected in the work of several important thinkers. Many of these people rank as major contributors to the development of management thought. Evidence of their prominence is indicated by the results of a survey reported in Figure 2-2. The survey, of fifty management scholars, showed that the overall impact of researchers such as Follett, Bernard, and Mayo from the behavioral school of management thought was clearly considered to be important in terms of their contributions to current management practice.

Mary Parker Follett (1868–1933) asserted that the hierarchical distinction between managers and subordinates (one worker viewed as "above" another) was artificial and that it obscured a natural partnership between labor and management. For example, Follett argued that management leadership should not be established according to traditional lines of authority but on the basis of the superior knowledge and ability of the manager.

The key to understanding Follett's work is to know that she promoted the notion of integration in all of her writings.[15] An early advocate of a "systems" approach, she stressed that organizations should emphasize interdependence among their parts, activities, and functions. A promoter of open communication between managers and subordinates, Follett is also remembered for her view of leadership as a group process and for her early recognition of the human factor in organizations.

Mary Parker Follett (Courtesy of Joan C. Tonn, University of Massachusetts, and the Urwick Management Center, Slough, England)

FIGURE 2-2
Major Contributions to
the Development of
Management Thought

Rank	Contributor	Number of Votes	Points	Total Points	First-Place Votes
1	Taylor, Frederick W.*	108	850	958	51
2	Barnard, Chester I.*	81	516	597	9
3	Gilbreth, Frank*	70	414	484	0
4	Mayo, Elton*	61	368	429	3
5	Gilbreth, Lillian*	61	348	409	2
6	Sloan, Alfred P., Jr.	55	313	368	3
7	Follett, Mary Parker*	55	302	357	2
8	Ford, Henry	48	262	310	4
9	Maslow, Abraham†	45	209	254	3
10	Gantt, Henry L.†	40	211	251	2

Source: From D. A. Wren and R. D. Hay, "Management Historians and Business Historians: Differing Perceptions of Pioneer Contributors," *Academy of Management Journal* (September 1977): 476. Reprinted by permission of the Academy of Management.

*Discussed in this chapter.

†Maslow's work is discussed at length in Chapter 14; Gantt's work is described in Chapter 19.

Oliver Sheldon
(Courtesy of Rowntree
Mackintosh)

Chester I. Barnard (UPI/
Bettmann Newsphotos)

Hugo Munsterberg
(Culver Pictures)

Oliver Sheldon (1894–1951) stressed the social obligation of business to treat its workers fairly. He also argued that business had an ethical responsibility to society beyond the efficient production of goods and services.[16] According to Sheldon, management must treat its workers honestly and fairly. Furthermore, it must attempt to use new technical advances not only to achieve greater production and profit but also to enhance the well-being of the whole community. For example, a factory that had the technical capacity to develop a new pollution-control device should do so for the benefit of the community, whether or not it could be done profitably.

Chester I. Barnard (1886–1961) argued that the needs and goals of a business organization must be balanced with the needs and goals of its individual members.[17] He emphasized that when they are formally organized to achieve goals, people can outperform individuals acting alone. Barnard also recognized the importance of the informal subgroups that form within every organization, arguing that managers must take these groups into account when making decisions and developing strategies. He built on Follett's appreciation for integration and for productive approaches to the resolution of conflict.

The focus on the workers themselves coincided with the birth of *industrial psychology*. The preeminent early figure in this movement was Hugo Munsterberg (1863–1916). Although Munsterberg died early in the twentieth century, many of his ideas have influenced the way modern managers attempt to deal with the psychological needs of workers.

Using techniques drawn from experimental psychology, Munsterberg searched for what he called "the best possible effect" to motivate workers. He suggested that ideas derived from learning theory should be applied to the training of workers.[18] Munsterberg's suggestions eventually led to tests administered to determine worker aptitudes in various areas, such as mechanics or mathematics. His ideas also encouraged industries to train new workers and to give workers an opportunity to advance themselves through company-sponsored training.

These telephone relay assembly-room workers became famous as the subjects of studies of the impact on productivity of various changes in their work environment. (Courtesy of Western Electric)

Elton Mayo (Courtesy of The Baker Library, Harvard University)

FOCUS ON WORKERS: THE HAWTHORNE EXPERIMENTS

The behavioral approach was more oriented toward the feelings and attitudes of workers than were the classical approaches. Hence it is somewhat ironic that these "subjective" factors in the work environment led to more scientific research on worker productivity. The best-known example was the Hawthorne Studies.[19] So named because they were conducted at the Western Electric Hawthorne plant in Cicero, Illinois, these studies were begun in an effort to examine the effects of changes in lighting on the productivity of workers. The early studies were conducted by company engineers in collaboration with the National Academy of Sciences. Problems posed by this initial research were later addressed by a team of researchers led by Elton Mayo, F. J. Roethlisberger, and W. J. Dickson of Harvard in studies conducted from 1927 to 1932.

F. J. Roethlisberger (Courtesy of The Baker Library, Harvard University)

One phase of the research was referred to as the "lighting experiments." Researchers divided workers into two groups: a control group and the experimental group. The control group was exposed to a consistently well-lighted workplace, while the experimental group worked under varied lighting conditions. The results of this study were not clear-cut. For example, when the experimental group's lighting was improved, productivity seemed to increase—but only in an uneven and inconsistent manner. On the other hand, production also tended to improve when the lighting conditions for the experimental group were subsequently made *worse*.

One conclusion drawn from these results was that no direct cause-and-effect relationship could be established between a single environmental factor (lighting) and worker productivity.[20]

W. J. Dickson

The "assembly test room" experiment, a second phase of the studies, involved six skilled female workers whose job was assembling telephone relays. The experiment was conducted in a test room, and detailed records were kept on such physiological states as the workers' blood pressure. Changes in such factors as the number and frequency of rest periods were noted. Clearly, this was a scientific study carried out along lines previously developed in the classical approach. Yet this phase of the Hawthorne research contained an important new variable. The six selected workers became "special." For example, they were consulted about proposed changes, and the changes were not instituted if the women rejected them.[21] Rather than feeling like guinea pigs impersonally observed through glass in a laboratory, these workers felt a sense of worth. They had a voice in decisions made about their work.

Worker morale remained high and productivity increased because the workers felt they were an important part of a group effort and participated in the decision-making process.[22] This phenomenon has been called the **Hawthorne effect**: Employees work harder when they believe management is concerned about their welfare and when managers pay special attention to them. Such "special" treatment of test subjects gave birth to the management notion of human relations.

Mayo is also credited with substituting the concept of "social worker" for the concept of "rational worker" in management thought. The rational worker had been assumed to be motivated by personal economic needs. Mayo discovered, on the contrary, that workers were motivated just as much by social needs (such as group approval), by the satisfaction of doing a worthwhile job, and by the need to respond to the challenge of a task rather than to managerial authority.[23]

By applying the scientific method, Mayo and his colleagues laid a firm foundation for the behavioral science approach to management thought. Later researchers, more thoroughly trained in anthropology, sociology, and psychology, were able to build on this foundation.

THE LEGACY OF THE BEHAVIORAL SCHOOL

The most important contribution of the behavioral approach has been our increased understanding of human motivation, of worker behavior in groups, of personal relationships at work, and of the satisfactions derived from work over and above monetary reward. Through increased and more sophisticated knowledge of human motivation, managers who adopt the behavioral approach have achieved new insights into such phenomena as leadership and communication.

Some practitioners, however, insist that the behavioral approach has not yet realized its full potential. At times the models and theories proposed by behavioral theorists seem too complicated or abstract to apply to actual work situations. Further, research and theory development have rarely considered diverse cultural influences on managers' performance, one of which is highlighted in Insights for International Managers 2. And behavioral scientists often differ widely in their suggestions on how to deal with employee problems. Nevertheless, the behavioral approach has made possible the development of a scientific approach that attempts to take into account the complexity of human behavior.

Managers who adhere to the behavioral school know that this approach emphasizes competence in human skills, such as leadership and communication. But this emphasis should not obscure the need for proficiency in other skills as well. For example, a production manager who deals well with people but cannot plan an effective production system is not fully effective.

━━━━━━━━━━━━━━ *Insights for International Managers 2* ━━━━━━━━━━━━━━

TRADITIONS OF ARAB AND AFRICAN DECISION MAKERS

Tribal leaders have practiced council meetings or "palaver" for milennia, and the consultation tradition is supported by the Koran and sayings of Mohammed. Senior members of the ruling families or the community are still consulted on matters of importance; in other matters the family is often asked for input. The consultation method is used almost to the exclusion of joint decision-making or delegation of decision-making responsibility. Arab executives say the practice continues because it works: it is a good human-relations technique, diffusing potential opposition, and it actually produces good input. Arabs prefer consultation on a person-to-person basis; they hate committees and group meetings. Arabs make decisions in an informal and unstructured manner. Some of our professional business approaches seem to them rigid and impersonal. Their heritage is not one of enclosed offices but of open spaces, tents, and generous hospitality. As a result, you may find your meetings interrupted by the constant commotion of people coming and going, telephone calls and servants offering beverages. If you insist on a more formal style, you may be at a disadvantage.

Source: From L. Copeland and L. Griggs, *Going International* (New York: Random House, 1985), p. 125.

The Management Science School

The **management science school** developed from knowledge that investigators gained in applying quantitative analysis to military and logistic problems. During World War II, researchers sought solutions to such complex problems as how to increase bombing accuracy and how to refine search procedures for the detection of enemy supplies. Much of the research was done by interdisciplinary teams of experts from such fields as statistics, engineering, economics, mathematics, and political science. When the war was over, many researchers saw enormous potential in applying this broad interdisciplinary approach to industry studies.

One good way to characterize the management science school is to describe some of the ways in which it differs from the classical and behavioral schools.

1. *An emphasis on decision making.* Scientific management focused on the efficiency of the manufacturing process. The management science school, however, regards technical efficiency as only a tool, rather than as an end in itself. It places greater weight on the overall decision-making process and on planning. It recognizes, for example, that the efficient production of size-8 ball bearings is of little value if the decision to make the part was unwise in the first place. In the classical school, the tendency was to be satisfied by the mere *ability* to be more efficient. In management science, technology is a tool that managers try to view with a cooler eye than their classical predecessors.

2. *The use of quantitative models.* The management science approach emphasizes the use of mathematical models in planning. (We will have more to say about mathematical models in Chapter 19.) Managers are always concerned, for example, about the relationship among inventory costs, lost sales, and angered customers when inventories are inadequate, ordering costs high, and total sales uncertain. By creating a mathematical model designed to take such variables into account, managers who avail themselves of management science tools become better able to control the production rates that affect the rate at which

surplus inventories accumulate. The key difference between this school and other schools of thought is that a science—mathematics—is being applied more to the decision-making process itself than to specific technical problems, such as the need to increase the speed of, say, inspectors on a tire assembly line.

3. *The use of computers.* Through the quantitative approach just described, the management science school has developed a highly abstract way of assimilating a wide variety of complex data and variables. In many cases it could not do this without the aid of the computer, which many believe has been the most important single factor in the rise of management science.[24] In a sense, the management science school has taken the essence of the scientific management approach and applied it at an abstract level to management decision making. For some good examples of computer application of management science, see "In Practice 2-2."

4. *Evaluation of effectiveness.* To back up its emphasis on decision making, management science has devised techniques for evaluating the effectiveness of models in terms of such factors as return on investment, revenue generated, and cost savings. Again, these models are set apart from those of earlier schools by the emphasis on their use in managerial decision making.

LEGACY OF THE MANAGEMENT SCIENCE SCHOOL

The management science school has had a considerable impact on management practice. Perhaps its greatest contribution is in the development of models to help managers analyze complex statistical data. Computers and quantitative analysis have made it possible to assess the effect of many variables in the workplace that might formerly have been overlooked.

Even so, managers should recognize the limitations of the management science school as an actual day-to-day tool of management. For example, using the sophisticated calculations of quantitative theory, managers might be able to obtain interesting and useful information about the use and misuse of sick leave among workers. They might be able to factor in many variables—such as the age of employees, how long they have been employed, the frequency of sick leave, the actual payment of medical benefits, and the occurrence of sick leave in close proximity to holidays, for example. Through the computer-assisted analysis of such variables, managers may be able to amass overwhelming evidence that sick leave is abused by workers, such as when workers consistently call in sick on the days before or after holidays. Yet such statistical evidence may be of little use in actually curtailing the abuse of sick leave. This might require the somewhat more comprehensive techniques of the behavioral school or the administrative management approach, which emphasizes a concern for the welfare of the worker and a conscientious search for the reasons behind certain human behavior.

Integrative Perspectives in Management

Two modern approaches to management thought have evolved in the 1970s and 1980s. The systems approach and the contingency approach are currently considered integrative perspectives employed to supplement the established schools of management thought.

In Practice 2-2

MANAGEMENT SCIENCE TODAY

Pat Raffee, a consultant, uses computer software to help companies train their salespeople. She had not thought software could help her manage more efficiently until she got a new computer software product called the "Management Edge."

A part-time employee in her Newport Beach, California, firm, the Raffee Company, was becoming undependable, and "my nervousness was rising as her dependability was lowering," says Raffee, who had a large new contract and needed the employee.

"I don't mind confrontation myself," Raffee says, "and I train managers in confronting directly to boost sales results." That wasn't working with her employee. The "Management Edge" program asked Raffee a series of questions to be answered with a "yes" or "no." Then it asked her for a few adjectives to describe the employee.

What the program then gave Raffee was a detailed $8\frac{1}{2}$-page printout that told her what kind of manager she was and what kind of employee she had, and suggested ways of handling the discipline problem—from the tone of voice Raffee should use to the kind of approach she should take.

For this employee, the program said, "a subtle word will have as much impact as direct discipline." Raffee sat down with the employee and explained her concern about the new project, saying she needed the employee to be dependable. The employee agreed and has been fine since.

Testimonials for computerized programs aimed at increasing individuals' productivity are becoming common in the business world as more companies augment training with software.

In the past, training programs were designed for mainframe computers and often cost $3,000 or more. Suddenly the personal computer has made possible software offering similar training for much less.

Thoughtware, Inc., of Coconut Grove, Florida, offers a line of programs that cost about $450 apiece. The programs carry titles like "Leading Effectively" and "Managing Time Effectively." Thoughtware products pose a number of questions, asking a manager how he rates himself in several areas relevant to the subject.

The manager can compare his own ratings with similar self-ratings by a national sample of managers. Because managers tend to rate themselves higher than do the people working for them, Thoughtware programs include a way for subordinates to rate the manager, who can compare those ratings with a national sample. The packages then recommend procedures for improving the manager's efficiency.

Although most managers cannot pinpoint measurable gains in productivity from using the various software packages, most are enthusiastic about the help they have gotten.

Johnson draws a sharp line between the products of companies like Thoughtware and his own line of packages, which includes the "Sales Edge" and the "Management Edge"—the ones Raffee uses—as well as the "Negotiation Edge" and the "Communication Edge," ranging in price from $195 to $295.

Human Edge software differs from others in that it uses "expert systems modeling," Johnson says. Instead of offering a menu of choices to the user, expert systems modeling takes information from a user and comes up with specific recommendations for a particular problem.

Such programs have been developed as software companies work toward developing artificial intelligence, the as-yet-unrealized dream of software so powerful that it allows a computer to solve problems by imitating human reasoning. Human Edge calls its products "business strategy software."

Source: Excerpted from M. Lewis, "Software That Improves Managers," *Nation's Business* (October 1984): pp. 45–46. Reprinted by permission from *Nation's Business*, October 1984. Copyright 1984, U.S. Chamber of Commerce.

The Systems Approach

Drawing freely on biology, psychology, sociology, and information theory, the **systems approach** attempts to view the organization as a single, integrated system of subsystems. Instead of dealing separately with individual parts of an organization, managers are advised to focus on what role each part plays in the whole organization. The general open-system model is depicted in Figure 2-3.

Managers who adopt the systems approach are encouraged to think beyond the areas of their own authority. For example, a production manager using the systems approach devises a production schedule only after considering how it will affect other departments, such as marketing and personnel. The systems approach further requires managers to consider the effects their decisions will have on other sectors and levels of the organization. For example, will the increased production of a certain product impinge on the test marketing of a newer, similar item the company is starting to promote? This is a question the production manager will have to answer by consulting marketing managers and other supervisors.[25]

The first great contributor to the systems approach was Chester I. Barnard (1886–1961). Also closely linked with the behavioral school of management, as we noted earlier in this chapter, Barnard is best known for his 1938 book *The Functions of the Executive,* which presented his application of sociological concepts to management and offered a comprehensive analysis of organization structure. His basic premise was that an organization is a "system of consciously coordinated activities, in which the executive is the most strategic factor."[26]

Barnard is credited with a more penetrating study of management than that of Taylor or Fayol because of his "analysis of the kinds and quality of forces at work and the manner of their interaction."[27] His studies emphasized more of the totality of the managerial environment than did the work of any of his predecessors or contemporaries. For Barnard, an executive could achieve excellence in his job only when he performed three critical duties:

1. Provided a system of communications.

2. Promoted the efforts needed to operate the system.

3. Formulated and defined the objectives of the system.

Barnard felt that the second of these duties was probably most important; unless workers could be induced to cooperate, managers' plans were doomed to failure.

In modern applications of the systems approach, managers are encouraged to remain aware of the importance of the following aspects of organizations:

FIGURE 2-3
Open-System Model

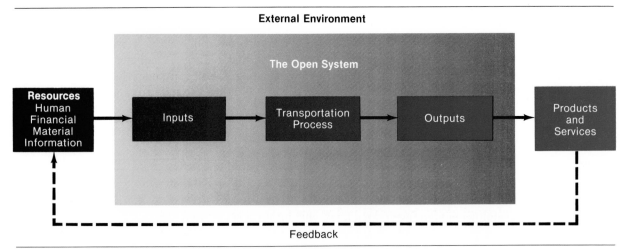

1. **Subsystems** are the individual parts that make up the whole organization. Each subsystem is part of a system that may in turn be a subsystem of a still larger system. For example, a department is a subsystem of a plant, which may be a subsystem of a conglomerate, which is in turn a subsystem of the particular industry itself. Finally, the industry is a subsystem of the entire economy.

2. **Synergy** reflects the concept that the whole is greater than the sum of its parts. This means that a whole organization cannot be defined merely by enumerating its various departments. Synergy emphasizes the interrelationship among all the parts of an organization. In terms of business, this means that separate departments within an organization are more productive when they cooperate and interact than when they act separately.

3. An **open system** is one that interacts with the environment; a **closed system** is one that does not. Actually, all organizations interact with their environment to some extent and the task is to determine the optimal degree of openness. Goodyear Tire engages in constant interaction with the external environment. On the other hand, Folsom State Prison has (by design) only a limited degree of contact with the outside.

4. **Boundaries** are the points at which an organization meets the outside environment. In a fairly closed system, such as a private catering business responsible for food service in one company, the boundary is fairly well defined. The interests of this business do not extend beyond a fairly regular number of customers, a particular location, and a single corporate client. For a coal mining company, however, the boundary between the firm itself and the outside environment is constantly changing. The coal company is always searching for resources in the outside environment. It has a legal responsibility not to abuse its mining privileges by failing to protect the environment. Moreover, because of the nature of its work, it must deal with government regulations concerning the welfare of its workers, who might be susceptible to lung disease.

5. **Flow** is the movement of materials and human energy through a system. Information enters a system as inputs (raw material), is transformed within the system (refined), and leaves the system as outputs (goods and services). Thus iron ore enters a steel refinery, is transformed into molten metal, and emerges as steel.

6. Getting **feedback** is the process of monitoring information about various systems in order to evaluate their operation and make corrections if necessary. For example, an employee wage-incentive plan is introduced to help increase production of "raw," or green, tires in a tire factory. The work involves a good deal of speed and skill in the operation of a tire-building machine. Obtaining feedback would consist of determining whether the wage-incentive plan was actually inducing the workers to make more tires.

The Contingency Approach

The **contingency approach** was developed through attempts to apply to real-life situations concepts drawn from various major schools of management thought. It holds that no approach is universally applicable and that different problems and situations require different approaches. The manager's past experience and the experiences of other firms are also carefully considered in "contingency management."

According to contingency theory, managers need to identify the approach that will serve them best in a given situation and that will most help them meet their managerial goals. For example, faced with the task of increasing production in a shoe factory, managers who subscribe to the contingency approach examine both the scientific management and the behavioral approaches. Then they would ask, "Which technique will be most efficient here?"

Next they might institute a time study of the operations on the shoe assembly line in the classic manner of Frederick W. Taylor or the Gilbreths, seeking a technical solution to the problem in terms of how labor is divided. But what if the need for an increase in production is temporary? In this case the managers might seek an administrative solution by organizing an overtime schedule for workers. Working overtime is not required, so they might devise a bonus plan as an incentive, depending on its cost compared to the benefits to be derived from the increase in production. Their approach, in short, is *contingent* on the specific factors involved in the problem they are dealing with.

It is important to remember that the contingency approach emphasizes diversity and that different problems require different solutions. For example, one study might reveal a wide variation between factors that motivate managers in nontechnical areas and those that motivate computer specialists. The nontechnical managers give high ratings to such traditional rewards as salary and status. The computer specialists, on the other hand, are more interested in acquiring new job skills. From a contingency point of view, the results of this study would have important implications for managers responsible for motivating both nontechnical and technical workers in a single environment.

As we saw in the example of the shoe factory, the contingency approach encourages the use of any method that answers the needs of the actual situation. The contingency approach also focuses managers' attention on the relationship between the internal environment and the external environment of an organization. The **external environment** consists of the social, political, and economic factors that might affect an organization. The **internal environment** is the environment inside the organization.

According to the contingency approach, managers must be aware of the relationship between these two environments. An automobile manufacturing plant has an internal environment consisting of all the departments involved in putting automobiles together. But the manager must also be concerned with the vast external environment that is affected by the manufacture of automobiles. For example, the public's concern about pollution has required auto makers to devise safe and effective fuel exhaust systems. The external environment, of course, is not limited to "environmental" concerns. It includes all factors (except those involved in the internal operation of the company) that might affect the firm, including the large body of government regulations.

Managers who plan on a contingency basis must be aware of limits, or constraining factors, that exist within their own organizations. The contingency approach acknowledges three basic constraints: technological, task, and human.

Technological constraints derive from the type and flexibility of an organization's means of producing its goods and/or services. Different kinds of organizations require different kinds of technological resources. The machinery and equipment needed in the making of steel, for example, are very costly. Because of these large capital expenditures, it is difficult for steel companies to change their technology quickly to meet new demands.

The kind of technology an organization uses also determines how much interdependence exists among its different segments. The higher the level of interdependence, the more coordination is required—and hence, the more managerial skill. For example, a plant that manufactures complex electrical component systems exhibits a great deal of interdependence among the departments that supply various parts. Considerable managerial skill is required in coordinating this firm's production.

Task constraints arise from the actual nature of the jobs performed by workers. Some employees may work in a methodical manner with little variation in the tasks required to perform their jobs, as is the case for many assembly line workers. Others may be involved in more complex, less predictable jobs, such as those performed in TV manufacturing inspection departments, wherein workers have to spot a variety of defects in the products.

Human constraints reflect the levels of competence of the people employed by an organization. One contingency factor here is what motivates a particular group of workers. Is the manager dealing with a work force primarily interested in salary and job security? Or are the workers more interested in advancement, personal development, and the respect of their peers?

CRITIQUE OF THE CONTINGENCY APPROACH

The systems approach emphasizes the interlocking relationships among the various parts of an organization. By focusing more closely on the nature of these relationships, the contingency approach has sharpened this perspective. As a result, the contingency approach is the foremost approach to management thought today.[28]

The contingency approach, however, is not without its critics.[29] Some maintain that it has little theoretical foundation, which means that it has no base of knowledge, lacks predictive ability, and is essentially intuitive. In rebuttal, defenders argue that one of the most useful answers to the questions "How do we do this?" and "What do we do next?" is "It all depends." In the contingency approach, each situation is examined to determine its unique attributes before a management decision is made. This contrasts markedly with earlier approaches that tended to deal in universal principles that were often not applicable in specific situations. Rather than apply hard-and-fast rules, contemporary managers are expected to analyze the situation and then to draw on all the various schools of thought to invoke whatever combination of managerial techniques appears to be most appropriate.

Review of the Learning Objectives

Having studied this chapter, you should be able to respond to the learning objectives with extensions of the following brief answers.

1. Describe three major schools in the evolution of management thought.

The three major schools in the evolution of management thought are the classical, the behavioral, and the management science schools.

The classical school can be divided into two basic approaches. The scientific management approach focused primarily on the tasks done by workers and sought ways to make production more efficient. The administrative management approach focused more on the overall task of managing large groups of people in complex organizations.

The behavioral school focused on the workers doing their jobs. This approach employed scientific methods derived from psychology, sociology, and other disciplines. Focusing attention on the behavior of workers led to a greater concern for their well-being and increased interest in what motivated them.

The management science school emphasized the need to systematize and quantify the managerial decision-making process. Two integrative perspectives have emerged: the systems approach and the contingency approach. The former advocates exploiting the interrelatedness of the parts of an organization as a means to more effective management. The latter stresses examining the particular situation and drawing from all the schools of management thought whatever techniques seem appropriate.

2. **Define the key attribute of the classical school in terms of its assumptions about human motivation.**

According to the classical model, the worker was motivated almost solely by a desire for financial gain. It viewed the worker as a rational, logical part of a whole system.

3. **Explain the role that time studies have played in scientific management.**

A cornerstone of scientific management was the search for increased productivity through increased worker efficiency. One of the ways devised to make workers more efficient was the time study. In a time study, the motions required for completion of a job could be broken down into their component parts, timed, and analyzed. Such analysis often yielded ways to increase efficiency by reducing time required for the completion of each piece of work.

4. **Discuss the ways in which the administrative approach differs from the scientific approach to management.**

The scientific approach focused on the management of tasks and the creation of greater efficiency among unskilled workers. The administrative approach focused more on the management of people in large, complex organizations wherein production tasks were only one component. Other functions included purchasing raw materials, marketing products, accumulating and investing capital, and designing products.

5. **Explain the significance of the Hawthorne experiments.**

The Hawthorne experiments were a milestone in the behavioral approach to management thought. Among many other discoveries, researchers found that no direct cause-and-effect relationship could be established between a single environmental factor and worker productivity. There also emerged from these experiments evidence of what came to be known as the Hawthorne effect. Productivity in the groups selected for testing seemed to increase merely because they were treated as "special" subjects who had a voice in how their work would be managed.

6. Cite the four key features of the management science school.

The four distinguishing features of the management science school are its emphasis on decision making, the use of quantitative models, the use of computers, and the key role played by the evaluation of a model's effectiveness.

7. **Describe the systems approach and the contingency approach, and explain how they are related to the early schools of management thought.**

Managers who adopt the systems approach view the organization as a single, integrated system of subsystems. The emphasis in the contingency approach is on dealing with problems and situations with an appreciation for their uniqueness. Highly compatible, these two approaches both incorporate the major elements of early schools of management thought.

Key Terms and Concepts

Having completed your study of Chapter 2 on "The Evolution of Management Thought," you should have mastered the following important terms and concepts:

management theories	bureaucracy	systems approach	flow	internal environment
classical school	behavioral school	subsystems	feedback	technological constraints
scientific management	the Hawthorne effect	synergy	contingency approach	task constraints
administrative management	management science school	open system	external environment	human constraints
		closed system		
		boundaries		

Questions for Discussion

1. Why is it important to understand the various management theories that have evolved?

2. What were some of the tools devised by Frederick W. Taylor to increase production? Did these methods take into account the subjective motivations of workers?

3. Which of Fayol's principles still apply today?

4. Explain the transition from the assumptions that characterize the classical school to those that are characteristic of the behavioral school. What were some important reasons for the rise of the behavioral school?

5. In what way can the behavioral school be seen as a synthesis of the two branches of the classical school?

6. Discuss the Hawthorne effect. What are the implications of this phenomenon for the practice of management?

7. What do you think are the major strengths and weaknesses of the three major schools of management thought?

8. Why is it difficult to understand contemporary management without knowing its history?

9. Discuss the limitations of the rational model of human behavior in terms of effective management in the workplace.

10. Why is the systems approach more appropriate today than it would have been in Fayol's time?

Notes

1. Excerpted from R. G. Greenwood, "Harold F. Smiddy: Manager by Inspiration and Persuasion," ed. R. C. Huseman, *Academy of Management Pro-* *ceedings*, pp. 12–15. Copyright © 1979 Academy of Management.

2. H. R. Towne, "The Engineer as an Economist," re-

printed from *Transactions of the American Society of Mechanical Engineers,* 7 (1886): 428–432, in *Papers Dedicated to the Development of Modern Management,* ed. D. A. Wren and J. A. Pearce, II (Atlanta, Ga.: Darby Press, 1986), pp. 3–4.

3. A. Smith, *An Inquiry into the Nature and Causes of the Wealth of Nations* (New York: Modern Library, 1937). Originally published in 1776.

4. A. C. Bluedorn, Review of *Scientific Management* by F. W. Taylor, New York: Harper & Brothers, 1947, *Academy of Management Review* 11, no. 2 (April 1986): 443–447.

5. C. D. Wrege and A. Perroni, "Taylor's Pig-Tale: A Historical Analysis of Frederick W. Taylor's Pig-Iron Experiment," *Academy of Management Journal* 17 (1974): 6–27; and A. C. Bluedorn, T. L. Keon, and N. M. Carter, "Management History Research: Is Anyone Out There Listening?" *Academy of Management Proceedings,* ed. R. B. Robinson, Jr., and J. A. Pearce, II (Atlanta, Ga.: Darby Press, 1985), pp. 130–133.

6. F. W. Taylor, *Scientific Management* (New York: Harper, 1911).

7. R. E. Flanders, *The Functions of Management in American Life* (Stanford: Graduate School of Business, Stanford University, 1929).

8. F. W. Taylor, *Principles of Scientific Management* (New York: Harper, 1911).

9. E. H. Schein, *Organizational Psychology* (Englewood Cliffs, N.J.: Prentice-Hall, 1970), pp. 52–72 and 93–101.

10. D. J. Brass, Review of *The Writings of the Gilbreths,* ed. W. R. Spriegel and C. E. Myers, Homewood, Ill.: Irwin, 1953, *Academy of Management Review* 11, no. 2 (April 1986): 448–451.

11. F. B. Gilbreth and L. M. Gilbreth, *Applied Motion Study* (New York: Sturgis and Walton, 1917).

12. L. M. Gilbreth, "Hiring and Firing: Shall the Calendar Measure Length of Service?" *Factory and Industrial Management* 79 (February 1930): 310–311.

13. J. D. Breeze, "The Harvest from the Archives: The Search for Fayol and Carlioz," ed. K. Chung, *Academy of Management Proceedings* (Atlanta, Ga.: Darby, 1983), pp. 116–120; and N. M. Carter, Review of *General and Industrial Management* by Henri Fayol (C. Storrs, trans.) London: Pitman, 1949, *Academy of Management Review* 11, no. 2 (April 1986): 454–456.

14. A. M. Henderson and T. Parsons, *Max Weber: The Theory of Social and Economic Organization* (New York: Free Press, 1947), pp. 329–333.

15. D. L. Ferry, Review of *Dynamic Administration,* The Collected Works of Mary Parker Follett, ed. H. C. Metcalf and L. Urwick, New York: Harper and Brothers, 1941, *Academy of Management Review* 11, no. 2 (April 1986): 451–454.

16. O. Sheldon, *The Philosophy of Management* (London: Pitman, 1924; reprinted 1965).

17. C. I. Barnard, *The Functions of the Executive* (Cambridge, Mass.: Harvard University Press, 1938).

18. H. Munsterberg, *Psychology and Industrial Efficiency* (New York: Arno Press, reprint of 1913 edition).

19. F. J. Roethlisberger, and W. J. Dickson, *Management and the Worker* (Cambridge, Mass.: Harvard University Press, 1939).

20. L. F. Urwick, "Elton Mayo—His Life and Work," in *Papers and Proceedings XII International Congress of Scientific Management* (Melbourne: CIOS, 1960).

21. A. S. Tannenbaum, *Social Psychology of the Work Organization* (Belmont, Calif: Wadsworth, 1966), pp. 22–24.

22. D. W. Organ, Review of *Management and the Worker* by F. J. Roethlisberger, and W. J. Dickson, New York: Wiley, Science Editions, 1964, *Academy of Management Review* 11, no. 2 (April 1986): 459–464.

23. E. Mayo, *The Human Problems of an Industrial Civilization* (New York: Macmillan, 1953).

24. J. W. Forrester, *Industrial Dynamics* (Cambridge, Mass: MIT Press, 1961).

25. S. Tilles, "The Manager's Job—A Systems Approach," *Harvard Business Review* 41, no. 1 (January–February 1963): 73–81.

26. C. S. George, Jr., *The History of Management Thought* (Englewood Cliffs, N.J.: Prentice-Hall, 1968), p. 133.

27. C. I. Barnard, *The Functions of the Executive* (Cambridge, Mass.: Harvard University Press, 1938), p. 4.

28. F. Luthans, "The Contingency Theory of Management: A Path out of the Jungle," *Business Horizons* 16, no. 3 (June 1973): 62–72.

29. H. Koontz, "The Management Theory Jungle Revisited," *Academy of Management Review* 3, no. 3 (July 1978): 679–682.

Cohesion Incident 2-1

Background for the Charles Richards Incidents

A special feature of this book is its two sets of "cohesion incidents." These short case studies create realistic management situations that are designed to provide practical examples of several of the major points presented in each chapter. The term cohesion reflects the fact that the objective of the two sets of incidents appearing at the end of each chapter is to tie together the management concepts by presenting integrated illustrations. To this end, each set of incidents recounts the managerial experiences of a single individual. Your challenge is to apply the material that you have just learned to these management situations, all of which are based on experiences that we (or our former students) have had early in our (or their) management careers.

There are several important advantages to this unique approach:

1. *You will have the opportunity to follow the careers of two new managers who you will come to know as "real people"; their backgrounds and initial management positions may well parallel your own.*

2. *Witnessing the management problems that they face may help prepare you to face similar problems that you are likely to encounter.*

3. *You will learn not only about people but also about how they are affected by the organizational environments in which they work.*

The cohesion incidents for this chapter provide the introductory backgrounds for subsequent incidents. The first set of incidents describes the management career of Charles Richards, a new college graduate employed in the development program for line managers of a corporation in a service industry. The second set of incidents, by contrast, focuses on Leslie Phillips, who has chosen to begin her management career in a staff position with a more traditional manufacturing firm. Though similar in age and education, these two new managers will encounter strikingly different problems because of differences in the people with whom they work, the companies that employ them, and the industries in which their companies compete. Read and study these two background incidents carefully. The information that they provide will frequently be valuable to you as you analyze the incidents appearing in future chapters.

Charles Richards, a recent university graduate with a B.S. degree in management, has been employed with Journey's End Inns, Inc., for three months. He spent his first month in a training program at the central headquarters of Journey's End, where he became familiar with the policies and procedures used by managers of the various motels. The first few days of his training program were spent discussing the overall objectives and goals of Journey's End and how managers of the various motels structured their day-to-day responsibilities to be consistent with these goals. He was also given examples of performance appraisals that showed how various managers were evaluated on the different aspects of their duties. He discovered that new trainees were first assigned as assistant managers at inns where they developed the skills needed to become managers. Charles viewed videos showing examples of problems a manager might encounter and, with the rest of the trainees, discussed possible ways of resolving such conflicts.

Charles thoroughly enjoyed meeting with the other trainees, learning more about Journey's End, and becoming acquainted with the various management techniques he would be using on the job. After one month's training, he was assigned to be the assistant manager at a large motel in Graniteville, North Carolina.

Graniteville is located in a mountain resort area, and the Journey's End Inn is one of the three national motel chains in the area. The majority of the guests stay at the motel for fewer than five days. During the summer months, the Journey's End Inn is also the site of three to four conventions. Graniteville is the home of the Customer Service Center of a major manufacturer of paper products, Cronor, Inc., and the local Journey's End has contracted with Cronor to provide rooms for its personnel and guests who visit the Customer Service Center.

The Journey's End motel in Graniteville has 450 rooms and has been operating for three years. The motel has two large meeting rooms used for convention purposes, a swimming pool reserved for guests, a restaurant operated by Journey's End that is open from 6:00 A.M. until 10:00 P.M., and a lounge that is open from 5:00 P.M. until midnight. Both the restaurant and the lounge are operated seven days a week.

In his position as assistant manager, Charles reports directly to the manager of the local motel, Roger Elliott. Roger has been with Journey's End for twelve years, having come to Graniteville three years earlier as the first manager of the local Journey's End Inn. Before coming to Graniteville, Roger had been an assistant manager for three years and manager for six years at a Journey's End in Virginia. Charles has found Roger to be extremely hard-working and most cooperative in helping Charles adjust to his role as assistant manager. Roger is innovative and appears to be well respected by the top management of Journey's End.

Roger usually arrives at the motel each morning at 8:30 and leaves around 6:00 P.M. Charles comes in at 2:00 P.M. and stays until the lounge closes at midnight. In addition to Roger and Charles, two other employees have some managerial responsibilities at the Journey's End in Graniteville. These are Susan McNaughton, who is the hostess in the restaurant, and Miles Allen, the bartender in the lounge. Susan is responsible for the operation of the restaurant and has three cooks and eight waitresses reporting to her. There are three waitresses in the lounge; they report to Miles. In addition, five clerks and ten maids report directly to Roger or, in his absence, to Charles.

Journey's End was formed in 1959 when C. H. Flynn, who is still president of the corporation, built one motel in Myrtle Beach, South Carolina. Encouraged by the success he had in Myrtle Beach, Mr. Flynn began building other motels in major resort areas throughout the United States. At first Journey's End followed other major chains into various resort areas, but recently it has taken the first step in building in areas that have the potential to become high-traffic vacation spots. Currently, there are 123 Journey's End Inns located throughout the United States. No attempt has been made to become international.

Top management of Journey's End attributes the firm's success to its properly training managers and giving each manager full responsibility for the operation of his or her motel. The one area in which corporate management retains some control is the setting of room rates. Although the local managers can suggest that room rates be changed for their particular motels, they must have the approval of corporate management before making such changes.

The corporation has been very successful in achieving growth in the industry. It uses current-year profits to build additional motels, and the recently released five-year plan calls for new inns to be built at the rate of five per year for the next five years.

Because most of the costs of the company are fixed (in the form of depreciation and interest expense on money borrowed), the room occupancy rate is a key figure for the firm. Bonuses are paid to individual managers when room occupancy exceeds 75 percent for their inns. Financial management has determined that it takes an overall occupancy rate of 68 percent for the firm to break even (no loss, no profits). Corporate figures on room occupancy, revenue, and profits for the past five years are shown in the following table:

	1988	1987	1986	1985	1984
Room Occupany	79%	76%	74%	76%	75%
Total Revenue*	$212,564	195,481	173,722	164,510	136,841
Total Profit* (after taxes)	$ 10,641	8,141	5,671	6,131	4,611

*Dollar values in thousands.

The corporate philosophy is as follows:

1. Journey's End will continue to expand into high-traffic resort areas as profits permit. The total debt-to-equity ratio will never be higher than 20 percent.

2. Each inn will be appraised on its individual performance, and the manager of each inn will be compensated accordingly. We realize that individual managers are the key to our success and will strive to keep their turnover to less than 5 percent annually.

3. The total average occupancy rate for our corporation will be no lower than 70 percent.

4. We believe our product to be "Service to the Customer" and will strive to treat all guests with respect and meet their needs in an efficient and courteous manner.

5. We consider our inns an integral part of the community in which they reside and expect our inns to conform to the values and needs of such communities.

Cohesion Incident 2-2
Background for the Leslie Phillips Incidents

At age twenty-three, Leslie Phillips is completing her second year with Travis Corporation where, six months before, she was promoted to the position of assistant market researcher in the Electronic Controls Division. The company manufactures and markets vehicular and industrial equipment such as drivetrains, engine and chassis parts, transmission products, and electronic accessories for four markets. These markets are automobiles, small trucks, large trucks, and heavy off-road equipment. Part of Travis Corporation's sales are to the "aftermarket"—that is, to retailers and distributors who specialize in sales and installation of accessories and replacement parts. In addition, Travis sells to manufacturers of original equipment such as General Motors, Ford, and Caterpillar.

Travis Corporation is an international firm with plants in twenty-four countries. Reorganization fifteen years ago reduced the number of corporate staff members from over 500 to 100 and created the decentralized structure shown in the following figure that presently characterizes the company:

Organizational Chart for
Travis Corporation

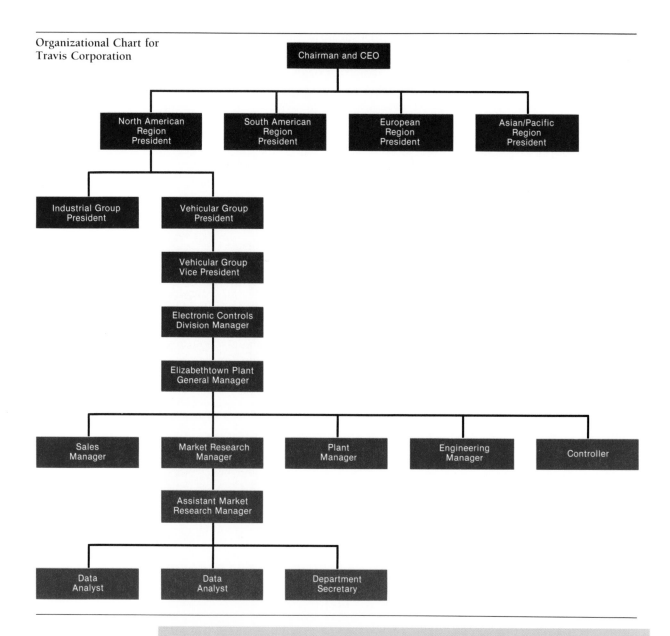

Four international regions (the North American, Central/South American, European, and Asian regions) operate relatively independently, each assessing and addressing the demands of its own markets. In the North American region, sales of equipment for large and small vehicles have steadily outpaced sales of industrial equipment. Vehicular markets now account for over 80 percent of net sales. Over 30 percent of these vehicular sales are made to two major original-equipment customers, General Motors and Ford.

The North American region includes seventeen product divisions that function more or less as independent companies. Each product division is responsible for its own market research, product development, manufacturing, sales, shipping, and financial control. Leslie Phillips is employed at the Elizabethtown plant, one of four in the Electronic Controls Division. This plant manufactures Cruise-o-Matic, a cruise control device, and Autoalarm, an antitheft device. Like other Travis plants, the Elizabethtown facility is run by a general manager who has considerable latitude and operates the plant in an entrepreneurial fashion.

Last year the Elizabethtown general manager, Peter Bostic, decided to divide the sales and market research functions of the plant into two separate departments. The Market Research Department, under the direction of the market research manager, is responsible for planning and conducting market research, maintaining product competition files, compiling and interpreting customer feedback, recommending changes in product lines, serving as liaison between the Sales and the Engineering Departments, and designing and implementing marketing strategy.

Eileen Thompkins, thirty-two, was hired as market research manager and given the task of organizing and staffing the department. Eileen has been with Travis Corporation for eight years. She has a college degree in accounting and a master's degree in library science. This combination led her into a job as assistant librarian for an accounting firm and then to a position as corporate librarian in Travis's Corporate Marketing Department. From that position she was recruited into the Trucking Division as a sales representative and became one of the first women to join that sales force in its midwestern and southern territories. Her sales performance was outstanding. Within two years her broad knowledge of the vehicular products and her research skills were noted by the manager of the Electronic Controls Division. As a result, she was recommended to the general manager of the Elizabethtown plant as a candidate for the newly created position of market research manager. Upon her arrival at the Elizabethtown plant, Eileen hired a staff of four: two data analysts and a department secretary, all of whom report to the assistant market research manager.

Leslie Phillips was hired as assistant market research manager with almost two years of experience with Travis Corporation. After graduating from college with a degree in psychology, Leslie worked for six months as data analyst in the Sales and Marketing Department of the Mt. Tipton plant of Travis's Electronic Controls Division. She then moved into the job of sales representative in the same department. Once she has settled into her new position in the Elizabethtown Market Research Department, she plans to enroll in an evening MBA program at State University. She hopes this additional education will help her advance further at Travis.

The two data analysts were hired immediately after their graduation from State University. Bill Sherman, twenty-two, signed on four months ago and has since worked conscientiously and accurately on all assigned tasks. He seldom initiates projects beyond the specific analyses assigned to him, however, and has shown minimal creativity in his work. Steven Macy, twenty-one, joined the department just one month ago and is still "in training." As data analysts, Bill and Steve have responsibilities that include programming, tabulating and analyzing data, and writing reports. As they become more experienced, their responsibilities will include other aspects of market research.

Rounding out the new Market Research Department is Harriet Wilcox, thirty-nine, the department secretary. She has worked at Travis's Elizabethtown plant for eight years. In that time she was promoted from the secretarial pool to secretary for the Engineering Department and then to secretary for the Sales Department. When the Market Research Department was created, she expressed interest in the position of data analyst but was not encouraged to apply for the job. The personnel manager recommended that she seek education beyond her high school degree if she wanted to pursue similar positions in the future. She then applied for the job of secretary to the new department and was hired. She hopes this experience will further expand her knowledge of the different departments and their functions. Harriet is extremely competent in her job. Her range of experience already gives her a broad understanding of the Elizabethtown plant and the Electronic Controls Division. Thus she is a major asset to the Market Research Department. Harriet is committed to Travis Corporation and has often been heard to describe working there as "like being part of a family." She seeks new challenges in her work, however, and would like to assume greater responsibilities at the plant.

As the Market Research Department gears up to meet its new responsibilities, there is an air of optimism about the plant. In its most recent annual report, Travis Corporation reported record sales of $4.5 billion (a 25 percent increase over the previous year) and net profits of $230 million (70 percent higher than the year before). This was welcome relief following a four-year slump that had seen sales, profits, plant utilization, and employment levels plummet. Improvements were attributed to cost reductions, greater productivity, penetration of new markets, and the commitment of Travis's employees. At the Elizabethtown facility, Leslie Phillips is optimistic about the coming year and sees the Market Research Department playing a major role.

Management Development Exercise 2
Modern Bureaucracy

The following exercise will enable you to determine how comfortable you are likely to be in a modern bureaucratic organization. Simply circle the number after each statement that reflects the extent to which you agree with it. After you have completed the exercise, your instructor will help you to calculate and interpret your score.

1. Goal setting should be a method for putting into practice the organization's strategic plan.   4   3   2   1

2. Training and development activities should provide a forum for instructing organization members in important policies and procedures.   4   3   2   1

3. Roles and responsibilities in an organization should be determined on the basis of tasks and situations.   4   3   2   1

4. Performance appraisals should be used to give rewards or administer sanctions, based on an individual's work activity.   4   3   2   1

5. The organizational chart should provide a simplified but helpful structure for examining and understanding the organization.   4   3   2   1

6. Problem solving should be a step-by-step rational process to resolve organizational issues.   4   3   2   1

7. Conflict should be best dealt with through rational examination of the issues and resolution by higher authority.   4   3   2   1

8. Strategic planning should be aimed at developing clear action plans that are recognized and understood by everyone.   4   3   2   1

9. Decision making should involve an accepted, rational sequence of steps that, if followed, will lead to a sound conclusion.

    4   3   2   1

10. Career planning should help the organizaton set up stable long-range plans based on the most efficient use of individuals' talents.

    4   3   2   1

11. People should be motivated to achieve by concrete rewards for performance.

    4   3   2   1

12. The most important function of organizational communication should be the development of a shared understanding of the nature of the organization.

    4   3   2   1

13. Meetings should be forums for organized discussion and, as appropriate, decision making.

    4   3   2   1

14. Clear rules and policies should be the basis for running a smoothly functioning organization.

    4   3   2   1

15. Promotions should be ways of recognizing effective task performance and rationally using human resources to the organization's best advantage.

    4   3   2   1

Source: This exercise was developed from materials presented in M. Sashkin and W. C. Morris, *Experiencing Management* (Reading, Mass.: Addison-Wesley, 1987), pp. 10–17. Reprinted with permission.

3

Managerial Decision Making

Your study of this chapter will enable you to do the following:

1. Explain the differences between programmed and nonprogrammed decisions.
2. Explain the difference between the centralized and decentralized approaches to decision making.
3. Define the concept of bounded rationality and explain why it is important to the decision-making process.
4. Explain why individual psychology is important in understanding people's conflicting styles of decision making.
5. List and describe the five basic steps in decision making.
6. Describe some of the conditions under which decisions are made.
7. Explain the value of several technical tools that enhance managerial decision making.

Managerial Decision Making at Citicorp

In 1987 Citicorp was among the most prestigious and powerful financial institutions in the world; its flagship, Citibank, was the largest bank in the United States. Yet top managers of the massive corporation, including its new chairman John S. Reed, knew that Citicorp would have to make daring or even controversial decisions to remain on top in the next decade.

There were many challenges to Citicorp's bold plan to become a global superpower in individual, institutional, and investment banking, in insurance, and in information technology—the Five I's. Nearly all Citicorp's markets had become more competitive, and the days of easy growth had gone. At home, Citicorp faced rising competition from financial-service companies, which were moving in on the sacred ground that banks once had to themselves. And there was increased competition from abroad—five Japanese banks were now among the top ten in the world. Amid these more general threats, Reed and his top managers faced more specific problems. Aiming to make Citicorp the largest bank in the world, the previous chairman, Walter B. Wriston, had skimped on capital to propel the bank into a rapid period of growth. The growth was grand but also dubious.

One result of this fast growth was a diminished safety cushion of capital— the corporation's primary capital equaled only 6.6 percent of its assets, below average for money-center banks. With $186 billion in assets, the corporation had a lackluster year in 1985. In 1986, earnings per share were down for the first nine months by 6 percent; profitability declined and expenses rose by 21 percent later in that year.

To deal with challenges to Citicorp's primacy, top managers knew they had to focus on the long haul, and their planning was fixed in terms of decades, not quarters or years. Managers said they did not feel compelled to exhibit short-term performance at the expense of long-term stability. Yet Citicorp officials remained worried about such pressing issues as defaults on their loans to troubled developing countries and write-offs on loans to corporate customers that were running twice the normal rate.

John S. Reed's dynamic and innovative decision-making style underlies his success as chairman of Citicorp. (David Burnett/Contact/ Woodfin Camp & Associates)

Reed's strategy was to strengthen the bank internally. Between the start of 1985 and the latter part of 1986, he increased Citicorp's total capital position by 70 percent to $20.3 billion, a figure three to five times the total capital of its major competitors. Reed hoped to build a capital base of $30.3 million. Instead of working toward this goal by selling off some of the corporation's more attractive assets, such as high-priced office buildings, Reed elected to build the capital more steadily out of income. This decision meant that earnings per share in 1986 dropped from $8.50 to about $7. In accordance with Reed's long-range goal of building up capital from income, he planned steps to make costly acquisitions designed to strengthen the bank on the deposit-taking side. Among the hoped-for acquisitions were large banks in Japan and Britain.

Although Reed was committed to nurturing all the Five I's, it was doubtful in 1986 that he would see significant returns from the institutional and investment areas, and the insurance and information industries in which the corporation was involved were still considered a long way from prosperity. He decided to stake his future on the individual, or consumer, bank. Some observers pointed out that Reed seemed to be walking on a tightwire, that the individual bank might have trouble growing because so many consumers were already carrying too much debt. In 1986, Citicorp had to write off nearly a billion dollars in consumer loans, most in credit-card balances.

Despite these liabilities, top management at the individual bank believed that the bank's earnings—$400 million or more in 1986—would be doubled in five years. They predicted that consumer losses would decline over the next several years. They also expected another big boost to come as barriers to interstate banking fell and Citicorp expanded into more and more states. Another reason for optimism on the part of managers was that Citicorp was increasingly becoming a global consumer bank, with a soaring portfolio of consumer loans that now accounted for more than half of its total portfolio.

Although other big New York City banks have discovered consumer banking, Citicorp's early push has put it well ahead of the competition. Today one in every five families in the United States does business with Citicorp. Citicorp's individual bank has grown bigger than any other U.S. bank except BankAmerica. For the past five years, consumer revenues have been growing at 30 percent a year, three times faster than the wholesale banking side, which lends to corporations and governments.

Reed bet his future on the success of the individual bank, since he believed risks are more satisfactorily predicted in that area than in other banking areas. His strategy seems to be paying off.[1]

Introduction

What Is Decision Making?

Decision making is the process of choosing a course of action from two or more alternatives. A **decision** is a conscious choice to behave or to think in a particular way in a given set of circumstances. When a choice has been made, a decision has been made.[2] Decision making cannot really be avoided, because explicitly to avoid making a decision is in itself to make a decision. It has been said that the only real problem in life is what to do next. In this sense, human beings make decisions at every interval in their lives when they are not preoccupied by a particular activity. When people finish their work and are presented with leisure time, for example, they may consider playing chess, going to a movie, or taking a walk. Choosing one of these alternatives is making a decision, just as much as Reed's choice among alternatives at Citicorp.

Decisions are part of everyday life. Most decisions are made reflexively; we do not pause to review the reasons for these decisions, to predict their effects, or to evaluate their results. However, the quality of management decisions is apparent in the effects they have on an organization. They are public decisions because their consequences extend far beyond the individual or the family to people in an organization. Deciding where to take a family vacation, on the one hand, is a private decision because it does not involve people outside the family. On the other hand, a managerial decision about a company vacation plan is a public decision because it affects the lives of people in a public workplace.

In this chapter we will explore the art and science of managerial decision making. The emphasis will be on proven approaches for addressing decision situations that will result in respected and effective organizational achievement.

Programmed and Nonprogrammed Decisions

All decisions fall into one of two basic categories. They are programmed decisions or nonprogrammed decisions.

Programmed decisions are made on the basis of established policies, rules, or procedures. For example, when a manager at General Electric receives a request for a raise from a machine operator, the decision whether to grant the request is programmed. As is the case in most large, complex organizations (and partly because of worker organization), GE has an established wage structure. Not only is the wage structure fixed for the organization, but it is also likely to be written into the organization's contract with a union, if the plant is unionized. The decision whether to grant the raise is likely to be answered in accordance with policy already set, or programmed.

Nonprogrammed decisions are not bound by policy, rules, or procedures. The nonprogrammed decision is usually made in cases of exceptional or novel problems, and it typically involves the broad use of managerial initiative and judgment. For example, in reviewing the request of the machine operator for a raise, managers might discover an ambiguity in GE policy regarding calculation of the time an individual has accumulated as an employee of GE. Let us say that the policy states that paid sick leave is included in the time accumulated as an employee but neglects to say whether an unpaid extension of this sick leave is also included. The machine operator is counting as accumulated time the time he spent on unpaid sick leave; his supervisor is not. In this situation, a nonprogrammed decision is required. Managers, in conjunction with union leaders, will have to make or negotiate important decisions clarifying the policy itself. Moreover, managers will have to make a decision on the individual request of the machine operator.

The categories of programmed and nonprogrammed decisions are not mutually exclusive. The line between a programmed and a nonprogrammed decision is sometimes a fine one. It may help to view decisions on a continuum between totally programmed decisions and totally nonprogrammed decisions.[3]

In the case of the machine operator, a routine request for a raise, which might have called for a programmed decision, brought to light an ambiguity in a company policy on wage scales. If the policy had specified exactly what constituted an employee's total accumulated time, the decision would have been programmed. But because the policy was ambiguous on this issue, a nonprogrammed decision was necessary.

Clearly, it is in the best interests of managers to avoid having to make nonprogrammed decisions on such routine matters as pay raises. The practical lesson to be learned from this example is that policies and procedures—from which programmed decisions are routinely made—should be as explicit as possible. Gaps in existing policies should be identified and eliminated. In this example, the managers would have profited by raising *before the fact* the questions of whether unpaid sick leave—and if so, how much of it—counted as accumulated time with the company. Such foresight would have saved the firm from having to make a time-consuming nonprogrammed decision later.

Types of Programmed and Nonprogrammed Decisions

Labeling and defining various kinds of decisions have an important practical value: Categorizing decisions suggests courses of action, and it helps managers frame their decisions and examine their motives in making particular choices. The types of decisions described in the following paragraphs are presented as opposite pairs of decision types. The type that appears first is typically a programmed decision; the second is more likely to be nonprogrammed.

ORGANIZATIONAL VERSUS PERSONAL DECISIONS

Organizational decisions are made by managers within the formal limits of their official roles and authority. *Personal decisions,* on the other hand, are made by managers as private individuals. Organizational decisions are frequently programmed in the sense that they are often delegated to subordinates. Personal decisions cannot, by definition, be delegated to others.[4] For example, a manager who fires a subordinate because of excessive absence from the job is making an organizational decision. However, if the manager fires the subordinate because of a fight the subordinate had with the manager's brother (who is not an employee), the manager is making a decision based on personal, not organizational, reasons. Thus it would be labeled a personal decision. The distinction between organizational and personal decisions helps define the interaction between subjective human factors (anger, resentment, a personal interest in an employee) and objective organizational goals and needs (harmony in the workplace, competitive productivity). The distinction helps managers focus on a basic question behind decision making: Is the decision in the interests of the organization or merely in my own interest?

OPERATIONAL VERSUS STRATEGIC DECISIONS

This distinction reflects the scope of the decision-making process. *Operational decisions* are made on a day-to-day basis and are often carried out by middle- to low-level management. They are generally part of short-range plans. For example, a manager who makes work assignments for employees is often guided by company policies and plans. This kind of decision lies at the programmed end of the continuum; it allows for limited initiative and discretion on the part of the manager. *Strategic decisions* are made in response to new and complex problems and often deal with such broad variables as the state of the economy, competition with competitors, or negotiations with labor unions.[5] A decision to engage in advertising that mentions a specific competitor (such as the Burger King ad making light fun of the "fixed" garnishes on McDonald's hamburgers) is a strategic decision.

RESEARCH VERSUS CRISIS-INTUITIVE DECISIONS

This distinction reflects the degree of urgency in the decision-making process. A *research decision* is one made under little time pressure. For example, say Procter & Gamble's product manager wanted to determine who would buy Head & Shoulders dandruff shampoo. The decision to use surveys to determine the nature of this market would be a research decision. A *crisis-intuitive decision* is a spontaneous decision made in response to a particular emergency. For example, the managers of a company that makes aluminum siding might suddenly decide to radically and temporarily increase production of their product in the wake of a devastating tornado in a particular region. The decision would be made quickly, on the assumption that massive rebuilding would create enormous short-term demand for the product. Caution: Crisis-intuitive decisions often contain an element of emotional response that may or may not be logically justified. And decisions based on the intuition (meaning the experience) of the manager may or may not be good ones.[6]

OPPORTUNITY VERSUS PROBLEM-SOLVING DECISIONS

This distinction reflects the degree of foresight in decision making. An *opportunity decision* is one made by managers who are looking for ways to reap future benefits for their organizations. A decision to branch out into a new area of product manufacture when a company is already earning a good profit with its current products is an opportunity decision. In many cases, when a company decides to diversify to get into new areas of production, its managers are making an opportunity decision. A *problem-solving decision,* on the other hand, is a decision made

---

Guidelines for Management Practice

Categorizing decisions is no mere academic exercise. In fact, it has important practical value.

1. By identifying some decisions as research decisions and others as crisis decisions, managers can compare the number of crisis decisions they are making to the number of research decisions.

2. Managers should plan ahead to reduce the incidence of crisis decisions. And often, allotting more time to research decisions pays off by reducing the number of crisis decisions that have to be made.

3. A large number of crisis decisions made over a relatively short period of time might indicate that managers have become so bogged down in "fire fighting" that their firm is no longer being guided by carefully developed, long-range plans. In this case the labeling of decisions could lead to notable improvements in the firm's decision making.

in response to a particular problem. For example, a breakdown of equipment on an assembly line presents a particular problem to be solved and therefore calls for a problem-solving decision.

Decision-Making Approaches

Just as managers have to make various types of decisions, organizatons exhibit a variety of approaches to the process of decision making.

The Centralized Versus the Decentralized Approach

In an organizational setting, the *centralized approach* to decision making calls for as many decisions as possible to be made by top management. For example, major decisions on the future of Citicorp were made by Chairman John Reed and a small group of top managers. Specifically, Reed's decision to strengthen the consumer banking area of Citicorp was a major, highly centralized decision. It was made by one man at the highest level of management.

Even under a highly centralized system, certain decisions about the operation of the consumer bank could be made at lower management levels at Citicorp. For example, a middle-level manager might be delegated the responsibility of engaging a consulting firm to determine, via a queuing study, how best to minimize the lines of customers that form at a number of the division's savings and loan institutions. In any corporation as complex as Citicorp, many decisions have to be made by middle management or at the supervisory levels. However, in the centralized approach, the tendency is to push as many decisions as practical to the highest levels.

The *decentralized approach* encourages managers to delegate responsibility, enabling decisions to be made at the lowest possible management level. This approach keeps top managers such as Reed from being bogged down in small details of everyday operations. Under a decentralized approach, the middle-level manager at the consumer bank who was assigned to oversee the queuing study would have had considerable leeway in solving any specific problems that arose. One obvious advantage of the decentralized approach is that it gives greater responsibility and decision-making power to people at the lower management levels. The extent of decentralization in decision making is a function of several influences. These include the preferences of individual managers, organizational dynamics, and, as evidenced in Insights for International Managers 3, even cultural influences.

The Group Versus the Individual Approach

In the *group approach* to decision making, a manager and one or more employees work together on the same problem. The *individual approach* is decision making by one manager. Research by J. K. Murninghan has helped clarify the advantages and disadvantages of these two approaches.[7]

The individual approach is often preferable when the time available for the making of a decision is short or the cost of a group decision is prohibitive. On the other hand, group decision making is often better when managers have enough time and resources to make and implement a group decision. An important advantage of group decision making is that it gives the decision makers a chance to gather more information to use in generating alternative solutions. The use of the

---

Insights for International Managers 3

CONTINUUM OF INTERNATIONAL DECISION-MAKING STYLES

Americans pride themselves on their ability to delegate effectively. Authority and responsibility are dispersed throughout the average U.S. organization. Moreover, delegation allows for flexibility. If an issue does not fall in a specific, prescribed area, some department will eventually take responsibility, even if only after some shuffling.

Actually, Americans seem to be about in the middle on a continuum of decision making/delegation styles, from totally authoritarian and centralized patterns on one extreme to the very participatory style of the Japanese on the other. In the center with us appear to be many Scandinavian and Australian concerns—in both countries, distance between those with authority and their subordinates is small. Nevertheless, American managers in those countries often find unexpected differences. For example, as far as Americans are concerned, Swedes violate the corporate chain of command. When Swedes need information, they'll go directly to the source, even if this means by-passing their immediate bosses. Managers in Sweden are much more conductors, planners or diplomats than their American counterparts. When managing Swedes, you need not feel threatened when an employee goes over your head.

Source: From L. Copeland and L. Griggs, *Going International* (New York: Random House, 1985), p. 123.

---

group approach is based on two assumptions: (1) groups make better decisions than individuals and (2) group decisions are easier to implement.[8] If group decision making is a managerial option, managers must decide, for each case, whether to involve others in making the decision.

The Participatory Versus the Nonparticipatory Approach

In the *participatory approach,* managers solicit input from the people who will be affected by the decision being made. A manager who is contemplating a change in shift schedules might ask for the opinions of the workers who work under the current schedule.

Research suggests that the success of the participatory approach depends on the nature of the problem.[9] Allowing employees to participate in decisions that directly affect them often boosts morale and increases the chance of their accepting the decision. On the other hand, if the decision does not result in changes that directly affect employees, the participatory approach may waste time and cause unnecessary concern and confusion.

The participatory approach is related to the group approach in that both involve more than one person in helping to make the decision. It is not the same as the group approach, however. In the group approach, the group makes the decision and a group of people actually meets. In the participatory approach, the manager may reserve the right to make the final decision. The manager solicits input from other people, but a group of people is not necessarily called together. The participatory approach can be seen as a process of consultation: The decision maker seeks information and suggestions but may or may not invite others to share directly in making the decision.

One of the weakest forms of participatory decision making is the suggestion box, in which employees are invited to give their views on a particular problem by dropping signed or unsigned written comments in a box for managers to read and consider. Those who sign their suggestions may be invited to offer direct input on the solution of the problem. On a higher plane, when a manager at Citibank must decide whether to hire a consulting firm to conduct technical studies in individual banks, he or she consults other bank officers who have made similar decisions, soliciting information and suggestions. These other people are part of a participatory approach. They know that they are contributing to the making of a particular decision, but they do not bear responsibility for actually deciding. For example, the Citibank manager might delegate to an operations manager the task of screening the group of consulting firms that submit proposals on the queuing study to determine what subgroup of firms the senior manager should consider further.

At one of the highest levels of participation, employees make up work teams that are largely self-managed. See "In Practice 3-1" for examples of such work teams. Managers who adopt the *nonparticipatory approach* prefer to gather information, assess the alternatives, and make decisions without relying directly on input from others.

The Democratic Versus the Consensus Approach

In the *democratic approach,* decisions are made on the basis of majority rule. This approach is rarely used in business organizations because it tends to polarize voting participants into "winners" and "losers" on any given question. Furthermore, the democratic approach is apt to conflict with the hierarchical arrangements of most organizations.

An alternative is the *consensus approach,* which involves many participants in the making of a decision but seeks agreement among all participants. The consensus approach is usually practiced as a form of the group approach. The focus is on soliciting viewpoints from as many as possible of the people affected by the decision and then attempting to forge general agreement. Voting is often prohibited

---

Guidelines for Management Practice

Managers should be aware that the use of group and participatory approaches offers the following obvious advantages:

1. The problem prevention capabilities of the group are enhanced because the causes and importance of problems are more widely understood.

2. The best solution alternatives are likely to be generated and selected because of the group's broader and deeper perspectives on a problem.

3. Employee motivation increases with a greater appreciation of the productivity-rewards relationships involved in a plan.

4. Resistance to change is reduced because of the reduced uncertainty for employees involved in organizational changes.

Despite these important advantages of group and participatory approaches, there are also some drawbacks. Among the disadvantages of group decision making that managers should keep in mind are the following issues:

1. The increased amount of time it takes to reach a decision.

2. The negative effects of participating managers' having to spend time away from their subordinates.

3. The frustration that participants may experience when their involvement does not lead to the outcomes they desired.[10]

━━━━━━━━━━━━━━━━━━━━━━━ *In Practice 3-1* ━━━━━━━━━━━━━━━━━━━━━━━

WHAT MAKES WORK TEAMS SUCCEED?

Work teams came to this country from the English coal mines and, for the most part, have not transplanted well. Quality circles, imported from Japan, are still only tenuously grafted onto American business methods. The failure of these and other participative movements to catch on widely in this country has little to do with results. When quality circles and autonomous work groups work, they show impressive results. Why, then, is there so much resistance to the notion of letting employees work smarter?

Experts such as Raymond E. Miles, dean of the University of California's business school at Berkeley, believe that "the problem with participative management is that it works."

General Electric has initiated almost ninety work teams in the past twenty years. Though the teams made productivity gains in nearly all instances, most have disappeared or dwindled. A survey of former team members found that they did not want to see the teams end but believed that general foremen, top management, and non-team members did. "The most important condition for the success of work teams," says management consultant Billie Alban, "is that the management above the plant understands and buys into the philosophy and values that are involved."

In addition, she points out, top management must demonstrate its commitment to a number of difficult changes: in work design, in organizational structure, and in information and measurement systems, to name just a few. There must be a reward system that recognizes team effort and values people's input to the team, and there must be performance appraisal of the team as a team.

It is the complexity and difficulty of achieving such changes that sink most work teams. Among the survivors, most started from scratch at new sites like Digital's Enfield plant or Exxon's Venetia refinery. TRW and Procter & Gamble have also had success with work teams at new plant sites.

Bill Byham, whose firm Development Dimensions International trains managers and others in participative skills, believes that work teams offer their members a strong psychological incentive to participate and benefit from the energy of group process techniques. But his chief condition for success is plenty of training for the workers and their supervisors. In a work team setting, both groups need particular skills. Workers may need training in taking initiative while supervisors need to learn nonmanagement leadership.

Wilson Learning Corporation recently surveyed twenty companies on the design of high performance work teams. Vice president for curriculum development, Steve Buchholtz, summarizes the following ingredients for success:

- Authentic participation

- Wide scope of activities (many problems to solve or many solutions to deal with)

- Ideas consistent with the organization's culture

- Perception of trust

- Rewards for participants spelled out clearly

in this process of seeking a consensus. Some observers have pointed out two negative phenomena that can arise in the group process: domination of the group by one or more individuals and "groupthink."[11] *Groupthink* is a process whereby, in response to social pressure, individuals go along with a decision even when they do not agree with it and, in order to avoid conflicts, do not even voice their reservations.[12] In these instances, the decision is usually made by a relatively small number of group members but is accorded the status of a legitimate consensus.

Group decision making is more open to conflicts of personality and other subjective obstacles than other approaches. In addition to monitoring the time and cost of the group decision-making process, managers should be aware that it sometimes discourages individual initiative.

Figure 3-1 offers a brief comparison of the eight approaches to decision making that have been discussed in this chapter.

Decision-Making Concepts

So far we have defined decision making and examined different types of decisions and various approaches to decision making. In this section we will discuss concepts that underlie the decision-making process itself.

Bounded Rationality

Bounded rationality refers to the limitations of thought, time, and information that restrict a manager's view of problems and situations. According to Nobel Prize laureate Herbert Simon, managers work within the concept of bounded rationality. They try to make the most logical decisions possible, given the limitations on information and their imperfect ability to assimilate and analyze that information.[13] To acknowledge bounded rationality is to guard against unproductive pursuit of "the perfect solution" and to recognize that problem solving is an ongoing process. Managers want to minimize the chances of creating unnecessary problems by making short-sighted decisions, but they must realize that the solution to one problem may not cover subsequent problems that may arise.

Ideally, decision making would be a completely rational, logical process in which all relevant information was acquired, all the time needed was available, and all managers involved attached the same importance to all the data collected. As suggested in Figure 3-2, however, completely rational decision making is constrained in the real world by limitations of time, money, materials, human resources, and incomplete information.

When managers acknowledge their bounded rationality, they no longer seek the ideal solution to every problem, nor do they expect to make ideal decisions. They seek a *satisficing* (satisfactory) solution[14] to each problem rather than searching for the maximizing (optimal, or best) possible solution.

Even when these constraints are minimal, managers may have to face major external constraints in working toward their objectives. One such constraint is

FIGURE 3-1
Summary of Decision
Approaches

Approach	Key Idea
Centralized	As many decisions as possible are made by top management.
Decentralized	The delegation of authority is encouraged.
Group	Two or more people work together to make decisions.
Individual	One manager makes the decisions.
Participatory	Managers solicit input from others.
Nonparticipatory	Managers do not solicit input from others.
Democratic	Decisions are made on basis of majority rule.
Consensus	Many participants are involved, but general agreement is sought.

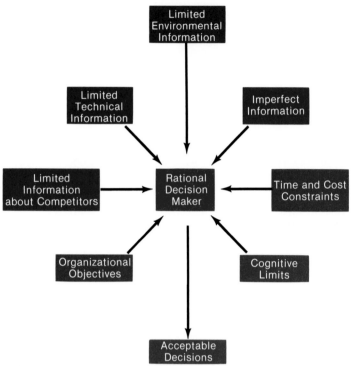

Source: Adapted from H. F. Frank, *The Managerial Decision-Making Process,* 2nd ed. Copyright © 1981 by Houghton Mifflin Company. Adapted with permission.

FIGURE 3-2
Factors Enforcing
Bounded Rationality

public or industry opinion. The ability to anticipate such major constraints is a key managerial skill. For example, George Keller, chairman of Chevron Corporation, made a public proposal for government support to "prop up" domestic oil prices, possibly by imposing import tariffs. However, Keller also explicitly recognized the consensus of opinion in the oil industry, which has long opposed government price intervention.[15] Although industry observers gave Keller's proposal little chance of being accepted by Congress, he may have increased his chances of being taken seriously by publicly acknowledging the constraint that the industry's opinion imposed.

Managers should beware of the conflicting pressures to find the best possible solution on the one hand and, on the other, to find a solution that will merely suffice. The theoretical impossibility of perfection expressed in the principle of bounded rationality should not be used as an excuse not to conduct a productive search for reasonable alternatives. Similarly, the principle of satisficing should not be used to thwart the search for a better solution.

The Practice of Decision Making

Irrespective of the approach a decision maker decides to follow, there are certain steps that managers take in the course of actually making decisions. As shown in Figure 3-3, the process can be broken down into six steps: (1) define the problem, (2) establish objectives, (3) generate alternative solutions, (4) select an alternative, (5) implement the decision, and (6) evaluate the effects of the decision. Let us examine each of these steps in turn.

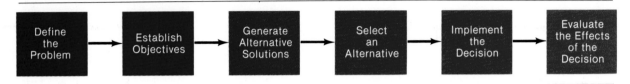

FIGURE 3-3
Steps in the Decision-
Making Process

Define the Problem

A problem is any deviation from a set of expectations.[18] The process of discovering a problem includes identifying and defining the problem. **Problem identification** is the process of establishing that some sort of problem exists. The sources from which a manager can learn of the existence of a problem include personal observations, analysis of available data and company documents, and the public, including customers and critics of the organization. A manager's peers and subordinates are also valuable sources of problem identification. An instrument that can help your employees point you in the right direction when it comes to identifying problems within your work unit is provided in "Management Development Exercise 3."

Managers often become aware of a problem from two or more of these sources. For example, the company that manufactures Nifty Flyer balsa wood toy airplanes might discover that a rubber band necessary for their use has been omitted from certain assembly kits. It is likely that the manager will learn of this problem from retailers of the toy, who have learned of it from dissatisfied customers.

Problem definition is the process of determining the scope and nature of a problem once it has been identified. Say that shortly after New Year's the president of the toy company that makes the balsa wood planes received a letter from a young boy in Topeka describing his disappointment on Christmas morning when his eagerly awaited Nifty Flyer plane was missing the crucial rubber band. A problem has been identified, but it remains to be defined. Is this an isolated incident? The company manufactured and packed nearly 800,000 Nifty Flyer model balsa wood plane kits before the Christmas season. To identify the scope of the problem, sales managers might make spot checks of retailers to see if there have been other complaints about missing rubber bands. Once managers determine whether or not the incident is isolated, the scope of the problem has been defined.

Note, however, that the cause of the problem has not been determined. Defining the scope of a problem is not the same as determining its cause or source; problem definition is only an estimate of the extent and the degree of seriousness of the problem. Even so, the results often dictate whether the investigation will proceed further.

Little benefit, for example, would be derived from having managers undertake a complete review of the Nifty Flyer package assembly process if the rubber band were rarely missing. On the other hand, if a pattern of missing parts emerged in retail outlets throughout the country, company managers would probably want to consider instigating an extensive review of the assembly packing system.

Consider a third scenario. Suppose very few of the planes lacked the rubber band but this one case garnered wide publicity in the newspapers as an example of the shortcomings of Santa Claus in an age of mass production. In the face of this public relations nightmare, top managers might make an opportunity decision: Let the company president fly to Topeka and present the boy with a brand new

Nifty Flyer. Thus a single defective item is deftly used to advertise the company's concern for quality and customer satisfaction—and much newsworthy goodwill is achieved at very little cost.

The important point is that discovering the scope of the problem helps define the company's response. In the late 1970s the general public was alarmed by defects in Firestone radial tires. Yet the "big picture" was much larger than the controversial and highly publicized safety issue and recall of the radial tire. Firestone Chairman John J. Nevin had been told to improve the balance sheet of the company, and by October of 1979 corporate debt had been cut by about half (to $504 million). To do so, however, required closing several tire manufacturing facilities, cutting back on inventory, and selling a subsidiary plastics company, all of which contributed to production difficulties such as those that plagued the corporation's radial tire production. In this case, the road to recovery involved a broad restructuring of the company, not just the elimination of a single product defect.

In January of 1987, Volkswagen, the parent West German makers of the Audi 5000S automobile, announced a recall of this car model because of extensive problems with the vehicle's acceleration system. Audi's first response was to disclaim responsibility for accidents alleged to have been caused by a malfunction in the car. Next they promised to install special locks on this and other models to prevent the sudden acceleration of the vehicle. However, as the full extent of the problem became known, company officials decided to recall the car.

The scope of the problem turned out to be larger than Audi had anticipated. Over 500 complaints were received, and four deaths were alleged to have been caused by defects in the car. Publicity over the problem in the United States media contributed to a 16 percent decline in U.S. sales (a decline equal to $3.3 billion). The problem was how to recall the Audi 5000S while maintaining rapport with possible customers. Before the recall, company officials announced a new Audi line called the 4000S; they simultaneously launched a huge ad campaign directed at selling customers and potential customers on the reliability of the Audi 5000S.

The process of identifying and defining a problem often helps managers determine how later steps in the process of decision making should be carried out. If only isolated malfunctioning of the Audi 5000S or of the Firestone radial tires had occurred, the managers might not have been compelled to take such a drastic step as recalling the product.

Establish Objectives

Defining the problem is followed by setting objectives that will serve as the basis by which the decision to solve the problem will be made. Managers should ask themselves, "What do I hope to accomplish by this decision? And what assumptions will be implicit in the decision I make?" Managers need to agree on their basic assumptions and objectives when evaluating decision options.

Consider Zenith Electronics Corporation's approach to a marketing problem. In 1979 Zenith acquired a large personal computer line with its $64.5 million purchase of Heath Company. Business customers were Zenith's target market for personal computers. But sales were poor. Most top Zenith executives were in favor of an expensive advertising and marketing campaign to wedge their wares into the computer stores where business people shopped. However, one executive (Jerry K. Pearlman, then a chief financial officer) argued that such a strategy was too risky. "If we spend $10 million dollars and sell 100,000 units, that's great. But what if we only sell 10,000 units?" he asked. Pearlman argued that Zenith would do better to cut its prices and concentrate on market sales to a few potential high-volume customers such as universities and government agencies. Such a strategy, he said, would not require expensive advertising.

The objective of making this decision at Zenith was the same for both Pearlman and his colleagues: to make a profit from the commercial computer line and to avoid allowing part of the Heath purchase to become a corporate albatross. Yet Pearlman and his colleagues differed in the means by which they thought this goal should be met. Most executives implicitly value high-powered advertising, such as the appeals to a mass market of individual computer dealers that most Zenith executives advocated. Pearlman wanted to rely instead on salesmanship: direct contact with potential buyers in specific markets ripe for the sales of personal computers. As it happened, Pearlman prevailed and the low-key approach proved successful for Zenith, which quietly built its computer sales into a $500 million business by 1987.

Generate Alternative Solutions

Alternative solutions are two or more ways to deal with a particular problem. The process of generating alternative solutions is designed to find the best possible solution within whatever constraints managers face. It helps prevent managers from grabbing the first available solution. Instead of being examined separately and accepted or rejected in a vacuum, alternatives are examined together. Managers may first measure one solution against another and choose the better of the pair. They may then repeat the process with two completely different solutions. Next the two better solutions arrived at in this manner are compared, and a final choice is made. The point is that each alternative should be evaluated against not only the decision objectives but also an alternative solution. This pairing process can be compared to the eliminations in a basketball tournament. And, just as in "consolation matches," temporarily discarded alternatives may be pitted against other discarded alternatives, enabling managers to construct a hierarchy of alternatives.

The process of generating alternative solutions is tied to gathering information relevant to a problem and analyzing it. Information can be gathered from many sources, such as customers, suppliers, outside critics, workers and management colleagues, the observations of the manager making the decision, technical publications and papers, and the data compiled through the organization's own research.

In gathering information, managers must recognize the limits of bounded rationality. No problem can be completely researched. Managers must decide when to stop gathering information and begin the process of selecting an alternative from among those that have been generated. As we have seen, the process of decision making is never completely rational, because all the relevant data on all possible variables are never available.

The executives at Zenith generated at least two alternative ways to solve the problem of poor sales of personal computers. Both alternatives suggested the need for more information: the cost of a mass advertising campaign targeting dealers of personal computers on the one hand and, on the other, the potential size of available "market niches," such as universities. Certain information was collected to help executives choose between the two alternatives, but in both cases some relevant information (as it always does) remained unknown. Could Zenith beat its competitors to the doors of many of the "market niches"? Would the mass advertising campaign be cost-efficient?

Select an Alternative

At this point, managers must ask themselves a crucial question about each alternative: Is this the best possible solution within the recognized constraints? To answer this question, managers must carefully evaluate a wide range of alternatives. The potential effects of each alternative should be considered, along with the estimated probability that these effects will occur. (In the next section, we will discuss techniques that make this process easier.) The positive and negative effects of each alternative should be compared. Managers can supplement this approach by asking the following series of questions about each alternative:

1. *Will the alternative be effective?* The effectiveness of an alternative can be measured by assessing two factors—how realistic the alternative is in terms of the objectives and resources of the organization and how well it will help solve the problem. Managers should keep in mind that the apparently ideal solution to a particular problem might not be a productive solution in the long run. For example, Zenith's Pearlman recognized that mass advertising would be fruitless without a huge corresponding increase in sales of personal computers to individual business people. In selecting an alternative, managers must try to minimize the risk of creating unnecessary new problems. Pearlman's response was to suggest that the firm not risk mounting an unprofitable advertising campaign that might make it even more difficult to turn a significant profit on the sale of personal computers.

2. *Can the alternative be implemented?* If an alternative cannot be implemented, it should be eliminated. Suppose Zenith had considered selling for $70 million the assets it acquired when it purchased the Heath Company for $64.5 million. Here implementation *would* have been an obstacle, and Zenith executives would have had to assess the likelihood that the sale could be made and their price met.

3. *What are the organizational consequences of the alternative?* As we have already seen, managers must determine whether the alternative will create unnecessary problems. They must also determine how subordinates and workers will react to the decision. Will it be carried out wholeheartedly, or will there be strong resistance to implementation of the decision? The fact that an alternative is controversial need not disqualify it. But subordinates' attitudes must be considered in weighing the alternative against other alternatives. Similarly, managers must consider what effect, if any, the alternative will have on other departments in the organization.[19]

Implement the Decision

Selecting an alternative triggers its **implementation**, the process of putting a decision into action. Several factors are involved in implementing a decision.

1. *Announcing the decision.* Managers should announce the decision clearly and without apology. If an alternative is worth selecting, it is worth supporting with confidence.

2. *Giving the appropriate orders.* Managers should communicate the selected alternative to subordinates and fellow managers involved in implementing the decision. The orders should be communicated clearly, and any change in current operations should be explained.

3. *Assigning specific tasks.* Implementing a decision involves assigning specific persons to specific tasks. Sometimes these assignments are only slightly different from the procedures already carried out routinely by subordinates; at other times they involve significant changes in the routine; and occasionally they entail the generation of novel tasks and new assignments. In most cases, managers who assign novel tasks to subordinates should explain the reasons underlying the new assignment.

4. *Allocating resources.* Implementation may demand a new allocation of both material and personnel resources. Managers should have become aware of what resources are needed to implement the decision in the step that involved generating alternative solutions.

5. *Monitoring the progress of the decision.* Managers must know whether the decision is being properly implemented. Many good decisions have unjustly been considered bad decisions simply because they were not implemented properly.

6. *Making follow-up decisions.* Implementation usually requires follow-up decisions based on how best to facilitate implementation of the main decision. Zenith had to decide specifically which potential high-market customers to target. But making follow-up decisions may also be a part of solving general problems that arise from the successful implementation of a decision. For example, Zenith managers may have faced the problem of reorganizing the firm's sales force to concentrate its efforts on certain high-volume markets.

Evaluate the Decision

After the decision has been implemented, managers should evaluate its effectiveness. Did the decision achieve the objective or objectives for which it was selected? Did the decision contribute to the long-range good of the organization? Was it cost-effective? Did it open up areas of growth for the firm? Did subordinates accept it as a productive decision? What difficulties were encountered during implementation of the decision?

If a decision is judged to have been a poor one, managers may be faced with having to select another alternative or to generate a new list of alternatives. If a decision emerges as a good one, managers should review the elements that made it successful. The experience of making and implementing every decision she or he selects becomes an invaluable part of that manager's decision-making background. It will be used repeatedly in making future decisions.

Techniques for Decision Making

In recent years, management scholars and practitioners have perfected a number of techniques that attempt to make decision making less subjective and more scientific. The steps in decision making help managers to be more systematic; decision-making techniques help managers to be more rational. Techniques have evolved that use decision models and precise mathematical calculations. All of these tools seek to render predictions and the weighing of alternatives more systematic and less intuitive.

All techniques for decision making are based on models. Models are scientific tools. A **model** is a representation of some real object or situation. Toy soldiers arranged on a coffee table are a model of real soldiers on a battlefield. A map is a model of a land area. Models need not (indeed they should not) represent *all* the varied details of the object or situation they represent, but they are expected to represent its essential features.

By omitting many details, the model offers a simplified view of the total reality it represents. Yet most details that are left out of a model are unnecessary to the making of the decision at hand. A profile of an ideal applicant for a job as a factory auditor, for example, is not likely to include details such as hair and eye color, height, and weight. These details would be irrelevant to the purpose of the model. On the other hand, such details would be relevant for a model profile of someone applying for an acting job. In short, the features and details included in a model are tailored to the overall purpose the model is designed for. One criterion for a successful model is that it contains an acceptable balance of real and abstract features. Too much detail mires the model in irrelevant aspects of the actual situation. Too much abstraction shifts the focus too far from the concrete situation.

There are three types of models: descriptive, analogue, and symbolic. A **descriptive model** represents an object or situation by showing us how it looks. Such models contain a high degree of detail or concreteness and include relatively little abstraction. For example, an architectural model of a new factory and an organization chart are descriptive models. This type of model is relatively simple to make, but it is not easy to change. It is difficult to manipulate the variables in a descriptive model because its elements are relatively concrete. They are designed to describe a particular situation. A scale model of a factory is a scale model of a particular factory; it is not a model whose features can be used to describe a great number of factories.

An **analogue model** represents an object or situation by substituting for various real elements different forms or properties. For example, a lake is represented on a map by the color blue. A picture that resembles a plumbing diagram but represents cash flow in a company is an analogue model. These models are easier to manipulate than descriptive models, because they exhibit a higher level of abstraction from the concrete situation.

A **symbolic model** represents the various properties or elements of a situation with symbols. An example of this type of model is the mathematical model, in which various elements of a situation are expressed in the form of an equation. Symbolic models are the easiest to manipulate because of their high level of abstraction.

Models can serve a number of managerial purposes. They can, for instance, help managers get an overall perspective on a concrete situation. The most obvious example of this function is a company organization chart, in which the management hierarchy is represented by a group of connected boxes. If a manager must follow a strict chain of command in delegating responsibilities, an organization chart is a quick and efficient reminder of where each individual stands in the chain.

Models can also help managers predict certain fluctuations in their organizations. For example, it is possible to predict, on the basis of past experience, what fluctuations in cash flow should result from planned changes in the production schedule.

In addition, models can be used to prescribe or dictate managerial decisions, which thereby become programmed decisions. If a manager can design a model that closely reflects the operations of some elements of the organization, analyzing and experimenting with the model may reveal an obviously preferred course of action. For example, knowing the initial costs of two alternative ice makers, along with their respective output volumes, useful lives, and expected maintenance costs, enables a manager systematically to calculate the most cost-efficient machine for the organization to purchase.

The Decision Tree

The **decision tree** is a model in the form of a graphic tool that charts the steps to consider in evaluating each alternative faced in decision making. The decision tree emphasizes two main points: (1) using the information acquired in preparing to make the decision and (2) recognizing the sequential nature of the decision-making process. The decision tree, then, is a graphic outline of what future choices the decisions made in the present will lead to. It helps managers evaluate and order information. It is introduced early in this book because it is a good example of a management tool that bridges the qualitative and quantitative aspects of decision making. Decision trees enable managers to introduce a degree of quantifiability into the often subjective task of making nonprogrammed decisions.

One way to think of the decision tree is to picture its various branches as forks in a road. Managers use this technique to estimate the paths along which various series of decisions will take them. Then, by studying the alternative paths, they attempt to determine which one it will be most to their advantage to follow.

Figure 3-4 shows how a manager faced with deciding whether to expand the company's marketing effort to one or the other of two different overseas markets might outline, on a decision tree, the various elements that make up the decision. Because the company cannot afford to enter both multinational markets at once, the manager must decide between the European and Asian markets. In this example, assume that the basic decision criterion is profit and that the major constraint is that the products cannot be introduced to both markets at the same time. In dealing with this problem, managers will have to consider the following factors (depicted in Figure 3-4):

1. The manager identifies the *possible actions* associated with each *decision point.*

2. The manager assigns a *probability of occurrence* to each key event that will bear on the consequences of possible actions. Each set of these probabilities of occurrence must total to 1.0, or 100 percent.

3. The manager estimates the *anticipated payoff* that should result from each action if each event occurs.

4. To calculate the *expected yield,* the manager estimates the monthly profit to be derived from introducing the product to each multinational market in year one. The calculation involves multiplying the anticipated payoffs by their associated probabilities of occurrence. Finally, the yields for each possible action are summed to provide a basis for decision making.

Managers faced with this decision not only must decide in which market to introduce their products first; they must also decide whether to approach the

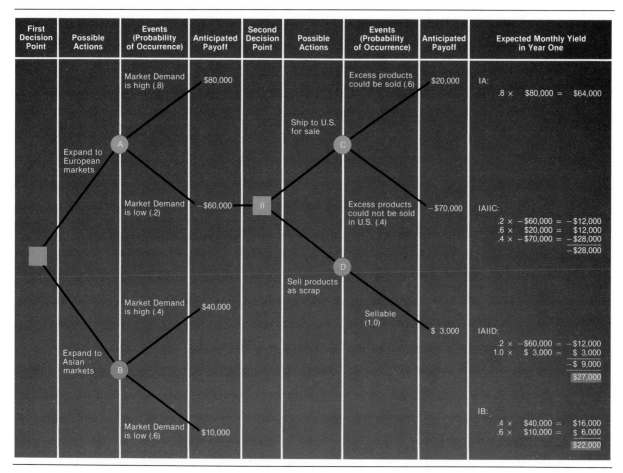

First Decision Point	Possible Actions	Events (Probability of Occurrence)	Anticipated Payoff	Second Decision Point	Possible Actions	Events (Probability of Occurrence)	Anticipated Payoff	Expected Monthly Yield in Year One

FIGURE 3-4
Decision Tree

second market at all. Each branch of the tree shows a possible sequence of decisions and consequences. The decision tree in Figure 3-5 is a simple one: It shows the best alternative as the top branches of the decision tree, to expand to European markets. It has an expected yield of $27,000. In terms of profit, it shows that managers should introduce the product to the European markets and that the Asian market also offers considerable profit potential.

Actual decision situations are usually more subjective. Perhaps none of the alternatives presented meets the goals. Perhaps two equally feasible alternatives present themselves. In addition, managers must be aware of any negative side effects of decisions that nevertheless look good on paper. For example, new market research may have already indicated that the European market for the product, though it is currently soaring, is expected to drop rapidly in the mid-1990s.[20] Finally, decision makers need to remember that the "expected yield" is a mathematical compromise; it is rarely the outcome that actually occurs.

The Break-even Technique

The **break-even technique** is another example of a decision-making model that helps managers determine whether a certain volume of output will result in a profit or a loss. The point at which "breaking even" occurs is the volume of output at which total revenues equal total costs. The technique can be further used to answer the question "What is the profit associated with a given level of output?" To use the technique, one needs only three types of information: fixed costs of operations, variable costs of production, and price per unit.

Fixed costs are expenses that do not change in the short run, no matter what the level of production and sales. For example, a piece of equipment that stitches shoes costs the same whether 2,000 or 3,000 or 4,000 shoes are assembled on the machine. *Variable costs* vary with the volume produced. They are usually expressed in terms of per-unit variable costs. For example, the raw leather used to produce shoes is likely to cost less per shoe as the volume of leather purchased is increased. *Total costs* are the sum of fixed and variable costs. *Price* is the total amount received from the sale of one unit of the product. Multiplying the price by the number of units sold yields the amount received by the company, which is known as its *revenues*. *Profit* is what remains when the total costs are subtracted from the total revenues. The **break-even point** is the level of output or sales at which total profit is zero—in other words, where total revenues equal total costs.

To determine whether a particular volume of production will result in profit or loss, managers can employ a break-even technique known as a break-even chart (Figure 3-5). Fixed costs remain the same regardless of production, so they are represented on the chart by a single horizontal line. In our chart the fixed costs are set at $20,000. The vertical line at the far left represents various amounts of revenues and costs, ranging from zero to $130,000. The horizontal line at the bottom represents the number of units of output produced or sold.

Because variable costs increase in proportion to production, they are represented by an upward-sloping line. The line representing total costs is equal to variable costs plus fixed costs at each level of production, so it slopes upward, from the $20,000 level, according to the increase in production.

The break-even point occurs where the total-revenues line intersects with the total-costs line. In the area above the intersection of these lines (the shaded area on the chart), total revenues exceed total costs. At any point above this production level, managers can expect to earn a profit. It is now apparent, then, that the break-even point in the example is 4,000 units. If under 4,000 units are sold, managers can expect a loss. For every unit produced and sold in excess of 4,000, a profit can be expected.

THE BREAK-EVEN FORMULA

A quicker way to calculate the break-even point is to use a formula. According to this formula, the price per unit (P) multiplied by the number of units sold (X) is equal to the fixed costs (F) plus the variable costs (V) multiplied by the number of units produced. That is,

$$P(X) = F + V(X)$$

In our example, the fixed costs (F) are $20,000. The variable costs per unit (V) are $15.00, and the price per unit (P) is $20.00. We find the break-even point (X) by plugging these values into the equation:

$$20(X) = 20{,}000 + 15(X)$$
$$20X - 15X = 20{,}000$$
$$5X = 20{,}000$$
$$X = 4{,}000 \text{ units}$$

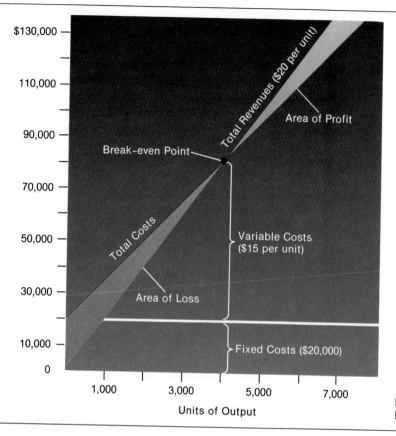

FIGURE 3-5
Break-even Chart

The major shortcoming of decision-making techniques is that their use depends on the managers' ability to provide quantification for the variables in the model. Because the ability to be precise is often very limited, managers need to have a method available for analyzing subjective information. Long-range environmental forecasting and trends in consumer preferences are just two examples among the hundreds of decisions that are characterized by uncertainty about the accuracy of the prediction variables. How managers can cope analytically with varying degrees of uncertainty is the topic of the following section.

Types of Decision-Making Conditions

Decision making does not happen in a vacuum. Rather, decisions are made under a variety of conditions and under different kinds of constraints. Consider John Reed's situation in the opening case. To make his decision about the proper strategic direction for Citicorp, he needed to consider such diverse constraints as the loan capacity of the corporation, the confidence of investors, and the loyalty of Citicorp employees.

We have already discussed the concept of bounded rationality, which reminds managers that they must work within certain limits. Now we will examine a general set of conditions under which decisions are made. These conditions fall on a continuum representing the degree of risk inherent in each type of decision. Overall, there are three general conditions under which decisions are made: The certainty condition is at one end of the continuum, the complete uncertainty condition is at the other extreme, and the risk condition occupies all points between.

The **certainty condition** exists when managers know *precisely* what the results will be if a certain decision is implemented. Certainty has a significant effect on the process of evaluating alternatives. When the outcome of each alternative can be reliably predicted, managers are likely to choose the alternative with the most acceptable predicted outcome. However, most organizational decisions are not made under conditions of certainty.

The **uncertainty condition** prevails when managers have *no* information that could help them predict the outcome of an implemented decision. In such conditions, decisions might as well be made by flipping a coin! Luckily, few organizational decisions are made at this extreme.

The **risk condition** exists when managers have enough information to estimate the probable outcome of an implemented decision. The element of risk varies from problem to problem. Managers usually operate under some sort of risk condition. A manager who hires three extra inspectors in an attempt to spot previously undetected defects in assembly-line products cannot be certain that the new inspectors will be able to eliminate *all* defective products. And there is some risk that the cost of the new inspectors will not be offset by the savings that their work

A manager responsible for the inspection of automotive air-conditioning pipes discusses their methods with a subordinate. (Brownie Harris/The Stock Market)

generates. However, the company's previous experience with using special inspectors as troubleshooters may nevertheless indicate that there is a reasonable probability that employing them in this new situation will be cost-effective. Such a decision situation, therefore, is characterized by a condition of risk.

It is difficult to determine exactly how much risk a decision entails. Managers can seldom determine that a particular decision has, say, one chance in four of being effective; the odds cannot generally be calculated like gambling odds. However, the risks inherent in alternative solutions to a problem can usually be compared in a relative sense, even though no absolute figures can be attached to them. Alternative A, for example, may clearly have a lower risk factor than alternative B. Thus, in most major business decisions, the process of screening alternatives includes considering how much chance each alternative has, relative to the other alternatives, to succeed.

Making Decisions Under Conditions of Risk

If managers could determine what strategies their competitors would adopt and knew how future conditions would affect their decisions, the decision-making process would be simple. Managers would calculate the return or payoff that each alternative would yield and then select the strategy that offered the highest return.

Unfortunately, managerial decisions are rarely made in the comfort of such certainty. A company cannot usually be sure what its competitors will do or what economic conditions will exist in the future. Instead it operates under assumptions about the probability that certain conditions, known as "states of nature," will occur. **States of nature** are the conditions under which a decision is being made. In these cases, managers make decisions under risk conditions. Various levels of GNP growth represent different states of nature, as do increases or decreases in industry competitiveness and the relative aggressiveness of government agencies in enforcing legislation affecting business operations. Various conceptual tools are available to help managers make decisions under conditions of risk. We will consider two of them here.

EXPECTED VALUE

In a risk-free environment, managers would be able to base their decisions on the worth they assigned to the predictable occurrence of an event. This worth, which is usually expressed in dollars, is known as the **conditional value**. However, because environmental conditions and competitive actions almost always have a bearing on the outcome of an alternative, managers need to employ the concept of expected value in their decision making. **Expected value** is the conditional value of an occurring event multiplied by the probability that it will occur. Expressed in the form of an equation, expected value (EV) is equal to the conditional value (CV) multiplied by the probability of its occurrence (p).

$$EV = CV \times p$$

Imagine a company whose profits depend on competitive bidding for construction contracts. This company is faced with deciding whether to bid on contract A or contract B. It can bid on only one of the two contracts. Contract A is worth $250,000 and the probability of securing it is estimated to be .25 (or one in four). Contract B is worth $175,000 and the probability of securing it is estimated to be .30 (or three in ten). The expected value (EV) for each alternative is worked out as follows:

$$\text{Contract A}\quad EV = \$250{,}000 \times .25$$
$$= \$62{,}500$$
$$\text{Contract B}\quad EV = \$175{,}000 \times .30$$
$$= \$52{,}500$$

The expected value of contract A exceeds the expected value of contract B by $10,000. Given that obtaining the maximum amount of sales dollars is the objective, the company should bid on contract A. Even so, managers should keep in mind that there is no guarantee of a $250,000 revenue if they bid on contract A. They could end up with $250,000 or they could end up with nothing, depending on whether the company is awarded the contract. Therefore, if the company's objective is simply to get the job *whatever* its value, management should choose alternative B because of its greater probability of occurrence (.30 is greater than .25).

THE PAYOFF APPROACH

The **payoff approach** is a technique for estimating the return on an investment under varying degrees of risk. This approach can be used to estimate the return on different investments under different conditions. It is an extension of the expected-value approach because it relies on the probabilities associated with the possible occurrence of events.

For example, an organization of fast-food outlets might be considering three possible growth alternatives: (1) build a new outlet, (2) lease additional space, or (3) expand an existing outlet.

In calculating the return on the original investment, managers who use the payoff technique consider various largely uncontrollable external factors referred to as states of nature. For example, the financial return to the fast-food restaurant would be expected to vary as shown in Figure 3-6 under the economic states of nature known as recession, stability, and upswing.

FIGURE 3-6
The Payoff Approach to
Decision Making
(in thousands)

Options	State of Nature N-1 RECESSION	State of Nature N-2 STABILITY	State of Nature N-3 UPSWING	Expected Payoff	Choice
O-1: Build new outlet	− $1,000[a]	$200	$700	− $10[b]	
O-2: Lease available space	− $ 500	$300	− $250	$45	✓
O-3: Expand current outlet	− $ 400	$200	$200	$20	
Probability of occurrence for each state of nature	.30	.40	.30		

[a]Expected effect on monthly net profit.
[b]$EP = -\$1{,}000(.30) + \$200(.40) + \$700(.30)$
$EP = -\$300 + \$80 + \$210$
$EP = -\$10$

FIGURE 3-7
Conditional Values for
the Restaurant's Growth
Options
(in thousands)

	State of Nature		
Option	N-1 RECESSION	N-2 STABILITY	N-3 UPSWING
O-1: Build new outlet	−$1,000	$200	$700
O-2: Lease available space	−$ 500	$300	$250
O-3: Expand current outlet	−$ 400	$200	$200

Two features of Figure 3-6 are important to notice. First, the decision makers must estimate the payoff that is likely for each option under each state of nature. Second, the managers must estimate the probability that each state of nature will occur. In the example, these probabilities are shown as N-1 = .30, N-2 = .40, and N-3 = .20. Although many more states of nature are conceivable than are seriously considered in the calculations, the listed states are usually treated as though they were the only options. Thus their probabilities of occurrence add up to 1.00.

To calculate the benefits to be derived from the selection of each option, the decision maker simply multiplies each payoff for an option by its probability of occurrence. The results are next summed to produce an expected payoff for that option. These total expected payoffs are then compared, and the most favorable option—given the estimated values that were originally assumed—is identified.

In the example in Figure 3-6, option 2 is the preferred choice; its payoff of $45,000 is better than those of options 1 (−$10,000) and 3 ($20,000).

Making Decisions under Conditions of Uncertainty

Techniques such as the payoff approach are valuable tools in decision making. However, after constructing various conditional values on a payoff chart, managers may find that they have no objective or solidly rational grounds on which to assign probabilities of occurrence. In such cases, managers can use one of four different selection criteria, in combination with a conditional-value table, shown in Figure 3-7, to calculate the option that best suits their decision-making style. (Note that the conditional-value table shown in Figure 3-7 is identical to the expected value table shown in Figure 3-6 minus the probabilities of occurrence and associated calculations.)

We will now examine the method for evaluating options under each of the four selection criteria.

THE LAPLACE CRITERION

The **Laplace criterion** (pronounced *lä pläz*) states that there is no defensible reason to believe one event is more likely to occur than another. This leads to the assignment of equal probabilities to each state of nature. In the problem that we used in constructing a payoff matrix, the probability was assumed to be variable for three different states of nature: recession, stability, and upswing. Using the Laplace criterion, however, managers would assign the same probability to each state of nature and then choose the option that yielded the highest expected value. With the probability of each state of nature set at one-third (.33), managers would choose option 2, the leasing of additional space. Under the payoff matrix formula used in Figure 3-6, this choice would have the highest expected value ($16,667), as shown in Figure 3-8.

THE PESSIMISM CRITERION

The **pessimism criterion** is used when managers wish to base a decision on the premise that the worst is going to happen. Under this criterion (Figure 3-9), the managers charged with determining the fate of the fast-food outlet would assume that they would be operating under a recession (N-1) if they were to choose to build (O-1), to expand (O-2), or to lease (O-3). Under this decision-making criterion (see Figure 3-5), managers would choose the option that was predicted to be most profitable (or least unprofitable). In this case it is option 3, the leasing of available space, which has an anticipated payoff loss of $400,000.

THE OPTIMISM CRITERION

The **optimism criterion** is selected when managers wish to act on the premise that the best will happen. In our example, this would mean assuming that if O-1 was chosen N-3 would occur, if O-2 was chosen N-2 would occur, and if O-3 was chosen either N-2 or N-3 would occur (see Figure 3-10). In this case, managers would choose option 1, building a new outlet, which has the highest payoff ($700,000).

THE REGRET CRITERION

The **regret criterion** offers a way of choosing an option that minimizes the maximum possible regret. The regret of an option is its payoff under any given state of nature subtracted from the maximum possible payoff that *could* have been realized under that condition. For example, if N-2 (stability) occurs in the example

---

FIGURE 3-8
Decision Making Under the Laplace Criterion[a]
(in thousands)

Option	Total Payoff × Equal Probability	Choice
O-1	$-$100 \times .33 = -33.33[b]	
O-2	$\$ 50 \times .33 = \$16.67$	√
O-3	$0 \times .33 = 0$	

[a]The object is to apply equal probability of occurrence to each state of nature.
[b]The formula for calculating this answer was as follows: $(-\$1,000 + \$200 + \$700) \times .33 = -\$33.33$.

FIGURE 3-9
Decision Making Under the Pessimism Criterion[a]
(in thousands)

Option	Worst Condition	Payoff	Choice
O-1	N-1	$-$1,000$	
O-2	N-1	$-\$ 500$	
O-3	N-1	$-\$ 400$	√

[a]The object is to choose the option that turns out best if the worst possible state of nature occurs.

FIGURE 3-10
Decision Making Under the Optimism Criterion[a]
(in thousands)

Option	Best Condition	Payoff	Choice
O-1	N-3	$700[b]	✓
O-2	N-2	$300	
O-3	N-2, N-3	$200	

[a]The object is to maximize the payoff.
[b]The figure $700 is more profitable than $200 or − $1,000.

FIGURE 3-11
Decision Making Under the Regret Criterion[a]
(in thousands)

Option	High minus Low Conditional Values			Maximum Regret	Choice
	N-1	N-2	N-3		
O-1	$600[b]	$100	0	$600	
O-2	$100	0	$450	$450	✓
O-3	0	$100	$500	$500	

[a]The object is to select the option such that no matter which state of nature occurs, the decision maker's regret over not having had the foresight to select the best option is minimized.
[b]Best outcome for a given state of nature minus the outcome being studied, or (− $400) − (− $1,000) = $600.

shown in Figure 3-7, the regret factor of option 1 is $100,000. This figure is obtained by subtracting the $200,000 payoff expected from option 1 under conditions of stability from the maximum possible payoff ($300,000) expected of option 2, leasing. The maximum regret of each option is determined by simply identifying the highest regret factor for each option and comparing them. In this example (see Figure 3-11), the maximum regret is $600,000 for option 1, $450,000 for option 2, and $500,000 for option 3. Seeking to minimize the maximum regret, managers would choose the option of least regret, which is option 2, expanding the current outlet.

Objective and Subjective Probability

Because probability is an important element in the foregoing equations, it is important to characterize it more distinctly. There are two kinds of probability, objective and subjective. **Objective probability** is that which is based on past experience. For example, managers may be able to estimate from past experience how well an employee will do at a certain job on the basis of the employee's score on a screening test. In some cases, however, managers are not able to judge the probability of an occurrence on the basis of past experience. Their estimates of probabilities in such a situation are subjective. **Subjective probability** is that which is based on a general assessment of a particular situation. Although less precise than objective probability, it should not be ignored as a part of the decision-making process.

████████████████████████ *Guidelines for Management Practice* ████████████████████████

Managers use mathematical equations as tools that provide inputs to help them make decisions. However, the decision is not automatically made when an equation is solved. Managers must be aware of the context in which the decision is being made. For instance, in our example of the construction contract, the company might prefer contract B to contract A for a variety of reasons. Perhaps there is a greater chance of winning future bids with the company offering contract B, if the first project is successfully completed. Perhaps the winning of contract B, although less profitable in the short run, will secure for the company a prestigious building project that offers valuable publicity. In short, the mathematical tools do not dictate decisions. They simply provide an important part of the data used in decision making.

Review of the Learning Objectives

Having studied this chapter, you should be able to respond to the learning objectives with extensions of the following brief answers:

1. **Explain the differences between programmed and nonprogrammed decisions.**

   Programmed decisions are made on the basis of established policies, rules, or procedures. They give managers relatively little opportunity to exercise their own initiative. In a programmed decision, a manager confronts a problem, consults the appropriate policy or rule, and then usually implements a decision prescribed by a fixed plan. Nonprogrammed decisions are not made on the basis of established policies, rules, or procedures. They give managers much more latitude.

2. **Explain the difference between the centralized and decentralized approaches to decision making.**

   In the centralized approach, as many decisions as possible are made by top management. In this approach the tendency is to push decisions to the highest level of management. The decentralized approach is precisely the opposite: As many decisions as possible are made by lower and middle management. The goal of the decentralized approach is to delegate authority and share responsibility for the total operation.

3. **Define the concept of bounded rationality and explain why it is important to the decision-making process.**

   This term refers to the limitations that restrict a manager's view of problems and situations. It reflects the notion that decisions can *never* be made under ideal conditions (unlimited resources, time, and information with which to generate alternatives and select the best one). This concept is important to decision making because it reminds managers that ideal decision making is impossible. It helps managers accept the limits or constraints on the decision-making process.

4. **Explain why individual psychology is important in understanding people's conflicting styles of decision making.**

Many management researchers believe there are two kinds of decision makers, systematic and intuitive, and that the differences between these two types of people may be neurologically based. A systematic decision maker tends to approach a problem via a structured method that is likely to lead to a solution. The intuitive decision maker uses a trial-and-error approach that involves experimenting with a number of techniques.

5. **List and describe the five basic steps in decision making.**

The five basic steps are (1) discovering the problem—the process of identifying and defining the problem to be solved; (2) generating alternative solutions—the process of coming up with at least two possible solutions to a particular problem; (3) evaluating the alternatives—the process of weighing various factors before deciding which alternative to select; (4) making and implementing the decision—the "action" part of the process, wherein an alternative is selected and the actions necessary to carry out the decision are taken; (5) evaluating the decision—the process of judging how well the decision worked out and determining whether it was a good or bad, an efficient or inefficient, decision.

6. **Describe some of the conditions under which decisions are made.**

The conditions under which decisions are made can be broken down into three categories: the complete certainty condition, the complete uncertainty condition, and the risk condition. Complete certainty exists when managers are sure what the results of a decision will be. Complete uncertainty exists when managers have little or no idea of what the results of a decision will be. A risk condition exists when managers have enough information to estimate the results of a given condition. Most decisions are made under some sort of risk condition, and it is often the task of managers to determine the degree of that risk as they evaluate proposed alternatives.

7. **Explain the value of several technical tools that enhance managerial decision making.**

Among the techniques used in decision making are various kinds of models that help to extract from the total situation those variables that most affect the decision that must be made. Models also help managers to get an overall perspective on the environment in which the decision is being made. Techniques for decision making include the break-even technique (used to determine whether a particular volume of sale will yield a profit or loss), the decision tree (used to map sequences of events and to predict the probable consequences of making each series of decisions), and the payoff approach (used to estimate the consequences that alternative decision choices will have under different states of nature and how likely those conditions are to occur.

Key Terms and Concepts

Having completed your study of Chapter 3 on "Managerial Decision Making," you should have mastered the following important terms and concepts:

decision making	nonprogrammed	problem	models	decision tree
decision	decisions	identification	descriptive model	break-even
programmed	bounded rationality	alternative solutions	analogue model	technique
decisions	problem definition	implementation	symbolic model	break-even point

certainty condition	risk condition	expected value	pessimism criterion	objective
uncertainty	states of nature	payoff approach	optimism criterion	probability
condition	conditional value	Laplace criterion	regret criterion	subjective
				probability

Questions for Discussion

1. Do you consider yourself a systematic or an intuitive decision maker?

2. From your own experience, cite two examples each of programmed and nonprogrammed decisions.

3. What role do goals play in the decision-making process?

4. What is the difference between problem finding and opportunity finding?

5. How could the concept of bounded rationality be used as a rationalization (excuse) for not seeking a better solution?

6. What three questions should managers ask themselves when presented with a problem? Are the answers to these questions all they need to know?

7. For what kinds of decisions are quantitative techniques most appropriate? For which are they least appropriate?

8. How do managers know when to stop gathering information in the decision-making process? How do they know when they have insufficient information?

9. What kinds of managerial decisions do you think it is best for the manager to make alone? What kinds are better made by the group process?

10. How is participative decision making different from group decision making?

11. What are the advantages of establishing decision criteria at the start of the problem-solving process?

Notes

1. Adapted from *Business Week,* December 8, 1987, pp. 90–96; "Citibank Wows the Consumer," *Fortune,* June 8, 1987; and "John Reed Builds His Dream House," *Institutional Investor,* March 1987.

2. J. W. Duncan, *Decision Making and Social Issues* (Hinsdale, Ill.: Dryden, 1973), p. 1.

3. H. A. Simon, *The New Science of Management Decision,* rev. ed. (Englewood Cliffs, N.J.: Prentice-Hall, 1977).

4. C. I. Barnard, *The Function of the Executive* (Cambridge, Mass.: Harvard University Press, 1938), p. 188.

5. H. Mintzberg, D. Raisinghani, and A. Theoret, "The Structure of Unstructured Decision Processes," *Administrative Science Quarterly* 21, no. 2 (June 1976): 250.

6. C. Smart and I. Vertinsky, "Designs for Crisis Decision Units," *Administrative Science Quarterly* 22, no. 4 (December 1977): 640.

7. J. K. Murninghan, "Group Decision Making: What Strategies Should You Use?" *Management Review,* February 1981, pp. 55–62.

8. T. V. Bonoma and G. Zaltman, *Psychology for Management* (Boston: Kent, 1981), pp. 60–62.

9. J. Bragg and I. Andrews, "Participative Decision Making: An Experimental Study in a Hospital," *Journal of Applied Behavioral Science* 9, no. 6 (1973): 727–735; and J. L. Cotton, D. A. Volbrath, K. L. Froggatt, M. L. Lengnick-Hall, and K. R. Jennings, "Employee Participation: Diverse Forms and Different Outcomes," *Academy of Management Review* 13, no. 1 (1988): 8–22.

10. E. A. Locke, D. M. Schweiger, and G. P. Latham, "Participation in Decision Making: When Should It Be Used?" *Organizational Dynamics,* Winter 1986, pp. 65–75.

11. J. A. Pearce, II, and W. A. Randolph, "Improving Strategy Formulation Pedagogies by Recognizing Behavioral Aspects," *Exchange,* December 1980, pp. 7–10.

12. I. Janis, "Groupthink," *Psychology Today,* November 1971, p. 44.

13. H. A. Simon, *Models of Man: Social and Rational* (New York: Wiley, 1957).

14. H. A. Simon, *The New Science of Management Decision,* rev. ed. (Englewood Cliffs, N.J.: Prentice-Hall, 1977).

15. *Business Week,* December 8, 1986, p. 72.

16. J. McKenney and P. Keen, "How Managers' Minds Work," *Harvard Business Review,* May–June 1979, pp. 74–90.

17. H. Mintzberg, "Planning on the Left Side and Managing on the Right Side," *Harvard Business Review,* July–August 1976, pp. 49–58.

18. C. H. Kepner and B. Tregoe, *The Rational Manager* (New York: McGraw-Hill, 1965), pp. 186–202.

19. T. Herbert and R. W. Estes, "Improving Executive Decisions by Formalizing Dissent: The Corporate Devil's Advocate," *Academy of Management Review* 2, no. 4 (October 1977): 662–667.

20. E. F. Harrison, *The Managerial Decision-Making Process* (Boston: Houghton Mifflin, 1975), pp. 26–35.

Cohesion Incident 3-1
Civitan Convention

While Roger was taking part of his vacation during the first week in May, Charles was left in charge of managing the Graniteville City Journey's End. After just three months on the job, Charles was pleased with how much he had learned and how easy it was to manage the motel that Roger had organized so well.

He was still in the process of patting himself on the back when the telephone rang. On the other end was Sam Ealy, the state president of the Civitans, a civic club. He told Charles that the Civitans were planning their annual state convention in Graniteville and that he was inquiring about the cost of holding their convention at Journey's End. He informed Charles that they would need approximately seventy-five rooms for the first weekend in June. They would arrive on a Friday night and spend two nights in the motel. In addition, they wanted to reserve the convention meeting room for three days.

Charles explained that he was the assistant manager and would be pleased to help but that he would prefer to check with his boss before making final commitments. Mr. Ealy responded that he understood Charles's predicament but that he had to have some estimates ready for a meeting of the Civitans board of directors in two days. He requested that Charles telephone him the following day with some information.

After hanging up the telephone, Charles reached for the policy manual. He flipped to the section entitled "Convention Groups" and read the following:

It is the policy of Journey's End to accommodate all convention groups when practical. To encourage such groups, we offer them a 10 percent discount on all rooms. Each manager has the discretion to offer up to an additional 3 percent discount to meet competition in the local area.

Charles wondered for a moment why a 10 percent discount was given, but then he realized that the $50 a day that the group paid for the meeting room, plus the additional use of the restaurant and lounge, should make up for the lowered room price.

Before calling Mr. Ealy back, Charles decided to check the books to determine what the occupancy rate had been at the Graniteville City Journey's End for the two prior years in the first weekend in June. He was somewhat surprised to find that last year every room was filled and that two years ago there were only ten vacant rooms.

Charles took out a pencil and began to jot down some numbers. He calculated that if the motel could be filled without the convention, total revenues would be greater by $75. (At the full price of $30 per room, the 75 patrons would pay $2,250. The convention guests, with their 10 percent discount, would pay $27 per room and would also pay meeting room rent of $150. Hence the Civitans would pay only [$27 × 75] + $150 = $2,175.) On the other hand, there was no assurance that the inn would be filled without the convention. Furthermore, if the Civitans were turned down this year, they might not even bother to check with Journey's End in future years. Charles was beginning to think, "Roger, where are you when I need you?"

Discussion Questions

1. Is the decision whether to offer a 10 percent discount to the Civitans programmed or nonprogrammed?

2. Is Charles working under conditions of certainty, conditions of risk, or conditions of uncertainty? Explain.

3. What would you suggest that Charles do?

Cohesion Incident 3-2
Two Heads are Better. . . Sometimes

In Chicago for two days, Leslie has been asked to represent the Elizabethtown plant at a meeting of Travis Corporation's marketing managers and assistant managers. A substantial part of the conference involves training in market research and in the availability and use of existing data bases. In addition, she has registered for a discussion group whose purpose is to generate ideas and formulate recommendations for top management regarding a specific problem the corporation faces. Several discussion groups were scheduled, each designed to address an issue related to the corporation's long-range goals. Leslie selected the discussion group entitled "Reducing Dependence on the U.S. Auto Industry." She hoped she could take some ideas from this discussion group back to her department, which had begun to explore possibilities for new product and new market development. The discussion was billed as a "brainstorming session."

Six others showed up besides Leslie and the leader, Ed Murray. To her surprise, Ed seemed to know most of the others in the group, and many of the participants seemed to know each other from previous meetings. It appeared that the discussion had already begun informally the night before in the bar, and it continued that morning at a lively pace even before Ed opened the meeting.

After brief introductions around the table, Ed announced the group's task: to list possible solutions to the problem of Travis's overdependence on U.S. auto manufacturers as its primary market. Leslie was relieved that the meeting was "officially" beginning so she could join in the discussion.

Ed: We'll be doing a little brainstorming to see if we can put our heads together and prove the old adage true once again. Tom, let's start with you and move around the table. What would you suggest as a solution?

Tom: Well, Ed, I think you summed it up pretty well last night. I don't think we have a problem, or at least not a problem of *over*dependence. The U.S. auto industry is our major customer and well it should be. I'm concerned about the feasibility of trying to develop new international markets as I've heard some others suggest. The Japanese have the electronic controls market all sewn up abroad. I think it's a waste of our resources to try to increase our share in those markets. The problem is not finding a new market, but strengthening the one we have.

Ed: (*chuckling*) Tom, I must say we see eye to eye on this. I suppose I should have asked you last since I already knew your views, but let's move on to the others in the group. Paul, what about you and the folks in your department? What's your approach to this situation?

Paul: Well, I have to admit we agree with you guys on this one. Not only do we think we're unlikely to be competitive in the foreign auto electronics market, but we also feel some obligation to our U.S. customers not to sell to their major competitors. Some of us just see these foreign-market proposals rumored to be hot with the top brass these days as practically unpatriotic, a breach of faith with our long-term customers in Detroit.

Ed: Allan, how about you? Where are you on this?

Allan: I just can't agree with you on this issue. I think we have to go for the foreign automakers to counter our domestic risks. When Detroit suffered a few years back, so did we. That was our worst slump in years, and it could, and probably will, happen again.

Tom: (shaking his head) That won't help us in the long run. . . .

Paul: (nodding and cutting Tom off in mid-sentence) Tom is right. If we lose our foothold in Detroit, we'll be worse off than we will ever be if we stick with Detroit through bad times as well as good.

Two of the other participants nod in affirmation and throw in anecdotes regarding their longstanding affiliation with Detroit as part of their territory.

Ed: Well, let's continue around the group. Leslie, do you have anything you want to add to this?

Leslie: Our department favors new product development with the possibility of new domestic market development outside the auto industry. I would like to know if any other departments have been considering new products that might better address new markets, either domestically or abroad?

Tom: Not a good plan! Our product development has been mainly geared toward new accessories for the traditional auto aftermarket and original-equipment markets. It's beyond Travis's marketing and distribution channels to move outside the automotive or industrial-equipment markets.

Others chime in, repeating what seems to be the position of the vocal majority, that the problem is not one of overdependence on the auto industry, but one of finding ways to help strengthen that industry in order to maintain its traditional role as Travis's strong market.

Leslie and one of the other participants, who had yet to enter the discussion, exchanged frustrated glances and shook their heads. "And to think I got up early for this," Leslie marvels to herself.

Discussion Questions

1. How could a knowledge of the various types of non-programmed decisions have helped Leslie to clarify the need to discuss Travis's problem in greater depth?

2. Which of the decision-making approaches was being used at the meeting? Was it the correct approach to use in addressing the problem at Travis?

3. How effectively was the decision-making process used in this case? What steps were omitted or ignored?

Management Development Exercise 3
Problem Identification Instrument

To what extent is there evidence of the following problems in your work unit?

	Low evidence		Some evidence		High evidence
1. Loss of production or work-unit output	1	2	3	4	5
2. Grievances or complaints within the work unit	1	2	3	4	5
3. Conflicts or hostility between unit members	1	2	3	4	5
4. Confusion about assignments or unclear relationships between people	1	2	3	4	5
5. Lack of clear goals or low commitment to goals	1	2	3	4	5
6. Apathy or general lack of interest or involvement of unit members	1	2	3	4	5
7. Lack of innovation, risk taking, imagination, or taking initiative	1	2	3	4	5
8. Ineffective staff meetings	1	2	3	4	5
9. Problems in working with the boss	1	2	3	4	5
10. Poor communications: people afraid to speak up, not listening to each other, or not talking together	1	2	3	4	5
11. Lack of trust between boss and members or between members	1	2	3	4	5
12. Decisions made that people do not understand or agree with	1	2	3	4	5
13. People feel that good work is not recognized or rewarded	1	2	3	4	5
14. People are not encouraged to work together in better team effort	1	2	3	4	5

Source: From W. Dyer, *Team Building* © 1977 Addison-Wesley Publishing Company, Inc., Reading, Mass. Reprinted with permission.

Environmental Forces

Your study of this chapter will enable you to do the following:

Learning Objectives

1. Identify and describe the three levels of environmental forces.
2. Distinguish between technology innovation and technology transfer.
3. Name the factors that intensify rivalry among industry competitors.
4. Identify the four principal types of information used in constructing a customer profile.
5. Cite the principal claims of a firm's major stakeholders.

Europe's Growing Debate over Ocean Incineration

Densely populated Europe is rapidly coming up against the problem of finding a place for its PCBs, dioxins, and all those other hazardous chemicals that have become household words in America. Companies producing them are running out of storage space. Many disposal sites have a year's backlog. The European Economic Community (ECC) continues to drag its feet over comprehensive regulatory legislation, while its member-states bicker. Holland claims that its upstream neighbors are polluting the Rhine. England and Italy support ocean dumping; Denmark fiercely opposes it. Even Belgium, historically Europe's apathetic chemical dumping ground, is refusing its neighbors' garbage.

One disposal option available to European countries but forbidden on the other side of the Atlantic, however, is ocean incineration. This method is hotly contested in America, where the Environmental Protection Agency is caught up in emotional crossfire between staunch conservation groups and industries desperate for acceptable ways to clean house. Recent test burns off the Texas coast have put whole communities up in arms, and it may be years before any decision is reached.

Not so in Europe, where ocean incineration has been conducted for more than fifteen years with relatively little controversy—which is not to say it doesn't have its opponents. Governmentally, England, Belgium, Holland, and Ireland stand by it, while Denmark, Germany, Norway, and Sweden oppose it. Spain and Por-

95

Conventional toxic waste disposal sites such as this one stimulate interest in ocean incineration. (Alon Reininger/ Contact/Woodfin Camp & Associates)

tugal, the EEC's newest members, are undecided, and France is neutral, though it doesn't take a very positive view of burning at sea.

Three ships, the U.S.-owned *Vulcanus I* and *Vulcanus II* and the German ship *Vesta,* are authorized to burn chemical wastes, and only at a very specific site: ninety miles off the coast of Holland in the North Sea, about halfway between England and Denmark. "Residence time" for chemicals within a ship's incinerator is one second at 1200 degrees centigrade. Rules require "stack probes" to assure a combustion efficiency of 99.9 percent.

On the topic of ocean incineration, European environmental groups clash head-on with Europe's industries, more and more of whom see such a disposal technique as the solution to overcrowded land-based storage facilities.

"PCBs [polychlorinated biphenyls, carcinogens used in the production of some electrical capacitators] represent a serious, hidden waste problem in Europe, of which the public is not yet fully aware," said Gert Heinemann, general manager of Ocean Combustion Services, N.Y., in Holland, "and there is a huge backlog of PCBs here." OCS, a subsidiary of Illinois-based Waste Management, Inc., the world's largest waste-disposal company, with annual revenues of more than $1.3 billion, owns and operates *Vulcanus I* and *II.* "Germany has about 100,000 tons; France, about the same," Heinemann says. "Most of Europe's wastes are stored in places unknown to the authorities. None of these states has sufficient land incineration capacity to get rid of them even within ten years."

Such a build-up makes everyone nervous, especially industry, which is putting pressure on governments to allow new incinerator facilities. "We are pretty sure that . . . through, say, 1995, there will be a shortage of land-based incinerators," says Louis Jourdan. He is director of the technical department at the European

Council of Federations of Chemical Industries (CEFIC), a private lobbying group similar to the National Association of Manufacturers in the United States. "We're already seeing temporary overloads as sites shut down for cleaning. Currently this is overcome by transportation to other facilities, but there will come a time when even this will not be feasible."

Jourdan states emphatically, "If incineration at sea were eliminated right now, there would be a grinding down of economic activity in Europe, not only within the chemical industry, but in general."

Greenpeace scoffs at such "hyperbole," taking the position that economically feasible disposal alternatives to sea incineration can be found. However, it won't specify exactly what those methods might be. "It's not our position to define the alternatives, but we will identify what [things nations] cannot do," says Karel Ameye of Greenpeace, "and ocean incineration is one of them."[1]

Introduction

What Are Environmental Forces?

Environmental forces are the external and largely uncontrollable factors that influence managers' decisions and actions and, ultimately, the internal structures and processes of organizations. Managers are asking about environmental forces whenever they address the question "Who and what outside of the firm will affect the success of our plans?"

Environmental forces are so numerous and interrelated that managers often find it difficult to isolate the factors that are most important in their decision making. After reading the opening case for this chapter, one might easily think that the problem of hazardous waste, coupled with the claim of twenty-five states that they are unable to dispose of any further garbage within their boundaries, must be a dominant consideration in the decision making of every organization. In fact, however, few managers give waste treatment serious consideration. They prefer to study the megatrends forecasted to affect the traditional profit equations. But after studying materials like those that "In Practice 4-1" presents, managers are often left with the feeling that their business is subject to powerful forces too complex and numerous to grapple with intelligently.

To put this problem in perspective, it is helpful to view the firm's general external environment as composed of three spheres of influence. As shown in Figure 4-1, these are the remote, the industry, and the operating environments. These environments, the forces that they create, and their impacts on managerial decision making are the central themes of this chapter.

The Remote Environment

The **remote environment** consists of a set of forces that originate beyond, and usually regardless of, any single firm's operating situation. Encompassing ecological, economic, political-legal, sociocultural, and technological factors, the remote environment presents opportunities, threats, and constraints for the firm. And rarely is the organization able to exert any meaningful reciprocal influence.

MEGATRENDS IN THE CORPORATE ENVIRONMENT

Among recent books on future developments in the corporate environment is the highly acclaimed *Megatrends: Ten New Directions Transforming Our Lives,* by John Naisbitt. On the basis of twelve years of analysis of hard-news items published in newspapers, Naisbitt distilled the following ten major trends that are affecting business:

1. The American economy is undergoing a "megashift" from an industrial to an information-based society.
   - Today 13 percent of the total U.S. workforce is employed in manufacturing, while 60 percent produce or process information. Those that use or convey information include teachers, clerks, secretaries, accountants, stockbrokers, lawyers, and insurance people.

2. As the society increases in high-tech, there will be high-touch reactions involving the sensitivity of employees.
   - Teleconferencing, a high-technology innovation, has not yet caught on because people enjoy the high-touch of face-to-face meetings.
   - Many companies try to add high-touch to their high-tech to increase the latter's acceptance. Thus Apple Computer chose the apple and a rainbow to symbolize its "user-friendly" nature. These companies search for "earth values" or "feather values" to soften their products.

3. The U.S. is moving away from isolation and self-sufficiency and recognizing its global interdependence. It is losing its dominance as an economic power.
   - Productivity growth in the U.S. fell to 1 percent per year between 1973 and 1977 and actually declined 2 percent in 1979. Japan is number one in productivity. However, Japan is being challenged by Singapore, South Korea, and Brazil.

4. U.S. corporate managers are beginning to think about the long term rather than the next quarter.
   - The short-term emphasis was due largely to pressure from shareholders and the fact that managers are rewarded for short-term rather than long-term planning.

5. We are beginning to build from the bottom up in our companies and are moving away from a centralized structure toward a decentralized structure. (See Chapter 3 for a discussion of the difference.)

6. We are returning to an emphasis on self-reliance and deemphasizing help from institutions.
   - No longer are people content to devote their lives to corporations. There has been an entrepreneurial explosion. In 1950, 93,000 new businesses were started; today 600,000 new businesses are forming per year.

7. Workers and consumers are demanding and getting a greater voice in government, in business, and in the marketplace.
   - Because of the availability of information today, it is possible for the average voter to know as much as or more than his or her representatives.

8. The computer is smashing the corporate organizational chart. We are moving from hierarchies to networks.
   - People are forming networks to share ideas, information, and resources, and the networks often cut across hierarchies.

9. Workers are moving from the North and Northeast to the South and Southwest.
   - The cities showing the greatest opportunity are Albuquerque, Austin, Dallas, Denver, Phoenix, Salt Lake City, San Antonio, San Diego, San Jose, Tampa, and Tucson.

10. People are demanding variety instead of "one size for all."
    - Only 7 percent of the population fits the old traditional family profile: working father, mother at home, two children.
    - Today there are 752 different models of cars and trucks, 2,500 types of light bulbs, and 200 different TV channels on cable networks.

Ecological Forces

As the opening case on ocean incineration illustrates, **ecological forces** have come to have a pervasive influence on managerial decision making. This concern for protecting and preserving the natural environment led in the 1970s to enactment in the United States of the Clean Air and Clean Water Acts. More recently—and perhaps more problematically for business in the 1990s—attention has focused on the Resource Conservation and Recovery Act (RCRA or "Reck-Rah").

Passed by Congress in 1976, RCRA was originally intended to regulate the 15,000 largest generators of hazardous waste, which are the major source of the 250 metric tons of hazardous waste produced in the United States annually.

As business and government learned more about waste management problems, however, it became clear that even small generators of hazardous waste could do long-term ecological damage by disposing of waste improperly. Consequently,

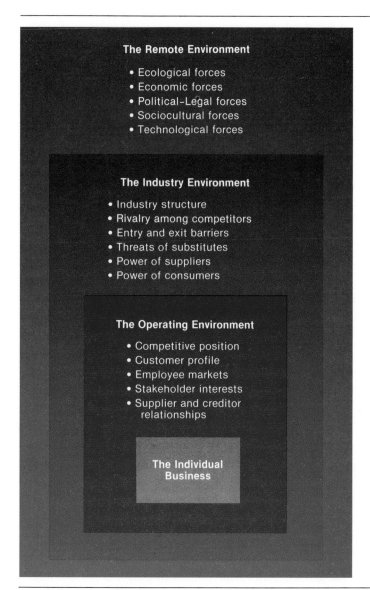

FIGURE 4-1
The Environmental
Forces Exerted on
Business

the Reagan administration broadened RCRA's responsibilities as of 1984. Companies that produce as little as 220 pounds of toxic waste a month (about half of a fifty-five-gallon drum) are now subject to the complete set of RCRA regulations. An estimated 190,000 businesses in the United States are currently held responsible under the Act.[2] Among the businesses affected are car dealerships that must dispose of motor oil and paint thinner (disposal cost, $400 per drum) and dry cleaners that must get rid of perchloroethylene, a suspected cancer-causing agent used to leach soil from clothing ($140 per drum).

The concern that managers must show for ecological balance is not limited to obeying government mandates. As responsible citizens, managers must consider several related but essentially unregulated issues in their decision making. Finite unrenewable resources such as coal, oil, silver, and numerous other minerals, for example, must be used judiciously until (if ever) substitutes can be created.[3] Finite renewable resources raise a second set of issues that deserve attention. The encouraging fact is that with careful management, such resources as forests and cultivatable land can be more than replenished; they can actually be expanded.

Economic Forces

Economic forces are the pressures on a business that result from the nature and direction of the production, distribution, and consumption of goods and services in the countries in which business operates. Because patterns of consumption are largely determined by the relative influence of various market segments of the population, it is essential that each firm understand the economic trends that affect its industry. A firm must consider, *on both national and international levels,* the general availability of credit, the level of disposable income, and the propensity of people to spend. Prime interest rates, rates of inflation, and trends in the gross national product are additional economic conditions that managers must take into account in decision making.

Frustrated by the tendency of economists to vacillate on their projections— Federal Reserve Board Chairman Alan Greenspan once changed from a doomsday prediction of recession to an optimistic prediction of United States currency appreciation in less than three months—most managers have learned to look only for a consensus among economic forecasters on general tendencies. They have found that painstaking analysis of finely detailed economic projections contributes little to the quality of their business decisions.

For example, our favorite economic forecasts for the 1990s include the following:[4]

1. The United States will create 13 million jobs in the decade. Ninety percent of these will be in service industries. Eighty percent will be filled by women, minorities, and immigrants.

2. The gross national product will rise at an average rate of 2.6 percent a year.

3. The decade will begin by emerging from a recession.

4. Five of six married couples will own their own homes.

5. The truest measure of economic well-being, per capita GNP, will rise by an attractive 2 percent a year.

6. Manufacturing productivity will rise by a strong 4 percent a year.

7. Corporate profits in the United States will rise to a healthy 9 percent a year.

8. Inflation will remain in the 5 percent range.

9. Federal deficits will fall as a consequence of other beneficial economic trends such as GNP growth, low inflation, and new consumption taxes.

Again, managers who study such economic forecasts as these should be trying to gain a general sense of the opportunities that exist for their firms. Will it matter to a business if inflation averages 6 percent rather than 5 percent in the 1990s? Yes, of course. But managers are unlikely to be able to predict the impact of the difference, so they are wise simply to anticipate that inflationary growth will be modest.

Political-Legal Forces

Political-legal forces are the constraints on decision making that result from the legal and otherwise governing parameters within which the firm must, or may wish to, operate. Constraints are imposed on each company through fair-trade decisions, antitrust laws, tax programs, minimum-wage legislation, pollution and pricing policies, administrative "jawboning," and many other actions aimed at protecting the consumer and the environment. These laws, practices, and regulations are most commonly restrictive in nature, so they tend to reduce the firm's potential profits. However, other political and legislative actions are designed to benefit and protect the company. Such probusiness activities lead to patent laws, government subsidies, and product research grants, for example. Thus the restrictions imposed through political and legal forces both limit and benefit the firms subject to their influence.

The legal obligations that permeate the business environment are so numerous and so intrusive on decision making that managers must do more than use their "good sense" in attempting to act as responsible corporate citizens. Indeed they must study the law and understand it thoroughly, often seeking the advice of the firm's attorneys on more technical points. (Strange things can happen; see "In Practice 4-2.") Figure 4-2 provides a list of the principal areas in which managers have legal obligations. The list is far from comprehensive, but it outlines many of the major legal problems that managers may have to confront.

Although federal laws that govern business activities number in the thousands, one can gain a good sense of how they affect management activities by studying a sample of the major federal agencies that regulate business practice.

The agency with the most extensive authority over business practice is the Federal Trade Commission. The mandate of the FTC is "to prevent the free enterprise system from being stifled or fettered by monopoly or anti-competitive practices and to provide the direct protection of customers from unfair or deceptive trade practices."[5]

The responsibilities of the FTC are presented in Figure 4-3, along with those of six other important and influential agencies. It is worth noting that whereas the powers of the FTC are very broad, the authority of the other agencies is restricted to specific products, services, or business activities that are subsets of the FTC's overarching mission.

Sociocultural Forces

Sociocultural forces are constraints on decision making deriving from the beliefs, values, attitudes, norms of behavior, opinions, and lifestyles of the members of the firm's external environment, as evolved from their history, traditions, and

---

In Practice 4-2

ANONYMOUS SOURPUSS CAUSES CLOSING OF LEMONADE STAND

The long arm of bureaucracy has forced two brothers to close a lucrative business that helped them buy a home computer and a trip to Disneyland.

Chip Merrick, 14, and J. J. Merrick, 7, had to close their lemonade stand, a neighborhood institution, because it violated a city zoning ordinance.

The business had slaked the thirsts of deputy sheriffs, city workers, paramedics, and moving van crews for three years, but it's gone now because of an anonymous caller.

The bad news was delivered last week by C. C. Smallwood, a city code enforcement official. The area is zoned for residences, the lemonade stand apparently is a business, and it costs $650 to apply for a zoning change.

"On my own, I wouldn't have done it." Smallwood said. "So many times I thought about stopping there and buying lemonade. It was cute."

But he said when a complaint is filed, city officials have to act.

"We were planning on vacationing and taking some bike tours in New England," Chip Merrick said. "It doesn't look like we will be able to now."

Bruce Merrick, the boys' father, said he wanted to teach them to follow rules. So he told them to close the stand. Then he called the mayor's office.

"Everyone we talked to said they support us, but their hands are tied because a complaint was filed," he said.

The boys gave part of their lemonade profits to their church and several hundred dollars for missionary work, their father said.

Source: From "Anonymous Sourpuss Causes Closing of Lemonade Stand," 1987. Reprinted
by permission of The Associated Press.

---

religious, educational, and ethnic conditioning. As sociocultural attitudes change, so does the demand for various clothing, books, leisure activities, and other products and services. Like the other forces in the remote external environment, sociocultural forces are dynamic. They constantly change as people try to control and adapt to the other environmental factors in order to satisfy their desires and needs. The opening case on ocean incineration presents an outstanding example of the effects of sociocultural forces. It was these forces, not the objective facts about the effectiveness of incineration in the treatment of PCBs, that resulted in international upheaval.

Sociocultural forces affect managers' decisions because they are known to influence the way customers and other outsiders react to the firm's operations and products. It is sociocultural forces that determine customers' perceptions of "good taste" in advertising, employees' views on equal employment opportunity, and competitors' beliefs about ethical business practice.[6] The accuracy of these notions is dramatically illustrated in Figure 4-4 (p. 106), which shows how several cultural attributes vary in five different countries and regions.

DEMOGRAPHIC FORECASTS

A popular and useful way to anticipate the emergence and decline of business opportunities is to employ demographic forecasts to project social forces that will prevail in the future. These demographic forecasts describe the population of those individuals who are possible consumers of the firm's products or services. Typically, demographic forecasts include such variables as age, sex, gender, marital status, housing, income, expenditures, and education. Most businesses that market

FIGURE 4-2
Legal Obligations in the
Business Environment

Legal Area	Type of Firm	Potential Problems
Environmental	Manufacturing; utility; mining; industrial developers; contractors	Excess pollutants; factory location; expansion; cost of equipment; business operation restrictions; limited areas of development; historical or archaeological sites
Employment, OSHA	All firms covered but high vulnerability in manufacturing, industrial construction, and mining companies	Changing guidelines; excessive and costly projections; OSHA inspections and citations; failure to follow guidelines
Workers' Compensation	Most employers covered in most states; covered accidents mostly in manufacturing, industrial construction, and mining firms	Inadequate coverage; product liability causation; disputes over compensation amounts
EEOC	Employers with fifteen or more employees	Discriminatory hiring, firing, promotion, salary increase practices; sexual harassment; invalid testing instruments
Fair Labor Standards	Nearly all businesses, with exceptions for farm, seasonal, and family businesses	Minimum wage; accurate overtime compensation; professional and executive exemptions
Union	All businesses with union workers; businesses that become unionized	Union elections; unfair labor practices; boycotts; slowdowns; pickets; strikes; collective bargaining; union rules (seniority and so forth)
SEC	Sales: Any corporation selling partnership or business interests that qualify as securities (*security* = investment in a common enterprise with profits to come solely from the efforts of others). Reporting: Any business with $1,500,000 in assets and 500 shareholders *or* listed on national exchange. Fraud: All businesses selling securities	Exemption filing; registration statements; inadequate disclosure; fraud; false information; faulty audit
State Blue Laws, Sky Laws	State exemptions vary; businesses selling securities are governed by some part of the states' securities laws	Failure to file; most merit review exemptions; fraud
Business Organization	All types: sole proprietorships, partnerships, corporations	Fictitious name registration; filing of partnership agreement; limited partnership requirement; incorporating requirements; annual reports; IRS elections; statutory agent
Patent	Firms with unique process or product	Patent registration; infringement
Tradename, Trademark	Firms with product name or symbol requiring protection	Registration; or avoiding generic use
Copyright	Literary or music publishing firms	Application; protection; enforcement
Product Liability	Firms selling any product or part	Consumer product safety division; Federal Regulation Compliance (Magnuson-Moss)
Warranty	Firms selling products (regardless of whether written warranty is given)	Uniform Commercial Code—Article II—express and implied warranties; efficacy of disclaimers; samples; models
Corporate Crime	All corporations	SEC, antitrust, tax crimes; fraud; check kiting; failure to correct regulatory violations
Crime, Officer and/or Director Liability	All corporations	Guilt through responsibility; nondisclosed activities; knowledge of violations

Continued

Legal Area	Type of Firm	Potential Problems
Contracts	All firms	Failure to perform; excuses for nonperformance; breach by other party; improper formation; fraud defenses; statute of frauds (written)
Torts	All firms	Defamatory remarks or publication; advertising defamation; interference with business relationships; collection torts (privacy and/or emotional distress); accidental harms (autos, slip, and/or fall)
Product Liability	Manufacturing firms; suppliers to manufacturers	Defective design; inadequate instructions or warnings; quality control; poor distribution system
Agency	All firms	Negligence by employees within scope of employment (auto accidents); employees exceeding their authority; apparent and implied authority; employees leaving to start work for competing firms
Property	All firms	Lease disputes; land ownership disputes; liability to customers on premises; nuisance (operation of plant)

Source: M. M. Jennings and F. Shipper, "Strategies and Tactics for the Public Arena," in *Strategic Planning and Management Handbook*, ed. W. R. King and D. I. Cleland (New York: Van Nostrand Reinhold, 1987), pp. 598–599.

FIGURE 4-2

to U.S. consumers are considering projections of the following demographic trends for the 1990s, which are based on data from the Bureau of the Census:

1. Females will outnumber males by nearly 52 to 48 percent.
2. Newborn females will have a life expectancy of 78 years, as opposed to only 71 years for males.
3. The median age of the population will rise from 31 to 36 years in 1985.
4. A record high 40 percent of all children will be first-borns.
5. Parents will spend $25,000 to raise one child to the age of five years.
6. Population growth will be greatest in the Mountain, South Atlantic, Southwest, and Pacific regions (see Figure 4-5, p. 107, for details).
7. Both disposable income (aftertax income for spending and saving) and discretionary income (for luxuries, after necessities) will rise, and real family income will reach $30,000.
8. Nearly 60 percent of all adult women will be in the workforce.
9. Less than 13 percent of the population will not have a high school diploma.
10. Illegal drug-related losses in worker productivity will cost business billions of dollars per year (see Figure 4-6, p. 108 for details).
11. The downward trend in average family size will stabilize at about 3.2 persons.
12. Of persons 65 or older, 80 percent will have incomes less than $25,000 a year.

Guidelines for Management Practice

Despite their obvious value, all types of data have their shortcomings. Managers should be particularly cautious in the use of demographic data. Although they are collected by the United States government from a very large "sample," Census Bureau data are nevertheless limited in value for three reasons:

1. Most demographic data are collected by the Census Bureau only once every ten years. Thus their "projective" value decreases at the end of every decade. Even the Bureau's selective updates are of somewhat limited value because of a two-year time lag between collection of the data and their publication.

2. Most census data are presented in an overly broad form and hence are too generalized for most firms to use. (Noncollapsed or "raw" data are available, but they are very time-consuming to analyze.)

3. Demographic data are "cold"; that is, they cannot be used to help managers understand the cultural, sociological, or psychological bases for consumers' behavior.

These shortcomings notwithstanding, demographic data are a potent source of information that is vital in forecasting environmental trends and pressures.

FIGURE 4-3
Major Federal Regulatory Agencies

Agency	Impact on Management Practice
Equal Employment Opportunity Commission (EEOC)	Responsible for administering and enforcing the Civil Rights Act; issued the Uniform Guidelines on Employment Selection Procedures
Occupational Safety and Health Act (OSHA)	Established an agency that creates standards to improve the safety of the workplace; conducts inspections of the workplace with the power to fine and imprison employers who do not keep the workplace environment "free from recognized hazards that are causing or likely to cause death or serious physical harm to . . . employees"
Federal Trade Commission (FTC)	Enforces law and guidelines regarding business practices; takes action to stop false and deceptive advertising and labeling
Food and Drug Administration (FDA)	Enforces laws and regulations to prevent distribution of adulterated or misbranded foods, drugs, medical devices, cosmetics, veterinary products, and particularly hazardous consumer products
Consumer Product Safety Commission	Ensures compliance with the Consumer Product Safety Act; protects the public from unreasonable risk of injury from any consumer product not covered by other regulatory agencies
Interstate Commerce Commission (ICC)	Regulates franchises, rates, and finances of interstate rail, bus, truck, and water carriers
Federal Communications Commission (FCC)	Regulates communication by wire, radio, and television in interstate and foreign commerce
Environmental Protection Agency (EPA)	Develops and enforces environmental protection standards and conducts research into the adverse effects of pollution
Federal Power Commission (FPC)	Regulates rates and sales of natural gas producers, thereby affecting the supply and price of gas available to consumers; also regulates wholesale rates for electricity and gas, pipeline construction, and U.S. imports and exports of natural gas and electricity

Source: Adapted in part from W. M. Pride and O. C. Ferrell, *Marketing*, 5th ed. Copyright © 1987 by Houghton Mifflin Company. Used with permission. p. 45.

Country/ Region	Body Motions	Greetings	Colors	Numbers	Shapes, Sizes, Symbols
Japan	Pointing to one's own chest with a forefinger indicates one wants a bath. Pointing a forefinger to the nose indicates "me."	Bowing is the traditional form of greeting.	Positive colors are in muted shades. Combinations of black, dark gray, and white have negative overtones.	Positive numbers are 1, 3, 5, 8. Negative numbers are 4, 9.	Pine, bamboo, and plum patterns are positive. Cultural shapes such as Buddha-shaped jars should be avoided.
India	Kissing is considered offensive and not seen on television, in movies, or in public places.	The palms of the hands are placed together and the head is nodded for greeting. It is considered rude to touch a woman or shake hands.	Positive colors are bold colors such as green, red, yellow, or orange. Negative colors are black and white if they appear in relation to weddings.	To create brand awareness, numbers are often used as a brand name.	Animals such as parrots, elephants, tigers, or cheetahs are often used as brand names or on packaging. Sexually explicit symbols are avoided.
Europe	Raising only the index finger signifies a person wants two items. When counting on one's fingers, "one" is often indicated by thumb, "two" by thumb and forefinger.	It is acceptable to send flowers in thanks for a dinner invitation, but not roses (associated with sweethearts) or chrysanthemums (associated with funerals).	Generally, white and blue are considered positive. Black often has negative overtones.	The numbers 3 and 7 are usually positive. 13 is a negative number.	Circles are symbols of perfection. Hearts are considered favorably at Christmastime.
Latin America	General arm gestures are used for emphasis.	The traditional form of greeting is a hearty embrace followed by a friendly slap on the back.	Popular colors are generally bright or bold yellow, red, blue, or green.	Generally, 7 is a positive number. Negative numbers are 13, 14.	Religious symbols should be respected. Avoid national symbols such as flag colors.
Middle East	The raised eyebrow facial expression indicates "yes."	The word "no" must be mentioned three times before it is accepted.	Positive colors are brown, black, dark blues, and reds. Pink, violets, and yellows are not favored.	Positive numbers are 3, 5, 7, 9, while 13, 15 are negative.	Round or square shapes are acceptable. Symbols of 6-pointed star, raised thumb, or Koranic sayings are avoided.

Sources: From J. C. Simmons, "A Matter of Interpretation," *American Way,* April 1983, pp. 106–111; and "Adapting Export Packaging to Cultural Differences," *Business America,* December 3, 1979, pp. 3–7; and W. M. Pride and O. C. Ferrell, *Marketing* 5th ed. Copyright © 1987 by Houghton Mifflin Company. Used with permission.

**FIGURE 4-4
Multinational Cultural
Variations**

Technology Forces

The history and projected rate of technological advancements are also a major consideration in a firm's remote environment. **Technology** consists of applications of new knowledge for practical purposes in any aspect of business conduct. Therefore, businesses must keep abreast of technological progress in how their raw

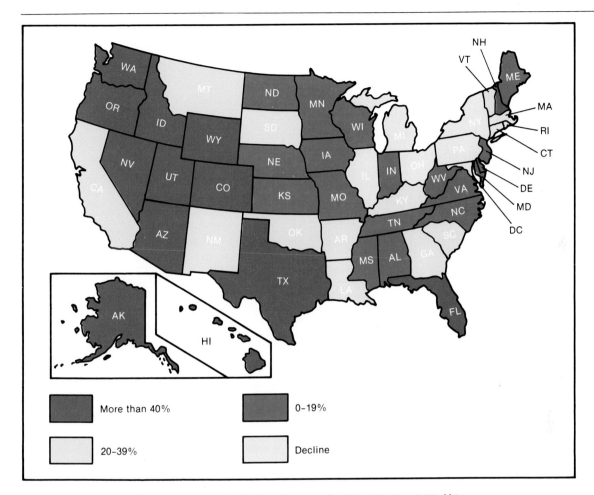

Source: *U.S. News & World Report,* September 19, 1983, p. 58. Copyright, 1983, *U.S. News & World Report.* Reprinted from issue of September 19, 1983.

FIGURE 4-5
Projected Population Growth Rates, 1980–2000

materials are prepared, how their own products are designed and manufactured, what functions those products serve, and how they are delivered to consumers.

Technology innovation and technology transfer are important issues in coping with technology. **Technology innovation** is the development of new methods, processes, products, and technologies by the basic sciences. It is sometimes known as research and development (R&D). Recent developments include laser technology, semiconductors, and ocean incineration as described in the opening case.

Technology transfer involves the conversion of basic scientific breakthroughs into useful products and applications. Examples include the use of fiber optic cables for telecommunications, the mass marketing of acetaminophen, and the use of microwave antennas to monitor long-distance phone calls.

Technological issues for the 1990s include the pending explosive growth in the use of robots. General Motors, for example, is currently reducing the numbers of its 37,000 workers by slowly phasing in robots to fill voids created when people resign or retire. By one account, GM will continue this program until more than 18,000 workers have been replaced by robots. The anticipated drop in cost per

FIGURE 4-6
Drug Abuse: The Cost
to the Economy

A government-sponsored study by the Research Triangle Institute shows the staggering economic toll of drug use in 1983 dollars.

Lost Productivity

Absenteeism, slowdowns, mistakes, and sick leave	$ 4.9 billion
Drug-related deaths	1.3 billion
Imprisonment	2.1 billion
Leaving jobs for criminal careers to support habits	8.3 billion

Medical Expenses

Treatment in rehabilitation centers, in hospitals, and by doctors	$ 1.9 billion
Administration of treatment programs, research training	365 million

Crime

Federal, state, and local expenditures for courts, police, and prisons	$ 5.2 billion
Alarm systems, locks, and other preventive steps for businesses and individuals	1.6 billion
Property destroyed during criminal acts	113 million
Total	**$25.8 billion**

Source: From "Drug Abuse: The Cost to the Economy," *Newsweek,* August 22, 1983, p. 55. Copyright 1983, Newsweek, Inc. All rights reserved. Reprinted by permission.

robot during the next decade from $50,000 to $10,000 each is expected to increase robot sales from their 1980 level of 3,500 to more than 200,000 per year in 1998.[7]

Obviously, technology's impact will be felt in many places. In 1987, one of every five new jobs was classified as "high-tech." Many new product successes will also result from new technologies. Promising forecasts have been made for biotechnology, camcorders, cellular phones, compact disk players, pocket televisions, and videocassette tapes.

Environmental Dimensions

When studied as a set, the five individual components of the remote environment provide a basis for comparing one industry's environment with those of others. This is done by using the components to rate the environment on its degree of change and degree of complexity.[8]

DEGREE OF CHANGE

In evaluating the extent of stability or dynamism in the environment, managers are measuring the **degree of change** that it exhibits. This gauge of the predictability of the environment is determined in part by the stage of the industry life cycle, technological advancements, economic influences, dramatic shifts in customers and markets, government policies, and the strategic posture of competitors.

DEGREE OF COMPLEXITY

The second dimension on which environments are commonly judged is their degree of complexity. Ranging from simple to complex, **degree of complexity** reflects (1) the number of "players" that operate and affect competitive operations and (2) the level of sophisticated knowledge that is required to operate successfully

One of the areas in which General Motors now uses robots is on its automotive chassis assembly lines. (Stephen Ferry/Gamma Liaison)

in that environment. An environment's players include not only competing firms but also their suppliers and the customer groups they serve.

An important element of complexity is the extent of sophisticated knowledge about players and products that a firm must possess in order to operate profitably. Manufacturers of the radar monitors used in air traffic control, for example, must cope with very sophisticated equipment and especially knowledgeable consumers.

AN ENVIRONMENTAL MATRIX

An intriguing way to study business environments is to place the dimensions degree of change and degree of complexity on horizontal and vertical axes, respectively, as shown in Figure 4-7. Next, simply bisect each axis. This creates four quadrants that represent all four of the possible "high/low" combinations of the two dimensions.

Quadrant I defines environments with low degrees of change and of complexity. These stable and predictable environments are typical of industries offering few products and services to limited numbers of consumers. Relying on relatively unsophisticated technologies, firms in these industries seldom have to deal with many suppliers or competitors. Examples include several basic industries such as coal mining, steel fabrication, and the manufacture of containers.

Quadrant II environments exhibit the same stability as those in Quadrant I, but they are complex in terms of the variety of products and services offered and in terms of the customer, supplier, and competitor pressures they must contend with. They also typically must exhibit sophisticated knowledge of products and technologies. Banks, brokerage houses, and appliance manufacturers compete in such industries.

Quadrant III environments are simple yet dynamic and unpredictable. Most similar to firms operating in Quadrant I environments, businesses in these environments offer a few products or services to a few customers. They also deal with a limited number of suppliers and competitors, and their need for sophisticated knowledge is minimal. However, turmoil is far more likely here than in Quadrant I, and frequent changes occur in numbers of competitors, styles or components of products, and production technologies. The classic example is clothing manufacturers, whose production and distribution systems are well established but whose product design characteristics change as often and as radically as fashions, styles, and people's preferences in fabrics.

Quadrant IV environments are characterized by uncertainty; they are both complex and dynamic. Businesses in these industries offer multiple products or services to diverse customer groups. Furthermore, the high level of sophistication needed to operate effectively in these environments is complicated by large numbers of suppliers and competitors. High-technology firms, medical equipment and computer software manufacturers, and many communications firms are characterized by such unpredictable environments.

Managers are often frustrated in their attempts to forecast the dynamic forces in the remote environment. These forces vary so much in their effect on the outcome of each decision that they often seem random and capricious. Such feelings are legitimate! The only certainty about the impact of the environment is that it will remain *uncertain* until the manager's decision is made and enacted.

This disconcerting reality leads many managers, particularly in comparatively small and less influential companies, to become **reactive** in their decision making. They wait for the environment to settle down, to become more predictable so that their decisions become less risky. They hope thereby to reduce environmental uncertainty and to commit resources only at times when the environment is less volatile and easier to understand and forecast. For some businesses, this "wait-and-see" approach can work well, particularly if, while waiting, managers invest in financial, human, and material resources that help keep their firms flexible so that they can quickly and decisively take advantage of whatever windows of opportunity eventually open. However, the trade-off associated with this reactive decision making should also be considered. The absence of a clear managerial commitment to an aggressive, goal-oriented approach to the marketplace can prevent the firm from assuming a leadership position in the competitive environment. Reactive companies are almost always forced to play by their competitors' rules.

To evaluate your understanding of the forces that make up the remote environment, complete "Management Development Exercise 4" at the end of this chapter.

The Industry Environment

Forces operating in the company's industry have an even more direct effect on the behavior of a firm than forces in the remote environment. In this context, the term **industry** refers to a set of businesses that produce products (or provide services) that are close substitutes for one another.

Degree of Change

	Stable	Dynamic
Simple	Stable, predictable environment Few products and services Limited number of customers, suppliers, and competitors Minimal need for sophisticated knowledge I	Dynamic, unpredictable environment Few products and services Limited number of customers, suppliers, and competitors Minimal need for sophisticated knowledge III
Complex	Stable, predictable environment Many products and services Many customers, suppliers, and competitors High need for sophisticated knowledge II	Dynamic, unpredictable environment Many products and services Many customers, suppliers, and competitors High need for sophisticated knowledge IV

Degree of Complexity (vertical axis label)

UNCERTAINTY (arrow)

Source: From R. Duncan, "What Is the Right Organization Structure? Decision Tree Analysis Provides the Answer," *Organizational Dynamics,* Winter 1979, p. 63. Reprinted, by permission of the publisher, from *Organizational Dynamics,* Winter 1979. © 1979 American Management Association, New York. All rights reserved.

**FIGURE 4-7
Dimensions for the
Assessment of
Environments**

The Nature of the Environment

As a starting point in the process of assessing their firm's position in its industry, managers should study the competitive structure of the industry. As Figure 4-8 suggests, industries can be broadly categorized as operating under conditions of monopoly, oligoply, monopolistic competition, or pure competition.

In a **monopoly**, a single firm serves the entire market. Such power is usually possible only when a company holds a critical patent (as Polaroid did on its Land camera film) or when a company operates as a public utility. Dominated as they are by a single seller, monopoly markets pay little heed to price or promotion considerations.

In an **oligopoly**, a few sellers control a large percentage of the supply of the product. One of the two most common forms of competition in the United States, oligopoly can exist for either differentiated products (such as televisions and refrigerators) or homogeneous products (such as steel and coal). Promotion is usually a key feature of competition in these environments, because companies attempt to avoid self-destructive price wars. They try instead to distinguish themselves on the basis of product features such as options, color, delivery, image, trademark, packaging, or advertising.

Among the easily identified oligopolists in the United States are General Motors, Ford, and Chrysler in the automobile industry; McDonald's, Kentucky Fried Chicken, Burger King, and Wendy's in the national fast-food industry; Gerber, Beech-Nut, and Heinz in the baby food industry; and Sears, J.C. Penney, and Wards in the department store chain industry.

The other form of competition common in the United States is **monopolistic competition**. In industries where monopolistic competition prevails, a relatively

Type of Competition	Number of Competitors	Knowledge of Competition	Concentration of Sales	Nature of Product	Barriers to Entry
Monopoly	None	Perfect	100 percent by one seller	No substitutes	Many
Oligopoly	Few	Imperfect	High percentage by each seller	Few substitutes	Some
Monopolistic competition	Many	Moderate	Small percentage by each seller	Many substitutes	Many
Perfect competition	Many	Perfect	Miniscule percentage by each seller	Few substitutes	None

FIGURE 4-8
Characteristics of
Competitive Situations

large number of companies offer similar products. Because each of the competitors in these industries controls a small market share (hence "monopolistic" competition) each has little control over price. Therefore, as in oligopolies, managers attempt to differentiate their products for customers within a narrow market segment. For example, Chiquita has skillfully differentiated its brand name in the generic banana industry.

Pure competition is the fourth category of environmental structure, but it rarely if ever exists anywhere in the world. Theoretically, it would involve a large number of sellers of homogeneous products. No competitor would control a significant market share, there would be easy entry to and exit from the industry, and any competitor could sell its entire output at the current market price. The closest real-world example is perhaps the agricultural industry in Third World nations.

Porter's Five-Forces Approach

Having examined the business environment from the perspective of the remote forces that shape it, and having noted the major differences among market structures, you can better understand how difficult it is for managers to "zero in" on the key factors they must address in their planning and decision making. In a highly regarded book for managers and scholars, Michael E. Porter offers an approach that focuses our understanding of the remote forces by stressing their impact on the specific industry in which a business firm operates. Many managers have found that the industry approach helps them identify the most critical environmental issues.

As shown in Figure 4-9, Porter's five-forces model argues that the nature of competition in an industry is determined by:

1. The potential entry of new competitors

2. The bargaining power of buyers

3. The threat of substitute products and services from companies in other industries

4. The bargaining power of suppliers

5. The rivalry among existing firms

████████ *Guidelines for Management Practice* ████████

Studying the nature of the competitive environment will enable you as a manager to do more than simply label a firm as operating in a monopolistic, oligopolistic, monopolistically competitive, or purely competitive industry.

1. The real payoff from analyzing the market structure that confronts their firms is that it makes managers better able to evaluate the strategies of their competitors and to understand how these firms, collectively, operate in the marketplace.

2. Managers must determine which market segments have unmet needs and which are saturated, where differentiation of products has been accomplished and where it has not, where customer satisfaction is high and where it is low.

3. Such analyses can help managers focus their decision making on the most profitable options available.

Porter believes that studying these five forces will help managers take into account the factors in the remote environment while continuing to concentrate on the reason for environmental assessment—namely, profitable competition.[9] We will briefly examine Porter's comments about each of the five factors that determine the nature of competition.

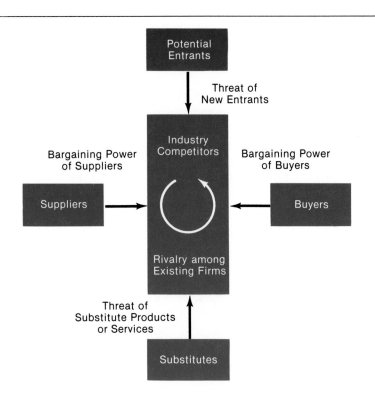

FIGURE 4-9
Five Forces Driving Industry Competitors

Source: Reprinted with permission of the Free Press, a division of Macmillan, Inc., from *Competitive Strategy: Techniques for Analyzing Industries and Competitors* by M. E. Porter. Copyright © 1980 by The Free Press.

THREAT OF ENTRY

When new companies enter an industry, they bring new resources for production and promotion. The result is often increased marketing costs and decreased sales per firm. New entrants are likely to appear, however:

- When there are many economies of scale, as there are in the manufacture of most mass-produced goods.

- When competitors' products are easy to distinguish from one another, as are specialty or differentiated products such as baby care products and cosmetics and services such as investment banking and public accounting.

- When there are large financial requirements for competing, as in mineral extraction and computer hardware manufacturing.

- When it is especially costly for a customer to switch from one industry competitor to another, as it was for IBM personal computer customers who wished to switch to Apple's Macintosh hardware.

- When existing competitors can bar new entrants' access to distribution channels, as many manufacturers have done by convincing their distributors to commit themselves to long-term contracts.

- When existing competitors can block access to new materials, as de Beers can to many South African diamond mines.

    Other advantages of currently competing firms can include proprietary product knowledge, favorable locations, and government subsidies and policies.

BARGAINING POWER OF BUYERS

Buyers from firms in an industry affect competition by forcing prices down and by demanding higher quality and more services. Industry competitors are weakened:

- When buyers purchase in large volumes relative to the capacity of the producer, thereby making the manufacturer dependent on one or few customers.

- When the products that the buyer purchases from the industry represent a significant fraction of the buyer's costs, thereby making the buyer inclined to shop for the best price.

- When the products that the buyer purchases are standard or undifferentiated, again placing the focus on price considerations.

- When the buyer faces few switching costs.

- When the buyer earns low profits.

- When the buyer could stockpile the supplies in order to better control its costs.

- When the industry's product is unimportant to the quality of the buyer's products or services.

- When the buyer has full information about the industry member's competitive position.

THREAT OF SUBSTITUTE PRODUCTS

Porter argues that "substitutes limit the potential returns of an industry by placing a ceiling on the prices an industry can charge. The more attractive the price-performance alternative offered by substitutes, the firmer the lid on industry profits."[10]

Thus, for example, securities brokers are concerned about infringement on their traditional markets by full-service banks, real estate firms, insurance companies, and money market funds.

The firms that are most likely to be threatened by substitute products are (1) those that earn high profits, thereby attracting producers of substitutes who are willing to undercut prices in exchange for gains in market share and (2) those that are vulnerable to technological advances that can dramatically alter the consumer's understanding of the major competitors in the industry.

BARGAINING POWER OF SUPPLIERS

The bargaining power of suppliers is largely determined by the ability of the buyer to pass along increased costs of supplies. Therefore, when industry prices are fairly fixed, suppliers gain influence by threatening to raise their prices or to lower the quality of the materials they supply.

Porter argues that a supplier group is powerful when the following conditions exist:

- It is dominated by a few companies and is more concentrated than the industry to which it sells.

- It does not face substitutes for sale to the industry.

- The industry is not an important customer to the supplier group.

- The suppliers' product is an important input to the industry.

- The suppliers' products are differentiated or entail switching costs.

- The supplier group has the potential to buy a major industry member, to whom it could offer "sweetheart deals."

RIVALRY AMONG EXISTING FIRMS

Rivalry within an industry derives from attempts by firms to win sales or market share from one another. In general, the more intense the rivalry, the less attractive the market is both to present and prospective competitors. Why? Because intense rivalry is most often associated with higher-than-normal costs and lower-than-normal profit margins.

In its most appealing form, rivalry is focused on advertising, which promotes the qualities of a product in general while emphasizing a particular brand. For example, advertisements by Cosco-Peterson that spell out the advantages of having children ride in safety car seats not only help the company sell its products but may also increase the number of customers interested in buying a car seat, Cosco brand or not.

Much more common, however, is rivalry that is manifested in profit-devouring price competition. Lowered prices are matched by competitors, and the principal effect is lost profits for the industry. Furthermore, customers come to expect that prices will remain low in the future. If prices rise even to prerivalry levels, the industry's customers seek substitutes more actively.

Rivalry is intensified by a number of factors:

- Numerous or equally strong competitors; in such situations, no firm is strong enough to "mediate" or suppress disputes between companies.

- Slow industry growth; competitors must win market share from one another in order to grow.

- Higher fixed or storage costs; strong needs to produce at capacity or to move the goods into customers' hands create intense price competition.

- Little differentiation or low switching costs; competition on price is accentuated as a consequence.

- Diverse competitors; different company needs can prompt actions that disrupt the "peace" among nonconfronting firms.

- High stakes; when the consequences of success or failure are so high that they may profoundly affect a corporation's overall performance, the competition becomes vigorous.

- High exit barriers; when it is extremely difficult for a corporation to leave a competitive arena, it often competes very hard to survive, even at low profit margins. Such exit barriers include specialized assets with low liquidation values, fixed costs of exit such as labor agreements or resettlement costs, strategic interrelationships with other units of the corporation, governmental and social restrictions, and management's emotional commitment.

Porter's five-forces model is extremely well conceived and clever, and it provides many managers with conceptual "handles" to use in assessing the forces that are active in their competitive environments. However, for just as many managers, the sophisticated issues Porter raises aggravate self-doubt about their ability to assess environmental trends intelligently. The goal of all managers, of course, is to be **proactive** in their decision making—that is, to make decisions whereby they help create the future environment that will enable them to achieve their objectives.

There is no doubt that planners experience numerous frustrations in conducting an analysis of environmental forces. However, they report that the greatest benefits of environmental assessment frequently derive not from fine-tuning business decisions, but from identifying and acting on fairly easily read signs of (1) growing impediments to the firm's future success and (2) emerging opportunities that warrant serious investigation. Thoroughly analyzing major industry environmental forces can yield significant insights to managers who are competent in making such assessments and who do so diligently. As managers work to evaluate the impact of industry forces on their organization, it is critically important for them to also assess the affects of governmental influences on potential for dramatic and unexpected changes in industry performance. As shown in "Insights for International Managers 4," the power of governmental control is felt most frequently by multinational firms.

The Operating Environment

More commonly seen to affect the success of a business than either the remote or industry environment is the operating environment. The **operating environment** consists of the forces in a firm's immediate situation that pose many of the challenges it faces when it tries to attract or acquire needed resources or to market its goods and services in a profitable manner. Also called the *task environment,* the operating environment represents the level at which the individual firm has the greatest influence. Its forces require quicker responses on the part of managers and demand more frequent assessments. In many respects, this is true because the operating environment is very much a "personalized" arena, wherein the general forces in the larger remote and industry environments are interpreted in terms of their specific relevance for an individual firm. Among the most prominent of these forces are a firm's competitive position, its customer profile, its stakeholder interests, its reputation among suppliers and creditors, and its accessible employee markets. These five forces will now be explored in detail.

Competitive Position

Coming to understand the firms with which one competes in an industry is an extraordinarily complex and often costly undertaking. Among the types of information that can be collected and assessed for each individual competitor are market share, breadth of product line, the effectiveness of its sales distribution, proprietary and key account advantages, price competitiveness, the effectiveness of its advertising and promotion, facility location and newness, capacity and productivity, place on the experience curve, costs of raw materials, financial position, relative product quality, R&D advantages, the caliber of its personnel, and its general image.[11] When the firm knows where its major competitors fall on all of these dimensions, it has a good grasp of its own **competitive position**.

Whereas general information about competitors is collected and evaluated in the assessment of forces operating at the industry level, more specifc information must be considered in the analysis of the operating environment. In theory all firms within an industry compete against each other, but in fact firms compete most directly against a relatively small group of others with whom they share some few key product, market, or technological characteristics. National fast-food chains such as Wendy's and McDonald's battle head-on, ignoring small chains like Rush's. Status-minded Woodward & Lothrup's worries about Bloomingdale's but not about T.J. Max. Presidential Airlines watches Piedmont Airlines in the East but seldom considers Western Airlines in the West. Thus a key to assessing the competitive element in the operating environment is to determine just who one's strongest competitors will be and what advantages they will enjoy as they launch their market plans.

Customer Profile

Perhaps the most valuable result of conducting an analysis of the operating environment is that it helps managers gain an understanding of the characteristics of their customers. By developing a **customer profile** of present and prospective buyers, managers become better able to plan the operations of the firm, to anticipate changes in the size of markets, and to reallocate resources in response to forecasted shifts in consumer demand patterns.

Insights for International Managers 4

GOVERNMENTAL INFLUENCES

Government influences all foreign business, although with varying degrees of control. Whether you are doing business in one of the twenty-four member countries of the Organization for Economic Cooperation and Development (OECD), such as Japan, or the countries of Western Europe, or trading in non-OECD countries, such as Mexico, Korea or Taiwan, your business abroad will be affected by the country's trade structure. Just as at home, business practices are restricted by law. You must play by a different set of rules, and it is your job to know the restrictions.

In the USSR, East European countries, and the People's Republic of China, you must find out from the Ministry of Foreign Trade which commodity group includes your product and which foreign trade organization is responsible. Foreign trade is a function of a state monopoly, and contracts are negotiated with foreign trade organizations (FTOs), a legal entity assigned by the state to serve as intermediaries between foreign and domestic organizations. The FTO is not an unbiased intermediary; it represents the domestic operation in negotiations and may act as its purchasing agent. The FTO is primarily responsible for evaluating the commercial aspects of a potential import—price, quality, quantity, delivery times, and payment terms—while the technical evaluations will usually be made by the end-user.

In the USSR, the German Democratic Republic (East Germany), Bulgaria, Czechoslovakia, and Rumania, an American firm is unlikely to have any direct access to the foreign company. Elsewhere, such as in the People's Republic of China, Poland, and Hungary, decision making has become somewhat more decentralized as a result of economic reform. This does not mean one may completely by-pass FTOs, but it does mean that contact with the end-user can be more direct once initial contact is made with the FTO.

In a centralized business environment it is best to establish how much authority any individual or department really has before wasting too much energy "barking up the wrong tree." And the more centralized the decision making (as in Russia but less so in China), the more negotiations or promotional techniques must be carefully adapted to the audience of decision makers and may even ignore the actual end-user or supplier. Once business is under way, promotion, market research, and conduct of business in general will continue to be restricted.

Source: From L. Copeland and L. Griggs, *Going International* (New York: Random House, 1985), p. 23.

Four principal types of information—geographic, demographic, psychographic, and buyer-behavior information—are useful in constructing a customer profile.

It is is important to understand the boundaries of the *geographic* area from which one's customers do or could come. Geographic locations are commonly defined by national, regional, county, city, or metropolitan boundaries, by population density, and by climate. Almost every product and service market exhibits some geographic quality that makes it variably attractive to buyers from different locations. Products such as snow skis, Hobie cats, and western-style boots have strong regional appeal but would not often be successful if they were marketed nationwide.

Demographic variables are the factors most commonly used for differentiating among groups of individual customers. Typically included in demographic studies are measures of age, sex, family size, stage in the life cycle, income, occupation, religion, education, race, nationality, and social class. Figure 4-10 gives a very specific example of how sales of over-the-counter drugs have been affected by demographic changes in the customer population.

Customer personality and lifestyle are often even better predictors of purchase behavior than geographic or demographic variables. In such situations, a psychographic study of customers is an important component of the total profile. *Psychographic* variables that are frequently used include compulsiveness, gregariousness, autonomy, conservatism, authoritarianism, leadership, and ambitiousness. Memorable soft-drink advertising campaigns by Pepsi Cola ("The Pepsi Generation") and 7 Up ("It feels so good comin' down") reflected management's attending not only to demographics but also to the psychographic characteristics of their largest customer segment—physically active, group-oriented nonprofessionals.

Another type of information that can be used in constructing a customer profile is *buyer-behavior* data. Such data reflect a set of factors used to explain or predict some aspect of customers' behavior. Information gathered by a business about such buyer-behavior factors as usage rate, benefits sought, and brand loyalty can significantly help managers design business strategies that are accurately and profitably targeted.

Employee Market

The ability of a firm to attract and retain capable employees is an undeniable key to success. Thus firms need to consider carefully three forces in the operating environment that most directly affect their attempts to compete successfully for talented, skilled, and committed employees.

1. *The business's reputation as an employer.* A firm that is seen as a permanent fixture in the community, is at least competitive in its compensation package, is concerned with employee welfare, is respected for its product or service, and is appreciated for its overall contribution to the general welfare is more likely to attract and retain valuable employees than is a rival firm that either exhibits fewer of these qualities or emphasizes one to the detriment of others.

2. *Local employment rates.* Depending principally on what stage of growth a business community has reached, the readily available supply of skilled and experienced personnel may vary considerably. A new manufacturing firm seeking skilled employees in a vigorous and established industrialized community obviously faces a more difficult problem than the same firm would if it were located in an economically depressed area where similar firms had recently cut back their operations.

3. *Ready availability of needed knowledge and skills.* Some people's skills are so specialized that they may be forced to relocate in order to secure appropriate jobs and the impressive compensation that their skills usually command. Examples include oil drillers, recognized chefs, technical specialists, and industry executives. A firm seeking to hire such an individual is said to have broad labor market boundaries. That is, the geographic area within which the firm might reasonably expect to be able to attract qualified candidates is quite large. On the other hand, it is much less likely that an individual with more commonly available skills would be willing to relocate from any considerable distance in order to get a modest raise or take a small step upward in his or her career. Thus the labor market boundaries are fairly limited for, say, unskilled laborers, clerical personnel, and retail clerks. Firms have to recruit them locally or face shortages.

FIGURE 4-10
Demographic
Characteristics of the
Over-the-Counter Drug
Industry

What factors are the major contributors to recently increasing sales in over-the-counter drugs? Is it the recent preoccupation of young adults with health and fitness? Is it the greater variety of drugs that are now available? A demographic study of over-the-counter drug purchasers indicates that the answer lies simply in an aging population. Notice in the percentages shown that older households (33.7 percent) account for a disproportionate share of drug sales (43.1 percent). Additionally, the data suggest that whereas education levels may be irrelevant to purchase patterns, income levels are not. Thus as real income continues to rise, increased sales in the over-the-counter drug industry appear to be very likely.

	Percent of Households	Percent of Drug Expenditures
Age of Household Head		
Under 25	11.8	4.3
25–34	23.5	18.0
35–44	16.0	17.0
45–54	15.0	17.6
55–64	14.8	20.1
65 and over	18.9	23.0
Household Income		
Under $5,000–$9,999	35.8	27.5
$10,000–$19,999	26.9	29.0
$20,000–$34,999	26.7	31.0
$35,000–$49,999	7.7	9.3
$50,000 and over	3.1	3.4
Education of Household Head		
Some high school or less	26.1	26.9
High school graduate	30.8	28.4
Some college	21.1	22.9
College graduate	22.0	21.8

Source: Adapted from F. Linden, "Over-the-Counter Drugs," *American Demographics*, April 1985, p. 4. Reprinted with permission of American Demographics, Inc.

Managers carefully monitor trends in employment opportunities. They provide solid clues to the skills, knowledge, and abilities that managers are most or least likely to have difficulty finding in job applicants in the future. "In Practice 4-3" provides an interesting example.

Stakeholder Interests

Influential persons and groups who are vitally interested in the actions of a business are called **stakeholders**. Included in the general category of stakeholders are several who are commonly recognized to exert forces on managers, such as competitors, customers, suppliers and creditors, employees, and government. We have already discussed these groups as they are active in the operating environment.[12] Also included as stakeholders are the following equally potent sources of influence on managers:[13]

1. *The general public.* This constituency demands that the firm participate in and contribute to society as a whole, that it bear a fair portion of the cost of maintaining government, that it charge fair prices for products and services, that it advance technology in its lines of business, and that it behave both legally and ethically.

2. *Local communities.* The local community demands that the firm provide productive and healthful employment, that company officials participate in community affairs, that the firm provide regular employment and fair pay, that it support the local government, that it participate in cultural and charity projects, and that it exhibit a sustained commitment to the community.

3. *Stockholders.* As the true owners of the business, stockholders demand to share in the distribution of profits, in additional stock offerings, and in assets upon liquidation. They are also legally entitled to "vote their shares" at the company's annual meeting, to inspect company books, to transfer their stock, and to elect and remove the board of directors.

4. *Unions.* Organized labor unions seek recognition as the negotiating agent for employees and desire to perpetuate the union's role as a participant in the business organization.

To summarize, then, the general public seeks some overall improvement in the quality of life as a consequence of the firm's existence, local communities want the company to be a responsible citizen, stockholders claim appropriate returns on their investments, and unions seek to negotiate benefits for their members in proportion to the latter's contribution to the company's success.

Supplier and Creditor Relationships

Smooth-running and dependable relationships between an organization and its suppliers and creditors are essential to the firm's prosperity. A company depends on such sources for financial support, services, materials, and equipment. Moreover, a business is occasionally forced to make special requests of its creditors and suppliers for such favors as quick delivery, liberal credit terms, or smaller-than-normal orders. Particularly at these times, it is essential that the business have developed an enduring and mutually beneficial relationship with its suppliers.

Given the importance of suppliers and creditors in making the operating environment attractive to a company, managers must assess what the suppliers and creditors seek from their relationship with the firm. In general:

1. Suppliers want timely repayment of the credit they have extended, and they value professional, dependable, and enduring relationships with the firm in terms of personal contacts and the business practices involved in the firm's purchasing and receiving of goods and services.

2. Creditors want timely interest payments and return of principal from their investment in the firm, security of their pledged assets, and relative priority among those who must be paid in event of the firm's liquidation.

In essence, then, suppliers and creditors eagerly provide the firm with resources it needs when they have reasonable assurance that, like other "investors," they will receive a fair financial return.

In Practice 4-3

JOBS OF THE NINETIES: FROM SUREFIRE HITS TO IMPOSSIBLE DREAMS

First, the good news: jobs requiring a college degree are expected to increase "significantly" by 1995, according to federal labor economists. Fields with dramatically rising employment rates include health services, computer sciences, and engineering. However, in sheer numbers of jobs, the Bureau of Labor Statistics states that job growth in the 1990s will be greatest for building custodians, cashiers, secretaries, general office clerks, and salesclerks.

To help you chart your career course, we've ranked future jobs for college graduates into four groups, based on federal statistics. The categories are: Surefire Hits, jobs that will increase rapidly by the 1990s, with little competition for openings; Growth Jobs, moderately increasing, some competition; The Combat Zone, increasing, but highly competitive; and The Impossible Dream, the same or declining numbers of jobs, very stiff competition.

Computer and engineering jobs are multiplying as new technology increases demand. Health-care jobs are burgeoning because there will be more of us in the 1990s, especially more older people, who generally need more medical care. Indeed, a gerontology specialization—whether as a doctor, nurse, or therapist—will boost employer interest in the next decade.

Within each category that follows, jobs are ranked by ease of hiring (the occupation with the highest level of employment for the future is first in each group). For example, the rankings show that, by 1995, it will be easier to find a job as an actress than as a lawyer. Some jobs, though not ranked high, are showing a revival in hirings—preschool teachers, for example.

Surefire Hits

- Computer systems analysts
- Computer programmers
- Electrical engineers
- Occupational therapists and physical therapists
- Health services administrators
- Mechanical engineers
- Podiatrists

Growth Jobs

- Registered nurses
- Nuclear engineers
- Civil and metallurgical engineers
- Bank managers
- Chemical engineers
- Travel agents
- Industrial engineers
- Aerospace engineers
- Accountants and auditors
- Preschool teachers and elementary schoolteachers
- Biological scientists
- Actuaries

The Combat Zone

- Actors, actresses, dancers
- Designers
- Architects
- Stockbrokers
- Writers and editors
- Physicians
- Lawyers
- Psychologists
- Real estate agents
- Veterinarians

The Impossible Dream

- Public relations
- Radio and TV announcers
- Chiropractors
- Economists
- Dentists
- Social Workers
- Urban and regional planners
- High school teachers
- College and university teachers (this field is expected to lose 111,000 by 1995)

Review of the Learning Objectives

Having studied this chapter, you should be able to respond to the learning objectives with extensions of the following brief answers:

1. **Identify and describe the three levels of environmental forces.**

   The remote environment is composed of ecological, economic, political-legal, sociocultural, and technological forces that originate beyond, and usually regardless of, any single firm's operating situation. The industry environment is composed of five forces—entry barriers, rivalry among existing firms, threats of substitutes, and the bargaining power of suppliers and buyers. These forces create opportunities and impose limits on firms that are in the same industry. The operating environment consists of factors in the immediate competitive situation that spawn many of the challenges a particular firm faces when it tries to attract or acquire the resources it needs or to market its goods or services in a profitable manner. Among the most prominent of these forces are a firm's competitive position, customer profile, stakeholder interests, reputation among suppliers and creditors, and employee markets.

2. **Distinguish between technology innovation and technology transfer.**

   Technology innovation involves the *development* by the basic sciences of new methods, processes, products, and technologies. Technology transfer involves the *conversion* of scientific breakthroughs into useful products and applications.

3. **Name the factors that intensify rivalry among industry competitors.**

   Rivalry among industry competitors is intensified when numerous, equally strong, or diverse competitors are present and under conditions of slow industry growth, high fixed or storage costs, little differentiation among competing products or low switching costs, high stakes, and high exit barriers.

4. **Identify the four principal types of information used in constructing a customer profile.**

   These types of information are geographic, demographic, psychographic, and buyer-behavior data.

5. **Cite the principal claims of a firm's major stakeholders.**

   A firm's general public seeks some overall improvement in the quality of life as a result of the firm's existence. Local communities want the company to be a responsible citizen. Stockholders claim appropriate returns on their investments. Unions seek benefits for their members in proportion to their contribution to the company's success. Customers want what they pay for, suppliers seek dependable buyers, governments expect obedience to laws, and competitors want fair competitors.

Guidelines for Management Practice

Looking at the three levels of the environment simultaneously can provide some interesting insights into managerial behavior and success. Frustrations occur at each level. The remote environment is too massive, complex, and powerful to be controlled (or usually even influenced) by a firm. The industry environment is often too political, uncertain, regulated, and confrontational to engender optimism and positive management action. The operating environment, where managers can have the most direct and constructive impact on organizational behavior, is frequently the least influential in determining the company's financial performance.

In general, then, how should managers behave in assessing these three difficult environments and steering the firm to success. Some suggestions follow.

1. With regard to the remote environment, try to keep abreast of major trends that are likely to affect your firm. Most first-hand data collection and analysis are far beyond the resources and talents of an individual business. Your task is to study the findings of others and attempt to interpret their significance for your firm. Look for major shifts or monumental events that might influence your company. Focus only on the "big negatives" and the "big positives" in the remote environment that can reasonably be expected to affect your industry and firm.

2. The magnitude of the task of monitoring and assessing the industry environment shrinks somewhat when a firm is involved in an industry association. These associations, which exist for every major industry, help firms interpret the effect of remote forces on the industry at large and of industry forces on various kinds of individual firms. Furthermore, industry associations maximize the influence of individual member firms by voicing their arguments collectively to industry stakeholders. Thus managers can increase both their understanding of the industry environment and their impact on it through active membership in their industry association.

3. The arena in which managers can make the most difference is the operation of their own businesses. The advantage that any one firm enjoys over another can usually be attributed to its managers' skill in understanding and maneuvering in the operating environment. To a large extent, the remote environment is essentially uncontrollable and the industry environment is essentially unmanageable. Still, some firms do better than others, generally as a consequence of better management within the operating environment. Thus the key to organizational success is to keep a weather eye out for the big events in the remote environment, anticipate their impact on your industry, and attempt to position your firm within its operating environment in such a way as to use those larger environmental forces to advantage.

Key Terms and Concepts

Having completed your study of Chapter 4 on "Environmental Forces," you should have mastered the following important terms and concepts:

environmental forces	sociocultural forces	degree of complexity	oligopoly	operating environment
remote environment	technology	reactive decision making	monopolistic competition	competitive position
ecological forces	technology innovation	industry	pure competition	customer profile
economic forces	technology transfer	monopoly	proactive decision making	stakeholder
political-legal forces	degree of change			

Questions for Discussion

1. In what ways does the analysis of environmental forces become more complex when multinational companies are involved, as in the case of ocean incineration?

2. Many management experts do not include ecological forces among those affecting the corporate environment. Do you believe they should be included? Explain.

3. Can you forecast an eleventh megatrend? On what data do you base your forecast?

4. Why is it practical for managers to analyze their environments in terms of three levels?

5. It is estimated that the United States will spend as much as $16 billion on the care of AIDS patients in 1991, that health insurance rates for employers and individuals are about to soar, and that AIDS-related problems on the job will be a major employee relations issue in the 1990s. How could paying close attention to the competitive environment help managers deal effectively with these issues?

6. Select a highly visible consumer product. Can you subjectively determine the demographic forecasts that might have shaped its advertising program?

7. Describe some of the corporate strategies that would be associated with each of the environments shown in Figure 4-8.

8. Give examples of how American firms in industries that operate under conditions of oligopoly differ from other U.S. firms in their competitive behaviors.

9. In what ways would an industry's barriers to entry also create barriers to exit?

10. Cite examples of proactive and reactive responses by industry competitors to the same event or trend.

Notes

1. From B. K. Tigner, *Management Review,* May 1986, pp. 14–16. Excerpted, by permission of the publisher, from *Management Review,* May 1986. © 1986 American Management Association, New York. All rights reserved.

2. J. Finegan, "Down in the Dumps," *Inc.,* September 1986, pp. 64–68.

3. *Seventeenth Annual Report of the Council on Environmental Quality* (Washington, D.C.: Government Printing Office, 1987).

4. M. Brody, "The 1990s," *Fortune,* February 2, 1987, pp. 22–24.

5. "Your Federal Trade Commission" (Washington, D.C.: Federal Trade Commission, 1977), pp. 8–9.

6. B. Rosen and T. H. Jerdue, "Sex Stereotyping in the Executive Suite," *Harvard Business Review* 52 (1974): 45–48.

7. "Robots Join the Labor Force," *Business Week,* June 9, 1980, pp. 62–78.

8. H. Mintzberg, *The Structuring of Organizations* (Englewood Cliffs, N.J.: Prentice-Hall, 1979).

9. M. E. Porter, *Competitive Strategy* (New York: Free Press, 1980), pp. 5–33.

10. M. E. Porter, "How Competitive Forces Shape Strategy," *Harvard Business Review* 57, no. 2 (March–April 1979): 142.

11. These items were selected from a competitive-position assessment matrix proposed by C. W. Hofer and D. Schendel in *Strategy Formulation: Analytical Concepts* (St. Paul, Minn.: West, 1978), p. 76.

12. R. E. Freeman, *Strategic Management, a Stakeholder Approach* (Boston, Mass.: Pitman, 1984), pp. 24–27.

13. W. R. King and D. I. Cleland, *Strategy, Planning, and Policy* (New York: Van Nostrand Reinhold, 1978), pp. 152–154.

Cohesion Incident 4-1
Cronor Contract

In Roger's first year as manager of the Journey's End in Graniteville, he circulated a survey asking the guests why they had chosen to stay at Journey's End. He discovered that every month, at least eight to ten rooms had been charged to Cronor Industries. Further research indicated that each month Cronor had personnel or customers from other cities visit its Customer Service Center located in Graniteville.

After gathering his information, Roger made an appointment to talk with the manager of the Customer Service Center. Over the next few weeks, Roger was able to negotiate a contract with Cronor in which ten rooms would be permanently assigned to Cronor to be used as Cronor needed them. Although the rate charged to Cronor was only 75 percent of the normal rate, Roger felt good about the deal; it ensured full occupancy in those rooms as far as his records were concerned. Cronor was willing to pay for days when the rooms were *not* used because it valued the convenience of the arrangement and the assurance of always having rooms reserved. The original contract was for a year's duration, and subsequent contracts were written for a year at a time.

During the first two years, both Roger and the management of Cronor were pleased, and renegotiating the contract was just a formality. However, Roger has just received a letter, which he shared with Charles, stating that a competitive inn in Graniteville was offering Cronor the same type of contract at a 10 percent lower cost than that charged by Journey's End. Because of the good relationship they have had with Journey's End, Cronor managers have offered to stay with Journey's End if the motel will lower its rates to match its competitor's bid.

"Charles, I've been expecting something like this to happen for the past few months. Ever since Happy Nights moved here, it has done everything possible to cut into our market share. I hate to lose our contract with Cronor, but if we cut the price this year, I feel sure that Happy Nights managers will just lower theirs again next year. And with all the new inns being built around Graniteville, we can expect more of these problems. Maintaining our 83 percent occupancy rate is going to be very difficult. What do you think we should do?"

Discussion Questions

1. What alternatives do Roger and Charles have? What are the possible consequences of each?

2. Besides competition, what other external factors do firms often encounter?

3. Which do you think are easier to control, internal or external factors? Why?

Cohesion Incident 4-2
Autoalarm: Effects of the External Environment on Marketing Decisions

The first problem Leslie Phillips was assigned when she joined the Marketing Research Department was the case of Autoalarm. The Elizabethtown plant designed, manufactured, and marketed this antitheft device. The alarm system was designed to detect both intrusion into parts of the vehicle, such as the hood, trunk, doors, and windows, and any motion such as that caused by vandalism to the body or paint job. First-year sales were disappointingly low, despite strong promotions directed at auto manufacturers and accessory distributors. In fact, sales were slow enough to cast doubt on the advisability of continuing to produce Autoalarm.

In analyzing sales patterns, Leslie found that auto manufacturers accounted for less than 30 percent of Autoalarm sales. The vast majority of sales were to the auto accessory aftermarket, but even these were only 75 percent of what had been forecast on the basis of initial market studies. Earlier research, conducted before the department was formed, had indicated that auto theft rates have more than doubled in the last ten years. Furthermore, there had appeared to be few strong competitors producing a quality alarm system. The opportunity to develop a market for the new product had seemed ripe. Leslie decided to pursue two lines of research to find out what went wrong. While she tried to determine why auto manufacturers were buying so few Autoalarms, she set Bill Sherman to work studying attitudes of aftermarket purchasers.

Bill interviewed aftermarket distributors who purchased Autoalarm and surveyed samples of "end users"—that is, consumers who had had Autoalarm installed in their cars. The interviews and surveys addressed three questions: What did users of Autoalarm like and what did they dislike about the product? For consumers who chose another brand over Autoalarm, why was the other brand preferred? Who was likely to buy the alarm system and for what purpose?

The interview and survey data provided ready answers to questions about consumers' likes and dislikes. Consumers were satisfied with the product's performance, but two features of the product were perceived as substantial liabilities—substantial enough to have accounted for the disappointing level of aftermarket sales. First, potential consumers reported that the device, which protruded several inches below the dash when installed, was ugly and got in the way of passengers in the front seat. Second, most consumers wanted either motion detection or intrusion detection, but not both features. Furthermore, they considered the second feature an unnecessary added expense. The survey also revealed that many people believe alarm systems are bought for "luxury" and "specialty" cars, not "family" cars. Bill concluded that increasing the aftermarket sales would require making design changes to improve the unit's appearance, reduce its intrusion into the passenger's space, and enable consumers to combine the motion and intrusion detection features *or* select one or the other. In addition, marketing would need to change the image of the alarm system from luxury item to standard accessory.

Leslie's study of auto manufacturers found them reluctant to invest in any type of auto alarm system, standard or optional, until the outcome of pending legislation was known. The Motor Vehicle Theft Law Enforcement Act would soon be introduced in Congress. If passed, the bill would require auto manufacturers to take one of two steps to deter auto theft. They would have to either label twelve major parts of each vehicle with a permanent identification number or equip each car with an effective antitheft system. The auto industry seemed to prefer the alarm option. Because some form of the bill seemed likely to pass, the auto industry planned to lobby heavily for the auto alarm system requirement.

Armed with this information, Leslie called Bill to arrange a meeting to discuss the results of their investigations and to draw up recommendations to include in their report to Eileen.

Discussion Questions

1. What type of variable in the external environment is most clearly illustrated in this case?

2. Why might the mere fact that this legislation is pending have dampened sales of Autoalarm to major automobile manufacturers?

3. What potential impact could passage of the Motor Vehicle Theft Law Enforcement Act have on future markets for Autoalarm?

4. Explain how an external environment variable such as pending legislation can create both opportunities and problems for an organization. Specifically, in what ways does the pending legislation in this case create opportunities for the sale of Autoalarm, and in what ways does it create problems?

5. What other types of external environment variables would Leslie Phillips be wise to consider in her analysis of Autoalarm's future?

Management Development Exercise 4
Environmental Forces

Mark the following trends to indicate what force in the remote environment each represents. Use EC for economic and SC for sociocultural.

_____ 1. People aged 55 and older spend 80 percent of all pleasure-travel dollars spent in the United States because they travel more often, go greater distances, and stay away longer than members of any other age group.

_____ 2. Men make up 71 percent of all passengers on North American airline flights, according to the World Airline Entertainment Association. Male flyers have a median age of forty-five and a median annual household income of $69,800.

_____ 3. Swimming remains the most popular American sport, according to the 1984 Gallup Leisure Activities Index. In 1984, 41 percent of American adults got wet, up from 33 percent in 1960 when the first survey of leisure activities was taken.

_____ 4. About 54 percent of Americans never studied economics in high school or college, and 55 percent of the population tends to feel uncomfortable because they do not know as much as they think they should about economics.

_____ 5. Half the people who live alone will move in with someone within five years. The median time that people spend alone is 4.77 years.

_____ 6. Single women bought 1.1 million homes in 1984, one out of every ten homes sold that year.

_____ 7. When people's incomes rise, they tend to consume more beef, cheese, oils, fruits, and alcoholic beverages and less poultry, eggs, cereal, pasta, and nuts.

_____ 8. As education increases, so does participation in sports. College graduates have the highest participation rate in nearly every sport. The martial arts are most popular with those who have less than a high school education.

_____ 9. More than eleven million Americans lived in mobile homes in 1982, up from 6.5 million in 1971. One-fourth of today's mobile home buyers are people aged fifty-five and older.

_____ 10. According to a 1984 study commissioned by *Newsweek* magazine, the majority of working women—56 percent—earn less than $15,000 annually. One-third earn between $15,000 and $24,999, and a mere 10 percent make $25,000 or more.

_____ 11. Nearly one of every five Americans has a college degree, up two percentage points since 1980—and up fully eight percentage points since 1970, when 11 percent had a college degree.

_____ 12. An average of 1.6 million college graduates will enter the labor force each year until 1995. One in five will have to take a job that does not require a college degree.

_____ 13. According to the 1980 Distress Index, the "least distressed" cities in the nation are Amarillo, Texas; Garden Grove, California; Honolulu, Hawaii; Huntington Beach, California; Independence, Missouri; Parma, Ohio; Torrance, California; and Virginia Beach, Virginia. This index measures unemployment, poverty, violent crime, age of area housing, and city taxes in large cities.

_____ 14. Among workers aged forty-five and older, 38 percent of men and 16 percent of women have been with their current employer for more than twenty years.

_____ 15. American families say they need at least $252 a week to get by. Those aged sixty-five and older say they need at least $198 a week. Those aged thirty to forty-nine need $301 a week. Republicans report that their families need $298 a week, Democrats $251.

_____ 16. The U.S. Department of Agriculture found that in 1983, 41 cents out of each dollar spent on food was spent away from home. That compares with 33 cents in 1970 and 27 cents in 1960. Dinner is the most popular meal when it comes to eating out, but lunch is right behind.

Source: Trends adapted from *American Demographics*, January–October, 1985. Reprinted with permission of American Demographics, Inc.

5

Social Responsibility and Management Ethics

Learning Objectives

Your study of this chapter will enable you to do the following:

1. Summarize the three basic philosophies of social responsibility.
2. Explain the differences among economic, legal, ethical, and discretionary social responsibilities.
3. List the main propositions of the Davis Model of social responsibility.
4. Discuss some arguments for and some against business's assuming social responsibility.
5. Explain the purpose of a social audit and the concept of social responsiveness.
6. Describe three main approaches to business ethics.

Johnson & Johnson's Reaction to Criminal Tampering

In October 1982, seven consumers died after swallowing cyanide-laced capsules of Tylenol. This highly publicized poison scare was expected to leave permanent scars on Johnson & Johnson. Immediately following the crisis, J&J stock fell from 45½ to 38¾, but a few months later it rose to a record 51¼. Industry analysts claim that the recovery occurred because management was able to protect and promote the product's credibility and because J&J was judged as having acted in the consumers' best interest.

James Burke, chairman of J&J, went against the advice of government agents and colleagues when he decided to recall 31 million bottles of Tylenol from store shelves across the country. Government officials feared such a decision would increase the panic that already existed in response to the deaths. Additionally, the FBI argued that this action would demonstrate to terrorists that they could bring a multibillion dollar corporation to bankruptcy. However, Burke prevailed and managed to regain the public's confidence in Tylenol.

Instead of becoming defensive about the deaths, Johnson & Johnson and its McNeil Consumer Products subsidiary, the manufacturer of Tylenol, opened their doors. Burke appeared on public television programs ("Donahue" and "60 Minutes") to explain what had happened and to answer questions. The company dedicated itself to the investigation and posted a $100,000 reward.

After the recall, which cost $50 million after taxes, Burke began campaigning for the new triple-sealed packages of Tylenol capsules. Sales representatives for the company made one million calls to physicians and pharmacists requesting their aid in reassuring consumers. The company also aired testimonial-style TV ads that promoted trust in the company's concern for public well-being.

Within one year Tylenol regained more than 80 percent of the market share it had held before the poisonings. During the three years following the 1982 Tylenol crisis, J&J earnings continued to increase beyond what investors expected. However, in February 1986 a cyanide-laced capsule of Tylenol caused another death. Initially, J&J treated this occurrence as a single isolated incident; however, a second tainted bottle of Tylenol capsules was found in the same vicinity where the Tylenol that killed the latest victim was purchased. In a dramatic response to these incidents, Burke decided that J&J was no longer going to sell any over-the-counter drugs in capsule form. This decision cost the company $150 million. In addition, according to market research, capsules were still preferred to tablets because of their ease of ingestion.

Even though apparent tampering incidents were very isolated, once aware of the problem, Johnson & Johnson immediately initiated a $50 million effort to strip Tylenol from shelves nationwide. (Susan Greenwood/ Gamma Liaison)

The company shifted to the production and sale of Tylenol in the form of caplets, which are smooth, elongated tablets. In an attempt to regain consumer confidence and to promote the use of caplets, Burke appeared both on TV and on radio to explain that capsules could never be safe. J&J was promoting the use of caplets in the interest of public safety. Some industry experts claimed that the company was converting a "J&J" problem into a "capsule" problem, but other drug-producing companies did not follow suit and abandon the manufacture of their capsules.[1]

Introduction

What Is Social Responsibility?

Social responsibility is an organization's obligation to benefit society in ways that transcend the primary business objective of maximizing profits. For example, the primary business objective of the hotel-motel industry is to maximize its profits through increased rental of rooms and sale of food in its restaurants. Yet in some areas of the country, associations of hotel and restaurant owners, in conjunction with United Way and similar charitable groups, have established programs to provide temporary shelter for the homeless. This is a prime example of industry attempting to fulfill its social responsibility.

The concept of social responsibility extends beyond simple stories of corporate charity. It also involves confrontations with controversial political and social issues. Smith and Wesson, a company that makes handguns, cannot avoid the highly charged issue of gun control. Beyond its basic concern with making a profit via the manufacture and sale of firearms, this company must confront the rising concern of society with the role of the handgun in violent crime. Similarly, executives of Trojan, a maker of condoms, encounter widespread social resistance to teenage sexual activity as they try to overcome objections to advertising their AIDS-deterring product on television. In the opening case, Johnson & Johnson risked losing its reputation as a provider of safe products to publicly acknowledge that its Tylenol products were the target of sabotage. As a consequence, Johnson & Johnson faced the possibility of needlessly endangering the psychological and physical well-being of millions of Tylenol users who would be otherwise unaffected by the isolated contaminations.

Business has never existed in a social vacuum. Yet the last two decades have seen a broadening of the public's perception of the responsibility business has to society beyond its responsibility to enhance economic growth. In the public view, the social responsibility of business has come to represent an obligation; business, it is widely felt, should help solve a broad agenda of social problems—from poverty to teenage pregnancy, from crime to environmental pollution.

Most definitions of social responsibility include some reference to corporations advancing the interests of society beyond the bounds of basic economic concerns. Yet the most basic corporate economic concerns *can* be construed as embodying an element of social responsibility, depending on the rationale and intentions of those who are making the decisions. For instance, some managers insist that by maximizing profits, expanding, and thereby creating more jobs, their companies are meeting a social responsibility to lower the unemployment rate.

Because there are various—and often conflicting—approaches to corporate social responsibility, managers should be aware of what approach their companies take. When the basic philosophy of the company is clearly defined, managers can use it to develop guidelines for their personal actions within the firm.

Historical and Philosophical Perspectives

History of Social Responsibility

That producing goods and providing services is not the only responsibility of business is not a new idea. Beginning in the last quarter of the nineteenth century, the rise of the first huge corporations (including the John D. Rockefeller and Andrew Carnegie business dynasties) gave industry tremendous new power that called public attention to the need for some corporate social responsibility. Observers of business at the beginning of this century recognized a need for some form of corporate social responsibility. In 1919 business scholars first warned that society would try to take over business if business neglected its social responsibilities.[2] Other management scholars, writing in the early 1920s, stressed the social responsibility of business.[3]

The public's perception of the social responsibility of business has gone through three phases in this century:

1. **Profit-maximizing management**. Although some observers in the early twentieth century saw a need for social responsibility, the public generally believed that business was responsible only to its own direct interests. This view prevailed from the turn of the century until the 1930s.

2. **Trusteeship management**. In the 1930s the Great Depression, coupled with the rise of labor unions, required business organizations to confront the issue of providing safe working conditions as a basic social responsibility. The labor unions pressured companies to consider factors other than profitability, such as worker benefits, pension plans, and working conditions. In this second phase, managers were required to maintain a balance among claims other than their obvious interest in maximizing profits. Also to be considered were the social complaints and concerns of a wide variety of disparate groups: employees, customers, creditors, and community.

3. **Quality-of-life management**. Since the 1960s managers and organizations have been operating under a third phase in the public's perception of corporate social responsibility. This phase stems from the philosophy that managers and companies should involve themselves directly in attempting to cure major social ills. It is characterized by increased social concern with the regulation of business activities and by the impact of the consumer movement.

Figure 5-1 provides an overview of attitudes associated with these three historical phases. In the form of simple but revealing statements that managers might make, this table characterizes each of the historical phases of social responsibility. Note, for example, the evolution of business attitudes toward aesthetic values. Phases 1 and 2 show, respectively, ignorance of and indifference to this social concern. In phase 3, managers have been willing to help preserve aesthetic values. For example, McDonald's often designs its fast-food restaurants so that they will

FIGURE 5-1
Historical Perspective on Managerial Attitudes toward Social Responsibility

Attitudes	Phase 1 Profit-Maximizing Management (1800 to 1920s)	Phase 2 Trusteeship Management (late 1920s to early 1960s)	Phase 3 Quality-of-Life Management (late 1960s to present)
Orientation	1. Raw self-interest.	1. Self-interest. 2. Contributors' interest.	1. Enlightened self-interest. 2. Contributors' interests. 3. Society's interests.
Economic values	What's good for me is good for my country. Profit maximizer. Money and wealth are the most important. Let the buyer beware (*caveat emptor*). Labor is a commodity to be bought and sold. Accountability of management is to the owners.	What's good for organizations is good for our country. Profit satisficer. Money is important, but so are people. Let us not cheat the customer. Labor has certain rights which must be recognized. Accountability of management is to the owners, customers, employees, suppliers, and other contributors.	What is good for society is good for our company. Profit is necessary, but . . . People are more important than money. Let the seller beware (*caveat venditor*). Employee dignity has to be satisfied. Accountability of management is to the owners, contributors, and society.
Technological values	Technology is very important.	Technology is important, but so are people.	People are more important than technology. We hire the whole person.
Social values	Employee personal problems must be left at home. I am a rugged individualist, and I will manage my business as I please. Minority groups are inferior to whites. They must be treated accordingly.	We recognize that employees have needs beyond their economic needs. I am an individualist, but I recognize the value of group participation. Minority groups have their place in society, and their place is inferior to mine.	Group participation is fundamental to our success. Minority group members have the same rights as everyone else.
Political values	That government is best which governs least.	Government is a necessary evil.	Business and government must cooperate to solve society's problems.
Environmental values	The natural environment controls the destiny of people.	People can control and manipulate the environment.	We must preserve the environment in order to lead a quality life.
Aesthetic values	Aesthetic values? What are they?	Aesthetic values are okay, but not for us.	We must preserve our aesthetic values, and we will do our part.

Source: Adapted from R. D. Hay, E. R. Gray, and J. E. Gates, *Business and Society: Cases and Text* (Cincinnati: South-Western, 1976), pp. 10–11.

not clash blatantly with a particular historical district. In a related spirit of corporate patronage of the arts, Mobil sponsors cultural programming on the Public Broadcast System.

Philosophical Justifications

Corresponding to the three historical phases of social responsibility are three basic philosophies that underlie and provide a rationale for each perspective.

TRADITIONAL PHILOSOPHY

The **traditional philosophy** corresponds to phase 1. According to this philosophy, the main concern of business should be maximization of profits and the long-term interests of the business organization. Social responsibility is defined as the production of goods and services at the lowest cost to society.[4]

Perhaps the best-known advocate of this view is economist Milton Friedman. He holds that business should serve the interests of its stockholders and that to use company resources in ways that do not directly advance stockholder interests is tantamount to spending the owners' money without their consent. This philosophy excludes the demands of groups other than stockholders to which the organization may be responsible.[5] According to the traditional concept, government rather than business is best equipped to deal with social problems.

STAKEHOLDER PHILOSOPHY

The **stakeholder philosophy** corresponds to phase 2. According to this philosophy, managers must be responsible to certain groups that are affected by, or can affect, the company's objectives and interests. Such groups include stockholders, customers, government agencies, competitors, unions, employees, trade associations, important suppliers, protest groups, and others.

Compared to the traditional approach, the stakeholder philosophy broadens the scope of social responsibility. It is often justified on grounds of enlightened self-interest: A better society creates a better setting for business. What is good for the company, it is argued, is good for society. The stakeholder philosophy also makes the accumulation of capital a management priority. Capital accumulation is seen as the basis of social responsibility because it is essential for the creation of future jobs.

A dramatic example of the application of the stakeholder philosophy is the Kellogg Company's reaction to a product tampering scare. Kellogg recalled 44,000 boxes of cereal after metal shavings were found in three boxes of cereal in April 1986. Despite medical opinion that the metal shavings were too small to cause serious injury, company officials initiated the recall as a precautionary measure. The recall involved boxes of Just Right fruit and nut cereal that had already been distributed to twenty-six grocery chains and food distributors in sixteen states. Customers who had already purchased the product could return boxes to stores, or mail box tops to the company, for replacement or refund.

This example and the example of the Johnson & Johnson Tylenol scare discussed in this chapter's opening case show corporate initiative in response to crises. They illustrate an important component of the stakeholder philosophy: social responsibility as a form of self-interest.[6] The responses of Johnson & Johnson and Kellogg were designed to protect consumers. By protecting consumers—an important stakeholder group—the company protected its corporate image and economic interests.

By protecting the interests of stakeholder groups, the corporation hoped to help ensure its long-term profitability, even though it incurred short-term losses. By exercising its own initiative in matters of social concern, these business organizations were governing themselves. Such self-imposed controls reduce the incidence of government intervention. This in turn can reduce conflict between business and government regulatory agencies.[7] In addition, it was clear from their openness and candor and the criteria applied in their decision-making processes that Johnson & Johnson and Kellogg executives placed a high priority on fulfilling their personal sense of moral obligation. Top-level managers consistently tried to keep customers informed of dangers. In the Tylenol case, Johnson & Johnson even helped customers identify competitors' products that could be used as near-substitutes until Tylenol could once again be safely purchased.

The stakeholder philosophy is a bridge between the traditional philosophy and the affirmative philosophy of social responsibility. Although it stops short of advocating a broad commitment to social issues, it nevertheless acknowledges groups to which business should be socially responsible.

AFFIRMATIVE PHILOSOPHY

The **affirmative philosophy** corresponds to the third historical phase. This philosophy of social responsibility is the broadest and most complex of the three. It holds that managers have a responsibility to promote the mutual best interests of the firm and its various stakeholders, including the general public.

The affirmative philosophy goes beyond the stakeholder philosophy in one significant way: It obligates managers to anticipate changes in the social environment in which they operate, and it requires them to blend the goals of the company with the general and diverse interests of society as a whole. For example, beginning in 1985, several major American-owned companies (including General Foods, Pepsico, and Pan American Airlines) voluntarily curtailed their business ventures in South Africa in order to protest that country's policies of racial separation. These companies not only anticipated changes in a society; they actively tried to effect such changes by bringing to bear the pressure of voluntary economic sanctions.

The affirmative philosophy holds that companies have a voluntary obligation to constituent groups other than stockholders. These obligations suggest what business "ought to do" to perform in a morally and ethically satisfactory manner. Management that adopts this philosophy must address the concerns of a wide range of groups as well as plan for the future needs of society.[8] The depth of the required commitment under this approach is apparent in Figure 5-2, which lists some managerial obligations under the affirmative philosophy.

Basic Concepts Applied to a Real Situation

In January 1985, Mack Trucks, Inc., announced its long-awaited decision to build a new $80 million truck plant near Winnsboro, South Carolina. Plant officials said the plant would employ 1,200 workers in the Winnsboro area. This was good news for financially depressed Fairfield County and for state officials who had spent time encouraging Mack to locate a plant in South Carolina.

Examples of Obligation Categories	Examples of Managerial Obligations
Search for legitimacy	Considers and accepts broader—extralegal and extramarket—criteria for measuring the firm's performance and social role.
Ethical norms	Takes a definite stand on issues of public concern; advocates ethical norms for all in the firm, industry, and business in general. These ethical norms will be advocated even if they seem detrimental to the immediate economic interest of the firm or are contrary to prevailing ethical norms.
Operating strategy	Maintains and improves current standards for protection of the physical and social environments; compensates victims of pollution and other corporate-related activities, even in the absence of clearly established legal grounds; evaluates possible negative effects of the firm's planned actions on other stakeholders, including the public, and attempts to eliminate or substantially reduce negative effects prior to implementation.
Response to social pressures	Accepts responsibility for solving current problems; willingly discusses activities with outside groups; makes information freely available to the public; accepts formal and informal inputs from outside groups in decision making; is willing to be publicly evaluated for its various activities.
Legislative and political activities	Shows willingness to work with outside groups for good environmental laws; does not pursue special-interest laws; promotes honesty and openness in government and in the firm's own lobbying activities.

FIGURE 5-2
Some Obligations of Managers under the Affirmative Philosophy

Source: Adapted from S. P. Sethi, "A Conceptual Framework for Environmental Analysis of Social Issues and Evaluation of Business Response Patterns," *Academy of Management Review* 8(1979): 63–74.

Plans to build the new plant corresponded with the closing of a Mack Truck plant in Allentown, Pennsylvania, so the new plant actually represented the relocation of Mack's manufacturing resources. The company also drastically curtailed its parts manufacturing in Hagerstown, Maryland, in favor of increased purchasing from vendors. The plants in Allentown and Hagerstown were both highly unionized, and thousands of union jobs were lost in both of these areas. Mack arranged to operate in Winnsboro with a nonunion labor force.

Groundbreaking for the new plant began in March 1986. But two months after the announcement of its intention to build the plant, Mack had made little information on the new plant available to the press and the public. It was believed that the company's "no comment" stance was related to its desire to avoid problems with the United Auto Workers union. The dearth of information about Mack's plans caused some concern in the Winnsboro community that the longstanding struggle between the UAW and Mack would continue in Fairfield County.

What were the obligations of Mack Truck to its employees, to its potential employees, and to the community in which it located the new plant? The answers to these questions depend on the philosophy of social responsibility that the firm's managers subscribe to. Under the traditional philosophy, Mack executives would be under no obligation to inform the public, or even its own employees and potential employees, about its long-term plans for the new plant. They would not, for example, have to inform Fairfield County officials how many of the expected 1,200 "new" jobs would be filled by current employee transfers (assuming that Mack had this information). Under the traditional philosophy, Mack had no obligation to inform the community of its long-term plans as long as the relocation served to further the economic interests of the company.

Under the stakeholder philosophy, Mack would have an obligation to share its plans for the new plant with those groups that had a direct stake in its operations. Obviously, employees in Allentown and potential employees in Winnsboro were two of these groups. For example, the company would be obligated to inform current employees who wanted to move with the company to Winnsboro of its intention to operate a nonunion plant.

The general public in South Carolina was also a stakeholder. Operating under a stakeholder philosophy, Mack would be obligated to inform the public of its intention to operate a nonunion plant. This would alert the public to possible conflicts. Did the company's relocation of the Allentown plant to Winnsboro depend on its being able to operate a nonunion plant? Under the stakeholder philosophy, the public would have a right to this information.

Under the affirmative philosophy, Mack would be obligated to predict changes in its new competitive environment and to examine them openly. If it was resolved that the plant be nonunion, it would be obligated to make this stance clear to the public. It would also be obligated to defend this stance in terms of its position on the balance of interests between labor and management in society. And rather than focusing solely on the economic advantages Winnsboro would realize from relocation of the plant, Mack would also have to consider any possible social problems the presence of the plant might occasion. Given the criteria we have outlined, Mack chose to operate under a stakeholder philosophy—clearly the prevailing choice of the 1980s.

Defining the Scope of Corporate Social Responsibility

Before planning corporate social programs, managers must be aware of their organization's philosophy on social responsibilities.[9] Many large corporations have some type of stated philosophy about what socially beneficial activities they wish to engage in, and many of these exceed the typical expectations of individuals. In fact, recent surveys have shown that corporate executives' concern with social issues equals, and in some cases surpasses, the concern of the general public.[10]

Figure 5-3 presents the results of a study conducted by Opinion Research Corporation, which surveyed members of the Public Relations Society of America, corporate executives, and officials in Washington, D.C. Each respondent was asked to rate the business community's performance on a variety of public issues. In addition to its obvious value as an index of current opinion, this table suggests areas in which organizations might well exhibit greater social responsibility. The table also highlights the fact that there is a "situational" component to social responsibility. This means that social responsiveness is a consequence not only of managerial values but also of the situation in which a firm operates. The environmental forces described in Chapter 4 account for many of the situational variables that affect the firm's choice among a range of socially responsible options.

Figure 5-4 emphasizes some of the limitations that business is subject to in dealing with social issues. It also suggests guidelines to help society determine

FIGURE 5-3
Perception of Corporate
Social Responsibility

Issues	PERCENT OF THE FOLLOWING RESPONDENTS RATING BUSINESS "EXCELLENT" OR "GOOD"			
	Public Relations Executives $n = 189$	Executives in Major Companies $n = 556$	Executives in Mid-Sized Companies $n = 502$	Washington "Thought Leaders" $n = 103$
Protecting the health and safety of employees	74	84	78	42
Supporting not-for-profit organizations	65	65	57	42
Managing the assets of pension funds in a responsible manner	61	81	62	40
Controlling costs to hold down inflation	40	60	56	29
Paying a fair share to have cleaner air and water	39	63	39	20
Developing adequate energy supplies for the future	37	43	37	32
Providing equal pay for equal work	36	58	49	20
Taking steps to ensure the future competitiveness of U.S. business in world markets	34	46	45	28
Working to effect fair international trade policies	27	38	36	27
Doing something to hold down the cost of health care	26	36	26	12
Improving the quality of public education in the United States	26	25	27	12
Paying a fair share to clean up hazardous industrial waste dumps	24	40	22	17
Paying a fair share to have an adequate supply of water for the future	24	35	23	17
Preventing the flow of proprietary technology from the United States to foreign countries	18	23	22	14
Retraining workers whose skills are obsolete	14	18	23	10
Supporting the rebuilding of roads, bridges, and tunnels in the United States	12	12	19	11
Doing something to preserve world peace	12	18	20	9
Helping Third World countries to improve their standards of living	11	20	19	12
Using their influence to prevent the flow of illegal drugs into the United States	3	4	7	4
Standing up for human rights in other countries	1	9	9	4

Source: From "Survey by ORC Reveals Practitioners' Views on Major Issues," *Public Relations Journal*, August 1984, p. 30. Reprinted with permission from the August 1984 issue of the *Public Relations Journal*. Copyright 1984 by the Public Relations Society of America.

what it should expect of business—and what it should *not* expect—in the area of social responsibility. In essence, it places the social responsibility of business in a social context and acknowledges the multifaceted constraints on business's actions.

FIGURE 5-4
Responsibility of
Society to Business in
the Shared Pursuit of
Social Obligations

1. *Set rules that are clear and consistent.* Society must define organizations' boundaries, minimum standards expected to be met or exceeded, and performance criteria. Society must be consistent in its expectations for corporate social responsibility throughout the various governmental regulations affecting this area.

2. *Keep the rules within the limits of technical feasibility.* Business cannot do the impossible. However, many of today's regulations are unworkable in practice. Extreme environmental restrictions have, on occasion, set standards surpassing those of Mother Nature.

3. *Make sure rules are economically feasible; recognize that society itself must be prepared to pay the cost—not only of their implementation by business, but also of their administration by government.* Ultimately, it is the people who must pay, either through higher prices or through taxes.

4. *Make rules prescriptive, not retroactive.* There is a present trend toward retroactivity in an attempt to force retribution for the past—to make today's rules apply to yesterday's ball game.

5. *Make rules goal seeking, not procedure prescribing.* Tell organizations to devise the best, most economical, and most efficient way to get there.

Source: Adapted from J. McAfee, "Responsibilities Shared by Corporations and Society," *Credit and Financial Management*, May 1978, p. 31. Copyright May 1978. Published by the National Association of Credit Management, 520 Eighth Avenue, New York, New York 10018-6571.

Guidelines for Management Practice

The social responsibility of business is controversial. Since organizations are likely to espouse varied attitudes toward dealing with social issues, managers are likely to encounter different approaches to social problems. However, as general guidelines for the operation of a socially responsible firm, we have found the following suggestions to be extremely valuable.[11]

1. When conflicts arise about how to approach a perceived social obligation, managers should recognize that management practice in the area of social obligations always grows out of some philosophical perspective, whether stated or unstated. Accordingly, it is best for the firm to formally express the philosophical perspective under which it wants its managers to operate.

2. The purpose of a business is to make a profit; thus managers should strive for the optimal profit that

can be achieved over the long run. But no true profits can be claimed until business costs are paid, since this includes all social costs. Managers must determine these costs by detailed analysis of the social balance between the firm and society.

3. Managers should encourage their employees to become involved in establishing standards of socially responsible behavior for the firm, and they should include a factor in their selling prices to cover the cost of behaving in a socially responsible manner.

4. When competitive pressure or economic necessity precludes socially responsible actions, managers should recognize that social capital is being depleted, which represents a loss to society. Managers should attempt to remove the barriers to social responsibility through better internal management or by advocating corrective legislation.

A Continuum of Social Responsibility

In an attempt to match philosophies toward social responsibility with plans that will lead to desired corporate behavior, managers can view the social responsibility

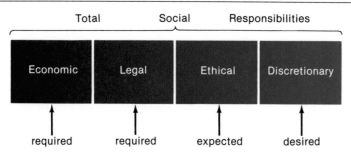

FIGURE 5-5
A Continuum of Social Responsibilities

Source: Adapted from A. B. Carroll, "A Three-Dimensional Model of Corporate Social Performance," *Academy of Management Review,* October 1979, p. 499.

of business on a continuum from the most to the least fundamental kinds of social commitment. As shown in Figure 5-5, these types include economic, legal, ethical, and discretionary social responsibilities.

Economic responsibilities are the most basic social responsibilities of business, especially from the traditional point of view. As we have noted, some economists (such as Milton Friedman) see these as the only legitimate social responsibilities of business.

Living up to their economic responsibilities requires managers to maximize profits whenever possible. The essential responsibility of business is assumed to be providing goods and services to society at a reasonable cost. In discharging that economic responsibility, the company also emerges as socially responsible, in some cases, by providing productive jobs for a segment of the work force.

Legal responsibilities reflect the firm's obligation to comply with the law. This includes both the general civil and criminal law that applies to the public and also the specific laws that regulate business activities.

The consumer and environmental movements have focused increased public attention on the need for social responsibility in business by lobbying for laws that govern business in the areas of pollution control and consumer safety. More consumer legislation has been enacted in the last fifteen years than in the previous 189 years.[12] In response and in anticipation, more than 600 corporations and trade associations have established consumer affairs departments to handle consumers' complaints and respond to their concerns.[13]

The intent of consumer legislation has been to correct the "balance of power" between buyer and seller in the marketplace. Among the most important of such laws are the Federal Fair Packaging and Labeling Act of 1966, which regulates labeling procedures for business; the Truth in Lending Act of 1967, which regulates the extension of credit to individuals; and the Consumer Product Safety Act of 1972, which protects consumers from unreasonable risks of injury in the use of consumer products.

The environmental movement has had a similar impact on the regulation of business. This movement, which became prominent in the early 1970s, achieved stricter enforcement of existing environmental protection laws and spurred the passage of new, more comprehensive laws.

One key piece of legislation was the National Environmental Policy Act of 1969, which was devoted to preserving the country's ecological balance and made environmental protection a federal policy goal. It requires environmental impact studies whenever new construction, for example, may threaten an existing ecosystem, and it established the Council on Environmental Quality to guide business development. Another result of the environmental movement was creation of the federal Environmental Protection Agency (EPA) in 1970. This agency interprets and administers the environmental protection policies of the U.S. government. Changing interpretations of the law by the EPA and complaints that its regulations are too costly to administer have made the agency's value a controversial issue among business organizations. Cumulative costs to business arising from the implementation of environmental legislation have been estimated to be $735 billion between 1979 and 1988.[14]

Ethical responsibilities reflect the company's notion of right or proper business behavior. Ethical responsibilities are obligations that transcend legal requirements; firms are expected, but not required, to behave ethically. Some actions that are legal might also be considered unethical. For example, the manufacture and distribution of cigarettes are legal. But in light of the often-lethal consequences of smoking, many consider the continued sale of cigarettes unethical, despite the warnings from the surgeon general that the law requires be printed on each package.

In many situations managers have an option that is obviously both legal and ethical. Here the legal mandate and the ethical norms of society are congruent and clearly understood. This is perhaps the easiest type of ethical situation to deal with. In other cases, however, there may be less agreement on what is ethical and what is unethical behavior.

Discretionary responsibilities are those that are voluntarily assumed by a business organization. They are of three types: public relations activities, good citizenship, and full corporate social responsibility.

Through *public relations* activities, managers attempt to enhance the image that their company and its products and services project by supporting worthy causes. This form of discretionary responsibility has elements of the self-serving. An example is the annual, highly publicized donation that Dow Chemical makes to the United Way campaign.

Companies that adopt the *good-citizenship* approach actively support ongoing charities, public-service advertising campaigns, or issues in the public interest. An example is an ad for Bartles & James wine cooler that warns against the dangers of driving when intoxicated. A second example is Dow Chemical's organ donor program.

A commitment to *full corporate social responsibility* requires managers to attack social problems with the same zeal with which they attack business problems. For example, teams in the National Football League provide time off for players and other employees afflicted with drug or alcohol addictions who agree to enter rehabilitation programs. Unfortunately, relatively few companies operate at this level.

The Davis Model of Social Responsibility

What is perhaps the most highly regarded model of social responsibility was developed by Professor Keith Davis. The Davis model is based on five propositions that describe how and why business should take action that enhances and protects the welfare of society. These propositions follow.[15]

1. Social responsibility arises from social power. Business is inevitably involved in the welfare of society as a whole, because it has a great deal of influence over such issues as minority hiring and environmental quality. Because business

Guidelines for Management Practice

The categories on the continuum of social responsibility cannot be understood in isolation. They overlap not only with each other, but also with other elements in the business environment. Managers dealing with issues of social responsibility should keep in mind the following examples.

1. Fulfilling the firm's legal responsibilities is in its economic long-term interests. A history of socially responsible actions both builds customer and societal support for the firm and provides a "goodwill buffer" that will help to minimize the damage done to the firm if it is ever implicated in improper conduct.

2. Many of a firm's legal responsibilities are also ethical responsibilities. For example, while maintaining a standard of product safety for the protection of consumers is clearly the right thing to do, such ethical responsibilities may help a company to avoid additional legal requirements.

3. Discretionary responsibilities often have an ethical component. McDonald's assumes the discretionary responsibility of providing free lodging for families of seriously ill children at the Ronald McDonald Houses because it believes this is the right thing to do.

In considering the overlap between various kinds of social responsibility, however, keep in mind the distinctions. Economic and legal responsibilities are required; ethical responsibility is expected; and discretionary responsibility is desired.

wields significant power in shaping social conditions, society must hold business responsible for the way it influences existing conditions.

2. Business shall operate as a two-way system with open receipt of inputs from society and open disclosure of its operations to the public. Honest and open communication must be maintained between business and society at large. Business must be willing to listen to input from citizens and social representatives. And it must be willing to issue regular reports on what it is doing to meet its social obligations.

3. Both the social costs and the social benefits of an activity, product, or service shall be thoroughly calculated and considered before it is approved for sale or use. Business must consider the long-term as well as the short-term social implications of its activities. Technical feasibility and profitability should not be the only factors affecting business decisions.

4. The social costs related to each activity, product, or service shall be passed on to the consumer. This proposition is a major factor in inducing business to switch from a traditional or stakeholder concept of social responsibility to an affirmative one. Simply stated, it posits that business should *not* be expected to absorb the full cost of expensive social programs. Rather, some of the cost of socially desirable activities should be passed along to the consumer.

5. Business institutions have the responsibility to become involved in addressing certain social problems that are outside their normal areas of operation. Business often has the expertise to help solve social problems. When it does, business has an obligation to do so, even if it is not directly affected by the problem at the time.

An example will help to demonstrate the model's value. Say the officers of Colonial Pancakes, a regional chain of short-order restaurants, are asked by a charitable organization to provide free breakfasts to destitute people. The proposed program is organized so that people who qualify for it are issued meal-redeemable meal tickets by the charitable organization. The participating restaurants are later reimbursed by the charitable organization for a nominal fraction of the menu price of the food. The program is designed as a continuing charitable function.

Following the logic of the Davis Model, the officers of Colonial Pancakes might decide to grant the request because such an activity benefits society by helping some disadvantaged people find jobs and become productive taxpayers. They might reason that few people have the energy to look for work when they are suffering from malnutrition. This would be the principle whereby compliance with the charitable organization's request is justified. The social responsibility of the officers of the restaurant chain derives from the fact that they have the power to influence society in a positive or negative way.

Having decided to engage in the socially responsible activity of feeding the destitute, the restaurant officers have an obligation to keep society informed of the progress of the program. In pursuing the program, they must be willing to gather input from citizens and social representatives. This is the second proposition of the Davis Model in action.

The managers of Colonial Pancakes must also consider the costs and benefits of their program of feeding the poor. Under the third proposition of the Davis Model, it is not sufficient to take part in the program merely to garner the favorable publicity attendant upon providing a charitable service. The plan must also be regarded as a business venture whose costs and social implications must be carefully reviewed.

Furthermore, suppose the program is instituted at all the restaurants in this particular chain. Other restaurant owners are participating in the program, but more destitute people than expected are redeeming their free-meal tickets at the restaurants in this particular chain. Participation in the free-meal program is so extensive that continuing it will constitute a significant expense for the restaurants. Guided by the fourth proposition in the Davis Model, the officers would then pass that expense on to their paying clients in the form of a price increase.

Let us say that the program devised by the restaurant owners is successful and becomes a permanent part of the chain's operation. No social problem, however, exists in isolation. Consequently, the chain's open and well-publicized interest in feeding the destitute leads it to consider, for example, the problem of urban decay in certain areas of cities near where its restaurants are located. This social problem has nothing immediately to do with financial interests of the Colonial Pancakes chain. However, the firm's officers might consider it their obligation to become involved in helping to solve it. This attitude is supported by the fifth proposition of the Davis Model.

The Davis Model offers a series of propositions that help guide managers in practical decision making. One of the chief advantages of such a model is that it helps managers think in long-range terms about the social programs they might elect to institute. Whereas the various philosophies of social responsibility help guide managers in a general way, the Davis Model helps managers deal with specific issues, such as the cost of social programs and how much of that cost they should pass along to their customers.

The Pros and Cons of Social Responsibility

Inasmuch as the issue is inherently controversial, managers must be aware of arguments for and against social responsibility. Arguments for and against social responsibility, as developed by Joseph Monsen, Jr., are listed in Figure 5-6. The major arguments also will be discussed in some detail in the next two sections.

Arguments Favoring Social Responsibility

1. *It is in the best interests of business.* This argument can best be summarized in two forms, positive and negative. The positive form is based on the concept that fulfilling the obligations that business organizations have to society as a whole will, in the long run, benefit business in particular.

    Even though the owners of a restaurant chain that supplies meals to the homeless incur a significant economic loss, they may reason that such an ex-

---

Major Arguments for Social Responsibility

1. It is in the best interest of the business to promote and improve the communities where it does business.
2. Social actions can be profitable.
3. It is the ethical thing to do.
4. It improves the public image of the firm.
5. It increases the viability of the business system. Business exists because it gives society benefits. Society can amend or take away its charter. This is the "iron law of responsibility."
6. It is necessary, to avoid government regulation.
7. Sociocultural norms require it.
8. Laws cannot be passed for all circumstances. Thus, business must assume responsibility to maintain an orderly society.
9. It is in the stockholders' best interest. It will improve the price of stock in the long run, because the stock market will view the company as less risky and open to public attack and will therefore award it a higher price-earnings ratio.
10. Society should give business a chance to solve social problems that government has failed to solve.
11. Business is considered, by some groups, the institution with the financial and human resources to solve social problems.
12. Prevention of problems is better than cures—so let business solve problems before they become too great.

Major Arguments against Social Responsibility

1. It might be illegal.
2. Business plus government equals monolith.
3. Social actions cannot be measured.
4. It violates profit maximization.
5. The cost of social responsibility is too great and would increase prices too much.
6. Business lacks social skills to solve societal problems.
7. It would dilute business's primary purposes.
8. It would weaken the U.S. balance of payments, because prices of goods will have to go up to pay for social programs.
9. Business already has too much power. Such involvement would make business too powerful.
10. Business lacks accountability to the public. Thus, the public would have no control over its social involvement.
11. Such business involvement lacks broad public support.

FIGURE 5-6
The Pros and Cons of Social Responsibility

Source: J. Monsen, Jr., "The Social Attitudes of Management," in *Contemporary Management: Issues and Viewpoints,* ed. Joseph W. McGuire (Englewood Cliffs, N.J.: Prentice-Hall, 1974), p. 616.

penditure will be good for their business in the long run. If, for example, there are many destitute people living on the streets near the restaurants, any action that might contribute to their being able to find work would help create a better environment in which the restaurants could operate. The short-term costs could therefore be seen as investments in long-run profitability.[16]

The negative form of the same argument is based on the assumption that it is in the best interest of business to engage itself in social issues because, inevitably, society will sooner or later require that it do so. According to this argument, if business fails to take the initiative in helping to solve social problems, society will retaliate by orchestrating product boycotts and protests. This argument also maintains that social responsibility is ultimately in the best interests of business because it helps to prevent further government intrusion.[17] When Kellogg and Johnson & Johnson took swift, socially responsible action to ensure that their products were safe to use, they were perhaps discouraging more government regulation of how their products are packaged and distributed.

2. *Responsible social actions can be profitable.* Although there is no clear evidence of a cause-and-effect relationship between business social action and profits, it is argued that supporting social causes contributes to the long-term profitability of the business organization. For example, donations to higher education might establish a perceived connection between a corporation and certain universities. Such a connection might help the corporation recruit the most promising graduates.

3. *It is the ethical thing to do.* This argument holds that companies should commit themselves to social concerns because they have a moral obligation to do so. Consider a company plant that is the source of an oil spill that has harmed the environment. The company may be legally required to correct the damage done by the oil spill, but even if this were not true, most of the public would still see correcting the damage as the *right* thing to do.

4. *Laws cannot be passed for all circumstances.* For this reason, business has a responsibility to maintain an orderly, legal society. This argument emphasizes the relationship between the legal and ethical aspects of social involvement, as they are described on the continuum of social responsibility. It holds that a predisposition to behave ethically is concomitant with a predisposition to behave legally. For example, the company that takes the initiative in voluntary programs is more likely to obey existing laws.

Arguments Against Social Responsibility

1. *Addressing social problems should be the province of government.* Those who subscribe to this argument hold that business discharges all its social obligations by earning profits, the taxes on which provide money for government to initiate social programs. Social programs initiated by business, so this argument goes, undermine the profit motive. Some even believe that business's participation in social concerns will eventually undermine the vital functional difference between business and government.[18]

2. *Social responsibility programs cannot be accurately evaluated.* Proponents of this argument hold that managers cannot accurately measure the effects of social programs. The problems involved in placing a monetary value on social in-

vestments are complex and open to numerous subjective considerations.[19] For example, it would be difficult to quantify the value to society of the restaurant chain's helping to feed the poor. And just how many free meals did it take to get how many destitute people off the welfare rolls?

3. *Social responsibility dilutes the primary purposes of business.* Any social activism that companies indulge in siphons human, material, and financial resources away from the primary purpose of business, which, according to this view, is to maximize profits for its shareholders.[20]

The arguments favoring and those opposing social responsibility highlight the controversial nature of the issue. Managers planning social programs may encounter resistance to such programs embodied in the arguments against social responsibility. It is up to managers to decide which arguments have merit—and which view their firm endorses—when making decisions about any particular social obligation.

Social Responsiveness and the Social Audit

To some degree, all organizations acknowledge some need to act in a socially responsible manner. To assure that their behaviors are consistent with their commitments, firms need to measure and evaluate the effectiveness of these socially responsive activities. Although such measurement is not so accurate and conclusive as the assessment of economic activity, managers should have a plan for evaluating *social effectiveness*. Without a plan, they have no way of determining the comparative worth or relative success of various social programs in which they participate.

Social Responsiveness

A *socially responsive approach* to meeting the firm's social responsibilities includes the following five elements:[21]

1. Incorporating social goals into the annual planning process. In other words, social responsibility is not to be a corporate afterthought or a mere stop-gap measure.

2. Examining existing norms of social responsibility in the industry. What are other companies doing in the area of social responsibility? How successful are their programs? What does the community expect in terms of corporate social responsibility?

3. Keeping stakeholders informed of the firm's socially responsive activities through regular reports. If social goals are incorporated into the annual planning process, stockholders should be regularly apprised of the effectiveness of these programs.

4. Experimenting with different approaches. Because corporate social programs are often "unfamiliar territory" for business organizations, managers must expect to have to try different approaches in carrying them out. The failure of a

particular approach does not necessarily mean that the social program in question is not worthwhile.

5. Attempting to measure the cost of the firm's investment in social programs. Managers should know how much is being spent on social programs and should attempt to make long-term assessments of the social impacts of the social programs they support.

What to Measure

This last consideration—assessing the impact of the firm's efforts to discharge its social responsibilities—warrants further discussion, because the results of social programs are so difficult to measure. Even so, companies should take social responsibility measurements in the following areas:[22]

1. *Economic function.* It is important to assess the economic contribution the company is making to society simply by creating jobs, providing goods and services, paying fair wages, and ensuring worker safety.

2. *Quality of life.* Is the company improving or degrading the general quality of life? Producing high-quality products and trying to avoid polluting the environment are two examples of efforts to improve the quality of life.

3. *Social investment.* Measures of this variable indicate the extent to which the company is investing money and human resources to solve social problems.

4. *Problem solving.* Is the company dealing with the causes of social problems rather than merely treating their symptoms?

How to Measure: The Social Audit

A specific management tool for evaluating a firm's social responsiveness, the **social audit** attempts to measure the impact of an organization on society. It is an inventory that identifies, describes, and gathers specific information on the current and prospective plans of an organization. The social audit tries to arrive at an organization's net contribution to social goals by comparing the social costs and social benefits of its programs.[23] The basic steps in a social audit are monitoring, measuring, and evaluating the performance of a company in its conduct of socially responsible activities. The information provided helps the organization to develop strategies to meet its future goals. Figure 5-7 offers an outline of the way the social audit is often organized by company personnel or an outside consultant. It also indicates what most social audits contain.

Management Ethics

Crucial to the idea that corporations should be operated in a socially responsive way for the benefit of all stakeholders is the belief that managers will behave in an ethical manner. In this section we will explore the complexities of management ethics. The term **ethics** is defined as a set of moral principles that governs the actions of an individual or a group. The values held by an individual, group, or society are the basic components of various ethical systems. And, of course, the values of one individual, group, or society may be at odds with the values of another individual, group, or society as is highlighted in "Insights for International Managers 5." Ethical standards, therefore, reflect not a universally accepted code

Part	Contents
1. A list of social expectations and the corporation's response	A summary of what is expected for each program area (consumer affairs, employee relations, physical environment, the corporation's local community development). A statement of the corporation's explanation of why it has undertaken certain activities and has not undertaken others.
2. A statement of the corporation's social objectives and the priorities attached to specific activities	For each program area, the corporation's report on what it will try to accomplish and what priority it places on the programs and activities it will undertake.
3. A description of the corporation's objectives in each program area of the activities it will conduct	For each priority activity and program, the corporation's statement of a specific objective (in quantitative terms when possible), describing how it is striving to reach that objective (such as making available ten qualified staff employees for a total of 400 hours of community service).
4. A statement indicating what resources have been committed to achieving social objectives	A summary report, by program area and activity, of the costs—direct and indirect—assumed by the corporation.
5. A statement of the accomplishments and/or progress made in achieving each objective	A summary describing the extent to which each objective has been achieved. When feasible, this description should be in quantitative terms. Objective, narrative statements should be used when quantification is not possible.

FIGURE 5-7
Outline for Social Auditing by Business Organizations

Source: Adapted from J. J. Carson and G. A. Steiner, *Measuring Business Social Performance: The Corporate Social Audit* (New York: Committee for Economic Development, 1974), p. 61.

of behavior, but rather the end product of a process of defining and clarifying the nature of human interaction.

Even when groups or individuals agree on what constitutes human welfare in a given case, the means they choose to enhance this welfare may differ. Hence ethics also involves the means used to attain defined goals (or ends) of human welfare. A fundamental example of the ethical problem of what ends justify what means concerns the value we call health. Most people would agree that health is a value worth seeking—that is, it enhances human welfare. But what if the means deemed necessary to attain this value for some include the denial or risk of health for others? This conflict arises in the production of health care products by pharmaceutical manufacturers. During production of these products, employees are sometimes subjected to great risk of personal injury and infection. For example, if contacted or inhaled, the mercury used in making thermometers and blood pressure equipment can cause heavy metal poisoning. If inhaled, ethylene oxide used to sterilize medical equipment before it is shipped to doctors can cause fetal abnormalities and miscarriages. Even penicillin, if inhaled during its manufacturing process, can cause acute anaphylaxis or shock. Thus, although the goal (customer health) might be universally accepted, the means (involving jeopardy to employees) may not be.

■ *Insights for International Managers 5* ■

IF YOU MUST GREASE PALMS, DO IT RIGHT

Bribe, mordida, dash, commission, tip, or back-sheesh—greasing of palms is a daily part of international business. Whether or not to do it is a question that inevitably confronts anyone who continues to work abroad. There is no single rule that will apply to all situations, because no two situations and countries are the same. However, there are laws. Some forms of payment are illegal, and you must know the laws and local practices.

American managers overseas complain most bitterly about U.S. laws: "We were doing well abroad before the Foreign Corrupt Practices Act. Our share of the business in Saudi Arabia has gone from 34 percent to 4 percent since then. Now we are losing to the Germans, Koreans, French, and anyone else who can let money flow in the customary ways. If a payment is acceptable in a foreign culture, it cannot be considered wrong, and your job is to help your overly moralistic company reconsider its ethnocentric values as they are applied to the foreign situation." The West Germans, for example, deduct bribes as legitimate business expenses. In many countries, government officials are not paid very well and "tips" are a way of compensating them. If you need government approvals or permits in those places, you had better

seriously think about legal ways of putting something into the right pockets.

Wherever they stand on the ethical questions, whether to make payments or not, people experienced in international business suggest that before you make a move, examine U.S. law and your company's policies, and talk with someone who has successfully done business in that country for a long time. Bribing is always a risky business, and penalties are severe, both for the individual briber, the company, and those accepting bribes. Even where bribery is local practice, laws may be invoked whimsically.

Often the bribery situation will not involve a monumental ethical or legal question, just a monumental nuisance. A typical scene: An American hands his passport over to the Jakarta customs official, who puts it up on a shelf. The American is asked to wait, and he does, until his patience gives out and he asks for his passport back. "I don't know what you are talking about," says the official. The American says, "It's right up there, I saw you put it there," but the official, who has all the time in the world, shrugs and maintains, "I don't know." Even the most naïve traveler will finally catch on and pass over some cash—if it is enough he gets his passport back. If he is unlucky, he is arrested by an unobserved policeman.

Source: From L. Copeland and L. Griggs, *Going International* (New York: Random House, 1985), pp. 177–179.

As we have noted, ethical concerns overlap legal concerns. Frequently, however, individuals are expected to exhibit ethical behavior above and beyond the basic requirement to obey the law. For example, an executive might be hired for a job at a firm that is interested in certain technical advancements made by the manager's former employer, a competitor. Soon this manager is asked to share knowledge she or he gained while working for the previous employer—information the former employer deemed confidential. It might not be illegal to divulge this information, but it might very well be unethical.

The ethical content of managerial decisions has come under increased public scrutiny in recent years. There is a growing perception among the public, and among business executives themselves, that business managers are being subjected to ever-greater pressure to act illegally or unethically. This perception is an outgrowth of publicity about white-collar crime in the upper echelons of management at respected companies. In a three-month period in 1985, the Bank of Boston, E.F. Hutton, General Electric, and LTV Corporation were found guilty of major white-

In Practice 5-1

ETHICAL QUESTIONS FOR GENERAL DYNAMICS

After cashing in on the Reagan administration's $1 trillion defense spending binge, contractors such as General Dynamics face a relatively stringent stretch, as the government struggles to bring the deficits down to size. That prospect, together with the Soviet peace offensive and the Reagan-Gorbachev summit meeting, have depressed defense stock generally.

Investors' sentiment hasn't exactly been buoyed up, either, by prospects of a crackdown on billing practices following recent accusations against General Dynamics as well as other contractors, including General Electric and Rockwell International. Or the fact that the Pentagon is seeking more competitiveness in weapons systems development.

Still more bad news hit GD last week when the Justice Department indicted one of its executive vice presidents, George A. Sawyer, on charges of hiding that he was negotiating to join the company while still serving as assistant secretary of the Navy in 1983. Sawyer is on leave from GD pending the outcome of the conflict-of-interest charges, but the company expresses confidence that he'll be cleared.

Nonetheless, as indicated, General Dynamics is still flying high. Its order backlog is a stratospheric $20 billion, twice the total five years ago. More important, General Dynamics is the only contractor turning out major weapons systems for the three services. It makes fighters and missiles for the Air Force, nuclear submarines and missiles for the Navy, and tanks for the Army.

Notwithstanding the furor over billings, General Dynamics and the Pentagon are like the couple who can't get along with each other but can't live without each other.

The history of defense contracting is replete with production goofs, weapons systems failures, and contract fraud (although there's a tendency to dwell on the warts and lose sight of the splendid successes).

Misfirings are in large part a by-product of the temptingly free flow of defense money and its sheer size. What's more, the growing complexity of weapons systems almost guarantees considerable instances of technological failure.

General Dynamics officials are bitter about what they consider distortions by critics and by the media. The main distorter, they contend, is P. Takis Veliotis, a former executive vice president and accused kickback-taker now hiding in Greece to avoid prosecution. Veliotis has been feeding material to investigators to embarrass his former employer and to promote his chances for winning immunity from prosecution.

Though Veliotis is suspect as an accuser, he supplied investigators with enough details to give General Dynamics more than a few highly uncomfortable moments in congressional hearings this year. The list ran from titillating tales of lavish executive expenditures billed to the Pentagon to such howlers as charging to the government the cost of a kennel for a dog accompanying a traveling executive. And there were nonsensical gifts, valued at $67,500, to an unreconstructed critic, retired Admiral Hyman Rickover.

To pacify the Pentagon, General Dynamics initially withdrew $23 million of overhead expenses, which it lamely pinned on sloppy bookkeeping. More serious was an extreme Pentagon action in April to hold up all payments to General Dynamics until the military could recoup a long string of overcharges. But things got back to near normal in August, with the lifting of the payments ban after General Dynamics adopted a new ethics code and tighter accounting procedures.

The company was fined $675,000 by the Navy for the Rickover gifts. A presumably chastened General Dynamics promptly received a whopping $900 million addition to Navy submarine and missile contracts.

Source: From Harlan S. Byrne, "Bloody But Unbowed," *Barron's,* November 4, 1985, pp. 6–8. Reprinted by permission of *Barron's,* © Dow Jones & Company, Inc., 1985.

collar crime schemes. E.F. Hutton, for example, was forced to pay fines and court costs in 1987 totaling $2.75 million after the discovery that it was involved in a giant check "floating" scheme. And as "In Practice 5-1" reveals, the problems at General Dynamics were even greater.

The trials of Ivan Boesky captured major news headlines in 1987 and 1988 because of his illegal role as an insider trader on Wall Street. (Stephen Ferry/Gamma Liaison)

According to surveys conducted by Gallup pollsters for *The Wall Street Journal,* 65 percent of Americans believe that the general level of business ethics declined in the decade between 1975 and 1985. When asked what suspect business practices have become more frequent in recent years, one manager stated, "Bribes, falsifying documents, improper financial statements, bid rigging, price collusion. . . ."[24]

In response to another survey, nearly 40 percent of the executives questioned said their superiors had, at some point, asked them to do something they considered unethical.[25] Generally, the public has adopted a cynical view of the ethical standards of executives. Only 18 percent rated the ethical standards and honesty of business executives high or very high. "In Practice 5-2" gives you an opportunity to "second guess" the ethics of one recent management decision at American Express. For another opportunity to judge your ethical standards, complete "Management Development Exercise 5," the "Management Ethics Questionnaire."

Ways to Approach Questions of Ethics

Deciding which actions are ethical and which are not is an extraordinarily difficult task. Managers find that the most critical quality of ethical decision making is consistency. Thus they often try to adopt a philosophical approach that can provide the basis for the consistency they seek. There are three fundamental ethical approaches for business managers: the utilitarian approach, the moral rights approach, and the social justice approach.[26]

■ *In Practice 5-2* **■**

AMERICAN EXPRESS SECRETLY FUNDED NEWSLETTER

American Express Company has for more than a year been secretly financing a newsletter that criticizes the interest rates charged by competing bank credit cards.

Bank Credit Card Observer, a frequently quoted publication produced in Kendall Park, N.J., has received—and will continue to receive until yearend—a subsidy "likely to approach $500,000," according to the *American Banker,* a trade publication that broke the story yesterday.

American Express began financing the newsletter a few months before it launched its own lower-interest Optima credit card to compete with Master-Card and Visa. The newsletter—like several similar publications—has given editorial credit to Optima for helping to drive down credit card interest rates.

Colleagues in the consumer credit and journalism fields expressed shock and dismay at the American Express link to *Bank Credit Card Observer,* although many defended the newsletter's contents.

"It raises doubts about conflict of interest," said Gary Serota, president of BankCard Holders of America, a consumer organization. "There is no indication the data are inaccurate, but it is inappropriate to receive money from any [bank] player."

Bank Credit Card Observer, which costs its 400 subscribers $290 a year, conducts a monthly survey of the largest credit card–issuing banks. It lists banks across the nation that charge the lowest interest rates on credit card balances, along with their annual fees. It also gives the rates charged by the largest banks, as well as the average rate, in eighteen major U.S. cities.

Bank Credit Card Observer was launched in April 1986, less than a year before the Optima card made its debut. The Optima card charges 13.5 percent on unpaid balances, whereas the national average for all bank cards is 17.3 percent.

During 1986 and early 1987 the newsletter's publisher, John C. Pollock, held news conferences in five cities denouncing high interest rates charged on bank credit cards. The publicity tour was secretly funded from the American Express grant.

American Express said it had furnished seed money and was progressively cutting back its subsidy. Asked why he had not revealed the link with the travel giant, Pollock replied, "No one ever asked about it."

He said there was no conflict of interest because he had complete editorial independence. "We're proud of the reliability of our data," he added. *The Wall Street Journal* and other publications regularly use BCCO tables of credit card charges.

Pollock denied knowing anything about the creation of the Optima card before the official announcement. At that time he told *The New York Times,* "This could open up a whole new competitive era in credit cards. Up to now, the really larger banks, which control 75 percent of the credit card business, just have not been competitive."

Two months later, Pollock's newsletter noted, "Curiously, the largest drops in [interest rates] came about after American Express announced its Optima credit card. . . . Nothing like a little competition from a national power."

Other publications expressed similar opinions at the time, as did consumer representatives.

Source: Reprinted from N. L. Ross, "American Express' Secretly Funded Newsletter," *The Washington Post,* September 19, 1987, pp. G1–2. © The Washington Post.

---

1. One who adopts the **utilitarian approach** judges the effects of a particular action on the people directly involved and does so in terms of what provides the greatest good for the greatest number of people. The utilitarian approach[27] focuses on *actions* rather than on the *motives* behind the actions. Potentially positive results of an action are weighed against potentially negative results. If the former outweigh the latter, the manager taking the utilitarian approach is

likely to proceed with the action in question. That *some* people might be adversely affected by the action is accepted, under this approach, as inevitable. For example, the Council on Environmental Quality conducts cost-benefit analyses when setting air pollution standards under the Clean Air Act.[28]

2. One who subscribes to the **moral rights approach** judges whether decisions and actions are in keeping with the maintenance of fundamental personal and group rights and privileges. Some of these rights and privileges are enumerated in such documents as the Bill of Rights (the first ten amendments to the United States Constitution) and the United Nations Declaration of Human Rights. The moral rights approach (also referred to as deontology) includes the rights of human beings to life and safety, a standard of truthfulness, privacy, freedom to express their conscience, freedom of speech, and private property.

3. One who takes the **social justice approach** judges how consistent actions are with equity, fairness, and impartiality in the distribution of rewards and costs among individuals and groups. These ideas stem from two principles known as the liberty principle and the difference principle. The *liberty principle* states that individuals have certain basic liberties compatible with similar liberties enjoyed by other people. The *difference principle* holds that social and economic inequities must be addressed so that there may be a more equitable distribution of goods and services.

In addition to these defining principles, three "implementing principles" are essential to the social justice approach. According to the *distributive justice principle,* individuals should not be treated differently on the basis of arbitrary characteristics, such as race, sex, religion, or national origin. This familiar principle is embodied in the 1964 Civil Rights Act.

The *fairness principle* holds that employees must be expected to engage in cooperative activities according to the rules of the company, assuming that the company rules are deemed fair. The most obvious example is that, in order to further the mutual interests of the company, themselves, and other workers, employees must accept limits on their freedom to be absent from work.

The *natural duty principle* points up a number of general obligations, including the duty to help others who are in need or in danger when to do so would not injure oneself, the duty not to injure another, the duty not to cause unnecessary suffering, and the duty to comply with the just rules of an institution.

Review of the Learning Objectives

Having studied this chapter, you should be able to respond to the learning objectives with extensions of the following brief answers:

1. Summarize the three basic philosophies of social responsibility.

The three basic philosophies of social responsibility are the traditional, the stakeholder, and the affirmative philosophies. According to the traditional philosophy, the main concern of business should be the maximization of profits

■ *Guidelines for Management Practice* ■

The three ethical approaches we have just discussed provide the moral standards that underlie the judgments managers use in decision making.[29] Managers should consider the following guidelines when trying to anticipate the circumstances under which these ethical approaches come into play.

1. Managers (and all of us) tend to rely on *utilitarian standards* when they lack the time, money, or other resources to collect information on all the issues and individuals who are involved in a given situation. Thus the manager's skill in estimating general benefits to be derived from a decision is most in demand. Managers faced with making decisions about pension plans and company-sponsored health insurance should realize that they will often be required to make utilitarian judgments.

2. The *moral rights approach* comes into play when managers must decide, for instance, about the employees' "right to know." How much disclosure of information is appropriate? Should managers tell their subordinates, before a final decision has been reached, that some layoffs may be required in their department? Should employees be informed about daily fluctuations in the perceived quality of their performance? Should employees be told whose names are "penciled in" on the managerial succession chart? Managers must answer these and thousands of similar questions on the basis of how they think such information will affect the welfare of the people involved. Specific attention must be given to the employees' right to freedom of choice, the validity of the information, and the implicit

and explicit understandings that the subordinates have with management about the nature and timing of information that they are to receive.

3. When managers' decisions pertain to how the benefits and burdens of employment in the organization should be shared, the basis for ethical judgment is *social justice*. Given that employees differ in skills, abilities, work orientations, aspirations, and contributions, in what ways should they be "treated the same"? Some argue for the following guideline: "From all according to their ability; to all according to their need." Others advocate strict adherence to a publicly announced input/output equation: The more employees produce, the more they are paid. The managers' decisions must ultimately stem from their judgment about what is fair, overall, to the individuals involved. For example, unequally productive employers may be equally paid but may not receive equal consideration for such "perks" as priority vacation times.

Ethical decision making is difficult not because of the need to consider unethical options but because "ethical" often implies "fully comprehensive." Managers must make decisions hampered by bounded rationality, limited resources, time pressures, and imperfect information. However, by keeping in mind that different ethical approaches are appropriate to different situations, they can substantially increase their chances of reaching good—and ethical—decisions.

---

and the long-term interests of the business organization. The stakeholder philosophy holds that the organization must be directly responsible to certain groups that have a stake in its operations, including employees, customers, shareholders, unions, trade associations, and even the general public. The affirmative philosophy obligates managers to predict social trends and to blend the goals of the organization with social goals.

2. **Explain the differences among economic, legal, ethical, and discretionary social responsibilities.**

Economic responsibility means the operation of an organization to the greatest economic advantage. This is a *required* responsibility. A second required responsibility is the legal responsibility to obey the law. Ethical responsibility is the *expected* behavior of doing what is deemed morally right in a given situation. Discretionary responsibility is the *desired* behavior of performing voluntary socially responsible actions.

3. List the main propositions of the Davis Model of social responsibility.

Social responsibility arises from social power. Business should receive inputs from society openly and should openly disclose its operations to the public. Both the costs and the benefits of social programs should be calculated and considered before the programs are approved.

4. Discuss some arguments for and some against business's assuming social responsibility.

Among the principal arguments *in favor* of social responsibility is that it is in the best interests of business: What benefits society will benefit business. Business initiative in this area will help prevent or forestall actions that might otherwise be taken by society against business, such as increased regulation. The basic argument *against* this proposition is that social programs are the responsibility of government. Business discharges its responsibility to society by advancing its own interest in increasing profits.

5. Explain the purpose of the social audit and the concept of social responsiveness.

Social responsiveness involves evaluating an organization's effectiveness in meeting its defined social responsibilities. The social audit, patterned after a financial audit, is the specific tool used to perform this evaluation.

6. Describe three main approaches to business ethics.

The three main approaches to business ethics are the utilitarian, the moral rights, and the social justice approaches. The utilitarian approach judges the effects of a particular action on a particular group in terms of what provides the greatest good for the greatest number of people. The moral rights approach judges whether actions are in accordance with accepted principles of moral and legal rights such as those enumerated in the Bill of Rights and the United Nations Declaration of Human Rights. The social justice approach judges actions in terms of whether they are consistent with the maintenance of fairness, equity, and impartiality in the distribution of rewards and costs among individuals and groups.

Key Terms and Concepts

Having completed your study of Chapter 5 on "Social Responsibility and Management Ethics," you should have mastered the following important terms and concepts:

social responsibility	traditional philosophy	economic responsibilities	discretionary responsibilities	moral rights approach
profit-maximizing management	stakeholder philosophy	legal responsibilities	social audit	social justice approach
trusteeship management	affirmative philosophy	ethical responsibilities	ethics	
quality-of-life management			utilitarian approach	

Questions for Discussion

1. Do you think a business organization in today's society can avoid defining some socially responsible role for itself? Why or why not?

2. Which of the three basic philosophies of social responsibility would you find most appealing as the chief executive of a large corporation? Explain.

3. Do you think society's expectations for corporate social responsibility will change in the next decade? Explain.

4. How much should social responsibility be considered in evaluating an organization's overall performance?

5. Is it necessary that an action be voluntary to be termed socially responsible? Explain.

6. Do you think an organization should adhere to different philosophies of corporate responsibility when confronted with different issues? Or should its philosophy always remain the same? Explain.

7. After reviewing arguments for and against social responsibility, which side do you find more compelling? Why?

8. Describe yourself as a stakeholder in a company. What kind of stakeholder role do you play now? What kind of stakeholder roles do you expect to play in the future?

9. What sets the affirmative philosophy apart from the stakeholder philosophy of social responsibility? In what areas do the two philosophies overlap?

10. Cite examples of both ethical and unethical behavior drawn from your knowledge of current business events.

11. How would you describe the contemporary state of business ethics?

12. What is business self-interest? How can this self-interest also serve social interests?

Notes

1. Based on S. Koepp, "A Hard Decision to Swallow," *Time* 127, no. 9 (March 3, 1986): 59; B. Powell and M. Kasindorf, "The Tylenol Rescue," *Newsweek* 107 (March 3, 1986): 52; and "Tylenol's Miracle Comeback," *Time* 122, no. 17 (October 17, 1983): 67.

2. H. L. Gantt, *Organization for Work* (New York: Harcourt, 1919), p. 15.

3. S. Oliver, *The Philosophy of Management* (Marshfield, Mass.: Pitman, 1966), p. xv. (This book was originally published in London in 1923 by Sir Isaac Pitman and Sons.)

4. W. F. Abbott and R. J. Monsen, "On the Measurement of Corporate Social Responsibility: Self-Reported Disclosures as a Method of Measuring Corporate Involvement," *Academy of Management Journal*, September 1979, pp. 501–515.

5. M. Friedman, "A Friedman Doctrine: The Social Responsibility of Business Is to Increase Its Profits," *New York Times Magazine*, September 13, 1970, pp. 32, 33, 122, 124, 126; and K. V. Ramanathan, "Toward a Theory of Corporate Social Accounting," *The Accounting Review*, July 1976, pp. 516–528.

6. H. Mintzberg "The Case for Corporate Social Responsibility," *Journal of Business Strategy*, Fall 1983, pp. 3–15.

7. D. A. Garvin, "Can Industry Self-Regulation Work?" *California Management Review* 25, no. 4 (Summer 1983): 37–52; J. E. Heard and W. J. Bolce, "The Political Significance of Corporate Social Reporting in the United States of America," *Accounting Organizations and Society* 6, no. 2 (1981): 247–252; and C. E. Spitzer, "Does Business Need a Social Responsiveness Index?" *Public Relations Journal* 34, no. 6 (June 1978): 8–11.

8. M. Dierkes and L. E. Preston, "Corporate Social Accounting Performing for the Physical Environment: A Critical Review and Implementation Proposal," *Accounting Organizations and Society*, 1977, pp. 3–22; and R. D. Hay, "Social Auditing: An Experimental Approach," *Academy of Management Journal* 18, no. 4 (December 1975): pp. 871–876.

9. F. Luthans, R. M. Hodgetts, and K. R. Thompson, *Social Issues in Business* (New York: Macmillan, 1987), pp. 26–30.

10. "Survey by Opinion Research Corporation Reveals Practitioners Views on Major Issues," *Public Relations Journal*, August 1984, p. 30.

11. G. Sawyer, *Business and Society* (Boston: Houghton-Mifflin, 1979), p. 401.

12. C. Barksdale, and D. Perreault, Jr., "Can Consumers Be Satisfied?" *MSU Business Topics*, Spring 1980, p. 17; and D. Greer, *Business, Government, and Society* (New York: Macmillan, 1987).

13. T. Hise, L. Gillet, and J. Kelly, "The Corporate Consumer Affairs Effort," *MSU Business Topics*, Summer 1978, p. 17.

14. Q. Alexander, "A Simpler Path to a Cleaner Environment," *Fortune,* Summer 1978, p. 17.

15. K. Davis, "Five Propositions for Social Responsibility," *Business Horizons,* June 1975, pp. 19–24.

16. M. E. Francis, "Accounting and the Evolution of Social Data," *The Accounting Review,* April 1973, pp. 245–257.

17. J. E. Heard and W. J. Bolce, "The Political Significance of Corporate Social Reporting in the United States of America," *Accounting Organizations and Society* 6, no. 2 (1981): 247–252.

18. T. Levitt, "The Dangers of Social Responsibility," *Harvard Business Review,* September–October 1958, pp. 41–50.

19. C. Churchill and B. Toan, Jr., "Reporting on Corporate Social Responsibility: A Progress Report," *Journal of Contemporary Business,* Winter 1978, pp. 5–17.

20. M. Friedman, "Does Business Have a Social Responsibility?" *Magazine of Bank Administration,* April 1971, p. 14.

21. A. Lipson, "Do Corporate Executives Plan for Social Responsibility?" *Business and Society Review,* Winter 1974–1975, pp. 80–81.

22. H. Casell, "The Social Cost of Doing Business," *MSU Business Topics,* October 1974, pp. 19–26.

23. S. M. Hunt, "Conducting a Social Inventory," *Management Accounting,* October 1974, pp. 15–16; B. Carrol and M. Beiler, "Landmarks in the Evolution of the Social Audit," *Academy of Management Journal,* September 1975, pp. 589–599; and R. W. Estes, "Socio-Economic Accounting and External Diseconomies," *The Accounting Review,* April 1972, pp. 284–290.

24. R. Rickleffs, "Executives and General Public Say Ethical Behavior Declining in the U.S." *The Wall Street Journal,* October 31, 1983, p. 25.

25. R. Rickleffs, "Public Gives Executives Low Marks for Honesty and Ethical Standards, *The Wall Street Journal,* November 2, 1983, pp. 29–33.

26. N. Bowie, *Business Ethics* (Englewood Cliffs, N.J.: Prentice-Hall, 1982), pp. 42–54; and J. Des Jardins, "Virtues and Corporate Responsibility," in *Corporate Governance and Institutionalizing Ethics,* ed. W. M. Hoffman, J. M. Moore, and D. A. Fedo (Lexington, Mass.: Lexington Books, 1983).

27. A. Sen and B. Williams, eds., *Utilitarianism and Beyond* (New York: Cambridge University Press, 1982); and H. B. Miller and W. Williams, eds., *The Limits of Utilitarianism* (Minneapolis: University of Minnesota Press, 1982).

28. Council on Environmental Quality, *Environmental Quality, 1987* (Washington D.C.: U.S. Government Printing Office, 1988).

29. M. G. Velasquez, *Business Ethics* (Englewood Cliffs, N.J.: Prentice-Hall, 1988).

Cohesion Incident 5-1
Play Ball!

When the corporate managers of Journey's End decided to build a motel in Graniteville, they bought the land on which to build it from an individual. Although only two acres of land were required for the proposed building and parking facilities, the owner of the land was reluctant to sell unless Journey's End bought his entire lot of four acres. Confident that the land would only become more valuable over time, the company purchased the entire lot.

The motel was built in such a manner that the two additional acres were located to the west of the motel. When Roger arrived in Graniteville as the first manager of the motel, this land was overgrown with small trees, honeysuckle, and weeds. At his suggestion, the area was landscaped and grassed over, providing an excellent play area for guests of the motel and for the children of Graniteville. Youngsters could often be seen flying kites and playing ball in the area.

Over the past three years, many businesses have approached Roger about buying the land. He relays all such offers to corporate headquarters. The offers have ranged from $8,000 to $15,000, but none has been accepted by Journey's End.

Late one afternoon, a Little League baseball coach approached Charles and asked whether he and his team could use the area behind the motel to practice. Charles gave him permission, but cautioned him that the motel could not be responsible for any injuries. The coach explained that all the boys had insurance, thanked Charles, and left. During the next few weeks, the team practiced on the park once or twice a week.

After the Little League season was over, Charles received a letter from the coach he had talked with, thanking him and Journey's End for the use of the field. In the letter, he went on to say that he had been chosen commissioner of youth baseball in Graniteville and that he would like to discuss with "your management" the possibility of the league's buying or leasing the land next to the motel to convert it into a Little League ball park. He ended the letter by stressing how much Graniteville needed another field to accommodate the growing number of teams in the city.

Charles showed the letter to Roger and asked what he should do. Roger glanced over it and replied, "Charles, I'm sure this motel has no reason to expand, and as long as we don't have any future need for that land, I'd love to see us lease it to the Little League for $1 a year. Of course, this would have to be approved by Mr. Flynn, and a formal contract would have to be drawn up. In our corporate goals and objectives, I know there's a section on how each motel is supposed to be a part of the community and help out in any way it can. I believe that Mr. Flynn would be in favor of something like this. Let me sit down and write him a letter suggesting we go ahead with a lease arrangement. And I'll suggest that, while we're at it, we also pay to have the park set up for a Little League field: regrading, putting up fences, bleachers, and dugouts, whatever else is needed. We can get us a nice article in the paper about what we're doing, and you can't beat that free promotional space!"

Discussion Questions

1. Did the Journey's End in Graniteville have any type of formal responsibility to landscape and make into a park the extra land it had? If not, why did it do so?

2. Of the list of arguments for and against social responsibility, which ones apply to this situation in Graniteville?

3. What is the opportunity cost of leasing the land to the city? What do you think Journey's End should do?

Cohesion Incident 5-2
Crisis and Responsibility

As Leslie Phillips answered the telephone one morning, she had no idea that the complaint she fielded about a defective electronic component, possibly in the drive shaft itself, was only the beginning of a problem that would rock corporate headquarters for more than a year and challenge the physical and mental limits of each and every employee in the organization.

During the past eight years, the demand for computerized vehicular equipment and electronic accessories had increased 75 percent. As a consequence, Travis Corporation had increased its electronic manufacturing department drastically. The accompanying technological upgrade placed great demands on the expertise and knowledge of individual workers.

Special training and retraining were necessary to keep the workers up to date on how to operate the highly sophisticated equipment. The corporation's strength in this area was put to its most severe test when a computerized component manufactured by Travis was found to be defective in 500,000 Ford Thunderbirds shipped from Detroit to distributors in the southwest region of the United States.

The call Leslie took was only the first of many thousands that Travis Corporation would receive. As complaints poured in from angry customers, distributors, and car dealers in a five-state region, Travis began an extensive, around-the-clock effort to determine what component was making the accelerator stick at various speeds, causing the car to veer, and forcing the driver to rely on the emergency brake to stop the vehicle. Accidents and personal injuries attributed to this defect led to several lawsuits. Worst of all, the fact that NBC, CBS, and ABC followed the story closely resulted in bad publicity and a loss of consumer confidence.

Travis Corporation executives held daily meetings with each department manager to discuss ways to deal with the situation. Every department—from electronics to consumer service and public relations—was to play a role in handling the crisis.

Obviously, the reputation of Travis Corporation was at stake. It would take many months for repairs to be made on all the individual vehicles recalled, but Travis Corporation was dedicated to the protection of its clients, workers, and consumers.

Discussion Questions

1. What are Travis Corporation's economic, legal, ethical, and discretionary responsibilities to its employees, its distributors, and its consumers?

2. Describe strategies that could be implemented by the public relations department, the operations department, and the marketing department to help restore employee and consumer confidence.

3. What does the consumer have a right to expect or demand from Travis Corporation?

Management Development Exercise 5
Management Ethics Questionnaire

First indicate how ethical or unethical *you* think each of the following behaviors is. Next indicate the views you would expect to be expressed by students in your business school classes, professors in your business school, and business managers. Place the number of your response on the line provided for each of the statements.

(1)	(2)	(3)	(4)	(5)
Very Unethical	Basically Unethical	Somewhat Unethical	Not Particularly Unethical	Not at All Unethical

	You	Other Students	Professors	Managers
1. Passing blame for errors to an innocent co-worker	_____	_____	_____	_____
2. Divulging confidential information	_____	_____	_____	_____
3. Falsifying time/quality/quantity reports	_____	_____	_____	_____
4. Claiming credit for someone else's work	_____	_____	_____	_____
5. Padding an expense account over 10 percent	_____	_____	_____	_____
6. Pilfering company materials and supplies	_____	_____	_____	_____
7. Accepting gifts or favors in exchange for preferential treatment	_____	_____	_____	_____
8. Giving gifts or favors in exchange for preferential treatment	_____	_____	_____	_____
9. Padding an expense account up to 10 percent	_____	_____	_____	_____
10. Authorizing a subordinate to violate company rules	_____	_____	_____	_____
11. Calling in sick to take a day off	_____	_____	_____	_____
12. Concealing one's errors	_____	_____	_____	_____
13. Taking longer than necessary to do a job	_____	_____	_____	_____
14. Using company services for personal use	_____	_____	_____	_____
15. Conducting personal business on company time	_____	_____	_____	_____
16. Taking extra personal time (lunch hour, breaks, early departure, and so forth)	_____	_____	_____	_____
17. Not reporting others' violations of company policies and rules	_____	_____	_____	_____

After you have completed this questionnaire, your instructor will compare your answers with those collected from large groups of students and business managers.

Planning

The most basic function of every manager is planning. To be effective, managers must know what they intend to accomplish. Managers who are successful planners can create the basis on which to organize, lead, and control the work of others. In other words, planning is the foundation for successful execution of each of the other basic management functions. This section is intended to increase your knowledge of the planning function and build your planning skills.

Setting and using objectives is basic to the planning function. Chapter 6 provides a thorough coverage of the concepts and skills you will need to set and use objectives effectively.

Every manager should appreciate how the long-term direction of a company is set in order to successfully plan their role in it. This process of managing the company's long-term direction, called strategic management, is presented in detail in Chapter 7.

The major planning responsibility of operating managers is to develop action plans that guide the day-to-day work of organization members. Chapter 8 describes the planning tools and skills of action planning.

Chapter 9 completes this section by explaining several quantitative techniques managers use in executing their planning responsibilities.

6

Setting Objectives

Your study of this chapter will enable you to do the following:

1. Explain why setting objectives will make you a better manager.
2. Identify three types of objectives and explain their role in the planning process.
3. Describe how to set effective objectives.
4. Identify five principles for successfully managing the objective-setting process.
5. Describe at least one popular objective-setting technique.

The Value of Objectives at Wal-Mart

On the sidewalk in front of the Merrill Lynch office on Wall Street, Sam Walton looked up nervously for a ray of sun. It was March 14 and he said he was glad it wasn't snowing.

"Let's go," Mr. Walton said. "We're going to get this thing over with quickly—28 degrees, goodness."

With that, Sam Walton, the sixty-five-year-old chairman of Wal-Mart Stores, donned a grass skirt, a gaudy shirt, and a lei. With the help of a Hawaiian duo, Mr. Walton did a hula dance in New York's financial district.

The hula was performed because Mr. Walton promised 65,000 employees he'd dance the hula on Wall Street if the company showed an 8 percent pretax net profit for 1983 in an industry where 3 percent profits were average. They did and he did. Wal-Mart's 642 stores in nineteen states wound up the year with a pretax return on sales of 8.04 percent.

Did his promise spur employees to higher profits? "I don't think it had all that much effect," he said, "but setting an effective objective surely did!"

Wal-Mart's 8 percent objective was the focal point around which several additional objectives were set throughout the Wal-Mart organization. Wal-Mart's top management invested considerable time refining and clarifying two broad objectives that told everyone in the Wal-Mart organization the purpose of Wal-

Mart and its basic mission. Wal-Mart's purpose was "to provide a convenient, retailing value to its customer in a manner that is both profitable for the company and filled with opportunity for every Wal-Mart employee." Its mission was to locate large, discount retail facilities in smaller towns and suburbs not currently served by mass merchandisers and to stock each store via a network of Wal-Mart distribution centers nationwide. These two broad objectives helped each employee know just what their organization existed to do.

More specific objectives were also set that tied into the 8 percent return on sales objective. First, Sam Walton and corporate managers worked with each of 642 store managers setting a realistic profit objective at each individual store. Second, objectives were set in other parts of the organization critical to profitability. Wal-Mart's purchasing department had a specific gross margin objective—48 percent—it was to meet in purchasing over $4 billion worth of merchandise to be resold in Wal-Mart outlets. Each of 12 regional warehouses had an objective to ensure a steady stock at every Wal-Mart outlet they served by averaging less than two days to fill any store's order and allowing no stores to be out of merchandise advertised for sale.

Sam Walton doing the hula as he had promised, in the heart of New York City's financial district. (UPI/Bettmann Newsphotos)

At the store level, each store manager was required to have every Wal-Mart employee identify two objectives for the year and two each month that they could accomplish that would contribute to Wal-Mart's 8 percent profit objective. The combination of all these objectives and objective-setting activities was what Sam Walton credited with making him do the hula on Wall Street.[1]

Introduction

What Are Objectives?

The 642-store Wal-Mart chain sought to lead the mass retailing industry in profitability by attaining a pretax net profit of 8 percent of sales. Holiday Inns seeks to remain the largest provider of lodging services worldwide. Wendy's aspires to an average revenue of $1 million per store by 1990. Lou Holtz wants to win a national football championship at Notre Dame. Mack Trucks is attempting to achieve higher profitability than its three largest competitors in the extremely competitive truck manufacturing industry. The American Cancer Society intends to find a cure for cancer. Barbara Potts, manager of the small-company practice of the Atlanta office of Big Eight accounting firm, Coopers & Lybrand, seeks to increase the firm's average annual revenue per client to $25,000 by 1991.

In each of these situations, an individual has identified an intended or expected end, and these ends are called **objectives**. Some people use the terms *objective* and *goal* interchangeably. Others use the word *goal* to refer to nonmeasurable, future ends and the word *objectives* to refer to specific, measurable ends. Furthermore scholars have recently distinguished between open-ended and closed-ended goals and have pronounced an objective a closed-ended goal. To avoid the confusion, we have decided to use only the term *objective*.

Objectives are recognized by effective managers as essential ingredients contributing to organizational performance. Simply stated, people must know where they want to go before deciding how to get there. As obvious as this seems, setting clear objectives and managing ongoing activities with those objectives continually in mind is one of the most difficult challenges managers face.

The objective of this chapter is to prepare you to face the challenge of managerial objective setting. First, however, we want to offer evidence that setting and using objectives will make you a better manager. To begin we present an overview of the planning process and describe the role of objectives in this process. Then we define and describe three different types of objectives and explain how to set objectives effectively. Next we introduce five important principles that managers should follow in order to manage the objective-setting process successfully. Finally, we describe two popular management approaches, management by objectives and one minute managing.

Will Objective Setting Make You a Better Manager?

Will learning to set and use objectives make you more effective as a manager and leader? The answer to this question is yes. Skillful objective setting should make you a better manager—and your organization more effective.

Evidence That Objective Setting Enhances Performance

The idea that objective setting should make you, your work group, and indeed your entire organization perform better is intuitively appealing. The opening story about Sam Walton and Wal-Mart illustrates a situation wherein the founder and chairman of a large discount retailing chain attributes the firm's achievement of outstanding performance to its managers' having set a clear objective. And, in fact, considerable research evidence supports this idea.

One relatively recent study compared the pretax profits of businesses that engage in formal objective setting to those of business firms that set objectives only informally.[2] Examining performance over a ten-year period, the study found that profits and the rate of increase in earnings over time were significantly higher for businesses that had adopted systematic objective-setting practices. Several recent studies have yielded the same conclusion: Systematic objective setting enhances organizational performance.[3]

In addition to organizational performance, studies have identified benefits accruing from systematic objective setting at the work-group and individual levels as well. One study examined various service-related jobs and found that objective setting improved performance. Another study focused on individuals and work groups in manufacturing firms. It showed that better performance resulted when individuals or work groups were given specific objectives than when they were just provided with informal or implicit work standards. A similar study, which included several work settings, indicated that productivity was higher and absenteeism lower when objective setting was used to structure and guide desired performance. Many other studies also suggest that enhanced performance is associated with objective setting.[4]

Why Objective Setting Enhances Managerial Performance

OBJECTIVES PROVIDE GUIDANCE

There are a number of reasons why objective setting improves performance. First, objectives give managers guidance in directing the efforts of individuals in organizations. A recent study investigated the relationship between objective setting and educational level in the performance of technicians entering an organization.[5] It showed that the more sophisticated people were, the more their performance was related directly to their setting objectives, either on their own or with their superiors. The less sophisticated people were, the more important it was for managers to make their objectives clear and provide them with regular feedback on their performance. The important point is that objectives provided the basis for guiding the efforts of quite different individuals and spelled higher performance all around. Similarly, Sam Walton's single profit objective served to guide 642 Wal-Mart store managers.

OBJECTIVES REDUCE UNCERTAINTY

A recent study identified a number of causes of common organizational problems.[6] Reduced productivity and poor task performance were caused primarily by uncertainty and lack of a clear-cut direction. When people agree on an objective, they reduce uncertainty by setting forth "what they believe can be made to work out." Objectives act as facts to guide behavior, thereby increasing the predictability of cause-and-effect relationships. Providing even a single sales objective in the face of environmental uncertainty—as Sam Walton did—creates a consistent premise to serve as a guideline for ordering materials, determining production schedules and hiring needs, directing sales efforts, and anticipating cash-flow requirements, at least in the short run. In reducing uncertainty, managers make a crucial contribution to organizational efficiency. Sam Walton's corporate officers, for example, work with each of the 642 Wal-Mart store managers every December to set a specific profit objective. This reduces any uncertainty about the performance they are expected to turn in for the upcoming year.

OBJECTIVES MOTIVATE PEOPLE

One of the fundamental principles of performance psychology is that setting objectives activates behavior. It enhances performance by focusing effort on specific ends. When people know their objectives, they become self-motivated because they have ever-present standards by which to measure the outcomes of their behavior. Setting objectives creates subtle discontent with the status quo, which often spurs creativity in an individual or organization and can stimulate new heights of individual as well as organizational accomplishment.[7] Furthermore, when individual and organizational objectives are clearly intertwined, a strong sense of involvement and commitment usually results and thus further motivates high performance. Sam Walton's hula dance on Wall Street occurred in response to the outstanding results of a work force highly motivated by a clear, shared objective.

OBJECTIVES FACILITATE LEARNING

Objectives and the process of setting them enhance both individual and organizational learning. The process of objective setting is more than simply agreeing to move from X to Y. For instance, the process of seeking to clearly understand X and Y helps managers and subordinates discover exactly where they are and where they might go. Understanding where one wants to go, why, and how makes the process of getting there more effective and efficient. Similarly, assessing actual performance in light of objectives can be a learning exercise. It enables a manager to assess what worked, what did not, what may have changed, and how future efforts can improve performance.

OBJECTIVES ALLOW COORDINATION

Objectives provide a **"linking pin"** to coordinate diverse organizational activities. Objectives and the process of setting them provide a mechanism for communication among individuals within the organization whose tasks and responsibilities are quite different but who depend on each other. For example, setting a basic sales objective requires input and agreement from the sales group, the operations group, and the personnel group, each of which plays a unique role in the organization and has very different priorities. Yet the success of each is totally dependent on the actions of the others. Sam Walton's precise objective served to focus the diverse activities of 642 Wal-Mart stores, 12 regional warehouses, the corporation's purchasing department, and its working-capital management into a coordinated effort directed toward one goal. Objectives allow coordination by providing a focal point that links parts of an organization into a profitable enterprise.

To ensure that these performance-enhancing characteristics of objectives are present in an organization, it is essential that objectives play a prominent role in the organization's planning process. The next section describes the role of objectives in the planning process.

Guidelines for Management Practice

The five ways in which objectives enhance performance can be applied in many different ways to improve performance. In *diagnosing poor performance,* for example, these five items can be used as indicators that the absence or misapplication of objectives is hurting performance:

1. Identify areas in which individuals or work groups are performing poorly. One way to accomplish this is to ask the people involved why performance is down.

2. Because objectives provide guidance, be sensitive to situations in which not knowing what to do or what the purpose is seems to be causing poor performance.

3. Be alert to identify situations wherein uncertainty has stymied performance—for instance, uncertainty about why a given job needs to be done. Simply providing objectives—and particularly eliciting participation in the objective-setting process—can significantly reduce uncertainty and its dysfunctional side effects.

4. Objective setting should also be considered when motivation appears to be lacking, especially within an otherwise knowledgeable work group. Be sensitive to such answers as "It's just a job," "No one else cares, so why should I?" and "We're not pulling together around here." Such answers reflect a lack of motivation.

5. Be especially alert to opportunities to use objective setting as a means to enhance individual and organizational learning; objectives provide a useful focus to help people learn about their role in organizational performance.

6. Finally, take advantage of the potential for coordinating diverse yet interdependent activities that can be derived from setting objectives jointly.

Managers who are attempting to improve performance by *structuring meaningful objectives* can use these same five items as a test of the value of the objectives set by subordinates:

1. Does the objective provide guidance by telling those responsible exactly what the intended result is? Do people receive the information they need in a timely fashion to monitor the accomplishment of that objective?

2. Does the objective reduce uncertainty by stating clearly what is to be accomplished, when it must be done, and how it will be measured? When outcomes need not (or cannot) be specified exactly, the manager can still provide a measurable range of acceptable performance.

3. Simply setting objectives should enhance employee motivation. As a manager, you can improve motivation further by encouraging subordinate participation in forming objectives, by reviewing and approving them, and by regularly monitoring progress toward them.

4. For objectives to be instrumental in enhancing long-term performance, the objectives must be a mechanism to facilitate individual and organizational learning. Your efforts to monitor and evaluate the accomplishment of objectives can facilitate individual and organizational learning if you spend time discussing the behaviors and resources necessary to meet them.

5. Every objective should be related in a clear, logical way to the objectives of those units above and below it. For example, a work group's objectives should clearly relate to unit and organizational objectives as well as to the objectives of individual group members.

The Role of Objectives in the Planning Process

The fundamental importance of objectives is readily apparent in the basic steps that characterize most planning processes. Figure 6-1 shows how objectives play a vital role in three phases of the planning process. During the first phase, managers assess the basic reasons for their company's existence. They typically agree on three broad objectives during this phase. First, managers identify or reaffirm the company's *purpose*—why the company exists. For example, Days Inns' management says that "Days Inns' purpose is to provide the best price/value lodging to its customers, career opportunities for its employees, and a high return to its stockholders." Second, managers usually agree on basic *values* for company personnel to uphold in pursuing this purpose. "Employees will make each individual customer their top priority anytime the opportunity presents itself" is one of ten companywide values espoused by Days Inns' managers. Finally, managers almost always set forth the company's *mission* as a general statement describing how the firm will seek to achieve its purpose. Days Inns' mission is to provide low-cost lodging accommodations to value-conscious travelers at convenient United States locations. This phase, then, establishes the foundation on which the rest of the company's planning activity rests. These three broad objectives provide open-ended statements that set basic parameters for the analyses, objectives, and plans that make up the remainder of the planning process. They provide a key mechanism through which top management shapes the specific plans and objectives that other managers will develop and implement. (These objectives will be discussed in more detail later in this chapter.)

The next phase of the planning process in which objectives play a prominent role occurs when managers seek to identify the specific, long-term ends their strategic plans are designed to accomplish. **Strategic plans** set forth the major actions and investments a firm will make over a five- to ten-year time horizon. Wal-Mart's strategic plan included a five-year commitment to open four regional, computerized warehouses and to implement a new megastore concept nationwide. Strategic plans are discussed more fully in Chapter 7. As you can see in Figure 6-1, long-term objectives are determined after managers have conducted a thorough analysis of both the opportunities and the threats presented by the company's external environment in relation to the company's strengths and weaknesses. Through this analysis, managers determine which market opportunities the com-

FIGURE 6-1
The Role of Objectives
in the Planning Process

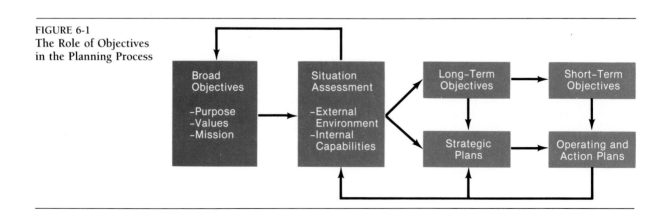

pany will pursue, what resource allocations and organizational commitments they must make to pursue these opportunities, and the performance outcomes they expect to achieve in three to five years as a result of these decisions. **Long-term objectives** are clear, simple, measurable statements of the specific outcomes the firm expects to achieve through companywide effort in three to five years.

Once long-term objectives and strategic plans have been established, operating personnel know what the fundamental thrust of their future activities (strategic plans) will be and have clear performance targets for three to five years (long-term objectives). A critical gap remains, however: What should the firm seek to accomplish this year or in its current endeavors? **Short-term objectives** play an essential role in filling this gap with specific, measurable performance objectives. These objectives specify what should be accomplished immediately in a way that links short-term results with long-term expectations and provides a basis for monitoring, controlling, and adjusting strategic decisions made earlier in the planning process by the company's top management. Thus the final phase of the planning process in which objectives play a prominent role occurs when managers identify specific, short-term results that represent both incremental steps in the accomplishment of long-term objectives and the ends that various operating plans are designed to achieve.

It should be clear that objectives play a critical role in the planning process. Objectives create an outline of what people in the organization intend to do. Furthermore, objectives that are set at different levels within the organization create a hierarchy of objectives that connect and relate diverse parts of the organization and various phases in the planning process. They provide both the foundation for the planning process and the central mechanism by which managers succeed at their most basic function, planning. For many participants, the planning process seems abstract or simply a discussion of future conditions or actions that may or may not come to pass. But when objectives are the focus of attention, these otherwise frustrated participants get a clear sense of what the planning effort is for—what will be accomplished when and by whom. In this way objectives are a central, concrete mechanism for making the planning process real, focused, and meaningful.

For objectives to serve this important role, they must be clearly and effectively stated. The next section explains how to set effective objectives.

How to Set Effective Objectives

Setting effective objectives requires an understanding of several issues. First, you need to know what topics managers typically cover when they set objectives in business organizations. Second, you should be familiar with the eight key characteristics that enhance the value and impact of effective objectives. Finally, you must be able to apply five key principles in setting and using objectives. These three aspects of effective objective setting are discussed in the following sections.

What Topics Should Be Covered?

BROAD OBJECTIVES

To guide the efforts and decisions of the enterprise at large, it is important that company executives establish broad objectives that communicate the fundamental reasons for the company's existence. We have noted briefly three topics that are implicitly or explicitly covered when managers set broad objectives: the organization's *purpose,* its *mission,* and its *values.*

Organizational Purpose. The **purpose** of an organization is defined as the fundamental reason for its existence. This definition is usually derived from the societal context in which the organization operates. A primary purpose of business organizations such as IBM, McDonald's, and CBS is to provide a favorable financial return to the company's owners. Higher educational institutions such as the University of Nebraska, San Diego Community College, and Boston University exist to discover and share knowledge. The United States government exists to provide national security, domestic order, and social services. The primary purpose of your local hospital is to furnish health care to your community.

In setting the broad objective that addresses organizational purpose, managers of business organizations typically focus on the constituencies served by the firm and on basic economic considerations. The primary constituencies of most business organizations that are cited in statements of organizational purpose are customers, employees, communities, and owners. The basic economic considerations set forth by managers of business organizations are survival, growth, and profitability. Examples of the organizational purpose objectives of two business firms appear in Figure 6-2.

The six elements of organizational purpose shown in Figure 6-2 seem rather self-evident. For example, survival would appear to be an obvious objective for any firm. However, like growth and profitability, survival is so easily taken for granted as an objective that it is often neglected as a focus of analysis and decision making. Apple Computers, preoccupied with the uniqueness of its atmosphere and the clever features that some of its products sported, demonstrated an arrogant attitude toward IBM's entry into the personal computer market in the mid-1980s; it even took a full-page ad in *The Wall Street Journal* to welcome IBM into the market. Within two years, IBM had captured over 40 percent of the PC market and dominated the PC business-user segment. Apple saw its market share drop more than 50 percent. The restructuring of the company that followed included the removal of Steven Jobs, Apple's co-founder, from Apple's board of directors. Addressing its problems cost Apple millions of dollars and hampered its growth. Genuine attention by management to the six elements of organizational purpose could perhaps have lessened the impact on Apple of IBM's entry into the PC market. (We will examine other reasons why setting broad objectives in the area of organizational purpose will make you a more effective manager in a subsequent section.)

While statements of organizational purpose are quite useful, they alone do not provide the organizationwide focus for which broad objectives are needed. Another type of broad objective, company mission, is very important in focusing organizationwide efforts.

Company Mission. **Organizational mission** is the broad objective that sets a business apart from other firms of its type and identifies the scope of its operations in product and market terms. A well-designed mission statement clearly and concisely communicates the objective of the company's management in structuring the basic business activity of the firm. Whereas societal considerations shape the organization's purpose, managers choose the path to take in order to achieve that purpose; that path is the company's mission.

	Holiday Inns	Hewlett-Packard
Constituencies		
Customers	To provide quality food and lodging services to business and vacation travelers	To provide products and services of the greatest possible value to our customers
Employees	To provide unlimited career opportunities for productive employees	To provide job security based on performance, recognition of achievement, and sense of accomplishment from their work
Owners	To provide a consistent, attractive return on investment	To generate a high level of profitable growth
Economic Considerations		
Survival	To manage and make investments that are in the long-term interest of the firm	To enter new fields only when the ideas we have assure that we can make a needed and profitable contribution to the field
Profit	To generate a return on investment that is consistently among the highest in our industry	To achieve sufficient profit to finance our company growth and to provide resources for other company objectives
Growth	To grow at a level that maintains our leadership position in the worldwide lodging industry	To let our growth be limited only by our profits and our ability to produce technical products that meet real customer needs

FIGURE 6-2
Excerpts from Statements of Organizatonal Purpose at Holiday Inns and Hewlett-Packard

Source: Developed from the 1985 and 1986 Annual Reports provided by Holiday Corporation and Hewlett-Packard, Inc.

Managers usually focus on three elements in stating a company's mission: basic product or service; primary market; and principal technology. All three of these components are indispensable, because only in combination do they adequately describe the business activity of the company. A good example of these three components of the organizational mission can be found in the business plan of ITT Barton, a division of ITT:

ITT Barton's mission is to serve industry and government with quality instruments used for the primary measurement, analysis, and local control of fluid flow, level, pressure, temperature, and fluid properties. This instrumentation includes flow meters, electronic readouts, indicators, recorders, switches, liquid level systems, analytical instruments such as titrators, integrators, controllers, transmitters, and various instruments for the measurement of fluid properties (density, viscosity, gravity) used for process variable sensing, data collection, control, and transmission. The unit's mission includes fundamental loop-closing control and display devices, when economically justified, but excludes broadline central control room instrumentation, system design, and turnkey responsibility.

Markets served include instrumentation for oil and gas production, gas transportation, chemical and petrochemical processing, cryogenics, power generation, aerospace, government and marine, as well as other instrument and equipment manufacturers.[8]

This mission statement clearly indicates to all readers—from company employees to potential investors—the basic products, primary markets, and principal technologies of ITT Barton, and it does so in only 129 words.

Organizational Values. There has been increased emphasis in recent years on the need for top managers to articulate the basic values of the company and its employees. **Organizational values**, as we noted in Chapter 5, are the philosophical and ethical standards explicitly and implicitly adhered to by company personnel in pursuit of the company's purpose and mission. In setting forth organizational values, top management seeks to provide its customers and other external groups with a description of the firm's operating standards. At the same time, top management is setting forth enduring objectives that employees are expected to keep in mind as they perform their daily tasks.

Figure 6-3 provides a description of the organizational values adhered to by Intel Corporation, a highly acclaimed innovator in the computer peripherals industry. Note that these statements of Intel's organizational values are addressed both to external groups (customers) and to company employees. Also note how clearly they communicate the specific standards of conduct that company personnel are expected to maintain.

Companies often communicate organizational values as part of their statements of purpose and mission. For example, the elements of organizational purpose shown to be basic objectives at Holiday Inns and Hewlett-Packard (Figure 6-2) serve the dual role of expressing selected organizational values and communicating elements of each company's purpose and mission. Whether communicated separately or intertwined with organizational purpose and mission statements, statements of organizational values accommodate three basic considerations in seeking better management of the firm:

1. Organizational values function to direct the behavior of people employed by the company.

2. Organizational values reflect management perceptions about the way society will respond to the company.

3. The actual responses of others to the company will in part determine organizational values.

LONG-TERM AND SHORT-TERM OBJECTIVES

Broad objectives that clarify a company's purpose, mission, and values provide important, open-ended guidelines for decisions that company personnel will make and actions that they will take in the future. Indeed, "Insights for International Managers 6" shows the importance of broad objectives to managers of European and Japanese firms. But although this guidance is essential, it is also incomplete. Company executives and managers of subunits within the company need to set specific, measurable objectives that communicate the ends that strategic actions are expected to accomplish over a three-to-five-year time period. These long-term

FIGURE 6-3
Statements of
Organizational
Values for
Intel Corporation

Public Image

We are sensitive to our IMAGE WITH OUR CUSTOMERS AND THE BUSINESS COMMUNITY [emphasis added]. Commitments to customers are considered sacred, and we are upset with ourselves when we do not meet our commitments. We strive to demonstrate to the business world on a continuing basis that we are credible in describing the state of the corporation, and that we are well organized and in complete control of all things that we do.

Organizational Environment

It is a general objective of Intel to line up individual work assignments with career objectives.

We strive to provide an opportunity for rapid development.

Intel is a results-oriented company. The focus is on substance versus form, quality versus quantity.

We believe in the principle that hard work, high productivity is something to be proud of.

The concept of assumed responsibility is accepted. (If a task needs to be done, assume you have the responsibility to get it done.)

Management Style

Intel is a company of individuals, each with his or her own personality and characteristics.

Management is self-critical. The leaders must be capable of recognizing and accepting their mistakes and learning from them.

Open (constructive) confrontation is encouraged at all levels of the corporation and is viewed as a method of problem solving and conflict resolution.

Decision by consensus is the rule. Decisions once made are supported. Position in the organization is not the basis for quality of ideas.

Management must be ethical. Managing by telling the truth and treating all employees equitably has established credibility that management is ethical.

Source: 1985, 1986 and 1987 Intel annual reports.

objectives provide a specific focus of both companywide and subunit efforts; a basis for ensuring organizationwide coordination; and standards against which to monitor the progress and success of strategic actions. The managers also set specific, measurable short-term objectives that identify what should be accomplished immediately (within one year or less time) if progress toward the long-term objectives is to be maintained. Long-term and short-term objectives are commonly established in one or more of eight areas. We will discuss each separately.

Survival and Growth. A fundamental concern of any organization is *survival and growth.* This concern is virtually always at the heart of the strategic plans guiding any business. Managers typically set objectives for sales volume, sales growth, and customer base on a companywide and a product-line basis.

In setting objectives related to their firm's "customer mix," managers draw on their fundamental assumptions about growth and long-term demand. Wendy's, for example, set the objective of having 10 percent of each store's revenue come from breakfast customers within five years of its 1985 decision to expand its menu to include breakfast items. And Whirlpool, which sold over 80 percent of the

━━━━━ *Insights for International Managers 6* ━━━━━

SETTING OBJECTIVES IN DIFFERENT COUNTRIES

The nature of management objectives in international companies is shaped by dimensions that vary in their importance across different countries. U. S. companies often differ from their European and Japanese counterparts in the importance they place on objective-related dimensions like time horizons, foreign sales, and the extent of product standardization. The following table summarizes the differences between U.S., European, and Japanese companies on seven dimensions that influence the nature or emphasis in their objectives.

Dimension	U. S.	European	Japanese	Implications for Objectives
Time horizon	Short < 3 yrs	Medium to long	Long >10 yrs.	European and Japanese firms place greater emphasis on the distant future than do U.S. firms. This in turn means that statements of mission, organizational purpose, and organizational philosophy would be the dominant type and language of objectives in European and Japanese companies.
Relative importance of foreign sales	Low	High	High	Expect a major emphasis on several objectives for foreign sales levels in European and Japanese firms—reaching through every organizational level. U. S. firm's foreign sales objectives are likely to arise only at the departmental level.
Technological sophistication	Low to high	High	High	Regular emphasis on technological objectives will be found in European and Japanese firms. This will vary in U.S. firms.
Importance of patents and copyrights	High	Medium	Low	One of the prominent interim objectives given considerable attention by U.S. managers for measuring progress in international growth of U.S. firms is often the receipt of international patents or copyrights. Japanese firms place far less emphasis here, particularly as a companywide objective or end.
Advertising intensity	High	Low	Low	Objectives measuring the impact of advertising in penetrating foreign markets get heavy emphasis in U.S. firms.
Level of diversification overseas	Low	Medium to high	High	U.S. firms will typically have only a few international objectives tied to narrow product lines. Japanese and European firms have a majority of the companywide objectives tied to international sales of a wide variety of product lines.
Extent of standardization in product design and marketing practices	High	Medium	Low	Output per hour, number of sales contacts per week—are typical objectives you will see in U.S. firms' international divisions. Quality control, general progress, local relations are but a few of the wide variety of objectives used to guide the production efforts in Japanese and European firms.

Source: Adapted from Anant R. Negandhi, *International Management,*
(Boston: Allyn and Bacon, 1987), p. 440.

appliances it made to one customer—Sears—in the early 1980s, has since sought to modify its customer mix such that Sears would represent no more than 30 percent of its sales base by 1990.

Companies occasionally select key "milestones" as objectives related to survival and growth. Newer, growth-oriented companies may establish going public within five years as a significant objective. Opening new facilities, reducing the firm's dependence on a lone supplier, and phasing out unprofitable product lines are other examples of survival and growth objectives.

Profitability. The capacity of any business to continue to operate depends on its attaining an acceptable level of **profitability**. Well-managed businesses characteristically have one or more profit objectives, which might include categories such as return on equity, return on sales, absolute amount of profit or profit relative to a previous time period or other standard, return on investment, and earnings per share. Sam Walton, for example, set a profit objective expressed as return on sales—8 percent—the accomplishment of which led to his dance on Wall Street.

Resource Allocation and Risk. Business organizations typically set objectives that communicate (1) priorities for the **allocation of resources** that the business generates and (2) targets for the level of **risk** that the managers intend to assume. Objectives that are related to the dividends the firm hopes to pay to shareholders communicate resource allocation priorities. Exxon has repeatedly set the objective of maintaining a dividend level equal to between 8 and 10 percent of its stock price. Risk is often expressed in objectives that set targets for a company's use of debt. Holiday Inns set the objective of achieving a 30 percent debt-to-equity ratio, seeking to keep its level of debt relatively low in case a major recession occurs in the 1980s.

Productivity. Managers constantly try to improve the **productivity** of their organizations. This has become a major concern in an increasingly global economic environment. Companies that can better the "input-output relationship" normally increase profitability. Productivity objectives are commonly expressed in terms of the number of items produced or sold per unit of input or in terms of the number of services rendered per unit of input. Examples include occupancy rates in hotels, number of "table turns" in restaurants, cost per unit in manufacturing firms, percentage of billable hours in accounting or other personal-service firms, and revenue per employee across a variety of companies. Productivity objectives can also be stated in terms of desired decreases in cost. For example, a company with high shipping costs may seek to reduce its transportation expense expressed either as cost per item or as a percent of sales. Another company may seek to reduce maintainence costs per unit, payroll as a percent of sales, or its current cost of goods sold. There is increasing emphasis in the United States on quality-related productivity measures. If accomplished, objectives that seek to improve product or service quality (reduced percentage of defective items, fewer returned purchases, fewer customer complaints, and the like) usually have a favorable impact on profitability.

Competitive Position. A widely applied measure of business success is share of a chosen market, or **competitive position**. Managers typically segment (divide) markets in product, customer, or geographic terms and specify what portion of that market segment they will try to "capture." Market share expressed in terms of percent of total dollar volume or number of units sold is often used to set a measurable objective. Rank relative to other competitors in terms of sales volume in specific markets is another frequently used measure for setting competitive position objectives. For example, Pepsi is reported to have set the objective of becoming the number-one seller of soft drinks through grocery stores by 1985 and the objective of achieving a 25 percent share of the nationwide soft drink market by 1989.

Employee Development and Relations. Employees value growth and career-development opportunities in their work. Well-managed companies often recognize the need for **employee development** by adopting specific career-development objectives for their employees. The company derives many benefits, including higher productivity, lower employee turnover, and clarification of the skills its employees must develop to execute strategic plans successfully.

Concern with **employee relations** is often communicated through the setting of long- and short-term objectives that are established specifically in the employees' interest. Such objectives reinforce the idea that management is interested in the workers' welfare and links the welfare of the work force to the planned pursuits of the company. Examples of areas wherein employee relations objectives are set include safety programs, promotion guidelines, employee involvement in management committees, and employee stock option plans.

Technological Activity. Managers must decide whether to lead or follow in the **technological development** of the processes and products they use to serve the markets in which they compete. Some companies (such as Polaroid) place great emphasis on maintaining technological leadership. Other companies (such as the container company Crown, Cork and Seal) deliberately choose not to be at the forefront of technological development, preferring to assimilate new technologies once they have been proved effective in the marketplace. Each approach can be very successful. Crucial to that success are specific objectives that spell out the firm's long-term and short-term expectations for technological research and development activities.

Public Responsibility. Finally, well-managed companies recognize their **public responsibilities** to customers and society at large. Managers in these companies set objectives that guide company efforts to function as responsible "corporate citizens" in their local, national, and international communities. Examples of topics such objectives might cover include charitable and educational contributions, recruitment of and special training for members of minority groups, community service, political activity, and economic development.

Figure 6-4 gives selected examples of long-term and short-term objectives that have been adopted in recent years at well-known companies operating in the United States. But knowing the appropriate areas to cover is just one aspect of setting such effective objectives. We will next look at eight characteristics of objectives that it is essential to incorporate if long-term and short-term objectives are to be effectively stated.

Characteristics of Effective Objectives

Effective objectives consistently exhibit a number of important characteristics. Figure 6-5 summarizes these eight essential characteristics.

OBJECTIVES SHOULD BE SPECIFIC AND UNDERSTANDABLE

Useful objectives unambiguously set forth exactly what outcome is desired. A major reason for setting objectives is to eliminate uncertainty about what the individual, work group, and organization is expected to accomplish. Any objective should be stated in specific terms so that it is understandable to all concerned. Consider the potential misunderstandings over the objective "to increase productivity in the administration department." Does this mean to increase the number

| Areas | OBJECTIVES | |
	Long-Term	Short-Term
	Chrysler's Eagle/Jeep Division	
Survival and Growth	To invest $2 billion in facilities, equipment, and tooling over the next five years for product development	To open the $675 million Bramalea plant (Brampton, Ontario) by mid-1987, one of the most modern and efficient auto plants, employing state-of-the-art automated manufacturing technology to produce the most advanced, best-built car in the industry
	Koppers Company	
Profitability	To achieve 18% return on equity by 1990	To improve return on equity by 2% per year from 10% starting in 1986
	Ford Motor Company	
Resource Allocation and Risk	To make a comprehensive and continuous effort to increase shareholder wealth	To equal or increase dividend payments from $2.40 per share average in 1985 to reflect improved profitability
	Alcan Aluminum Limited	
Productivity	To achieve the lowest break-even point in the manufacture of aluminum by 1990	To continue emphasis on cost savings through better raw material contracts, improved labor agreements, and replacement of obsolete facilities in 1986
	AT&T (technologies sector)	
Competitive Position	To be among the top three suppliers of computer and communications gear outside the U.S. by 1995	To increase revenues from outside the U.S. from 5% in 1985 to 25% by 1995 with increases of 2% per year
	Dow Chemical Company	
Employee Development and Relations	To continue firm commitment to improving safety records	To match or improve the 0.11 frequency rate of lost-time injuries per 1,000,000 work hours achieved in 1985
	Hitachi	
Technological Development	To develop long-range products for applications in the twenty-first century through pioneering research in such technologies as biotechnology, software science, and materials science	To devote $1 billion a year to research using the talents of 16,000 research and development personnel
	Dow Chemical Company	
Public Responsibility	To continue commitment to environmental protection programs	To increase capital expenditures on environmental control projects to $82 million in 1985

FIGURE 6-4 Examples of Long-Term and Short-Term Objectives in the Eight Key Areas for Several Well-Known Companies

---

◼◼◼◼◼◼◼◼◼◼ *Guidelines for Management Practice* ◼◼◼◼◼◼◼◼◼◼

When choosing the areas their objectives should cover, managers must address several areas as suggested in the preceding section. Regardless of the specific area for which a manager is setting an objective, the following basic tips are always useful in guiding a manager's objective setting.

1. Make sure objectives start at the top of the organization. Without top-management objectives, lower organizational levels lack direction, and people at those levels may assume that objective setting is not important.

2. Include a clear statement of mission as a pervasive organizational objective. Subordinates often become so enmeshed in activities that the mission that invests the work with meaning becomes secondary. Managers must systematically keep key objectives in people's minds by asking, "What are we in business for?" "What is the focus of this organization?"

3. Make sure every person, work group, and unit in the organization has at least one clearly understood, regularly monitored objective.

4. Do not assign anyone more than six to nine objectives. Overwhelming subordinates with too many objectives diffuses their efforts and undermines their effectiveness.

---

of administrative employees or to decrease the number of administrative employees? Or does it mean to computerize the administrative function? And if so, by how much and in which aspects of administrative work? As this simple example illustrates, objectives must be prepared in specific and understandable terms in order to reduce uncertainty about what performance is expected. "Increasing sales per administrative employee by 10 percent in 1990 over 1989 sales" and "decreasing the average age of accounts receivable from 42 to 25 days in 1990" are specific, understandable objectives.

OBJECTIVES SHOULD BE MEASURABLE

Measurable objectives (which usually means objectives that can be quantified, or expressed numerically) are easier to understand. Measurable objectives provide managers with a way to monitor and evaluate performance, interpret feedback, and achieve control. Measurability focuses attention on outcomes and results; the lack of it often causes managers to devote an inordinate amount of attention to processes and activities that are not related to desired outcomes.

Consider the objective "to improve the operations and administrative groups' support of the sales effort." Now imagine a manager's intermittent efforts during

---

FIGURE 6-5
Characteristics of Effective Objectives

Effective objectives are . . .
- Specific and understandable
- Measurable
- Given a time frame
- Concise
- Above standard
- Realistic
- Flexible
- Acceptable

the year to accomplish it and his or her later efforts to evaluate whether it had been accomplished at the end of the planning period for which it was set. What comes to mind? Perhaps several debates among managers with varied responsibilities about whether a current decision, activity, or issue is or is not related to the sales support objective; a sales manager interrupting the invoicing of an accounts receivable staff member to get something else done "because the objective says you're supposed to"; overall, much ado about individual activities, what is and what is not relevant, and who tells whom what to do.

Now consider some alternative, measurable objectives: (1) to reduce the time lapse between order date and delivery date by 12 percent (three days) by July 1, 199X; (2) to reduce the costs of goods produced by 6 percent to support a price decrease of 2 percent by January 15, 199X; (3) to increase by 5 percent the rate of before- and on-schedule delivery by July 1, 199X. Do these objectives improve people's understanding of what is expected? Do they provide a basis for monitoring and evaluating performance? Do they facilitate control? Supply useful feedback? Your answer to each question should be "yes"—effective objectives must be measurable.

OBJECTIVES SHOULD INCLUDE A TIME FRAME

The three measurable objectives just cited are effective not only because they are quantified but also because each specifies a time frame for accomplishment of the objective. It is much better to state that performance will increase by some amount within a certain period of time. Doing so helps the manager determine at what intervals progress checks should be scheduled in order to ensure that any adjustments necessary to keep things on schedule are made in plenty of time. Finally, recognizing a time frame helps different individuals and units know when certain stages on which their own work depends will be completed.

Recognizing a time frame is critical for long-term and short-term objectives. A time frame is less frequently recognized in setting broad objectives of purpose, mission, and organizational values.

OBJECTIVES SHOULD BE CONCISE

Long-term and short-term objectives are most effective when they are brief and to the point. Consider the objective "to increase and expand our market coverage and share during the next year (January 1, 199X–December 31, 199X) to a level that is 8 percent to 10 percent above the previous year, with particular emphasis on increased advertising, direct-mail efforts, discount pricing, and sales incentives." This objective is too wordy. "To increase our market share by 10 percent in 199X" is more concise—and hence more effective.

Managers are often tempted to violate the need for concise objectives and to include descriptions of the methods that will be used in pursuing objectives rather than simply stating the desired outcomes. The means or methods that will be employed to pursue objectives are better spelled out as part of the plans managers intend to implement.

OBJECTIVES SHOULD CALL FOR ABOVE-STANDARD PERFORMANCE

In most jobs, the *standard* is the minimum level of acceptable performance by an individual, a work group, or a subunit of an organization. Standards typically reflect the lowest level of performance the organization will tolerate. Objectives are targets or desired outcomes that are above standard. Thus if standard means 2 percent rejects per month, a worthy objective might be to reduce that figure to 1 percent rejects per month.

OBJECTIVES SHOULD BE REALISTIC

Objectives must be realistic. Objectives that are consistently set too high become frustrating. Yet when objectives are set too low, achieving them yields no feeling of accomplishment and, over time, meeting objectives simply provides reinforcement of risk avoidance rather than a reward for risk-taking behavior. Studies have repeatedly shown that people are most productive when objectives are set at a motivational level—one high enough to challenge but not so high as to frustrate or so low as to be easily attained.

What is high enough may differ from one individual or work group to another. For example, the objective "to increase profitability from 2 percent to 8 percent of sales in 199X" may challenge one group, frustrate another, and barely interest a third. One solution is to develop multiple objectives targeted at different groups. Customizing objectives requires extra time and involvement on the part of planners, but the outcome is usually more realistic, motivational objectives.

OBJECTIVES SHOULD BE FLEXIBLE

Objectives should be modifiable in the event of unforeseen or extraordinary changes in the firm's situation. But flexibility is usually accomplished at the expense of specificity—an important characteristic of effective objectives. The way to resolve this dilemma is simply not to treat objectives as all-or-nothing criteria. If the objective is to increase sales by 12 percent, for example, attaining an 11.6 percent increase hardly represents a failure or a job badly done. Otherwise, people would avoid taking any risk and would gravitate toward conservative objectives that they could always meet.

OBJECTIVES SHOULD BE ACCEPTABLE

An objective is more effective when it is acceptable to the people responsible for accomplishing it. When an objective reflects outcomes consistent with their personal perceptions and preferences—and especially when they participated in setting it—it is even more vigorously pursued.

Objectives that meet all the criteria set forth here tend to be acceptable, particularly when they are also consistent with the values and assumptions of the managers who are to oversee their accomplishment. One way in which managers try to make objectives acceptable is to get those responsible for accomplishing the objectives to read and formally agree to them. Management by objectives, discussed later in this chapter, incorporates this idea.

Objectives that incorporate these eight characteristics are more effective than those that do not (see "In Practice 6-1" for an account of how good objective setting in a crisis helped save a company). "Management Development Exercise 6" gives you an opportunity to test your ability to recognize these characteristics in typical objectives. But the way objectives are stated is not the last consideration. Managers should also concern themselves with five key aspects of setting and using objectives in order to maximize the effectiveness of those objectives. These five concerns are so important that we will devote the entire next section to them.

Guidelines for Management Practice

Managers often pay attention to objectives. They are frequently discussed on an annual basis. They are often addressed orally; less so in written form. Managers can make sure they state objectives in an effective, useable fashion if they keep these tips in mind.

1. State every objective in terms of an outcome, not an activity.

2. Make sure that every objective includes a time frame during which it is to be accomplished.

3. Make sure that everyone involved in meeting the overall objective has measurable objectives, even

if they are arbitrarily set. But be prepared to adjust the overall objective to keep it realistic.

4. When setting objectives in the face of uncertainty, define them in terms of a range of acceptable outcomes.

5. When objectives are conditional, state the relevant conditions.

6. When objective setting is a joint effort, do not balk at minor variations from what your judgment tells you would be a more precise objective. Misplaced precision can stifle initiative.

Setting and Using Objectives: Five Key Principles

Knowing what areas objectives should cover and what characteristics good objectives share is important, but stating good objectives does not by itself make you a better manager. If all the benefits that objective setting can offer are to be realized, five principles in using objectives should be incorporated in every manager's approach to objective setting. These five principles are summarized in Figure 6-6.

Negotiating Objectives

Objectives are much more effective when the subordinates who are responsible for their accomplishment participate in setting them. Objectives are based on analysis, assumptions, premises, and intuitions about future events. As such, their appropriate level, time frame, and so on are subject to differences of opinion. Allowing subordinates to "negotiate" the objectives they are responsible for accomplishing tends to secure their greater commitment and turns what could be a negative situation into a positive situation for managers.

On the individual level, participation in setting objectives for one's performance gives a person a heightened sense of responsibility for accomplishing that objective. At the group level, negotiating about the level of performance and the time frames associated with key objectives facilitates coordination between interdependent subunits of any organization. Finally, vertical negotiation across management levels within an organization helps ensure consistency among mission, long-term objectives, and short-term objectives.

---

1. Objectives should be *negotiated*.
2. Objectives should accurately reflect organizational *priorities*.
3. Regular *feedback* is essential to effective objectives.
4. Objectives should be linked to the *reward system*.
5. Avoid *means-end inversion*.

FIGURE 6-6
Five Principles for Managers in Setting and Using Objectives

━━━━━━━━━━━━━━ *In Practice 6-1* ━━━━━━━━━━━━━━

KEY OBJECTIVES IN CHRYSLER'S TURNAROUND STRATEGY

When Lee Iacocca came to Chrysler, the Michigan State Fairgrounds were jammed with thousands of unsold, unwanted, rusting Chryslers, Dodges, and Plymouths. Foreign operations were leeching the lifeblood out of the company. And worst of all, cars were coming off the assembly line with loose doors, chipped paint, and crooked moldings.

According to Iacocca, the Chrysler experience highlighted four painful realities:

1. The quality of Chrysler products had declined.

2. Work practices had shortchanged productivity.

3. The government had become an enemy instead of an ally.

4. Foreign countries that the United States had defeated in war and rebuilt in peace were beating this country in its own markets.

Chrysler was faced with a choice. The company could go under—the suggestion of not a few—or efforts could be made to save the company, and with it, according to Iacocca, "the American way of doing business—with honesty, pride, ingenuity, and good old-fashioned hard work."

In charting Chrysler's turnaround strategy, Iacocca identified six key objectives essential to a successful turnaround. Careful, systematic attention was given to monitoring progress on each objective as a key indicator of desired execution of the turnaround strategy.

1. Reduce wage and salary expenses by half the 1980 level. (Chrysler ultimately reduced its work force from 160,000 to 80,000 and received over $1.2 billion in wage and benefit sacrifices.)

2. Reduce fixed costs by over $4 billion. (Chrysler closed twenty plants and modernized the remaining forty with state-of-the art robot and computer technology.)

3. Reduce the number of different parts by one-third. (Chrysler reduced the number of parts from 75,000 to 40,000, shaking $1 billion out of inventory in the process.)

4. Improve its weak balance sheet. (Chrysler retired its U.S. bank debt by converting much of it to stock.)

5. Improve the quality of its components and finished products. (Chrysler reduced warranty costs by 25 percent in 1982; it reduced scheduled maintenance costs to a level $20 to $200 below those of the competition.)

6. Implement a $6 billion product improvement program. (Chrysler has a lead in front-wheel drive technology; it has the best economy car in the industry; it offers the industry's most extensive warranty.)

The benefits associated with negotiating objectives can be enhanced by two additional features: "sign-off" and accountability. The sign-off technique has the participants who are involved in setting objectives sign or initial the final objectives. This act acknowledges a contract of sorts about what is to be done, how it will be accomplished, and what resources are needed to achieve the agreed-upon outcomes. The sign-off usually promotes clearer objectives and reduces ambiguity, primarily because individuals will not contract to ends or means that are ambiguous or imprecise. Whether through the sign-off activity or as a separate undertaking, managers should always ensure clear accountability when setting objectives. This simply means clarifying who is responsible for accomplishing each objective that is set.

Establishing Priorities

Organizations, and the managers who lead those organizations, set multiple objectives. Consider McDonald's, a large but relatively simple company. The company starts with approximately ten broad objectives for the next decade, which are set by corporate executives. From these broad objectives, division, area, and unit managers develop several long-term and short-term objectives that reflect what they intend to do within the next one to five years. McDonald's has 8 divisions, 16 areas worldwide, 6,500 units, and over 150,000 employees, so the number of objectives generated throughout the McDonald's organization is considerable. Accordingly, effective managers set priorities among the objectives for which they are accountable. They focus their attention on objectives in areas where the results are crucial. Rather than getting caught in the trap of *doing things right,* they concentrate on *getting the right things done.* Research on objective setting has shown that the most effective managers are those who set challenging objectives for which they "have a clear sense of priority."[9]

Providing Regular Feedback

Research has repeatedly shown that significantly higher performance results when feedback on progress toward objectives is provided than when progress goes unmonitored. We are a society of scorekeepers, and people like to know where they stand. This simple principle is violated by managers who are content to set objectives during the annual planning phase and not return to examine them until the beginning, a year later, of the next cycle.

Setting and using objectives is one of the central ways in which managers get their jobs done. This manager is conducting an objective-setting meeting with a subordinate. In this and other ways, she is applying the five principles for setting and using objectives. (Stacy Pick/Stock, Boston)

Not only are people more likely to meet their objectives and to be better motivated when they are given regular feedback, but they may also become more productive. The best course is to set interim steps in the accomplishment of objectives and to provide feedback (either orally or via routine reports) on the group's or individual's progress at each step of the way.

Linking Objectives to a Reward System

The effectiveness of objective setting is enhanced when objectives are integrated into the organization's reward and review system. A system that rewards the accomplishment of mutually agreed-upon objectives inspires exceptional commitment to those objectives. More is needed, however, to ensure the long-term integrity of the reward system.

The reward system should also recognize effective objective setting whether or not the objectives are met. Say a maintenance director manages three supervisors whose performance she is currently reviewing. One supervisor has not performed satisfactorily, and it appears that he may not have established appropriate objectives to begin with. His review should focus on how he can do a better job of setting the objectives against which his performance will be measured in the next review period. The second supervisor set effective objectives but did not meet them because an unexpected interruption occurred in the supply of certain maintenance materials. This supervisor's review should focus on why such an interruption was not foreseen and how it can be avoided in the future. This diagnosis should then be used to improve the supervisor's analytical skills. And the basic soundness of the second supervisor's original objectives should be rewarded. The final supervisor set effective objectives, met them, and should be rewarded accordingly.

Avoiding Means-End Inversion

Sometimes people forget that the means chosen for achieving an end (or objective) is not the end itself. This situation, called *means-end inversion,* can be quite dysfunctional for a manager, work group, or organization. Consider the experience of Don Dicus, marketing manager for a regional provider of hazardous waste management services (see Chapter 18). Dicus set an objective of adding 175 customers per year for two years through 199X in each of two states that represented new markets for his firm. One of the means that staff members employed to pursue this objective was telemarketing. They quickly began talking about how many calls they made per day and, caught up in the spirit, Dicus started giving small monetary awards for the highest number of customers called during a week. When the performance review period for the first year arrived, Dicus was surprised to find several telemarketing staff members expecting substantial pay increases while the actual numbers of new customers added for the year in the two states were 103 and 89, respectively. The employees' reasoning was always the same: "I called a substantial number of prospects, and I got the award for calling the largest number of prospects during certain weeks." What happened to Dicus and his staff? The answer is means-end inversion. The number of telemarketing calls made (a means) replaced the number of new customers (the original end) as the objective guiding the staff's efforts.

Applying these five principles will enhance your success in the use of objectives as a management tool. Indeed, these principles underlie two management

---

Guidelines for Management Practice

Attending to the five principles for using objectives that we have just described should serve people well as future managers. The following tips provide nine ideas for putting those principles into action as managers set objectives with their subordinates:

1. Have the people who are responsible for achieving objectives participate in setting them.

2. Begin objective setting with brief statements of future objectives. Allow for brainstorming before fine-tuning objectives in later meetings.

3. Make sure objectives reflect true organizational priorities. Test every objective by asking, "How is it related to the reason we're in business?"

4. Prioritize objectives. Divide them into three cate-

gories: essential, desirable, and "time permitting." Accomplish them accordingly.

5. Regularly (at least quarterly) review and discuss progress toward objectives.

6. Be sure to link all subordinates' objectives to the organization's reward system.

7. Avoid "activity" objectives. Objectives that describe things to do rather than results to be achieved are dysfunctional.

8. Make sure that the means employed to achieve objectives do not become ends in themselves.

9. Setting effective objectives gets easier the more often one does it.

---

techniques that are very popular in today's business environment. The next section briefly introduces these two techniques.

Popular Objective-Setting Techniques in Management

Objective setting in the management process is so important that several techniques have been designed to ensure that managers use objective setting. Two of the techniques that are widely used to highlight objective setting in the process of managing are "management by objectives" and "one minute managing." This section introduces you to these two techniques.

Management by Objectives

Management by objectives (MBO) is a popular technique that organizations use to integrate objectives into the activities that managers engage in. We will examine the background of MBO, its essential elements, and its strengths and weaknesses.

THE BACKGROUND OF MBO

Peter Drucker, perhaps the most widely read management author of the twentieth century, is generally credited with popularizing MBO as an integrated approach to planning. His book *The Practice of Management*[10] was published in 1954. Since that time others have served up versions of MBO called "management by results," "goals and controls," "goals management," "objectives management," and "work planning and review."

MBO is a formal, or a quasi-formal, procedure that begins with objective setting and ends with performance appraisal, usually on an annual cycle. Managers and their subordinates work together to establish, for the subordinates, objectives that will later be applied when the subordinates are evaluated and rewarded for their performance. Employee participation in setting objectives, the integration of objectives across organizational levels, and the linking of objectives to performance appraisal are the three essential features of any MBO program. (These features are identical to several of the principles for effective objective setting that we have already noted in this chapter.) Figure 6-7 is a diagram of a typical MBO process.

KEY ELEMENTS IN THE MBO PROCESS

When introducing an MBO program, it is important to set aside a period of time to acquaint managers and subordinates with MBO: what it is, what their role in it will be, and how serious the organizational commitment to MBO is.[11] For managers, MBO is a tool to boost subordinate participation in objective setting and decision making. For subordinates, it is a program to create better synergy between organizational and individual objectives and to improve communication about what they are expected to do and how well they are doing it.

Several studies of MBO programs have concluded that clear and visible top-management support of the MBO program and participation in it are key determinants of the program's success or failure.[12] Top managers set the tone that inspires commitment throughout the organizational hierarchy.

The MBO process starts with top managers setting preliminary organizational objectives after consulting with other organizational members. The objectives are

FIGURE 6-7
The Cycle of
Management by
Objectives

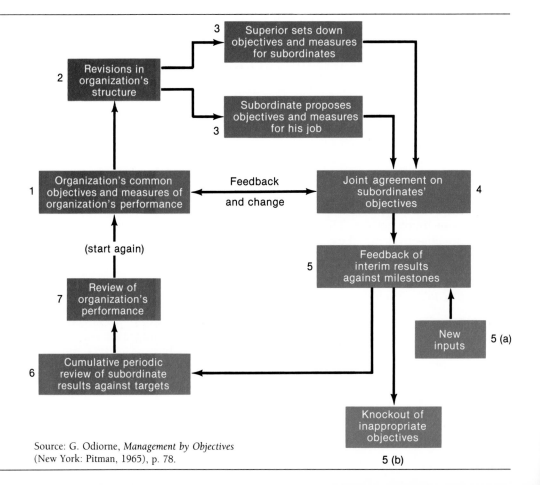

Source: G. Odiorne, *Management by Objectives*
(New York: Pitman, 1965), p. 78.

preliminary because they are subject to change as the ideas and objectives of managers throughout the organization are discussed and fine-tuned.

Collaborative objective setting is the essence of MBO; it involves a manager and subordinate collaborating to set the subordinate's objectives for the planning period.[13] Such collaboration ensures that subordinates will help managers set realistic objectives; they are the ones who know best their capabilities and resource needs. Collaboration affords managers the opportunity to encourage high levels of achievement and to foster improvement by becoming aware of ways in which they can better support their subordinates' efforts. The collaboration process usually involves several distinct steps:

1. Managers and their subordinates have an initial meeting in which the managers outline preliminary organizational and unit objectives. Subordinates are asked to think about these objectives and about what their objectives should be in supporting unit and organizational objectives.

2. Managers next meet with their subordinates on an individual basis to set objectives that both the subordinate and the manager have helped develop.

3. In most MBO programs, major emphasis is placed on quantifying objectives and on including a specific time frame for their accomplishment. The objectives are generally written down, and both manager and subordinate usually sign or initial this document. (You should recognize in this element several of the characteristics of effective objectives identified earlier in this chapter.)

4. Another important element in the objective-setting phase of MBO is the manager's role as coach and counselor. Managers are urged to use these meetings as training and development sessions wherein they make subordinates aware of critical issues, suggest ways of doing their job more effectively, and place the subordinates' role in the "broader" context of the organization or division at large.

5. A final element in the objective-setting phase of MBO programs in many organizations is an emphasis on spelling out the key resources a subordinate can expect to utilize in accomplishing the objectives. For example, the accounting department manager might commit himself to reducing the average age of accounts receivable from 62 to 31 days in 199X *if* he can add a new billing or accounts receivable clerk. That condition should be formally stipulated as part of the objective, and the manager should be informed promptly whether the additional person can be hired.

Manager and subordinate usually meet regularly for periodic reviews of the subordinate's progress toward objectives during the time period for which the objectives were set. Usually this means quarterly meetings associated with annual objectives. During each review they discuss what problems, if any, are inhibiting achievement of the objectives they agreed on and what they can do to resolve these problems. They also modify objectives when different objectives are appropriate for the next review session or when a change in unit or organizational objectives has occurred. These periodic reviews serve to keep managers better informed and give them opportunities to inform, coach, and motivate subordinates.

Managers meet with individual subordinates at the end of the MBO cycle (usually annually) to review the extent to which the objectives were met. They focus on the reasons why specific objectives were met or were not achieved.

This final performance evaluation also serves as a starting point to begin the next MBO cycle.

Evaluation of the MBO Approach

Approximately 40 percent of *Fortune* magazine's list of the 500 largest industrial firms in the United States use some form of MBO. General Electric, General Motors, General Foods, DuPont, and Alcoa are but a few examples. Research on some of these organizatons and reports from others suggest that the MBO approach exhibits certain strengths and certain weaknesses.

STRENGTHS OF MBO

Perhaps the best summary of the strengths of well-run MBO programs appears in a survey of managers by Henry L. Tosi and Stephen J. Carroll:[14]

1. MBO lets individuals know what is expected of them.

2. MBO aids in planning by forcing managers to establish objectives and target dates.

3. MBO improves communication between managers and subordinates.

4. MBO makes individuals more aware of organizational objectives.

5. MBO makes the performance review and evaluation process more equitable by focusing on specific results. It also improves the review process by providing systematic feedback during the time period these results are expected.

WEAKNESSES OF MBO

Criticisms of the MBO approach are generally associated with attempts to implement the approach that neglect key features of the MBO process. The two most common mistakes are:

1. *Lack of top-management support.* Top management may decide to use the program but may relegate its implementation solely to lower management personnel. Under these conditions, the people charged with implementing the program become disenchanted, question the value of making the effort, and grow suspicious of upper management's motives in initiating the program.

2. *Overemphasis on quantitative objectives.* Firms fall into this trap when they seek to quantify every possible objective and require excessive paperwork and recordkeeping to manage the MBO process. This approach tempts managers to assign objectives to or request objectives from their subordinates rather than sitting down and working objectives out with them. Again, suspicion and resentment or disenchantment with the program may result from overemphasis on quantitative objectives and obsessive recordkeeping.

When it is properly implemented, MBO can be an effective program that takes advantage of the payoffs associated with objective setting. It can clarify expectations, improve communication between successive sets of managers and subordinates, and help both get more out of performance reviews and evaluations.

MBO has been well recognized for three decades as a management technique based on objective setting. A more recent approach to receive similar acclaim is one minute managing. This is described in the next section.

One Minute Managing

The One Minute Manager is a succinct account of how a manager can effectively apply three basic ideas about planning.[15] Kenneth Blanchard, who studies organizational behavior, wanted to condense the field into a few simple ideas or, as he called them, secrets for effective managing. His three "secrets" are: objective setting, praising, and reprimanding (Figure 6-8). We will briefly discuss each of these aspects of **one minute managing**.

In one minute objective setting, managers and subordinates agree on basic objectives and the behaviors for achieving them. A critical part of this step is to write down each objective in fewer than 250 words and then read it over frequently.

After the objectives have been set, managers must recognize the positive behavior of their subordinates. The basic point, according to Blanchard, is that managers readily give negative feedback in the course of day-to-day work activities but usually forget to give positive feedback or feel it unnecessary. To overcome this tendency, he includes one minute praising as a second important step. First,

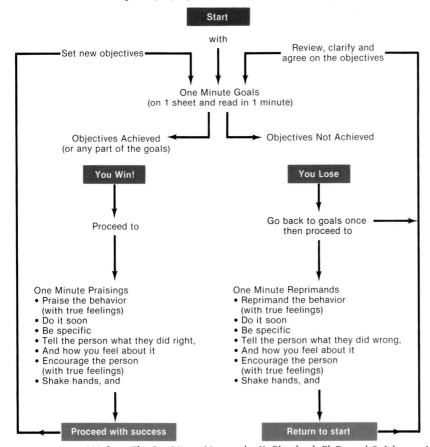

A very brief summary of
The One Minute Manager's "Game Plan"
How to give yourself & others "the gift" of getting greater results in less time.
Set objectives; praise and reprimand behaviors; encourage people;
speak the truth; laugh; work; enjoy
and encourage the people you work with to do the same as you do!

FIGURE 6-8
The One Minute
Manager's Game Plan

Source: Excerpt page 101 from *The One Minute Manager* by K. Blanchard, Ph.D., and S. Johnson, M.D. Copyright © 1981, 1982 Blanchard Family Partnership and Candle Communications Corporation. By permission of William Morrow and Company.

managers are to tell subordinates directly that they will let them know how they are doing. This step prepares them to receive more frequent feedback from the manager, positive or negative. Next, managers are to praise people, as often as possible, immediately after they have done something right. They are to be specific in describing what the people did right. The effect is to encourage productive behavior by reinforcing it. Finally, managers are to personalize their sincerity. A manager should tell subordinates how good their behavior makes her or him feel and how much it helps the company. Allowing a moment of silence will help subordinates "feel" how good the manager feels, and shaking hands or otherwise touching them helps spur them on to more of the same good performance.

After subordinates have been prepared to expect frequent feedback, Blanchard recommends that, in cases of faulty performance, a two-part reprimand be given to people as soon as possible after managers learn what they did wrong. First, they are to be told specifically what they did wrong. Then they are to be told briefly how the manager feels about their wrongdoing, followed by a few seconds of uncomfortable silence to let them "feel" how the manager feels. Next, the manager is expected to shake hands or otherwise touch the subordinates in a way that lets them know that the manager is on their side, reminds them how much they are valued, and demonstrates that once the reprimand is over, it is truly over.

AN EVALUATION OF ONE MINUTE MANAGING

The one minute manager approach enjoyed widespread acclaim in industry and government organizations during the 1980s, but it has not yet received much research attention. Testimonials from managers suggest several basic strengths: It is simple and easy to understand; it is universally applicable; and it offers a positive, caring approach to the process of setting objectives and providing feedback.

Weaknesses or possible problems have also been suggested. For example, one minute is often an unrealistically short time; the propensity for openness and touching are not so easily developed as the guidelines for application would imply; and it is not altogether clear how to tie one minute managing in with other organizational objectives or reward systems.

Review of the Learning Objectives

Having studied this chapter, you should be able to respond to the learning objectives with extensions of the following brief answers:

1. **Explain why setting objectives will make you a better manager.**

   Setting objectives accomplishes five things that will make you a better manager because of their important impact on organizational, work-group, and individual success. Objectives provide guidance, reduce uncertainty, motivate, facilitate individual and organizational learning, and coordinate diverse activities.

2. **Identify three types of objectives and explain their role in the planning process.**

   Broad objectives provide open-ended statements that express the direction the organization is moving in and describe the reason for its existence. Long-term objectives identify the specific, measurable ends that the company's strategic plans are designed to achieve, usually over a three-to-five-year time span. Short-term objectives are specific, measurable ends that are to be achieved within a year or sooner and that reflect progress toward the accomplishment of long-term objectives and the ends the specific operational plans are designed to achieve.

3. **Describe how to set effective objectives.**

The first concern in setting objectives is to be sure that the appropriate topics are covered. Three topics that are usually covered when managers set broad objectives are the organization's purpose, its values, and its mission. Up to eight areas are typically covered when managers set long-term and short-term objectives. These are survival and growth, profitability, resource allocation and risk, productivity, competitive position, employee relations and development, technological activity, and public responsibility.

The second concern in creating statements of objectives is to make sure those statements incorporate eight characteristics of effective objectives. Objectives should be specific and understandable, measurable, concise, realistic, flexible, and acceptable; they should specify outcomes that exceed the standard, or minimal expected, performance; and they should incorporate a time frame.

4. **Identify five principles for successfully managing the objective-setting process.**

To derive the benefits that objective setting offers, managers should keep in mind five principles as they manage the objective-setting process. They should derive objectives through participation and negotiation, prioritize objectives, provide regular feedback evaluating the subordinate's progress toward objectives, link objectives to the organizational reward system, and avoid means-end inversion.

5. **Describe at least one popular objective-setting technique.**

Management by objectives (MBO) is a formal or quasi-formal procedure used by many organizations. It begins with objective setting in management-subordinate pairs throughout the organization and continues with performance appraisal on an annual cycle. Key elements in MBO include careful introduction of the program, top-management commitment to the MBO philosophy, establishment of preliminary objectives, collaborative setting of objectives, periodic reviews, and final performance evaluation.

One minute managing is an approach to the practice of management developed by Kenneth Blanchard, who advocates the use of three "secrets" to make you a better manager: one minute objectives, one minute praisings, and one minute reprimands. The essence of one minute managing is to set clear and meaningful objectives and to provide regular feedback on the subordinate's progress toward and accomplishment of those objectives. Though little research on this technique has yet been completed, it has been widely endorsed by leaders of business firms and other organizations.

Key Terms and Concepts

Having completed your study of Chapter 6, "Setting Objectives," you should have mastered the following important terms and concepts:

objectives	long-term objectives	organizational purpose	organizational values	profitability
linking pin	short-term objectives		survival and growth	resource allocation and risk
strategic plans		organizational mission		

productivity	technological	public	management by	one minute
competitive position	development	responsibility	objectives (MBO)	managing
employee relations and development				

Questions for Discussion

1. Briefly describe several situations in which a manager might need to set objectives.

2. Consider a competitive sporting event in which you were involved. What effect did objective setting or the lack of it have on the outcome of that event? Why?

3. Consider the first job you had wherein your objectives were clearly explained to you. Contrast that with another job you held in which no explanation of the purpose of your work was offered. In which setting were you more productive? Why?

4. Devise an example in which objective setting provides guidance. In which it is motivational. In which it reduces uncertainty. Increases individual learning. Increases organizational learning. Increases organizational coordination.

5. Why should top management be primarily concerned with broad objectives and long-term objectives, whereas first-line supervisors should be primarily concerned with short-term objectives? Illustrate your reasons by referring to a business with which you are familiar.

6. List three long-term objectives for your academic program or the job you currently hold. Now list three short-term objectives associated with the same endeavor. Evaluate each of these six objectives for compliance with the eight characteristics of effective objectives.

7. Describe a means-end inversion that you have experienced or witnessed and explain its impact.

8. Compare management by objectives and one minute managing. Which approach do you think would be more likely to help you as a manager attempting to take advantage of the benefits of objective setting? Why?

Notes

1. From "How Sam Walton Does it," *Forbes,* August 16, 1983, pp. 42–44. Adapted by permission of *Forbes* magazine, August 16, 1982, pp. 42–44. © Forbes, Inc., 1982.

2. D. W. Karger, "Integrated Formal Long-Range Planning and How to Do it," *Long-Range Planning* 6, no. 4 (1973): 31–34.

3. Early studies include D. Herold, "Long-Range Planning and Organizational Performance: A Cross Validation Study," *Academy of Management Review,* March 1972, pp. 91–102; D. Krager and Z. Malik, "Long-Range Planning and Organizational Performance," *Long-Range Planning,* December 1975, pp. 60–64; Z. Malik and D. Karger, "Does Long-Range Planning Improve Company Performance?" *Management Review,* September 1975, pp. 27–31; L. Rue and R. Fulmer, "Is Long-Range Planning Profitable?" *Academy of Management Proceedings,* 1972; S. Schoeffler et al., "Impact of Strategic Planning on Profit Performance," *Harvard Business Review,* March–April 1974, pp. 137–145; S. Thune and R. House, "Where Long-Range Planning Pays Off," *Business Horizons,* August 1970, pp. 81–87; and D. R. Wood, Jr., and R. L. LaForge, "The Impact of Comprehensive Planning on Financial Performance," *Academy of Management Journal* 22, no. 3 (1979): 516–526. More recent studies are summarized in C. B. Shrader, L. Taylor, and D. R. Dalton, "Strategic Planning and Organizational Performance: A Critical Appraisal," *Journal of Management* 10 (1984): 149–171.

4. J. S. Kim and W. C. Hamner, "Effect of Performance Feedback and Goal Setting on Productivity and Satisfaction in an Organizational Setting," *Journal of Applied Psychology* 61 (1976): 48–57; J. M. Ivancevich, "Different Goal Setting Treatments and Their Effects on Performance and Job Satisfaction," *Academy of Management Journal* 20 (1977): 406–419.

5. J. M. Ivancevich and T. J. McMahon, "Education as a Moderator of Goal Setting Effectiveness," *Journal of Vocational Behavior* 11 (1977): 83–94.

6. T. Barry et al., "Productivity Decline," *Industrial Engineering,* November 1980, pp. 22–26.

7. L. G. Hrebiniak and W. F. Joyce, *Implementing Strategy* (New York: Macmillan, 1984), p. 105; M. Nash, *Managing Organizational Performance* (New York: Jossey-Bass, 1984).

8. From the 1985 ITT Annual Report.

9. S. J. Carroll and H. L. Tosi, *Management by Objectives: Applications and Research* (New York: Mac-

millan), 1973; J. S. Kim and W. C. Hamner, "Effect of Performance Feedback and Goal Setting on Productivity and Satisfaction in an Organizational Setting," *Journal of Applied Psychology* 61(1976): 48–57; J. F. Bryan and E. A. Locke, "Goal Setting as a Means of Increasing Motivation," *Journal of Applied Psychology* 51 (1967): 274–277; J. F. Bryan and E. A. Locke, "Parkinson's Law as a Goal-Setting Phenomenon," *Organizational Behavior and Human Performance* 2 (1967): 258–275; D. M. Dale, *How to Manage by Results* (New York: AMA, 1983), p. 24.

10. P. F. Drucker, *The Practice of Management* (New York: Harper & Row, 1954).

11. G. Odiorne, *Management by Objectives* (New York: Pitman, 1965), p. 78.

12. The most frequently cited works are those by G. S. Odiorne, a major proponent of MBO and contributor to its development, and H. Weihrich, author of many articles on the application of MBO to a variety of situations. See especially Odiorne's *MBO II: A System of Managerial Leadership for the 80's* (Belmont, Calif.: Fearon Pitman, 1979) and *The Ef-*

fective Executive's Guide to Successful Goal Setting (Westfield, Mass.: MBO, Inc., 1980); and Weihrich's "Goal Setting by the OK MBO Boss," *S.A.M. Advanced Management Journal* 42, no. 4 (Fall 1977): 4–13 and "Getting Action into MBO," *Journal of Systems Management* 28, no. 11 (November 1977): 10–13.

13. S. J. Carroll and H. Tosi, *Management by Objectives*, pp. 1–19; and J. M. Ivancevich, "Different Goal-Setting Treatments and Their Effect on Performance and Satisfaction," *Academy of Management Journal* 20, no. 3 (September 1977): 406–419. See also G. P. Latham and T. P. Steele, "The Motivational Effects of Participation versus Goal Setting on Performance," *Academy of Management Journal* 26, no. 3 (September 1983): 406–417.

14. H. L. Tosi and S. J. Carroll, "Managerial Reaction to Management by Objectives," *Academy of Management Journal* 11, no. 4 (December 1968): 415–426.

15. K. Blanchard and S. Johnson, *The One Minute Manager* (New York: Berkley Books, 1982).

Cohesion Incident 6-1
What Is the "Objective" of Happy Hour?

During the three years the Journey's End motel has been in Graniteville, the surrounding area has shown tremendous growth. When the Journey's End was first built in Graniteville, it was one of five motels in the area, only two of which were nationally known. Although demand for the rooms in the area has grown, Roger has noticed that his total revenue and profits have slowly dropped as he cut his room rates to meet the competition. He has been successful in maintaining a high occupancy rate, but he wonders how much lower corporate management will allow him to reduce room rates. Key operating and financial data for the past three years are shown in the following table.

	1984	1983	1982
Occupancy Rate	82.7%	83.1%	84.1%
Total Revenue	$4,075,000	$4,252,000	$4,351,000
Total Profits (before taxes)	285,000	306,000	321,000
Profit Percent	7.0%	7.2%	7.4%
Average Price per Room	$30.00	$31.15	$31.50

Although Roger was aware that his financial data were extremely strong compared with those of other inns in the Journey's End organization, he was concerned about the rate reductions at Graniteville Journey's End. He was reluctant to ask for further decreases in room rates, and the restaurant business was so competitive that at first he did not see any way to increase profits in that segment of the business. Then he remembered an action that had had favorable results in the motel he had managed just before moving to Graniteville. When he started a free hors d'oeuvres Happy Hour in the lounge at that motel, he achieved a significant increase in profits. Hoping for similar results, Roger decided to initiate a free hors d'oeuvres campaign in Graniteville. He advertised it widely, emphasizing the interval during which all hors d'oeuvres in the lounge would be free: 5:00 P.M. until 6:00 P.M. each day. Roger was convinced that enough customers would stay in the lounge after 6:00 to compensate for the free hors d'oeuvres during Happy Hour. He remembered that many customers at the prior inn moved over to the restaurant for dinner. And he further believed that the Happy Hour might also attract guests to the motel.

After a slow start, the new idea began to work well. The lounge was usually filled between 5:00 P.M. and 6:00 P.M., and Roger noticed that many of the customers stayed at the lounge after 6:00. At the end of the first month, a slight improvement showed up in his overall profit margin (0.3 percent), and Roger attributed most of it to the happy effects of Happy Hour. Roger was quite proud of his idea.

During the second month, however, Charles (who worked from 2:00 P.M. until midnight) observed that a rising number of customers in the lounge were not guests of the motel but rather young people from the community who were coming for the Happy Hour and staying well into the night. At times they became somewhat rowdy, and Miles, the bartender, had even had to ask two to leave one night, threatening to call the police if they did not. Charles also overheard some of the motel guests complaining about the noise coming from the lounge.

After one particularly rowdy night in which a fight broke out, Charles decided to suggest to Roger that the Happy Hour be canceled or limited to a few nights a week. As he drove to work the next day, Charles practiced what he wanted to say to Roger about the situation.

Discussion Questions

1. Roger has successfully achieved his objective of increasing the profit margin but is he doing so in a way that conflicts with other organizational objectives? See "Cohesion Incident 2-1: Background for the Charles Richards Incidents" for a list of the business's objectives.

2. Cite several areas in which objectives might be set for the Journey's End organization.

3. Why is it necessary for Journey's End to have more than a profit-margin objective?

4. What additional objectives would you set at Journey's End?

Cohesion Incident 6-2
Management by Whose Objectives?

Travis Corporation described its people as its greatest asset. Its management philosophy stressed the importance of open and clear communication at all levels of the organization. Employees were encouraged to offer suggestions, and supervisors were expected to solicit and respond to input from their subordinates. Accordingly, all supervisors were expected to provide performance feedback to their employees every six months. Management by objectives (MBO) was strongly recommended as a method for setting objectives and evaluating performance.

Leslie Phillips was responsible for conducting semiannual performance appraisals and providing feedback for two data analysts. She was familiar with their duties because she had once held that position at another plant. However, she had never used MBO to set objectives for herself or for others.

She made her first attempt at developing objectives for an MBO program in preparation for Bill Sherman's next six-month evaluation. Bill recalled a textbook definition of MBO, but that's all he knew about the procedure. As he went into Leslie's office to discuss his MBO plan, he felt somewhat in the dark about the whole process and was relieved that Leslie took charge.

"Bill, as you know, we have begun to implement MBO as the basis for our semiannual performance evaluations. The purpose is to state as clearly as possible what you're expected to accomplish in the next six months. Then we'll use those objectives as the standard to evaluate your work performance. I've listed what I consider the most important objectives for you in the coming months. I hope this clarifies things for you."

She handed him the following list of objectives:

Employee: Bill Sherman
Evaluation Period: July 1–December 31

1. Interviewing and surveying
   a. Reduce costs of interviews by 10 percent by December 31.
   b. Conduct at least ten interviews per week with at least 95 percent usable data.
   c. Report validity checks for 5 percent of the interview sample by October 31 and December 31.
   d. Increase return rate of mail surveys to at least 60 percent.
2. Tabulation and input of data
   a. Tabulate and input data with 100 percent accuracy.
   b. Meet 100 percent of the deadlines for preparation of data for analysis.
3. Analysis and report preparation
   a. Meet 100 percent of the deadlines for report preparation.
   b. Increase effectiveness of graphs for purposes of summarizing data.
   c. Increase creativity in consideration of alternative interpretations of results.
4. Special projects
   a. Construct cruise-control end-user sample by September 1.
   b. Complete and report results of search of potential and completed legislation relevant to cruise-control by October 1.

"Are there any objectives here that you have questions about or need me to clarify further?"

Bill, a little puzzled, looked over the objectives and was surprised by some of them. For example, he did not realize that he was expected to generate alternative explanations for the results of his analyses. He thought that was up to management. He was also uncertain about what he was expected to do to "increase creativity." Leslie's presentation had made it clear that she perceived these tasks as part of his job, however, so he replied, "No, no questions so far. I guess this does point out parts of the job I need to work extra hard on."

Discussion Questions

1. Describe the steps involved in implementing an MBO plan. For each step, evaluate Leslie's implementation of the plan. What problems are she and Bill likely to encounter when it comes time to evaluate his performance in trying to achieve the stated objectives?

2. What are the characteristics of well-stated objectives? Evaluate the objectives Leslie has set for Bill.

Management Development Exercise 6
Setting Management Objectives

Good objectives require specific statements that display the key characteristics discussed in this chapter. Listed below are six poor objectives and six good objectives addressing the same end. You should match the letter of the appropriate "good" objective with the number of its "poor" counterpart. After you have completed this test your instructor will tell you how to evaluate your answers.

Poor Objectives	Good Objectives
1. Improve our customer relations.	A. Adherence to a courtesy standard; answer within three rings, speak politely and pleasantly, use caller's name, limit "hold" time to one minute, ensure that customer reaches someone who will take responsibility for action; full compliance with courtesy standard achieved within thirty days from now.
2. Increase our share of the market.	
3. Improve employee morale.	
4. Improve job opportunities for women.	
5. Improve our responsiveness to our client agencies.	
6. Improve telephone courtesy to customers who call our office.	
	B. Complaints and call-backs less than 1 percent by the end of this year.
	C. 50,000 units of product A sold by the end of this year.
	D. Absentee rate 5 percent of working hours or less by the end of the next fiscal quarter.
	E. X (number) qualified women placed in management positions at all levels (in the work-force population) by ——— (date).
	F. Work-order response time reduced to less than four hours on Type-A requests, less than sixteen hours on Type-B requests, by the end of this month.

Source: Adapted from K. Albrecht, *Successful Management by Objectives* (Englewood Cliffs, N.J.: Prentice-Hall, 1978), pp. 78–79. Karl Albrecht, Ph.D. *Successful Management by Objectives,* © 1978. Reprinted by permission of Prentice-Hall, Inc., Englewood Cliffs, N.J.

Strategic Management

Your study of this chapter will enable you to do the following:

1. Define the term *strategy*.
2. Explain why formulating a strategy should make your organization more effective.
3. Distinguish among three levels of strategy.
4. Cite several conceptual tools that can be used as a basis for setting forth specific corporate and business-level strategies.
5. Describe the key elements of the strategic planning process, and explain how they can be used to formulate effective strategies.

Learning Objectives

The Wendy's Story

After completing his education and a three-year tour of duty in the U.S. Army, R. David Thomas went to work for Harland Sanders selling special chicken recipes and cooking utensils to restaurants. Soon thereafter Sanders started Kentucky Fried Chicken and Thomas prospered, owning three KFC franchises in Columbus, Ohio. In 1971, Thomas initiated a lifelong dream: opening the first of what he hoped would be a nationwide chain of hamburger restaurants named after his youngest daughter, Wendy.

Analysts for *The Wall Street Journal* and *Business Week*, citing a "competitively saturated fast-food hamburger industry," predicted in the early 1970s that the Wendy's venture would not succeed. As they saw it, market saturation and rising commodity prices, fuel costs, and labor costs were already plaguing the industry.

Despite such comments, Thomas remained convinced that his strategy was sound, saying that "there is a vast opportunity in the United States for a hamburger chain that provides a limited menu of fresh food daily primarily to adult and young adult consumers in a fast, efficient manner during lunchtime at a reasonable yet profitable price."

Contrary to analysts' predictions, Thomas's well-thought-out strategy was overwhelmingly successful. Wendy's opened an average of one restaurant every

This Wendy's outlet is like most in the Wendy's chain. It is conveniently located to high-traffic areas. It is compact in design, yet sensitive to the dining preferences of adult diners. It is attractively landscaped in a manner that minimizes maintenance costs. Finally, it is situated so as to maximize ease of traffic flow to its drive-in window. Each of these features is a part of Wendy's carefully constructed strategy. (Courtesy of Wendy's)

two days between 1971 and 1980, becoming the first restaurant chain to top $1 billion in its first ten years, the fastest-growing restaurant chain in the world, and (by 1980) the third-largest hamburger chain in the world.

Thomas was recently asked to explain Wendy's phenomenal success against such sizable odds. His answer: "We were committed to a specific objective, we developed a sound strategy that served us well for over fifteen years, and we have motivated people who have made our strategy work." Mr. Thomas then proceeded to describe Wendy's strategy and specific objective.

"First, we had an overall objective for our company—some people call it a mission; that was to become the largest hamburger chain in America providing fresh food daily primarily to adult patrons in high-traffic, urban locations, using a store operation that could fill their orders in less than one minute." To achieve this mission, Wendy's executives committed the company to a market development and differentiation strategy. This strategy included seeking to "grow the business" by rapidly opening new locations in cities throughout the United States (market development) and making the Wendy's store concept distinctly different from current fast-food outlets in terms of offering an upscale, fresh product and atmosphere that commanded a premium price (differentiation).

Wendy's implemented numerous functional strategies designed to accomplish this competitive strategy. Food was bought fresh daily by each local store manager from a local vendor, rather than being bought frozen from regional distributors by corporate purchasing departments. Each store was designed to maximize work-flow efficiency, and a drive-in window (Wendy's was the first hamburger chain to use one) was included to increase speed, sales per square foot, and the convenience of adults on thirty-minute lunch breaks. One person worked the cash register while another person filled the order, again reducing customer waiting lines. Hamburgers were all one size, which cut inventory cost, and were square, which gave the appearance of more "beef" inside the bun. Attendants picked up customer plates, giving a more "upscale service atmosphere" than McDonald's. Chili was a menu item that eliminated high waste costs (hamburgers not sold in three minutes are usually thrown out by most fast-food chains); at Wendy's, unsold hamburgers became the meat in tomorrow's chili. Stores were located close to downtown areas and office buildings, rather than in the residential, school, and shopping center-adjacent locations chosen by McDonald's and Burger King.

"One of my best functional strategies, a financial one really, accelerated our growth tremendously while seemingly violating traditional norms in fast-food franchising," offered Thomas. He continued, "we sought out wealthy franchisees that wanted to buy the franchise for large areas, say a whole state, and required that they open a certain number of stores within a specified time. This allowed us to expand our size at an unprecedented rate since companies like McDonald's had a corporate policy only to sell a franchise for one store location at a time." It also allowed Wendy's, in its early frugal years, to get more cash up front in the form of franchise fees. And whereas McDonald's and Burger King preferred franchisees who were not involved with other restaurant or franchise businesses, Wendy's actively encouraged such people as franchisees, reasoning that they would bring more experience and know-how to each franchise location.

Concluding his comments, Thomas offered, "I could go on and on about various functional strategies we used, or the change in our business strategy when we decided to start the Sister's Chicken 'n Bisquits chain. But the important thing to see is that creating sound strategies and using them to guide our efforts *throughout* the company created the fastest-growing restaurant chain in the history of commercial endeavor." It was clear that Wendy's strategies, designed to guide both the overall business and different functional areas within each store, proved that the industry analysts who predicted the Wendy's chain would never work had not done their homework.[1]

Introduction

What Is Strategic Management?

Sears, once a Chicago-based mail order company, has become the nation's largest retailer of dry goods and soft goods and is rapidly becoming the nation's largest provider of financial services. Woolworths, once a dominant force in the retailing of dry and soft goods, with locations nationwide, recently went bankrupt. Delta Airlines, once a small regional airline, has for ten years been the most profitable national airline in the highly competitive airline industry. Pan Am, TWA, Eastern, and Braniff once took in, among them, over 50 percent of all industry receipts. Only one remains to compete with Delta today. Dairy Queen and its Brazer Burger had a twenty-year headstart on Wendy's in selling hamburgers and offering drive-in service. Yet Wendy's has grown faster than any food chain in history, while Dairy Queen languishes as a marginal competitor.

Sears and Woolworths competed in the same industry but achieved dramatically different results. Delta and Braniff, Pan Am and TWA competed in the same industry; again the outcomes were dramatically different. And the same can be said of Wendy's and Dairy Queen. Why? Perhaps General Robert E. Wood, the chief executive officer and architect of Sears's retailing success, provides the best answer: "Business is like a war in one respect, if its grand strategy is correct, any number of tactical errors can be made and yet the enterprise proves successful."[2]

Years ago, the managerial emphasis in a typical business firm fell squarely on operations. The primary challenge managers faced was how to make efficient use of the limited resources at their disposal in producing goods and services at prices customers were willing to pay. Successfully doing this, it was believed, would maximize the firm's profitability. Today, although the efficient use of limited resources certainly remains a major concern of managers in any business, the ability of the firm to adapt properly to its environment has become more critical to the firm's survival because that environment tends to be turbulent and to change rapidly. As General Wood suggests, a company may overcome the inefficient use of internal resources if its basic strategy is effective, but it is not likely to overcome the ill effects of choosing the wrong strategies, even if its operations are extremely efficient.[3] Peter Drucker said it another way: "It is increasingly important that managers should be first concerned with being effective and then with being efficient. Effective means doing the right things; efficient means doing things right."[4]

This chapter is about how managers help their businesses focus on "doing the right things." To play this role of business strategist, managers must understand the concept of strategy and the process of formulating a strategy—strategic planning. For these managers, **strategy** means large-scale, future-oriented plans for competing in designated products and markets to achieve organizational objectives. Thus a strategy represents a firm's "game plan" for how to compete against whom, when, where, and for what. **Strategic planning** is the process of formulating this strategy and guiding its execution by members of the organization.

After reviewing the evidence that strategic planning enhances a firm's performance and exploring some of the reasons why, we will define and explain the concept of strategy. Next we will consider key elements in the process of formulating strategy, or strategic planning. Finally, we will describe strategic planning in different organizational settings.

The Value of Strategic Planning

Strategic planning confers several advantages on organizations that use it effectively. First, studies suggest that many businesses have benefited financially from the use of strategic planning. Second, strategic planning has been credited with bringing about numerous behavioral improvements in businesses that use it. This section examines the value of strategic planning in greater detail.

Financial Benefits

Does strategic planning enhance financial performance? Yes, according to the results of several studies that have addressed this question. One of the earliest such studies examined ninety-three U.S. manufacturing firms and found that strategic planners outperformed nonplanners in sales growth, asset growth, earnings per share, and earnings growth. The strategic planners investigated in this study were also found to be more accurate in predicting the outcome of major strategic actions.[5] A second study (reviewed in the same publication) examined the performance of matched pairs (thirty-six firms) of businesses in six different industries and found that strategic planners significantly outperformed nonplanners. This study also compared strategic planners' performance before and after they adopted strategic planning and found poststrategic planning performance significantly higher than preplanning performance. A follow-up study examining firms in two of the six industries (drugs and chemicals) yielded similar results, including the observation that the disparity between the financial performance of strategic planners and that of nonplanners increased over time.[6] Several studies of the financial benefits of strategic planning conducted since these pioneering studies have generally continued to report that financial benefits are associated with strategic planning.[7]

The overall pattern of results reported across all of these studies generally supports the value of strategic planning as measured in financial terms. On the basis of the research evidence now available, we can safely say that managers who engage in strategic planning can expect that the effort will lead to improved financial performance.

Behavioral Benefits

Wendy's grew faster than any chain in restaurant history. Wendy's success in such a rapid-growth environment hinged on coordinated planning and interaction among an increasingly large number of managers. Strategic planning emphasizes the interaction of managers at all levels of the organizational hierarchy. As a result, strategic planning has certain behavioral consequences that are also characteristic of participative decision making. Therefore, a full appreciation of the value of strategic planning requires awareness of the behavioral improvements that strategic planning fosters. It can be argued that the manager who is trained to promote these behavioral effects is for that very reason in a good position to generate the financial benefits we have noted. However, regardless of the profitability of *particular* strategic plans, several behavioral effects of applying *any* strategic plan can be expected to improve the welfare of the firm.

1. *Strategic planning should enhance the problem-prevention capabilities of the firm.* As a consequence of encouraging and rewarding subordinates for giving their attention to planning considerations, managers are in a position to detect potential problems and plan how best to resolve them.

2. *Group-based strategic decisions are most likely to reflect the best available alternatives.* Group interaction usually generates more alternatives. And the screening of alternatives and ultimate choice of a strategy are improved because group members bring specialized expertise to the decision process.

3. *Employee motivation should improve as employees participate in developing the strategic plan.* Employees gain a better understanding of organizational priorities and the reasons behind the strategy by which the firm will pursue them. Employees become personally committed to strategies they help develop.

4. *Gaps and overlaps in activities among diverse individuals and groups should be reduced* as participation in strategic planning clarifies everyone's responsibilities.

5. *Resistance to change should be reduced.* Perhaps the most common reason why people resist change is uncertainty about its ramifications for them. One of the fundamental concerns of strategic planning is reducing uncertainty about the future consequences of decisions made today.

The existence of a clear strategy and the process of formulating it (strategic planning) both appear to offer significant behavioral as well as financial benefits to the organizations that use them. Therefore, managers who understand the concept of strategy and grasp the key elements in the process of formulating a strategy are more likely than others to enhance organizational effectiveness. The remainder of this chapter is intended to provide you with this understanding. We will first examine what a strategy is.

▰▰▰▰▰▰▰▰▰▰ *Guidelines for Management Practice* **▰▰▰▰▰▰▰▰▰▰**

Strategic planning is not something that happens once and for all. In fact, managers should examine their company's strategy and consider initiating a strategic planning process when any of the following conditions exist:

1. There seems to be a need to change the direction of the company.

2. There is a need to step up growth and improve profitability.

3. There is a need to develop better information to help top managers make better decisions.

4. Managers are concerned that resources are not concentrated on important things in the company.

5. Managers express a need for better internal coordination of company activities.

6. The industry in which the company competes is rapidly changing.

7. There is a sense that company operations are out of control.

8. Managers in the company seem tired or complacent.

9. Managers are cautious and uncertain about the company's future.

10. Managers are more concerned about their own "shops" than about the overall well-being of the firm.

The Concept of Strategy

What Is a Strategy?

Every firm competing in an industry has a strategy, whether explicit or implicit. Wendy's may have developed its strategy explicitly through a strategic planning process, or its strategy may have evolved implicitly through the activities of the firm's various departments.

For a firm with an **explicit** (or "**intended**") **strategy**, its strategy is the plan or program that formally states how the organization defines its objectives and how it will achieve them and implement its mission. In firms of this type, managers take an active, deliberate approach in formulating the organization's strategy. Wendy's founder R. David Thomas's description in the opening case of the strategy that company management used to guide the early growth of Wendy's constitutes an intended, explicit strategy.

In firms with an **implicit** (or "**realized**") **strategy**, on the other hand, the strategy is "the pattern of the organization's responses to its environment over time."[8] Every organization has an implicit strategy based on its relationship with its environment, which can be examined and described. Some strategies are reactive and informal, and managers simply respond and adjust to the environment when the need arises. Hardees, one of the fast-food chains that Wendy's surpassed to become third-largest in its market, did not have a formal, intended strategy guiding its response to the Wendy's challenge (nor did McDonald's or Burger King) during the 1970s and early 1980s. Only after it was acquired by Spartan Foods did Hardees abandon its reliance on an implicit, informal strategy and adopt a formal, intended strategy to guide its future growth.

Even in firms with planned strategies, the actions taken by managers may reflect a somewhat different, "realized" strategy. Most firms have both kinds of strategies. They set forth an explicit, intended strategy that is based on conditions known or predicted at the time. Subsequent efforts for implementing that strategy, however, become the firm's realized strategy, which may differ in subtle ways from the intended strategy—or even in major ways if conditions change. Tylenol had a very thoroughly developed, explicit strategy for its growth during the 1990s that included the investment of over $1 billion in equipment for making and filling capsules. This intended strategy was excellent, but two bizarre, random poisoning incidents that involved the capsules and resulted in several deaths occurred in the early 1980s (as described in the opening case to Chapter 5). Consequently, Tylenol shifted to a very different, realized strategy and virtually stopped making capsules.

Although both kinds of strategies have their place, we will emphasize the actively formulated, explicit strategy. The research we reviewed earlier suggests that managers who take this perspective on their role as strategists achieve greater effectiveness than those who rely solely on hitting upon the right strategy as the firm moves along.

In addition to understanding the distinction between explicit and implicit strategies, you must realize that strategy is formulated at three different levels in the decision-making hierarchy of most major business organizations. At the top is the corporate level, composed principally of members of the board of directors and the chief executive and administrative officers. The next level comprises business and division managers. The third level is made up of functional, product, and geographic managers. Each level needs its own specific strategy or "game plan" that clearly specifies what must be done at that level to support the accomplishment of organizational objectives. Effective organizations have found that meeting this need for "level-specific" direction calls for three types of strategies (see Figure 7-1).

Corporate-Level Strategy

Corporate strategy is formulated by the top management of multibusiness companies to oversee the interests and actions of the total organization. The need for corporate strategy arose as industrial organizations became complex, often subsuming numerous businesses under one corporate umbrella. **Corporate strategy** is concerned with two basic questions: What kind of businesses should the company be engaged in? And how should resources be allocated among those businesses? Originally built on one business (lodging), Holiday Corporation had become a travel-related, multibusiness corporation by the early 1980s. Delta Steamships, Trailways, and Perkins Restaurants were just a few of the businesses it operated in addition to its Holiday Inns chain. The Holiday Corporation board of directors and its top management then selected a corporate strategy for the 1990s that had the company divesting all transportation businesses and reallocating those resources to new lodging chains (Hampton Inns, Crown Plaza Hotels), its Harrah's casino business, its Perkins restaurant business, and its traditional Holiday Inns chain (see "In Practice 7-1," page 211).

CONCEPTUAL TOOLS FOR ESTABLISHING AND DESCRIBING CORPORATION-LEVEL STRATEGIES

One of the earliest paradigms for thinking about corporate strategies was codified by William F. Glueck, an early strategic management researcher.[9] He suggested that all corporate strategies represent one of four basic types:

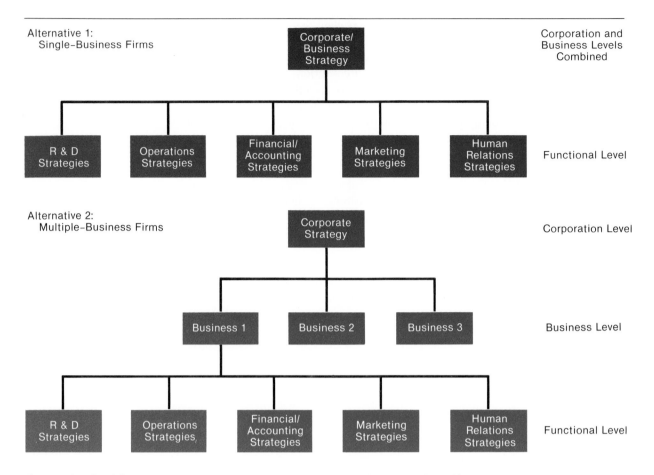

Alternative 1:
    Single–Business Firms

Corporate/
Business
Strategy

Corporation and
Business Levels
Combined

R & D
Strategies

Operations
Strategies

Financial/
Accounting
Strategies

Marketing
Strategies

Human
Relations
Strategies

Functional Level

Alternative 2:
    Multiple–Business Firms

Corporate
Strategy

Corporation Level

Business 1

Business 2

Business 3

Business Level

R & D
Strategies

Operations
Strategies,

Financial/
Accounting
Strategies

Marketing
Strategies

Human
Relations
Strategies

Functional Level

Corporation-level Strategy addresses what businesses an organization will be in and how resources will be allocated among those businesses.

Business-level Strategy focuses on how to compete in a given business.

Functional-level Strategy is concerned with the activities of the different functional areas of the organization and with what short–range, step–by–step methods will be used (tactics).

FIGURE 7-1
The Levels of Strategy
in Different Business
Settings

1. **Growth strategies** are appropriate when an organization seeks to expand (as expansion is gauged in terms of sales, product lines, or other measures of size) at a rate greater than the growth in GNP and inflation. Firms can grow via internal growth, merger or acquisition, market development, or product development. The corporation is resolved to commit as much as possible of its current resources—profit, leverage (borrowing power), and so on—to increasing its future size. Carl Icahn used high leverage, mergers, and acquisitions to rapidly expand TWA from a $250 million company primarily in airlines into a $2.5 billion company involved in a wide variety of businesses.

2. **Stability strategies** are adopted when an organization is satisfied with its current courses of action (markets, products, and the like), and management seeks to maintain a steady, profitable growth that is equivalent to the growth in GNP or inflation. Stability-oriented firms usually have strong positions in slow-growth markets and are primarily concerned with maximizing current return to the company's stockholders. After years pursuing rapid growth in various energy and office equipment businesses, Exxon has adopted a stability strategy

and is seeking to consolidate and concentrate the focus of the world's largest energy company.

3. **Defensive strategies** are emphasized in companies with poorly performing lines of business. TransAmerica, a widely diversified firm in certain financial service, lodging service, auto rental, and airline service businesses, found itself performing poorly in virtually every sector in the mid-1980s. Corporate officers sold off several businesses, cut back others, and reorganized several more as part of a corporationwide "defensive" strategy to reorient the company in a more profitable direction. Such defensive strategies tend to be of short duration; they are usually maintained for three years or less.

4. Glueck suggests that many multibusiness companies pursue a combination of several strategies across the different businesses in which they are involved. Within one company, certain businesses might follow growth strategies while others might adopt stability strategies and still others might use defensive strategies. Holiday Corporation, when it was simultaneously phasing out transportation businesses, increasing its casino business, and achieving stable high payoffs in lodging, illustrates the application of a corporate **combination strategy**.

Glueck's typology is conceptually quite useful, because it enables us to categorize virtually any corporate strategy. But therein lies its weakness as well: It is so general that it provides corporate managers with only limited guidance.

THE CORPORATE PORTFOLIO APPROACH

The **portfolio approach** to corporate strategy views a company as a "portfolio" of business investments which managers must balance by expanding investment in some while reducing investment in others. It is currently used in some form by many multibusiness companies as a means of establishing and communicating corporation-level strategy. One of the earliest frameworks for using this approach is often referred to as the **BCG matrix** or the **growth–share matrix**.[10] (BCG stands for Boston Consulting Group, the firm that devised the growth–share matrix.) Figure 7-2 depicts the growth–share matrix.

Corporate managers found the growth–share matrix particularly useful in addressing three questions: What businesses should we be in? What basic mission should each pursue? And how should we allocate corporate resources across those businesses? Managers who used the growth–share matrix plotted each business (or potential business) on a diagram like the one shown in Figure 7-2 on the basis of (1) its relative market share and (2) the growth rate of its primary market. *Relative market share* is determined by dividing the business's market share by that of its next-largest competitor. *Growth rate* is the projected growth rate of that primary market, usually over the next five years. Once these variables were calculated for each business the firm was in (or was considering entering), each business was assigned to one of the four quadrants shown in Figure 7-2.

The arrangement of businesses that emerged within the matrix gave corporate managers a means of establishing and describing corporate strategy. First, corporate managers could look at the balance of businesses within the matrix. An ideal balance was thought to be a few *star* businesses, a few *question mark* businesses, a reasonable level of *cash cow* businesses, and a few *dog* businesses. Corporate managers who saw that their set of businesses did not conform to this "ideal" would then have some idea of which businesses to keep, which to divest

FIGURE 7-2
The BCG or
Growth–Share Matrix

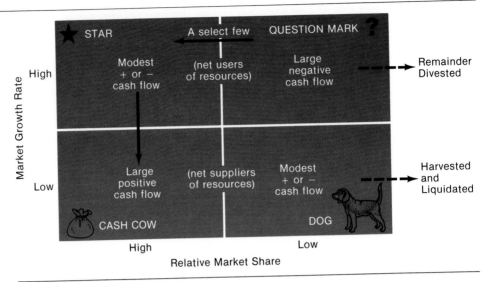

Source: Reprinted by permission of A. C. Hax and N. S. Majluf, "The Use of the Growth–Share Matrix in Strategic Planning," *Interfaces* 13, no. 1 (February 1983). Copyright 1983, The Institute of Management Sciences, 290 Westminster Street, Providence, R.I. 02903.

themselves of, and which to acquire in order to achieve a balanced portfolio of businesses that would optimize corporate objectives.

A second feature of the matrix gave managers guidance in how to allocate corporate resources as well as assistance in making divestiture and acquisition decisions. This was the "ideal flow of resources" suggested by the matrix. The cash cow and dog businesses were slated to be "milked" or "divested" as sources of cash to support the high-potential businesses (stars) and the question marks that managers believed might develop into stars. In other words, businesses in the lower half of the matrix (those with low market growth rates) were to be used as sources of excess cash to pump into those businesses that represented the companies best opportunities for future growth and survival (those with high market growth rates, and particularly those with an already established high market share).

Finally, the growth–share matrix enabled corporate managers to provide strategic guidance to managers of business units in establishing business-level strategies consistent with corporation-level portfolio strategy. "Star" businesses were expected to develop strategies to rapidly increase their market share. This usually meant substantial investment in physical plant and marketing. "Cash cow" managers were told to pursue strategies that maximized near-term profitability. That usually meant keeping capital and marketing investments to the minimum necessary to maintain market share in order to "harvest" as much cash as possible. "Dog" managers were directed to minimize expenditures and investment so as to "harvest and eventually divest" parts or all of their business operations. Managers of each "question mark" business were directed to justify rather quickly the future potential of their business (its ability to increase its relative market share) or, failing that, to prepare it for possible divestiture.

A similar portfolio approach to corporate strategy was pioneered by General Electric to reduce the complexity that managing a diverse set of businesses entails and to improve on the growth–share matrix. Figure 7-3 shows what they came up with. GE managers sought to improve on the growth–share matrix by incorporating multiple measures of each dimension in their **GE planning grid** and by

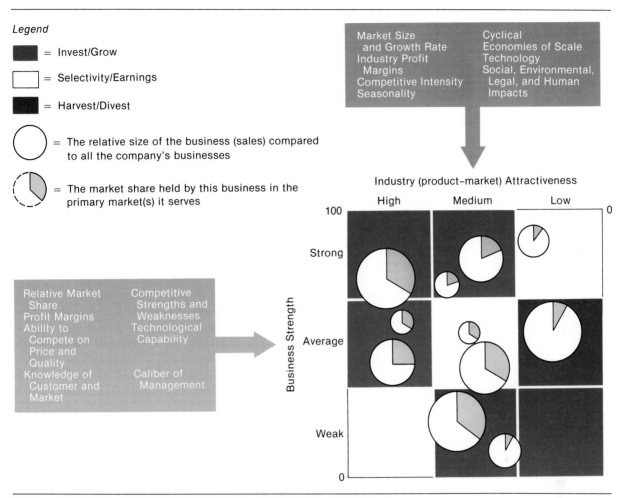

Legend

■ = Invest/Grow

□ = Selectivity/Earnings

■ = Harvest/Divest

○ = The relative size of the business (sales) compared to all the company's businesses

◔ = The market share held by this business in the primary market(s) it serves

Market Size and Growth Rate
Industry Profit Margins
Competitive Intensity
Seasonality

Cyclical
Economies of Scale
Technology
Social, Environmental, Legal, and Human Impacts

Industry (product–market) Attractiveness

High   Medium   Low

100   0

Strong

Relative Market Share
Profit Margins
Ability to Compete on Price and Quality
Knowledge of Customer and Market

Competitive Strengths and Weaknesses
Technological Capability

Caliber of Management

Business Strength

Average

Weak

0

FIGURE 7-3
General Electric's Nine-Cell Planning Grid

increasing the number of cells within the grid so as to enhance their ability to differentiate individual businesses.

The growth–share matrix's "relative market share" dimension was replaced in the GE grid by a composite measure of "business strength," whereas the "market growth rate" was replaced by a composite measure of "industry (product–market) attractiveness." As in the growth–share matrix, different (in this case, three) basic strategy guidelines emerged to assist corporate and business unit managers: *invest/ grow, selectivity/earning,* and *harvest/divest.* Corporate managers used the planning grid as a basis for selecting an appropriate portfolio of businesses, to guide decisions on resource allocation, and to provide business managers with strategic direction that was consistent with corporation-level strategy.

Both the growth–share matrix and the GE planning grid have been criticized as relying on the assignment of values to variables that are difficult to measure accurately, being insensitive in the terminology used to describe business-level strategic directives, overly simplified in assessing the needs of high-potential businesses, and unsuccessful in capturing the long-term potential of businesses slated for "harvest or divest" roles in the corporate portfolio. Nonetheless, thousands of multibusiness companies, including most of the *Fortune* 500 companies, incorporate a portfolio approach in some form as a means of establishing and describing their corporation-level strategy.

While the portfolio approach helps corporate-level managers make basic decisions about increasing and decreasing investments in various businesses, it provides minimal guidance to the managers of each business about the strategy of that business. The development of business-level strategy is described in the next section. "In Practice 7-1" provides a useful distinction between a new corporate strategy at Holiday Corporation (market segmentation) and the business-level strategies for each of its five product lines.

Business-Level Strategy

Business strategy is formulated by business managers to oversee the interests and actions of a particular business in such a way as to accomplish its long-term objectives. It seeks to answer these questions: How will the business compete within its market? What products and/or services will it offer? What customers will it serve? How will resources be distributed within the business? What technologies will be emphasized and what key synergies (opportunities for cooperative action or benefit) can be obtained across departments? In single-business companies, corporate strategy and business strategy are handled as one level.

Comparing IBM and Apple Computer in the early stages of growth of the personal computer industry yields an interesting example of two different business-level strategies used with the same basic product. IBM's PC division adopted an early business-level strategy in the personal computer market of offering dual-floppy disk, ten-megabyte disk, and twenty-megabyte disk computers to business and government segments of the worldwide computer market. Apple, on the other hand, focused on selling inexpensive single- and dual-floppy disk computers to individuals and elementary school systems. IBM felt its worldwide reputation for supplying high-quality computer products and service would give it a major competitive advantage in support of its PC strategy. Apple felt its founding role in the industry, its low price, its association with children through education-oriented software, and its impact in the elementary school market conferred on it major competitive advantages in support of its PC strategy. IBM's PC strategy placed major emphasis on the synergy available through its strong presence in, and knowledge of, business and government computer markets. IBM was also able to count on cost-related and technological synergy between its existing computer operations and its entry into the PC market. Apple lacked such an established presence in business and government segments, leading it initially to concede these segments to IBM until it could arrange to make its products tie in electronically with those of Digital Equipment Corporation and to sell its Macintosh computers along with those DEC products.

CONCEPTUAL TOOLS FOR ESTABLISHING AND DESCRIBING BUSINESS-LEVEL STRATEGIES

Corporate-level mandates such as "grow," "hold," "harvest," and "divest" give some sense of direction to business-level strategy. But they provide none of the comprehensive guidance managers need to assess the scope, resource deployments, competitive advantages, and synergy a specific strategy entails for a particular business. This section discusses three conceptual frameworks that enable managers to describe a business-level strategy in clear, comprehensive terms. The first framework, product–market evolution, is based on the idea that different business strategies are appropriate across stages in the product–market life cycle. The second framework, generic strategies, suggests that there are three basic business strategies

In Practice 7-1

A NEW STRATEGY AT HOLIDAY CORPORATION

At the end of the 1970s, Holiday Corporation was a diversified corporation involved in lodging (Holiday Inns), food (Perkins Restaurants), steamships (Delta Steamships), buses (Trailways), and casino gaming. Top management saw its corporate mission as being in travel-related businesses.

In the early 1980s, however, top management chose a completely different corporate strategy: to be in the lodging businesses only. By the end of the 1980s, the company had sold all of its original businesses except Holiday Inns and Harrah's casinos and had added four lodging chains serving different niches in the overall lodging industry (see the accompanying chart).

Corporate-Level Strategies:

Business-Level Strategies:

Lodging and Gaming Products

In response to changing customer needs, Holiday Corporation developed a market segmentation strategy in the early 1980s and introduced two new hotel brands—Embassy Suites, an all-suite product, and Hampton Inn, a limited-service chain. In 1985, the company acquired a 50-percent interest in its third new hotel product, The Residence Inn hotels, targeted to extended-stay guests. Each new brand serves the needs of a distinct market niche and was designed to complement the company's core Holiday Inn hotel brand.

	Holiday Inn	Embassy Suites	Hampton Inn	Residence Inn	Harrah's
Product Description	Foremost among our brands is Holiday Inn hotels. With nearly two and one half times more hotels worldwide than the nearest competitor, Holiday Inn hotels are the recognized leader in the full-service, mid-priced market. Holiday Inn Crowne Plaza hotels are top-of-the-line Holiday Inn hotels featuring extra services and amenities, located in major metropolitan areas. Typical price range: $40-70* $80-100* (Holiday Inn Crowne Plaza)	The leader in the all-suite hotel segment, the Embassy Suites hotel brand offers the business and leisure traveler a two-room suite and extra amenities, like a complimentary breakfast, for the price of a "single" at a typical upscale hotel. Typical price range: $79-119* Typical weekend rate: $59-89*	The fastest growing limited-service hotel chain in the country offering travelers high-quality guest rooms and select services at a superb price/value. Typical price range: $30-40*	The Residence Inn hotels appeal to guests staying five or more consecutive nights. The ambience of these all-suite facilities is residential, they feature townhome units with fireplaces and fully equipped kitchens. The Residence Inn hotels clearly are the leader in the extended-stay suite market. Typical price range: $60-90*	The world's premier casino gaming company recognized for the quality of its service, entertainment, facilities and fine dining.
Customer Profile	The familiar Holiday Inn hotel brand fits the needs of the majority of travelers on a variety of travel occasions, from managers attending a teleconference to families traveling on vacation. 96 percent of all U.S. travelers have stayed at a Holiday Inn hotel.	On weekdays, Embassy Suites hotels attract the upscale frequent business traveler including a high proportion of businesswomen. On weekends, these hotels appeal to a wide range of guests, mostly couples, who seek a luxurious getaway.	Hampton Inn hotels appeal to the value-conscious business or leisure traveler who does not need nor want to pay for such amenities and services as on-premises restaurants, large meeting rooms or banquet facilities.	The Residence Inn hotels appeal principally to travelers who will be away from home for an extended period of time. Many stay while their entire family when relocating to a new city. The average length of stay is 12 consecutive nights.	Harrah's attracts a broad range of customers, with each hotel/casino occupying a strong leadership niche within its respective market.
Features	• Restaurant, lounge and banquet facilities • Pool • Meeting Rooms • Non-smoking rooms • Room and valet service • Exercise facilities (Holiday Inn Crowne Plaza) • Executive boardroom (Holiday Inn Crowne Plaza) • Lobby bar, where permitted (Holiday Inn Crowne Plaza)	• Two-room suites, with living room, galley kitchen, separate bedroom and bath • Free cooked-to-order breakfast • Complimentary evening cocktails (where permitted) • Recreational facilities, such as pool, steambath, whirlpool • Free airport transportation at most locations	• Free continental breakfast • Free local phone calls • Free in-room movies • Non-smoking rooms • No restaurant • No lounge • No large meeting space	• One- and two-bedroom suites • Fully equipped kitchen • Woodburning fireplace • Sport Court, swimming pool, whirlpool/spa • Grocery shopping service • Maid service, which includes kitchen cleanup • Free continental breakfast • Complimentary hospitality hour (where permitted)	• 515 total table games • 7,474 total slot machines • 247,600 total square feet casino space • Big name entertainment • Fine dining
Market Share	39% share of mid-scale chain supply which includes Best Western, TravelLodge, Howard Johnson, Rodeway, Quality Inn, and Ramada hotels, among others.	52% of total all-suite chain supply, which includes Lexington Suites, Quality/Royale Suites, Guest Quarters, Park Suites and Amberley Suites hotels, among others.	11% of limited-service chain supply, including LaQuinta, Days Inn and Comfort Inn hotels, among others.	89% of total extended-stay chain supply which includes Lexington Suites, Hawthorne Suites and Guest Suites hotels.	Harrah's accounts for nearly 10% of total gaming revenues nationwide.
Locations	1,641 hotels worldwide located in 51 countries and all 50 states. 70 hotels were under construction at year end.	73 properties located in 22 states, primarily in major U.S. metropolitan markets. 17 hotels were under construction at year end.	106 properties located in 29 states. As a rule, properties are situated near restaurants. 45 hotels were under construction at year end.	87 properties in 33 states, primarily near major metropolitan markets. 17 hotels were under construction at year end.	Hotel/casinos in the four major U.S. gaming markets: Reno, Lake Tahoe, and Las Vegas, Nev., and Atlantic City, N.J.
Distribution					
	*Based on single occupancy at a majority of hotels, although prices may vary significantly depending on season and market.	*Based on single occupancy at a majority of hotels, although prices may vary significantly depending on season and market.	*Based on single occupancy at a majority of hotels, although prices may vary significantly depending on season and market.	*Based on single occupancy at a majority of hotels, although prices may vary significantly depending on season and market.	

Source: 1986 Holiday Corporation Annual Report.

that businesses should choose from. The third framework, the product–market matrix, says that appropriate business strategies differ according to the combination of the nature of the products a firm intends to offer and the nature of the market for which those products are intended.

Product–Market Evolution. One of the earliest frameworks used by managers to develop business-level strategies in the key products they offer and the markets they serve has been the idea of the product life cycle, or the stages that characterize the evolution of a product and market. What business strategy is appropriate depends on what stage of the **product–market evolution** the business's major product and market have reached.

Figure 7-4 is a graphical representation of the rise and fall of a product's sales and profit in a particular market. This "rise and fall" can be divided into at least four stages, each of which suggests different strategic guidelines. The four stages parallel the four cells in the growth–share matrix: Question mark businesses are typically in the introductory stage, stars in the growth stage, cash cows in the maturity stage, and dogs in decline. Question marks typically have low sales volumes and are in newly emerging products or markets. Stars have strong sales volumes in rapidly growing products or markets. Cash cows have strong yet stable revenues in maturing products or markets, and dogs are experiencing stagnant or declining sales in mature products or markets.

In using the stages of product–market evolution to formulate effective business strategies, business managers need to keep two important points in mind. First, *the four stages do not last the same length of time.* This is true both for the evolution of a single product–market and across different product–markets. For example, IBM's highly successful 360 series of mainframe computers enjoyed a growth period of several years following a comparatively short introductory period of only a few years. On the other hand, IBM chose not to enter the PC market until that market reached the growth stage, because it correctly anticipated that the introductory stage required to develop the market would take over ten years. Other examples of the way product–market stages vary emerge when we compare fad items such as hula hoops, pet rocks, and CB radios with breakfast cereals, automobiles, and televisions.

The second point managers must keep in mind when using the stage framework is the lead time necessary to formulate a stage-related strategy. We have seen that the "life" of each stage varies within and across products and markets. Thus *managers must be sensitive to the emergence of the next stage* so as to plan the appropriate strategy in advance of the need to implement it. It is very shortsighted of a management team to wait for profits to start heading downward (thus signaling the end of the growth stage) before plotting a more defensive strategy for the maturity stage.

Bearing in mind the variability in length of the stages and the importance of anticipating the arrival of the next stage, let us examine the four stages in the product–market evolution.

Introductory stage strategies should focus on confirming that the perceived market niche and customer base truly exist and that the initial product characteristics are indeed compatible with the needs of that customer group. In addition to refining and confirming the scope of the strategy, managers introducing products should seek a competitive advantage by achieving simplicity in both product design and production processes. They must also deploy company resources in such a way as to maintain flexibility in the use of people and equipment, because

Stage of Product–Market Evolution:				
	Introduction	*Growth*	*Maturity*	*Decline*
Basic Business Strategy:				
	Build 2 Position	Enhance Position	Consolidate and Defend the Position	Exploit the Position
Basic Strategic Concerns:				
Marketing	Resources/skill to create widespread awareness and find acceptance from customers; advantageous access to distribution	Ability to establish brand recognition; find niche; reduce price; solidify strong distribution relations and develop new channels	Skill in aggressively promoting products to new markets and holding existing markets; pricing flexibility; skills in differentiating products and holding customer loyalty	Cost-effective means of efficient access to selected channels and markets; strong customer loyalty or dependence; strong company image
Production/ Operations	Ability to expand capacity effectively; limit number of designs; develop standards	Ability to add product variants; centralize production or otherwise lower costs; improve product quality; seasonal subcontracting capacity	Improve product and reduce costs; ability to share or reduce capacity; advantageous supplier relationships; subcontracting	Ability to prune product line; cost advantage in production, location, or distribution; simplified inventory control; subcontracting or long production runs
Finance	Resources to support high net cash overflow and initial losses; ability to use leverage effectively	Ability to finance rapid expansion; still have net cash outflows but increasing profits; resources to support product improvements	Ability to generate and redistribute increasing net cash inflows; effective cost control systems	Ability to reuse or liquidate unneeded equipment; advantage in cost of facilities; control system accuracy; streamlined management control
Personnel	Flexibility in staffing and training new management; existence of employee with key skills in new products or markets	Existence and ability to add skilled personnel; motivated and loyal work force	Ability to cost effectively reduce work force; increase efficiency	Capacity to reduce and reallocate personnel; cost advantage
Engineering and Research and Development	Ability to make engineering changes; have technical bugs in product and process resolved	Skill in quality and new feature development; state developing successor product	Reduce costs; develop variants to differentiate products	Support other growth areas or apply to unique customer needs
Key Functional Area and Strategy Focus	Engineering; market penetration	Sales; consumer loyalty; market share	Production efficiency; successor products	Finance; maximum investment recovery

Sources: Adapted from P. Doyle, "The Realities of the Product Life Cycle," *Quarterly Review of Marketing,* Summer 1976, pp. 1–6; H. Fox, "A Framework for Functional Coordination," *Atlantic Economic Review,* November–December 1973; C. W. Hofer, *Conceptual Constructs for Formulating Corporate and Business Strategy* (Boston: Intercollegiate Case Clearing House, 1977), p. 7; P. Kotler, *Marketing Management* (Englewood Cliffs, N.J.: Prentice-Hall, 1988); and C. Wasson, *Dynamic Competitive Strategy and Product Life Cycles* (Austin, Tex.: Austin Press, 1978).

FIGURE 7-4
Tying Business Strategy to the Stage of Product–Market Evolution

changes may occur and problems may arise with the product or the means of producing it. And they must ensure that the firm has the financial capacity to ride out a period during which cash outlays significantly exceed revenues. Negotiating the introductory stage successfully is a tall order! Genetech is one of a few businesses in the newly emerging genetic engineering industry that is seeking to standardize its product characteristics and carve out a clear market niche for what is said to be the technological breakthrough of the 1990s—all the while making public stock offerings and engaging in selected joint ventures with large drug companies to support a substantial negative cash flow.

The basic concern in a *growth stage strategy* is to confirm the size and potential of the major market niche while searching for opportunities to broaden the customer base by reaching related customer groups. Competitive advantages should be sought through brand identification, distribution strength, price and/or quality, and the ability to respond to a rapidly growing market. Rapid expansion should be supported through the deployment of financial resources, the addition and placement of personnel, and optimal development of facilities. IBM's PC strategy in the mid-1980s incorporated several of these key tactics, enabling the firm rapidly to become the market-share leader in the PC market.

Maturity stage strategies start with a rather clear scope (product and market). For businesses facing increasingly competitive conditions in low-growth markets, a major concern is sustaining and improving their competitive advantages through intense marketing, cost efficiency, and special relationships with buyers and suppliers. Resource allocation focuses on tight control, internal financing, and redeployment of resources toward future opportunities. Airlines provide good examples of companies attempting to formulate effective maturity stage strategies.

Decline stage strategies seek to emphasize the most cost-effective offerings in the product line to customers who are particularly sensitive to price or to special product or service features in the market targeted by the strategy. Competitive advantage is sought through special customer relationships, intense marketing, or cost advantages in an extremely competitive setting. Crown, Cork and Seal has carved out an extremely successful decline stage strategy in the market for cans by focusing on customers with hard-to-hold commodities and providing them with regular technical assistance, quick shipment, and low prices.

The stage of product–market evolution provides a useful framework within which to formulate specific, detailed business-level strategies. But it is not the only possible approach, and several more are worth examining closely.

Generic Strategies. Michael Porter, a professor of economics and business strategy at Harvard University, proposed another framework for describing business-level strategies that became very popular among business managers in the 1980s.[11] Porter contends that all business strategies are one of three kinds. Porter suggests that business managers should develop an understanding of the competitive dynamics of their industry and then define a competitive niche within that industry by adopting one of the three **generic strategies** shown in Figure 7-5.

Managers who adopt the **overall cost leadership** strategy try to maximize sales by minimizing costs per unit and charging low prices. The idea is to outperform competitors by selling at a lower price and doing so profitably by exploiting the firm's lower costs. Normally this means investing extensively in production or service facilities to achieve economies of scale and continuing to emphasize productivity improvements. Businesses that have successfully followed the cost leadership strategy include BIC in writing instruments, K Mart in retailing, and Nissan and Toyota in automobiles. The concern for low costs should permeate

Strategic Advantage

FIGURE 7-5
Porter's Generic
Strategies

		Uniqueness perceived by the customer	Low–cost position
Strategic Target	Industrywide	Differentiation Strategy	Overall Cost Leadership Strategy
	Particular segment only	Focused Differentiation Strategy	Focused Cost Leadership Strategy

Source: Modified with permission of the Free Press, a Division of Macmillan, Inc. from *Competitive Advantage: Creating and Sustaining Superior Performance* by Michael E. Porter. Copyright © 1985 by Michael E. Porter.

every area of the company—purchasing, overhead, advertising, research, selling, and personnel—not just production. A relatively large market share is usually required to support this high-volume, low-margin business strategy.

Following a **differentiation** strategy requires managers to emphasize competitive methods that ensure that most of the customers in the industry perceive the company's product or service as unique. The basis for differentiation may be quality, design, accompanying service, or other attributes of major importance to the customer. Successful differentiation enables the company to charge a higher price (and therefore to produce a higher margin, or more profit, per unit) because of the brand loyalty of customers who believe the firm's product or service is superior. Examples of products that have been successfully differentiated include Calvin Klein jeans (unique design), BMW automobiles (high quality), Cross writing instruments (quality and image), and Curtis Mathis televisions (quality and long product life).

Business managers use a **focus** strategy when attempting to gain a competitive advantage within a narrower market through some combination of cost leadership and differentiation. The narrower market is some segment of a larger market defined in terms of geographic location, customer characteristics, or the like. These segments are often inefficient for cost-leadership–oriented firms to pursue and can be successfully defended (via a well-designed focus strategy) from differentiation-oriented firms serving larger markets. Examples of businesses that have successfully applied focus strategies include Johnson Cosmetics (cosmetics for blacks), Valic Annuities (IRAs for educators), and numerous small businesses, particularly personal service firms, serving local or regional markets.

One of the few criticisms of Porter's generic strategies is leveled at his claim that each strategy is distinct and that each business follows only one of the strategies. Recent research suggests that, on the contrary, successful firms often emphasize cost leadership and differentiation simultaneously.[12] It appears that many of the firms in these studies may be simply following focus strategies combining elements of cost effectiveness *and* differentiation. And for that matter, of course, managers who rely on differentiation must still be concerned about costs, and cost leaders must remain concerned about customer relations.

The Product–Market Matrix. A third approach to describing business-level strategies is derived from the **product–market matrix** shown in Figure 7-6. Managers who

FIGURE 7-6
The Product–Market
Matrix Grand Strategy
Typologies

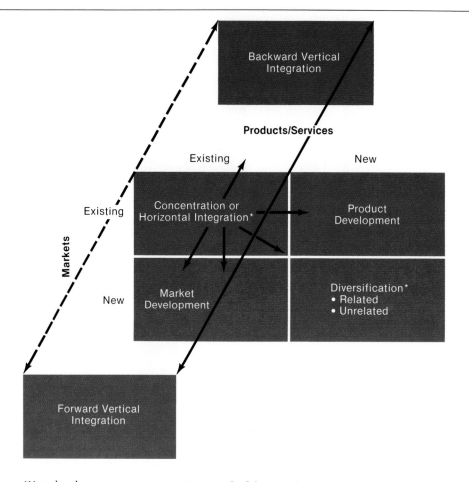

*Note that there are two strategy options in each of these two boxes.

follow this approach can choose among eight "grand strategy options" at the business-unit level that reflect management decisions about the future product and market focus of the business. We will comment on each of these grand strategies individually.

The most common grand strategy is **concentration** on the current business— that is, continuing to sell the business's present products or services to its existing customer base. Managers who choose this strategy emphasize one or more of three basic ideas:

1. Increase the present customers' rate of usage.

2. Attract competitors' customers.

3. Attract nonusers to buy the product.

Airlines place major emphasis on "frequent flyer membership" as a cornerstone of concentration strategies seeking to increase their customers' rate of usage as well as to attract competitors' customers. Burger King used the "Where is Herb?" promotional campaign as part of a concentration strategy designed to encourage people who had never tried Burger King to do so. Concentration is a popular business strategy because it lowers the firm's immediate risk while enabling it to gain competitive advantages over more diversified competitors in production skill, marketing know-how, customer sensitivity, and reputation. These competitive advantages result from concentrating on one product, in one market, with one technology, over time.

Geographic expansion is a frequently employed **market development** strategy: Start locally, next expand regionally, then go national. Wendy's heavy emphasis on rapid expansion throughout the United States via area franchising is a good example of a market development strategy. Market development strategies can also focus on attracting new markets to existing products through new channels of distribution, different advertising media, and slightly different versions of the product that appeal to other market segments. In its movement from mail order to national retail outlets to multiprice points (for example, Kenmore refrigerators at five different prices) for each product line, Sears offers an example of a market development strategy that has guided a business for over seventy-five years.

Product development involves the substantial modification of existing products or the creation of new but related items that can be marketed to current customers through established channels. The product development strategy is often used either to prolong the life cycle of current products or to take advantage of favorable reputation and brand name. The idea is to attract to new products customers who have been satisfied with the company's earlier product offerings. A major strategy followed by McDonald's and other fast-food chains has been product development whereby they seek continually to come up with new menu items that encourage satisfied customers to try still other of their offerings. For years cereal companies have modified accepted brands to bring forth new products for their loyal customer base. Thus sprung, for example, Honey Nut Cheerios from the old standby Cheerios.

Another strategy that has been used by many businesses as a means both to grow and to secure scarce resources or control distribution channels is a **vertical integration strategy**. There are two types of vertical integration strategies. **Backward vertical integration** occurs when a business acquires an operation that plays a role earlier in the production and marketing process. This strategy was employed

Product development strategies are perhaps most easily seen in the way cereal makers try to stay on top in the breakfast market. General Mill's mainstay in this market, Cheerios, has been a favorite for several generations. Yet, as competition has expanded and General Mills has sought avenues to grow, product adaptations like Honey Nut Cheerios have been developed as a means for General Mills to expand sales. (Courtesy of General Mills)

by Anheuser Busch when it sought to guarantee quality sources of yeast and barley for its brewery operation; in the process, it became the largest producer of yeast in the United States. **Forward vertical integration** occurs when a company moves up the distribution chain—through investment or other activity—in order to be closer to the consumers of its products or services. In the late 1980s, for example, Xerox and Texas Instruments experimented with owning their own retail stores to sell their products and services.

Horizontal integration strategies were very popular with many companies during the 1980s. A firm following this strategy grows by acquiring similar businesses that represent the same link in the production and marketing chain—in short, its competitors. Such acquisitions may provide access to new markets, eliminate some competitors, or enable the acquiring firm to achieve greater economies of scale. Deregulation of interstate banking has made mergers and acquisitions among banks committed to horizontal integration the quickest way to enter new markets and to build an organization large enough to compete with sizable financial service organizations. Figure 7-7 illustrates the three different integration strategies.

Diversification strategies, the seventh and eighth "grand strategy options," are perhaps the most difficult to execute successfully because they generally require a management team to move the farthest afield from its proven area of expertise. Taking on new products and new markets at the same time represents a big challenge for business managers.

When a diversification involves the addition of a business that is related to the firm in terms of technology, markets, or products, it is called a *concentric,* or *related, diversification.* Philip Morris's skill in consumer marketing led it to acquire the ailing Miller Brewing Company and eventually to make that firm number two in the beer industry. Both products (beer and tobacco) are consumer products used by similar customers as leisure-time products. They are also sold through

FIGURE 7-7
**Vertical and Horizontal
Integration Strategies**

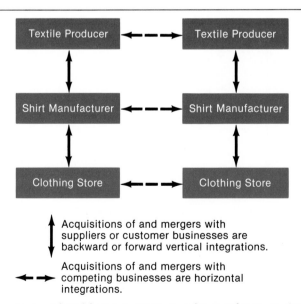

Source: Adapted from J. A. Pearce, II, and R. B. Robinson, Jr., *Strategic Management: Strategic Formulation and Implementation,* 3rd ed. Richard D. Irwin, Inc. © 1988.

similar outlets and subject to similar regulation. This was a most successful concentric diversification for Philip Morris.

When firms grow by acquiring businesses in products and markets that are unrelated to their core business, they are engaging in *conglomerate,* or *unrelated, diversification.* The principal concern for companies following this strategy is the profit pattern of the target venture. Such companies are seeking to balance cyclical sales patterns, high-cash/low-opportunity and low-cash/high-opportunity businesses, debt considerations, and tax considerations. ITT, Fuqua Industries, Litton, and TransAmerica are a few companies that have engaged in conglomerate diversification for several years.

When Prosperity Eludes the Firm. The eight grand strategies of the product–market matrix are focused on making a business grow. For any of a great many reasons—economic recessions, production inefficiencies, and competitive pressures, to mention a few—a business can find itself with declining profits. Managers facing these conditions occasionally choose one of three additional strategies: retrenchment/turnaround, divestiture, and liquidation.

A firm seeking to fortify its basic competencies through cost reduction (employee attrition, decreased expense accounts, reduced promotions) or asset reduction (the sale of land, buildings, or "perks" such as cars or beach condominiums not essential to the business) is following a **retrenchment/turnaround** strategy. In the 1980s, U.S. automobile manufacturers used employee attrition, reduced perks, and union wage concessions as part of a retrenchment/turnaround strategy designed to make them more competitive in the worldwide automobile industry.

A **divestiture** strategy, wherein managers sell a business or a major component of a business, is often followed when retrenchment fails to accomplish the desired turnaround. Chrysler Corporation sold its air-conditioning business as a means of raising cash to support the turnaround strategy it had adopted for its automobile business.

When the grand strategy is **liquidation**, the business is typically sold in parts for its tangible assets, not as a going concern. Because of its staggering potential liabilities resulting from the effects of asbestos, Johns Manville Corporation chose a liquidation strategy—rather than slowly depleting its assets in an endless series of legal encounters—in order to give stockholders the best return possible under the circumstances.

Function-Level Strategy

Whereas corporate and business strategies are concerned with "doing the right things," functional strategies provide guidance to ensure that functional areas "do things right." **Functional strategies** create the framework for the immediate-term management of basic business *functions*—marketing, finance, production, accounting, personnel, and research and development—in a manner that is consistent with and supportive of business-level strategy. IBM's decision to first market PCs through established computer retailers (such as Computerland) and its decision to assemble its PC from subcontracted parts rather than manufacturing its own parts are functional strategies that supported IBM's PC business in its early years.

As we move from corporate to business to functional strategies, the time horizon shortens and specificity increases. Each level seeks to give guidance to, and set parameters for, the next-lower level. The three levels of strategy closely parallel the three types of objectives: Broad objectives are linked to corporation-level strategy, long-term objectives to business-level strategy, and short-term objectives to function-level strategies.

▰▰▰▰▰▰▰ *Guidelines for Management Practice* ▰▰▰▰▰▰▰

The value of a well-developed strategy is very significant in guiding organizational members toward long-range objectives. Managers contribute most effectively to the use of strategy when they remember these important guidelines.

1. Discourage top-management domination of the creation of each level of strategy. Encourage the development of corporate strategies by top corporate management with input from business managers; the development of business strategies by top business managers with input from functional managers; and the development of functional strategies by functional managers, subject to the review of business managers.

2. Corporate managers should anticipate that most business managers would prefer that their busi-

nesses be designated "growing" businesses. Make a special effort to express appreciation for the contributions of "hold" or "harvest" businesses.

3. Insist that business strategies become themes reflected in everything that goes on in the business. If differentiation is the business strategy, make sure every employee understands what it means, how it is centrally achieved, and what her or his area contributes to differentiating the business. Always subject the activities in each functional area to the test of consistency with the strategic theme.

4. Carefully monitor functional strategies regularly. This is where changes that are inconsistent with the overall business strategy usually emerge first.

The last several sections of this chapter have described several frameworks through which managers can establish and describe a strategy. Corporate strategy is necessary to guide decisions in a company that has several businesses. Techniques such as the growth–share matrix and the GE planning grid portray the company's businesses as a portfolio of investments and thereby help *corporate* managers conceptualize an overall strategy for the company and decide how to allocate resources among the members of their portfolio. Once these decisions are made, each *business* must similarly chart its overall competitive strategy and allocate resources to support that strategy. The product–market evolution framework helps business managers target the strategic context they face, and such constructs as Porter's generic strategies and the product–market matrix provide an array of competitive strategies from which to choose. Once the business strategy has been chosen, *functional* strategies complete the strategic cycle, becoming comprehensive guides to short-term action in each area of the business that functions to implement the business strategy.

But how do managers formulate these strategies? This process, which is known as strategic planning, is discussed in the next section.

Strategic Planning: The Process of Strategy Formulation

Businesses vary in the processes they use to formulate strategies. Sophisticated planning organizations such as General Electric, IBM, and Exxon have developed more detailed processes than less formal planners. Small businesses that rely on the strategy formulation skills and limited time of an entrepreneur typically exhibit very basic planning that contrasts sharply with the planning of larger firms in their industries. It should not be surprising that firms whose operations are diverse because they depend on multiple products, markets, or technologies also tend to rely on more complex strategic planning. Multinational companies, because of their involvement in diverse overseas markets, must engage in strategic planning that is sophisticated in scope yet flexible, as discussed in "Insights for International Managers 7." However, despite differences in detail and in degree of formality, the essential components of any approach to strategic planning are very similar.

Broad Objectives

The starting point of strategic planning is reconfirmation of the business's purpose, values, and mission—concepts you became familiar with in Chapter 6. (For a review, see Figure 7-8.) These three fundamental concepts define the "strategic playing field" for managers' strategic planning activity. Top-level managers initiate strategy formulation by reviewing their current mission; debating whether it reflects the basic product, market, and technological focus they think the company should have; adjusting the mission on rare occasions; and providing the rest of the organization with a clear mission statement (and purpose and values) to guide managers when they grapple with each of the elements of strategic planning. Wendy's top managers, after ten years of initial success, reviewed their mission of providing fresh food to adults in urban locations in under a minute. They decided that the basic mission was still viable but became concerned that its exclusive emphasis on adults and on a limited, hamburger-based menu deserved serious examination. Every organization must define its mission before it can formulate effective strategies.

Insights for International Managers
STRATEGIC PLANNING IN INTERNATIONAL OPERATIONS

Claus Halle, president of Coca-Cola's international softdrink business sector, says: "The key to developing our international business lies not in the rigid application of a global strategy, but in a *flexible* planning system, heavily reliant on input from the market and able to respond quickly to shifts in local growth and competitive conditions."

Hans Becherer, senior vice president of Deere & Company's Overseas Division, says much the same: in two words, the key to international success is "planned flexibility." "A company needs all the attributes and qualities that make it successful in its home market," Becherer says. "In addition, it must take into account differences in culture and marketplace, as well as international realities such as shifting currencies and political relationships." The international company and its managers need to be adaptable to succeed abroad.

Words such as "flexible" and "adaptable" should not suggest managers or a company that is weak, malleable, compliant, a pushover. Successful American companies and their executives abroad are not pushovers. They do not bend to every wind, nor adapt like chameleons to each circumstance—quite the contrary. But neither are they rigid, immovable or unimpressionable. They are what the Japanese would call "hard like water." Water goes with the flow, bending with the turns in the riverbed, but it's water that carved out the Grand Canyon. Water is soft and takes the shape of its container, but water can carry the load of a thousand-ton ship. So strategic planning systems in international divisions must be active and allow rapid changes so that executives abroad can remain flexible, adaptable, and "hard like water."

Source: From L. Copeland and L. Griggs, *Going International,* (New York: Random House, 1985) p. 210.

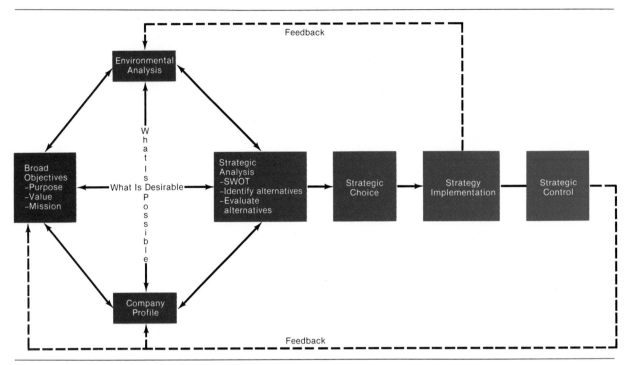

FIGURE 7-8
Strategic Planning:
The Process of Strategy
Formulation

Once the mission is identified, the obvious next question should be, "Is it appropriate in today's and tomorrow's environment?" The next section describes how strategic managers should answer this question by conducting an environmental analysis.

Environmental Analysis

A critical aspect of the process of formulating a strategy is environmental analysis. **Environmental analysis** is the systematic assessment of information about the firm's external environment during the strategic planning process to identify strategic opportunities for the company as well as major threats, problems, or other possible impediments. Such analysis is used by managers both to shape and (subsequently) to evaluate strategic options. It is also used to confirm and reevaluate key determinants of success in the markets a business serves. The following examples illustrate the role of environmental analysis.

1. Holiday Corporation saw the budget (lower-price) segment of the lodging industry as the fastest-growing and most profitable segment going into the late 1980s and early 1990s. That led the firm to adopt a product development strategy and start a completely new lodging chain, Hampton Inns, as a means of competing in that market segment. Another lodging chain, Days Inn, pioneered this budget segment. Conducting their own environmental analysis, Days Inns executives' analysis of the intentions of Holiday Inns led them to pursue an aggressive market development strategy in order to expand rapidly from a regional to a national budget chain in anticipation of much stiffer competition in the 1990s.

2. The development of microelectronic circuitry at Texas Instruments spurred TI executives to search their environment for new markets they might enter with

such proprietary technology. Adopting a related diversification strategy, TI moved rapidly into the watch industry with a low-priced digital watch. Reacting to TI's move, many traditional watch makers adopted defensive strategies in an effort to minimize TI's impact on their low-priced products.

3. After years of cost-containment activity, Winnebago managers used what appeared to be a steady drop in the price of oil in the late 1980s as the basis for an aggressive concentration strategy to rebuild sales of their large recreational vehicles. Most observers of the RV industry consider the price of fuel to be the single largest determinant of industry sales volume.

In the first two examples, managers analyzed environmental factors to determine how any opportunities or threats they presented would affect their companies' strategic options. In the third example, managers continually monitored a key determinant of market success (oil prices) and altered their strategy in accordance with changes in that factor.

An organization's environment plays a major role in shaping strategy, which is, in fact, a large-scale plan for interacting with the firm's environment. Proactive managers are always scanning and analyzing the environment, and the information they glean from these activities becomes critical to the strategic planning process.

Top managers must know what is going on in business, government, and society at large if they are to shape an effective strategy. Executives charged with formulating business-level strategy must carefully monitor information about their particular industry—buyers, suppliers, substitutes, potential entrants, and direct competitors—in order to shape and compare strategic options. In Chapter 2 we noted the key elements in a firm's remote and operating environments.

Managers get information from four sources: outside personal contacts, outside impersonal sources, inside personal contacts, and impersonal sources inside the organization. Figure 7-9 offers several examples of each of these four sources. Research suggests that strategic decision makers use personal contacts much more widely than impersonal sources.[13]

Company Profile

Managers engaged in the strategic planning process also carefully profile their company's resources and skills. It is the creative and thoughtful matching of this company profile with the environmental analysis that ultimately generates appropriate strategic options.

A **company profile** depicts the quantity *and* quality of a company's principal resources and skills in three broad areas: financial; physical, organizational, and human; and technological. A company profile simply seeks to determine the firm's performance capabilities on the basis of its existing and accessible resources and skills.

Managers look at the profile to pinpoint their firm's strengths and weaknesses. First they answer the question "What are our capabilities?" Then they ask two additional questions: "How do our capabilities compare to those of existing or potential competitors?" and "How do those capabilities support what we would like to do?"

Once a profile of the company's resources and skills has been developed, managers are ready to move to the decision-making phase of the strategic planning process: strategic analysis and choice.

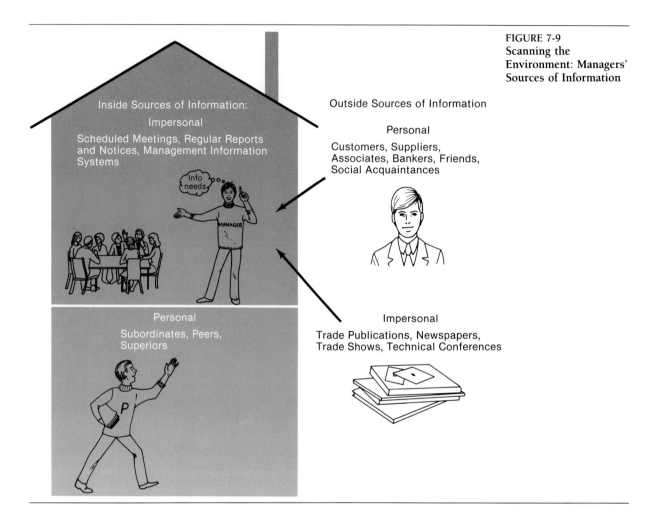

FIGURE 7-9
Scanning the Environment: Managers' Sources of Information

Strategic Analysis and Choice

When managers have completed their environmental analysis and company profile, they are in a position to begin to make decisions about what the firm's strategy for the future should be. This phase is the heart (and, to some, the most exciting phase) of the strategic planning process. Strategic analysis can be broken down for purposes of discussion into the four steps presented here. But in reality, managers usually perform each step several times as they identify, evaluate, and choose among strategic options.

SWOT ANALYSIS

SWOT is an acronym for **s**trengths and **w**eaknesses, **o**pportunities and **t**hreats. At this step of the strategic planning process, managers juxtapose their environmental analysis and their company profile to see what interactive opportunities and threats emerge, given the firm's strengths and weaknesses. Managers are trying to accomplish two things during this **SWOT analysis:**

1. Compare the profile of the company's resources and skills to the opportunities, threats, and key requirements for success in the product/market segments where

they might compete. The object is to bring to light any major strengths on which an effective strategy could be based and any major weaknesses that must be overcome.

2. Compare the organization's strengths and weaknesses with those of its major competitors to identify which of its resources and skills are sufficient to yield competitive advantages in key product/market segments.

Two examples will serve to illustrate the SWOT step in strategic analysis. IBM examined the PC market in the 1980s and determined that its name recognition, technological skills, and service capabilities represented major strengths in this new market. It also determined that its lack of direct retail contact with individual buyers constituted a serious weakness in any attempt it might make to move into this market. Comparing itself to other competitors, such as Apple and Tandy (Radio Shack), IBM designed an initial strategy of entering the PC market by selling primarily to business and institutional customers through its current sales organization. At the same time, it would gradually overcome its weak retail position by licensing the sale of IBM PCs through selected computer retailers while it built its own retail operation (IBM Product Centers) as a basis for broader market penetration at a later time.

General Electric observed the rapidly growing trend toward computerization in the 1970s and determined that its skills in electronic technology, combined with its financial resources, provided key strengths on which to base an aggressive strategy for entering the computer industry, particularly the mainframe segment. After the firm suffered early setbacks, managers who conducted subsequent SWOT analyses determined that GE's lack of special sales skills, distribution channels, and any extensive service organization was a weakness that gave GE's major competitors the advantage. Ultimately determining these deficits to be major obstacles to success that GE managers did not feel they could easily overcome, GE concluded that its technological and financial strengths were not sufficient for it to compete effectively in the mainframe computer market. It subsequently divested itself of its computer operations.

IDENTIFICATION OF STRATEGIC ALTERNATIVES

Once the SWOT analysis is complete, managers seek to identify different strategies the firm might pursue to take advantage of the interactive opportunities available to them. Managers first look to the existing strategy and perform what is called **gap analysis**. Here they simply seek to determine whether a performance "gap" exists between what their existing strategy can realistically be expected to accomplish (in terms of sales, productivity, and profitability) and the objectives that have been established in these performance areas. Where no gaps exist, managers have good reason to conclude that the current strategy is the appropriate strategic alternative. Where serious gaps appear to exist, managers concentrate on identifying alternatives that can eliminate or compensate for substandard performance. In the latter case, a significant change in the firm's strategic approach is often called for.

EVALUATION OF STRATEGIC ALTERNATIVES

In the next step of the strategic planning process, managers sytematically evaluate the strategic options, applying four broad criteria as they assess the merits of each.

1. Is the option compatible with the broad objectives—purpose, values, and mission—of the company? Or will it necessitate a major departure from (and therefore a major change in) these fundamental objectives?

2. Does the strategy focus on and exploit key opportunities and critical success factors in the product or market for which it is intended?

3. Does it take advantage of the company's established internal strengths and minimize the impact of deficits in areas wherein the firm is known to be weak?

4. Finally, is the strategy realistic? That is, what is the risk that it will not work?

The demanding task of managers charged with evaluating alternative strategies, then, is to scrutinize each strategy and determine what competitive advantages the firm would have to enjoy to make that strategy successful and how likely the firm is to either have or be able to create the competitive advantages essential to each strategy's success.

STRATEGIC CHOICE

Strategic choice is usually interwoven with the evaluation of alternatives. Managers experienced in strategic planning try to separate the two, however, in order to ensure that each alternative gets a fair evaluation before the final decision is made. Effective managers realize, for example, that organization members have vested interests that may or may not be enhanced by certain strategic options. For example, the vice president in charge of sales who has built a large direct-sales organization may strongly oppose a strategic option that entails a move toward telemarketing or new distribution channels. Likewise, a production vice president may enthusiastically support a backward-integration option that solves a problem she has had in purchasing critical supplies, even though the added commitment to a particular product is not in the long-term best interest of the company as a whole.

After the alternatives have been fully evaluated and discussed, managers choose the firm's strategy, attempting as they do so to balance the risk associated with the strategy and its potential for achieving the firm's long-term objectives. This decision-making process usually involves ranking and voting on various options after an extended period of discussion and debate among managers. Once the decision is reached, wise managers close ranks behind it and focus on ensuring that the newly formulated strategy and its accompanying long-term objectives are clearly spelled out so that the implementation phase can begin.

Strategy Implementation

The newly formulated strategy must now be incorporated into the daily activities of the company. This means that the strategy must be translated into action and guides to action on the part of organizational members. **Strategy implementation** first involves developing short-term plans, covering one year or less, that provide immediate guidelines for each area of the company. These short-term plans are linked directly to the strategic plan in order to ensure consistency between formulated strategies and actions taken. Also needed are short-term objectives throughout every area of the organization—again linked directly to the long-term objectives identified in the process of strategy formulation. Finally, budgets, time schedules, and "one-time" project plans must be developed to guide organizational actions. (Chapter 8 will examine strategy implementation in greater detail.)

Strategic Control

The success of any strategy depends in part on the manager's diligence in controlling progress in key areas as well as monitoring changes in critical resources, skills, and competitive, market, or other environmental factors. Managers must regularly check progress against the strategic plan—especially at key milestones and critical stages—to assess whether the organization is moving apace toward its long-term objectives. Usually achieved via a formal control system, this activity continuously seeks the answer to three questions: "Is the strategy being implemented as planned?" "Are the critical assumptions on the basis of which we selected it still valid?" "Is the strategy achieving the intended results?"[14] (Strategic control will be discussed in greater detail in Chapter 8.) For a sample of the kinds of questions a firm should continually ask about its strategic planning system, see "Management Development Exercise 7".

Strategic planning as a process to formulate an organization's strategy is appropriate for any organization. Subtle differences may apply across different size organizations and profit versus nonprofit organizations. Strategy formulation in these different organizational settings are discussed in the next section.

Strategy Formulation in Different Organizational Settings

Different types of organizations often go about formulating strategy in different ways. This section examines those differences in three types of organizations: large businesses, small businesses, and not-for-profit organizations.

Large Businesses

Large organizations need a formally staffed planning department. Strategic planning in these organizations has become too complex for their managers to handle in a timely fashion without the help of planning staffs. The time horizons and financial investments associated with the strategic decisions they must regularly make render the support and expertise of specialized planning personnel indispensable. Planning staffs in large businesses help top managers scan the environment, forecast future developments, analyze environmental and company profile information, and evaluate strategic options. Although top managers remain responsible for making strategic decisions, planning staffs have traditionally played key roles as information gatherers, analyzers, and organizers of the planning process for top managers in large businesses facing increasingly complex environments.

Hence planning staffs play a dominant role in shaping and directing the creation of strategic plans in many large organizations. Several organizations, however, have failed to plan effectively by this means and have become disenchanted with it, primarily because planning staffs were often removed from regular contact with customers, markets, and operations.[15] As a result, the role of formal planning staffs has changed in recent years. Their function has become that of supporting and assisting line managers in strategic planning and of serving as catalysts for change rather than dictating plans in isolation from corporate headquarters. For many large firms, membership on the planning staff is a revolving assignment for younger managers as part of their management development.[16] This approach is said to improve the link between planning analysis and operating issues. It has also led to a more active planning role for top managers in large business organizations.

Small Businesses

The nature of and need for strategy formulation activities is substantially different in small business organizations. Several researchers have observed key ways in which small businesses differ from large businesses. Some of these help explain the need for different strategy formulation activities.[17]

1. Small businesses provide relatively few products or services.

2. Their resources and skills are comparatively limited.

3. A key competitive advantage is their ability to change quickly.

4. They generally do not have formal procedures for monitoring the environment, making forecasts, or evaluating and controlling strategies that are currently being pursued.

5. Most management personnel have been trained on the job and therefore tend to rely on experience and intuition rather than on systematic procedures.

6. Time for planning is at a premium, because managers tend to be intimately involved in day-to-day operations.

7. Management positions and large blocks of stock are often held by relatives or friends of the founder(s).

Because of these differences, the procedures for formulating strategies in small businesses are less formal, systematic, and regular than that observed in larger firms.[18] This is not to say that small firms do not plan well. Indeed, very effective strategic planning can take place in small firms, even when it is informal, often qualitative, and relatively simplified. As an expert in small-firm planning has capably argued, "Strategy should be formulated [in small firms] by the top management team at the conference table. Judgment, experience, intuition, and well-guided discussions are the key to success, not staff work and mathematical models."[19]

Not-for-Profit Organizations

As the name implies, not-for-profit organizations differ in a fundamental way from profit-seeking ones. Not-for-profit organizations also differ dramatically from each other. Organizations such as the Red Cross, the Republican Party, Vanderbilt University, the Airline Pilots Association, and the United Methodist Church have very different reasons for being. One recent study listed six ways in which not-for-profit organizations differ from profit-seeking firms.[20]

1. The service they provide is often intangible and hard to measure.

2. "Customer" influence may be weak.

3. Strong employee commitment to professions or to a cause may weaken their allegiance to the organization.

4. Resource contributors may intrude into internal management.

5. Restraints on the use of rewards and punishments result from considerations 1, 3, and 4 above and from the heightened regulatory guidelines that are usually imposed.

6. Charismatic leaders (if they exist in the organization) and/or the "mystique" of the organization may be the only real means of resolving conflicts and overcoming restraints.

Perhaps because of these differences, strategic planning is less prominent in not-for-profit organizations. One recent study found that these organizations tended to be "managed much more in a short-term operations sense than in a strategic sense."[21] Another review of this issue reported that "there is some evidence that some of these [not-for-profit] organizations have no strategies at all. Rather, they seem motivated more by short-term budget cycles and personal goals than by any interest in reexamining their purpose or mission in light of altered environmental circumstances."[22]

Nevertheless, it appears that strategic planning in some form may be increasing in selected not-for-profit organizations. Pressures such as funding cutbacks, the presence of business people on boards of trustees, and demands for greater accountability may be creating the impetus toward strategic planning. Reports of strategic planning efforts in colleges, churches, local governments, hospitals, and libraries are no longer a rarity.

▮▮▮▮▮ *Guidelines for Management Practice* ▮▮▮▮▮

The strategic planning process is basically a straightforward, logical approach to deciding an organization's future. Yet managers frequently encounter problems making it work well. These guidelines offer you suggestions on how to deal with several problems that detract from strategic planning efforts.

1. Managers should make sure that the process of strategic planning involves six basic activities: setting broad objectives, conducting environmental analyses, analyzing company resources, performing an analysis of the strategic alternatives and selecting one, implementing the chosen strategy, and exerting strategic control.

2. It is important to recognize the *unit* for which the plan is being developed. The most important unit is a particular business, although the unit is at times the overall corporation (in multibusiness companies), a division, a major product line or market area, a department, a task force, or other organizational group. Planning can fall victim to misunderstanding, a dearth of relevant perspectives, or a lack of authority if care is not taken to define the unit at the outset.

3. Managers should agree on a common "language" in strategic planning and on a specific timetable for the current planning effort and for the ongoing planning process. This agreement on language, or terminology, ensures that everyone will use such words as *objectives, acceptable,* and *strategies* to mean the same thing. The agreement on terminology usually includes agreement on the conceptual tools used to generate and evaluate strategy alternatives.

4. The full support of senior management and its involvement in the planning process are critical to the success of strategic planning. Planning teams should include enough members so that planning skills, industry knowledge, and skills in financial, marketing, and operations management are represented on the team.

5. Remember that planning officers and staffs do not develop strategic plans. Rather, they assist line managers in the planning process. In the medium-sized or small company, a top executive frequently directs the strategic planning process, approaching it as a joint effort with others in senior management. The level of detail and formality may be different, but the planning process is similar in all such firms, regardless of their size.

6. Managers in finance, marketing, and operations should be given an active role in the planning process so that the plan reflects their input and they gain a thorough understanding of the role their functions will play in implementing the strategic decisions the group reaches.

Review of the Learning Objectives

Having studied this chapter, you should be able to respond to the learning objectives with extensions of the following brief answers:

1. **Define the term** *strategy*.

   By strategy, managers mean their large-scale, future-oriented plans for interacting with the competitive environment to optimize achievement of organizational objectives.

2. **Explain why formulating a strategy should make your organization more effective.**

   The existence of a clear strategy and the process of formulating it—strategic planning—appear to bestow significant behavioral as well as financial advantages on the organizations that use them. Several studies have examined the financial performance issue, and the results support the notion that financial performance is enhanced in firms that engage in formal strategic planning. Engaging in the process of strategy formulation also appears to provide five "behavioral" benefits: improved problem prevention capabilities, group-based strategic decisions, improved motivation via participative decision making, better intraorganizational coordination, and a lessening of resistance to change.

3. **Distinguish among three levels of strategy.**

   Corporate strategy is concerned with two basic questions: What kind of businesses should the company be engaged in? And how should resources be allocated among those businesses? Business strategy is concerned with the following five questions: How will the business compete within its market? What products and/or services will it offer? What customers will it serve? How will resources be distributed within the business? What technologies will be emphasized and what key synergies obtained across functional areas? Functional strategies create the framework for immediate-term management of the basic business functions in a manner consistent with and supportive of business-level strategy.

4. **Cite several conceptual tools that can be used as a basis for setting forth specific corporate and business-level strategies.**

   Two basic conceptual tools are available at the corporate level: Glueck's four strategy categories and the portfolio approach. The most popular conceptual tools at the corporate level have been the two portfolio approaches—the BCG or growth–share matrix and the GE planning grid. Three conceptual tools were described at the business level: the stages of product–market evolution model, Porter's generic strategies, and the product–market matrix. All three are widely used in formulating business strategies.

5. **Describe the key elements of the strategic planning process, and explain how they can be used to formulate effective strategies.**

   The starting point of the strategic planning process is the determination or reconfirmation of the business's purpose, values, and mission—its broad objectives. These define the "strategic playing field" for managers' planning activities. The next critical element is environmental scanning and analysis. This step provides strategists with information about key environmental factors that will influence the firm's future and, through the managers' analysis, pinpoints key determinants of success in selected product/markets. The next critical element is a profile depicting the quantity and quality of the company's principal resources and skills in three broad areas: financial; physical, organizational, and human; and technological. Once these three elements are available, managers use them as a basis for determining what key opportunities and threats face the business and which of the company's resources and skills are sufficient to yield competitive advantages in key product/markets. Once this SWOT analysis is complete, managers identify different strategies the firm might pursue, evaluate these alternatives, and ultimately choose the firm's future strategy. The implementation phase follows, wherein specific actions are planned and executed and systems for monitoring and controlling execution of the strategy are put into place.

Key Terms and Concepts

Having completed your study of Chapter 7, "Strategic Management," you should have mastered the following important terms and concepts:

strategy
strategic planning
explicit ("intended") strategy
implicit ("realized") strategy
corporate strategy
business strategy
functional strategy
growth strategy

stability strategy
defensive strategy
combination strategy
portfolio approach
BCG matrix
growth–share matrix
GE planning grid
product–market evolution

generic strategies
overall cost leadership
differentiation
focus
product–market matrix
concentration
market development
product development

vertical integration
diversification
backward vertical integration
forward vertical integration
divestiture
horizontal integration
retrenchment/turnaround

liquidation
environmental analysis
company profile
SWOT analysis
gap analysis
strategic choice
strategy implementation
strategic control

Questions for Discussion

1. For what reasons would you expect strategic planning to be beneficial to your organization and to enhance your effectiveness as a manager?

2. Define the term *strategy* and give a current example.

3. Explain the difference between an intended and a realized strategy.

4. Explain the three basic levels of strategy. How are they different?

5. Compare the Glueck framework with the portfolio approach as alternative ways of conceptualizing corporate strategy. Which do you find more effective and why?

6. Describe Porter's generic strategies and illustrate each one using a company you are familiar with.

7. Compare the product/market evolution framework and the product–market matrix as methods for generating business strategies.

8. What is the difference between a functional strategy and a business strategy?

9. What are the key steps in the strategic planning process and how do they differ?

10. Consider the opening case in this chapter. What was Wendy's strategy and why does it appear that strategy played a central role in Wendy's success? Consider Wendy's today. What changes do you see at Wendy's and what grand strategies do those changes reflect?

Notes

1. Adapted from "Wendy's International, Inc. (B)," in J. A. Pearce, II, and R. B. Robinson, Jr., *Strategic Management: Strategic Formulation and Implementation,* 3rd ed. Richard D. Irwin, Inc. © 1988, pp. 487–509.
2. Quoted in A. D. Chandler, Jr., *Strategy and Structure: Chapters in the History of the American Industrial Enterprise* (Cambridge, Mass.: MIT Press, 1962), p. 235.
3. G. A. Steiner, *Strategic Planning* (New York: Free Press, 1979), p. 5.
4. Peter F. Drucker, *Management: Tasks, Responsibilities, Practices* (New York: Harper & Row), p. 611.
5. H. I. Ansoff, R. Brandenberg, F. Portner, and R. Radosevich, *Acquisitions Behavior of U.S. Manufacturing Firms, 1946–65* (Nashville: Vanderbilt University Press, 1971).
6. S. Thune and R. House, "Where Long-Range Planning Pays Off," *Business Horizons,* August 1979, pp. 81–87.
7. D. Herold, "Long-Range Planning and Organizational Performance: A Cross Validation Study," *Academy of Management Review,* March 1972, 60–64; and L. Rue and R. Fulmer, "Is Long-Range Planning Profitable?" *Academy of Management Proceedings,* 1972. For a comprehensive review of numerous studies, see C. B. Shrader, L. Taylor, and D. R. Dalton, "Strategic Planning and Organizational Performance: A Critical Appraisal," *Journal of Management* 10 (1984):149–171.
8. The distinction we make between "intended" and "realized" strategies draws heavily on earlier work by H. Mintzberg, "Patterns in Strategy Formulation," *Management Science* 24 (1978): 934–948.
9. W. F. Glueck, *Business Policy* (New York: McGraw-Hill, 1976).
10. A. C. Hax and N. S. Majluf, "The Use of the Growth–Share Matrix in Strategic Planning," *Interfaces,* 13 (1983): 8–21; and "The Use of the Industry Attractiveness–Business Strength Matrix in Strategic Planning," *Interfaces,* 13 (1983): 54–71.
11. M. E. Porter, *Competitive Strategy* (New York: Free Press, 1980).
12. Several recent studies examining Porter's generic strategies include G. G. Dess and P. S. Davis, "Porter's (1980) Generic Strategies as Determinants of Strategic Group Membership and Organizational Performance," *Academy of Management Journal* 27, no. 3: 467–488; R. B. Robinson, Jr., and J. A. Pearce, II, "The Structure of Generic Strategies and Their Relationship with Business Unit Performance," *Academy of Management Proceedings,* San Diego, 1985; C. C. Woo and K. Kool, "Porter's (1980) Generic Competitive Strategies: A Test of Performance and Functional Attributes," Krannert School of Management working paper, Purdue University, West Lafayette, Ind., 1985.
13. F. J. Aguillar, *Scanning the Environment;* J. A. Pearce, II, and R. B. Robinson, Jr., "Environmental Forecasting," *Business,* February 1985.
14. See D. A. Aaker, "How to Select a Business Strategy," *California Management Review* 26, no. 3 (Spring 1984): 167–175. Aaker suggests that the accuracy of a strategy's evaluation can be increased by including factors beyond sales and profit forecasts, such as judgments of its flexibility, feasibility, consistency with the firm's mission, and responsiveness to the environment.
15. "The New Breed of Strategic Planner," *Business Week,* Sept. 17, 1984, pp. 62–68.
16. See C. D. Burnett, D. P. Yeskey, and D. Richardson, "New Roles for Corporate Planners in the 1980s," *Journal of Business Strategy* 4, no. 1 (Summer 1983): 64–68.
17. T. P. van Hoorn, "Strategic Planning in Small and Medium-Sized Companies," *Long Range Planning* 12, no. 2 (April 1979): 84–91; and R. B. Robinson, Jr., and J. A. Pearce, II, "Research Thrusts in Small Firm Strategic Planning," *Academy of Management Review* 9, no. 1 (January 1984): 128–137.
18. R. B. Robinson, Jr., "The Importance of 'Outsiders' in Small Firm Strategic Planning," *Academy of Management Journal* 23, pp. 217–229.
19. F. F. Gilmore, "Formulating Strategies in Smaller Companies," *Harvard Business Review* 49, no. 3 (May–June 1971): 81; G. A. Steiner, "Approaches to Long-Range Planning for Small Businesses," *California Management Review* 10, no. 1 (Fall 1967): 3–16; and Robinson and Pearce, "Research Thrusts." See also G. H. Rice, Jr., "Strategic Decision Making in Small Business," *Journal of General Management* 9, no. 1 (Autumn 1983): 58–65.
20. M. S. Wortman, Jr., quoted in *Strategic Management* ed. D. Schendel and C. W. Hofer (New York: Little, Brown, 1979), p. 314.
21. C. W. Hofer, *Strategy Formulation: Issues and Concepts* (St. Paul, Minn.: West, 1986), pp. 25–29.
22. Wortman, p. 315.

Cohesion Incident 7-1
The Strategic Implications of Bud Dunkin's Retirement

Once a year, Roger and the managers of the 122 other Journey's End Inns are invited to corporate headquarters. There they review the past year's operations, prepare budgets for the coming year to meet organizational objectives, and have an opportunity to discuss ideas they have implemented successfully in their particular inns.

Charles was left completely in charge of the Graniteville inn while Roger was away and felt very comfortable about his duties. A couple of minor problems arose, however, and he was looking forward to Roger's return so that they could discuss the problems. Upon Roger's arrival at the inn after the corporate meeting, Charles casually inquired, "How was your meeting?"

"Charles, as far as our past year was concerned, everything looked great. Overall, the occupancy rate was up, profits were slowly rising, and top management was generally pleased with our efforts. We also had a great retirement party for Bud Dunkin. Bud has been with Journey's End since 1960, and he has always been responsible for choosing new sites for Journey's End Inns. He's done a fantastic job and is one of the biggest factors in the success of this corporation. It's amazing the feel he has had about certain areas and how well Journey's End would fit into those locations."

"Who's going to replace Mr. Dunkin?" Charles asked.

"Now you'll hear about what the other managers and I did not like about the trip. Instead of replacing Bud with another person, top management has created a whole new department, Strategic Planning, to be operated by a three-person staff. Charles, sometimes our managers remind me of little boys with money burning a hole in their pockets. We had a good year and profits were up, so they had to find some new department to spend that money on."

Charles listened as Roger told him about the three high-priced (to use Roger's phrase) planners being added to the payroll. They were introduced at the meeting and will assist management in determining the best locations for new inns. By using market research and surveys, they were said to be able to predict what locations would be the most rational and risk-free options for new inns built by Journey's End.

"Charles, we've never needed any group like this before. All I see them accomplishing is adding to the corporate overhead already in my budget and taking some of the fun out of picking a new site. And even with their fancy models and research forms, I bet Bud could have done just as good a job. Sometimes we built our most profitable inns in high-risk areas that turned out to be top resort attractions. We were the first ones there and made plenty of profit before our competitors hit. I just hope they know what they're doing."

Discussion Questions

1. How might strategic planning at a Journey's End differ from the era of Bud Dunkin to the era after Bud Dunkin?

2. Do you think Roger's concern is justified? Why or why not?

3. If you were one of Journey's End's top managers, what would you expect this new planning department to do?

Cohesion Incident 7-2

Star Gazing

"So, are we 'stars' yet," Leslie asked Eileen jokingly, "or are we headed for the doghouse?"

Eileen, Leslie, Bill, and Steve were surveying the latest data on the sales and market-share performance of Travis's major product divisions (see the following table).

Annual Report of Travis Market Share and Growth in Sales	Product Division	Relative Market Share	Growth in Sales
	Automotive Parts	large	high
	Industrial Equipment	small	low
	Large Highway Vehicles	large	low
	Mobile Off-Highway Equipment	large	high
	Electronic Controls	small	high

As they looked over the figures, they speculated about the corporation's future plans for the Electronic Controls Division. "Looks like it'll be a busy year for us in Market Research," Eileen said, smiling. "I hope you like a challenge; there could be a new star on the horizon."

Seeing the puzzled look on Bill's face, Leslie offered a brief explanation. She told Bill that Travis's approach to strategic planning now included the use of a market-share–market-growth matrix to look at the strategy alternatives appropriate to each product division. "As a result," Leslie explained, "we can use this market-share and growth-in-sales information to plot the position of our division on a share–growth matrix and thereby get a pretty good idea of what is in store for our division."

Leslie then drew a share–growth matrix (as shown below). She explained the origin of the share–growth (or BCG) matrix, the four categories, and their strategic implications. She then turned to Bill and said, "Now you plot the five divisions and tell us what's in store."

Share–Growth Matrix

Relative Market Share

Large   Small

Growth in Sales

Low   High

Discussion Questions

1. Complete Travis Corporation's share–growth matrix (above) including the following information: For each cell in the matrix, indicate which product divisions would fit in that classification. In general terms (high or low) indicate what each product line would be expected to generate in terms of cash and to require in terms of investment.

2. What is the purpose of this type of portfolio analysis?

3. Where does the Electronic Controls Division's product line fall in the matrix? Given its classification, what strategies might be considered for it? Why does Eileen predict that her department will face a challenging year?

4. What strategies are likely to be considered for product divisions in the other three cells?

5. What are the limitations of this type of portfolio analysis?

Management Development Exercise 7
Evaluating a Company's Strategic Planning System

Managers need to be prepared to help their firm assess the effectiveness of its strategic planning system. What follows, then, is an exercise for an organization to assess its strategic planning practices. You can use this form as a useful exercise in a future job assignment. You should practice it now by using it as a guide to interview a manager in an organization of your choosing about the organization's strategic planning system.

Answer each question by circling 1, 3, or 5.

	No	Sometimes	Yes
1. Top management spends very little time on strategic planning—usually sporadically.	1	3	5
2. There is too much foot-dragging about planning. It is paid lip service, but too many line managers really do not accept it.	1	3	5
3. Line managers generally spend very little time with other line managers and/or staff in developing strategic plans.	1	3	5
4. The planning process usually proceeds on a random basis without an acceptable set of procedures.	1	3	5
5. The planning procedures are not well understood in the company.	1	3	5
6. The work requirements and assignments to complete the plans are not very acceptable to managers and staff.	1	3	5
7. The process encourages routine responses rather than inducing in-depth thinking.	1	3	5
8. Too much attention is paid to putting numbers in boxes. The process is too "proceduralized," too routine, too inflexible.	1	3	5
9. New ideas are generally discouraged or ignored.	1	3	5

10. Too many managers are not willing to face up to company weaknesses in devising plans.

1   3   5

11. Divisions or departments do not get enough guidance from headquarters for effective planning.

1   3   5

12. Divisions or departments are too restrained by headquarters for effective planning.

1   3   5

13. The ability of managers to do effective strategic planning is seldom taken into consideration when they are measured for overall performance.

1   3   5

Total the numerical values of your thirteen answers and ask your instructor for further instructions.

Planning and Implementation

Your study of this chapter will enable you to do the following:

1. Describe the role of action plans in implementing strategic decisions.
2. Identify and describe three types of action plans.
3. Cite important guidelines for the effective use of one-time plans and standing plans.
4. Identify barriers to effective action planning.
5. Summarize the key guidelines for overcoming barriers to planning.

Sherwin-Williams Implements a New Plan

In the early 1980s, many experts thought that the Sherwin-Williams Company, a firm principally known for its paint products, was destined for bankruptcy. But its new chief executive officer, Jack Breen, had other plans. He committed the Sherwin-Williams Company to a turnaround strategy that focused on the installation of a strategic planning process, development of a manpower planning process, and implementation of a management accounting system. He refocused the company on the paint and decorating market. Breen's emphasis on cost-cutting and planning meant that activities at the division level had to be well thought out before they were implemented. Managers at Sherwin-Williams developed internal action plans to guide division level activities.

Breen scrapped his predecessor's management strategy, which he characterized as management from the top, and shifted considerable power and responsibility to his operating managers. And he put seventy-five top executives, including himself, on a salary program of base pay plus incentive as a means of stimulating profit-oriented thinking.

The turnaround effort began in the Personnel Department. A personnel operating plan was developed to reduce the managerial work force by 20 percent in year one and 10 percent in year two through a coordinated emphasis on early retirement, dismissals, and more intensive performance appraisal. A "one-time" plan was put into effect to help departing managers find other employment by providing desks, telephones, and administrative assistance from the Personnel

Jack Breen's intensity, evident even at home, has enhanced his ability to make sure that every detail of his turnaround strategy at Sherwin Williams was properly executed. (Courtesy of Sherwin Williams)

Department. Once the reduction in management personnel had been completed, a standing plan or policy of promoting from within was instituted to reassure high-performing members of the Sherwin-Williams organization and to serve as an incentive.

A functional plan in the financial area included imposing strict controls on over 1,400 retail stores and effecting a substantial reduction in long-term debt. (Before Breen took over, the firm had borrowed heavily to fund expansion in a market that was not growing as had been expected.) Breen also ordered that accounts payable be stretched from thirty days to sixty days, first as a temporary measure (a one-time plan) for six months, and later as a permanent standing policy. Strict attention was given to the development of budgets and their use at the corporate and store levels to carefully monitor sales, expenditures, and financial position.

Marketing and operations were also affected. Two hundred new decorating centers were opened. Dutch Boy paints was purchased, and its products became an alternative product line promoted heavily through the home decorating centers.

Results indicate that Breen's tactics were successful. Sales have doubled and return on equity has more than tripled since the turnaround was implemented.[1]

Introduction

What Are Action Plans?

When Jack Breen became the new CEO of Sherwin-Williams, he quickly saw that Sherwin-Williams had to follow a turnaround strategy to improve its performance. But his planning did not stop there. Breen instigated the development of several very specific plans to guide the implementation of his turnaround strategy.

The manager's planning role does not end when objectives have been identified and long-term strategies selected that chart the business's future course in achieving those objectives. Managers, particularly operating managers, must develop detailed guidelines that initiate and control organizationwide action. These guidelines, or **action plans**, are designed to ensure that the people responsible for accomplishing long-term and short-term objectives have clear guidance on what they need to do and how they are to achieve those objectives. Action plans also provide a mechanism by which top managers can satisfy themselves that what the firm is doing is consistent with the intent of their strategic plans.

Managers implement strategy through action plans; but other considerations—organizational structure, rewards, and control systems—also have a major impact on the successful implementation of a business's strategy.

Surprisingly, there is little research on how the use of action plans affects organizational performance. Of the studies available, all support the idea that the use of action plans enhances organizational performance. For example, one study in the retailing industry showed that firms that developed specific guidelines for marketing, operations, finance, and personnel significantly outperformed their counterparts. A second study showed that firms with strategic and functional plans significantly outperformed their counterparts that used strategic plans only.[2]

Entry-level managers can expect to be called on early in their careers to develop plans. A fundamental objective of this chapter is to prepare you for this planning role. First we will explain the role of action plans in the overall planning process used by most business organizations. Then we will examine the three types of action plans with which operational managers must be concerned: functional (or functional-area) plans, plans designed for one-time use, and standing plans. Related to these plans is the use of budgets and employee participation to link the expenditure of resources to the actions being planned. Finally, to make their action plans effective, operational managers must be able to recognize and overcome barriers that might otherwise reduce managerial success in implementing organizational action.

The Role of Action Plans

Although they are mainly concerned with implementation, action plans are tentatively developed at the formulation phase of the strategic planning process to serve as input to business and corporate managers attempting to make strategic decisions. They provide "front line" information to decison makers who are not involved in the day-to-day activities of the firm. They also help ensure consistency between top-management decisions and operating action. Sherwin-Williams's line managers were a major source of information that CEO Jack Breen needed as he began to formulate the company's turnaround strategy. Having just joined the company, Breen had to assess the situation within the company, get an authentic sense of what was possible, and see how "in touch with the problem" his line managers were. The input they supplied by providing their action plans enabled him to do this. Figure 8-1 illustrates a typical planning cycle in a multibusiness company.

Action plans have several distinct features. For instance, they are primarily the responsibility of operating managers and department managers. This requirement ensures that those responsible for implementing a strategic plan are involved in developing it. Final action plans grow out of the corporate and business strategies and the broad objectives of the firm. They become the "approved guidelines"

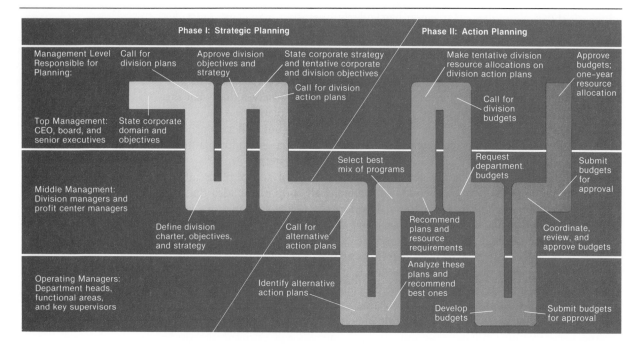

FIGURE 8-1
The Role of Action Plans in the Overall Planning Cycle*

*During the planning cycle, plans and objectives are hammered out by the three levels of managers as the planning process moves from strategic planning to the shorter-term action planning.

Sources: Reprinted by permission of the *Harvard Business Review*. An exhibit from "Strategic Planning in Diversified Companies," by R. Vancil and P. Lorange (January/February 1975). Copyright © 1975 by the President and Fellows of Harvard College; all rights reserved; and G. Dressler, *Management Fundamentals* (Reston, Va.: Reston Publishing, 1985), p. 35.

to organizational action that is consistent with the business strategy. Thus creating action plans is the beginning of the implementation phase of the strategic planning process.

Another important characteristic of action plans is that they are usually accompanied by detailed budgets. Indeed, in some organizations, budgets serve as the principal means by which action plans are communicated. Budgets perform two important functions. They link resource allocations to action plans and indicate which people, funds, and other resources are available for implementing any particular action plan. They also provide a means for monitoring and evaluating the implementation of strategy. "Management Development Exercise 8" provides a basis for evaluating action plans.

Three Types of Plans That Guide Organizational Action

Operating managers must develop three different types of action plans for guiding the day-to-day activities that are intended to implement strategic decisions. *Func-*

tional plans are always needed to guide decisions and actions in the various functional areas of the business. *One-time plans* are often created for special projects or programs that must be undertaken in support of the business's strategy. For example, personnel managers at Sherwin-Williams developed a one-time plan to help managers who were dismissed during implementation of Breen's turnaround strategy to find new jobs. *Standing plans* or policies are usually needed to set specific guidelines for carrying out certain recurring activities. Sherwin-Williams's management policy of trying to fill all job openings by promoting a qualified person from within the company is an example of a standing plan. These three types of action plans, summarized in Figure 8-2, are discussed more fully in the next three sections.

Functional Plans

Suppose you are the assistant manager of the Operations Department for a regional distributor of consumer electronic products serving five southeastern states. Your boss, the operations manager, has just informed you that top management is finalizing a five-year plan that seeks to double sales volume by expanding services into five midwestern states and by adding two lines of industrial electronics products. She then indicated that you would be in charge of developing an inventory and logistics plan to add the new product line and to expand into at least two new states during the next year. Two of your friends, who hold similar positions in the Finance Department and the Marketing Department, received similar in-

Type of Action	Primary Role of the Plan	Form the Plan Takes	Examples
Functional plans	To guide implementation of the company's strategic plan	Key short-term objectives and immediate tactical approach in each functional area	BIC Pen Corp.'s plan to sell directly to large mass merchandisers rather than use regional distributors
One-time plans	To carry out activities that are not intended to be repeated after the one-time plan is executed	1. Programs 2. Projects	BIC's task force and plan to manage the discontinuation of relationships with regional distributors
Standing plans	To standardize decisions about routine activities that are encountered regularly over time	1. Policies 2. Standard operating procedures 3. Rules and regulations	BIC's pricing policies to be used by BIC salespersons in selling to local mass merchandisers

FIGURE 8-2
Three Types of
Action Plans

structions from their respective managers. Each of you has been given two weeks to develop a tentative plan.

As assistant operations manager, you would be expected to develop a plan that set forth how you would handle such issues as warehousing, purchasing, shipping, keeping track of inventory, and reordering for both your existing product lines and the new industrial product lines. For example, you might need to establish a new warehouse facility, reorganize purchasing, and revise your computerized inventory and reordering system. Your friend in marketing would be concerned with such issues as organizing the sales force, establishing sales offices and territories, and beginning to devise tactics to announce the availability of the new product lines, promote them, and establish the company's presence in the two new states. Your friend in finance would be busy planning the capital expenditures, cash requirements, and financial control systems necessitated by the expanded product line and increased territorial coverage. In each case, the task is to develop detailed guides to action in a specific functional area.

A useful way to envision what functional plans contain is to view each plan as the source of answers to the question "What should we do in our area or department to implement the business strategy?" In that a **functional plan** describes the specific actions to be taken in the immediate future by people responsible for that particular functional area, it usually sets forth short-term objectives, the actions to be taken to achieve those objectives, and a time frame for the accomplishment of each action. The types of actions, of course, vary widely among functional areas, several of which we will discuss here.

MARKETING

Managers in the marketing area are responsible for creating **marketing action plans** that tell sales and marketing personnel who will sell what, where, when, to whom, in what quantity, and how. Sherwin-Williams's marketing action plans usually describe what products are stocked for sale in each store, how they should be priced and promoted, and what customer services the store should include. Figure 8-3 illustrates the types of questions that a marketing plan usually addresses.

A simple example of issues that managers consider in developing part of a marketing action plan can be found at Giorgio, a company that sells very exclusive women's fragrances and perfumes. The company's flagship product, also named Giorgio, is a fragrance that sells for $150 an ounce and dominates the $1 billion expensive perfume market in the United States. The keys to Giorgio's success are its vintage Beverly Hills pedigree (it originated and was once sold only in Beverly Hills) and its "snob appeal." Recently adopting a strategy to increase its sales rapidly by expanding its market coverage, top management asked Giorgio marketing managers to create a marketing action plan that would accommodate rapid growth while maintaining the product's aura of exclusivity so that women would still pay its premium price. After debating the merits of several ways to introduce the product rapidly to new market areas, Giorgio marketing managers decided on a plan that protects the product's unique image by limiting the sale of the fragrance to a single store or chain in each city where Giorgio was to be sold. This exclusive distribution approach is a fundamental component of the marketing plan now followed by Giorgio's sales personnel.

Just as Giorgio's marketing managers had to come up with a unique marketing action plan, international marketing managers are often faced with developing

FIGURE 8-3
The Focus of Functional
Plans in Marketing

Key Areas	Typical Questions That Should Be Answered by the Functional Plan
Product (or service)	Which products do we emphasize? Which products/services contribute most to profitability? What is the product/service image we seek to project? What consumer needs does the product/service seek to meet? What changes should be influencing our customer orientation?
Price	Are we primarily competing on price? Can we offer discounts or other pricing modifications? Are pricing policies standard nationally or is there regional control? What price segments are we targeting (high, medium, low, etc.)? What is the gross profit margin? Do we emphasize cost/demand or competition-oriented pricing?
Place	What level of market coverage is necessary? Are there priority geographic areas? What channels of distribution are key? What are the channel objectives, structure, and management? Should the marketing managers change their degree of reliance on distributors, sales reps, and direct selling? What sales organization do we want? Is the sales force organized around territory, market, or product?
Promotion	What are key promotion priorities and approaches? Which advertising/communication priorities and approaches are linked to different products, markets, and territories? Which media would be most consistent with the total marketing strategy?

Source: Adapted from J. A. Pearce, II, and R. B. Robinson, Jr., *Strategic Management: Strategic Formulation and Implementation*, 3rd ed., Richard D. Irwin, Inc. © 1988, p. 338.

marketing approaches that are different from those used in domestic markets. "Insights for International Managers 8" provides several illustrations of the need for different marketing approaches that U.S. managers encounter when taking their products and services abroad.

FINANCE/ACCOUNTING

Managers responsible for the financial resources of a firm devise **financial action plans** that spell out how these resources are to be used and controlled. Financial managers are usually concerned with plans to acquire capital, plans to allocate capital resources, and guidelines for the management of working capital. The financial position of Sherwin-Williams when Jack Breen first took over was precarious. Under Breen's direction, financial managers formulated a plan that care-

---

Insights for International Managers 8

HOW TO SELL IN NEW, OVERSEAS MARKETS

A British buyer for Marks & Spencer's, one of England's major department store chains, says: "If you want to sell to the British, write a nice, clear, nonexaggerating letter explaining the simple facts of your business, and ask for an appointment to come over and see me. I will be busy, but British buyers, unlike American buyers, *will* see you. I will give you half an hour to persuade me, and if you are flamboyant, I will reject most of what you say. If you are not as aggressive as most Americans, I will probably take you more seriously and may even believe you. Then, of course, the final decision has to do with expected profits, not whether or not I care for you as a person." Indeed, some British companies have tried to eliminate the personal aspects of buyer-seller relations by disallowing wining and dining. Nonetheless, marketers need to sell themselves before buyers will be receptive to the product.

Compared to their foreign competition, many American companies do not put nearly enough effort into direct, personal communication. Japanese success in displacing the United States as Saudi Arabia's leading supplier is instructive: Japanese exporters send small teams to meet with Saudi importers; they go to Saudi workshops, travel to secondary towns, meet with sub-agents. The Americans, on the other hand, invite all their Saudi agents together for a luncheon, do not have private meetings, do not get their hands dirty, and never travel to secondary towns—they tend to stick to the three market centers. Saudis complain that U.S. effort is misdirected: American personnel devote infinitesimal detail to making arrangements for visiting executives, going so far as to specify rooms overlooking a certain view from a hotel.

Compared to most other cultures, particularly non-Western cultures, Americans are extraordinarily preoccupied with the tangible aspects of a product. We round up all our sales agents and give a product presentation instead of putting our energies into the more important conponent of international marketing—people. In America and only a few other countries it is normal to do business from a distance, between strangers, by mail or telephone.

Source: From L. Copeland and L. Griggs, *Going International* (New York: Random House, 1985) pp. 53–54.

---

fully preserved working capital by negotiating sixty-to-ninety-day terms on accounts payable, rapid payment of the firm's accounts receivable, and refinancing of its current monthly debt payments. Figure 8-4 illustrates the types of questions that a financial plan often addresses.

Celanese Corporation, an international manufacturer of chemical products, offers a good example of a financial plan. When it experienced drastically declining earnings during the recession of the early 1980s, it instituted a number of measures as part of a retrenchment strategy to streamline the company. (In Chapter 7, retrenchment strategies were defined as strategies whereby the company cuts back on the scope of its operations to invest most of its resources in its areas of greatest strength.) A key objective of this strategy was to increase stockholder wealth. Financial managers developed a two-year financial plan to generate cash by selling certain assets and businesses and to use excess cash to buy back up to 30 percent of its outstanding stock during this time. The idea was to reduce the total number of shares of stock outstanding, while improving profitability; this was expected to boost the value of Celanese stock. And indeed, the value of Celanese stock advanced from about $70 per share in 1984 to over $200 per share in 1986.

FIGURE 8-4
The Focus of Functional
Plans in Finance/
Accounting

Key Areas	Typical Questions That Should Be Answered by the Functional Plan
Capital acquisition	What is an acceptable cost of capital? What is the desired proportion of short- and long-term debt, preferred and common equity? What balance is there between internal and external funding? What risk and ownership restrictions are appropriate? What level and forms of leasing should be used in providing assets?
Capital allocation	What are the priorities for capital allocation projects? On what basis is final selection of projects to be made? What level of capital allocation can be made by operating managers without higher approval?
Dividend and working-capital management	What portion of earnings should be paid out as dividends? How important is dividend stability? Are things other than cash appropriate as dividends? What are the cash-flow requirements? minimum and maximum cash balances? How liberal/conservative should credit policies be? What limits, payment terms, and collection procedures are necessary? What payment timing and procedure should be followed?

Source: Adapted from J. A. Pearce, II, and R. B. Robinson, Jr., *Strategic Management: Strategic Formulation and Implementation,* 3rd ed., Richard D. Irwin, Inc. © 1988, p. 341.

PRODUCTION/OPERATIONS

Production/operations management (POM) is a core function in any business firm. POM consists of planning and overseeing the process of converting inputs (raw materials, supplies, people, knowledge, and equipment) into value-enhanced output. This function is widely associated with manufacturing firms, but it is equally important in all other types of businesses, including service and retail firms. For example, **POM action plans** must guide decisions about the basic nature of the firm's POM system, the efficiency of operations, the location and design of company facilities, and day-to-day process planning. Figure 8-5 lists the types of questions that POM plans typically address.

Jack Breen's success at Sherwin-Williams involved a three-part POM plan. Rather than invest in expanding current manufacturing capacity and equipment in order to add a needed new line of paint, he acquired another paint company (Dutch Boy). This enabled him to add the new line immediately and to exploit the customer awareness that Dutch Boy enjoyed and its reputation for quality. The second part of the Sherwin-Williams POM plan was to evaluate the location,

FIGURE 8-5
The Focus of Functional
Plans in Production/
Operations

Key Areas	Typical Questions That Should Be Answered by the Functional Plan
Facilities and equipment	How centralized should the facilities be? (One big facility or several small facilities?) How integrated should the separate processes be? To what extent will further mechanization or automation be pursued? Should size and capacity be oriented toward peak or normal operating levels?
Purchasing	How many sources are needed? How do we select suppliers and manage relationships over time? What level of forward buying (hedging) is appropriate?
Operations planning and control	Should work be scheduled to order or to stock? What level of inventory is appropriate? How should inventory be used (FIFO/LIFO), controlled, and replenished? What are the key foci for control efforts (quality, labor cost, downtime, product usage, other)? Should maintenance efforts be preventive or breakdown-oriented? What emphasis should be placed on job specialization? plant safety? use of standards?

Source: Adapted from J. A. Pearce, II, and R. B. Robinson, Jr., *Strategic Management: Strategic Formulation and Implementation,* 3rd ed., Richard D. Irwin, Inc. © 1988, p. 345.

customer flow, and sales volume of every Sherwin-Williams retail outlet over a thirty-day period. This led to the closing of 275 old retail outlets. The third element of its POM plan was to open 200 new outlets as complete decorating centers, rather than simply paint stores, so that Sherwin-Williams could accommodate customer needs in a more convenient and efficient manner.

Functional plans are also frequently developed in the areas of personnel and research and development. For example, as it began transforming itself from a stock brokerage business into a diversified financial services institution, Merrill Lynch implemented an extensive early-career training plan and ongoing career-development plan designed to meet an expanding need for personnel who could work in several areas.

In summary, regardless of the area for which they are developed, functional plans share three distinct characteristics. First, the period of time that they cover is usually one year or less. Second, a functional plan is often more specific than a strategic plan. Functional plans tell operating personnel responsible for accomplishing short-term objectives how to meet such objectives. Third, devising functional plans is the responsibility of operating managers.

Anheuser-Busch occupies a dominant position in the highly competitive U.S. beer industry. Many people attribute that success to Anheuser-Busch's emphasis on detailed functional plans, particularly in marketing. "In Practice 8-1" describes several of the marketing plans Anheuser-Busch has used.

In Practice 8-1

FUNCTIONAL PLANS AT ANHEUSER-BUSCH

It is early evening at the sprawling Missouri farm of August A. Busch, III, and his after-work ritual is just beginning. In the family room, the fifty-year-old chief executive of Anheuser-Busch samples beer shipped in that day from his eleven breweries. He looks for proper mixtures of barley malt, hops, rice, corn, yeast, and water. Then he calls in his assessments to his chief brewmaster, Gerhardt Kraemer.

Although per capita beer consumption has been declining for years, Busch sells twice as much beer as he sold a decade ago, more beer than his two largest rivals combined, more beer than anyone else in the world. The company's secret is to apply venerable marketing techniques more vigorously and imaginatively than the competition.

The company's most important technique is target marketing—segmenting the market with a vengeance. Anheuser-Busch sponsors events and runs advertising specifically aimed at all sorts of different consumers: blacks, whites, blue-collar workers, computer buffs, auto racing fans, the military, and even immigrants.

The company divides the United States geographically into 210 markets and concentrates its resources on Los Angeles, New York, Boston, and the thirty-three other markets that account for 75 percent of all beer sales. The regional strategy makes sense because Anheuser-Busch faces different competitors in different markets—a lot of local brands, a popular Miller in the central states, Coors in the West.

Anheuser-Busch's distribution is the strongest in the business. The company wants its wholesalers to feel personally attended to, so it puts top executives in charge of the most important target states. Busch handles California, the biggest-volume state, and he visits each of the distributors there at least twice a year. The distributors love it.

The company also demands more from distributors than any other brewer. Each year every wholesaler is asked to suggest a special local promotion for each brand. Anheuser-Busch often covers half the cost, and it almost always outdoes its rivals.

The marketing machine that has become the legend of the beer business did not look so fierce when Busch took over from his father at age thirty-seven, in 1975. Until then Anheuser-Busch sold beer the old-fashioned way, relying on one sort of national advertising that targeted the general beer-drinking audience. "Anheuser-Busch was a $700 million company that was run like a corner grocery store."

Anheuser-Busch didn't revolutionize the beer business; Philip Morris did when it acquired Miller in 1971, pouring millions into the High Life brand, applying sophisticated market research, and gobbling up most of the commercial time on TV sports programs. Philip Morris relentlessly pursued the typical beer drinker, the male blue-collar worker, by dumping High Life's image as "the champagne of bottled beer" and pitching it as a reward to enjoy after a hard day's work—at "Miller Time." Busch's father, who was chief executive, and others at Anheuser-Busch opposed jacking up marketing spending to compete. His son persisted and won. So began the modern Anheuser-Busch.

Even competitors agree that chairman Busch's obsession with quality has been a main reason why Anheuser-Busch has stayed ahead. He claims his company invests more capital to produce a bottle of beer than any competitor, and he notes that it makes Budweiser and Michelob beers by supplementing the traditional barley malt with rice instead of with the cheaper corn that most rival brewers use.

Secure at the pinnacle of its industry, Anheuser-Busch is making sure no one gets too close. Coors has been expanding eastward but has damaged Anheuser-Busch least. A month before Coors moved into the huge New York and New Jersey market, an Anheuser-Busch wholesaler received a 300-page "Coors Defense Plan" and money for buying into promotional opportunities that might interest Coors (Hispanic parades, for example). Coors could not cut a good deal with a major beer wholesaler, so it is distributing through a Canada Dry soft drink bottler. In retaliation, Anheuser-Busch's wholesalers are promoting especially hard in the arena the soft drink people know best, the supermarkets.

One-Time Plans

Although functional plans are developed to cover a short period of time, they generally outline a course of action that is likely to be repeated several times in the future. Managers often find themselves called on to develop another type of plan, a one-time plan, as part of their managerial duties. **One-time plans** are developed to guide the carrying out of activities that are not intended to be repeated. There are two types of one-time plans: program plans and project plans.

PROGRAM PLANS

A **program plan** is a one-time plan designed to coordinate a diverse set of activities that are necessary to carry out a complex endeavor. Sherwin-Williams used a program plan to chart and carry out its effort to help departing managers find new jobs. Managers are often confronted with the need to develop a program when planning such activities as introducing a new product or service, installing a management information system, restructuring a department, opening new facilities, or similar undertakings that require input and action on the part of several different sources.

An example of a new-product program is Bankers Trust's introduction of a sophisticated cash management account service designed to make it more competitive with traditional brokerage businesses in the increasingly deregulated financial-services industry. Numerous features and services, such as money market rates, discount stock purchases, checking, and assorted investment fund options, would now be offered to old and new customers who were accustomed to simple checking and savings services. The program required market research, design of the service, arranging the technical aspects of the service, coordinating contributors both inside and outside Bankers Trust, pricing and packaging, promotion, and entry into the marketplace. The program was coordinated by a task force that included representatives from different divisions within Bankers Trust and, intermittently, representatives from outside organizations including computer companies and a nationwide brokerage organization.[3] The service took two years to bring to market and is now sold to other banks in addition to Bankers Trust.

PROJECT PLANS

A **project plan** is made to guide and control completion of a one-time activity that is typically less involved and complex than a program. A project plan may be part of a larger program plan or a self-contained one-time plan. Either way, project plans always involve a specific time frame and go into far more detail than is found in the average functional plan.[4]

Typical of project plans are plans to build a new office or facility, complete a maintenance shutdown in a manufacturing plant, arrange distribution in a new territory, design an advertising campaign, or develop an employee benefit package. When Holiday Corporation's management decided to diversify into the low-priced segment of the lodging industry, it assembled a project team to plan the appropriate concept and facility layout for its new Hampton Inn lodging facilities. That effort necessitated a project plan that set forth activities, decisions, responsibilities, and deadlines in a detailed fashion.

Guidelines for Management Practice

While managers routinely develop program and project plans, some of them frequently encounter difficulty in getting started. Managers attending project planning seminars that are comfortable with project planning have offered several guidelines to their less confident counterparts. Their advice has been condensed into the following eight guidelines:

1. Identify the total set of activities involved in completing the program or project, and specify a tentative deadline for its completion.

2. Divide the total set of activities into meaningful steps.

3. Examine each step and identify any relationships among the steps. Be especially careful to identify any steps that must take place in a specific sequence.

4. Assign responsibility for each step to the appropriate managers and units.

5. Determine what resources will be needed to complete each step.

6. Obtain a realistic estimate of the time that will be required to complete each step.

7. Estimate starting and completion dates for each step, taking into account any sequencing requirements and resource procurement requirements.

8. Assign target dates for the completion of each step, and allocate the resources needed for each step.

Managers who use these guidelines usually conclude with a detailed plan describing each step, a list of the activities involved in each step, a timing sheet displaying starting and completion dates, and a budget explaining how resources are to be allocated. Generally, the plan also identifies the people assigned to and responsible for each step. And it often suggests key checkpoints for evaluation of progress during the time covered by the program or project and stipulates any provisions that have been made for changing the plan if necessary.

The specific techniques that help managers develop program and project plans—Gantt charts, milestone scheduling, PERT (program evaluation and review technique), and CPM (the critical path method)—are explained in Chapter 9.

Standing Plans

One important aspect of the manager's role is to establish, from time to time, standing plans designed to guide the thinking, decisions, and actions of organizational personnel in the day-to-day execution of their responsibilities. **Standing plans** are directives that serve to increase organizational effectiveness by standardizing many routine decisions. This frees managers from having to be involved in every decision and lets employees get on with their jobs. Standing plans differ from functional plans primarily in that they are not intimately linked to overall strategy. (Functional plans are directly linked to business strategy; their purpose is to implement it.) Standing plans are focused on guiding daily behavior within the organization. There are three types of standing plans that managers may be called on to develop: policies, standard operating procedures, and rules and regulations.

POLICIES

A **policy** is a statement intended to set parameters for making recurring decisions. Policies offer a general guide to action and, in fact, represent the most general type of standing plan. For example, a company may establish a policy requiring a minimum educational level for applicants to qualify for certain jobs.

Policies can be externally imposed or internally derived. For example, a company may embrace an equal employment opportunity policy in order to comply with external (government) requirements. A policy setting credit terms for customers (such as 1 percent off on invoices paid within ten days or the net amount due within thirty days) is an internally derived policy. Policies may also emerge informally, over time, from a consistent set of decisions on the same issue. For example, if vacation time or office space is repeatedly assigned on the basis of seniority, that often becomes an informal policy within the organization. Examples of policies are provided in Figure 8-6.

STANDARD OPERATING PROCEDURES

A **standard operating procedure**, or SOP, is a standing plan that outlines a series of steps to be followed in accomplishing a specific activity or discharging a specific responsibility. More specific than a policy, an SOP performs a similar function: It frees the manager or supervisor from routine decision making and gives the subordinate freedom to act within certain guidelines. In fact, many SOPs often arise out of the need to provide detailed guidelines to employees responsible for abiding by a particular policy.

A good example of an SOP is the guidelines given to a motel desk clerk for registering new customers. The desk clerk might be told that when a person arrives to check in, he or she should (1) welcome the customer to the facility; (2) ask the customer whether payment will be by cash, check, or credit card; (3) have the customer fill out the registration form; (4) ask for a major credit card (if the customer specified that method of payment) and process the card while the customer is filling out the form; (5) review the form once the customer has completed it and add any missing information, and so on. Such detailed procedures guide the employees who perform a specific activity and help ensure a consistent approach in the execution of that activity without direct managerial involvement. Examples of SOPs are provided in Figure 8-6.

RULES AND REGULATIONS

Rules and regulations are guidelines stating that specific actions may or may not be taken in a given situation. Rather than "guiding" decisions, rules and regulations substitute for decision making or discretion in a specific situation. For example, the motel desk clerk may be given a rule that no guest can be provided with a room and room key until he or she either prepays the room charge or signs a validated credit card voucher. Rules and regulations are often accompanied by punitive consequences that befall anyone who violates the rule. For example, the desk clerk may be informed that he or she will be personally responsible for the room charge of any guest who does not pay if the clerk fails to follow the prepayment or credit card voucher rule. Although rules constitute rigid, generally irrevocable procedures, a manager at a high enough level can suspend or "bend" the rules.

FIGURE 8-6
Standing Plans in
Several Well-Known
Companies

Policies: Guidelines to recurring decisions

1. General Cinema has a *financial policy* that requires that annual capital investment in movie theaters not exceed annual depreciation. (By keeping capital investment no greater than depreciation, this policy supports General Cinema's financial strategy of maximizing cash flow—in this case, all profit—to growth areas of the company. It also reinforces General Cinema's financial strategy of leasing as much as possible.)

2. Crown, Cork and Seal Company has a *research and development policy* of not investing any financial or human resources in basic research. (This policy supports Crown, Cork and Seal's functional strategy that emphasizes customer service, not technical leadership.)

Standard operating procedures: Detailed guidelines to performing a particular activity

1. Wendy's has a *purchasing SOP* for local store managers that gives them the authority to buy fresh meat and produce locally rather than from regionally designated or company-owned sources. (This SOP supports Wendy's objective of cooking fresh, unfrozen hamburger daily.)

2. Holiday Inns has a *personnel SOP* that ensures that every new innkeeper attends a three-week innkeeper program at Holiday Inns University within one year of being hired. (This SOP supports Holiday Inns' commitment to consistent operating standards at every Holiday Inn location by ensuring standardized training of every new innkeeper at every Holiday Inn, whether company-owned or franchised.)

Rules and regulations: Parameters establishing standards of conduct for specific activities

1. First National Bank of South Carolina has a strict regulation that requires an annual revision of the financial statement of every personal borrower. (This regulation supports First National's efforts to maintain a loan/loss ratio below the industry norm and ensures compliance with federal banking laws.)

2. IBM originally made it a firm rule not to give free IBM personal computers (PCs) to any person or organization. (This rule was imposed to support IBM's image as a professional, high-value, service business as it sought to dominate the PC market.)

Rules and regulations are useful to managers and their subordinates in "programming" routine activities. But having to remember and follow too many rules and regulations, with little room for exercising initiative, may adversely affect employee morale. The "Guidelines for Management Practice" that follow offer suggestions for avoiding this problem. Examples of selected rules and regulations appear in Figure 8-6.

We have seen in Chapters 6 and 7 that planning serves an important role in guiding organizational action. Indeed, standing plans provide a useful mechanism to program day-to-day actions. The preceding section has described the essential link between planning and a manager's control function. Given the many important roles of planning, it would seem that planning is universally accepted as an important activity. Unfortunately, this is not always the case. Managers often encounter barriers to planning that limit its impact.

━━━━━━━━━━ *Guidelines for Management Practice* ━━━━━━━━━━

New managers often feel the need to establish standing plans wherever possible to make their jobs "easier." Subordinates sometimes find an onslaught of standing plans frustrating. Experienced managers counsel selective use of standing plans. They suggest that new managers use these eight guidelines to aid in selectively choosing where standing plans are appropriate.

1. *Establish indirect control over independent action* by making a clear statement about how things are now to be done. By limiting discretion, standing plans in effect control decisions and the conduct of activities without direct intervention by top management.

2. *Promote uniform handling of similar activities.* This facilitates coordination of work tasks and helps reduce friction arising from favoritism, discrimination, and inconsistent handling of similar issues.

3. *Ensure quicker decisions* by standardizing answers to previously unanswered questions that would otherwise recur and be pushed up the management hierarchy again and again.

4. *Help institutionalize basic aspects of organizational behavior.* This minimizes conflicting practices and establishes consistent patterns of action in terms of how organizational members attempt to make the strategy work.

5. *Reduce uncertainty in repetitive and day-to-day decision making,* thereby providing the foundation necessary for coordinated, efficient efforts.

6. *Counteract organizational members' resistance to or rejection of chosen strategies.* When major strategic change is undertaken, unambiguous standing plans help clarify what is expected and facilitate acceptance, particularly when operating managers and their subordinates participated in development of the standing plan.

7. *Offer a predetermined answer to routine problems,* giving managers more time to cope with nonroutine matters. Dealing with ordinary *and* extraordinary problems is greatly expedited when the former can be resolved by referring to established standing plans and the latter by drawing on the manager's time.

8. *Afford managers a mechanism for avoiding hasty and ill-conceived changes.* Standing plans can always be used as a reason for not yielding to emotion-based, expedient, or temporarily valid arguments for altering procedures and practices.

The level of discretion needed in the problem or activity is the main basis on which a manager should determine which type of standing plan is most appropriate. When it is essential that no discretion be allowed, a rule or regulation is called for. When some discretion is permissible within an otherwise highly routinized situation, a detailed SOP is often most effective. When discretion is acceptable and even necessary, within certain basic parameters, a policy is the best standing plan for the manager to employ.

Barriers to Planning

Barriers to planning fall into two categories. The first category is the anti-planning bias of individuals toward engaging in planning activity. Individuals are often unwilling or unable to plan because of personal barriers to meaningful participation in planning. The second type of barrier is found at the organizational level. Organizational barriers arise out of constraints on resources, the limited information usually available, and the organizational implications of decisions associated with the planning process. Both kinds of barriers to planning are discussed below.

Individual-Based Barriers

Effective planning requires the input and active participation of individual members of the organization. These individuals—especially those involved in developing action plans at the operating level of the business—often harbor anti-planning biases that present major barriers to effective planning.[5]

PRIORITY OF DAY-TO-DAY PROBLEMS

Managers, particularly those at the operating level, spend most of their time solving problems, making decisions, and otherwise ensuring that the concerns of that day are dealt with effectively. (One recent study found that managers at this level spend an average of only eight minutes on any one activity or decision during a typical day![6]) As a result, these managers are action-oriented, moving briskly from one problem or decision to the next. They tend to view planning as an unnecessary luxury that does not contribute to solving the many problems that exist today or are "just around the corner." Planning represents the unnecessary expenditure of a valuable commodity—time—which diverts that person's attention from pressing problems it is his or her job to solve. And spending time planning also means that those immediate problems or decisions mount up or, even worse, cut down on subordinate productivity until the manager can resolve them.

LACK OF PLANNING SKILLS

Managers, again most notably those at the operating level, often lack training in how to plan. They enter an organization at the operating level where planning beyond one day or one week is seldom if ever a part of their job assignment. Consequently, as they move up in the organization, they get minimal on-the-job training in planning skills. Planning is often viewed as something everyone innately possesses the skill to do. And because they hesitate to admit their lack of proficiency, managers are often asked to assume greater planning responsibility without really being prepared for it.[7]

RELUCTANCE TO SET FORTH OBJECTIVES AND PLANS

Another barrier to effective planning is the reluctance of some managers to commit themselves and their units of responsibility to specific objectives or plans. A major reason for this reluctance is often fear of failure or lack of confidence on the part of an individual manager. Success or failure is more readily determined when a manager sets forth a clear-cut objective and plan. And to risk failure is often to jeopardize one's self-esteem, one's sense of having the respect of others, and even one's job security. Thus some managers consciously or subconsciously try to avoid such a specific level of accountability—and hence erect a major barrier to effective planning.[8]

PERSONAL RESISTANCE TO CHANGE

Planning almost by definition implies making decisions and commitments to future changes. The process of planning involves new interpersonal encounters, which may lead to discussions that mount new challenges to individual values, underscore the need to face new facts and ideas, and raise the prospect of changing established ways of doing things. When planning is under way, people entertain new ideas about the future and about how their group or unit should respond. These new ideas may lead to changes in the way things are done, how relationships are organized, and what priorities are adhered to in the future. Overall, planning often changes so many things in units and organizations that it raises all sorts of doubts, misunderstandings, frustrations, and insecurities—and that creates considerable uncertainty, which is not something many people like.[9]

Organization-Based Barriers

The anti-planning bias felt by individuals can present a significant obstacle to effective planning. Other barriers often emerge at the organizational level out of environmental and other constraints, limitations on the information available to support planning, certain negative effects of group dynamics, and the implications for various units of decisions being made in the planning process.

DYNAMIC AND COMPLEX ENVIRONMENTS

When businesses operate in environments that are complex and change rapidly, the very complexity of the environment can impair planning. In Chapter 4 we saw that the rate of change and the complexity of factors contributing to that change have increased substantially for business organizations. Because the planning process usually requires some form of environmental assessment or prediction about future conditions, the rate and complexity of environmental change can create a major barrier to meaningful planning. Examples abound: A rapid decline in interest rates in the mid-1980s necessitated significant changes in businesses' capital investment plans. Most sought to accelerate those plans, which in turn changed other functional plans within those companies. Terrorist actions in the

Because of the risk associated with international travel in the mid-1980s, many college students chose to take advantage of the special stand-by programs offered by domestic airlines and to spend their summer vacations exploring the United States instead of traveling abroad. (Chuck Fishman/ Woodfin Camp)

mid-1980s dramatically altered worldwide business and vacation travel, which spelled major changes for lodging and travel businesses worldwide. And the 1986 amendments to the Resource Conservation and Recovery Act increased the number of businesses classified as generating some regulated form of hazardous waste from 200,000 to over 2.5 million in the United States alone. In each case, a rapid change in an environmental factor radically altered the plans of many businesses or obstructed their planning processes.

CONSTRAINTS AND LACK OF INFORMATION

Constraints on what an organization or work unit can do are another major barrier to effective planning. For example, Apple had a limited sales force and distribution system around which to plan an effective response to IBM's entry into the personal computer market. A product design group within an organization may be required to "buy" its component parts from a specific company subsidiary, even though more effective parts are available on the open market.

Lack of information can also constrain effective planning. For example, a financial management team developing plans to improve cash flow would be inhibited by incomplete information on sending invoices and receiving payments from specific customers. A marketing and operations group seeking to redesign and price certain services would be more effective in that planning effort if it were in possession of systematically collected information on the prices charged by relevant competitors and the buyer response to those competitors' services than if it had only sporadic information about its own costs. When the firm or unit is constrained by limited information, inaccuracy hampers the planning effort. When limited organizational capabilities plague the firm, the result is often a reduction in the options available, which dampens the motivation of the participants.[10]

GROUP DYNAMICS

Groups are common vehicles for planning. They are good for encouraging the airing of diverse views, shared decision making, and commitment. But the group approach can also generate planning problems.

1. There is a tendency for individuals in groups to be willing to accept high-risk decisions they would not have endorsed singly.

2. Interacting groups often become fixed on one train of thought for long periods of time, to the exclusion of alternatives.

3. Individuals tend to participate in discussions only to the extent that they view themselves as equally competent with others.

4. Even though the more expert group members may not express criticism, others tend to expect that they will and thus hold back their own ideas.

5. Lower-level managers often are inhibited and go along with the ideas of their superiors, even though in their own minds they have better solutions.

6. Group pressures for conformity and the implied threat of some kind of punishment for deviation are almost inevitable.

7. More dominant individuals tend to monopolize and control the group with the result that the ideas of others are lost.

8. Groups tend to devote time to their own maintenance and survival and to the members getting along with each other; this detracts from the effectiveness of their decision making.

9. Groups have a tendency to move to quick decisions, short-circuiting the search for further relevant information.[11]

Certainly groups will remain important in planning, but managers should remember that certain dynamics associated with group decision making represent potential barriers to effective planning.

ORGANIZATIONAL RESISTANCE TO CHANGE

Planning implies that changes may be made in the way things are done, priorities set, resources distributed, decisions made, and influence exerted within an organization. The prospect of such fundamental changes to the status quo can make people apprehensive. Work groups uneasy about the outcome of planning decisions may go to great extremes to shape those decisions in ways that protect their special organizational interests, regardless of the need to make the best decision from an overall organizational viewpoint. This resistance to change is a major obstacle to effective planning.

In addition to threatening present power relationships within an organization, planning may highlight conflicts caused by struggles for power and/or capital allocations. For example, there is a natural conflict among the needs of various functional groups—production, sales, finance, and so on. Similar conflicts arise between staff groups at different levels in an organization, between divisions and headquarters, and between "competing" divisions (where they are even encour-

---

Guidelines for Management Practice

Action plans may appeal to most operating managers, but often these managers do not use them. There are two main reasons for this. Either such plans are not linked to the unit's day-to-day activities, or there are formidable barriers to planning. Fortunately, operating managers can overcome both of these problems if they are aware of the barriers to the effective creation of action plans and do everything possible to overcome them. It is important that managers learn to recognize the common symptoms of the following barriers:

1. *Priority of day-to-day problems.* This barrier is often present when subordinates always talk about daily problems but seldom concern themselves with progress against a plan.

2. *A lack of planning skills.* Ask your subordinates to provide copies of recent plans. If they cannot, or if you find their plans inadequate, they probably have weak planning skills.

3. *Reluctance to set objectives and plans.* Reluctance to set objectives and plans is certainly an indication of a barrier. Subordinates who hesitate to plan usually are unsure of their planning responsibilities, do not know how to plan, or prefer to avoid distinct and visible accountability.

4. *Organizational resistance to change.* Preference for preserving the status quo gets stronger at the organizational level.

Managers who anticipate and watch carefully for signs of these barriers are in a better position to prevent or overcome them.

aged). These sources of conflict make managers reluctant to plan, because they fear that the results will put them at a disadvantage. Change, and the management of it, are examined in detail in Chapter 12.

Overcoming Barriers to Planning

The individual and organizational barriers to planning can be significant, but planning is any manager's most important role, and fortunately, it is possible to overcome barriers to planning. Several ways in which managers can overcome barriers to planning are discussed below.

1. *Top-management support and involvement.* Effective planning must start at the top of the organization. Top managers must visibly and concretely take the lead in establishing the importance of planning through their involvement in planning activities. They must be sensitive to (or be made aware of) the presence of barriers to planning within their organization and take action to remove any obstacles. In fact, a visible and serious commitment to planning on the part of top managers serves in and of itself to remove or reduce many of the barriers to planning.

2. *Leadership in planning.* An objective is met when someone is personally responsible for meeting it. This managerial truism suggests an important strategy for overcoming planning barriers: Someone needs to be specifically responsible for each planning effort. The CEO may take responsibility for strategic planning, and other managers need to be similarly identified as responsible for specific plans throughout the organizational structure.

3. *Training in planning.* Finding effective planning "leaders" and overcoming anti-planning biases are encouraged when managers are trained in planning skills. Barriers associated with fear of failure, lack of confidence, or unwillingness to relinquish attractive alternatives are reduced in companies that have well-communicated planning processes and that offer systematic training in the skills necessary to planning.

4. *A communication system.* Barriers to planning are lowered when procedures are in place to help people obtain and share information relevant to planning. For example, a guideline calling for information sharing—to include such practices as distributing critical, decision-related information or analyses one week in advance of each meeting—reduces conflict and improves understanding among the members of a planning group. The same is true on a broader, organizational level. Companies that organize information and make it available to managers for planning and decision-making purposes generate more effective plans. (Chapter 20 discusses information management systems in detail.)

5. *Link planning to the reward system.* Individual biases against planning are reduced when planning commitments are a regular component of the company's reward system. Linking individual and unit rewards to the accomplishment of objectives that were set in the planning process increases the attention paid to planning activities. Commitment to planning is further enhanced when rewards are partially allocated merely on the basis of participation in planning, regardless of the degree to which goals were met. For example, Jack Breen had department managers provide recognition (wall plaques, newsletter reports) and

small bonuses to supervisors who made an active, substantive contribution in their departmental planning efforts to determine the best ways to cut costs and increase productivity, regardless of whether these objectives were actually achieved.

6. *Encourage participation and develop group management skills.* Managers and operating personnel are usually more fully committed to plans that they have helped to shape than to those that are simply imposed on them. They often have important information to contribute, and it usually becomes their responsibility to implement the plan, so their involvement and participation prove critical. Because participation connotes a group process, it is also important to overcome barriers associated with group dynamics. Managers responsible for the group effort should encourage information sharing within the group, ensure that each group member has an opportunity to contribute, establish a norm of constructive comments, and allow time for people to generate creative ideas and express them without fear of criticism. (A thorough discussion of group dynamics and techniques for managing groups effectively appears in Chapter 16.)

7. *Develop contingency plans.* A contingency plan is an alternative course of action that would be appropriate and practicable in the face of a specific event or set of events that the original plan assumed would *not* occur. Contingency planning is particularly useful when the firm operates in a highly complex and dynamic environment. For example, many oil companies suffered serious problems as a result of overcommitments in domestic oil exploration and drilling when oil prices plummeted in 1986. As a result, several of these companies have had financial and operating managers develop specific contingency plans for moving into and out of exploration commitments depending on future trends in the volatile price of oil.

    Many companies have expanded the idea of contingency planning. For example, Heinz, United Airlines, Dow Chemical, and Waste Management have recently devised new "crisis-management" plans and set up "SWAT" (Special Work Action) teams that can swing into action when disaster strikes.[12] Not only do these companies have a preset contingency plan, but they also designate certain people as members of a team that immediately moves into action when a crisis occurs, coordinating the company's response and adjusting the contingency plan as necessary.

8. *Address resistance openly.* Perhaps the worst way to reduce resistance to planning is to ignore that resistance. Ignoring it communicates a sense of disinterest or disregard for what may be legitimate concerns or misunderstandings. Effective managers seek to bring resistance to planning out into the open and deal with it constructively.

9. *Recognize the limitations of planning.* Planning cannot solve all of an organization's problems. Often, some resistance to planning comes from individuals who have experienced the limitations of planning without also experiencing its benefits. They can represent a significant barrier to planning when they look on the current planning effort as just another "pie in the sky" exercise. Managers should recognize that good planning does not ensure success and should make their subordinates and other participants in planning aware that planning has its limits.

Guidelines for Management Practice

Here are a few specific ways in which managers can put into effect the techniques we have noted for overcoming anti-planning tendencies.

1. *Obtain top-management support and involvement.* Ask your boss to okay your work group's plans. Have your boss attend planning meetings occasionally and specifically recognize what subordinates have accomplished in their planning efforts.

2. *Ensure leadership and accountability for planning.* Make sure someone is responsible for each major planning task or project plan. Regularly review his or her results.

3. *Provide training in planning skills.* Personally assist subordinates in planning. Send subordinates to training programs on planning.

4. *Set up a planning communication system.* Make sure everyone in your work group is familiar with all key objectives, understands the plans the group has generated, and knows who is responsible for each key assignment.

5. *Link planning to the reward system.* Make sure that "results-compared-to-plan" is an important criterion in reviewing and rewarding subordinate performance.

6. *Encourage participation and develop group skills.* Ask people to participate. Insist that they do. Help them overcome any hesitation to speak up in a group.

7. *Develop contingency plans.* Recognize potential contingencies and indicate in some way how the plan would change if each such contingency occurred.

8. *Address resistance to change openly and directly.* Provide ample opportunity for subordinates to express their views. Raise questions in planning meetings about how your subordinates feel about proposed changes and how their subordinates feel.

9. *Recognize the limitations of planning.* Planning is only one aspect of producing results. Make sure everyone knows this.

Review of the Learning Objectives

Having studied this chapter, you should be able to respond to the learning objectives with extensions of the following brief answers:

1. **Describe the role of action plans in implementing strategic decisions.**

   Once objectives have been identified and long-term strategies have been selected, managers (particularly operating managers) must develop detailed guidelines that initiate and control organizationwide action. These guidelines, or action plans, ensure that people responsible for accomplishing long-term and short-term objectives understand what they need to do and the parameters within which they should operate to achieve those objectives. Action plans also provide a mechanism by which top managers obtain reassurance that organizational action is consistent with the intent of their strategic plans.

2. **Identify and describe three types of action plans.**

   A *functional plan* is a description of the specific actions to be taken in the immediate future by personnel responsible for that particular functional area. *One-time plans* are plans developed to carry out a course of action that is not likely to be repeated in the future, usually a special program or project. The third type of action plan is called a standing plan. *Standing plans* are designed to guide the decisions and actions of personnel involved in frequently recurring activities.

3. Cite important guidelines for the effective use of one-time plans and standing plans.

Managers develop more effective *one-time plans* when they (1) identify the total set of activities involved in completion of the program or project and specify a tentative deadline for completion, (2) divide the total set of activities into meaningful steps, (3) identify any steps and activities that must occur in a specific sequence, (4) assign responsibility for each step to appropriate managers and groups, (5) determine what resources are needed for each step, (6) obtain a realistic estimate of the time necessary to complete each step, (7) estimate starting and completion dates, and (8) assign target dates for completion of each step and allocate the necessary resources. Managers should use *standing plans* when there is a need to (1) establish indirect control over independent action, (2) promote uniform handling of similar activities, (3) ensure quick decisions, (4) help institutionalize basic aspects of organizational behavior, (5) reduce uncertainty in repetitive and day-to-day decision making, (6) counteract resistance to or rejection of chosen strategies by organizational members, (7) offer a predetermined answer to routine problems, or (8) afford managers a mechanism for avoiding hasty and ill-conceived decisions in changing operations.

4. Identify barriers to effective action planning.

Five key barriers to planning are the tendency to give priority to day-to-day problems, a lack of planning skills, the reluctance of some to set objectives and commit themselves to plans, dynamic and changing environments, personal resistance to change, constraints and lack of information, certain aspects of group dynamics, and organizational resistance to change.

5. Summarize the key guidelines for overcoming barriers to planning.

Nine basic guidelines through which managers can overcome planning barriers are as follows: (1) Ensure top-management support *and* involvement. (2) Assign leadership and accountability for planning. (3) Provide training in planning skills. (4) Set up a planning communication system. (5) Link planning to the reward system. (6) Encourage participation and develop group skills. (7) Develop contingency plans. (8) Address resistance to change openly and directly. (9) Recognize the limitations of planning.

Key Terms and Concepts

After having completed your study of Chapter 8, "Planning and Implementation," you should have mastered the following terms and concepts:

action plan	financial plan	program plan	policy	rules and
functional plan	POM plan	project plan	standard operating	regulations
marketing plan	one-time plan	standing plan	procedure	barriers to planning

Questions for Discussion

1. How are action plans different from strategic plans? How are they related?

2. Explain the differences between functional plans, one-time plans, and standing plans. Give an illustration of each type of plan.

3. What guidelines in the use of standing plans would you recommend to a practicing manager?

4. Describe several major barriers to planning. Illustrate each one.

5. Describe nine ways to overcome barriers to planning. Illustrate each one.

Notes

1. "The Tough So-and-So Who Saved Sherwin-Williams," *Business Week,* May 5, 1986, p. 88.

2. R. B. Robinson, Jr., J. Logan, and J. A. Pearce, II, "Planning Activities Related to Independent Retail Firm Performance," *American Journal of Small Business* 11, no. 1 (1987): 1–12; R. B. Robinson, Jr., J. Logan, and M. Salem, "Strategic versus Operational Planning in Small Retail Firms," *American Journal of Small Business* 10, no. 3 (1986): 7–16. For a review of related studies, see R. B. Robinson, Jr., and P. McDougall, "Patterns of Operational Planning," *Academy of Management Proceedings,* San Diego, 1985.

3. Based on discussions with Bankers Trust executives in charge of the product development team.

4. A. Randolph and B. Z. Posner, *Effective Project Planning and Management: Getting The Job Done* (Englewood Cliffs, N.J.: Prentice-Hall, 1988).

5. P. Meising and J. Wolfe, " The Art and Science of Planning at the Business-Unit Level," *Management Science* 31 (1985): 773–781.

6. H. Mintzberg, *The Nature of Managerial Work* (New York: Harper & Row, 1973).

7. D. Gray, "Uses and Misuses of Strategic Planning," *Harvard Business Review* 64, no. 1 (1986): 89–97.

8. R. K. Bresser and R. C. Bishop, "Dysfunctional Effects of Formal Planning: Two Theoretical Explanations," *Academy of Management Review* 8 (1983): 588–599.

9. G. Steiner, *Strategic Planning* (New York: Free Press, 1979). A useful recent treatment of this issue is found in D. J. Power, M. J. Gannon, M. A. McGinnes, and D. M. Schweiger, *Strategic Management Skills* (Reading, Mass.: Addison-Wesley, 1986).

10. C. B. Shrader, L. Taylor, and D. R. Dalton, "Strategic Planning and Organizational Performance: A Critical Appraisal," *Journal of Management* 10 (1985): 149–171.

11. A. H. Van de Ven and A. L. Delbecq, "Nominal versus Interacting Group Processes for Committee Decision-Making Effectiveness," *Academy of Management Journal* 14, no. 2 (June 1971).

12. "How Companies Are Learning to Prepare for the Worst," *Business Week,* December 23, 1985, p. 74.

Cohesion Incident 8-1
Developing an Action Plan for Maid Turnover

Because of Roger's experience in the motel industry, few problems arose in the first few months after Charles's arrival in Graniteville. In fact, Charles was truly impressed by how well-organized Roger was and how casual and relaxed he was in handling any problem that arose. One day over coffee, Charles mentioned to Roger that he admired Roger's ability to get things done with what looked like a minimum of effort. Roger replied, "Charles, I've always remembered what I saw in the paper a few years ago. It went something like this: 'Those who fail to plan, plan to fail.' In fact, I've discovered that the more time I spend planning, the more time I seem to have to complete my plan."

Roger continued to elaborate on the importance of planning and explained how he usually spends the first hour of each day planning exactly what he hopes to accomplish that particular day and trying to anticipate any problems that may occur.

He suggested that Charles work with him to formulate a plan to address a situation that had recently grown more serious and could eventually become a real problem area: the rate of turnover among the maids.

Because of the size of the Journey's End Inn, ten maids were kept busy each day changing linens and cleaning rooms. During the past year, it had grown increasingly difficult to keep the same staff of maids. None of the current maids had been on the job for more than six months, and the rates of turnover for the past six months had been as follows:

	Feb.	March	April	May	June	July
Rate of Turnover	22%	24%	38%	30%	32%	32%

Very little training was involved, so the high turnover rate was more of a nuisance than anything else. And Roger had a stack of applications in his file of potential employees. However, the paperwork that hiring entailed was time-consuming, and occasionally overtime had to be paid when the staff was not at full strength and some maids were asked to work extra hours.

Roger asked Charles to formulate a plan that would help solve the high turnover rate among the maids. "Charles, between now and next week, go through the four basic steps in the planning process and jot down a few items to get us started. I'll do the same and we'll compare our notes before we draw up our plan."

As Charles went about his duties for the rest of the day, he contemplated how to begin his new assignment.

Discussion Questions

1. List the basic steps in planning, and identify the type of action plan Charles should develop.

2. Comment on the statement Roger quoted: "Those who fail to plan, plan to fail."

3. What is the relationship between objectives and planning? Will objectives be important in Charles's plan? Give an example.

4. Outline what elements you think Charles's plan to solve the maid turnover problem should contain.

Cohesion Incident 8-2
A New Planning Assignment

Leslie Phillips had just returned from a two-day seminar in New York on "Developing Action Plans—Getting Results Through Careful Implementation." Her boss had suggested that she attend. On her desk lay a note from her boss, Eileen Thompkins, asking her to set aside Wednesday morning for the two to meet. Leslie wondered what she wanted to talk about.

On Wednesday Leslie went to Eileen's office immediately upon arriving at work. She welcomed her, closed the door, and opened their meeting with this comment: "Leslie, I sent you to that seminar for several reasons. First, I wanted to reward you for work well done. Second, I wanted to develop your skills. Finally, I wanted to provide some background to help you with a specific planning assignment I have for you."

They talked for a while about the seminar, and then Eileen told Leslie about the particular assignment she had in mind. "Leslie, I've got several issues that I want you to help me solve. I think the solutions involve plans of one sort or another. I hope the seminar helped prepare you to help me and our department solve these problems and issues. Let me tell you about them."

Eileen then described five basic problems she wanted Leslie to work on: "First, several departments, such as engineering and production, want to be involved more fully in our market research activities. Specifically, they would like to be involved—often in an 'approving' capacity—in every step from design through execution and interpretation of our market research. I'm not sure how to accommodate them and still avoid disruption of the good work our people do.

"Second, as you know, Leslie, our people are often required to travel to key cities in conducting our market research. I've become increasingly concerned about reports that several people are inviting their spouses or partners and taking a 'half vacation' at the company's expense. How can we stop that?

"Third, John Shuford, our accountant, continually complains in our manager meetings that employee expense vouchers are not being filled out properly. He seems particularly concerned about people in sales and market research getting $200 to $1,000 advances and subsequently turning in poorly documented expense vouchers. I'm tired of his gripes. What can we do?

"Fourth, Jackson Stafford in the Industrial Division has urgently requested a crash market research effort to use in a presentation one month from now in which he hopes to persuade the executive committee to come up with another $1.5 million for his new diesel injector system. I told him you and I would provide a full outline of a proposed research program and a preliminary budget next Monday.

"Finally, the annual planning cycle is under way, and in one month I'm due to present our plan for the role of the Market Research Department in the overall marketing area for next year. Would you please give me your initial thoughts by next Tuesday?"

That said, Eileen asked Leslie whether she had any questions. After asking a few questions, Leslie returned to her office to open her mail and start the day.

Discussion Questions

1. What types of plans would be best suited to each of these five assignments?

2. Explain what you think each plan would look like.

3. What questions would you ask Eileen in getting guidance for completing these assignments?

Management Development Exercise 8
Evaluating Action Plans

Experience suggests that there are ten key considerations in developing effective action plans. Use them to evaluate the effectiveness of your action plans by circling Y (yes) or N (no) for each criterion.

1. Upper management supports the action plan.   Y   N

2. The action plan is integrated into the company's strategic plan.   Y   N

3. Responsibility for the action plan is fixed and understood.   Y   N

4. The action plan leaves room for managers to exercise judgment.   Y   N

5. Accounting and planning jargon is held to a minimum.   Y   N

6. Care has been taken to ensure that the action plan does not become
   complex, cumbersome, or restrictive.   Y   N

7. The action plan clearly defines standards against which performance
   is to be measured.   Y   N

8. The action plan has been developed with input from all who must
   implement it.   Y   N

9. The action plan is a meaningful document.   Y   N

10. The action plan is referred to in performance evaluation and reward.   Y   N

Your instructor will explain how to score and interpret this exercise.

Managerial Planning Techniques

Your study of this chapter will enable you to do the following:

1. Define the term *forecasting*.
2. Cite two basic types of forecasting, and identify five forecasting techniques that managers often use.
3. Describe linear programming (LP), and explain how managers use it to assist in planning.
4. Describe two fundamental techniques used by managers in scheduling key activities.

Learning Objectives

Mack Truck Moves for Efficiency

Mack Truck started construction of its major North American production facility in 1987 in Winnsboro, South Carolina. Mack executives had decided to close down their Pennsylvania plant and build in South Carolina because of its convenient location, support industries, and favorable local wage structures.

Mack's decision was hardly unexpected. High wage levels and other costs had contributed to Mack's declining position in an increasingly competitive worldwide truck market. After months of talks with the United Auto Workers failed to produce the concessions that Mack named as its price for remaining at its facility in Allentown, Pennsylvania, the company announced that a move out of state was imminent. Mack executives said that the company would produce more trucks per week in the South Carolina facility—seventy, compared with fifty-two at Allentown—with 800 fewer employees! Mack executives expected to combine new technology with basic management planning techniques (programming and scheduling) to achieve near optimal productivity.

Cost savings further supported the move to Winnsboro. There were no automobile manufacturing businesses in South Carolina for direct comparison, but the average hourly wage for a production worker in the state was $7.62, compared

Mack Truck's new production facility in Winnsboro, S.C., is one of the world's most modern truck manufacturing plants. (Courtesy of Mack Truck)

with a national average of $9.54 an hour. Fringe benefits were estimated to add another 35 percent of those totals. Members of the United Auto Workers union at Mack's Allentown plant made $23 an hour, including fringe benefits.

Another advantage of the move for Mack was lower costs for electricity. The Edison Electric Institute estimated that Mack would pay a $274,405 electric bill in Pennsylvania. It would pay $224,593 in South Carolina.

Karen Ubelhart, a capital goods analyst who follows Mack for Oppenheimer & Co., believes the lower labor costs and the modernization that go with Mack's move to the Winnsboro facility bode well for the company. "It'll certainly make them a more viable long-term player," she says. Mack forecasts annual pre-tax savings of $80 million from the relocation, says Ubelhart, or about $57 million after taxes. "That's over a dollar a share—a pretty big number, if they can execute it well." "Executing it well" will require, among other things, sound application of such basic managerial planning techniques as forecasting, linear programming, and scheduling.

In deciding to relocate a major truck manufacturing facility to Winnsboro, South Carolina, Mack Truck executives designed the plant to produce two different kinds of trucks. One truck, actually called a "tractor," and the mainstay of the industry, is designed to pull the freight-hauling trailers commonly seen on highways across America. The second truck, actually called a "short-haul bus," is designed to transport goods and people on short, intracity routes. As construction of the facility neared an end and a new work force was being trained to start production in 1990, Mack executives faced several decisions. First, they needed to decide how many tractors and how many short-haul buses to produce each year. Second, they needed to carefully coordinate the production process to ensure efficiency in receiving supplies, producing vehicles, and distributing finished trucks to their international network of dealers.[1]

Introduction

The previous three chapters have described three fundamental planning responsibilities shouldered by managers at Mack Truck and every other company. These managers must repeatedly chart the strategic direction of their company, set objectives that reflect those strategic plans, and formulate short-range action plans to guide the implementation of strategic decisions at the operating level. Mack Truck's decision to relocate to Winnsboro and its time table for implementing this decision provide a specific example of the execution of these planning responsibilities. In discharging these planning responsibilities—particularly those associated with efficiently and effectively operating the Winnsboro plant—Mack managers enlisted specific planning tools and techniques. This chapter discusses three basic quantitative and qualitative techniques that are necessary to effective planning.

Managers at the Winnsboro plant relied on these three basic planning techniques to address key decisions described in the opening case. They first used *forecasting* to predict the level of demand for each type of Mack truck. In so doing, they tried to take into account competitive conditions, technological changes, economic conditions, and historical demand levels experienced by Mack Truck. Second, they used *linear programming* to select the most profitable "mix" of the two types of trucks on the basis of the different costs associated with each and the range of demand forecasted for each vehicle. The use of these two techniques enabled them to make their first decision: how many tractors and how many short-haul buses to produce in 1990. Once this decision was made, plant managers needed to organize and coordinate each step in the process of producing and delivering the tractors and short-haul buses to be manufactured in 1990. To accomplish this, plant managers relied on a variety of *scheduling techniques* that yielded useful charts; targeted critical, interrelated activities; and specifically set forth the responsibilities everyone would have to assume and the time constraints they would have to honor to accomplish every step in producing their 1990 quotas of tractors and short-haul buses.

Forecasting, linear programming, and scheduling are techniques managers frequently use to accomplish their planning responsibilities. Entry-level managers regularly encounter the need to use one or more of these techniques in their routine operational planning and their development of unit plans for the upcoming year. Each technique is fully explained and illustrated in this chapter, starting with forecasting.

Forecasting

What Is Forecasting?

Forecasting is attempting to state beforehand what will happen in the future. A **forecast** is a prediction or estimate of future conditions. Many decisions that managers make require that they "factor in" forecasts about future conditions. Nissan's decision to build a $1 billion plant in Smyrna, Tennessee, was based in part on its management forecast of the future demand for small trucks in North America. McDonald's decision to invest heavily in the development of highly automated restaurants was based in part on management's forecast of a future scarcity of minimum-wage labor. General Motors's $2.6 billion acquisition of Electronic

Data Systems was based in part on expert forecasts of the extensive use of computer technology in the manufacture and operation of automobiles.

What Do Managers Forecast?

Managers forecast in order to arrive at premises on the basis of which they develop plans, make decisions, and solve problems. So managers forecast future events or the future condition of key factors that will affect the outcome of actions they must plan and decisions they must make in the present. The western regional manager for Holiday Inns may forecast business travel and leisure travel activity through 1992 in key western cities to help her decide where to locate new inns in her territory over a three-year period. Executives at Mack Truck Company forecasted the labor force that would be available before building a new production facility in Winnsboro, South Carolina.

These examples suggest the variety of factors for which managers develop forecasts. Managers are particularly concerned with forecasting the future state of key environmental forces such as those we noted in Chapter 4. Three types of forecasts that many business organizations rely on are technological, economic, and demand (sales) forecasts.[2]

TECHNOLOGICAL FORECASTS

Technological forecasts usually focus on the rate of technological progress or the nature of technological developments in areas related to a business's core technologies. Computer manufacturers want to know how fast the capacity of memory chips is increasing. Manufacturers whose production processes generate toxic wastes or by-products want to keep abreast of new developments in the reduction and disposal of hazardous waste.[3]

Technological changes will provide many companies with new products and materials to offer for sale, and other businesses will face competition from those companies. The incorporation of digital electronics into watches opened up a whole new market for semiconductor firms such as Texas Instruments. At the same time, traditional watch companies lost over 30 percent of their watch market to these new competitors. And even if the product remains unchanged, technological changes in production processes can render large capital investments obsolete. Virtually the entire U.S. steel industry has seen new technologies (developed primarily abroad) render it noncompetitive as a world steel supplier.

ECONOMIC FORECASTS

The future state of the economy, inflation rates, and interest rates are factors that profoundly influence the success of future business activities. Current decisions about whether to invest in new facilities, to step up or cut back on plant capacity, and to expand or contract the work force are shaped by these **economic forecasts**.

DEMAND FORECASTS

The **demand forecast** (or **sales forecast**) gives the expected level of demand for the company's products or services throughout some future period. It is fundamental to the company's planning and control decisions. A company's demand forecast affects all its decisions about where to allocate resources, expand capacity, reduce or increase investment, and develop people, just to mention a few areas in which demand is critical. "In Practice 9-1" illustrates hospital bed demand infor-

---

In Practice 9-1

STUDY: ONE IN TEN OF NATION'S HOSPITALS TO CLOSE BY 1995

One out of every ten U.S. hospitals is likely to close by 1995 because of declining admissions and shorter stays, according to a study by one of the nation's largest accounting firms. The study released recently by Arthur Andersen & Co. also predicted a decline in doctors' incomes in the next eight years and continued problems in providing health care to the nation's poor.

The survey polled more than 1,600 leading officials in the fields of medicine, government, insurance, and consumer affairs about trends in the U.S. health-care system through 1995.

Andersen officials said their predictions on hospital closings was based on a continuing drop in hospital admissions and a decline in the length of the average hospital stay.

Nationwide, a 10 percent closing rate for hospitals would mean that 700 hospitals would close by 1995. That would be a 69 percent increase over the 459 U.S. hospitals that closed from 1976 to 1986, said Tom Bradley, a health-care specialist in Andersen's Miami office.

The report also predicted that:

- Future health policy will be driven more by cost than by quality.
- Consumers will pay more for the level of health care they now receive.
- Employers will be forced to provide health insurance for all their workers.

"Our national health-care system clearly will be driven by dollar concerns, rather than by people concerns," said Stanley Wesbury, president of the 21,000-member American College of Healthcare Executives, which co-sponsored the study.

Robert Clyde, a partner at Anderson and co-chairman of the study, said successful marketing will determine which hospitals survive. "The hospitals that most effectively communicate the quality of their care will be the ones that succeed in the 1990s," Clyde said.

According to a related Associated Press report, officials at several rural Georgia hospitals say their institutions are threatened by the same pressures that may shut down 10 percent of the nation's hospitals by 1995.

"I do agree that there will be [hospital closings] in Georgia within the next five years," Vernon Griffin, administrator of Turner County Hospital in Ashburn, said Wednesday. "They will have to affiliate with larger facilities or close the doors." His hospital, a forty-bed facility in Ashburn, faces a low patient census and rising bills and has begun negotiations on a management contract with a not-for-profit subsidiary of Tift General Hospital, a 168-bed facility in neighboring Tift County.

LaVilla Bryan, administrator of the fifty-bed Putnam County Hospital, said proposed Medicare rules reducing what hospitals are paid for outpatient services could damage rural facilities. "You will see rural hospitals close. At least 50 percent of their patients are Medicare or Medicaid," she said. "Our census is down somewhat, but our outpatient services have filled in the gap. . . . We're not closing, but if they keep cutting, I don't know what's down the road."

Federal cutbacks, increasing technological costs, and competition are forcing hospitals to improve their business practices, said Steve Johnson, administrator of Perry Hospital. The public also must decide how much tax support a hospital is worth, he said. Another administrator agreed that a hospital's health depends on community support.

Source: Adapted from *Courier Herald*, July 28, 1987, p. 1. Reprinted courtesy of the *Courier Herald* (Dublin, Georgia).

mation generated by the Big-Eight accounting firm, Arthur Andersen, for selected hospital clients.

Numerous factors influence the demand for a company's products or services; Figure 9-1 shows some of them. To develop a demand forecast is to predict the future impact of some (or all) of these factors and to translate that prediction into a forecast of future demand. Other factors, such as previous demand and demographic changes, are often used by company managers as a basis for developing demand forecasts.[4]

The techniques that managers can use to develop forecasts are broadly classified into two types: qualitative and quantitative. Because of the importance of demand forecasts in every business, our discussion of forecasting techniques will focus on their use in generating demand (or sales) forecasts.[5]

Qualitative Forecasting Techniques

Forecasts can range from spur-of-the-moment hunches to the solutions of complex mathematical equations.[3] Often the simplest (and not the least accurate) are those methods that involve only subjective judgment and no mathematical formulas whatever. Three such **qualitative forecasting techniques** that managers have found most useful are considered in this section. Each method uses a different source for the subjective information it relies on.

JURY OF EXPERT OPINION

The **jury of expert opinion**, also referred to as the **Delphi technique**, involves soliciting opinions or estimates from a panel of "experts" who are knowledgeable about the variable being forecasted. In attempting to develop a sales forecast, a manager in charge of generating a forecast might solicit the opinions of a group ("jury") of company executives about what they think demand for the company's products will be. Then the manager might take the average of these estimates or circulate the various responses to executives involved in the process and seek revised estimates independently or via a group discussion. Regardless of the specific steps involved, this approach relies on the subjective judgments of a knowledgeable group of individuals to forecast or predict what will happen in the future.[7]

In addition to being useful in the creation of a sales or demand forecast, this approach is often involved when managers try to predict future technological developments. For example, venture capitalists who are attempting to evaluate the attractiveness of investing in start-up companies often conduct a series of interviews with a panel of four to six independent experts knowledgeable in the technology underlying the products made by the company under consideration. Again, managers are relying on the informed, subjective judgments of a knowledgeable group of individuals to forecast or predict future conditions.[8]

A major advantage of this approach is that it can provide a forecast in a relatively short time. It also brings a variety of viewpoints to bear on the subject and can foster a team spirit.

It has the disadvantage of often requiring the time of highly paid executives or experts and it is subject to biases that spring from individual attitudes and situations.

SALES FORCE ESTIMATES

An approach frequently used in many companies to forecast sales is to have each sales representative estimate sales in his or her territory for the next year. These

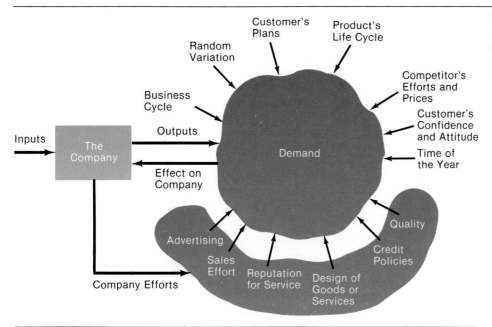

FIGURE 9-1
Some Factors That Affect Demand for a Company's Product or Service

Source: J. B. Dilworth, *Production Operations Management,* 3rd ed. (New York: Random House, 1986), p. 90. Copyright 1986. Reprinted by permission of Random House.

estimates are combined and reviewed at successive levels of the management hierarchy in order to incorporate the opinions of the district managers and the sales management.[9]

Forecasts of this nature have several advantages. They are easily divided by territory, branch, sales representative, or product. Input is provided from company personnel who are directly in touch with the customer. Sales representatives may be more highly motivated when they participate directly in the planning process. And the forecast can be accomplished quickly.

This approach has some disadvantages, however. It is subject to individual biases, such as a personal preference for selling certain types of products. And sales representatives may be unduly influenced by recent market responses. But perhaps its greatest weakness emerges when sales performance objectives are based on the forecast; this may tempt sales representatives to underestimate. Another distortion may arise when the forecast is used as the basis for allocating scarce products, which tempts sales representatives to overestimate in making sales forecasts.

Firms engaged in international business often utilize several of these forecasting techniques to predict some of the basic risks inherent in the countries in which they operate that will affect future demand. Forecasting in an international setting is discussed in "Insights for International Managers 9."

CUSTOMER EXPECTATIONS

A third qualitative technique for forecasting sales is to go outside the company and seek subjective opinions from customers about their future purchasing plans.

━━━━━━━━━━ *Insights for International Managers 9* ━━━━━━━━━━

INTERNATIONAL ENVIRONMENTAL FORECASTING

International managers need regularly to analyze the opportunities and threats to international business in the countries in which they have interest. Their fundamental concern is to forecast the risks associated with protecting their assets and investments in each country as well as risks that might affect their operating profits and cash flow. The following diagram shows the nature and causes of two basic types of international business risks international managers try to forecast:

	Causes	Nature	
Macro Causes	Competing political philosophies (capitalism, socialism, communism) Armed conflicts and internal rebellions Social unrest and disorders New international alliances	Confiscation Nationalization expropriation Damage to property or persons Loss of transfer freedoms ($, ownership, people, goods)	Asset protection/ investment recovery risks
Micro Causes	Changing social mores and values Unstable/depressed economic conditions Vested interest of local quasi-political groups Vested interests of local business groups	High inflation and currency instability Breaches of or unilateral revisions to contracts Discrimination (taxes, subcontracting, etc.) Operating restrictions (Market share, product characteristics, employment, etc.)	Operational profitability/ cash flow risks

Five forecasting approaches are used to predict these two types of international risks. These five forecasting approaches are:

1. Grand Tours—tours of the country or region under consideration by an executive or team of executives from the domestic operations of the company.
2. Old Hands—the use of analyses and forecasts prepared by businesspeople, journalists, educators, and others with years of firsthand experience in the area or country of interest.
3. Delphi Forecasts—Multiple, repeated sampling of a knowledgeable panel of "experts" familiar with the area or country that rank different factors affecting risk.
4. Quantitative Models—Statistical techniques that attempt to predict future conditions of several factors relevant to the area or country based on historical data.

Sales representatives may poll their customers or potential customers about their future needs for the goods and services the company supplies. Direct-mail questionnaires or telephone surveys may be used to obtain the opinions of existing or potential customers.

This method lets managers in on some of the reasoning behind the customers' intentions. Forecasters may obtain user viewpoints on the product's advantages and weaknesses as well as insight into the reasons why some customers are buying, and others failing to buy, the product.

One potential disadvantage of the customer expectations method is that it may annoy some highly valued customers. And, because customer buying expectations are also subject to judgment and error, the method may also instill more confidence than managers really should place in it.

5. Systems Analysis—Constucting a systematic causal chain of actions and events leading from the present to the projected future of the area or country of interest.

The following table shows when use of each forecasting approach is more likely to help the international manager predict the influence of each type of risk on either asset protection or profitability and cash flow.

	Asset Protection and Investment Recovery Opportunities and Threats[a]	Operating Profitability and Cash Flow Opportunities and Threats[a]
Macro risks	grand tours OLD HANDS DELPHI FORECASTS QUANTITATIVE MODELS Systems Analysis	grand tours Old Hands delphi forecasts Quantitative Models Systems Analysis
Micro risks	Grand Tours Old Hands Delphi Forecasts Quantitative Models SYSTEMS ANALYSIS	GRAND TOURS old hands — quantitative models systems analysis

[a]Note: ALL CAPS indicate areas of primary applicability; Initial Caps indicate areas of secondary applicability; no caps indicates areas of tertiary applicability.

Sources: Adapted from H. V. Wortzel and L. H. Wortzel, *Strategic Management of Multinational Corporations: The Essentials* (New York: Wiley, 1985), pp. 149–157; and S. H. Robock, "Political Risk: Identification and Assessment," *Columbia Journal of World Business* 6 (July-August 1971), p. 162; reprinted by permission of the *Columbia Journal of World Business,* Trustees of Columbia University.

Quantitative Forecasting Techniques

Quantitative forecasting techniques use a mathematical expression or model to show the relationship between demand and some independent variable or variables. There are two major types of quantitative forecasting techniques: time-series analysis and causal models.[10]

TIME-SERIES ANALYSIS

A *time series* is a sequence of data points plotted at constant intervals of time. A chain of daily, weekly, or monthly sales data, for example, is a time series. The underlying assumption of time-series analysis is that the past is a good predictor of the future. So a chain of monthly sales figures over several years, for example, is assumed to be a valid basis on which to forecast future sales levels. Time-series analysis is most frequently used when managers have available a lot of historical data and when stable trends and patterns are readily apparent.

A **time-series analysis** "plots" sales (or any other variable under consideration) across specific time intervals and then computes a "best-fit" line describing the sales pattern over time. Extension of this "best-fit" line becomes the basis for the manager's forecast of future sales. Figure 9-2 shows how a forecast based on a three-year time-series analysis might look for Mack Truck.

The process of computing a forecast based on a time-series analysis is much more complicated than simply drawing a line on graph paper to approximate the pattern apparent in historical sales data. Rather, a time-series analysis attempts to identify at least two key components: the trend component and the seasonal component. The *trend component* in a time-series analysis is the general upward or downward movement of the "average" (for example, quarterly sales) over time. The *seasonal component* in a time-series analysis is a recurring fluctuation of demand above and below the trend component that is reliably exhibited each year. For example, demand for Head snow skis has followed a generally upward trend (the trend component) for many years, and that demand has repeatedly been highest in the fall of each year and lowest in the spring (the seasonal component).

You can see from Mack's historical truck sales in Figure 9-2 that a truly accurate time-series analysis should forecast seasonally high demand in the spring and summer. Mathematical techniques are available that enable managers to adjust their forecasts for seasonality. You should be aware that they exist, but detailed coverage of these techniques is beyond the scope of this book. Forecasts allow managers to make both strategic decisions, like whether or not to expand the facility, and operating decisions, such as when to schedule personnel, use temporary student employees, and even take a vacation. Effective managers often find

FIGURE 9-2
A Time-Series Forecast
of Mack Truck Sales

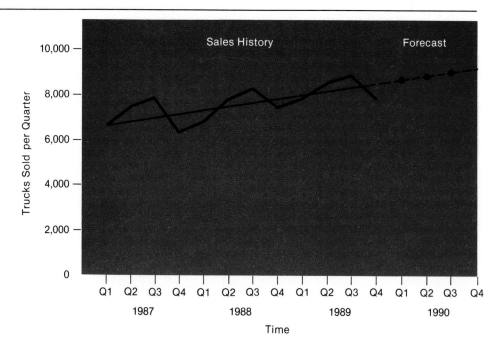

time series analysis incorporating trend and seasonal components to be a useful technique for forecasting future demand.

CAUSAL MODELING

The time-series analysis we described used time as the only independent variable in developing a forecast. Indeed, sales are forecasted solely on the basis of a trend over time. But other variables may also be useful in helping forecasters estimate future demand. For example, the amount of snow predicted to fall in the Colorado Rockies may be as important a "predictor" of demand at Colorado ski resorts as are trends based on historical (time) patterns. **Causal modeling** consists of mathematical techniques by which we use independent variables other than time to develop forecasts. Figure 9-3 summarizes three of the more useful causal modeling techniques. Causal modeling enables forecasters to quantify some of the factors (independent variables) they would probably consider if they were making subjective forecasts.

Causal modeling depends on regression analysis. **Regression models** are statistical equations designed to estimate some variable (such as sales volume) on the basis of one or more "independent" variables believed to have some association with it. For example, marketing managers might develop a regression model to predict the sales volume associated with different advertising expenditures and price levels for key products. The following is a typical regression equation a marketing manager might come up with:

$$y = ax_1 + bx_2 + d$$

where: y = the dependent variable (sales)

x_1 and x_2 = independent variables (such as interest rates and price level)

a and b = weights for the independent variables calculated while developing the regression equation or model

d = a constant calculated at the same time

FIGURE 9-3
A Summary of Causal Modeling Forecasting Techniques

Technique	Purpose of the Technique	Example
Regression models	A statistical procedure used to predict a single variable on the basis of the known or assumed value of one or more other, "independent" variables	Forecast sales of Mack's short-haul trucks on the basis of interest rates, GNP growth, and urban population growth
Econometric modeling	A statistical procedure that uses a series of regression equations to predict major economic trends and conditions	Forecast the level of the 1991–1992 balance of payments in the U.S.
Economic indicators	A regularly repeated regression procedure to predict variables of interest to business and government; usually done monthly by the U.S. Bureau of Statistics	Forecast future increases or decreases in the cost-of-living index

Once the model is developed, a manager can plug in various alternatives for advertising expenditures and price level to compute sales volume (y). The value of y represents the forecast. The regression model is developed on the basis of the past experience of the company.[11]

Econometric modeling is a second type of causal modeling used in managerial forecasting. **Econometric models** use regression techniques at a much broader level in an effort to predict major economic shifts and the potential impact of those shifts on the company. For example, Sears might use changing demographic patterns and regional income levels to predict levels of demand and variation in demand for its retail products and financial services. Econometric models are increasingly used by large brokerage houses and insurance companies to predict trends in various industrial sectors and the future values of specific investment alternatives. A complete econometric model of this sort may require hundreds or even thousands of equations; it is a complex and costly approach to forecasting.

Economic indicators, a third approach to causal modeling, are population statistics or indexes that portray the economic well-being of a specific population. Examples of widely used economic indicators include the rate of inflation, the unemployment rate, and the prime interest rate. Firms such as Mack Truck follow each of these indicators and have generally found that rises in any one are associated with subsequent decreases in demand. Many firms develop regression models to predict future demand on the basis of economic indicators found consistently to be associated with demand for their products or services.[12]

Once managers have forecasted future demand, for example, they often need to answer such questions as, "What is the optimum combination of products we should produce?" or "What mix of resources would maximize profitability?" Questions like these can be answered more effectively with techniques like linear programming. The next section provides a basic overview of linear programming.

Guidelines for Management Practice

We have examined several techniques that managers find useful in developing forecasts of future conditions. The availability of an accurate forecast is often critical to effective managerial planning and decision making.

A key question, of course, is when to use each technique. To answer this question, the manager must ponder a number of issues associated with time, resources required, input available, and output desired. Eight guidelines to help managers choose the best forecasting technique follow.

1. If a forecast is needed urgently, a sales force composite is usually the quickest qualitative forecast technique.

2. A time-series analysis is the quickest quantitative forecast technique as long as past data is available.

3. If managers are asked to compare new and past forecasts on a regular basis, quantitative techniques using computers will make the task easiest.

4. Accuracy can be a problem in any forecast.

5. When using a qualitative technique, managers should be aware that personal bias from a salesperson or customer is the main source of inaccuracy.

6. When using a quantitative technique, accuracy is most affected by the reliability and validity of the quantitative measures the manager employs.

7. Qualitative techniques should be used for only short-to-medium time frames. Quantitative techniques are appropriate for any time frame.

8. The financial costs of quantitative techniques are usually greater than for qualitative techniques.

Linear Programming

What Is Linear Programming?

Linear programming (LP) is a mathematical procedure used to determine the best combination of those resources and activities that are necessary to optimize some objective. LP is one of the most widely used quantitative planning tools for determining how to optimize sales, profits, or the use of resources or time. LP employs graphical methods or algebraic expressions to identify the optimal combination of resources or other factors to achieve a specific objective.

The LP approach requires that a manager identify two quantifiable elements. First, a quantifiable goal or objective to be minimized (such as time, costs, or resources used) or maximized (such as sales, profit, or output) must be identified. And the LP approach requires a set of constraints (such as resources, capacity, or time) that express in quantifiable terms what is available to the manager in her or his efforts to accomplish the objective.[13]

Once the objective to be optimized (or minimized) has been determined, it must be expressed as a linear algebraic equation. The constraints on the resources, capacity, or time available to accomplish that objective must be expressed as a series of linear inequalities. The objectives and constraints are expressed algebraically or diagrammed in graphical form in order to provide a means for the manager to "solve" the problem. Perhaps the best way to explain LP is through a simple example.

Sarina Smith, a recent graduate of Clemson University, took a management trainee position with Mack Truck at the new Winnsboro plant. A production/operations management (POM) major at Clemson, Smith had joined the production planning staff at Mack. One of her first assignments was to use linear programming to determine the "optimal" level at which to produce Mack's two types of trucks—tractors and short-haul buses—per week. Figure 9-4 shows the information that Smith had available in solving this problem.

Each truck has a known profit margin and a demand well in excess of the capacity at Mack's Winnsboro plant. Two critical resources that constrain the Winnsboro plant's capacity to produce these trucks are body metal and work crew time. So Smith's assignment is to identify the number of tractors (T) and buses (B) that should be produced each week to maximize Mack's profit (P). This assignment can be expressed algebraically via the following *objective function*:

$$\text{Profit}_{\text{maximize}} = \$10{,}000T + \$12{,}000B$$

where: T = number of tractors to be produced
   B = number of short-haul buses to be produced

The $10,000 and $12,000 are the profit margins on each tractor and short-haul bus, respectively.

The challenge for Smith, of course, is to maximize profits *within* the constraints portrayed in Figure 9-4. In this example, the two constraints she must plan for are the amount of body metal available per week and the number of work crew hours available to spread across each tractor. Using the information given in Figure 9-4, she created the following algebraic statements, or linear inequalities, to quantify these constraints:

Body metal:	$40T + 20B \leq 400$
Work crew hours:	$8T + 12B \leq 200$

FIGURE 9-4
Production Data for
Mack Truck

	Requirements per Truck		AMOUNT AVAILABLE PER WEEK
ITEM	TRACTORS	BUSES	
Body metal	40 feet	20 feet	400 feet
Work crew hours	8 hours	12 hours	200 hours
Profit margin	$10,000	$12,000	

And because she will recommend producing something at or above zero trucks of each type, these two constraints also apply:

$$T \geq 0$$
$$B \geq 0$$

At this point, Smith can "solve" the problem either graphically or algebraically (by solving a series of linear equations and inequalities). Let's look briefly at both methods.

The Graphical Solution

The graphical method for solving LP problems is used mainly to solve problems involving two decision variables. In the graphical method, we plot the constraints on a graph, as illustrated in Figure 9-5. We would graph the Mack problem by first assuming that the production of each type of truck is maximized when production of the other type is zero. The resulting "solution" or production level is then plotted on a set of coordinate axes.

If no tractors were produced ($T = 0$), then the number of buses (B) that could be produced with the 400 feet of body metal available each week would be found as follows:

$$40T + 20B \leq 400$$
$$40(0) + 20B \leq 400$$
$$20B \leq 400$$
$$B \leq 20$$

And with the same material available, if no buses were produced ($B = 0$), then

$$40T + 20B \leq 400$$
$$40T + 20(0) \leq 400$$
$$40T \leq 400$$
$$T \leq 10$$

These "solutions" or points, ($B = 20$, $T = 0$) and ($B = 0$, $T = 10$), are then plotted on the graph and connected by a line representing the body metal constraint, as shown in Figure 9-5.

The next step in the graphical solution is to deal similarly with the second constraint, work crew time. If no tractors were produced, then

$$8T + 12B \leq 200$$
$$8(0) + 12B \leq 200$$
$$12B \leq 200$$
$$B \leq 16.66$$

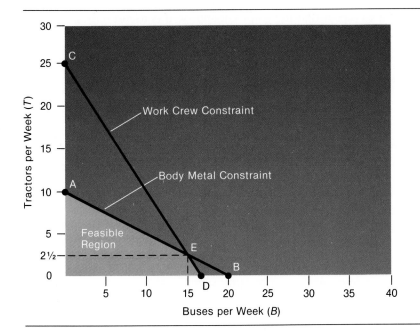

FIGURE 9-5
The Graphical Solution
of a Linear
Programming Problem

And with the same work crew hours available, if no buses were produced, then

$$8T + 12B \leq 200$$
$$8T + 12(0) \leq 200$$
$$8T \leq 200$$
$$T \leq 25$$

These "solutions" or points, $(B = 16.66, T = 0)$ and $(B = 0, T = 25)$, are then plotted and connected by a line representing the work crew hours constraint on weekly production of Mack trucks.

Figure 9-5 shows how the final graphical solution to the Mack plant would look. The shaded area in the graph created by the intersection of the two constraint lines and the two axes, as shown in Figure 9-5, identifies an area that is common to both constraints. This area, known as the *feasible region*, is bounded by points A, E, D, and the zero-point on the axes. Returning to the Mack example, any combination of tractors and buses within that region is "feasible" for the Winnsboro plant to produce each week. The optimal number of tractors and buses that maximizes Mack's profit margin will be defined at one of the four corners of the feasible region. At point B the plant would produce $16\frac{2}{3}$ buses each week ($16.66 \times \$12,000 = \$180,000$ in profit). At point C the plant would produce 10 tractors each week ($10 \times \$10,000 = \$100,000$ in profit). At point E, the intersection of the two constraint lines, the plant would produce $2\frac{1}{2}$ tractors and 15 buses each week ($2.5 \times \$10,000 + 15 \times \$12,000 = \$205,000$ in profit). This last point yields the optimal weekly profit at the Winnsboro plant. It entails using 400 feet of body metal [$2.5(40) + 15(20)$] and 200 work crew hours [$2.5(8) + 15(12)$] each week. The intersection point is usually the optimal solution, but managers might choose a feasible solution for other reasons. For example, corporate management at Mack might insist on a specific number of tractors at Winnsboro, regardless of the optimal combination in terms of plant profitability.

It is important to repeat that the graphical approach is useful only when just two dimensions (such as tractors and buses) apply. If more than two dimensions apply (such as three or more types of Mack trucks), the graphical approach is not practical and the manager must use an algebraic approach. An algebraic approach to solving our simple example is explained in the next section.

The Algebraic Approach

Sarina Smith can also use the series of algebraic expressions she created early in her analysis of the problem to represent the objective function and the two constraints as a basis for determining the appropriate number of tractors and buses to produce each week in order to maximize Mack's weekly profit from the Winnsboro plant.

The first step is to state the two constraint inequalities as a set of simultaneous equations (equations whose variables can simultaneously satisfy all the equations in the set).

$$
\begin{array}{ll}
\text{Body metal:} & 40T + 20B = 400 \\
\text{Work crew hours:} & 8T + 12B = 200
\end{array}
$$

At this point Smith has two equations and two unknowns, but she can use them to create one equation that has one unknown and is easily solved. Once this first unknown is found, it can be substituted into one of the constraint equations, enabling Smith to determine the value of the second unknown. This process is called solving a series of simultaneous equations.

The first step we usually take in solving a series of simultaneous equations is to modify one or both of the equations in such a way that we obtain one pair of variables with the same coefficients. This enables us to subtract one equation from the other and have only one variable in the resulting equation. Continuing with our example,

$$
\begin{array}{lll}
(1) & 40T + 20B = 400 \\
(2) & 8T + 12B = 200
\end{array}
$$

Smith multiplies equation (2) by 5 (to make the coefficients of T equal) and subtracts the new equation, equation (2'), from equation (1).

$$
\begin{array}{lll}
(1) & 40T + 20B = 400 \\
-(2)' & \underline{-40T - 60B = -1000} \\
& \quad\;\; -40B = -600 \\
& \qquad\;\; B = 15
\end{array}
$$

Solving for B as the first unknown shows her that 15 is the optimal number of buses to produce each week. The second step is to substitute this value into either equation (1) or equation (2) by way of solving for the optimal number of tractors. She chooses equation (1) and proceeds as follows:

$$
\begin{array}{ll}
40T + 20(15) = 400 \\
40T + 300 \;\;\;= 400 \\
40T \qquad\quad= 100 \\
T \qquad\quad\;\;= 2\tfrac{1}{2}
\end{array}
$$

Thus the optimal number of tractors to produce each week is $2\tfrac{1}{2}$.

████████████████████ *Guidelines for Management Practice* ████████████████████

Linear programming (LP) is a quantitative technique widely used by operations managers to help them make decisions. You should always consider using LP when making one of the following three types of decisions:

1. *Determining a product or service mix that will maximize company profits under specified conditions.* Say you are faced with this problem: "We can produce or provide A, B, and C (products or services), but we are uncertain what mix would be most profitable." You should use LP to help find the answer.

2. *Determining transportation strategies to move people and goods in a least-cost manner.* When you are faced with several transportation options—rail, air, or truck—for shipping products, purchasing supplies, or using your people, you should enlist LP to help shape an answer.

3. *Determining what combination of worker assignments will maximize worker efficiencies under certain specified conditions.* For example, a sales manager might use LP to help determine the "optimal" levels at which to use an outside, direct-contact sales force and an inside, telephone-contact sales force.

In order to use LP, you *must* be able to do two things:

1. Represent decision alternatives as mathematically expressed "decision" variables.

2. Identify the major limitations and constraints (resources, demand, and so on) *and* be able to express them mathematically.

Finally, we can substitute these two values into the original objective function to determine the optimal level of profitability associated with these two quantities:

$$
\begin{aligned}
\text{Profit}_{\text{maximize}} &= \$10,000T + \$12,000B \\
&= \$10,000(2.5) + \$12,000(15) \\
&= \$205,000 \text{ per week}
\end{aligned}
$$

Just like the result yielded by the graphical approach, the algebraic approach suggests that Mack can achieve an optimal weekly profit margin of $205,000 in Winnsboro by producing $2\frac{1}{2}$ tractors and 15 buses each week.

Once managers have programmed production levels or resource utilization, their planning responsibility does not end. A major, repetitive planning task they must execute effectively to make all the other planning pay off is scheduling. They must schedule the use of people, equipment, resources, and time so that the projects they are executing meet expectations. The next section explains two scheduling techniques useful to managers in meeting these types of expectations.

Scheduling Techniques

A planning responsibility that managers frequently encounter at every organizational level is the need to schedule and coordinate the activities of people and units and the use of resources to get a specific project or task done. When Mack Truck executives decided to introduce a new line of trucks, a large and varied number of tasks, projects, and activities were required. Marketing managers needed to obtain, from potential customers, clearer information about what their transportation needs would be in the 1990s and how they viewed Mack as a source of equipment to meet those needs. Engineering and technical managers needed to undertake the design and development of the new truck. Advertising managers needed to develop a promotional program for introducing the product. As in other organizations, the more effectively and efficiently Mack managers could coordinate the use of people, money, and time, the more successful their new product would be.

Two scheduling techniques that are popular among skilled managers as aids in effectively and efficiently coordinating the use of people, money, and equipment *over time* are Gantt charts and PERT (the program evaluation review technique). Gantt charts are typically used for general scheduling needs. PERT is used to schedule one-time projects. Both respond to the recurring need of every manager to schedule and monitor often complex sets of interrelated activities under resource and time constraints.[14]

Gantt Charts

One of the earliest techniques employed by managers to help them schedule the use of people, resources, and time is the Gantt chart. Developed by Henry Gantt in the early 1900s, the **Gantt chart** is a control chart on which time appears in the horizontal dimension and activities or tasks appear in the vertical dimension. Horizontal bars represent planned schedules and time required for each task, and additional markings on each horizontal bar indicate actual task accomplishment; all are plotted against time.

An example of a Gantt chart developed to control the fabrication of a stand and the installation of an industrial compressor is shown in Figure 9-6. It illustrates the common symbols associated with the use of Gantt charts. The brackets ([and]) show when a task is scheduled to occur. A solid bar shows the extent of actual progress. The "current date" pointer at the bottom of the chart indicates

Both Gantt charts and PERT networks were used extensively by NASA managers in developing the United States space program. (Courtesy of The Johnson Space Center, NASA)

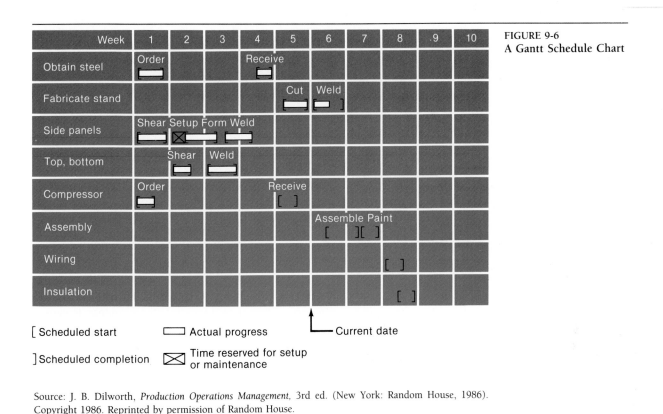

FIGURE 9-6
A Gantt Schedule Chart

[Scheduled start   ⬜ Actual progress   └─ Current date

] Scheduled completion   ⊠ Time reserved for setup
                               or maintenance

Source: J. B. Dilworth, *Production Operations Management,* 3rd ed. (New York: Random House, 1986). Copyright 1986. Reprinted by permission of Random House.

what week (or other unit of time) has already been reached, enabling any manager to look at the chart and determine the current status of the project. For example, the date pointer in Figure 9-6 suggests that progress on the stand is ahead of schedule whereas receipt of the compressor is behind schedule.

Gantt charts can show the plan for, and progress on, virtually any conceivable project or planned performance over time. Kept up to date, they reveal any discrepancy between planned and actual achievement at any given date. Armed with this knowledge, managers can act speedily to make additional resources available to a project that has fallen behind schedule. The Gantt chart can also show degree of conformity between budgeted and actual costs and changes in tasks or activities. Today Gantt charts often include identification of the person(s) responsible for each task to further help managers use the chart as an effective scheduling and control device.

PERT

PERT (the program evaluation review technique) was developed during the late 1950s to help managers schedule and monitor large-scale projects. For example, the construction of a house can be viewed as a project in which the various activities to be completed include pouring the foundation, installing the plumbing and electrical wiring, building the frame, painting the interior, and so on. Developed by the U.S. Navy in an effort to speed up the work of the several thousand contractors involved in creating the first Polaris submarine, PERT is credited with cutting more than two years off the length of time required for the Polaris project![15]

PERT is a planning technique that enables a manager to create an accurate estimate of the time required to complete a project. Managers who use PERT identify all the distinct *activities* necessary to complete a project, *events* that signal completion of those activities, and the *time* necessary to complete each activity. This information is used to create a network diagram, which displays all the activities, events, and times that are involved from the start of the project to its completion. The five fundamental steps in any application of PERT are as follows:[16]

1. Make a list of all activities necessary to the project and the events that will signal completion of each activity.

2. Construct a network diagram that displays the relationships among these activities and events. The key concern here is that the diagram show which activities must precede or follow other activities (what *sequences* must be honored).

3. Calculate the time needed to accomplish each activity.

4. Determine the total time necessary to complete the project and the key sequence of activities that accounts for this amount of time (this key sequence is called the *critical path*).

5. Use the PERT diagram to direct and control the project.

A simple example at the Mack plant serves to illustrate the use of PERT for project planning. Take the case of Fritz Pickens, a Mack manager assigned to establish a four-person personnel recruitment office in Winnsboro prior to construction of the Mack plant. That office's role was to create a visible Mack presence before the plant was built and to generate a large group of potential employees whom Mack managers (in production, administration, maintenance, and so on) could contact as time to open the plant drew nearer.

Pickens decided to use PERT to plan and execute this project. His first step was to create the table of activities and events shown in Figure 9-7. The second thing he did was to create the network diagram shown in Figure 9-8a. Once the diagram was completed, Pickens needed to estimate the time required for each activity. These time estimates are usually calculated by averaging the manager's *most optimistic* estimate of the time required to complete the activity, his or her *most pessimistic* estimate, and the time he or she believes is *most likely* to be required (this estimate is given four times as much weight as either of the others). Expressed mathematically, this estimate of expected time for each activity is

$$\text{Expected time} = \frac{O + 4L + P}{6}$$

$$\text{where:} \quad O = \text{optimistic time estimate}$$
$$L = \text{most likely time estimate}$$
$$P = \text{pessimistic time estimate}$$

The expected time for each activity in Fritz Pickens's project is shown in parentheses in Figure 9-8a; the estimates that these expected times were derived from are given in the accompanying table (Figure 9-8b).

The fourth step Pickens took was to determine how long the entire project should take and what critical sequence of activities (the critical path) would have to be accomplished without any delays for the project to be completed within that

Activity	Description	Events	Immediate Predecessor
		A. Start	
1	Locate office	B. Lease is signed	Start (A)
2	Interview	C. Three people are hired	Start (A)
3	Order furniture	D. Office is furnished	B
4	Develop recruitment material	E. Material is developed	B
5	Train employees	F. Employers know how to recruit	C, E
6	Start recruiting	G. First recruit is hired	D, F

FIGURE 9-7
Activities and Events for Completing Mack's Winnsboro Personnel Office

time. A path in a diagram is a sequence of activities and events that leads from the start to the finish. Three paths can be found in Pickens's diagram. They are the following sequences:

1. A–B–E–F–G

2. A–B–E–F–G

3. A–C–F–G

The length of time each path will take can be determined by summing the times consumed by all the activities on the path. The path with the *longest* time

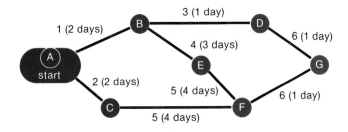

FIGURE 9-8
(a) Mack Project Network Diagram

(b) Activity Time Estimates

Activity	OPTIMISTIC	MOST LIKELY	PESSIMISTIC	$\frac{O + 4L + P}{6}$ Estimate
1	1	2	3	2
2	1	$1\frac{3}{4}$	4	2
3	$\frac{1}{2}$	1	$1\frac{1}{2}$	1
4	2	$2\frac{1}{2}$	6	3
5	$2\frac{1}{2}$	$3\frac{1}{2}$	$7\frac{1}{2}$	4
6	$\frac{1}{2}$	1	$1\frac{1}{2}$	1

■■■■■■■■■■■■■■ *Guidelines for Management Practice* ■■■■■■■■■■■■■■

New managers often come to their jobs trained in linear programming and the use of Gantt charts or PERT. All too frequently, they seem to get immersed in daily pressures and fail to use these planning tools. The following guidelines, condensed from interviews with several such managers, reflect applications and techniques that helped them regain the use of linear programming and scheduling techniques.

1. Except in the most routine, controlled situations, use linear programming as a tool to narrow your range of expectations or to set parameters for decisions.

2. Do not use any planning tool for the sake of the tool. Use it as a means to manage toward a clear, important objective.

3. Do not start diagramming schedules before you have identified a clear objective, listed the activities necessary to accomplish that objective, and estimated the time for each activity.

4. Refer to local office supply stores and catalogs for scheduling boards. They are very convenient to use for Gantt charts.

5. Several excellent software programs are now available to aid you in using linear programming, Gantt charts, and PERT on a regular basis.

---

is the critical path—the least time that *must* be invested to complete the project. For Pickens, the critical path is path 1, which requires ten days to complete.

The PERT diagram is an effective tool to enhance managerial control. For example, Pickens can use this diagram to monitor the progress of his project and the time necessary to complete each activity. Doing so may alert him to problems jeopardizing the timely achievement of certain events or to opportunities to save time in certain activities. Although Pickens's diagram is rather simple, a project involving hundreds of activities becomes quite complicated—a compelling reason to use PERT both to plan the project and to control its execution.

Another network method similar to PERT is CPM (the critical path method). CPM was developed by DuPont managers about the time PERT was being developed by the Navy. The main difference is that CPM is based on the use of known time requirements for activities necessary to a project.

PERT applications can become much more sophisticated than our simple example. Numerous computer programs are available to create PERT diagrams. Some incorporate probability estimates, cost considerations, and complex network capabilities. "Management Development Exercise 9" gives you the opportunity to apply PERT to an unusual project planning assignment.

Review of the Learning Objectives

Having studied this chapter, you should be able to respond to the learning objectives with extensions of the following brief answers:

1. Define the term *forecasting*.

Forecasting is attempting to state beforehand what will happen in the future.

2. **Cite two basic types of forecasting, and identify five forecasting techniques that managers often use.**

Managers use two basic types of forecasts—qualitative forecasts and quantitative forecasts—to predict technological, economic, and sales trends. Three qualitative techniques that managers use to forecast are juries of expert opinion, sales force estimates, and customer expectations. Two quantitative techniques that managers use to forecast are time-series analysis and causal modeling.

3. **Describe linear programming (LP), and explain how managers use it to assist in planning.**

Linear programming incorporates the use of graphical methods and algebraic expressions to identify the optimal product mix or minimal cost, subject to quantifiable constraints that influence product mix or costs. LP first requires a goal or objective to be maximized or minimized. Second, LP decision variables must be identified and quantifiably expressed. Third, LP constraints that restrict solution parameters have to be identified. And finally, all of the first three components must be graphically portrayed or expressed as a series of algebraic equations.

4. **Describe two fundamental techniques used by managers in scheduling key activities.**

Two fundamental scheduling techniques often used in managerial planning are Gantt charts and PERT network diagrams. A Gantt chart is a control chart that displays time on the horizontal dimension and activities on the vertical dimension. Activities are plotted across time with various symbols that make it possible to track plans, progress, and results. PERT is a network technique frequently used in managerial planning. The user must first identify the necessary activities, the events that signal their completion, the time each activity requires, and any sequences of interdependent activities. This information is then portrayed as a network chart so that managers can visualize, monitor, and (if necessary) adjust the activities that make up the overall project.

Key Terms and Concepts

After completing your study of Chapter 9, "Managerial Planning Techniques," you should be able to explain the following terms and concepts:

forecasting	sales forecast	Delphi technique	time-series analysis	economic indicator
forecast	qualitative	quantitative	causal modeling	linear programming
technological	forecasting	forecasting	regression model	Gantt chart
forecast	technique	technique	econometric model	PERT
economic forecast	jury of expert			
demand forecast	opinion			

Questions for Discussion

1. Why do managers need to forecast? Give examples drawn from current business practices to support your answer.

2. Identify and illustrate three types of forecasts.

3. Describe three qualitative forecasting techniques, and explain when you might use each technique in a career you may enter.

4. What are the basic components of a time-series analysis? Is each component essential in any forecasting situations?

5. What are the strengths and weaknesses of time-series analysis and of causal modeling? When would these forecasting techniques be most useful? When would they be least useful?

6. What types of planning situations benefit most from linear programming? Provide a simple example of the use of LP in a business of interest to you.

7. What is a Gantt chart and how might you use one in this course?

8. Explain PERT. What advantages does it offer a manager? How you might use it in a job you may hold?

Notes

1. Adapted from "MACK comes to Winnsboro," *The State* (Columbia, S.C.), May 6, 1986, p. C8.
2. J. B. Dilworth, *Productions and Operations Management* (New York: Random House, 1986).
3. J. P. Martino, *Technological Forecasting for Decision-Making* (New York: Elsevier, 1983).
4. R. F. Reilly, "Developing a Sales Forecasting System," *Managerial Planning*, July-August 1981, pp. 24–30.
5. M. Moriarty, "Design Features of Forecasting Systems Involving Management Judgments," *Journal of Marketing Research* 22, no. 11 (1985): 353–364.
6. D. M. Georgoff and R. G. Murdick, "Manager's Guide to Forecasting," *Harvard Business Review* 64, no. 1, (1986): 110–120.
7. N. Dalkey, *The Delphi Method: An Experimental Study of Group Opinion* (Santa Monica, Calif.: Rand, 1969); and T. Spinelli, "The Delphi Decision-Making Process," *Journal of Psychology* 113, no. 1 (1983): 73–80.
8. F. J. Parente, J. K. Anderson, P. Myers, and T. O'Brien, "An Examination of Factors Contributing to Delphi Accuracy," *Journal of Forecasting* 3, no. 2 (1984): 173–182.
9. J. Duncan, "Businessmen Are Good Sales Forecasters," *Dun's Review*, July 1986.
10. M. J. Lawrence, "An Exploration of Some Practical Issues in the Use of Quantitative Forecasting Models," *Journal of Forecasting* 2, no. 2 (1983): 169–179.
11. R. L. Schultz, "The Implementation of Forecasting Models," *Journal of Forecasting* 3, no. 1 (1984): 43–55.
12. S. G. Makridakis, S. C. Wheelwright, and V. E. McGee, *Forecasting Methods and Applications,* 2nd ed. (New York: Wiley, 1983).
13. J. Byrd and L. Moore, "The Application of a Product Mix Linear Programming Model in Corporate Policy Making," *Management Science* 24, no. 9 (1978): 1342–1350.
14. D. I. Cleland and W. R. King, *Systems Analysis and Project Management,* 3rd ed. (New York: McGraw-Hill, 1983).
15. J. D. Wiest and F. K. Levy, *A Management Guide to PERT/CPM* (Englewood Cliffs, N.J.: Prentice-Hall, 1969).
16. J. L. Riggs and C. D. Heath, "Guide to Cost Reduction Through Critical Path Scheduling," *Business Horizons* 15, no. 6 (1972): 16–20; and R. J. Schonberger, "Custom Tailored PERT/CPM Systems," *Business Horizons* 15, no. 6 (1972): 64–66.

Cohesion Incident 9-1
Keeping the Pool Clean

Because an increasing number of competing motels in the Graniteville area have swimming facilities for their guests, the Graniteville Journey's End has decided to enlarge its swimming pool to olympic size. Corporate management had to approve the expansion of the pool, but then Roger and Charles were given the authority to oversee the construction and make the new pool operational.

In the middle of May the pool was completed. Because Roger has given Charles the responsibility for operating the pool, Charles is making every effort to do an outstanding job. He has placed a large sign at two locations in the pool area: "Journey's End Inns, Inc., will not be liable for injuries due to the carelessness of our patrons." Included in the list of regulations posted on the inside of each door are the days and the times of day that the pool will be open to Journey's End guests.

As Charles looks forward to the day the pool will open, he is anticipating exactly what he will be doing in connection with the pool. The maids have been assigned the duties of cleaning the area around the pool daily and removing debris from the pool every other day. The major responsibility that Charles has is that of adding the correct chemicals to the pool each day to keep it safe. The installers of the pool recommend that chlorine and another chemical for cleaning the pool be added each day. Charles has estimated that over the course of the swimming season, at least 480 pounds of chlorine and at least 500 pounds of the cleaning agent will be required. He has learned that neither of these can be bought in the pure form.

Charles calls a local distributor of pool supplies and is told that two types of mixtures are available, both sold in ten-pound bags, that contain the chlorine and cleaning agent. The bag of EZ Clean sells for $3 and has the equivalent of four pounds of chlorine and eight pounds of the cleaning agent. The bag of X-TRA Clean sells for $5 and has the equivalent of seven-and-one-half pounds of chlorine and five pounds of the cleaning agent.

The dealer told Charles that a discount was given for large purchases but that he should not purchase too far ahead, because some of the chemicals could lose their potency in storage over the winter and, if stored in a moist place, would become very difficult to use in the following summer. He also suggested that Charles could buy both products and mix them to improve operating costs.

Charles's objective, of course, is getting at least the minimal amounts of chemicals he needs at the lowest cost.

Discussion Questions

1. How many bags of each product should Charles purchase? Solve by using graph paper and a linear programming model. Assume that any discounts in price will not affect the ratio between the costs of EZ Clean and X-TRA Clean.

2. What will be the total amount paid for the chemicals before any discount is subtracted? (Use the quantities you obtained in question 1.)

Cohesion Incident 9-2
What's the Plan?

As Leslie Phillips left Eileen Thompkins's office, she studied the problem she had been assigned. Eileen was preparing a proposal to develop a mail survey of end users of Cruise-o-matic. She needed the results of the study for a presentation she would make in twenty weeks to the sales manager, engineering manager, and general manager. Eileen had asked Leslie to plan the research and to set up a schedule that could be used to direct and monitor its progress. And as soon as possible, she wanted an estimate of the total number of weeks it would take to complete the project.

Leslie returned to her office and constructed the table shown on the next page. In it she listed in sequence all the steps involved in the project, along with her estimates of how long it would take to complete each activity. She also indicated which activities she thought could be performed simultaneously. The big question that remained was whether the project could be completed in time for Eileen to present the results in twenty weeks.

Project Activities and Time Estimates

Sequence of Activities	Estimated Time in Weeks	Simultaneous Activities
1. Proposal and budget approval	1	
2. External background research (such as technical and trade journals)	2	3, 4
3. Internal background research (such as sales records and sales and service reports)	2	2, 4
4. Construction of samples for pre-test and survey	1	2, 3
5. Drafting of questionnaire for pre-test	1	
6. Training the coders	1	7
7. Collection of pre-test data	2	6
8. Coding and input of pre-test data	2	last week of 7
9. Analysis of pre-test data	1	
10. Preparation of pre-test report	1	
11. Revision of questionnaire on the basis of pre-test results	1	
12. Data collection	3	13
13. Coding and input of data	2	last week of 12
14. Analysis of data	1	
15. Preparation of final report	1	

Discussion Questions

1. Develop a project plan that Leslie might construct from the information given in the table above.

2. How many weeks will the entire project take to complete? Is it possible to have a report of the results in hand for the meeting twenty weeks from now?

Management Development Exercise 9
Ross Perot's EDS Executive Rescue Team

BACKGROUND: You are a member of Ross Perot's secret executive rescue team at EDS sent to Iran to rescue three EDS executives from an Iranian prison. It is essential that your rescue effort be well planned. You are assigned to plan the prison break aspect of this mission. Your surveillance reports inform you that once the alarm has sounded, it will take the Iranian police seven minutes and thirty seconds to reach the prison. You must now determine whether the prison break can be completed successfully in that time.

To complete the prison break, two members of your team (a rifleman and a locksmith) will be dropped off behind the prison and will be responsible for picking the lock on the rear door. The rest of the team will be driven to the front of the prison to wait. Once the alarm has sounded, the rest of the team will enter the prison. The riflemen will point their weapons at the guards and the prison personnel, while the demolitions person will blast into the inner prison and seal off the inner prison guards. Meanwhile, the locksmith will walk to the cell block where the three executives are being held and then unlock or blow open the cell doors. Once the executives have been found, all team members will meet at the front door and leave together.

Your task is to determine whether the prison break can be accomplished in the allotted time (before the Iranian police arrive). Determine the critical path. Explain whether you would or would not attempt this prison break.

Team members include two riflemen, one locksmith, one demolitions person, one driver, and of course, yourself.

Step 1: Identify the activities and events associated with this project.
Step 2: Arrange these activities in their logical order.
Step 3: Create a PERT network diagram.

ACTIVITIES

A. One rifleman and the locksmith are dropped off in the alley behind the prison (they will pick the lock).
B. The other team members are dropped off in front of the prison.
C. The riflemen take up their positions and point their weapons at the guards.
D. The demolitions person blasts into the inner prison.
E. The demolitions person seals off the inner prison guards.
F. The locksmith walks to the cells.
G. The locksmith gets the executives' cell block open.
H. The locksmith finds the executives and returns with them to the front of the prison.
I. All members of the team leave the prison at the same time.
J. The driver meets the rest of the team in front of the prison when the break is completed, and they drive away.

TIMING

1. It takes 2 minutes to pick the lock on the rear door.
2. The alarm goes off when the back door is picked; the Iranian police arrive in 7 minutes and 30 seconds.
3. It takes 45 seconds to drive from the alley to the front of the prison.
4. It takes 30 seconds for the riflemen to enter the prison and take up their positions.
5. It takes 60 seconds for the locksmith to reach the cells from the back door.
6. It takes 30 seconds for the demolitions person to enter the prison and blast into the inner prison.
7. It takes 3 minutes to seal off the inner prison guards.
8. It takes 2 minutes to open the executives' cell block.
9. It takes 2 minutes to find the executives and assemble them.
10. It takes 45 seconds to exit from the prison and reach the car at the front curb.

Once you have developed your PERT diagram and answered the question posed, your instructor will provide you with information useful in interpreting your answer.

Source: Adapted from L. D. Goodstein and J. W. Pfeiffer, eds., *The 1983 Annual Handbook for Facilitators, Trainers, and Consultants* (San Diego, Calif.: University Associates, Inc., 1983). Used with permission.

Organizing

One of the most challenging and significant functions managers must execute is organizing the work of individuals, teams, departments, and entire organizations. This section presents key aspects of the organizing function and the skills or concepts necessary to execute them effectively.

Chapter 10 builds a foundation for understanding the organizing function by examining four fundamentals of organizing. It describes how work is divided, authority, and responsibility are balanced and shared, coordination is achieved, and organizational purpose is maintained at the work-group level.

Chapter 11 examines how organizations are designed and structured at the organizational level. It explains five basic dimensions that shape sound organizational design decisions.

Keeping work groups and organizations organized often means accommodating to the inevitable force of change. Chapter 12 examines the nature of change and its impact on organizations. Selected techniques that have become popular for managing planned change are examined in this chapter.

Organizing is ultimately people-centered. Chapter 13 concludes this section by providing you with a thorough examination of human resource management and labor relations. It examines the key concepts and skills necessary to successfully manage both human resources and labor relations.

10

Fundamentals of Organizing

Learning Objectives

Your study of this chapter will enable you to do the following:

1. Define the term *organizing*, identify the four elements of organizing, and discuss why organizing is important to effective managing.
2. Explain specialization as a basis for organizing, and discuss some of the advantages of specialization.
3. Define the term *departmentalization*, and explain several key ways in which managers implement departmentalization as a basis for organizing.
4. Define the term *authority*, and describe at least two foundations of authority in organizational settings.
5. Define the term *delegation*, and explain the differences among responsibility, accountability, and authority.
6. Explain the difference between decentralization and delegation, and discuss the factors that affect an organization's degree of decentralization.
7. Define the term *coordination* as an element of organizing, and explain three basic principles underlying coordination.

Getting Gummy Bears Organized

A successful business is built on a good product, good planning, and, as Peter De Yager has learned, on talented and productive employees. De Yager, president and CEO of Foreign Candy Corporation of Hull, Iowa, saw his firm grow rapidly and its productivity increase considerably when be began to spend less time concentrating on growth and more focusing on the fundamentals of organizing. Foreign Candy, sole U.S. distributor of the Black Forest brand of Gummy Bear candy made in West Germany, boosted sales by 545 percent in five years. (Sales reached $13 million in 1987.) As a result, De Yager was named Iowa Small Business Person of the year by the Small Business Administration.

De Yager now regards employees as the company's greatest asset, but he admits that for several years he gave low priority to their concerns. "Our rapid growth put a great deal of pressure on everyone," he says. "I didn't take enough time to address fundamentals of organizing, assess employee needs, or seek employee opinion on how to improve the firm. Company growth received all my attention." De Yager began to reassess his attitude following a personnel survey conducted by John Cain, the firm's accountant. "He did an excellent job of eliciting frank comments from employees," said De Yager. "Then he came to me with a long list of areas needing improvement. It took us one and one-half years to accomplish everything on that list."

De Yager's top priority was to put employees before growth. One thing this involved was creating a detailed organization chart to define the company's personnel structure. Employees wanted clarity in their job design, accountability, responsibility, and avenues for coordination. Previously, "employees hadn't really known what their jobs were, or how they fit into the grand scheme of things," said De Yager.

To remedy the situation, Bill Van Horssen was hired as general manager and assigned the task of improving the link between employees and top management. "Employee morale was very low when I started here," Van Horssen recalled. "Employees didn't know where to go with problems, or whether they would ever receive feedback about their ideas."

Van Horssen improved the company's information channels, making management more available to employees and clarifying the chain of command. Work was divided in a logical fashion, departments were identified on a functional basis, and efforts to improve coordination were implemented. The system was also adjusted to ensure that employees received responses to suggestions or complaints.

Learning to delegate responsibility and authority and to use managers effectively was an important lesson for De Yager. As the company grew, he was performing an increasing number of tasks. But because he lacked the expertise—most

Peter De Yager joins a group of his employees in front of their Foreign Candy Corporation headquarters. (Courtesy *Small Business Report*)

notably financial skills—necessary for long-range planning, De Yager recruited a new management team and gradually distanced himself from internal activities. "I'm just reaching the point where I can let go. We have excellent managers, but they haven't been here long."

De Yager underestimated the difficulties of adopting a hands-off style, particularly the time it would take to put together a management team he trusted. "Developing a strong group of managers was my greatest challenge," he says. "When we began, I thought I could simply appoint people to managerial positions and let them work. It's not that easy. I've found that not all employees with outstanding talent make good managers." Van Horssen added, "Department heads now have the authority to make decisions. And people respect those decisions, whereas in the past they knew the managers had little power."

After years of being virtually a one-person management staff, De Yager now wants to be in the background, allowing managers to take charge of daily matters. "I'm the idea person for the company," he said. "I love to look for future possibilities. This company's growth will intensify even more when I don't have to concern myself at all with day-to-day activities."[1]

Introduction

What Is Organizing?

Organizing is the process of defining the essential relationships among people, tasks, and activities in such a way that all of the organization's resources are integrated and coordinated to accomplish its objectives efficiently and effectively. It is not often that "getting organized" becomes newsworthy, especially in an organizational context. Yet in Chapter 1 we recognized organizing as one of the essential managerial functions. One reason we do not hear much about organizing is that it is an ongoing process that typically requires subtle changes in how work is accomplished. Only intermittently—perhaps every three to five years in many organizations—is a major reorganization effort mounted. Such was the case for the Foreign Candy Corporation and its founder, Peter De Yager. The Foreign Candy Corporation was an outgrowth of De Yager's entrepreneurial talent and creative genius, but because the organization had grown so rapidly, the need for managerial organizing ability had become acute. Faced with increasing sales and an organizational structure that had become unwieldy for De Yager and confusing and frustrating for his employees, De Yager made "getting organized" his number-one priority.

This chapter examines the fundamental elements of the organizing function. The *division of work* is the first element to be addressed. Managers must look at the need for specialization in the types of work in which individuals engage to produce the products of the business. Five different task characteristics of jobs are discussed that provide the basis for making specialization decisions. *Departmentalization*, the next element of the organizing function, was a major issue facing Peter De Yager. This chapter examines five types of departmentalization that are fundamental to the way managers organize the work their subordinates do. Distribution of *authority* is another critical element managers like De Yager must address in organizing what people do. Emphasis is placed on the importance of the delegation process. Delegation is the main way managers distribute authority to ensure that the work they are responsible for is well organized. The final fundamental element of organizing examined in this chapter is *coordination*. Managers must ensure that the work activities of the firm are coordinated if the benefits of good organization are to be truly realized.

Before turning to the fundamental elements of the organizing process, we will first look at some reasons for organizing, some of the characteristics of organizational relationships, and some procedures that underlie the organizing process.

Reasons for Organizing

As the very relationship between the two words suggests, organizing lies at the heart of organizations. Organizations are created and continue to exist because a given goal cannot be achieved by a single person or even by several people working independently. Managers engage in organizing activities in order to accomplish three things. First, organizing improves the efficiency and quality of an organization's work. When the organization's diverse tasks are skillfully meshed, opportunities to achieve synergies are created. That is, groups of people working together effectively can accomplish more than just the sum total of their individual efforts.

The second reason for organizing is to establish accountability. Participants in any effort are more effective when they understand their specific responsibilities. In addition, it is important that all employees know to whom they must answer and who will assign and supervise their work. It is also helpful for everyone to be familiar with the entire authority structure of the organization. Authority relationships should be clear from the workers at the base of the organizational pyramid to the CEO at the top.

The final reason for organizing is to facilitate communication. Formal communication directly follows the organization's authority structure. At the very least, when a person knows who his or her boss is and what subordinates he or she directs, formal lines of communication have been established in two directions. This process continues throughout the entire organization so that an unbroken line of communication exists from top to bottom and across the firm.

De Yager's motivation to reorganize his company reflected these three reasons. First, the company's rapid growth had created pockets of people working independently in ways that simply evolved "during the heat of battle" to get the job done. The company's diverse activities needed to be defined and efficiently meshed. Second, the number of people had expanded rapidly, yet almost everyone in the organization still felt that only one person, De Yager, was "the boss." Clearer lines of responsibility and accountability needed to be established. And finally, throughout the organization, actions were often being taken without key people knowing what was happening and why. Foreign Candy needed a better communication system from the top of the organization to the bottom, as well as from the bottom to the top.

Organization Charts

The outcome of a firm's organizing effort can be depicted on an **organization chart**, a simple drawing of lines and boxes that shows how the firm is organized. Boxes represent the firm's activities and the people who perform these activities. Lines indicate the relationships among them. People whose jobs are near the top of the chart have more authority and responsibility than those below them. The number of horizontal rows of boxes is an indication of how many levels of management an organization has. In the Foreign Candy Corporation, for example, Peter De Yager intended to convert the firm from one level of managers to two or three managerial levels.

An organization chart is really a "blueprint" of what formal relationships are intended to exist at a particular time (Figure 10-1). The organization is dynamic, however, and in action every day. Accordingly, it is subject to subtle or even overt deviations from what the "blueprint" says the structure of relationships was intended to be.

A major way in which the dynamic nature of the organization emerges is often called the "informal" organization. The organization chart depicts the planned, formal relationships that are necessary to get the work of the organization accomplished. But getting the work of the organization done often requires unplanned actions and decisions and relies on informal relationships among members of the organization. These unplanned relationships and activities among people in an organization that emerge to expedite the organization's work are called the **informal organization**.

The informal organization may arise spontaneously, or it may be the result of political savvy and careful strategizing among some of the organization's members. The organization chart is a static drawing of horizontal and vertical lines. The informal organization is dynamic, and all the possible relationships within are very difficult to draw. The informal organization has no managers, but it does have leaders. It has no authority hierarchy; its relationships are social. It has no formal rules but is governed loosely by social norms. Figure 10-2 depicts the contrast between the formal organization chart and the informal organization at Foreign Candy Corporation.

The communication system of the informal organization is called the *grapevine*. Whereas the organization chart depicts formal channels of communication, getting the work of the organization accomplished often requires unplanned communication between organization members, such as the links depicted

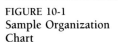
FIGURE 10-1
Sample Organization
Chart

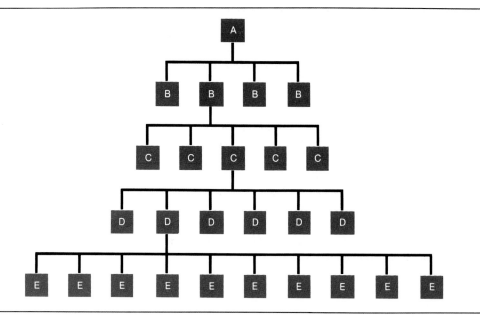

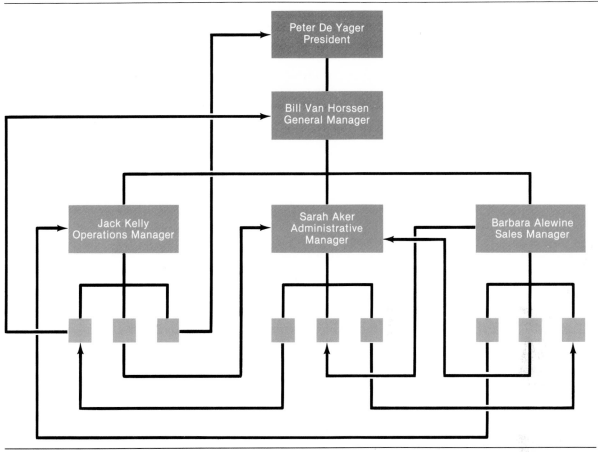

FIGURE 10-2
The Informal
Organization at Foreign
Candy Corporation

in Figure 10-2. The grapevine analogy is a good one; the channels of informal communication weave their way up, down, around, and through the formal structure of the organization.

The Foreign Candy Corporation has a formal procedure through which orders are processed, filled, and shipped to the appropriate customers. Several salespersons who have been with the company for a long time, particularly two who handle school (fund-raising) accounts, have been with the company since its inception and have close personal relationships with people in packing and shipping. Over the years they have frequently made exceptions and expedited last-minute requests for additional Gummy Bears to schools that have run out of the product as their fund-raising programs were in their final stages. These individuals constitute an informal organization, and the communication necessary to sustain it is part of Foreign Candy Corporation's grapevine.

Steps in Organizing

Experience suggests that managers who follow the sequence of steps outlined here are the most effective organizers.

1. *Determine the essential jobs to be done by dividing the total organizational task into work assignments each of which can logically be done by one person.* It is

critical that the total work load in an organization be broken down into individual job assignments for each of the organization's workers. Imagine the chaos if eleven people were sent onto a football field with only the vague directive "Win the game!" Here the total task is first divided between an offensive unit and a defensive unit. Further, each player has a very specific job to do that depends on the position played. The quarterback, the linebackers, and the tackles all contribute to winning the game, but none of them can do the entire job alone. John Cain, De Yager's consultant in the opening case, started his assignment by interviewing every person in the Foreign Candy organization. One of his objectives in these initial interviews was to determine the essential jobs to be done at Foreign Candy and to get a clear idea how they might best be broken down into work assignments to be done by one person.

2. *Group the individual tasks into meaningful units that can work together effectively.* Working units function more smoothly when their activities are complementary or occur in some logical sequence. For example, Cain found that the two Foreign Candy employees responsible for billing and collections were assigned to the sales manager. He recommended that people working in accounts receivable be located in the Accounting Department, along with people performing other accounting activities, rather than in the Marketing Department.

3. *Decide who should be responsible for managing each of the groups of activities, and delegate those responsibilities.* The assignment to subordinate managers of responsibility for the accomplishment of certain tasks makes clear who is accountable for the work and who has the authority to see that it is done. This **delegation** of responsibility also has the effect of designating the formal lines of communication in an organization. One of the major organizational problems that Cain sought to remedy at Foreign Candy Corporation was the need to designate several functional-area managers *and* to make sure they were given the authority and freedom they needed to execute these assignments. He was able to convince De Yager that De Yager himself made too many decisions, stifling the company's ability to grow.

4. *Provide the means to integrate the work of each group or department into a coordinated effort designed to achieve the organization's objectives.* Once the individual work has been grouped into departments, these departments must be integrated to ensure that the organization gets its work done effectively. The efforts of one department or group often depend on the efforts of another. The success of the company as a whole certainly depends in part on coordinating the work of such interdependent units. So organizing must create ways in which coordination can be achieved. Cain knew this element would be critical to the success of his reorganization of Foreign Candy Corporation. The result was a rather dramatic recommendation: De Yager must step aside as "chief operating officer" and hire a person with extensive distribution experience (as a top executive) to run the newly organized company. This person would have the perspective and experience necessary to understand the coordination needs of the different departmental managers at Foreign Candy Corporation.

These four steps point up four essential elements of the organizing function: division of work, departmentalization, distribution of authority, and coordination. If managers are to be effective in their organizing function, they must address each of these elements as they structure organizational activities. Figure 10-3 summarizes the reasons behind the four elements of organizing. Each of these elements

Key Steps	Associated Organizing Element	Reason
1. Determine the essential jobs that need to be done.	Division of work	To divide the total organizational task into work assignments that can logically be done by one person
2. Group individual tasks into units.	Departmentalization	To combine jobs in some meaningful way so that the activities complement each other or occur in sequence
3. Distribute authority across units and between individuals.	Distribution of authority	To assign responsibility for the completion of tasks and to delegate the authority necessary to get them done
4. Integrate all people and activities so that the objectives of the organization are achieved.	Coordination	To integrate all of the people and activities in a way that facilitates achievement of organizational objectives

FIGURE 10-3
The Organizing
Function

is supported by a number of basic managerial principles. The remainder of this chapter examines the four essential elements of the organizing function and the major management principles associated with each function.

The Division of Work

Even in very primitive cultures, people recognized that there are advantages to be gained by dividing up the jobs to be done. Some people were hunters, others were food gatherers, and still others worked as makers of tools and weapons. In these cultures, people understood that their survival was enhanced by assigning each member of the group specific responsibility for the job that she or he did best.

Organizations are like cultures in that they, too, must accomplish the effective **division of work** in order to survive in a competitive environment. They must divide the work of the organization into specialized tasks. The advantages of assigning workers to specialized tasks was illustrated in a famous account written by Adam Smith, in which he described the efficiency achieved by workers manufacturing pins.[2] One worker drew the wire, another straightened it, another cut it, a fourth ground the point, a fifth polished it, and so on. This **specialization** enabled ten people to produce 48,000 pins a day, according to Adam Smith, whereas each man could produce only 20 pins per day if he worked alone and performed all the tasks himself! Perhaps the most prominent advocates of the specialization of tasks were scientific management theorists such as Frederick W. Taylor and successful industrialists such as Henry Ford, who analyzed even the simplest repetitive tasks and tried to break them down into their basic motions.

The Rationale for Specialization

The logic of the argument in favor of specialization seems clear. When the total organizational task is divided among individual members in such a way that each person has a special job to do, people become experts at what they do and consequently the efficiency and productivity of the organization increase. All of the following have been touted as advantages of specialization:

1. *Less-skilled workers can be used.* Because the complex task has been simplified into smaller jobs, the workers who do these jobs do not have to be highly trained. And workers with fewer skills are paid less.

2. *Selection and training are easier.* Because the skills required for the specific job are minimal, it is easier to identify applicants who already have those skills. In addition, training new workers takes less time and is not so difficult.

3. *Proficiency is gained more quickly.* Because a specialized task is repetitive, the worker gets a lot of practice and becomes an expert rather quickly.

4. *There is an increase in efficiency.* Workers do not waste time moving from one task to another. Also, it is more efficient to use each worker's best skills.

5. *There is greater availability of labor.* More potential workers are available because fewer specialized skills are required. The size of the pool of available labor is increased.

6. *The speed at which work is done increases.* More work is done by each worker, so the task gets finished sooner.

7. *Concurrent operations are possible.* Because one worker is not assigned to more than one task, there is no delay in a second task while he or she completes the first.

8. *Specialization increases choice.* There is a large variety of tasks to choose from, so the worker can choose, or be assigned, on the basis of his or her preference or particular skill.

Specialization has been a major tenet guiding American industry for the last 150 years. The advantages associated with the division of work led to many large, highly successful American companies that dominated their respective industries. The last ten years, however, have seen several companies question and modify this extreme emphasis on specialization. (This new trend will be examined in a subsequent section.) Even so, specialization remains a central organizing concept used by effective managers.

Measuring Specialization

One way in which managers attempt to determine how much specialization is appropriate is by assessing the work involved in the job along two dimensions: job depth and job scope.

JOB DEPTH

Job depth is the level of control the worker has over her or his job. Depth is associated with the freedom to plan and organize one's own work, to work at one's own pace, to circulate about the workplace, and to interact with others. Where rules are strict, work is highly routinized, standards are rigid, and workers are closely supervised, on the other hand, job depth is low. For employees at a McDonald's restaurant, job depth is low, as "In Practice 10-1" suggests.

JOB SCOPE

Job scope consists of the length of time required for the job cycle and the number of operations involved in the job. A job that entails fewer repetitions and more

---

In Practice 10-1

AN EXAMPLE OF LOW JOB DEPTH

To find out how a McDonald's restaurant works, correspondent Kathleen Deveny spent a lunch hour behind the counter. Her report:

On my way down Chicago's Magnificent Mile, past Tiffany's and Gucci, to the McDonald's restaurant, I keep thinking back to the Tastee Treet in Minneapolis. That was my first job, making ice cream cones and flipping burgers for the high school students who swarmed into the converted gas station during the short summers.

McDonald's is nothing like Tastee Treet. Here every job is broken down into the smallest of steps, and the whole process is automated. The videotape that introduces new employees to French fries, for example, starts with boxes of frozen fries rolling off a delivery truck. Stack them in the freezer six boxes high. Leave one inch between the stacks, two inches between the stacks and the wall. Cooking and bagging the fries is explained in even greater detail: 19 steps.

Anyone could do this, I think. But McDonald's restaurants operate like Swiss watches, and the minute I step behind the counter I am a loose part in the works. By noon the place is mobbed. I keep thinking of the McDonald's commercial that shows former Raiders Coach John Madden diagramming the precision moves of a McDonald's crew in action. I imagine a diagram of my own jerky movements, zigzagging wildly behind the counter because I keep forgetting the order.

I bag French fries for a few minutes, but I'm much too slow. Worse, I can't seem to keep my station clean enough. Failing at French fries is a fluke, I tell myself.

Condiment detail sounds made to order. First comes the mustard, one shot of the gun, five perfect drops centered on the bun. Next, the ketchup: one big shot. Quite a difference from Tastee Treet, where I used to measure out the ketchup by writing my boyfriend's initials on each hamburger bun.

I try to speed up. Now a quarter-ounce of onions and two pickles—three, if they're small. Cover them with a slice of cheese, slap on the burger. Another slice of cheese.

I am happy with the tidy piles I am making, but the grillman is not as pleased. I move too slowly, and he could cook the patties and dress the buns a lot faster without my help.

Disheartened, I move on to Filet-O-Fish. I put six frozen fish patties into the fryer basket and drop them into the hot grease. When the red light flashes, I put the buns in to steam. After a few minutes, the square patties are done. I line them up in neat rows and center the cheese on each. I try to move faster, but my coworkers are playing at 45 rpm, and I'm stuck at $33\frac{1}{3}$.

Debbie, the crew member who rescued my French fries earlier, comes back to see how I'm doing. It's my last chance to shine. I pull out more cooked fish, slap on the buns, and pinch my finger in the tartar sauce gun. "You're doing O.K.," she somehow says. That's all I wanted to hear. The regimented work is wearing on my nerves. The strict rules, which go so far as to prescribe what color nail polish to wear, are bringing out the rebel in me. I can't wait to get back to my cluttered office, where it smells like paper and stale coffee and the only noise is the gentle hum of my personal computer.

Source: K. Deveny, "Bag Those Fries, Squirt That Ketchup, Fry That Fish," *Business Week,* October 13, 1986, p. 88. Reprinted from October 13, 1986 issue of *Business Week* by special permission, copyright © 1986 by McGraw-Hill, Inc.

operations has higher scope. A tailor's job, which involves taking measurements, designing a pattern, cutting fabric, sewing, and fitting the finished garment, is higher in scope than that of a sewing machine operator who stitches the seams in men's suits. The cycle for stitching the seams in a suit is much shorter than the time required to create and tailor a suit, and the tailor has a far greater variety of tasks to perform than the sewing machine operator.

Different parts of a job can vary in depth and scope. For example, job depth is higher when the tailor is designing a pattern than when he or she is cutting fabric. How specialized a job is depends on its overall depth and scope. The lower the depth and the lower the scope, the more specialized the job is or can be.

Managers who wish to apply the principle of specialization in attempting to create a better division of work can examine the scope and the depth of the jobs they are concerned with and use the results as one basis for determining the appropriate level of specialization. Where job depth, job scope, or both are *high,* there is probably room for reorganizing the work to exploit specialization. Foreign Candy Corporation originally had the same people assorting, packing, and shipping Gummy Bear candies. They found that efficiency could be enhanced and training simplified when they divided those tasks into separate jobs.

Where both scope and depth are low, however, the manager must often take steps to deal with certain troublesome consequences that are likely to mar an otherwise ideal application of specialization. These consequences may include boredom, frustration, and lack of interest in the job, which can lead to high levels of turnover, absenteeism, or mistakes. McDonald's has avoided the ill effects its extraordinary specialization might otherwise have had by hiring largely part-time, unskilled workers—often high school students—who are interested in supplemental earnings, have little previous work experience, and intend to move on to other jobs rather than to build a career with McDonald's. Dealing with the dysfunctional consequences of specialization is discussed in a subsequent section of this chapter.

A second and more comprehensive way in which managers can gauge opportunities for reaping the benefits of specialization is by examining the work's task characteristics.

Task Characteristics

Several researchers have attempted to describe **task characteristics**, or core dimensions, of jobs in order to guide managers in determining the content of individual tasks. The five dimensions they have come up with are skill variety, task identity, task significance, autonomy, and feedback.[3]

1. **Skill variety** is the spectrum of talents required on a job. Jobs that require creativity and are intellectually challenging have more skill variety than jobs that require minimal creativity and pose no intellectual challenge.

2. The extent to which a job involves the production of a complete product determines its **task identity**. Crafts that involve doing all aspects of a job, from start to finish, and producing a tangible product have a greater degree of task identity than jobs that represent small parts of an overall effort to produce a product or service.

3. A job's **task significance** is the extent to which it affects others. Jobs that affect the well-being, safety, or survival of people inside or outside the organization have more task significance than jobs that have no such impact.

Characteristic	High Degree	Low Degree
Skill variety—the extent to which several skills and talents are required to accomplish tasks	Engineer	Doorman
Task identity—the degree to which a job involves completing an entire assignment or piece of work	Hair stylist	Worker on an assembly line
Task significance—the degree to which a job affects the well-being or work of other people inside and outside the organization	Physician	Chain store clerk
Autonomy—the degree of freedom and discretion the job holder can exercise in carrying out the job	Marketing manager	Accounts payable clerk
Feedback—the level of specific information about successful task execution provided to the job holder	Securities analyst	Hotel maid

FIGURE 10-4(a)
Task Characteristics

FIGURE 10-4(b)
Task Characteristics and Work Outcomes

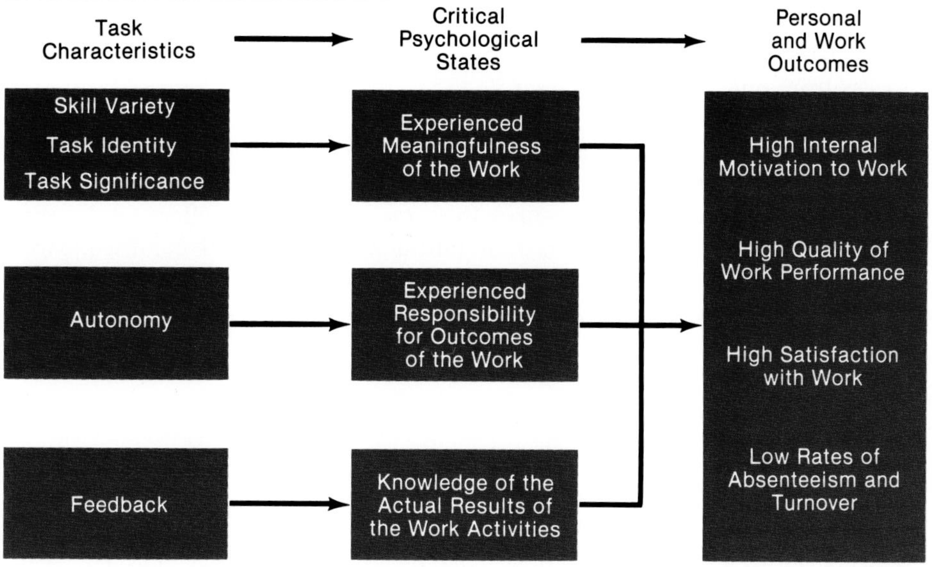

Source: Adapted from J. R. Hackman, "Work Design," in J. R. Hackman and J. L. Suttle, eds., *Improving Life at Work* (Santa Monica, Calif.: Goodyear, 1977), p. 129.

4. The **autonomy** inherent in a job is the extent to which the individual who performs it has the freedom to plan and schedule the tasks to be carried out. The more responsibility an individual assumes for the success or failure of a job, the more autonomy the job offers.

5. **Feedback** reflects the extent to which an individual receives information about the effectiveness of his or her work. The more specific the evaluation of job performance, the greater the feedback.

Figure 10-4 summarizes these five task characteristics and describes how each might be incorporated into a job. The table also gives examples of jobs with high and low degrees of each characteristic. As the bottom of Figure 10-4 suggests, a high level of each of these five characteristics is generally associated with favorable personal or work outcomes.

Managers analyze task characteristics for two reasons. First, when they can bring about work specialization in such a way as to achieve high levels of all five task characteristics, they can expect favorable outcomes. Second, where specialization reduces the level of one or more of these task characteristics (which is certainly more common), managers must recognize that they are trading satisfaction for productivity and must consider ways to minimize the ill effects of the trade-off.[4]

The Effects of Specialization

Traditionally, most of the benefits derived from specialization have been economic in nature. Although the principles of specialization were initially focused on operating-level jobs, they have since been extended to management and professional jobs.

The effects of specialization are not always favorable. Particularly when human considerations are taken into account, there is considerable concern that overspecialized jobs can be boring and even degrading. Overspecialization can lead to such behavioral problems as high absenteeism and turnover, low productivity, and even sabotage. Specialization can also create loss of time in moving work in process from one worker to another.

Although specialization can have negative as well as positive effects, some degree of specialization is fundamental to managers' efforts to organize work activities. Hence the challenge managers face in making organizing decisions is to incorporate specialization and benefit from the advantages it offers while being careful to avoid extreme specialization and its attendant negative consequences. Managers are able to achieve this balance in specialization by "measuring" the degree of specialization appropriate to various jobs and then carefully structuring its use.

Satisfaction-Productivity Trade-offs

Specialization may contribute to greater productivity, but overspecialization can lead to employee dissatisfaction. The complexity of organizational tasks makes some specialization necessary, but beyond a certain point the increases in efficiency are overshadowed by the disadvantages that emerge on the human side. Two ways have been suggested to help managers redesign jobs in order to combat the behavioral difficulties brought on by a numbing routine. These methods are known as job enlargement and job enrichment.

JOB ENLARGEMENT

The idea of **job enlargement**, which was developed by industrial engineers, is to increase the number of activities that a worker performs. Often job enlargement is accomplished by combining several very routine jobs. In short, the scope of the job is increased. In a variation of job enlargement called *job rotation*, the worker moves around from one job to another. In both cases, the sense of challenge is heightened and the worker gains some relief from boredom.

When the Volvo Company in Sweden built a new automobile engine assembly plant, its management decided to try a new system of enlarged jobs instead of the traditional "Detroit-type" assembly line. Figure 10-5(a) represents a traditional assembly system wherein seven specialists put together an engine every 12.6 minutes. During an eight-hour shift, each worker faces a new automobile part over 700 times. Volvo engineers thought that if each worker were allowed to assemble engines from start to finish, the work might be more challenging and interesting, and efficiency might be improved as well. Efficiency at Volvo indeed did improve significantly after these changes were made. Figure 10-5(b) represents the enlarged job of engine assembly.[5]

JOB ENRICHMENT

Whereas job enlargement is essentially an increase in job scope, job enrichment involves an increase in job depth. **Job enrichment** attempts to increase job depth by allowing more autonomy. Employees are given more responsibility for deciding how their jobs will be done and are also allowed to participate in making decisions that affect their work unit. Often, attempts at job enrichment involve organizing

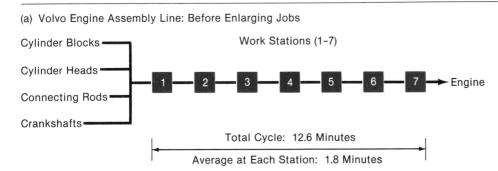

(a) Volvo Engine Assembly Line: Before Enlarging Jobs

FIGURE 10-5
An Example of Job Enlargement

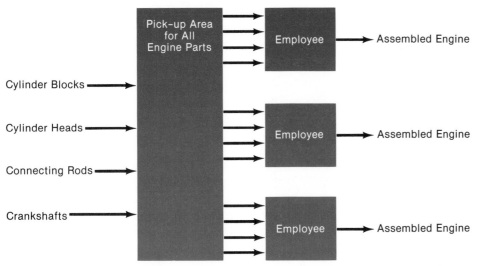

(b) Volvo Engine Assembly: After Enlarging Jobs

Source: Adapted from J. L. Gibson, J. M. Ivancevich, and J. H. Donnelly, Jr., *Organizations: Behavior, Structure, Processes,* 5th ed. (Dallas, Tex.: BPI, 1985), p. 333.

workers into teams that are charged with some group-productivity goal. The team is allowed some autonomy in deciding how it will go about achieving its assigned task.[6]

Foreign Candy Corporation encountered one problem in its reorganizing efforts that was solved through a form of job enlargement. School systems across the country that sold the Gummy Bear candies every year frequently needed to reorder rapidly during their fund-raising efforts. They would often call the company headquarters and talk to someone in shipping or packing to request an immediate shipment. Foreign Candy's procedure was to route all sales through designated territorial salespeople. Unfortunately, these people were often on the road, and it was not unusual for two days to go by before they filled out the appropriate order and sent it to headquarters for packing and shipping. This was frustrating for the customers and for the packing and shipping personnel who

---

■■■■■■■■■■ *Guidelines for Management Practice* ■■■■■■■■■■

In making decisions about specialization, managers may find it helpful to think of jobs in terms of the following 2 × 2 matrix:

Job Specialization Matrix

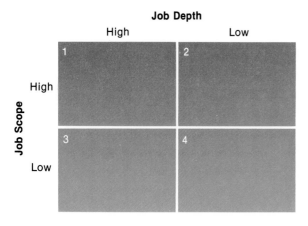

The horizontal axis of this matrix is *job depth*, the amount of control the individual has over his or her work activities. The vertical axis is *job scope*, the amount of variety and repetition involved in the job. Each axis is divided into high and low categories.

Cell 1. Where job depth and job scope are both high, the manager should look for ways to increase spe-

cialization, such as reducing the variety and/or degree of control associated with the job or increasing the amount of repetition.

Cell 2. Where job scope is high but job depth is low, the manager should reduce the job scope by eliminating some of the required operations involved in the task so that the remaining ones are repeated more frequently. In addition, a program of job enrichment should be launched to counteract the dysfunctional effects of low job depth.

Cell 3. Where job scope is low but job depth is high, a program of job enlargement should be installed that increases the variety of the required tasks and reduces the repetitiveness of the job cycle. Be more specific about standards and expectations, and provide more structure to reduce the uncertainty attendant upon high job depth.

Cell 4. Where job scope and job depth are both low, the manager should institute a program that includes both job enrichment and job enlargement. Jobs that can be classified in this cell have become much too specialized. When job redesign is not possible, managers should monitor such jobs carefully to detect and correct such undesirable outcomes as excessive absenteeism and poor performance. In addition, special care should be taken to assign to these specialized jobs workers who are better able than others to cope with tedium.

████████████████ *Guidelines for Management Practice* ████████████████

The following list provides some guidelines to job enrichment.[7] However, managers who decide to enrich or enlarge jobs should keep two caveats in mind. Although productivity may be increased by eliminating much of the oppressiveness of overspecialized positions, neither job enrichment nor job enlargement is intended to increase productivity. Managers should not expect too much from these methods. Second, designing and implementing these programs can be expensive. Careful consideration should be given to whether the anticipated results justify the costs.

1. *Form natural work units.* Apportion tasks on the basis of (1) the workers' training and experience and (2) the job's meaningfulness and importance to workers.

2. *Combine tasks.* Encourage the development of several skills by combining a number of specialized functions into one whole task.

3. *Establish client relationships.* Provide workers with opportunities to (1) receive direct feedback on their work output, (2) develop interpersonal skills and self-confidence, and (3) assume responsibility for managing relationships by interacting with clients (users of the firm's product or service).

4. *Increase employees' autonomy.* Give workers more responsibility and control by allowing them to (1) decide what work methods they will use, (2) advise and train less experienced workers, (3) schedule overtime, (4) assign work priorities, (5) manage their own crises rather than relying on a supervisor, and (6) control budgetary aspects of their own projects.

5. *Open feedback channels.* Provide workers with feedback while they are performing their tasks instead of after the fact. Such feedback can be derived from (1) direct relationships with clients, (2) workers' responsibility for quality control inspections, and (3) frequent and standard reports on individual performance.

usually talked with them. Eventually the problem was solved by enlarging the job responsibilities of those who worked in packing and shipping, allowing them to accept and process refill orders from established fund-raiser customers.

Summarizing the Work Division Element

A fundamental organizing decision that confronts every manager is how to design or structure jobs. Determining the degree of specialization appropriate to effective job design is the central issue the manager faces. The narrower the job scope and the shallower the job, the greater the level of specialization and potential efficiency—but the lower employee satisfaction in some cases. The higher the level of five task characteristics, the higher employee satisfaction tends to be. Job enlargement and job enrichment are popular ways to reincorporate expanded scope or depth into highly specialized jobs in order to realize substantial "human" payoffs.

In organizing work activities, the effective manager seeks to balance the effects of specialization with the human considerations often associated with narrowing or broadening job scope and depth. Once managers have divided individual work based on opportunities for specialization, the work of individuals needs to be organized. The fundamental element of organizing that does this is departmentalization. The next section examines five ways managers departmentalize work activities.

Departmentalization

What Is Departmentalization?

The second element in the organizing function involves deciding how to group jobs into logical work units. **Departmentalization** is the grouping of jobs, processes, and resources into logical units to perform some organizational task.

One useful way to understand departmentalization as a basis for organizing decisions is to consider a small but growing business such as Foreign Candy Corporation. Although at first the owner-manager (De Yager) supervised employees performing every activity, this became ineffective when the firm reached a certain size. At this point, additional management positions were created and activities assigned to them. Activities and jobs were not assigned randomly; rather, De Yager grouped activities and jobs in a logical fashion. In so doing, the owner-manager used *departmentalization* as a basis for making an organizing decision. And as Foreign Candy Corporation continues to grow, activities and jobs may again need to be regrouped to keep the company effectively organized. Some of the most common ways of grouping jobs, or departmentalizing, are described in the following sections.

Types of Departmentalization

FUNCTIONAL DEPARTMENTALIZATION

Functional departmentalization[8] is the grouping of jobs and resources within the company in such a way that employees who perform the same or similar activities are in the same department. The groups of activities focus on the basic business functions. In a typical manufacturing business, departments are usually set up to carry out the functions of production, finance, and marketing. For a retail store the departments might be merchandising (acquiring and selling the store's goods), promotion (advertising, displays, and the like), operations (security, inventory, and customer service), and finance. The functional departmentalization at Foreign Candy Corporation is shown in Figure 10-6.

Functional departmentalization is the most common approach to grouping jobs and resources. It is particularly prevalent among smaller organizations. Functional departmentalization affords the firm the opportunity to improve internal operating efficiencies, develop expertise, and simplify or specialize work. The main

FIGURE 10-6
Functional
Departmentalization
at Foreign Candy
Corporation

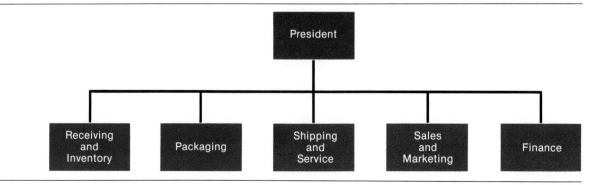

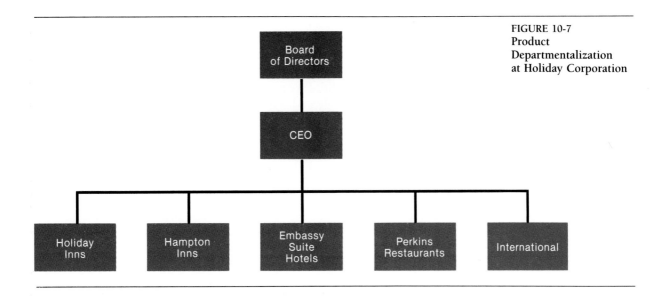

FIGURE 10-7
Product Departmentalization at Holiday Corporation

advantages of functional departmentalization, then, are that (1) focusing on one functional area encourages employees to become experts in their particular area, (2) supervision and coordination are easier because the manager needs to understand and integrate only a narrow range of functional skills, and (3) functional departmentalization is well suited to stable situations.

Functional departmentalization also has some disadvantages: (1) Employees lose sight of the organization's goals because they concentrate so narrowly on their own department and expertise. (2) Overall decision-making time begins to expand to accommodate the time required for each functional area to make its separate decision. (3) Narrow expertise fosters conflict between functional departments. (4) Bottlenecks can occur when work flows from one department to another.

In Chapter 11 we will examine organizational design based on functional areas in more detail. The important thing to note at this point is that departmentalization by functional area is perhaps the most fundamental basis for organizing work activity in business organizations. An alternative type of departmentalization that arises as firms become larger, and offer many products or services, is product departmentalization.

PRODUCT DEPARTMENTALIZATION

Product departmentalization is the grouping of jobs and resources around the products or product lines that a company sells. In large conglomerate organizations with diverse product lines, the functional needs associated with each product are likely to be quite different. For example, besides making beer, Anheuser-Busch also operates family amusement parks, manufactures aluminum cans, and owns a major league baseball team. People skilled in marketing its beer are not likely to be equally skilled in serving its industrial customers for aluminum cans. Figure 10-7 illustrates how Holiday Corporation divides its operations into its major product groups: the familiar Holiday Inns, its budget-priced Hampton Inns, the upscale Embassy Suite Hotels, Perkins Restaurants, and the company's international lodging operations.

Product departmentalization has several advantages: The product becomes the central focus, and all tasks can be coordinated around it. Decision making can be faster and more effective than in the functionally organized company. Responsibilities can be clearly defined and the performance of individual products easily assessed. Because responsibilities are more varied, the training of general managers with broad experience is facilitated. Finally, product departmentalization is well suited to a dynamic environment, because it keeps the firm flexible and able to respond rapidly to changing conditions.

Product departmentalization has disadvantages, however. Departments tend to focus only on their own product and fail to recognize the needs of the whole organization. Coordination among divisions suffers because each department operates somewhat autonomously. Firms structured this way are more costly to run than functionally organized companies, because each department must have its own set of specialists. Product-based organizational structures will be discussed further in Chapter 11.

CUSTOMER DEPARTMENTALIZATION

Customer departmentalization is the organizing of jobs and resources in such a way that each department can carefully understand and respond to the different needs of specific customer groups. Foreign Candy Corporation is currently using functional departmentalization, but it may well have to move to customer departmentalization as its two basic (and different) customer groups—schools raising funds and department stores—increase in size and diversity.

The success of customer departmentalization depends on the ability of the organization to identify unique categories of customers and to recognize each category's special needs. One particular advantage of customer departmentalization is that it enables specialists to become very sensitive to the needs of the particular customer group they serve. Often this gives the organization an edge in anticipating new customer needs and meeting them better and faster than the competition. A very common method of departmentalizing on the basis of customer groups is to designate one department for retail customers, one for industrial customers, and one for government agencies. Figure 10-8 provides another good example. The lending activities at Denver Savings Bank are departmentalized in terms of the needs of different kinds of loan customers. An individual who applies for a personal loan is served by the consumer loan department, whereas a business customer is served by the commercial loan department. The skills a consumer loan specialist needs to examine an individual's credit record and determine

FIGURE 10-8
Customer
Departmentalization at
Denver Savings Bank

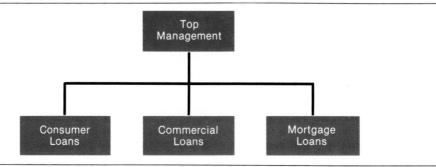

whether the bank should lend him or her money to purchase an automobile are quite different from those a commercial loan officer exercises in deciding whether the bank should supply the capital for a new business venture.

The greatest advantage of customer departmentalization is that it encourages the development of highly skilled specialists to deal with unique customers. But a large staff group is necessary to coordinate and integrate the activities of all these specialists.

GEOGRAPHIC DEPARTMENTALIZATION

Geographic departmentalization is the grouping of jobs and resources around particular locations. For example, Ted Turner's Cable News Network relies on geographic departmentalization. As Figure 10-9 shows, the Cable News Network uses western, midwestern, eastern, and international divisions as a basis for organizing camera crews, news journalists, and editorial jobs and resources.

Geographic departmentalization is often seen where a company's operations or markets are widely dispersed. But it is also used in a single city by organizations such as real estate firms, police departments, and school districts. Departmentalization based on geographic location is primarily used where logistic restrictions or distinct customer requirements vary from one location to another.

The main advantage of geographic departmentalization is that it makes the organization more responsive to the needs of particular customers and to the unique features of various regions. A disadvantage of having the organization's departments so dispersed is that control and coordination become difficult and require more administrative staff.

OTHER TYPES OF DEPARTMENTALIZATION

Departmentalization by function, product, customer, and location are seen the most frequently, but three other methods are occasionally used.

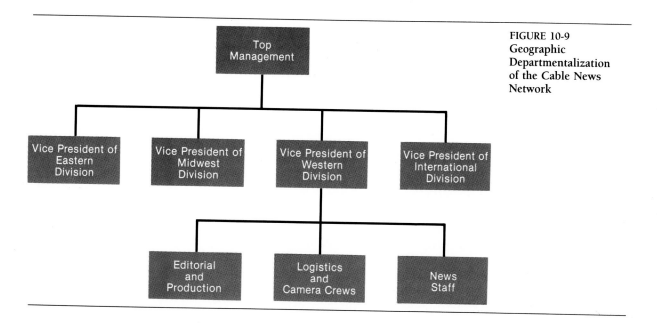

FIGURE 10-9
Geographic Departmentalization of the Cable News Network

In departmentalization by *time*, jobs are organized in terms of periods of time. Many factories and hospitals divide their work by shifts. Organizations that find it efficient (factories) or essential (hospitals) to operate around the clock often divide their work into three eight-hour shifts: first shift (7:00 A.M.–3:00 P.M.), second shift (3:00 P.M.–11:00 P.M.), and third or "graveyard" shift (11:00 P.M.–7:00 A.M.).

In departmentalization by *process*, activities are organized on the basis of the various processes necessary to produce a finished product. For example, a furniture manufacturing firm might be departmentalized by processes such as woodcutting, lathing, assembling, sanding, and finishing. One reason for choosing the process method of departmentalization is that the physical location of equipment and materials in the workplace often makes division in terms of process a logical approach.

In departmentalization by *size*, work is organized on the basis of numbers of people doing the same job. The U.S. Army, for example, is organized into squads, platoons, companies, and so on. Often departmentalization by size is chosen because it makes it easier to manage large numbers of people, especially when the most important key to success is having large numbers of workers.

Other Considerations

It is not unusual for organizations to employ several types of departmentalization as a basis for organizing. They typically use different forms of departmentalization at different levels in the company. Figure 10-10 shows such a combination of organizing principles at Time, Inc., a publisher of several popular magazines. At the first level, the organization is divided into its major product categories, each magazine being a unique product. Next each magazine is organized by function; then each function is broken down into special departments on the basis of its particular needs—the circulation department, for example, is divided in terms of customer groups (individual and corporate).

Figure 10-11 summarizes several of these basic forms of departmentalization and describes the basis on which the work is defined in each case. A skeleton organization chart depicting each form of departmentalization is also shown.

One final observation about departmentalization: Managers use many different terms when grouping tasks or jobs. They are equally likely to designate groups of jobs and resources as units, divisions, departments, sections, teams, sectors, or groups.

Once departmentalization is complete, the organizing role of managers turns to how authority must be distributed within each department. The next section examines the concepts of authority and delegation as fundamental ways managers distribute authority.

Authority

A third element central to most organizing decisions is the distribution of authority across people and units within the organization. The distribution of authority across people flows from a manager to his or her subordinates. This distribution of authority from a manager to a subordinate is usually called **delegation**. Authority is also distributed across units or departments at different levels within an organization. The distribution of authority across organizational levels is fre-

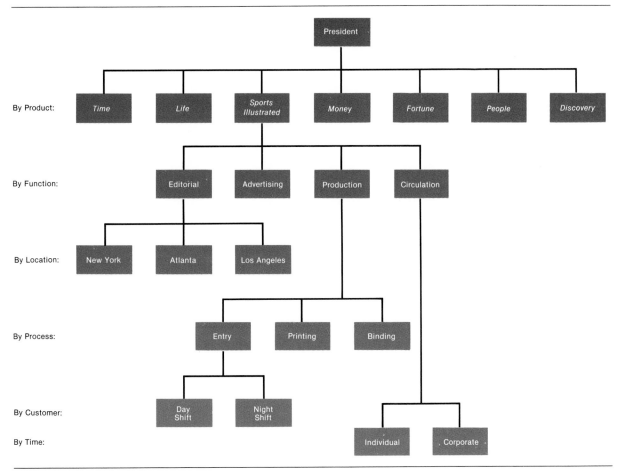

FIGURE 10-10
Combined
Departmentalization
at Time, Inc.

quently called **decentralization**. Before treating these two ways in which authority is distributed, however, we must examine the nature of authority itself.

What Is Authority?

Authority is the organization's legitimized power that is linked to each position within the organization. It typically involves the right to command, to perform, to make decisions, and to expend resources.

Any discussion of the concept of authority requires an understanding of the relationship of authority to power. People often talk about power and authority as though they were the same thing. But whereas **power** is the ability to act or exert influence, authority is the *right* to do so. Authority is derived from one form of power—legitimized power—as the foregoing definition implies. A person may have the power to do something even though he or she has no authority to do it. For example, a bank teller has the authority to handle large amounts of cash; and he or she also has the power to keep some of that cash, but not the authority. Power is derived from the control of various types of resources and thus is not totally dependent on a person's position in an organization. Position in the organization endows a person with a particular type of power known as *legitimate power*. Other types of power are discussed in Chapter 16.

FIGURE 10-11
The Major Kinds of
Departmentalization

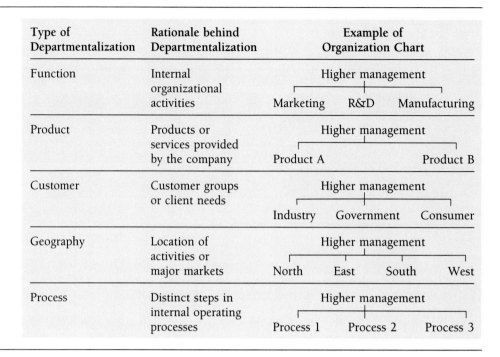

FIGURE 10-11
The Major Kinds of Departmentalization

Type of Departmentalization	Rationale behind Departmentalization	Example of Organization Chart
Function	Internal organizational activities	Higher management — Marketing, R&D, Manufacturing
Product	Products or services provided by the company	Higher management — Product A, Product B
Customer	Customer groups or client needs	Higher management — Industry, Government, Consumer
Geography	Location of activities or major markets	Higher management — North, East, South, West
Process	Distinct steps in internal operating processes	Higher management — Process 1, Process 2, Process 3

Theoretical Foundations

Four management theories have attempted to explain the nature of authority.

The classical theory of authority is based on the organizational hierarchy concept. Authority flows from the top down and is a function of the position held. When removed from her or his position in the organization, the person no longer has the authority that is associated with that position. Figure 10-12 shows how, in the classical or formal view, authority flows into and down through an organization. This classical theory of authority has its roots in the concept of ownership; that is, the owner has the right to vest in certain others the power to make certain decisions and to act in certain ways.

The acceptance theory of authority was first proposed by Mary Parker Follett[9] but was popularized by Chester Barnard.[10] According to acceptance theory, or what Barnard called the "zone of acceptance," a manager's authority rests with his or her subordinates. The manager has no authority unless subordinates choose to accept his or her commands. Subordinates have the power to deny authority to a manager by refusing to act on his or her directives. Figure 10-13 illustrates the acceptance theory of authority. It shows that subordinates determine whether a manager actually has any authority. After the manager makes a request (as shown in the first block), the subordinate has two choices: either acknowledge the manager's authority by yielding to the request or deny the manager authority by refusing to act on the request.

A third theory of authority was suggested by Follett.[11] She believed that the nature of the situation should be the force that grants authority. This idea is easiest to understand when applied to a crisis situation, wherein a person assumes authority in order to avert a catastrophe. For example, if a fire started in a workplace, the worker nearest the telephone might legitimately assume the authority to call the fire department even though she or he had not specifically been directed to do so.

Finally, another theory holds that the person who is the most knowledgeable in a given situation has authority by virtue of his or her expertise. For example, the president of Foreign Candy Corporation, Peter De Yager, often deferred to one or more of his territorial sales managers to make critical decisions on geographic expansion that would affect Foreign Candy's future success, because they had the necessary specialized knowledge about certain regions of the country.

Any manager who makes organizing decisions finds that the distribution of authority is central to effective organization. And these four perspectives on the nature of authority help managers appreciate different considerations that arise in distributing it effectively. Authority is primarily distributed through positions designated by the manager. For example, the general manager of a local automobile dealership may let her or his new car and used car departments have the authority to reduce prices by 5 percent before having to discuss the transaction with top

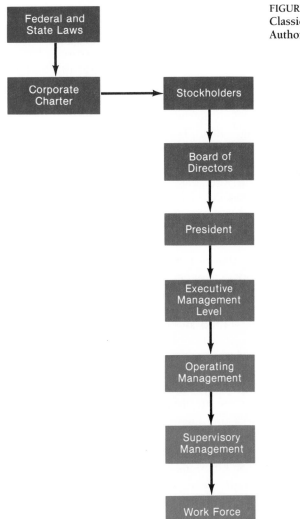

FIGURE 10-12
Classical View of Authority

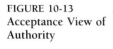
FIGURE 10-13
Acceptance View of
Authority

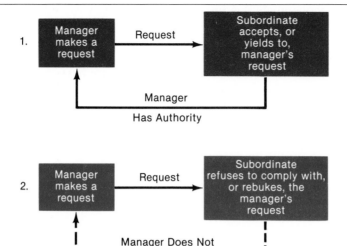

management. Yet if one department has a manager with extensive experience in pricing and costs, the general manager may grant *this* manager greater pricing discretion on the basis of that person's experience or knowledge. And *each* department manager might be allowed to exercise authority in making pricing decisions on those occasions when a customer offers a trade-in, wants a maintenance agreement, is buying several vehicles, or is otherwise creating a unique situation. Of course, a department manager's authority as the final word on pricing decisions for his or her salespeople depends on their accepting that authority rather than insisting that they can make pricing decisions independently or go over their manager's head to others in top management for approval.

Types of Authority

Authority relationships are specified in an organization to facilitate the carrying out of assigned responsibilities. Because there are different types of responsibilities, at least three different types of authority have been identified. These are line authority, staff authority, and functional authority.

Line authority is the most fundamental type of authority assigned in an organization. It is concerned with making decisions and giving instructions that have a direct bearing on the accomplishment of organizational goals. A line manager has the authority to command immediate subordinates. The delgation of line authority sets up the organization's management hierarchy or chain of command.

Staff authority is granted to those units that are assigned responsibility for assisting line units. Staff units serve an auxiliary role and are located outside the organizational chain of command. For example, in a manufacturing organization, the Production Department and the Sales Department are thought of as serving line functions because their responsibilities are closely related to the core mission of the firm. The Data Processing Department, on the other hand, serves a staff function because it helps the line departments accomplish organizational goals. In practice, the separation of line and staff in terms of primary work versus assistance often does not hold. Many times, staff functions are every bit as vital as line functions. For this reason, the line–staff distinction is frequently made only in terms of the chain of command.

Functional authority is assigned to complement line or staff authority in order to accomplish a specific task. Often a special assignment requires that certain managers have control over some individuals outside the area encompassed by their normal authority. For example, a manager in Foreign Candy Corporation's Finance Department charged with instituting cost-cutting measures may have to issue various directives to departments outside his or her normal sphere of authority in order to fulfill the specific responsibility that was assigned.

Managers who establish patterns of authority are concerned about distributing authority across organizational subunits (decentralization) and among subordinates (delegation). Managers face decentralization decisions on an occasional basis, such as when they are reorganizing a firm, expanding a business, or creating a committee or task force. Managers encounter delegation decisions on a regular basis, as they seek to accomplish their objectives while supervising and developing their subordinates. The next few sections examine delegation and decentralization in greater detail.

The Delegation Process

WHAT IS DELEGATION?

Perhaps the most crucial organizing concept that you will face as a new manager is the ongoing need to delegate authority among your subordinates and the ongoing delegation of authority to you from your superior. **Delegation** is the process by which a manager assigns tasks and authority to subordinates who accept responsibility for those jobs.

The need for delegation arises because one person cannot do all the work of the organization. Peter De Yager found this to be a central problem at Foreign Candy Corporation. Any critical task that a manager fails to delegate to a subordinate, that manager must do personally. Management itself is commonly described as getting work done through others; it is clear that delegation lies at the heart of the managerial task.

Delegation is important for at least four reasons. First, it extends the capability and capacity of a manager. By delegating various tasks to key employees, a manager is able to take on more ambitious projects or responsibilities as well as to "oversee" those currently assigned. In other words, the manager can spread himself or herself further. Second, delegation provides excellent training and testing for potential managers. When their superior delegates certain managerial responsibilities, subordinates get an opportunity both to learn more about unit operations and to develop their management skills. A third reason for delegation exists when the subordinate has greater knowledge or expertise in a particular area than the manager. And a fourth reason why delegation is important is that it is a way to introduce specialization of the manager's job. In other words, delegation provides a way to break down the responsibilities of a manager and assign them across several subordinate managers based on their specialized capability.[12]

ELEMENTS OF THE DELEGATION PROCESS

Delegation from a manager to a subordinate involves three essential elements:

1. Assign responsibilities (tasks) to immediate subordinates.

2. Grant the authority the subordinates need to fulfill these responsibilities.

3. Create an obligation (accountability on the part of the subordinate) to the manager to perform the duties satisfactorily.

Figure 10-14 depicts the three elements in the delegation process. Though they are shown as distinct steps, these elements occur simultaneously when a manager is delegating. And it is important to understand the differences among these elements in order to appreciate what is necessary for effective delegation.

Assigning responsibilities is the first element of the delegation process. A **responsibility** is a duty, task, activity, or decision that a manager or other organizational member is expected to accomplish. So the first step in delegation is for the manager to assign this responsibility to a subordinate. It is important to realize that a manager cannot actually abdicate a responsibility assigned to a subordinate. Rather, even though the manager obtains the subordinate's acceptance of the responsibility, he or she remains the one ultimately responsible for the assignment's being carried out.

Authority, as we saw earlier, is the right to command, to perform, to make decisions, and to expend resources. The second step in delegation is that the manager grants authority to the subordinate who assumes the delegated responsibility. The subordinate must have the authority to make the decisions and expend the resources that are necessary to accomplish the new responsibility.

The balance between authority and responsibility is central to effective delegation. This balance is often referred to as the **parity principle**, which states that responsibility and authority must be equal. When a duty is delegated to a subordinate, sufficient authority must also be granted to that subordinate if the duty is to be effectively accomplished. Conversely, a subordinate cannot be expected to assume responsibility for tasks beyond the scope of his or her delegated authority. Although it sounds simple enough, achieving an appropriate balance between authority and responsibility is often very difficult for managers.

Accountability, the third element of delegation, is the clear awareness on the subordinate's part that the outcome of the delegated task or activity will be attributed to his or her efforts. Two things are important to remember in understanding accountability. First, make sure that your subordinate understands *and* agrees that he or she is accountable for the successful (or unsuccessful) execution of a newly assigned responsibility. That sense of obligation helps ensure subordinates' attention to the duty, encourages them to ask questions that clarify "gray areas" of responsibility or authority, provides a basis for performance evaluation, and en-

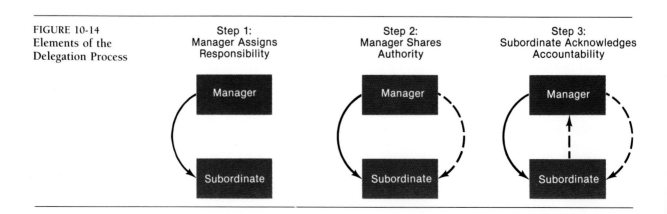

FIGURE 10-14
Elements of the
Delegation Process

Step 1:
Manager Assigns
Responsibility

Step 2:
Manager Shares
Authority

Step 3:
Subordinate Acknowledges
Accountability

Manager

Subordinate

Manager

Subordinate

Manager

Subordinate

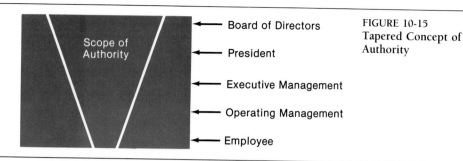

FIGURE 10-15
Tapered Concept of Authority

ables the manager to gauge their level of confidence or control. Second, managers cannot delegate accountability. A manager may delegate responsibility for a task to a subordinate and hold that person accountable, but the manager cannot abdicate accountability. Because the division of work proceeds down through the chain of command, the manager remains accountable to her or his superior for accomplishment of the task whether she or he performs it personally or delegates it to a subordinate. Figure 10-15 depicts this continuity of accountability throughout the organization.

PROBLEMS OF DELEGATION

Although the value of delegation seems fairly obvious, a variety of obstacles hinder effective delegation. The sources of these obstacles include the supervisor, the subordinate, and the organization. Supervisors or managers create obstacles to delegation when they harbor any one or more of the following unenlightened attitudes: (1) They like having power and do not wish to relinquish any of it to subordinates. (2) They view delegation as a sign of weakness indicating that they cannot handle their job. (3) They feel insecure in their job and are afraid that a subordinate who performs well will "show them up." (4) They feel that the only way to get something done right is to do it themselves. (5) They do not want to take the time to teach the subordinate to do the task.[13] "Management Development Exercise 10" lets you examine your delegation orientation or style.

Subordinates may present obstacles to delegation when: (1) they lack confidence in their ability to accept additional responsibility, (2) they are afraid of failing, (3) they view additional responsibility as extra work with no additional reward, (4) they lack the information or resources required to do the job, or (5) they find it easier to ask their supervisor than to try to solve the problem themselves.

Finally, the organization's characteristics or culture may block effective delegation when: (1) because of its small size, there are very few jobs to be delegated, or (2) it has no history of delegation, so there is no behavioral precedent for subordinates to follow. De Yager's early attempts to "reorganize" the Foreign Candy Corporation encountered this problem—subordinates were not accustomed to having De Yager delegate. International managers frequently encounter different cultural orientations toward delegation as well, as illustrated in "Insights for International Managers 10."

In addition to delegation from a manager to a subordinate, effective organizing requires that authority be disbursed among different organizational units. The distribution or delegation of authority among organizational units involves the decision of how centralized or decentralized the organization will be. This issue is examined in the next section.

■■■■■■■■■■■■■ *Insights for International Managers 10* ■■■■■■■■■■■■■

AUTHORITY AND DELEGATION IN INTERNATIONAL SETTINGS

Americans pride themselves on their ability to delegate effectively. Authority and responsibility are dispersed throughout the average U.S. organization. Actually, Americans seem to be about in the middle on a continuum of delegation/decentralization styles, from totally authoritative and centralized patterns on the one extreme to the very participatory style of the Japanese on the other. Scandinavian and Australian companies have a mid-range style similar to the Americans, with the distance between those in authority and their subordinates being small. Nevertheless, American managers in those countries often encounter unexpected differences. Swedes, for example, violate the chain of command as far as Americans are concerned. When Swedes need information, they go directly to the source even if that means bypassing their bosses. So, when managing Swedes, you need not feel threatened when an employee goes over your head.

South American, European, and European-influenced countries tend to require multilevel approval for authorization of routine items. Companies are often run where everything must trickle up to the top executive level. Even where efforts have been made to delegate authority within the organization, local business people continue to insist on seeing the head person, and employees continue to seek the approval of their superiors.

French, Italian, and German executives generally believe that a tight rein of authority is needed to obtain adequate job performance, and managers feel there is more prestige in directing than in persuading.

Far Eastern countries (Japan, Korea, China) emphasize group approaches to problem solving. As a result, managers share authority with their work group and the exercise of authority is often discussed in a group context. Arabic and African executives keep authority at the top, but effectively share it in a consultation-oriented approach. Deriving from their culture, where senior members of a family or community were usually consulted about major decisions, Arab executives prefer to share authority with subordinates while expecting them to regularly consult back on a one-to-one basis about the use of that authority.

Source: From L. Copeland and L. Griggs, *Going International* (New York: Random House, 1985), pp. 123–125.

Centralization and Decentralization

CENTRALIZATION AND DECENTRALIZATION DEFINED

The concepts of centralization and decentralization refer to the degree to which authority is disbursed throughout an organization. Just as authority is delegated from an individual manager to a subordinate, organizations distribute authority across numerous units, departments, and levels of management. **Decentralization** indicates that authority has been widely distributed throughout the organization, whereas **centralization** means that authority has been retained at the top of the organization. The tapered concept of authority is often used to help explain centralization and decentralization. This idea, pictured in Figure 10-15, is simply that the scope of authority becomes narrower at lower levels in the organization—how much narrower depends on the degree of decentralization. Figure 10-16 compares the extents to which authority is tapered in centralized and decentralized organizations.

Absolute centralization or decentralization seldom exists in organizations. Rather, an organization's distribution of authority should be thought of as falling somewhere on a continuum between highly centralized and highly decentralized,

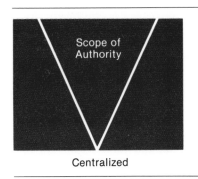
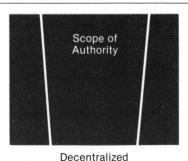

Board of Directors

President

Executive
Management

Operating
Management

Employee

Centralized

Decentralized

FIGURE 10-16
Centralized versus
Decentralized Authority

as shown in Figure 10-17. As Figure 10-17 indicates, many successful and well-known companies employ different levels of decentralization as a basis for distributing authority. Even firms in the same industry, such as Sears and K mart or Burger King and McDonald's, employ different levels as a basis for organizing. Sears relegates many decisions about merchandise to the department manager within a local store. K Mart makes the merchandising decisions for all its stores at corporate headquarters. DuPont and Dow Chemical, two successful chemical products companies, manage their research and development very differently. Most of DuPont's research and development is assigned to one or another of its major product divisions. Dow Chemical undertakes virtually all its research and development at one central facility that is a part of its corporate headquarters. GM allows each major product division (Buick, Chevrolet, for example) to operate as a separate business, whereas Ford maintains several product lines but centralizes many decisions about marketing, promotions, and product development. Finally, McDonald's and Burger King have both grown as worldwide chains by selling franchises to build and operate restaurants using their name and format. McDonald's has always maintained tight, centralized control over franchisees by granting franchises for only one store at a time. Burger King has taken a decentralized approach, selling franchises for as many as four states at once. So whereas every McDonald's must do exactly what corporate headquarters mandates, Burger King once had several franchise groups that were almost as large as the parent company and that were allowed to make many purchasing, promotion, and operating decisions on their own.

For managers, the relevant question is what point on the centralization-to-

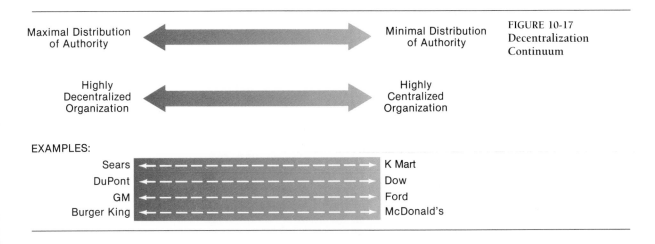

FIGURE 10-17
Decentralization
Continuum

decentralization continuum is right for their firm. The answer is contingent on a number of factors.

FACTORS THAT INFLUENCE DECENTRALIZATION DECISIONS

Factors that affect decentralization decisions can be categorized as either external factors or internal factors. External factors include issues involving the organization's environment, characteristics of its market, and the competitive arena it operates in. Some external considerations are the dispersion of customers, the dispersion of suppliers, the homogeneity of product line, and the volatility of the competitive environment. Generally speaking, the more spread out a firm's buyers or suppliers are, the greater the need for decentralization. Decentralization also becomes more appropriate as the firm's product line grows more diversified. Finally, in volatile competitive environments where rapid changes dictate the need for quick, flexible decision making and creativity, a more decentralized structure is desirable.[14]

Internal factors are related to the firm's characteristics and culture. Some important considerations include the company's size, attitude toward cost control, desire for policy uniformity, and management philosophy, as well as the differences among functional areas. As an organization gets larger, the need for decentralization becomes greater. Generally, the greater the cost involved, the higher up in the organization the decision is made; and where there is greater concern for strict cost control, there tends to be more centralization. When the top management of a firm wants its policies to be standardized throughout the organization, there is likely to be a greater degree of centralization. Similarly, many firms have a history or culture of centralization or of decentralization, and the philosophies of its top and lower-level managers reflect that culture. Finally, because of the unique nature of their activities, some functional areas tend to be more decentralized than other areas that require more central control.

A DuPont scientist performs laser experiments to develop new product variations. Rather than conduct this search for applications across DuPont's wide range of products, this scientist focuses his efforts within a single product division. DuPont managers believe that this way of organizing research and development encourages greater focus, expertise, and success. (Courtesy the DuPont Company)

■■■■■■■■■■■■■■■ *Guidelines for Management Practice* ■■■■■■■■■■■■■■■

For beginning managers, the challenge of deciding between centralization and decentralization and of assigning responsibility and authority is most immediately felt in the act of delegation. Delegation is one of the most important management skills a beginning manager must develop. For many new managers, it is also the most difficult to master.

Here are eight key guidelines that new managers should follow if they are to be effective delegators.

1. When delegating, specify clearly and completely the expected level of performance, the constraints under which the subordinate will be operating, the level of initiative expected, and the type of action required.

2. Set a time at which the subordinate should report the results of her or his efforts to accomplish the delegated task.

3. Inform all who will be affected by the delegation that delegation has occurred.

4. Provide all information that is relevant to task accomplishment at the time delegation occurs, and pass on other information as it becomes available.

5. Allow subordinates to participate, as appropriate, in determining what tasks are delegated to them and when.

6. Avoid accepting "upward" delegation by requiring subordinates to propose solutions and not ask for your solutions first.

7. Evaluate primarily in terms of results, not means or methods.

8. Delegate consistently, not just when you are overloaded or when tasks are unpleasant.

Decentralization concludes organizing decisions that ensure well-organized work activities by segmenting individual and group efforts. The final organizing element is coordination. It is concerned with tying work efforts together.

Coordination

The final element in the organizing process is coordination. The object of coordination is to unify all of the manager's organizing efforts and ensure that the organizing process contributes to the achievement of organizational objectives.

Coordination Defined

Coordination is integration of the activities of individuals and units into a concerted effort that works toward a common aim. James D. Mooney, who wrote one of the landmark classics of management literature, *The Principles of Organization*,[15] believed that it was the duty of management to devise an appropriate organization, and his first principle of organization was coordination. He defined coordination as "the orderly arrangement of group effort to provide unity of action in the pursuit of a common purpose."

Individuals in an organization can be assigned only a small part of a total task. Consider the forty-five individuals working at Foreign Candy Corporation. Those people play several different roles. Some order the candies from Germany; others receive, unpack, and store the candies. Still other people call on customers, sell the candy, and develop new customers. Someone must also process the orders, pack and ship them, and provide follow-up services. Yet other people must pay bills, collect sales revenues, manage the firm's money, and plan for the future. For Foreign Candy Corporation to be a successful, lasting organization, all of these activities must be coordinated. Without such coordination, the various efforts of individual workers or departments within Foreign Candy Corporation would become haphazard, disjointed, and ineffective. Much like members of a symphony orchestra or workers in a factory, the individuals and work units at Foreign Candy must be integrated in a unified effort to advance a common aim.

Common to both definitions is the idea that coordination rests on three notions: "group effort," "unity of action," and "common purpose." Coordination helps to ensure that the endeavors of individual workers are integrated as a group effort. Managerial coordination seeks to ensure the efficiency of this group effort by unifying the actions of the various groups or departments within the organization. And the effectiveness of these collective efforts is "coordinated" by maintaining a link between the common purpose of the enterprise and all individual or group work activities. Coordinating, then, is similar to building effective teamwork.

Fundamentals of Coordination

How do managers ensure that their organizing efforts incorporate the element of coordination? What can they do when they structure work activities in order to be sure that those work activities will be effectively coordinated on a daily basis? The answer lies in three basic fundamentals of coordination: unity of command, chain of command or the scalar chain, and span of management. Managers who understand and use these concepts when making organizational decisions incorporate the element of coordination into the work structures they fashion.

UNITY OF COMMAND

According to the principle of **unity of command**, no subordinate should be responsible to more than one superior. The idea that workers cannot work for more than one boss was recognized by people in ancient cultures, and the Bible mentions the fact that no one can serve two masters. As noted in Chapter 2, Henri Fayol[16] is credited with explicitly stating the concept of unity of command in business settings. In his classic work, which appeared in French in 1916 and was later translated into English, Fayol laid out fourteen principles of management, one of which was the unity of command. Fayol believed strongly in unity of command: "A body with two heads in the social as in the animal sphere is a monster and has difficulty surviving."

Unity of command has been criticized in recent times as being too rigid for today's complex managerial settings. Modern managers need more flexibility. In larger organizations, horizontal communication is essential, especially in highly technical organizations where many types of very specialized expertise are needed. The conglomerate nature of corporate giants has spawned a need for new organizational forms that allow for more flexibility in superior–subordinate relationships. However, the spirit of the principle is still preserved as much as possible because the conflicts caused by violating it are well documented. (Some of the structures designed to allow more flexibility are discussed in Chapter 11.)

SCALAR CHAIN

The scalar chain is another of Fayol's principles of management. It is often referred to as the chain of command. The idea of the **scalar chain** is that the line of authority in an organization begins at the top, and authority is scaled down through the organization in an unbroken chain. As an organization chart illustrates, most authority resides at the top of the pyramid. At successively lower levels, authority is dispersed among more people. The legs of the pyramid that has been super-imposed on the organization chart in Figure 10-18 illustrate the unbroken chain. Note also that there is only one line passing through each level. Hence an employee at position H is connected to the top manager at position A through managers at F, D, and B.

The scalar chain serves to define the formal lines of communication between subordinates and immediate superiors throughout the organization. The chain of command also serves to reinforce unity of command.

The chain of command facilitates coordination, because managers who know the reasons behind key decisions or the role of another work unit serve as a "chain" through which subordinates channel information. However, as Fayol recognized, following the chain should not mean that a manager has to move up and then down the chain just to communicate with others at the same managerial level. Fayol maintained that short cuts in the communication process could be used to ease and speed communication. He proposed the "gangplank" or "Fayol Bridge" for communication on one level. In Figure 10-18, the manager at F might com-municate with a manager at position G (without sending a message all the way up one side of the pyramid and back down the other) by crossing the "gangplank" indicated by the dotted line. The gangplank is a kind of informal organization. It is used when communication necessary to coordinate two units does not need to flow through higher management levels.

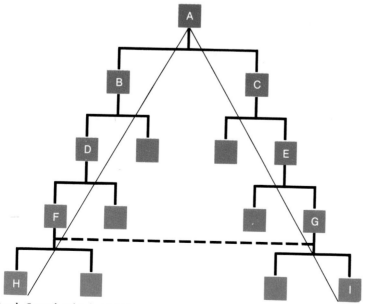

FIGURE 10-18
Scalar Chain and the "Gangplank"

Source: From H. Fayol, *General and Industrial Management*, trans. C. Storrs (London: Sir Isaac Pitman and Sons, 1963), p. 34. Copyright © 1987 by David S. Lake Publishers, Belmont, Calif. 94002.

SPAN OF MANAGEMENT

In an organizational framework, a manager has several subordinates under his or her direct supervision. The president of the firm, for example, has two or more vice presidents, each vice president has several managers under his or her direct supervision, each of those managers has several supervisors reporting directly to him or her, and so on. **Span of management** (or span of control, as it is often called) is the number of people or units a manager supervises. The number of people a manager supervises is an important consideration in that manager's ability to coordinate the activities of those subordinates and to integrate their activities with those of other work units in the organization. So choosing the correct span of management is important.

Sometimes span of management is referred to as span of control. This is because one thing that helps determine the appropriate span of management is how many subordinates a manager can effectively "control." But the term *span of management* seems to be preferred; control is only one managerial function, and the concept is intended to apply to all aspects of managerial activity.[17]

Spans of management are often described as "narrow" or "wide," depending on whether the manager at each level has few or many immediate subordinates. In addition, the "width" of the span helps to determine the "height" of the organization. For example, Figure 10-19(a) illustrates a narrow span of management, and such a firm is characterized as having a "tall" organization structure. Figure 10.19(b) shows a relatively wide span of management and a relatively "flat" organization. Factors that affect the choice of an appropriate span—and consequently determine the organization's "shape"—are discussed in the following paragraphs.

Optimal Span. Many early management writers hazarded suggestions about the ideal number of employees who should report to one manager, but a consensus has never been reached. Personalities as diverse as military strategist Sir Ian Hamilton and classical management writer Lyndall Urwick proposed ideal spans that ranged from three to six.[18] The idea of finding the ideal number of subordinates has attracted attention since ancient Roman and biblical times, and in the 1930s an accountant, V. A. Graicunas,[19] developed a mathematical formula to analyze superior-subordinate relationships. Graicunas based his thesis on the notion that humans have a limited attention span and can attend to only a few relationships at any one time. His formula showed that as the number of subordinates increased arithmetically, the complexity of the manager's job increased exponentially. Graicunas based his reasoning on the number of direct relationships and cross relationships that are introduced when one subordinate is added. The number of possible relationships was calculated via the formula

$$R = n(2^{n-1} + n - 1)$$

where: R = total number of relationships

$\quad\quad n$ = number of persons reporting directly to a supervisor

When a manager who has one subordinate gets another, the number of relationships grows from one to six. When the number of subordinates is increased to ten, the number of calculated relationships becomes 5,210!

Graicunas's formula helps us calculate the number of relationships involved in different spans of management, but it does not tell us what the optimal span is. Perhaps the fact that this question has been debated since ancient times means that there is no single optimal span of management. Rather, the number of rela-

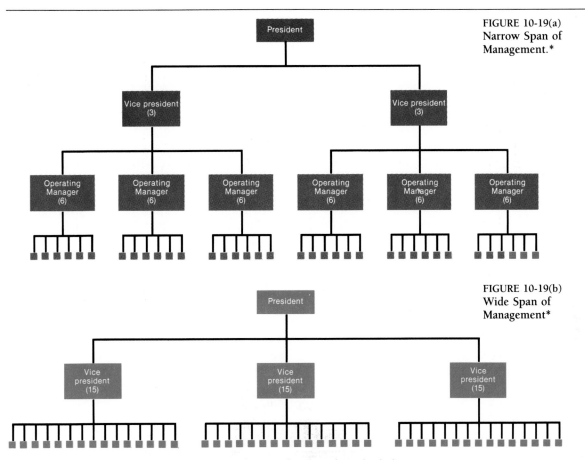

FIGURE 10-19(a)
Narrow Span of
Management.*

FIGURE 10-19(b)
Wide Span of
Management*

*The numbers in parentheses indicate how many people report directly to that individual.

tionships a manager can effectively coordinate depends on several factors associated with the work situation.

Factors That Affect Choice of Span. Recently, management researchers have begun to recognize that what span of management is appropriate depends on the work situation. That is, the coordination demands of a given managerial situation should dictate the most productive span of management. Evidence suggests that at least three sets of factors contribute to determining an appropriate span: factors associated with the activities supervised, with the manager, and with the subordinates.[20]

"Activity factors" include the similarity of the functions being performed, the complexity of the functions being performed, the degree of interdependence among organizational units, how often new problems arise in the unit, the extent to which procedures are standardized, and the efficiency of the total organization.

For example, the span of management conducive to effective coordination at a typical McDonald's hamburger restaurant is rather large. One store manager can easily coordinate twenty or more employees, because their work assignments are very routine and standardized. An account manager for an advertising agency requires a much narrower span of management, perhaps three or four people, to effectively coordinate the very creative and somewhat unpredictable process of working with a unique client situation.

"Manager factors" include the capability of the manager, the degree to which the manager is responsible for nonmanagerial tasks, the amount of time required for the manager to coordinate the activities of workers, the amount of time the manager must spend developing and integrating plans and objectives, how much of the manager's time is demanded by other people and other units, and how much organizational assistance the manager receives.

For example, sales management trainees with Procter & Gamble are initially given responsibility for one product in a narrow geographic area with only two or three subordinates to coordinate. Once they "prove" themselves over the course of twelve to eighteen months, they may be made responsible for ten or more subordinates who are involved in selling and distributing that same product across several geographic areas.

"Subordinate factors" include the competence of subordinates, the degree of interaction among subordinates, the physical proximity of subordinates, and the amount of direction and control required by subordinates.

The number of restaurants assigned to area managers for the Steak 'n Ale restaurant chain is regularly adjusted depending on the background and experience of individual unit managers. One area manager may have ten stores because they are all headed by experienced restauranteurs; another area manager may be responsible for only four stores because the local operators are inexperienced.

Figure 10-20 summarizes the relationship of some of these factors to the span of management. Inverse relationships indicate the need for narrower spans, whereas direct relationships signal that wider spans can be permitted.

Summarizing the Coordination Element

As managers confront organizing decisions, one critical element is the need to integrate individuals' and work units' activities into a concerted effort that advances a common aim. This element—coordination—is achieved by structuring the organization in such a way as to ensure vertical coordination between hierarchical levels of management and horizontal coordination across individuals and work units at similar levels. Managers try to ensure coordination by incorporating unity of command, a chain of command (the scalar chain), and a span of management appropriate to the situation as they make organizing decisions.

FIGURE 10-20
Factors Affecting Span
of Management

Factor	Description	Relationship to Span of Management
Complexity of the work activities	Job scope Job depth	Inverse: As complexity increases, the span must narrow.
Variety of the work activities	Number of different types of jobs being managed	Inverse: As variety increases, the span must narrow.
Proximity of the work activities	Physical dispersion of jobs being managed	Direct: If work activities are close, the span can increase.
Quality of subordinates	General quality of the subordinates being managed	Direct: If you have qualified subordinates, the span can increase.
Quality of the manager	Ability to perform managerial duties	Direct: A talented manager can accommodate a broader span.

Review of the Learning Objectives

Having studied this chapter, you should be able to respond to the learning objectives with extensions of the following brief answers.

1. **Define the term** *organizing,* **identify the four elements of organizing, and discuss why organizing is important to effective managing.**

   Organizing is the process of defining the essential relationships among people, tasks, and activities so that all of the organization's resources are integrated and coordinated to accomplish its objectives effectively. The four elements of organizing are as follows: (1) Determine the essential jobs to be done by dividing the total organizational task into work assignments each of which can logically be done by one person. (2) Group the individual tasks into meaningful units the members of which can work together effectively. (3) Decide who should be responsible for managing each of the groups of activities, and delegate those responsibilities. (4) Examine the objectives of the organization to determine the work that must be done to achieve those goals. Organizing is important to effective managing because it helps improve the efficiency and quality of an organization's work, it establishes an authority framework, and it facilitates communication throughout the organization.

2. **Explain specialization as a basis for organizing, and discuss some of the advantages and disadvantages of specialization.**

   Specialization involves dividing the work of the organization into separate tasks. As the organization grows, its total task becomes larger and the need to break the total task into smaller parts becomes greater. Some of the advantages of specialization include gains in worker efficiency and proficiency, easier selection and training of employees, use of more specialized equipment, and greater availability of the less-skilled labor required. Some of the disadvantages of specialization include worker boredom and dissatisfaction (which result in absenteeism and turnover), reduced quality of work, and loss of time in moving work in process from one worker to another.

3. **Define the term** *departmentalization,* **and explain several key ways in which managers implement departmentalization as a basis for organizing.**

   Departmentalization is the process of grouping jobs and resources into logical units to perform some organizational task. Four of the most commonly used bases for departmentalization are functional, product, customer, and geographic bases. *Functional departmentalization* groups jobs and resources within the company so that employees who perform the same or similar activities are in the same department. *Product departmentalization* groups jobs and resources around products or product lines that the company sells. *Customer departmentalization* groups jobs and resources around specific customer groups. *Geographic departmentalization groups* jobs and resources around different locations.

4. **Define the term** *authority,* **and describe at least two foundations of authority in organizational settings.**

   Authority is the right to command, to perform, to make decisions, and to expend resources. The *classical theory* of authority holds that authority flows from the top down through the organization and is a function of the position held in the organization. The *acceptance theory* of authority maintains that authority flows upward in an organization to the degree that subordinates are willing to act on a superior's directives. A third theory of authority states that the nature of the situation should be the force that grants authority. A final theory of authority holds that the person most knowledgable in a given situation has authority by virtue of his or her expertise.

5. **Define the term** *delegation,* **and explain the differences among responsibility, accountability, and authority.**

Delegation is the process by which a manager assigns tasks and authority to subordinates who accept responsibility for those jobs. Responsibility, accountability, and authority are three interrelated elements of the delegation process. *Responsibility* results from the assignment of tasks to immediate subordinates. *Accountability* is the subordinate's obligation to the manager to perform the assigned duties satisfactorily. *Authority* commensurate with assigned duties must be granted so that the accepted responsibility can be fulfilled.

6. **Explain the difference between decentralization and delegation, and discuss the factors that affect an organization's degree of decentralization.**

Delegation is the process of assigning tasks and granting sufficient authority for their accomplishment. *Decentralization* refers to the degree to which that authority is distributed throughout the organization. Factors that influence decentralization include dispersion of customers; dispersion of suppliers; homogeneity of the product line; volatility of the competitive environment; the company's size, attitude toward cost control, desire for uniformity of policy, and management philosophy; and the differences among functional areas.

7. **Define the term** *coordination* **as an element of organizing, and explain three basic principles underlying coordination.**

Coordination is the integration of activities of individuals and units into a unified effort that works toward a common aim. Three principles underlying coordination are *unity of command* (no subordinate should be responsible to more than one superior), the *scalar* chain (the line of authority in an organization begins at the top, and that authority is scaled down through the organization in an unbroken chain), and *span of management* (the number of people that a manager supervises).

Key Terms and Concepts

After completing your study of Chapter 10, "Fundamentals of Organizing," you should be able to explain the following terms and concepts:

organizing	skill variety	functional	authority	accountability
organization chart	task identity	departmentalization	power	decentralization
informal	task significance	product	line authority	centralization
organization	autonomy	departmentalization	staff authority	coordination
division of work	feedback	customer	functional authority	unity of command
specialization	job enlargement	departmentalization	delegation	scalar chain
job depth	job enrichment	geographic	responsibility	span of
job scope	departmentalization	departmentalization	parity principle	management
task characteristics				

Questions for Discussion

1. Why is organizing considered one of the essential functions of management?

2. Describe the trade-offs that a manager might face in trying to decide what degree of specialization is appropriate for his or her organization.

3. "One form of departmentalization is just as good as another." Comment on this statement.

4. Is there any relationship between authority and power? Explain why or why not.

5. Explain how the delegation process might be different in such settings as an accounting firm, a garment factory, and a department store. Be sure to consider all three elements of the delegation process: responsibility, accountability, and authority.

6. Describe the hypothetical cases of completely centralized and completely decentralized organizations. Why do such organizations not exist in reality?

7. What are some of the factors a manager should consider in deciding what span of management is appropriate for her or his organization?

Notes

1. Adapted from "The Foreign Candy Corporation," *Small Business Reports,* November 1987. *Small Business Reports* is a monthly management journal published for top executives in small and mid-sized companies by Business Research and Communications, 203 Calle del Oaks, Monterey, Calif. 93940.

2. A. Smith, *The Wealth of Nations* (New York: Modern Library, 1937). Originally published in 1776.

3. J. R. Hackman and E. E. Lawler, "Employee Reactions to Job Characteristics," *Journal of Applied Psychology Monograph 55* (1971): 269–286; J. R. Hackman and G. R. Oldham, "Development of the Job Diagnostic Survey," *Journal of Applied Psychology* 60, no. 2 (April 1975): 159–170.

4. J. R. Hackman and J. L. Suttle, eds., *Improving Life at Work* (Santa Monica, Calif.: Goodyear, 1977).

5. J. H. Donnelly, Jr., J. L. Gibson, and J. M. Ivancevich, *Fundamentals of Management: Functions, Behavior, Models,* 4th ed. (Plano, Tex.: Business Publications, 1981), pp. 331–333; N. M. Tichy, "Organizational Innovations in Sweden," *The Columbia Journal of World Business,* Summer 1974, pp. 18–27.

6. W. F. Dowling, "Job Design in the Assembly Line: Farewell to the Blue-Collar Blues?" *Organizational Dynamics,* Spring 1973, pp. 51–67; and P. G. Gyllenhammer, *People at Work* (Reading, Mass.: Addison-Wesley, 1977).

7. J. R. Hackman, "Work Design," in J. R. Hackman and J. L. Suttle, eds., *Improving Life at Work* (Santa Monica, Calif.: Goodyear, 1977), pp. 136–140.

8. The word *function* is used here to refer to the basic "business" activities—marketing, POM, finance, personnel/human resources, engineering, and R&D—found in any business enterprise. It is not to be confused with the basic "functions" of management: planning, organizing, directing, and controlling.

9. M. P. Follett, *Freedom and Co-ordination* (London: Management Publication Trust, 1949), pp. 1–15.

This lecture was first delivered in 1926 and was later reproduced in *Freedom and Co-ordination.*

10. C. I. Barnard, *The Functions of the Executive* (Cambridge, Mass.: Harvard University Press, 1938), p. 163.

11. H. C. Metcalf and L. Urwick, *Dynamic Administration—The Collected Papers of Mary Parker Follett* (New York: Harper and Brothers, 1940).

12. "Delegation," *Small Business Report,* June 1986, pp. 38–43; and D. Caruth and T. Pressley, "Key Factors in Positive Delegation," *Supervisory Management,* July 1984, pp. 6–11.

13. T. J. Erin, "How to Improve Delegation Habits," *Management Review,* May 1982, p. 59.

14. R. B. Chase and D. A. Tansik, "The Customer Contact Model for Organization Design," *Management Science* 29 (1983): 1037–1050.

15. J. D. Mooney, *The Principles of Organization* (New York: Harper and Brothers, 1947).

16. H. Fayol, *General and Industrial Administration* (London: Sir Isaac Pitman and Sons, 1947), p. 26.

17. Arthur G. Bedeian, "A History of the Span of Management," *Academy of Management Review* 2 (1977): 356–372.

18. I. Hamilton, *The Soul and Body of an Army* (London: Edward Arnold, 1921); and L. Urwick, "Scientific Principles and Organizations," *Institute of Management Series No. 19* (New York: American Management Association, 1938).

19. V. A. Graicunas, "Relationship in Organization," *Bulletin of the International Management Institute* (Geneva: International Labour Office, 1933). Reprinted in L. Gulick and L. F. Urwick, eds., *Papers on the Science of Administration* (New York: Institute of Public Administration, 1937).

20. D. Van Fleet, "Span of Management Research and Issues," *Academy of Management Review* 26 (1983): 546–552.

Cohesion Incident 10-1
Changes at the Top

"Charles, I guess I can look for my corporate overhead expense to increase again!" These were Roger's first words as Charles entered his office and saw him reading a recent memorandum from corporate headquarters.

"When I first started with Journey's End twelve years ago, we had sixty-five motels and all the managers reported directly to Will Gardner, the vice president of motel management. Just six years before I started, all managers reported straight to President Flynn himself. Will was a manager himself for fifteen years and used to visit each motel about once a year—more often if we had a problem—and then report back to Mr. Flynn. Now I see where they are going to redesign the organization chart to include four vice presidents of motel management, one for each of four geographic regions. Looks like we are going to wind up in the southeastern region with Alex Jordan as our vice president. The other regions will be the southwestern, northeastern, and northwestern. At least they're putting former managers in those positions as vice presidents. In fact, I started work for Journey's End as an assistant to Harold Cummings, who is going to be the vice president over the southwestern region. Here you go, Charles. You might want to look over the rest of this." With that he handed the memo over to Charles.

As Charles looked over the revised organization chart, he noticed a few differences from the chart he had seen at the training session six months earlier. At the top of the chart he now saw the president of the corporation. Reporting directly to him were the vice presidents of the functional departments of research and development, marketing, finance, and personnel. Charles remembered that the chart he had looked at a few months earlier had a fifth functional department, motel management, whose vice president also reported to the president.

The new organization chart also showed a new group of four vice presidents of motel management, all reporting to the president. Shown beneath them in the chart were the 123 Journey's End motels, grouped in terms of the territory in which each was located. In the southeastern region, Charles found the Graniteville motel along with twenty-seven other motels.

"Well, Charles, what do you think? I can remember my dad always telling me, 'If it ain't broke, don't fix it.' We've had such success with our original setup. I wonder why they're changing it now."

Discussion Questions

1. Draw the new organization chart. Include only the president and the vice presidents mentioned, plus the position of manager of Journey's End in Graniteville.

2. What is the main purpose of an organization chart? List some advantages and disadvantages of such charts.

3. Journey's End has changed its organizational structure from purely functional departmentalization to a functional/territorial structure. Explain each principle of organization, and give reasons why you think Journey's End decided to make this change.

Cohesion Incident 10-2
The Travis Policy Manual

When Steve came to work for Travis Corporation, he expected to receive a thick stack of policy manuals—the rules and regulations, so to speak. At least, that has been the experience of several of his college friends who had gone to work for two other large manufacturing firms. His friend Charlie, a management trainee at a nearby pharmaceutical company, even found a dress code, right down to white shirt and solid tie, included in the employee manual. Instead of a manual of detailed policies and procedures, however, Steve received a single page entitled "Travis Policy." It began:

> We believe that our people are our most important asset and we are committed to encouraging them to contribute and to grow as they desire and are capable. . . . We are committed to challenging and training our people and to supporting their educational needs. General managers and division presidents are responsible for the education of people in their organizations. Every effort will be made to provide opportunities for people to develop their skills and expertise further through on-the-job training and our managerial resource training programs.

Now that he's been with Travis several months, several experiences and observations that at first surprised Steve now seem consistent with the "Travis way of life" as it was described in that one-page statement. For example, at regularly scheduled department meetings, he and Bill are routinely asked for their suggestions about departmental functioning. Eileen and Leslie both seek out their ideas about current and future projects, as well as their evaluations of completed projects. At first Steve thought these requests were just to allow him and Bill to let off steam. But ever since his suggestions about revising the department's data management procedures were implemented, he has taken the requests more seriously. He enjoys approaching his job with an eye for improvement.

Steve has noticed similar things happening at other levels of the plant. A new market research strategy that the division marketing team is preparing to implement originated at the Elizabethtown plant as a result of Leslie's and Eileen's collaborative work. Eileen will be presenting it to other marketing managers at this month's division meeting. Steve's biggest surprise came when he toured the shop floor of the plant during orientation and learned that the supervisors had been elected by each work team and shift. In addition, ideas for recent design modifications of some of the equipment used in the plant came from the people who operate that equipment.

Though brief, the one-page policy statement addresses other key activities within the organization, such as planning:

> We believe in planning at all levels of the organization. Global regions are responsible for developing their own goals and strategies, and divisions are responsible for formulating and implementing their own one- and five-year plans, consistent with the overall corporate objectives.

responsibility of management:

> We believe in minimizing unnecessary layers of management, and to that end, division presidents and plant managers have responsibility for performance in these organizations and for setting and developing the means to accomplish their goals. We have no corporate procedures but leave those to the discretion of the division presidents and plant managers.

and communication:

> We believe the most important skill for Travis people is communication, and we will strive to develop our technology and our people's interpersonal skills to provide optimal communication one-to-one, among divisions, and around the world.

From others who have been with Travis for many years, Steve learned that prior to the company's reorganization fifteen years ago (before the Elizabethtown plant was even on the drawing board), policies and procedures were spelled out in much more detail, and key decisions were, without exception, made in the home office. Reorganization transformed the company from one departmentalized by function to one organized around product divisions in each geographic area. Each product division became a relatively independent profit center. Decisions that were once made at company headquarters (often after taking months to move through the company hierarchy) now are made at the division or plant level in much less time. The present policy statement was written to reflect the company philosophy that underlay this reorganization.

Sometimes Steve and Bill laugh about the new "club" they joined when they came to work for Travis—"Travistites," they called themselves. They had a hunch the name would never catch on as part of the official Travis policy statement; nonetheless, it wasn't unusual at all to hear people talk about the "Travis way" of doing things. For most of the people they worked with, the "Travis way of life" summed up company policy, much as the one-page policy manual did in its last phrase: ". . . participation, flexibility, commitment, and identity."

Discussion Questions

1. Distinguish between centralized and decentralized organizations. Which term best characterizes Travis Corporation? Explain why.

2. List several factors that affect the extent of centralization or decentralization in an organization.

3. Discuss how three of the factors you listed in question 2 affect centralization and decentralization in Travis Corporation.

Management Development Exercise 10
Assessing Your Orientation toward Organizing

This exercise is designed to help you understand the assumptions you make about people and human nature. These assumptions will influence the decisions you make, as a manager, about work division, departmentalization, delegation, and coordination. Ten pairs of statements follow. Assign a weight from 0 to 10 to each statement to show the relative strength of your belief in that statement. The points assigned for each pair must always total 10. Be as honest with yourself as you can, and resist the tendency to respond as you would like to think things are. There are no right or wrong answers to this exercise. It is designed to stimulate personal reflection and discussion.

1. It's only human nature for people to do as little work as they can get away with.   a. _____

   When people avoid work, it's usually because their work has been deprived of meaning.   b. _____

2. When employees have access to any information they want, they tend to have better attitudes and behave more responsibly.   c. _____

   When employees have access to more information than they need to do their immediate tasks, they generally misuse it.   d. _____

3. One problem in asking for the ideas of employees is that their perspective is too limited for their suggestions to be of much practical value.

    e. _____

    Asking employees for their ideas broadens their perspective and results in the development of useful suggestions.

    f. _____

4. If people don't use much imagination and ingenuity on the job, it's probably because relatively few people have much of either.

    g. _____

    Most people are imaginative and creative but may not show it because of limitations imposed by supervision and the job.

    h. _____

5. People tend to raise their standards if they are accountable for their own behavior and for correcting their own mistakes.

    i. _____

    People tend to lower their standards if they are not punished for their misbehavior and mistakes.

    j. _____

6. It's better to give people both good and bad news because most employees want the whole story, no matter how painful.

    k. _____

    It's better to withhold unfavorable news about business because most employees really want to hear only the good news.

    l. _____

7. Because a supervisor is entitled to more respect than those below him in the organization, it weakens his prestige to admit that a subordinate was right and he was wrong.

    m. _____

    Because people at all levels are entitled to equal respect, a supervisor's prestige is increased when she supports this principle by admitting that a subordinate was right and she was wrong.

    n. _____

8. If you give people enough money, they are less likely to be concerned with such intangibles as responsibility and recognition.

    o. _____

    If you give people interesting and challenging work, they are less likely to complain about such things as pay and supplemental benefits.

    p. _____

9. When people are allowed to set their own goals and standards of performance, they tend to set them higher than the boss would.

    q. _____

    When people are allowed to set their own goals and standards of performance, they tend to set them lower than the boss would.

    r. _____

10. The more knowledge and freedom a person has regarding his job, the more controls are needed to keep him in line.

    s. _____

    The more knowledge and freedom a person has regarding his job, the fewer controls are needed to ensure satisfactory job performance.

    t. _____

Scoring: To determine your scores, add up the points you assigned as follows:

Sum of a, d, e, g, j, l, m, o, r, and s = X score
Sum of b, c, f, h, i, k, n, p, q, and t = Y score

Your instructor will tell you how to interpret your scores once you have completed this exercise and scored your answers as suggested above.

Source: Adapted from M. Scott Myers, *Every Employee a Manager*, 2nd ed. (New York: McGraw-Hill, 1970). Used by permission of the author.

11

Organization Design

Your study of this chapter will enable you to do the following:

1. Define the term *organization design,* and discuss why it is important to the organizing function.
2. Identify five basic elements of organization design, and explain why it is important that these elements fit together.
3. Explain the meaning of the term *contingency,* and describe the major variables on which organization design is contingent.
4. Describe five organization design alternatives, and cite their principal advantages and disadvantages.
5. Identify four dimensions that reflect the future of organization design.

Redesigning the Apple Organization

Apple Computer was founded by Steven Jobs, a believer in new technology and a man destined to become a celebrated visionary in the computer industry. Co-founder Steve Wozniak, a brilliant engineer, designed the original Apple computer. Soon after its modest beginning, Apple began to be recognized in the business world as a rare corporate phenomenon, an entrepreneurial idea that had achieved extraordinary success driven by a special spirit and vision. Its employee teams were noted for their near fanaticism about the product groups for which they worked.

Unfortunately, success exacted a high price. Frequently companies that are superstars in the arena of new ventures do not survive in the long run because their founders are dreamers and geniuses like Jobs and Wozniak, not professional managers. To Jobs's credit, he recognized the need for managerial expertise. He hired John Sculley away from PepsiCo to become Apple's chief executive officer. From the beginning, Sculley saw revamping the Apple organization as his mission. In 1985, the Apple began to lose some of its polish, and Sculley realized that drastic action was necessary. The company experienced its first-ever quarterly loss, its stock price dropped to a three-year low, and sales (especially in the Macintosh Division) had been disappointing. Sculley felt that Apple needed to improve its marketing techniques and its responsiveness to retailers and customers. A part of his plan included redesigning Apple's basic organizational structure and systems.

As Figure 11-1(a) shows, Apple's structure had grown to encompass nine divisions. Each division was highly decentralized, and most of the divisions were organized primarily around a product line. This product focus was consistent with the emphasis that the founders, especially Jobs, had placed on products. However, the product structure had become a problem for at least two reasons. First, as Sculley noted in his memo (Figure 11-1a), the product divisions had gained too much independence and were being run almost as stand-alone companies. Second, the two major product divisions were at odds with each other. Jobs headed the Macintosh Division and treated his managers as the company's superstars. He regarded the Apple II Division as "dull and boring." But Macintosh sales had fallen short of expectations, and the Apple II Division was carrying the company. It was this sort of rivalry that had caused co-founder Wozniak to leave the firm.

Sculley's reasons for the proposed new structure, as enumerated in Figure 11-1(b), seemed sound: They included a lower breakeven point, simplified internal

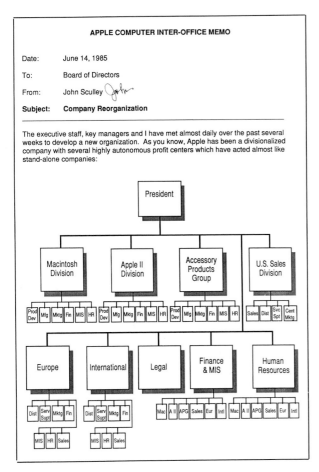

FIGURE 11-1(a)
Apple's Former
Organization Design

Source: Apple Computer, *Annual Report*, 1985, p. 4.

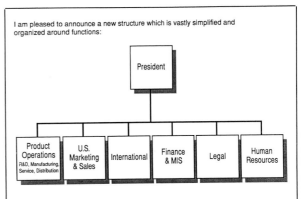

FIGURE 11-1(b)
The New Structure
at Apple

Source: Apple Computer, *Annual Report*, 1985, p. 5.

Steven Jobs and Steve Wozniak started the Apple Computer Company in a garage with the wooden framed computer shown here. Their invention grew quickly into a large computer company that was the beginning of the personal computer industry. Eventually, Apple had to confront the need for major organizational changes as the industry matured and became very competitive. (Jim Wilson/Woodfin Camp and Associates)

communications, and greater consistency in implementation. As Sculley pointed out, his reorganization might cost the company in the short run but should improve its viability in the long term. Industry experts indicated that Apple's success depended on its ability to develop more breakthrough products.[1]

Introduction

Chapter 10 presented principles that managers keep in mind when organizing specific parts of an organization. In this chapter we consider organization design—the structure of the entire organization. Considering organization design requires an overarching perspective, because it involves combining all the elements of the organization in a way that best implements the organization's strategy. Apple Computer CEO John Sculley took such an overarching perspective and saw redesigning Apple as essential to its future. He then recast virtually every part of the Apple organization into a new design more consistent with future market needs. In doing so, John Sculley was engaged in organization design.

This chapter will explain what managers must deal with as they shape organization design. After explaining what organization design is and why it is important, the chapter examines the fundamental role of strategy in shaping organization design. Next, the chapter introduces you to five basic elements incorporated into organization design. This is followed by an examination of five organization design alternatives and factors that affect organization design.

What Is Organization Design?

Organization design is the process of finding the fit between an organization's key elements (structure, people, tasks, decision and reward systems, and informal organization and culture) and its strategy that results in successful performance. The process of designing an organization is not a matter of choosing a single optimal design, and it is not a one-time decision. Organizations constantly change, and their designs must change with them. Some changes are incremental and occur gradually over relatively long periods of time; other changes are swift and dramatic. For both types of change, an organization must adjust its design so that it can continue to operate effectively.[2]

Why Organization Design Is Important

Designing the organization is an important part of effective management for at least four reasons. As an organization increases in size, its designs must become increasingly decentralized in order for managers to delegate decision-making authority to those parts of the organization best positioned to make the decisions. Second, different kinds of work require different designs, and the kinds of work that an organization emphasizes change over time. Third, the organization's design must be consistent with its chosen strategy. When the organization's strategy is changed, that new strategy's chances for success are enhanced by a supportive organization design. Finally, technology is an important part of every organization. As an organization's technology changes, its needs for information change. In addition, changes in decision making are made, and some of the organization's functions may have to be eliminated in favor of new ones. All of these technology-based changes suggest a need for corresponding changes in design.[3]

In short, any time there is a change in the way managers go about making decisions, the organization's design must be modified. The dynamism of today's management environment suggests that such changes will be occurring more and more often. Therefore, managers' interest in developing and refining the concepts and methods of organization design should continue to be strong.

Symptoms of Design Problems

A large part of any manager's job is to identify and solve problems. The manager is constantly bombarded with a host of symptoms that suggest organizational problems. It is not easy to decide whether such symptoms point to a need for design modifications or call for some other solution. However, there are several organizational problems that typically indicate the need to redesign.

One problem that often arises as a result of design failure is conflict, especially when the conflict is large-scale—that is, between groups or departments rather than individuals. Organizational conflict over basic goals and objectives is also a sign of design problems.

John Sculley noted in introducing Apple's new organization design that "Apple has been a divisionalized company with several highly autonomous profit centers which have acted almost like stand-alone companies." This was a polite way of alluding to several serious problems at Apple that led to Sculley's decision to reorganize the company. First, Sculley discovered fundamental disagreement over just what the company's overall mission and long-term goals should be. The Apple II group felt the company should focus on educational markets, emphasize affordable prices, and increase sales while boosting profitability by steadily developing software and hardware improvements over the basic Apple II computer. The Macintosh group, on the other hand, felt that Apple's success lay in being a technology leader and creating products that were always years ahead of the competition. Wanting most of all to be personally satisfied with their technical accomplishments, the members of this group were certain that profitability and market acceptance would follow. Both products were sold through the same retail outlets, and Sculley learned that retailers were increasingly frustrated with the different priorities, pricing, and logistical support emanating from the two divisions of Apple. This conflict was also seen in continual skirmishes between top managers of both divisions over what the other division's salespeople should and should not do to avoid interfering with their efforts to sell their product to national retail networks. Sculley recognized this conflict as symptomatic of the need to reorganize the firm.

A second indicator of design problems is managers' beginning to get involved in decisions that should be made at lower levels. A well-designed organization should be equipped to handle most problems that arise at lower levels in the organization. Only when a major crisis arises should top levels become involved. Problem-handling mechanisms should be a part of every effective design.

Sculley found himself and the top managers of the Apple II Division and the Macintosh Division meeting regularly to resolve how territorial salespeople from each division were to interact with local retailers. Similar negotiations were required over which accessories would be provided by the Accessory Products Group and how they would be priced, packaged, and shipped. Hence the top manager of the Accessory Products Group had to be present at these discussions. Sculley quickly became frustrated; he and two or three of the company's other top managers were regularly spending considerable time making decisions that should have been handled at lower organizational levels. This frustration was yet another symptom of the need to reorganize Apple.

A third problem that signals design flaws is difficulty in coordinating work between groups. Such a situation could be the result of any one of a number of organizational changes, or it could be due simply to normal growth. During the time Apple had separate product divisions, the firm's Accessory Products Group had an employee turnover rate twice that of the company as a whole.

One of the first things Sculley did upon arriving at Apple was to have Apple's Human Resources Department conduct exit interviews with every departing employee of the Accessory Products Group. The interviewers quickly learned that the main complaint of these employees was that they did not know whether to respond to the demands of the Apple II Division or the Macintosh Division when time was limited. They reported constant conflict and difficulty in coordinating the work between themselves and the demands these two "separate" businesses placed on them.

Fourth, when an organization begins to neglect critical areas of its operations or allows its technical expertise to decline, some design problems probably need to be corrected. Such neglect usually suggests that areas of responsibility have not been clearly delineated. This situation often results in the organization's being less sensitive to opportunities and threats than it should be.

Perhaps one of Sculley's greatest reasons to be frustrated, at first, with Apple was its virtual absence from the business computer market. Apple in effect conceded this market to IBM, and Sculley did not fully understand why. What he quickly found was that neither the Apple II Division nor the Macintosh Division considered itself responsible for studying the computer needs of the business market in order to design a product to meet them.

Finally, when organizational members are unclear about what their assignments are, design problems may be the cause. Such a situation often results in people working hard but working on the wrong things. That is, they may be efficient but not effective. One symptom of this condition is people having to ask where to concentrate their efforts, what goals to focus on, and where to locate required information. Signals such as these point to a need for a more sharply defined design, especially in terms of responsibilities. Sculley's initial reorganization reduced the number of jobs at Apple by 1,200 people—a telling indication of the level of unclear assignments, overlapping assignments, and duplication of effort that existed under the old Apple organization.

Shaping the proper organization design is an exciting and rewarding task. The foundation of effective organization design is its consistency with a company's strategy.

Strategy and Organization Design

The primary consideration in designing an organization is that organization's strategy. A well-developed design enhances the accomplishment of strategic objectives, and these strategic objectives should have been carefully selected to ensure successful organizational performance. Apple CEO John Sculley's strategy was for Apple products to become stronger in business markets and for Apple's overall market responsiveness to increase as its costs declined. Integrated functional areas handling all products were more consistent with this new strategy than the separate product divisions that characterized Apple's old organization design. Organization designs are overall plans for organizing the work, goals, relationships, and decisions of an organization in such a way that people can perform to the best of their abilities. Thus the ultimate goal of organization design is to facilitate performance. A poorly conceived design can prevent high performance. In a well-managed organization, the connection among strategy, design, and performance is strong. John Sculley's revamped organization design appears to have been well suited to Apple's new strategy—witness Apple's reemergence as an industry leader in sales growth and profitability, as well as its increasing presence in the business market of the 1990s.

This connection among strategy, design, and performance was first documented by Alfred Chandler,[4] whose phrase "structure follows strategy" is well known. He traced the development of some of the largest and best-known businesses in the United States and observed that as these organizations adopted new strategies to cope with waning performance due to increasing complexities, they found that their old designs could not accommodate the new strategies effectively. They had to devise new designs that facilitated the effective implementation of their new strategies.

Researchers have pointed out that an organization's existing design also affects its strategy. For example, the design places power in the hands of a certain group of people, so there is a tendency among the members of this group to formulate strategies that preserve the status quo. It is not necessary to figure out whether strategy or design came first, or which has more impact, but it is critical to acknowledge the strong reciprocal relationship that exists between strategy and design.[5]

Basic Elements of Organization Design

Our earlier definition of organization design identified five elements that are the focal points in designing organizations. Figure 11-2 portrays these five elements and the key factors that shape their role in the organization's design. Organization designs differ according to the nature of these five basic elements and the "fit" among them.

Figure 11-2 illustrates three important points. First, as we have just noted, a firm's strategy has a major impact on the nature of an organization's design. Second, organization design is also influenced by three critical factors: the external environment, the technology necessary to do the organization's work, and the size of the organization. Finally, it is important for managers to ensure an adequate "fit" among the five elements of organization design so that the link between strategy and performance will be achieved.

We turn now to a brief examination of the basic elements of organization design and the idea of fitting these elements together. This section is followed by

FIGURE 11-2
Key Considerations in
Designing Organizations

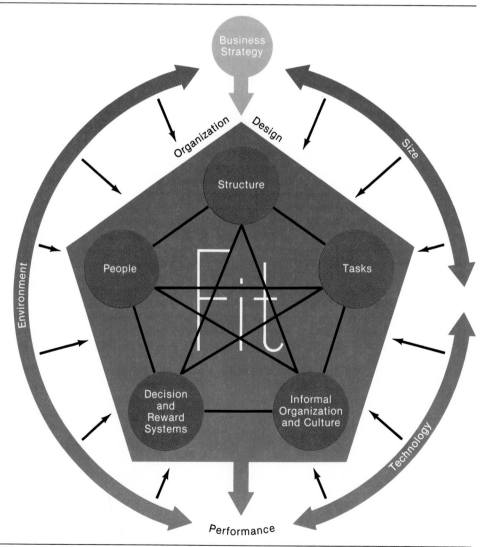

a broader discussion of fundamental structural alternatives in shaping organization design and by an examination of each of the three factors (environment, technology, and size) on which organization design is contingent.

Structure

Sometimes people use the term *structure* synonymously with *organization design*. As Figure 11-2 suggests, organization design encompasses more than just structure, but structure is a major manifestation of the organization's design. John Sculley's redesign of the Apple organization involved changes in each of the five basic elements, but it was primarily in the context of structure that management described and explained the changes in Apple's organization design.

Structure is the formal arrangement of the parts of an organization. An effective structure divides the organization's work into relevant subunits and at the same time provides the formal coordinating relationships that integrate each subunit's efforts into the organizationwide mission. An organization's structure builds on the concepts of coordination and specialization that were discussed in Chapter 10. What structure contributes to the design of the organization is a definition of each person's job and his or her formal relationships within the organizational framework. Because of its important role in communicating organization design, structure is discussed in greater depth in a subsequent section of this chapter.

Tasks

In terms of organization design, *tasks* are those activities that the organization must perform especially well in order to implement its strategy successfully and achieve its goals. For example, in an industrial organization, efficient manufacturing is a critically important task. In a retail firm, marketing and selling are of primary importance. Whereas product development and engineering/design were the critical tasks in the old Apple organization, John Sculley identified production and marketing as essential and structured the new Apple organization accordingly. He sought to shift Apple's emphasis to efficiency in production and effectiveness in marketing.

Identifying the organization's critical tasks is a key step in selecting a design alternative. In Chapter 10 we examined several aspects of job (task) design. That coverage will not be repeated here. Rather, the effects of the three contingencies (see Figure 11-2), particularly technology, on the task element of organization design are examined in a subsequent section.

People

The *people* who constitute an element of organization design are not only the current employees of the organization but also those who will be hired in the future. This element involves decisions about the number of people to be employed, their skill and ability levels, their personal characteristics, and their career expectations. Chapter 13 addresses the "people element" in greater detail.

One of John Sculley's early concerns upon joining Apple was the firm's overemphasis on technical, creative-oriented people and the comparative dearth of specialists in traditional cost control and sales, particularly in management positions. A major step in his redesign of the Apple organization was nearly to reverse these patterns.

Decision and Reward Systems

Decision and reward systems prescribe where and how decisions are made in the organization, the way information is to flow through the organization so that people can make these decisions, and how organization members are rewarded for making correct decisions. Decision and reward systems include formal planning and control mechanisms; the degree of decentralization allowed in the organization; and performance measurement, evaluation, and reward systems.[6]

Decision making and reward systems are covered primarily in other chapters. Chapter 3 describes the nature of decision making. Rewards are discussed in Chapter 13. The design of information systems to support decision-making and reward systems is treated in Chapter 20.

The central design consideration related to decision and reward systems is the degree of openness and centralization or decentralization they should display, which is largely contingent on the environment, technology, and size of the organization. This relationship is examined in a subsequent section of the chapter.

John Sculley was frustrated by two problems in Apple's old organization structure. Marketing decision making was highly decentralized in each product division and was guarded rather than open to scrutiny. And rewards were allocated solely at the discretion of product division managers. Sculley's new design sought to centralize decision making by function while making the substance and rationale of those decisions, particularly marketing decisions, fully open to employees and customers alike. He also encouraged a reward system for sales success that was straightforward and similar across product lines.

Informal Organization and Culture

The informal organization, which we discussed in Chapter 10, consists of the personal relationships and means of communication that are often necessary to accomplishing the work of the organization but are not a part of the formal organization structure. A related concept is the organization's **culture**: the shared beliefs, attitudes, and opinions about the company and what it stands for. The informal organization and the organization's culture are created by people throughout the company rather than being controlled by top management.

Informal organization and culture are important considerations in the overall design of an organization because of their influence on the behavior and performance of employees. In designing or redesigning an organization, management must always take the informal organization and the prevailing culture into account. If the organization's design clashes with its culture, it is most unlikely that the design will be effective. And where the design specifically attempts to frustrate part of the informal organization, harmful conflict may result.[7]

Apple was famous for its informal organization and its creativity-nurturing culture. John Sculley had to reorient both as part of his reorganization plan. Knowing full well the enormity of this undertaking, he sought gradually to introduce both a new reward system and changes in key people as his new strategy took hold. (One outcome was the eventual departure of Apple's co-founder, Steven Jobs.)

Fit

As Figure 11-2 suggests, all five of the design elements are interrelated. It is important that a match be achieved between each pair of elements. These matches should emphasize consistency and reinforcement. Some of the critical matches are illustrated below.

People/Decision and Reward Systems. The organization must employ people who have the skills and abilities necessary to make the types of decisions that the nature of the organization's work calls for. Also, reward systems must be designed so that they motivate people to perform effectively. John Sculley sought the best production people and the best sales and marketing people. He rewarded cost-effective production and sales penetration in existing retail channels as well as new business channels.

Tasks/People. The organization must employ people who have the skills necessary to perform its critical tasks.

Tasks/Reward Systems. It is true that organizations usually get what they are willing to reward. Therefore, organizations must design their reward systems such that they focus employees' efforts on the critical tasks that need to be accomplished.

People/Structure. Structure defines not only the specific jobs that need to be done but also how these jobs are grouped. People must be able to function effectively within the work groups defined by the formal structure. John Sculley wanted functional specialists expert in their particular areas and comfortable sharing as well as coordinating decisions that affected Apple's overall efforts.

Informal Organization/People. Every organization has its own culture or "personality." It may emanate from top management, but it represents those things that employees believe the organization values. An effective design is one wherein employees accept and support the organization's values.

Tasks/Structure. The technology of an organization dictates, to a considerable extent, what the critical tasks of the organization are. The formal structure of the organization must be chosen to accommodate its technology. John Sculley wanted a structure that allowed high task specialization and provided for control of the marketing function across products rather than within different product divisions.

Although the examples presented here do not exhaust all of the possible combinations of design elements, they should make it clear that successful organization design must take into consideration the relationships among these elements. This is particularly true in international settings, as illustrated in "Insights for International Managers 11."

Alternatives in Organization Design

When John Sculley made decisions about incorporating the five elements of organization design to create Apple's new organization, he found the element of structure the best medium for explaining the new organization design at Apple. This is not unusual. As we have noted, structure is the primary manifestation of an organization's design. So in our discussion of design alternatives, we will follow the lead of so many practicing managers and describe key design alternatives in terms of different structures. (The other design elements are treated in considerable detail in the separate chapters that we identified when we introduced those elements.)

■ *Insights for International Managers 11* ■

DESIGNING WORK GROUPS AND TEAM BUILDING IN OVERSEAS LOCATIONS

Some peoples, such as Saudis and South Americans, tend not to be experienced or comfortable with the requirements of teamwork, nor do they necessarily appreciate joint credit. Arabs and Latins are extremely individualistic, and their characters will have to be recognized when organizational structure and group dynamics are considered. If teamwork is vital to the work done in the overseas location, you must give considerable attention to changing work habits and providing models for group behavior.

Team building may be impossible in places where different hostile tribes or long-term national rivals cannot work together, or where groups of dif-ferent status cannot be forced into the same work situations. This problem often arises in India, for example, where Indians of different castes are very uncomfortable being trained together, even though the caste system is officially banned.

On the other hand, in countries where teamwork is traditional, most American managers need to allow more time for the team approach—in Korea and Japan, for example. A Coopers & Lybrand executive observed: "If you have to debug a program, an American will go off alone to solve the problem, but the Chinese will do it in a group, often at the top of their voices."

Source: From L. Copeland and L. Griggs, *Going International* (New York: Random House, 1985), p. 153.

Most contemporary organizations exhibit one of five structures: simple, functional, divisional, strategic business unit (SBU), or matrix. We will briefly describe each structural type and explain its strengths and weaknesses.

Simple Structure

The **simple structure** exists in firms that have just one manager and a general group of employees. It prevails in the smallest organizations, and the manager is usually the owner of the business. All strategic and operating decisions are made by the owner-manager. The primary strategic concern in small organizations is usually survival, and one bad decision could seriously threaten that survival. Hence a structure that maximizes the owner's control is appropriate. It also makes possible rapid responses to product/market shifts and enhances the firm's ability to accommodate unique customer demands without difficulties in coordination. Simple structures encourage employee involvement in more than one activity and so protect the small firm from becoming too dependent on a single specialist. This design works especially well for businesses that serve a localized, simple product/market, as many service businesses do. However, the simple structure can be very demanding on the owner-manager, and, as volume increases, he or she feels pressured to pay more attention to day-to-day concerns rather than to long-range management activities. Figure 11-3 shows a model of a simple structure and summarizes its advantages and disadvantages.

Functional Structure

The functional structure predominates in firms that concentrate on one or a few related product/markets. **Functional structures** group similar tasks and activities (such as those of production/operations, marketing, finance/accounting, research

FIGURE 11-3
Advantages and
Disadvantages of Simple
Structure

Advantages	Disadvantages
1. Facilitates control of all the businesses's activities.	1. Very demanding on the owner–manager.
2. Rapid decision making and ability to change with market signals.	2. Increasingly inadequate as volume expands.
3. Simple and informal motivation/ reward/control systems.	3. Does not facilitate development of future managers.
	4. Tends to focus owner–manager on day–to–day matters and not on future strategy.

Source: J. A. Pearce, II, and R. B. Robinson, Jr., *Strategic Management: Formulation and Implementation of Competitive Strategy,* 3rd ed., Richard D. Irwin, Inc. © 1988, p. 360.

and development, and personnel) as separate units within the organization. This specialization encourages greater efficiency and refinement of particular expertise, and it enables the firm to seek and foster distinct competencies in one or more functional areas. Expertise is critical to single product/market companies and to firms that are vertically integrated. The functional structure helps a firm fine-tune its particular competitive advantage and focus on whichever departments are the core of its strategy. John Sculley's new organization at Apple used the functional structure. Sculley saw Apple as a simple computer company with a very limited product line. He felt Apple needed to build a competitive advantage in production and another in marketing if it was to grow and prosper. Apple boosted its production efficiencies and marketing skill by creating separate functional departments for each of those areas. These departments handled both Apple II computers and the Macintosh line at the same time. A model of a functional structure is shown in Figure 11-4.

Divisional Structure

When a firm diversifies its product or service lines, covers broad geographic areas, utilizes unrelated market channels, or begins to serve customer groups distinctly different from those it has served before, a functional structure rapidly becomes inadequate. For example, functional managers may wind up overseeing the production or marketing of numerous and vastly different products or services, and top management may have to coordinate activities that it is beyond their capacity to monitor with a functional structure. When this happens, some form of divisional structure is necessary to meet the coordination and decision-making requirements resulting from increased diversity and size. A **divisional structure** organizes the company into distinct divisions that operate with considerable autonomy from other divisions and that usually perform their own marketing and operations activities.[8] Divisional structures are usually organized in terms of products, geographic areas, distinctly different marketing channels, or customer groups. For

FIGURE 11-4
Advantages and
Disadvantages of
Functional Structure

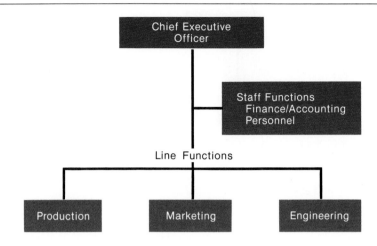

Advantages

1. Efficiency through specialization.
2. Improved development of functional expertise.
3. Differentiates and delegates day-to-day operating decisions.
4. Retains centralized control of strategic decisions.

Disadvantages

1. Promotes narrow specialization and potential functional rivalry or conflict.
2. Difficulty in functional coordination and interfunctional decision making.
3. Staff–Line conflict.
4. Limits internal development of general managers.

Source: J. A. Pearce, II, and R. B. Robinson, Jr., *Strategic Management: Formulation and Implementation of Competitive Strategy,* Richard D. Irwin, Inc., © 1988, p. 360.

example, Apple's international growth may one day make it advisable for Apple to organize into domestic and international divisions. Similarly, Sculley could have found that selling to businesses was so different from selling to schools that the company needed to be organized into a Business Division and a School Division. The typical divisional structure is depicted in Figure 11-5.

A divisional structure enables corporate management to delegate authority for the management of a distinct business entity. This arrangement can expedite critical decision making within each division in response to varied competitive environments, and it leaves corporate management free to concentrate on decisions with companywide implications. The divisional structure helps clarify accountability by facilitating the accurate assessment of profit and loss so that top management can single out poorly performing divisions for closer scrutiny. Although the divisional structure offers several advantages, the Apple experience suggests that it can be costly and inefficient when distinctly different products, geographic areas, or customer groups do not truly exist.

Strategic Business Units

Some firms have difficulty controlling their divisional operations as the diversity, size, and number of these units continue to increase. It becomes increasingly difficult for corporate management to evaluate and control the many, often multi-industry divisions. Under these conditions, it may be necessary to add another layer of management in order to improve strategy implementation, promote syn-

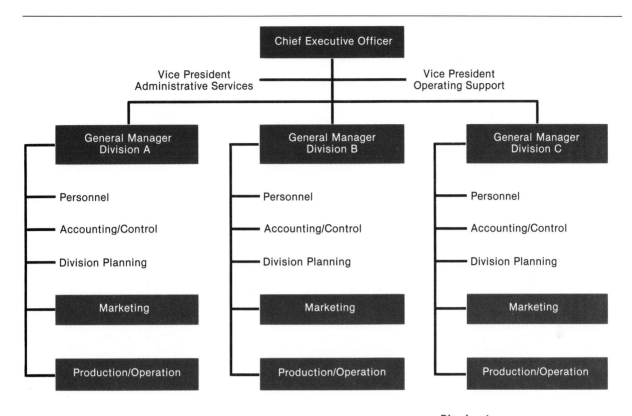

Advantages

1. Forces coordination and necessary authority down to the appropriate level for rapid response.
2. Places strategy development and implementation in closer proximity to the divisions' unique environments.
3. Frees chief executive officer for broader strategic decision making.
4. Sharply focuses accountability for performance.
5. Retains functional specialization within each division.
6. Offers good training ground for strategic managers.

Disadvantages

1. Fosters potentially dysfunctional competition for corporate–level resources.
2. Problem with the extent of authority given to division managers.
3. Potential for policy inconsistencies between divisions.
4. Problem of arriving at a method of distributing corporate overhead costs that is acceptable to different division managers with profit responsibility.

Source: J. A. Pearce, II, and R. B. Robinson, Jr., *Strategic Management: Formulation and Implementation of Competitive Strategy,* Richard D. Irwin, Inc., © 1988, p. 366.

FIGURE 11-5
Advantages and Disadvantages of Divisional Structure

ergy, and gain greater control over the diverse business interests of the organization. An effective way to build an additional management layer into the structure is to group various divisions (or parts of some divisions) in terms of common strategic elements. The structure of these groups, which are often called **strategic business units (SBUs)**, is usually based on the independent product/market segments served by the firm.

A diagram of the SBU structure is shown in Figure 11-6. General Electric pioneered the SBU organization structure. Faced with having little profit growth to match its massive growth in sales, GE restructured over forty-eight of its divisions into six SBUs. For example, three separate divisions that made food preparation appliances were merged into a single housewares market. General Foods has designed its SBUs along menu lines: breakfast foods, beverages, main meals,

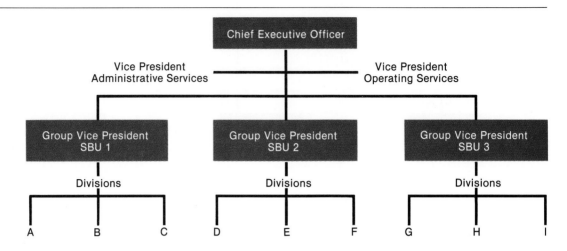

Advantages	Disadvantages
1. Improves coordination between divisions with similar strategic concerns and product/market environments.	1. Places another layer of management between the divisions and corporate management.
2. Tightens the strategic management and control of large, diverse business enterprises.	2. Dysfunctional competition for corporate resources may increase.
3. Facilitates distinct and in-depth business planning at the corporate and business levels.	3. The role of the group vice president can be difficult to define.
4. Channels accountability to distinct business units.	4. Difficulty in defining the degree of autonomy for the group vice presidents and division managers.

Source: J. A. Pearce, II, and R. B. Robinson, Jr., *Strategic Management: Formulation and Implementation of Competitive Strategy,* Richard D. Irwin, Inc., © 1988, p. 367.

FIGURE 11-6
Advantages and Disadvantages of Strategic Business Unit Structure

desserts, pet foods, and so on. (See "In Practice 11-1" for a description of General Foods's SBU organization.) Such a configuration enables General Foods to target specific markets more effectively.

Matrix Organization

In large companies, increased diversity leads to numerous product and project efforts, all of which have major strategic significance. The result is a need for an organizational form that provides and controls skills and resources where and when they are most useful. The matrix organization, pioneered by such firms as defense contractors, construction companies, and large CPA firms, has increasingly been used to meet this need. The list of companies now exhibiting some form of matrix organization includes Citicorp, Digital Equipment, General Electric, Shell Oil, Dow Chemical, and Texas Instruments.

The **matrix organization** is an organization structure that establishes dual channels of authority, performance responsibility, evaluation, and control. Job holders are typically assigned to both a basic functional area and a project or product manager, as shown in Figure 11-7.

A hypothetical example at Apple Computer will help illustrate the matrix approach. Say that, in the interest of expanding more fully into the business and school markets, John Sculley assigns two trusted managers as product development coordinators for each of these markets. Each manager is designated project manager for the product development project in his or her distinct market.

In Practice 11-1

GENERAL FOODS TO REORGANIZE

The General Foods Corporation, a part of the Philip Morris Companies, recently eliminated most of its corporate staff and created separate operating companies to run its three lines of business, as shown in the following table:

The Split-Up at General Foods

Under the corporate restructuring plan, each of the company's three product sectors would become a separate operating company reporting directly to Philip Morris.

Philip Morris Companies

↓

General Foods Corporation
The White Plains-based food producer with 1986 sales of $9.66 billion was acquired by Philip Morris in 1985.

General Foods U.S.A.
Formerly the domestic grocery sector. Products include Jell-O, Birds Eye, Kool-Aid, Entenmann's, Crystal Light, Ronzoni pasta, and Post cereals.
Sales: $3.3 billion.

General Foods Coffee and International
Formerly the worldwide coffee and international sector. Products include Maxwell House, Yuban, Sanka, Brim, Maxim, and General Foods International coffees. Also other items distributed outside the U.S.
Sales: $4.3 billion.

Oscar Mayer Foods
Formerly the processed meat sector. Products include Louis Rich turkey products, Claussen pickles, luncheon meats, bacon, sausage, and hot dogs.
Sales: $2.1 billion.

General Foods, whose brand names include Kool-Aid, Maxwell House coffee, Jell-O gelatin, and Entenmann's baked goods, said the reorganization is intended to reduce the number of layers of management so that its division can make faster and more flexible decisions. "This decentralization will make our businesses more formidable competitors because they will be able to move quickly and aggressively," said Philip Smith, president and chief executive of General Foods and head of the three product sectors.

Smith acknowledged the need to improve the company's sales, especially in the coffee and domestic grocery products sectors. "The business environment has become increasingly competitive," he said, "and by redesigning our organization our sectors will become more responsive and faster afoot."

"This is the beginning of . . . changes designed to make General Foods a more dynamic organization," said Lawrence Adelman, a food and beverage analyst at Dean Witter Reynolds, Inc.

Each of General Food's three basic lines of business (or "product sectors" as General Foods calls them) was restructured as a separate strategic business unit within the parent company, Philip Morris's, portfolio of businesses. The organization design within each SBU would then vary depending on the SBU's strategy and the basic design elements within each SBU.

Oscar Mayer Foods will use a functional type of organization. Its meat and pickle products are processed in two centralized locations and then sold through standard food distribution channels. A simple functional design will maximize efficiency. General Foods Coffee and International will use a matrix type of structure, with product managers and territorial managers jointly managing product sales in separate territories in a manner best suited to each domestic or international territory. General Foods U.S.A. will use a geographic divisional type of structure, with major warehouses in five geographic territories forming the center of each division's operations.

Source: Adapted from "The Split-Up at General Foods," *New York Times,* August 18, 1987.
Copyright © 1987 by The New York Times Company. Reprinted by permission.

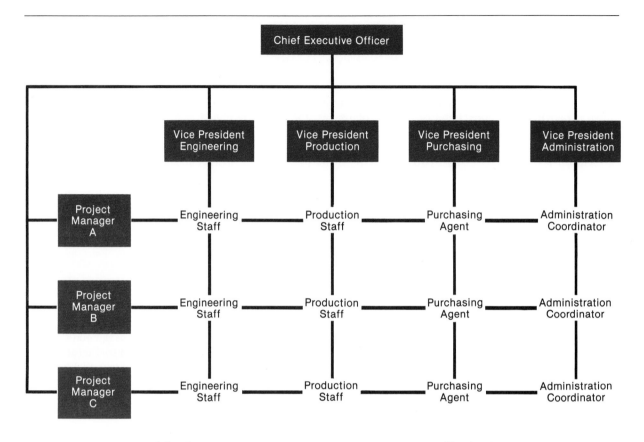

Advantages

1. Accommodates a wide variety of project–oriented business activity.
2. Good training ground for strategic managers.
3. Maximizes efficient use of functional managers.
4. Fosters creativity and multiple sources of diversity.
5. Broader middle–management exposure to strategic issues for the business.

Disadvantages

1. Dual accountability can create confusion and contradictory policies.
2. Necessitates tremendous horizontal and vertical coordination.

Source: J. A. Pearce, II, and R. B. Robinson, Jr., *Strategic Management: Formulation and Implementation of Competitive Strategy*, Richard D. Irwin, Inc., © 1988, p. 369.

FIGURE 11-7
Advantages and Disadvantages of Matrix Structure

These two project managers need virtually the same type of five-person team. They need an Apple II product engineer, a Macintosh product engineer, a software technician, a production specialist, and an administrative coordinator. John Sculley, after ascertaining their needs, would probably authorize the temporary assignment of ten people from their respective functional areas—five for each project manager. Each such person would be given specific tasks in connection with the project to which she or he was assigned and would be accountable to the project manager for completing them. Indeed, they would probably work very closely with their project manager. At the same time, they would remain accountable to their functional manager for their work on this project as well as for other responsibilities they retained in their functional areas.

The matrix structure is intended to combine the advantages of functional specialization and product or project specialization. A "matrix-based" work group specializes in a narrowly defined project while retaining the ties that members of that work group have to the permanent functional structure of the company. In theory, the matrix is a conflict resolution system through which strategic and operating priorities are negotiated (the strategic need for a new product or project, for instance, versus the routine operating needs of the various functional areas), power is shared, and resources are allocated internally on the basis of what is best for the unit as a whole.

The matrix increases the number of middle managers who exercise general management responsibilities and broadens their exposure to organizationwide strategic concerns. Thus it can accommodate a shifting focus on varied projects, product/markets, or technologies and increase the efficient use of functional specialists who might otherwise be idle.

Although the matrix structure is easy to design, it is difficult to implement. Dual chains of command challenge fundamental principles of effective organization. Negotiating shared responsibilities, the use of resources held in common, and priorities can create misunderstanding or confusion among subordinates.

To overcome the deficiencies that might be associated with a permanent matrix structure, some firms use a "temporary" or "flexible" overlay structure to accomplish each individual strategic task. Our Apple example could easily represent such a temporary structure. This approach is meant to take temporary advantage of a matrix-type team while preserving the shape and spirit of the underlying divisional structure. Thus the basic idea of the matrix structure is to sharpen a group's focus and concentrate its resources on a narrow but strategically important product or market. It appears to be an important structural alternative in large, diverse organizations.

Choosing among these five design alternatives is a challenging assignment for any manager. It is important to consider how selected factors have important implications on organization design. These factors are discussed in the next section.

Guidelines for Management Practice

The need to redesign the organization does not arise every year, but neither is it rare, given today's rapidly changing markets and environments. Managers who hope to assist effectively in organization design should remember the following guidelines:

1. It is acceptable to use more than one organization design alternative within the same organization. For example, a company's core technology may be organized functionally, whereas product management and marketing may be organized divisionally or in a matrix format.

2. Once an organization's design has been selected, it is often useful to try to minimize key disadvantages associated with that structure. For example, cross-functional problem-solving teams or forums can help overcome the "territorial" problems associated with functional structures.

3. Changing from one structure to another is a major challenge to any organization. Changes in organization structure should therefore be undertaken only after careful deliberation. Focusing on making the advantages of the new structure evident to members of the organization eases resistance to structural change.

Factors That Affect Organization Design

Three factors have been found to have an effect on the design of an organization. The most appropriate design for an organization seems to be contingent on such variables as the state of its environment, the complexity of its technology, and its size. The organization's environment is an external variable; its technology has internal as well as external aspects; and its size is principally an internal factor.

Environment

As we noted in Chapter 4, organizations are influenced by the broader environment in which they exist. Government policy, societal values and social norms, economic trends, and the rate of technological change and innovation are general environmental factors that can affect virtually any organization. And every business must adjust daily to its customers, competitors, suppliers, and creditors—all are part of its immediate environment.

Managers of businesses design their organizations to take advantage of opportunities that arise in their environment and to respond to changes in this environment. Most studies investigating the relationship between an organization's design and its environment have concluded that the best design for a given organization is contingent on the characteristics of its environment.[9]

In the early years of the personal computer industry, Apple grew rapidly, while maintaining a highly decentralized, divisional structure that was really a confederation of many different product-centered businesses. As the PC industry became more competitive and structured, Apple eventually found it necessary to adopt a more centralized, functional structure in order to achieve greater control over its sales and marketing efforts and to enhance its operating efficiency.

ENVIRONMENTAL VARIABILITY

In assessing the possible impact of the environment on its design, an organization must consider the amount of variability in its environment—that is, the degree of change with which it must be prepared to cope. It must consider the frequency of change, the magnitude of change, and the predictability of change. An organization's environment may be stable, changing, or turbulent. As Figure 11-8 shows, these degrees of variability can be arranged on a continuum. Figure 11-8 lists some of the characteristics common to stable and to turbulent environments, which represent the theoretical end points of the continuum.

Stable Environments. A **stable environment** is one that experiences little or no unexpected or sudden changes. Products require only minor changes, if any, and the market shows very few fluctuations. For whatever reasons, the product attracts neither regulatory attention nor technological innovation. Consequently, the organizations in a stable environment can remain virtually the same for a long time. But stable environments are becoming more scarce. It is difficult to think of many organizations that have made the same product with the same process and sold it in essentially the same way for the last century.

Arm & Hammer is one organization with a stable environment. It has been providing baking soda to similar markets for over one hundred years. The markets have grown, outlets for selling baking soda have changed, and additional uses for the product have been found, but the overall level and rate of change in the product and its markets have been minimal.

Dimensions of Variability	Environmental Types		
	Stable	Changing	Turbulent
Frequency of Changes	Seldom, never	Often	Constantly
Magnitude of Changes	Small, incremental		Large
Predictability of Changes	Highly predictable	Follows trends	Erratic

FIGURE 11-8
Continuum of Environmental Variability

Source: Reprinted by permission from *Management,* 2nd ed., by E. F. Huse. Copyright © 1982 by West Publishing Company. All rights reserved.

Changing Environments. **Changing environments** are defined by trends that are predictable. Thus the organization can be prepared to adjust to the changes when they occur. For example, the environment of many service firms could be characterized as changing. Trends in demand for services often depend on the social fabric of society. Values and tastes certainly change over time, but these changes do not usually occur so unexpectedly or so rapidly that service firms cannot adjust to them. The characteristic flexibility of service firms helps them adapt readily to such changes. Firms that produce products can also predict trends in changing environments. For example, Apple's decision to position itself more strongly in the business computer market was motivated in part by the overall decline in the student population (Apple's traditional strength), which resulted from changes in demographic trends that were apparent well before they actually affected the numbers of students.

Holiday Inns is another example of a company that is adjusting its business to predictable changes—in this case, changes in the social characteristics of potential lodging customers. Specifically, the rising number of women in the work force has created a need to ensure that lodging facilities accommodate female as well as male executives. And the declining number of families has reduced the emphasis on family-centered accommodations.

Turbulent Environments. **Turbulent environments** are marked by swift, frequent, and radical changes that occur with little or no warning. In the early stages of development of an industry, its environment is often turbulent as a new technology quickly emerges to replace an older one, new products or models are rapidly introduced to supersede yesterday's, and (often) regulations are imposed to reign in the rapidly changing industry. Usually this turbulence is temporary, and the industry and its surviving organizations soon settle down into a less volatile state. The computer industry, however, is an exception. It has operated in a turbulent environment for several decades now.[10]

Consumer electronic products constitute one of the most rapidly changing industries worldwide. A model introduced in the fall of the year, such as a VCR camera, is often rendered obsolete by new models—and even new technologies—available the next spring.

DESIGNING ORGANIZATIONS TO MATCH THEIR ENVIRONMENTS

Some of the pioneering work on the relationship between organization design and environment was done by Tom Burns and G. M. Stalker.[11] They found that successful organizations were designed differently in different environments. They distinguished between two types of organization designs: a mechanistic design and an organic design. The characteristics of both these designs are summarized in Figure 11-9.

Mechanistic Designs. A **mechanistic design** follows Weber's bureaucratic model (discussed in Chapter 2) very closely in that it is characterized by specialized activities, specific rules and procedures, an emphasis on formal communication, and a well-defined chain of command. Because mechanistic designs tend to be inflexible and resistant to change, this type of design is more successful in a stable environment. The U.S. Army offers a good example of a mechanistic design.

Organic Designs. In an **organic design**, task activities are loosely defined, there are very few rules and procedures, and great emphasis falls on self-control, participative problem solving, and horizontal communication. Organic designs are more successful in dynamic, rapidly changing environments that require adaptability to change. Apple's early organization design was organic. The personal computer industry (which Apple pioneered) was rapidly changing, and this design was well suited to those early days of a new industry.

Burns and Stalker did not suggest that organizations could make one of only two design choices on the basis of their environment. They recognized that the

---

Guidelines for Management Practice

Responding to environmental factors by adjusting organization design is a challenging undertaking. The following guidelines provide some useful, fundamental considerations managers should incorporate into the organization design efforts they are responsible for initiating.

1. One of the strongest sources of resistance to a new strategy comes from people who prefer the firm's current organization design. There are at least two effective ways to deal with this resistance: (1) Early in the planning process, discuss the design implications of different strategies. (2) Remove or transfer key managers who are not willing to accept the new design. This is not to say that no "intermediate" solutions are possible, but it should be obvious which of these two approaches is less disruptive to the firm.

2. One of the key environmental factors to consider in designing an organization is the markets served by the firm. Regular monitoring of customers, end users, and channels of distribution helps alert managers to needs that may require changes in design.

3. Small firms make design changes (particularly structural changes) more frequently than large firms. Small, growing firms typically shift from a functional to a divisional structure to accommodate the management of increasing product lines—and then from a divisional back to a functional structure as the needs for better control and greater profitability become more acute.

FIGURE 11-9
Comparison of
Mechanistic and
Organic Organizations

Mechanistic	Organic
1. Tasks are highly fractionated and specialized; little regard paid to clarifying relationship between tasks and organizational objectives.	1. Tasks are more interdependent; emphasis on relevance of tasks and organizational objectives.
2. Tasks tend to remain rigidly defined unless altered formally by top management.	2. Tasks are continually adjusted and redefined through interaction of organizational members.
3. Specific role definition (rights, obligations, and technical methods prescribed for each member).	3. Generalized role definition (members accept general responsibility for task accomplishment beyond individual role definition).
4. Hierarchical structure of control, authority, and communication. Sanctions derive from employment contract between employee and organization.	4. Network structure of control, authority, and communication. Sanctions derive more from community of interest than from contractual relationship.
5. Information relevant to situation and operations of the organization formally assumed to rest with chief executive.	5. Leader not assumed to be omniscient; knowledge centers identified where located throughout organization.
6. Communication is primarily vertical between superior and subordinate.	6. Communication is both vertical and horizontal, depending on where needed information resides.
7. Communications primarily take form of (1) instructions and decisions issued by superiors and (2) information and requests for decisions supplied by inferiors.	7. Communications primarily take form of information and advice.
8. Insistence on loyalty to organization and obedience to superiors.	8. Commitment to organization's tasks and goals more highly valued than loyalty or obedience.
9. Importance and prestige attached to identification with organization and its members.	9. Importance and prestige attached to affiliations and expertise in external environment.

Source: Adapted from T. Burns and G. M. Stalker, *The Management of Innovation* (London: Tavistock, 1961), pp. 119–122. Used with permission.

environment surrounding each firm is unique and that each firm must design its structure accordingly. The mechanistic and organic designs are not two "either-or" design options; rather, they exist at opposite ends of a continuum along which an organization's design is characterized.

Later work by Paul Lawrence and Jay Lorsch[12] supported Burns and Stalker's findings. Lawrence and Lorsch studied several firms in three different industries and found that more effective firms had designs that matched their environments in a manner suggested by Figure 11-10. The most effective firms in stable industries had mechanistic organization designs, whereas the most effective firms in turbulent industries had organic designs.

FIGURE 11-10
Suggestions about
Organization Design
from the Work of Burns
and Stalker and of
Lawrence and Lorsch

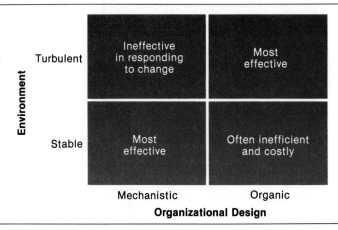

While the nature of a firm's external environment has a strong influence (or should have) on the firm's organization design, other influences must be considered. Another important factor to be taken into account in organization design decisions is the nature of the firm's technology.

Technology

As we have said, technology has internal as well as external dimensions. There is a tendency to associate technology only with factories and machines, but in terms of organization design, its meaning is much broader. **Technology** encompasses all the tools, equipment, processes, actions, materials, and knowledge required to convert an organization's inputs into outputs that can be distributed as useful goods or services. This definition makes it possible for such diverse activities as teaching students, dry cleaning clothes, and assembling automobiles all to be considered technologies. In this sense, technology is an internal dimension; it is the way the organization goes about doing the work it exists to do.[13] A professor can teach a course with three hundred students in one class; another course might be restricted to thirty-five students. The former would probably require the lecture format, or technology, whereas the thirty-five–student class could be taught via several technologies, including the case method, lectures, and group projects. Similarly, a dry cleaner can choose among several ways to provide dry cleaning services. In either example, the "technology" whereby the work is done can vary. And different technologies affect the degree of specialization or standardization necessary, the types of coordination mechanisms needed, the levels at which decisions should be made, and the optimal size of organizational units.[14]

An organization is more effective when it is designed to accommodate its technology. John Sculley's redesign of Apple into a functional structure enabled the Apple organization to achieve greater economies of scale in production by combining responsibility for the production of all computer products within one unit. This design better accommodated the precise, assembly-line process used for manufacturing personal computers. And his decision to combine all marketing into one department gave Apple a design more consistent with the "technology," or the way computers were sold, in the late 1980s. Two scholars who have contributed significantly to our understanding of the impact of technology on organization design are Joan Woodward and James Thompson.[15] Their contributions are discussed below.

JOAN WOODWARD

Much of the pioneering work on the relationship between technology and organization design was done by Joan Woodward. She found that differences in technological complexity accounted for differences in the way effective organizations were designed. Her scale for measuring technological complexity consisted of three major categories: unit and small-batch technology, large-batch and mass-production technology, and continuous-process technology. Woodward assigned a firm's technological complexity to one of these three categories on the basis of the extent to which its manufacturing processes were automated and standardized.

Unit and Small-Batch Technology. **Unit and small-batch technology** is consistent with the notion of a job shop. Custom-made items (such as tailored clothing) and items only one of which is produced (such as portraits) are examples of unit production. Small-batch technology is the production of small quantities of items with each production run. Print shops wherein each customer's order must be set and run separately utilize small-batch technology. Unit and small-batch technology is the least complex of Woodward's categories because it offers little opportunity for using automated and standardized techniques. Most of the work done by professionals such as doctors, lawyers, and managers could be considered unit technology.

Large-Batch and Mass-Production Technology. The most common example of **large-batch and mass-production technology** is an assembly line, where large numbers of the same product are produced. This kind of production utilizes mechanization and standardized parts. Almost all consumer durable goods, such as automobiles and appliances, are produced in this manner. Apple's technology for producing Apple II and Macintosh personal computers is large-batch and mass-production.

W. A. Krueger is a well-known quality printer used by business clients nationwide. The company has a small-batch technology, providing printing in separate, intense runs for each client. This type of organization requires procedures to ensure that design, marketing, and production personnel coordinate services for each individual client. (Sepp Seitz/Woodfin Camp and Associates)

Continuous-Process Technology. A **continuous-process technology** utilizes fewer workers than does mass production, because most of the process is automated. A continuous stream of raw-material input is actually transformed into a continuous flow of output, not into separate, definable units. The process often changes the material composition of the inputs. Most refinery operations, such as that of petroleum, chemicals, or sugar, are considered continuous-process technologies. This category is the most complex in Woodward's scheme, because the processes involved are almost always completely automated.

Woodward found that several design components varied with the organization's type of technology. As technological complexity increased, the number of levels of management increased (that is, the organization structure became taller), the span of control of top management increased, and the ratio of line to staff workers increased. However, the span of control for lower-level managers was greatest for technologies intermediate in complexity. This is probably because large-batch and mass-production technologies require greater numbers of workers than do either unit or continuous-process technologies.[16]

Woodward's findings indicated that organizations characterized by the most complex (continuous-process) and the least complex (unit and small-batch) technologies tended to have more organic designs. Organizations exhibiting technologies in the middle range of complexity (large-batch and mass-production technologies) had more mechanistic designs. Most important, she found that the most successful organizations followed this pattern. It appears that technology is an important determinant of appropriate structure. Woodward's findings are summarized in Figure 11-11.

JAMES THOMPSON

Several years after Woodward's British studies, the American James D. Thompson divided technologies into three categories on the basis of years of observation in different organizations. He labeled technologies as long-linked, mediating, or intensive.

Long-Linked Technology. Thompson's **long-linked technology** is characterized by a series of sequential tasks that must be performed in a specified order. The assembly line is an example of long-linked technology. Thus this category closely parallels Woodward's large-batch and mass-production technology.

Mediating Technology. A **mediating technology** is a process that brings together groups that need to be interdependent for the desired action to take place. For example, banking is a mediating technology; it facilitates the interaction between depositors and borrowers. Employment and other talent search agencies connect suppliers of specialized labor with buyers. This type of technology is intermediate in flexibility. It allows for some standardization but can also adjust its output in response to variations in the needs of the parties it seeks to link.

Intensive Technology. An **intensive technology** involves the application of specific skills, techniques, or services in order to make a change in an input. This type of technology describes custom work and is consistent with Woodward's unit production technology. The value of an intensive technology is its maximal flexibility.

ORGANIZATIONAL CHARACTERISTICS OF WOODWARD'S SAMPLE[a]

| Technology Category | NUMBER OF | | | Ratio of Production Workers to Administrative Workers | Implications for Organization Design |
	Management Levels	Workers per Supervisor	Supervisors per Executive		
Unit or small-batch	3	23	4	8:1	Organic
Large-batch or mass-production	4	48	7	5:1	Mechanistic
Continuous-process	6	15	10	2:1	Mechanistic

[a]The numbers in this table are the medians for the organizations in each technology category in Woodward's sample.

FIGURE 11-11
Woodward's Findings on Technology and Organization Design

Although the categories proposed by Thompson are similar to Woodward's, several differences arise because the writers' aims were different. Woodward sought to categorize manufacturing organizations; Thompson was trying to devise a typology that would take all kinds of organizations into account.

Thompson's work suggested that the character of an organization's design should vary with the category in which the technology of the organization fell. Firms having long-linked technologies were seen as most effective when structured in accordance with mechanistic designs. Firms with intensive technologies were expected to be most effective when organized in terms of organic designs. And firms based on mediating technologies were seen as needing mechanistic designs for part of their operations and organic designs in other areas of the firm. Using banks as an example, Thompson was saying that a bank might need a mechanistic design for its routine depositing and borrowing services but a more organic design in the parts of the organization that handled investments and services for large depositors and borrowers. An important result of Thompson's observations is this recognition that many organizations require different technologies to get their work done. Therefore, organization design may have to vary within a firm to accommodate these differences in technology.[17]

Environment and technology are not the only critical factors shaping organization design decisions. The sheer size of an organization often plays a central role in organization design. The next section examines the size consideration in greater detail.

Size

The impact of the sheer size of an organization on its design has attracted a great deal of research attention. It seems obvious that organizations change as they get larger and that more complex designs become necessary, but the research results are not unanimous. This may be due in part to the fact that size has been measured in a variety of ways, including criteria as diverse as number of employees, sales, total assets, and scope of operations. However, the variety of measures does not explain away the different outcomes. Most of these measures are highly correlated and thus should produce similar results. Figure 11-12 illustrates the point that although there may be a series of structures that organizations typically progress through as they grow, there are clearly several alternative paths as well. This figure

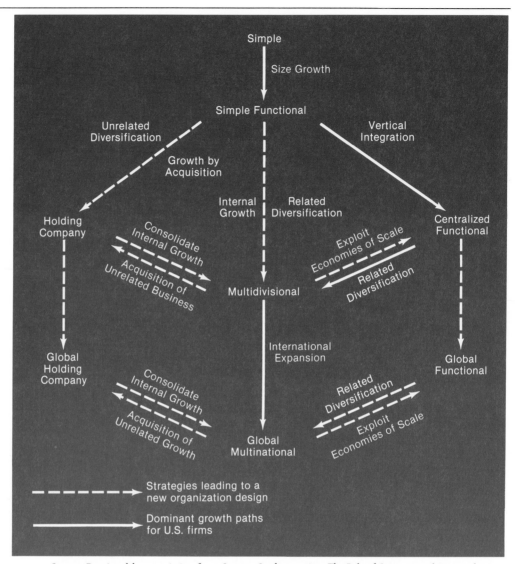

Source: Reprinted by permission from *Strategy Implementation: The Role of Structure and Process,* by J. R. Galbraith and D. A. Nathanson. Copyright © 1978 by West Publishing Company. All rights reserved.

FIGURE 11-12
Growth and Changing
Organization Design

also suggests that the chosen path is not necessarily unidirectional; that is, organizations may decide to revert to simpler structures at some point along the way.[18]

Joan Woodward's work inspired much of the research on the relationship between size and most effective design. Her findings indicated that there was no such relationship. However, a research team known as the Aston Group[19] argued that Woodward found no effect for size because all the firms in her sample were similar in size—mostly rather small. The members of this team designed a study that included a variety of firms that were different in size and examined the relationships among size, technology, and organization design. Their study suggested that the sheer size of an organization has a major impact on the nature of its organization design. In fact, they found size to be much more important than technology in accounting for differences in organization design. Figure 11-13 sum-

	Small ←————————————→ Large	
Job Specialization:	Less—people do many tasks	More—seek efficiency through specializing
Standardization:	Less—primary need just to get by	More—significant need to keep things simple
Decentralization:	Less—the boss can see all and decide all	More—many varied, complex decisions regularly required

FIGURE 11-13
Relationships between Organization Size and Organization Design

marizes what we know from these and other studies about the relationship between organization design and size.

The roles of environment, technology, and size are central to most decisions about organization design. The pace of change in our society, the level of education, and individual expectations are also shaping organization designs of the future. The final section of this chapter examines key trends in the way future organizations will be designed. "Management Development Exercise 11" provides a checklist for evaluating new designs.

Guidelines for Management Practice

When managers are called upon to help make decisions about the design of their organization (or a part of it), they face a challenging but fascinating task. Perhaps some of the most important guidelines for success in organization design involve keeping an open mind. To that end, remember the following suggestions:

1. Managers tend to choose organization structures that they are familiar with. For example, a sales manager trained in a territorial organization in which each salesperson sold every product would be likely to prefer this structure to a product divisional one in which each salesperson sold just one product line. Because of this inclination, be sure to challenge the rationale behind suggestions for structural change.

2. "Power" in organizations is sometimes thought of negatively. Yet managers must often look at alternative organization designs from the perspective of how they provide a source of power to get work done. Do not automatically think of power in negative terms.

3. If you are assigned to help design the organization of part of your company, be sure to consider several forms, even when they are different from the structure of the overall company or that of other parts of the company. Companies frequently include more than one structure in their overall organization design. For example, Corning Glass Works adopted one structure (a centralized, organic structure) to manage its operating system and another (a "product × territory" matrix structure) to manage its marketing function.

4. Consider using temporary structures, such as project groups and crisis teams, to cope with rapidly changing environments, technologies, and markets. Personnel can move in and out of assignments within these temporary structures several times a year.

5. If your firm faces rapid change, consider incorporating outsiders in your organization design. For example, using key customers in product development teams or suppliers in technology/process development and quality teams often pays big dividends.

Organization Design in the Future[20]

For many years the fundamental structure underlying organization design has been the classic pyramid. Although it still plays a major role, some authors are beginning to suggest that organization design in the future will be characterized by four basic differences from today's pyramid-oriented structures and will exhibit:

1. A small number of management levels

2. Adhocracy and porous departments

3. Systems decoupled from structure

4. The sharing of resources rather than the dividing of them

Small Number of Management Levels

The distance between the point where an organization experiences the forces of change—especially in its markets, technologies, and products—and the point where strategic decisions are made to redesign the company in response to these forces is often five or more levels of management. As a result, the time it takes to respond to major change may be much longer than necessary, causing organizations to be reactive rather than proactive (at the forefront of change). Requests for changes carry a heavy burden of documentation, justification, presentation, and timing requirements as they move up and down each of these five or more levels of management.

Organizations of the future will seek to reduce the physical and psychological distance from the top to the bottom of their structures. The authority, responsibility, and power necessary to deal effectively with rapidly changing conditions will be vested in the lowest level of the organization, where the factors relevent to decisions about change are most readily apparent and best understood. John Sculley at Apple moved in this direction by adjusting Apple's design so that territorial managers have greater discretion in deciding how Apple can meet the needs of major customers (educational or business) in their areas. Sculley also created rapid-response teams composed of the territorial manager, a production manager, and an ancillary products manager. This team has authority to make significant decisions about how Apple will price, produce, and supply products for customers whose needs exceed certain levels.

Adhocracy and Porous Departments

As organizations get larger, they begin to stifle the ability of subunits to make decisions and respond autonomously to change. One of the major reasons for the success of the corporate raiders of the 1980s was the efficiencies to be gained by simply buying highly diversified companies and breaking them apart into their individual, separate businesses. The resulting freedom and flexibility often produced much more profitable businesses.

Organizations of the future will accept adhocracy: federations of relatively autonomous units each of which can operate entrepreneurially. And within each unit, the structure will be more fluid or porous. Arbitrary barriers between and within departments will be less important—may even be removed—to allow people to "float" more between units, contribute to decisions, and get key jobs done.

Apple's rapid-response teams are an example of such units. Indeed Apple managers have begun to allow these teams the freedom to assign software and hardware engineers to their unit temporarily when meeting a special customer need also promises to be fertile ground for new-product development. In Chapter 21, these types of entrepreneurship within large organizations are discussed in greater detail.

Systems Decoupled from Structure

Most organization structures are quasi-permanent. They stay in place for many years. It is not surprising that most of the systems that help "manage" the company—compensation, promotion, accounting, communication, and planning, to mention a few—are fitted to the structure of the organization.

If flexible structures such as adhocracy and fewer levels of management evolve, the supporting systems will have to stand alone. Promotions must be more than movements between slots in units and levels. Compensation must be linked to more than unit-related criteria. The key will be tailoring the systems to individuals rather than to organization units. Systems generally exist today to protect the company from human error. Systems of the future must enhance innovation, which probably means that systems must decouple from structures and serve to enhance individual initiative, not limit it.

When he resigned from Apple, founder Steven Jobs said that he feared John Sculley's changes would improve profitability by making the organization's design respond to the needs of its departments and functional areas, rather than stimulating individual initiative as he had designed Apple to do. Indeed Sculley's redesign of Apple has proved effective partly because it imposed systems and structures that answered the needs for greater standardization and control in production and marketing. This profitable redesign of Apple's systems has served Apple's organizational units well during the last half of the 1980s. But what if Apple and other computer companies become dependent on rapid innovation that must spring from individual creative effort? Will Steven Jobs's warning come back to haunt Sculley— or his successor—then?

Sharing Rather Than Dividing Up Resources

The system that many organizations use to make decisions about the future and to commit resources to support those decisions is budgeting. Hence many managers are preoccupied with determining what resources they have to work with. Then, on the basis of that, they decide what they can do in the future. They ask, "What resources do we have under our control and what options do they allow us to pursue?" The central theme in this orientation is the need to identify and control the resources available.

Another system or orientation that many organizations are beginning to take seriously looks at the opportunities dictated by changing environments as the true starting point for making future decisions. Managers with this orientation ask, "What opportunities are available to us?" Only after settling on a range of opportunities do they address the issue of resources: "What resources do we need [not "'control"] in order to pursue favorable opportunities?" The manager who takes this approach seeks to borrow or temporarily use resources, not to own and control them. Resources are viewed simply as a means of pursuing attractive opportunities, not as things to accumulate as a source of organizational power. Managers in firms that employ this type of system use company resources (people, facilities, money, capacity, technology, marketing capability) only as long as they are needed. And because it is critical to make resources available in time for managers to seize the opportunities they discover, this system encourages access to resources in a manner that reduces paperwork, the levels of management through which decisions must travel, and the extent of "political" activity necessary to secure resources. Many people feel that this orientation—sharing rather than owning resources—will be the most effective orientation for organization designs of the future.

John Sculley's changes at Apple have certain characteristics of a shift from a resource-owning orientation to a resource-sharing orientation. The product divisions in Apple's old organization were very independent and were adamant in asserting their control over resources provided them. Lab facilities, people, marketing capacity, and money were staunchly "claimed" by each group of product division managers. Within the sprawling Apple complex, for example, Macintosh managers designed and flew a Macintosh flag over their facility for almost three years—a visible symbol of what was in effect their territory and resource base. Sculley's redesign of Apple dramatically changed this. Production, marketing, and engineering resources were centralized, and product managers for the Apple II and the Macintosh lines were accorded access to these resources on the basis of comparisons among the business opportunities presented by both groups.

The "network" character of emerging organizations of the future has also been frequently discussed. Organizations operating as networks place minimal emphasis on centralized coordination; rather, the units participating in the organizational network coordinate themselves and respond to environmental change when and if needed. The network idea is consistent with the four characteristics we have identified: fewer levels of management, porous departments, the decoupling of systems, and the sharing of resources. These basic characteristics, or organizing principles, may well shape the way future managers design their organizations.

Review of the Learning Objectives

Having studied this chapter, you should be able to respond to the learning objectives with extensions of the following brief answers:

1. **Define the term** *organization design*, **and discuss why it is important to the organizing function.**

   Organization design is concerned with finding the most appropriate structure to accommodate the interrelationships among numerous characteristics of an organization, such as its strategy, technology, environment, size, and people. Organization design is important to the organizing function of management, because it integrates the principles of organizing the various parts of an organization. An overarching view of the design of the whole organization is taken.

2. **Identify five basic elements of organization design, and explain why it is important that these elements fit together.**

   Five basic elements of organization design are tasks, people, structure, decision and reward systems, and the informal organization. It is important that each of these elements fits together because they are all related. Each pair of elements must match in order to ensure design consistency; and all of the elements must fit together in order to reinforce organizational objectives.

3. **Explain the meaning of the term** *contingency*, **and describe the major variables on which organization design is contingent.**

Briefly, to be contingent on something means to be determined by it. In the case of organization design, managers must consider variations in such factors as environment, technology, and size. Variations in any of these factors influence what design is most effective. An organization's *environment* is described in terms of its degree of variability, which can be represented on a continuum ranging from stable to turbulent. *Technology* encompasses all the tools, equipment, processes, actions, materials, and knowledge required to convert an organization's inputs into outputs that can be distributed as useful goods and services. Technology is often described in terms of how automated and standardized an organization's activities are. Organization *size* has been measured in a number of ways, including sales volume, number of employees, total assets, and scope of operations. The effects of size on an organization's structure seem to be most prominent when considered in conjunction with other factors such as strategy.

4. **Describe five organization design alternatives, and cite their principal advantages and disadvantages.**

The five organization design alternatives are simple structure, functional structure, divisional structure, strategic business units, and matrix organization. (The advantages and disadvantages of each alternative are summarized in Figures 11-3 through 11-7.)

5. **Identify four dimensions that reflect the future of organization design.**

The four dimensions that reflect the future of organizational design are: (1) a smaller number of management levels; (2) adhocracy, porous departments; (3) systems decoupled from structure; and (4) sharing resources rather than dividing them up.

Key Terms and Concepts

After completing your study of Chapter 11, "Organization Design," you should be able to explain the following important terms and concepts:

organization design	matrix organization	mechanistic system	large-batch and	long-linked
culture	stable environment	organic system	mass-production	technology
simple structure	changing	technology	technology	mediating
functional structure	environment	unit and small-	continuous-process	technology
divisional structure	turbulent	batch technology	technology	intensive
strategic business	environment			technology
unit (SBU)				

Questions for Discussion

1. What is organization design? Why is it important?

2. Describe three symptoms of organization design problems.

3. Explain the link between strategy and organization design.

4. What are the basic elements in organization design? Explain and illustrate each element.

5. Identify five alternatives for structuring organizations.

6. In what way is the design of an organization contingent on the organization's environment?

7. In what way is the design of an organization contingent on the organization's technology and on its size?

8. Explain the difference between a mechanistic design and an organic design.

9. If Alfred Chandler had studied four different organizations other than Sears, GM, Standard Oil, and DuPont, do you think his conclusions about strategy and structure might have been different?

10. Consider a local pharmacy, a national grocery store chain, and a large manufacturing firm. What contingency factors are likely to be most important in each case? Which design alternative might be chosen in each case?

11. Why do organizations change their designs? How do the contingency factors contribute to these changes?

12. Describe a situation wherein a matrix organization structure would be appropriate. What problems would you anticipate?

13. If you were the owner-manager of a small business, what factors might indicate the need for a change in your organization's design?

14. Why are managers concerned with organization design?

15. Why is the organization's size alone not a sufficient indicator of the appropriate design for that organization?

Notes

1. Adapted from B. Uttal, "Behind the Fall of Steve Jobs," *Fortune*, August 5, 1985, pp. 20–24. ©1985 Time, Inc. All rights reserved.

2. H. Mintzberg, *The Structuring of Organizations: A Synthesis of the Research* (Englewood Cliffs, N.J.: Prentice-Hall, 1979), pp. 215–297; and H. Mintzberg, "Organizational Design: Fashion or Fit?" *Harvard Business Review* 59 (January–February 1981): 103–116.

3. M. Yasai-Ardekani, "Structural Adaptations to Environments," *Academy of Management Review* 11 (1986): 1–21.

4. A. D. Chandler, Jr., *Strategy and Structure: Chapters in the History of the American Industrial Enterprise* (Cambridge, Mass.: MIT Press, 1962).

5. J. R. Galbraith and D. A. Nathanson, *Strategy Implementation: The Role of Structure and Process* (St. Paul, Minn.: West, 1978).

6. L. G. Hrebiniak and W. F. Joyce, *Implementing Strategy* (New York: Macmillan, 1984).

7. P. J. Stonich, *Implementing Strategy* (Cambridge, Mass.: Ballinger, 1982).

8. B. Yavitz and W. H. Newman, *Strategy in Action* (New York: Free Press, 1982).

9. In addition to the work of Burns and Stalker and of Lawrence and Lorsch cited below, others who have written on the relationship between structure and the environment include J. Child, "Organizational Structure, Environment and Performance: The Role of Strategic Choice," *Sociology* 6 (January 1972): 2–22; and R. Duncan, "What Is the Right Organization Structure? Decision Tree Analysis Provides the Answer," *Organizational Dynamics* 7, no. 3 (Winter 1979): 59–80.

10. P. Lawrence and D. Dyer, *Reviewing American Industry* (New York Free Press, 1983).

11. T. Burns and G. M. Stalker, *The Management of Innovation* (London: Tavistock, 1961).

12. P. R. Lawrence and J. W. Lorsch, *Organization and Environment: Managing Differentiation and Integration* (Homewood, Ill.: Irwin, 1967).

13. L. W. Fry, "Technology-Structure Research: Three Critical Issues," *Academy of Management Journal* 26 (1982): 532–552.

14. D. M. Rousseau and R. A. Cooke, "Technology and Structure: The Concrete, Abstract, and Activity of Organizations," *Journal of Management* 10 (1984): 345–361.

15. J. Woodward, *Industrial Organization* (London: Oxford University Press, 1965); and J. D. Thompson, *Organizations in Action* (New York: McGraw-Hill, 1967).

16. P. D. Collins and F. Hall, "Technology and Span of Control: Woodward Revisited," *Journal of Management Studies* 23 (March 1986): 143–164.

17. W. A. Randolph and G. G Dess, "The Congruence Perspective of Organization Design: A Conceptual Model and Research Approach, *"Academy of Management Review* 9 (1984): 114–127.

18. W. G. Astley, "Organizational Size and Bureaucratic Structure," *Organizational Studies* 6 (1985): 201–228.

19. See, for example, D. S. Pugh and D. J. Hickson, *Organization Structure in Its Context: The Aston Programme I* (Lexington, Mass.: D.C. Heath, 1976).

20. This section draws heavily from the pioneering work of S. Brandt, *Entrepreneurship in Mature Organizations* (Homewood, Ill.: Dow Jones–Irwin, 1986).

Cohesion Incident 11-1
Organization Design at Journey's End

Roger and Charles returned from their visit to corporate headquarters both puzzled and excited by their new planning assignment. Both had been asked to be part of an eleven-person committee formed to examine the organization design of Journey's End and make recommendations about any changes available in the 1990s. The committee's specific assignment was to recommend the best organization structure at the individual location level, the regional level, and the national level. The committee was asked to justify its recommendations and to state the strengths of the designs they recommended and any potential problems those designs might cause. Part of the information that they were given follows:

1. Competition in this industry is getting more intense, and business is certain to be very competitive in the 1990s at the national, regional, and local levels.

2. A key concern at the local level will be operating efficiency. Pressures on profitability will be intense, and each facility must be able to run its lodging, restaurant, and lounge businesses carefully and tightly.

3. Regionally, a key concern will be adapting to regional competitive pressures as well as detecting and moving to exploit under-served markets. Chain development is quite concentrated in the southeast, northeast, and Pacific Coast regions. It is less developed in the southwest and Rocky Mountain regions. The other concern here is variability in the nature of market needs. The West Coast has a strong tourist demand and convention demand. The southeast is heavily oriented to the business traveler. The northeast is a blend of downtown convention facilities and airport business facilities.

4. Internationally, Journey's End has only a few locations, in western Canada and Puerto Rico. Other chains are gearing up for major international expansion, and Journey's End management does not want to miss an opportunity to participate in the industry's next growth area.

5. Corporate managers are concerned with several things. First, they want to provide key support services to the Journey's End network—mainly reservations, assistance in site selection, and quality control. Second, they want to increase systemwide effectiveness through research, education (Journey's End University), and idea sharing. Third, they want to manage the system's pool of resources well. And fourth, they want to explore avenues for diversification beyond the lodging business.

   Roger and Charles spent the first night after their return contemplating their assignment. They had been asked to draft preliminary recommendations about the structure of the company at each level that they deemed appropriate and to be sure to include the local and corporate levels.

Discussion Questions

1. Assume that you have been asked to help Roger and Charles design the local organization. Diagram the structure you would suggest. Would it be the same at each location? What are the advantages and disadvantages of the design you recommend?

2. How would you organize Journey's End at the national and international level? Make sure you take into account all the requirements above the local level that are identified in management's directives to the committee.

3. Select two different organization structures that you think would work at the local, regional, or national level. What differences would they lead to in the way work is done, priorities set, and problems created?

4. Do any of the considerations we noted when we discussed organizations of the future apply in your analysis of Journey's End? Explain.

Cohesion Incident 11-2
Organization Redesign at Travis Corporation

Leslie Phillips could hardly contain her enthusiasm. She had been asked by the division marketing manager to be his aide at the corporate strategic planning retreat. The retreat was now over, and Travis Corporation's top executives had decided to commit the company to a product development and market development strategy for the year 2000. The basic idea, Leslie explained to some friends, was to continue strong research in the firm's basic product areas (drive trains, brake assemblies, and engine components), leading to continued positioning as a regular provider of new-product offerings. This was supplemented by a desire to significantly expand the company's market presence and penetration in North America and Europe, as well as among various customer groups (auto manufacturers, truck manufacturers, equipment reconditioners, and such new-customer areas as industrial machinery, power machinery, and farm machinery). Leslie was asked to provide a memo outlining her choice among three structural alternatives discussed at the planning retreat:

Structure 1 would divide North America into two regions and treat Europe as a third region. Each region would have its own manufacturing capacity and sales force. Financial administration would be coordinated out of the corporate offices. Otherwise, each region would be much like its own separate company.

Structure 2 would divide the company into three product divisions. Each product division would produce its main product line (such as drive trains) and would have its own specialized sales force to sell this product line worldwide. Again, financial administration would be centralized at corporate headquarters.

Structure 3 would be less clear-cut than the first two alternatives. Financial administration and product R&D would be centralized under corporate control—that is, functionally organized. Three product divisions would oversee product planning and sales for their respective product lines. Approximately twenty regions would be set up in which each regional manager would oversee company facilities (production plants and warehouses) and marketing efforts (especially key customers) in his or her region. A form of matrix organization would be superimposed on the product divisions and regional areas, wherein sales personnel and production people would be jointly responsible to product division managers and territorial managers.

Travis managers saw several trends emerging that would be relevant to their chosen strategy and might be relevant to the choice of structure. Manufacturing technology in each product line was rapidly becoming automated, and robotics was becoming a key factor. Product design was rapidly changing; there was a continuing trend toward smaller product designs and toward the continual introduction of new metals and alloys, which created radically new or improved performance capabilities.

Another important trend was the increasing number of foreign companies that were becoming Travis' prime customers. And finally, virtually every industry Travis sold components to was becoming more competitive and, in turn, placing more pressure on suppliers of components, such as Travis.

Discussion Questions

1. What specific advantages and disadvantages do you see in each design alternative for Travis Corporation? Give examples of both.

2. Which structure would you choose? Why?

3. Create a fourth structural alternative that you think might work as well as, or better than, any of the three proposed by Travis managers.

Management Development Exercise 11
A Consistent Organization Design?

Peter F. Drucker, the well-known management author, has proposed seven criteria by which to judge the effectiveness of an organization design. These seven criteria serve as a checklist for evaluating new designs before they are adopted or as a means of analyzing the problems or potential deficiencies of a company's (or work unit's) current organization design.

INSTRUCTIONS: Select an organization in which you work, have recently worked, or are actively involved. Seven criteria for assessing the effectiveness of organization design are identified below. Accompanying each is a question that you should answer about your organization's design. Check one of the three possible responses to each question. Each "no" or "unsure" answer may suggest a potential problem in your organization design. Once you have completed these questions, your instructor will provide you with further interpretive information.

CLARITY

Does the design clarify your position as well as the positions of those around you? For example, do you know where to go to find information?

_____ yes   _____ unsure   _____ no

ECONOMY

Does the design minimize the effort that must be expended to reduce friction and maintain control?

_____ yes   _____ unsure   _____ no

DIRECTION OF VISION

Does the design focus attention on the end user, on products, and on performance rather than on the means to achieve performance?

_____ yes   _____ unsure   _____ no

UNDERSTANDING

Does the design enable you to understand how your work fits into the total picture?

_____ yes   _____ unsure   _____ no

AN AID TO DECISION MAKING

Does the design encourage making decisions at the lowest possible level, thereby allowing managers to make the decisions that they are most qualified to make?

———— yes   ———— unsure   ———— no

STABILITY AND ADAPTABILITY

Is the design stable in the face of adversity but adaptable to changes in the environment, the firm's strategy, or both?

———— yes   ———— unsure   ———— no

PERPETUATION AND SELF-RENEWAL

Does the design develop managers from within yet allow new ideas, such as innovations in technology or sales, to be applied?

———— yes   ———— unsure   ———— no

Source: P. F. Drucker, "New Templates for Today's Organizations," *Harvard Business Review,* January–February 1974, p. 51.

12

Change and Organization Development

Your study of this chapter will enable you to do the following:

1. Define the term *organization development* (OD).
2. Explain the nature of change in organizations, particularly planned change.
3. List four reasons for resistance to change and five ways this resistance can be overcome.
4. Outline the organization development process.
5. Identify the key skills exhibited by successful organization development practitioners.
6. List several approaches to organization development.
7. Cite the conditions that contribute to the success of organization development.

A Need for Change and Organization Development at Frenolt

John Walker, president of the Frenolt Technical Corporation, called James Holton, an organization development consultant, to arrange a meeting. At the start of their meeting, Walker told Holton that he had a problem with his executive staff. The staff numbered four vice presidents and one assistant to the president. Walker said it was a problem of communication.

Walker said that people were reluctant to discuss the issues facing the company and that when they did have discussions, staff members never seemed to focus on the "real" issues as he saw them. He also sensed that the staff might be keeping information from him. But, he said, he knew he had an outstanding group of people. They were bright, worked hard, and sincerely cared about the organization and its future.

Among the members of the group were the following people: The chief financial officer had taken early retirement from a Fortune 500 firm and brought a tremendous amount of experience to Frenolt, but at times he appeared to act as though others were inferior to him. The vice president of operations was an old

This chapter was written by the authors and Mark E. Sandberg.

When Frenolt's top management team meets to discuss production problems and other decisions facing Frenolt, they try to determine which to discuss with John Walker, Frenolt's president, and which they can act on without consultation. (Dick Luria/Science Source/ Photo Researchers)

timer who had come up through the ranks and was highly respected by his people. But sometimes he seemed to fear new methods. The newest person was the vice president of human resources, who had been named by a leading business magazine as "a woman to watch" in the corporate world. She seemed knowledgeable and well organized. Though she had been aboard for only three weeks, she got along well with the others. The vice president of marketing had had his own small corporation, built it up, and sold it. He had all the money he would ever need. He had joined Frenolt after getting tired of playing golf every day, and he loved the challenge of his job. However, he was so independent that Walker was occasionally irritated by his unwillingness to compromise. The fifth member of the team, the assistant to the president, was a young MBA who previously had been a customer relations officer with Frenolt's principal bank. He viewed Walker's personal invitation to join the company as an opportunity to "get in on the ground floor" and have a real chance of assuming the Frenolt presidency one day.

Walker further mentioned to Holton that he had already brought in two previous consultants. One was a traditional management consultant, the second a communications expert. Both had written fine reports, but nothing had really been done with those reports. The staff had not seemed to feel that the reports were relevant.

Walker said that he had learned about organization development from a friend in another corporation. He sensed there was a need to change things at Frenolt. He was not sure what should be changed or how, and he did not know how his people would react. He was hoping that the organization development approach might help bring about a successful planned change that would solve his communication problem.[1]

Introduction

The Role of Change and Organization Development

To explore the area of change in organizations is to come face to face with the intricacies of human behavior. Otherwise, bringing about change in organizations might be as easy as computing a few basic formulas. But because human nature is what it is, creating successful change in any organization can be very difficult. John Walker sensed the need for change at Frenolt Technical Corporation. He knew the executive staff could function more effectively. But two efforts to change things for the better had had little (if any) positive impact.

In days past, an owner or manager could just announce a change and fire anyone who did not conform. But in most organizations, those days are over. Union grievance procedures, affirmative action regulations, and stockholder lawsuits are just a few of the constraints on executives today. But even if executives *could* order people to change, the results might be less than effective. People might feel they had to do what they were told, but they would resent it. They might lose enthusiasm and turn in a merely adequate performance. In today's competitive world, adequate is not good enough.

For managers to be effective in today's organizations, they must understand change and be ready to effect it. The purpose of this chapter is to examine the nature of change in organizations and some of the conditions and managerial skills that make it easier to accomplish successfully.

One of the major events in the evolution of a skilled approach to bringing about organizational change is the emergence of the field of management called **organization development (OD)**. OD offers a framework and a perspective that managers can draw on to facilitate planned change. Change is the one constant among people and within organizations. Many managers find themselves reacting to change, or the need for it, often without understanding either the need for change or its positive side. Effective managers look on change as necessary and beneficial. They seek to effect planned change, and OD is an important way to do just that.

The remainder of this section provides a brief introduction to OD and defines several key terms. It is followed by a section explaining the nature of change and the idea of planned change. The next two sections explain the key steps in the OD process and the specific skills and techniques that are useful to the OD practitioner. The final section identifies some conditions critical to the success of OD programs.

What is Organization Development?

Any manager who has ever tried to introduce changes has quickly learned that people resist change. Consequently, the need to help people make changes—changes in attitudes, perceptions, behaviors, or expectations—is many times the focal point of organization development. Basically, OD concentrates on how to bring about change via people.

Organization development can be defined as "an effort (1) *planned,* (2) often *organizationwide,* and (3) *managed from the top,* to (4) increase *organization effectiveness* and *health* through (5) *planned interventions* in the organization's process, using *behavioral science* knowledge."[2]

This definition says that OD is planned, not haphazard. In many cases, to be effective it needs to be organizationwide. Unless the people at the top of the corporation support and manage the OD effort, it can be undermined at critical junctures. OD's purpose is to increase the effectiveness and health of the organization. The definition further emphasizes that OD involves planned interventions: activities or techniques employed to help make things happen. In one sense, OD can be viewed as an elaborate problem-solving process.

Organization development, of course, is not the only field of study that addresses organizational change. For example, on the quantitative side of modern management, systems engineers labor to analyze and redesign work. OD is a part of the modern behavioral school of management generally known as *organizational behavior*. Most large corporations today have an OD department. It is usually found in the personnel/human resources area, along with the departments of Management Development and Training, Employee Relations, Recruiting, and the like.

Anyone, whether manager or consultant, who is skilled in OD and able to implement approaches to OD is referred to as an *OD practitioner*. OD practitioners tend to be called on when people in an organization cannot work through many of the interpersonal issues preventing them from making changes that the organization needs in order to maintain or improve its effectiveness. So it was at Frenolt Technical Corporation.

The OD practitioner's role is to recognize the need for change and to bring it about in a way that enhances organizational effectiveness. So before examining the OD process, we need to understand change—especially the notion of planned change.

Change in Organizations

Change is all around us. In fact, it has been said that change is the only constant in organizational life. Hence managers who wish to manage effectively must understand change and people's reactions to it.

Two Types of Change

There are essentially two types of change in organizations. **Reactive change** is change brought about by a sudden or unplanned event. The 508-point drop in the Dow Jones Industrial Average on October 19, 1987, necessitated unplanned, reactive change in many businesses nationwide. Perhaps most notably, several major stock brokerage firms reorganized their operations, laid off thousands of people, and altered the way they used computers to buy and sell stocks. These major changes were primarily reactive—changes made in response to the sudden events on Wall Street.[3]

The second type of organizational change is planned change. **Planned change** is a systematic, deliberate change in the way part or all of an organization functions. Planned change usually focuses on processes, people, or technology and can involve one person, a work team, a department, or the entire firm. Planned change will result from efforts to correct the "communication" problem at Frenolt Technical Corporation. Another example is Merrill Lynch's effort to reorient its "stock brokers" from selling stocks and bonds to acting as "financial advisors" selling a wide range of financial services.[4] A manager's decision to change her or his management style from a low to a high level of delegation to subordinate managers is planned change on a personal basis. Milliken, a worldwide leader in the textile industry, has rapidly moved from a labor-intensive textile producer to one whose production process is fully mechanized and heavily robotic is another example of planned change. International Paper Corporation's move to change the compensation program for wood-yard work crews from salaries to a work group piece-rate method is an example of planned change.[5] So is any small company's decision to switch from a manual accounting system to a computerized accounting system. Common to all of these examples of planned change are (1) identifying a problem or opportunity that necessitates change, (2) deciding what changes are needed, and (3) making those necessary changes. And although planned changes vary from the technological changes at Milliken to those in communications or management style at Frenolt Technical Corporation, all types of planned change usually involve some changes in what individual people do—their behaviors at work. Managing these changes in people's behaviors at work presents a major challenge to managers.

The Change Process

Kurt Lewin developed a model modified by Edgar Schein that is quite helpful in describing the change process.[6] This model suggests that change occurs in three phases: unfreezing, changing, and refreezing.

The **unfreezing phase** begins when an individual or a group senses the need to do things in a different way. Typically, persistent problems signal the need for change, and these problems begin to be discussed in the context of the need to change. John Walker's contact with James Holton was the beginning of the un-freezing phase at Frenolt Technical Corporation.

This phase usually evolves into a discussion of what changes might resolve the underlying problems. Milliken managers recognized the need to automate their production process. Merrill Lynch managers perceived the need to change the role of the broker. As the label suggests, this phase involves the "unfreezing" of the status quo; the need for change is recognized, and alternatives for implementing that change are proposed and considered.

The second phase of the change process begins as initial changes are made. During this **change phase**, planned changes are made in individuals' behavior or in organizational processes. For example, a manager starts delegating more tasks to her or his subordinate managers. Or the administrative staff in a small company begins a program of computer training and starts to keep daily records by using the computer.

The change phase can begin experimentally, as changes are made subject to participant scrutiny to determine whether they produce the desired results. Adjustments are usually necessary to make the changes work as planned. The purpose of the change phase is to both introduce and adjust the new ways of doing things.

Most people will "try on" change, but the tendency to revert to the old ways of doing things or to resist some changes is strong. The third phase of the change process, **refreezing**, is the time when the changes are accepted as the new status quo. The people most affected by the change accept it as the way they will work or behave in the future. Former Merrill Lynch "stockbrokers" accept their new identity as "financial advisors" and find selling IRAs, insurance, and financial planning just as logical and appropriate as selling stocks and bonds. Or an employee in a small company who would prefer to balance the bank accounts manually nevertheless accepts the responsibility of balancing the accounts with a computer, using the company's new accounting software.

Most people resist change. Thus managers must spend time dealing with situations arising from resistance to change. Managers can deal more effectively with these situations when they understand why people resist change and develop some basic ways to overcome this resistance.

Resistance to Change

Managers seeking to implement changes often encounter subordinates and even other managers who are unenthusiastic about the changes. These people often seem to prefer to maintain the status quo rather than accept the new methods, programs, or ideas being proposed. Such **resistance to change** arises for a number of reasons. Understanding those reasons and the ways to overcome them helps managers implement change more effectively.

UNCERTAINTY

Employees often resist change because they are uncertain about the impact the change will have on their lives. They may worry about job security, their ability to adjust to new expectations, or they simply may be nervous and anxious in the face of the ambiguity associated with a new way of doing things. Administrative employees in small companies often resist computerization because they are uncertain how it will change the way they do their work and because they fear being replaced by a machine.

LACK OF UNDERSTANDING AND TRUST

Some people resist change because they do not understand the need for it. Or they may mistrust the initiators of the change, fearing that they are being manipulated or that the "real" reasons for the change have not been disclosed. A manager's decision to reorganize work teams by changing individual assignments may encounter employee resistance because one or more subordinates doubt the underlying reasoning behind the change or they suspect that the manager may have other reasons in mind such as splitting up problem subordinates.

SELF-INTEREST

Managers and employees usually resist change they think will take away something of value to them. The Eastern Airlines Pilot Association went to court on several occasions to block the implementation of decisions by Texas Air (Eastern's parent company) president Frank Lorenzo that the pilots feared would reduce their bargaining power within Eastern.[7] Changes in structure, in technology, or in the way things are done can often lead to the perception that one might lose financial benefits, power, or prestige.

DIFFERENT OPINIONS ABOUT OUTCOMES

Judgment is often the basis for assessing the need for change and the best method for meeting that perceived need. Managers involved in making these assessments or designing the necessary changes can legitimately reach different conclusions. Such differences, often strongly felt, can be a major source of resistance to change.

Overcoming Resistance to Change

Managers should not be overwhelmed when resistance to change is encountered. Instead, they should consider any one of several approaches that appear to lower resistance to change. The following approaches, summarized in Figure 12-1, have been shown through research to be successful for some managers.[8]

FIGURE 12-1
Some Approaches for
Dealing with Resistance
to Change

Approach	When to Use the Approach
Communication and Education	When the change involves how jobs are performed or other technical considerations; when accurate information is needed to understand the change; and when time is available before the change must be made
Participation	When the actual "best" design of the change is uncertain; when the people affected by the change can offer useful ideas; and when those affected by the change have considerable reason to resist
Negotiation	When a key group has significant power over the successful implementation of the planned change; and when that group will clearly lose something in a change
Coercion	When managers initiating changes are powerful; when time is of the essence; and when other approaches have failed or would take too long
Top Management Support	When the planned change will affect several different departments or divisions within the company in terms of work processes, resource allocation, or both; and when interdepartmental self-interests might block change

Source: An exhibit from "Choosing Strategies for Change," by J. P. Kotter and L. A. Schlesinger, *Harvard Business Review,* March–April, 1979, pp. 106–114. Copyright © 1979 by the President and Fellows of Harvard College.

COMMUNICATION AND EDUCATION

When the change is anticipated well in advance, resistance to it can be reduced by preparing individuals and work groups for it and educating them about the change. The decision by the International Paper Company to switch to autonomous work groups in their wood yards was preceded by a three-month educational program explaining why the change was planned and how it would be implemented. This program greatly reduced resistance to this rather dramatic change at International Paper.

PARTICIPATION

Several research studies have shown that resistance to change can be reduced by having the people involved in the change participate in planning and designing the change.[9] The reasons are straightforward. Individuals who participate in planning change are more likely to understand the need for it, feel a part of it from the beginning, and have less uncertainty about its impact on their lives or their role in the organization.

NEGOTIATION

It is not unusual for managers to negotiate with others involved in or affected by change as a means of reducing their resistance to it. Where key individuals, work groups, or departments are known or would be expected to strongly resist a planned change, formal bargaining to win approval of a planned change is a feasible approach. The negotiation approach often involves exchanging support for change for other guarantees or concessions. For example, auto workers at Ford Motor Company agreed to several major changes in work processes and compensation packages in return for specific profit-sharing formulas.[10]

COERCION

Coercion occurs when managers use their formal power to dampen or ignore resistance to change and to force individuals, work groups, or departments to implement the desired change. Job reassignments, dismissals, compensation adjustments, and the denial of promotions are but a few examples of ways managers can coerce others into accepting change. Coercion works best in crisis situations when other efforts have not proven successful. It is often a choice of last resort because using coercion risks making future efforts to implement change even more difficult.

TOP MANAGEMENT SUPPORT

Most people in organizations recognize the power that resides with top management and generally are willing or feel a duty to accommodate such expectations. Thus when top managers are visibly supportive of a planned change, resistance to that change is usually reduced. Particularly when the changes affect more than one department or division of the company, top management support is often crucial to overcome resistance based on the self-interests of individual departments.

Understanding the sources of resistance to change and some ways to overcome them helps managers deal effectively with change. Managers can further improve their ability to manage change effectively by recognizing three different types of change in organizations.

Approaches to Planned Change

There are three approaches to planned change that managers take in most business organizations: structural, technological, and people changes. These three approaches to change are illustrated in Figure 12-2. They are shown as being interconnected because a change in one area of the organization often necessitates change in another.[11] "In Practice 12-1" illustrates planned change at two well-known companies. This section examines each of these approaches to change.

Structural Change

Structural change involves altering organizational design, the level of decentralization, lines of communication, and distribution of authority within an organization. Apple Computer's shift from a divisional structure to a functional structure (Chapter 11) is an example of a major structural change. Fundamental organizing components and organizational design considerations were discussed in detail in

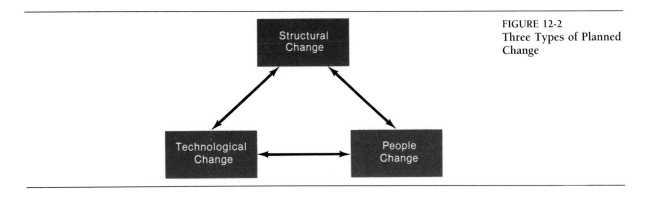

FIGURE 12-2
Three Types of Planned Change

Chapters 10 and 11; here we will review briefly their relevance as means to improve organizational performance by making desired changes.

Structural changes can be made in the basic components of organizations. The level of decentralization is often an area where planned change is necessary to improve organizational performance. Apple's change to a functional structure sought to increase centralization. Philip Morris divided its General Foods subsidiary into three autonomous product divisions seeking to introduce greater decentralization (see "In Practice 11-1"). Both changes led to improved performance. Structural change also includes adjustments in distribution of authority, span of management, job design, and scheduling of activities.

Shifts in overall organizational design would be considered structural changes. Corning Glass Works's decision to adopt the matrix framework (see Chapter 11) to organize and coordinate its marketing activities across eight major product lines and worldwide geographic territories was a classic structural change.

Technological Change

Technology, as we have defined it, includes all the tools, equipment, processes, actions, materials, and knowledge with which an organization creates and provides its products or services. **Technological change** refers to changes in any of these factors. Technological changes might involve changes in the equipment used to produce the organization's products or services. Mack Truck's robotic-intensive plant in South Carolina represented a major change in the equipment used to produce their trucks. That change encountered strong union resistance as well as the need for significant employee training or retraining due to the dramatically different skills necessary in a robotic-intensive factory (Chapters 5 and 9).

Technological change also takes place when work processes are altered. For example, a company that changes from an assembly-line approach to an approach in which a work team focuses on an entire product would be experiencing a major technological change. A decision to subcontract activities formerly done by the company, such as when Ford Motor Company decided to purchase rather than manufacture over 40 percent of a typical car's parts, is another type of technological change.

The need for technological change is often recognized first at lower levels within an organization when people directly engaged in the work process recognize the need to do things differently and initiate change. The *bottom up approach* describes the concept of changes being developed at lower organizational levels

---

In Practice 12-1

PLANNED CHANGE AT HONEYWELL AND MOUNTAIN BELL

Honeywell

After going head-to-head with IBM for eleven years, Honeywell Information Systems Division had not made much progress by 1981. They were, nevertheless, a large organization bringing in $2 billion of Honeywell's $5 billion, with 25,000 people. They held 8 percent of the market. However, revenues growing at a slower rate and increasing expenses had brought operating profits below the previous year. Employee morale was sagging. The corporate culture was one of infighting. Something needed to change!

In the planned change that followed, members of the organization went through sessions in which they analyzed the politics and culture of the organization as well as challenges to leadership. They decided what changes would be necessary to produce the culture wanted and learned about trust, teamwork, and cooperation. They then tied the corporate culture to values and business strategy. The primary vehicle was a five-day conference. This conference was repeated a number of times for each group of participants with follow-up discussions over a two-year period.

Two years later, revenues hit an all-time high and profits were up substantially. A new organization was in place, with free-standing divisions and independent profit and loss accountability. The culture was dramatically different, and planned change had succeeded at Honeywell.

Mountain Bell

Imagine more than 100 unionized employees working in a seven-day, twenty-four-hour telephone company facility with a budget of $2.4 million to service seven states. Further, imagine employees at this office having responsibility for training, service quality, productivity improvements, miscellaneous expenses and overhead, office practices and procedures, and attendance. Finally, imagine this office operating without any direct supervisors.

How did it happen? It started with the belief of a district manager, Ed Murdock. It required the involvement of the union president, the establishment of a committee of employees, and a systematic effort to plan and implement a major change in this 100-person office of Mountain Bell. One of the first challenges was to train the committee in team building, problem solving, and how to run meetings.

As the committee made decisions and learned to operate, many problems had to be overcome, such as the filing of seventy grievances. But the committee remained committed to its goal—to establish a successful self-managed office. But the real change occurred along the way. As events unfolded and as the committee attempted to operate and problems were resolved, a learning process occurred. Over 20 percent of the work force rotated through the committee. And they learned how to operate without a supervisory level at this Mountain Bell office. The planned change to a self-managed work group was successful.

Absenteeism and grievances fell to low levels, while productivity improved and employee morale soared.

Sources: Adapted, by permission of the publisher, from "Operating Without Supervisors: An Experiment," by D. Friedman and D. Couture, from *Organizational Dynamics* 15, no. 3 (Winter 1987): 26–38. © 1987 American Management Association, New York. All rights reserved; and from J. J. Renier, "Turnaround of Information Systems at Honeywell," *The Academy of Management Executives* 1, no 1, (February 1987): 47–55.

---

and being sent up through the organization for approval. Structural change is often just the opposite. The *top down approach* to structural change involves ideas for change that are generated at the top of the organization and passed down to lower levels for implementation.

Whether top down or bottom up, technological change and structural change often occur together. For example, changes in the way the organization's work is done—a technological change—necessitates change in reporting relationships or grouping of work units—a structural change.

People Change

People change refers to changes in the behaviors, attitudes, skills, and expectations of employees so as to increase organizational performance. Pepsico was for years a distant second to Coke in the soft drink industry. Pepsico's top management decided in the 1970s to become more aggressive and to try to eventually surpass Coke as the worldwide soft drink leader. This shift in corporate strategy required major changes in the work habits, norms, expectations, skills, and attitudes of virtually every PepsiCo employee, but particularly the route sales people.[12]

People changes are usually undertaken in three ways. First, employee training and development might be used to instruct people in newly desired behaviors, attitudes, or expectations. Second, employee recruitment and hiring may be the major focus of an effort to get the desired personnel into the organization. The intent of this approach is to effect a people change by hiring people with the skills or attitudes wanted to replace (usually by attrition) those not wanted. Pepsico relied heavily on both approaches to successfully create a totally different culture within Pepsico in just five years. Pepsico's people change included the turnover of over 90 percent of its salespeople. Overseas operations are often affected by people changes, as shown in "Insights for International Managers 12."

■■■■■ *Insights for International Managers 12* ■■■■■

MAKING PLANNED CHANGES IN OVERSEAS OPERATIONS

One feature of change in American operations overseas has been the lack of a long-term perspective. Whenever bad news reaches headquarters, the standard solution is to send in a new "general." Predictably, new management brings changes. Projects are shelved. New methods are instituted. New directions are taken. When projects are ended, local personnel have to withdraw from commitments, causing loss of trust and "face," which makes it difficult for staff to maintain working relationships in the local community. New management may be totally unaware of these repercussions, while employee morale may be devastated.

When there is constant turnover at the top, the local management and workers become skeptical about the solidity of new policies. Commitment will be low and participation half-hearted. When the top management is changed, the cast must have a sense that the show must go on. Without a script, they will begin to make up their own lines. Consistency in direction is vital, and to ensure it, management at home must hire people who are sure to be around a long time, then take good care of them.

Consistency is important not only in management, but also in any function dependent on personal relationships—virtually all international positions. Foreign buyers, suppliers, agents and distributors, government officials and almost any other foreign business associates simply do not want to do business with someone who will be gone tomorrow. When you do have to move personnel, don't take all your people out at once. Stagger the changes so that you always have continuity in foreign country expertise as well as continuity of relationships.

Source: From L. Copeland and L. Griggs, *Going International* (New York: Random House, 1985), p. 191.

Another major approach to people change is organization development (OD), which is discussed in detail beginning in the next section. OD often involves large-scale people changes across an entire organization, and it can easily take five or more years to achieve its results. Some OD programs involve structural and technological change as well as people change. The distinguishing characteristic of OD efforts is that the focus is on planning for comprehensive change through people-focused programs.

The Process of Organization Development

The **organization development (OD) process** can be viewed as a series of six steps. OD experts repeatedly emphasize that organization development is most successful when the six steps shown in Figure 12-3 and explained in the following sections are faithfully adhered to.

Step 1: Recognizing a Problem

Recognition of the need to change is a strong driving force for change. This is particularly true when the need for change is recognized by the manager responsible for the work group, department, or organizational unit.

When John Walker realized that a problem existed among the executive staff members at Frenolt Technical Corporation and that change might be necessary to resolve it, he started the OD process. Acknowledging that a problem exists by calling in an OD practitioner not only initiates the process but also alerts others affected by this problem that the manager recognizes and is affected by it too. In a sense, it legitimizes or sanctions explicit awareness that a problem exists.

Step 2: Diagnosing the Situation

After assuming responsibility for facilitating planned change, one of the first things the OD practitioner must do is make a personal assessment of potential problems. The manager may state the problem one way, but that does not mean that she or he has identified the real problem. Managers frequently focus on symptoms, rather than on the underlying problem.

John Walker's situation at Frenolt Technical Corporation provides a useful example. The president said he had a problem in communication with his executive staff. Generally speaking, when people say that they have a communication problem, they do. But the people involved here (Walker's executive staff) would certainly have been able to figure out how to institute a new reporting system or whatever else might have been appropriate to enhance communication. More than likely, this "communication problem" stems from other issues. Are people so overworked that when they make a decision, they remember to notify only three other departments and forget a fourth department that should also be notified? Has a member of the team become so threatening to some other members that in order to protect themselves, they have stopped communicating any bad news? Many other reasons could be at the root of the problem, but that problem is certainly something other than poor communication. Here, as in step 2 of any organization development effort, the OD practitioner must first diagnose the situation and determine what the underlying problems really are.

How do OD practitioners diagnose problem situations? Four approaches are

STEP 1: The manager who perceives a problem calls in an OD practitioner and defines the problem to be addressed.

STEP 2: The OD practitioner makes an initial personal diagnosis of the problem and the need for change.

STEP 3: The OD practitioner gets everyone involved in the problem to recognize, "own," and diagnose it.

STEP 4: Those involved in the problem search for solutions and agree to support some solution. The solution inevitably involves "changing" one or more current organizational practices, people, or processes.

STEP 5: The solution (the prescribed change) is planned and implemented.

STEP 6: The impact of the solution (change) in producing the intended results is evaluated.

FIGURE 12-3
The Organization Development Process

common. They can interview people, which offers the advantage of direct contact with people involved in the situation. The disadvantage of interviews is that some people are hesitant to reveal much information face to face. A second diagnostic approach that OD practitioners often use is surveys or questionnaires. This approach allows participants to remain anonymous. It also ensures that all respondents answer questions in the same format, which provides the OD practitioners with a consistent basis for diagnosing problems. Some OD practitioners prefer simple observation as a means of diagnosing problems. A fourth approach is to read records, files, reports, and any other material that is relevant. In each approach, the OD practitioner seeks objective information and insight into the people and processes that make up the firm.[13]

Step 3: Identifying the Problem and Admitting It Exists

Once OD practitioners discover what a situation *appears* to be, they must get all key people affected by the problem to recognize it, "own" it, and talk about it. This is a bit tricky. OD practitioners operate differently from traditional management consultants. The latter would write a report and present it to the client. But most problems necessitating planned changes stem from obstacles preventing people and departments or units in an organization from cooperating fully. And many of these obstacles exist because people do not trust each other. If people are fearful enough, they ignore the consultant's report even if it is accurate. The OD practitioner makes a broader commitment to ferreting out and solving organizational problems. Frequently this requires getting the people involved to "own" the problem—not just read a report about it. And it requires a lot of time, too.

The rationale behind this step is simple. If people refuse to believe that a problem exists, they certainly will not see any need to work at solving it. If they agree that a problem does exist, OD practitioners say that the people have begun to "own" the problem. The concept of *ownership* in OD means that the people involved accept that they are a part of the problem, share responsibility for its consequences, and must participate in identifying and implementing the changes necessary to solve it. Many managers try to force people to solve problems before they know whether the people involved have actually owned the problem. The result is that these people, at best, pretend to solve the problem. One can imagine the outcome.

Step 4: Selecting and "Owning" a Solution

In addition to owning a problem, people can own a solution. Many times, individuals or departments recognize that a problem exists but cannot agree on a solution. There are two possible outcomes in this situation. If the people involved have a professional attitude and respect one another, the dissenters say, "Okay, I disagree with the rest of you, but if this is the decision, I'll go along with it." They acknowledge that they could be wrong and their colleagues could be right, and they realize that if the planned change is to have any chance to succeed, it must have everyone's support. Therefore, they resolve to support the decision in any way they can. The other option is to sit back and do nothing to help the solution become successful. People who make no commitment to the solution may even secretly delight in seeing it fail. These people do not "own" the solution.

Managers who begin implementing changes without getting people to indicate whether they "own" the solution take the very real risk of assuming people are behind them, only to be frustrated by people "forgetting" to do the assignments they have been given. All managers should be aware of the OD practitioner's mental concept of ownership and ask themselves, "Do my people own the problem? Do my people own the solution?" If the answer to either question is no, in most cases the manager needs to stop right there and resolve the issues of ownership before going any further.

For OD practitioners, the concept of ownership plays a major part in how they present themselves. Once they diagnose what is wrong, what should they do? Facilitating ownership of both the problem and the solution is a fundamental part of the answer to that question.

Consider what the OD practitioner who diagnosed the problem at Frenolt discovered. Walker, the firm's president, thought he had a problem in communication with his executive staff. In fact, he had a different problem. He had a highly talented group of people but refused to delegate responsibility to them, so they were frustrated. And because he could not handle everything himself, mistakes were occurring. His staff was working behind the scenes to minimize the mistakes but could not tell the president they were doing so; he had never officially given them the power to do many of the things they were doing! An OD practitioner, in an effort to facilitate constructive planned change, would first get Walker and his staff to "own" an accurately described problem. Ownership occurs when people openly recognize that a problem exists, when they accept their contribution to the problem or the impact it has on them, or when they commit to the need to identify the problem and to do something about it. Then the determination and ownership of an appropriate solution could be achieved.

Step 5: Planning and Implementing the Change

Once the solution has been selected and "owned," it must be implemented. What processes will be changed? According to what timetable? Who is responsible for each phase? These questions must be answered and acted on via a planning approach such as that described in Chapter 8.

The reason why OD practitioners always get several people involved in diagnosing the problem and selecting solutions becomes quite apparent in this implementation phase. When the solution is implemented, it usually means changing one or more organizational practices. Once the new practices start, problems that were not anticipated may occur. People who are committed to the solution are more likely than uncommitted participants to make effective adjustments in the plans that have been implemented. Solutions, much like new computer programs, must be "debugged." This adjusting and fine-tuning is a key part of the implementation of planned change.

Step 6: Evaluating the Change

A planned change generated by the OD process is usually undertaken in the hope that the organization will become more effective in some specific way. Reduced absenteeism, improved morale, increased efficiency, and better customer relations are four examples of improvements that an OD-generated change might be intended to produce. The executive group at Frenolt Technical Corporation sought better communication, greater delegation, and more freedom in decision making.

Any OD process should include an objective evaluation that answers the question "Did the changes produce the desired results?" If the answer is yes, then the changes are working. If the answer is no or is uncertain, then adjustments or a new diagnosis may be called for.

We can conveniently summarize the OD process by briefly outlining its application at Frenolt Technical Corporation. Step 1, management's preliminary diagnosis, was rather straightforward. President Walker called in James Holton and told him what the problem was or, as we realize now, *what he thought* the problem was.

How did the OD practitioner discover, in step 2, that the underlying problem was that the president did not delegate? He held a series of interviews with each member of the executive staff. Over the course of a few interviews, the people being interviewed decided to trust the OD practitioner and to tell him what they thought was going on in the organization. These interviews were meetings wherein the OD practitioner talked with a single member of the staff in a private setting (his or her office or a conference room). Each staff member was interviewed about three times over a period of several weeks. During those meetings, the people being interviewed had to decide whether they believed the OD practitioner was knowledgeable, was politically astute, and could be trusted not to get them in trouble if they confided in him. Not every member of the staff took such risks. But when many of the members opened up, and they seemed to identify many of the same problems, it became possible for the OD practitioner to draw tentative conclusions.

In step 3, getting appropriate members involved in problem diagnosis, the president and the group agreed to prepare confidentially, on an individual basis, a list of problems facing the organization. The OD practitioner wrote these newly generated data on large easel sheets, which were posted on the wall of the conference room for the next group meeting. The group did agree that a series of problems existed. Included in this list was the fact that the president did not delegate. Even the president agreed that this was a problem.

Step 4, determining and owning a solution, involved a series of meetings at which various solutions were determined and accepted (owned) by the group. Among these was a decision that the president, working with the OD practitioner, would create a list of responsibilities that he would be willing to delegate. Next he would decide which tasks on his list should be delegated to whom.

Step 5, the planning and implementation stage, found Walker deciding that he would meet individually with each executive staff member to whom a task was being delegated. In that meeting (at which the OD practitioner was present), he

---

■■■■■■■■■■■■ *Guidelines for Management Practice* ■■■■■■■■■■■■

USING THE OD PROCESS

In effecting change through organization development, the manager is responsible for deciding who (himself or herself or an outside specialist) spearheads the effort. But in either case, that manager needs to remain actively involved. The following guidelines suggest how.

1. Use an outside OD practitioner when you feel too deeply involved in a problem or too uncertain about its origin to analyze it effectively. When in doubt, call someone else in.

2. Ask for references when considering a particular OD practitioner, and check out those references before starting.

3. Make sure that any effort to use OD in facilitating planned change omits none of the steps in the process except in rare situations where time doesn't permit it.

4. Use time frames (how long for each step?) and expected results along the way to monitor the progress of the organization development process.

---

and the subordinate would determine how to follow up and see that the delegated task was being successfully accomplished, how to expand the delegation of responsibilities over time, and how to guard against a return to past practices.

Step 6 was complete when the OD practitioner surveyed the executive team one year later to determine whether the level of delegation had remained satisfactory.

The OD process is a proven, logical approach to planned change. But for the process to work, particularly in facilitating major change, the OD practitioner should have four critical skills. These skills are covered in the next section.

Skills Useful to the OD Practitioner

OD practitioners need certain basic skills to make the OD process work. These skills can be grouped into four categories: interpersonal, problem-solving, group dynamics, and political skills.

Interpersonal Skills

Critical to the OD process are **interpersonal skills**—the ability to facilitate clear communication between people in a situation that is often tense and emotionally charged. These conditions can make people guarded in what they say, so an OD practitioner must be skilled in recognizing and understanding nonverbal behavior. Learning to understand nonverbal behavior means learning to notice and interpret the subtle tightening of muscles around the mouth or the slight shift back in the chair when the conversation turns to something that makes the person uncomfortable. Recognizing these behaviors helps the OD practitioner understand what people are "saying," even when they are purposely concealing their thoughts or are unsure themselves how they feel.

OD practitioners must also know how to construct feedback. A large part of this skill is the ability to depersonalize the feedback they are giving. Feedback tends to be personal, but it must be communicated in such a way that it is non-

threatening and can be disputed without anyone's losing face. One way OD practitioners can do this is to describe the *behavior* they observed that caused them to
draw the conclusions they have drawn. Finally, feedback should be constructed
in such a way as to enable the parties to reflect on what was said. Reflection puts
people in the proper frame of mind to explore various viewpoints jointly and
search for ways to solve problems together.

Problem-Solving Skills

We have described OD as a problem-solving process, so it should come as no
surprise that **problem-solving skills** are vital to the effective OD practitioner. First
among these skills is the ability to sort out the issues being discussed and to
recognize which issues are crucial. Next is the ability to maintain a detached
perspective. It is easy to get caught up in the dynamics of the situation and to
respond emotionally. Remaining objective is very difficult for some people until
they are trained to do so. In addition, an OD practitioner must learn to express
unspoken concerns that group members may have in a way that others can acknowledge. Finally, an OD practitioner needs to know how to maintain her or his
composure and control, even when other people do upsetting things. It is probably
evident by now that interpersonal skills and problem-solving skills are not quickly
learned. But every person *can* learn them. Not only in OD, but also in management
in general, a person who has developed interpersonal and problem-solving skills
is much more effective.

Skills in Group Dynamics

Most people in organizations spend a lot of their working lives as part of small
problem-solving groups. But the dynamics that shape people's behavior in such
groups do not always enhance their performance. For instance, when people in
groups get their turn to speak, they often simply restate the position they expressed
the last two times they spoke. Everybody is so busy reiterating their positions that
nothing of a constructive nature seems to happen. An OD practitioner (or a manager) with good **group dynamics skills** knows when to let a group drift and when
(and how) to intervene and help it focus its efforts better. Group skills also include
knowing how to help people confront each other in appropriate and productive
ways.

Political Skills

OD practitioners who were oblivious to the political interaction in an organization
would rarely know when they were putting people at risk by what they said or
did. It is not that OD must operate in an environment of total openness and trust.
But to the extent that people *can* come to be open and to trust each other, OD is
more successful. In fact, one of the functions of OD is to help people become
better able to be frank with each other. If the members of the group view the OD
practitioner as politically naïve, they will not be willing to take risks. It is up to
OD practitioners (and effective managers) to establish their credibility by the way
in which they present issues, discuss issues, and refer to the political ramifications.

To the extent that a group believes an OD practitioner has adequate political
awareness, and to the extent that the members realize the OD practitioner wants
them to be open but not to be foolish about it, they begin to respond with some

■■■■■■■■■■■■■■■■■■■■■■■■■■ *Guidelines for Management Practice* ■■■■■■■■■■■■■■■■■■■■■

Although managers should seriously consider enlisting outside OD practitioners to guide any OD process, they should also be prepared to incorporate some OD-related skills into their regular management practices. Doing so helps them in two ways. First, it makes them better able to contribute to an outsider-directed OD program if one is instituted. Second, it helps them and their subordinates be alert to issues and problems that may necessitate an OD program. These guidelines offer some practical tips that managers can incorporate into their own behavior at work to create an OD-responsive environment.

1. Create a climate in which members of the work group can raise problems and issues in front of each other at meetings. One good way to do this is to discuss an issue, in private and on an individual basis, with key people involved prior to an upcoming meeting. This makes discussing the issue in an open group meeting easier and also builds in group members the trust and confidence they need to raise issues and problems in the future.

2. Ask questions and raise issues in an impersonal manner. People usually respond more openly to such a question as "What are the key aspects of this problem?" than to "Why is that a problem for you?"

3. Allow subordinates private access to you on a regular basis. For example, take each one to lunch every six months. Then encourage them to share problems and issues.

4. Use group meetings as an opportunity to confirm what you think problem areas are. Saying "I think we have a problem with [whatever]," enables you to find out whether what you think is going on is what others think is going on. If the group agrees, the members confirm your assessment *and* "own" the problem, too.

5. Be sure you can tell whether people really agree with your description of a problem or are just saying so. As a way of removing your doubts and increasing their ownership of the problem, ask people who you suspect may not really agree to illustrate how the problem affects them.

6. Ask quiet people to state their opinions. This gets them involved, encourages their ownership of problems, and generates better solutions.

initial attempts to express the critical problems as they see them. The group continues to assess the political savvy of the OD practitioner and observes his or her skill at working with the group. As the OD practitioner's credibility grows, more members of the group start to address the issues that damage the effectiveness of the department. To establish this credibility, the OD practitioner has to learn what to say, what not to say, and how to handle various situations. This is all part of the **political skills** that the OD practitioner must acquire.

Being familiar with the steps in the OD process and cultivating these four key skills help the OD practitioner guide planned change successfully. In addition, several implementation techniques are often essential to an effective OD intervention or planned change. Selected OD techniques are briefly described in the next section.

OD Techniques

To make the organization development process work, OD practitioners often rely on several techniques for facilitating planned change. This section briefly explains selected OD techniques, some used in diagnosing the problem confronting the organization and others applied in the OD practitioner's attempt to help group members work together to find and implement a solution.

Diagnostic Techniques

Survey feedback is frequently used by OD practitioners. A survey or questionnaire is used to solicit information about problem areas so that organization members offer their opinions and attitudes anonymously. The survey approach makes it possible to obtain input from large numbers of people quickly and in a standardized format. Survey feedback is generally used to get a better idea where change may be needed or to assess the overall impact of changes after some time has passed. The results are often consolidated and shown to the people surveyed as a basis for in-depth discussions about what problems exist and what solutions are possible.

The **nominal group technique** (NGT) is another method that some OD practitioners use to identify problem areas, pinpoint the need for change, and generate suggested ways to implement change. The nominal group technique is a group discussion method in which the intermember interaction is carefully controlled. But it attempts to get the benefit of the ideas and opinions of people who tend *not* to speak out during a highly charged group interaction. Hence all group members are first asked to write down comments or suggestions and then to respond in writing as the group leader reads the list of suggestions. Typically, group members are asked to list key problems facing the work group. Their confidential lists are then consolidated by the group leader and copied onto a blackboard or easel for the group to see. No one is identified with a particular item. Next the group members are asked—again without discussion—to identify the most important problems. The group leader again consolidates the information and lists it for the group. At this point, problems or items are usually categorized and members are asked to list possible solutions on another sheet of paper—once again without interaction. The group leader consolidates *this* information, lists it for all to see, and does not reveal any member's association with any item. Now group interaction may be allowed, but only after major progress has been made in identifying the problem and generating possible solutions without any discussion.

Force-field analysis (FFA) is a technique used to diagram key forces in a situation characterized by conflict or planned change and then to use it (in the latter case) to plan the change more effectively.[14] According to the theory behind FFA, in any conflict or political situation, opposing forces are at work. This idea is applied to Frenolt Technical Corporation's problem in Figure 12-4. In force-field analysis, the first step is to identify the key forces promoting the shift to a new, desired situation (driving forces) and those inhibiting such a change (restraining forces). The second step is to estimate the strength or importance of each such force and represent it via the size of its arrow (see Figure 12-4). When the diagram is complete, logic suggests that a change from the status quo to a new situation can be achieved only when the driving forces are greater than the restraining forces. Following this logic, the third step is to devise specific changes that would have the effect of increasing the driving forces, decreasing the restraining forces, and/or changing restraining forces into driving forces. At Frenolt Technical Corporation, the subordinates' desire for delegation was recognized, John Walker's fear of delegating was reduced, and uncertainty about what tasks to delegate was transformed into a clear understanding. FFA is a simple but powerful technique to aid in diagnosing the dynamics of a problem situation and developing a strategy for planned change.

The diagnosis of problems is often used to stimulate discussion and analysis of ways to make meaningful change. This interaction itself is facilitated by an additional set of OD techniques, which are described in the next section.

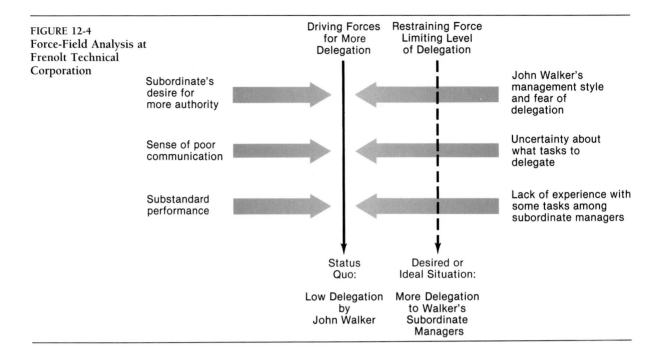

FIGURE 12-4
Force-Field Analysis at
Frenolt Technical
Corporation

Driving Forces for More Delegation

Restraining Force Limiting Level of Delegation

Subordinate's desire for more authority

John Walker's management style and fear of delegation

Sense of poor communication

Uncertainty about what tasks to delegate

Substandard performance

Lack of experience with some tasks among subordinate managers

Status Quo:

Desired or Ideal Situation:

Low Delegation by John Walker

More Delegation to Walker's Subordinate Managers

Interaction-Facilitating Techniques

Team building is a group-oriented OD technique designed to increase the level of trust, openness, and cohesiveness in work groups or management teams. In team building, the OD practitioner encourages team members to reveal more information (job-related and personal) within the group than is currently shared. Thus each group member risks providing some previously unknown information and is reinforced when another member does the same thing, which can build a greater level of trust among group members. As the level of trust increases, OD practitioners expect the effectiveness of the team to increase as well.

Figure 12-5 (which is also called the *Johari window*) illustrates the typical focus of team building—to increase information and understanding about what is known or shared among team members. As the dotted lines in Figure 12-5 indicate, the information that is "known to self" and "known by others" is increased (1) when one obtains information known to others but not to oneself (such as "You come across as too stiff and formal on a sales call") and (2) when one reveals information known to oneself but not known to others ("The reason I've been such a pain the last six months is that my marriage is in trouble"). As the arrows suggest, the basic purpose of team building is to increase the amount of relevant information that is known to oneself *and* to others by sharing and revealing that information. The desired payoff is greater understanding, which should increase the level of trust and make planned change more successful. The events at Frenolt Technical Corporation reflected a form of team building. John Walker revealed to the group his difficulty in deciding what tasks to delegate after he learned that the group thought he did not delegate enough tasks or authority.

Team-building is often fostered by using exercises that help team members see the potential for better decisions when information is shared within the group.

A San Francisco-based neighborhood development organization, Tenderloin, sought the assistance of an OD practitioner to help promote team building within the organization. As a first step, a meeting of citywide managers was scheduled to allow the OD practitioner to explain the OD team-building process. (Charles Vergara/Photo Researchers)

One such exercise to illustrate this, the Lost at Sea exercise, is provided as "Management Development Exercise 12" at the end of this chapter.

Process consultation is another interaction-facilitating OD technique. In **process consultation**, an OD practitioner examines some organizational process, develops ideas on how to improve it, and then leads participants in that process through a discussion of those ideas. The process at issue might be a work team, a production operation, or a manager-subordinate relationship. At Frenolt Technical Corporation, the OD practitioner's decision to sit in as Walker discussed what tasks to delegate and the nature of authority granted and to attend subsequent meetings between Walker and members of his executive team exhibits process consultation aimed at improving Walker's management process.[15]

Grid OD is the last organization development technique we will describe. **Grid OD** is a comprehensive program for (1) evaluating the management styles of managers within an organization on the basis of their concern for people and

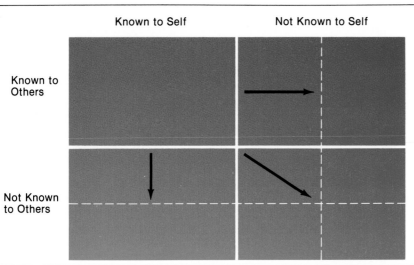

FIGURE 12-5
Team Building

their concern for production and (2) then using training activities to move them toward a preferred management style. It is based on the Managerial Grid®, which was developed by Robert Blake and Jane Mouton[16] (Chapter 15).

Grid OD first assesses a manager's style via a survey that determines how concerned that manager is for people and for production (getting the work done). This assessment could apply to the manager of one work group, or the OD practitioner might combine it across several managers to get a feel for unitwide or organizationwide management style.

Grid OD is usually based on the assumption that a high concern for people *and* production is the ideal management style individually and collectively. So once the managers' styles have been assessed, a training effort is undertaken to help managers understand their style, other styles, the value of moving toward an ideal style, and how to do so. For example, John Walker at Frenolt Technical Corporation might have been assessed as having a strong concern for getting the job done and little concern for the people doing it. After making this assessment, the practitioner using a grid OD approach would involve Walker in examining the positive and negative ramifications of this style, in examining alternative styles, and in searching for ways to boost his concern for people so that he could move toward the ideal style. If the complete top management team at Frenolt were involved, individual styles would be determined and compared (usually anonymously). The ramifications of all the different styles, but particularly those found at Frenolt, would be discussed. And ways to move toward the ideal style, both individually and collectively, would be explored and acted on.

The use of grid OD is accomplished by a six-phase process described by Blake and Mouton:[17]

1. *The grid seminar.* This phase consists of a one-week program that provides participants with an opportunity to analyze their managerial style and to learn team methods of problem solving. Top management attends the seminar first. They assess themselves through case studies and questionnaires, then participants receive feedback on their styles from other group members.

2. *Teamwork development.* This phase of the grid program allows managers to practice team development in two or more different groups. These groups consist of their present boss and their immediate subordinates. Like the seminar phase, the team-building phase, conducted in an off-the-job-premises setting, provides the team members with uninterrupted time and usually begins with top management—the managers and their corporate staffs or the managers and their department, division, or plant staffs.

3. *Intergroup development.* In order to achieve organizational excellence, every organization must function as a whole, even if it is made up of different sections with specialized tasks and different goals. To improve intergroup relations the following steps are necessary: (1) before each session, each participant prepares a written description contrasting the actual working relationship with the ideal working relationship; (2) groups then summarize their perceptions of the actual and ideal relationships in isolated environments over a period of several days; (3) the groups later meet using a spokesperson and limiting their exchange to comparing their perceptions; and (4) the groups work to make relationships more productive. When the groups have a definite understanding of the specific actions each will take and how the actions will be followed through, this phase is complete.

4. *Developing an ideal strategic organization model.* This phase emphasizes the following basic rules that top managers in an organization work toward to achieve organizational excellence: (1) development of clear definitions of minimum and optimum organizational financial objectives; (2) development of clear, concise definitions of the character and nature of organizational activities; (3) development of clear, operational definitions of the character and scope of markets, customers, or clients; (4) the development of an organizational structure to integrate operations for synergistic results; (5) the development of basic policies for organizational decision making; and (6) the development of approaches to implement growth capacity and avoid stagnation or obsolescence.

5. *Implementing the ideal strategic model.* If the first four phases have been successfully completed, many of the barriers to implementation will already have been reduced, leaving managers with a good understanding of what the communication blocks are and how to resolve them. Implementing the ideal strategic model then becomes a matter of applying the following strategies: (1) defining the business segments in terms of the nature of the organization and its market or environment; (2) identifying specific organizational units, such as cost centers or profit centers; (3) appointing planning teams for each autonomous unit; and (4) establishing an overall headquarters organization that has the ability to develop executive talent, to develop investment capital, and to provide service to the entire organization more cheaply or efficiently than can be done by local decision centers or autonomous units.

6. *Systematic critique.* The systematic examination of the organization's progress toward the ideal model, including formal and informal measurement and evaluation of direction, rate, quality, and quantity of progress, is the last phase in achieving ideal organizational excellence. This phase also provides for the systematic planning of future development activities. This critique becomes increasingly crucial as an organization proceeds through the grid process, since Blake and Mouton see lack of communication and planning as the greatest barriers to organizational excellence.

Grid OD offers OD practitioners two advantages. First, it provides a concrete measurement tool for comparing management styles. Second, it can be applied at both individual and organizational levels.

This section treated only a few of many OD techniques, all of which rely on the basic skills identified in the preceding section and have the same goal: successful planned change. Although organization development has emerged as a prominent force in facilitating planned change, OD programs have often failed. The next section examines why OD programs fail by identifying nine conditions that must be present if OD programs are to bring about planned change successfully.

Conditions Contributing to the Success of OD

Past efforts to assess the value of organization development as a means of bringing about planned change have yielded mixed results. This is perhaps due to the difficulty of evaluating the total impact of an OD program.

Over the years, OD practitioners have examined OD programs that have failed in order to learn why. Two prominent OD scholars have examined numerous OD programs and concluded that failure is usually attributable to an absence of "en-

▬▬▬▬▬ *Guidelines for Management Practice* ▬▬▬▬▬

Once a manager becomes interested in using OD to initiate planned change, he or she usually needs to find and select an external OD practitioner. "How do I know that I am hiring a good OD practitioner?" and "Where do I find several OD practitioners to choose from?" are two questions that managers must be able to answer.

In talking with an OD practitioner whom he or she might hire, a manager should make a personal judgment about the following issues:

1. Can the two of them communicate well? Are they direct in their discussions? Does each of them say what needs to be said? It is necessary for the manager and the OD practitioner to work together well. That is something only the two of them can judge.

2. Is the OD practitioner insightful about organizational politics? If the OD practitioner is naïve, he or she is likely to create problems by assuring people that it is appropriate for them to do or say things that, in fact, could get those people in trouble.

3. Does the OD practitioner seem to know what he or she is talking about when he or she describes how groups work together (or fail to do so)?

4. Does the OD practitioner seem to have the interpersonal skills required to be successful? How does he or she proceed when the discussions between manager and OD practitioner get serious?

5. Experience is a very important consideration. Managers usually want to know where the OD prac-

titioner was trained, but most really good OD practitioners pick up their skills over time, not in any particular program. If one tries to assess the OD practitioner only through traditional means, one may hire a person who meets prescribed academic criteria but does not have the applied skills to be successful "in the trenches." What is important is whether the OD practitioner has the insight to figure out what needs to be done and how to do it and has the skill to make it happen through the commitment of others. Reviewing the OD practitioner's past OD programs, perhaps by calling managers who were involved in them, is a good way to find out whether he or she has this sort of insight.

6. Unfortunately, inferior OD practitioners have fooled many a prospective client. For this reason, much hiring in this field is done on a referral basis. Managers should ask other managers. In a corporation, many times the internal staff knows how to find OD consultants for the manager to interview. Managers can tap another important source of potential OD practitioners by contacting colleagues with whom they have a good relationship in their own firm or other organizations.

Managers who need help in finding an OD practitioner, can get information and referrals from several professional associations whose members are active OD consultants. Specifically, managers can contact The National OD Network, P.O. Box 69329, Portland, Oregon 97201; or the OD Institute, 11234 Walnut Ridge Road, Chesterland, Ohio 44026.

---

abling conditions" within the organization or to faulty execution of the OD program.[18] They have condensed these conclusions into nine conditions necessary for OD success.

1. *Recognition by managers, particularly top managers, that the organization or unit has problems necessitating change.* Where top managers do not recognize the need for change, they are unlikely to be committed to change. And without this commitment and the resources and support that go with it, organization development is doomed to failure.

2. *Use of an outside OD consultant.* Internal change agents are often perceived as having a vested interest in the outcome, as offering little experience, as lacking

objectivity, or as not having the power to make a major program of change stick.[19]

3. *Visible support of top management right from the start.* People take change more seriously when top management is clearly behind it.

4. *Early success with the OD effort.* When the first planned change is made and proves successful, organization members gain confidence that the OD process is working and merits their support. (Early failure, of course, has just the opposite effect.)

5. *Education of organization members about OD.* Change is difficult for most people. Efforts to manage planned change can appear manipulative. Making sure people understand what the OD process involves reduces this perception that they are being manipulated.

6. *Acknowledgment of members' strengths.* Planned change often involves good, talented members of the organization. Such people may resent the OD practitioner's status as the expert or teacher. Periodically acknowledging their talent and value to the firm reduces this problem.

7. *Development of internal OD practitioners.* Internal OD expertise and skill, particularly among line managers, help sustain and refine planned changes after the external OD practitioner has become less involved.

8. *Effective management of the OD program.* Planned change needs to be just that, *planned,* to be most effective. Organization members lose faith in an approach that seems poorly coordinated, loosely controlled, and erratic in its progress.

9. *Measurement of the impact and results.* OD practitioners are better able to manage and adjust the OD process in a timely fashion when data on the impact of the effort to change are obtained regularly.

Review of the Learning Objectives

Having studied this chapter, you should be able to respond to the learning objectives with extensions of the following brief answers.

1. **Define the term** *organization development* **(OD).**

   OD can be defined as a planned effort (often organizationwide), managed from the top, to increase the organization's effectiveness and health through planned interventions in organizational processes via behavioral science knowledge. OD focuses on bringing about change in people and processes through very involved problem solving.

2. **Explain the nature of change in organizations, particularly planned change.**

   Change is an inevitable part of organizational life. *Reactive change* occurs in response to a sudden or unplanned event. *Planned change* is a systematic, deliberate change in the way part of all of an organization functions. Either type of change usually involves three phases: unfreezing, change, and refreezing. There are three approaches to organizational change: structural change, technological change, and people change.

3. **List four reasons for resistance to change and five ways this resistance can be overcome.**

   Resistance to change arises because individuals and groups are *uncertain* about the impact of change, *lack trust* or *understanding* about the need for change, have *self-interests* that are hurt by the change, or have *different opinions about the outcomes* of the proposed changes. Resistance to change can be overcome by *communication and education, participation* in planning change, *negotiation* to mediate the impact of change, *coercion* to force acceptance of change, or strong and visible *top management support.*

4. **Outline the organization development process.**

   The OD process can be viewed as a series of six steps intended to manage planned change. The first step occurs when a manager perceives a problem and calls in or acts as an OD practitioner. In step 2, the OD practitioner makes an initial personal diagnosis. In step 3, the OD practitioner gets everyone who is involved in the problem to recognize and "own" it. Step 4 has participants searching for solutions and agreeing to support the solutions that are chosen. The solution, which consists of planned changes, is devised and implemented in step 5. In step 6, OD practitioner and participants evaluate the impact of the changes they have implemented.

5. **Identify the key skills exhibited by successful organization development practitioners.**

   Successful OD practitioners must possess four important skills. They need *interpersonal skills* to facilitate clear communication between people in a situation that is often tense and emotionally charged. *Problem-solving skills* are essential as they sort out issues and seek solutions. *Group dynamics skills* are necessary as the OD practitioner observes, interprets, and facilitates group interaction and problem solving. *Political skills* are critical if the OD process is to be viewed as realistic and if the OD practitioner is to be trusted and respected.

6. **List several organization development techniques.**

   Three techniques that are important to effective diagnosis are survey feedback, the nominal group technique, and force-field analysis. Interaction-facilitating techniques include team building, process consultation, and grid OD.

7. **Cite the conditions that contribute to the success of organization development.**

   These conditions are (1) recognition by managers that the organization or work unit has problems that necessitate change, (2) the use of outside OD consultants, (3) visible top management support, (4) early success with the OD effort, (5) the education of organization members about OD, (6) acknowledgment of the participating managers' strengths, (7) the development of internal OD practitioners, (8) a well-run OD program, and (9) measurement of the impact and results of the OD program.

Key Terms and Concepts

After having completed your study of Chapter 12, "Change and Organization Development," you will have mastered the following important terms and concepts.

organization development (OD)	change phase refreezing phase resistance to change	people change OD process interpersonal skills	group dynamics skills political skills	force-field analysis (FFA) team building
reactive change	structural change	problem-solving skills	survey feedback	process consultation
planned change	technological		nominal group	grid OD
unfreezing phase	change		technique	

Questions for Discussion

1. Explain the nature of organization change and two ways it might come about.

2. Explain the unfreezing, change, and refreezing steps in the process of change.

3. What are the main sources of resistance to change? Provide an illustration of one such source from your personal experience.

4. Describe three ways managers can overcome resistance to change and illustrate one of them.

5. Explain how OD might play a role in organizational change.

6. Describe the typical OD process.

7. Why are interpersonal skills necessary for an OD practitioner?

8. Explain how a lack of group dynamics skills might detract from an OD practitioner's effectiveness.

9. Why are problem-solving skills and political skills important for OD practitioners? How are they different?

10. Explain and illustrate survey feedback, the nominal group technique, and force-field analysis.

11. What is team building? Process consultation? Grid OD?

12. Identify and illustrate at least five conditions that enable OD programs to be successful.

Notes

1. Adapted from the client files of Mark Sandberg, OD consultant and associate dean, Rider College.
2. R. Beckhard, *Organization Development: Strategies and Models* (Reading, Mass.: Addison-Wesley, 1968), p. 9.
3. F. Norris, "The Crash of 1987: Men and Machines Wreak Havoc on Wall Street," *Barrons,* October 26, 1987, p. 8.
4. "Feast and Famine: Trading Income," *Economist,* May 9, 1987, p. 72.
5. "IP Replaces Striking Workers at Two of Its Mills," *Pulp and Paper,* August 1987, p. 25.
6. K. Lewin, *Field Theory in Social Science* (New York: Harper and Bros., 1951); K. Lewin, "Group Decision and Social Change," in G. E. Swanson, T. M. Newcomb, and E. L. Hartley, eds., *Readings in Social Psychology* (New York: Holt, 1952), pp. 459–473; and E. Schein, *Coercive Persuasion* (New York: Norton, 1961).
7. P. Engardio, "Why Eastern is Backing Off from a Union Showdown," *Business Week,* October 12, 1987, pp. 108–109.
8. J. P. Kotter and L. A. Schlesinger, "Choosing Strategies for Change," *Harvard Business Review,* March–April, 1979, pp. 106–114.
9. L. Coch and J. French, Jr., "Overcoming Resistance to Change," *Human Relations* 1, no. 4 (1948): 512–532; S. Hinckley, "A Closer Look at Participation," *Organizational Dynamics* 13, no. 3 (Winter 1985): 57–67; and P. Lawrence, "How to Deal with Resistance to Change," *Harvard Business Review,* January–February 1969, pp. 4–12, 166–176.
10. J. B. Treece, "Can Ford Stay on Top?" *Business Week,* September 28, 1987, pp. 78–82.
11. S. E. Seashore, E. E. Lawler, III, D. Mirvis, and C. Cammann, *Assessing Organizational Change: A Guide to Methods, Measures, and Practices* (New York: Wiley, 1983).
12. S. Caminiti, "Pepsi and Coca-Cola: The All-American Worldwide War," *Fortune,* October 26, 1987, p. 56.
13. K. Brown, "Diagnosing Poor Work Group Performance," *Academy of Management Review* 9, 1 (1984): 54–63.
14. K. Lewin, *Field Theory in Social Science.*
15. R. E. Walton, *Managing Conflict: Interpersonal Dialogue and Third Party Roles* (Reading, Mass.: Addison-Wesley, 1987); and E. Schein, *Coercive Persuasion.*

16. R. Blake and J. Mouton, *The Managerial Grid III* (Houston: Gulf, 1985).

17. R. Blake and J. Mouton, *Corporate Excellence Through Grid Organization Development: A Systems Approach* (Houston, Texas: Gulf, 1968); and R. Blake and J. Mouton, *Building a Dynamic Corporation Through Grid Organization Development* (Reading, Mass.: Addison-Wesley, 1969).

18. W. L. French and C. H. Bell, *Organization Development: Behavioral Science Interventions for Organization Improvement,* 3rd ed. (Englewood, Cliffs, N.J.: Prentice-Hall, 1984), pp. 54–62.

19. R. Kanter, "Dilemmas of Managing Participation," in M. Beer and P. Spector, eds., *Readings in Human Resource Management* (New York: Free Press, 1986), pp. 196–226.

Cohesion Incident 12-1
Starting Over in Gainesville

"Charles, you caught me right in the middle of my yearly desk cleaning. I must be feeling inspired by all the talk about reorganization going on at the corporate level.

Charles has just walked in on Roger, who is bent over cleaning out one of his desk drawers, putting half of the items in a trash can and the other half back into the drawer. He pulls out a business card, glances at it, and passes it over to Charles. "Charles, I hope you never need to use this outfit, but they're fantastic at helping overhaul an operation such as ours. I called them in once to help me over at Journey's End in Gainesville, and they really got us straightened out."

Glancing at the card, Charles sees the name "Thurman, Arnold, and Berry— Management Consultants" highlighted on the card. "Why were you using a firm like this?" he asked.

"When I arrived in Gainesville about three years ago, it was my second experience working here. I had been in Gainesville about twelve years ago for my initial month-long training program when I first joined Journey's End. Charles, they had one of the finest motels around. The occupancy rate always averaged 90 to 93 percent. Everyone associated with the motel was high-spirited, and they just had a grand time. Twice in my first three years with the Journey's End organization they got the "Most Profitable" plaque at the annual meeting.

"About nine years ago, though, things began to go downhill. In fact, when I returned three years ago, I was the third manager in five years. I could tell there was a definite lack of spirit in the employees. Even our guests seemed to have lost their spark! As I walked through the dining room, the lounge, and the lobby, I could sense that things just weren't right. And the staff meetings might as well have been held in a funeral parlor. Things had been so vibrant and alive in the past that I could hardly believe the change. I'm sure I was sent back there in hopes of rekindling the old spark.

"After about six months, I couldn't see where I was making any progress. The lack of communication was appalling, no one wanted to take on any type of extra responsibility, and a complete lack of innovation stifled the place. That's when I called in Thurman, Arnold, and Berry."

"Did they get Gainesville turned around?" Charles asked.

"Boy, did they ever. They spent three months with us, but when they were finished, we had regained the spirit and enthusiasm that had been missing.

"They call it OD, organization development. Our practitioners started by diagnosing exactly where we were when they arrived. They handed out numerous questionnaires and surveys to everyone in the organization . . . from the maids to me. They held meetings with various groups of employees, and I gave them free access to our records. Then they relayed all these data to me and to everyone else involved. There were no secrets. Next they instituted a series of meetings to help us see what we could do to meet our goals. They provided certain individuals with sensitivity training to help them develop interpersonal skills. Others attended group change and team-building conferences to improve the functioning of their individual teams. They even made one change in the organization chart at the Gainesville Journey's End.

"Keep that card. As I said, I hope you never need it, but if you do, they can fix you up."

Questions for Discussion

1. How was organization development undertaken at Journey's End?

2. Why was this OD effort successful?

3. What needs to be done to maintain the improvements that OD made possible at the Gainesville Journey's End?

Cohesion Incident 12-2
Implementing Strategic Change

On October 15, 1988, Alonzo Fulmer, chief executive officer of Travis Corporation, reviewed three notes he had exchanged with Charlotte Robinson, president of a company owned by Travis. The two executives were going to meet in a few minutes to discuss problems that had recently surfaced. During the past decade, Travis had aggressively pursued a growth objective based in part on a strategy of acquiring companies in distress. Chairman Fulmer's policy was to appoint a new chief operating officer for each acquisition, with instructions to facilitate a turnaround. Fulmer reviewed two of the notes he had written to Charlotte Robinson.

DATE: January 15, 1987: Memorandum

TO: Charlotte Robinson, Director of Fiscal Affairs, Travis Corp.

FROM: Alonzo Fulmer, Chairman, Travis Corp.

SUBJECT: Your Appointment as President, Lee Medical Supplies

You are aware that Travis Corporation recently acquired Lee Medical Supplies. John Lee, founder and president of the company, has agreed to retire, and in line with our earlier discussions, I am appointing you to replace him. Our acquisitions group will brief you on the company, but I want to warn you that Lee Medical Supplies has a history of mismanagement. As a distributor of medical items, the company's sales last year totaled approximately $300 million, with net earnings of only $12 million. Your job is to make company sales and profits compatible with Travis standards. You are reminded that it is my policy to call for an independent evaluation of the company's progress and of your performance as president after eighteen months.

DATE: September 10, 1988: Memorandum

TO: Charlotte Robinson, President, Lee Medical Supplies

FROM: Alonzo Fulmer, Chairman, Travis Corp.

SUBJECT: Serious problems at Lee Medical Supplies

In accordance with corporate policy, consultants recently conducted an evaluation of Lee Medical Supplies. In a relatively short period of time, you

Source: Adapted from "Implementing Strategic Change," in *Critical Incidents in Management*, J. M. Champion and J. H. James, eds., Richard D. Irwin, Inc. © 1985, pp. 120–126.

have increased sales and profits to meet Travis's standards, but I am concerned about other aspects of your performance, as revealed by the consultant's report. I am told that during the past eighteen months, three of your nine vice presidents have resigned and that you have terminated four others. An opinion survey conducted by the consultants indicated that morale is low and that your managerial appointees are regarded by their subordinates as hard-nosed perfectionists obsessed with quotas and profits. Employees report that ruthless competition now exists among divisions, regions, and districts. They also note that the family-oriented atmosphere fostered by Mr. Lee has been replaced by a dog-eat-dog situation characterized by negative management attitudes toward employee feelings and needs. After you have studied the enclosed report from the consultants, we will meet to discuss their findings. I am particularly alarmed by their final conclusion that "a form of corporate cancer seems to be spreading throughout Lee Medical Supplies."

As Fulmer prepared to read the third note, written by Charlotte Robinson, he reflected on his exit interview with the consultants. Whereas Fulmer himself considered Robinson a financial expert and a turnaround specialist, her subordinates characterized her as an autocrat, a hachet woman, and better suited to be a Marine boot camp commander!

DATE: September 28, 1988: Memorandum

TO: Alonzo Fulmer, Chairman, Travis Corp.

FROM: Charlotte Robinson, President, Lee Medical Supplies

SUBJECT: The so-called serious problem at Lee Medical Supplies

I have received your memorandum dated September 10, 1988, and have reviewed the consultant's report. When you appointed me to my present position, I was instructed to take over an unprofitable company and make it profitable. I have done so in eighteen months, although I inherited a family-owned business that by your own admission had been mismanaged for years. I found a group of managers and salespeople with an average company tenure of twenty-two years. They believed their jobs were guaranteed for life. Mr. Lee had centralized all personnel decisions so that only he could terminate an employee. He tolerated mediocre performance. All employees were paid on a straight-salary basis, and seniority was the sole criterion for advancement. Some emphasis was given to increasing sales each year, but none was given to reducing costs and increasing profits. Employees did indeed find the company a fun place to work. They did indeed express undying loyalty and love for Lee. And a feeling of being a part of a family did permeate the company. Such attitudes were, however, accompanied by mediocrity, incompetence, and poor performance.

I found it necessary to implement immediate strategic changes in five areas: the organization's structure, employee rewards and incentives, management information systems, allocation of resources, and managerial leadership style. As a result, sales areas were reorganized into divisions, regions, and districts. Managers who I felt were incompetent or lacked commitment to my objectives and methods were replaced. Unproductive and mediocre employees were encouraged to find jobs elsewhere. Authority for staffing and compensation decisions was decentralized to units at the division, region, and district levels. Managers of those units were informed that along with their authority went responsibility for reducing costs and for increasing sales and profits. Each unit was established as a profit center. A new department was established and charged with reviewing the performance of those units. Improved accounting and control systems were implemented. A management-by-objectives program was developed to establish standards and monitor performance. Performance appraisals are now required for all employees. To encourage more aggressive action, bonuses and incentives are offered to managers of units that show increased profits. A commission plan based on measurable sales and profit performance has replaced straight salaries. Resources are allocated to units on the basis of their performance.

My own leadership style has probably represented the most traumatic change for employees. Internal competition is a formally mandated policy throughout the company. It has been responsible for much of the progress achieved to date. Progress, however, is never made without costs, and I was employed to achieve results, not to ensure that employees remain secure and happy in their work. Don't let a few cry-babies unable to adjust to changes lead you to believe that problems take precedence over profits. I believe it is unlikely that a spirit of aggressiveness and competitiveness can coexist with an atmosphere of cooperativeness and family orientation. Does that mean I am not people-oriented? Do you feel we owe our employees a family orientation? Frankly, I thought I had your support in doing whatever was necessary to get this company turned around. In our meeting, tell me whether you think my approaches have been wrong, and if so, tell me what I should have done differently.

Just as Fulmer finished reviewing the third memorandum, his secretary informed him that Charlotte Robinson had arrived for their scheduled meeting. He realized that he was not certain how to communicate to Robinson his ideas and beliefs about how changes in an organization are best implemented. He knew he did not appreciate the way Robinson expressed her views in her memo, but he realized he should probably set emotions aside and respond as best he could to the issues Robinson raised.

Questions for Discussion

1. What appear to be the key dynamics of the organizational change situation at Lee Medical Supplies? Use force-field analysis to diagram what you think the situation was before and after Charlotte Robinson's first eighteen months at Lee Medical.

2. How could OD have been used to guide change at Lee Medical? How can it be used now?

3. If you were advising Fulmer, what would your recommendations be?

Management Development Exercise 12
Lost at Sea

One of the challenges facing OD practitioners is the "time versus quality of decision" trade-off involved in deciding between individual and group approaches to planned change. Individuals can assess problems and generate solutions more quickly and efficiently than groups. Yet although they take more time, groups can often generate better solutions because of the varied perspectives represented in a group, the discussion that is possible, and the trust that develops. As a manager, you will often encounter this time–quality trade-off in deciding how to plan change in your organization.

The following exercise will help illustrate this trade-off. Complete the exercise individually. Then your instructor will assign you to a group to repeat the exercise. After both phases are complete, your instructor will explain how to score and interpret the results.

Instructions: You are adrift on a private yacht in the South Pacific. As a consequence of a fire of unknown origin, much of the yacht and its contents have been destroyed. The yacht is now slowly sinking. Your location is unclear because of the destruction of critical navigational equipment and because you and the crew were distracted trying to bring the fire under control. Your best estimate is that you are approximately 1,000 miles south-southwest of the nearest land.

Below is a list of fifteen items that remain intact and undamaged after the fire. In addition to these articles, you have a serviceable rubber life raft equipped with oars and large enough to carry yourself, the crew, and some of the following items. The total contents of all survivors' pockets are a package of cigarettes, several books of matches, and five $1 bills.

Your task is to rank these fifteen items in terms of their importance to your survival. Place the number *1* by the most important item, the number *2* by the second most important, and so on through number *15*, the least important.

_____   Sextant

_____   Shaving mirror

_____   Five-gallon can of water

_____   Mosquito netting

_____   One case of U.S. Army C rations

_____   Maps of the Pacific Ocean

_____   Seat cushion (flotation device approved by the Coast Guard)

_____   Two-gallon can of oil–gas mixture

_____   Small transistor radio

_____   Shark repellent

_____   Twenty square feet of opaque plastic

_____   One quart of 160-proof Puerto Rican rum

_____   Fifteen feet of nylon rope

_____   Two boxes of chocolate bars

_____   Fishing kit

Source: Reprinted from J. W. Pfeiffer and J. E. Jones, eds., *The 1975 Annual Handbook for Group Facilitators* (San Diego, Calif.: University Associates Publishers, 1975). Used with permission.

Human Resource Management and Labor Relations

Your study of this chapter will enable you to do the following:

1. Define the term *human resource management* and list the activities it involves.
2. List the groups protected under equal employment opportunity regulations, and explain the criteria that employment practices must meet in order to be considered nondiscriminatory.
3. Explain what job analysis is and cite three products of job analysis.
4. Define the term *human resource planning* and describe the steps it involves.
5. List the basic steps in the employee selection process.
6. Explain four purposes of performance appraisal.
7. Describe three major pieces of legislation that have defined the rights of labor and management in the United States.
8. Trace the steps involved in the unionization process.

Employee Recognition Programs at Diamond Fiber Products

Poor working relationships between management and employees can contribute to high absenteeism, low productivity, and lack of communication within a company. Diamond Fiber Products in Thorndike, Massachusetts, has successfully addressed this industrial relations problem by instituting an employee recognition program.

Daniel Boyle, co-owner of the company, proposed the idea in 1980 after a grievance meeting with union representatives. The meeting underscored the deteriorating communication and cooperation between management and labor. "Only a few of the items discussed at the meeting were true grievances," Boyle recalls. "The other issues were minor matters that escalated into grievances because of the poor working relationship."

Cartoon reminders about the 100 Club at Diamond Fiber Products appear throughout employee work areas. (Courtesy of Diamond Fiber Products)

At the time, the Thorndike plant was part of Diamond International and had one of the lowest efficiency ratings in the corporation's Fiber Division. To improve morale, communication, and productivity throughout the company, Boyle suggested instituting a program that would recognize and then reward those employees who were doing their jobs well. "Corporate managers gave us the go-ahead for the program," he says. "They were willing to try anything to turn things around."

Representatives from every department assisted in designing and developing what Boyle named "The 100 Club." Still, most managers and line employees remained skeptical. "At first, employees didn't believe they would be rewarded simply for doing their jobs properly. They thought there had to be some strings attached to the program," recalls Boyle.

Responding to employees' concerns, Boyle explained the concept behind The 100 Club at a union meeting. In describing the plan, he reemphasized that the company wanted to recognize employees for doing their current jobs well. He assured them that there would be no increase in their present workload.

As part of the recognition program, employees receive "points" for achieving pre-established goals. All employees have an equal opportunity to earn points, but the criteria vary depending on the needs of each department. Achievements are weighted in order of importance. For example, maintenance department employees received the highest number of points for reducing equipment failures, production workers for increased efficiency, and employees in accounts payable for utilizing all available discounts.

Additionally, all company employees can earn points for good attendance and punctuality, work safety, suggestions that promote savings and safety, and community involvement. Nominally priced gifts based on the number of points earned are then awarded to employees. Those earning 100 points receive "The 100 Club" jackets, and additional gifts are awarded at fifty-point increments.

The 100 Club was an immediate success. Managers and employees who had originally criticized the program became strong supporters. At the end of the first year, the cost savings to the company totaled $1.6 million, "most of it resulting from a productivity explosion of 14.7 percent," explains Boyle. Although the program cannot be credited with all the savings, he feels strongly that The 100 Club was the catalyst for ongoing improvement, including a 40 percent decrease in production errors, reduced absenteeism, and a productivity increase averaging 2 percent each year.

Despite the phenomenal cost savings, Boyle says the most significant aspect of The 100 Club program has been improved communication between management and labor. In the past, he explains, employee recommendations were often ignored. Now, however, suggestions are both encouraged and implemented. "There is a new team spirit in the company that has had a positive effect on all aspects of production." For an annual cost of approximately $20 per employee, Diamond Fiber Products has netted a return of more than 250 times its original investment, measured in terms of increased productivity, reduced absenteeism, and improved worker safety.[1]

HUMAN RESOURCE MANAGEMENT

Introduction

What Is Human Resource Management?

Much has been written in recent years about the importance of people as a key to increasing and maintaining the productivity of organizations. Dana Corporation, for example, included a statement of that principle in its annual report, declaring that "People are our most important and productive asset."[2] In their study of outstanding companies, *In Search of Excellence,* Thomas Peters and Robert Waterman suggest that one characteristic of excellent companies is their tendency to "treat people . . . as the primary source of productivity gains." As they conclude, "If you want productivity and the financial reward that goes with it, you must treat your workers as your most important asset."[3] In large part, this is the task of human resource management. **Human resource management** (HRM) is the process of ensuring that competent people are available, that they are able to achieve organizational objectives, and that their energy and abilities are used effectively. Successful HRM can yield the kinds of exceptional employee contributions that are apparent at Diamond Fiber Products.

In this chapter, after discussing the impact of governmental regulation on human resource management, we will deal with the HRM activities of knowing the job, planning, staffing, and developing human resources. Large companies often have a separate human resources or personnel department consisting of an HR manager and staff charged with carrying out these activities. But all managers need to be familiar with HR activities. In smaller organizations there may be no HR department, in which case the responsibility for HR activities in each department falls on the manager of that department.

Governmental Impact on HRM

Among the external institutions with the greatest impact on human resource activities are the federal and state governments. Every manager must be aware of federal and state regulations that seek to ensure **equal employment opportunity** (EEO) and of their implications for human resource activities. Equal employment opportunity consists of the right of all employees and job applicants to be considered for employment, promotion, compensation, termination, and other conditions of work only on the basis of job-related qualifications or performance.[4] Since the 1960s, several key laws and executive orders have been enacted to promote EEO and to prevent and correct discriminatory personnel practices. Figure 13-1 summarizes the most important of these.

Under these laws, the following groups are protected employees:

- Members of minority groups

- Women

- People over forty years of age

- Differently abled

FIGURE 13-1
Laws Protecting Equal
Employment
Opportunity

The Equal Employment Opportunity Commission (EEOC) is the federal agency most directly responsible for enforcing EEO regulations. Another agency, the Office of Federal Contract Compliance Programs (OFCCP) oversees the HR

Equal Pay Act	1963	Requires equal pay for men and women performing work that requires similar skill, effort, responsibility, and working conditions.
Title VII, Civil Rights Act	1964	Prohibits discrimination in employment on the basis of race, religion, color, sex, or national origin.
Executive Orders 11246 and 11375	1965 1967	Requires federal contractors and subcontractors to eliminate employment discrimination and the effects of prior discrimination through affirmative actions.
Age Discrimination in Employment Act Mandatory Retirement Act	1967 1978	Prohibits discrimination against persons ages 40–70 and restricts mandatory retirement requirements, except where age is a "bona fide occupational qualification."
Executive Order 11478	1969	Prohibits discrimination in the Postal Service and in the various government agencies on the basis of race, color, religion, sex, national origin, handicap, or age.
Vocational Rehabilitation Act Rehabilitation Act of 1974	1973 1974	Prohibits employers with federal contracts over $2,500 from discriminating against handicapped individuals.
Vietnam-Era Veterans Readjustment Act	1974	Prohibits discrimination against Vietnam-era veterans by federal contractors and the U.S. government and requires affirmative action.
Pregnancy Discrimination Act	1978	Prohibits discrimination against women affected by pregnancy, childbirth, or related medical conditions. Requires that they be treated as all other employees are treated for employment-related purposes, including benefits.

Source: Reprinted by permission from *Personnel: Human Resource Management,* 4th ed., by R. L. Mathis and J. H. Jackson, p. 87. Copyright © 1985 by West Publishing Company. All rights reserved.

policies of companies that are federal contractors or subcontractors to ensure that they comply with EEO regulations and that they initiate affirmative action to eliminate the effects of prior discrimination. These two agencies, along with the Department of Justice and the Office of Personnel Management, have set forth the Uniform Guidelines on Employee Selection Procedures. These guidelines apply to most HR activities, including

- Hiring (qualifications, application blanks, interviews, tests)

- Promotions (qualifications, selection process)

- Recruiting (advertising, availability of announcements)

- Demotions (why made, punishments given)

- Performance appraisals (methods used, how used for promotions and pay increases)

- Training (access to training programs, development efforts)

- Labor union membership requirements (apprenticeship programs, work assignments)

- Licensing and certification requirements (job requirements tied to job qualifications)[5]

The Uniform Guidelines set forth two major criteria that employment practices must meet in order to meet EEO requirements: (1) Employment practices must have no adverse impact on a protected class. And (2) employment tests must be valid and job-related. The EEOC and the courts often use the **four-fifths rule** (4/5 rule) to determine whether discrimination has occurred. The *selection rate* is the proportion of applicants who are actually hired for a job. To avoid charges of discrimination, a company's selection rate for any protected group must be at least 4/5, or 80 percent, of the selection rate for a majority group. For example, if Sunline Electronics hired 20 percent of the women who applied for its management trainee positions but hired 40 percent of the male applicants, the selection rate for women would be only 50 percent of that for men. Sunline would not have met the 4/5 rule and thus could be open to charges of discrimination. To meet the 4/5 rule, Sunline would have to hire at least 32 percent of its female applicants if it continued to hire 40 percent of its male applicants.

The Uniform Guidelines further require that if adverse impact on a protected class has resulted from the use of specific employment selection criteria, such as tests, application blanks, or interview procedures, then the selection criteria must be shown to be valid and job-related. A test or other selection procedure is *valid* if it actually measures what it is intended to measure. *Job-related* selection criteria are those that measure skills, abilities, and characteristics that are necessary to perform a particular job satisfactorily. Consider the case of a textile company that uses a manual dexterity test with written instructions as a screening device to select employees for its weaving plants. To conform to the Uniform Guidelines, the test must be valid; that is, it must actually measure manual dexterity—not, for example, just the applicant's ability to read or understand the instructions for the test. In order to be job-related, the test must be designed in such a way that people who score higher on it generally perform better as weavers than those whose score is low.

EEO regulations and the Uniform Guidelines affect virtually every activity involved in HR management. Therefore, it is important that every manager keep up to date on EEO requirements.

Job Information and Human Resource Planning

Job Analysis

Human resource managers need a good deal of specific information to describe and distinguish among the jobs that are performed in their organization. They need this information to develop hiring plans, to select and train employees, to provide appropriate compensation, to develop valid performance appraisals, and to comply with federal legislation. Job analysis provides this information. **Job analysis** is identification of the specific activities performed in a job and the characteristics of the person, the work situation, and the materials or equipment necessary for performing the job effectively. Data for a job analysis can be collected in a number of ways: by direct observation, by holding structured interviews, by administering questionnaires to jobholders, or by soliciting information from "expert juries"—people with previous experience in performing or supervising the job.

Figure 13-2 presents three types of information that a job analysis yields: job description, job specification, and job evaluation. It also illustrates the relationship of job analysis to several other HRM activities.

Products of Job Analysis

A **job description** specifies the tasks, duties, and responsibilities that a jobholder has and describes briefly how, when, and where these activities are to be per-

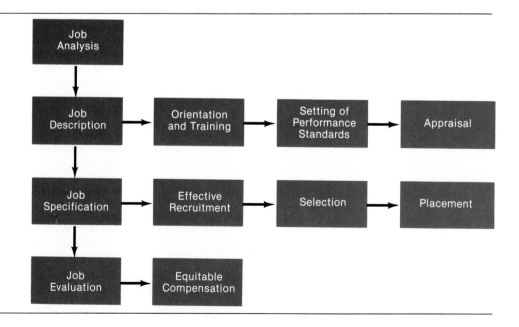

FIGURE 13-2
Relationship of Job Analysis to Other HRM Activities

formed. Accurate job descriptions are necessary for specifying standards of performance, for judging performance, and for designing training programs that accurately communicate the firm's expectations. Figure 13-3 provides an excellent example of a properly prepared job description.

A **job specification** describes the skills, knowledge, and abilities that a person needs in order to perform that job satisfactorily. Accurate job specifications are particularly important in the firm's efforts to recruit, select, and place new employees as well as to respond to the training and development needs of those employees who are interested in changing jobs or advancing within the organization. Figure 13-3 presents a job specification, as well as a job description, for an HR manager.

Job evaluation is a systematic process for determining the relative worth of jobs within an organization. One major application of job evaluation is its use in formulating equitable pay structures. In a job evaluation, all jobs in an organization are compared and classified in terms of their relative importance, the skills needed to perform them, their relative difficulty, and the relative stressfulness of the working conditions.[6] Jobs rated higher in these factors are assigned more points and often command higher compensation. In addition, many companies use the point system to determine the *comparable worth* of jobs. The concept of comparable worth has grown out of legal proceedings; it requires that women and men be compensated equally for jobs that require comparable knowledge, skills, and duties, even if those jobs do not involve identical activities. Companies such as Westinghouse have responded to comparable-worth suits with undisclosed out-of-court settlements. The states of Minnesota and Washington have established funds to equalize the wages of female state employees and those of males in comparable jobs. At least fifteen other states now incorporate comparable-worth standards into their wage structures; these states are Alaska, Arkansas, Georgia, Hawaii, Idaho, Kentucky, Maine, Maryland, Massachusetts, Nebraska, North Dakota, Oklahoma, South Dakota, Tennessee, and West Virginia.[7]

Human Resource Planning

Once accurate descriptions and specifications of jobs have been developed, the next step in the staffing process, **human resource planning**, begins. In order to meet their objectives, all organizations try to anticipate their future staffing needs and the future labor supply so that they can have the right number of the right people doing the right jobs at the right times. Imagine, for example, that a regional grocery chain plans to increase its number of stores by 50 percent over the next five years and, further, that it plans to increase its number of twenty-four-hour stores from 10 percent to 50 percent of all its stores. The staffing needs of the new stores will have to be determined, and plans will have to be made for hiring some new employees, training or retraining some present employees, and transferring and/or promoting others. Furthermore, because this grocery chain presently employs a large number of part-time, teenaged workers, the demographics of the labor force in the next five to ten years will need to be considered. A drop in that age group is expected in coming years, so this company may need to reformulate its recruiting, selection, and training plans.

In general, HR planning involves comparing the organization's forecasted personnel needs with the number *and the skills* of its present and anticipated labor supply. Plans are then made to increase, decrease, or reorganize the organization's work force. The need for HR planning is clearly represented in a statement made

Job Description

General description

Performs responsible administrative work managing personnel activities of a large state agency or institution. Work involves responsibility for the planning and administration of a personnel program which includes recruitment, examination, selection, evaluation, appointment, promotion, transfer, and recommended change of status of agency employees, and a system of communication for disseminating necessary information to workers. Works under general supervision, exercising initiative and independent judgment in the performance of assigned tasks.

Examples of work performed

Participates in overall planning and policy making to provide effective and uniform personnel services.

Communicates policy through organization levels by bulletin, meetings, and personal contact.

Interviews applicants, evaluates qualifications, and classifies applications.

Recruits and screens applicants to fill vacancies and reviews applications of qualified persons.

Confers with supervisors on personnel matters, including placement problems, retention or release of probationary employees, transfers, demotions, and dismissals of permanent employees.

Supervises administration of tests.

Initiates personnel training activities and coordinates these activities with work of officials and supervisors.

Establishes effective service rating system and trains unit supervisors in making employee evaluations.

Maintains employee personnel files.

Supervises a group of employees directly and through subordinates.

Performs related work as assigned.

Job Specification

General qualification requirements

Experience and training
    Should have considerable experience in personnel administration.
Education
    Graduation from a four-year college or university, with major work in education and personnel administration.
Knowledge, skills, and abilities
    Considerable knowledge of principles and practices of personnel administration, selection and assignment of personnel, and job evaluation.

Source: W. F. Glueck, *Personnel: A Diagnostic Approach*, rev. ed., Richard D. Irwin, Inc., © 1978, p. 108.

by Reginald Jones, former chairman of General Electric, in which he describes factors that contributed to the difficulty that GE had moving into new products and technologies in the 1970s. "I didn't realize it at the time," he said, "but we were a company with 30,000 electromechanical engineers becoming a company that needed electronics engineers. We didn't plan for change in 1970 and it caused big problems by the mid-1970s." By the late 1970s GE managers were involved in HR planning.[8]

There are at least three reasons for an organization to undertake formal HR planning: (1) to use its human resources effectively and efficiently, (2) to create better satisfied and more highly developed employees, and (3) to more effectively plan equal employment opportunities.[9] Figure 13-4 illustrates the steps involved in HR planning.

The grocery chain's plans to increase its number of stores is a good illustration of the impact an organization's strategic planning can have on HR planning. In order to bring about this planned expansion, new objectives will be developed for all the departments in the organization, including the human resource department.

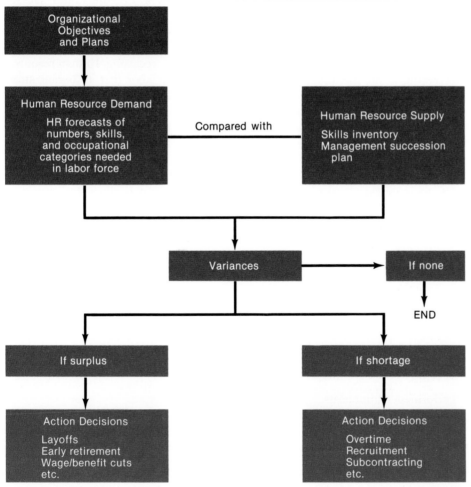

FIGURE 13-4
The Human Resource
Planning Process

Source: Adapted from W. F. Glueck, *Personnel: A Diagnostic Approach,* rev. ed., Richard D. Irwin, Inc., © 1978, p. 89.

If the expansion calls for fifty new store managers, plans need to be made to develop and promote present employees and/or to hire and train additional managers. In addition, issues that affect staffing and labor supply may need to be considered in the development of the organization's strategic plans. For example, if part-time, teenaged employees are in short supply, perhaps the company should consider the financial implications of hiring more full-time employees, for whom benefits such as insurance must be provided. If several large companies nearby have just opened new facilities and hired sizable work forces, it may be difficult to find suitable employees and, as a result, much more difficult to achieve the company's objectives.

The next step in HR planning is to identify and assess the internal and external factors that will influence the need for and availability of competent employees. The opening of new plants, the expansion of product lines, and the introduction of new technology all require more personnel, often with new skills. Conversely, plant closings, the reduction of product lines, and the phasing out of old technology may require a reduction in personnel or a shift in the skills that workers need to be competent in their jobs. Organizations have much less control over the external factors that affect HR planning. Yet, as Figure 13-5 illustrates, factors from many different sources in the organization's external environment affect human resource activities. The figure also provides specific examples of the types of effects these external factors can have on HR planning.

The next step in HR planning is human resource forecasting. **Human resource forecasting** is the attempt to predict the demand for labor that an organization will experience if it is to accomplish its objectives in a specified period of time, usually from six months to more than five years. Forecasting techniques range from simple intuition and rules of thumb to sophisticated computerized management inventory and decision support systems.[10] In developing these forecasts, HR managers consider such information as projected sales, anticipated expansion or reduction of operating facilities, expected changes in technology, economic forecasts, the base-rate level of turnover to be expected even if other factors do not change, and the composition, skills, and status of their present labor force.

To describe the organization's current labor force, a human resource audit is conducted. The HR audit compiles information about the skills and performance history of all the employees in the organization. An **employee skills inventory** collects the following types of information about an organization's employees.[11]

- Previous jobs held
- Length of time in present job
- Educational and training qualifications
- Specific knowledge and skills
- Performance appraisals
- Past and current compensation and benefits
- Capacity of the individual (for example, test scores and health information)
- Special preferences of the individual (such as location or job preferences)

Skills inventories range in sophistication from simple checklists to much more detailed computerized human resource information systems. The information they

Source of Influence	Examples	HR Decisions Affected
Government laws and policies	Civil Rights Act, Title VII, and Equal Employment Opportunity Act	Recruiting, selection, promotion, layoffs
	Automobile import restrictions	More employees needed than without the restrictions
Economic conditions	Decrease in unemployment	Fewer qualified job applicants
	Economic growth, lower inflation	More employees needed to staff expanded facilities and increase production
Shifts in population and work force	Reduction in total work force mid-1980s to mid-1990s, fewer workers aged 16–24, more aged 25–54	Fewer applicants for entry-level jobs
	Greater proportion of labor force will be women (⅓) mid-1980s to mid-1990s, greater percentage of women with children under 18 working (60% in 1984 vs. 50% in 1974), greater number of two-career couples	Revisions of benefits to include employer-supported child care, maternity/paternity leave
Geographic and competitive conditions	Increased labor demand from competing employers with new plant openings	Greater pool of job applicants
	Net migration of people to the "Sunbelt"	More qualified job applicants
	Lower wages and benefits than competing employers in the area	Fewer qualified job applicants

Sources: Reprinted by permission from *Personnel: Human Resource Management,* 4th ed., by R. L. Mathis and J. H. Jackson, pp. 211–213. Copyright © 1985 by West Publishing Company. All rights reserved; also from H. N. Fullerton and J. Tschetter, "The 1995 Labor Force: A Second Look," *Monthly Labor Review,* November 1983, pp. 3–10; and from "Miscellany," *Labor Law Journal,* March 1986.

FIGURE 13-5
External Factors Affecting Human Resource Planning

provide enables HR managers to compare anticipated personnel needs with existing resources. Because the information on specific individuals is useful in making decisions about selection, promotion, layoff, and termination, it must meet all the EEOC requirements of job-relatedness and nondiscrimination.[12] In addition to a skills inventory, an HR audit at the managerial level often includes a management succession plan. Its purpose is to summarize the availability of talented managers, to evaluate their readiness for promotion, and to identify those in need of further training or development programs.

The overall HR plan, which includes forecasting information and the HR audit, summarizes this information, states the conclusions drawn from it about surpluses and shortages, and proposes what action the organization should take to bring HR demand and supply into balance. A well-developed HR plan should answer the following questions:

1. What specific skills do current employees have?

2. How many current employees will stay with the organization?

3. In what EEO categories do current employees fall?

4. What jobs now exist?

5. What changes in current jobs will occur?

6. What is the potential for upward movement among current employees?

7. What new skills must current employees have in the future?

8. How many and which types of people (in terms of EEO categories) will be needed in the future?

9. What jobs will exist in the future?

10. How must company policies and practices change to be compatible with meeting future employee requirements?

11. Where will the organization obtain needed future employees?[13]

As Figure 13-4 suggests, the last two questions involve action decisions that the firm must make to deal with anticipated surpluses or shortages of qualified workers. When a *surplus* of employees is predicted, several alternative courses of action are possible, including not filling positions vacated by natural attrition (retirement, resignation, or death); offering early retirement; and demoting, transferring, laying off, or terminating some employees. Many organizations consider layoffs and terminations so disruptive that they take these actions only as a last resort. In addition, organizations may accelerate production or expansion plans or transfer activities from understaffed to overstaffed units. In anticipation of the opposite situation, labor *shortages,* companies may decelerate expansion plans, hire subcontractors to do part of the work, and use temporary labor to fill some vacancies. In the last few years, temporary workers have accounted for almost 20 percent of the labor force.[14] Using temporary help is a means of managing labor shortages in ways that will not contribute to future labor surpluses in an organization.

Staffing: Obtaining Human Resources

Staffing is the process of obtaining and keeping the number and type of workers necessary to accomplish an organization's objectives. It involves both recruitment and selection, and its success depends in part on the effectiveness of previous job analysis and HR planning.

Recruitment

When HR planning indicates that more employees will be needed because of either expanded production or attrition, decisions must be made about how to recruit people to fill these jobs. **Recruitment** is the process of obtaining qualified applicants for a job. Even during times of labor surplus, many companies continue their recruitment programs in order to remain in touch with outside recruiting

Guidelines for Management Practice

The practicing human resource manager wants to know what the "best" HR strategies are. Is there a best plan for compensation? Is there a best staffing, training, or development plan? Is there a best way to forecast HR needs? There is no one "best" HRM strategy. The effectiveness of any HRM strategy depends on many factors, such as the amount of uncertainty and complexity in the environment and the content of the organization's long-range plans. Managers are wise, therefore, to evaluate the impact such factors can have on the planning. Some examples are:

1. Researchers have found that only organizations that face complex environments require sophisticated mathematical and computerized techniques to predict their future HR needs and, further, that these techniques work only when important aspects of the environment remain more or less stable over time.[15]

2. The maturity, or stage of development, of the organization and its strategy can also affect HRM strategies.[16] For example, a new business faces such uncertainty about its share of the market and expected growth rate that it is likely to make little attempt to forecast long-term HR needs or to lock itself into any long-term compensation or benefit plan. Instead of pensions, which have fixed, long-term costs, employees are more likely to be offered more flexible benefits, such as profit-sharing plans.

By contrast, the high-growth business is trying to increase its already healthy market share and is more confident that it can anticipate continued growth. Forecasts of HR needs are more important for this firm than they are for the new business. Even so, compensation and benefit plans in the high-growth business are likely to remain flexible and to be linked to organizational performance. Mature and aging businesses fall in still another category. They are more interested in keeping operating costs down; neither is in a stage of growth anymore. Their human resource forecasts are more likely to be used to identify areas where employees can be trimmed than areas where they must be added, and plans stressing early retirement, the reassignment and retraining of displaced workers, or layoffs may be the outcome of such forecasts.[17]

3. The practicing manager cannot formulate HRM strategies and plans without considering the overall strategic plans of the organization. These strategic plans reflect the demands of both the external and internal environments within which the organization operates.[18] In turn, the success of corporate or business strategy depends largely on its human resources. For this reason, some researchers recommend that HRM should figure prominently in decisions about corporate and business strategy.[19]

sources, keep internal recruiting channels open, and see that employees enroll in career-development programs that prepare them to fill positions that become available.[20]

The recruitment process generally begins with an employee requisition, which is sent to the HR manager from the manager of the department requesting the employee. The requisition includes a job description, job specifications, pay scale, and starting date. The HR office then attempts to locate, through either internal recruiting or external recruiting, a job applicant who is qualified.

Internal recruiting draws from a pool of applicants who are already working in the organization. Many organizations post or circulate announcements of anticipated job openings among employees before they attempt to recruit applicants externally. Current and past employees, who are familiar with the organization's specific goals and operations, often know of people who would fill the organization's needs. Many organizations (including RCA, Wang Laboratories, and Mutual of Omaha) offer cash or other bonuses to employees who recommend job candidates who are hired and satisfactorily complete a probationary period.[21] Internal job-training or career-development programs are another source of applicants from within the organization.

External recruiting involves attracting applicants from outside the organization. Schools, colleges, and universities may be tapped by announcing job openings or conducting interviews in conjunction with career guidance and placement offices. State and private employment agencies are sometimes engaged to list job openings and do the preliminary screening of applicants. Temporary employment agencies provide employees who contract to do clerical and semi-skilled labor for a specified period of time. In unionized organizations, the labor union often plays an active role in providing the organization with qualified applicants. Other professional and trade associations provide employment listing services at their meetings and in their publications. Newspapers and radio stations sometimes run announcements for recruiting employees.[22]

Though internal recruiting is usually considered a desirable practice because of its positive impact on employee morale and its utility in recognizing good work and professional development, it can encourage a sort of "inbreeding." This can be a particularly serious hazard for organizations that face rapidly changing technological or competitive environments. In such environments, people who have been recruited from outside an organization may bring innovative perspectives unlikely to be taken by those already inside the firm. Also, in rapidly changing environments, organizations may find that their staffing needs develop and change more rapidly than internal training and development programs can handle. For these reasons, organizations that function in relatively stable environments may find internal recruiting to be more advantageous than those that operate in rapidly changing environments.[23]

Selection and Placement

Once a business has recruited a pool of applicants from which to hire, it must go through the processes of selection and placement. **Selection** is the process of choosing which people would best fill specific jobs. **Placement** is the process of deciding which of several jobs is best suited to an individual who has been selected and hired.[24] In some circumstances, a person is selected and hired for a specific job, and in that case, placement occurs simultaneously with selection. In other cases, an individual may be hired and trained and only then placed in a specific job, perhaps on the basis of his or her performance in the training program. In small organizations with fewer than one hundred employees, selection and placement may be conducted by the managers of the particular departments that have job openings. In larger organizations, however, these staffing functions are often performed by specialists in the human resource or personnel department. Selection responsibilities may then be divided between the HR staff and the operating managers.

There are several advantages of having a specialized HR department to coordinate employee recruitment and selection in large organizations.[25]

1. The application process is simpler for applicants if they need apply to only one office.

2. Contact with outside recruitment sources can be coordinated more easily by a single office.

3. Operating managers are free to concentrate on their operating responsibilities and are brought into the selection process when their expertise is most useful.

4. Staffing specialists may provide for better employee selection.

5. The applicant is more likely to be considered for a greater variety of jobs.

6. Selection costs can be reduced by avoiding unnecessary duplication of effort and recordkeeping.

7. With increased government regulation affecting the selection process, it is important that people who know about these rules handle a major part of the selection process.

The steps that are typically involved in personnel selection include (1) reception, (2) preliminary interview, (3) application form, (4) selection interview, (5) pre-employment tests, (6) realistic job preview, (7) background check, and (8) medical report. Their relative importance of these steps and the sequence in which they are performed depend on the job that is being filled. For example, a physical examination might be an earlier and more important screening device in selecting and hiring airline pilots than it would be for computer programmers. We will illustrate all these steps by outlining the experience of one applicant, Janet Carlson, as she applies for a job as a bank clerk.

Carlson follows the directions she has been given to the personnel office of a large bank. She first encounters the department receptionist, who asks her to complete an application form and refers her to a personnel specialist. In some organizations, this first stage, reception, also includes a preliminary screening interview in which a member of the personnel staff—sometimes the receptionist, sometimes a personnel specialist—asks a series of questions to determine whether the person has certain minimal qualifications, such as a high school diploma. Though structured interviews (in which the interviewer asks the same, job-related questions of all potential applicants) are generally viewed as preferable to unstructured interviews, many organizations conduct rather haphazard preliminary screening. If the firm's minimal qualifications are met, the applicant is asked to fill out an application form. The reception stage can significantly affect the applicant's perception of the organization and its products or services. This is true regardless of whether there are any job openings or whether the applicant is qualified for any openings that do exist.

In Janet Carlson's case, the preliminary screening interview was conducted as the personnel specialist reviewed the application blank she had just completed. Application forms are commonly used in organizations to collect job-related information and information on the applicant's personal and professional background. Well-constructed application forms often serve as many as three different functions: (1) to provide a record of the applicant's interest in the job, (2) to provide an interviewer with a profile of the applicant that can be used during the interview, and (3) to serve as a personnel record for applicants who become employees.[26] The EEOC requires that application forms ask for only job-related information. The EEOC also requires that employers keep records of the race and sex of their applicants, but it prohibits firms from collecting this information as part of the application form unless those characteristics can be shown to be job-related. To comply with EEOC regulations, more and more organizations are collecting this information on forms that are kept separate from application files and employee records. Despite EEOC regulations and the requirements of the

Uniform Guidelines, two surveys conducted in the early 1980s reported widespread use of application forms that contained items of questionable legality. In one study of ninety-four organizations, 73 percent included such items on their applications; in a second study of fifty national corporations, 96 percent included application items that violated the Uniform Guidelines.[27] Inappropriate questions asked about applicants' age, sex, marital status, legal difficulties, race, disabilities, children, dependents, and pregnancy.

The personnel specialist who met with Carlson used her application as a structured guide to the preliminary screening interview. The questions asked were designed primarily to determine whether the organization should move her application into the next phase of the selection process. Carlson was found to be interested in and qualified for the types of positions the bank had open or anticipated having open in the near future. As the next step in selection, Carlson was scheduled to take several pre-employment tests, including a mathematics aptitude test, the California Personality Inventory, and a polygraph test.

Pre-employment tests are used to screen and select potential employees. Pre-employment tests fall into three general categories: (1) psychological and personality tests, (2) aptitude and ability tests, and (3) other employment screening devices (such as polygraph tests, drug tests, and genetic screening). These tests must also meet the EEOC Uniform Guidelines requirements of validity and job-relatedness. The validity and legality of many tests in the last of the three categories are hotly debated. For example, the validity of polygraph tests as a measure of honesty or a means of lie detection is questionable. Polygraphs are good at measuring levels and patterns of physiological arousal, but there are many causes of physiological arousal besides lying, and not all people experience arousal when they attempt to deceive. For these reasons many states prohibit requiring polygraph tests as a condition for employment.[28] Similarly, the validity, job-relatedness, and legality of drug testing are current topics of debate in HRM.[29]

The information from Carlson's application form and her test results were then combined with information obtained in a more in-depth selection interview. This interview can vary greatly, depending on the job in question, and it can serve several purposes. For example, the interviewer who spoke with Carlson observed and rated her interpersonal communication skills while they discussed various aspects of her application. The interviewer also probes for further information about any issues that the responses to the application form or the test results seem to raise. Carlson, for instance, was asked why she had left her last two jobs after less than a year in each. The interview can also be used to give the applicant information about the organization. Finally, the interview can be used to "sell" the organization to the applicant and to try to persuade a desirable candidate to accept a job offer.[30]

Interviews are sometimes unreliable selection devices. They are particularly susceptible to the cognitive and perceptual biases of the interviewer. Unless interviewers are trained specifically to be aware of such biases, they are likely to give too much weight to first impressions, to negative information, to information that supports their unexamined expectations, and to applicants' degree of composure and way of speaking. Even so, interviews are the most frequently used selection device. When they are conducted by trained interviewers, they can provide useful and reliable selection information.[31]

Interviews used in recruiting are generally structured or unstructured. In *structured interviews,* the interviewer asks the same questions of all applicants. Such interviews consist of obtaining the answers to a set of questions the organization considers to provide job-related information. Questions are always asked in the same order and in the same way; they seldom allow for extended, open-ended responses by the interviewees. *Unstructured interviews,* in contrast, are not based on a systematic list of questions to be asked of all applicants. Questions are much more likely to be open-ended, increasing the probability that some crucial information will not be obtained and that information that is not clearly job-related will be revealed in the interview. The structured interview is generally considered a better selection device than the unstructured, because it is less subject to interviewer bias in question selection or information recording, and because it is easier to demonstrate that information obtained in the structured interview is job-related.[32]

During the selection interview, Carlson was given a realistic job preview, in which the interviewer and other bank employees tried to paint as accurate a picture as possible of what her job would be like. Carlson also saw a short film about the day-to-day aspects of a bank clerk's job. In some organizations the realistic job preview provides opportunities for the job applicant to talk with people who are already working in the organization or to observe someone actually doing the job. Advocates of realistic job previews maintain that they help job candidates develop accurate expectations about the job and thereby help reduce turnover and dissatisfaction that result from disenchantment and unrealistic expectations.[33]

The next step in the bank's consideration of Carlson's application was a reference check and background investigation. Carlson provided the personnel office with the name of a supervisor at each of her previous jobs who could evaluate her work, and she signed forms requesting that copies of her college transcript and a current credit report be sent to the personnel office. Reference checks usually seek information from people who have had direct experience with the applicant's employment, educational, and/or personal history. Of these, personal references are generally the least helpful in selection decisions; they seldom provide any negative information, and the information they provide is not always clearly job-related. For these reasons, many organizations do not ask for information from personal references.

Background investigations sometimes tap other sources of information about the applicant's personal life, such as records of criminal convictions. These types of information are, however, subject to the requirement that they be job-related. For example, conviction for embezzlement or forgery might be considered a valid reason for a bank to reject a job application, though some courts have ruled that only job-related convictions that occurred within five to seven years are valid grounds for rejection.[34]

Information about a person's employment and educational history is often obtained through telephone calls, letters of reference, and transcripts from educational institutions. The Family Educational Rights and Privacy Act of 1974 guarantees students and former students the right to examine and challenge any of their educational records and requires that the individual's consent be obtained before such documents as transcripts are released to prospective employers. Under the Act and subsequent legislation and judicial rulings, people have a legal right to see letters of reference written about them unless they waive that right in writing.[35] Some organizations send the person supplying the recommendation a form whereon he or she rates the applicant on scales designed by a job analyst. This approach ensures that the information contained in letters of reference is job-related and that similar information is available for all applicants.[36]

The last step in the selection process for Carlson's application at the bank was a medical report. This step is usually taken if the applicant meets all other selection criteria. In Carlson's case, the medical report required her to complete a medical questionnaire, sometimes referred to as a pre-employment health checklist. Some organizations require a physical examination instead of, or in addition to, the questionnaire. Information derived from a medical report may be used to:

1. Assign workers to jobs for which they must be physically and emotionally fit.

2. Provide data about an individual as a basis for future health guidance.

3. Safeguard the health of present employees through the detection of contagious disease.

4. Protect applicants who have health defects from undertaking work that could be detrimental to themselves or might endanger the employer's property.

5. Protect the employer from workers' compensation claims that are not valid because the injuries or illnesses were present when the employee was hired.

Like other selection requirements, the physical requirements for jobs must be justifiable as job-related.[37]

An increasing number of companies are also requiring pre-employment drug tests. It is estimated that almost one-third of the Fortune 500 companies now require such tests. IBM routinely screens every job applicant for drug use, and other companies (such as Ford Motor Co., Alcoa, Boise-Cascade, American Airlines, and the *New York Times*) administer drug tests to at least some of their applicants and employees. However, questions about the legality of such tests and the purposes for which they can be used are still being debated in the courts.[38]

Guidelines for Management Practice

It is in the best interests of any organization to have an effective and legal selection process. How can managers accomplish this?

1. It is necessary to definitively establish what constitutes satisfactory performance of specific jobs. This requires clear job descriptions and job specifications based on competent job analysis. It is impossible to design a selection system or to evaluate its effectiveness or legality without this type of information.

2. All components of the selection process need to be viewed as selection devices or "tests," in the broadest sense of the word, and to meet the EEOC's requirements for employment tests. For example, questions asked in a preliminary interview may determine whether a person is invited to complete an application form. Preliminary interviews are much more likely than later steps in the selection process to be conducted by employees (such as receptionists) who may be relatively unfamiliar with EEO regulations. Unsystematic screening at any stage of selection can result in the loss of qualified applicants and can increase the chances that charges of discrimination will be leveled at the firm.

3. All selection tests should be validated and shown to be job-related. The method of validation depends on the nature of the test. The assistance of a specialist in job analysis and test validation may be required.

4. Any selection devices that are not job-related or that cannot be validated should be scrapped. They leave a company vulnerable to discrimination charges and do little to increase the effectiveness of selection.

Performance Appraisal and Development

After they have carefully selected and placed their employees, managers turn to the issues of appraising the employees' performance and further developing subordinates' skills. Performance appraisal and development are two complementary human resource activities. **Performance appraisal** is the process of determining how well someone is performing in his or her job; it involves measuring performance and comparing it with an established standard. **Human resource development** is long-term training designed to increase an employee's job effectiveness and to develop his or her ability to assume greater job responsibilities.

Training and Human Resource Development

Because performance appraisals point out specific strengths and weaknesses of employees, they are useful sources of information about the need for, and the effectiveness of, job training and HR development. **Training** usually refers to programs designed to teach specific job skills or techniques. For example, a secretary may be trained in the use of various word-processing software packages, and assembly line workers may undergo training in a specific assembly process. Training is often conducted in order to improve productivity, improve the quality of performance, lower scrap loss and/or reduce inefficiency, minimize accidents, reduce turnover and absenteeism, and make sure employees' skills keep pace with innovations in the equipment and techniques they work with. Three steps are generally involved in carrying out a training program: assessment, implementation, and evaluation. The first and the last of these are closely tied to performance appraisal. *Assessment* involves determination of training needs, identification of training objectives, and development of criteria for evaluating the effectiveness of the training. In the *implementation* step, trainees are pre-tested, training methods selected, and training sessions conducted. *Evaluation* consists of monitoring the training sessions and evaluating them by comparing the performance of the trainees with the standard of performance established in the objectives of the training program. Often the success of HRM training depends on how valuable the workers and their managers expect it to be. To better understand your own biases toward training, complete "Management Development Exercise 13."

Like these accounting executives, managers are frequently involved in continuing professional development activities. (Allen Green/Photo Researchers)

In contrast to job training, professional development programs are designed to improve the interpersonal, problem-solving, and decision-making skills of managers. At General Foods, performance appraisals, combined with HR audits and management succession plans, are used to determine what types of skills need to be developed in current managers or potential managers.[39] **Assessment centers** provide a specialized type of performance appraisal for managers. An assessment center brings together groups of managers who participate in simulated decision-making and problem-solving situations. Their performance on these tasks is appraised, and they and their supervisors receive information about their management abilities. This information can serve as feedback about management skills they need to develop and as data on which to base selection and promotion decisions.

Performance Appraisal

Performance appraisal serves several purposes. First, information about the quality of job performance can provide feedback, not only to the employees, but also to HR managers and to operating managers. A well-designed appraisal system pinpoints an employee's strengths and weaknesses in such a way that he or she can plan to correct the deficiencies while maintaining the strengths. The information communicated in a periodic evaluation should come as no surprise to an employee who has received frequent praise and constructive criticism.[40] Another type of feedback that performance appraisals provide goes to HR and operating managers. When designed appropriately, appraisals can offer feedback on the effectiveness of recruitment, selection, training, motivation, and compensation practices. A second purpose of performance appraisal is to provide information that managers can use to make decisions about promotions, transfers, demotions, terminations, compensation, and training needs and to select employees who might benefit from development programs. Third, performance appraisals provide a data base for documenting the grounds for various HR decisions. Such documentation is valuable for four reasons: (1) It increases the likelihood that personnel decisions will be made wholly on the basis of the job-related, nondiscriminatory criteria required by EEOC guidelines. (2) It is necessary information for validating selection tests and showing that they are job-related. (3) It provides a useful data base for an organization that is charged with discrimination to use in investigating or refuting that charge. Finally, performance appraisal enables managers to assess how efficiently they are utilizing human resources and to take corrective action when it is called for.[41] The importance of carefully designing performance appraisals for multinational firms is demonstrated in "Insights for International Managers 13."

Characteristics of Effective Performance Appraisal

Effective methods of performance appraisal share several characteristics. First, they are *valid;* that is, they measure the aspect of job performance they are designed to measure, rather than personality characteristics or how much the evaluator likes the person being evaluated. An effective appraisal method provides the information that a supervisor needs to appraise a particular performance. For example, if the purpose of the appraisal is to select one of a group of employees to receive an award for top performance, the appraisal has to provide information that makes it possible to compare the performances of all the employees. If the appraisal is intended to serve as the basis for counseling employees individually about ways to improve their performance, then how the employee has performed compared

---

Insights for International Managers 13

AVOID BLAME, AVOID SHAME

According to Exxon executive Paul Makosky, a key to success in managing foreign employees is patience and the willingness to permit them to make some mistakes. "You can't operate in an environment where your people fear you will cut their heads off when they make a mistake," he says. If your employees are going to participate in decision making, they need to feel secure in taking a risk that they may make a wrong decision. At first they may need to be right only 51 percent of the time.

Nobody likes to be criticized, especially in front of others. But Americans sometimes fail to take the sting out of "helpful" comments and in the United States one is supposed to accept criticism as valuable feedback. An employee might even thank a manager for being frank. It is a big mistake to behave this way anywhere else in the world, however—with the possible exception of Australia.

To Arabs, Africans, Asians and Latin Americans, the preservation of dignity is an all-important value. Those who lose self-respect, or the respect of others,

dishonor both themselves and their families. Public criticism is intolerable. If you use harsh words, or even contradict a person, foreigners will unite in antagonism against you. The result of a confrontation with employee or servants will be such a shock that they may leave the job. In a unionized work situation there might be some kind of employee action. When irreconcilable positions are reached, a third-party mediator is often crucial.

Experienced travelers say that reward systems aside, the only way to enforce a standard of performance is by courteous exhortation, lots of explanation and conversation, humor and an appeal to the foreigner's sense of cooperation. Jim Kelso, after twenty-two years with Occidental Petroleum in Indonesia and Libya, says: "Keep telling them, 'Good try . . . That's great . . . What would happen if you tried it this way?' Never make it personal or emotional." If you fail and cause loss of face, enmity will be undying.

Source: From L. Copeland and L. Griggs, *Going International* (New York: Random House, 1985), pp. 131–132.

---

to others is not nearly so important as specific information about that employee's strengths and weaknesses.

Second, effective methods of performance appraisal are *reliable;* that is, they consistently measure the same aspects of performance and are likely to yield similar results even if they are administered by different evaluators. Reliable performance appraisals are not very susceptible to rater bias. Several types of rater bias can reduce the reliability and validity of performance appraisals. The **halo effect** is the tendency to assume that a person who performs well in some areas is also good in other areas. Thus to assume that someone who is a good salesperson is also good at organizing and managing the sales department is to fall victim to the halo effect. The opposite of the halo effect, sometimes called the *horns effect,* can also occur. In the horns effect, performance appraisal is biased by the assumption that a person who performs poorly in one area of the job also performs poorly in other areas. An evaluator who uses only a small region of a rating scale to evaluate everyone being rated is subject to the bias known as **restriction of range**. When raters give uniformly positive evaluations to everyone, regardless of their performance, their bias illustrates a type of restriction of range called the *leniency effect.* Other types of restriction of range take the form of the *severity effect,* in which a rater gives very low ratings to everyone, and the *central tendency effect,* in which a rater gives moderate or average ratings to everyone, again without regard to their actual performance.

███ *Guidelines for Management Practice* ███

The effectiveness of any performance appraisal system as a source of feedback depends not only on the choice of technique but also on the manner in which the results of the appraisal are communicated to the person whose work has been evaluated. Personnel specialists have recommended to supervisors the following "Do's and Don'ts" to increase the effectiveness of the discussion of performance appraisals.[45]

Do:

1. Prepare in advance.
2. Focus on performance and development.
3. Be specific about the reasons for ratings.
4. Decide on specific steps to be taken for improvement.
5. Consider your role in the subordinate's performance.
6. Reinforce the behavior you want.
7. Focus on future performance.

Don't:

1. "Lecture" the employee.
2. Mix performance appraisal for the purpose of feedback with salary or promotion issues.
3. Concentrate only on the negative.
4. Do all the talking.
5. Be overly critical or "harp on" a failing.
6. Feel it is necessary for both of you to agree on everything.
7. Compare the employee to others.

Finally, a mutually agreed-on time should be arranged to discuss the appraisal; "hallway" appraisal reports and other impromptu discussions do not allow for appropriate preparation and interaction. The employee can make better use of the appraisal information if he or she knows prior to the meeting that the performance appraisal will be the topic of discussion.

Finally, effective performance appraisals are well timed. Good appraisals provide continuous and ongoing feedback.

Methods of Performance Appraisal

There are several methods for conducting performance appraisals. Some evaluate an employee individually by measuring his or her performance against some predetermined standard of performance. Some compare an employee's performance with the performance of other employees. The comparative approach may take the form of straight ranking, alternation ranking, forced distribution, or forced choice (paired comparison).

Consider the case of a sales manager who is going to appraise the performance of each of her ten sales representatives. To use **straight ranking**, she would rank-order the ten people on a single dimension, such as their overall sales performance. The best salesperson would be ranked "1," the second best "2," and so on. The salesperson whose performance was least satisfactory would be ranked "10."

Alternation ranking is similar, but the rater first picks the best and the worst sales representatives, ranking them "1" and "10," respectively. Next, she picks the second best sales representative, whom she ranks "2," and the next-to-worst, whom she ranks "9," and so on until all ten have been ranked.

To understand the **forced-distribution method**, imagine that the sales manager has been asked to identify which category each salesperson belongs in, on the basis of sales performance. She has been given five categories and is asked to assign a specific percent of her sales representatives to each category. For example, she might be asked to name those excellent sales representatives whose performance puts them in the top 10 percent of her sales staff. Because there are ten people on the sales staff, this means that only one person can be named an excellent performer. She might also be asked to name the 20 percent (two employees) who are above average, the 40 percent who are average, the 20 percent who are below average, and the 10 percent who are poor in sales performance.

In the **forced-choice method**, each person being evaluated is compared with every other person. For example, if the ten sales representatives were labeled A through J, then the rater would compare A with B, C, D, and so on, until all possible comparisons had been made. For each pair, the rater indicates which of the two sales representatives is the better. The person chosen the better most frequently is then judged best—the person with the top performance appraisal.

Comparative methods generally avoid the pitfall of grouping everyone at more or less the same level, because raters are forced to rate some people high, some average, and some low. There are several disadvantages of comparative methods of performance appraisal, however. First, comparative methods are cumbersome if large numbers of people are to be ranked. For example, it is very difficult to rank-order thirty people; most raters would have difficulty distinguishing between the performances of the employees ranked 19 and 20. Comparative methods also require that one rater be familiar with everyone's performance. Comparative methods usually evaluate people on a single dimension of global performance rather than on multiple, specific aspects of performance. Therefore, they are susceptible to halo and horns effects because the rater is not required to consider specific behaviors, and they provide very little feedback to employees about specific behaviors that they need to change or improve. Finally, comparative appraisal methods exaggerate differences in performance and fail to reflect similarity. For example, if all employees in the group being evaluated are performing at similar levels, this similarity is obscured by any rank ordering, forced-choice comparison, or forced-distribution method.

A second major category of performance appraisal methods include techniques for comparing an individual's performance against some predetermined standard of performance. **Graphic scales** are probably the most common method of performance appraisal because they are fairly easy to construct and to use. The individual being evaluated is rated on a series of job-related dimensions as $5 =$ outstanding, $4 =$ above average, $3 =$ average, $2 =$ below average, or $1 =$ unsatisfactory. Highly specific job-related behaviors can be included in such a scale, so it can be used to provide information about training and development needs as well as to give the person being evaluated some specific feedback about areas in need of improvement. Several problems can arise with graphic rating scales, however. First, they assume that every rater uses the rating scale in the same way—for example, that all the raters using the scale would consider the same behavior or performance level "excellent." Often this is not the case. As a result, graphic rating scales are highly susceptible to restriction-of-range errors. Given the relative convenience of using them, however, graphic rating scales are often helpful if one is aware of these potential biases and takes steps to avoid them. Rater training programs have proved effective in increasing the reliability and validity of graphic rating scales when the training (1) involves raters in discussions of common biases in performance appraisal ratings, (2) develops agreement among the raters about standards of performance, and (3) gives them practice in improving the accuracy of their ratings. Such training programs have been successful at R. J. Reynolds, Nestlé, and Florida Power and Light.[42]

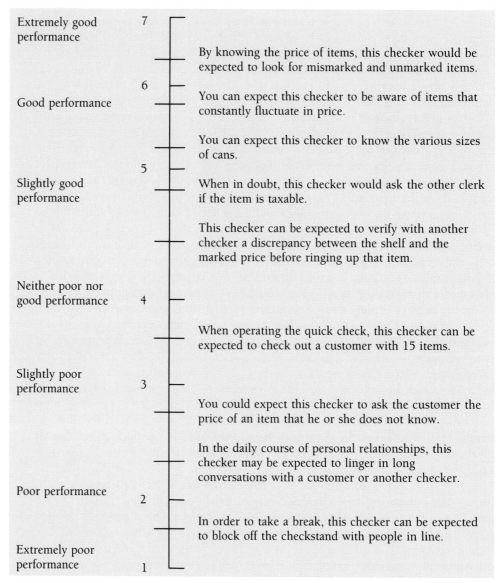

Source: L. Fogli, C. Hulin, and M. Blood, "Development of First-Level Behavioral Job Criteria," *Journal of Applied Psychology* 55, no. 1 (1971): 6. Copyright © 1971 by the American Psychological Association. Reprinted by permission of the author.

FIGURE 13-6
Behaviorally Anchored Rating Scale to Appraise Grocery Checkers' Use of Knowledge and Judgment

A second method of individual appraisal is the **essay evaluation**, which often takes the form of a paragraph or letter of evaluation. Essays can be a rich source of information about an employee's performance, but they are subject to two major sources of bias. Essays are based on the free recall of the writer, so they are particularly susceptible to selective recall and halo effects. Furthermore, because the evaluator selects the content, essays often contain information that is irrelevant to actual job performance. Research suggests, however, that the accuracy of essay evaluations can be increased by training evaluators to keep a critical-incident diary during the period of time to be covered in the essay.[43] The critical-incident diary specifies categories of job-related behaviors, and the evaluator records all instances of those behaviors as they occur. At the end of the evaluation period, the diary becomes the basis for the essay. This type of training helps reduce bias that is attributable to selective recall and halo effects. It also helps reduce the amount of irrelevant information in the essay.

Behaviorally anchored rating scales (BARS) are a third type of individual performance appraisal method. This type of rating scale is based on the results of a job analysis that specifies the behaviors required to do the job. Specific examples of behaviors that are judged to represent all levels of performance from very low to very high are used to "anchor" the points on the rating scale. Figure 13-6 presents an example of a BARS used to appraise the performance of a grocery clerk.

Raters are often involved in developing the BARS scale, so they are more likely to use the scale in similar ways and, therefore, more likely to avoid restriction-of-range errors. Because they participate in developing the scale, appraisers may also be more likely to accept the scale as an appraisal tool. The major liability of BARS is that such scales are difficult to construct and generally require the assistance of someone trained in job analysis and in the construction of behavioral scales. Furthermore, because highly specific behaviors are included as the anchor points for the scale, a BARS may need to be revised frequently as job procedures or technologies change.[44]

LABOR RELATIONS

Introduction

What Are Labor Relations?

To this point in the chapter, human resource management has been treated as involving a complex but direct relationship between managers and subordinates. This generally accurate portrayal is complicated, however, when employers are represented by a union. When a union acts as an intermediary between employees and their supervisors, managers must acquire additional HRM skills in labor relations. **Labor relations** consist of the ways in which managers relate to employees who are represented by a union. Principally as a consequence of the emergence of foreign competitors in markets traditionally dominated by U.S. firms, American management has been sternly challenged to defend its labor relations practices. As suggested by "In Practice 13-1," there are many new HRM alternatives that managers in the United States must understand and consider.

Although labor relations in this country are guided by governmental regulation, they are essentially the consequence of management's interaction with the labor unions of an organization's employees. A **labor union** is "a formal association of workers that promotes the welfare of its members" by engaging in collective bargaining to determine wages, benefits, and other working conditions.[46] Labor unions affect HRM activities in important ways. In particular, decision-making processes and power are distributed differently in companies in which employees are represented by unions. In the absence of labor unions, managers are often free to make unilateral decisions about wages, benefits, working conditions, hours, hiring, firing, and promotions. Employers who have an organized labor force,

■ *In Practice 13-1* ■

THE JAPANESE APPROACH TO LABOR RELATIONS

Because the Japanese have been the industrial super-stars of the last several years, many observers are closely studying the Japanese approach to labor relations to find out whether it can be applied in this country. They are paying special attention to the concept of lifetime employment.

Lifetime employment is a concept that we associate with Japanese companies, yet it is often misunderstood by Americans. Indeed, the term itself is a misnomer. Employment does not last a lifetime, nor does "lifetime employment" apply to all Japanese workers. Better termed "career employment," the practice is much more prevalent among the larger companies than among the small to medium-sized companies that employ the majority of workers in Japan. Even in large companies, it does not apply to the approximately 20 percent of Japanese workers who are temporary. Women, who are expected to leave the company when they get married to raise families, are also not considered lifetime employees.

"Newcomers" undergo intensive training and are thereafter expected to work for the company until they retire, usually at age fifty-five to sixty. They are not laid off during this period and are rarely fired. At worst, in times of significant slowdown, they may be sent to training school or dispatched to one of the company's suppliers, subcontractors, or even customers. For example, steel workers are often dispatched to the automobile manufacturers that their companies supply, because the auto companies have had a greater demand for workers in the last several years than the steel producers.

Traditionally, although this is changing somewhat, workers in companies with lifetime employment systems do not look for jobs with other companies during the course of their careers. They do not, for example, seek advancement by looking for a better position with another employer. Indeed, in large Japanese companies such casual movement would be met with social disapproval, and any worker who left his or her company would almost never be rehired except on a temporary basis.

Lifetime employment, however, is not a legal commitment in Japan. There is no contract between employer and employee guaranteeing the worker's employment throughout his career, nor does a collective bargaining agreement between a Japanese corporation and its workers' union include a contractual guarantee of lifetime employment. Rather, lifetime or career employment is a goal—it results when employer and employee work together to ensure the company's success.

Secure, well-educated, and highly trained employees are expected to be flexible as well as productive. Workers in Japan are expected to perform any job that will help the company and to work overtime or weekends when necessary. Even white-collar workers join the assembly line when the need arises. Workers understand that if they demand job security, they must do everything possible to maximize the efficiency of the company in order to maintain its competitive edge in the marketplace.

however, must involve union representatives in these decisions, which then become bilateral decisions.[47] Regardless of whether their own employees are unionized, effective managers need to understand why people join unions, how labor unions operate, what laws govern the actions of unions and those of employers vis-à-vis unions, and how to negotiate with labor organizations.

Union Membership

The total number of people who belong to unions has increased since the mid-1930s. Yet union membership as a percentage of the private nonagricultural labor force declined from almost 25 percent in 1970 to 15.5 percent in 1984.[48] Several factors have contributed to this decline in unionization of the work force. A major factor is that the composition of the work force is changing. Groups that traditionally have not been unionized, such as women and white-collar workers, now make up larger percentages of the work force. Layoffs, plant closings, and other reductions in the work force have hit heavily unionized industries such as the steel and automobile industries particularly hard and have reduced union membership. Two rulings by the Supreme Court, along with recent actions of Congress and the **National Labor Relations Board** (NLRB), have also made it easier for companies to terminate their relationship with a union by declaring bankruptcy or by closing and moving their plants. As a result of such rulings, for example, Continental Airlines was able to rid itself of an expensive union by declaring bankruptcy and then continuing to operate legally with nonunion employees. And Otis Elevator legally moved its research and development operations to a different state without bargaining with employees over the decision.[49] These factors and others have led to the types of attitudes revealed in the *Washington Post* survey shown in Figure 13-7.

Motives for Unionization

There are many reasons why people join unions. Three reasons were frequently mentioned by the workers who were surveyed in a 1945 study of unionization:

1. Unionization increases economic and job security.

2. Union membership provides some opportunities for leadership, prestige, and status.

3. Unionization gives workers greater control over decisions that affect their work life.

People join unions, then, mainly to improve their standard of living through higher wages and better benefits, to achieve job security, and to secure protection from unfair treatment. They also join union for status or leadership opportunities.[50] Employees generally do *not* join unions under the following conditions:[51]

1. They identify with management and view a union as an adversary. (However, if they experience enough dissatisfaction, this identification with management may diminish.)

2. They do not agree with the goals of the union. For example, professionals tend to define fair pay in terms of individual performance, whereas blue-collar workers define fairness in terms of seniority and equality.

3. They see themselves as professionals and view unions as inappropriate for professionals. Some studies indicate that the attitudes of white-collar employees toward unions are becoming more favorable than they were in the past.

Labor Legislation

A body of legislation often referred to as the National Labor Code governs the activities of unions and employers. Three major pieces of legislation are included

FIGURE 13-7
Public Attitudes Toward Unions

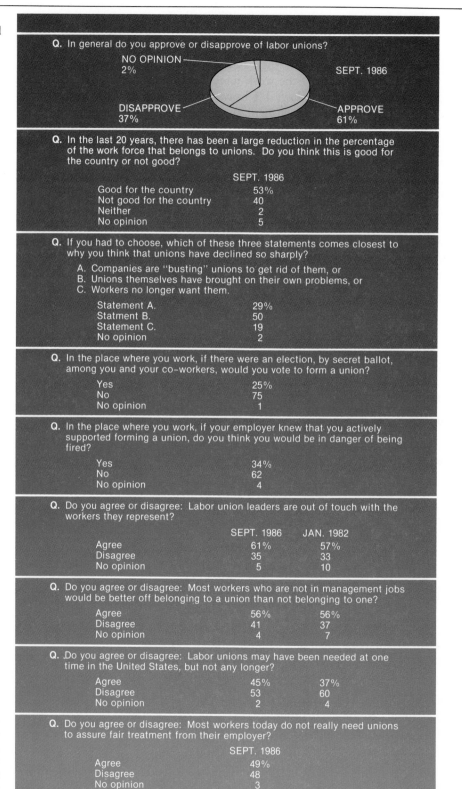

Q. In general do you approve or disapprove of labor unions?

NO OPINION — 2%   SEPT. 1986

DISAPPROVE — 37%   APPROVE — 61%

Q. In the last 20 years, there has been a large reduction in the percentage of the work force that belongs to unions. Do you think this is good for the country or not good?

	SEPT. 1986
Good for the country	53%
Not good for the country	40
Neither	2
No opinion	5

Q. If you had to choose, which of these three statements comes closest to why you think that unions have declined so sharply?

A. Companies are "busting" unions to get rid of them, or
B. Unions themselves have brought on their own problems, or
C. Workers no longer want them.

Statement A.	29%
Statment B.	50
Statement C.	19
No opinion	2

Q. In the place where you work, if there were an election, by secret ballot, among you and your co-workers, would you vote to form a union?

Yes	25%
No	75
No opinion	1

Q. In the place where you work, if your employer knew that you actively supported forming a union, do you think you would be in danger of being fired?

Yes	34%
No	62
No opinion	4

Q. Do you agree or disagree: Labor union leaders are out of touch with the workers they represent?

	SEPT. 1986	JAN. 1982
Agree	61%	57%
Disagree	35	33
No opinion	5	10

Q. Do you agree or disagree: Most workers who are not in management jobs would be better off belonging to a union than not belonging to one?

Agree	56%	56%
Disagree	41	37
No opinion	4	7

Q. Do you agree or disagree: Labor unions may have been needed at one time in the United States, but not any longer?

Agree	45%	37%
Disagree	53	60
No opinion	2	4

Q. Do you agree or disagree: Most workers today do not really need unions to assure fair treatment from their employer?

	SEPT. 1986
Agree	49%
Disagree	48
No opinion	3

Source: From "The Washington Post Poll," *Washington Post,* September 13, 1987, p. 1. © The Washington Post. The figures are from a *Washington Post* national survey of 693 adults, September 2–8, 1986.

in the National Labor Code: the Wagner Act, the Taft-Hartley Act, and the Landrum-Griffin Act.

Prior to 1935 there was very little legal protection for labor unions engaged in disputes with employers. A congressional investigation in 1936 documented widespread anti-union activities among some employers (including infiltration and discrediting of unions, attacks on union leaders, and strike breaking) and company unions that did not adequately represent workers' interests.[52] In 1935 the Wagner Act, also known as the National Labor Relations Act, was passed in order to protect unions from these types of employer actions and to reduce the economic disruption caused by lengthy and sometimes violent labor disputes. The Wagner Act encouraged union growth by (1) guaranteeing unions the right to organize and engage in collective bargaining without management interference, (2) defining unfair labor practices on the part of employers, and (3) creating the National Labor Relations Board (NLRB) to enforce the legislation. According to Section 7 of the Wagner Act,

> Employees shall have the right to self-organization, to form, join, or assist labor organizations, to bargain collectively through representatives of their own choosing, and to engage in concerted activities, for the purpose of collective bargaining or other mutual aid or protection.

In order to protect unions' right to organize without interference from employers, the Wagner Act prohibited employers from engaging in five unfair labor practices. These are presented at the top of Figure 13-8.

By 1946 there was widespread feeling that unions had too much power. For example, in the twelve months following the end of World War II and the lifting of wartime restrictions on strikes, an unprecedented 4,985 strikes caused the loss of over 116 million worker-days of production.[53] In 1947 the Taft-Hartley Act, also known as the Labor Management Relations Act, was passed. Whereas the Wagner Act was considered pro-union, the Taft-Hartley Act was designed to be pro-management. The Taft-Hartley Act included a "right to work" provision in all areas of employment except construction-related occupations. This provision made illegal the *closed shop,* which required that individuals join a specific union before they could be hired. It also prohibited unions from engaging in the seven unfair labor practices listed in the middle section of Figure 13-8.

The third piece of legislation in the National Labor Code is the Landrum-Griffin Act, also known as the Labor/Management Reporting and Disclosure Act. It was passed in 1959 to fight corruption in unions and to protect individual members of unions. Several of the provisions of the Landrum-Griffin Act are presented at the end of Figure 13-8.

The Landrum-Griffin Act guaranteed union members the right to nominate and vote for officers, the right to attend and participate in union meetings, and the right to review the financial records of the union and to have pension funds properly managed.

The Process of Union Organizing

In order for a union to represent a group of employees, it must be certified as their representative by the National Labor Relations Board (NLRB). The process of unionization includes six steps: (1) gathering information, (2) organizing internally, (3) collecting authorization cards, (4) conducting a representation hearing, (5) conducting a representation election, and (6) negotiating a contract.

FIGURE 13-8
Labor Practices

As a result of the *Wagner Act,* it is an unfair labor practice for an employer to:

1. Interfere with, restrain, or coerce employees in the exercise of their rights to organize, bargain collectively, or engage in other concerted activities for their mutual aid or protection.

2. Dominate or interfere with the formation or administration of any labor organization or contribute financial or other support to it.

3. Encourage or discourage membership in any labor organization by discrimination with regard to hiring or tenure or conditions of employment, subject to an exception for valid union security agreements.

4. Discharge or otherwise discriminate against an employee because he or she filed charges or gave testimony under the Act.

5. Refuse to bargain collectively with representatives of the employees.

As a result of the *Taft-Hartley Act,* it is an unfair labor practice for a union to:

1. Restrain or coerce employees or employers in the exercise of their rights under the Act.

2. Cause or attempt to cause an employer to discriminate against an employee on account of membership or nonmembership in a labor organization.

3. Refuse to bargain collectively in good faith with an employer if the union has been designated as bargaining agent by a majority of the employees.

4. Induce or encourage employees to stop work to force an employer or other persons to stop doing business with any other person (boycott provisions).

5. Induce or encourage employees to stop work to force an employer to assign particular work to members of one union instead of to members of another union (jurisdictional strike).

6. Charge an excessive or discriminatory fee as a condition of becoming a member of the union.

7. Cause or attempt to cause an employer to pay for services that are not performed or are not to be performed (featherbedding).

As a result of the *Landrum-Griffin Act,* union members are protected in the following ways:

1. Every labor organization is required to have a constitution and bylaws containing certain minimum standards and safeguards.

2. Reports on the union's policies, procedures, and the annual financial report must be filed with the Secretary of Labor and must be disclosed to the union's members.

3. Union members must have a bill of rights to protect their rights within the union.

4. Standards are established for union trusteeship and union elections.

5. Reports on trusteeships must be made to the Secretary of Labor.

6. A fiduciary relationship is imposed on union officers.

7. Union leaders are required to file reports with the Secretary of Labor on conflict-of-interest transactions.

8. The Secretary of Labor, as a watchdog on union conduct, is a custodian of reports from unions and their officers and has the power to investigate and prosecute violations of many of the provisions of the Act.

First, union organizers try to collect information about employee dissatisfaction with company policies—perhaps with wages and benefits, job security, or their treatment by supervisors.[54] Then they set about explaining what the union can do to address these complaints. This often involves the distribution of hand-bills outside the plant and, subsequently, the formation of an inside organizing committee comprised of employees who support unionization. The primary goal of the inside committee is to move the unionization process to the next step, collection of authorization cards.

Authorization cards are signed by employees to indicate that they favor holding an election to determine whether they will be represented by the union. The NLRB requires that authorization cards be signed by at least 30 percent of a bargaining group before an election can be held. There are many reasons why employees sign authorization cards. Some are in favor of electing the unions as their representative; others are undecided but want the question put to a vote; others simply want to send management the message that they are dissatisfied. For this reason, not everyone who signs an authorization card can be expected to vote for the union, so union organizers generally try to get more than 30 percent of the employees to sign authorization cards before they hold an election.

At this point, if the company does not contest union representation, a **consent election** is held immediately. Majority support for the union in this election establishes the union as the legal representative of the employees. If, as is usual, the company contests, a hearing is held to determine whether there is evidence that at least 30 percent of the employees signed authorization cards and that the appropriate bargaining unit has been defined. The group of employees that the union could be authorized to represent is called the *bargaining unit* and a **representation election** is held to see if the union will be confirmed as the agent of the bargaining unit. The representation election is supervised by the NLRB, and both the union and the employer must follow certain rules. A successful charge of unfair labor practices by either side can prompt the NLRB to require a new election. (Suggestions for avoiding unfair labor practices during a campaign are discussed later.) To win an election, the union must get over 50 percent of the votes that are actually cast in the election. For example, if only 100 of the employees in a plant that employs 400 vote in a representation election, fifty-one votes are required for the union to win.

Collective Bargaining

After a successful union election, a contract is negotiated via **collective bargaining**. Contracts cover union security, management rights, wages and benefits, job rights, and grievance procedures.[55]

Union security may be protected by specifying that the bargaining unit will be a *union shop;* that is, all employees must join the union and pay dues within a specified period of time after beginning employment. An *agency shop* requires all employees to pay union dues but does not require them to join the union. In a *maintenance-of-membership agreement,* employees who are union members must maintain their membership in the union for the period of time covered by the labor agreement, but other employees are not required to join the union or to pay dues. An *open shop* is one in which workers are not required to join the union or to pay dues; it offers the least union security.

Management is concerned about the degree to which a labor agreement will allow it to have exclusive rights over activities such as product pricing, accounting methods, directing employees, and establishing job content. In addition, the degree of management and union input in decisions about work standards, discipline, work scheduling, work assignment, and promotions are specified in the agreement. For their part, unions are generally interested in controlling policies that affect transfers, promotions, demotions, terminations, layoffs, and other job rights and in participating in decisions that affect job security.

Wages and benefits are crucial issues addressed by labor agreements. Specific wage and benefit issues include job evaluation and classification policies, wage adjustments, premium pay, cost-of-living increases, and fringe benefits such as health care, child care, and employee stock plans.

Guidelines for Management Practice

What should managers do when faced with a unionization attempt? Any campaign opposing the union must be conducted in accordance with the guidelines for fair elections specified by the NLRB.[56] A successful charge of unfair labor practices by either side can lead the NLRB to require a new election. According to these guidelines, an employer may conduct a campaign opposing the union, but that campaign may not intimidate or coerce employees in any way. Specifically, a manager must be aware that an employer may not:

1. Threaten economic retaliation if the union wins, or promise promotions or pay increases if the union is defeated.

2. Threaten to close or move a plant or threaten employees with loss of jobs if the union wins.

3. Grant wage or benefit increases during the campaign unless they can be demonstrated to be wholly unrelated to the campaign against the union.

4. Visit employees in their homes or meet with them in places that are associated with "special" unionization efforts.

5. Ask individual employees how they plan to vote, whether they have signed authorization cards, or what their general attitude toward the union is.

6. Spy on union meetings or enlist someone to spy on them.

7. Deliver a speech to employees within twenty-four hours of the union election.

8. Urge employees to persuade others to vote against the union.

Within the NLRB guidelines, however, employers may openly oppose the union and communicate to employees what they believe the disadvantages of belonging to the union will be. Specifically, employers may:

1. Tell employees they will use all legal means to oppose the union.

2. Forbid unions to distribute literature in working areas during work hours.

3. Provide employees with information about negative experiences other groups of employees have had with unions.

4. Explain the unionization process accurately to employees.

5. Provide employees with information about how their current wages and benefits compare to those at other companies.

6. Describe the disadvantages of union membership (such as the cost of union dues and any limits on personal freedom that accompany membership).

7. Present information on the direct and indirect costs that unionization and collective bargaining may have for both employer and employees.

8. Enforce previously existing disciplinary policies and rules consistently and fairly.

Finally, labor agreements specify grievance procedures. In the typical grievance procedure, the employee first discusses the grievance with his or her immediate supervisor. If there is no satisfactory resolution at that level, the union becomes involved and the grievance proceeds through the following channels until it is resolved: (1) discussion with the union steward and the supervisor, (2) discussion between the union steward and the supervisor's manager, (3) meeting of the union grievance committee with the unit plant manager or the industrial relations department, (4) meeting of the national union representative and the company executive or corporate industrial relations officer, (5) arbitration by an impartial entity.[57]

In recent years an increasing number of nonunion companies have established formal "employee due process" procedures to deal with grievances and thus tried to avoid unionization attempts built on grievances. Tektronix, an electronics manufacturer, has established a five-step grievance procedure, and McDonald's has provided an ombudsman whose job it is to mediate employee grievances.[58]

Union Decertification

Decertification is the process by which employees can remove a union as its representative. As in the certification process, employees sign authorization cards to indicate their desire to vote on whether to separate from the union. An election is called if authorization cards are signed by at least 30 percent of the employees in the bargaining unit. The NLRB prohibits management from funding or otherwise assisting in this process.

Review of the Learning Objectives

Having studied this chapter, you should be able to respond to the learning objectives with extensions of the following brief answers:

1. **Define the term *human resource management* and list the activities it involves.**

   Human resource management is the process of ensuring that competent people are available, that they are able to achieve organizational objectives, and that their energy and abilities are used effectively. HR management includes the following activities: job analysis, HR planning, recruitment, selection, placement, orientation, training, development, appraisal, compensation, labor relations, safety, and HR records and research.

2. **List the groups protected under equal employment opportunity regulations, and explain the criteria that employment practices must meet in order to be considered nondiscriminatory.**

   Women, members of minority groups, people over the age of forty, and disabled people are all protected classes under EEO regulations. In order to be nondiscriminatory, employment practices must have no adverse impact, as defined by the 4/5 rule, on any protected group; they must be valid; and they must be job-related.

3. **Explain what job analysis is and cite three products of job analysis.**

Job analysis identifies the specific activities that are performed in a job and the characteristics of the person, the work situation, and the materials or equipment that are required for the job to be performed satisfactorily. Three products of job analysis are job description, job specification, and job evaluation.

4. **Define the term *human resource planning* and describe the steps it involves.**

Human resource planning is the process of (1) anticipating the future staffing needs of the firm and the supply of labor that will be available and (2) developing plans to meet those staffing needs. HR planning involves the following steps: The staffing implications of factors internal and external to the organization are considered, and staffing needs are forecasted; forecasts of the labor supply are developed and are compared with the anticipated staffing needs; and plans are made to deal with any expected surplus or shortage of personnel.

5. **List the basic steps in the employee selection process.**

Most selection procedures include the following steps, though the sequence in which they are performed may vary: reception, preliminary screening interview, evaluation of the completed application form, pre-employment testing, selection interview, realistic job preview, reference and background checks, and medical report.

6. **Explain four purposes of performance appraisal.**

Performance appraisal can provide feedback to employees about the quality of their performance and to managers about the effectiveness of the firm's selection and training programs. They can provide information to be used as a basis for decisions about promotion, termination, compensation, and the selection of candidates for development or training opportunities. They can also serve to document and support specific personnel decisions. Finally, performance appraisals provide feedback to HR managers about how effectively they are utilizing available human resources.

7. **Describe three major pieces of legislation that have defined the rights of labor and management in the United States.**

The Wagner Act guaranteed unions the right to organize and engage in collective bargaining. It also defined unfair labor practices and created the NLRB. The Taft-Hartley Act made closed shops illegal and protected management as well as unions from unfair labor practices. The Landrum-Griffin Act guaranteed union members full participation and protection in their own unions.

8. **Trace the steps involved in the unionization process.**

The six steps in the unionization process are information gathering, organizing internally, collecting authorization cards, conducting a representation hearing, conducting a representation election, and negotiating a contract.

Key Terms and Concepts

After completing your study of Chapter 13, "Human Resource Management and Labor Relations," you should be able to explain the following important terms and concepts.

human resource management	human resource forecasting	human resource development	forced-choice method	National Labor Relations Board
equal employment opportunity	employee skills inventory	training	graphic scales	consent election
four-fifths rule	staffing	assessment center	essay evaluations	representation election
job analysis	recruitment	halo effect	behaviorally anchored rating scales (BARS)	collective bargaining
job description	selection	restriction of range		
job specification	placement	straight ranking	labor relations	decertification
job evaluation	performance appraisal	alternation ranking	labor union	
human resource planning		forced-distribution method		

Questions for Discussion

1. In what ways is a thorough job analysis necessary in order to effectively carry out other HR activities, such as HR planning, recruitment, selection, training, development, and performance appraisal?

2. Why do some researchers suggest that HR planning must take into consideration the strategic plans of the organization? What are some examples of the impact a company's strategic plans have on HR planning?

3. What are the advantages and disadvantages of internal recruiting? of external recruiting? In what ways might the environment in which the organization operates affect the relative merits of internal and external recruiting for that organization?

4. Consider all of the steps that are usually involved in the selection process. Give examples of discriminatory practices that could occur, either intentionally or unintentionally, at each step.

5. How does job training differ from development? What skills might each address?

6. What are the major types of rater biases that can affect performance appraisal? How can rater bias reduce both the reliability and the validity of a performance appraisal instrument?

7. What are the relative advantages and disadvantages of comparative methods of performance appraisal and individual performance appraisal methods?

8. What are some potential biases that can affect appraisals based on the use of graphic rating scales? How can some of these biases be avoided?

9. Students are often asked to evaluate the performance of their professors. What specific behaviors could serve as critical incidents to anchor a behaviorally anchored rating scale that evaluates the effectiveness of the professors' presentation of material in class?

10. Why might it be a bad idea to hold a single conference with an employee in order to report salary, raise, or promotion decisions that had been made on the basis of a performance appraisal *and* to provide feedback about the employee's strengths and areas in need of improvement?

11. In what ways are the human resource activities discussed in this chapter involved in such general functions of management as planning, organizing, staffing, leading, and controlling?

Notes

1. Excerpted from "Case History: Employee Recognition Programs," *Small Business Report,* October 1986, p. 98. Diamond Film Products, Thorndike, Mass. David C. Boyle and Associates, Chicopee, Mass. Co-owners; Product: Molded pulp egg cartons; Territory: National; Number of employees: 308.

2. *Commitment: Dana 1984 Annual Report* (Toledo, Ohio: Dana Corporation, 1984), p. 14.

3. T. J. Peters and R. H. Waterman, Jr., *In Search of Excellence* (New York: Harper & Row, 1982), p. 238.

4. U. S. Equal Employment Opportunity Commission, *Affirmative Action and Equal Employment* (Washington, D.C.: U.S. Government Printing Office, 1974).

5. R. L. Mathis and J. H. Jackson, *Personnel: Human Resource Management,* 4th ed. (St. Paul, Minn.: West, 1985), p. 96.

6. D. P. Schwab and R. Grams, *A Survey of Job Evaluation Practices Among Compensation Specialists* (Phoenix: American Compensation Association, 1984.)

7. G. Magnum and S. Magnum, "Comparable Worth

Confusion in the Ninth Circuit," *Labor Law Journal* 37 (June 1986): 351–365; and G. P. Sape, "Coping with Comparable Worth," *Harvard Business Review* 63 (1985): 145–152.

8. D. Q. Mills, "Planning with People in Mind," *Harvard Business Review* 63 (1985): 97.

9. D. P. Schwab and R. Grams, *A Survey of Job Evaluation Practices.*

10. K. H. Chan, "Decision Support System for Human Resource Management," *Journal of Systems Management,* April 1984, pp. 17–25.

11. W. F. Glueck, *Personnel: A Diagnostic Approach,* rev. ed. (New York: Business Publications, 1978), p. 89; and T. H. Patten, *Manpower Planning and the Development of Human Resources* (New York: Wiley, 1971), p. 243.

12. Mathis and Jackson, *Personnel,* p. 215.

13. R. L. Mathis, "Managing and Planning Human Resources," in *Ideas in Management* (Cleveland, Ohio: Association for Systems Management, 1979), p. 104.

14. A. O. Manzini, "Human Resources Planning and Forecasting," in W. R. Tracey, ed., *Human Resources Management and Development Handbook* (New York: American Management Association, 1985), pp. 507–529; and L. C. Megginson, *Personal Management,* 5th ed. (Homewood, Ill.: Irwin, 1985).

15. T. H. Stone and J. Fiorito, "A Perceived Uncertainty Model of Human Resource Forecasting Technique Use," *Academy of Management Review* 11 no. 3 (1986): 635–642; and J. Fiorito, T. H. Stone, and C. R. Greer, "Factors Affecting Choice of Human Resource Forecasting Techniques," *Human Resource Planning,* 1985, pp. 1–17.

16. E. C. Smith, "Strategic Business Planning and Human Resources: Part 1," *Personnel Journal* 61, no. 8 (1982): 606–610; "Part 2," pp. 680–682; and L. Dyer, "Studying Human Resource Strategy: An Approach and an Agenda," *Industrial Relations* 22, no. 2 (1984): 156–169.

17. E. C. Smith, "Strategic Business Planning, Part 1," pp. 606–610.

18. L. Dyer, "Studying Human Resource Strategy: An Approach and an Agenda," *Industrial Relations,* 1984, pp. 156–169.

19. E. C. Smith, "Strategic Business Planning, Part 2," pp. 680–682; and S. M. Nkomo, "The Theory and Practice of HR Planning: The Gap Still Remains," *Personnel Administrator* 31 (August 1986): 71–84.

20. Mathis and Jackson, *Personnel.*

21. P. Brownstern, "Recommend a Worker, Get a Bonus," Associated Press, March 25, 1984.

22. E. Hartzell, "Remember the Classifieds," *Personnel Journal* 58 (November 1979): 736; R. Stoops, "Radio Advertising as an Effective Recruitment Device, *Personnel Journal* 60, no. 1 (1981): 21; and

J. A. Breaugh, "Relationships Between Recruiting Sources and Employee Performance, Absenteeism, and Work Attitudes," *Academy of Management Journal* 24, no. 1 (1981): 142–147.

23. Mathis and Jackson, *Personnel.*

24. F. J. Landy and D. A. Trumbo, *Psychology of Work Behavior,* (Homewood, Ill.: Dorsey, 1980).

25. Mathis and Jackson, *Personnel,* pp. 238–239.

26. Mathis and Jackson, *Personnel,* p. 243.

27. R. S. Lowell and J. A. DeLoach, "Equal Employment Opportunity: Are You Overloading the Application Form?" *Personnel* 59, no. 4 (1982): 40–55.

28. D. T. Lykken, "The Case Against the Polygraph in Employment Screening," *Personnel Administrator* 30, no. 9 (1985): 58–65.

29. R. T. Angarola, "Drug Testing in the Workplace: Is It Legal?" *Personnel Administrator* 30, no. 9 (1985): 79–89.

30. R. W. Mondy, A. Sharplin, R. E. Holmes, and E. B. Flippo, *Management Concepts and Practices,* 3rd ed. (Boston: Allyn and Bacon, 1986).

31. R. Wagner, "The Employment Interview: A Critical Summary," *Personnel Psychology,* 1949, pp. 17–46; L. Ulrich and D. Trumbo, "The Selection Interview Since 1949," *Psychological Bulletin* 63, no. 2 (1965): 100–116; M. D. Hakel, "Similarity of Post-Interview Trait Rating Intercorrelations as a Contributor to Interrater Agreement in a Structured Employment Interview," *Journal of Applied Psychology* 55, no. 5 (1971): 443–448; M. Snyder and S. W. Uranowitz, "Reconstructing the Past: Some Cognitive Consequences of Person Perception," *Journal of Personality and Social Psychology* 36, no. 9 (1978): 941–950; J. G. Hollandsworth, Jr., R. Kazelskis, J. Stevens, and M. E. Dressel, "Relative Contributions of Verbal, Articulative, and Nonverbal Communication to Employment Decisions in the Job Interview Setting," *Personal Psychology* 32, no. 2 (1979): 359–367; Bureau of National Affairs, *Personnel Policies Forum,* Survey No. 114, 1976.

32. E. D. Pursell, M. A. Champion, and S. R. Gaylord, "Structured Interviewing: Avoiding Selection Problems," *Personnel Journal* 59, no. 11 (1980): 907.

33. P. Popvich and J. P. Wanous, "The Realistic Job Preview as a Persuasive Communication," *Academy of Management Review* 7, no. 4 (1982): 570–578; J. A. Breaugh, "Realistic Job Previews: A Critical Appraisal and Future Research Directions," *Academy of Management Review* 8, no. 4 (1983): 612–619; and R. A. Dean and J. P. Wanous, "Effects of Realistic Job Previews on Hiring Bank Tellers," *Journal of Applied Psychology* 69, no. 1 (1984): 61–68.

34. E. Matusewitch, "Employment Rights of Ex-offenders," *Personnel Journal* 62, no. 12 (1983): 951–954.

35. D. Shaffer, P. V. Mays, and K. Etheridge, "Who Shall

Be Hired: A Biasing Effect of the Buckley Amendment on Employment Practices," *Journal of Applied Psychology* 61, no. 5 (1976): 571–575.

36. C. C. Kessler, III, and C. J. Gibbs, "Getting the Most from Application Blanks and References," *Personnel* 52, no. 1 (January–February 1975): 53–62.

37. Mathis and Jackson, *Personnel*, p. 264; and M. A. Champion, "Personnel Selection for Physically Demanding Jobs: Reviews and Recommendations," *Personnel Psychology* 36, no. 3 (1983): 527–550.

38. A. Brown, "Employment Tests: Issues without Clear Answers," *Personnel Administrator* 30 no. 9 (September 1985): 43–51, 56.

39. R. S. Courtney, "A Human Resources Program that Helps Management and Employees Prepare for the Future," *Personnel* 63, no. 5 (May 1986): 32–40.

40. K. Blanchard and S. Johnson, *The One Minute Manager* (New York: Morrow, 1982).

41. R. Albanese and D. D. Van Fleet, *Organizational Behavior: A Managerial Viewpoint* (Chicago: Dryden, 1983); and R. W. Griffin and G. Moorhead, *Organizational Behavior* (Boston: Houghton Mifflin, 1986).

42. D. E. Smith, "Training Programs for Performance Appraisal: A Review," *Academy of Management Review* 11, no. 1 (1986): 22–40; and M. R. Edwards and J. R. Sprooll, "Rating the Raters Improves Performance Appraisal," *Personnel Administrator* 28, no. 8 (August 1983): 82.

43. H. J. Bernadin and M. R. Buckley, "Strategies in Rater Training," *Academy of Management Review* 6, no. 2 (1981): 205–212.

44. L. L. Cummings and D. P. Schwab, *Performance in Organizations: Determinants and Appraisal* (Glenview, Ill: Scott, Foresman, 1973).

45. Mathis and Jackson, *Personnel*, p. 358.

46. Mathis and Jackson, *Personnel*, p. 555.

47. D. J. Cherrington, *Personnel Management* (Dubuque, Iowa: Brown, 1983).

48. U.S. Bureau of the Census, *Statistical Abstract of the United States: 1986*, 106th ed. (Washington, D.C.:

U.S. Department of Commerce, 1986).

49. L. M. Apcar, "Unions Press Congress to Reverse Decision by High Court on Bankrupt Firm's Pacts," *Wall Street Journal*, March 21, 1984, p. 31; and J. S. Lubin, "NLRB Rules Employers Needn't Bargain with Unions Before Moving Operations," *Wall Street Journal*, April 11, 1984, p. 16.

50. E. W. Bakke, "Why Workers Join Unions," *Personnel*, July 1945, pp. 37–46; and K. S. Warner, R. F. Chisholm, and R. F. Munzenrider, "Motives for Unionization Among State Social Service Employees," *Public Personnel Management* 7, no. 3 (1978): 181–191.

51. W. F. Glueck, *Personnel: A Diagnostic Approach*, 2nd ed. (Dallas, Texas: Business Publications, 1978), p. 643; P. Feville and J. Blandin, "Faculty Job Satisfaction and Bargaining Sentiments," *Academy of Management Journal* 17, no. 4 (1974): 678–692; F. S. Hills and T. Bergmann, "Professional Employees: Unionization Attitudes and Reward Preferences," *Personnel Administrator* 27, no. 7 (July 1982): 50–73; and B. Bass and C. Mitchell, "Influences on the Felt Need for Collective Bargaining by Business and Science Professionals," *Journal of Applied Psychology* 61, no. 6 (1976): 770–773.

52. La Follette Committee, *Report on Industrial Espionage*, report no. 46, parts I to XXI, 75th Congress.

53. B. J. Taylor and F. Whitney, *Labor Relations Law* (Englewood Cliffs, N.J.: Prentice-Hall, 1979).

54. J. M. Brett, "Why Employees Want Unions," *Organizational Dynamics* 8, no. 4 (Spring 1980): 47–59.

55. J. P. Yaney, *Personnel Management: Reaching Organizational and Human Goals* (Columbus, Ohio: Merrill, 1975), p. 180.

56. "The Anti-Union Grievance Ploy," *Business Week*, February 12, 1979, pp. 117–120.

57. Mathis and Jackson, *Personnel*, pp. 576–577; and D. J. Cherrington, *Personnel Management* (Dubuque, Iowa, 1983), pp. 552–553.

58. Mathis and Jackson, *Personnel*, p. 597.

Cohesion Incident 13-1
Performance Appraisals

"Charles, one of our most important tasks each year is conducting the annual appraisals of those employees who report to us. In my case, I'm talking about you, Miles, Susan, and the five desk clerks. Our philosophy at Journey's End is to base salary increases on these performance appraisals. Every year, I fill in the appraisal and then have each employee review it with me and sign it. We then go ahead and talk about that person's salary for the coming year. The salary increase depends on the composite of the various categories in the appraisals. To give you some experience in appraising, I thought we would both fill out a form on the people

I mentioned and then compare our results. This will probably help me as well as you, since you've been around each of these people long enough to have formed some type of opinion. Here, look over this form and ask me any questions you have about it." With that, Roger handed Charles the form shown below:

**Rating Scale for
Performance Appraisal
at Journey's End**

Name _____   Position _____

	(5) Outstanding	(4) Good	(3) Satisfactory	(2) Fair	(1) Poor	Not Observed
Job Knowledge						
Quality of Work						
Relationships with Subordinates						
Initiative						
Personal Appearance						
Cooperation						
Reliability						
Career Potential						

Composite Score _____   Appraised by _____ Date _____

Reviewed with Employee on _____

Employee's Signature _____

During the next few days, Charles carefully considered the categories as they pertained to each employee and completed the form on each. When he and Roger compared their results, they discovered a couple of surprising discrepancies. They were in almost total agreement on the ratings of the five clerks. In fact, the average composite ratings by Roger and Charles were within eight-tenths of a point on each of the five desk clerks. But their appraisals of Miles and Susan were quite different.

Concerning Miles, Charles had given him an average composite rating of 4.5, marking either "Outstanding" or "Good" in every category. This contrasted sharply with Roger's appraisal of Miles, which showed a composite rating of only 3.2.

"Charles, I know that you think a lot of Miles and that you two have become good friends, which is fine, but are you sure that you were being completely objective in his evaluation? I agree with you that his job knowledge and quality of work are 'outstanding,' but we differ quite a bit on the rest. I notice that you rated his reliability as 'outstanding,' compared to the 'fair' I gave him. Why just last week, he was late two days."

Looking at Susan's appraisal, they noticed just the opposite situation: Roger's evaluation of her was much higher than Charles's. As he listened to Roger explaining what an excellent job Susan had done in the restaurant, Charles began to think that maybe Roger was guilty of rating Susan high on *all* categories because she was excellent in several. Charles, however, was still convinced that her relationships with subordinates could use some definite improvement, as could her initiative.

Discussion Questions

1. Discuss at least three ways in which the performance appraisal technique at Journey's End could be improved.

2. Is there evidence of the halo effect in this case?

3. Roger suggested that Charles evaluate the employees as part of his training and also said that Charles's evaluations would help him (Roger) as well. What did he mean by that?

Cohesion Incident 13-2

What Exactly Is Job Discrimination?

Helen Johnson, personnel director for Travis Corporation, had placed an ad in the local paper announcing an opening in the Marketing Research Department. This particular job required a degree in either business or marketing plus at least one year of related experience. One of the applicants was Bill Reeves, a recent graduate of the state university with a degree in business management.

Bill had maintained a B average throughout college and had helped meet his college expenses by working part-time for a local marketing research firm. He was eager and energetic, and he saw this position as a promising career opportunity.

Helen Johnson took the résumé and placed it on a large stack of applications. "Are all those applications for the marketing position?" asked Bill. "Yes, Mr. Reeves. You should be notified by the end of next week," explained Helen.

Bill went home and waited. He jumped each time the telephone rang. Finally, seven days later, he received a call from Helen. She told him that he was one of the three finalists for the position and that she wanted to arrange for an interview.

Arriving fifteen minutes early for his scheduled interview with the marketing director, Bill sat in the waiting area as one of the other applicants came out of the director's office. The other candidate had obviously made a good impression—he even seemed to be on a first-name basis with the director. Bill's confidence was shaken. He knew he was qualified, but now he had to convince the director.

Bill's interview also seemed to go well. As he left the director's office, he realized he had a chance but nothing was certain. He was young, qualified, and eager. He felt he should get the job.

Several days passed before Bill finally received a letter thanking him for his interest but explaining that he had not been selected. Naturally disappointed, he called the personnel office and asked which candidate had been chosen. The secretary who answered the phone told Bill that Henry Burgess had been offered the job.

"Wasn't he the older gentleman?" asked Bill.

"Yes," said the secretary. "They were really looking for someone more mature to fill the position."

Discussion Questions

1. Could Bill file a job discrimination complaint against Travis Corporation on the basis of the secretary's statement?

2. Would the 4/5 rule apply in this case?

3. Has Travis Corporation violated the Uniform Guidelines set forth by the Equal Employment Opportunity Commission (EEOC)?

Management Development Exercise 13
"Opinionnaire" on Assumptions
About Human Relations Training

A number of assumptions about "personal growth groups" and participants in human relations training are listed. Report your reaction to each item in the space to the left of the item number. Use a five-point scale; 5 = strongly agree; 4 = agree; 3 = uncertain; 2 = disagree; and 1 = strongly disagree.

_____ 1. The behavior emitted in the group is sufficiently representative of behavior outside the group so that learning occurring within the group will carry over or transfer.

_____ 2. Psychological safety can be achieved relatively quickly (in a matter of a few hours) either among complete strangers or among associates who have had varying types and degrees of interpersonal interaction.

_____ 3. Almost everyone initially lacks interpersonal competence; that is, individuals tend to have distorted self-images, faulty perceptions, and poor communication skills.

_____ 4. Negative feedback is conducive to change.

_____ 5. People love and trust others to the extent that they love and trust themselves.

_____ 6. Self-revelation is necessary for change.

_____ 7. People in the helping professions tend to underestimate the strength and resilience of normal people.

_____ 8. People can be seriously hurt by their experiences in a personal growth group.

_____ 9. The trainer who participates in the group to satisfy his own needs prevents the group from completing its development.

_____ 10. The conditions leading to behavior change require the person to feel frustrated or fearful.

_____ 11. People who usually are quiet in the personal growth group sessions do not get as much out of the experience as people who participate more actively.

_____ 12. The members of a personal growth group generally can be trusted to stop short of a participant's breaking point.

_____ 13. The value of a personal growth group experience can be justified on whatever grounds seem appropriate to any participant.

_____ 14. The personal growth group experience may decrease a person's sense of individual responsibility for what he or she does.

_____ 15. Personal growth group training sponsored by an institution should not produce outcomes inconsistent with the stated goals of the supporting institution.

_____ 16. Almost everyone can profit from a personal growth group experience.

_____ 17. Through the personal growth group experience, you can see that all people are deserving of your love.

_____ 18. The trainer, to be effective or useful, should feel free to interact and participate just like any other participant in the group.

_____ 19. Without the introduction of theory units—either in separate sessions or, as appropriate, in personal growth group meetings—the laboratory method of teaching produces little generalizable information for the participant.

_____ 20. Data-based decisions are better than intuitive (instinctive) ones.

_____ 21. Democratic decision making results in the most effective action.

_____ 22. With regard to decision making in groups, efficiency is less important than effectiveness.

_____ 23. The final arbiter of the rightness of any collective judgment or arrangement is the procedure of consensual validation.

_____ 24. Motive analysis is to be avoided in the personal growth group.

_____ 25. Empathic understanding is a necessary condition for giving help.

_____ 26. The effectiveness of the trainer is more a function of his personality than it is a function of his academic preparation.

_____ 27. Competition within a group generally produces better decisions.

_____ 28. Conflict should decrease in the human relations group as the members come to know one another better.

Source: This structured experience from "Opinionnaire on Assumptions about Human Relations Training," was prepared by John E. Jones, University Associates, San Diego, California, with the assistance of Jim Dickinson, University of South Florida, Tampa, and of Carla Dee, University of Iowa, Iowa City. The normative data were derived from a survey of the membership of the Midwest Group for Human Resources conducted by John E. Jones and B. Howard Arbes, University of Wisconsin, Madison. Reprinted from J. W. Pfeiffer and J. E. Jones, eds., *A Handbook of Structured Experiences for Human Relations Training*, Vol. I. San Diego, Calif.: University Associates, Inc., 1974. Used with permission.

Directing

The management function of directing involves the responsibility of managers for communicating to others what their roles are in achieving the company plan. Directing also includes providing an organizational environment in which employees can become motivated to perform at their best. In this section you will learn about four critical components of the directing function: motivating, leadership, managing groups, and interpersonal and organizational communication.

The topic of motivating is covered in Chapter 14, which explains the motivational process and describes the manager's role in developing a motivated work force.

The study of leadership in Chapter 15 focuses on leadership as a process that achieves its greatest results when managers have learned to use their social powers in a manner that reflects the contingencies of the work environment.

The theme of Chapter 16 is managing groups. This chapter emphasizes how group processes relate to the functions of management. Among the topics covered are the types of groups, socialization, group performance, and organizational conflict.

Finally, in describing interpersonal and organizational communications, Chapter 17 covers the basic communications process, its pathways, and the types of information that are carried. It also provides the most up-to-date information on ways to increase your personal communications effectiveness.

14

Motivating

Learning Objectives

Your study of this chapter will enable you to do the following:

1. Explain the motivational process and describe the manager's role in developing a motivated work force.
2. Compare and contrast the three leading content approaches to motivation, and explain how they can best be implemented by managers.
3. Evaluate the relative strengths of the four most prominent process approaches to motivation in terms of their application by managers to typical work situations.
4. Describe the relationship between job performance and job satisfaction.
5. Explain the potential of money as a motivator.

Motivation at Digital Equipment

"People manage their own families and finances," said Bruce Dillingham, plant manager with Digital Equipment Corporation. "Work is a natural extension of their home lives and should be no different." It was with this philosophy in mind that he developed the electronic-module assembly plant in Enfield, Connecticut, that, compared with traditional Digital plants, requires 40 percent less time to build products, has lower inventory levels, maintains a quality level two to three times higher, and moves parts through the operation twenty times faster. In short, it is 40 to 50 percent more effective. The plant has no walls, no offices, and few managers, because the authority and responsibility for all functions (from assembling parts to fixing equipment to preparing budgets to hiring, training, and evaluating employees) are in the hands of fourteen- to eighteen-member teams.

Dillingham remembered that when he was first asked to design and then run a new plant in Enfield, he decided that a participative structure giving people responsibility for an entire product would benefit the company in more ways than an assembly line structure that assigned people narrow, repetitive tasks ever could. "Typical manufacturing plants tend to put people into jobs without any regard for their past experiences, interests, and hobbies. They do not make use of the total person." Further, he said, narrow job assignments limit a company's flexibility: When a few people in one function are absent, productivity necessarily drops.

Products such as these are assembled at Digital Equipment's highly innovative Enfield, Connecticut, plant, which was designed to enhance employee motivation. (Digital Equipment Corporation)

With a general idea of what he wanted to create, he began working with people in Digital's organization design area. They drew up a set of values and norms to govern the plant. These included trust, acceptance of responsibility, openness, self-direction, flexibility, initiative, risk taking, creativity, a focus on "the big picture," employee development, team spirit, participation, a balance of work and family, simplicity, and fun. Then they worked out the physical design of the plant and the logistics of setting it in motion. From throughout the corporation, Dillingham recruited employees with different functional skills who wanted to give the idea a try. Within a year, the Enfield plant was open for business.

Today, said Dillingham, the 180-employee plant is made up of two business units; a third is on the way. Both of the units have four operating teams, each of which controls and performs every activity that goes into building a product. (There are two support groups as well—engineering and administration—that also operate according to team-management principles.) The plant runs on two shifts, and teams meet at the beginning of each shift to discuss problems and priorities, determine work schedules (which may even involve changing the number of work days per week), and assign tasks and responsibilities. "Teams have financial, materials, and personnel responsibilities," said Dillingham, "but no one has a narrow job. The team members decide who does what, because they know each other's strengths and weaknesses and respect one another's decisions."[1]

Introduction

What Is Motivation?

Motivating, in an organizational context, is the process by which a manager induces others to work to achieve organizational objectives as a means of satisfying their own personal desires. **Motivation** is the outcome of this process.

Even when employees seem to be satisfying others' goals, they do so because they believe that is the best way to achieve their own aims. Workers perform hard physical labor, supervisors accept long working hours, and executives endure great stress because they believe that these negative aspects of their work are acceptable in view of the rewards that they reap for themselves and for others who are important in their lives.

Some managers misconstrue the intensely personal nature of the motivational process. They believe that their actions as role models, company cheerleaders, goal setters, task masters, or stern disciplinarians will inspire or coerce subordinates to act in accordance with managerial expectations. In the short run, it may appear that such managerial behaviors are indeed the keys to motivation. But managers soon notice that their subordinates seem uninspired, uncommitted, and unwilling to do more than is absolutely necessary. As one jaundiced manager moaned in assessing his workers' performance, "They don't do what is expected, only what is inspected!"

What this manager and others have failed to realize is that unenthusiastic job performance is most frequently attributable to workers' lack of personal involvement. Workers want a sense of "partnership" with the company and its management. They need to understand how their personal success is tied directly to the success of the company, and they need confidence that the extra energy they voluntarily invest will eventually be reflected in the benefits they receive from the firm. And they need some of the opportunities to exercise autonomy that are offered by Digital at Enfield. This chapter explores the topic of motivation: what it comprises and how it can be managed for the mutual achievement of individual and organizational goals.

A Simple Model of Motivation

As Figure 14-1 shows, a simple model of the motivational process has just three elements: needs, goal-directed behavior, and need satisfaction. People behave in ways that they feel are most likely to satisfy their needs. These **needs** are wishes, wants, or desires for certain tangible or intangible outcomes. People need such tangible items as clothes, homes, stock portfolios, large offices, and company cars; they need such intangibles as feelings of achievement, recognition, and personal growth.

People engage in **goal-directed behavior** in an attempt to satisfy their needs. Working for a company is one kind of goal-directed behavior. Working toward a promotion in one's company and making an effort to be named an official of one's church are other types of goal-directed behavior designed to meet one's need for recognition. To earn either of these advancements, the individual has to direct considerable personal energies toward achievement of the particular organization's goals. Thus the task of a manager who must motivate workers is to provide them with opportunities to satisfy their personal needs in exchange for notable job performance. Managers have the further task of helping subordinates recognize

FIGURE 14-1
The Motivational Process

and appreciate the advantages that their job and company have to offer so that the workers' goal-directed behavior will be voluntarily channeled toward the achievement of company objectives.

The term **need satisfaction** refers to the positive feelings of relief and well-being that an individual enjoys when he or she has met a need. Getting the promotion, being named church deacon, completing a project, being thanked by a co-worker for valuable training, and receiving a pay raise for meeting assigned objectives are all typically associated with a sense of need satisfaction.

Levels of Motivation

Although researchers rarely talk about levels of motivation, practicing managers do. At the level of **satisfying behavior**, workers do the minimum that will be acceptable to management. They often seem adept at the subtle art of balancing a desire to minimize the quantity and quality of the effort they expend with the desire to stay out of trouble. Several management approaches motivate workers to perform at this functional level, and as we have already noted, employees who do so believe simply that their current job, like almost any job, requires an exchange of their time and energies for the money that they need to live. When this is the extent of their motivation, it signals a failure of management to help subordinates "connect" with the goals of the firm. Employees motivated only at this level are likely to have high rates of absenteeism and turnover and to feel little satisfaction with their jobs, managers, or companies.

Work is a much more desirable, rewarding, and satisfying part of the lives of employees who are motivated at the level of **excellence behavior**. Researchers have estimated that employees hold in reserve about 20 percent of their normal performance ability, releasing it only when they believe that their extra efforts will be rewarded. At this level, the rewards that employees seek are psychological and intangible; they reflect a broader spectrum of potential need satisfactions than are sought by less motivated co-workers. The obvious task for managers is to create opportunities for subordinates to satisfy the full spectrum of their needs on the job in exchange for excellent performance. It is with these ideas in mind that Digital Equipment undertook the team concept described in the opening case.

Theories of Motivation

This chapter focuses principally on theories of motivation. Unfortunately, the word *theory* often connotes unreal and untested notions. In the context of our discussion of motivation, the term should suggest none of these ideas. We have carefully selected the most useful and practical managerial approaches to motivation. When a theory has been shown to have weaknesses, we caution you about its shortcomings, but in general we believe that familiarity with these theories will make you a better manager.

The great strength of a theory lies in its utility as a general model for handling issues and problems. Although theories of motivation cannot prescribe how a manager should behave in any given situation, they provide guidelines on the issues that should be considered in making decisions, and they suggest what process is most likely to yield the desired results.

Theories of motivation can be divided into two categories. **Content theories** address the question of what causes motivation. Often referred to as need theories, they are concerned with identifying the reasons underlying employees' behavior. **Process theories** deal with the question of how behavior is started, directed, sustained, and stopped.

Content Theories of Motivation

There are three major content theories of motivation: Abraham Maslow's hierarchy of needs, the two-factor theory of Frederick Herzberg, and the achievement motivation theory of David McClelland. Though the details of these theories differ, all three approaches can help managers develop better working environments for their subordinates by making available as compensation the specific types of rewards that their employees seek. And taken together, these models of motivation provide practical guidelines for improving managers' efforts to motivate employees effectively.

Hierarchy of Needs

Abraham Maslow believed that all motivation occurred in response to an individual's perception of one of five basic types of needs.[2] Every person was seen as having every type of need at one time or another, but the strength of any particular need at any particular time was believed to depend on the individual's personal set of priorities, or **hierarchy of needs**. Maslow argued that five basic needs were almost always experienced in the order shown in Figure 14-2. A manager who knew the level in the hierarchy at which a subordinate was currently motivated would be able to anticipate the sorts of needs that the person would *next* be motivated to fulfill.

The five levels of needs in Maslow's hierarchy are as follows:

1. *Physiological needs.* The **physiological needs** consist of basic and essentially unlearned, primary needs. Sometimes called the biological needs in the modern work environment, they include the desire for pay, vacations, pension plans, break periods, comfortable working environments, heating, lighting, and air conditioning.

2. *Safety needs.* Once the physiological needs are met, safety needs, or security needs, come to the fore. **Safety needs** reflect a desire to preserve the rewards already achieved and to protect oneself from danger, harm, threat, injury, loss, or deprivation. In organizations, these needs are seen in the employee's desire for job security, seniority systems, unions, safe working conditions, fringe benefits, insurance and retirement benefits, savings and thrift plans, and severance pay.

3. *Social needs.* Once the satisfaction of his or her physiological and safety needs is secured, the individual's attention turns to a desire for companionship, love, and belonging. As "social animals," people like to be liked, and they pursue the satisfaction of **social needs** on the job by supporting formal and informal work groups, cooperating with co-workers, and taking part in company-sponsored activities.

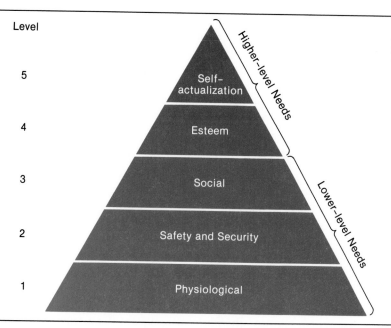

Level

5   Self-actualization

4   Esteem

3   Social

2   Safety and Security

1   Physiological

Higher-level Needs

Lower-level Needs

FIGURE 14-2
Maslow's Hierarchy of Needs

4. *Esteem needs.* At the fourth level of the hierarchy are an individual's **esteem needs**, or ego needs. These needs take two different forms. The first is the need for self-esteem—that is, satisfaction with oneself. Self-esteem is tied to feelings of achievement, competence, knowledge, maturity, and independence. The second is the need to be held in esteem by others. This need revolves around personal reputation, recognition, peer-group status, and appreciation. In an organization, rewards that can satisfy people's needs for esteem include titles, recognition, praise, status symbols, responsibility, and promotions.

5. *Self-actualization needs.* When all four lower levels of needs are satisfied, individuals often focus on meeting the need for self-fulfillment. In doing so, they try to realize their full potential, to increase their abilities, to be creative, and to "be the best that they can be." Such **self-actualization needs** are the highest of human needs.

IMPLICATIONS OF THE HIERARCHICAL NATURE OF NEEDS

The fact that needs can be arranged in a hierarchy has several important implications for managers. First, needs at the lower levels must be satisfied first; only then can higher needs be addressed. If a manager tries to motivate an employee whose safety needs have not been met by offering a social reward, the desired goal-directed behavior will not take place.

A second important implication is that lower-level needs form a foundation on which the higher levels are built. Only when lower-level needs remain satisfied can managers hope to motivate workers via the satisfaction of higher-level needs. For example, when an employee whose lower-level needs have been satisfied suddenly faces a threat to her or his job security, that employee's attention will immediately shift to the lowest level of needs.

A third implication revolves around Maslow's notion of **prepotency**, according to which individuals are assumed to progress from motivation by needs at lower levels in the hierarchy to motivation by needs at higher levels. Thus, if a subordinate is currently motivated principally by the pursuit of safety needs (level 2), the manager can be confident that, once those safety needs are met, the person will next seek to satisfy social needs (level 3).

A fourth implication is the idea of **sufficiency**. A person almost never feels that a need is *totally* satisfied. Most people want more money, security, friends, esteem, and self-confidence, no matter how much they have achieved. Thus individuals move up the hierarchy not when a need is totally satisfied, but when it is *sufficiently* satisfied.

CRITIQUE OF MASLOW'S HIERARCHY

Maslow's hierarchy of needs has great intuitive appeal, which perhaps best explains its popularity as a way of thinking about the causes of motivation. However, from the viewpoint of managerial action, the Maslow approach presents some difficulties.[3] First of all, most of us reorder the levels of the hierarchy at some time in our lives. We may accept a first full-time job, for example, that pays less than an acceptable salary (level 1) because we believe that our performance on that job will soon provide excellent opportunities for prestigious career moves (level 4).

Second, it is extremely difficult to determine the level of needs at which an individual is currently motivated. The problem stems in part from how hard it is to distinguish between the fairly insignificant fluctuations in needs that all people experience every day (when they get hungry, for instance, or perceive the need to retreat to the curb in the face of oncoming traffic) and the more meaningful, less frequent shifts in people's needs.

A third difficulty arises in the measurement of a person's needs. Most of us have enough trouble identifying and prioritizing our own needs. Managers charged with the creation of motivating environments for many different subordinates face a complex task indeed.[4]

Finally, individuals differ in the extent to which they feel that a need has been sufficiently satisfied. Construction workers walking on steel beams fifteen stories high may feel safe enough, but most people would probably find such a job too threatening. Similarly, employees differ in the extent to which they are motivated to pursue a given amount of money, recognition, autonomy, or other need satisfiers. "Management Development Exercise 14" presents one of the best aids available for measuring individual needs. You may wish to use it now as a self-assessment tool and later, as a manager, to assess the needs of your subordinates. In either case, remember that the priorities assigned to different levels of needs change and that an individual's personal insights almost always help to improve the evaluative quality of a measurement instrument.[5]

Two-Factor Theory

Frederick Herzberg's need-based model of motivation was derived not from clinical observation, as was Maslow's, but from field research involving two hundred engineers and accountants.[6] These employees of a large paint company were asked two questions: "Can you describe, in detail, when you felt exceptionally good about your job?" and "Can you describe, in detail, when you felt exceptionally bad about your job?"

Maslow would have expected Herzberg to receive answers consistent with the five levels of the hierarchy of needs. But instead, Herzberg found in his respondents' answers two distinct sets of needs. He labeled one set **hygiene factors**, or *maintenance factors* or *dissatisfiers*. This set consisted of factors or conditions on the job that, when they were not met, operated to make employees dissatisfied. When they were met, these factors prevented dissatisfaction but did not increase either motivation or job satisfaction. The hygiene factors included company policy and administration, supervision, relationship with supervisors, work conditions, salary, relationship with peers, personal life, relationship with subordinates, status, and security (Figure 14-3). These factors had value only in the sense of being external rewards that accrued after the job was done.

The second set of factors Herzberg labeled **motivators**, or *satisfiers*. They were job conditions that, when they were met, were associated with high levels of employee motivation and job satisfaction. When these conditions were not met, both motivation and job satisfaction were prevented. The motivators included

FIGURE 14-3
Categorization of
Herzberg's Motivators
and Hygiene Factors

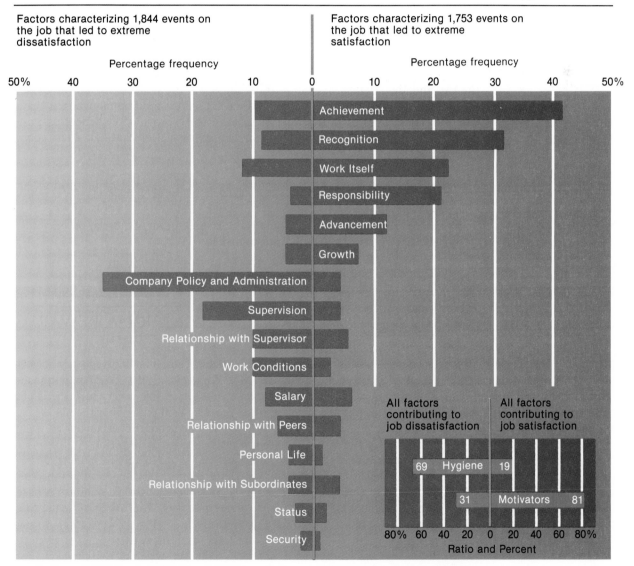

Source: Reprinted by permission of the *Harvard Business Review*. An exhibit from "One More Time: How Do You Motivate Employees?" by F. Herzberg (January–February 1968). Copyright © 1968 by the President and Fellows of Harvard College; all rights reserved.

achievement, recognition, the nature of the work itself, responsibility, advancement, and opportunities for personal growth (Figure 14-3). Note that these factors had intrinsic value. That is, they had motivational potential because the job that exhibited them had inherent worth. Reflecting back on the opening case about Digital Equipment, it is apparent that the company's motivational program was intended to take advantage of the potential of Herzberg's satisfiers. Japanese managers are often credited with taking optimal advantage of the motivational potential of Herzberg's satisfiers. "Insights for International Managers 14" provides some concrete examples of the Japanese approach.

A COMPARISON OF HERZBERG AND MASLOW

There are notable similarities between the theories of Maslow and Herzberg. Both men arranged needs in a hierarchy, and both recognized physiological, safety, social, esteem, and self-actualization needs (although Herzberg used different labels).

From a managerial viewpoint, there are also important differences between the two theories. Figure 14-4 shows that Maslow's work was based on the belief that the same factors led to satisfaction (and therefore could be motivating) that, when absent, led to dissatisfaction. Herzberg's work provided evidence that, on the contrary, there are two fairly distinct types of factors that can elicit goal-oriented behavior:

1. Hygiene factors that can be used to elicit a satisfying level of motivation, at best.

2. Motivators that can serve to stimulate an excellent level of motivation once the hygiene needs have been sufficiently satisfied.

Insights for International Managers 14

CARROTS ARE NOT GREEN—DON'T FORGET NONFINANCIAL REWARDS

Many observers say the reward that seems to work best in many places is appreciation. In Taiwan the most highly sought reward is affection and social recognition from the top. Cash bonuses are given out across the board, but departments compete for top management's public praise at the annual celebration.

Japanese companies do offer cash rewards to individuals, but payments are nominal. Matsushita Electric gave a factory worker $13 for suggesting a device to stop solder from dripping down the endplates of television sets and causing short circuits. Another worker received $100 for sixty suggestions accepted in a year. At Mitsubishi Electric, ten members of a quality circle jointly received a cash reward of $200 for suggesting the best cost-reduction idea of the year. Most companies prefer to rely on nonfinancial rewards. At some plants, rectangular cards are hung from the ceiling directly above some of the workers, showing the production count or marking the group for its excellent performance.

There are many alternatives to money: job security, vacations, parties, gifts, sports or health facilities, services, prestigious titles, and public or private praise, to mention a few. The rule is to match the reward with the values of the culture. The wrong reward can be as insulting as extra time off given to the American manager who still hasn't taken last year's vacation.

Source: From L. Copeland and L. Griggs, *Going International* (New York: Random House, 1985), p. 131.

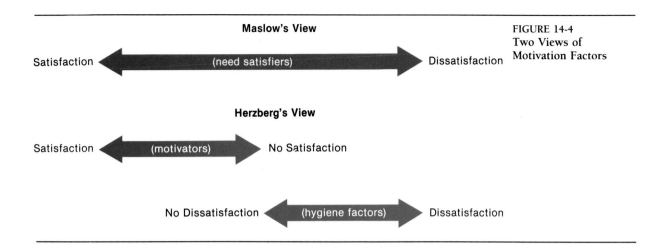

FIGURE 14-4
Two Views of
Motivation Factors

An important implication of the two-factor theory is that managers must be careful not to emphasize hygiene factors as the basis of need satisfaction when such lower-level needs are already satisfactorily met. Likewise, they should not waste the resources associated with offering motivators as incentives before hygiene needs appear to be satisfied.

HERZBERG'S FINDING ON THE MOTIVATIONAL POWER OF MONEY

Perhaps the most surprising and disconcerting discovery that Herzberg's research yielded is that money is principally a dissatisfier, or hygiene factor, not a motivator. But remember that Herzberg's research dealt with money as an established salary, not as an incentive that varied with daily performance. (Salaries are rarely altered except at predictable intervals.) Thus it is unlikely that the white-collar workers surveyed in Herzberg's research thought of money as a cause of immediate satisfaction. Blue-collar workers on a piece-rate plan, however, might! A "sufficient" amount of money might have been more readily available to Herzberg's respondents than it is to nonprofessionals.

Money *is* very important to most employees, either for its purchasing power or because of the status that it can confer. However, managers do themselves and their organizations a disservice when they treat money as an all-powerful surrogate for the wide range of need satisfiers that employees seek.

CRITIQUE OF HERZBERG'S THEORY

It must be noted that the support for Herzberg's theory is more anecdotal than research-based. In fact, much of the research that has been done to further test Herzberg's ideas has failed to confirm his findings.[7] Nevertheless, numerous companies have adopted recommendations stemming from Herzberg's research.

Nabisco, Eaton Corporation, AT&T, Texas Instruments, Procter & Gamble, IBM, the U.S. Air Force, and American Airlines have all reported considerable success in their efforts to motivate employees by applying the two-factor theory. Specifically, they have followed Herzberg's recommendation to develop job enrichment programs (see Chapter 10). In these programs, employees' jobs are redesigned, expanded, and upgraded in scope, challenge, and responsibility. At one production plant, for example, janitors' jobs were enriched when they were permitted to handle all housekeeping problems themselves. The new responsibilities included making personal work assignments, interviewing jobbers and ordering cleaning supplies, and responding to all complaints about their work. Not only did the janitors' motivation levels improve with their increased feelings of responsibility and status, but their absenteeism and turnover rates also declined, perhaps because they enjoyed the most rewarding janitorial jobs locally available.

Managers might also peruse an *Industry Week* study reported by pollsters Daniel Yankelovich and John Immevwahr for more information about how to motivate employees. As shown in Figure 14-5, the results lend moderate support to Herzberg's distinction between motivators and hygiene factors or satisfiers. Note especially that the survey respondents felt that those conditions that best motivated and those that best satisfied were essentially different.

FIGURE 14-5
Employee Ratings of Potential Motivators and Satisfiers

	Motivators	Satisfiers	
	WOULD CAUSE ME TO WORK HARDER	MAKES JOB MORE AGREEABLE	BOTH
Factors That Enhance Productiveness			
Good chance for advancement	48%	22%	19%
Good pay	45	27	22
Pay tied to performance	43	31	16
Recognition for good work	41	34	17
Job enabling me to develop abilities	40	27	20
Challenging job	38	30	15
Job allowing me to think for myself	37	33	17
Great deal of responsibility	36	28	14
Interesting work	36	35	18
Job requiring creativity	35	31	20
Factors That Make Job More Agreeable			
Good fringe benefits	27%	45%	18%
Fair treatment in workload	24	45	18
Being informed about what goes on	21	49	16
Flexible work pace	20	49	12
Getting along well with my supervisor	19	52	12
Working with people I like	17	54	13
A job without too much rush and stress	15	61	13
Workplace free from dirt, noise, and pollution	12	56	12
Convenient location	12	56	12

Source: D. Yankelovich and J. Immevwahr, "Let's Put the Work Ethic to Work," *Industry Week,* September 5, 1983, p. 35. Reprinted with permission from *Industry Week,* September 5, 1983. Copyright, Penton/IPC., Cleveland, Ohio.

Guidelines for Management Practice

Managers who want to develop job enrichment programs should remember six elements that are essential to their success:[8]

1. People need frequent feedback on their performance results.

2. They need opportunities for psychological growth.

3. They need to be able to schedule their own work.

4. They need to be responsible for some job costs.

5. They need to be able to enjoy open communication with superiors at many levels of management.

6. They must be held accountable for productivity over which they have control.

Achievement Motivation

In a theory that he and his colleagues have been developing for decades, David McClelland argues that organizations offer individuals opportunities to satisfy three higher-level needs: the need for achievement, the need for power, and the need for affiliation. His most widely reported findings are that the need for achievement is positively associated with managerial performance and success and that a need for achievement can be developed in aspiring managers.[9]

NEED FOR ACHIEVEMENT

The **need for achievement** lies on Maslow's hierarchy between esteem and self-actualization needs. Individuals who exhibit high achievement orientations are characterized by moderately high levels of risk taking, a desire for concrete feedback on their performance, a desire for problem-solving responsibility, and a tendency to set moderate goals. They also tend to possess strong organizational and planning skills.

　　Managers who want to understand, manage, and create a motivating environment for subordinates with high achievement needs should know that they derive satisfaction principally from the process of initiating, conducting, and completing a job—and less from the rewards that *follow* a job well done.[10]

NEED FOR POWER

Like the need for achievement, the **need for power** lies between the needs for esteem and self-actualization on Maslow's hierarchy. This need is an expression of an individual's desire to control and influence others. Seen as a positive attribute, as McClelland intended, the need for power is closely related to the desire to assume a position of leadership.

　　McClelland believes that there are several stages in the development of an individual's idea of the purpose of power and that managers can be trained to reject the view that one should not try to influence others. Rather, an effective leader and manager is selfless, altruistic, personally committed to the goals of the organization, and concerned with developing a strong sense of company loyalty among subordinates. He or she exhibits low affiliation needs and high self-control.

NEED FOR AFFILIATION

McClelland's **need for affiliation** is essentially identical to Maslow's. It reflects the desire to have close, cooperative, and friendly relations with others. Individuals with high affiliation needs most often succeed in jobs that require high levels of social interaction—jobs wherein interpersonal relationships are especially critical to performance.

RESEARCH RESULTS

Though individuals throughout the organization probably experience some need for achievement, for power, and for affiliation, McClelland has used the results of his research to identify three types of managers:

1. *Institutional managers* have greater needs for power than for affiliation and exhibit high levels of self-control.

2. *Personal-power managers* have greater needs for power than for affiliation but are more open and socially interactive than institutional managers.

3. *Affiliation managers* have greater needs for affiliation than for power and are also open and socially interactive.

Research suggests that personal-power managers and institutional managers have more productive departments than affiliation managers, principally because of their greater need for power.[11]

McClelland's work has shown that the need for achievement can be developed in managers and that the probable outcome is improved managerial and organizational performance. Organization development that stresses competitive methods for achieving task goals and the importance of goal achievement has been found to increase managers' goal-oriented behavior.[12]

Managers need to give and to be given difficult but achievable goals and tasks that they can see through to completion. Finally, although high-achievement–oriented individuals appear most likely to be high achievers as well, organizations can benefit from a combination of all three of the types of managers McClelland described.

A comparison of the three leading content theories is given in Figure 14-6. It shows that the theories are comfortingly similar. It is true that McClelland chose to address only the higher-level needs and that the focus of the authors' analyses differed (Maslow was concerned with general life needs, whereas Herzberg and McClelland were specifically concerned with motivation on the job). Even so, the theories support many of the same recommendations.

One group of managers who share an appreciation of the content approach to motivating subordinates are those at the St. Regis Grocery Bag Plant. See "In Practice 14-1" for a description of how they implement their ideas.

Process Theories of Motivation

Process theories of motivation try to explain how goal-oriented behavior is started, directed, sustained, and stopped. Regardless of how the content of motivation is classified, supervisors need to understand how to manage it, in themselves and others. There are four major process theories of motivation: the expectancy theory

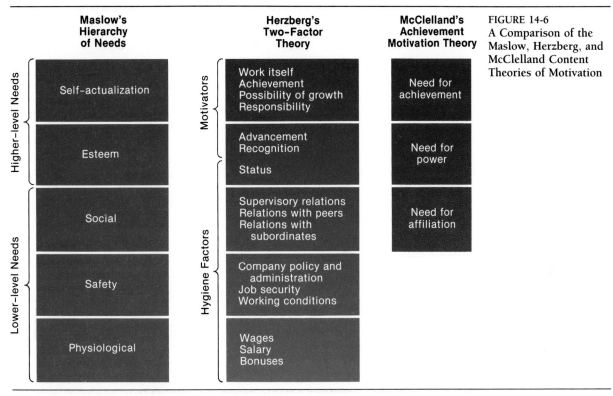

FIGURE 14-6
A Comparison of the Maslow, Herzberg, and McClelland Content Theories of Motivation

Maslow's Hierarchy of Needs

Higher-level Needs
- Self-actualization
- Esteem

Lower-level Needs
- Social
- Safety
- Physiological

Herzberg's Two-Factor Theory

Motivators
- Work itself
  Achievement
  Possibility of growth
  Responsibility
- Advancement
  Recognition
- Status

Hygiene Factors
- Supervisory relations
  Relations with peers
  Relations with subordinates
- Company policy and administration
  Job security
  Working conditions
- Wages
  Salary
  Bonuses

McClelland's Achievement Motivation Theory
- Need for achievement
- Need for power
- Need for affiliation

In Practice 14-1

ST. REGIS GROCERY BAG PLANT

Masterpieces by Van Gogh, Cézanne, and Picasso adorn not only the walls of the Louvre, the Tate Gallery, and New York's Metropolitan Museum but also the walls of the St. Regis Grocery Bag Plant in Vernon, California.

To satisfy workers complaining about the shoddy appearance of the manufacturing department, production supervisor Ray Young decided to expose them to some of the world's finest art. Twenty-five employees volunteered to help him recreate these masterpieces on the factory walls on their own time. Young and his volunteer artists selected the paintings to be duplicated, then presented the idea to management. When the proposal was approved, their creative endeavor began.

A grid pattern was drawn on a print of the artwork, which was then flashed onto a wall from a projector placed on a forklift. Seated on a second forklift against the wall, a volunteer then began to sketch the image. Painting the mural started after necessary adjustments were made and the proper paints mixed. It took an average of two to three months to complete a reproduction in either of two formats: 5 × 7 feet or 12 × 14 feet.

A company spokesperson says the project has improved workers' productivity and morale by making them more pleased with their surroundings. "Management can see improvements in general housekeeping on the plant floor," she says. "The workers care about how it works."

Seven "originals" have been completed thus far, including Picasso's *Man in a Straw Hat,* Cézanne's *Still Life with Basket of Apples,* Van Gogh's *Sunflowers,* and Modigliani's *Portrait of a Young Girl.* Currently the group is working on a Monet and a Toulouse-Lautrec.

of Victor Vroom, the extended expectancy model of Lyman Porter and Edward Lawler, the equity theory of J. Stacy Adams, and reinforcement theory, popularized by B. F. Skinner.

Expectancy Theory

Most modern process theories of motivation are built on Victor Vroom's view of motivation as a process that governs individual choice. He believed that people are in a nearly constant state of motivation. Thus, to Vroom, the key to being a successful manager is to show subordinates how focusing their efforts on the achievement of organizational goals will lead to the greatest achievement of their personal goals. According to Vroom's **expectancy theory**, subordinates are most productive when they believe there is a high probability that the following three relationships will hold:[13]

1. Their efforts will lead to high levels of productivity; this belief is called *effort-performance expectancies*.

2. Their high levels of productivity will result in desired outcomes; this belief is called *performance-outcome expectancies*.

3. The desired outcomes will, in fact, satisfy their deepest needs; this effect is called *instrumentality*.

EFFORT-PERFORMANCE EXPECTANCIES

When an individual asks, "To what degree can I expect my efforts to result in the quantity and quality of performance that my manager desires?" the answer is expressed in terms of an **effort-performance expectancy**. The greater the expectancy that one's effort will produce the desired performance, the greater the probability that one will perform a particular task. For example, say an employee has the option of accepting either of two promotions. Given that the jobs are equal in all other ways, expectancy theory argues that the employee will choose the job at which he or she feels there is the greatest likelihood of success.

PERFORMANCE-OUTCOME EXPECTANCIES

Once employees have assessed the probability that they can do the job successfully, they ask themselves (often subconsciously) the following question: "If I perform the job as desired, to what degree can I expect to receive the outcome or reward that I desire?" Uncertainty is always involved when workers must rely on others to deliver promised rewards. The higher the subjective probability in the workers' minds that the manager can and will deliver the rewards promised, the greater the likelihood that the workers will pursue the task requested by the manager. In the expectancy model, this probability is called the **performance-outcome expectancy**.

Many factors play a role in determining how much confidence workers place in a manager's promise to deliver the desired outcomes. First, confidence is increased by the explicitness of the manager's promise. Managers need to learn that they must be specific in expressing their promises and in the conditions that affect them. Second, confidence is increased by the workers' knowledge that the manager actually has the power to provide, or influence the delivery of, the desired rewards. Thus managers must remember that, by their actions, they create reputations and images that should be protected or improved if they are to succeed in influencing their subordinates' choices.

INSTRUMENTALITY

Even when employees have a high degree of confidence that they can do the job the manager desires and that the manager will deliver the promised reward, they still must ask themselves perhaps the most difficult question of all: "If I get the reward that I seek, will it be instrumental in helping me to satisfy the major needs that I currently have in my life?" According to expectancy theory, the answer to this question provides a measure of instrumentality.

Instrumentality, which is a statement of probability, is a critically important notion in the study of motivation, and yet it is often slighted by managers. For example, managers often assume that the instrumentality of money is perfect (1.00) for satisfying subordinates' needs. This means that they believe that no matter what the needs of their subordinates, money will satisfy those needs. Such managers are likely to think that if employees are unhappy with their jobs or express interest in joining a union, they must want more money. Your knowledge of the wide spectrum of human needs revealed in the content theories of motivation should alert you to the fallacy of this belief.

A very real problem raised by the issue of instrumentality is that people rarely take the time to assess and evaluate their needs thoroughly. Furthermore, because money can indeed buy so many things that are in some ways need-satisfying, subordinates often mislead *themselves* into believing that money is the desired outcome. Few ideas can lead to greater frustration and dissatisfaction. Employees who derive job satisfaction only from the pay that they receive are likely to suffer from a lack of fulfillment, feelings of low self-esteem, and a sense of stagnation of intellect, skills, and abilities.

VALENCE

Maslow used the term *prepotency* to indicate the general level of needs that an individual would next seek to satisfy. But how can a manager judge which of many outcomes or rewards an employee will seek as the means of satisfying those needs? To answer this question, Vroom applied the term *valence* to the strength of the individual's preference for a particular outcome. Thus valence is a measure of value or priority. The valence of an outcome can range from highly positive (1.00) to highly negative (−1.00). Though the notion of valence is abstract, it enables people to compare their options. For example, if a job with a "Big 8" accounting firm merits a valence score of 0.90, how much is a job in a regional bank management program worth? Of course, answering this question involves considering many issues, but stating the answer in valence terms makes it easier to compare one's options.

THE EXPECTANCY THEORY MODEL

The four concepts we have just discussed form the basis of the expectancy theory model. As shown in Figure 14-7, an individual's motivational force is directed

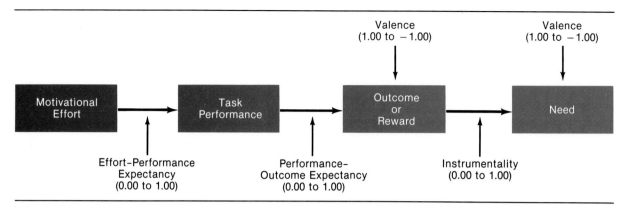

FIGURE 14-7
Expectancy Theory
Model

toward that combination of expectancies, instrumentalities, and valenced outcomes which is expected to provide the greatest overall satisfaction of needs. The
relationship shown in the model can be expressed as follows:

$$ME = (E/P\ E)(P/O\ E)(V_o)(V_n)$$

where

$$ME = \text{motivational effort}$$
$$E/P\ E = \text{effort-performance expectancy}$$
$$P/O\ E = \text{performance-outcome expectancy}$$
$$V_o = \text{valence of the outcome}$$
$$V_n = \text{valence of the need}$$

Figure 14-8 offers an example of how the model actually works. In this
example, the preferable option under conditions of rational decision making would
be path 1 (A,A,Q), because it offers the highest expected need satisfaction.

LIMITATION OF THE EXPECTANCY MODEL

Although most of the research on the use of the expectancy model has shown that
it can improve the relationship among individuals' motivation, performance, and
need satisfaction, it also seems to pose great difficulties for managers who try to
apply it directly.[14] This means that whereas the ideas behind the model are valid,
calculating all the different valences, instrumentalities, and expectancies necessary
to make a single decision is so complex and time-consuming that busy managers
cannot hope to use the model *in its mathematical form.*

Extended Expectancy Model

Psychologists Lyman Porter and Edward Lawler have developed a model of motivation that combines ideas drawn from the content theories of Maslow, Herzberg,
and McClelland with those of Vroom's process theory.[15] As shown in Figure 14-9,
their integrative approach, which we call the **extended expectancy model**, includes
consideration of the relationship between satisfaction and performance.

The numbers on the boxes in Figure 14-9 indicate the path (from 1 to 9) of
motivation and its effects. In theory, the model operates in the following manner.
The individual combines the value of the expected reward (1) with his or her

---

Guidelines for Management Practice

Although expectancy theory can be difficult to apply, the ideas on which it is based can help managers understand that individuals differ in the extent to which particular options are attractive to them.[16] It further reminds us that the process of making a decision to work toward the attainment of a particular need consists of several steps, many of which are often taken subconsciously and all of which have a very large subjective component. Vroom's expectancy theory suggests several practical guidelines for improving managerial action.

1. The process of matching subordinates' needs and organizational rewards can be systematic, though it is rarely completely rational. Subordinates should be encouraged to think their needs through and to help their managers design programs by which the organization can help see that the individual's specific requirements are met.

2. Employees often need assistance grasping the link among efforts, outcomes, and need satisfaction. They gain confidence when managers show their awareness of these links and encourage their subordinates to pursue particular courses of action.

3. Because individual subordinates differ in the needs to which they give highest priority, and consequently in the value that they place on different potential organizational rewards, managers can maximize the benefits of the rewards they have to confer by carefully matching subordinates and incentives.

4. Managers must reinforce the appropriateness of their encouragement of specific undertakings in their subordinates and must demonstrate their ability as managers consistently to deliver meaningful rewards when organizational objectives are achieved.

---

perception of the effort that will be required to achieve that reward (2). The resulting effort that is actually made (3) combines with the individual's abilities and traits (4) and perceptions of the role that he or she must perform (5) to help accomplish the desired performance (6). This performance is associated with both intrinsic (7a) and extrinsic (7b) rewards. The **intrinsic rewards** are those that are inherent in performance of the task itself, such as a sense of pride in one's accomplishments. **Extrinsic rewards** are those that are expected to be conferred by management as a direct consequence of the employee's accomplishing the desired level of performance. Note the jagged line between the boxes for performance and for extrinsic rewards. It reminds us that the "delivery" of extrinsic rewards is uncertain; receiving them depends both on the manager's evaluation of the satisfactoriness of the job performance and on the organization's willingness and ability to follow the manager's recommendation that the desired reward be given. Finally, to the extent that the combination of the two types of rewards is seen as equitable (8) by the individual, given the effort exerted, they result in the individual's overall sense of satisfaction (9). The individual later uses the results of this motivational experience in assessing the value of the rewards that she or he is likely to earn by performing well in the future.

The idea that performance leads to satisfaction is perhaps the most important contribution of Porter and Lawler's model. It contrasts sharply with some work of early behavioral scientists, particularly Herzberg, who believed that satisfaction leads to better performance—that is, that "happy employees are productive employees." Research, however, has substantially supported Porter and Lawler's idea that "productive employees are satisfied employees." This belief is now shared by most researchers and practicing managers.[17]

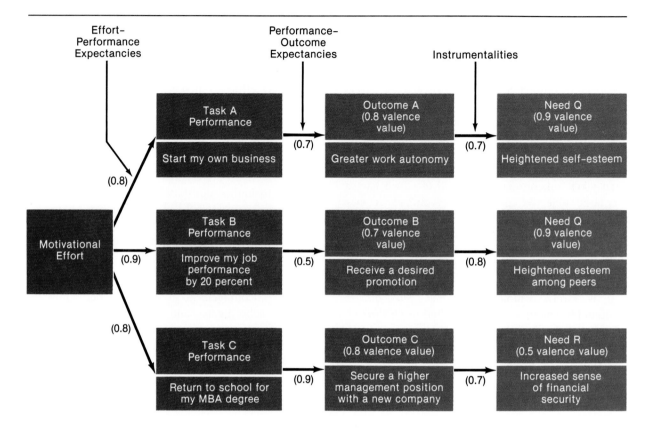

PATH 1 (A,A,Q) = (0.8)(0.7)(0.8)(0.7)(0.9) = .2822 (Preferable Option)
PATH 2 (B,B,Q) = (0.9)(0.5)(0.7)(0.8)(0.9) = .2268
PATH 3 (C,C,R) = (0.8)(0.9)(0.8)(0.7)(0.5) = .2016

FIGURE 14-8
Example of the Operation of the Expectancy Theory Model

The extended expectancy model of Porter and Lawler gives managers even more motivational elements to consider than the Vroom model did, yet it is no less subjective or difficult to put into practice. Still, important benefits accrue to managers who ponder this model in trying to understand and increase their employees' motivational levels. Essentially, they can feel that they have been very thorough in tackling the problem. Managers who use these models as frameworks for analysis are less likely than their counterparts to overlook a critical element in their subordinates' decision making.

Equity Theory

A third prominent process approach to motivation is **equity theory**, as popularized by J. Stacy Adams.[18] It addresses the issue of whether a person believes that he or she is being fairly treated compared to the treatment of others who are in a similar situation. This theory is based on the belief that in determining the focus of their goal-directed behavior, employees make two fundamental *evaluations*:

1. "What am I giving to the organization?" Inputs that are considered include effort, experience, education, skill, and training.

2. "What outcomes will I receive—especially in comparison with the outcomes enjoyed by other employees who perform similar tasks in the organization?"

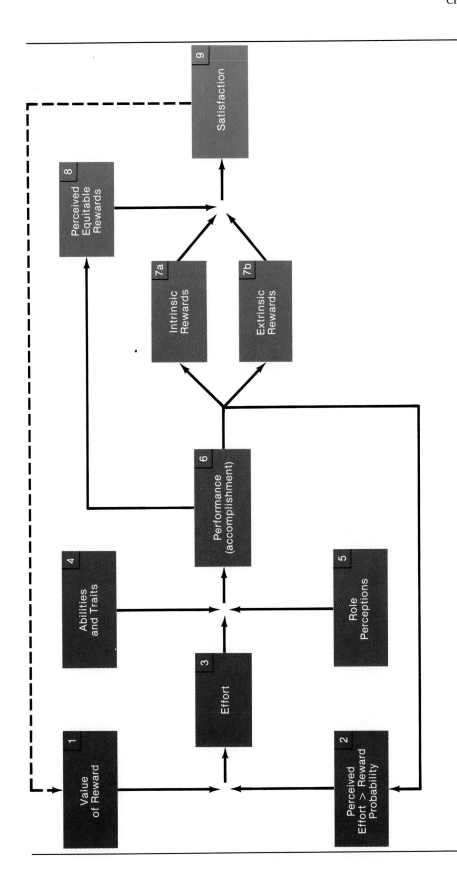

Source: L. W. Porter and E. E. Lawler, III, *Managerial Attitudes and Performance,* Richard D. Irwin, Inc., © 1968, p. 165.

FIGURE 14-9
Porter and Lawler's Extended Expectancy Model

Outcomes that are considered include such rewards as pay, fringe benefits, bonuses, working conditions, and status indicators.

In making these two evaluations, individuals create mental *ratios* to assess the equity inherent in their work situations. The individual feels that equity exists when she or he judges these two relationships between inputs and outcomes to be mathematically equal in value:

$$\frac{\text{Personal outcomes}}{\text{Personal inputs}} = \frac{\text{Others' outcomes}}{\text{Others' inputs}}$$

When inputs exceed outcomes, the person feels dissatisfied, angry, or unappreciated. When outcomes exceed inputs, the person feels a sense of guilt at having "cheated" his or her employer.[19] Supporters of equity theory believe that either of the two negative feelings affects motivation and induces the individual to behave in such a way as to establish a sense of equity.[20] Such behaviors include working less hard to overcome feelings of being undercompensated or working harder to overcome guilt. Other workers who perceive inequity may attempt to change the work behaviors of their *fellow employees* in order to restore equity. Finally, employees may simply change their perceptions of the relative values of the inputs and outcomes, either through a conscious reevaluation of their initial assessments or through such mental defense mechanisms as rationalization. Therefore, managers who believe that less deserving peers received higher annual raises might work harder to be more certain of raises in the next review, might work less

Guidelines for Management Practice

Equity theory is perhaps the easiest of the motivational models to comprehend, and it is one of the most powerful in helping managers understand the motivations of their subordinates. The old saying "Fool me once, shame on you. Fool me twice, shame on me!" applies especially well to employee-manager relationships. Having studied this chapter, you know that a critical element in any motivational process is the manager's ability to offer and deliver the rewards that subordinates deserve in exchange for their performing behaviors directed at the achievement of organizational goals. Keeping faith with those commitments to all, and in so doing helping to ensure the equity of everyone's performance/reward ratios, is essential. Even if the inequitable treatment of employees is unintentional, subordinates rarely allow a manager to "fool them twice."

Some key points for managers to remember about equity theory follow.

1. Employees' attitude and performance problems arise from their feelings of having been inequitably treated.

2. Because it is so hard to tell how their subordinates perceive the relationship between what they are putting into their job and what they are getting out of it, managers must systematically monitor their employees' sense of being equitably treated.

3. Managers' standards for measuring subordinates' inputs and for determining the appropriate level of their rewards should be announced, before work is undertaken, in as explicit a form as possible.

4. Employees are principally concerned with the relative—not the absolute—level of their rewards. Managers can use this fact to their advantage even when only small amounts of resources are available to reward behavior just by carefully allotting marginally greater amounts to outstanding performers.

because to do otherwise would be to be paid less than they deserved, might harass the better paid peer for being "rate busters," or might reassess the equity of the raise decisions.

Reinforcement Theory

B. F. Skinner is a behavioral psychologist whose theories of behavior have been applied to the motivation of employees. According to Skinner, people are *conditioned* by the outcomes of their past responses to similar situations.[21] Skinner's reinforcement theory is offensive to some people, because it implies that an employee's future behavior is largely predetermined, thus contradicting the belief in free choice.

Skinner's position, however, is that employees learn from prior work experience to perform tasks that lead to desirable outcomes and to avoid tasks that lead to undesirable outcomes. Such firms as Procter & Gamble, Michigan Bell, GE, Chick-fil-A, Standard Oil, Emery Air Freight, and many other organizations have undertaken to change employees' behavior by the systematic application of reinforcement theory.[22]

Reinforcement theory is based on a simple four-step model:[23]

Stimulus → Behavior → Consequences → Future Behavior

In this model, an employee's voluntary response (behavior) to a particular situation or event (stimulus) is the cause of specific outcomes (consequences). If the outcomes are positive, the employee will tend to repeat the behavior in similar future situations. If they are negative, the employee will avoid the stimulus or act differently in the future.

The key to applying the reinforcement model is to understand the need to manage the consequences of subordinates' behavior. A manager has four options:

1. In **positive reinforcement**, the manager encourages a specific behavior by providing desirable consequences when the employee behaves in a desirable manner. For example, college textbook publishing companies typically lease cars for the use of their sales representatives. Often, the model of the car and the extent of its option package are determined by the salesperson's previous-year sales. The desired consequence (a better-equipped, more appealing car) is used to encourage desired behavior—in this case, higher sales.

2. **Negative reinforcement**, sometimes called avoidance learning, also involves the encouragement of a specific behavior—but this time via the removal or elimination of an outcome that the individual feels is undesirable. By this means, employees are guided to behave in certain ways in order to avoid undesirable consequences. For example, because most subordinates dislike being closely watched, a manager who gives high-performing workers greater autonomy is reinforcing their improved productivity.

3. In **extinction**, the manager tries to weaken a particular behavior by failing to provide a desired outcome or even by ignoring the behavior altogether. For example, say a supervisor expects a bonus because his or her group improved its productivity. When she or he is not given that raise because greatly increased levels of defective items resulted, the future probability of that manager's going for productivity at any cost is decreased.

4. **Punishment** is an attempt to weaken and discourage a specific behavior by providing an undesirable consequence. For example, a manager who suspends a subordinate for two working days without pay as a punishment for violating rules against taking company equipment from the workplace is attempting to dissuade the subordinate from repeating the act.

USING REINFORCEMENT THEORY

Reinforcement theory has been attacked on several grounds. Some believe that it is too rigid and ignores social processes. Others say that it is too simplistic and ignores individual differences. Still others feel that it is potentially manipulative and that it insults employees by assuming that they will overemphasize external rewards and overlook intrinsic satisfactions.[24] Nevertheless, in most of its popularized forms, reinforcement theory has proved desirable to employees and productive for the organization.[25]

Perhaps the best set of guidelines on reinforcement theory available to managers comes from W. Clay Hamner. These guidelines are shown in Figure 14-10.

Money as a Motivator

Because many people see money as the principal reward with the power to stimulate goal-oriented behavior, it seems deserving of special attention. This is particularly true because the only motivational theorist to have considered money directly was Herzberg—and he concluded that money at best merely prevented dissatisfaction and was not a motivator to excellence in performance. How can Herzberg be right, when most people seem to feel that even they themselves are motivated largely by money?

The key to understanding this paradox is to remember that money has no intrinsic value. If others would not accept our money as a medium of exchange or did not covet it because of what it is or what it represents, our money would have little value to us. Virtually everyone knows this; certainly, Herzberg did. So what did his interview respondents mean when they indicated that money was not a principal motivator? We believe that they were reporting that they much preferred directly receiving the satisfaction of needs rather than having to accept

Guideline	Comment
1. Don't reward all individuals equally.	To be effective behavior reinforcers, rewards should be based on performance. Rewarding everyone equally in effect reinforces poor or average performance and ignores high performance.
2. Failure to respond can also modify behavior.	Managers influence their subordinates by what they do not do as well as by what they do. For example, failing to praise deserving subordinates may cause them to perform poorly the next time.
3. Tell individuals what they can do to receive reinforcement.	Setting performance standards lets individuals know what they should do to be rewarded; they can then adjust their work patterns to get these rewards.
4. Tell individuals what they are doing wrong.	If managers withhold rewards from subordinates without indicating why they are not being rewarded, the subordinates may become confused about what behaviors the manager finds undesirable. The subordinates may also feel that they are being manipulated.
5. Do not punish in front of others.	Reprimanding subordinates might sometimes be a useful way of eliminating an undesirable behavior. Public reprimand, however, humiliates subordinates and may cause all members of the work group to resent the manager.
6. Be fair.	The consequences of a behavior should be appropriate for the behavior. Subordinates should be given the rewards they deserve. Both failing to reward subordinates properly and overrewarding those who are not deserving reduce the reinforcing effect of rewards.

Source: Adapted from W. C. Hamner, "Reinforcement Theory and Contingency Management in Organizational Settings," in H. L. Tosi and W. C. Hamner, eds., *Organizational Behavior and Management: A Contingency Approach,* rev. ed. (New York: Wiley, 1977), pp. 93–112.

FIGURE 14-10
Guidelines for the Use of Reinforcement Theory

only money, which it might *or might not* be possible to "exchange" for genuine satisfaction of their needs.

Consider the person who seeks peer-group recognition. Would such a person rather have a chance to prove his or her ability on a group project or receive a $.25 an hour pay raise that co-workers might interpret as a reason to hold the person in higher esteem? Herzberg's respondents were more often motivated by the chance to prove themselves, but to us that does not indicate that money would not have motivated excellence in performance under different circumstances. If an employee wants to buy a new car, the extra money that could be earned by working overtime might keep that worker's motivational level high through many weeks of sixteen-hour days!

■■■■■■■■■■■ *Guidelines for Management Practice* ■■■■■■■■■■■

The effective manager should keep in mind the following key points about money as a motivator:

1. The desire for money does motivate—at particular times—almost every individual.[26]

2. Money is not sought as an end in itself but rather as an indicator of some positive personal attribute.

3. Relative levels of money typically matter far more to individuals than do absolute amounts.

4. There are many needs for which money is an inadequate or inefficient source of satisfaction. In such cases, managers should seek more direct ways of satisfying needs.

Review of the Learning Objectives

Having studied this chapter, you should be able to respond to the learning objectives with extensions of the following brief answers:

1. **Explain the motivational process and describe the manager's role in developing a motivated work force.**

   The motivational process consists of three basic elements: an individual's perception of an unsatisfied need, goal-directed behavior intended to satisfy that need, and need satisfaction that reinforces the appropriateness of the person's choice of behaviors. For managers to have motivated subordinates, they must create a work environment in which their employees can understand how the achievement of organizational goals will simultaneously satisfy a full range of their personal needs.

2. **Compare and contrast the three leading content approaches to motivation, and explain how they can best be implemented by managers.**

   As best shown in Figure 14-6, the theories of Maslow, Herzberg, and McClelland all address the question of what causes motivation. The hierarchy of needs and the two-factor theory present means of classifying a full range of human needs, whereas achievement motivation theory intentionally focuses only on the higher level, the more intrinsic bases of need satisfaction. In all three cases, the key to successful implementation is for the manager to recognize that preferred rewards vary widely among employees and to be flexible in rewarding desired performance.

3. **Evaluate the relative strengths of the four most prominent process approaches to motivation in terms of their application by managers to typical work situations.**

   Expectancy theory and the extended expectancy model receive high ratings for thoroughness in the elements and relationships that they incorporate. However, they deserve only low ratings for practicality—the degree to which they can be applied in everyday work situations—because of the high levels of subjectivity and complexity involved. In contrast, the somewhat less complex equity theory and reinforcement theory are easier to understand and to communicate. Although both these models of motivation also demand a high degree of subjective evaluation by managers, practical guidelines have been developed to assist managers in their application (see, for example, Figure 14-10).

4. **Describe the relationship between job performance and job satisfaction.**

   Thanks to research results supporting the extended expectancy model, managers can now be confident that performance leads to satisfaction, not the reverse. Consequently, managers can best ensure a highly motivated work force by helping to provide employees with the resources, work environment, and incentives they need to perform well in their tasks. A desired by-product of the resulting high performance is almost certain to be high employee satisfaction.

5. **Explain the potential of money as a motivator.**

Money is a desired and pursued outcome whenever employees believe that receiving money will enhance their ability to achieve satisfaction of their needs. However, managers must be aware that money is often weakly linked to ultimate need satisfaction, especially for higher-level needs. In such cases, managers must work either to demonstrate how money can be more effectively used in satisfying needs or to provide alternative nonmonetary rewards.

Key Terms and Concepts

After completing your study of Chapter 14, "Motivating," you should be able to explain the following important terms and concepts.

motivation	safety needs	need for	instrumentality	positive
needs	social needs	achievement	extended	reinforcement
goal-directed	esteem needs	need for power	expectancy	negative
behavior	self-actualization	need for affiliation	model	reinforcement
need satisfaction	needs	expectancy theory	intrinsic rewards	extinction
satisfying behavior	prepotency	effort-performance	extrinsic rewards	punishment
excellence behavior	sufficiency	expectancy	equity theory	
hierarchy of needs	hygiene factors	performance-outcome	reinforcement	
physiological needs	motivators	expectancy	theory	

Questions for Discussion

1. In what situations might a manager effectively motivate by behaving as a role model, "company cheerleader," or stern disciplinarian for subordinates?

2. Under what circumstances have you seen people behave at what appeared to be an "excellence level"? Could you bring about these or similar circumstances in a managerial position that you would like to have?

3. How do union organizers benefit from an understanding of Maslow's hierarchy?

4. Prepare a list of ten low-cost or no-cost incentives that a manager could use as motivators.

5. What finding most surprised you about the results of Herzberg's research (see Figure 14-3)? Do such counterintuitive results strengthen your belief in the value of academic research?

6. How would you interpret Herzberg's finding on the motivational power of money? Under what circumstances do you plan to use money as a motivator for your subordinates?

7. Can you think of any serious negative aspects of introducing a job enrichment program? Hint: If there are none, then why do so few firms try job enrichment?

8. Using McClelland's terminology, explain what kind of manager you are likely to be. What, then, will probably be your strengths and weaknesses as a manager?

9. How could you productively use expectancy theory as a manager?

10. Describe how Vroom integrated the work of Maslow and Herzberg into the expectancy theory model.

11. Can you explain why Porter and Lawler might believe that intrinsic rewards directly follow successful completion of a task, whereas extrinsic rewards might not?

12. In what ways are equity theory and expectancy theory compatible?

13. Can you think of a time when someone successfully used a form of reinforcement theory on you? Did you find the experience dehumanizing or insulting? Explain.

Notes

1. Adapted, by permission of the publisher, from B. Solomon, "A Plant That Proves That Team Management Works," *Personnel* 62, no. 6 (June 1985): 6–8. Copyright © 1985 American Management Association, New York. All rights reserved.
2. A. Maslow, "A Theory of Human Needs," *Psychological Review,* 1943, pp. 370–396; and A. Maslow, *Motivation and Personality* (New York: Harper & Row, 1954).
3. J. B. Miner, *Theories of Organizational Behavior* (Hinsdale, Ill.: Dryden, 1980), pp. 18–43; and E. Locke, "The Nature and Causes of Job Satisfaction," in M. Dunnette, ed., *Handbook of Industrial and Organizational Psychology,* (Chicago: Rand McNally, 1976), pp. 1297–1349.
4. E. Betz, "Two Tests of Maslow's Theory of Need Fulfillment," *Journal of Vocational Behavior,* April 1984, pp. 204–220.
5. H. Schwartz, "Maslow and the Hierarchical Enactment of Organizational Reality," *Human Relations,* October 1983, pp. 933–956.
6. F. Herzberg, B. Mausner, and B. Snyderman, *The Motivation to Work* (New York: Wiley, 1959); and F. Herzberg, *Work and the Nature of Man* (Cleveland, Ohio: World, 1966).
7. D. Schwab, H. DeVitt, and L. Cummings, "A Test of the Adequacy of the Two-Factor Theory as a Predictor of Self-Report Performance Effects," *Personnel Psychology,* Summer 1971, pp. 293–303; M. Dunnette, J. Campbell, and M. Hakel, "Factors Contributing to Job Satisfaction and Job Dissatisfaction in Six Occupational Groups," *Organizational Behavior and Human Performance,* May 1967, pp. 143–174; and C. Hulin and P. Smith, "An Empirical Investigation of Two Implications of the Two-Factor Theory of Job Satisfaction," *Journal of Applied Psychology,* October 1967, pp. 396–402.
8. F. Herzberg, "Orthodox Job Enrichment: A Common-Sense Approach to People at Work," *Defense Management Journal,* April 1977, pp. 21–27.
9. D. McClelland, *The Achieving Society* (Princeton, N.J.: Van Nostrand, 1961); and D. McClelland, "Business Drive and National Achievement," *Harvard Business Review,* July–August 1962, pp. 99–112.
10. J. Nicholls, "Achievement Motivation: Conceptions of Ability, Subjective Experience, Task Choice, and Experience," *Psychological Review,* July 1984, pp. 328–346.
11. D. McClelland and D. Burnham, "Power Is the Great Motivator," *Harvard Business Review,* March 1976, pp. 100–110.
12. D. McClelland, "Toward a Theory of Motive Acquisition," *American Psychologist,* May 1965, pp. 321–333.
13. V. Vroom, *Work and Motivation* (New York: Wiley, 1964).
14. L. Reinharth and M. Wahba, "Expectancy Theory as a Predictor of Work Motivation, Effort Expenditure, and Job Performance," *Academy of Management Journal* 18, no. 3 (1975): 520–533; T. Connolly, "Some Conceptual and Methodological Issues in Expectancy Models of Work Performance Motivation," *Academy of Management Review* 1, no. 4 (1976): 37–47; and H. Sims, A. Szilagyi, and D. McKemey, "Antecedents of Work Related Expectancies," *Academy of Management Journal* 19, no. 4 (1976): 547–559.
15. L. Porter and E. Lawler, *Managerial Attitudes and Performance* (Homewood, Ill.: Irwin, 1968.)
16. T. Mitchell, "Expectancy Models of Job Satisfaction, Occupational Preference, and Effort: A Theoretical, Methodological, and Empirical Appraisal," *Psychological Bulletin* 18, no. 12 (1974): 1053–1077.
17. See, for example, D. G. Kuhn, J. W. Slocum, and R. B. Chase, "Does Job Performance Affect Employee Satisfaction?" *Personnel Journal,* June 1971, pp. 455–459; J. R. Schuster, B. Clark, and M. Rogers, "Testing Portions of the Porter and Lawler Model Regarding the Motivational Role of Pay," *Journal of Applied Psychology,* June 1971, pp. 187–195; J. B. Miner, *Theories of Organizational Behavior* pp. 160–161; and R. S. Bhagat, "Conditions under Which Stronger Job Performance–Job Satisfaction Relationships May Be Observed: A Closer Look at Two Situational Contingencies," *Academy of Management Journal,* December 1982, pp. 772–789.
18. J. S. Adams, "Inequity in Social Exchange," in L. Berkowitz, ed., *Advances in Experimental Social Psychology,* vol. 2 (New York: Academic Press, 1965), pp. 267–299.
19. R. Vecchio, "Predicting Worker Performance in Inequitable Settings," *Academy of Management Review,* January 1982, pp. 103–110.
20. R. Cosier and D. Dalton, "Equity Theory and Time: A Reformulation," *Academy of Management Review,* April 1983, pp. 311–319; M. Carrell and J. Dittrich, "Equity Theory: The Recent Literature, Methodological Considerations, and New Directions," *Academy of Management Review,* April 1978, pp. 202–210; and R. J. Mowday, "Equity Theory Predictions of Behavior in Organizations," in R. M. Steers and L. W. Porter, ed., *Motivation and Work Behavior* (New York: McGraw-Hill, 1979).
21. B. F. Skinner, *Science and Human Behavior* (New York: Free Press, 1953).
22. "Where Skinner's Theories Work," *Business Week,* December 2, 1972, pp. 64–65; and "New Tool: Reinforcement for Good Work," *Psychology Today,* April 1972, pp. 68–69.

23. B. F. Skinner, *Contingencies of Reinforcement* (New York: Appleton-Century-Crofts, 1969).
24. F. Luthans and P. Smith, "Organizational Behavior Modification," in B. Karmel, ed., *Point and Counterpoint* (Hinsdale, Ill.: Dryden, 1980), pp. 45–93.
25. D. Cherrington, H. Reitz, and W. Scott, "Effects of Contingent and Noncontingent Reward on the Relationship Between Satisfaction and Performance," *Journal of Applied Psychology* 55, no. 6 (1971): 531–536; J. Fossum, "The Effects of Positively and Negatively Contingent Rewards and Individual Differences on Performance, Satisfaction, and Expectation," *Academy of Management Journal* 22, no. 3 (1979): 577–589; and F. Luthans and M. Martinko, "An Organizational Behavior Modification Analysis of Absenteeism," *Human Resource Management* 15, no. 3 (Fall 1976): 11–18.
26. R. Denzler, "People and Productivity: Do They Still Equal Pay and Profits?" *Personnel Journal,* January 1974, pp. 59–63; and E. Lawler, III, *Pay and Organizational Effectiveness* (New York: McGraw-Hill, 1971).

Cohesion Incident 14-1
Get Me to the Bar on Time

Although it is against Journey's End policy for any employee to drink while on duty, Charles generally goes by the lounge each night to talk with Miles Allen, the bartender, and to see how things are going in there.

Miles started with Journey's End in Graniteville the night they opened three years ago and has enjoyed working with Roger. Miles is also well liked by the waitresses he supervises, and the lounge is frequented by the local citizens of Graniteville as well as by motel guests. Charles enjoys talking with Miles, catching up on the latest news, and discussing sports.

Knowing that Miles spends a lot of time listening to other people's problems, Charles kiddingly said to Miles one night,"Do you ever feel like going to another bar or lounge and spilling all your problems to someone else?"

"Charles, now that you mention it, there is one problem that perhaps you can help me with. It has to do with getting my three waitresses to show up on time. You know we open the lounge at 5:00 P.M., but some days it's almost 6:00 P.M. before any of them show up. I can usually handle the first few minutes by myself, but it gets tough mixing drinks, taking orders, and making change all by myself. I've threatened to fire them if they continue to come in late, and after that they'll be on time for about two or three weeks. Then they slowly get back into the same old habit. I think they know, down inside, that I would really hate to lose them. Except for their tardiness, all three of them are super waitresses. I bet they make more in tips than any other waitresses in the city, which is probably one reason why they feel they don't need to come in until after six. The big tippers are usually those who come in late at night."

"Miles, have you mentioned this to Roger? I know he believes in letting you make your own decisions and doing what you think is needed, but if this has been going on for as long as you say, maybe it's time to get his ideas."

"Actually, I did mention it to Roger a few weeks ago. I told him the same thing I just told you, and he came up with a bonus plan for each waitress who arrived no later than 5:00 P.M. for two straight weeks. A $20 bonus at that! He planned on keeping it in effect for a couple of months and then slowly phasing it out."

"Well, how did it work?" asked Charles.

"Would you believe that not a single one even made it past the *first* week! Money must not mean that much to them. I think if we could think of something else that they would really work hard for, and offer them *that,* maybe we could improve their time of arrival on the scene each night."

"Give me a couple of days to work on it, Miles, and I'll get back to you. I agree that the key is finding out what these women want and setting up a plan to enable them to get it *if* they get here on time."

Discussion Questions

1. According to expectancy theory, what would be one way to establish a reward for these waitresses that would be guaranteed to have a high positive valence?

2. Once the reward was established, what would be the next step to ensure success?

3. In applying expectancy theory, would it be necessary to establish the same reward for all three waitresses? Why or why not?

Cohesion Incident 14-2
The Coffee Lounge

"I work with slobs," Bill muttered to himself as he dropped the remains of what might once have been a sandwich into the trash can.

Bill thought the "coffee lounge"—a small couch, a refrigerator, and a table with coffeemaker, supplies, and occasional snacks—was a great addition to the office. At least, he had thought so until recently. As the newness wore off, so did his co-workers' neatness. In the beginning it had been agreed that everyone would clean up his or her own mess. But these days, by 4:30 P.M. the coffee lounge was filled with dirty cups and spoons, dried coffee grounds, overflowing ashtrays, and foods that were no longer subject to positive identification.

He tried jokes first, then polite requests, then sarcastic comments. Each was effective for a day or two. Then, once again, Bill would find himself a one-man clean-up crew. Even nagging had not worked. He had promised to stop nagging as soon as people started cleaning up, but when Harriet and Steve started avoiding him, he stopped nagging. "It's not worth being shunned," he thought at the time.

A month ago he had decided to try a new strategy. Thinking back to a psychology course he once took, he had speculated, "Maybe I've just been reinforcing those pigs all this time by cleaning up after them. From now on, I'm going to completely ignore their mess, and I'll drop the snide comments as well. They'll get no response from me."

Despite his best intentions, every now and then he could not stand it. Sometimes once a week, sometimes twice a week, sometimes as infrequently as every other week, he broke down and cleaned up everyone's mess. "That's okay," he told himself. "I'm happy to clean up once a week or so if the others will take their turns. Maybe this will serve as an example."

Still, in the month since he implemented his new plan, he saw practically no improvement in the others' behavior. As a last resort he was ready to try yet another plan. "Each day that there's a mess left in the coffee lounge, I'll leave some of the trash in a prominent location on each person's desk," he thought. "Simple as that." But on the second day, Bill was shocked to find all the trash "reminders" piled on *his* desk. And there was little or no change in the condition of the coffee lounge.

"So much for behavior modification," he muttered. "I guess it only works with rats." Then he resignedly pulled out a red thermos of coffee from his briefcase and began a boycott of the office coffee lounge.

Discussion Questions

1. In what way might Bill have been reinforcing his co-workers' sloppy behavior? Is this an example of positive or negative reinforcement?

2. What type of reinforcer was Bill applying when he nagged until they cleaned up the mess? What techniques of reinforcement theory did he use when he left trash on each person's desk after finding the lounge a mess? What major disadvantage of these two techniques is illustrated by Steve and Harriet's avoidance of Bill?

3. How might Bill have used the principles of reinforcement theory more effectively in this situation?

Management Development Exercise 14
How You Motivate Subordinates

How will you attempt to motivate subordinates? This exercise is designed to provide you with some answers. Respond honestly and thoughtfully to the twenty questions below, then your instructor will help you interpret your scores.

Part I

Directions

The following statements have seven possible responses:

Strongly Agree	Agree	Slightly Agree	Don't Know	Slightly Disagree	Disagree	Strongly Disagree
+3	+2	+1	0	−1	−2	−3

Please mark one of the seven responses by circling the number that corresponds to the response that fits your opinion. For example, if you "Strongly Agree," circle the number "+3."

Complete every item. You have about ten minutes to do so.

1. Special wage increases should be given to employees who do their jobs very well.

    +3 +2 +1   0 −1 −2 −3

2. Better job descriptions would be helpful so that employees will know exactly what is expected of them.

    +3 +2 +1   0 −1 −2 −3

3. Employees need to be reminded that their jobs are dependent on the company's ability to compete effectively.

    +3 +2 +1   0 −1 −2 −3

4. A supervisor should give a good deal of attention to the physical working conditions of his or her employees.

    +3 +2 +1   0 −1 −2 −3

5. The supervisor ought to work hard to develop a friendly working atmosphere among his or her people.

    +3 +2 +1   0 −1 −2 −3

6. Individual recognition for above-standard per-   +3 +2 +1   0 −1 −2 −3
   formance means a lot to employees.

7. Indifferent supervision can often bruise feelings.   +3 +2 +1   0 −1 −2 −3

8. Employees want to feel that their real skills and   +3 +2 +1   0 −1 −2 −3
   capacities are put to use on their jobs.

9. Company retirement benefits and stock programs   +3 +2 +1   0 −1 −2 −3
   are important factors in keeping employees on
   their jobs.

10. Almost every job can be made more stimulating   +3 +2 +1   0 −1 −2 −3
    and challenging.

11. Many employees want to give their best in every-   +3 +2 +1   0 −1 −2 −3
    thing they do.

12. Management could show more interest in em-   +3 +2 +1   0 −1 −2 −3
    ployees by sponsoring social events after hours.

13. Pride in one's work is actually an important   +3 +2 +1   0 −1 −2 −3
    reward.

14. Employees want to be able to think of them-   +3 +2 +1   0 −1 −2 −3
    selves as "the best" at their own jobs.

15. The quality of the relationships in the informal   +3 +2 +1   0 −1 −2 −3
    work group is quite important.

16. Individual incentive bonuses would improve the   +3 +2 +1   0 −1 −2 −3
    performance of employees.

17. Visibility of upper management is important to   +3 +2 +1   0 −1 −2 −3
    employees.

18. Employees generally like to schedule their own   +3 +2 +1   0 −1 −2 −3
    work and to make job-related decisions with a
    minimum of supervision.

19. Job security is important to employees.   +3 +2 +1   0 −1 −2 −3

20. Having good equipment to work with is impor-   +3 +2 +1   0 −1 −2 −3
    tant to employees.

15

Leadership

Your study of this chapter will enable you to do the following:

1. Define the term *leadership* and explain the process of leadership.
2. Explain how leadership involves a self-fulfilling prophecy.
3. Identify and evaluate the major trait theories of leadership.
4. Identify and evaluate the major behavior theories of leadership.
5. Identify and evaluate the major contingency approaches to leadership.
6. List and explain the importance of the sources of leaders' power.

Harry Quadracci of Quad/Graphics, Inc.

Harry Quadracci founded Quad/Graphics in 1970, using capital from a second mortgage on his summer home. Believing that magazines would soon use only color photos, Quadracci bought a state-of-the-art, full-color printing press. He housed it in a former warehouse in a rural area outside Milwaukee.

After some lean years, the business started to prosper. Fourteen years later Quad was printing more than 100 different national magazines and catalogs, including the Midwest edition of *Newsweek;* advertising pages for *Time, U.S. News & World Report,* and *Playboy;* and regular monthly issues of *Black Enterprise, True Story, Beauty Digest, Mother Jones,* and *Four Wheeler.* The work force has grown from eleven to 1,400. The one web press was joined by nine others in a printing plant now the length of five football fields. And the one plant was joined by two others—one in nearby Sussex, another in Saratoga, in upstate New York. In 1984 the firm was named one of the 100 Best Companies to Work for in America.

From the outset, Quadracci, a former lawyer, structured his company like a typical law firm. He speaks of his employees as "partners," and like a law firm, which is owned by the partners, Quad is mostly employee-owned. Quadracci considers all employees "students" hired by "sponsors" and directed by "mentors" rather than by bosses.

What seems to tie much of Quadracci's thinking together is his belief that a successful business is built on trust. Once a year Quad demonstrates this faith in what is called the "Spring Fling and Management Sneak." All managers leave the plant to have meetings and then go to the Milwaukee Art Museum. For twenty-

The owner-employees of Quad/Graphics are well-lead, in fact, almost self-led. (Quad Graphics)

four hours, normal printing operations continue with no managers present. "We trust them," Quadracci explained. "But we also hope the mistakes will be small ones." *Inc.* called the technique "management by walking away."

Quad's managers have an unusual amount of latitude. Each division operates as its own business. For instance, Quad's fleet of ten Peterbilt trucks hauls most of the printed magazines. Several years ago, Quadracci suggested that the truckers find loads for their return trips. When the truckers asked what they should carry, Quadracci reportedly shrugged and told them to figure it out for themselves, saying they were now a separate division, DuPlainville Transport, Inc.

"Believe me, it was a big challenge for everybody," fleet manager Larry Lynch told *Inc.* "We got stung a few times by loads and destinations that were not as promised, but we got rolling."

When the new entrepreneurs are operating, Harry Quadracci is loath to intervene. There are stories of how he has been reprimanded with his own philosophy when he has tried. Quadracci once urged the rehiring of an employee who had been fired with four others who were smoking marijuana during lunchtime. Quadracci argued with the bindery managers that the employee in question should not have been dealt with so harshly because he had been an innocent bystander. The managers disagreed, saying the young man had "violated their trust," the worst possible offense. Quadracci backed off.

The following is Quadracci's formal organizational statement on trust:

- The Trust of Teamwork. Employees trust that together they will do better than they would as individuals apart.

- The Trust of Responsibility. Employees trust that each will carry his or her fair share of the load.

- The Trust of Productivity. Customers trust that work will be produced to the most competitive levels of pricing, quality, and innovation.

- The Trust of Management. Shareholders, customers, and employees trust that the company will make decisive judgments for the long term rather than pursuing only short-term goals or today's profits.

- The Trust of Think Small. We all trust in each other: We regard each other as persons of equal rank; we respect the dignity of the individual by recognizing not only the individual's accomplishments, but the feelings and needs of the individual and family as well; and we all share the same goals and purposes in life.[1]

Introduction

What Is Leadership?

Leadership is the process of influencing others to work toward the attainment of specific goals. In a business setting, a manager is a leader when he or she is able to influence subordinates, peers, or superiors to direct their work effort toward the achievement of organizational goals.

A brief discussion of the three key elements of our definition of leadership will make the process easier to understand. First, saying leadership is a *process* implies that the way a person exercises leadership can be broken down into a systematic series of actions directed toward a particular aim. Such a process can be learned. All of us are capable of leadership.

Second, the notion of *influence* implies that others must be willing to accede to the preferences of the leader. This willingness is prompted by explicit or implicit trade-offs. It means that others conditionally assign their rights of self-direction in exchange for the rewards that they expect achieving the leader-directed goals will provide for them personally. The level of subordinates' confidence in this exchange and the level of motivation with which they execute their roles depend on the power held by the manager. It is clear that Harry Quadracci has the power to make changes at Quad/Graphics. And just as important, he continues to increase his power of leadership because he is willing to share it with those subordinates from whom it was derived. The topic of personal power will be a major theme later in this chapter.

Third, one needs *followers and appropriate goals* in order to be a leader. As we learned in our study of motivation in Chapter 14, the self-centered goals of subordinates enable a manager to exercise leadership only when the achievement of organizational goals can be demonstrated to coincide with the achievement of the individual worker's goals. Thus leaders and followers must share common goals. For example, a series of angry contract negotiations took place in 1986 between a number of U.S. airlines and various union groups—most notably the flight attendants. The central issue was the airlines' demands for wage concessions similar to those that had been won from pilots and maintenance unions. The repeated failure of the negotiations stemmed from management's inability to convince the flight attendants that their concessions were necessary to bring about a mutually desired goal: the survival of the airlines.

In this chapter you will learn about various approaches to the practice of leadership. We will consider the possibilities that leaders are determined by their personal traits, by specific behaviors in which they engage, and by the situations in which they operate. The goal is to equip you to know when and how your personal leadership style is most likely to result in superior subordinate productivity. We will begin our study by considering the idea that leadership results are a self-fulfilling prophecy.

Leadership's Self-Fulfilling Prophecy

Theories X and Y

One of the greatest contributions to our understanding of leadership was made by Douglas McGregor.[2] His studies of practicing managers disclosed that to a great extent, subordinates behaved as their managers had expected them to behave. Unfortunately, this did not mean that the managers were good predictors. It meant that subordinates responded to their managers' expectations and acted as the managers believed that they would. Which came first, the behaviors or the beliefs? McGregor's research revealed that it was the managers' beliefs. When managers believed that their workers would perform well, objective measures showed that they later did. When expected to perform poorly, subordinates fulfilled that expectation, too, and did perform below par.

The key to understanding the strength of the self-fulfilling prophecy is to realize that the managers *themselves* behaved in accordance with their personal expectations about their subordinates.[3] When they thought that their subordinates would perform well, the managers unwittingly supervised them in a way that enhanced the likelihood of high performance. On the other hand, lower expectations caused managers to behave in ways that actually inhibited the performance of the subordinates they were trying to motivate. McGregor's work can thus be used to guide managers in the "creation" of high-performing groups. McGregor described the potential for leadership in terms of two opposing sets of assumptions that managers might hold about their subordinates.[4] For simplicity's sake, these two views are presented as opposite ends of a continuum. One extreme position is labeled Theory X, and the other Theory Y.

THEORY X

Theory X managers tend to take a very directive and authoritative approach to leadership, because they take a very dim view of their subordinates. Among the more commonly held assumptions of Theory X managers are the following:

1. The average person inherently dislikes work and, where possible, avoids it.
2. People have little ambition, tend to shun responsibility, and prefer to be directed.
3. Above all else, people want security.
4. In order to get people to attain organizational objectives, it is necessary to use coercion, control, and threats of punishment.

Managers who view people in general, and their subordinates in particular, as fitting the Theory X mold are likely to limit the degree of freedom, autonomy, and discretion that they allow their subordinates. They are likely to set subordinate objectives unilaterally, to be very control-oriented, and to insist on rigid adherence to organizational hierarchies and information channels. They are also likely to emphasize the satisfaction of subordinates' lower-level needs and to be very autocratic in their management style.

THEORY Y

At the opposite end of McGregor's continuum is **Theory Y**, which was meant to represent a completely optimistic view of how subordinates might approach their work in an idealized environment. Theory Y assumptions include the following:

1. Work is a natural phenomenon, and under the right conditions, people not only accept responsibility but also seek it. (This idea is often reported as "Work is as natural as play.")

2. If people are committed to organizational objectives, they will exercise self-direction and self-control in pursuing these aims.

3. Commitment to organizational objectives is a function of the rewards associated with goal attainment. The more the organization is willing to give its people, the harder they will work in pursuing its goals.

Guidelines for Management Practice

Research suggests that managers with both Theory X and Theory Y orientations can achieve high-quality and high-quantity results from their subordinates. However, when you, as a manager, see a Theory Y organizational environment in existence or perceive that bringing such an environment about is possible, this orientation is likely to yield the most productive results for you and your organization. Managers should be aware of what kinds of organizational environments are conducive to Theory Y management, as well as what the effects may be of applying Theory X management in these situations.

1. They are environments wherein Theory Y is already practiced. Because assumptions are typically reinforced by top management, it is important that workers and lower-level managers see top managers as "trend setters." Lower-level managers can hold views different from their superiors, but they must realize that their relationships with subordinates will suffer if their views are significantly at odds with those of top management. For example,

a Theory Y manager might try to permit subordinates to set their own reasonable deadlines when they are scheduling several jobs at the same time. However, imagine the problem that will result when a Theory X top manager insists on accelerating the deadline for a specific customer only days prior to the delivery date the subordinates had set!

2. The Theory Y approach works best in situations in which the subordinates are accustomed to that kind of leadership. Subordinates in such professions as science, teaching, medicine, and engineering are typically accustomed to Theory Y management and respond to it productively. Workers in unskilled jobs tend to produce best under the close supervision that is characteristic of Theory X management.

3. Promising Theory Y environments are frequently ones that require a high level of creativity, demand variety in job skills, have a flexible work pace, reward teamwork, and place a premium on a high level of skill and competence.

4. The capacity for ingenuity and creativity is widespread throughout the population, but under conditions of modern industrial life, this potential is only partially tapped.

Managers such as Harry Quadracci, who embrace the Theory Y perspective, are likely to work jointly with subordinates to determine work goals and the individual or small-group strategies that can be used to achieve them. They tend to communicate frequently and openly with their subordinates, encouraging them to accept greater autonomy and to discipline themselves in the sense of using their own mistakes as the basis for improving future performance. Theory Y managers also try to use higher-level need satisfiers in their efforts to create the optimal environment for their subordinates.

Approaches to Understanding Leadership

Most attempts to understand leadership, beyond the notion that it is often the consequence of the individual's personal predisposition toward others, have followed one of three approaches. The first approach to be devised, known as **trait theory**, attempts to identify the characteristics, or traits, of successful leaders in order to help predict the futures of untested managerial candidates. In **behavior theory**, the second approach, emphasis is placed on identifying what behaviors are characteristic of effective leaders. The more recently emerged **contingency theory** is based on the belief that a manager's success is situationally determined and therefore not attributable to any universally desirable set of leadership qualities. The remainder of this chapter will explore these approaches. We will try to extract from each approach the ideas that have proved valuable in promoting managerial success.

Trait Theories

Attempts to identify what personal characteristics leaders exhibit, in order to predict who will be a good manager, form the basis of trait theory. Researchers have focused on physical characteristics and on personality and intelligence.

PHYSICAL TRAITS

The results of studies on physical characteristics are fairly unambiguous; no physical traits clearly distinguish leaders from nonleaders. Not height, weight, age, sex, personal appearance, or physique has been found to be systematically related to managerial performance.[5] Although we may be attracted to individuals because of their appearance, and may on first impression believe that they look like leaders, whatever managerial success they eventually achieve proves to be unrelated to these superficial qualities. Researchers have confirmed what most of us know instinctively: There are no "born leaders."

PERSONALITY AND INTELLIGENCE TRAITS

Efforts to identify special sets of personality and intelligence traits associated with successful leadership have met with only limited success. This area of investigation was dominated by Edwin Ghiselli, who conducted studies on leadership personality traits for over twenty years, despite the lack of enthusiasm that his work, his

	Importance Value[a]
Supervisory ability (A)	100
Occupational achievement (M)	76
Intelligence (A)	64
Self-actualization (M)	63
Self-assurance (P)	62
Decisiveness (P)	61
Lack of need for security (M)	54
Working-class affinity (P)	47
Initiative (A)	34
Lack of need for high financial reward (M)	20
Need for power (M)	10
Maturity (P)	5
Masculinity–femininity (P)	0

FIGURE 15-1
Ghiselli's Managerial Traits

Source: Reprinted by permission of the publisher from "A Test of Ghiselli's Theory of Managerial Traits," by J. F. Gavin, *Journal of Business Research,* February 1976, p. 46, as adapted from E. E. Ghiselli, *Explorations in Managerial Talent.* Copyright 1976 by Elsevier Science Publishing Co., Inc.
Note: A = ability trait; P = personality trait; M = motivational trait.
[a]Importance value: 100 = very important; 0 = plays no part in managerial talent.

approach, and the general topic inspired. [6] Figure 15-1 summarizes the results of Ghiselli's research. It shows the relative importance of thirteen personality, ability (intelligence), and motivational traits in terms of their value in identifying potentially successful managers. Not surprisingly, Ghiselli concluded that managers with strong supervisory ability are more likely than managers with low supervisory ability to be successful in their jobs. To lesser degrees, occupational achievement, intelligence, self-actualization, self-assurance, and decisiveness are important.

In one of the few other significant research projects on the topic of personality and intelligence traits, Fred Fiedler concluded that successful managers are more perceptive and more psychologically distant from their subordinates than are their less successful counterparts. They are also better able to distinguish between high- and low-performing subordinates.[7]

Perhaps the most valuable finding to emerge from all the trait theory research is that individual managers' traits do not determine success. And as a consequence, traits are inappropriate for making most managerial selection decisions. It is important, however to match a manager's characteristics carefully with the traits of the work group. Research has shown that managers who are well matched with their subordinates are likely to be more successful than those who are not.[8]

An additional significant finding is that male and female managers are perceived as equally effective by their subordinates.[9] This finding should further help to erase sexist stereotypes.

Despite the research findings on physical, personality, and intelligence traits, it is important to realize that managers typically must "fit in" in many ways. As highlighted in "Insights for International Managers 15," the idea of looking and acting like a leader is of recognized importance for managers assigned to overseas appointments.

■ *Insights for International Managers 15* ■

AUTHORITY FIGURES MUST LOOK AND ACT THE PART

The respect of subordinates depends on appearance of strength and competence, but what comes across as strong and competent is not the same everywhere. In Mexico, machismo is important. In Germany, polish, decisiveness and breadth of knowledge give a manager stature. This is not to say that you should adopt without restraint any of the more blatant symbols of power in a country; it is foolish to appear arrogant or superior to local subordinates. The point is, you should behave appropriately for your role, or your employees may be confused.

Americans are peculiar in their concentration of interest and effort into a few activities. With few exceptions, industrial leaders in the United States are known only for their corporate identity. Latin American management emphasizes the total person. Leaders are respected as multidimensional social beings who are family leader, business leader, intellectual and patron of the arts. Appreciation for "high culture" is a mark distinguishing the upper classes. French and Italian industry leaders are social leaders. Mr. Dreyfus, who runs Renault, Mr. Michelin, owner of the tire company, the Agnelli family, who own Fiat, and the Olivettis of the typewriter company are industry leaders, but in addition, they have high social prominence and sharp political power. In Germany,

power can be financial, political, entrepreneurial, managerial, or intellectual; of the five, intellectual power seems to rank highest. Many of the heads of German firms have doctoral degrees and are always addressed as "Herr Doktor."

In most countries, power is more visible than it is in America, where great pains seem to be taken by the most powerful to appear ordinary. Abroad, people are often shocked when they see American executives pushing a shopping cart or mowing a lawn, or when they see American children working in summer jobs. Local personnel gets confusing signals from our behavior.

To communicate rank or to estimate the power of a foreigner you have to know the local accouterments of success or position. Style of dress, possessions, office setting, even titles do not all mean the same in different countries. Appearance and clothing are extremely important to the Latin Americans. Arab and American businessmen seem to value large offices, expensive automobiles, and magnificent homes. British offices of important people may be quite cramped and much more conservatively appointed. Ostentatious displays of power are considered bad form by the Germans.

Source: From L. Copeland and L. Griggs, *Going International* (New York: Random House, 1985), pp. 120–121.

Behavior Theories

The failure of trait research to provide a wealth of important insights into the question of how to predict the future success of managers led to the development of behavior theory. In this approach to understanding leadership, attention focused on learning how successful and unsuccessful managers *behave* differently. If important behaviors could be identified, then prospective managers who possessed appropriate behavioral orientations could be hired, and current managers could be trained how to behave in such a way as to increase group productivity.

THE OHIO STATE UNIVERSITY AND UNIVERSITY OF MICHIGAN STUDIES

Two largely parallel sets of leadership studies were begun in the mid-1940s at the Ohio State University and the University of Michigan in attempts to determine what leader behaviors were meaningfully associated with organizational productivity.

The two studies, under the initial leadership of Ralph Stogdill at Ohio State[10] and of Rensis Likert at the University of Michigan,[11] both concluded that there were two principal dimensions of leader behavior:

1. *Concern for people.* The dimension of **concern for people** involves a manager's concern for developing mutual trust with subordinates, for promoting two-way communication, and for being sensitive to their feelings and preferences. Managers with this concern are often characterized by their personal warmth, approachability, friendliness, and concern for group welfare. The groups they lead usually exhibit cohesion and harmony. Other terms associated with this orientation are "consideration," "employee-centered," and "commitment-oriented."

2. *Concern for production.* The dimension of **concern for production** involves a manager's concern for actively directing subordinates in order to get the task done with optimal efficiency. Managers who score high on this dimension tend to be characterized by an overriding concern for completing the task according to the plan. They tend to be highly directive and oriented toward rules, regulations, policies, and procedures. Other terms associated with this orientation are "initiating structure," "job-centered," and "task-oriented."

Research on the importance of these two dimensions has provided useful information.[12] For example, managers who worked in manufacturing situations and who exhibited high concern for production and low concern for people were rated by their superiors as more proficient than more employee-centered managers. In service organizations, including colleges, accounting and CPA firms, hospitals, and restaurants, just the reverse was true. That is, the most highly rated managers were those with a high concern for people and a lower concern for production.[13] It was also found that greater concern for production and less concern for people were related to the highest levels of accidents, grievances, absenteeism, and turnover. However, in groups that lack structure and cohesiveness, a strong managerial concern for production can lead to a sense of job clarity among subordinates, to self-perceptions of productivity, and to high levels of job satisfaction.[14]

MANAGERIAL GRID

The success of the Ohio State and the University of Michigan studies led to the development of a matrix method for depicting managerial leadership styles. Created by Robert Blake and Jane Srygley Mouton, the **Managerial Grid**® enables us to identify a wide range of styles that represent various combinations of concern for people and concern for production.[15] As shown in Figure 15-2, a manager is rated on two 9-point scales to indicate the extent to which the manager demonstrates concern for each of the two central leadership dimensions. When these two scores are plotted on coordinate axes, their point of intersection falls on a grid of 81 (9 × 9) possible points. This point is then used as a basis for comparing the manager's behaviors with those of other managers whose orientations have been measured in the same manner—and whose behaviors have already been studied. Of course, an attempt to define every one of the 81 positions on the grid would fail; researchers' abilities to distinguish leader behaviors in work situations are far from that well developed. Instead, Blake and Mouton prefer to describe five "extreme" positions on the grid.

1. (9,1) *"Authority-obedience" or "task" leadership.* This position characterizes managers who place a high priority on a concern for productivity and little emphasis

FIGURE 15-2
The Managerial Grid

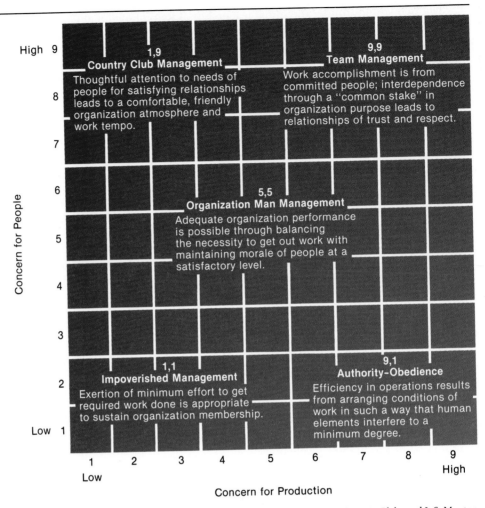

Source: From *The New Managerial Grid III: The Key to Leadership Excellence,* by R. R. Blake and J. S. Mouton (Houston: Gulf Publishing Company). Copyright © 1985, page 12. Reproduced by permission.

on a concern for people. Such managers often believe that group-centered action is likely to result in mediocrity. Thus they stress the quality of the decision over the desires of the subordinates. At their best, 9,1 managers tend to be extremely conscientious, hard-working, loyal, responsible, and personally capable. However, their concern for excellence on their own terms often alienates them from subordinates, resulting in a "satisficing" level of group performance.

2. (1,9) *"Country club" or "good neighbor" leadership.* This position characterizes managers who place a high priority on a concern for people and little emphasis on a concern for productivity. Such managers often believe that the most important leadership activity is to secure the voluntary cooperation of group members, without which, they feel, no productivity would occur. At best such managers are well liked by their subordinates, who are willing to support their boss in times of need. The subordinates of 1,9 managers report generally high levels of job satisfaction and display low levels of absenteeism and turnover. Unfortunately, as an unintended consequence of trying to create a participative en-

vironment, such managers are sometimes seen as abdicating responsibility for decision making. They are also likely to be targets of abusive subordinates who see them as "soft touches."

3. (5,5) *"Organization man" or "middle-of-the-road" leadership.* This position characterizes managers who place moderate priority both on a concern for people and on a concern for productivity. Such managers believe that compromise is at the heart of good leadership and that decisions must be sound, but also endorsed by subordinates, in order to be implemented. This style of management reflects the leaders' willingness to trade off a degree of control over the decision-making process in exchange for greater involvement and greater commitment from subordinates. At best, 5,5 managers are steady, dependable, and unlikely to deviate from previous patterns or traditional performance levels. Unfortunately, they are also unlikely to provide any dynamic new leadership or the initiative that responding to internal constraints or external competition often demands.

4. (1,1) *"Impoverished," "default," or "retired-on-the-job" leadership.* This position characterizes managers who place low priority on both concern for people and concern for productivity. They believe that it is best for managers to rely on precedent or on experts outside the group in order to avoid the disagreements and emotional reactions that they believe are inevitably associated with group dynamics. This sort of manager is clearly never a leader in a positive sense and at best serves as a "place keeper" until the group's problems can be attended to seriously.

5. (9,9) *"Team" or "eye-to-eye" leadership.* This position characterizes managers who place high priority on both concern for people and concern for productivity. Unlike the 5,5 managers who believe that optimal outcomes result from compromise, 9,9 managers believe that concerns for people and production are compatible. They think that the best way to have an excellent production plan is to involve subordinates in the decision-making process, which, in turn, leads to heightened levels of employee commitment. Even Blake and Mouton hesitate to claim that any one leadership style is superior in all cases, but in "typical" business situations, the 9,9 style is preferable to all others.[16]

The Managerial Grid® is by far the most popular approach taken by executive trainers to help teach managers about leadership. Not only does this approach combine important contributions from other research, but it also provides an informative and convenient "shorthand" for managers to use in communicating about their leaderships styles and those of others. In order to help you learn about your own potential leadership style, we have provided a copy of a "Leadership Styles Questionnaire" as "Management Development Exercise 15."

CATEGORIES OF LEADER BEHAVIOR

Perhaps the most important recent contribution to the study of leader behavior was made by Gary Yukl,[17] who documented the nineteen categories of leader behavior shown in Figure 15-3. This list, which is an extremely complete description of managers' actual on-the-job behaviors, can be used to train managers and prospective managers to recognize what the managerial component of their jobs should actually entail. The specificity of Yukl's categories has been shown to help managers get a clearer picture of managerial behaviors that result in effective leadership.

FIGURE 15-3
Categories of Leader
Behavior

1. *Performance Emphasis:* The extent to which a leader emphasizes the importance of subordinate performance, tries to improve productivity and efficiency, tries to keep subordinates working up to their capacity, and checks on their performance.

> Example: My supervisor urged us to be careful not to let orders go out with defective components.

2. *Consideration:* The extent to which a leader is friendly, supportive, and considerate in his or her behavior toward subordinates and tries to be fair and objective.

> Example: When a subordinate was upset about something, the supervisor was very sympathetic and tried to console him.

3. *Inspiration:* The extent to which a leader stimulates enthusiasm among subordinates for the work of the group and says things to build subordinates' confidence in their abilities to perform assignments successfully and attain group objectives.

> Example: My boss told us we were the best design group he had ever worked with and that he was sure this new product was going to break every sales record in the company.

4. *Praise-Recognition:* The extent to which a leader provides praise and recognition to subordinates with effective performance, shows appreciation for their special efforts and contributions, and makes sure they get credit for their helpful ideas and suggestions.

> Example: In a meeting the supervisor told us she is very satisfied with our work and said she appreciated the extra effort we made this month.

5. *Structuring Reward Contingencies:* The extent to which a leader rewards effective subordinate performance with tangible benefits such as a pay increase, promotion, more desirable assignments, a better work schedule, more time off, and so on.

> Example: My supervisor established a new policy that any subordinate who brought in a new client would earn 10 percent of the contracted fee.

6. *Decision Participation:* The extent to which a leader consults with subordinates and otherwise allows them to influence his or her decisions.

> Example: My supervisor asked me to attend a meeting with him and his boss to develop a new production schedule, and he was very receptive to my ideas on the subject.

7. *Autonomy-Delegation:* The extent to which a leader delegates authority and responsibility to subordinates and allows them to determine how to do their work.

> Example: My boss gave me a new project and encouraged me to handle it any way I think is best.

8. *Role Clarification:* The extent to which a leader informs subordinates about their duties and responsibilities, specifies the rules and policies that must be observed, and lets subordinates know what is expected of them.

> Example: My boss called me in to inform me about a rush project that must be given top priority, and he gave me some specific assignments related to this project.

9. *Goal Setting:* The extent to which a leader emphasizes the importance of setting specific performance goals for each important aspect of a subordinate's job, measures progress toward the goals, and provides concrete feedback.

> Example: The supervisor held a meeting to discuss the sales quota for next month.

10. *Training-Coaching:* The extent to which a leader determines training needs for subordinates and provides any necessary training and coaching.

> Example: My boss asked me to attend an outside course at the company's expense and said I could leave early on the days it was to be held.

FIGURE 15-3 (continued)

11. *Information Dissemination:* The extent to which a leader keeps subordinates informed about developments that affect their work, including events in other work units or outside the organization, decisions made by higher management, and progress in meetings with superiors or outsiders.

    Example: The supervisor briefed us about some high-level changes in policy.

12. *Problem Solving:* The extent to which a leader takes the initiative in proposing solutions to serious work-related problems and acts decisively to deal with such problems when a prompt solution is needed.

    Example: The unit was short-handed due to illness, and we had an important deadline to meet; my supervisor arranged to borrow two people from other units so we could finish the job today.

13. *Planning:* The extent to which a leader plans how to efficiently organize and schedule the work in advance, plans how to attain work-unit objectives, and makes contingency plans for potential problems.

    Example: My supervisor devised a shortcut that allows us to prepare our financial statements in three days instead of the four days it used to take.

14. *Coordinating:* The extent to which a leader coordinates the work of subordinates, emphasizes the importance of coordination, and encourages subordinates to coordinate their activities.

    Example: My supervisor had subordinates who were ahead in their work help those who were behind so that the different parts of the project would be ready at the same time.

15. *Work Facilitation:* The extent to which a leader obtains for subordinates any necessary supplies, equipment, support services, or other resources; eliminates problems in the work environment; and removes other obstacles that interfere with the work.

    Example: I asked my boss to order some supplies, and he arranged to get them right away.

16. *Representation:* The extent to which a leader establishes contacts with other groups and important people in the organization, persuades them to appreciate and support his work unit, and uses his influence with superiors and outsiders to promote and defend the interests of the work unit.

    Example: My supervisor met with the data processing manager to get some revisions made in the computer programs so they will be better suited to our needs.

17. *Interaction Facilitation:* The extent to which a leader tries to get subordinates to be friendly with each other, cooperate, share information and ideas, and help each other.

    Example: The sales manager took the group out to lunch to give everybody a chance to get to know the new sales representative.

18. *Conflict Management:* The extent to which a leader restrains subordinates from fighting and arguing, encourages them to resolve conflicts in a constructive manner, and helps to settle conflicts and disagreements between subordinates.

    Example: Two members of the department who were working together on a project were having a dispute about it; the manager met with them to help resolve the matter.

19. *Criticism-Discipline:* The extent to which a leader criticizes or disciplines a subordinate who shows consistently poor performance, violates a rule, or disobeys an order; disciplinary actions include an official warning, reprimand, suspension, or dismissal.

    Example: My supervisor was annoyed that a subordinate kept making the same kinds of errors and warned him to make a more concerted effort.

Source: G. Yukl, *Leadership in Organizations,* © 1981, pp. 121–125. Adapted by permission of Prentice-Hall, Inc., Englewood Cliffs, New Jersey.

Contingency Theories

The most recent and most highly regarded approach to the understanding of leadership builds directly on the behavior theories. It argues that the appropriateness of leaders' actions depends on the situation in which the actions are taken. For example, a highly autocratic leadership approach that proves very effective for the supervisor of a crew of day workers may prove most ineffective for the manager of a research and development department. Known as the contingency or situational approach, this school of leadership thought has spawned five basic models that have been of great value to managers.

LEADERSHIP CONTINUUM

Robert Tannenbaum and Warren Schmidt found that managers were often unsure how certain types of leadership problems should be handled.[18] Specifically, they worried about how to distinguish between those types of problems that they should handle by themselves and those that should be resolved jointly with their subordinates. After studying the problem, Tannenbaum and Schmidt concluded that to make the appropriate choice of how autocratic or democratic to be in decision making, a manager needed to consider three sets of issues:

1. *Personal concerns.* Managers need to consider their own values, leadership inclinations, feelings of relative security, and the level of confidence they have in their subordinates.

2. *Subordinate concerns.* Managers need to consider their subordinates' needs for independence and responsibility, their interest in and knowledge of the problem, and the level of their desire to be involved in problem solving.

3. *Concern for the situation.* Among the most important situational concerns are the nature of the problem, the group's competence in handling this type of problem, the time pressures on the decision-making process, and the type and history of the organization.

Tannenbaum and Schmidt combined these concerns in developing what they labeled the **leadership continuum**. This continuum encourages a manager to consider a full range of options from very boss-centered **autocratic leadership** to very employee-centered **democratic leadership**. And, as Figure 15-4 suggests, in those situations wherein all employees, including the manager, are equally accountable and influential in the decision process, problems may be handled best via **laissez-faire leadership**, wherein the manager is essentially uninvolved in the functioning of the work group.

"In Practice 15-1," on the leadership style of Manufacturers Hanover CEO John McGillicuddy, provides an interesting study of shifts in a leader's management style. The leadership continuum can help you analyze this example, as can the other theories covered in this chapter.

The experiences of many managers have provided a basis for offering some recommendations about the conditions that make autocratic, democratic, and laissez-faire management, respectively, appropriate. A useful list of such recommendations is provided in Figure 15-5.

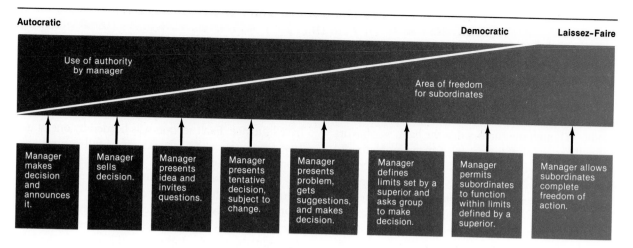

FIGURE 15-4
Continuum of
Leadership Behavior

THEORY OF LEADERSHIP EFFECTIVENESS

Fred Fiedler is credited with being among the first of all management experts to advocate the contingency approach to leadership.[19] Fiedler believed that the appropriateness of a leader's style could be determined only by understanding how well the style "fit" the situation in which the manager was operating. He argued that a successful or effective leadership style depended on three factors: leader-member relations, the task structure, and the leader position power.

1. *Leader-member relations.* The most important determinant of leader effectiveness is the degree to which the leader enjoys the acceptance, confidence, support, and loyalty of subordinates. When **leader-member relations** are strong, the leader has a full range of personal and organizational bases of influence to use in trying to gain subordinates' support. When leader-member relations are weak, however, the leader's influence is often reduced to the impersonal power granted by the company.

2. *Task structure.* The degree to which subordinates' jobs are routine (simple and highly defined), as contrasted to nonroutine (complex or unique), is the measure of **task structure**. Highly structured tasks, such as those requiring a great deal of repetition, confer much authority and power on managers, because there are likely to be very specific performance criteria that managers can use to enforce desired subordinate behavior. On the other hand, complex tasks that give subordinates problem-solving responsibility of a nonroutine nature usually necessitate a more democratic, less dominant leadership style.

3. *Leader position power.* The extent of formal and informal power granted to the manager by the organization is the measure of the **leader position power** the leader exerts. Such power is indicated by the manager's authority, vested in him or her by the top management of the firm, to reward and punish subordinates. High position power allows for the use of more autocratic leadership styles; low position power usually requires a more democratic, or even a laissez-faire, approach.

In Practice 15-1

MANNY HANNY'S MCGILLICUDDY

Early in May 1984, rumors surfaced that Manufacturers Hanover Corporation (Manny Hanny) was in trouble. Though the rumors that the bank was having difficulty raising funds were false, many problems did in fact exist for the bank and John F. McGillicuddy, chairman and CEO. The bank's stock value declined continuously from 1984 through 1988 despite actions by the company to shore-up public confidence. The decline was blamed largely on a $7.5 billion liability of the bank in Latin America and because of a ratings drop.

Although Manny Hanny has undergone some changes since 1984, the company's rate of change has been dangerously slow, even though the bank has received excellent marks in the area of expense control through the consolidation of related facilities, the elimination of unprofitable activities, and a reduction in personnel. Although basic steps were taken to control expenses and accelerate changes, the risk continued to remain high that the bank's diverse holdings could either be sold or broken up or that the company could be taken over by another financial institution when the banking industry nationalizes in the early 1990s.

Recognizing these threats and having met extensively with consultants from McKinsey and Company, McGillicuddy undertook to change the bank's method of operation through decentralization. In April 1985, McGillicuddy announced that line managers would be compelled to make decisions on their own and that they would be rewarded according to their performance. Remaining true to his word, he divided the bank into five sections: retail, investment banking, international, corporate lending, and asset-based finance. Each section was headed by one of his best employees and each was given full control and responsibility for a section.

For Manufacturers Hanover Corporation and for John F. McGillicuddy this operational change was revolutionary. Manny Hanny had always been run like a family-owned and operated business with one and only one leader, John F. McGillicuddy, who had been with the bank for twenty-eight years and had inspired tremendous loyalty. McGillicuddy had the ability to motivate weak managers as well as a reputation for being fair but firm. However, because McGillicuddy had previously required that he be consulted on every issue, the division of power among five leaders was a dramatic departure from traditional managerial behavior.

McGillicuddy's greatest obstacle was to overcome an outdated, strongly centralized corporate culture. For many years Manny Hanny boasted of a friendly environment with more competition on the golf course than in the boardroom. Even by the end of 1986, McGillicuddy was still finding it difficult to persuade managers to make their own decisions without the help of senior management. Finally, he warned all of his managers that if they could not accept greater autonomy, they should leave.

Manny Hanny's problem, then, was less operational than psychological. Changing human behavior, however tedious, had become the key to the bank's future as well as its greatest challenge.

Sources: T. Kreuzer, "Manny Hanny: The Next BofA?" *Bankers Monthly*, June 1987, pp. 23–28. J. Bartlett, "The Turnaround Trauma at Manufacturers Hanover," *Business Week*, August 24, 1987, pp. 68–70. S. Andrews, "Can Manufacturers Hanover Get Its Act Together?" *Institutional Investor*, December 1986, pp. 187–194.

Fiedler believed that these three variables combined to suggest the leadership style that would work most effectively. To measure leadership style, Fiedler developed a unique and somewhat controversial method.[20] He asked managers to describe their least preferred co-worker (LPC)—that is, the subordinate with whom they would *least* like to work. The research instrument used to arrive at an LPC score is shown in Figure 15-6.

FIGURE 15-5
Appropriate Leader
Behavior, Situationally
Defined

Consider Being Autocratic When . . .	**Consider Being Democratic When . . .**	**Consider Being Laissez-Faire When . . .**
LEADER/MANAGER:	LEADER/MANAGER:	LEADER/MANAGER:
Has complete power and no restraints on its use. Has a way of saving matters in an emergency. Has some unique knowledge. Is firmly entrenched in his or her position.	Has limited power and authority. Has restraints on use. Group might reject his or her authority and succeed at it. Has *some* existing time pressures. Has *limited* sanctions he or she can exert.	Has no power to compel action. Has no time pressures. Possesses tenure based on pleasure of the group. Has no sanctions to exert. Has no special knowledge.
FOLLOWERS:	FOLLOWERS:	FOLLOWERS:
Are leader-dependent persons. Are rarely asked for an opinion. Have low educational background (not always). Recognize emergencies. Are members of a "labor surplus" group. Are autocrats themselves. Have low independence drives.	Expect to have some control over methods used. Have predominantly middle-class values. Are physicians, scientists, engineers, managers, or staff persons. Possess relatively scarce skills. Like system, but not authority. Have high social needs.	Have more power than the leader. Dislike orders. Will rebel successfully if they so choose. Choose their own goals and methods. Are volunteers, loosely organized, or in short supply. Are physicians, scientists, or others with rare skills.
WORK SITUATION:	WORK SITUATION:	WORK SITUATION:
Features tight discipline. Is characterized by strong controls. Is marked by low profit margins or tight cost controls. Includes physical dangers. Requires low skills from workers. Requires that frequent changes be made quickly.	"Umbrella" organization objectives understood. Involves shared responsibility for controls. Has some time pressures. Consists of gradual changes or regularly spaced changes. Involves actual or potential hazards occasionally. Is one in which teamwork skills are called for.	Has no clear purpose apparent except as the individual chooses. Is unstructured. Is one in which only self-imposed controls exist. Has no time pressures. Features few or only gradual changes. Takes place in a safe, placid environment. Requires high individual skill or conceptual ability.
Effect of Autocratic Leadership if Carried to Extreme or Overused:	**Effect of Democratic Leadership if Carried to Extreme or Overused:**	**Effect of Laissez-Faire Leadership if Carried to Extreme or Overused:**
May result in poor communication, rigidity of operation, slow adaptation to changing conditions, and stunting of the growth of people.	May result in loss of ability to take individual initiative when necessary (in favor of group decisions); also may result in slow decision making in emergencies.	May result in organization fragmentation, member isolation, chaos, and anarchy.

Fiedler's thesis was that managers who described their LPC in rather favorable terms were managers who had great concern for human relations. They had strong, positive, supportive, and caring emotional bonds with their subordinates. Fiedler labeled these managers *relationship-oriented leaders*. In contrast, managers who described their LPC in essentially unfavorable terms were assumed to be low in human relations orientations and to have a strong tendency to place task demands above subordinate preferences. Labeled *task-oriented leaders,* they exhibited many of the same characteristics as Tannenbaum and Schmidt's autocratic leader: They monitored workers' behaviors closely, provided structure, and promoted rules and policies.

Figure 15-7 assembles most of Fiedler's ideas to depict the situational determinants of effective leadership. The figure presents the eight possible combinations of the three variables (leader-member relations, task structure, and leader power position) in order of attractiveness for the leader from 1 (high) to 8 (low). Each of these combinations is then matched with the leadership style—relationship-

FIGURE 15-6
Fiedler's Least Preferred
Co-Worker Scale

Throughout your life you will have worked in many groups with a wide variety of different people—on your job, in social groups, in church organizations, in volunteer groups, on athletic teams, and in many other situations. Some of your co-workers may have been very easy to work with in attaining the group's goals, while others were less so.

Think of all the people with whom you have ever worked, and then think of the person with whom you could work *least well*. He or she may be someone with whom you work now or with whom you have worked in the past. This does not have to be the person you liked least well, but it should be the person with whom you had the most difficulty getting a job done, the *one* individual with whom you could work *least well*.

Describe this person on the scale by placing an X in the appropriate space.

Look at the words at both ends of the line before you mark your X. *There are no right or wrong answers.* Work rapidly; your first answer is likely to be the best. Do not omit any items, and mark each item only once.

Now describe the person with whom you can work least well.

			Scoring[a]
Pleasant	8 7 6 5 4 3 2 1	Unpleasant	___
Friendly	8 7 6 5 4 3 2 1	Unfriendly	___
Rejecting	1 2 3 4 5 6 7 8	Accepting	___
Tense	1 2 3 4 5 6 7 8	Relaxed	___
Distant	1 2 3 4 5 6 7 8	Close	___
Cold	1 2 3 4 5 6 7 8	Warm	___
Supportive	8 7 6 5 4 3 2 1	Hostile	___
Boring	1 2 3 4 5 6 7 8	Interesting	___

oriented or task-oriented—that Fiedler believes is likely to be the most effective under those circumstances.

As Figure 15-7 shows, combinations 1, 2, 3, and 8 are most likely to prove successful for task-motivated leaders. The situation depicted by combination 1 is so favorable to the leader that subordinates will accept directives almost without question in order to maintain their good standing with the leader. Although the leader's organizational power is diminished in combination 2, the strength of the leader's personal power, combined with the limited discretion allowed by a structured task, provide opportunities for the task-oriented manager to excel. In combination 3, the strength of the leader's personal and organizational power makes forceful leadership possible. In combination 8, the conditions facing the leader are so unfavorable that a "show of force," as contrived as it may be, offers the most promising option for salvaging a desperate situation. In the remaining four combinations (4, 5, 6, and 7), a relationship-oriented style is likely to be most effective. The nature of these situations demands a greater array of skills, knowledge, and

FIGURE 15-6 (continued)

	1	2	3	4	5	6	7	8		
Quarrelsome	1	2	3	4	5	6	7	8	Harmonious	——
Gloomy	1	2	3	4	5	6	7	8	Cheerful	——
Open	8	7	6	5	4	3	2	1	Guarded	——
Backbiting	1	2	3	4	5	6	7	8	Loyal	——
Untrustworthy	1	2	3	4	5	6	7	8	Trustworthy	——
Considerate	8	7	6	5	4	3	2	1	Inconsiderate	——
Nasty	1	2	3	4	5	6	7	8	Nice	——
Agreeable	8	7	6	5	4	3	2	1	Disagreeable	——
Insincere	1	2	3	4	5	6	7	8	Sincere	——
Kind	8	7	6	5	4	3	2	1	Unkind	——

Total_____

Source: Adapted from F. E. Fiedler, M. M. Chemers, and L. Mahar, *Improving Leadership Effectiveness*, p. 7. Copyright © 1976 John Wiley & Sons. Reprinted by permission of John Wiley & Sons, Inc.

[a]Scoring: 64 and above   High LPC
          63–58   Medium LPC
          57 and below   Low LPC

FIGURE 15-7
Situational
Determinants of
Effective Leadership

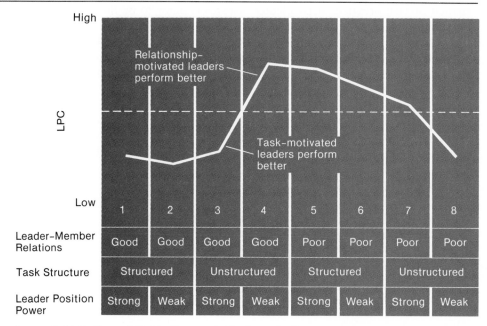

Source: F. E. Fiedler and M. M. Chemers. *Leadership and Effective Management* (Glenview, Ill.: Scott, Foresman, 1974), p. 80.

talents than almost any manager could provide. Thus by working closely with subordinates, as the relationship-oriented leader does, the manager improves the probability of designing and implementing effective plans of action.

PATH-GOAL THEORY

A third contingency approach is the path-goal model developed by Robert House.[22] **Path-goal theory** got its name from the belief that effective leaders need to perform

Lee Iacocca led Chrysler to profitability from near bankruptcy through a combination of good corporate strategies and governmental and stakeholder confidence in the effectiveness of his flexible leadership style. (Dick Durrance/Woodfin Camp and Associates)

Guidelines for Management Practice

The manager can often change situational factors in order to improve the chances of creating a productive work environment. The following are some suggestions that Fiedler and his colleagues Martin Chemers and Linda Mahar believe managers should use to improve the effectiveness of their leadership in the three different situations.[21]

MODIFY LEADER-MEMBER RELATIONS

1. Spend more or less time with your subordinates (at lunch, coffee breaks, etc.).

2. Organize activities outside of work that include your subordinates (social get-togethers, bowling teams, etc.).

3. Volunteer to direct difficult or troublesome subordinates.

4. Transfer particular subordinates into or out of your unit.

5. Increase or decrease your availability to subordinates (open-door policy, rap sessions).

MODIFY TASK STRUCTURE

If You Wish to Reduce Task Structure, You Can:

1. Ask your boss to give you, whenever possible, new or unusual problems and the freedom to figure out how to get them done.

2. Take the problems and tasks to your subordinates and invite them to work with you.

3. Where possible, define the task in relatively vague form.

4. Delegate more to subordinates.

If You Wish to Create More Highly Structured Tasks, You Can:

1. Ask your superior to give you, whenever possible, tasks that are well defined.

2. Give subordinates more detailed instruction and guidance.

3. Break the job down into smaller subtasks that can be better defined.

MODIFY POSITION POWER

To Increase Position Power, You Can:

1. Show your subordinates who is boss by more fully exercising the power you have.

2. Make sure that information coming to your group is channeled through you; require more approval rights.

To Decrease Your Position Power, You Can:

1. Play down your status as "the boss."

2. Involve subordinates more often in important decisions.

3. Delegate more responsibility to your subordinates.

4. Give subordinates greater access to those higher up in the organization.

---

three tasks. They must identify and communicate to subordinates the path that those subordinates should follow in order to achieve personal and organizational goals. They must help subordinates to make progress along that path. And they must clear away any obstacles on the path that might slow or prevent subordinate achievement of the goals. This model differs from the others we have discussed in that it does not attempt to specify a "best" leadership style for a particular set of circumstances. Instead, path-goal theory argues that a manager needs to be flexible enough to exhibit several different styles of leadership. Specifically, the manager should be prepared to emphasize whichever of the following four options the situation dictates:

1. In **directive leadership**, the leader sets goals, timetables, work methods, and performance standards for the subordinates.

2. In **supportive leadership**, the leader stresses human relationships by treating subordinates with respect and equality, by being friendly and approachable, and by attending to any of their social needs that can appropriately be satisfied on the job.

3. In **achievement-oriented leadership**, the leader establishes challenging expectations for subordinates, places a high degree of emphasis on constantly improving the quantity and excellence of the subordinates' output, and attempts to provide the supportive and rewarding environment in which exceptional performance can be achieved.

4. In **participative leadership**, the leader solicits subordinates' recommendations, ideas, and evaluations before making or implementing decisions.

As shown in Figure 15-8, the four types of leader behavior (which parallel the task and relationship-oriented styles that we have studied) combine with situational contingencies to determine leader effectiveness. By incorporating situational variables, the model warns managers of the need to consider task and employee characteristics before choosing their leadership style. For example, House would argue that directive leadership is likely to be the most effective option when tasks are unique and unstructured. Supportive leadership is often the preferred choice when the tasks are routine and highly structured. When subordinates are productivity-minded, an achievement-oriented leadership style is most appropriate; when they are highly talented, well-educated, and experienced professionals, participative leadership will probably be most effective.

PARTICIPATIVE DECISION MODEL OF LEADERSHIP

Another model that views managerial decisions as situationally defined, and therefore argues that managers should adopt whichever of several different leadership styles is most appropriate to the demands of the particular problem at hand, is

FIGURE 15-8
Path-Goal Model of Leader Effectiveness

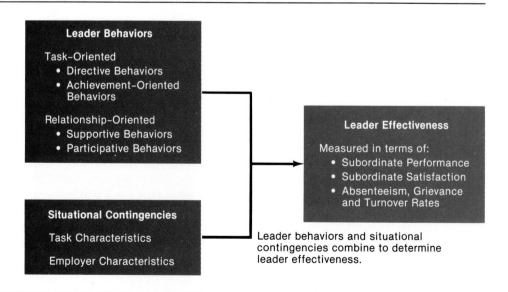

Leader behaviors and situational contingencies combine to determine leader effectiveness.

the **participative decision model** of Victor Vroom and Philip Yetton.[23] Sometimes referred to as a normative theory of leadership (because it suggests how decisions "ought" to be made), this model directs the manager to one of five leadership styles depending on her or his responses to seven diagnostic questions. The questions are arranged in the form of a decision tree.

Vroom and Yetton's five leadership styles are defined in terms of the degree of participation by subordinates that each style solicits.

Autocratic I (A I). The manager solves the problem or reaches the decision alone, using available information.

Autocratic II (A II). The manager obtains information from subordinates before making the decision. The role of subordinates is to provide information for decision making; they may or may not have been informed about the nature of the issue under consideration.

Consultative I (C I). The manager shares problems with subordinates *individually* and then solicits their ideas and information. Subordinate input may or may not be used further in the decision-making process.

Consultative II (C II). The manager shares problems with subordinates *as a group* and then solicits their ideas and information. Subordinate input may or may not be used further in the decision-making process.

Group Participation (G). The manager shares problems with subordinates as a group. Together, with the manager coordinating the process, they generate and evaluate alternatives before trying to reach a consensus decision.

Before deciding on an appropriate leadership style, managers need to ask themselves the following seven diagnostic questions:

A. Is there a quality requirement such that one solution is likely to be better than others?

B. Do I have sufficient information to make a high-quality decision?

C. Is the problem structured?

D. Is acceptance of the decision by subordinates critical to effective implementation?

E. If I were to make the decision by myself, is it reasonably certain that it would be accepted by my subordinates?

F. Do subordinates share the organizational goals to be attained in solving this problem?

G. Is conflict among subordinates likely in preferred solutions?

These seven questions serve as decision points on the tree diagram shown in Figure 15-9. By the time managers have answered these questions by responding "yes" or "no," they have been led to Vroom and Yetton's recommendation about the degree to which they should involve their subordinates in the decision under consideration.

SITUATIONAL LEADERSHIP MODEL

Once known as the life-cycle model of leadership, the **situational leadership model** developed by Paul Hersey and Kenneth Blanchard (of *One Minute Manager* fame; see Chapter 6) has been enhanced and refined over time to become one of the most popular applied models available for use by practicing managers.[24] As presented in Figure 15-10, the model is in the form of a 2 × 4 matrix with "Relationship Behavior" on the vertical axis and "Task Behavior" on the horizontal axis. The most important variable in determining the leadership style that the manager should adopt is the maturity level of the followers. Hersey and Blanchard define

FIGURE 15-9
Participative Decision Model

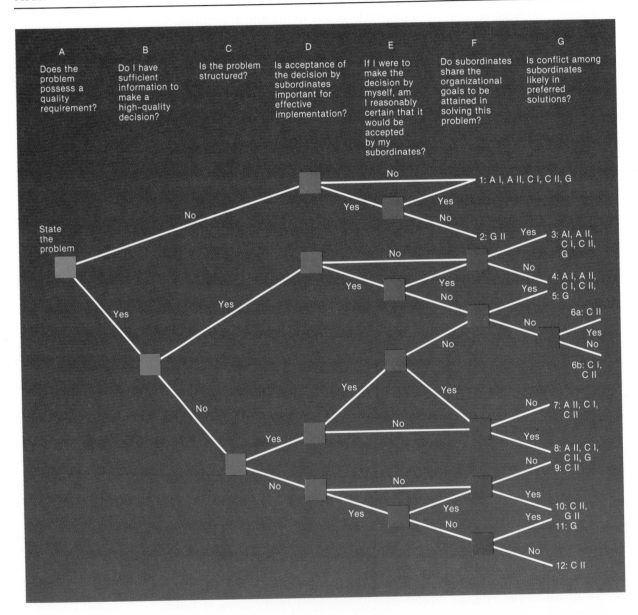

Source: Reprinted from *Leadership and Decision Making* by V. H. Vroom and P. W. Yetton by permission of the University of Pittsburgh Press. © 1973 by University of Pittsburgh Press.

FIGURE 15-10
Situational Leadership
Model

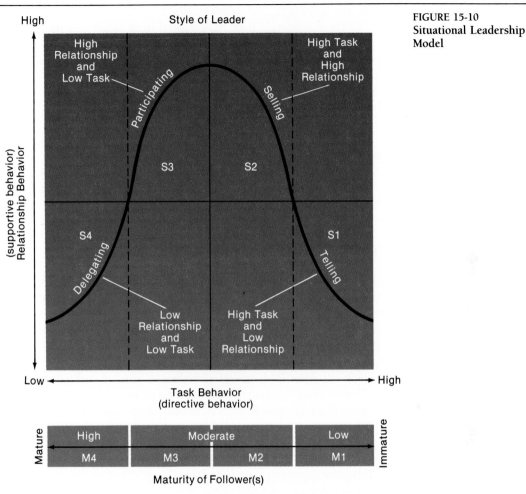

Style of Leader

High

High
Relationship
and
Low Task

High Task
and
High
Relationship

Participating

Selling

S3

S2

(supportive behavior)
Relationship Behavior

S4

S1

Delegating

Telling

Low
Relationship
and
Low Task

High Task
and
Low
Relationship

Low ←————————————————→ High

Task Behavior
(directive behavior)

Mature	High	Moderate		Low	Immature
	M4	M3	M2	M1	

Maturity of Follower(s)

Source: P. Hersey and K. H. Blanchard, *Management of Organizational Behavior: Utilizing Human Resources,*
4th ed., © 1982, p. 248. Reprinted with permission of Prentice-Hall, Inc., Englewood Cliffs, N.J.

maturity as task-relevant training, ability and experience, the desire for achievement and a sense of accomplishment, and the willingness to accept responsibility.

For simplicity's sake, the model shows only four maturity levels, from low
(M1) to high (M4). Each of these levels is associated with a recommended leadership style. In the case of M1, Hersey and Blanchard suggest that the manager
adopt a *telling* leadership style, which is characterized by a high-task and low-
relationship orientation. This style is most often seen among successful managers
of new employees, who appreciate the structure that such a leader brings to an
uncertain and anxiety-arousing learning situation.

Once subordinates have learned their task and have become acclimated to
their work environment—though they have not yet really mastered either—they
have reached the M2 maturity level. At this point a *selling* leadership style is
recommended. Until subordinates are prepared to accept full responsibility for
their tasks, they need and appreciate close supervision, frequent feedback, and
encouragement. At this stage, followers feel a strong need to be accepted as contributing and personally welcome members of the group. Thus highly supportive,
relationship-oriented behaviors on the part of the leader are frequently associated
with manager effectiveness.[25]

By the M3 stage, the subordinates begin to seek greater responsibility as a result of the confidence they have gained from mastering their task assignments and their feelings of acceptance into their work group and the organization. A *participating* leadership style is most effective at this stage of subordinate development. The need for close supervision and direction has been replaced by a need for a high-relationship–oriented, low-task–oriented leader who provides support and encouragement.

Finally, as subordinates achieve the high levels of task and interpersonal competence that characterize the M4 stage, the manager is usually most effective when followers are in essence allowed to manage themselves. In pursuing a *delegating* leadership style, the manager acts as a group sponsor and facilitator, someone who performs the administrative role and who eases the way for largely self-motivating and self-directing subordinates.

Sources of Leaders' Power

Leadership theories help us to understand managers' propensities to behave in particular ways, and they provide meaningful clues as to how subordinates and peers will respond to managers' leadership initiatives. However, it is also important to understand the sources of power that managers have and must further develop in order for them to gain and maintain follower support. A leader's ability to influence others is largely determined by the power that the leader is able to exert in a given situation. This power of managers over subordinates is known as **social power**, to remind us that it is derived from the social interaction of leader and follower and that without the willingness of the subordinate to follow, managers would have little power to lead. The combined works of John French and Bertram Raven and of Paul Hersey and W. E. Natemeyer provide important insights into the seven bases of a leader's social power.[28]

Coercive power is based on subordinates' fear of the manager. Leaders who rely on coercive power use their ability to punish as their primary means of influencing others. Specifically, coercive leaders may threaten to punish by giving undesirable work assignments, by administering reprimands, or by dismissing non-compliant subordinates.

Expert power is based on the leader's possession of expertise, skill, or knowledge that convinces subordinates that the leader's views should serve as a basis for their action. Leaders who rely on expert power use their perceived ability to improve the job performance of others as their means of controlling decision making.

Legitimate power is based on the perception of the manager's subordinates that because of the manager's position in the organizational hierarchy, they should accede to his or her influence. Typically, the higher the managers' positions in the organization hierarchy, the greater their legitimate power. Managers who enjoy a high degree of legitimate power are seen by their followers as having the right, as a result of their position in the company, to dominate decision making.

Referent power is based on the magnetism of the leader's personal traits. Leaders who have high referent or charismatic power are liked and admired by others, who typically accede to the leaders' influence in order to increase identification with them.

Reward power is based on the leader's ability to provide rewards for followers. Managers with high reward power are perceived by their subordinates as being

Guidelines for Management Practice

Perhaps the most intriguing of the seven sources of social power is referent power. The recognizable but intangible quality attributed to great leaders, referent power (which is often referred to as charisma or personal power), is apparently a critical element of every great manager's leadership. The following are some recommended guidelines for increasing your referent power. Although many of these ideas seem obvious and easily accomplished, busy managers frequently ignore such recommendations—at least the less powerful ones do![30]

1. Realistically assess the power you already hold.

2. Gain the support of other people.

3. Develop specializations and expertise in areas where others need help.

4. Create a need for your specialized resource.

5. Form a wide range of working relationships and associations, and make them known.

6. Conceal the extent to which others' responses reward or punish you.

7. Minimize the pain of criticism.

8. Get complete information about the motives, knowledge, understanding, and attitudes of those with whom you are trying to increase your power.

9. Ingratiate yourself.

10. Become a part of the group before initiating innovations.

able to provide positive rewards—such as pay, promotion, and recognition—to followers who comply with their wishes.

Connection power is based on the leader's relationships with influential persons both inside and outside the organization. Followers accede to the preferences of a leader with high connection power, because they wish to gain favor with such a well-connected person, or at least to avoid her or his disfavor.

Information power is based on the leader's knowledge of or access to information that is believed to be valuable to others. A leader who has high information power is willingly followed by those who need the leader's information or who simply enjoy "being in on things."

Recent studies have taught us a great deal about the effectiveness of different sources of social power in the workplace.[29] A frequent finding is that most effective managers rely more on the use of personal powers such as expert, connective, and referent power than on the positional powers that include legitimate, reward, coercive, and information power.

Review of the Learning Objectives

Having studied this chapter, you should be able to respond to the learning objectives with extensions of the following brief answers.

1. Define the term *leadership* and explain the process of leadership.

Leadership is the process of influencing others to direct their productive energies toward the attainment of specific goals. The three key underpinnings of this definition are leadership's nature as a process, the need for power with which to influence others, and the need for followers and appropriate goals.

2. **Explain how leadership involves a self-fulfilling prophecy.**

As best explained by the philosophy behind Theories X and Y, research has shown that leaders often (though perhaps unwittingly) influence followers to perform as the leaders believe they will or can perform. It appears that subordinates tend to become what their leaders think they are.

3. **Identify and evaluate the major trait theories of leadership.**

Research on the physical, personality, and intelligence traits of leaders has essentially failed to distinguish effective from ineffective managers on any of these bases.

4. **Identify and evaluate the major behavior theories of leadership.**

Studies at the Ohio State University and at the University of Michigan, work by Blake and Mouton on the Managerial Grid, and Yukl's categorization of leader behaviors have helped managers understand the need to work to encourage high levels of employee commitment and task excellence in order to elicit superior task performance.

5. **Identify and evaluate the major contingency approaches to leadership.**

Tannenbaum and Schmidt's leadership continuum, Fiedler's contingency model, House's path-goal theory, Vroom and Yetton's participative decision model, and Hersey and Blanchard's situational leadership model have all made meaningful contributions to our understanding of ways in which managers can improve their leadership performance. Perhaps most important have been the findings that the work situation greatly affects what leadership style is appropriate and that managers can alter their leadership styles in order to better match the situation.

6. **List and explain the importance of the sources of leaders' power.**

Seven sources of social power have been identified: coercive, expert, legitimate, referent, reward, connection, and information power. Derived either from the manager's position in the organization or from his or her interpersonal behavior, these social powers principally determine the manager's effectiveness as a leader.

Key Terms and Concepts

After completing your study of Chapter 15, "Leadership," you should be able to explain the following terms and concepts.

leadership	concern for people	autocratic	leader-member	directive leadership
Theory X	concern for	leadership	relations	supportive
Theory Y	production	democratic	task structure	leadership
trait theory	Managerial Grid	leadership	leader position	achievement-
behavior theory	leadership	laissez-faire	power	oriented
contingency theory	continuum	leadership	path-goal theory	leadership

| participative leadership | situational leadership model | coercive power | referent power | information power |
| participative decision model | social power | expert power legitimate power | reward power connection power | |

Questions for Discussion

1. Is a manager a leader? Is a leader a manager?

2. If a manager assumes that subordinates possess qualities that make Theory Y management appropriate, when in fact they have been conditioned to respond in Theory X ways, how effective is the manager likely to be?

3. Is it possible to treat some subordinates in a manner consistent with Theory X and others in a manner consistent with Theory Y? Is it desirable?

4. Despite the failure of the trait theory approach to detect meaningful differences between effective and ineffective leaders, researchers continue to be intrigued by the possibility that traits relevant to leadership exist. Why do you think this is true?

5. How would you account for the fact that a leader's intelligence is not correlated with his or her effectiveness?

6. Cite five management behaviors that suggest a concern for people and five that suggest a concern for production.

7. Describe situations in which each of the five extreme styles appearing on the Managerial Grid might not be effective.

8. Of what benefit to practicing managers is knowing Yukl's nineteen categories of leader behavior?

9. If managers move up and down on the leadership continuum in order to be flexible enough to treat every leadership situation individually, will subordinates not see them as unpredictable?

10. Give two examples each of high task structure and low task structure.

11. Managers with high-LPC scores are judged to be relationship-oriented. Is it possible, however, that they are simply not capable of critically evaluating their employees?

12. Is it not possible and desirable for a leader to exhibit more than one of the path-goal leadership styles simultaneously?

13. Describe the major differences between the two most popular applied models of leadership, that of Blake and Mouton and that of Hersey and Blanchard.

14. In general, which of the bases of social power should a manager rely on most? Why?

Notes

1. Adapted from R. Levering, M. Moskowitz, and M. Katz, *The 100 Best Companies to Work for in America*, © 1984, Addison-Wesley Publishing Co., Inc., Reading, Massachusetts. Pages 295–299. Reprinted with permission.

2. D. McGregor, *The Human Side of Enterprise* (New York: McGraw-Hill, 1960).

3. M. Gent, "Theory X in Antiquity, or the Bureaucratization of the Romans' Army," *Business Horizons* 27, no. 1 (January–February 1984): 52–56.

4. McGregor, *The Human Side of Enterprise,* pp. 33–34, 47–48. We wish to point out that McGregor saw Theory X and Theory Y as but two leader philosophies among several available. The notion of a continuum, with these two theories as end points, reflects the portrayals of authors other than McGregor.

5. R. Stogdill, "Personal Factors Associated with Leadership," *Journal of Applied Psychology* 32, no. 1 (January 1948): 35–81.

6. E. Ghiselli, "Managerial Talent," *American Psychologist* 18, no. 10 (October 1963): 631–641; and E. Ghiselli, *Explorations in Managerial Talent* (Santa Monica, Calif.: Goodyear, 1971). For a notable exception, see J. Gavin, "A Test of Ghiselli's Theory of Managerial Traits," *Journal of Business Research* 4, no. 1 (February 1976): 45–52.

7. F. Fiedler, "The Leader's Psychological Distance and Group Effectiveness," in D. Cartwright and A. Zander, eds., *Group Dynamics,* (New York: Harper & Row, 1968).

8. D. Cartwright and A. Zander, eds., *Group Dynamics* (New York: Harper & Row, 1968).

9. R. Rice, D. Instone, and J. Adams, "Leader Sex, Leader Success, and Leadership Process: Two Field Studies," *Journal of Applied Psychology* 69, no. 1 (February 1984): 12–31; and S. Donnell and J. Hall, "Men and Women as Managers: A Significant Case of No Significant Difference," *Organizational Dynamics* 8, no. 4 (Spring 1980): 60–77.

10. R. Stogdill and A. Coons, *Leader Behavior: Its Description and Measurement* (Columbus: Ohio State University, Bureau of Business Research, 1957).

11. R. Likert, *New Patterns of Management* (New York: McGraw-Hill, 1961); and R. Likert, "From Production- and Employee-Centeredness to Systems 1–4," *Journal of Management* 5 (Fall 1979): 147–156.

12. E. Fleishman, "The Measurement of Leadership Attitudes in Industry," *Journal of Applied Psychology* 37, no. 3 (June 1953): 153–158; E. Fleishman and D. Peters, "Interpersonal Values, Leadership Attitudes, and Managerial Success," *Personnel Psychology* 15, no. 2 (Summer 1962): 127–143; A. Korman, "Consideration, Initiating Structure, and Organizational Criteria—A Review," *Personnel Psychology* 19, no. 4 (Winter 1966): 349–361; and C. Schriesheim and B. Bird, "Contributions of the Ohio State Studies to the Field of Leadership," *Journal of Management* 5 (Fall 1979): 135–145.

13. E. Fleishman, E. Harris, and H. Burtt, *Leadership and Supervision in Industry* (Columbus: Ohio State University, Bureau of Educational Research, 1955).

14. S. Kerr and C. Schriesheim, "Consideration, Initiating Structure, and Organizational Criteria—An update of Korman's 1966 Review," *Personnel Psychology* 27, no. 4 (Winter 1974): 555–568; J. Schriesheim, "The Social Context of Leader-Subordinate Relations: An Investigation of the Effects of Group Cohesiveness," *Journal of Applied Psychology* 65 no. 2 (April 1980): 183–194; and C. Schriesheim and C. Murphy, "Relationships Between Leader Behavior and Subordinate Satisfaction and Performance: A Test of Situational Moderators," *Journal of Applied Psychology* 60, no. 5 (1976): 634–641.

15. R. Blake and J. Mouton, *The New Managerial Grid* (Houston, Texas: Gulf Publishing), 1978.

16. R. Blake and J. Mouton, "Should You Teach There's Only One Best Way to Manage?" *Training HRD,* April 1978, pp. 25–29; and R. Blake and J. Mouton, "How to Choose a Leadership Style," *Training and Development Journal* 36, no. 2 (February 1982): 38–45.

17. G. Yukl, *Leadership in Organizations* (Englewood Cliffs, N.J.: Prentice-Hall, 1981).

18. R. Tannenbaum and W. Schmidt, "How to Choose a Leadership Pattern," *Harvard Business Review* (May–June 1973): 162–180.

19. F. Fiedler, "A Contingency Model of Leadership Effectiveness," in L. Berkowitz, ed., *Advances in Experimental Social Psychology,* vol. 1 (New York: Academic Press, 1964), pp. 149–160; and F. Fiedler, *A Theory of Leadership Effectiveness* (New York: McGraw-Hill, 1967).

20. J. Kennedy, "Middle-LPC Leaders and the Contingency Model of Effectiveness," *Organizational Behavior and Human Performance,* 30, no. 1 (August 1982): 1–14; B. Kabanoff, "A Critique of the Leader Match and its Implications for Leadership Research," *Personnel Psychology,* 34, no. 4 (Winter 1981): 749–764; R. Rice, "Leader LPC and Follower Satisfaction: A Review," *Organizational Behavior and Human Performance,* 28, no. 1 (1981): 1–26; and R. Singh, "Leadership Style and Reward Allocation: Does Least Preferred Co-worker Scale Measure Task and Relations Orientation?" *Organizational Behavior and Human Performance* 32, no. 2 (1983): 178–197.

21. F. Fiedler, M. Chemers, and L. Mahar, *Improving Leadership Effectiveness* (New York: Wiley, 1976), pp. 154–158.

22. R. House, "A Path-Goal Theory of Leadership Effectiveness," *Administrative Science Quarterly* 16, no. 3 (September 1971): 321–339; and R. House and T. Mitchell, "Path-Goal Theory of Leadership," *Journal of Contemporary Business* 3, no. 4 (Autumn 1974): 81–98.

23. V. Vroom and P. Yetton, *Leadership and Decision Making* (Pittsburgh: University of Pittsburgh Press, 1973); and V. Vroom, "Can Leaders Learn to Lead?" *Organizational Dynamics* 4, no. 3 (Fall 1976): 17–28.

24. P. Hersey and K. Blanchard, *Management of Organizational Behavior: Utilizing Human Resources,* 4th ed. (Englewood Cliffs, N.J.: Prentice-Hall, 1982).

25. P. Hersey and M. Goldsmith, "A Situational Approach to Performance Planning," *Training and Development Journal* 34, no. 11 (November 1980): 38.

26. J. Schriesheim and C. Schriesheim, "Test of the Path-Goal Theory of Leadership and Some Suggestions for Research," *Personnel Psychology* 33, no. 2 (Summer 1980): 349–371; and J. Falk and E. Wendler, "Dimensionality of Leader-Subordinate Interactions: A Path-Goal Investigation," *Organizational Behavior and Human Performance* 30, no. 2 (October 1982): 241–264.

27. C. Graeff, "The Situational Leadership Theory: A Critical View," *Academy of Management Review* 8, no. 2 (April 1983): 285–291.

28. J. French, Jr., and B. Raven, "The Bases of Social Power," in D. Cartwright and A. Zander, eds., *Group Dynamics: Research and Theory* (New York: Harper & Row, 1960), pp. 607–623; and report by P. Hersey and W. Natemeyer, available through the Center for Creative Leadership, Greensboro, N.C.

29. G. Yukl and T. Taber, "The Effective Use of Managerial Power," *Personnel* 60, no. 2 (March–April 1983): 37–44; and J. Pearce, II, and R. Robinson, Jr., "A Measure of CEO Social Power in Strategic Decision Making," *Strategic Management Journal* (May–June 1987): 297–304.

30. W. Reichman and M. Levy, "Personal Power Enhancement: A Way to Execute Success," *Management Review* 6, no. 3 (March 1977): 28–34.

Cohesion Incident 15-1
Follow the Leader

After his first six months at the Journey's End in Graniteville, Charles felt good about himself and the progress he was making in his position. When he was first assigned to Graniteville, he had been told that he was fortunate to be working with Roger Elliott and that he would be given an immediate opportunity to manage parts of the motel. Charles, in fact, had been given more and more responsibility for management of the motel. When he had encountered problems, Roger had urged him to solve them himself. Charles really appreciated his freedom to try new ideas, and Roger's confidence and support gave him even more incentive to do his best.

Although he did not object to working the shift from 2:00 P.M. until midnight, Charles was eager to be assigned to the morning hours, so he was pleased when Roger called him into his office one afternoon.

"Charles, I think it's time for us to change shifts for a while so you can get to know what goes on around here in the morning. For the next month, you'll come to work around 8:30 and leave at 6:00, and I'll take the time slot you've been filling. You've done such a super job in the first six months that I'm positive you'll have no problems. In fact, few people would have any problems managing this motel. That's because of the type of people we have working for us. As you already know, Susan rarely comes to me with problems she may be having in the restaurant. She enjoys being responsible for that restaurant and is doing a fantastic job. The two clerks you'll be supervising have both been here for two years and are also extremely hard-working. I've told them that any time they can answer or solve any questions or problems that our guests may have, they should go ahead and do it. Very seldom has a guest been dissatisfied with one of their decisions and insisted on talking with me. I'm seriously thinking about asking them both if they would like to go through our management training program.

"Charles, if you should have any problems, solve them yourself. Don't feel that you need to call me. You wouldn't have been hired into management with Journey's End if we didn't think you could handle it. The best way for you to learn this business is by doing it."

Roger continued, "When you leave here and have a motel of your own to manage, you'll discover that upper management will also leave you pretty much alone. Sure, we have our annual meetings to discuss goals and analyze our budgets, but after that, unless you deviate substantially from budget, you'll never hear from top management. So you end up being your own boss, making your own decisions, and getting paid according to how well you have performed. I think it's a great way to run our motels, and I'm trying to handle you and the other employees in the same way."

Discussion Questions

1. Would you characterize Roger as a Theory X or a Theory Y leader? Why?

2. It is often said that "Leaders lead by example." Explain how this saying is related to Roger's style of management.

3. Under what circumstances would Theory X be the more effective management style at Journey's End? Under what circumstances would Theory Y be recommended?

Cohesion Incident 15-2

Is Everybody Happy?

In the past week, Leslie has had growing concerns about the performance of her staff members. On more than one occasion she has found herself working weekends to redo data analyses or rewrite portions of reports that did not meet her expectations. Even Harriet's work in preparing reports and visual aids seemed to have suffered. Her work remained accurate, but she did not necessarily follow the format or the timetable Leslie had hoped for.

As she reflected over the past six months, Leslie wondered whether the performance problems had not been there all along. It dawned on her that even now she might not have labeled the situation a problem if Eileen had not called it to her attention. Eileen seemed particularly concerned that Leslie was spending too much time "tidying up" after her staff had completed their work on an assignment. Leslie had found the meeting with Eileen stressful but, on reflection, thought-provoking.

Until Eileen had conveyed her concerns, Leslie had been pleased with the way her part of the department was shaping up. Bill had moved smoothly through training, and Steve seemed to be doing likewise. They were both consistently willing to take on the tasks she delegated to them with few questions. She intentionally gave them little guidance in the execution of their work, because she believed they would appreciate the challenge and be more satisfied with their work if they organized the tasks themselves. She saw her role as that of encourager, supporter, counselor, and facilitator.

Leslie had been pleased to see that Harriet, Bill, and Steve worked so well together as a team. That was part of what puzzled Leslie now. Why was their performance a problem when everything else was running so smoothly? After a few weeks together, the three had created their own atmosphere in the office. Furniture was gradually rearranged—a bookcase moved to open up more space between desks, a desk turned to allow easier eye contact, some files shifted to create the "coffee lounge." Friendly joking was the norm. To Leslie, there was a relaxed but professional air that should have ensured satisfied staff members and good performance. "After all," she thought to herself, "these people all know best how to do their jobs. All they need is the right atmosphere in which to work and the opportunity to feel challenged in what they do." She had oriented her management style toward achieving those ends.

Following her conversation with Eileen, however, she had begun to wonder whether her strategy had been the wisest. She wondered whether she had provided enough direction in objectives, timetables, and standards for completed work. She was also uncomfortable about approaching her staff with these concerns. There was certain to be some conflict, because she had not communicated any of her dissatisfactions until now. She realized, nonetheless, that she could not continue to spend her time "tidying up" when their work was not up to par. As Eileen had made clear, Leslie's performance in other areas was starting to suffer as a result.

Discussion Questions

1. Which of the five management styles on the Managerial Grid best characterizes Leslie's style of leadership? Cite examples from the case to support your answer.

2. According to the Managerial Grid theory, what is the most desirable management style for Leslie? According to the assumptions underlying contingency theories of leadership, what management style would be the most desirable for her to adopt?

Management Development Exercise 15
Leadership Styles Questionnaire

The following items describe aspects of leadership behavior. Respond to each item according to the way you act as the leader of your work group. Circle A if you behave in the described way always or frequently; circle S if you behave that way seldom or never. (You can ignore the fact that some of the question numbers are circled.)

As the leader of a work group . . .

A   S   _____   (1.) I act as the spokesperson of the group.

A   S   _____   2. I encourage overtime work.

A   S   _____   3. I allow members complete freedom in their work.

A   S   _____   (4.) I encourage the use of uniform procedures.

A   S   _____   5. I permit the members to use their own judgment in solving problems.

A   S   _____   6. I stress being ahead of competing groups.

A   S   _____   (7.) I speak as a representative of the group.

A   S   _____   8. I strongly urge members to greater effort.

A   S   _____   9. I try out my ideas in the group.

A   S   _____   10. I let the members do their work the way they think best.

A   S   _____   11. I work hard for a promotion.

A   S   _____   12. I am able to tolerate postponement and uncertainty.

A   S   _____   (13.) I speak for the group when visitors are present.

A   S   _____   14. I keep the work moving at a rapid pace.

A   S   _____   15. I turn the members loose on a job and let them go to it.

A   S   _____   16. I settle conflicts when they occur in the group.

A   S   _____   (17.) I get swamped by details.

A   S   _____   (18.) I represent the group at outside meetings.

A   S   _____   (19.) I am reluctant to allow the members any freedom of action.

A   S   _____   (20.) I decide what shall be done and how it shall be done.

A   S   _____   21. I push for increased production.

A   S   _____   22. I let some members have authority that I should keep

A   S   _____ (23.) Things usually turn out as I predict.

A   S   _____ 24. I allow the group a high degree of initiative.

A   S   _____ 25. I assign group members to particular tasks.

A   S   _____ 26. I am willing to make changes.

A   S   _____ 27. I ask the members to work harder.

A   S   _____ 28. I trust the group members to exercise good judgment.

A   S   _____ (29.) I schedule the work to be done.

A   S   _____ (30.) I refuse to explain my actions.

A   S   _____ (31.) I persuade others that my ideas are to their advantage.

A   S   _____ 32. I permit the group to set its own pace.

A   S   _____ 33. I urge the group to beat its previous record.

A   S   _____ (34.) I act without consulting the group.

A   S   _____ (35.) I ask that group members follow standard rules and regulations.

T_____   P_____

After you have completed this questionnaire, your instructor will help you score and interpret your answers.

Source: Adapted from G. H. Goldhaber, et al., *Instructor's Manual T/A Organizational Communication*, 4th ed. Copyright 1986 William C. Brown Publishers, Dubuque, Iowa. All rights reserved. Reprinted by permission.

Managing Groups

Your study of this chapter will enable you to do the following:

1. Explain how group processes are related to each of the management functions.
2. Define the term *group* and distinguish between formal and informal groups.
3. Describe three types of changes that occur during socialization of an individual into a group, and explain what a manager can do to facilitate the orientation and socialization of new employees.
4. Explain how characteristics of the group and of the task can interact to affect group performance.
5. Define the term *intergroup conflict* and describe five styles of conflict management.

Learning Objectives

"Workstyle" at Data Design Associates

Back in the glory days of Silicon Valley, companies like Data Design Associates, Inc., seemed to be the wave of the future. It was one of those high-flying, high-tech, high-touch outfits—a software developer in Sunnyvale, California, to be exact—and, for more than a decade, it sailed along with revenues and profits growing at a rapid pace, rising to $11 million and $2 million, respectively, in fiscal 1985.

Nobody benefited from this growth more than the company's one hundred employees. In fact, it often seemed that founder and president David Lowry was intent on giving away his own share of the corporate riches. He offered all of the employees stock and bought memberships in fancy health clubs. He set up a bonus system and let the employees determine the size of the bonus pool. They settled on 20 percent of pretax profits—whereupon Lowry boosted the total, adding 50 percent of all profits above the stated goal. The employees seemed delighted with all of this, as well they might, but Lowry was still not satisfied. He continually sought their advice on ways to make the work environment even better.

Which is how it came to pass that Data Design's managers found themselves jumping out of airplanes, plunging over waterfalls, scaling mountains, and sleeping in the snow.

Data Design Associates employees enjoy a 10-day trek through the Rocky Mountains as part of their workstyle program. (Data Design Associates)

The idea of a workstyle program originated with the managers themselves, who felt that the company's growth was making it more and more difficult to maintain their *esprit de corps*. Meetings over lunch, they said, just didn't do the trick anymore. Someone suggested that the managers try going away together, maybe spending a little time out in the wilderness. The next thing they knew, they were barreling down the Yuba River on white-water rafts, one of which shot out over a ten-foot waterfall and capsized, nearly drowning Lowry's thirty-three-year-old assistant, Ola Harris.

Then there was the grueling, ten-day trek through the Rocky Mountains under the auspices of Outward Bound. Before it was over, the managers had to climb a 13,000-foot mountain with forty-pound packs strapped to their backs and camp out in the snow. The director of marketing, an IBM Corporation veteran named Desmond Crain, proved to be a source of inspiration, often hoisting the weight that others couldn't carry. But when Crain declined to participate in the six-mile run at the end of the expedition, he was denied his Outward Bound diploma. Lowry broke down and wept. So did Crain.

Next they took up skydiving.

Oddly enough, this stuff seemed to work. To a person, the managers swore that they had never felt closer or worked together more effectively. Meanwhile, sales and profits continued to soar. And at a time when turnover rates among small technology companies often approached 50 percent, Data Design's was less than 5 percent.

To be sure, Data Design wasn't the only high-tech company with a slightly bizarre corporate culture back then. The Valley was filled with legends about companies doing extraordinary things to promote a better, more productive work environment. Rolm Corporation had its steam rooms and saunas. Tandem Computer, Inc., held Friday afternoon beer busts. Activision, Inc., sponsored ski trips to Lake Tahoe and took its entire staff to Hawaii. At one point, Apple Computer, Inc., even hired masseurs for the workers in its Macintosh Division. That idea appealed so much to Apple Computer president and chief executive officer (and former PepsiCo senior vice president) John Sculley that he started getting massaged, too. "I'm a cerebral person," he explained. "This lets me meditate and clear my head."

Clearing heads was only one of the goals of such programs, however. The real payoff, proponents argued, lay in high productivity, low turnover, and soaring profits. This stuff was not just fun; it was smart business. Even if you couldn't measure the benefits of, say, having your chief financial officer take a roll on the rapids, the results eventually showed up where they counted: on the bottom line.[1]

Introduction

What Are Groups?

How do committees, boards of directors, quality circles, carpools, work groups, softball teams, and a group of co-workers who regularly get together for a beer on Friday afternoons differ from collections of people who are dining in the same restaurant, sitting in a receptionist's office waiting to be interviewed for a job, standing in line to buy concert tickets, working in the same building, or riding in an elevator together? In a word, the first list is made up of groups and the second comprises aggregates of people. We will use the term **group** to refer to "two or more people who interact with one another, are psychologically aware of one another, perceive themselves to be members of the group, and work toward a common goal."[2] Group members have reciprocal influence on one another—that is, each person in the group influences and is influenced by the others. Hence people in groups, unlike those in aggregates, develop mutual perceptions of one another, emotional ties, patterns of interdependence, roles, and norms.[3]

This chapter discusses these and other characteristics of groups and examines factors that affect how well group members work together. It then explores the effects that groups have on the way an organization functions. In total, this chapter will help you to understand why the group development activities at companies like data design associates provide psychological and economic benefits for both managers and their employees.

The Need to Understand Groups

Why does a manager need to understand how groups work? While attending to the technical and task-related aspects of their jobs, many managers either overlook or fail to understand the significance of such interpersonal aspects of their jobs as group dynamics. Yet how effective a manager is in planning, organizing, staffing, leading, and controlling often hinges on how well he or she can manage groups. Figure 16-1 illustrates how each of these management functions is related to group processes.

Managers should be aware that their actions affect group processes, which in turn affect organizational outcomes. As Figure 16-1 illustrates, one aspect of a manager's responsibility to organize is to design work groups, work spaces, and jobs. Because these actions have an effect on the structure of group communication

FIGURE 16-1
Impact of Management Functions on Organizational Outcomes via Groups

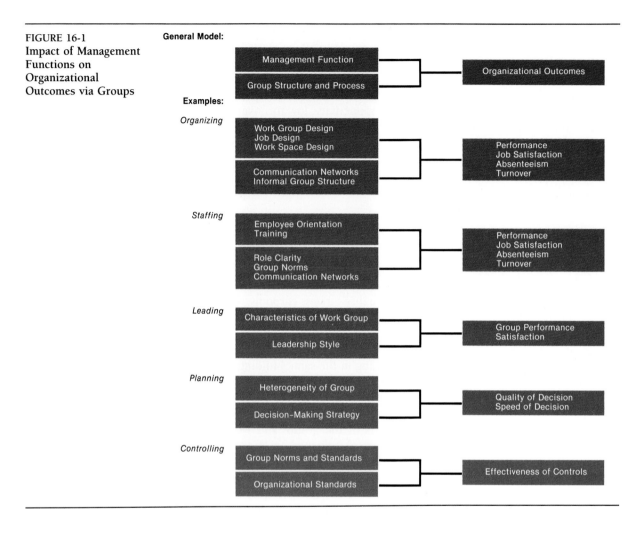

networks and informal group structure, they can influence such organizational outcomes as performance and job satisfaction. Similarly, the type of orientation a manager provides for new employees can affect performance, satisfaction, absenteeism, and turnover through its effect on role clarity and group norms.

Whether a particular way of carrying out a management function has positive or negative effects on organizational functioning depends on characteristics of the groups involved. Three examples should suffice to illustrate the importance of the nature of the group.

1. A participative leadership style may be more effective for groups that have goals and norms consistent with those of the organization than for groups that do not.

2. Making decisions about which course of action a group should take to meet its objective is part of the planning function of management. Whether such decisions should be made by a group or an individual depends in part on aspects of the group's structure, such as its heterogeneity and cohesiveness.

3. Whether the standards a manager sets for group performance will be effective as performance controls can depend on whether the group's norms and performance standards are consistent with those set by the manager.

Groups: Their Characteristics and Value to Members

Why Do People Join Groups?

To understand how groups function, it is necessary to understand why people join groups in the first place. Many researchers assume that our behavior in groups is motivated by the desire to satisfy individual needs or to achieve goals that cannot be achieved alone.[4] As we noted when we discussed motivating in Chapter 14, groups may help an individual satisfy the social and esteem needs described in Maslow's hierarchy, and they can contribute to both the hygiene factors and the motivators described in Herzberg's two-factor theory.[5] Groups are the major means for satisfying what McClelland calls the need for affiliation and are often a means for satisfying the need for achievement and the need for power.[6] From a behavioral perspective, groups are major sources of secondary reinforcements such as status,[7] and they offer members an opportunity to exchange a wide range of interpersonal resources, as described in equity theory and social exchange theory.[8]

Let us assume, then, that we join groups in order to meet our personal needs and goals. It remains to consider why people join *particular* groups. The reasons tend to fall into two categories. First, a person may expect that the group itself will satisfy some of his or her needs. These are called *internal reasons* because the source of need satisfaction is located within the group itself. On the other hand, a person who joins a group for *external reasons* does not expect that the group itself will meet his or her needs directly, but sees membership in the group as a way of getting needs met by sources outside the group.[9] In most cases, there are probably many internal and external reasons why a person becomes a member of a particular group.

INTERNAL REASONS FOR JOINING A GROUP

There are four ways in which a group itself can satisfy group members' needs: interpersonal attraction, group activities, group goals, and group membership itself. These four sources of need satisfaction provide four internal reasons for joining a group. Let us consider each of the specific different reasons that four people gave to explain why they joined a local chapter of the Jaycees.

Stan Rubenstein, after attending a few of the meetings, decided to join because he has much in common with the group and enjoys the company of the group members. It is obvious that we join many groups because we like the *members of the group* and enjoy interacting with them. Research on interpersonal attraction indicates that we are particularly attracted to people who are similar to ourselves in important ways—that is, those who embrace similar attitudes, values, and beliefs. Interaction with similar others has been demonstrated to be rewarding, and it constitutes one major positive outcome for individuals in groups. Informal groups often form among people who live or work in close proximity to one another. Frequent interaction provides opportunities to learn more about any similarities that exist, and frequent exposure often increases interpersonal attraction.[10]

Some members of a group may be more attracted by the *activities of the group* than by the other members. One member of our chapter of the Jaycees, John Brewster, indicated that he joined the Jaycees primarily because he enjoys their community service activities and the programs at the monthly meetings.

Support for *group goals* may be another reason why one joins a group. For example, Jean Berkowitz joined the Jaycees because she values the group's goals of promoting local business and industry and developing leadership skills in young business people. Even though she does not particularly enjoy the people who belong to the chapter and does not have time to participate in many of the activities they sponsor, she continues to participate as a group member because of the goals she holds in common with the group.

Finally, some people join a group primarily for *group membership* itself: to satisfy affiliation needs and feel a sense of belonging. Social psychologists have suggested that one important consequence of affiliation is that other group members provide us with information about ourselves and our performance through a process called **social comparison**.[11] Particularly when we find ourselves in novel or ambiguous situations, we are inclined to compare ourselves to others in order to evaluate and revise our behavior. There is substantial evidence that we would rather engage in social comparison with similar others than with dissimilar others; groups often provide this opportunity. Groups may also help to reduce anxiety in stressful or threatening situations, particularly when other group members are also experiencing, or have experienced, the stressful event.[12]

EXTERNAL REASONS FOR JOINING A GROUP

People may also choose to join a group for reasons that are not intrinsic to the group. Two external reasons are common: (1) Membership in the group increases one's chances for interaction with people to whom one is attracted who are *outside* the group, and (2) group membership can help one achieve personal goals that are unrelated to the group goals. As an example of the first of these, Ed Mandes joined the local Jaycees hoping to get to know the community business leaders who often speak at the meetings and to become more involved in the local business network. Ellen Cheung's motivation illustrates the second external reason: she had been strongly encouraged by her employer to get involved in local civic and service organizations and joined the Jaycees in order to meet that goal. Note that membership in any one of several community organizations would have served Ed Mandes and Ellen Cheung just as well. A group one joins for external reasons is not necessarily unique in its ability to help one reach one's goal.

At this point, it would be valuable to look back to the opening case to try to reassess the reasons why Data Design's group-building efforts were so successful. Were group members motivated by external reasons only?

Types of Groups

An individual in an organization is likely to be a member of many different groups, and these are likely to vary in lifespan and degree of formality. It is useful to consider how each of these dimensions can affect the structure and functioning of a group.

Lifespan of the Group

Groups differ in their longevity. Some groups, such as departments within an organization and friendship groups, exist on a long-term, indefinite basis. Other groups, such as task forces and special-interest groups are established to accomplish a particular goal and are disbanded when that goal is reached. Because of the relatively short time frame within which these latter groups operate, they are more effective when members have similar reasons for being part of the group and when those reasons are to a large extent task- or activity-oriented.

Formality

Groups also differ in whether their membership and goals are mandated by the organization or are chosen by group members. Within any organization, some groups are formed at the direction of the organization in order to accomplish organizational goals. These are called **formal groups**. Departments, committees, task forces, work teams, and quality circles are all formal groups. **Informal groups**, by contrast, are created by the choice of their members for the purpose of goals defined by the group. Figure 16-2 illustrates four different types of groups that the four possible combinations of formality and lifespan generate.

Permanent formal groups that consist of managers and their subordinates are called **command groups**. They are likely to be represented in the formal structure of the organization, as the solid lines in Figure 16-3 illustrate. A functional department or a product department is a good example of a command group.

Relatively impermanent formal groups, called **task groups**, are less likely to follow the structure of the organization chart. That, in fact, is one of their strengths. A task force or ad hoc committee can be formed for just as long as it is needed to accomplish a specific purpose and, because of its temporary nature, can include people who represent several different command groups. The National Aeronautics and Space Administration (NASA) is well known for its use of temporary project groups. Using task groups enables an organization to respond flexibly to its changing environment.

In an organization, membership in several formal groups is usually required or at least strongly encouraged. Members of a formal group, such as a committee, may choose to serve on that particular committee for internal reasons. For example, they may believe in its goals and want to try to help the committee accomplish them, or they may enjoy working with the other members of the committee. Yet required membership can also constitute an external reason for membership, as when a person serves on a committee to obtain the positive regard of his or her manager. Despite the existence of such external reasons for membership, the fact that personal needs are also met in formal groups can affect the group's functioning. For example, a person who consented to serve on a personnel grievance committee primarily to satisfy social, self-esteem, and belongingness needs might impair the group's performance by being reluctant to disagree with other group members or to take a stand on a controversial issue.

Informal groups often develop within and across the boundaries of formal groups. Because informal groups come into being by the choice of the members rather than in response to an organizational mandate, they are often affected by

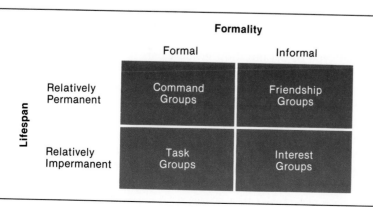

FIGURE 16-2
Types of Groups in
Organizations

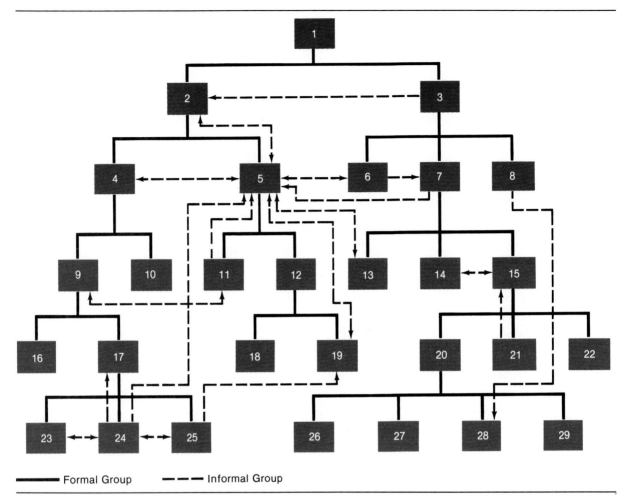

FIGURE 16-3
Formal and Informal
Groups

people's attraction for one another and individuals' perceptions that they share common interests or goals. They may also be affected by factors that are to some extent controlled by the organization, such as physical proximity and organization design. Relatively permanent informal groups such as these are called **friendship groups.** For example, in an organization that is functionally organized, informal friendship groups are more likely to develop among individuals who work in the same functional area, whereas in an organization that exhibits a structure based on product line, informal groups are more likely to contain people from different functional areas of the organization.

The final type of organization group exists because of a shared concern of members at any level or area in the firm. Called **interest groups,** they develop or become active when members believe that their special concerns are receiving insufficient managerial attention. Usually informal, interest groups form around issues such as working conditions, equitable treatment, and concern for employee welfare.

Figure 16-3 contrasts the formal structure of an organization (shown by solid lines) with the informal network (shown by dashed lines) that, in many cases, crosses those formal lines. This latter type of diagram, called a **sociogram,** is constructed by asking members of the organization to report how frequently they interact with each other member, as well as by observing and recording their actual patterns of interaction.

The structure of informal groups can significantly affect interactions within an organization's formal groups. Specifically, people who become highly active as communicators within the informal network can increase their power and influence within the formal structure of an organization.[13] Many researchers believe that informal interactions are valuable in that they yield information and support, two resources that increase one's opportunities to exert influence in the formal organizational structure and to move upward in that structure.[14] For these reasons, the U.S. Army often tries to preserve informal groups in its assignment of military personnel.

Several factors can make an individual more central in an informal group. These include: (1) informal access to influential members of the formal group, (2) thorough integration with one's work group, (3) a physical location that places one in frequent interaction with people inside and outside one's work group, and (4) a job that is nonroutine and provides access to information useful in dealing with conditions of uncertainty. In Figure 16-3, person 5 appears to be central in the informal network, as illustrated by her or his relatively high number of informal contacts. Studies of informal group dynamics in both supervisory and non-supervisory settings have indicated that individuals who are most central in the informal group structure and who have greater access to communication with the dominant coalition are perceived by others in the organization as more influential and are more likely to be promoted.[15]

Informal groups may seem threatening to some managers because they develop and change outside the manager's direct control. But the distinct benefits they offer outweigh their negative qualities when the manager knows how to make effective use of the informal network and is willing to risk some of the negative effects that accompany the benefits. These benefits and negative effects are listed in Figure 16-4.

FIGURE 16-4
Benefits and Negative Effects of the Informal Work Group

Benefits

- Assists in accomplishing work
- Helps to remove weaknesses in the formal organizational structure
- Widens the effective span of management
- Compensates for violations of principles of the formal organization
- Provides an additional channel of communication
- Provides emotional support for employees
- Encourages better management

Negative Effects

- May work counter to the purpose of the formal organization
- Reduces the degree of predictability and control
- Reduces the number of practical alternatives
- Increases the time required to complete activities

Source: Adapted from R. W. Mondy, A. Sharplin, R. E. Holmes, and E. B. Flippo, *Management Concepts and Practices,* 3rd ed. (Boston: Allyn & Bacon, 1986), p. 222.

=============== *Guidelines for Management Practice* ===============

The potential benefits listed in Figure 16-4 suggest the following guidelines for the manager who wants to make best use of informal groups:

1. *Be aware of the conditions under which informal group structure can help accomplish objectives of the more formally defined groups.* Specifically, when informal groups share the goals and the performance norms of the formal organization, allow them more flexibility in determining how to accomplish the objectives. Because of faster information flow and less rigid procedure, the informal group can often adjust its work to cope with the unexpected more efficiently than the formal group can. Of course, relying on informal groups entails some risk if the norms or goals of the group are inconsistent with those of the organization.

2. *Use the informal group structure to fill in gaps in the formal structure.* A newly promoted manager may draw on the expertise of more experienced members of the informal group in a way that he or she could not within the formal organization because of its more rigid assignment of roles and responsibility.[16]

3. *Use some types of informal groups to increase the sphere of the manager's influence.* Groups whose goals and norms are consistent with those of the formal organization and whose members are highly attracted to the group often apply normative group pressure that can reduce the need for supervision. Effective group control can increase the number of employees a manager can effectively supervise.

4. *When appropriate, use the informal group structure to compensate for breakdowns or violations of the formal group structure.* Individuals who have influence because of the information and support available to them by virtue of their central position in the informal group, rather than because of any authority attached to their position in the formal group, may be able to get things done with remarkable efficiency, despite the fact that they are not part of the usual "channels."

5. *Allow the informal group to provide social and emotional support for employees.* Research on whether the negative effects of work-related stress are reduced by social support at work have yielded inconsistent results, but employees who feel they get social support from their supervisors or their co-workers seem to report less job dissatisfaction and less anxiety over work-related matters.[17]

6. *Learn more specifically what motivates individuals and subgroups* within the formal organization by observing the informal groups that form and determining what needs they satisfy. In some cases work groups, committees, and task forces can be organized around informal groups, allowing people to work in formal groups with people they like and work well with. The results of research wherein this approach was applied to the formation of construction crews suggest that it reduced turnover, fostered greater job satisfaction, and lowered production costs.

8. *Finally, there are certain extra time costs associated with employees' involvement in informal groups.* Managers must accept that informal groups take longer than formal groups to complete some activities. Furthermore, a healthy group needs to spend some time in interaction that is not directly task-related but is nonetheless necessary to maintain good "socio-emotional" functioning in the group.

Group Structure

Group structure consists of the norms the group develops and conforms to in order to reach its goals, the roles that are played by various people within the group, and the group's cohesiveness (its network of communication and interpersonal attraction).[18] There are, then, three properties of group structure that it is particularly important for managers to understand: norms, roles, and cohesiveness. Let us look at each component.

Norms

A **norm** is a standard of behavior to which group members expect each other to adhere. As a standard, a norm provides a basis by which the appropriateness of an individual's work behavior can be judged. Group norms serve several functions. They increase the group's chances for survival and for successful goal attainment. They increase group members' ability to predict their fellow members' behavior and simplify individuals' decisions about their own behavior. They minimize the number of embarrassing situations that arise within the group and, as a result, reduce the likelihood of decreasing the rewards that individuals' derive from group membership. They also express the core values of the group, displaying and increasing the group's sense of identity.[19]

Norms function as a means of social control within a group and keep the group moving toward its goal with minimum conflict, but unlike the formal social control imposed by an organization's rules and regulations, group norms are usually enforced by subtle group pressure to conform. Production norms typically exist in work groups, for example, and they can either enhance or depress production. Such norms are often strongly influenced by the informal relationships within the formal group. Say a certain work group in Company A has a norm of working steadily but not too hard. How will it react to a new member of the work group whose output consistently runs 10 percent higher than the group average? She may well find herself closed out of much social interaction with the group on and off the job. In contrast, in Company B a work team is recognized each month if it has the highest overall work-team performance or if one of its members has the top production record in the plant. If the comparable work group in Company B has a norm of striving to have the highest individual and the highest group production, the same employee who was shunned in Company A for producing "too much" will probably be welcome in Company B's work group.

What happens to group members who violate group norms? That depends on what type of norm is violated and on who the group member is. **Pivotal norms** are those that are closely related to the group's identity and goals. Adherence to this type of norm is a requirement of group membership and is typically expected of all members of the group, regardless of their status. For example, IBM has a pivotal norm prescribing that high-quality customer service always be given first priority. A sales representative who regularly deviated from that norm when interacting with customers would probably not be with the company for long. **Peripheral norms** describe what the group expects as desirable behavior, but they are less crucial to the preservation of group identity or the achievement of group goals. One is not likely to be expelled from the group if one violates peripheral norms, though other sanctions may result, such as warnings or negative evaluations of work habits or performance. The same sales company that values customer service as a pivotal norm may also expect its sales representatives to dress in conservative business suits when calling on customers. Though a sales representative who deviates from that norm might be reprimanded for "unprofessional appearance" and might even be passed over for a promotion, violation of this type of peripheral norm would not necessarily result in loss of group membership.[20]

How does a group respond to one of its members who does not adhere to group norms? Research has indicated that the group first increases the amount of communication that is directed toward the "deviant" individual in an attempt to clarify the norm, to identify the basis for the person's violation of the norm, and to step up the pressure to conform. In an organization, such communication might take the explicit form of a reprimand or warning from one's supervisor or the more subtle form of a "Dutch uncle talk" initiated by a co-worker or pointed teasing and joking from peers. If the person persists in deviating from the group norm, however, other group members are likely to exclude him or her gradually from their interactions, and the frequency of communication directed toward that person dramatically decreases. This is particularly likely to occur in a highly cohesive group.[21] (Group cohesiveness is discussed a little later in this chapter.) It is partly for this reason that organizations such as Data Design Associates invest in team-building programs. Quarterback-turned-consultant Fran Tarkenton expresses similar support for teambuilding in "In Practice 16-1."

In Practice 16-1

TARKENTON ON TEAMBUILDING

"We've taken skills in motivating and managing people for granted too long in this country," said Fran Tarkenton. "We've felt that technical solutions would win the battle, but they never do. People win the battle of business. You could have the best technical solutions in the world, but if people don't join in and feel like part of the team, you just don't get anywhere."

Teamwork is familiar ground for Tarkenton, known to millions as the legendary quarterback who led the Minnesota Vikings to the Superbowl. "What does teamwork mean? It's when people say, 'I want input. I want a say in what's going on. I have good ideas that will help this company run better.'" After twelve years in management consulting, Tarkenton is now also known to such companies as General Motors, Exxon, and American Express as the chairman of Tarkenton & Company, the Atlanta-based consulting firm.

"Teamwork sounds wonderful. Everyone can abide by that. But teamwork means that we recognize the value of the members of the team beyond just doing their work, that we want them to become involved in our strategizing. It means pushing the level of creativity and decision making further and further down."

The first step in building a team, according to Tarkenton, is to think about what we want out of the team and how we want it to be structured. The next step is to get the input of the future team members as to the format and structure of the team. Tarkenton emphasized that none of this means giving up managerial authority to the members of the team. "Certainly Jim McMahon is not going to tell Mike Ditka how to run the Chicago Bears. But he does and should have input as to what type of passes he runs, what kind of offense, and so forth. This is what teamwork is about."

Another quality of good team leaders is that they realize that a great deal can be accomplished if they don't care who gets the credit for a success —that credit can come through the success of the team, rather than from being the individual in charge of the team. "You can't say, 'Sure, I had help from the people on the team, but I accomplished this. I'm the leader, I'm the manager, I'm the quarterback.'" Tarkenton warned. "The fact is the quarterback didn't win. His guards and tackles kept the people off him, the receivers caught the ball, the special teams got field position, the defense got him the ball, and the runners ran the ball. That's all teamwork. The important thing is that the team do well, and if it does, the team leader will get credit without having to shout it to the world."

Every team leader should expect a certain amount of conflict since encouraging people to share ideas inevitably results in a wealth of different opinions. "We are so accustomed to managing computers and technology that we want people to act like machines and make decisions like them, in the same consistent manner." according to Tarkenton. "That doesn't happen and we shouldn't encourage it to happen. We should encourage these differences of opinions and ideas, and with that comes conflict."

High-status members who are considered very valuable to the group may be allowed more latitude in their behavior, particularly when they violate peripheral norms, than group members with lower status. It has been suggested that high-status members of the group may earn "idiosyncrasy credits" for making particularly valuable contributions to the group—credits that earn them more indulgence when their everyday behavior deviates somewhat.[22] Consider, for example, the members of a sales department who generally honor the norm of dressing conservatively yet regularly allow their top salesperson to wear loud ties without any negative reactions. A new person in the department, however, would be ill-advised to sport flashy colors.

Roles

The term **role** describes the way group members expect a person in a particular position within a group to behave.[23] In one sense, roles define the jobs that need to be performed in order for the group to be successful. In another sense, roles define people's expectations about those jobs. **Role differentiation** refers to the way a group divides up the behaviors it needs its members to perform. One useful model of role differentiation distinguishes between *task-oriented roles,* which must be played in order for the group to accomplish its task-related goals, and the *group maintenance roles* necessary to maintain the socio-emotional well-being of the group. A third category, *self-oriented roles,* consists of behaviors that further the needs of individual group members, often to the detriment of the group's task accomplishment, its socio-emotional well-being, or both.[24] In a well-functioning group, both task-oriented and group maintenance roles are represented and self-oriented roles are minimized.

Group Cohesiveness

A group's level of **cohesiveness** is the degree to which group members want to remain in the group and the amount of pressure to remain that the group brings to bear on its members.[25] Groups with high levels of cohesiveness generally retain a stable membership. Cohesive groups exert a considerable amount of influence on the behavior of their members. In particular, because members of cohesive groups desire to remain in the group, they are more likely to conform to group norms than are members of groups with little cohesiveness. In many countries, the desire for cooperation promotes cohesiveness even more than does between-group competition, as demonstrated in "Insights for International Managers 16."

What effect does cohesiveness have on the performance of groups in organizations? The answer depends in large part on how closely the cohesive group's goals and norms correspond to those of the organization and to commonly accepted ethical principles. Highly cohesive groups are very effective in reaching their own goals and enforcing their own norms. Cohesive work groups that perceive a high level of compatibility between their goals and the organization's goals and that perceive management as generally supportive of their goals perform at higher levels than less cohesive groups in the same organization.[26]

But when a cohesive group develops norms and goals that run counter to those of the organization or of society, group cohesiveness can be quite detrimental. In part of the classic Hawthorne studies, Mayo documented just such an effect. In spite of financial incentives for increased performance, a highly cohesive work group developed a norm of working slowly and quitting work early in order to restrict performance. Interviews revealed that several members of the group believed that if they increased their performance levels, still higher levels would soon

---

■■■■ *Insights for International Managers 16* ■■■■

THERE'S NO RACE IF NOBODY WANTS TO RUN

In America, competition is the name of the game: everyone wants to be a winner. Elsewhere, competition in the workplace means everyone loses, either because people go off in their own directions or because they stop dead in their tracks. The international manager must know where to encourage individual effort or group collaboration.

In Greece they say: "Two Greeks will do badly what one will do well." Greek teams work well only when a strong leader is available to set goals and settle conflicts. In South America a team is likely to get stuck in power play among equally strong-willed individuals. Generally speaking, in countries where people are inexperienced in cooperative working relationships, leadership and responsibilities should be clearly delineated. If class, race and other social divisions are strong, it is important to be sensitive to inter-group hostilities and social practices.

In countries where competition is the norm, the objective of the competition must be clear, with measures of what constitutes "winning" firmly understood. If goals and rules are not clear, employees' competitive moves may not be good for the company.

Where cooperation is an art form, as in Japan, Taiwan, and other Asian countries, creating competition can bring work to a halt. The goal is to maintain group harmony, but you can effectively stir competition against those outside the group. Needless to say, Japanese concern for harmony does not keep Japanese companies from competing all-out with U.S. firms. In Communist countries such as the USSR, even workers who have no personal ambition can be stirred to compete to prove the excellence of their country, as in the sciences or athletics.

Source: From L. Copeland and L. Griggs, *Going International* (New York: Random House, 1985), pp. 128–129.

---

be expected.[27] Though it is doubtful that all the group members believed this, social pressure from the group was enough to restrict everyone's performance. Not just the organization, but also individuals and society at large can fall victim to cohesive groups with norms that diverge from ethical standards. For forty years, Manville Corporation (then Johns Manville) suppressed information from its own medical department that asbestos inhalation was a cause of lung disease, cancer, and deaths among its employees. Manville's senior management and its corporate medical directors collaborated in the cover-up. In the face of multimillion-dollar lawsuits from employees and their survivors, Manville filed for protection under the bankruptcy statutes. Intense but misapplied company loyalty was probably one of the factors that contributed to Manville's downfall.[28]

The rank-ordering in Figure 16-5 shows how level of cohesiveness of the group and degree of congruence between group and organizational goals and norms interact to affect the performance of groups. Some characteristics of groups that tend to increase cohesiveness and that tend to reduce it are listed in Figure 16-6.

Groups are more cohesive or less cohesive for various kinds of reasons.[29] For example, *incentive properties* make membership in a group attractive. The group may confer high status on its members, reward their interactions, or provide access to people who have similar attitudes and values. Groups are also attractive when they satisfy the needs of and motivate group members. A friendly group atmosphere is particularly attractive to someone motivated by social, self-esteem, and belongingness needs. For someone who is not motivated by those needs, however, a friendly atmosphere may be irrelevant in determining level of attraction to the group. Cohesiveness depends, then, on the right "fit" between group characteristics and group members' needs.

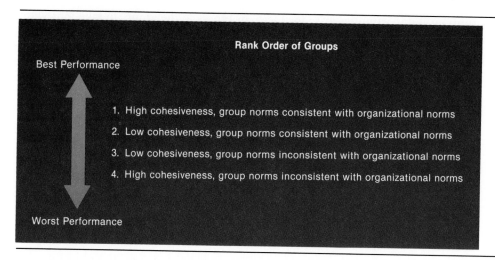

FIGURE 16-5
Effects of Group Norms
and Cohesiveness on
Performance

Groups are attractive to people—and therefore cohesive—so long as the members receive a satisfying level of good outcomes. Groups are also attractive and cohesive so long as they provide *better* outcomes than any alternative groups that people might belong to.[30] Consider the case of Ann Fiero, an accountant, who is most satisfied with her present job and the group with whom she works. The group includes people with similar beliefs and values; it strives to reach goals that enable her to meet many of her personal and professional goals; it is small, friendly, and cooperative; and it confers high status on its members. This is a fairly cohesive

FIGURE 16-6
Factors That Increase or
Decrease Group
Cohesiveness

Increase Cohesiveness

- Attractiveness of members: high status, rewarding interactions
- Similarity of members' attitudes, beliefs, values, and interests
- Attractiveness of group goals: explicitly stated, similar to members' goals; high consensus on how to reach goals
- Cooperative interdependence among group members
- Enjoyable group activities
- Leadership style consistent with members' preferences
- Group small enough to facilitate personal communication
- Friendly group atmosphere
- Threatening external environment that crystallizes group goals and identity

Decrease Cohesiveness

- Unattractive members: low status, unpleasant group interaction
- Lack of similarity among members' beliefs, attitudes, values, and interests
- Disagreement over group goals or means of reaching them
- Competition within the group
- Lack of enjoyable group activities
- Leadership style inconsistent with members' preferred style
- Group so large as to impair personal communication
- Membership or rewarding involvement in other groups or activities outside the group
- Threatening internal environment that fosters competition for resources within the group

Source: Table from *Group Dynamics* by D. Cartwright and A. Zander. Copyright © 1962, 1968 by Dorwin Cartwright and Alvin Zander. Reprinted by permission of Harper & Row, Publishers, Inc.

group until opportunities arise for Fiero, or others in the group, to take jobs with other accounting firms that offer an additional positive outcome: the chance eventually to become a partner in the firm. Fiero's present job and work group become less attractive to her because they suffer by comparison with another alternative. The other job and group are more attractive. A group's cohesiveness, then, depends not only on the level of positive outcomes provided by that group, but also on how those benefits compare with those available in alternative groups.

Socialization in Groups

Socialization is the process by which individuals are incorporated into a group, introduced to its norms and role structure, and trained to perform specific task-oriented and/or group maintenance roles. In large part, socialization occurs in order to protect and promote the cohesiveness of a group.

The potential benefits of effective orientation and socialization are many. A socialization process that helps new employees better understand and fit into the formal and informal groups in an organization increases the likelihood that these employees will carry out their role assignments dependably and effectively and will remain in the organization. It also boosts the chances that they will spontaneously engage in innovation and cooperation to achieve organizational objectives that transcend the requirements of their specific roles. Effective socialization can increase people's job satisfaction, their motivation to work, and their commitment to and involvement with their jobs. As you might imagine, many of Data Design's group development efforts were obvious and intentional extensions of the managers' socialization efforts in behalf of all employees.

Researcher Daniel Feldman's model of organizational socialization describes the process as unfolding in three phases: anticipatory socialization, encounter, and change and acquisition.[31] During each phase, role behaviors appropriate to the group are acquired, the work skills and abilities the employee needs to further the group goals are developed, and adjustment to the work group's norms and values occurs. Feldman's model of socialization suggests that in planning the orientation and socialization of new employees, a manager should see that certain information and experiences are provided during each of the three phases of socialization. We will examine each individually.

ANTICIPATORY SOCIALIZATION

During this first phase, a prospective employee learns about the organization and obtains the information he or she needs in order to decide whether to join it. This phase of socialization is enhanced when a realistic job preview gives the prospective employee

1. *Realistic information about the organization:* A full and accurate picture of the goals and climate of the organization.

2. *Realistic information about the job:* A full and accurate picture of what the employee's duties will be.

3. *An opportunity to assess congruence of skills and abilities:* The chance to determine whether one has the appropriate skills and abilities to complete task assignments successfully.

4. *An opportunity to assess congruence of needs and values:* The chance to determine whether one shares the values of the new organization and has personal needs that the organization can meet.

ENCOUNTER

Once someone joins the organization, he or she gets an early "inside look" at what the organization is really like and undergoes some shifting or adaptation of values, skills, and attitudes. During the encounter phase of socialization, the new employee should experience

1. *Management of outside-life conflicts:* Progress in dealing with conflicts between personal life and work life (such as scheduling, demands on the employee's family, and preoccupation with work).

2. *Management of intergroup role conflicts:* Progress in dealing with conflicts between one's own group and the demands of other groups in the organization.

3. *Role definition:* Clarification of one's own role within the immediate work group; crystallization of job duties, priorities, and the time allocated for tasks.

4. *Initiation to the task:* The learning of new tasks at work.

5. *Initiation to the group:* The establishment of new interpersonal relationships and the learning of group norms.

CHANGE AND ACQUISITION

The third phase may overlap the end of the encounter phase. It involves relatively long-lasting changes in abilities, skills, roles, norms, and values, including mastery of new skills, successful performance of new role behaviors, and adjustment to the organization's norms and values. This last phase of the socialization process should include

1. *Resolution of role demands:* Agreeing implicitly or explicitly with the work group on what tasks to perform and on task priorities and time allocation; resolving, or deciding how to deal with, both conflicts between personal life and work life and intergroup role conflicts at work.

2. *Task mastery:* Learning the tasks of the new job; gaining self-confidence and attaining consistently positive performance levels.

3. *Adjustment to group norms and values:* Developing mutual liking and trust with co-workers, understanding the group's norms and values, and making a satisfactory adjustment to the group culture.

Socialization with regard to roles, abilities, and norms and values occurs at each of the three phases. All too often, managers assume that the orientation of new employees should merely introduce the tasks that must be done and indicate what information and technical skills the employee will require in order to do them. Feldman's model—indeed, this entire chapter—suggests that orientation should also include effective socialization into the organization's group structure.

Performance of Groups

"Common sense" sayings about whether groups or individuals are better at getting a job done are often contradictory. "Two heads are better than one," but then again, "If you want a job done right, do it yourself." "Many hands make light the work," but then again, "Too many cooks spoil the broth." There is no simple answer to the question "Do groups outperform individuals?" It depends on the nature of the task, the characteristics of the groups or individuals involved, and the situational context in which the task is performed. A more appropriate set of questions is "Under what conditions does group performance exceed individual performance? Under what conditions is individual performance better? And under what conditions does it make no difference?" We will first distinguish among several kinds of tasks and then evaluate the performance of groups on a specific task, problem solving.

Nature of the Task

The tasks that groups perform can be usefully described as additive, conjunctive, compensatory, or disjunctive. These four kinds of tasks differ in how the work of the group members is combined to form a group product.[32] A definition and example of each are presented in Figure 16-7.

In principle, a group could do quite well on any task, and for any task there are unique ways in which group dynamics can contribute to good performance. But the group dynamics associated with any kind of task also can *weaken* group performance. The performance of a group can usually be explained as the result of the combined effects of (1) the resources available to, and used by, group members and (2) the quality of the group dynamics or the interaction within the group.

Let us take a look at several types of tasks and at how well groups usually perform them, compared with individuals. (This is most readily apparent in the results of research comparing the group's performance on each task with the performance of the group's best member and that of its worst member.) Then we will examine the group dynamics that affect the group's performance of each of

FIGURE 16-7
Four Types of Group Tasks

Nature of the Task	The Group Product Amounts to . . .	Example
Additive	The sum of all the members' performance	Number of phone calls made in a fund-raising phonathon
Conjunctive	The performance of the worst member	Time it takes a work group to complete a company report when each section is prepared by a different group member
Compensatory	The average of all the members' judgments	Average of hiring committee members' ratings of a job candidate
Disjunctive	The performance of one (often the best) member	One member's proposal about how to solve a work group's problem meeting quality standards

the four types of tasks we have described. In the course of this analysis, we will note certain pitfalls that can adversely affect group performance of each kind of task.

Group Dynamics for Each Type of Task

On *additive tasks,* the group product is the sum of the individual members' contributions. Loading a truck and making phone calls for a fund-raising event, for example, are additive tasks. Such tasks can often be performed by individuals working simultaneously yet independently. No group member has to depend on the work of another in order to complete his or her part of the task, but they all have to coordinate their work with that of the others so that, for example, they do not run into one another while loading a truck or solicit donations from the same person. On additive tasks, the groups studied in experimental laboratory settings generally performed better than even their best members.[33]

Additive tasks increase the likelihood that group members will engage in *social loafing,* which is the tendency to reduce personal effort and let others do most of the work. Research has indicated that as group size increases, so does social loafing (this does not necessarily occur with other kinds of tasks).[34] Social loafing can be reduced by increasing individuals' perceptions that they are making a unique and identifiable contribution to the total outcome. This can be done by making the overall task more challenging and difficult, by giving each person a different task to do, or by making public each individual's contribution to the group effort.[35] It appears, however, that the productivity advantages of groups persist for additive tasks, even when larger size promotes social loafing, because increasing the group size increases the resources available to the group (the number of hands available to work).

A *conjunctive task* is one for which the group outcome is defined as the performance of the worst member of the group. For example, when performance is defined as the time it takes for the entire group to complete a task the members are working on independently, its completion time will be the time the slowest member requires. A daily newspaper cannot go to press until all the features, stories, and ads are turned in by all the contributing staff members. Because group

Even in a trading room, group dynamics have a role in determining the productivity of individuals. Additive tasks may be acceptably performed, but conjunctive and compensatory tasks would clearly be complicated by such a work environment. (Catherine Ursillo/Photo Researchers)

performance on conjunctive tasks can be no better than the worst member's performance, individual performance usually exceeds that of the group. This problem is rooted not so much in group dynamics as in group resources. In many groups, however, the performance of the worst member is not much lower than that of the best members. In a fairly homogeneous group that includes highly trained or highly skilled members, group performance on a conjunctive task does not necessarily suffer the way it does in a group whose members exhibit a wide range of skill levels.

Compensatory tasks are usually judgment or evaluation tasks for which the group product represents the average judgment of all the group members. For example, when hiring or promotion decisions are made by a committee, the group often makes its decision by averaging its members' individual ratings of each of the candidates. On this type of task, group performance is usually equal or superior to the individual performance of the best member. This may be partly because the "averaging" nature of this task facilitates a type of compromise between any extreme (and presumably erroneous) responses in the group.[36] The group judgment benefits from resources available in the form of all the group members' judgments. This does not necessarily mean that a group should always be convened to make such judgments. And, of course, group averaging cannot make up for a lack of knowledge or expertise. In situations in which the "best judgment" is represented by the rating of only a minority of group members, the compensatory task offers no means for those minority members to try to sway the judgments of the rest of the group. As a result, the group's average judgment is still likely to be a poor one.

If the judgment task is changed somewhat, such that the group is forced to reach a single unanimous decision rather than taking an average, it becomes more like a disjunctive task. In a *disjunctive task*, the performance of one group member is taken as the measure of the group's performance. For example, on a disjunctive task, group performance can be as good as individual performance if the member whose performance is chosen to represent the group product is also the best member of the group. In peforming disjunctive tasks, group members must agree on what they think is a single best judgment, decision, or approach to a problem. Reaching consensus in this manner is probably one of the most common tasks people in work groups are asked to perform. Yet certain dynamics of group behavior can prevent the group from identifying or accepting the best judgment, decision, or solution.

In a judgment task, the requirement that the group select a single correct outcome (for example, "We should promote Jones rather than Smith") changes the group dynamics, and the decision becomes susceptible to group polarization effects. **Group polarization** is the tendency of groups to make more extreme decisions and judgments than individuals. Specifically, if most of the individuals in a group lean toward a conservative judgment *before* group discussion, the final group decision is likely to be still *more* conservative *after* group discussion. The same polarization effect occurs if the group leans toward a risky judgment before discussing an issue; its final decision after group discussion is still riskier. Group polarization is in part the result of conformity to group pressure and in part the result of the group's tendency to deal primarily with arguments that support the position of most of the group members.[37] As an example of the latter effect, one study reported that in groups trying to reach consensus about a decision, 76 percent of the arguments discussed by the groups were arguments that supported the decision favored by the majority of the group.[38]

A problem arising out of the dynamics that operate when a group tackles a disjunctive decision-making or problem-solving task is groupthink. **Groupthink** is a way of thinking that characterizes cohesive group members whose concerns for unanimity take precedence over the needs they feel to objectively evaluate alternative courses of action. In the case of groupthink, group dynamics created by high cohesiveness can adversely affect the group's decision by restricting the informational resources available to the group.[39] Groupthink on the part of Morton Thiokol managers and NASA project directors may have been partially responsible for the disastrous explosion of the space shuttle *Challenger* in 1986. Figure 16-8 presents a model that illustrates the group characteristics and the circumstances that foster groupthink, the symptoms of groupthink, and some of the negative consequences it can have on group decision making.

There are a number of steps that can be taken to minimize groupthink and its effects within a group. First the likelihood that the group will be biased by its leader should be minimized. For example, some group members should act as "devil's advocates" or should ask the group to respond to "worst-case scenarios." These roles can also be useful in taking the second step to prevent groupthink; they can be used to challenge premature group consensus. A "second-chance" meeting is another way to avoid premature consensus. This type of meeting follows one at which tentative consensus has been reached and enables group members to air any doubts or second thoughts about their decision. Next, the leader can try to minimize the group's isolation from other viewpoints. Deliberate attempts to bring in and deal with alternative points of view are crucial in minimizing

FIGURE 16-8
A Model of Groupthink

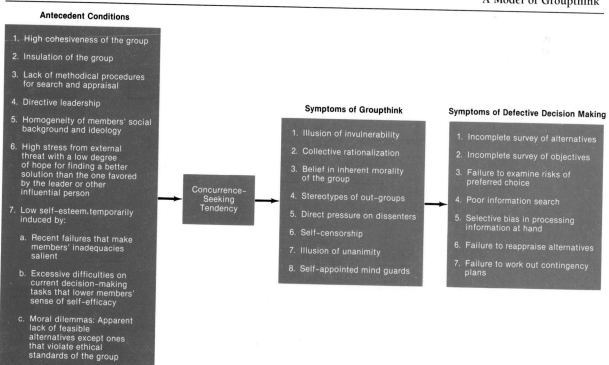

Source: From I. L. Janis, *Groupthink*, 2nd ed. Copyright © 1982 by Houghton Mifflin Company. Adapted with permission.

groupthink in a highly cohesive group, because members of a cohesive group are likely to hold similar viewpoints.

To assess your own perceptions of and feelings about a group of which you are a member, use the special self-diagnostic scale that we have included as "Management Development Exercise 16" at the end of this chapter.

Generally, groups take longer to solve problems than the average group member working alone. In most problem-solving groups there are some members who can solve the problem by themselves and some who cannot. Yet, if the group problem-solving process involves allotting each group member time to present his or her ideas, some of that time is wasted on proposed solutions that will not be selected. Group members who can see a good solution must also spend time convincing the rest of the group that their idea is the one that should be accepted.

When one considers the wages or salaries paid for the personhours expended by groups to perform tasks that an individual could perform, it is easy to see why problem-solving and decision-making groups can be costly to an organization. Even so, there are certainly situations in which it is worth investing the extra time and expense that group meetings entail. For example, group decision making is often chosen to maximize the chances that the best decision or solution will be reached or in order to involve group members directly in decisions that affect the group. It is important for a manager to understand when to make a decision alone and when to assemble a group, and incur the associated costs, in order to make an effective decision.

Vroom has suggested that a manager should invoke a group decision-making process under the following conditions:[40]

1. A quality decision is required.

2. The leader does not have all information necessary to make a quality decision.

3. The problem is an unstructured one.

4. Group acceptance of the decision is critical.

5. An autocratic decision is not likely to be accepted.

6. Subordinates share personal goals.

7. Conflict over the decision is likely.

8. No severe time pressures exist.

9. The development of subordinates is desired.

10. Professionalism is high.

Intergroup Conflict

The effectiveness of a group within an organization often depends on the nature of its interactions with other groups. This is because groups are often interdependent and therefore have the ability to affect each other's outcomes. Conflict between groups occurs when each of the groups involved perceives that the other group has interfered with (or will interfere with) the accomplishment of its goals.[41] **Intergroup conflict** is characterized by a mutually perceived incompatibility of goals as well as by mutual interference in goal attainment. For example, in a labor dispute, union representatives may strive for higher wages and better benefits for the union membership, whereas management representatives may attempt to cut operating expenses by reducing wages and benefits. Their goals are clearly incompatible, and each group's insistence on its preferred outcome blocks the other group's movement toward its goal.

Conflict can have both positive and negative consequences. On the negative side, conflict can interfere with intergroup communication, increase negative stereotyping of the other group, reduce coordination between groups, shift group leadership toward an autocratic style, and reduce group members' ability to take the perspective of members of the other group. On the positive side, conflict can lead to more careful consideration of new ideas, focus attention on key problems, increase the likelihood of innovation, and lead to the improved monitoring of performance.[42] Some of these positive outcomes develop as a result of a group's attempts to improve its position relative to that of the other group; some of them result from the groups' attempts to resolve or reduce the conflict.

Conflict Management

There are many different ways to handle intergroup conflict. The model presented in Figure 16-9 presents five approaches to conflict resolution. These five approaches represent different combinations of two dimensions of intergroup interaction. The first dimension is degree of cooperativeness—that is, concern for the other group's interests. A high level of cooperativeness is accompanied by the perception that the two groups' goals are compatible. The second dimension is degree of assertiveness, or concern for one's own group's interests. High levels of assertiveness are likely to be accompanied by the perception that one's own group's goals are very important.

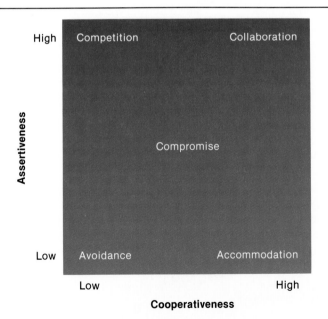

FIGURE 16-9
Approaches to Managing Intergroup Conflict

Source: Adapted from K. W. Thomas, "Conflict and Conflict Management," in M. D. Dunnette, ed., *Handbook of Industrial and Organizational Psychology*. Copyright © 1976 John Wiley & Sons. Reprinted by permission of John Wiley & Sons, Inc.

None of these approaches to conflict management is the best strategy for all situations, and both advantages and drawbacks are associated with each. When two groups' goals are incompatible, but are not particularly important to them, their interaction is likely to take the form of *avoidance*. This may be a satisfactory mode of interaction for a while, but because the source of conflict has not been dealt with, competition or conflict may eventually result if the goals remain incompatible, but become more important to the groups. For issues that are trivial and remain so, however, avoidance may be a useful way of dealing with conflict.

Collaboration occurs when groups have important goals that are compatible with one another and are considered important and in the best interests of each group. Some argue this is the best method for handling intergroup conflict and that collaborative groups are more creative and innovative than others.[43] This advantage seems to be limited, however, by the groups' collaborative skills and the likelihood that they will actually be able to collaborate.

In some cases, the goals of two groups are compatible and each group has a good deal of cooperative concern for the other group's needs. If these goals are of little importance or there is little assertiveness on the part of either group in pursuing its own interests, *accommodation* is likely to be the approach that the two groups take to conflict management. Accommodation makes for pleasant interaction, but if incompatible goals develop, it may later be perceived as a position of weakness.

Guidelines for Management Practice

Though the five approaches to conflict resolution may be useful for categorizing styles of conflict management, they do not specify steps to take to direct groups through the process of conflict resolution. For this managers will find more useful a conflict-solving model devised by R. R. Blake and J. S. Mouton, which suggests the development of *superordinate* organizational goals.[44] These are goals that are accepted by both groups and that allow each group to attain its individual goals in the process of reaching the shared superordinate goals. Commitment to superordinate goals has been demonstrated to increase collaboration between conflicting groups and to reduce conflict and hostility between groups.[45] The development of superordinate goals is designed to overcome three problems that often intensify conflict between groups: the tendencies of each group to (1) perceive itself more positively than its opponent, (2) emphasize group loyalty over other considerations, and (3) focus on its own group goals rather than on broader organizational objectives.

To use the conflict-solving model, managers need to follow a sequence of six steps:[46]

1. *Develop the optimal model.* Independently, each side describes what *ideal* relations between the two groups would be like.

2. *Consolidate the optimal relationship.* The two sides meet to integrate their views and arrive at a common picture of their optimal relationship.

3. *Describe the actual relationship.* Independently, each group describes the current relationship between the two groups.

4. *Consolidate the actual relationships.* The two groups meet to integrate their views and arrive at a common picture of their present relationship.

5. *Plan for change.* A specific plan is designed to bring the actual group interaction more in line with the groups' joint view of their optimal interaction. A date is set to review progress in three to six months.

6. *Review progress and update plans.* At a specified future date, progress is reviewed and plans for change are modified as necessary.

When two groups have goals that are incompatible and are very important to each, *competition* is likely to characterize their interaction. Although competition can be effective in increasing cohesiveness within each group, it can also boost the likelihood of future intergroup conflict by alienating the other group.

Compromise involves intermediate levels of cooperativeness and assertiveness. There is a moderate level of goal compatibility and interest in the other's goals, and a moderate level of importance is attached to pursuing one's own goals. This approach to conflict management tends to produce somewhat less overall satisfaction than the collaborative style, because both parties are required to make concessions.

Review of the Learning Objectives

Having studied this chapter, you should be able to respond to the learning objectives with extensions of the following brief answers.

1. **Explain how group processes are related to each of the management functions.**

   Some of the management functions, such as organizing and staffing, can affect aspects of group structure and process, which, in turn, can influence organizational effectiveness. For other management functions, such as leadership, planning, and control, whether or not a particular style of carrying out that function will be effective depends in part on the structure of and dynamics within relevant groups.

2. **Define the term *group* and distinguish between formal and informal groups.**

   A group is a collection of two or more people who interact with one another, are aware of one another, perceive themselves to be members of the group, and work toward a common goal. Formal groups are mandated by the organization and usually have a goal specified by the organization. Informal groups are formed voluntarily and develop their own goals.

3. **Describe three types of changes that occur during socialization of an individual into a group, and explain what a manager can do to facilitate the orientation and socialization of new employees.**

   During socialization into a group, the new member acquires role behaviors appropriate to the group, develops work skills necessary to pursue group goals, and adjusts to the group's norms and values. To facilitate a new employee's socialization, a manager can provide the person with a realistic job preview, clear definitions of the roles and responsibilities expected of him or her and of the roles and responsibilities of others in the group, and feedback and support as the new employee adjusts to new roles, tasks, and group norms.

4. **Explain how characteristics of the group and of the task can interact to affect group performance.**

   There are four types of tasks a group can perform: additive, conjunctive, compensatory, and disjunctive. These differ in terms of how the group product is defined. There are unique group dynamics associated with each that can impair performance, but whether these dynamics actually hamper performance depends in part on the nature of the group. For example, disjunctive decision-making tasks are susceptible to groupthink when the group is highly cohesive, is isolated, and has a norm of censoring dissent. Groups with norms that encourage dissent and debate and that invite outside opinions are much less likely to make decisions marred by groupthink.

5. **Define the term *intergroup conflict* and describe five styles of conflict management.**

Intergroup conflict exists when each group perceives that the other group has interfered with, or will interfere with, its attaining its goals. Five styles of conflict management represent five combinations of the levels of assertiveness and cooperativeness exhibited by the groups experiencing conflict. *Competition* reflects high assertiveness and low cooperativeness, *avoidance* reflects low assertiveness and low cooperativeness, *accommodation* reflects low assertiveness and high cooperativeness, *collaboration* reflects high assertiveness and high cooperativeness, and *compromise* reflects moderate levels of both.

Key Terms and Concepts

After completing your study of Chapter 16, "Managing Groups," you should be able to explain the following important terms and concepts.

group	command group	sociogram	peripheral norm	socialization
social comparison	task group	group structure	role	group polarization
formal group	friendship group	norm	role differentiation	groupthink
informal group	interest group	pivotal norm	cohesiveness	intergroup conflict

Questions for Discussion

1. List as many specific examples as you can of ways in which work groups meet the personal needs of their members.

2. Consider an organization with which you are familiar. Describe one informal group that you think has considerable influence within the organization. How does it overlap or cross the boundaries of formal groups? What are the norms of this informal group? What effect does it have on the organization's functioning?

3. How do formal and informal groups communicate their norms to their members?

4. How can a manager encourage group cohesiveness? Under what conditions would it be advisable for a manager to try to do this? Under what conditions would it be inadvisable?

5. How might "idiosyncrasy credits" contribute to innovation within a group?

6. Consider a group of which you are a member. Which of the task-oriented roles and group maintenance roles are effectively played in your group and which are not? What self-oriented roles are played? What are the consequences for group functioning? Which roles do *you* usually play? Which could you play more often?

7. Under what conditions might a person stay in a group or a job with which he or she is dissatisfied? Under what conditions might someone join a new group or take a new job, leaving another even though it was satisfying?

8. What information would you like to obtain during a job interview in order to begin to understand the norms and roles of the groups in which you would be working?

9. Even when its norms are similar to those of the organization, a highly cohesive group can be at a

disadvantage in performing decision-making tasks. What is the nature of this disadvantage and in what ways does cohesiveness contribute to the problem?

10. Consider two groups that are in conflict with one another and are dealing with that conflict by using avoidance. If one of the groups suddenly took much greater interest in the goal it perceived the other group as thwarting, how would that change the groups' approach to dealing with the conflict? How would both groups' adoption of superordinate goals affect their conflict management styles?

Notes

1. Excerpted from G. Stove and B. Burlingham, "Workstyle," *Inc.,* January 1986, pp. 45–46. Reprinted with permission, *Inc.* magazine, January 1986. Copyright © 1986 by *Inc.* Publishing Company, 38 Commercial Wharf, Boston, Mass. 02110.

2. H. L. Tosi and W. C. Hamner, *Organizational Behavior and Management,* 4th ed. (Columbus, Ohio: Grid Publishing, 1985), p. 275.

3. M. E. Shaw, *Group Dynamics: The Psychology of Small Groups,* 3rd ed. (New York: McGraw-Hill, 1981).

4. S. Schacter, *The Psychology of Affiliation* (Stanford, Calif.: Stanford University Press, 1959).

5. A. Maslow, *Motivation and Personality* (New York: Harper & Row, 1954); and F. Herzberg, B. Mausner, and B. Synderman, *The Motivation to Work* (New York: Wiley, 1959).

6. D. C. McClelland and R. E. Boyzatzis, "Leadership Motive Pattern and Long-Term Success in Management," *Journal of Applied Psychology* 67, no. 6 (1982): 737–743.

7. B. F. Skinner, *Contingencies of Reinforcement* (New York: Appleton-Century-Crofts, 1969).

8. H. H. Kelly and J. W. Thibaut, *Interpersonal Relations: A Theory of Interdependence* (New York: Wiley-Interscience, 1978).

9. Shaw, *Group Dynamics.*

10. D. Byrne, *The Attraction Paradigm* (New York: Academic Press, 1971); and C. A. Insko and M. Wilson, "Interpersonal Attraction as a Function of Social Interaction," *Journal of Personality and Social Psychology* 35, no. 12 (1977): 903–911.

11. L. Festinger, "A Theory of Social Comparison Processes," *Human Relations* 7, no. 2 (1954): 117–140.

12. Schacter, *The Psychology of Affiliation.*

13. J. P. Kotter, "What Effective General Managers Really Do," *Harvard Business Review* 60, no. 6 (1982): 156–167.

14. S. L. Albrecht, "Informal Interaction Patterns of Professional Women," in J. R. Gordon, ed., *A Diagnostic Approach to Organizational Behavior* (Boston: Allyn & Bacon, 1983), pp. 287–290.

15. D. J. Brass, "Men's and Women's Networks: A Study of Interaction Patterns and Influence in an Organi- zation," *Academy of Management Journal* 28, no. 2 (1985): 327–343.

16. K. E. Kram, "Phases of the Mentor Relationship," *Academy of Management Journal* 26, no. 4 (1983): 608–625.

17. R. S. Bhagat, "Effects of Stressful Life Events on Individual Performance Effectiveness and Work Adjustment Processes Within Organizational Settings: A Research Model," *Academy of Management Review* 8, no. 4 (1983): 660–671; and D. C. Ganster, M. R. Fusilier, and B. T. Mayes, "Role of Social Support in the Experience of Stress at Work," *Journal of Applied Psychology* 71, no. 1 (1986): 102–110.

18. A. P. Hare, *Handbook of Small Group Research,* 2nd ed. (New York: Free Press, 1976).

19. J. H. Davis, *Group Performance* (Reading, Mass.: Addison-Wesley, 1964), p. 82; and D. C. Feldman, "The Development and Enforcement of Group Norms," *Academy of Management Review* 9, no. 1 (1984): 47–53.

20. E. H. Schein, *Organizational Psychology,* 3rd ed. (Englewood Cliffs, N.J.: Prentice-Hall, 1980).

21. R. W. Napier and M. K. Gershenfeld, *Groups: Theory and Experience,* 3rd ed. (Boston: Houghton Mifflin, 1985).

22. E. P. Hollander, "Competence and Conformity in the Acceptance of Influence," *Journal of Abnormal and Social Psychology* 61, no. 3 (1960): 365–370.

23. A. P. Hare, *Handbook of Small Group Research* (New York: Free Press, 1976), p. 101.

24. K. D. Benne and P. Sheats, "Functional Roles of Group Members," *Journal of Social Issues* 4, no. 2 (1948): 41–49.

25. D. Cartwright, "The Nature of Group Cohesiveness," in D. Cartwright and A. Zander, eds., *Group Dynamics: Research and Theory,* 3rd ed. (New York: Harper & Row, 1968).

26. J. F. Schriescheim, "The Social Context of Leader-Subordinate Relations: An Investigation of the Effects of Group Cohesiveness," *Journal of Applied Psychology,* 65, no. 2 (1980): 183–194.

27. E. Mayo, *The Social Problems of an Industrial Civilization* (Cambridge, Mass.: Harvard University Press, 1933).

28. S. W. Gellerman, "Why 'Good' Managers Make Bad Ethical Decisions," *Harvard Business Review* 64, no. 4 (1986): 85–90.
29. Cartwright, "The Nature of Group Cohesiveness.
30. Kelly and Thibaut, *Interpersonal Relations: A Theory of Interdependence.*
31. D. C. Feldman, "The Multiple Socialization of Organization Members," *Academy of Management Review* 6, no. 2 (1981): 309–318.
32. I. D. Steiner, *Group Process and Productivity* (New York: Academic Press, 1972).
33. I. D. Steiner, "Task-Performing Groups," in J. W. Thibaut, J. T. Spence, and R. C. Carson, eds., *Contemporary Topics in Social Psychology* (Morristown, N.J.: General Learning, 1976).
34. B. Latané, K. Williams, and S. Harkins, "Many Hands Make Light the Work: Causes and Consequences of Social Loafing," *Journal of Personality and Social Psychology* 37, no. 6 (1979): 822–832.
35. S. Harkins and R. E. Petty, "Effects of Task Difficulty and Task Uniqueness on Social Loafing," *Journal of Personality and Social Psychology* 43, no. 6 (1982): 1214–1229.
36. Steiner, *Group Process and Productivity.*
37. D. G. Myers and H. Lamm, "The Group Polarization Phenomenon," *Psychological Bulletin* 83, no. 4 (1976): 602–627.
38. D. G. Myers and G. D. Bishop, "Enhancement of Dominant Attitudes in Group Discussion," *Journal of Personality and Social Psychology* 20, no. 3 (1971): 286–391.
39. I. L. Janis, *Victims of Groupthink* (Boston: Houghton Mifflin, 1972), p. 9.
40. V. H. Vroom, "Can Leaders Learn to Lead?" *Organizational Dynamics* 4, no. 3 (1976): 17–28.
41. K. W. Thomas, "Conflict and Conflict Management," in M. Dunnette, ed., *Handbook of Industrial and Organizational Psychology* (Chicago: Rand McNally, 1976), pp. 889–935.
42. R. A. Baron, *Behavior in Organizations,* 2nd ed. (Boston: Allyn & Bacon, 1986).
43. R. R. Blake, H. A. Shepard, and J. S. Mouton, *Managing Intergroup Conflict in Industry* (Houston, Texas: Gulf, 1964).
44. R. R. Blake and J. S. Mouton, *Solving Costly Organizational Conflicts* (San Francisco: Jossey-Bass, 1984).
45. M. O. Sherif, O. J. Harvey, B. J. White, W. E. Hood, and C. W. Sherif, *Intergroup Conflict and Cooperation: The Robber's Cave Experiment* (Norman, Okla.: University of Oklahoma, 1961).
46. Blake and Mouton, *Solving Costly Organizational Conflicts.*

Cohesion Incident 16-1
Restaurant Turnover

As Charles was walking into Roger's office late one afternoon, he met Susan McNaughton coming out with a folder of applications for employment in her hand. Susan has been the hostess in the Graniteville Journey's End since it opened and has done an excellent job. She was thirty-nine years old and had been a waitress for twelve years when she applied for the hostess position at Journey's End when the motel opened. She attended a training program for hostesses sponsored by Journey's End and had impressed Roger by how well she had handled her responsibility of managing the restaurant.

Of the eight waitresses who report to Susan, five have been at Journey's End for over a year and get along extremely well with each other, both on and off the job. Four of them attended high school together; all are married and have young children. They often trade shifts and days off with each other when it is necessary for one of them to be away. They have been so loyal to Journey's End that Susan has given them permission to make these changes without consulting her as long as the correct number of waitresses shows up for each meal. All are cheerful, enjoy each other's company, and are excellent waitresses.

Filling the other three waitress positions has been an ongoing problem for Susan. Over the past year, thirteen different waitresses have been hired to fill those three slots. Most of them left to work in other restaurants in the area, saying merely that they had prospects for a better job.

So, as Charles met Susan with her folder of applicants, she smiled and said, "Here we go again. Becky left this morning, making number thirteen in the past twelve months. Am I that hard to work for? I just wish I could find three more like Betsy, Carolyn, Peggy, Linda, and Hannah. Maybe if I interview enough new applicants, I can find someone who will stay with us for a while. Oh well, back to the drawing board."

Says Roger as Charles enters the room, "I was just going to ask you to come see me. Did you happen to see Susan as she was leaving?"

"Yes, I did, together with her usual folder of applications. I can't understand why she has such a problem with those other three spots. As far as I can tell, she's an excellent person to work for. And I know the wages and tips these women make are as good as anywhere else in the area."

"Charles, I think her favorite five may be the source of Susan's problem. I've suggested that she include them in her interviewing process when she hires the next waitress. Maybe as a group they can come up with someone who will stick with us."

Discussion Questions

1. Why do you think Roger suspects that the five reliable waitresses may be causing the high rate of turnover in the other three spots?

2. What do you think of his suggestion? Explain.

3. State three advantages and three disadvantages of group problem solving. How might each of these work in favor of (or against) the success of Roger's plan?

4. Who makes up the formal group of waitresses here? Who constitutes the informal group?

Cohesion Incident 16-2
Group Roles

Each Monday afternoon Eileen Thompkins meets with the marketing staff and several others who comprise the product development team to discuss their on-going research. Others who attend the meetings are Leslie Phillips; the two data analysts Steve and Bill; Bob Turnow and Alice Whittier, liaisons from the sales and engineering departments; and Harriet Wilcox, the department secretary. When Eileen first began to hold the weekly department meetings, everyone seemed to think they were a good idea, but after a few months they were dreaded by all involved, Eileen included. In fact, after what she observed at last week's meeting, Eileen decided something had to be done to improve their effectiveness. Instead of increasing efficiency, improving communication, and building cohesiveness within the work group, the weekly meetings seemed to be undermining the group members' ability to work together. She was beginning to worry that key members from other departments would decide not to participate any more. But she was at a loss to find a solution to the group's problem. It wasn't until she overheard the following conversation between Bill and Leslie in the coffee lounge last Monday afternoon that she decided she should analyze the behavioral roles of the group members.

Bill: I don't know about you, Les, but I've had it with these meetings. I've about given up trying to get an idea in.

Leslie: I noticed you've really withdrawn during the last few meetings. That's not like you, Bill. Is it because of Turnow?

Bill: You got it. I can't get a word in once that guy gets going.

Leslie: Yeah, poor Alice. Did you notice that every time she opened her mouth today, he interrupted her? I thought she had some good ideas, too.

Bill: Why didn't you jump to her defense then? We never did get back to the points she was making.

Leslie: By that time I was as fed up with the whole process as you were, and halfway through the meeting I realized that it wasn't altogether clear to me what our ultimate goal was. From what Eileen said at the end of our last meeting, I thought we were trying to decide how to construct the survey for the new vehicle control panel. That's why I prepared my presentation as I did. But then Eileen's comments and Turnow's remarks led us in a completely different direction, as though the issue of whether to use a survey method were still to be decided. And as usual, Steve was ready to agree with anything Eileen said. For once I'd like to know what *he* thinks rather than what he thinks will make him look good.

Bill: You know, even though we're a small group, circulating an agenda before the meeting would help. We've been playing "guess the agenda" for too long now.

Leslie: I wonder why no one brings any of these questions up in the meeting. If we don't address this soon as a group, we may as well forget these team meetings. In principle they're a good idea, but in practice they're a disaster. You heard Alice today; I bet she won't be back on Monday if she can convince the folks in engineering that her time is being wasted. Then we'll lose an important liaison with that department.

Bill: Well, I nominate you to discuss this with Eileen before our next meeting. All in favor, say aye.

Leslie: Sure, send me to do the dirty work. But you're right, Bill. Someone's got to talk to her soon. I should have done it earlier, but I knew she saw the problems, too, and was discouraged by them. I thought she would have come up with some workable solutions by now. I'll see if I can catch her to discuss it before I go home today. As I see things, it would be a marked improvement if she would give us a clearer statement of our task and our progress toward it, prevent someone like Bob from dominating the meeting, make sure that everyone gets a chance to air his or her views— including contradictory ones—and find ways of resolving conflicts like this when they come up.

Bill: Along with all that, it might be good to tell her what she does well in the group so far. She always has the information we need or knows who in the group meetings can supply it. She's also good at initiating new ideas. But all that needs to be balanced with more focus on our task and with some strategies for getting people to work better together as a group.

Discussion Questions

1. How are the task-oriented role, the group maintenance role, and the self-oriented role exemplified in this group?

2. On the basis of the conversation Eileen overheard, how could the difficulties of this work group be explained in terms of one or more of the group roles?

3. What changes in these role-related behaviors would improve this group's functioning?

4. As formal leader of the group, what is Eileen's responsibility with regard to the performance of these role-related behaviors?

Management Development Exercise 16
TORI Group Self-Diagnosis Scale

The TORI Group Self-Diagnosis Scale yields eight scores: four depicting how you see yourself in this group in terms of the four core growth processes (trust, openness, realization, and interdepencence—hence TORI) and four capturing your sense of the group itself on the same four dimensions. Think about a particular group of which you are a member. In front of each of the following items, write SD, D, A, or SA to indicate the extent to which that statement accurately describes the group itself and your feelings about it.

SD = strongly disagree   **D** = disagree   **A** = agree   **SA** = strongly agree

_____ 1. I feel that no matter what I might do, this group would understand and accept me.

_____ 2. I feel that there are large areas of me that I don't share with this group.

_____ 3. I assert myself in this group.

_____ 4. I seldom seek help from this group.

_____ 5. Members of this group trust each other very much.

_____ 6. Members of this group are not really interested in what others have to say.

_____ 7. The group exerts no pressures on the group members to do what they should be doing.

_____ 8. Everyone in this group does his or her own thing with little thought for others.

_____ 9. I feel that I have been very cautious in this group.

_____ 10. I feel little need to cover up things when I am in this group.

_____ 11. I do only what I am supposed to do in this group.

_____ 12. I find that everyone in this group is willing to help me when I want help or ask for it.

_____ 13. The members of the group are more interested in getting something done than in caring for each other as individuals.

_____ 14. Members of this group tell it like it is.

_____ 15. Members do what they ought to do in this group, out of a sense of responsibility to the group.

_____ 16. This group really "has it together" at a deep level.

_____ 17. I trust the members of this group.

_____ 18. I am afraid that if I showed my real innermost thoughts in this group, people would be shocked.

_____ 19. In this group, I feel free to do what I want to do.

_____ 20. I often feel that I am a minority in this group.

_____ 21. People in this group seem to know who they are; they have a real sense of being individuals.

_____ 22. Group members are very careful to express only relevant ideas about the group's task or goal.

_____ 23. The goals of this group are clear to everyone in the group.

_____ 24. The group finds it difficult to get together and do something it has decided to do.

_____ 25. If I left this group, the members would miss me very little.

_____ 26. I can trust this group with my most private and significant feelings and opinions.

_____ 27. I find that my goals are different from the goals of this group.

_____ 28. I look forward to getting together with this group.

_____ 29. People are playing roles in this group and not being themselves.

_____ 30. In this group we really know each other well.

_____ 31. This group puts pressure on each member to work toward group goals.

_____ 32. This group would be able to handle an emergency very well.

_____ 33. When I am in this group, I feel very good about myself as a person.

_____ 34. If I have negative feelings in this group, I do not express them easily.

_____ 35. It is easy for me to take risks in this group.

_____ 36. I often go along with the group simply because I feel a sense of obligation to it.

_____ 37. Members seem to care very much for each other as individuals.

_____ 38. Members often express different feelings and opinions outside the group than they express inside.

_____ 39. This group really lets people be where they are and who they are.

_____ 40. Members of this group like either to lead or to be led, rather than to work together with others as equals.

TORI Group Self-Diagnosis Scale Score Sheet

Instructions: The scoring is simple, even though it looks complicated. Look back at the items for one of the eight scales on the instrument to see how you responded. (The first scale shown below, for example, consists of items 1, 9, 17, 25, and 33.) On the score sheet, circle the number directly below your response for each item. Then sum the item scores for that scale. Do the same for each scale. Your instructor will help you to interpret your score.

Trust Item Score					Openness Item Score					Realization Item Score					Interdependence Item Score				
Item	SD	D	A	SA	Item	SD	D	A	SA	Item	SD	D	A	SA	Item	SD	D	A	SA
1.	0	1	2	3	2.	3	2	1	0	3.	0	1	2	3	4.	3	2	1	0
9.	3	2	1	0	10.	0	1	2	3	11.	3	2	1	0	12.	0	1	2	3
17.	0	1	2	3	18.	3	2	1	0	19.	0	1	2	3	20.	3	2	1	0
25.	3	2	1	0	26.	0	1	2	3	27.	3	2	1	0	28.	0	1	2	3
33.	0	1	2	3	34.	3	2	1	0	35.	0	1	2	3	36.	3	2	1	0

How I See Myself in This Group   T ☐   O ☐   R ☐   I ☐

Trust Item Score					Openness Item Score					Realization Item Score					Interdependence Item Score				
Item	SD	D	A	SA	Item	SD	D	A	SA	Item	SD	D	A	SA	Item	SD	D	A	SA
5.	0	1	2	3	6.	3	2	1	0	7.	0	1	2	3	8.	3	2	1	0
13.	3	2	1	0	14.	0	1	2	3	15.	3	2	1	0	16.	0	1	2	3
21.	0	1	2	3	22.	3	2	1	0	23.	0	1	2	3	24.	3	2	1	0
29.	3	2	1	0	30.	0	1	2	3	31.	3	2	1	0	32.	0	1	2	3
37.	0	1	2	3	38.	3	2	1	0	39.	0	1	2	3	40.	3	2	1	0

How I See This Group   T ☐   O ☐   R ☐   I ☐

Source: Abstracted from J. R. Gibb, TORI "Group Self-Diagnosis Scale," pp. 75–81. Reprinted from: J. W. Pfeiffer and J. E. Jones, eds., *The 1977 Annual Handbook for Group Facilitators*. San Diego, Calif.: University Associates, Inc., 1977. Used with permission.

17

Interpersonal and Organizational Communication

Learning Objectives

Your study of this chapter will enable you to do the following:

1. Describe the basic communication process and define each of its components.
2. Explain what display rules are and how they can affect the decoding of nonverbal messages.
3. Describe three characteristics of communicators that can influence the effectiveness of communication.
4. Give two types of technical factors that can interfere with effective communication.
5. Distinguish among three pathways of formal communication, and describe the types of information carried by each.

Communication at Baker Supermarkets

Two-way communication between management and employees is an effective way to control costs and increase productivity. This type of communication helped Baker Supermarkets, a nine-store chain in Omaha, Nebraska, accomplish both of these goals and increase its market share.

During 1984, competition from larger grocery chains in the Omaha area resulted in a decline in Baker's 40 percent market share. To communicate the urgency of the situation, management met with all 1,700 employees. At this meeting, the company announced that to remain competitive and prevent further decline in profit margins, annual pay raises would be cancelled. To management's surprise, employees responded not with dissatisfaction over lost raises, but by expressing concern for job security. "We were happy that employees knew Baker Supermarkets already paid higher wages than competitors," says Darryl Wikoff, Baker vice president.

The impressive growth of Baker Supermarkets is attributed by its executives to active communications among managers and other employees. (Rudy Smith)

To keep their jobs, employees asked management how they could increase productivity. Together, management and employees held a series of meetings to identify areas of operations in which costs could be reduced and [to consider] how sales might be increased. The meetings were not typical "bull sessions"; instead, employees came prepared to offer recommendations.

According to Wikoff, employees' recommendations enabled the company to regain its competitive edge. One idea involved damaged inventory. Use of the "mini-knife" for opening cartons was damaging food. Employees recommended another method for opening and shelving inventory and management adopted the idea. Baker now reports no waste due to damaged food, which previously had amounted to several tons daily.

An employee in one of Baker's store restaurants noted that bread heels were being discarded. The employee suggested using the heels to make pudding and even supplied management with a recipe. The item became the restaurants' best-selling dessert.

Another example of employee initiative involved changes in employees' work schedules. Baker's shelves must be stocked before stores open. This required a large number of employees in the stock departments for short periods of time. After the stores opened they were often assigned miscellaneous duties just to fill the remainder of the workday. Employees provided the solution—a six-day work-week consisting of fewer hours per day.

These and other employee suggestions dramatically improved Baker's bottom line. As a reward to employees, the company offered a one-time cash bonus. Then, to ensure continued employee involvement, future rewards were tied to performance and made part of the company's profit-sharing plan.

Management also developed Operation G.R.O.W. (Get Rid of Waste), a quality-circle approach modified to accommodate Baker's specific needs. G.R.O.W. reduces waste, increases productivity, and provides Baker with a method of communication between management and employees. Employees share their ideas for productivity improvements and cost-saving techniques at weekly meetings with managers, held on company time. They also participate in an ongoing dialogue with management to help set short-term goals.

Wikoff stated, "Employees have identified problems in operations that management wasn't even aware of. They also help solve problems that have been puzzling management for quite a while." He describes G.R.O.W. as a two-way communication process that involves talking—but mostly listening—to employees.

Wikoff believes Baker Supermarkets' increase in market share and profit margins can be traced to tapping employee ideas. "Two-way communication has resulted in employees realizing that not just their raises, but their very jobs, depend on how well the company performs," concludes Wikoff. "By allowing employees to help management plan the future, we're telling them we care about them and value their roles in the company."[1]

Introduction

What Is Communication?

Communication is the process by which one person or group transmits information to another person or group. The opening case on Baker Supermarkets describes executives and managers talking with employees and among themselves in the process of resolving shared problems. To understand the central role communication plays in a manager's effectiveness, consider the activities of Irene Wilson, manufacturing sales manager, in a typical workday. By noon she has

- Finished writing a budget report to be sent to her plant manager
- Met with the director of human resource development to discuss a development program that is being planned for the sales staff
- Interviewed an applicant for a position as sales representative
- Written several memoranda
- Had several conversations on the telephone
- Engaged in casual conversation at the office coffee pot

Her afternoon schedule includes

- A sales staff meeting at which she will present new departmental sales goals and plans for reaching them
- A telephone call to a customer who has complained about the performance of a sales representative
- A regularly scheduled meeting of all department managers and the plant manager
- A meeting with a sales representative whose job performance has taken a sudden nosedive

Research indicates that managers spend as much as 80 percent of their workday engaged in communication—either speaking or writing to others or listening to or reading others' messages.[2]

Communication is intimately related to the structure and dynamics within any group.[3] Groups, organizations, and other social systems are created and operate through communication. In turn, the structure of an organization affects the communication among its members. It influences how frequently they communicate, who communicates with whom, and what type of information is available to various members.

Good communication skills are necessary to the five general functions of management. For example, planning and organizing cannot be carried out effectively unless managers have the communications skills they need to acquire information on which to base decisions and develop plans. Furthermore, well-conceived plans and organizational structures are useless unless managers can successfully communicate them to others. Successful staffing and leading also depend on effective communication. No successful manager can carry out all of his or her responsibilities alone; he or she must rely on the cooperation and assistance of a coordinated and motivated staff. And coordinating and motivating personnel require good communication on the part of the manager. Recognizing that communication is the foundation of good management, Chester Barnard, an early management theorist, suggested that the very existence of an organization depends on the ability of its members to communicate. He insisted that the first responsibility of the executive is to develop and maintain an effective communication system.[4]

This chapter describes the process of communication. It then examines how the characteristics of individuals and of organizational structure can influence communication and, hence, organizational effectiveness.

The Communication Process

Communication is a social process that involves a shared system of rules along with the goals and expectations of the individual participants.[5] Figure 17-1 presents a model of this dynamic process of exchange and feedback.[6]

The **sender** is the source, or originator, of the message. Characteristics of this person or group, such as status or position in the organization, may affect the sender's credibility or access to certain means of communication. Hence they can affect the outcome of the communication. Sometimes called the **transmitter**, the sender casts the message in a form that can be sent to the receiver via the chosen medium. When electronic devices and computers are used, this transmission, or **encoding**, involves transforming the message into electronic impulses or into a computer language. When people convey the message, encoding involves converting the sender's ideas into words or nonverbal expressions that are appropriate

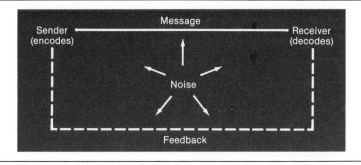

FIGURE 17-1
The Communication
Process

for the medium and interpretable by the receiver. An example of encoding is seen in the game of charades, in which people must encode and transmit linguistic messages in terms of gestures and other nonverbal expressions. The **message** is the expressed information that the sender hopes will convey the intended meaning to the receiver. The message can take the form of writing, speech, or gestures through such communication channels as memoranda, speeches, and handshakes. The **receiver** is the person who is the destination point for the message. The receiver must work to decode the message, which requires trying to interpret it as the sender intended. In the electronic transmission of communications, a decoding device re-converts the message into a form that is understandable to the receiver.

Finally, the receiver provides feedback to the person who was the source of the original message. **Feedback** conveys the receiver's reaction to the sender's message. At any point in this process, "noise" may distort the message. **Noise** is anything that interferes with transmission of the message. It may originate in the external environment, as when loud conversations make it difficult to hear or understand what someone is saying, or it may originate within the sender or receiver. Receivers' stereotypes, emotional states, and expectations can generate noise that may affect their attention to, as well as their decoding and interpretation of, a message. Likewise, the sender's expectations about the receiver may cause the message to be encoded in such a way that the receiver will not be able (or motivated) to understand it.

"Management Development Exercise 17" at the end of this chapter offers an instrument you can use to assess your own skills in providing feedback.

Forms of Communication: Combining the Channels

Communication **channels** include verbal language, which is the semantic content (meaning) of the words we speak or write; paralanguage, which refers to the intonation, pitch, and rhythm of speech; nonverbal communication, such as eye contact, facial expression, body movements, touch, and interpersonal distance; and visual symbols, such as pictures, diagrams, and graphs. Communication can take many forms that employ several different channels. It can be written or oral; it can occur face to face or across some distance. One study of first-level managers at DuPont revealed that the amount of time they spent communicating was divided among several forms (see Figure 17-2) and that over half of their communication time was spent in personal contact with others in one-to-one and group meetings.[7]

Some communication forms are considered to have greater *information rich-*

FIGURE 17-2
Percentage of Communication Time That Managers Use Various Forms of Communication

Form of Communication	Percentage of Communication Time
One-to-one and group meetings	53.0
Writing	15.5
Reading	14.9
Telephoning	8.0
Other	7.7

Source: Table from *The Dynamics of Organizational Communication*, by J. E. Baird, Jr. Copyright © 1977 by John E. Baird, Jr. Reprinted by permission of Publishers, Inc.

ness, or potential to convey information, than others.[8] Information richness depends on how many communication channels remain open during the communication and on the immediacy of feedback (the speed at which the two-way exchange of information takes place). Face-to-face conversation, for example, is highest in information richness. All of the communication channels are potentially open, and feedback can be immediate. (Note that, according to the data given in Figure 17-2, managers spend most of their communication time engaged in forms of communication that are high in information richness.) Telephone conversations are next in level of information richness. Nonverbal cues are lost over the telephone, but verbal and paralinguistic information can be exchanged, and immediate feedback is possible. Dialogue between people via computer terminals is also characterized by quick feedback for both parties, but it is less rich in information because it cannot benefit from tone of voice and most other paralinguistic cues.

Unlike forms of communication that provide immediate feedback, most forms of written communication, if they stimulate two-way communication at all, provide relatively slow feedback to a message. An informal, personally addressed letter or memo is considered to have moderate information richness; more formal, impersonally addressed written documents are relatively low in information richness. Formal numeric documents, such as computer printouts or balance sheets that carry little or no evaluative interpretation of the data, are considered very low in information richness.[9]

Different types of communication media are therefore appropriate for different types of situations and different communication purposes. Consider the problems that might arise if someone tried to communicate a fairly technical and detailed new job procedure by describing it to you orally in a single conversation. Though you would have an opportunity to ask questions, you would have no written source to consult to remind yourself of the details of the procedure once the conversation was over. Likewise, if you received a letter stating that you had been performing at a below-average level, you would not have an opportunity to seek feedback about how to improve. One study obtained supervisors' ratings of oral, written, and combined media to determine which are the most and which the least effective media for communicating with employees in different types of situations. The results are presented in Figure 17-3.

A communication that is high in information richness because it combines information from several communication channels may be more ambiguous than simpler, single-channel messages. This is because the information from various channels may conflict. A smile may accompany the words of a harsh reprimand. A person's words may sound friendly, but his or her body movements may communicate tension and anger. How do we interpret such mixed signals? One line of research into this question systematically combined conflicting vocal, facial, and verbal cues and studied the relative emphasis people who received the message placed on each type of cue in interpreting the message. For example, the study asked whether, when a positive facial expression and positive tone of voice accompanied negative words, the receiver interpreted the message any more positively than when the facial expression was negative. The results of this research suggest that people combine information from these three channels according to the following formula:

$$\text{Perceived attitude communicated in the message} = \text{verbal } 7\% + \text{vocal } 38\% + \text{facial } 55\%$$

Facial expressions, then, seem to carry the most weight in perceivers' inter-

Purpose of Communication	Most Effective Medium	Least Effective Medium
1. Communicating information requiring immediate employee action	Oral followed by written	Written only
2. Communicating information requiring future employee action	Written only	Oral only
3. Communicating information of a general nature	Written only	Oral only
4. Communicating a company directive or order	Oral followed by written	Oral only
5. Communicating information on an important change in company policy	Oral followed by written	Oral only
6. Communicating with your immediate supervisor about work progress	Oral followed by written	Oral only
7. Promoting a safety campaign	Oral followed by written	Oral only
8. Commending an employee for noteworthy work	Oral followed by written	Written only
9. Reprimanding an employee for work deficiency	Oral only	Written only
10. Settling a dispute among employees about a work problem	Oral only	Written only

Source: D. A. Level, Jr., "Communication Effectiveness: Method and Situation," *Journal of Business Communication* 10, no. 1 (Fall 1972): 19–25.

FIGURE 17-3
Effectiveness of Different Methods of Communicating with Employees

pretation of the sender's attitude when the channels bear conflicting information.[10] Additional research suggests that facial expression carries more weight than verbal information for messages that convey evaluation, but not necessarily for other kinds of messages. Specifically, this occurs when receivers are trying to decide whether messages convey like or dislike but not when they are trying to interpret messages that communicate status or dominance.[11]

There are some situations in which facial expressions clearly carry less weight in the receiver's interpretation of the message than information from other channels. For example, the type of information one is trying to glean influences choice of channel. When the person receiving the message is trying to determine whether the sender is lying, paralinguistic cues such as pitch, hesitation, and body movements other than facial expression are generally the most informative channels.[12]

The Effect of Cultural Differences on Communication

Cultural differences may also exist in the frequency or the manner in which senders transmit conflicting information in different communication channels. Though there is evidence that some nonverbal expressions—particularly facial expressions of emotion—are in part innate, cultural **display rules** determine the situations in which senders find it appropriate to display some nonverbal expressions.[14] For example, in some cultures it is customary to exhibit very little facial expression of emotion, whereas in others the facial expression of emotion is not only common but expected. Research on nonverbal behavior in Japan illustrates that Japanese often display laughter and smiles when they are experiencing anger, sorrow, or disgust in public settings. In private settings, when they believed that

Guidelines for Management Action

Managers should keep in mind that, in general, written media such as memoranda, reports, charts, and diagrams are most effective for communicating large amounts of detailed information, particularly when documentation of what has been communicated is needed or when the receivers are likely to need to reread the material in order to understand it or make use of it. Compared with oral media, written media have the following advantages:[13]

1. They give readers the opportunity to achieve understanding at their own rate using their own methods, including rereading.

2. Because they allow readers to receive the information at their own pace, they can go into much more detail.

3. They make it possible to convey ideas over distance and time.

4. They are easy to store and retrieve for use as input in future decision making and as documentation.

5. They can be made to be more precise, because they are open to the scrutiny of more than one individual.

Oral media, on the other hand, are most effective when immediate feedback and dialogue are desired. They are characterized by the following advantages:

1. They are particularly effective when rapid transmission of information and immediate feedback are desired.

2. They are especially appropriate for handling sensitive or confidential matters because their transitory nature makes discussion of "ticklish" matters more acceptable.

3. They convey a measure of personalness that is difficult to achieve through written media.

4. They are better suited to communicate feelings and some kinds of ideas than written media because oral discussion provides a better opportunity for interaction based on both verbal and nonverbal cues.

Combinations of media (such as oral and written media, oral and visual media, and visual and written media) are most effective when important policies or policy changes need to be communicated or when both feedback and documentation are desired.

---

they were not being observed, however, the participants in one study showed the more negative facial expressions that their display rules prohibit in public. Understanding of a culture's display rules and experience in interpreting conflicting information are important but often-neglected aspects of communication training for managers who are planning to work with people from another culture. Likewise, as discussed in "Insights for International Managers 17," cultural preferences dictate the extent to which it is wise for managers to be direct in their styles of communication.

Characteristics of Effective Communicators

The effectiveness of any communication depends not only on the communication process, but also on how the people who are communicating encode and decode messages. Several characteristics of communicators can influence the effectiveness of their communication. First, their *personalities* affect their ability to communicate—personality being the relatively stable set of traits or characteristics that influence a person's behavior. *Perceptual differences* also affect people's ability to communicate; they include the individual differences in selective attention to particular aspects of a message that result from stereotypes or expectations. People's

Insights for International Managers 17

THERE IS NO POINT IN GETTING STRAIGHT TO THE POINT

Getting straight to the point is a uniquely Western virtue. In the West we try to get a deal; others try to know us. We like facts, while others like suggestions. We specify, while others imply.

Cross-cultural consultant George Renwick says: "If we want to communicate with people, we have to understand the patterns of their thinking, and we can get glimpses of that by looking at how they talk." When Americans talk, they take the most direct route, one step at a time in a straight line to the finish. Not so the Arabs. They talk about other things before business. Then after they have talked about business for a while, they will loop off to talk about more social things, and eventually loop back to the business at hand. They will continue in this manner forever, and if forced by an impatient American to stay on what the American insists is the subject at hand, will become very frustrated. Renwick says forcing our linear thinking on Arabs only "cuts off their loops," causing resentment and ultimately loss of productivity.

Europeans don't go straight to the point either. An American who wants to talk business with a Frenchman over dinner will find that his French colleague wants to enjoy his meal. He may venture a few business remarks but is unlikely to entertain a business proposition at the dinner table. You need to build up slowly to new proposals, allowing time for the French to digest information and ideas. Indirectly, you can work into any conversation the background or credibility that must be established. French written communication will also be tentative and cumulative. An American will write a detailed letter with all the facts and plans and a sense of completion or finality. The Frenchman will write quite a different letter. It will be the first in a series, full of subtleties that will be elaborated upon in future correspondence. Both will be confused and each will try to second-guess what the other is really trying to say.

Africans, too, are suspicious of American directness. Nigerians complain that Americans have an "espionage mentality," asking for detailed information. Africans also feel that Americans talk too much, especially in public places. Many Africans consider it foolish to talk too much because "people may work against you if they know your plans."

As a general rule, business travelers and expatriates need to learn to slow down and sneak up on information, asking questions indirectly or obliquely, as a courtroom lawyer might. In most places it is best to get information conversationally or "educationally" by asking broader (even hypothetical) nonspecific questions and circling in gently on what is wanted. As anthropologist Tom Rohlen says, you have to learn to "mine for information." In other places, such as China, building a good rapport may be the only way to get people to give you information. Certainly, the direct question will be appropriate in some places, but most often you will need to learn how to beat around the bush.

Source: From L. Copeland and L. Griggs, *Going International* (New York: Random House, 1985), p. 103.

communication skills also affect their communication abilities; they are individuals' skills at encoding and decoding certain types of information and at providing feedback to the person with whom they are communicating. These three categories are not mutually exclusive: Different perceptual processes may be associated with different personality types, and perceptual processes may influence communication skills. Nonetheless, the three categories have been studied independently as factors that may affect communication.

Personalities of the Communicators

Two personality traits that have been found to affect communication are self-monitoring and self-esteem. **Self-monitoring** is the tendency to be aware of the characteristics of the social environment and to adapt one's behavior to the demands of the situation.[15] Figure 17-4 presents examples of the types of statements that people high in self-monitoring would be likely to make about themselves.

Individuals who are high in self-monitoring are adept at reading social cues, many of which are paralinguistic and nonverbal. In other words, they are very good at decoding other people's messages. In addition, they have a high degree of control over their own verbal and nonverbal communication.[16] Thus high self-monitors are skilled at encoding and transmitting messages that present them to others as they want to be seen. These strong encoding and decoding skills can be very useful in an organization.

People who are high self-monitors may be particularly effective in positions that require them to communicate with many different groups, each of which may have its own norms about communication. Research on the level of self-monitoring in boundary spanners has supported this hypothesis. **Boundary spanners** are people whose jobs require them to communicate across internal or external organizational boundaries, to represent their group or organization to external groups, and to transmit important information from the external environment back to their own group or organization. The boundary spanners studied were field representatives for a large franchise organization. The results showed that boundary spanners who were high in self-monitoring received higher performance ratings from their superiors than those who were low in self-monitoring.[17] This may have been attributable in part to their greater ability to communicate effectively with all of their constituents.

Self-esteem is a second personality characteristic that can affect one's ability to communicate effectively. In particular, low self-esteem may interfere with decoding messages received from other people. A considerable body of research suggests that a person's level of self-esteem can affect how he or she organizes new information and, as a result, which parts of that information he or she is later able to recall. Specifically, people who are low in self-esteem learn and remember negative information or information they dislike more readily than information they like.

The opposite is true for people with high self-esteem; they learn and remember positive or liked information more readily.[18] This has important implications for understanding the way the low-self-esteem individual encodes and responds to evaluative messages from other people. Consider the situation in which a manager is communicating the results of a performance appraisal to an employee who has relatively low self-esteem. First, this research suggests that the employee would register more of the negative comments and either miss or place less weight on the manager's positive comments. One common reaction to what is perceived as overwhelmingly negative feedback is to try to protect the image one presents to oneself and to others. This is called *defensiveness*. It is particularly common in individuals who do not have enough self-esteem to accept that they have made

---

FIGURE 17-4
Statements Likely to Be Endorsed by a High Self-Monitoring Person

1. In different situations and with different people, I often act like very different persons.
2. I am not always the person I appear to be.
3. I may deceive people by being friendly when I really dislike them.

Source: M. Snyder, "The Self-Monitoring of Expressive Behavior," *Journal of Personality and Social Psychology,* 1974, pp. 526–537. © 1974 by the Board of Trustees of the University of Illinois. Reprinted by permission of the University of Illinois Press.

mistakes or performed poorly. Defensiveness negatively affects communication in two ways. First, it interferes with listening to and decoding the message; instead of listening, the person is often desperately casting about for a way to respond to the criticism. Second, the verbal and nonverbal expression of defensiveness often elicits defensive responses from the other party, further interfering with communication.[19]

Perceptual Differences

Each participant in communication brings a different set of experiences to the situation and, as a result, may perceive the communication differently. These perceptual differences may affect the way people encode and decode messages. One particularly important perceptual barrier to communication is **selective perception**, people's tendency to pay attention to only part of a message. This results in the loss of information and decreases the chances that the source of the message and the person receiving it will interpret it the same way. In the Baker Supermarkets case, the company's executives openly expressed their concern that the financially mandatory cost-cutting measures would be misperceived by the employees. Fortunately for the company, a history of frequent, open, and productive manager-employee communications led Baker's workers to try to understand management's viewpoint on the company's problems.

One of the major causes of selective perception is expectation. What one perceives in a situation is often affected by what one expects. Such expectations are often contained in cognitive schemata. A **cognitive schema** is a body of knowledge based on past experience that affects not only our recall of the past (via selective recall) but also our perception and organization of new experiences (via selective perception).[20] For an example of how a schema works, look at the picture of the young woman shown in Figure 17-5. To decode and interpret this drawing, you called upon your schema of "young women," which includes information about what young women look like. Now look at the picture again and see if you can see an old woman. To make this perceptual change, you must decode the visual image differently. For example, the black line that had been the young woman's necklace becomes the old woman's mouth, and the young woman's chin becomes the old woman's nose.

FIGURE 17-5
An Ambiguous Picture: Whose Face Do You See?

Source: E. G. Boring,
"A New Ambiguous Figure,"
American Journal of Psychology, 1930, p. 444.

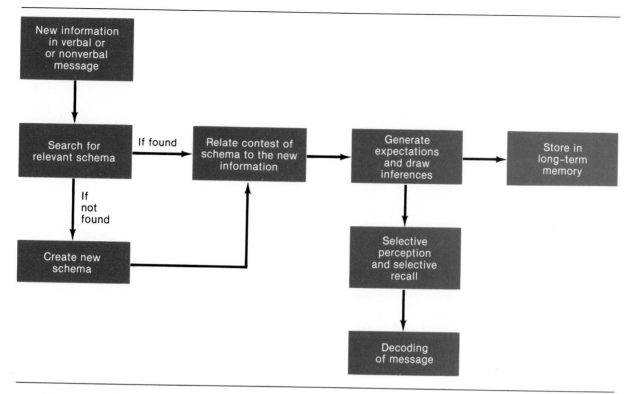

FIGURE 17-6
The Role of Cognitive
Schemata in the
Communication Process

Figure 17-6 illustrates how a schema affects our attempts to decode a message. When a person receives a message, he or she searches for a relevant schema with which to interpret the incoming information. Once that schema has been activated, the person is able to call up related information from past experiences with similar situations. As a result, the meaning of a message as it is decoded by the person who receives it may be changed and elaborated on as the receiver brings his or her own experience to bear on it. Finally, the receiver stores his or her interpretation of the new information with the relevant schema, which itself is now changed somewhat by this new information. Research suggests that information that is either very congruent with or very incongruent with a person's schemata is easier to store in memory and to recall at a later time. Information that is unrelated to any existing schemata often seems irrelevant and is selectively ignored and forgotten, unless it is information the person has to deal with repeatedly, in which case a new schema is created to include it.[21]

Stereotypes are a type of schema that can have a particularly detrimental impact on communication. A **stereotype** is a schema that contains a set of incoming information that is expected to describe all members of a group. When a person holds a stereotype, information that is unrelated to that stereotype is likely to be ignored and forgotten. For example, when a supervisor assumes that women are not expected to be assertive in their business dealings, the assertive behavior that female subordinates communicate both verbally and nonverbally might be either ignored or decoded and interpreted in terms of some other category that fits the supervisor's stereotype of women's behavior.

Communication Skills

The communication skills of both the person sending and the person receiving a communication affect how well the message is communicated. There are wide individual differences in verbal, nonverbal, and listening skills.

Both employees and their managers like to share their expertise and perceptions, but the value of such exchanges is largely predicated on the nonverbal and listening skills of the communicators. (Diamond Printing and Mailing, Inc.)

VERBAL SKILLS

Verbal skills involve many components. People may differ in their fluency in a language, particularly if it is not their first language; in their vocabulary; in their ability to read; and in their ability to write clearly. Communicators who do not consider the verbal skills of the person they are trying to communicate with will probably not convey their message effectively.

Messages must be encoded with the verbal skills of the recipient in mind. In the case of written communications (such as memoranda, written announcements, and employee manuals), this means that managers must know the range of reading levels of the employees they are trying to reach and must write the material at the lowest level in that range. One study of employee handbooks in fifty companies reported that, on the average, they were written at the reading level typical of those who have completed three years of college, though most of the employees for whom they were written read at a level substantially below that.[22] In some cases, illustrations and diagrams may be effective supplements or substitutes for written material.

NONVERBAL SKILLS

Because people differ in their ability to send and receive nonverbal messages, some communicate more effectively face to face. Likewise, someone who can notice and decode other people's nonverbal expressions is more likely to understand the entire message that the sender is trying to communicate. Women generally have been found to be better than men at encoding and sending nonverbal signals and at receiving and decoding nonverbal messages, especially facial expressions, from other people.[23] People who perform well in "helping professions" that require strong communication skills, such as counseling and social work, also appear to excel in encoding and decoding nonverbal messages, regardless of whether they are female or male. One study of counselors found that those who had high ability to decode others' facial expressions were also more likely to be rated high in effectiveness by their supervisors.[24] Given the importance of face-to-face communication for most managers, *nonverbal skills* would seem to be vital communication skills to develop. Furthermore, they seem to be skills that one *can* develop.

LISTENING SKILLS

Listening skills require people to integrate verbal and nonverbal skills. Listening involves much more than just hearing a message.[25] It involves attending to, decoding, and interpreting another person's verbal and nonverbal messages, as well as providing the responses and feedback that facilitate smooth interaction. Although we devote nearly half of the time we spend in conversation to listening, on the average we listen effectively to only one-quarter of what we hear. Sperry Corporation is one of many organizations that has trained its employees in listening skills.[26]

Listening skills involve attending, following, and reflecting (see Figure 17-7). Listening first requires *attending*—focusing on the other person and communicating that she or he has one's full attention. Eye contact and body posture are particularly important in communicating attention, as is physical activity. Someone who is shuffling papers or glancing through the mail while another is talking communicates a far different level of attention from someone who makes eye contact and pays undivided attention. A nondistracting environment communicates to the speaker that he or she has the listener's full attention, makes it easier for the listener to keep his or her attention focused, and increases the chances that the speaker will pay attention when the time comes for him or her to listen.

Following skills encourage the sender of a message to communicate. One communication specialist has said that "one of the primary tasks of a listener is to stay out of the other's way" so the listener can discover how the speaker views his or her own situation.

Reflecting skills communicate back to the speaker what the listener has received. They provide a way for the listener to check the accuracy of what he or she has received and for the speaker to tell whether his or her message has been

FIGURE 17-7
Three Categories of Listening Skills

Skill Category	Specific Skills
Attending Skills	A posture of involvement Appropriate body motion Eye contact Nondistracting environment
Following Skills	Door openers Minimal encouragers Infrequent questions Attentive silence
Reflecting Skills	Paraphrasing Reflecting feelings Reflecting meanings (tying feelings to content) Summative reflections

Source: From R. Bolton, *People Skills*. Copyright © 1979 by Simon & Schuster, Inc. Reprinted by permission of Simon & Schuster, Inc.

interpreted accurately. Reflecting may involve paraphrasing the message as it has been received, labeling and communicating back to the speaker the feelings that the listener has perceived the speaker to be communicating, indicating what events or ideas those feelings have been associated with in the communication, and summarizing what the listener understands the main themes or points of the speaker's message to have been.[27]

Listeners also provide the speaker with another important type of feedback called back channel feedback. **Back channel feedback** consists of the subtle vocal and visual responses the listener makes without taking over the speaking turn.[28] These include verbal responses such as "Uh-huh," "M-hmm," and "Really," which encourage the speaker to continue, as well as short questions asking for clarification or repetition, such as "What?" "Huh?" and "Say that again." Smiles, nods, frowns, and shakes of the head also communicate encouragement. Smooth conversation is marked by nonverbal gestures, eye contact, and body movements coordinated between speaker and listener.[29] Back channel communication is necessary in order for the speaker and listener to take turns smoothly. It also gives the speaker important information. In the absence of effective back channel feedback, speakers often become more wordy and their messages are less well directed for the specific listener.[30] This is because the speaker misses five important kinds of information about the listener: (1) whether the listener has relevant prior knowledge the speaker need not repeat, (2) whether the listener understands a point already so that the speaker can abbreviate or move on to another point, (3) whether the listener has misinformation that the speaker needs to try to correct, (4) whether the listener is confused or needs clarification, and (5) whether the listener is bored and the speaker should change topics or stop talking.[31]

Figure 17-8 summarizes the key steps in developing good listening skills.

Effective communicators must be aware of their own abilities and perceptual biases as communicators, and they must have empathy for those with whom they communicate. Self-awareness can eliminate perceptual biases and raise one's awareness of the need to seek information that may have been selectively filtered out.

FIGURE 17-8
Do's and Don'ts of Effective Listening

Do:	Don't:
1. Eliminate distractions.	1. Interrupt the speaker.
2. Find something of interest or value in the message.	2. Criticize or become distracted by the speaker's mannerisms or delivery.
3. Express empathy verbally and nonverbally.	3. Miss part of the message because you're busy thinking of your response.
4. Put the speaker at ease.	4. Engage in other activities.
5. Pay attention to nonverbal cues.	5. Daydream.
6. Paraphrase key points and feelings.	6. Become distracted by emotion-laden words.
7. Be patient, allow plenty of time.	7. Avoid difficult material.
8. Ask short questions to seek clarification or give encouragement.	8. Assume you know what the other is going to say.
9. Temporarily suspend judgment.	9. Fake attention.
10. Be silent when appropriate.	10. Listen just for facts.

■ *Guidelines for Management Practice* ■

Managers can help their employees develop effective communication skills. One particularly important skill is the ability to give feedback on the performance of others and to make constructive use of the feedback one receives oneself.[32] Effective feedback should be

1. Descriptive rather than evaluative

2. Specific rather than general

3. Directed toward behavior the person has some control over rather than toward general characteristics

4. Presented at a time when the person is ready to receive and consider it and as close in time to the behavior being evaluated as possible

5. Checked with the receiver (through paraphrasing, for example) to see whether he or she received the feedback message as it was intended

6. Ideally, communicated within a climate of trust in which the feedback can be seen as direction for growth rather than as punishment

Managers should keep in mind that enhancing people's self-esteem seems to increase their ability to use feedback constructively. People who make constructive use of critical feedback seem to recognize and set aside their own defensive tendencies; they realize that having made errors does not mean they are incompetent. They have sufficient self-esteem to tolerate errors in themselves, and they are able to admit their mistakes.[33]

Empathy enables communicators to understand the abilities and communication needs of others and to encode messages more appropriately.

Technical Issues in Communication

The effectiveness of communication is profoundly affected by technical factors, such as characteristics of the physical, social, and informational environment in which the message is transmitted and characteristics of the medium used to transmit the message.

Physical and Social Environment

The physical environment can facilitate or hinder communication. Social interaction and informal communication, which follows friendship ties rather than the organizational hierarchy, are greatly affected by the physical design of a building. This has been demonstrated in research on friendship, communication, and rumor transmission in apartment buildings and offices.[34] In these studies, the greatest amount of informal communication was found to occur between those people whose apartments or offices were closest to one another. One of the studies revealed the amount of communication between people whose offices were more than twenty-five feet apart to be minimal.

Many companies have developed environmental settings planned to foster informal communication. They provide places outside of people's offices where they can congregate and that are conducive to communication (such as a coffee lounge), they encourage some degree of informality (such as use of first names), and they design and arrange furnishings and office equipment to facilitate face-to-face interaction and communication. At Dana Corporation, Hewlett-Packard, and United Airlines, executives practice a policy of "management by walking around." They make it a point to get out of their offices to interact personally with employees. At all company functions at Walt Disney Productions, everyone (including the president) wears a tag displaying only his or her first name. At Hewlett-Packard, a company that employs an open office design, employees are expected to perform work that demands intense concentration at computer terminals. It is little wonder that the corporate nurse stocks earplugs! And in designing a new building for its engineering division, Corning Glass installed escalators rather than elevators in order to increase the amount of face-to-face interaction.[35]

Information Overload

Too much communication can overwhelm people's information processing capabilities. An optimal level of interpersonal interaction exists for each organizational setting. Too little, and there is not enough opportunity for informal communication networks to flourish. Too much, and communication is impaired because people are confronted with more information than they can deal with effectively. **Information overload** occurs when a person receives more information than he or she can deal with. It can result in the loss or distortion of information. People typically respond to information overload in one or more of the following ways:

1. Incoming messages are ignored.

2. Errors in incoming messages are overlooked or uncorrected.

3. Incoming messages are handled in an incomplete manner.

4. Incoming messages are inappropriately delegated to subordinates.

Almost all of these responses to overload have negative consequences for communication and for job performance. Information may be lost, the error rate may increase, or delays may occur. It is better to design information systems and communication networks in ways that minimize information overload than simply relying on individuals in the organization to cope with the overload.[36] Some suggestions for dealing with problems of information overload, distortion, and omission are presented in Figure 17-9.

FIGURE 17-9
Dealing with Overload, Distortion, and Omission in Organizational Communication

Problem: Overload
Solutions: 1. Use *gatekeepers*—individuals responsible for controlling the flow of information
2. Make *filtering* decisions—decide what information will be attended to and what will not
3. Use *queuing*—assigning priorities to incoming information

Problem: Distortion and Omission
Solutions: 1. Make messages *redundant*—transmit messages in another form or over another channel
2. *Verify* messages—test their accuracy
3. *Bypass* intermediaries—send the message directly to the intended party

Source: From R. A. Baron, *Behavior in Organizations* (Boston: Allyn & Bacon, 1983), p. 334.

Organizational Structure and Communication Patterns

Communications within an organization can only be fully understood if they are studied with an understanding of the organizational context or setting in which they occur. Therefore, it is important for managers to look at the informal and formal communication systems within their organization as a means to better understand and manage the flow of information in their company. *Informal communication* follows patterns of contact based on proximity and friendship as well as organizational structure. The *grapevine* is a good illustration of an informal communication network. Typically, a grapevine operates within and among all levels of the informal organization. It ignores formal chains of command; it spreads rumors, truths, lies, partial information, selective facts, and misunderstandings. The grapevine is the mechanism in an organization by which "everyone knows everything." At Safeco Land Title of Dallas, managers use the grapevine to gauge employee attitudes toward company policies and rules and to release favorable information that has not yet been confirmed or that they do not wish to be part of their records.[37] *Formal communication* follows the lines of the firm's organization chart and can move in any of three directions: upward, downward, or horizontally.

Downward Communication

Downward communication carries information from people in positions of higher authority to people in positions of lower authority. There are five general types of information that are communicated downward:[38]

1. Information about how to do a job

2. Information about the rationale for doing jobs

3. Information about the organization's policies and practices

4. Information about an employee's performance

5. Information to develop a sense of mission

As information is communicated downward, it is often distorted. Information distortion is the loss or addition of information as the message is transmitted. As information moves across boundaries in the formal system, from division managers to plant managers to supervisors and so on, it is especially likely to be distorted. One study of downward communication in one hundred companies showed that as a message was transmitted across five levels in the organization, 80 percent of it was lost.[39]

Information is lost, added, or exaggerated as a result of a variety of causes. Each person who transmits the information condenses it somewhat by summarizing it, leaving out certain words and details. People also tend to fill in missing details and to reduce the ambiguity of the message, often in misleading ways. They decode and encode the message according to their own expectations and perceptual biases. And they mistakenly assume that events that have occurred in the past will occur in exactly the same way again. As a message is relayed across levels in the formal organizational structure, all four of these causes of distortion often come into play.

Upward Communication

Upward communication occurs when someone at a lower level in the organization sends information to someone at a higher level. A message that travels upward in the formal communication system usually does one or more of the following:[40]

1. Reports what subordinates are doing—their work, achievements, progress, and plans for the future.
2. Describes unsolved work problems on which subordinates may need or would like some type of assistance.
3. Offers suggestions or ideas for improvements within the unit or the organization as a whole.
4. Reveals how subordinates think and feel about their jobs, their co-workers, and the organization.

When a message travels upward through many people, it may be distorted just like downward communication. But in upward communication, this distortion most often consists of the omission of parts of the message. Omissions happen for several reasons.[41]

1. Sometimes employees want to conceal their thoughts from managers out of distrust.
2. Employees may feel that supervisors and managers are not interested in their problems.
3. There may be no rewards for upward communication.
4. The feeling that supervisors and managers are too inaccessible and unresponsive to what employees say may inhibit subordinates.
5. Employees may be reluctant to communicate bad news to their superiors.

Horizontal Communication

Horizontal communication is the process of sending information to someone who is at the same level in the formal organizational structure. Horizontal communication serves at least six functions:[42]

1. To coordinate work assignments
2. To share information about plans and activities
3. To solve problems
4. To secure common understanding
5. To conciliate, negotiate, and arbitrate differences
6. To develop interpersonal support

Horizontal communication is often impeded if there are no formal horizontal channels to link different individuals, units, or departments at the same organizational level. In such cases, coordination between departments must depend on people in higher positions who receive information from and send directives to

▰▰▰▰▰▰▰ *Guidelines for Management Practice* ▰▰▰▰▰▰▰

Several characteristics of organizational structure can reduce the effectiveness of communication. Some researchers have suggested that organizations can build in practices that help to reduce the amount of distortion in communication. The four guidelines that follow are examples of steps that managers can take to increase the effectiveness of communication.

1. Identify more than one source of information pertaining to any communication that is suspected of being distorted. Multiple sources allow managers to verify messages and to try to identify and remove sources of distortion.

2. Develop procedures for counterbalancing distortions. If individual, technical, or organizational sources of distortion can be identified, then stand-ard ways of adjusting messages to correct for the typical distortions can be developed and applied. (If the source and extent of distortion cannot be determined, however, this technique can itself become a possible source of distortion.)

3. Eliminate or reduce the number of intermediaries between the decision maker and those who provide information. This practice is more common in organizations with a flat structure.

4. Develop distortion-proof messages—messages that cannot be altered in transmission. This practice is applicable only to the few messages that can be quantified or coded without substantial information loss. This last recommendation is not particularly useful for messages that are high in information richness.[43]

---

the lower-level units that are trying to coordinate their activities with one another. Competition for resources and lack of trust between departments can also obstruct horizontal communication. Yet effective horizontal communication is particularly important for highly specialized departments, such as engineering and market research; their activities affect one another, and they must share information or cooperate in other ways to accomplish their goals. Several strategies have been developed to provide channels for horizontal communication when problems require coordination across many departments. These include task forces and committees whose members are drawn from several departments. Another approach is the inclusion of an individual known as a *bridge,* who is a member of two departments or work units and serves to communicate the interests of each group to the other.

Multiple Communication Flows

The best communication networks are those wherein information is sent and received from several directions at nearly the same time. For example, Baker Supermarkets saw improved performance when information flowed in all three directions:

- Baker executives communicated downward to subordinates their recognition that corrective action was needed to deal with a problem.

- Baker employees communicated horizontally among themselves and with managers about the nature and causes of their problems.

- The employees communicated upward to the Baker executives their suggestions about solutions to the company's problems, including such specific ideas as the G.R.O.W. program.

Good ideas can originate at all levels of the organization. Converting ideas into productivity improvements typically requires an exchange of ideas generated at many levels. Management practices in a joint venture by GM and Toyota testify to the value and practicality of multiple forms of communications employed across and within multiple layers in an organization. For details, see "In Practice 17-1."

In Practice 17-1

NUMMI: TEAMWORK IN ACTION

If you phone the general manager for human resources at New United Motor Manufacturing, Inc. (NUMMI), for information, your call might be answered by a representative of the International United Automobile Workers—a clue that this is no ordinary auto plant. What happens between labor and management in Fremont, California, promises to have a major impact on U.S. industrial relations. At NUMMI, a joint venture of GM and Toyota (and, in a real sense, the UAW), the bosses and the workers are a team—and that teamwork is the key to resurrecting the U.S. auto industry and the U.S. economy as well.

In the beginning, the relationship stemmed from a desire on the part of each company, GM and Toyota, to learn more about the inside operations of the other. Just as GM wanted to understand Japanese production and management systems, Toyota needed to understand how to work with U.S. suppliers. In February 1983, the two companies formed a partnership. After seven months, a letter of intent was signed by NUMMI and the UAW to replace the traditional bargaining process with a more progressive and ongoing team of problem solvers from labor and management. This new process was designed to find options for mutual corporate gains while instilling trust in the workers by improving communication efforts.

The 15 concise pages of the letter of intent sharply contrasted with the legalese set forth in the 433-page contract that had previously existed between GM and the UAW. The letter clearly reflected the influence of Japanese industrial relations philosophies, including the constant search for improvement. The letter served not only as the basis for the original NUMMI/UAW one-year interim relationship, but it also provided the foundation for the formal, long-term collective bargaining agreement completed in the summer of 1985.

NUMMI's corporate culture of shared vision and common goals is reinforced in company literature, meetings, training sessions, and day-to-day operations. The company's democratic structure is built around teams that provide the framework for collaborative problem solving—a way of finding "win-win" solutions to problems that arise in engineering, on the shop floor, in executive decision making, or in labor relations. Open offices, a single parking lot, a common cafeteria, and the wearing of uniforms reinforce the feelings of unity between labor and management. Unlike traditional U.S. corporations, NUMMI views quality and productivity, cost containment and profitability, and job security and quality of work life as interdependent.

The collective bargaining agreement reflects a view of the worker as a professional partner committed to NUMMI's values. Employees are expected to act as members of a team, participating in setting and meeting team goals, looking for opportunities to make the company more efficient, and helping meet production goals and schedules. (Currently, 2,500 workers on two shifts produce 850 cars per day.) In contrast, the prior agreement between GM and the UAW defined only the "rights" of the corporation and made no mention of mutual or shared interests or responsibilities.

"If you ask the workers why they want to be there, they'll tell you it's because they are treated with respect," says a company spokesman. "The people are proud of what a good job they're doing." A low rate of absenteeism (3 percent) supports the company's optimism.

Source: Adapted from R. R. Rehder and M. M. Smith, "NUMMI: Teamwork in Action," *Newmanagement* 4, no. 2 (Fall 1986): 47–49. Copyright © 1986. Reprinted with permission of John Wiley & Sons, Inc.

Review of the Learning Objectives

Having studied this chapter, you should be able to respond to the learning objectives with extensions of the following brief answers.

1. **Describe the basic communication process and define each of its components.**

   In the process of communication, the sender (the person who wants to communicate the message) transmits information to the person who is the destination point. In order to be communicated, the message must be encoded by a transmitter. To encode is to cast the information in a form that can be transmitted. The encoded message is then transmitted to the receiver, who (or which) decodes the message, converting it into a form that is understandable to the person who is the destination point. Feedback occurs when the person who received the message transmits a return message to the sender indicating how she or he interpreted the message.

2. **Explain what display rules are and how they can affect the decoding of nonverbal messages.**

   Display rules are the rules by which each culture regulates nonverbal behavior. They define which nonverbal behaviors are appropriate and which are inappropriate in specific situations. One must understand a culture's display rules in order to decode its members' nonverbal messages. For example, a nonverbal behavior such as prolonged eye contact may signal friendliness or attraction in one culture and hostility or aggressiveness in another.

3. **Describe three characteristics of communicators that can influence the effectiveness of communication.**

   Three characteristics of communicators that can influence the effectiveness of communication are personality, perceptual differences, and communication skills. For example, people who are high in the trait known as self-monitoring are more accurate than others at decoding nonverbal messages and controlling their own nonverbal behavior. Perceptual differences include expectations and selective attention that result from cognitive schemata. Finally, people differ in their abilities to communicate verbally and nonverbally and in their listening skills.

4. **Give two examples of technical factors that can interfere with effective communication.**

   The use of an inappropriate medium of communication is one technical factor that can interfere with effective communication. Highly detailed information and information that needs to be documented and stored are not well suited to the medium of oral communication. Information overload is a second example of a technical communication barrier. It occurs when an individual is faced with more information than he or she can handle.

5. **Distinguish among three pathways of formal communication, and describe the types of information carried by each.**

   Formal communication flows upward, downward, and horizontally in an organization. Upward communication is more likely to carry information about what subordinates are doing, work problems, suggestions, and subordinates' attitudes. Downward communication carries directives, feedback on performance, information on company policies, and information about the mission of the organization. Horizontal communication carries messages pertaining to the coordination of groups, the sharing of information, problem solving, negotiation, and interpersonal support.

Key Terms and Concepts

After completing your study of Chapter 17, "Interpersonal and Organizational Communication," you should be able to explain the following important terms and concepts:

communication	feedback	self-esteem	information	upward
sender	noise	selective perception	overload	communication
transmitter	channels	cognitive schema	downward	horizontal
encoding	display rules	stereotypes	communication	communication
message	self-monitoring	back channel		
receiver	boundary spanner	feedback		

Questions for Discussion

1. What do we mean when we say that communication both shapes and is shaped by the organization or social system in which it occurs?

2. In what ways is communication a fundamental skill for managers? How can a manager's communication skills affect his or her ability to carry out each of the traditional functions of management?

3. Why does high information richness sometimes facilitate and sometimes impair communication?

4. How can a stereotype lead to errors in decoding a message from a member of the stereotyped group?

5. What are some examples of organizational structure that build in horizontal pathways of communication?

6. What are some examples of the three types of listening skills (attending, following, and reflecting) that you see in your own or others' conversations?

7. What types of problems might you encounter if you tried to converse with someone who is unskilled in providing back channel feedback?

8. What are some ways in which you can become better aware of the communication abilities and perceptual biases that affect your own conversation?

9. Why would someone high in self-esteem be better able than someone low in self-esteem to use criticism constructively?

10. Several solutions for dealing with information overload and with distortion and omission are presented in Figure 17-8. If these recommendations for dealing with overload were followed, what effect would they have on the distortion and omission of information in that organization? If the recommendations for dealing with distortion and omission were followed, what effect would they have on the amount of information overload?

11. What are the relative advantages of oral and of written media? Under what circumstances would it be best to use both?

Notes

1. Excerpted from D. Wikoff, "Case History: Employee Feedback Helps the Bottom Line," *Small Business Report,* August 1986, p. 98.
2. J. J. Cribben, *Effective Managerial Leadership* (New York: American Management Association, 1972).
3. H. Mintzberg, *The Nature of Managerial Work* (New York: Harper & Row, 1973); and D. Berlo, *The Process of Communication* (New York: Holt, 1980).
4. C. I. Barnard, *The Functions of the Executive* (Cambridge, Mass.: Harvard University Press, 1938).
5. R. L. Scott, "Communication as an Intentional, Social System," *Human Communication Research* 3, no. 3 (1977): pp. 258–267.
6. C. Shannon and W. Weaver, *The Mathematical Theory of Communication* (Urbana: University of Illinois Press, 1949); and B. A. Fisher, *Perspectives on Human Communication* (New York: Macmillan, 1978).
7. J. E. Baird, *The Dynamics of Organizational Communication* (New York: Harper & Row, 1977).
8. R. L. Daft and R. H. Lengel, "Information Richness: A New Approach to Managerial Behavior and Organization," in B. M. Staw and L. L. Cummings, eds., *Research in Organizational Behavior,* vol. 6 (Greenwich, Conn.: JAI Press, 1984), pp. 191–233.
9. D. Hellriegel, J. W. Slocum, and R. W. Woodman, *Organizational Behavior* (New York: West, 1986).
10. A. Mehrabian and S. R. Ferris, "Inference of Attitudes from Nonverbal Communication in Two Channels," *Journal of Consulting Psychology* 31, no. 3 (1967): 248–252; and A. Mehrabian and M. Weiner, "Decoding of Inconsistent Communications," *Journal of Personality and Social Psychology* 6, no. 1 (1967): 109–114.
11. B. M. DePaulo, R. Rosenthal, R. A. Eisenstat, P. L. Rogers, and S. Finkelstein, "Decoding Discrepant Nonverbal Cues," *Journal of Personality and Social Psychology* 36, no. 3 (1978): 313–323.
12. R. E. Kraut, "Verbal and Nonverbal Cues in the Perception of Lying," *Journal of Personality and Social Psychology* 36, no. 4 (1978): 380–391; and A. S. R. Manstead, H. L. Wagner, and C. J. MacDonald, "Face, Body, and Speech as Channels of Communication in the Detection of Deception," *Basic and Applied Social Psychology* 5, no. 4 (1984): 317–332.
13. A. Bedeian, *Management* (New York: Dryden, 1986), p. 531.
14. P. Ekman, "Universal and Cultural Differences in Facial Expressions of Emotions," in J. K. Cole, ed., *Nebraska Symposium on Motivation, 1971* (Lincoln: University of Nebraska Press, 1972), pp. 207–283; and H. Morsbach, "Aspects of Nonverbal Communication in Japan," *Journal of Nervous and Mental Diseases* 157 (1973): 262–277.
15. M. Snyder, "Self-Monitoring Processes," in L. Berkowitz, ed., *Advances in Experimental Social Psychology,* vol. 12 (New York: Academic Press, 1979).
16. R. Lippa, "The Effect of Expressive Control on Expressive Consistency and on the Relation Between Expressive Behavior and Personality," *Journal of Personality* 46, no. 3 (1978): 438–461.
17. D. F. Caldwell and C. A. O'Reilly, III, "Boundary Spanning and Individual Performance: The Impact of Self-Monitoring," *Journal of Applied Psychology* 67, no. 1 (1982): 124–127.
18. J. F. Rychlak, *The Psychology of Rigorous Humanism* (New York: Wiley, 1977).
19. J. Gibb, "Defense Level and Influence Potential in Small Groups," in L. Petrullo and B. M. Bass, eds., *Leadership and Interpersonal Behavior* (New York: Holt, 1961), pp. 66–81.
20. H. Markus, "Selective Self-Schemata and Processing Information about the Self," *Journal of Personality and Social Psychology* 35, no. 2 (1977): 63–78.
21. R. Hastie, "Schematic Principles in Human Memory," in E. T. Higgins and M. P. Zanna, eds., *Social Cognition: The Ontario Symposium,* vol. 1 (Hillsdale, N.J.: Erlbaum, 1981).
22. D. L. Heflich, "Developing Readable Employee Handbooks," *Personnel Administrator,* March 1983, pp. 80–84.
23. J. A. Hall, "Gender, Gender Roles, and Nonverbal Communication Skills," in R. Rosenthal, ed., *Skill in Nonverbal Communication: Individual Differences* (Cambridge, Mass.: Delgeschlager, Gunn & Hain, 1979), pp. 32–67; and C. Gallois and V. J. Callan, "Decoding Emotional Messages: Influence of Ethnicity, Sex, Message Type, and Channel," *Journal of Personality and Social Psychology* 51, no. 4 (1986): 755–762.
24. R. Rosenthal, J. A. Hall, M. R. DiMatteo, P. L. Rogers, and D. Archer, *Sensitivity to Nonverbal Communication: The PONS Test* (Baltimore: Johns Hopkins University Press, 1979).
25. R. Bolton, *People Skills* (Englewood Cliffs, N.J.: Prentice-Hall, 1979); R. G. Nichols, "Do We Know How to Listen? Practical Helps in a Modern Age," in J. DeVito, ed., *Communication Concepts and Processes* (Englewood Cliffs, N.J.: Prentice-Hall, 1971); and M. P. Rowe and M. Baker, "Are You Hearing Enough Employee Concerns?" *Harvard Business Review* 62, no. 3 (1984): 127–135.
26. D. L. DiGaetani, "The Sperry Corporation and Listening: An Interview," *Business Horizons,* March–April 1982, pp. 34–39.
27. Bolton, *People Skills,* p. 40.
28. H. A. Michener, J. D. DeLamater, and S. H. Schwartz, *Social Psychology* (New York: Harcourt, 1986).

29. A. Kendon, "Movement Coordination in Social Interaction. Some Examples Described," *Acta Psychologica* 32, no 2 (1970): 100–125.

30. R. E. Kraut, S. H. Lewis, and L. W. Swezey, "Listener Responsiveness and the Coordination of Conversation," *Journal of Personality and Social Psychology* 43, no. 4 (1982): 717–731.

31. Michener, DeLamater, and Schwartz, *Social Psychology,* p. 164.

32. R. V. Rasmussen, "Interpersonal Feedback: Problems and Reconceptualization," in J. W. Pfeiffer and L. D. Goodstein, eds., *The 1984 Annual: Developing Human Resources* (San Diego, Calif.: University Associates, 1984), pp. 262–266.

33. E. Aronson, *The Social Animal,* 3rd ed. (San Francisco: W. H. Freeman, 1980).

34. L. Festinger, S. Schachter, and K. Back, *Social Pressures in Informal Groups* (Stanford, Calif.: Stanford University Press, 1950); and T. J. Allen, "Performance Information Channels in the Transfer of Technology," *Industrial Management Review* 8, no. 1 (1966): pp. 87–98.

35. J. P. Stone and R. Luchetti, "Your Office Is Where You Are," *Harvard Business Review* 63, no. 2 (1985): 102–117; and T. J. Peters and R. H. Waterman, Jr., *In Search of Excellence: Lessons from America's Best-Run Companies* (New York: Warner Books, 1982).

36. D. D. White and D. A. Bednar, *Organizational Behavior: Understanding and Managing People at Work* (Boston: Allyn & Bacon, 1986).

37. D. D. White and D. A. Bednar, *Organizational Behavior: Understanding and Managing People at Work* (Boston: Allyn & Bacon, 1986).

38. D. Katz and R. Kahn, *The Social Psychology of Organizations* (New York: Wiley, 1967).

39. R. G. Nichols, "Listening Is Good Business," *Management of Personnel Quarterly* 1, no. 2 (1962): 2–10.

40. R. W. Pace, *Organizational Development: Foundations for Human Resource Development* (Englewood Cliffs, N.J.: Prentice-Hall, 1983).

41. J. Sharma, "Organization Communications: A Linking Process," *Personnel Administrator* 24, no. 7 (1979): 35–43.

42. Pace, *Organizational Development.*

43. A. Downs, *Inside Bureaucracy* (Boston: Little, Brown, 1967).

Cohesion Incident 17-1
Alex Jordan Comes to Visit

"Charles, do you remember my telling you about the new organizational structure? I just got a telephone call from Alex Jordan, who is the vice president of the southeast region. He's trying to visit all the motels under his supervision and will be in Graniteville next Monday. He said this will just be an informal visit to let us know that he'll work with us on any problem we may have in the months ahead. You know, Alex always seemed like a stuffed shirt in our annual meetings, but he really came across as a friendly person over the telephone. Maybe this new position has changed him."

A week later, Charles and Roger are in Roger's office when Jordan arrives. "Roger, it's good to see you again. I'm really looking forward to working with you in our new set-up. You notice now that I said 'working *with* you.' We both came through this organization together, and I want you to think of me more as a consultant than as your new boss," Jordan said smiling.

"Alex, did you have a good flight in?" questions Roger.

Ignoring the question, Jordan moves over to Charles and shakes his hand. Charles notices how overly firm the handshake is. "Charles, stay with Journey's End and you can go a long way. We've got some great plans for the future. If you ever need anything, let me know. Now let's see how things have been going here in Graniteville."

Roger asks Jordan how he is adjusting to his new position but is once again ignored as Jordan picks up his briefcase and moves into Roger's chair behind his desk. Roger offers to take his coat, but Jordan replies that he believes he'll leave it on, mentioning something about the air conditioning. As he opens his briefcase to remove some papers, he looks over Roger's cluttered desk and rolls his eyes as he slides all of Roger's papers to one side.

"O.K., Roger, I'm looking at your actual results for the first six months of this year compared to budget and to last year. Except for the high wages in the area of maid service, everything else looks great. Can you tell me what you're doing to get that back under control?"

As Roger explains what has been done, Jordan sits behind the desk, his fingers in a steeple position.

"Roger, I knew there had to be a reason for what had happened and that you had already taken corrective action. Charles, you follow Roger Elliott around for a while, and you'll know this business inside out."

Jordan goes over the other areas of interest and asks Roger and Charles if they have any questions for him. Roger asks, "Alex, I've heard that because of the downturn in the economy, most of our motels are operating in the red this year. Is there any truth to that?"

Jordan removes his glasses, and a strained silence falls over the room as he slowly cleans them. "Roger, as far as I know, we're still in good condition. Occupancy rates are down a little, but the motels are still profitable, though not as much as last year."

As he glances at his watch and begins to put folders back into his briefcase, Jordan continues, "Do you have any more questions? I'll be happy to sit and talk as long as you wish." He glances at his watch once more.

A few seconds pass before Jordan stands. "Roger, it was good to see you again and I'm really looking forward to working with you in the years ahead. Charles, I hope to see you as a full manager of one of our motels in the near future. By the way, could you give me a lift to the airport, Roger?"

Moving toward the door, Jordan pauses, allowing Charles to open it for him as he leaves.

Discussion Questions

1. Several examples of nonverbal communication appear in Jordan's behavior. List them, and explain what message each communicated to Roger and Charles.

2. What was the significance of nonverbal communication in the interpersonal communication among Jordan, Roger, and Charles?

3. Did Jordan's actions really speak louder than his words? Explain.

Cohesion Incident 17-2
Good News Travels Fast

It was Wednesday at 11:15 A.M.

"No problem, Harvey. I'll make those additions to your usual order today. Let's see—I thought so; your standing order's due to be shipped Friday. We can send it along with that."

Jan Michaels, one of the senior sales representatives at Travis Corporation's Elizabethtown plant, is winding up a phone conversation with Harvey Weinstadt. Harvey is the purchasing manager for one of Travis Corporation's best auto aftermarket customers. She talks with him at least once a month to keep tabs on current and upcoming orders.

"Thanks, Jan. I knew if anyone could help me out on such short notice, you could. I didn't want to leave any loose ends when I go on vacation next week. By the way, I hear you folks at Elizabethtown deserve some congratulations."

"Oh yeah? Besides surviving the monsoon season, what have we done lately?"

"Oh, I thought surely you'd heard—but since I've opened the bag, I'll go ahead and let the cat out. My regional manager just returned from the National Distributors meeting this morning and he said that your plant was named number one in quality of sales and service. But I'm sure you'll get the official word soon. Quite a plum for you folks and for Travis. And all this time I thought you just gave me special treatment! Seems like your other customers feel the same. Good job!"

"Well, that's great news. Always nice to hear about what we're doing right. Sounds like we've got a reputation to live up to now. I'd better get to work on your order before the celebrating begins. I'll be in touch next month, but give me a call if there's anything I can do for you in the meantime. And enjoy that vacation; you deserve it."

A half-hour later Jan called Carol Morgan, secretary to Tom Bradley, the Sales Department manager, to ask her to find out whether the rumor was true. Bradley was out of the office for the morning, so Carol called Helen Liu, executive secretary to Peter Bostic, general manager of the plant. After a moment of hesitation, Helen confirmed the good news. She had received official word from Travis headquarters in a phone call that morning. Peter Bostic was out of town and she was not sure whether he knew yet or not, but she decided that because the rumor was true and it was such good news, she would go ahead and confirm it "off the record."

Word spread quickly. At lunch Jan shared the news with her usual lunchtime companions, Stan Clark and Jerry Garza, also sales representatives, with Leslie Phillips from Marketing Research, and with Phil McNair from Engineering.

Leslie returned from lunch and passed the word along to her office crew, Eileen, Bill, Steve, and Harriet. Eileen asked Harriet to call Helen to confirm the story. By now Helen had received similar calls from Engineering and Accounting, all in less than three hours.

At 3:00 P.M. Peter Bostic returned from his trip eager to share the news of the plant's award. He called a meeting of the department managers for 4:00 P.M. When he walked into the conference room he was surprised to find that everyone but he himself and Ed Perkins, head controller, was wearing a button with a big red "Number 1" on it. Apparently Ed was the only one at the meeting who needed to be told. "Well," said Peter, as he too fastened a button onto his jacket, "I see good news travels fast!"

Discussion Questions

1. Explain the role of each of the following in the Elizabethtown plant and identify a person who played the role of boundary spanner or gatekeeper.

2. What roles best describe those of Ed Perkins, Jan Michaels, and Harvey Weinstadt?

3. How might the pattern of communication have differed if the news had been bad instead of good?

Management Development Exercise 17
Feedback Skills Questionnaire

Circle the number that best represents your own behavior in giving feedback. Try to be as honest as you can; you will not be asked to disclose specific responses or scores. Your responses are for your own analysis and will be worth more the more accurate you can be. Your instructor will help you to interpret your scores.

1. To what extent do you use terms like "excellent," "good," or "bad" when you give someone feedback?

1	2	3	4	5	6	7
always use such terms			sometimes use such terms		rarely or never use such terms	

2. How often do you provide specific examples or concrete details when giving feedback?

1	2	3	4	5	6	7
rarely give specific details			sometimes give specific details		always give specific details	

3. Do you generally first ask whether the other person wants feedback?

1	2	3	4	5	6	7
assume feedback is wanted			sometimes check to see if feedback is wanted		always check to see if feedback is wanted	

4. When you give someone feedback, is it generally because you want to get a load off your chest?

1	2	3	4	5	6	7
generally I "unload" with feedback			sometimes I "unload" by giving feedback		I rarely "unload" when I give feedback	

5. Do you generally give feedback as soon as possible or do you usually wait for an appropriate time, such as an appraisal session?

1	2	3	4	5	6	7
generally I wait for a good time			usually I give feedback close to the time of the behavior		I always give feedback immediately	

6. When you give feedback, is it quite clear what that person could actually do to make effective use of your feedback?

1	2	3	4	5	6	7
feedback I give is not usually focused on applications			feedback I give is sometimes focused on applications		feedback I give is always focused on applications	

Source: This exercise was developed from materials presented in M. Sashkin and W. C. Morris, *Experiencing Management*, © 1987, Addison-Wesley Publishing, Co., Inc., Reading, Massachusetts. Pages 10–17. Reprinted with permission.

Controlling

Perhaps one of the most visible functions of a manager is control. Corporate charters proclaim top management's primary responsibility to be controlling the use of corporate resources. Practicing managers continually search for ways to control the outcomes produced by subordinates. Quality control is popular as an explanation of German and Japanese preeminence as successful global competitors. This section is designed to increase your knowledge of the control function and your skill in executing it.

Common to any control effort is the idea of a control process and the basic steps it includes. Chapter 18 uses the idea of a control process to introduce you to the fundamentals of control.

Managers are particularly sensitive to the need for control as they seek to manage the production or operations core of their organization. Chapter 19 is designed to familiarize you with key concepts in production-operations management and ways in which control, particularly quality control, is managed.

Finally, managers are increasingly realizing that timely information is central to their control function. Chapter 20 provides you with a thorough, contemporary explanation of the information management skills and concepts necessary to manage information effectively.

18

Principles
of Control

Learning Objectives

Your study of this chapter will enable you to do the following:

1. Understand what control is, its focus, and its link with the planning function.
2. Recognize and explain feedforward control, concurrent control, and feedback control.
3. List and explain the four key phases in any control process.
4. Cite several barriers to control, and describe some of the ways in which managers can try to overcome them.
5. Identify mechanisms for controlling three key aspects of organizational behavior: organizational direction, financial resources, and human resources.

Bryson Industrial Services, Inc.: A Crisis of Control on the Road to Going Public

One of the most rapidly growing industries in the United States is the hazardous waste management industry. Every year, the manufacturing and chemical processes necessary to provide the typical American household with the products and amenities for the "the good life" generate approximately seventy-three 55-gallon barrels of hazardous or toxic waste per household. Past abuses in the disposal of these wastes have led to the enactment of strict federal and state regulations for the environmentally sound disposal of these materials. These regulations in turn have created a $50 billion annual market in the clean-up, removal, and disposal of these wastes. One company that provides such transportation and clean-up is Bryson Industrial Services in Atlanta, Georgia.

Companies able to offer such services have become the darlings of Wall Street. Bryson, a small entrepreneurial company, aspired to grow rapidly into a public company. An investment banker advised Bryson's owner-managers that they needed $10 million in annual sales and 12 to 15 percent in net profit before going

Asbestos, once the most used substance for insulating commercial and residential buildings, ships, furnaces, and water heaters, has been found to cause cancer and lung disease. Its removal from schools, offices, and homes across North America is estimated to cost several trillion dollars. It is but one of thousands of hazardous substances that have given rise to the hazardous-waste management industry. (John Chiasson/Gamma Liaison)

public. She also said that they needed five years of steady and consistent growth toward these objectives.

Between 1985 and 1988, Bryson's sales steadily grew from $1 million to $7.5 million while profits grew from 1.2 percent of sales to 12.8 percent by 1988. Sales were expected to reach $10 million and profit to reach 15 percent by 1989. The first two months of 1989 were right on schedule; revenues were approaching $800,000 per month and profits were at 18 percent. But March and April revenues plummeted to less than half the desired level, and profits dropped. The majority owners decided to lay off 20 percent of the Bryson work force. They called a meeting of the company's telemarketing staff to find out why sales had dropped so drastically. They contacted friends in the industry to determine whether similar drops were occurring in other companies. They uncovered several explanations.

First, they found that new federal legislation requiring manufacturers who generate hazardous waste to file annual reports detailing quantities of waste, the implementation of specific waste-minimization programs, and active state encouragement of waste reduction were rapidly reducing the volume of waste generated. Second, they learned that their telemarketing team was spending too much time solving minor customer problems and did not know what specific levels of business from existing and new customers they needed to obtain in order to meet the firm's $10 million sales objective. Third, they found that weekly sales meetings were devoted to the logistics of coordinating activities with outside salespeople instead of focusing on specific sales results. Finally, they learned that several major customers had other waste that the salespeople responsible for those territories did not even know about.

Armed with this information, the four major owners met to design a solution to the problem. They reviewed their plans and found them sound and realistic. They were sure they had competent and motivated people and that their company was logically organized. They concluded that their problem was a lack of control. Management of their sales efforts was focused on reviewing activities rather than controlling results. Systematic investigation of customer needs was simply assumed rather than monitored and controlled. In short, these managers had been successful planners, leaders, organizers, and motivators—but they had overlooked the vital importance of effective control. And their lack of attention to the control function now threatened their dream of going public.[1]

Introduction

What Is Control?

As the description of Bryson Industrial Services shows, it was a company without systematic controls. The founders built a viable business in a rapidly growing industry, but their lack of control threatened to keep them from going public. Externally, an environmental change with major implications for the future of the business was under way, yet the business was merely reacting to its impact, rather than having planned strategically to benefit from the change. Internally, the marketing arm of the company was focusing on routine, autonomous activities rather than being monitored and adjusted via a control system linked to Bryson's plans and objectives.

You will face just such questions in your career as a manager. This chapter is designed to provide meaningful answers to these fundamental questions about control.

Managerial **control** is the process of monitoring and adjusting organizational activities in such a way as to facilitate accomplishment of organizational objectives. Effective managerial controls are created in conjunction with the strategic planning process. They provide a basis on which to monitor actions intended to implement strategic plans so that management can determine how well the plan is working and where adjustments or changes need to be made.[2] For example, Tandem Computers, Inc., hit the minicomputer market in 1975 with a bang, offering a system for almost faultlessly handling rapid-fire transactions, such as bank account debits or airline reservations, as they occurred. That caused the company's revenues and profits to double every year until the early 1980s. Then something changed. Tandem's narrow product line began to limit its appeal. Organizational objectives for revenue growth and profits went unmet. Management recognized this trend and, by the late 1980s, had virtually replaced Tandem's line of products with a broader array, revamped its marketing strategy by working with outside software companies, honed manufacturing efficiencies, and tightened financial controls.[3]

At Tandem, the revenue and profit levels the firm hoped to achieve were key organizational objectives. Only because Tandem's top managers were intent on monitoring performance did they become aware of subpar performance in accomplishing those objectives in time to do something about it. And Tandem's expansion of its product line, redesign of its marketing approach, and improvement in its manufacturing efficiencies were all adjustments of organizational activities intended to support the firm's objectives of increased revenue and improved profitability. Tandem managers engaged in a process of monitoring and adjusting organizational activities in such a way as to facilitate the accomplishment of their organization's revenue and profit objectives. In other words, they practiced managerial control. And they did so successfully: Profits were up 113 percent by 1987, revenue was up 23 percent to $768 million, and their stock price reached an all-time high.

We will begin our study of management control by first examining the fundamentals of control. Specifically, this will include an examination of the link between planning and control, the focus of control, and the basic need for control. Three types of control that managers often use are considered in this chapter, as well as the phases common to any control process. The chapter then turns to two considerations important to the success of managers in using controls. First, barriers and resistance to control that managers can expect to encounter are identified and remedies examined. Second, ways managers control specific aspects of organizational behavior are examined, including guidelines managers can use to apply these key ideas.

The Link Between Planning and Control

In its broadest sense, control is making something happen the way it was planned to happen. Planning and control should be virtually inseparable, the "Siamese twins of management."[4] Figure 18-1 illustrates the sustained link between planning and controlling.

A comment made by an entrepreneur-manager involved in Bryson Industrial Services helps illustrate the relationship between planning and control:

> Our management team recognized early on the importance of planning if we were to grow effectively. Unless we had a soundly charted course of action, we would continually be distracted and uncertain of what should be emphasized if our objective of growing to go public was to be achieved. We needed a map identifying the timing and nature of all necessary actions and decisions.
>
> But investment in a thorough plan was not enough. It gave us a false sense of security. For if we didn't follow it, or faced a major change or made a wrong turn along the way, our ultimate objective might never be achieved. We now see that the plan was only as good as our ability to make it happen. And that means we must also invest in developing a system for monitoring deviations from plans when they are occurring so that adjustments and corrective action can be taken.[5]

As we said in Chapter 1, planning is usually the first part of the management process. This process continues as the manager organizes and directs people and

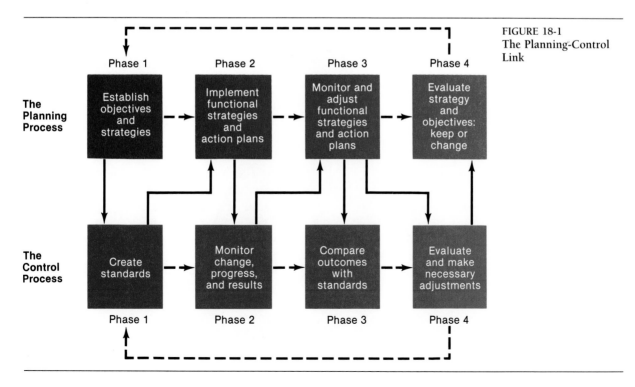

FIGURE 18-1
The Planning-Control Link

resources to get the actual work of the organization done. The process then comes full circle with the need for a control function that is tied directly into planning, whereby managers seek to monitor results achieved along the way toward fulfillment of the plans made earlier.[6] An effective control system at Bryson would have told managers what things were going according to plan and what things were not proceeding as planned and needed modification. And it would have alerted them that fundamental changes in the environment necessitated a totally new plan.

The Focus of Control

Managerial control is generally exercised at two organizational levels. **Operating control** is exercised at the operating level, where managers are concerned with using physical, financial, human, and information resources to accomplish organizational objectives (see Figure 18-2).

Control of physical resources includes purchasing (obtaining appropriate quality, price, and time of delivery), inventory management (stocking appropriate levels of items), equipment control (securing the proper kinds of facilities, machinery, and the like), and quality control (maintaining appropriate output quality). Control of human resources includes proper selection, training, appraisal, and compensation of the people in the organization. Control of information resources seeks to ensure the availability of enough timely and accurate information to support all organizational activities. Control of financial resources entails the

FIGURE 18-2
The Focus of
Managerial Control

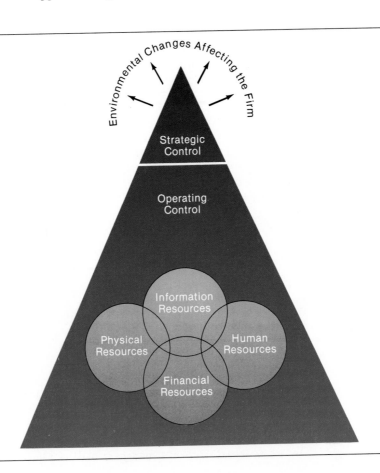

effective use of the capital available to the company. In Figure 18.2, financial and information resources are shown interconnected with other resource areas because they are related to all other resources. The costs associated with each type of resource (such as maintenance costs, computer costs, and salaries) become a top concern of managers as they examine different types of resources. And the data necessary to provide the information needed for effective control are part of the organization's information resources.

The second focus of managerial control is external. Managers responsible for corporate or business-level strategies typically oversee this type of control. Because of the level at which it takes place in the organization, this control is often referred to as **strategic control**. As we noted in Chapter 7, these top managers gather information about competitors, customers, suppliers, government, technology, and community and seek to monitor developments that may affect company plans so that the firm can adapt appropriately. As the Bryson example illustrated, the top managers of many companies need to monitor government regulation closely and adjust the organization's actions or direction as necessary. Kodak recently has assigned a four-person research team to constantly monitor and chemically analyze all Fuji film products because of the dramatic impact this Japanese film manufacturer has had on Kodak's market share.[7] In both examples, external factors may have a major impact on company plans. So managerial control must focus on these factors as well as on internal factors if organizational objectives are to be met.

The Need for Control

There are several reasons why managerial control is necessary. The most fundamental is the need to monitor what people are doing and to be sure they know what they should be doing. Small mistakes may not seem significant, but their cumulative effect, over time, may result in performance much below potential.[8] Bryson's telemarketing staff had grown accustomed to taking waste transportation orders and doing little "extras" for their customers, but they had never thought it was their job to explore different types of needs with these customers or to consider the cost to the company of the time they spent providing those "extras." This misunderstanding about what Bryson's telemarketers should do compounded over time and eventually resulted in significant lost revenue, excessive personnel costs, and a major control crisis. Monitoring what people and work units do—and especially the results of what they do—is a universal reason why managers need controls.[9]

Another reason for managerial control is the ongoing changes that organizations and their managers face. This dynamic quality of the firm's internal and external environments amplifies the importance of the link between planning and control. Managers develop plans and objectives that take time to achieve. During the time it takes to accomplish those objectives, many changes can occur in the organization and the environment in which it operates. Some of these changes may necessitate changes in the firm's plans and may even render some of its objectives inappropriate. Well-designed controls help managers predict, monitor, and adjust to changing conditions.[10]

After plans had been initiated to position the company to go public, Bryson's managers saw the Dow Jones Industrial Average for 500 companies listed in the New York Stock Exchange drop over 1,000 points in three days during mid-October 1987. This sudden change significantly altered the conditions affecting the initial public offering of new stock issues. Bryson's managers had to adjust their plans as a result, and they recognized the need for some type of control to help them plan for future events in the stock markets.

The increasing complexity of business organizations as they grow in size and in product-market scope is a third reason why managerial control is essential. When an organization is small, its managers are close to every activity undertaken. But as the business increases in size and scope, the managers responsible for the overall performance of the organization can no longer personally monitor every activity and all changing conditions or decide themselves what adjustments are necessary. They need a formal control system.[11]

Bryson's early days saw the two founders running and controlling virtually every aspect of the business on a totally personal basis. One managed the operations side of the business; the other was responsible for marketing and administration. They were generally present every day, involved in almost every decision, and available to every employee, supplier, and customer. As Bryson grew, that began to change. Particularly as Bryson expanded the types of services it offered, the day-to-day operation of the business became increasingly complicated. The mounting stress and frustration of these two owners ultimately led them to acknowledge their need for a formal control system.

Types of Control

When we view organizational activities as a system of taking inputs, transforming those inputs, and creating outputs, it becomes apparent that different managerial controls are needed for each phase of the system (see Figure 18-3).

Feedforward Control

Feedforward control (also called *steering control* and *preliminary control*) is an approach to control that uses inputs to a system of organizational activities as a means of controlling the accomplishment of organizational objectives. In feedforward control, managers identify the early inputs or issues in the organizational process that are critical to the success of the process. They then focus the control effort on choosing the best inputs, avoiding problems before they arise, and monitoring change.[12]

At the operating level, feedforward control usually means control via the careful selection of inputs or the development of policies and procedures to head off anticipated problems.[13] For example, Mack Truck carefully inspects the transmissions to be installed in its trucks to be sure that each truck's complicated gear mechanism (in which the transmission is used) works according to specifications. Focusing on controlling its future supply of management talent, General Foods hires only college graduates for its product management training program, because college graduates have consistently been more successful than others in managing product territories. Likewise, the National Football League recently implemented a policy requiring mandatory drug testing before each annual college draft to identify athletes who might be using drugs.

At the strategic level, feedforward controls are designed to alert managers to key changes in the environment that may affect the accomplishment of long-term organizational objectives. Ryan Builders, a nationwide residential development company, carefully monitors changes and trends in prime rates because of the dramatic effect a change upward (reducing the demand for housing) or downward (increasing the demand for housing) can have on the accomplishment of Ryan's

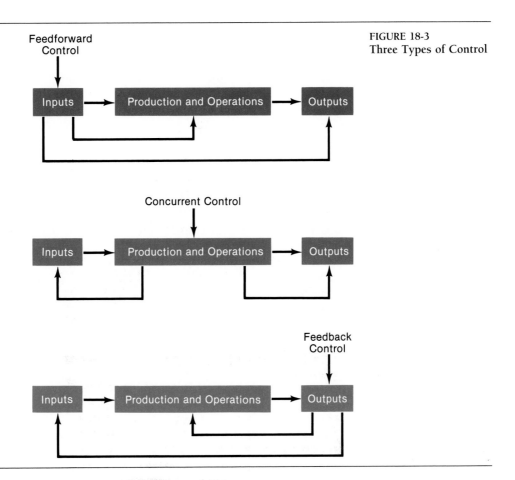

FIGURE 18-3
Three Types of Control

organizational goals. Bryson managers realized that they needed to monitor (1) federal and state regulations pertaining to hazardous materials and (2) trends in the stock market as two factors that would affect their plan to become a publicly owned company.

Concurrent Control

Concurrent control (also called *screening control* and *yes/no control*) is an approach to control that seeks to effect control while work is being performed. Compaq Computer Company has thirty-four checkpoints along the assembly line for its highly successful portable computer. As the product moves along, these periodic checks ensure that the product is working properly up to that point in the production process. Bryson waste technicians have a twenty-eight-item checklist they must initial. It covers every key step in the process of picking up hazardous waste from an industrial customer, transporting it to a licensed disposal facility, and releasing the material to that facility.

Concurrent control at the operating level seeks to ensure that work is being performed appropriately or that events are unfolding as planned. A floor supervisor at a Steak 'n Ale restaurant spends a significant amount of time each evening moving from the customer area, to the kitchen, to the cashier area. He or she monitors the serving of food as it is taking place and gauges customer satisfaction, making whatever adjustments are necessary to ensure proper service.

Managers engaged in concurrent control at the strategic level typically focus on quarterly results and on key milestones in order to monitor organizational progress and make any necessary adjustments. An area manager at Steak 'n Ale monitors the monthly sales levels of area restaurants as well as the building and opening of Steak 'n Ale restaurants in new locations in order to be sure that progress in his or her territory is consistent with key milestones on the yearly plan.

Feedback Control

Feedback control (also called *post-action control*) is the approach to control that focuses on the outputs of organizational activities after the production or operation process has been completed. The Honda lawnmower plant in Cary, North Carolina, has what it calls the "Barbara Foster" test that each of its mowers must pass before being shipped around the country to Honda dealers. Barbara Foster checks twelve key items on each mower and then gives the mower a single pull on its crank rope. If it starts immediately, it goes to shipping. If it doesn't, it goes back for further inspection. This is one type of feedback control.[14]

Feedback control at the operating level plays three roles. First, it provides operations managers with the information they need to evaluate the overall effectiveness of the organizational activities for which they are responsible. For example, the floor supervisor at Steak 'n Ale who gets several complaints one evening that certain cuts of steak were excessively tough uses this information to examine suppliers, as well as food-preparation activities in the kitchen, in order to improve the quality of the steak. Second, feedback control is often used as a basis for evaluating and rewarding employees. The Field Services manager at Bryson reviews the final cost on every clean-up job a Bryson crew completes for an industrial customer. He then uses this information to evaluate each crew and to award bonuses at the end of the year. A third role of feedback control at this level is to alert managers who are responsible for inputs or for the production process to any need to adjust their activities. The Steak 'n Ale supervisor's investigation of complaints about tough steak may lead to a change in the input—a new supplier or a different type of steak from the current supplier. The Bryson field services manager may use his information to change the operations process or the way clean-up jobs are done.

Feedback control at the strategic level provides top management with information to use in adjusting or changing the firm's future plans. Organizationwide results help top management gauge the success of current plans. Feedback control provides information on the appropriateness of those plans and on any need to adjust or redesign future actions across the organization. The erosion of IBM's market share in the personal computer market in the late 1980s alerted IBM's top management to the need to reconsider its basic IBM-PC product line and ultimately to introduce a whole new, less "cloneable" line of personal computers for the 1990s.

Using Multiple Types of Control

Many organizations exercise all three types of controls: feedforward, concurrent, and feedback. For example, Holiday Inn prides itself on offering quality accommodations at reasonable prices to travelers worldwide. Holiday Inn employs a staff of over one hundred inspectors who travel to Holiday Inn locations for three unannounced inspections a year, when they evaluate over five hundred items related to customer service. Their job is to make sure that each location is ready to provide high-quality services to future customers. This is a form of feedforward control. Each Holiday Inn has a "housekeeper" who inspects each room for cleanliness and monitors the work of the hotel staff daily to ensure superior service for present customers. This is a form of concurrent control. And finally, every guest is given two opportunities to evaluate Holiday Inn's lodging services (via cards placed in each room and at every restaurant table). This is a form of feedback control.

International managers also face the need to use each type of control in managing overseas operations. "Insights for International Managers 18" illustrates four specific controls popular among international managers.[15]

Phases in the Control Process

Control processes of every type and at every level seem to comprise four general phases. Figure 18-4 traces the typical flow of a basic control process through these phases. In this section we will examine each of the four phases in the control process.

Create Standards

The first phase of any control process is the creation of standards. A **standard** is a desired outcome or expected event with which managers can compare subsequent activities, performance, or change. Standards should grow out of organi-

---

Insights for International Managers 18

ESTABLISHING CONTROL OF INTERNATIONAL OPERATIONS

International managers exercise control over overseas operations in four basic ways: 1) ownership structure, 2) personal control, 3) personal visits, and 4) method of entry into overseas operations.

Ownership refers to the level of ownership a multinational company maintains in each overseas operation. U.S. multinational companies typically prefer to have wholly-owned or majority-owned overseas subsidiaries. Japanese and European multinational companies have a strong preference for joint ventures or joint ownership of foreign subsidiaries.

Personal contact is when the parent company involves its overseas subsidiary managers in the headquarter's formal and informal structures, such as serving on important companywide committees. European and Japanese firms have a long tradition of integrating their subsidiary managers in corporate and decision-making and policy-making structures. By contrast, U.S. and German firms do this less frequently.

Control through personal visits, whereby headquarters executives travel regularly to overseas operations, is a logical way of controlling overseas subsidiaries. U.S. executives use this method extensively. Japanese and European executives, often thought to be extensive travelers, use this method less frequently.

Method of entry refers to the method a firm uses to enter international markets. Firms often enter international markets by exporting from a home country, which trades off control for low risk. The next option is licensing with a private or state-owned enterprise in the host country. Jointly owned manufacturing facilities are the next approach, evolving at the last stage to acquiring or forming a wholly-owned subsidiary in the host country. The first and last options provide the highest levels of control to the parent company.

Source: Adapted from Anant R. Negandhi, *International Management* (Boston: Allyn & Bacon, 1987), pp. 142–152. Copyright © 1987 by Allyn & Bacon, Inc. Reprinted with permission.

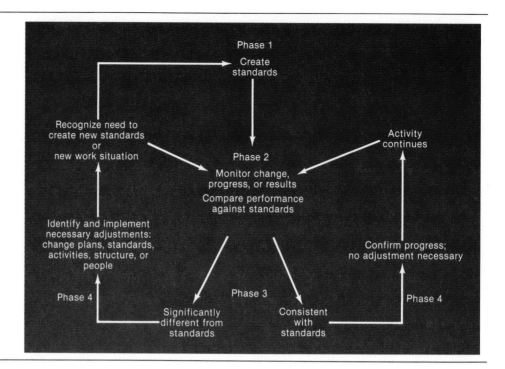

FIGURE 18-4
Phases in the Control Process

zational objectives. The clearer the link between organizational objectives and the standards applied for control, the more likely it is that the control process will be accepted, understood, and even self-regulating. Because objectives focus on results (the outcomes of activities, rather than activities themselves), they can be used in the creation of standards that also focus on results rather than activities.

The standards used in the feedforward control process at Holiday Inn that involved unannounced inspections included the following:

1. Each inn must pass 98 percent (490) of the 500 items examined during the inspector's visit.

2. Meal service must be prompt, courteous, and proper.

3. Each room must include a full complement of fresh towels, sheets, pillows, and other linen.

4. Check-in and check-out must take no longer than two minutes for customers with reservations.

The standards at Holiday Inns reflect specific performance targets that Holiday Inn personnel are expected to meet. By identifying these specific standards, managers establish a relevant basis against which to monitor and adjust the performance that employees turn in—in other words, to control the result of organizational activities. For example, the housekeeper at the Boise, Idaho, Holiday Inn uses as a standard the number of rooms cleaned per six-hour shift by each maid. This standard is linked to her two primary objectives: (1) pass four annual inspections conducted randomly by headquarters, and (2) maintain weekly cleaning costs at no more than 6 percent of room revenue.

Monitor Change, Progress, or Results

Once standards are created, the second phase of the control process begins: Managers monitor change, progress, or results against the standards they have established. A marketing manager for a national electronics distributor may monitor orders shipped into each territory on a weekly and monthly basis as a means of controlling annual sales production. A product development manager may monitor progress via key milestones in the development and market testing of a new product idea. A member of the planning staff of Ryder Truck company may monitor the changes in oil prices and interest rates over time as part of a feedforward control system designed to alert top management to any need to adjust key assumptions underlying the firm's future expansion plans. Bryson's field services manager might monitor weekly progress against a planned schedule as one type of concurrent control on a key clean-up project. In each example, these managers are monitoring key factors linked to standards underlying the control system.

The challenge in this second phase of the control process is twofold. Monitoring change, progress, or results first requires identification of the appropriate measures or indicators to monitor—not an easy task in many jobs. The second challenge is to monitor systematically. Many managers rush to document progress and results after the fact, neglecting to regularly and systematically monitor progress, change, or performance as it takes place. Sometimes this is attributable to information management problems (several of which are examined in Chapter 20). But more often the fault lies in the manager's lack of initiative. Unsystematic monitoring often results in crisis management or in the gradual disregard of control among a manager's subordinates.

Compare Performance Against Standards

The third phase in the control process is to compare the change, progress, or results that managers have been monitoring with the standards created in the first phase of the control process. These outcomes may meet the standard, or they may be lower or higher than the standard. The manager's job in comparing outcomes to standards is to decide how much deviation from standards is acceptable.

When standards for performance are straightforward and absolute, managers usually find making this comparison relatively easy. For example, Bryson's sales manager holds a monthly contest among his six salespeople wherein the person who books the largest number of waste transportation loads during the month receives a weekend, all-expenses-paid trip to the city of her or his choice during the next ninety days. In this example it is relatively simple to determine whether the standard (the largest number of waste transportation loads) has been met. Al Davis, general manager of the Los Angeles Raiders football team, applies "making the play-offs" as the critical standard for evaluating the coaching staff's performance. The standards for comparison in both of these examples are straightforward and absolute, making comparison relatively easy.

Comparison is more difficult when standards are not absolute and are open to some interpretation. With feedforward controls, for example, monitoring changes against certain standards is often difficult because long-term trends emerge only gradually. Bryson's board of directors considered the establishment of Bryson's new venture into handling infectious waste for hospitals an important standard in its evaluation of Bryson's management team in 1989. Yet although the threat of AIDS fueled concern over infectious waste disposal, legislation regulating the nature of disposal was slow to emerge in virtually every state and at the federal level as well. In the absence of such legislation, many hospitals choose the least expensive way to dispose of infectious waste, rather than the safer but more expensive Bryson approach. Bryson had only three accounts by the end of 1989. Bryson's board of directors would find comparison of the firm's performance with its target rather subjective, given the uncertainty that pending state and national legislation introduces into the operating environment. As another example, contracting businesses that rely on borrowing money (or on their customers' ability to borrow money) are subject to the influence of the prime rate on everyone's ability to borrow. But changes in the prime rate frequently move slightly up and down on a monthly basis, and only after some time is a trend clearly evident. So comparison of performance against standards linked to the prime rate is often open to considerable interpretation after tentative standards are set.

With post-action controls, the challenge in comparing results to standards often arises when results are close to expectations. For example, Bryson's transportation division was experiencing a high level of absenteeism (around 8 percent per week) among its drivers. The manager of Bryson's transportation division decided to evaluate his three shift supervisors against a new standard of 4 percent average weekly absenteeism and to evaluate them quarterly. At the end of the first quarter, one supervisor's work crew had a 4.2 percent absenteeism rate, a second crew had a 4.5 percent rate, and a third crew had a 5.2 percent rate. How should this division manager decide whether each team performed adequately? The effective manager takes into account many relevant factors, including the absolute absenteeism rate and any mitigating circumstances. No supervisor met the standard, but one was off by only a very small amount and another was relatively close. Furthermore, only one quarter had passed, and there may have been extenuating circumstances. The important point is that making comparisons against standards and subsequently interpreting the results often require that managers consider other relevant information in addition to the outcomes themselves.

Take Corrective Action and Make Adjustments

The Bryson transportation manager described above must ultimately decide what to do about the first-quarter results achieved by his three shift supervisors. That is, he must decide whether none, some, or all of the supervisors are reducing absenteeism effectively. He must further decide whether the actions they are taking to reduce absenteeism are appropriate or need to be changed. And he must decide whether the standard of 4 percent average weekly absenteeism is still appropriate or needs to be adjusted upward or downward. Bryson's transportation division manager has arrived at the fourth phase of the control process.

Concluding the evaluation of outcomes and taking corrective action or making adjustments where the manager deems them necessary is the final phase of the control process. Its purpose is to ensure that future organizational activities under the manager's control achieve the continuing or adjusted outcomes expected from them. Corrective actions or adjustments usually take one of three forms.

1. *Maintain current status.* Where outcomes are consistent with standards, the appropriate response is to recognize acceptable performance and maintain the status quo. This situation usually reflects organizational activity that is right on track, so little change is necessary. The key concern of the responsible manager is to make sure that positive feedback—recognition that the outcome is on target and expressions of appreciation—is provided so that subordinates are

clearly aware that their efforts are important and are monitored. The Bryson shift supervisor who achieved a 4.2 percent average weekly absenteeism rate was thanked and congratulated. He was also encouraged to stick with his approach to handling absenteeism among his drivers; it seemed to be working quite well.

2. *Make adjustments.* When outcomes deviate from standards, adjustments in what is being done or how it is being done are usually needed. If the occupancy rate for an Atlanta Holiday Inn is expected to average 72 percent per month and averages only 65 percent during the first six months, then corrective action may be in order. Adjustments in the advertising programs, convention sales approach, pricing, or customer service may be necessary to bring performance in line with the standard established by top management.

   Adjustments may also be appropriate when standards are far exceeded. If the Holiday Inn mentioned above experienced a 97 percent average occupancy for the first six months, and seasonality was not a major cause, then Holiday Inn management might consider several adjustments: increasing its prices, adding additional facilities, hiring more personnel to ensure a sufficient level of customer service, or perhaps building another inn nearby.

3. *Change the standards.* Where outcomes deviate significantly from standards, another adjustment that may be called for in the control process is to change the standard or plan. Bryson's standard that sales should grow at 15 percent annually may no longer be appropriate as a means of evaluating the sales staff when the company starts to face mature, heavily competitive market conditions. Expecting Bryson's transportation division drivers to average 550 miles per day (10 hours × 55 mph) in cross-country travel is no longer a sufficiently high standard, now that most states have reverted to a 65-mph speed limit on interstate highways. In both examples, changing the standard that is used in the control process would seem to be appropriate.

Once the manager implements any of the three corrective actions or adjustments, the control process repeats itself. As portrayed in Figure 18-4, managerial control is an ongoing process that recycles through the four phases we have examined in this section.

Guidelines for Management Practice

A useful way to practice strategic control is to ask key questions. The questions most often used to initiate strategic control follow.

1. Is the organization or unit moving in the proper direction?

2. Are key factors and actions falling into place?

3. Are assumptions about major trends and changes proving correct? What are the implications when they are not accurate?

4. Are the critical things we need to do being done?

5. Do we need to adjust or abort the current strategy?

6. How are we performing? Are we meeting objectives and milestones?

7. How well are overall costs, revenues, and cash flows matching projections?

Use of the control process goes a long way toward effecting managerial control, but managers must anticipate and overcome barriers and resistance to control. The next section examines key barriers and sources of resistance to control and offers guidelines to managers for overcoming them.

Barriers and Resistance to Control

Even though control is a crucial management function, resistance to control often arises among subordinates and other people within the organization. It is important for managers to understand why people resist control and to know how to overcome that resistance.

Too Many Controls

Organizations or managers may simply try to control too many activities or parts of activities. In the interest of trying to ensure that a job is well done or to avoid mistakes, controls are designed to "govern" virtually every activity undertaken on the organization's behalf. Some organizations have even found it necessary to control otherwise personal decisions by individual workers, such as how they dress, what hair styles they choose, and other personal habits. Military organizations usually insist on this extensive level of control over the daily activities and appearance of military personnel. But in this country, members of other organizations, particularly business organizations, would certainly resist a similar level of control.

To avoid the pitfall of excessive control, effective managers focus controls on outcomes and results, not on activities and appearances. Controls should be explained in such a way that they are understood to be a corrective process or means of monitoring progress rather than a pressure tactic, a way to restrict freedom, or an end in themselves. And controls should be periodically reevaluated to determine whether the need for each specific control still exists.

Aversion to Accountability or Loss of Flexibility

When control standards are accurate, timely, and objective, some people resist them because they realize that the control will make it easier to determine whether or not they are doing a good job. Among poor performers, this threat of being clearly responsible for their poor performance creates resistance to control. Even good performers sometimes resist controls that are clearly on target because they fear loss of the flexibility or freedom they view as necessary to their high-level performance.

The efforts to solicit employee participation outlined in Chapter 13 and the MBO programs described in Chapter 6 provide useful ways of dealing with an aversion to accountability or loss of flexibility. These techniques enable poor performers to participate in setting targets, to air their concerns, and to confront the fact that their subsequent rewards will be tied to the results they achieve, not just to their physical presence. Those who want to do well thus have an opportunity to seek guidance in improving; those who do not can consider changing their attitudes or seeking another place to work. MBO gives good performers an opportunity to raise their fears about loss of freedom and to structure their authority and use of control information in such a way as to alleviate those fears.

Inaccurate or Arbitrary Controls

Most people like to do an effective job, and most accept controls that provide feedback they can use in doing their job well. But they do resist controls they view as inaccurate, arbitrary, or poorly focused. For example, a telemarketing team may regard a control based on number of calls made per day as arbitrary. Customer availability varies from one day to another, so their preferred measure may be customers sold per week. Likewise, they may argue that number of calls per day is simply a conveniently quantifiable measure, whereas time spent building good-will with the customer is more important to the eventual sale and to long-term sales.

Bryson managers found that the budgeting process created resistance to control among several good employees. These employees felt that the budgetary "estimates" that served as standards for evaluating their efforts were inaccurate or arbitrary. Bryson's sales manager's estimate for travel expense, for example, was viewed by several salespeople as no longer reflecting the current cost of making sales contacts in broader territories. Yet each salesperson's monthly performance was judged in part on the basis of the individual's staying "within budget" on travel expenses. In each of these examples, otherwise productive employees began to resist controls they viewed as inaccurate, arbitrary, or poorly focused.

The grave danger is that employee resistance to these types of controls may both discourage good employees and undermine the purpose behind the control. For example, members of the telemarketing team may start making more calls but may put less effort into making the sale so that they can move rapidly on to the next call. Or they may give current customers poorer service than before, hastily explaining that they must spend more time trying to get new customers—an explanation that is likely to damage relations with current customers. The concern over budgeted travel expenses at Bryson could encourage inefficiencies. Salespeople might retaliate by overspending in areas with arbitrarily high standards. They might even resort to falsifying reports and "padding" their expense accounts because they are convinced that the control system is inappropriate.

Guidelines for Management Practice

Our analysis of the effective use of controls suggests the following guidelines for managers:

1. Always remember that control should be approached and designed as *a positive activity* that is necessary for focusing people, time, and money on organizational objectives.

2. Keep your subordinates involved in their own control. Self-control is often the best control.

3. Focus controls on outcomes and results, not on activities and appearances.

4. Regularly reevaluate controls to make sure they are still necessary and appropriate.

5. Involve subordinates in designing and monitoring controls.

6. Remember that some deviation from standards is normal. Use ranges to guide control of regular work standards.

7. Watch for positive as well as negative deviations. Be certain to recognize and reward positive deviations.

8. Watch out for subordinates who argue against controls because they don't want to be overly restricted or "lose their freedom." Their resistance may really spring from a desire to avoid being clearly accountable for results.

Effective managers make controls flexible to avoid their becoming inaccurate, arbitrary, or poorly focused. Remember that when outcomes vary significantly from standards, the problem may be in the standard as well as in the way work is being done. Effective managers always check and reexamine standards when a significant deviation occurs.

Effective managers also use participation to gauge the continued appropriateness of sensitive standards in each control cycle. Chapter 12 discussed the importance of participation as a means of reducing resistance to change. By the same token, when subordinates are involved in designing and implementing a control system, they are more likely to consider it accurate and focused—or at least to understand the logic behind the standards it employs.

It is also possible that choosing the "control style" that is best under the circumstances may help overcome people's resistance to control. "Management Development Exercise 18" at the end of this chapter explains what control style is and poses four questions that managers can ask in order to determine what approach to control may be best for them.

Controlling Specific Aspects of Organizational Behavior

Now that we have examined the basic concepts and ideas associated with managerial control, it is time to consider specific forms of control. The control mechanisms needed to effect strategic control of the organization itself are different in many ways from those needed to control financial resources, human resources, and selected operations that are going on within the firm. Figure 18-5 summarizes the control mechanisms used to control organizational direction, financial resources, and people.

Controlling Organizational Direction

Strategic control is concerned with monitoring and adjusting the direction of the overall firm—tracking the strategy that is being implemented, detecting problems

FIGURE 18-5
Control Mechanism for Different Organizational Settings

THREE TYPES OF CONTROL	ORGANIZATION FOCUS OR SETTING		
	Organizational Direction	Financial Resources	Human Resources
Feedforward	Premise Control Strategic Surveillance Special Alerts	Budgets	Selection MBO Constructive Delegation
Concurrent	Implementation Control Milestone Review Special Alerts	Budgets Ratios	Performance Appraisal Quality-Control Checkpoints On-the-Job Training Constructive Delegation
Feedback	Results Special Alerts	Budgets Audits Ratios	Performance Appraisal MBO

or changes in underlying premises, and making necessary adjustments. A general description of strategic control as part of the strategic management process was provided in Chapter 7. Looking more closely at strategic control, we discover that it is exercised through three specific mechanisms: premise control, strategic surveillance, and implementation control. These mechanisms are described below.

Premise control is a feedforward control designed to check systematically whether the premises underlying the company's plans are still valid. When a vital assumption (or premise) on which the plans were built is no longer valid, the strategy may have to be changed. For example, Bryson's plans for offering a transportation-based way to dispose of hazardous waste is based on two assumptions. One is that federal regulations severely restricting where and how waste can be treated (mainly at a few central sites nationwide) will remain in effect for at least ten years. The second is that inexpensive technologies for handling this waste at the plant will not be forthcoming for at least ten years. If changes take place that render either of these assumptions invalid, Bryson's current strategy could be in serious jeopardy. So Bryson's management should assign to specific organizational members the responsibility of monitoring trends in federal legislation, Environmental Protection Agency regulations, and new technology offerings from companies and research organizations interested in burning, treating, or recycling hazardous waste. This would be a form of premise control at Bryson.

The process of instituting premise controls begins when managers identify key premises during the planning process. The premises should be recorded, and responsibility for monitoring them should be assigned promptly to the appropriate person or department. Finally, managers should identify areas within the company or aspects of the strategy that changes in these premises would significantly affect so that contingency plans can be launched rapidly if necessary.

Strategic surveillance is another type of feedforward control designed to monitor a broad range of events inside and outside the company that could make changes in the firm's strategy advisable. The basic idea behind strategic surveillance is that some form of general monitoring of many information sources should be encouraged in order to uncover any important yet unanticipated information.

One of the major officers in Bryson Industrial Services, for example, always attends the Environmental Protection Agency's annual seminar on trends in waste management technologies and regulations in order to obtain any new information that may be pertinent to Bryson's future plans. A panelist on one of the programs in the 1986 EPA seminar commented that emerging controversy surrounding the AIDS virus may create a massive new category of regulated hazardous waste. She was referring to the trash—paper, needles, refuse, throw-away containers, gloves, and garments—deposited in dumpsters by hospitals and taken to local landfills. This comment led Bryson to investigate medical waste disposal practices and to make adjustments in its strategy that facilitate diversification into the market for medical waste transportation and disposal services. This is an example of strategic surveillance.

Implementation control is a concurrent control designed to assess whether the overall strategy should be changed in light of unfolding events and results associated with the sequence of steps and actions involved in implementing the company's strategy. Bryson recently terminated that part of its growth strategy which was based on having numerous regional waste-services offices. The updating of cost and revenue projections during the implementation phase began to suggest that the strategy was not working as planned. The cost of maintaining a full complement of services at each regional office was not being justified by a steadily increasing revenue base within each targeted territory. Rather, Bryson managers found that it was more cost-effective to keep overhead low at the regional transportation terminals and to base other services (such as clean-up crews, chemical laboratories, and special equipment) in a central location.

Implementation control is exercised two ways. One way is to monitor key strategic actions or programs that are central to a new strategy. Bryson's monitoring (and later phasing out) of its full-service regional offices is a good example. A second means of implementation control, the **milestone review**, usually involves the major reassessment of a firm's progress at critical junctures (milestones) in the process of implementing the strategy. These milestones are usually associated with the completion of a set of important activities or the end of a specific time period. "In Practice 18-1" offers examples of the three methods of strategic control.

Controlling Financial Resources

A key aspect of the planning process and the ongoing management of any organization involves the allocation of financial resources to various subunits within the organization for their use in getting the work of the organization done. From a control perspective, managers are interested in monitoring the use that each unit or subunit makes of these financial resources to ensure that they are being spent effectively and efficiently. This section highlights three basic mechanisms for controlling financial resources: budgets, ratio analysis, and financial audits.

BUDGETING

Budgeting is a control process that involves expressing the future activities of an organization or subunit in dollar or other quantitative terms. Budgets are typically drawn up for one year, and they are the foundation of most control systems. Figure 18-6 illustrates a typical budgeting system for controlling future expenditures that are designed to implement the organization's strategy.[16]

There are several types of budgets that managers use to control financial resources. Financial managers are involved with generating and reviewing virtually every budget, but they are especially concerned with three. *Cash flow budgets,* which break down the flow of the firm's incoming and outgoing cash into monthly, weekly, and even daily periods are used primarily to control the firm's ability to meet its current obligations. Financial managers are also primarily responsible for *capital expenditure budgets,* which establish how the company will procure and use funds the firm needs to acquire such major assets as land, equipment, and facilities. Finally, financial managers are usually responsible for monitoring *balance sheet budgets* that set forth what the company's future financial structure will look like on the basis of the results projected in all other budgets.

Operating managers use three types of operating budgets. Sales managers are particularly concerned with *sales or revenue budgets.* These budgets project the revenue the organization expects to generate in annual, quarterly, monthly, and even daily terms. Sales and operations managers—indeed all managers—regularly encounter the need to establish and subsequently monitor an *expense budget.* This budget helps control levels of expenditures, the timing of those expenditures, and the coordination of those expenditures with higher-level budgets such as the companywide cash flow budget. Finally, the *profit and loss budget* provides the basis

===== In Practice 18-1 =====

EXAMPLES OF STRATEGIC CONTROLS

Premise Control at Citicorp

Citicorp has been pursuing an aggressive product development strategy geared to achieving growth in earnings of 15 percent annually while becoming an institution capable of supplying clients with any kind of financial service anywhere in the world. A major problem Citicorp is attempting to deal with in achieving this earnings growth is its exposure because of earlier, extensive loans to economically troubled Third World nations. Thus Citicorp remains sensitive to the wide variety of predictions about impending Third World defaults.

Citicorp established a basic planning *premise* that 10 percent of the Third World countries would default annually over the next five years. Yet it maintains active *premise control* by having each of its international branches monitor daily announcements from key governments and by using inside contacts. When the premise is challenged, management attempts to adjust Citicorp's posture. For example, when Peru's president Alan Garcia stated that his country would not pay interest on its debt as scheduled, Citicorp raised its default charge to 20 percent of its $100 million Peruvian exposure.

Implementation Control at Days Inns

As Days Inns pioneered the budget segment of the lodging industry, its strategy placed primary emphasis on company-owned facilities and it insisted on maintaining roughly a 3-to-1 company-owned–to–franchise ratio. This ratio assured the parent company total control over standards, rates, and the like.

As other firms moved into the budget segment, Days Inns saw the need to expand rapidly throughout the United States, and it decided to reverse its conservative franchise posture. This would rapidly accelerate its ability to open new locations. At that time, executives concerned about potential loss of control over local standards instituted *implementation controls* requiring both regular franchise evaluation and annual milestone reviews. Two years into the program, most executives were convinced that a high franchise–to–company-owned ratio was manageable, and they accelerated the growth of franchising by doubling the franchise sales department.

Strategic Surveillance at IBM

In the early years years of its attempt to make and sell computers (in addition to its staple typewriters and adding machines), IBM's strategy was targeted toward the scientific and research markets in government, universities, and industry. The company's early experience was not encouraging: It appeared that money was too scarce among these organizations for them to buy IBM's large, expensive mainframe computer. Yet no other organization or setting had a need for as much computing capacity as IBM's mainframes offered—or at least that was IBM management's assumption.

Fortunately for IBM, one sales executive's reading included *Librarian,* a trade magazine circulated among librarians at the time. He noticed one article about the number of transactions handled in large libraries and the need for automated solutions. This led to a suggestion that libraries be investigated as a market for IBM's early mainframes. The libraries were relatively "flush" with recent, generous funding from the New Carnegie Foundation. This market proved to be the basis for IBM's early success, and some say its survival, in the mainframe computer business. The discovery of this early, important niche has been attributed to an IBM manager's regular reading. This piece of *strategic surveillance* was the only source of information that turned out to be critical to IBM's ability to "steer" its mainframe computer strategy in a successful direction.

Sources: Adapted from "Citicorp: What the New Boss Is Up To," *Fortune,* February 17, 1986, p. 40; conversations with selected Days Inns executives; and excerpts from *Innovation and Entrepreneurship* by P. Drucker (New York: Harper & Row, 1986) Copyright © 1985 by Peter F. Drucker. Reprinted with permission of Harper & Row Publishers, Inc.

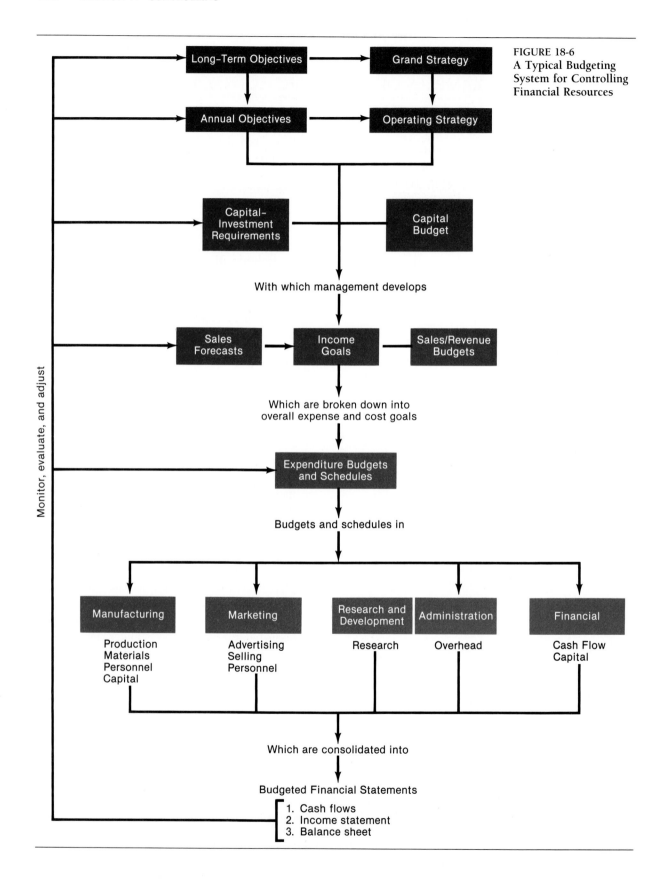

FIGURE 18-6
A Typical Budgeting
System for Controlling
Financial Resources

The development of annual budgets often involves several people. Here a manager is going over several points in a budget her staff has proposed for 1990. Each individual has played a key role in developing various aspects of the budget. (Ray Ellis/Photo Researchers)

for unit and department managers, as well as top management, to monitor expected differences between revenue and expenses and hence to adjust in a timely fashion to unprofitable situations.

Budgets can be developed in two ways. The most common approach for developing a budget is called *bottom-up budgeting*. Organizations using this approach have managers and supervisors at the operating level develop initial budget requests. These requests are then forwarded to the next management level for review, adjustment, and consolidation with other initial budget requests. The consolidated budget requests are usually forwarded to a budget committee, which evaluates the consolidated requests in terms of the company's strategy and available resources. It then makes budgetary recommendations to the top management of the organization. Once the organization's top managers make *their* decisions, the final budget is communicated down through the organization. It is then employed as a guide and a control mechanism for the use of financial resources.

This approach is called bottom-up budgeting because the initial budget requests originate at the operating level of the organization. In the second approach, called *top-down budgeting,* the initial budget is developed at the top of the organization and then circulated throughout the firm for evaluation, refinements, or requests for changes. Well-documented changes may be made, and a final, revised budget is communicated to all.

Both approaches to budgeting offer unique advantages. In the bottom-up approach, the operating managers, who are most familiar with their unit's specific needs, develop the initial budget requests. It also can create a psychological obligation on the part of these operating managers to "live with" budgets that they were largely responsible for developing. The top-down approach, on the other hand, minimizes the time necessary to complete the budgeting process.

Budgets are an important mechanism for establishing effective control. You will certainly have to use them as a manager. Budgets are a natural link between planning and control. They facilitate effective control by translating activities carried on throughout the organization into common, financial terms. Developing them can serve as a forum for constructive communication, debate, and coordi-

Ratio	How Calculated	What It Measures
Liquidity Ratios		
Current Ratio	$\dfrac{\text{Current assets}}{\text{Current liabilities}}$	The extent to which a firm can meet its short-term obligations
Quick Ratio	$\dfrac{\text{Current assets} - \text{inventory}}{\text{Current liabilities}}$	The extent to which a firm can meet its short-term obligations without relying on the sale of its inventories
Leverage Ratios		
Debt-to-Total-Assets Ratio	$\dfrac{\text{Total debt}}{\text{Total assets}}$	The percentage of total funds that are provided by creditors
Debt-to-Equity Ratio	$\dfrac{\text{Total debt}}{\text{Total stockholders' equity}}$	The percentage of total funds provided by creditors versus by owners
Long-Term-Debt-to-Equity Ratio	$\dfrac{\text{Long-term debt}}{\text{Total stockholders' equity}}$	The balance between debt and equity in a firm's long-term capital structure
Times-Interest-Earned Ratio	$\dfrac{\text{Profits before interest and taxes}}{\text{Total interest charges}}$	The extent to which earnings can decline without the firm becoming unable to meet its annual interest costs
Activity Ratios		
Inventory Turnover	$\dfrac{\text{Sales}}{\text{Inventory of finished goods}}$	Whether a firm holds excessive stocks of inventories and whether a firm is selling its inventories slowly compared to the industry average
Fixed-Assets Turnover	$\dfrac{\text{Sales}}{\text{Fixed assets}}$	Sales productivity and plant and equipment utilization
Total-Assets Turnover	$\dfrac{\text{Sales}}{\text{Total assets}}$	Whether a firm is generating a sufficient volume of business for the size of its asset investment

FIGURE 18-7
Summary of Key
Financial Ratios

nation. And they serve a useful purpose by linking detailed information on the use of financial resources to overall company performance.[17]

Budgets also have potential disadvantages. They can be applied too rigidly, which detracts from their ability to generate constructive communication and managerial support. Creating them takes time, and asking key players in the organization's operation to take time for budgeting may mean they have less time for producing results. Budgets also have a way of allocating funds for existing activities that may limit the funds available for innovation and change. And when amounts budgeted for prior years are used as a starting point for determining next year's budget, managers may be tempted to make sure they spend everything in this year's budget, even if the expenditure is not necessary, so that they will not lose that amount from next year's base![18]

Ratio	How Calculated	What It Measures
Accounts-Receivable Turnover	$\dfrac{\text{Annual credit sales}}{\text{Accounts receivable}}$	(In percentage terms) the average length of time it takes a firm to collect on credit sales
Average Collection Period	$\dfrac{\text{Accounts receivable}}{\text{Total sales/365 days}}$	(In days) the average length of time it takes a firm to collect on credit sales
Profitability Ratios Gross Profit Margin	$\dfrac{\text{Sales minus cost of goods sold}}{\text{Sales}}$	The total margin available to cover operating expenses and yield a profit
Operating Profit Margin	$\dfrac{\text{Earnings before interest and taxes (EBIT)}}{\text{Sales}}$	Profitability without concern for taxes and interest
Net Profit Margin	$\dfrac{\text{Net income}}{\text{Sales}}$	After-tax profits per dollar of sales
Return on Total Assets (ROA)	$\dfrac{\text{Net income}}{\text{Total assets}}$	After-tax profits per dollar of assets; this ratio is also called return on investments (ROI)
Return on Stockholders' Equity (ROE)	$\dfrac{\text{Net income}}{\text{Total stockholders' equity}}$	After-tax profits per dollar of stockholders' investment in the firm
Earnings per Share (EPS)	$\dfrac{\text{Net income}}{\text{Number of shares of common stock outstanding}}$	Earnings available to the owners of common stock
Growth Ratios Sales	Annual percentage growth in total sales	Firm's growth rate in sales
Income	Annual percentage growth in profits	Firm's growth rate in profits
Earnings per Share	Annual percentage growth in EPS	Firm's growth rate in EPS
Dividends per Share	Annual percentage growth in dividends per share	Firm's growth rate in dividends per share
Price-Earnings Ratio	$\dfrac{\text{Market price per share}}{\text{Earnings per share}}$	Faster-growing and less risky firms tend to have higher price-earnings ratios

Source: J. A. Pearce, II, and R. B. Robinson, Jr., *Strategic Management: Strategic Formulation and Implementation,* 3rd ed. Richard D. Irwin, Inc. © 1988, pp. 238–239.

The "Guidelines for Management Practice" following the end of this section offer several suggestions that you should keep in mind when using budgetary controls.

RATIO ANALYSIS

Ratio analysis is a second mechanism by which managers exercise financial control. Figure 18-7 lists and briefly explains many of the financial ratios that managers use to monitor and adjust the allocation of financial resources.

These ratios are divided into four groups, and each group focuses on a different type of financial control. *Liquidity ratios* are indicators of a firm's ability to meet its short-term obligations. They monitor the availability of current assets to pay off or reduce current liabilities. *Leverage ratios* identify the source of a firm's capital—the owners or outside creditors. A key concern is the extent to which long-term capital is provided by creditors. *Activity ratios* indicate how effectively a firm is using its resources. By comparing sales (or revenues) with the resources used to generate them, it is possible to assess the firm's efficiency of operation. *Profitability ratios* indicate how effectively the firm as a whole is being managed. Profitability is the net result of a large number of policies, decisions, activities, and individual efforts. Comparing profits to sales, assets, or net worth is a useful way to gauge the true pay-off generated by the organized endeavor that the firm represents.

In order for ratio analysis to be a useful control mechanism, managers must have a basis for comparison. These bases for comparison, which become "standards" in a ratio-based control process, are generated in two ways. One way is to compare the firm's ratios for a current time period with its ratios for past time periods. This lets managers gauge the firm's improvement in targeted areas. A second way in which managers use ratios is to compare the company's ratios with those of other companies or with averages across several companies (industry averages). This approach is frequently used by top management to pinpoint areas of weakness and then encourage improvement.

FINANCIAL AUDITS

The **financial audit** is the third type of mechanism used to control financial resources. The two major types of audits are external audits and internal audits.

Guidelines for Management Practice

Budgets are a regular part of most managers' control activities. Their regularity, however, creates occasional resistance from subordinates intent on overcoming budgetary restrictions. The following guidelines can help managers devise and use budgets effectively:

1. Involve your key subordinates in the development of any budgets for which you are responsible. Participation will increase their stake in making the budget work and will make them better aware of the costs associated with their work.

2. Do not make your budget a once-a-year exercise. Refer to it on a regular basis, at least monthly. Require the same of your subordinates.

3. Break your budgets down into monthly amounts and year-to-date (cumulative) totals. Compare your actual revenues and expenditures with the amounts budgeted in each of these categories.

4. Although you should communicate freely about budgets and ratios with subordinates and with your manager, do not leave detailed budgets lying around for all to see. They can be misinterpreted by casual readers. They can also fall into the wrong hands.

5. Allow for some flexibility in your budget. Do not cast it in stone.

6. Set aside a small portion in your budget for unspecified innovations and unexpected events. Then use it when that opportunity or that unexpected event occurs, to seize the opportunity and move quickly.

7. Become very familiar with the key ratios for your type of business. Apply this knowledge in your regular evaluation and interpretation of the ratios in your company and unit.

8. When you have your subordinates develop budgets and generate ratios, tell them how much time to allocate for the task so that they will not waste time.

External audits are conducted by experts, usually CPAs, who are not employees of the organization. They are extremely thorough in seeking to document the authenticity of every item on a firm's financial statements.[19] They act as a post-action control certifying to the board of directors, the stockholders, the investment community, and regulatory bodies such as the Securities and Exchange Commission the accuracy of management's statement of financial condition. *Internal audits* serve a similar purpose. The main difference is that they are conducted by company personnel and are intended to answer management's need for authentication as much as that of external groups.

Controlling Human Resources

Effective management and control of human resources has received increased attention in the last decade as a critically important focus for improved performance.[20] Chapter 13 discussed this trend, and several of the control approaches outlined below, in greater detail. Our purpose here is to review those human resource management mechanisms that are especially relevant to the control function: selection, performance appraisal, constructive delegation, and human resource ratios.

SELECTION

The **selection** of people entering an organization, or a unit within that organization, is an important control mechanism for ensuring the effective use of human resources. Selection is an example of a feedforward control in the human resource area. Obviously, selecting the right person for a task or activity increases the probability that the task will be performed well. Bryson Industrial Services is very careful to hire extroverted individuals with prior work experience for its telemarketing positions. In the manager's experience, these qualities tend to be exhibited by those members of the current staff who are most successful at selling services over the phone.

PERFORMANCE APPRAISAL

Performance appraisal is an essential mechanism that managers use to control human resources in an organization. As we noted in Chapter 13, the performance appraisal process parallels the control process. It identifies standards to be achieved, monitors and compares to those standards the performance of individuals and work groups, and makes any adjustments that those comparisons suggest are necessary.

Effective managers use performance appraisal as both a concurrent control and a feedback control. Periodic reviews of performance and occasional spot checks of performance serve as a basis for timely control and adjustment during the regular year. And annual performance reviews or appraisals serve as a feedback control wherein the previous year's performance is evaluated and standards for the coming year are set.

Unfortunately, performance appraisal is often underused as a means of controlling human resources. First, managers find it easy to avoid periodic appraisals during the year. The annual review becomes an empty ritual that contributes little to the monitoring and adjusting of current human resource use. Second, meaningful performance criteria are difficult to establish or monitor in many job settings. This causes some managers to avoid paying serious attention to individual performance appraisal.

HUMAN RESOURCE RATIOS

Certain **human resource ratios** are also used as a means of monitoring and adjusting the use of human resources throughout the organization. *Employee turnover,* the number of employees leaving the company in a particular time period divided by the total number of employees, is a ratio used to monitor and adjust such variables as pay and hiring policies. *Absenteeism,* the number of employees absent in a particular time period divided by the total number of employees, is a ratio used to detect and address problems related to the use of a firm's human resources. Heavy turnover or excessive absenteeism usually means reduced efficiency and effectiveness in a firm's operations; these quickly translate into reduced profitability. Finally, larger companies usually monitor various *work force composition ratios* to guard against discrimination. The percentage of their work force made up of females and the percentage made up of members of minority groups are two prominent composition ratios that many firms monitor.

Review of the Learning Objectives

Having studied this chapter, you should be able to respond to the learning objectives with extensions of the following brief answers.

1. **Understand what control is, its focus, and its link with the planning function.**

   Control is the process of monitoring and adjusting organizational activities in such a way as to facilitate the accomplishment of organization objectives. *Operational control* is concerned with controlling the use of the four basic inputs—physical, financial, human, and information resources—necessary to accomplish organizational objectives. *Strategic control* monitors developments in the external environment that may affect company plans and initiates any adjustments that are required.

2. **Recognize and explain feedforward control, concurrent control, and feedback control.**

   Viewing organizational activities as a system that receives inputs, transforms those inputs, and creates outputs suggests that different managerial controls are needed for each phase of the system. *Feedforward control* concentrates on inputs to a system of organizational activities as a means of controlling the accomplishment of organizational objectives. *Concurrent control* seeks to ensure that work is being performed appropriately or is progressing as planned. *Feedback control* focuses on the outputs of organizational activities to evaluate the effectiveness of final products and completed work.

3. **List and explain the four key phases in any control process.**

   The first step in the control process is the *creation of standards.* A standard is a desired outcome against which subsequent activities, performance, or change can be compared. The second step in the control process is to *monitor performance, change, and results*—that is, the outcomes the manager wishes to control. The third step is to *compare outcomes with established standards.* Outcomes may be lower than, higher than, or the same as the standard. The challenge for the manager is deciding how much outcomes may deviate from the standard and still be acceptable. The final step in the control process is *corrective action or adjustment.* Managers must do one of three things—maintain the status quo, make adjustments, or change the standard—to complete the control process, which then cycles back to phase 1.

4. **Cite several barriers to control, and describe some of the ways in which managers can try to overcome them.**

   Three barriers to control that managers should be sensitive to are: too many controls, aversion to accountability or loss of flexibility, and inaccurate or arbitrary controls. The pitfall of excessive controls can be avoided by focusing on outcomes, not activities. Encouraging subordinate participation helps overcome aversion to accountability. And making controls flexible avoids inaccurate, arbitrary controls.

5. **Identify mechanisms for controlling three key aspects of organizational behavior: organizational direction, financial resources, and human resources.**

   Control of organizational direction (strategic control) is accomplished through four control mechanisms: premise control, strategic surveillance, implementation control, and special alert control. Control of financial resources is accomplished through three mechanisms: budgets, ratio analysis, and financial audits. The mechanisms that help control human resources include selection, performance appraisal, constructive delegation, and human resource ratios.

Key Terms and Concepts

After having completed your study of Chapter 18, "Principles of Control," you should have mastered the following important terms and concepts.

control	concurrent control	strategic	milestone review	selection
strategic control	feedback control	surveillance	budgeting	performance
operating control	standard	implementation	ratio analysis	appraisal
feedforward control	premise control	control	financial audit	human resource ratio

Questions for Discussion

1. What is control? Give specific examples of controls exercised in organizations where you have worked or gone to school.

2. Distinguish between strategic and operating controls. How are they similar? How are they different?

3. Why is forging and maintaining a link between planning and controlling so important? Give several examples that support your answer.

4. Identify and explain the similarities and differences among the three basic types of control. Which type of control would you find easiest to use? Which do you think would be most effective at controlling?

5. Describe the four phases of the control process and their application to a set of work activities you might undertake.

6. Why do people resist control? How would you overcome that resistance?

7. Describe three ways in which strategic control can be achieved. Provide a description of how you assume a company currently in the news has used, or has not used, strategic control.

8. Describe three ways of controlling the use of financial resources. Illustrate how they might be implemented.

9. Explain three mechanisms for controlling the use of human resources. Offer an example of each in a work setting of your choosing. Which is the most effective control mechanism for that setting?

Notes

1. Based on author's conversations with owners and managers of Bryson Industrial Services, Inc.

2. R. L. Daft and N. B. Macintosh, "The Nature and Use of Formal Control Systems for Management Control and Strategy Implementation," *Journal of Management* 10, no. 1 (Fall 1984): 43–66.

3. "How Jim Treybig Whipped Tandem Back into Shape," *Business Week,* February 23, 1987, p. 124.

4. D. C. Mosley and P. H. Pietri, *Management: The Art of Working with and through People* (Encino, Calif.: Dickerson Publishing, 1975), p. 32.

5. Conversations with Joel E. Stevenson, president of Bryson Industrial Services.

6. Vijay Sathe, "The Controller's Role in Management," *Organizational Dynamics 11,* no. 3 (Winter 1983): 31–48.

7. "Kodak Fights Fuji," *Business Week,* February 23, 1987, p. 138.

8. D. J. Cockburn, "Another Way of Looking at Internal Control," *CA Magazine* 117, no. 11 (November 1984): 75–77.

9. H. R. Jessup, "Front Line Control," *Supervisory Management,* October 1985, pp. 12–20.

10. K. A. Merchant, *Control in Business Organizations* (Boston: Pitman, 1985).

11. N. K. Oballe, II, "Organizational/Managerial Control Processes: A Reconceptualization of the Linkage Between Technology and Performance," *Human Relations* 37 (1984): 1047–1062.

12. For useful discussions of feedforward control, see W. H. Newman, *Constructive Control* (Englewood Cliffs, N.J.: Prentice-Hall, 1975); B. Yavitz and W. H. Newman, *Strategy in Action* (New York: Free Press, 1982), Chapter 7; and P. Lorange, M. S. S. Morton, and S. Ghoshal, *Strategic Control* (St. Paul, Minn.: West, 1986).

13. E. P. Gordner, "A Systems Approach to Bank Credentials Management and Supervision: The Utilization of Feedforward Control," *Journal of Management Studies* 22 (1985): 1–24.

14. Based on Honda's U.S. television advertising program in 1987.

15. For another perspective on control issues in an international setting, see B. R. Baligia and A. M. Jaeger, "Multinational Corporations: Control Systems and Delegation Issues," *Journal of International Business Studies,* Fall 1984, pp. 25–40.

16. E. G. Flamholtz, "Accounting, Budgeting, and Control Systems in Their Organizational Context: Theoretical and Empirical Perspectives," *Accounting, Organizations, and Society* 8 (1983): 153–169.

17. N. C. Churchill, "Budget Choice: Planning vs. Control," *Harvard Business Review* 62 (July–August 1984): 150–164.

18. P. J. Carruth and T. D. McClandon, "How Supervisors React to Meeting the Budget Pressure," *Management Accounting* 66 (November 1984): 50–54; and see a classic related to this topic, C. Argyris, "Human Problems with Budgets," *Harvard Business Review* 31 (January 1953): 97–110.

19. See, for example, J. J. Welsh, "Pre-acquisition Audit: Verifying the Bottom Line," *Management Accounting,* January 1983, pp. 32–37.

20. R. E. Walton, "From Control to Commitment in the Workplace," *Harvard Business Review* 63 (March–April 1985): 76–84.

Cohesion Incident 18-1
Too Much Overtime

At the end of each month, Roger and Charles sit down together and review the operations of the Graniteville Journey's End Inn for the prior month. Their budget report shows the expenses budgeted for the month, the actual expenses for the month, and the actual expenses for the same month last year. It also shows room occupancy rate. If any major discrepancies exist, Roger takes steps to correct them.

As they examine the expense data, they find that every item is close to budget except "Maid Services." This expense, which is the payroll cost for the maids, is $3,800 over budget for the month of June.

"Charles, how about checking the payroll register to see how much overtime we paid the maids last month? I know we've got the same number of maids on the payroll as we had last year and the number of maids we had budgeted for this year. Our actual number of maids is right in line with the number we budgeted for. So the amount of overtime has got to be causing this problem."

As usual, Roger is correct. In fact, by jotting down some information from the payroll register and the budget, Charles is able to show Roger the following data:

	June 1988	June 1989	Budget
Number of Maids	10	10	10
Hours Worked	2,152	2,865	2,000
Total Wages	$8,177	$11,300	$7,500

"Charles, it's obvious to me that our maids are just getting lazy. Our occupancy rate this year is almost identical to last year's (83.1 percent versus 83.3 percent). There's no reason they can't clean the rooms just as quickly. This overtime is killing us. Since February, they've been more and more over budget each month. This year that one area is already more than $8,000 in the red!"

The next afternoon when Charles arrives at work, he notices a memorandum on his desk. It is addressed to the maids and states that, effective the following Monday, no overtime will be paid to any maid. It goes on to say that any rooms that cannot be cleaned in the allotted time should be left as they are and will not be rented for the night. Management will then find employees who can clean the rooms in the time allowed.

Although most of the maids grumbled about the new procedures when they saw the memorandum, none of them quit. During the first week after the new policy was introduced, no overtime was paid and all rooms were cleaned.

Discussion Questions

1. How does the monthly statement that Roger receives help him control his operation?

2. Although the maids are the ones who continued to build up overtime, who is really responsible for the slow but steady increase? Why?

3. Did Roger handle the problem correctly?

Cohesion Incident 18-2
Quality Control in the Market Research Interview

The Elizabethtown plant of Travis Corporation is considering developing and producing a new product, an electronic monitoring system for passenger cars and light trucks. The system would monitor and report the status of a number of processes and events in the vehicle and would provide a much wider range of information than systems currently on the market. The Market Research Department has been asked to conduct a large-scale market survey in order to determine whether there is a market for this type of system and, if so, which combination of items is preferred by potential users. For example, in addition to the usual reports on engine temperature, oil and water levels, doorlocks, and ignition key, the proposed system could also report the indoor and outdoor air temperature, air pressure in the tires, whether the hood and trunk or hatchback are closed and locked, cleanliness of the oil, and how many miles since the last oil change, lubrication, or other maintenance was performed.

For this type of large-scale survey, many part-time telephone interviewers have been hired and trained. Given the number of part-time, temporary employees assisting with the interviews, Leslie Phillips thinks it will be important to do random spot checks or validity checks to verify that the interviews have been completed as reported and that the interviewers are conducting the interviews and recording the data accurately.

Leslie uses the results of these validity checks to identify interviewers who are not performing their job effectively so that they can be retrained or replaced and to identify any interviews that have produced "suspect" data. Each interviewer is expected to complete eight 15-minute interviews during a 3-hour shift; if all eight are completed in less than 3 hours, additional interviews may be conducted for bonus pay. If an interviewer completes fewer than seven interviews in the 3-hour shift, however, his or her pay is docked. Leslie assumed this policy would discourage lingering on calls that do not produce usable data. On the average, each completed interview costs $4.50. On a weekly basis during the four weeks when the interviews are being conducted, Bill and Steve randomly check 10 percent of those completed by each interviewer. They ask several short questions for which answers can be easily coded, to verify the date and time of the interview, the identity of the person interviewed, and the reliability of responses to several of the items in the survey. The average cost of each validity check is $1.50. So far, these validity checks suggest that less than 1 percent of the interviews conducted have been falsified or have contained other flaws that rendered the data useless.

Discussion Questions

1. Define control as a management function. Explain how the spot checks serve this function in the present case.

2. Describe the requirements of effective controls. To what extent do the spot checks described in this case meet these requirements?

3. Are the spot checks described in this case feedforward controls or feedback controls? Explain.

Management Development Exercise 18
Choosing a Control Style

In the *Harvard Business Review* Cortlandt Cammann and David Nadler provided what is now a time-tested guide for managers to use in shaping their approach to control. They suggest that the choice of your approach to control, or your control style, should be based on four factors: your managerial style, the organization's style, relevant performance measures, and your subordinates' desire to participate. To choose a control style, first answer the following four questions:

1. In general, what kind of managerial style do I have?

    Participative. I frequently consult my subordinates on decisions, encourage them to disagree with my opinion, share information with them, and let them make decisions whenever possible.

    Directive. I usually take most of the responsibility for and make most of the major decisions, pass on only the most necessary job-relevant information, and provide detailed and close direction for my subordinates.

2. In general, what kind of climate, structure, and reward system does my organization have?

    Participative. Employees at all levels of the organization are used in decisions and influence the course of events. Managers are clearly rewarded for developing employees' skills and decision-making capacity.

Nonparticipative. Most important decisions are made by a few people at the top of the organization. Managers are not rewarded for developing employee competence or encouraging employees to participate in decision making.

3. How accurate and reliable are the measures of key areas of subordinate performance?

Accurate. Measures are reliable, all major aspects of performance can be adequately measured, changes in measures accurately reflect changes in performance, and measures cannot be easily sabotaged or faked by subordinates.

Inaccurate. Not all important aspects of performance can be measured, measures often do not pick up important changes in performance, good performance cannot be adequately defined in terms of the measures, and measures can be easily sabotaged.

4. Do my subordinates desire to participate and respond well to opportunities to take responsibility for decision making and performance?

High desire to participate. Employees are eager to participate in decisions, can make a contribution to decision making, and want to take more responsibility.

Low desire to participate. Employees do not want to be involved in many decisions, do not want additional responsibility, and have little to contribute to decisions being made.

Once you have answered these four questions, you can apply them in the accompanying diagram to generate suggestions about the control style that should serve you best. That style will be somewhere on a continuum between what Cammann and Nadler call an "internal motivation strategy" for control and an "external control strategy." Where an internal motivation strategy is suggested, they suggest you rely heavily on subordinates' self-regulation and control, assuming that intrinsic factors such as a sense of accomplishment, responsibility, achievement, and self-worth will motivate subordinates to manage their own control. Where an external control strategy is suggested, you would take a more active role in monitoring and adjusting subordinate activity and would rely on such extrinsic rewards as pay, promotion, and privileges to encourage subordinates to meet their control standards.

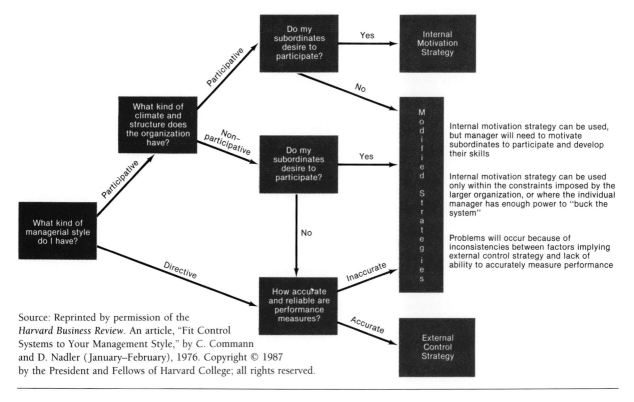

Source: Reprinted by permission of the *Harvard Business Review.* An article, "Fit Control Systems to Your Management Style," by C. Commann and D. Nadler (January–February), 1976. Copyright © 1987 by the President and Fellows of Harvard College; all rights reserved.

19

Operations Management

Your study of this chapter will enable you to do the following:

1. Explain the differences between a good and a service.
2. Distinguish among the three levels of operations management decisions, and give examples of each.
3. Describe the various production processes, and cite the conditions under which each is appropriate.
4. Explain what role inventory plays in manufacturing and how inventories are managed and controlled.
5. Identify four steps in designing a quality control system.

P/OM in Two Settings

Nissan Motor Manufacturing Corporation U.S.A. stands on some 782 acres in Smyrna, Tennessee, that were used to graze cattle in the early 1980s. By the late 1980s, $660 million had been invested to construct a more-than-80-acre manufacturing facility—the most modern in the world—to build light trucks and Sentra automobiles.

The Nissan plant is shaped like a giant E; its long edge extends about three-quarters of a mile, and each of the three shorter branches is a quarter of a mile long. Approximately seventeen miles of conveyors move parts through the plant as managers and supervisors coordinate assembly, painting, and finishing trucks and Sentras.

Delta Airlines started in Atlanta, Georgia, over fifty years ago as a provider of crop dusting services and a regional passenger carrier. Delta has become an international airline and a dominant force in the airline industry. It has long been the most profitable domestic airline.

A major contributor to the steady profit picture at Delta Airlines is its operations management orientation. First, Delta managers have to decide carefully which cities and routes Delta will serve. Along with this goes the need to locate selectively Delta's "hubs"—connection points on the Delta route system where passengers can transfer from flight to flight easily.

Nissan's vast facility in Smyrna, Tennessee, is one of the most modern automobile manufacturing facilities in the world. All the trucks and Sentras sold in North America are manufactured, assembled, and painted here. (Courtesy of Nissan)

Many operating decisions follow: What types of aircraft to use. Flight times. Food service on board. Are gate areas large enough? Are additional personnel required during peak periods? The list goes on and on. It is clear that operations managers at Delta have several decisions to make and make well if Delta is to remain profitable.

Delta provides a service—the use of a seat to fly from one destination to another. Nissan's Smyrna plant provides a product—trucks or Sentras. But each constitutes an operational system that needs sound management to operate effectively.[1]

Delta's Atlanta location is the largest hub for a single airline in the world. This concourse is just one of four used by Delta to service a daily average of ten thousand passengers from all over the world who travel through the Atlanta facility. (Courtesy of Delta)

Introduction

What Is Operations Management?

In the broadest sense, operations management includes all the decisions made in an organization that involve the production of goods and services.[2] **Operations management (OM)** is the designing, planning, controlling, and scheduling of any production system that converts required inputs into desired outputs.

OM is essential in the management of a production system for Nissan automobiles, and it is essential in the production or operations system that provides services such as air transportation. An operations manager is perhaps most easily visualized as a supervisor on a Nissan assembly line, but an operations manager is also responsible for scheduling the arrivals and departures for Delta Airlines.

Decisions made by an airline manager, who is one type of operations manager, are very different from those made by the assembly line supervisor, who is another type. An operations manager at Delta Airlines is concerned with scheduling employee shifts, making sure customers don't have to wait too long for their baggage, and providing timely transportation. The assemby line supervisor at Nissan Motors is not only concerned with employee scheduling; he or she must also make sure that parts are available when they are needed for production—and yet that inventory is not excessively high. The manager at Delta is concerned primarily with a production system that supplies a service. The assembly line supervision at Nissan motors is concerned with a production system that supplies a good such as an automobile. To be successful, both managers must apply sound OM practices and techniques.[3]

To understand the importance of OM in production systems providing either a good or service, managers must be familiar with the difference between a good and a service. A **good**, once produced, can be stored in inventory for use at a later date. A **service**, on the other hand, is used as soon as it is produced. It cannot be stored in inventory to be used at a later date. Delta Airlines uses the good known as an aircraft to provide the service of fast transportation. Once a plane takes off, transportation is being provided to all passengers on board. If a space is empty, Delta Airlines cannot remove the unused space and store it for use at a later date when demand is higher. Delta is providing a transportation service; customers buy the use of a seat for a specific day and time. The planes that Delta flies were made by Boeing, which manufactured the seat—a good—and held it in inventory until the planes were assembled and sold to Delta. Despite this difference, many of the same operations management decisions are made in the manufacture of goods and the provision of services.[4]

Understanding the OM Function

How can managers become more effective in their OM function? Whether producing goods or services, what must they do to ensure that their production systems create competitive advantages linked both to cost effectiveness and to quality of output? The answers to these questions lie in recognizing key decisions that are repeatedly addressed in the OM function and in understanding basic techniques available to help managers who must make those decisions. In our discussion of decisions that confront managers in the operations function, we have categorized them on the basis of the frequency with which the decisions are made and the impact of the decision on the organization. In the sections that follow, we have grouped together (1) decisions that are made only intermittently yet have tremendous impact on the organization, (2) decisions that are made more often and have less far-reaching effects, and (3) decisions that are made daily but may have less impact on the firm. These same three groups consist, respectively, of long-range, intermediate-range, and short-range decisions (see Figure 19-1).

Long-range decisions include where to locate a new plant, what product to produce by what process, and how to arrange the physical layout of facilities. These decisions are major yet intermittent; they are usually made in the context of fundamental competitive changes in the industry or the environment in which the firm operates. Decisions made at lower levels are constrained by the results of these long-range decisions. The next level of OM decisions consists of intermediate-range decisions. These include purchasing equipment, allocating financial resources, planning quality levels, and developing medium-range production plans. Intermediate-range decisions normally result in shorter-term effects than

FIGURE 19-1
Hierarchy of Operations Management Decisions

Level	Key Decisions	Example
Long-range	1. Facility location	McDonald's decision to place a restaurant at one location and not another.
	2. Product/process selection	McDonald's decision to offer such new products as salads and McRib sandwiches via a make-to-stock process.
	3. Facility layout	McDonald's decision to locate the French fries cooker, Coke machines, and ice cream machines at certain strategic locations.
Intermediate-range	1. Production planning	McDonald's decision to produce twice as many French fries as normal for lunch hours.
	2. Production and inventory	McDonald's decision to stock at least four Big Macs at all times.
	3. Quality planning	McDonald's decision to allow a hamburger to sit in inventory for a maximum of ten minutes and then to throw it away.
Short-range	1. Order scheduling	Deciding to make one customer's special order before another customer's.
	2. Worker assignments	Deciding which workers will wait on customers and which workers will prepare food.
	3. Quality control	Making sure French fries are hot and not overcooked.

long-range decisions. They often involve a time horizon of about one year. Finally, the most frequent OM decisions, short-range decisions, are the routine, operating decisions made by operations managers. These decisions typically involve the scheduling of orders, worker assignments, and quality control.[5]

Long-Range OM Decisions

Long-range OM decisions are made on an intermittent basis but are critical in determining the fundamental nature of a company's production system. They are made as a part of the strategic planning process discussed in Chapter 7. Once made, long-range OM decisions are seldom changed, and they constrain subsequent intermediate-range and short-range decisions by determining the context in which such decisions are made. There are three main types of long-range OM decisions. **Product/process design** is concerned with designing a product to meet a forecasted demand and a process by which to produce the product in the desired quantities. Decisions involving **facility location** determine the geographic location of new warehouses and production facilities. And **facility layout** decisions are related to the location of machinery, inventory storage areas, customer waiting rooms, and receiving docks within a facility. Before discussing these types of long-range decisions, however, we should outline the different classes of production processes that can be used to manufacture a product or provide a service.

Types of Production Processes

Manufacturing processes can be described in two ways. First, they can be classified in terms of the stage at which the company plans to hold inventory to meet customer demand. A company that carries finished-goods inventory that is used to fill customer demand employs what is called a "**make-to-stock**" **system**, because the goods produced are stocked in finished-goods inventory. McDonald's offers an example of a make-to-stock production system. Hamburgers are made and then stored in bins by hamburger type. When an order is placed for a hamburger, it is taken from this stock and given to the customer. On the other hand, a company that waits until a customer order is placed before making the product to fill the order employs what is called a "**make-to-order**" **system**. At Wendy's, hamburgers are not made until a customer places an order. All inventory in a make-to-order system is either in raw materials or work in process (WIP).

A second way in which manufacturing processes can be classified is by the degree of standardization in materials flow. There are three types: continuous flows, line flows, and intermittent flows. The organizational design implications of processes or technologies similar to these were discussed in Chapter 11. The operational considerations will now be briefly discussed. A **continuous flow** is a process wherein the work stations are arranged in order of the steps required to produce the product. An oil refinery is an example of a continuous flow. As oil is being refined, it is continuously flowing from one stage in the production process to another. The machines in a continuous flow are connected by some type of device that allows for constant movement of materials through the production process. In a refinery, the movement of materials is accomplished via pipes and pumping stations.

The second type of flow, which is also called *repetitive manufacturing*, is a **line flow**. Here, as in a continuous flow, the work centers are arranged in order of the steps required to produce the product. The assembly line that is used by

Nissan Motors to produce cars is an example of a line flow. An example of a line flow for the production of a service is the standardized process that a dry cleaner uses for cleaning customers' clothes. The primary difference between a line flow and a continuous flow is that the products produced on a line flow can be measured as discrete units, whereas the continuous flow produces products that can better be described as substances than as units. A car is assembled in distinct steps (chassis, body, motor, wheels, and so on), whereas oil refining is a steadily flowing process. In a continuous flow, the materials are frequently liquids, gases, or powders and are measured in units of volume.

The third type of flow is the intermittent flow, which is also called *job-shop manufacturing*. In an **intermittent flow**, the product being produced may follow a variety of routes through the shop, unlike the one fixed route found in a line-flow or continuous-flow production process. Machines in a job shop are arranged by grouping together machines that perform similar functions. For example, all the drilling machines would be located together, and all the sanding machines would be somewhere else. Companies that produce many different and unique end products, such as certain medical equipment manufacturers and certain machining shops, have an intermittent flow. An accountant who performs the service of preparing people's taxes has an intermittent flow, because each taxpayer's tax return requires different forms and calculations. Figure 19-2 summarizes these three types of processes and their characteristics.

Design of Products and Processes

One of the basic decisions top managers must make is what goods or services to produce. The nature of the product determines in what niche in the market the company will compete. Decisions on such factors as design specifications, ease of production, and product quantity directly affect the manufacturing process required. Close coordination between the product design engineers and the manufacturing department is necessary if a high-quality product is to be produced at a low cost. A tool that enhances this coordination is **computer-aided design (CAD)**.[6]

FIGURE 19-2
Characteristics Associated with Types of Materials Flows

Type of Flow	Type of Product	Typical Process Characteristics
Continuous	Make-to-stock	Totally automated process producing a completely standardized product at high volume. Very little work-in-progress (WIP) inventory because materials are always moving.
Line (repetitive)	Make-to-stock to replenish inventory levels	Highly automated process producing large batches of several products. Finished-goods inventory is high, but WIP has decreased from job shop.
Intermittent (job shop)	Make-to-order on customer demand	Highly flexible process producing small quantities of many different products on general-purpose machinery. Very little finished-goods inventory but WIP inventory is high.

The computer can evaluate the consequences of several designs by simulating the product's appearance and/or performance under various real-life scenarios. Thus engineers can evaluate a design from several angles without having to construct actual prototypes. CAD is discussed in Chapter 20.

Over the life of the product, many changes may take place in its design. These changes can be costly, because they may require the purchase of new machinery and may bring about the obsolescence of existing machinery. Operations managers must always balance the need for product changes with the cost of making them. Two practices that help managers reduce the number of changes they are likely to have to make are simplification and standardization. *Product simplification* is the practice of designing a product so that all unnecessary parts and components are removed. The smaller the number of parts on a product, the fewer the number of possible design changes. *Product standardization* is the practice of minimizing product variety and ensuring that components are used on more than one product (an example is using the same engine in several models and styles of automobiles).

Designing a service is much more difficult than designing a good. This is because many services are unique and thus standardization is impossible. Although Delta Airlines can provide the simple and highly standardized service of air transportation, a hair stylist provides a different service to each customer.[7]

AN APPROACH TO PRODUCT/PROCESS DESIGN DECISIONS

The environment in which product/process design decisions are made is dynamic in the sense that as the product evolves through the various stages in its life cycle, the process used to manufacture the product must also evolve. One way to appreciate this evolution is to view process and product as the two dimensions of the matrix shown in Figure 19-3. On the process side of the matrix is the type of process characterized by materials flow. On the product side of the matrix is the product life cycle of a firm whose product output ranges from a low-volume, high-variety product to a high-volume, standardized product.[8]

As Figure 19-3 suggests, most firms fall along the diagonal of the matrix. In the upper left-hand corner is the printing firm that produces many jobs to customer order on general-purpose machinery. Moving down the diagonal, we find the heavy-equipment manufacturer that produces in batches; the product is more standardized and the process a disconnected line flow. Further down the diagonal is the typical automotive assembly line, which produces large batches of a standardized product via an automated process. At the lower right-hand corner of the matrix is the sugar refinery, representing the continuous-flow process. A company that wishes to be the market leader for a particular product tends to position itself below the diagonal. Companies positioned below the diagonal have a production process that is further evolved than the product. This is a high-risk strategy because large amounts of capital are required to purchase the necessary equipment, and a product that suddenly becomes obsolete could result in a shutdown of the less flexible, more mature process.

A less risky strategy is for a company to position itself above the diagonal, where the product is more mature than the process. If the demand for such a product increases, the company can purchase the equipment necessary to meet the demand. The disadvantage, of course, is a longer start-up time: The company with a mature process already in place has the capability to meet the increased demand right away. This matrix helps illustrate the interaction between product and process and the dynamics of the evolution of both.

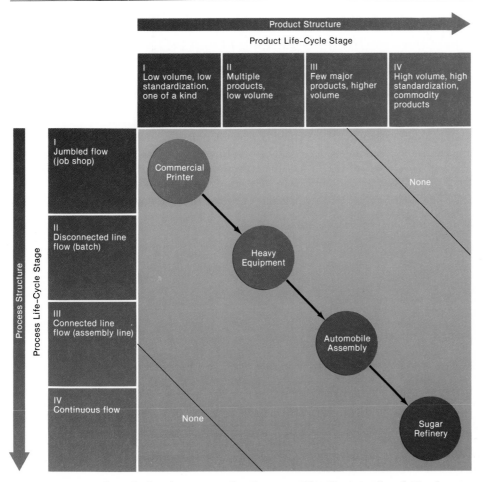

FIGURE 19-3
A Product/Process
Matrix

Source: R. Hayes and S. Wheelwright, *Restoring Our Competitive Edge: Competing through Manufacturing* (New York: Wiley, 1984), p. 209.

Location of Facility

A second long-range decision made by the operations manager is where to locate the facility. Nissan's managers spent several *years* choosing its new U.S. location: Smyrna, Tennessee. Delta managers have expanded the number of the airline's "hub" locations from two to six in the last ten years. The choice of each "hub" city was made only after careful, lengthy deliberation. The facility location decision is one of the most important and constraining decisions made by operations managers. This is particularly true when multinational companies attempt to select overseas locations, as illustrated in "Insights for International Managers 19."

The broader in scope the mistake made in locating a facility (restaurant, factory, or whatever), the more costly it will be and the less likely the decision is to be changed.[9] As a result, managers must consider many factors before choosing a location. These factors include fixed costs, such as land purchases and construction costs, and variable costs, such as local tax rates, labor costs, utilities, and transportation costs. Other factors may also play a part: population demographics, the availability of labor, the attitude that prevails in the local government, and any applicable environmental protection laws.

■■■■■ *Insights for International Managers 19* ■■■■■

SELECTING OVERSEAS PLANT LOCATIONS

Selecting overseas locations for business facilities involves two basic decisions: (1) Choosing a country, and (2) choosing a site within a country. Most international plant location research indicates that multinational companies are rather subjective and unsystematic about the long-term ramifications of overseas plant locations. But given the increasing independence of nation-states in economic relations, uncertainties in political and economic conditions, the increasing role of governments in economic matters, and the intense competitiveness of world market-

places, multinational firms will have to pay closer attention to plant location decisions.

International Business Machines (IBM) has pursued a general policy of manufacturing abroad for many years. In selecting a specific country or location for manufacturing, IBM managers assign weights to specific factors deemed relevant for evaluating alternative locations. The following table shows the weighted criteria method for plant location decisions at IBM.

Criteria	Assigned maximum value	SITES					
		A	B	C	D	E	F
Living conditions[a]	100	70	40	45	50	60	60
Accessibility[b]	75	55	35	20	60	70	70
Industrialization[c]	60	40	50	55	35	35	30
Labor availability[d]	35	30	10	10	30	35	35
Economics[e]	35	15	15	15	15	25	15
Community capability and attitude[f]							
Prestige effect on company reputation[g]	30	25	20	10	15	25	15
	35	25	20	10	15	25	15
Total	370	260	180	165	225	280	265

[a]General appearance of community, availability of housing, community services and education facilities, attractiveness of climate and environment, freedom from disruptive problems, living costs for transferred employees.

[b]Accessibility to markets, suppliers, services and other company facilities, quality of local transportation and of facilities for visitors, availability of communication networks.

[c]Level of industrialization, desirability of industrial and nonindustrial neighbors, potential for area's industrial growth.

[d]Wage rates, population within commuting radius, size of local labor force and level of employment, availability of skills and training programs, history of local labor problems.

[e]Relative cost of construction and site development, local costs of doing business, e.g., corporate and personal tax structure, utility rates.

[f]Quality and types of schools, adequacy of public services, local issues, attitudes toward industry and possible effect of introducing new facility into community, evidence of community planning for future growth.

[g]General reputation of area, especially, reputation which may relate to the type of facility planned, freedom from special problems which would create unfavorable reputation; desire of community to welcome type of activity planned.

Sources: Adapted from A. R. Negandhi, *International Management* (Boston: Allyn & Bacon, 1987), pp. 363–364. Copyright © 1987 by Allyn & Bacon, Inc. Reprinted with permission. And from E. S. Groo, "Choosing Foreign Locations: One Company's Experience," *The Columbia Journal of World Business* 6, no. 5 (September–October 1971): 77.

The objective of the facility location decision for a system producing a good is to minimize both the distribution costs associated with getting the product to the customer and the total production costs associated with making the product. The objective of the facility location decision for a service organization is to minimize the distance between the facility and its customers. Two different strategies for locating a new facility exist. The first is to locate it near the suppliers of raw materials or key inputs in order to reduce (1) the time it takes to place and receive an order and (2) the associated costs. The second is to locate the facility near key customers to reduce the time and distribution costs associated with getting the finished product to the customer. Service organizations normally adopt the latter strategy.

Layout of Facility

A third long-range decision that operations managers make is how to arrange various departments within a plant in the way that is most consistent with key cost and quality considerations. The layout of facilities at Delta Airlines involves the spatial arrangement of all departments, such as baggage claim areas, fuel storage areas, customer waiting rooms, ticket counters, and administrative offices.

Layouts are generally characterized as either process layouts or product layouts. In a **process layout**, all machines or workers of a similar type or function are grouped together. All the drilling machines would be located together, for example, as would all the sanding machines, punch presses, and welding machines. A hospital, which provides the service of health care, also exhibits a process layout. Orthopedic, x-ray, pediatric, and surgical services are all grouped separately by function. Because of its grouping together of machines and/or people who perform similar functions, a process layout is also known as a *functional layout*. A job shop has a process layout. A process layout is preferred when a high degree of process flexibility is required. In fact, one major characteristic of job-shop manufacturing, or intermittent flow, is a process layout.

In a **product layout** or *flow layout,* machines are arranged according to the sequential steps involved in the production of a part. For example, the assembly line that Nissan Motors uses to make automobiles has a product layout. The machine or work station next in the process is the one that is required to perform the next operation on the product. The painting department is located right next to the sanding department because painting is the next operation after the car has been sanded. A product layout is normally used when the product is well standardized, process flexibility is not required, and high volumes are desired. Line flows and continuous flows usually have a product layout. The advantages and disadvantages of a product layout and of a process layout are summarized in Figure 19-4.

A third type of layout, which tries to capture the benefits of both a process and a product layout, is a layout by group technology (GT).[10] A **group technology layout** requires the identification of a group of products called a *product family,* all the members of which are similar in shape, size, or material and require similar processing. A department called a *cell* is then designed with a product layout and dedicated to producing only this product family. The principal benefits of GT are that it speeds up the production process and reduces work-in-process inventories. This is accomplished by reducing the time that parts spend moving from one work station to another. In a typical job shop, a product may spend as much as 95 percent of its time in production waiting for a machine to become available. GT

Product Layout

Advantages
1. Reduced materials handling.
2. Small amounts of work in process.
3. Reduced total processing time.
4. Simplified production planning and control systems.
5. Simplification of tasks, enabling unskilled workers to learn tasks quickly.

Disadvantages
1. Lack of process flexibility: A change in product may require modification of the facility.
2. Lack of flexibility in timing: The product cannot flow through the line faster than the slowest task can be accomplished, unless that task is performed at multiple stations.
3. Large investment: Special-purpose equipment is used, and duplication is required to offset lack of flexibility in timing.
4. Dependence of the whole on each part: A breakdown of one machine or the presence of too few operators to staff all work stations may stop the entire line.
5. Worker monotony: Workers become bored by the endless repetition of simple tasks.

Process Layout

Advantages
1. Flexibility of equipment and personnel.
2. A smaller investment in equipment is possible, because duplication is not necessary unless volume is large.
3. Expertise: Supervisors for each department become highly knowledgeable about the lower number of functions under their direction.
4. Diversity of tasks: Work assignments make work more satisfying for people who prefer variety.

Disadvantages
1. Lack of materials-handling efficiency: Backtracking and long movements may occur in the handling of materials.
2. Lack of efficiency in timing: Work must wait between tasks.
3. Complication of production planning and control.
4. Cost: Workers must have broader skills and must be paid higher wages than assembly-line workers.
5. Lowered productivity: Because each job is different, it requires different setups and operator instruction.

is able to move parts more quickly because work stations are located closer together. This also makes it possible to bring many of the operations under the control of a computer. The result is called **computer-aided manufacturing (CAM)**.

The most advanced state of CAM is the *flexible manufacturing system* (FMS). An FMS is a group of computer-controlled machines connected by automated materials-handling equipment. Parts are automatically loaded on and off each machine by the materials-handling equipment. Such equipment includes carts guided and controlled by a computer. The computer tells the cart what part to move and where to move it. A typical FMS may also make use of robotics to

---

Guidelines for Management Practice

Long-range operations decisions are made by top management. Entry-level managers, if they get involved, do so in supporting roles—usually to research the issues and obtain information. The following guidelines are intended to assist managers in giving top management such support:

1. Location decisions usually involve collecting information about, examining, and comparing a few local areas. One of the best places to start getting relevant information is at Chambers of Commerce at the state and local levels. Every state has a State Economic Department Office, which is another good source; it often volunteers to do research at minimal cost for companies that are considering setting up shop in the state.

2. Location decisions always attract a lot of interest among prospective suppliers of services or products. They can be good sources of research assistance. But pursue location research cautiously and quietly; once "the word is out," your company can be innundated with solicitations.

3. Key location concerns vary with the type of business. If you work for a manufacturer, concentrate on the costs and availability of a skilled work force, raw materials and suppliers, and transportation. If you work for a distributor, focus on transportation costs. In retail and service firms, be concerned with level of customer concentrations.

4. It is usually helpful to involve supervisors in production process decisions and facilities layout decisions. Their day-to-day involvement and their awareness of problems that can arise often lead to useful adaptations of process and layout plans.

---

perform many of the manufacturing operations. Robots are ideally suited for the "pick and place" movement of materials. With an FMS, it is possible to produce a wide variety of products in small quantities and to achieve high levels of quality.

Long-range operations are an essential ingredient in a company's future success. They set parameters for all the operations decisions that follow. That does not diminish the importance of the latter decisions. Intermediate range OM decisions—planning and controlling production—are among the most important responsibilities of operations managers. These intermediate decisions are examined in the next section.

Intermediate-Range OM Decisions

Intermediate-range decisions are also made by operations managers. These decisions are made intermittently and may cover periods of time ranging from several days to a year. Intermediate-range decisions address three key areas:

1. Production planning

2. Controlling production and inventory

3. Quality planning

Operations managers address these intermediate-range decisions as a part of their development of functional strategies (Chapter 7) and, subsequently, action plans (Chapter 8) to implement those strategies.

Consider the challenge faced by Ernie Wardlaw, a production manager for the plant in Tennessee operated by Nissan Motor Company. Wardlaw is responsible for the week-to-week production planning for the different models produced by the plant. One key concern he faces is making sure that all materials used in manufacturing the different cars are available when they are needed. He must also plan how many of each model of car to produce each day.

Consider also the challenge faced by W. Clyde Morton, a manager for Delta Airlines. Morton is responsible for the planning of capacity to ensure that as many Delta customers as possible are able to get a seat on the flight they desire. Capacity in Morton's case is the number of seats flying to each city. Thus he must plan for both periods of low demand and periods of high demand.

Production Planning

Wardlaw's and Morton's main objective when planning production is to develop a plan to satisfy customer demand through a least-cost production strategy. Two production strategies are available for meeting customer demand: a chase strategy and a level-work-force strategy. In the **chase strategy**, the number of employees is adjusted to meet demand. When demand increases, a company employing a chase strategy hires more workers so that production output can meet demand. When demand declines, workers are fired or laid off to reduce expenses. Inventory is not needed, because the changing work force absorbs all changes in demand. A service organization such as Delta Airlines is forced to use a chase strategy; a service cannot be inventoried. In the **level-work-force strategy**, the production output is constant. The number of employees is fairly constant and does not vary when demand changes. Maintaining a constant level of production output causes inventory to build when demand is low. When demand increases, this inventory is used to help meet the unusually high demand. All fluctuations in demand are met by carrying a finished-goods inventory.

In practice, most operations managers choose a combination of the chase and level-work-force strategies. For example, Wardlaw may decide to run the plant on Saturdays during months of high demand, using overtime instead of hiring more employees. This is not a pure chase strategy, nor is it a pure level-work-force strategy.

AGGREGATE PRODUCTION PLANNING

One of the techniques that operations managers use to set production levels is aggregate production planning. **Aggregate production planning** is concerned with matching production levels with the demand for the product over an intermediate range of time. The term *aggregate* reflects the fact that production is planned for a single overall measure of whatever is produced, such as cars or meals. For example, an aggregate production plan for Nissan Motors may call for the production of 10,000 cars, whereas an aggregate production plan for Delta may call for the availability of 1,150,000 seats on flights. It would not call for the production of 2,000 Sentras, 4,500 300 ZXs, and 3,500 Maximas. Likewise it would not call for the provision of 50,000 seats to Cleveland, 30,000 seats to Nashville, and 100,000 seats to Atlanta. Massing all final products into a generic (aggregate) measure of the production system's output makes production planning easier. Thus the objective of aggregate planning is to develop a production plan to meet a normally uncertain demand in a least-cost manner over a time horizon of six to twelve months.

Again, consider W. Clyde Morton at Delta as he tries to plan how much capacity he will need to meet the demand projected for the upcoming year. Morton does not know beforehand exactly how many customers will request a seat to each of the different cities where Delta flies. He decides, therefore, to base his capacity plan on the average demand over the next few months.

Then consider Ernie Wardlaw at the Nissan plant as he tries to plan production levels for the next twelve months. Wardlaw knows that forecasting exactly how many Sentras or 300 ZXs will be sold each month over the next year is very difficult at best. Instead, he decides to use aggregate production planning to set production levels for the plant. Rather than trying to set production levels for each model to match an uncertain demand, Wardlaw sets a production level for an aggregate measure of production. The aggregate measure represents not an actual car to be produced, but an "average" car in terms of capacity requirements and materials used. Wardlaw then has to determine only how many cars are to be produced; he need not be concerned with the demand for specific models. Figure 19-5 offers an example of what an aggregate plan for Nissan Motors would look like.

THE MASTER PRODUCTION SCHEDULE

Another example of planning the production of a good is called master production scheduling. Before the aggregate plan can be used to make detailed scheduling and control decisions, it must be "disaggregated" into a **master production schedule (MPS)**. Recall that the aggregate plan is stated in terms of an overall output measure, such as cars. The MPS, on the other hand, is stated in terms of the actual end products the company produces. Instead of specifying a number of cars, the MPS would call for the production of, say, 400 Sentras and 100 300 ZXs. Figure 19-6 presents a possible MPS for the month of March, showing how the overall level of production planned for March (2,200 cars) is broken down into planned production levels for specific models. (Compare Figure 19-6 to Figure 19-5.)

Before the MPS is released to the plant for execution, its feasibility must be determined. An MPS is feasible if there are sufficient resources, materials, and capacity to meet it. The operations managers must determine whether they have the capacity to produce what the schedule calls for. They must therefore determine the total capacity requirements for each resource. Operations managers must also

FIGURE 19-5 Aggregate Production Plan (1989)	Month	Jan.	Feb.	Mar.	April	May	June
	Days	22	20	22	22	21	22
	Output	2,200	2,000	2,200	2,200	2,100	2,200

FIGURE 19-6 Master Production Schedule (March)	Week	9	10	11	12
	Sentra	400	—	100	250
	300 ZX	100	500	400	250
	Total	500	500	500	500

determine the availability of materials called for in the MPS (this process is discussed later in the chapter). If operations managers find that they have the necessary resources, the MPS is released to the shop for execution. For example, the requirements for machine capacity at all work centers, requirements for materials, and labor requirements for producing the 400 Sentras and the 100 300 ZXs for week 9 are calculated. These needs are then compared to the available supply of plant capacity. In Figure 19-7, the relationships among these steps are shown.

Control of Production and Inventory

After a production plan has been determined, the operations manager must control the operations function in an effort to meet this plan as closely as possible. The decisions made in order to meet the plan involve the control of production levels and inventory levels within the organization. Controlling the production and inventory of both services and goods entails making all the decisions involved in providing the materials needed for producing the planned production levels at the desired levels of quality, while minimizing production costs. Implementing effective materials control or inventory control procedures requires the operations manager to be familiar with several key ideas. First, the operations manager must understand why it is necessary to maintain inventories of materials. Familiarity

FIGURE 19-7
The Use of Master
Production Scheduling
(MPS)

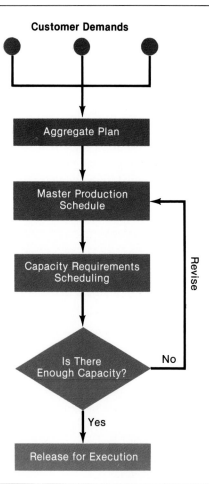

with these reasons helps managers focus their inventory management efforts. Second, managers need to be familiar with several costs associated with maintaining inventories. This knowledge helps them evaluate the true benefits of various inventory levels and options. Finally, operations managers need to be familiar with the different "types" of demand made on inventories and the techniques available for managing each.

CONTROLLING INVENTORIES

Ideally, the operations manager provides the exact amount of all necessary materials exactly where they are needed in the production process at exactly the time they are needed. The operations manager then supplies the right amount of raw materials used in the production process, the right amount of work in process (materials partially completed), and the right amount of finished goods, which are used to satisfy customer demand. As usual, however, reality differs somewhat from the ideal. Controlling inventories is a difficult task because the demand for materials is seldom known in advance. Dramatic fluctuations occur in both the quantity demanded and the timing of demand. Consider the Nissan MPS shown in Figure 19-6. In the month of March, it calls for the production of 400 Sentras in week 9, no Sentras in week 10, 100 in week 11, and 250 in week 12. This production plan results in a widely varying demand on the inventory of all the components and materials needed to manufacture Sentras. When any of the materials are not available, the Sentra cannot be assembled. This includes both expensive components such as the engine and relatively inexpensive items such as the rear-view mirror. Also consider the task of providing the materials Delta Airlines needs. There must always be an ample supply of the peanuts, drinks, ice, and meals required by the passengers on each flight, to say nothing of enough fuel! The objective of the operations manager is to provide the necessary materials at the right place and the right time as often as possible without greatly increasing production costs.

REASONS FOR MAINTAINING INVENTORIES

The primary reason why an operations manager would want to carry inventory is to make sure the necessary materials are available for all the stages in the production process. By carrying inventory, the operations manager "decouples" each production stage from the others. To "decouple" means to remove the dependency between the various stages. Consider that the demand for raw materials is dependent on the planned production of the plant, whereas the demand for plant production is dependent on final customer demand. Within the plant, the demand placed on a particular work center depends on the production schedule at the next work center. For example, Nissan Motors maintains finished cars at all its dealerships and at regional distribution centers in order to decouple the demand for cars from Nissan's production process. The company also stocks all the tires, windshields, and other components that go into making its cars in order to decouple its production process from the suppliers of these components.

When we view a production process as a system transforming raw materials into finished goods, we see that inventories are useful at three points in this process. Figure 19-8 provides a simple illustration. The finished-goods inventory decouples the production facility from customer demand; the raw-materials inventory decouples the production facility from suppliers; and the work-in-process inventory decouples the work centers within the facility from one another.

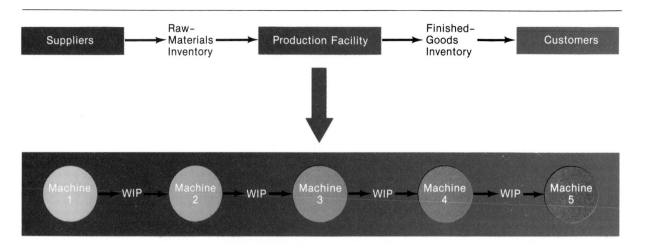

FIGURE 19-8
Inventory as a
Decoupler

Independent Versus Dependent Demand

It is very important for operations managers charged with determining an inventory policy to understand the nature of the demand to which their inventory is subject. Understanding this demand is also necessary for deciding on the total level of inventory and the quantity for each individual item in inventory. Demand involves both how many (or how much) of the inventoried items will be needed and when that need will arise.

There are essentially two types of demand: **independent demand** and **dependent demand**. When the source of demand is beyond the control of the company, the demand is said to be independent. Finished goods and distribution inventories generally experience independent demand, because the customer directly determines the demand. The expected demand for items subject to independent demand must be forecasted by using one of numerous forecasting techniques available. When the demand for an item is within the control of the company (such as a manufacturing company), the demand is dependent. The overall demand for items subject to dependent demand does not have to be forecasted but can be derived by examining planned production levels. For example, Nissan Motors would have to forecast the number of Sentras it expects to sell in a particular week because the sales of Sentras are based on customer orders. Once Nissan has determined that it will produce 500 cars to meet this forecasted demand, however, the demand for the components that are assembled to make each car does not have to be forecasted but can be derived. For example, the production of 500 cars requires that 500 engines, 500 windshields, 2,000 tires, and so on be available when needed.

INDEPENDENT DEMAND

An operations manager faced with controlling an inventory that is subject to independent demand can choose between two inventory control systems: the fixed-order quantity system and the fixed-order period system. Each of these control systems answers the fundamental inventory control questions (what to order, when to order, and how much to order) in different ways. Each uses a replenishments approach to inventory control in that each tries to maintain a state of inventory fullness. In other words, some inventory is always carried.

The Fixed-Order-Quantity System In the **fixed-order-quantity system** (also known as the Q-system), the size of the order for items to be placed in inventory is always the same. The operations manager places an order when the inventory level reaches a minimum level or *reorder point.* Because independent demand can fluctuate widely, the time that elapses between orders in a fixed-order-quantity system varies. Over the course of one year, a fixed order size of Q units may last for several months during periods of low demand—but for only several days during high-demand periods. Constant monitoring of the inventory level is required to determine when the reorder point has been reached. For this reason, the system is also referred to as a *continuous review system.*

The Fixed-Order-Period System The second type of control system for inventory subject to independent demand is the fixed-order-period system. Instead of the order quantity being fixed, as in a Q-system, in the **fixed-order-period-system** (or P-system) the time period between orders is kept constant while the order quantity is allowed to vary. In the P-system, an order is placed at predetermined intervals—for example, every two weeks. The quantity ordered is determined by subtracting the current inventory level from a target inventory level. This target inventory is the amount of inventory required to cover demand during the fixed period plus the order lead time. *Lead time* is the amount of time between when the order is placed and when the order is received. Lead times are usually not within the control of the operations manager; thus they are not constant and tend to vary from one order to the next.

DEPENDENT DEMAND

The fixed-order-quantity and fixed-order-period control systems are used primarily for inventory subject to independent demand, such as finished-goods inventories. Inventories of raw materials and work in process, however, experience dependent demand. In other words, the demand for raw materials and work in process depends on the items scheduled for production in the master production schedule.

In practice, the manufacture of most products involves the assembly of various component parts at different stages in the production process. When a higher-level product, such as a car, is assembled from several lower-level components, such as engines and tires, the demand for such components depends on the quantity of higher-level products to be made. If this end product is intended for customer use (is not a component for a still higher-level product), *its* demand is independent and has to be forecasted. Consider the MPS of Nissan Motors for week 12 (Figure 19-6); 250 Sentras are scheduled to be produced. For these Sentras to be assembled, 250 engines, 1,000 tires, and 250 steering wheels are required. The demand for engines, tires, steering wheels, and all other required lower-level components is dependent on the planned production of the higher-level products, the automobiles.

The relationship between components that are to be assembled in various stages of the production process can be illustrated by a product **bill of materials (BOM)**. A BOM is a structured parts list showing in what different production stages all lower-level components are needed for production. Figure 19-9 shows a BOM for the sound system of a Nissan automobile. A *parent item* in a BOM is the next-higher-level item on which a component at a lower level is dependent. For example, the sound system is the parent item for rear speakers, front speakers, and AM/FM cassette stereos. To compute the demand for such components, operations managers need know only the demand for the parent item.

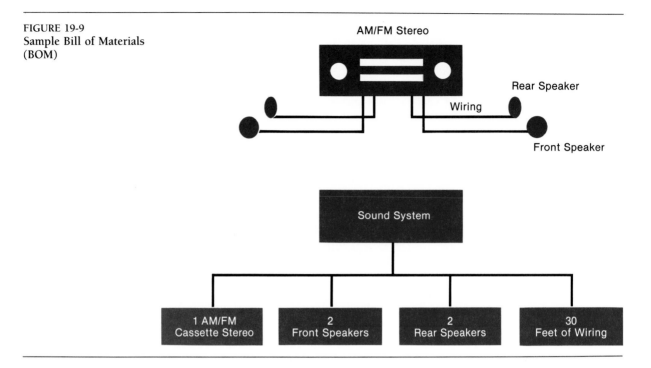

FIGURE 19-9
Sample Bill of Materials
(BOM)

Materials Requirements Planning

Materials requirements planning (MRP) is a system developed for controlling and planning inventories subject to dependent demand.[11] The primary input into an MRP system is the master production schedule, which specifies the planned production for each end item. The MPS is then converted into the demand for all lower-level components in the BOM. The process of computing the demand for lower-level items on the basis of the demand for parent items is called *MRP explosion*. The result of the explosion process is a complete list of all parts that are needed, when they are needed, and when they must be ordered so that the MPS can be met.

During the explosion process, all current inventories are considered before an order is released. The current inventories are then subtracted from the total requirements, or gross requirements, for each component; this yields the net requirements for each component. These net requirements are the actual quantities that must be ordered. For example, to make 100 of the sound systems represented in Figure 19-9 results in gross requirements of 200 rear speakers, 200 front speakers, 100 AM/FM cassette stereos, and 3,000 feet of stereo wiring. The order for each component is placed as far in advance of the time it is needed for production as the expected lead time for delivery of the order dictates.

Materials requirements planning is one of the most widely used planning techniques. It has been estimated that as much as $10 billion has been spent on the implementation of MRP systems in industry.[12]

The Just-in-Time System

The **just-in-time system (JIT)** is an operations technique that was developed in Japan and is gaining tremendous support in the United States and Europe. JIT seeks to eliminate all waste (and the expense it entails) by providing the right part at the right place in the exact quantity and at the exact time it is to be used.[13] JIT is often called a philosophy, because it goes far beyond inventory control to encompass quality planning and control and production scheduling. The just-in-time system was developed in, and is best suited for, repetitive production such as that on an automotive assembly line. Repetitive production implies large-volume production of batches of a small number of similar products.

In JIT, the MPS is planned one to three months into the future to enable work centers to plan their schedules. Over the course of one day, the production schedule is balanced in the sense that the same quantity of each product is produced each day for each month. This requires the production of small lots, or batches, in order to smooth production. The advantage of this production "leveling" is that it makes nearly constant demand on all work centers.[14]

High quality is essential in a JIT system. Defects create waste and may also bring the manufacturing system to a halt (when bad parts are produced, no others are available because of the reduced inventory levels associated with JIT). Little or no inventory is allowed, so defects are quickly spotted and the problem is immediately corrected. As a result, quality gains plantwide attention. The Japanese approach to quality is often referred to as *total quality control* or *zero defects*.

Because of the stellar success of the Japanese in areas once dominated by the United States (such as the steel industry, consumer electronics, textiles, and the automotive industry), JIT is becoming a rallying cry for many domestic manufacturers. It is widely believed that the United States must adopt a JIT-like philosophy if it wishes to remain competitive in the high-volume repetitive industries.

Quality Planning

Other intermediate-range decisions made by the operations manager fall in the area of quality planning. **Quality planning** involves the decisions made about the desired level of quality prior to actual production. As we use the term in this chapter, *quality* means fitness for use. In other words, does the product do what it is supposed to do? Effective quality planning requires the operations manager to understand what quality the consumer expects. The level of quality it plans often confers a major strategic advantage on the organization and helps to determine the particular market in which the company will compete.[15] Quality control involves the decisions made to ensure that the production process is generating a product that conforms to the level of planned quality. (Quality control involves short-range OM decisions and will be discussed in a later section.)

Two costs are normally recognized during quality planning. *Conformance costs* include all the costs associated with inspection to make sure the product conforms to planned quality levels. And *failure costs* include all the costs incurred when a customer finds a product of unacceptable quality. In Figure 19-10 these two costs are graphically depicted. To achieve higher levels of quality requires more investment in conformance costs, whereas the cost of failure increases dramatically as the numbers of failures increase. Traditionally, the objective of the operations manager has been to balance the two costs and produce at a level of quality where the total cost is lowest.

However, the JIT concept of total quality has convinced many traditional manufacturers that this view of quality is incorrect. In other words, if operations

FIGURE 19-10
Costs of Quality

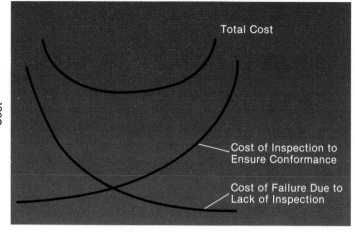

Total Cost

Cost of Inspection to
Ensure Conformance

Cost of Failure Due to
Lack of Inspection

Cost

Extent of Inspection

managers wish to compete with the Japanese, they can allow no level of defects. Manufacturers must try to produce 100 percent good-quality products. (See "In Practice 19-1" for evidence of U.S. managers' increased commitment to quality.)

Operations managers also face short-range, day-to-day decisions that are necessary to managing operations. Daily scheduling, worker assignments, and quality control are three areas in which operations managers must regularly make decisions. The next section examines these short-range decisions, and how operations managers can make them effectively.

Guidelines for Management Practice

Newer managers soon find themselves involved in intermediate-range operations decisions. These guidelines are intended to help operations managers address these intermediate decisions effectively.

1. If your company experiences seasonal demand for its product, expect pressure to consider a "chase" production strategy when cost cutting is a major management concern.

2. When trying to use a "chase" production strategy, develop a pool of part-time employees who can remain available for long periods of time and prefer part-time work. Older people, retired people, and students are three such valuable resources.

Keeping the same people on the job cuts training costs.

3. Also use "temporary" services when implementing a chase strategy. Here again, you can generally use the same person repeatedly.

4. Use suppliers to help reduce inventory costs and implement just-in-time programs. Make it your responsibility to customize their product services to your needs.

5. Regularly solicit customer comments about the quality of your products or services. Customers can help considerably in quality planning. Be personally involved in this effort; it shows your customers that you are serious about quality.

MAKE QUALITY YOUR TOP PRIORITY

We asked a smattering of purchasing managers across the country to pinpoint the most important demand that top management is now making on their buying organizations. The finding of our spot check: Quality is still number one, 100 percent of the time.

Some paused for a moment, mentally screening their choices to eliminate the least critical, and replied "quality"—end of conversation. Others, after that same pause, said something like, "I could spend the afternoon telling you what they [management] expect, but if I have to pick one, I guess it's got to be quality." And others went a step further, ranking management demands in terms of importance. Quality, delivery, and pricing emerged the top three.

"Quality is free. It doesn't hurt to get it right the first time around," says Stephen D. Morton, purchasing manager at Bendix Field Engineering Corporation in Columbia, Maryland. He says the big push is to move quality from dock to dock. "We're trying to instill a preoccupation with quality that goes beyond quality systems, that extends to a quality consciousness in employees." Morton adds that the only way a faulty part should get out of a supplier's plant is via the scrap heap. Morton is most apt to buy from "more highly automated, more capital-intensive, less people-intensive suppliers."

Thomas F. Bonnoil, purchasing manager at the magnetic tape division of Ampex Corporation in Opelika, Alaska, likens quality's rise in importance to triangles. "It used to be an equilateral triangle—with pricing, service, and quality the same. Now it's an isosceles triangle with quality right at the top," he says. There is "immense pressure" on Ampex suppliers to meet specs, and quality meetings are held regularly to ensure that they do, Bonnoil adds.

Although he puts quality performance first, Douglas M. Pedder, director of purchasing for the residential group at Aluminum Processing Corporation in Fall River, Massachusetts, feels management pressure in other areas too: cost reduction/avoidance, supplier delivery performance, improved contracting, and negotiation. To get "better pricing and more leverage," he is trying to centralize negotiations with national contracts to service the three divisions for which he is responsible. He is also concerned with long-term contracts so "the company won't be hurt by any snafu—supply/demand or strikewise."

Charles Adams, director of procurement at Wright Line in Worcester, Massachusetts, says quality, delivery, and cost are "all vital concerns." Because the plant is operating at full capacity, however, the pressure is more on production, with "purchasing gearing up to support them," says Adams. With the constant pressure to get materials in on schedule, Adams notes it has been difficult to concentrate on cost reduction. "The demands on the plant are just too great right now," he says. There have been some problems in corrugated packaging particularly; Wright Line requires big, bulky boxes and strives for just-in-time delivery to avoid having to store them.

J. Robert Connell, purchasing manager at the Coca-Cola Foods Division in Auburndale, Florida, says continuity of supply, quality of supply, and pricing are the top three concerns but that quality is "uppermost in our minds, while it may not be in theirs [management]."

In addition to quality, Joe Viva, procurement manager of the test systems group at Fairchild Camera and Instrument Corporation in Latham, New York, says this industry is having problems with demand changes and getting products in a hurry. Fairchild is also working to reduce costs and find more innovative ways to control inventory. "We're trying to maintain inventory while not showing it on the books. We've developed in-house stores and have distribution stock materials there. It's basically entering into a closer partnership with distribution. And we're still looking for the assurance that a product will be here on the day that it's due," Viva says.

Vern Sawyer, director of international purchasing for PPG Industries in Pittsburgh, Pennsylvania, says, "Top management is asking purchasing to establish even closer ties with our key suppliers to ensure that they understand our basic strategies and our dependence on them to provide us with (1) products meeting quality requirements on a consistent basis, (2) technological support as we strive to anticipate changing requirements in our marketplace, (3) timely deliveries to optimize inventory dollars, and (4) pricing that helps us remain competitive."

Source: Adapted from *Purchasing*, October 4, 1984, p. 23. Reprinted with permission of Cahners Publishing Company, Inc.

Short-Range OM Decisions

Short-range decisions are made by operations managers on a day-to-day basis, and they account for the great majority of all operations decisions. Short-range decisions include

1. Order scheduling

2. Worker assignments

3. Quality control

Order Scheduling

Short-range decisions dealing with scheduling in both service and goods industries are concerned with the efficient allocation of an organization's existing resources in order to meet demand at the least cost. The scheduling of customer orders involves setting times and dates for the start and completion of the various stages in the production life of a product. Clyde Morton at Delta must determine the time at which each plane is supposed to arrive and depart in such a manner that ground crews are not overloaded by too many planes.

Similar decisions and objectives are involved in scheduling for services and for goods. The scheduling procedures used by the operations manager in a job shop are very different, however, from those used in a line-flow production process. The procedures are different because the materials flow is intermittent in a job shop but linear in an assembly line. In a job shop producing a good, the orientation of the operations manager is toward order control, because numerous small batches of a large variety of products move through the shop on different routes or paths. In a job shop providing a service, the operations manager is concerned with the movement of customers. The decision to choose a particular order or customer from a waiting queue is called *dispatching*. Orders are chosen on the basis of a dispatch rule. For example, the dispatch rule *first-come, first-served* assigns a higher priority to orders that arrived at the shop first. First-come, first-served is usually the rule in banks, fast-food restaurants, and grocery stores.

In a line flow, the emphasis is on monitoring and controlling the materials and customers flow, because management is concerned primarily with plant output. This output, called *throughput,* is measured in units produced over some time period. All orders follow the same route through the shop, so controlling the flow is primarily a matter of setting output levels per period of time, such as 250 cars produced per day or 1,500 students registered before lunch.

Worker Assignments

Another short-range decision made by the operations manager is the assignment of workers to perform the various tasks necessary to manufacture a good or provide a service. The operations manager must understand several key principles if she or he is to be effective in making these decisions.

1. Assign workers to the job they are best qualified to perform. This implies that workers should be assigned tasks on the basis of their individual preferences and the differences among them in education, training, and abilities.

2. Set standards for performance evaluation. A standard specifies what a worker is expected to accomplish. If standards are not set, workers become confused about their responsibilities and may require excessive supervision to perform their tasks.

3. Workers who perform well should be rewarded. When a standard is set, it becomes a benchmark to evaluate a worker's performance. Any worker who performs above standard should be rewarded in order to encourage continued good performance.

Chapter 13 discussed human resource management in greater detail. The important point here is that worker assignment is a routine operations management responsibility.

Quality Control

Some of the most important short-range decisions are those the operations manager makes to ensure that the product being produced meets specified quality standards. **Quality control** can be defined as ensuring conformance to specifications.[16] To guarantee this conformance, a well-designed quality control system is necessary. "Management Development Exercise 19" provides a checklist some managers use to assess their quality control system. The design of such a system involves four basic steps.

The first step in the design of a quality control system is to *identify critical points in the production process where inspection is needed*. This includes the inspection of raw materials to ensure that suppliers are complying with raw-materials specifications, the inspection of work in progress to ensure that the process is running correctly, and the inspection of finished goods to ensure that low-quality products are not shipped to customers.[17]

In service businesses, inspection points are more difficult to identify, because services are produced and delivered to the customer *simultaneously*. Inspecting the raw materials used in the provision of a service is similar to inspecting the raw materials used in the production of a good. Inspecting work in progress for a service requires that the service be inspected while it is being performed.[18] Despite these differences, many of the decisions made to ensure the quality of a service are similar to those made to ensure the quality of a good.

Jet airplanes have no margin for error in their parts, which makes quality control at the parts manufacturing stage a critical process at Pratt Whitney. If any flaw is found in this engine turbine gear, it will automatically be melted down and reformed rather than risk a possible future engine failure. (Ray Ellis/Photo Researchers)

■■■■■■■■■■■■■■■■■■■■■■■■ *Guidelines for Management Practice* ■■■■■■■■■■■■■■■■■■■■■■■■

Short-range operating decisions are made continually, on a daily or weekly basis. They are often the direct responsibility of lower-level, newer managers. These guidelines should be helpful to managers who find making short-range operating decisions among their early management assignments.

1. Order scheduling and worker assignments often appear at first glance to have quirks or unnecessary aspects that could be eliminated. If you are tempted to revamp such procedures, do not act immediately. Before changing them, take some time to understand why they are the way they are.

2. Order scheduling, worker assignments, and quality control are three good candidates for delegation to subordinates. Things that seem routine to you may strike your ambitious subordinates as opportunities to grow and to demonstrate what they can do.

3. Reexamine order scheduling and worker assignments regularly.

The second step in designing a quality control system is to *determine the type of measurement to be used.* One of two types of measurements is generally used: "measurement by variable" or "measurement by attribute." Measurement by variable is used for physical characteristics of the product, such as depth, width, weight, height, and even temperature. Measurement by attribute focuses on general characteristics of the product or service that suggest an acceptable or an unacceptable level of quality. Discrete factors such as number of broken threads per square yard of cloth, number of bad light bulbs per box, and number of times each month that customers complain about lodging services are examples of measurement by attribute.

The third step in the design of a quality control system is to *determine the degree of inspection.* The operations manager could decide to inspect 100 percent of the items or to inspect a smaller sample drawn from the larger "population." Traditionally, cost has been the determining factor in deciding on the degree of inspection. If the cost of failure is much higher than the cost of inspection, 100 percent inspection may be justified. A smaller sample is usually inspected when the cost of inspection is large compared to the cost of failure. In the JIT system, the emphasis on total quality often dictates 100 percent inspection.

The final step in designing a quality control system is to *determine who will do the inspection.* The Japanese have demonstrated that workers trained in quality control techniques and given the responsibility of ensuring quality generally produce higher levels of quality, at a lower cost, than an extensive program of inspection of finished goods. The training of workers is normally carried out in *quality circles,* groups of workers who meet periodically to discuss manufacturing problems. Quality circles are based on the idea that the workers themselves can best identify and solve the problems encountered during the production process.[19]

Review of the Learning Objectives

Having studied this chapter, you should be able to respond to the learning objectives with extensions of the following brief answers.

1. **Explain the differences between a good and a service.**

   The primary difference between a good and a service is in the tangibility of the product. A good is tangible in the sense that it can be stored in inventory and used at a later date to help meet customer demand. Despite this major difference, some of the same operations management decisions are made for production systems supplying services and those supplying goods.

2. **Distinguish among the three levels of operations management decisions, and give examples of each.**

   The three levels of operations management decisions are long-range, intermediate-range, and short-range. Long-range decisions are made on an intermittent basis, and they normally affect an organization for several years. Examples of these decisions include plant location, plant layout, and product and process design. Intermediate-range decisions are also made intermittently, but they affect the organization for a much shorter time. Intermediate-range decisions may be made as often as every few months or as seldom as every one or two years. Intermediate-range decisions include inventory control, quality planning, and production planning. The decisions made on a routine, daily basis are short-range OM decisions. These decisions demand most of the operations manager's attention. The scheduling of orders, the assignment of workers, and quality control are all examples of short-range OM decisions.

3. **Describe the various production processes, and cite the conditions under which each is appropriate.**

   The different manufacturing processes can be described in terms of the nature of materials flow within the plant. The three processes are continuous flow, line flow, and intermittent flow. In a continuous flow, the material is in a constant state of movement. The product is usually measured by volume rather than in discrete units. Continuous-flow processes are highly efficient and are most appropriate for high-volume, highly standardized production. A line flow is also suited for high-volume, highly standardized production. In a line-flow process, however, the product can be measured in discrete units, such as 1,000 cars. The automobile assembly line is an example of a line flow. An intermittent flow is best suited for low-volume, nonstandardized products. It offers a high degree of production flexibility, because the production process can be adjusted to changes in product design, demand, or technology with no major interruption of the flow of materials.

4. **Explain what role inventory plays in manufacturing and how inventories are managed and controlled.**

   In manufacturing, the purpose of inventory and the associated inventory control system is to provide the necessary materials at the correct time to ensure that production is not interrupted. A manufacturing inventory that is subject to dependent demand is best controlled and managed via a materials requirements planning system. A distribution inventory that is subject to independent demand is best controlled by a fixed-order-quantity system or fixed-order-period system.

5. **Identify four steps in designing a quality control system.**

   The first step is to identify the points in the process at which inspection should be performed. The second step is to determine what type of measurement to use. The third step is to determine the degree or scale of inspection. The final step is to select the people who will do the actual inspecting.

Key Terms and Concepts

After having completed your study of Chapter 19, "Operations Management," you should have mastered the following important terms and concepts.

operations management (OM)	make-to-order system	computer-aided manufacturing (CAM)	independent demand	bill of materials (BOM)
good	continuous flow	chase strategy	dependent demand	materials
service	line flow	level-work-force	fixed-order-quantity	requirements
product/process	intermittent flow	strategy	system	planning (MRP)
design	computer-aided	aggregate	(Q-system)	just-in-time system
facility location	design (CAD)	production	fixed-order-period	(JIT)
facility layout	process layout	planning	system	quality planning
make-to-stock	product layout	master production	(P-system)	quality control
system	group technology layout	schedule (MPS)		

Questions for Discussion

1. Compare and contrast production using a line-flow process with production using a job-shop process.

2. How does the operations function seek to ensure the success of a company's strategy?

3. What is aggregate planning?

4. Describe the difference between a chase production strategy and a level-work-force strategy.

5. Why are items that are subject to dependent demand often managed by a different type of inventory system from that used for items that are subject to independent demand?

6. What are some of the costs that increase with the size of inventory?

7. Is capacity requirements planning important? Give some reasons for your response.

8. Explain the differences among the four steps in the design of an effective quality control system. Provide an illustration of each step.

9. What are four advantages and disadvantages of layout by product (flow line)?

10. What are the advantages of a group technology layout?

11. Discuss the just-in-time system philosophy of manufacturing. Why is it so successful?

12. Discuss how inventory serves as a buffer and a decoupler in the production process.

Notes

1. Developed by the authors based on generally available information.

2. J. B. Dilworth, *Production and Operations Management*, 3rd ed. (New York: Random House, 1986).

3. C. G. Andrew and G. A. Johnson, "The Crucial Importance of Production and Operations Management," *Academy of Management Review* 7 (1982): 143–147.

4. E. E. Adam, "Towards a Typology of Production and Operations Management Systems," *Academy of Management Review* 8 (1983): 365–375.

5. H. C. Meal, "Putting Production Decisions Where

They Belong," *Harvard Business Review* 62 (March–April 1984): 102–111.

6. M. P. Groover, *Automation, Production Systems and Computer-Aided Manufacturing* (Englewood Cliffs, N.J.: Prentice-Hall, 1980).

7. H. D. Sherman, "Improving the Productivity of Service Businesses," *Sloan Management Review* 25 (Spring 1984): 11–23.

8. R. Hayes and S. Wheelwright, *Restoring Our Competitive Edge: Competing through Manufacturing* (New York: Wiley, 1984).

9. J. A. Fitzsimmons and R. S. Sullivan, *Service Oper-*

ations Management (New York: McGraw-Hill, 1982).

10. K. Suzaki, *The New Manufacturing Challenge* (New York: Macmillan, 1987).

11. J. Orlicky, *Materials Requirements Planning* (New York: McGraw-Hill, 1975).

12. S. C. Aggarwol, "MRP, JIT, OPT, FMS?" *Harvard Business Review* 63 (September–October 1985): 8–16.

13. R. W. Hall, *Zero Inventories* (Homewood, Ill.: Dow Jones–Irwin, 1983).

14. R. C. Walleigh, "What's Your Excuse For Not Using JIT?" *Harvard Business Review* 64 (March–April 1986): 38–54; and D. Hutchins, "Having a Hard Time with Just-in-Time," *Fortune,* June 9, 1986, pp. 64–66.

15. H. S. Gitlow and S. J. Gitlow, *The Deming Guide to Quality and Competitive Position* (Englewood Cliffs, N.J.: Prentice-Hall, 1987).

16. E. L. Grant and R. S. Leavenworth, *Statistical Quality Control* (New York: McGraw-Hill, 1980).

17. D. A. Garvin, "Quality on the Line," *Harvard Business Review* 60 (September–October 1983): 65–75.

18. G. B. Northcraft and R. B. Chase, "Managing Service Demand at the Point of Delivery," *Academy of Management Review* 10 (1985): 66–75.

19. E. E. Lawler, III, and S. A. Mohrman. "Quality Circles after the Fad," *Harvard Business Review* 63 (January–February 1985): 65–71.

Cohesion Incident 19-1
A New Restaurant Layout

Journey's End recently has decided to construct new restaurants at twenty of its top fifty motels. Roger and Charles have been assigned to a task force that is responsible for determining how these new facilities will be arranged. Several requirements must be satisfied by the new layout:

1. There must be a private dining room that is large enough to hold 150 people (about one-sixth of the space in the new facility).

2. There must be a reception and waiting area.

3. There should be two distinct public dining rooms to eliminate the auditorium effect associated with large dining rooms.

4. The kitchen must be large enough to handle dinner for a maximum of 450 people (about one-fifth of the space in the new facility).

5. The lounge must be able to seat 100 customers (about one-third of the space in the new facility).

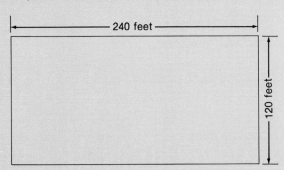

In addition, the top management of Journey's End has determined that all new restaurants will adhere to the following guidelines: The private dining room should not be near the other dining rooms, because private parties tend to be noisy. The private room should be relatively close to the lounge to allow the private diners easy access to beverages. The lounge should also be close to the reception area so that customers will be tempted to order a cocktail if they have to wait for a table. The two public dining rooms should be near the kitchen (so food can be delivered easily) and near the reception area (so customers can be seated easily).

The task force has scheduled a meeting in two months in Washington, D.C. Each member, including Roger and Charles, has been asked to suggest a layout that will meet the aforementioned objectives and bring it to this meeting. Charles and Roger are to work with the accompanying diagram. Charles and Roger agree to meet in one week and bring their tentative recommendations on how to lay out a restaurant facility that measures 240 feet × 120 feet and satisfies the requirements we have noted.

Discussion Questions

1. How would you lay out the restaurant facility?

2. What advantages does your layout have over other alternative layouts?

3. What objections might Roger or Charles make to your layout?

Cohesion Incident 19-2
An MRP at Travis Corporation

Leslie Phillips's friend Bob Taylor was Leslie's lunch companion once or twice each week at the Travis Corporation cafeteria. They met no oftener than that, because Leslie enjoyed "getting away" from work during lunch whereas Bob always talked about work. Bob was a product analyst and was developing quite a reputation for uncovering ways to improve efficiency and control costs in various Travis operations. As Leslie and Bob walked through the cafeteria line one Tuesday, Bob was describing his most recent assignment.

"One of the products manufactured by Travis Corporation is axle bearings. Each axle bearing is composed of one outside cover, one inside cover, and one bearing assembly. Each bearing assembly is composed of two bearing cases and thirty-six tapered roller bearings." As Leslie tried to find a seat where other people could share the listening burden, Bob continued. "Each tapered roller bearing is

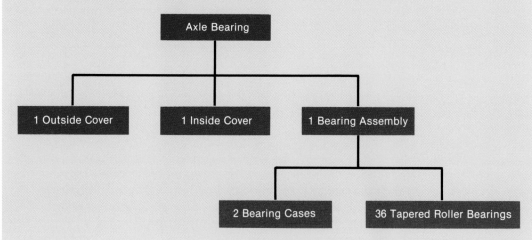

cut from steel wire that is stored as raw material. All parts except the tapered roller bearings are purchased outside the plant." Then Bob started drawing on a paper napkin, saying, "The bill of materials could be illustrated as follows:"

Growing somewhat impatient, Leslie said, "Well, what did they want you to do, Bob?"

"Travis sells approximately 100 axle bearings every month," Bob said, "and the managers feel we have been carrying excess inventory in the materials necessary to build them. Would you believe we were keeping over 360 outside covers in stock?" Sensing Leslie's fading interest, Bob said that his assignment was to develop a materials requirement plan for setting monthly inventories for axle bearing parts. "They even threw me a curve," Bob said proudly, "by asking me to assess two situations. The first situation would assume Travis had no bearing assemblies in stock. The second would have an outside supplier providing Travis with fifty bearing assemblies into stock each month."

Discussion Questions

1. What would be the monthly MRP for Travis's axle bearing components if sales of 100 each month were forecasted and no outside supplier was supplementing Travis's stock of bearings assemblies?

2. What would be the monthly MRP with the same forecast if fifty bearings assemblies were in stock each month from an outside supplier?

Management Development Exercise 19
A Manager's Quality Checklist

Ensuring that quality products and services are produced by the company's operations is the implicit responsibility of all company managers. An interesting study at Gates Rubber Company in Galesburg, Illinois, presents a typical dilemma that often confronts managers when they address the issue of quality. When forty Gates managers were surveyed about the source of quality problems, the following results were obtained:

1. Every department in the plant was identified at least once as the greatest contributor to product defects.

2. About 75 percent of the managers named a department other than their own as the department on which they would concentrate their efforts if they were given full responsibility for reducing defects.

In other words, every manager's area was identified as needing greater quality control, yet managers typically singled out departments other than their own as the source of these problems. Regardless of whether one area causes more such problems than another, every manager should accept responsibility for quality in his or her own department. This is the best way to ensure overall quality. Responsibility for quality is shared by all departments and not concentrated in any one department.

The checklist that follows should help you as a manager apply this concept of shared responsibility for quality control, rather than finding false comfort (like the Gates managers did) in assuming that the problem lies elsewhere. Your instructor will provide you with instructions on the use and interpretation of this checklist.

The contribution of other departments:	Yes	No
Do materials and components meet the standards?	☐	☐
Is machine and tool maintenance done on schedule?	☐	☐
Are schedule changes received on time?	☐	☐
Do I have ample lead time on changes and rush orders?	☐	☐
Do I make noise immediately when the answer to any of the foregoing questions is "No"?	☐	☐
Does Quality Control give me early warning when problems begin to show up?	☐	☐

The contribution of your people:		
Have I explained the "shared accountability for quality" concept?	☐	☐
Have I listened to their questions and objections?	☐	☐
Do I get their help in spotting and correcting quality problems?	☐	☐
And act on suggestions received?	☐	☐
Do they receive recognition and credit from me, for high-quality performance?	☐	☐

And *your* contribution:		
Do I work continually at maintaining a high level of training?	☐	☐
Do I evaluate the performance of each person?	☐	☐
And discuss my findings, either good or bad?	☐	☐
Do I give as much advance notice as possible of any changes that will affect quality, unless special action is taken?	☐	☐
Do I attempt to forecast such changes, so as to be ready for them?	☐	☐
Am I ready and willing to accept the share of the accountability for quality that is "spread" to me?	☐	☐

Source: Adapted from L. Avery, "Defect Control Is Your Responsibility," *Supervision* 40 (February 1978): 6–7; and F. Lippert, "Spreading the Quality Buck," *Supervision* 41 (June 1979): 18–19.

Information Management

Your study of this chapter will enable you to do the following:

1. Make the important distinction between data and information.
2. Describe seven types of information, and explain which types are used at the various organizational levels.
3. Define the term *information management system* (IMS), and describe four types of IMSs that managers encounter.
4. Describe how information management systems are developed, and summarize the role of the manager in creating IMSs.

Lundy Fields and General Foods

Lundy Fields is a young manager who shares with other managers the responsibility for making General Foods's Maxwell House coffee successful. Not long ago, Fields graduated from the University of Southern California's undergraduate business administration program. Five years later, he received an MBA from the University of South Carolina.

Lundy Fields joined General Foods as a management trainee in 1985 and has since held several managerial positions. In each position, he has found it increasingly important to understand information in organizations and to be personally involved in managing information to meet his own needs. "Understanding different types of information," says Fields, "appreciating their role in my managerial responsibilities, and helping design the best system to manage my information needs are three of the most important skills in my success as a manager."

Fields recently was promoted to the position of cost/capital coordinator for the Maxwell House Coffee Company, a division of General Foods. His position is defined by the following roles and responsibilities:

- Act as primary resource/liaison for plants to assure timely and accurate reporting of manufacturing costs and capital expenditures.

- Coordinate analysis of general cost trends and provide analysis to management. Support analysis of business propositions.

Lundy Fields in his office at the start of a typical day reviewing the first information of the day. On his desk may be reports from several General Foods locations. Shortly he will turn to his computer to both analyze and manage the flow of information to appropriate people in the General Foods organization. (Courtesy General Foods Corporation)

- Supervise the development of annual manufacturing cost data for incorporation into annual operating plan. Structure development capital program with operations manager.

- Provide counsel to operations function to assure compliance with cost and financial policies.

As we follow Lundy Fields through a typical day, we see many useful examples of a manager's needs for information. When Fields gets up in the morning, he goes outside his suburban home to retrieve the *Wall Street Journal*. During breakfast and on the bus he takes to work, he informs himself about general business and economic events. Armed with knowledge about the business environment, Fields enters his office. On his desk he finds a stack of mail, which sometimes includes the monthly financial performance report of the Maxwell House Division. On his credenza rests a personal computer. He turns it on and checks for messages in the electronic mail system. One message requests an update on his progress on a report analyzing the financial feasibility of a large project proposal. He puts this on his list of things to do.

Soon Lundy Fields leaves his office to attend several meetings. On his way back, he meets Sarah Barnwell, a financial analyst who reports to him. Barnwell tells him that the cost figures for his project analysis have not yet arrived, though they had been promised for that morning. Field calls the project manager and arranges for the figures to be delivered by 2:00 P.M.

After lunch, Fields meets with Walter Schroeder. They discuss a problem that has arisen with the new financial reporting procedures they are implementing for the Maxwell House Division and decide what steps to take to address the problem. They agree to meet again in two weeks. Then Fields compares the figures for two proposed projects. The current year's budget can support only one of them, and after an hour of analyzing the figures, he decides which project to recommend.

Meanwhile, the Maxwell House division manager is having a meeting to discuss entry into a new market; Fields is among those assigned to examine the financial risks and opportunities the new venture would entail. A successful decision depends heavily on people like Lundy Fields and their ability to obtain and use information effectively.

Introduction

What Is Information Management?

Information is knowledge of a particular fact, event, or situation. Managers in organizations use information to analyze and resolve problems. They depend on information. People used to think of information much as they thought of air: It was everywhere, it was free, and people took it for granted. Then environmentalists began making the public aware that air is not free—at least not clean air. And managers, likewise, are becoming aware that information is not free either. Just as people must manage the things that influence the quality of the air they breathe, managers must manage the things that influence the quality of their information.

As the opening case illustrates, Lundy Fields spends most of his time using information. He often wishes he had more information; sometimes the information he receives is not very useful; and sometimes he finds himself overwhelmed with information. Although he probably does not realize it, he needs to manage his own information better. If he manages it well, he increases his chances of being a successful manager. If he manages it poorly, he increases the chances that he will fail.

Fortunately, Lundy Fields manages his own information better than most, and he is successful. That is why he has been asked to serve as the financial analyst of a venture in a market new to General Foods. Like many—if not most—managers, Lundy Fields does not think of himself as an information manager. Nonetheless, he manages information every day. He would be even more effective if he made a conscious effort to manage his own information.

The Difference Between Data and Information

People often do not distinguish between *information* and *data*. **Data** are records of facts and events; they are a source of information. But by themselves, data have no meaning. They are just so many marks on paper or so many bits on a computer disk or tape or in computer memory. The stock and bond pages in just about any newspaper—columns and columns of numbers—serve to illustrate the difference between data and information. The columns of numbers are simply data to many people. These people either do not read the stock pages or pass over them because they do not know what the numbers mean. To other people the stock page is essential information—the first page they turn to when receiving each morning's paper. This is because the data on the stock page have meaning for such readers and provide information they want to know.

Two characters from the popular TV show, *Family Ties,* should serve to illustrate this distinction. Mallory Keaton, the artistically oriented sister would readily dismiss the stock page as meaningless rows of numbers. Yet Alex Keaton, the ambitious young capitalist played by Michael J. Fox, finds hours of pleasure in persuing the stock page each day. To one it is meaningless data; to the other it provides priceless information.

This chapter examines how managers obtain and use information. It is first important to understand how information is used in organizations as the foundation of managers' information management responsibilities. We then look at four types of information management systems and how they are used in managing organizations. Finally, this chapter introduces you to the basic steps in building an information system.

The Use of Information in Organizations

To understand how Lundy Fields and other managers use information in organizations, it helps to characterize information needs along two dimensions: the level at which information is used in the organization and the type of information used. Managerial activities at different levels in organizations sometimes require different kinds of information.

Level at Which Information Is Used

Figure 20-1 suggests four levels at which managers need and use information. At the *strategic management level,* managers need information that helps them plan and make decisions about the long-term direction the firm will take. They must carefully analyze the environment outside the organization and seek to make and implement decisions that position the organization effectively within this environment over time. Information needs at this level are complex, nonroutine, and oriented toward the future. For example, strategic managers at Pillsbury's headquarters, in trying to decide how to position the company for the twenty-first century, must determine the long-term implications of an aging population for their Burger King subsidiary.

Information needs at the *division/unit management level* are concerned with guiding and controlling the actions of subunits within the organization. For example, Burger King's advertising department creates ad campaigns that reflect the needs of an aging population and chooses, schedules, and monitors the use of different media—TV, radio, magazines—to get that message across.

Managers at the *operations level* are concerned with the day-to-day execution of various tasks within their area of responsibility. They plan, organize, and control the day-to-day work within the organization. At Burger King's headquarters, one manager in the advertising department is responsible for coordinating all TV advertisements during the week. At the same time, shift managers at Burger King outlets around the world are coordinating activities during their eight-hour shifts at local Burger Kings.

The fourth level is that of *transaction processing and reporting.* Recorded transactions are the foundation of the organization's internally generated information. In the past, these transactions were recorded on paper—in ledger books, on ledger cards, in log books, and the like. As computers have become commonplace in most organizations, this fourth level of information is increasingly recorded and stored on computers. For example, a shift manager at Burger King takes one hundred pounds of French fries out of the food locker to start the shift and logs this action on the computer: one transaction. A shift employee records a customer order on the computer cash register: another transaction. Many transactions are generated by internal activities, such as changes in inventory levels. However, critical to the survival of the organization are transactions with outside entities, such as customers and suppliers. While a substantial amount of effort goes into recording transactions, doing so is essentially a mechanical process that requires little direct management supervision. But transaction processing and reporting "capture" data that are often used to meet selected management information needs at each level within the organization. The characteristics of the data that yield information vital to each type of activity are different. Some generalizations are offered in Figure 20-2.

Levels	Information use
Strategic Management	Primarily external information used to chart the organization's future
Division/Unit Management	External and internal information needed to guide and control the actions of subunits within the organization
Operations Management	Primarily internal information used to plan, execute, and control day-to-day work activities
Transaction Processing and Reporting	Collection of data recording the multitude of individual transactions occurring in an organization's daily activities

FIGURE 20-1
Levels of Information Use

As we have seen, transaction processing obtains its data both internally and from transactions that the firm engages in with entities outside the organization. Operations management works largely with internal data. As we move toward strategic management, more of the vital data are external. Whereas the scope of transaction data is narrow—each piece of data refers to a specific transaction— the scope of strategic management data is very wide. As a result, the level of aggregation (the degree of summarization performed on the data) is low (none at all) at the transaction processing level, but at the strategic management level the

FIGURE 20-2
Data Characteristics by Managerial Activity

Characteristics of Data	Transaction Processing	Operational Management	Division/Unit Management	Strategic Management
Source	External Internal	Internal ←————————————→		External
Scope	Narrow ←——————————————————————→			Wide
Aggregation	Detailed ←—————————————————————→			Aggregated
Time Horizon	Historical ←————————————————————→			Future
Currency	Very Current ←——————————————————→			Old
Accuracy	Very High ←—————————————————————→			Moderate
Precision	Very High ←—————————————————————→			Low
Frequency	Very High ←—————————————————————→			Low

Source: Adapted from "A Framework for Management Information Systems," by G. A. Gorry and M. S. Scott Morton, *Sloan Management Review* 13, no. 1 (Fall 1971): 59 by permission of the publisher. Copyright © 1988 by the Sloan Management Review Association. All rights reserved.

figures represent large numbers of transactions in the form of total sales, average costs, or the like.

Transaction data record facts about transactions. Therefore, transaction data are historical; they record events that occurred in the past, even when the past is only seconds old. Strategic management, on the other hand, addresses the future: events that have not yet happened. Transaction processing captures data as soon after the event as possible; they are very current. Time passes, of course, as these data are processed to make them suitable for other managerial activities. Data may well be a day old when operations managers see them, a week or a month old when unit or division managers see them, and three to six months old when they come to the attention of managers at the strategic level.

At the transaction processing level, data must be highly accurate. At the strategic management level, data must be reasonably accurate, but small errors are not critical. *Precision* is related to *accuracy*. Transactional data must be very precise, down to the last penny on a sales transaction. If someone purchases a hamburger for $1.65 and the cashier rings it up as $16.50, what the cashier rings up is precise but not accurate. Precision is much less important at the strategic level. Numbers are frequently rounded off to the nearest million or hundred thousand. Recently, Leaseway Transportation Corporation purchased 2.2 million of its own shares from its largest shareholder at a price of $48.125. The amount of this transaction was reported in the *Wall Street Journal* as about $106 million.[2] This type of number is seen in corporate financial statements and is used at the strategic management level. It is accurate but not precise.

Finally, transactions occur and are processed frequently; there may be thousands per day. At the strategic level, by contrast, a particular piece of data may be used only once a year or less.

Type of Information

As information is processed, managers encounter or have a need for different types of information. As Lundy Fields moved through his typical day in the opening case, he demonstrated needs for different types of information. This section describes seven types of information[3] (see Figure 20-3).

The first type of information is general. **General information** is information that arises incidentally or in response to nonspecific inquiries or searches. It answers such questions as "What do you want to know?" "Is anything interesting?" When Lundy Fields reads the *Wall Street Journal*, he does so to acquire *general information*. When strategic managers at General Foods, or IBM, or ITT perform environmental scanning, they are scanning for general information. A strategic planner for Exxon takes note of news items about unrest in the Middle East but not of those about toy safety in the United States.

Because general information is so broad that it is difficult to define in advance, it is hard to support through computer systems. General information is more likely to be used at the strategic level than at the operations level. By its very definition, general information is not used at the transaction processing level.

Transaction processing is entirely concerned with **specific information**, information that meets particular requirements. Specific information may be requested, as when you verify what the balance is in your checking account at an automated teller machine. Specific information may be unsolicited, as when you receive notice that your telephone rates have increased. When Lundy Fields reads

**FIGURE 20-3
Seven Types of
Information**

Type of Information	Purpose	Example(s)
General	Increase general knowledge	Newspaper
Specific	Answer specific question	Response to request for information
Trigger	Initiate action	Telephone bill
Exception	Initiate preprogrammed corrective action	Report that employee has exceeded allowed days tardy
Control-decision	Assist in planning for exceptions; assist in dealing with unplanned exceptions	Optimal mix of ingredients on the basis of cost; present value of replacing broken piece of equipment vs. repairing
Allocation-decision	Assist in deciding between competing projects	Net present value
Direction-decision	Assist in deciding on new products to offer	Population trends

a report on the Maxwell House Division's financial performance, he receives specific information.

Trigger information is like specific information in that it too is specific. Whereas specific information simply makes the receiver aware of something, however, trigger information requires action. The action required is almost automatic; it is preprogrammed. When Lundy Fields received the request for an update on his progress toward goals, he automatically put the request on his list of things to do. He did not analyze the situation or compute the net present value of doing the report versus that of not doing it. He arranged to do it. Trigger information may be solicited or not, and the action triggered may be of any type.

Exception information is similar to trigger information in that it triggers an action. It is difficult because it triggers a specific type of action and because it is solicited by a general request to be notified when the exception occurs. When Sarah Barnwell told Lundy Fields about the late project figures, she was providing exception information, and Fields immediately took corrective action. Neither trigger information nor exception information requires complex decision making, and when we talk about managerial decision making, these are not usually the types of decisions we are talking about.

The four types of information described so far involve a simple response from the person informed. General and specific information simply tell a person something he or she did not know before. For example, when Lundy Fields sees that the prime rate is 9 percent, he knows that the prime rate has not changed. And in response to trigger information and exception information, the person takes some action that has been determined beforehand; she or he does not have to make a newly thought-out decision. Although much of what managers do involves simply informing themselves and taking predefined actions, that is not what makes managerial work important. Managers must often make difficult decisions to correct problems, allocate resources, or choose future objectives and direction.

When a plan has been set in motion, managers exert control to ensure that the plan is followed. The fifth type of information, then, is **control-decision information**: the information necessary for correcting deviations from plan when these corrections have not been specified in advance. This quality sets control-decision information apart from trigger information. In Lundy Fields's case, the financial reporting problem was not anticipated. He had to discuss the problem with Walter Schroeder and devise a solution tailored to the specific situation.

Weyerhaeuser Company is a forest products company. One of its objectives is to use its log mills to extract the maximum value from logs.[4] Because each log that enters the mill is different, no predetermined decision can be made about how to cut it. And because the prices of lumber and paper vary, the way to maximize the value of each log—and consequently of overall mill production—changes. Therefore, supplying accurate data on prices, costs, and log characteristics in a usable format and at the right time helps managers make the control decisions that maximize profits from the logs.

The sixth type of information is allocation-decision information. **Allocation-decision information** is information useful for deciding how to assign people, time, equipment, or money to computer projects. When Lundy Fields gathered data about the two proposed projects, he had to decide how to allocate the resources at his disposal. Here, he needed data so that he could generate information about the relative costs and profits of the two projects.

Finally, when top managers at General Foods weighed the pros and cons of entering a new market, they were pondering **direction-decision information** in order to make a decision about a very broad area of the firm's economic commitments. In order of occurrence, then, direction-decision information is applied before allocation-decision information (used in committing resources to projects), which is applied before control-decision information (used in correcting deviations from plan).

Use of Information in the Basic Management Functions

Managers, as we have seen throughout this book, are responsible for planning, organizing, and controlling the activities of organizations. Figure 20-4 indicates the frequency with which each type of information is used at each level of managerial activity.

PLANNING ACTIVITIES

Managers engaged in planning use the most different types of information, and they make use of the most general information. Information is used most heavily at the strategic level, less at the division/unit level, and least at the operations level. For example, John Naisbitt runs a consulting service that scans newspapers looking for trends that may enable the firm to make predictions about the future. This is almost a pure pursuit of general information. Naisbitt sells the findings to large corporations, which use them for strategic planning. At the division/unit level, plant managers at Chrysler watch trade publications for indications of new technologies or management techniques that may help them make their factories

Transaction Processing	Operational Management	Division/Unit Management	Strategic Management
General Information			
	PLANNING: Used, but not much.	PLANNING: Used a moderate amount.	PLANNING: Used much, especially in environmental scanning.
Specific Information			
ACTION: Execution of transaction processing is capturing and processing data for specific information.	PLANNING: Uses much specific information.	PLANNING: Uses a moderate amount of specific information.	PLANNING: Uses specific information, but not in large amounts.
Trigger Information			
ACTION: Transactions initiated by trigger information.	ACTION: Triggered often.	ACTION: Triggered less often than operational level.	ACTION: Triggered least often.
Exception Information			
CONTROL: Exceptions generated frequently.	CONTROL: Exceptions recognized frequently.	CONTROL: Exceptions occur less frequently.	CONTROL: Exceptions occur infrequently.
Control–Decision Information			
	CONTROL: Unanticipated exceptions handled moderately frequently.	CONTROL: Major part of job is planning for anticipated exceptions and handling unanticipated exceptions.	CONTROL: Occurs only when lower levels cannot handle exceptions.
Allocation–Decision Information			
	PLANNING: Few opportunities passed down.	PLANNING: Major part of this job.	PLANNING: Done here sometimes; often delegated to division level.
Direction–Decision Information			
	PLANNING: Low-level direction decisions made at this level, but not often.	PLANNING: Strategic choices made at this level on how to implement corporate strategies.	PLANNING: Major part of this job.

FIGURE 20-4
Frequency with which Information Is Used at Each Level for Various Managerial Activities

more productive and increase the quality of their automobiles. At the operations level, foremen at Monsanto's Port Plastics Division read trade magazines. Their hectic days may not allow them to read much, but occasionally they find something that helps them manage their crews.

Specific information is used for planning, but the pattern of its use in planning is the reverse of that for general information. At the operations level, foremen and supervisors are flooded with reports and statistics about their operations. At Monsanto, monthly reports detail how many pounds of plastic each production line is producing. Foremen set specific goals for each shift, using specific information on orders and previous shifts (such as which extruders are down for maintenance). When the plant managers at Chrysler see something interesting about a new product or tool in the trade literature, they often call a sales representative to obtain more specific data. By contrast, Naisbitt, who provides information to those engaged in strategic management, almost never reports on specific items in the newspapers that his company monitors.

Allocation-decision information is also used for planning. At the operations level, most allocation decisions have already been made—but not all. For example, when the manager of deposit systems in the information systems department at Banc One in Ohio determines which of the people who work for him will go to training classes, he is allocating the use of training funds. Strategic managers, who focus most of their attention on direction decisions, also make allocation decisions: more than are made at the operational level and fewer than are made at the division/unit level. At Apple Computer, the amount of the research and development budget is decreed by top management. Allocation-decision information is used most heavily at the division/unit level. Plant managers at General Motors decide how much to put into maintenance and how much to put into the purchase of new machinery.

Direction-decision information is used the least for planning at the operational level. Although the opportunities for direction decisions at the operational level are limited, they do exist. For example, the team leaders at Monsanto's Port Plastics Division decided whether team members should specialize in a single job or should learn several jobs. Division/unit managers make more direction decisions. Plant managers at Saab factories in Sweden decided to experiment with radical new methods of building cars that eliminated the traditional assembly line. Direction-decision information is used most heavily, however, at the strategic level. Making this type of decision is the main job of top management. General Motors has used direction-decision information to guide its acquisition strategy. When General Motors looked at the growing importance of information technology, it decided to buy companies such as EDS, a large information services company.

IMPLEMENTATION ACTIVITIES

Once plans are made, they must be carried out, and this implementation of plans depends largely on trigger information. Transaction processing is initiated by trigger information, and it also generates trigger information that initiates further transaction processing and other activities. The purpose of transaction processing is to handle specific data that can support specific information. For example, when a customer walks up to a Bank of America automated teller machine (ATM) and inserts a VISA card, trigger information is transmitted. The ATM and the computer use specific data such as the customer's account number and the amount of cash requested to process the transaction. The computer then sends trigger information to the customer in the form of a message and a beep to tell her or him to remove the cash from the machine.

At the operations level, trigger information is generated at a tremendous rate. One study showed that foremen were confronted with over 500 separate tasks a day.[5] In the quality control laboratory at Monsanto, new requests for tests on plastic pellets come in all during the shift. At the division/unit level, the pace of trigger information slows. Whereas trigger information arrives minute by minute for the foremen at Monsanto, it slows down to half-hourly or hourly for the plant manager. Trigger information reaches managers at the strategic level much less frequently. As top management at American Airlines monitors the environment for moves made by competitors, information that galvanizes them into action comes to light only daily or weekly.

CONTROLLING ACTIVITIES

As plans are executed, the process must be monitored and corrective action taken when it is needed. The purpose of exception information is to initiate corrective action. Transaction processing is usually the source of the data that makes it possible to extract exception information, and it generates such data with high frequency. In a large VISA card processing operation like that of Banc One, the bank card transaction processing system generates hundreds of late notices and hundred of lines of overdue account reports daily. The actions taken to correct these deficits are fairly automatic until the account becomes overdue by more than about six weeks.

The reports generated by transaction processing are read by people at the operations level. The credit manager or the collection manager at Banc One receives the reports on the level of delinquencies. Individual collectors also receive electronic copies of the reports on specific accounts. This gives them exception information and initiates action on their part: either a personalized letter or a phone call, depending on the stage of delinquency.

Exception information occurs less frequently at the division/unit level. When the warehouse manager at Square D (a large manufacturer and distributor of electrical parts) receives a monthly budget report that tells him he is over budget, he quickly tracks down the source of the problem and takes corrective action. Because managers at the strategic level deal with plans and actions that take a long time to complete, exceptions at this level occur least frequently. When Citicorp lends money to Brazil, a long time passes before it is known whether Brazil intends to postpone payment of the interest on the loan, as it did in 1987. At the strategic level, it is harder to preplan for exceptions. Citicorp, however, had anticipated the problem with Brazil, so part of its response was automatic.

Many deviations from plan are not anticipated. One use of control-decision information involves responding to unanticipated problems. Citicorp carefully analyzes Brazil's action to determine how to minimize its impact on Citicorp's financial position. The planning that Citicorp did before Brazil postponed interest payments illustrates the other use of control-decision information: in planning for anticipated problems. Control-decision information is used most frequently at the division/unit level. The director of information systems at Corning Glass Works uses control-decision information when he or she plans steps in recovery from potential disasters (first type) and when sudden increases in user demand result in long

---

Guidelines for Management Practice

Just as managers need to be aware of the different ways in which information is used in different managerial activities, they should bear in mind the following further guidelines.

1. Information, the meaning extracted from data, is integral to a manager's job.

2. Information management cannot be delegated. Delegating information management to the data processing department is abdicating an important part of a manager's responsibilities. This is not to say that the technical aspects of managing information technology cannot be delegated, but managers should be very active in managing their own information and supporting data.

3. Computer systems handle only data, not information. Furthermore, they do not perform magic. The

manager is essential in extracting information from data. Computers can be viewed as tools that extend managers' capabilities. They do not replace managers, but they certainly can replace clerks and "managers" who actually perform only clerical functions.

4. Managers must think about how they are using information. The use to which information will be put, like level of managerial activity, has a strong effect on the type of information system that should be used. Lower-level managers use specific, trigger, and exception information most often. Higher-level managers use control-decision, allocation-decision, and direction-decision information more often than trigger and exception information.

---

waiting times on computer jobs (second type). At the operations level, control-decision information is used less often and primarily in responding to problems. For example, when an extruder goes down at Monsanto, the line foreman uses control-decision information to decide how to "work around" the problem until the extruder is fixed. Regardless of the type of information or data being used, international managers often face unusual difficulties in generating and applying information across national borders. "Insights for International Managers 20" discusses the increased involvement of governments in data flows across borders.

The next section of the chapter describes types of systems that support the various uses of the information that we have examined here.

Computer-Based Information Management Systems

Clearly, people use information very frequently in organizations. Thus far, we have explored the different aspects of information. In passing, we have noted that computers manage data and make it possible to derive information. As the following discussion will show, computers are very useful for supporting some types of information use, but not others.

Although there are other types of information management systems, this chapter is concerned with computer-based information management systems. These systems consist of people; computers and their supporting hardware; the programs that make the computers run; data; and procedures for operating the system, preparing input, and interpreting output. Together these components make up an **information management system (IMS)**, a system that enables people to use information in support of the organization's operations, control, and planning.

This section of the chapter discusses four types of information management systems: transaction processing systems, management information systems, decision support systems, and knowledge-based systems.

Transaction Processing Systems

Day-to-day operations generate the most data in organizations, and **transaction processing systems** do basic data processing. Although they do not help much with operational, planning, or control decision making, they make handling the ever-increasing mass of necessary transactions a manageable task. In addition, they provide much of the data needed by systems that do directly support operational, planning, and control decision making.

At one time, clerical personnel regularly recorded these transactions in ledgers. Because recording these transactions was tedious and error-prone, but still straightforward, this activity was one of the first commercial applications of computers. Typical transaction processing systems handle general ledger accounting, accounts payable, accounts receivable, payroll, order entry, and inventory updating.

Strictly speaking, many accounting applications do more than transaction processing. For example, in addition to transaction processing, the accounts receivable system produces management information in the form of statistical summaries such as reports that show the total amount in delinquent accounts, arranged by the length of time they are delinquent.

Although managers like Lundy Fields benefit from transaction processing systems (they are paid through a payroll system, for instance), they seldom work directly with the transactions themselves. Fields's report on the financial performance of the Maxwell House Division, however, is an example of a summary report produced by a transaction processing system.

Transaction processing systems are built on a standard model, a diagram of which appears in Figure 20-5. When a transaction occurs, it must be "captured" and prepared for processing. For example, when you use your bank card in a small store, you are likely to receive one copy of the transaction slip, and the store

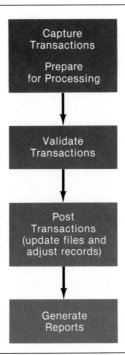

FIGURE 20-5
Standard Transaction
Processing Model

▰▰ *Insights for International Managers 20* ▰▰

MANAGING INFORMATION ACROSS INTERNATIONAL BORDERS

Most corporate managers take for granted the sharing of information between a company's many plants and offices. Data transfer and exchange are essential tools for financial management, inventory control, planning, production, sales, marketing, and customer service. Yet managers in today's multinational companies have found that transfering data across national borders is increasingly subject to restriction and regulation by host governments. Transborder data flow is not as easy and instantaneous as domestic managers might expect.

Concerns regulating the collection and flow of data vary from nation to nation. In Sweden, for example, certain lifestyle information is banned from collection by anyone, while it is illegal in France to document religious or union affiliation. Such legal guarantees and rights to privacy as well as a person's right to obtain and correct such information vary from country to country. Assume that information about a person is collected in Belgium, transmitted via a private telecommunications network owned by a corporation in the United States, processed in West Germany, stored in a file in France, and requested by a firm in England. You can quickly see that the legal aspects of transborder data transfer could become very complicated.

The table to the right summarizes the current status of various personal privacy regulations and issues from twenty-two nations and four supranational organizations you as an international manager are likely to encounter. The table covers such key regulatory concerns as type of regulation, protected persons, name-linked data, control, right to access/challenge, level of government regulating data collection, regulated sector, and enforcement. International managers should be increasingly attentive to the regulation of transborder data flow if they are to be successful in executing their managerial responsibilities.

Note that the countries studied will differ in degree of "regulatedness" or in strength of laws and diligence of enforcement. A "√" denotes the existence of a condition, not its strength. LP = legislation pending; L = legislation in force; R = report; G = guidelines
[a] European Economic Community   [c] Organization for Economic Cooperation and Development
[b] Council of Europe   [d] Intergovernmental Bureau for Informatics

---

Source: Adapted from R. T. Wingand, C. Shipley, and D. Shipley, "Transborder Data Flow, Informatics, and National Policies," *Journal of Communication* 34, no. 1 (1984): 167. © 1984 *Journal of Communication*. Reprinted by permission.

---

sends another copy to the bank that issued your card. Here the transaction has been captured on paper. After quite a bit of manual processing, it is prepared for computer processing. It may be keyed into special data entry equipment such as a keydisk system; it may be processed by an optical scanner; or it may be keyed into a computer terminal and stored directly on the main computer's files. By contrast, when you buy something in a large store such as Federated Department Stores' Gold Circle chain, the checkout clerk enters your bank card number into the cash register. You still receive a paper copy of the transaction, but Gold Circle uses an electronic copy. The *capture* of the transaction and its *preparation for processing* have been accomplished in a single step.

The second part of the transaction processing model is *transaction validation*. One type of validation checks for errors in individual transactions, such as missing data and the exceeding of allowable values. For example, the bank card transaction must have a non-zero amount. It must also have one (and only one) of several allowable transaction codes: sale, credit, payment, or adjustment.

Personal Privacy Regulations and Issues	Australia	Austria	Belgium	Canada	Denmark	Finland	France	Hungary	Iceland	Israel	Japan	Luxembourg	Netherlands	New Zealand	Norway	Portugal	Spain	Sweden	Switzerland	United Kingdom	United States	West Germany	EEC[a]	COE[b]	OECD[c]	IBI[d]
Type of regulation	LP	L	LP	L	L	LP	L	LP	L	L	R	L	LP	L	L	LP	LP	L	LP	R	L	L	R	R	G	R
Protected persons																										
Natural persons	√	√	√	√	√	√	√			√		√	√	√	√		√	√		√	√	√	√	√	√	√
Citizens/residents only				√																	√					
Legal persons		√	√		√							√		√	√										√	
Name-linked data																										
Electronic data processing/ automated data processing	√	√	√	√	√	√	√			√		√	√	√	√		√	√		√	√	√			√	
Manual data processing	√	√		√	√		√						√		√		√			√	√			√	√	
Collection/flow/storage	√	√				√	√			√		√			√									√	√	√
Control																										
Data control boards		√	√	√	√		√					√	√		√		√	√		√		√				
Registration/licensing		√	√	√			√			√		√			√					√	√					
Right to access/challenge	√	√	√	√	√		√			√		√		√	√					√	√	√				
Freedom of information	√	√		√	√	√	√					√	√		√					√	√					
Level of government																										
Local	√			√													√		√	√	√					
National	√	√	√	√	√		√		√	√		√	√	√	√	√	√	√		√	√					
International							√						√	√	√		√						√	√	√	√
Regulated sector																										
Public		√	√	√	√		√					√	√	√			√			√	√	√	√			
Private		√	√		√							√					√			√	√	√				
Self-regulation						√																√				
Enforcement																										
Fine							√					√														
Victim compensation													√	√							√					
Data confiscated/destroyed				√									√				√									

Through validation, certain aspects of groups of transactions are also checked. Transactions are often processed in batches, and the total amount of the transactions in the batch should be equal to the total provided with the batch. This ensures that no transactions are lost once the batch total has been calculated. Batches may contain only one type of transaction. (For example, Banc One in Columbus, Ohio, maintains a department just to process VISA card payments.) The validation process makes sure that all the transactions in those batches are payments.

The third part of the model is *transaction posting*. Here the transaction is used to adjust the appropriate records. For example, each entry in the accounting chart of accounts has a record that contains the current balance. When the firm sells on credit, each credit customer has an accounts receivable record. When it buys on credit, each creditor has an accounts payable record. Each inventory item has a record that contains the current level of that item. Hence a transaction recording the sale of a pair of shoes lowers the count of that style and size of shoe by one.

Finally, transaction processing systems include *reporting*. As we noted earlier, some of this reporting may "fit" better under management information for operations control or division/unit decision making, but a large part of it is simply transactional in nature. Reporting confirms the recorded event, or it directs another transaction to take place.[6] An example of the first type of report is a transaction register; of the second type, a billing invoice.

Transaction processing systems run in two modes: batch and real-time. A *batch system* saves transactions until some predetermined time and then processes all the accumulated transactions in a batch. A *real-time system* processes each transaction as it encounters it. Although real-time systems often have very fast processing times, any system that can accept transactions, process them, and return the results to the initiator quickly enough to affect the current activity can be called a real-time system. For example, a missile tracking system might require a response time of less than a second, but a response within one or two minutes might be adequate for a stock price inquiry.[7]

Transaction processing systems frequently incorporate both modes. Our example of a bank card transaction in a small store employs real-time mode for capture but batch preparation for processing. A sales clerk "captures" the customer's purchase by immediately filling out a bank card form and imprinting it with the customer's bank card. This step in the transaction is executed in real time, as the purchase is made. The store owner saves bank card slips until the end of the day (some small stores accumulate them longer) and deposits them at the bank. There they are collected with the paper transactions deposited by other stores and are eventually prepared for processing via keying or perhaps optical scanning. These final steps in this transaction processing system have been conducted in the batch mode.

The Gold Circle transaction we outlined earlier is captured and prepared for processing in real time via a computer cash register at the checkout line. When the transaction reaches the bank electronically, it does not require further preparation for processing.

Even when transaction processing systems capture and prepare transactions for processing in real-time mode, they often run transaction posting and reporting in batch mode. The captured and prepared transactions are collected until some predetermined time and then posted by the system all at once. Often, a convenient time is daily. For example, Sears captures, partially validates, and accumulates transactions in local store computers during the day. At the end of the business day, the transactions are transmitted to a central computer for further validation, posting, and reporting in batch mode. Payroll systems, on the other hand, run once a week or twice a month, depending on the pay schedule in the organization.

Transaction processing systems directly support the use of specific and trigger information. Some managers may view transaction processing systems as boring. This is a mistake! Transaction processing systems have provided vehicles for important strategic initiatives. For example, automated teller machines (ATMs) capture, prepare, and validate transactions in real-time mode. They usually accumulate transactions for later posting in batch mode. Banks that offered ATMs early hoped to gain an advantage over their competitors. Though that has not happened, *not* having ATMs has become a disadvantage.

McKesson Corporation has used a transaction processing system that places special terminals in its customers' locations—usually drugstores—to assist with order entry and inventory management.[8] This provides the customer with enhanced levels of service and (not insignificantly) creates a closer tie between McKesson and its customers.

As new technology becomes available and makes point-of-transaction capture, preparation, and validation more economically feasible, more ways will be found to make transaction processing systems important strategic tools. While it is true that transaction processing systems are among the oldest uses of computers, they are also on the cutting edge of profitable new applications.

Management Information Systems

The term *management information systems* sometimes has been defined to include all types of information systems, but in this chapter we will use it to denote a specific type of information system. A **management information system (MIS)** is an integrated reporting system specifically designed to help managers plan, execute, and control the organization's activities. It generates reports with data obtained from many transaction processing systems and perhaps from outside the organization. An MIS is usually designed to condense *selected* data from transaction processing systems and external sources to make these data more suitable for informing managers.[9] For example, Lundy Fields receives a monthly profit-and-loss statement for the Maxwell House Division. This is one type of MIS report condensed from various transaction data. Some managers ask that such reports include information on industry standards with which to compare their own company's performance.

Management information systems address problems that are known and understood in advance (such problems are said to be *structured*). Therefore, the relevant information requirements can be determined, reports designed, and programs written in advance. These systems are run on a recurring basis.[10] The Maxwell House Division's monthly profit-and-loss report is one such report. Furthermore, data items can be defined in advance and accessed with on-line queries or through report generators (programs that make it easy to create reports). Many managers have personal computers with which they can obtain certain predefined reports at any time during the day. For example, an MIS in the Maxwell House Division might produce a monthly report showing the monthly sales, costs, profit, and rate of return for each of its products. The general manager of the division could use this report in making control decisions for the division. Lundy Fields could use this report to monitor the performance of each product in the division and that of the division as a whole. He could also use the information in making financial recommendations for projects related to these products.

Management information systems tend to be limited to "read only" data that cannot be manipulated. For example, Lundy Fields cannot use the MIS to obtain *projected* profit-and-loss figures or to try out different assumptions based on different amounts of sales. This limitation does not undermine the value of MISs. Because managers have recurring information needs, an MIS is an important tool for providing regular reports that enhance the effectiveness of managerial planning and control.

Decision Support Systems

Many problems that managers encounter are not anticipated or understood in advance, and the MISs we have described are not helpful with these problems. Because of this, many systems that might once have been called management information systems have evolved into decision support systems.

Decision support systems (DSS) are computer-based systems that help decision makers deal with ill-structured problems by interacting with data and analysis models.[11] DSSs are focused on decisions; emphasize flexibility, adaptability, and quick response; are user-controlled; and can be adapted to various decision-making styles.[12]

This description emphasizes that DSSs *help* decision makers rather than replace them. They are designed to assist in the solution of problems for which there are no predefined solutions. Therefore, the decision maker must rely to a great extent on experience to make the decision. The DSS extends the decision maker's ability to manipulate relevant data in search of solutions. DSSs have proved helpful in providing support for analyzing data used in making control and allocation decisions.

A good example of a DSS is one used by Ben Heineman, CEO of Northwest Industries, a conglomerate with holdings in many different businesses. Heineman used a specially tailored system that drew on an extensive data base of reports, operating statistics, and industry statistics. He used the reports to detect deviations from expected performance in subsidiaries (control decisions). He also used the system's modeling capabilities to decide how to allocate financial resources to different subsidiaries by trying out different forecasts of economic activity (allocation decisions) and to decide whether to purchase new subsidiaries and whether to divest Northwest Industries of existing subsidiaries (direction decisions).[13]

DSSs are being used increasingly as aids in day-to-day operational decisions. Weyerhaeuser's log mill problem, which was described earlier, provides an example of a DSS used in a dynamic situation. Weyerhaeuser's system takes a large amount of data (including costs, sales prices, and the characteristics of the particular log) and makes a recommendation about how to cut up the log. The mill operator then decides whether or not to follow the recommendation. Norfolk Southern Corporation uses a DSS to assist in train dispatching. During an eight-hour shift, a train dispatcher might control the movement of twenty to thirty trains. This responsibility includes scheduling trains on single tracks where the use of passing sidings is required, and it includes coordinating train movement with the movement of roadway maintenance gangs, signal maintenance crews, industrial switch engines, and motor car inspection crews. Using this DSS helped dispatchers reduce the amount of delay time experienced by trains.[14]

DSSs make it possible for the decision maker to try out different approaches to solving the problem. They are designed under the assumption that the decision maker has the necessary expertise, and the system is there as a flexible tool. Ever since computers were invented, however, some researchers have looked for ways in which the computer can *replace* the decision maker. This effort has given rise to knowledge-based systems.

Knowledge-Based Systems and Expert Systems

As the banking industry was deregulated in the late 1980s, the number of financial institutions seeking to enter the commercial lending business—lending money on a six-month to five-year basis to various business borrowers—rapidly increased. This is an area of regular, profitable business for most banks. Knowledgeable, experienced commercial lending officers are critical in choosing which loans to make (in order to earn money) and which not to make (in order to avoid losing money).

The rapid move by thousands of banks into commercial lending created an enormous demand for good commercial loan officers. With the supply of such people running far short of the demand, one major bank initiated a joint venture with an experienced computer team to develop a computer software system that would emulate the decision process and logic applied by experienced loan officers as they evaluated applications for commercial loans. What they were doing was creating a "knowledge-based" system. Over an intense, two-year period, they were able to design a software system that could receive a wide variety of data about an applicant's situation, connect with numerous potentially relevant data bases inside and outside the bank, generate further questions to be answered, and eventually set forth a detailed assessment of the applicant's request. They had created a software program that contained knowledge and the power to reason; it was artificially intelligent.

The foregoing example describes a **knowledge-based system**, an artificial intelligence program that depends for its performance on knowledge, rather than on ingenious computations. Some knowledge-based systems are called *expert systems* when the standard for their performance is that to which we would hold a human expert.[15] For our purposes an *artificial intelligence* program takes on ill-defined, constantly changing problems—problems that were once thought too difficult to approach with computer programs.[16] There are many knowledge-based/ expert systems.[17] Schlumberger, a large oil drilling company, has developed a system called the DIPMETER ADVISOR that analyzes core samples to determine whether an oil well should be drilled on that site. One of the most glamorous successes has been a system called XCON that configures computer systems for Digital Equipment Corporation. Only around 10 percent of all the systems configured by XCON require human correction! A program called PROSPECTOR assisted in the discovery of an extension to a molybdenum deposit in Washington state.

The ultimate objective of a knowledge-based system is to replace the decision maker, but in reality, that is more than these systems can do. They may take over a part of the decision maker's job, but they cannot completely replace the decision maker. It will be some time before knowledge-based systems can replace managers, if it is ever possible. In this regard, knowledge-based systems have been oversold.

═══════ *Guidelines for Management Practice* ═══════

Judiciously applied, information management systems can be used as effective management tools. Nevertheless, we will phrase these guidelines for new managers as a warning, or caution, about using each of the four systems.

1. Do not underestimate the importance of transaction processing systems. They are the bread-and-butter applications that make other types of computer systems workable.

2. Management information systems are much more narrow in scope than was once envisioned. Look to MISs to supply you with trigger and exception information. MISs are most effective when designed to generate summary reports that consolidate routine data. MISs will always be important sources of information in your management career, but the higher you go in management, the less help MISs will provide in the decision making you need to do.

3. Take a careful look at decision support systems. When you have problems that can be addressed by one of several well-known techniques, decision support systems may be useful to you, but only if you understand which techniques to apply. When your problem cannot be addressed by known techniques and when it calls for intuition or judgment, decision support systems do not help much. Managing people is one of these problems. Use decision support systems only where they are appropriate.

4. Keep a level head about knowledge-based systems. They are being oversold today. Undoubtedly they will become more useful, and more readily available, in the future.

The most impressive developments over the next ten years are likely to be those achieved by software companies that are working on ways to incorporate knowledge-based techniques into conventional transaction processing applications. As a manager, you will be dealing with knowledge-based systems more and more, but you are in little danger of being replaced by a computer.

See "In Practice 20-1" for one example of the successful use of an information management system to promote good customer relations.

The Use of Information Systems

Each of the four types of information systems we have discussed is appropriate for a specific purpose. None is appropriate for all types of information use at all managerial levels.

Although not so glamorous as decision support systems or knowledge-based systems, transaction systems are essential. They receive data into the overall information system, they keep data organized and updated, and they move data to where they are needed. But by themselves, transaction systems are limited to supplying specific data (and thus supporting the derivation of specific and trigger information).

The types of management information systems discussed in this chapter expand on the capabilities of transaction processing systems, but they still condense and manipulate data on known and recurring problems to make them suitable for use in arriving at trigger and exception information. This information is used most frequently at the operations level, less at the unit or division level, and least of all at the strategic level.

Decision support systems help managers solve less structured problems. They are more suitable than MISs for generating control-decision, allocation-decision, and direction-decision information. DSSs are more complex to build and maintain than MISs, and although DSSs can solve trigger and exception information problems, MISs yield these solutions more economically.

DSSs offer easy and flexible access to an array of components. When they are well designed, it is easy to change how components are accessed and to add new components.[18] Like other powerful tools, DSSs are only as good as the skill with which they are used.

Knowledge-based systems, on the other hand, are intended to contain the skills. Currently, however, knowledge-based systems have limited and narrowly

Physicians now have available on computers both decision support and knowledge-based systems that allow them to, among other things, schedule patient medication, plan daily patient therapy programs, and consult international data bases for diagnostic assistance. (Mark Seliger)

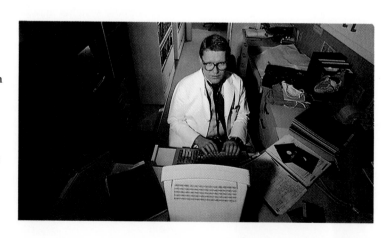

In Practice 20-1

INFORMATION MANAGEMENT AND AMERICAN AIRLINES

Esther Dyson, a newsletter publisher recently said, "As far as brand names go, I'm not much of a loyalist. But I am a loyal customer of American Airlines. American has won me with ten years of only an occasional slipup."

How does American achieve excellence in the details that constitute superior service? Dyson says that she has always suspected that it has something to do with the company's skilled use of computers. American led the industry in the seventies with its Sabre reservation system, a $350-million project that has since grown to encompass crew and flight scheduling, maintenance and parts-tracking, and other minutiae of airline operations. In the eighties, the company again led the industry with its Advantage frequent-flier program.

Dyson offered the following assessment of American's success: Automation lets American benefit from economies of scale without losing the personal touch. It may be just a computer trick, but isn't it nice to talk to someone who knows where you have flown to lately, knows your preferred seat, and, best of all, can answer your question, "What's the chance that the seat next to me on the overnight will be empty, so that I can stretch out and get some sleep?" The personal touch, lost in economies of scale, can be recovered with smart use of computer information. Automation and management depth also let American absorb AirCal during the summer of 1987 with hardly a glitch.

One more bonus to American—if not to the traveler—is that American's excellent yield management forces people like me to pay full fare when a less-well-managed airline will often give me a discount ticket—in spite of the fact that, like most business travelers, I am highly price-insensitive.

Dyson says, "I took special pleasure recently in visiting the shrine where my reservations are guarded and my miles are counted, American's headquarters in Dallas-Fort Worth. Senior vice president Max Hopper described American's extensive computer operations and some related businesses, which together turned in a profit of $122 million in 1986. By monitoring advance bookings, American can maximize (more or less) its revenues by adjusting the flow of tickets to fill seats at prices as high as the market will bear ("yield management").

"Yet I learned something that surprised me, but shouldn't have: It wasn't the computers per se that made American work well, but the human organization that utilized the computers. For example, I asked Hopper about the storms that had closed Chicago's O'Hare airport in the fall of 1987 and left thousands of travelers stranded. American felt little impact; it had rerouted most of its through customers around O'Hare through Dallas. I thought he would explain how computerized decision systems had advised the rerouting. 'That wasn't it at all,' Hopper responded. 'It was a human decision, made early that afternoon.' As it flew passengers out of Chicago, American flew extra personnel in to help with the commotion. Computers certainly helped management cope with reassigning people and flights, but only after the humans made the decision."

Source: Esther Dyson, "Secret Formula," *Forbes*, October 5, 1987, p. 242. Reprinted by permission of the author.

---

focused skills. For example, MYCIN is good at diagnosing bacterial infections, but it cannot deal with the symptoms of cardiac arrest. People are more flexible.

In the Northwest Industries example, Ben Heineman understood how to interpret forecasts and financial statements, compare data across operating companies, size up an acquisition (an evaluation that changes with each new situation), and evaluate proposed divestments. Each of these activities requires a different skill, and no knowledge-based system yet devised has that many different complete skills. Even a successful system such as XCON is not considered "complete."[19] At the present time, knowledge-based systems are powerful but limited tools that address control, allocation, and direction decisions. And given the complexity of direction decisions, control and allocation decisions are more appropriate targets for knowledge-based systems.

You may have noticed that we have said nothing about the role of computers in supporting the use of general information, though our discussion suggests that the four types of information management systems support the use of all the other types of information. Indeed, it seems best to leave the processing of general information in the hands of a skilled manager. This is not to suggest that the only source for the other six types of information is the computer. In fact, much information processing in organizations does not involve the computer at all. Nonetheless, computer-based information is an integral part of organizations.

Information systems are not necessarily immediately available for use, and managers often must build the information systems they need. The next section examines how to build information systems.

Building Information Systems

When computers were very new in the late 1940s and early 1950s, programming them was a daunting and difficult task, so it seemed natural to leave it to specialized programmers. It soon became apparent, however, that leaving the building of computer software systems entirely to technicians was not satisfactory.[20] Since then, *user involvement* has become an important issue in building systems. There is a lot of debate about when, how, and even whether users of information systems should be involved in their development. In this book we take the position that users should be involved. Users are managers who apply information systems. They do not want just any information system. They want one that solves problems for *them*.

System Development Life Cycle

In the early days of computer systems, especially in organizations that had not given the process much thought, developing computer programs was a haphazard affair. For example, many programmers started program coding as quickly as possible—often before it was clear what the program needed to do. Because that created problems, people began to impose some order on the process. This produced a model called a **system development life cycle (SDLC)**. Figure 20-6 shows a typical system development life cycle.

THE DEFINITION STAGE

The *definition stage* offers a critical opportunity to shape the information system. The *proposal submission* phase is critical, because the first exposure to the problem determines much of what follows. The *feasibility assessment* phase includes two basic tasks. The first is problem definition. The second is deciding whether building the system is feasible. Feasibility assessment takes place early in the system development life cycle, which usually means decisions are made with a minimum of information. This can cause problems, such as the omission of important considerations.[21]

During *system analysis,* time is spent determining what information the user wants to obtain from the system. The next step is to determine what data are needed to supply this information. During this process, the procedures are developed that will be needed to obtain the data and to make use of the information. Finally, it is learned where the data will come from and how they will move through the system.

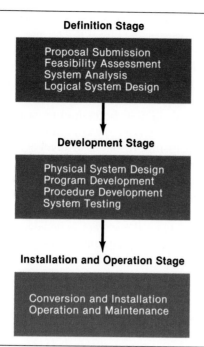

FIGURE 20-6
A Typical System
Development Life Cycle

In the next phase, *logical system design,* the task is to develop the concept for the system, including how the data will be collected, what will be done with the data, and what reports will be generated by the system. With the conclusion of logical system design, the definition stage is completed. The definition stage is critical to successful system development. It is also difficult. During system analysis many things seem abstract, and it is hard to imagine how they will look when they are built.

THE DEVELOPMENT STAGE

The *development stage* is critical too—but with a difference: A poor development stage can ruin good work done in the definition stage, but even outstanding work done at the development stage cannot salvage poor work done at the definition stage. In the *physical system design* phase, the logical design is translated into specifications for subsystems, programs, procedures, files, and data bases. Physical system design requires well-developed technical skills. If the tasks of the definition stage have been done well, extensive user involvement in designing the physical system is not necessary.

During *program development,* the project team designs the programs specified in the physical system design. They also write the programs and test them.

Procedure development involves designing and writing the procedures the users will follow to collect and prepare data for entry into the reporting system as well as the procedures for interpreting the reports. When the programs are written and tested, it is time for *system testing.* System testing has two parts: making sure the individual programs work together and testing the computer system's performance when the procedures specified in the user's manual were followed.

INSTALLATION AND OPERATION STAGE

In the *installation and operation stage,* the project moves from development to application. The *conversion and installation* phase is usually a critical time. The *conversion* process creates the files needed for the new system. This often requires a special subsystem that converts data from the format required by the old system to a new format. Temporarily deprived of any computer system, employees may enter a large amount of data manually, validating them as far as possible, and storing them in the new file format. Also during this time, the users must be trained in the procedures for using the new system.

The *installation* process moves the computer programs from the computer libraries used by the programmers to the computer libraries used when running the system for actual processing. It may also involve the physical installation of new terminals or computers.

Once the system has been successfully converted and installed, the development project is over and the *operation and maintenance* phase begins. During system *operation*, the system is run and the users provide input and use the output. The work is not complete when the system is developed. Systems contain errors that need to be fixed, and changing circumstances often dictate other changes to the system. So work on the system, called *maintenance*, continues.

User-Developed Systems

Managers are very likely to be involved in the development of new information systems during their careers. Therefore, they need to know something about the process so that they can participate intelligently. Many users also build their own

◼ *Guidelines for Management Practice* ◼

To a significant extent, success in management may depend on the manager's ability to contribute to the effective design of information management systems that serve his or her needs at a reasonable cost. To that end, remember the following guidelines.

1. Always invest considerable time analyzing and discussing specific information needs and problems before designing or acquiring information systems. The biggest mistake managers make in information management is buying hardware or software before the need for it is well established.

2. Information requirements—and the supporting data requirements—are different for different levels of managerial activity. Therefore, the information management systems that support these levels are different. When you build a system to support a specific level, you must tailor the system to meet the needs of that level. Do not be misled into trying to satisfy all information requirements with one type of system.

3. Remember that the higher you go in management, the more you depend on general information. As your career progresses, you will be faced with more problems that the computer does not solve well.

4. Manage your own information. Do not abandon your own role in building information systems. Most people check on their contractor when they have a house built, and you should work closely with your information systems specialist when you are "commissioning" an information system.

5. If you build your own information systems, use good system-building practices. Working meticulously may seem cumbersome, but it will pay off later.

6. You need to be careful about defining your own information requirements. A small system does not require *much* logical or physical design, but ignoring these steps entirely could cause your system to be less effective and efficient than it should be.

7. Test your program. Nothing—well, not much anyway—is worse than making decisions based on erroneous numbers.

systems. As new programming languages come along that are easier to use, it becomes more feasible for users to do this.

Certain risks arise with **user-developed systems**, however.[22] Users may have a one-sided view of the system and may not realize what its impact on the overall organization's information resources will be. They may not be trained to identify information requirements. Furthermore, users are often impatient with quality assurance procedures. And they may build private systems that duplicate formal organizational systems.

Responsible managers and users want to minimize these risks, and understanding the system-building process helps them to do that. When managers build systems themselves, they lose the benefit of outside opinions. This makes them more likely to make mistakes. To compensate, they need to be sensitive to the actual feasibility of building the system with the technology available to them. It does not make sense today for users to build large-scale transaction processing systems themselves, and perhaps it never will. But it does make sense for managers to build their own decision support systems and other small systems.

One of the challenges managers face when doing this is to find computer software that meets their needs. "Management Development Exercise 20" provides a checklist useful to managers in trying to select appropriate software.

Review of the Learning Objectives

Having studied this chapter, you should be able to respond to the learning objectives with extensions of the following brief answers.

1. **Make the important distinction between data and information.**

   Data are the records of facts and events. They are stored as marks on paper or bits in a computer storage device, and to have meaning, they must be interpreted. The meaning that is extracted from data is called information. In general, people are necessary for the extraction of information to take place.

2. **Describe seven types of information, and explain which types are used at the various organizational levels.**

   There are seven types of information. Acquiring *general information* increases one's general knowledge. Getting *specific information* consists of adding to one's knowledge about a specific issue in response to a question or a need to know. *Trigger information* is knowledge that stimulates, or triggers, a preprogrammed response. *Exception information* reveals a deviation from expected conditions and signals the need for corrective action. *Control-decision information* is used either to respond to an unanticipated problem or to plan a response to an anticipated problem. *Allocation-decision information* helps one decide how and where to commit scarce resources. *Direction-decision information* helps one make decisions about overall company goals and objectives.

   The four levels of managerial activity are the strategic, division/unit, operations, and transaction processing levels. At the strategic, division/unit and operations levels, general, specific, allocation-decision, and direction-decision information are used for planning. Execution at the transaction processing level consists of processing the data that support specific information. Trigger information occurs at all four levels as an essential part of execution. Exception information occurs at all four levels and is used for the control of anticipated problems that occur during execution. Control-decision information occurs at the operations, division/unit, and strategic levels as part of the control function.

3. **Define the term** *information management system* **(IMS), and describe four types of IMSs that managers encounter.**

Information management systems consist of people, computers, programs, procedures, and data that facilitate information use in support of the organization's operations, control, and planning. *Transaction processing systems* support the processing of the large numbers of transactions that are generated by an organization's day-to-day operations. *Management information systems* are integrated systems that enable managers to derive information that supports structured decision making for planning, operations, and control. *Decision support systems* help decision makers deal with ill-structured problems by interacting with data and analysis models. *Knowledge-based systems* are artificial intelligence programs that depend on knowledge rather than on ingenious computations to make or recommend decisions; their ultimate objective is to replace the decision maker.

4. **Describe how information management systems are developed, and summarize the role of the manager in creating IMSs.**

Information management systems are developed in several stages. It is first necessary to define a problem. The symptoms must then be sorted out and the real problem pinpointed. Next a desired solution must be defined and its feasibility assessed, and the information required to arrive at the solution must be defined. Once these things are accomplished—and they are difficult tasks—system design begins. A logical design is translated into a physical design. The necessary files and data bases must be designed. The actual programs must be designed, coded, and tested; and procedures must be designed and written for the user's manual. All the components of the system must be tested. Then the system must be put into operation and used. If the system is reasonably well understood, these tasks can be accomplished in the order listed. When the problem is not well understood, a more experimental approach may be more effective. In that case, these tasks are repeated as long as it takes everyone involved to fully understand the problem.

The manager has a critical role during the early definition tasks and during the final testing and operations tasks. The manager also has an important role during the design tasks, although her or his involvement is not quite so critical then as during the definition tasks. During the technical design and programming tasks, the manager's role is mainly one of clarifying any details that were not made entirely clear during earlier tasks. Managers do not use their time effectively when they try to become actively involved in programming.

Key Terms and Concepts

After having completed your study of Chapter 20, "Information Management," you will have mastered the following important terms and concepts.

information	control-decision	information	management	knowledge-based
data	information	management	information	system
general information	allocation-decision	system (IMS)	system (MIS)	system development
specific information	information	transaction	decision support	life cycle (SDLC)
trigger information	direction-decision	processing	system (DSS)	user-developed
exception	information	system		systems
information				

Questions for Discussion

1. Why is it important to distinguish between data and information? Give some examples of data in business and in your own life. Give some examples of information in business and in your own life. How do your examples illustrate the differences between data and information?

2. Discuss some problems that might arise from confusing data and information.

3. Cite the different levels of managerial activity. Are they strictly a function of the part of the organization that a manager is in? Explain.

4. Explain why data have different characteristics at different levels of managerial activity.

5. Discuss how distinguishing among the various types of information can help managers to better manage information.

6. Give examples of each type of information in your life at home, in school, and at work.

7. List several transaction processing systems that you come into contact with frequently.

8. Where do you think knowledge-based systems could be most useful? Most harmful? Explain.

9. The steps in the system development life cycle are often carried out sequentially. What kinds of problems can arise from insisting on this procedure?

Notes

1. Adapted from interviews with Lundy Fields, at General Foods in White Plains, New York, in 1988.
2. "Leaseway Buys 18.6% Holding of Its Common," *Wall Street Journal,* December 24, 1986, p. 3.
3. J. R. Weitzel, "Strategic Information Management: Targeting Information for Organizational Performance," *Information Management Review* 3, no. 1 (Summer 1987): 9–19.
4. M. T. Hehnen, S. C. Chou, H. L. Scheurman, G. J. Robinson, T. P. Luken, and D. W. Baker, "An Integrated Decision Support and Manufacturing Control System," *Interfaces* 14, no. 5 (September–October 1984), pp. 47–56.
5. H. Mintzberg, *The Nature of Managerial Work* (Englewood Cliffs, N.J.: Prentice-Hall, 1973), 82.
6. G. B. Davis and M. H. Olson, *Management Information Systems,* 2nd ed. (New York: McGraw-Hill, 1985), p. 135.
7. J. A. Senn, *Information Systems in Management,* 2nd ed. (Belmont, Calif.: Wadsworth, 1982), p. 215.
8. R. H. Sprague and B. C. McNurlin, eds., *Information Systems Management in Practice* (Englewood Cliffs, N.J.: Prentice-Hall, 1986), p. 53.
9. Senn, pp. 296, 303.
10. Senn, p. 303.
11. R. H. Sprague and E. D. Carlson, *Building Effective Decision Support Systems* (Englewood Cliffs, N.J.: Prentice-Hall, 1982).
12. R. H. Sprague, Jr., "A Framework for the Development of Decision Support Systems," *MIS Quarterly* 4, no. 4 (June 1980): 1–26.
13. J. F. Rockart and M. E. Treacy, "The CEO Goes On-Line," *Harvard Business Review* 16, no. 1 (January–February 1982): 82–88.
14. R. L. Sauder and W. M. Westerman, "Computer-Aided Train Dispatching: Decision Support through Optimization," *Interfaces* 13, no. 6 (December 1983), pp. 22–29.
15. R. O. Duda and E. H. Shortliffe, "Expert Systems Research," *Science* 220, no. 4594 (April 1983): 261–268.
16. J. S. Brown, "The Low Road, the Middle Road, and the High Road," in P. H. Winston, and K. A. Prendergast, eds. *The AI Business: The Commercial Uses of Artificial Intelligence* (Cambridge, Mass.: MIT Press, 1984), p. 82.
17. P. Harmon and D. King, *Expert Systems: Artificial Intelligence in Business* (New York: Wiley, 1985).
18. P. G. W. Keen, "Decision Support Systems: A Research Perspective," in J. F. Rockart and C. V. Bul-

len, eds. *The Rise of Managerial Computing* (Homewood, Ill.: Dow Jones–Irwin, 1986), Chapter 2, 47–52.

19. F. L. Luconi, T. W. Malone, and M. S. Scott Morton, "Expert Systems and Expert Support Systems: The Next Challenge for Management," *Sloan Management Review* 27, no. 4 (Summer 1986): 63–67.

20. F. Mann and L. Williams, "Observations on the Dynamics of the Change to Electronic Data Processing Equipment," *Administrative Science Quarterly* 5 (1960): 217–256.

21. Davis and Olson, *Management Information Systems*, p. 575.

22. Davis and Olson, pp. 430–431.

Cohesion Incident 20-1
Arrival of the Computer

As Charles arrives at the motel one afternoon, he sees a note on his desk asking him to stop by Roger's office. As he enters Roger's office, he has to walk around a large box that is sitting on the floor.

"Charles, what you see is our new computer terminal. I had heard at our last annual meeting that we had hired a group of IMS consultants to plan and implement a management information system for our motels. I thought the box was big until I saw this user's manual that goes with it! Just look at this thing. It must be 150 pages thick. They sent me two copies, so I guess this other copy is for you."

Looking through the manual, Charles sees examples of the various reports that the system will generate and information on how to input the data it will need. There is also a section on instructions for running the various reports.

Roger continues, "I suppose we can use some of the information off this terminal. I know it will help us store our budget information, and we will also be able to generate our income statement and our statement showing actual expenses versus budgeted expenses much more quickly each month. As you know, it's usually toward the end of the next month when we get all the information regarding the prior month. According to this manual, we'll have that information about four days after the end of the month. That will really help us set up controls on a more timely basis for those areas that need it.

"But some of these other reports I just don't know about. Look on page 57. There's a copy of a report that will show room occupancy rate for every room at the end of each month. Why do I need to know the occupancy rate of room 236 or room 309? That seems like a waste of money. Looking on page 61, you'll see another report showing how many guests were registered by each clerk. It makes no difference to me whether David or Earl registers more guests. They don't have any control over the time of day people stop in to register. Now a report that I could *really* use would be one showing a breakdown of our guests as vacation guests or business guests. The information is on the card that they fill out when they register. Each month, I go through those cards one by one to see what type of customer we are attracting and the trend involved. That really helps me in my advertising plan. But do we have a report like that from our computer? No!"

A few days later, the terminal is installed. At the end of the first month of operations with the computer in place, Roger and Charles produce their first computerized income statement and statement of actual versus budgeted expenses. Although they feel sure that they have followed all the instructions correctly, the statements are obviously wrong. Occupancy rate is shown to be 145 percent, clearly in error, and all actual expenses have been entered with no decimals. The total utilities expense, for example, is shown as $398,234 instead of the correct

$3,982.34. The budgeted items are correct, but all those were even dollar amounts. The income statement was also incorrect; again, all decimals had been omitted.

"Charles, I sure am glad we've got this computer," Roger sarcastically comments. "In just one month, our occupancy rate is up to 145 percent and our net income is about 100 times as great as what we've been experiencing. Oh well, at least I still know how to push a pencil."

Discussion Questions

1. What is an IMS and is it needed in this situation?

2. Explain how some steps that could have been followed in the design of the IMS system might have prevented some of the problems Roger has.

3. It has been said that the application for which it is intended should drive the technology of IMS, not the reverse. Is the application driving the technology at Journey's End?

Cohesion Incident 20-2
Designing an Information System

Eileen Thompkins, Leslie's boss, called her into her office late Thursday afternoon to talk. "Leslie," she said excitedly, "I've been thinking. Essentially, our department [market research] exists to create, interpret, and use information. We examine markets, ask questions, and do background research. Then we consolidate this information to answer questions posed by various marketing, product, and area managers. It has occurred to me that we continually respond to requests for this type of information as though we were firefighters—one survey here, another there, and all seem to start from scratch each time. If we could manage our department as an information source, rather than simply managing the day-to-day mechanics of doing market research, I think our department could become significantly more valuable to Travis Corporation as well as more efficient."

Sensing Leslie's increased interest, Thompkins elaborated. "We could keep every survey and piece of research in the computer. We could add key data about each survey or project: for whom it was done, type of product, time involved, customer characteristics, product characteristics, cost, region, unexpected findings, and so on. This information could be used to supplement future studies, to report how much our department is used by other parts of the company, to encourage longitudinal studies to monitor changes over time, and sometimes to answer questions with data collected already rather than having to do another study."

Leslie then interrupted. "Basically, you're suggesting that we structure all the data and information generated by what we as a department do into some sort of fully integrated data base? To structure such a data base would mean that common types of data—data on basic characteristics of the markets or customers being studied—would have to be gathered each time we did a research project so that we could cross-reference multiple research projects using such basic characteristics as location, age, and income of our customers."

Virtually jumping out of her chair, Thompkins shouted, "Yes, yes! Can you imagine giving Sandy Murrah in heavy equipment sales a printout summarizing the different preferences for Travis's product pricing or service characteristics between male and female purchasing agents in the United States and Canada? Why, we could even. . . ."

But Leslie interrupted again. "Eileen, you'd better slow down; that may be too specific! Anyway, I see where you are headed and I think the idea has merit."

Feeling encouraged by Leslie's comment, Thompkins concluded the meeting by saying, "Leslie, I want you to assume the responsibility for investigating and shaping this idea. Take one week to jot down a plan for how we might proceed. Talk with me about it—say next Thursday? And keep in mind that I would like to have the whole thing in final form to take to next year's corporate planning kickoff retreat that starts in three months."

Discussion Questions

1. Assume you are Leslie's information management consultant. Advise her about what to include in her preliminary plan.

2. What types of information systems would be needed to realize Eileen Thompkins's vision?

3. What key problems would you expect Leslie to encounter as she tries to design this information system?

Management Development Exercise 20
A Checklist for Software Purchases

One of the critical information management assignments you will face early in your management career is the need to purchase computer software that supports the information management needs of your work group or department. Experienced managers report that shopping for software that *specifically* meets their needs is one of their most challenging assignments. This self-test provides you with a checklist recommended by the Information Center Institute to guide managers in this difficult assignment. Your instructor will give you specific instructions on how to use it in this course and you would be well-advised to save it for your future use on the job.

There is no comparison shopping for software. As most vendors are happy to point out, software programs are unique. Unfortunately for those who want a simple selection process, they are right. Comparing software packages (even comparing those ostensibly designed to perform the same function) is a lot like comparing apples and oranges. On the other hand, your needs are unique as well, and knowing what they are will narrow down your market choices considerably. The only workable strategy for software purchases is to assess the market in terms of your own organization's needs. The following checklist was prepared by the Information Center Institute. Use it as a way of walking through your organization's needs and systematically assessing your requirements before you begin evaluating the tools that are available.

No. Item	Yes	No	N/A	Comments
Equipment Requirements				
1. Has the vendor verified that your present computer configuration is minimal or better?	___	___	___	_____
2. Has the vendor verified that your release of the operating system is correct for the application?	___	___	___	_____

Programming Language Used

3. Is the program written in a standard version of a higher-level language with which your systems programmers are familiar?   ___ ___ ___ _____

4. If the source language is unavailable in the contract, are there sufficient assurances that vendor personnel will be available to make modifications and extensions during its expected life?   ___ ___ ___ _____

5. Has the vendor made clear what the costs will be for any necessary modifications and extensions?   ___ ___ ___ _____

Generality

6. Is the package flexible and driven by parameter tables, such as screens?   ___ ___ ___ _____

7. Can the package handle a change in your organizational structure without extensive modifications?   ___ ___ ___ _____

8. Can the package handle future requirements that have been foreseen by your system analysis?   ___ ___ ___ _____

Input/Output, Control, and Efficiency

9. Do system files readily interface with other existing systems you are using?   ___ ___ ___ _____

10. Are there satisfactory data element codes and sufficient space for expansion?   ___ ___ ___ _____

11. Are there adequate controls built into the system?   ___ ___ ___ _____

12. Are there sufficient, documented error messages or error codes?   ___ ___ ___ _____

13. Are the CRT screens clear, effective, and user-friendly?   ___ ___ ___ _____

14. Are all the reports produced that were determined to be required in the system analysis?   ___ ___ ___ _____

15. Are sufficient options available with each output report?   ___ ___ ___ _____

16. Are adequate edit reports produced for both the control personnel and the users?   ___ ___ ___ _____

17. Are the available output reports sufficiently flexible to handle the needs of different groups?   ___ ___ ___ _____

Modifiability

18. Does the package appear to be designed to be readily modifiable and expandable in the future?   ___ ___ ___ _____

19. Has the vendor discussed future extensions and modifications?   ___ ___ ___ _____

Expandability

20. Has there been an analysis of the largest possible files expected in the use of the package? ___ ___ ___ _____
21. Does the package appear to be realistically expandable without too much difficulty? ___ ___ ___ _____

Package Installation Experience

22. Has the package been proven in commercial operation for at least a year? ___ ___ ___ _____
23. Does the vendor readily supply a list of users of the package who are willing to talk about their experiences with it? ___ ___ ___ _____
24. How do the other users compare the package with competitive packages? ___ ___ ___ _____

Pricing

25. Is the combination of the base price, plus modifications, plus extra charges for features on an optional basis, likely to remain within budget limitations? ___ ___ ___ _____
26. Are all the details of purchase, additional features, documentation, training, installation, and future support spelled out in the contract price statement? ___ ___ ___ _____

Processing Rates

27. Has it been estimated how long it will take the package to process the programs that are needed? ___ ___ ___ _____
28. Have present users of the package been contacted as to their experience with processing rates? ___ ___ ___ _____
29. Does the vendor claim any specific response time under defined conditions? ___ ___ ___ _____

Documentation Quality

30. Does the documentation appear to be satisfactory and done in a professional manner? ___ ___ ___ _____
31. Does the documentation sufficiently describe the data input, operations, report output, and audit controls? ___ ___ ___ _____

Estimated Package Life

32. Does the useful life appear to be five years if an application package, or up to thirty months if a system software package?   ___ ___ ___ _____
33. Is the package close to the mid-point of its life cycle for the vendor and not approaching the end?   ___ ___ ___ _____
34. If the package is several years old, will the vendor affirm that it will be enhanced in the near future to extend its useful life?   ___ ___ ___ _____

Contract Terms

35. Does the contract clearly state what is provided relative to the programs, documentation, maintenance, and support?   ___ ___ ___ _____
36. Is the contract consistent with the representation of the software package made by the supplier?   ___ ___ ___ _____

Source: Information Center Institute, "Checklist for Software Purchases," 1986.

Special Perspectives on Management

Two strikingly different yet powerful and pervasive forces are dramatically altering the bases of competition for firms worldwide. They are the forces of innovation-based entrepreneurship and international management. In this final section of the book, we will explore in depth the nature of these two competitive challenges; we will see how they constitute important, legitimate, and potent perspectives for organizational managers; and we will discuss ways by which you can best prepare yourself as a manager to benefit from the managerial opportunities that each perspective offers.

In Chapter 21, the importance of entrepreneurship and innovation to the American economy is described. The chapter explains the entrepreneurial process as it affects both new ventures and established firms. Finally, it describes the competencies and characteristics that are exhibited by successful entrepreneurs.

International management is the unifying theme of Chapter 22. The importance of an international orientation for managers is discussed, basic types of international activity are investigated, and organizational strategies are evaluated for use in the global marketplace.

21

Entrepreneurship and Innovation

Learning Objectives

Your study of this chapter will enable you to do the following:

1. Define the term *entrepreneurship* and explain why entrepreneurship is important in our economy.
2. Identify five key elements in the new-venture development process.
3. Cite the special competencies and characteristics that successful entrepreneurs exhibit.
4. Explain the key elements of a new-venture business plan.
5. Define the term *intrapreneurship,* and list at least five factors that facilitate it in large organizations.

Entrepreneurship Personified

Take creative genius, business acumen, entrepreneurial talent, and an accompanying fretfulness with the slow-grinding wheels of bureaucracy. Add flair, a touch of exhibitionism, and old-fashioned patriotism seasoned with an old-boy, down-home persona. Bake in the Texas heat, and out pops Ross Perot, fifty-seven, the founder of Electronic Data Systems (EDS), a company that had revenues in 1987 of around $4.4 billion—and that now, perversely enough, belongs to the biggest, most bureaucratic company in America.

The son of a Texas cotton broker at whose knee he says he learned his first business principle (treat the customer right), Perot started to work at the age of seven, making an honest buck breaking horses at $1 each. He acquired the habit of square dealing from his father and an appreciation of charity's blessings from his mother. President of his senior class at the U.S. Naval Academy, Perot disliked the Navy's seniority system, and left to work for IBM in 1957. Five years later he quit to found EDS with $1,000 in savings. He was unable to sell stock in the shaky-looking venture, but that early blow to a salesman's pride had its salve: Perot had to keep all the stock himself, which goes a long way toward explaining his present worth of around $2.5 billion.

Ross Perot stands among several Electronic Data Systems computers similar to those used in thousands of customer installations worldwide. Perot's achievements in building the multi-billion dollar EDS have made him one of today's best-known entrepreneurs. (Louie Psihoyos/Contact Press Images/Woodfin Camp & Associates)

EDS's rapid growth came from its skill at designing large computer systems for government agencies, including the Social Security Administration and the Department of Defense. In 1984, Perot sold out to General Motors, which wanted EDS primarily for its ability to integrate diverse computer systems. Perot accepted a chunk of stock in partial payment, and took his place on GM's board. The Dallas-Detroit marriage was stormy and short-lived. In 1987, Perot sold his GM shares back to the company for $700 million—about twice their 1984 value—and blazed away at his former partner. Among his more barbed thrusts, "Anyone who needs a chauffeur to drive him to work is probably too old to be on the payroll." Harking back to that old paternal lesson, Perot says that GM must learn again that "the customer is king!" Apparently trying to make a point about the importance of entrepreneurship in large companies, Perot offered to buy back his former company, EDS, for more than GM paid for it. GM refused, and Perot is now backing numerous start-ups, including a new computer company called Next, headed by Apple co-founder Steven Jobs.[1]

Introduction

What Is Entrepreneurship?

Ross Perot is a classic example of the manager as an entrepreneur. First, he had the creative vision and the managerial capability to start a new business venture—EDS. He had the insight to recognize a solid market need and the management ability to pull financial and human resources together into a business that was soon able to meet that rapidly growing need. Second, he shepherded EDS from a successful start-up venture to a major business enterprise. And after selling that venture to GM, he quickly became a major entrepreneurial force within one of the largest corporations in the world to reshape it into a more successful, innovative company. Combining his creative and managerial talents and skills, Ross Perot has spent a working lifetime practicing *entrepreneurship.*

Entrepreneurship is the process of bringing together creative and innovative ideas and actions with the management and organizational skills necessary to mobilize the appropriate people, money, and operating resources to meet an identifiable need and create wealth in the process. Whether the process is undertaken by a single individual or a team of individuals, there is mounting evidence that growth-minded entrepreneurs possess not only a creative and innovative flair but also solid management skills and business know-how.[2] Figure 21-1 helps illustrate the fundamental skills associated with entrepreneurship and compares them with those applied by inventors, promoters, and administrators.

Inventors are noted for their creative and innovative abilities. But their innovations seldom become commercial or organizational realities because many inventors lack the motivation or the management and organizational skills to bring products or services to the market effectively. Promoters, in contrast, may be skilled at devising creative schemes and programs, but their initiatives are usually aimed at nothing more than a quick payoff.

Administrators develop certain strong management skills and specific business know-how. They take pride in overseeing the smooth functioning of operations *as they are.* Their administrative skills are focused on maintaining efficiency, and creative or innovative behavior may actually be counterproductive within the organizations they operate.

But the entrepreneur has that unusual combination: strength in *both* creativity and management. In a new venture, these strengths enable the entrepreneur to conceive and launch a new business as well as to make it grow and succeed. Because these strengths so rarely coexist in one individual, entrepreneurship is often found in teams of people who combine their strengths. Apple Computer was successful largely because its 21-year-old founder Steven Jobs combined his creative skills with the skills of experienced business managers.[3]

FIGURE 21-1
Who Is the
Entrepreneur?

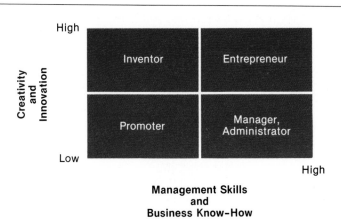

Source: From J. A. Timmons, L. E. Smollen, and A. L. M. Dingee, Jr., *New Venture Creation: A Guide to Small Business Development,* 2nd ed. (Homewood, Ill.: Richard D. Irwin, Inc., 1985), p. 144. © Jeffrey A. Timmons, Leonard E. Smollen, and Alexander L. M. Dingee, Jr., 1977.

Today entrepreneurship is enjoying a lot of attention in many sectors of our society. The best seller *Megatrends* suggested that entrepreneurship, in the form of self-employment, will be one of the ten most important trends to shape the future of American society.[4] *In Search of Excellence* and its sequel, *A Passion for Excellence,* both best sellers, extol entrepreneurship as the key to revitalizing corporate America.[5] Politicians tout the importance of entrepreneurship in creating jobs, overcoming discrimination, and sustaining a healthy economy. Business schools across the country are adding courses in entrepreneurship. All students of management should appreciate the role of entrepreneurship in our economy.

This chapter offers an overview of entrepreneurship in the United States and of entrepreneurs in new ventures, small businesses, and corporations. Specifically, the chapter examines three types of new ventures, timing considerations in pursuing new ventures, characteristics of successful entrepreneurs, and the nature of a new-venture business plan. Intrapreneurship, the practice of entrepreneurship and innovation in large companies, is examined in the last part of the chapter, with an emphasis on how to make it work.

The Role of Entrepreneurship in Our Economy

A study by Karl Vesper found that every year the number of new firms incorporated in the United States is approximately 600,000, and another 400,000 unincorporated start-ups are also estimated to take place each year.[6] Figure 21-2 illustrates the flow of these firms into our economy. As it shows, the majority of these start-ups survive as small businesses. A few grow into medium-sized or large businesses. Others fail or are discontinued within five years.

There are approximately 15 million businesses in the United States, a figure that includes part-time self-employed persons, farms, and franchises. Virtually 99 percent of these 15 million firms are small firms with fewer than 100 employees.

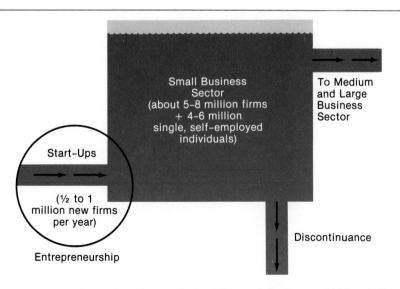

FIGURE 21-2
Entrepreneurship and
the U.S. Economy

Small Business
Sector
(about 5–8 million firms
+ 4–6 million
single, self-employed
individuals)

To Medium
and Large
Business
Sector

Start-Ups

(½ to 1
million new firms
per year)

Discontinuance

Entrepreneurship

Source: K. H. Vesper, *Entrepreneurship and National Policy* (Chicago: Heller Institute, 1983), p. 2. Copyright © Walter E. Heller, International Corporation. Sponsored by the Graduate School of Industrial Administration, Carnegie Mellon University.

So by their sheer numbers, start-ups and small businesses are a vital part of our economy. It is estimated that these firms employ 58 percent of the nation's work force and produce over half of all goods and services sold by the private sector. They also serve essential supplier and distribution roles for the relatively few large firms that comprise the remainder of our economy.

Job Creation

One of the most vital roles played by new-venture entrepreneurship is the creation of new jobs in our economy. One study showed that companies with fewer than twenty employees created 66 percent of *all* new jobs in the nation and 99 percent of all new jobs in the New England area during the last decade. As the researcher concluded, "It appears that the smaller corporations . . . are aggressively seeking new opportunities, while the larger ones are primarily redistributing their operations."[7]

The results of a study similar to Karl Vesper's are given in Figure 21-3a, which suggests the impressive potential of new-venture entrepreneurship to create jobs. Also shown, in Figure 21-3b, are the results of a U.S. Department of Commerce study that found that small, young, high-technology businesses create new jobs at a very high rate.

Innovation

Another achievement attributed to new-venture entrepreneurship is fostering innovation and the commercialization of new technologies. Two recent studies suggest that major inventions or innovations are more likely to derive from individuals or small companies than from large companies.[8] Recent examples include the personal computer, instant photography, Federal Express, Wendy's, Nike shoes, the game of Trivial Pursuit, and lasers.

Productivity and Economic Efficiency

Entrepreneurial start-ups have to be efficient and productive to prevail. They must overcome the advantages that their competitors enjoy: established facilities, brand names, and ongoing business relationships. In so doing, they often create better convenience or quality at lower prices for their buyers. Compaq computers, for example, managed to break into the booming microcomputer industry, but only after offering a high-quality computer that outperformed current products and was also portable.

Start-up firms often spur other companies to better performance, efficiency, and pricing through competition. Federal Express's entry into mail services influenced the availability and price of express mail services through the U.S. Postal Service. MCI's challenge to AT&T in long-distance telephone services resulted in expanded options and lower prices for both business and individual consumers.

Members of Minority Groups and Women in Business

Entrepreneurship has offered members of minority groups and women a way to enter the economic mainstream in recent years. The number of businesses owned by women has increased 9.4 percent a year since 1977—well above the annual 4.3 percent increase in businesses owned by men. And the annual growth rate in

FIGURE 21-3
Entrepreneurship and
Job Creation

(a) Job Creation in Selected Entrepreneurial Ventures

Individual Ventures	Year Founded	Number of Jobs Generated	Source of Information
Wendy's	1969	100,000	*Venture,* 5/82, p. 38
Hospital Corporation of America	1968	75,000	*Venture,* 5/82, p. 38
Chart House (Burger King)	1963	16,000	*Venture,* 5/82, p. 38
Godfather Pizza	1973	14,000	*Inc.,* 12/81, p. 41
Data General	1968	14,000	*Venture,* 5/82, p. 38
Federal Express	1971	11,000	*Venture,* 5/82, p. 38
Advanced Micro Devices	1969	10,000	*Venture,* 5/82, p. 38
Gap Stores	1969	7,800	*Venture,* 5/82, p. 38
Pizza Time Theaters	1977	7,000	*Venture,* 5/82, p. 38
Golden Corral Restaurants	1973	5,300	*Inc.,* 12/81, p. 41
Rolm	1960	5,000	*Venture,* 5/82, p. 38
Apple Computer	1974	4,000	*Venture,* 5/82, p. 38
Tandem Computer	1974	3,200	*Venture,* 5/82, p. 38

Source: Adapted from K. H. Vesper, *Entrepreneurship and National Policy* (Chicago: Heller Institute, 1983), p. 16.

(b) Job Creation Potential in Technology-based Firms

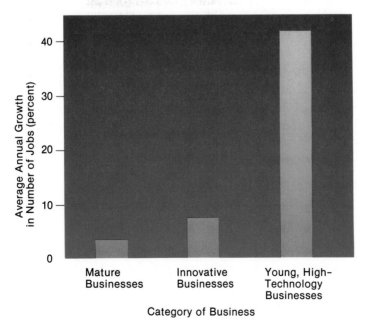

Source: U.S. Department of Commerce, *Recommendations for Creating Jobs Through the Success of Small, Innovative Businesses* (Washington, D.C.: U.S. Government Printing Office, March 1980), p. 88.

sales receipts of businesses owned by women was almost three times that of businesses owned by men in the same period of time. Minority self-employment has increased by 64 percent since 1975, compared to less than half that amount of growth in white and overall self-employment.[9]

In sum, entrepreneurs strongly affect our economy:

> Entrepreneurs introduce competition, which spurs productivity and efficiency. Some "established" businesses that prosper tend to become complacent and less dynamic, competitive, and risk-taking. Entrepreneurs are just the opposite. They increase competition, challenging the existing firms. They seek niches where there are unsatisfied needs in the marketplace, transfer technology, create new ideas and implement them, induce investment and with it new jobs. Entrepreneurs provide an important public service. They increase choices for the consumer and generate employment not only for "ordinary" workers, but also for the less formally trained, less conforming and less typical potential employees, including minorities, first-time job seekers, the old and the handicapped.[10]

New Ventures and Small, Growth-Oriented Businesses

A poll conducted by *USA Today* found the desire to be "an entrepreneur" or "president of my own company" a personal objective of over 55 percent of a nationwide group of working men and women.[11] A survey of business school programs suggests that the desire to be an independent entrepreneur is widespread among today's college students.[12] Entrepreneurs need to know how to start a business and must understand the key determinants of the success of such an undertaking.

"In Practice 21-1" offers an example of one individual's successful founding and development of a new venture.

An Opportunity versus an Idea

The most frequent cause for the failure of new ventures, as reported by Dun & Bradstreet in its yearly *Failure Record,* is lack of sales; the second most frequent cause is competitive weakness. Both causes of failure stem from a lack of appreciation of the necessity for a *marketing orientation* as the basis of any new venture. These causes suggest that new businesses are built around ideas rather than distinct needs or "opportunities" in a specific market. Hundreds of aspiring entrepreneurs have attempted to start data processing companies by purchasing a computer and offering to serve the payroll or billing needs of organizational customers. Unfortunately, their focus has typically been on gearing up to offer their service rather than identifying and examining a customer base that needs it. Ross Perot was the exception. He spent years selling large computers to large organizations and learned firsthand the difficulties they had in using them. He then designed his company around meeting their need for someone to run their computer operations—and saw his data processing company reach over $2.5 billion in annual sales.

All too frequently, entrepreneurs conceive an idea for a product or service and immediately become enamored of it. They invest time, money, and energy in developing the idea into a commercial reality. And, tragically, they make only a

In Practice 21-1

SPOKESWOMAN

There was nothing astonishing about the idea. In 1985, Georgena Terry, then a 34-year-old M.B.A. whose career path might charitably be described as eclectic, decided to start building bicycles.

After Wharton Terry had joined PPG Industries, Inc., as a financial analyst "like I was supposed to. But I hated it. All I did was push numbers around." So she moved to Merrill Lynch as a stockbroker. That was "boring." Worried that she would never find a job she liked, Terry took an aptitude test that showed she would make a terrific engineer. Two years later, she had a science degree from Carnegie-Mellon University and a job at Xerox Corporation in Rochester, New York. Two years after that, she was miserable again.

"I finally understood I don't like working for other people," says Terry. "I like to be in control. I hate flying because someone else is the pilot. On dates, I like to bring my own car."

So she simply stopped working for other people. "I headed off to my basement with my blowtorch and started making bicycle frames." She spent a lot of time trying to find a comfortable riding position. "The standard bicycle—even a woman's bike—is designed for a man. To fit women, who have relatively longer legs and shorter torsos, bike shops shove the seat forward and tilt the handlebars back." That did not help the five-foot-two, ninety-eight-pound Terry. She began wondering whether shortening the frame would improve comfort. So she went down to her basement with a blowtorch.

To her credit, she then moved deliberately. Her major innovation was the frame, so she concentrated on that and did not set out to reinvent the (bicycle) wheel or change anything else.

Her marketing plan was equally careful. As word spread, people would call up and ask to buy a bike. "We were thrilled, but we always asked the name of their local bicycle shop. We'd then call the shop and say, 'Congratulations, you just sold a Terry bike.'" Retailers, who found themselves making a quick couple of hundred dollars just for answering the phone, usually were intrigued enough to ask for one or two more bikes, and that is how Terry put together a dealer network.

With virtually no money for advertising—indeed, her entire operation is capitalized at $600,000 (half bank loans, half from private investors)—Terry concentrated on promotion. She hired a Manhattan public relations agency that was quick to position her as a female David taking on bicycling's Goliaths.

The approach paid off. The bicycle press discovered Terry. "This is a high-performance machine for serious training, racing and long-distance fitness rides," said *Bicycling* magazine.

But even as the marketing plan got her up and pedaling, Terry was moving to forestall competition. Recognizing that the high price would scare off many customers, she almost immediately started to segment. Terry now sells two models made in her East Rochester plant that retail at $910 and $1,560. To preempt the foreign competition that she knew would come, she signed two Asian companies to build a version of her bike that retails for $570 and approved a licensing deal that will retail a yet-more-basic version of her bicycle for $319.

At some point, Terry may have to think about selling out or joining forces with a bigger company to survive. But that is still a way off. For now, "this is wonderful."

minimal investment in identifying the customers, the customers' needs, and their willingness to buy the product or service as an answer to those needs. Such entrepreneurs are focused inward, perhaps satisfying their own personal ego needs. The result is often a product or service that few customers will buy.

The more successful approach is to assume a marketing orientation and look outward at a target market to identify the presence of a specific need. Here the entrepreneur is focused on potential customers and on seeking to understand a customer need. The entrepreneur seeks to confirm an opportunity defined by what the customer wants and is willing to pay for. The design of the product or service idea comes *in response to this opportunity,* rather than the other way around.

In the late 1970s, Adam Osborne conceived of the idea of building an inexpensive, portable computer that business people could easily carry and use. He focused on building an inexpensive device with simple software so that it would, from his point of view, be a good deal. Shortly thereafter, Osborne Computer Company was born in New York and was soon selling its new portable computer. But by 1982, just three years after starting up, Osborne Computer Company was bankrupt. In 1981 three entrepreneurs in Houston, Texas, introduced a portable computer that met what they believed to be a significant need among computer users at that time. It was fully IBM-compatible, ran most popular business software, contained advanced microchip technology for instant command processing, could be assembled or disassembled readily for both home and office use, and was to be sold through conventional retail and wholesale computer outlets at premium prices. Their Compaq Computer Company brought in revenues of $100 million in its first full year. Compaq joined the *Fortune* 500 by 1985, following the most rapid growth in the history of American business. Compaq took a marketing orientation and focused on an opportunity; Osborne Computer Company took a product orientation and focused almost exclusively on an idea.[13]

Where do new-venture entrepreneurs derive their visions of profitable opportunities? Karl Vesper has identified eight sources of new-venture opportunities.[14]

1. *Invitation as a source of venture opportunities.* Visions of profitable opportunities may come from someone wanting a collaborator. For example, a young man skilled in light manufacturing was approached by a delegation of creditors of a failing business. They offered him a salary to take over the company, but after checking out the company, the young man decided the firm was too far gone. Instead, he recommended forming a new firm to buy the assets and start over. Generating opportunities from this source usually requires cultivating contacts who might make such an invitation and performing in such a way that one is seen as an attractive potential partner.

2. *Venture opportunities conceived or derived from prior employment.* Many venture opportunities come in some way from former jobs held by entrepreneurs. Ross Perot developed his vision of the opportunity that became EDS while working as an IBM salesperson. Steven Jobs created the Apple personal computer while an employee of Hewlett-Packard and decided to pursue what he saw as a profitable opportunity after Hewlett-Packard declined interest in his creation. Mary Kay Ash was involved with the sale of Avon products before she started Mary Kay Cosmetics. All of these entrepreneurs applied knowledge and experience gained during prior employment to their creation of new ventures.

3. *Obtaining rights to profitable opportunities.* Ray Kroc was a restaurant equipment salesman when he called on the McDonald brothers in their busy hamburger restaurant in southern California. Amazed at the efficiency of their operation, he entered into an agreement to sell their name and restaurant procedures to other hamburger restaurants across the country. Two years later he bought them out for $6 million and continued to develop McDonald's restaurants worldwide. Ray Kroc had created the most successful restaurant business in the world by obtaining the rights to what he viewed as a profitable opportunity.

Franchising has become a popular way for aspiring entrepreneurs to initiate a venture. Franchising is simply obtaining the rights to an opportunity—often a proven business concept—and it has become an increasingly common way to enter various service or retail businesses.

4. *Venture opportunities arising from hobbies.* Occasionally, venture opportunities arise out of hobby activities. Pete Siebert learned to ski as a soldier in World War II. He continued to enjoy skiing as a hobby, particularly cross-country skiing, once he returned to Colorado. His cross-country skiing brought him in contact with a farmer who owned more than 2,000 acres in the Rocky Mountains outside Vail, Colorado. Siebert thought some of the farmer's terrain looked ideal for downhill skiing and, after buying an option on the land, started to develop what has become one of the most popular ski resorts in North America: Vail and Beaver Creek. Pete Siebert's hobby and his enthusiasm for it were central ingredients in the development of his entrepreneurial venture.

5. *Venture opportunities from social encounters.* Connections valuable to the new venture most often grow out of work relationships, but they can also come about socially. The genesis of the nationwide Jiffy Lube chain was attributed to a social occasion. Its eventual founder listened to a discussion between one friend who had experienced major difficulties getting routine service on her automobile and a second friend who, as an owner of several gasoline service stations, was describing the headaches involved in providing such low-margin service. Jiffy Lube solved these problems by providing only these low-margin services. It streamlined the process, made it more profitable, and made it quicker.

   The crude design of what became the Compaq portable computer was drawn on a paper napkin during a lunch that turned into a brainstorming session for three business friends who eventually founded the Compaq Computer Company.

6. *Pedestrian observations.* Occasionally, the idea for a successful new product or service derives simply from direct observation of a need in daily living. Again, as with opportunities that spring from social encounters, it is necessary that entrepreneurs first be alert to specific needs and then have the initiative to do something about them. Lewis Salton's wife asked him to give her something to keep food hot at the table. An RCA engineer, Salton solved this problem by designing an electrically heated tray on which to place serving dishes. This solution served as the basis for a manufacturing company that grew to a steady volume of $10 million per year.

7. *Self-employment as an idea source.* Persons currently engaged in self-employment are often more sensitive than others to new, profitable opportunities. R. David Thomas, a Columbus, Ohio, Kentucky Fried Chicken franchisee, felt he perceived a need for a fast-service restaurant providing fresh hamburger meals to adults on a tight schedule. That vision became Wendy's. Elmer Winter and Aaron Scheinfeld, self-employed attorneys, repeatedly had difficulty finding temporary typists. They first hired extra typists and farmed them out, as needed, for a fee. Then they formed Manpower, Inc., to oversee that function. That company now produces over $500 million in revenue in fifty-two countries.

8. *Deliberate search.* An increasing preference among aspiring entrepreneurs seeking new-venture opportunities is to engage in a deliberate search for venture ideas. Several sources available to aid in such searches are provided in the following Guidelines for Management Practice.

Guidelines for Management Practice

Potential entrepreneurs are often stymied by an inability to conceive of a solid venture idea. This is particularly true among nontechnical people. The aspiring entrepreneur should consider using the following sources for new-venture opportunities.[15]

1. A good way to generate ideas for profitable venture opportunities is to examine *product licensing opportunities* available from universities, corporations, and independent investors. Several computerized data sources provide this information for a fee. Examples include

   - American Bulletin of International Technology Transfer
     554 Wilshire Blvd.
     Los Angeles, Calif. 90036

   - Technology Mart
     Thomas Publishing Co.
     250 West 34th St.
     New York, N.Y. 10001

   - Government Inventions Available for Licensing
     National Technical Information Service
     U.S. Department of Commerce
     P.O. Box 1533
     Springfield, Va. 22151

   - International New Product Newsletter
     Box 191
     Back Bay Annex
     Boston, Mass. 02116

2. *Patent brokers* specialize in marketing patents owned by individuals, corporations, universities, or other organizations. Selected brokers include

   - University Patents
     875 N. Michigan Avenue
     Chicago, Ill. 60611

   - National Patent Development Corp.
     375 Park Ave.
     New York, N.Y. 10022

   - New Product Development Services, Inc.
     P.O. Box 8424
     900 State Line Rd.
     Kansas City, Mo. 64114

   Product and patent licensing opportunities are also available from many universities, major corporations, and not-for-profit research organizations.

3. Ideas for new-venture opportunities can spring from talking with potential customers, distributors, and wholesalers and from observing competitors and others in industries or markets the observer is familiar with.

4. *Franchise* companies account for over 35 percent of all retail sales. Franchising is an excellent way for a budding entrepreneur to get into business. Sources of information on available franchising opportunities include

   - *Franchise Opportunity Handbook*
     U.S. Department of Commerce
     Superintendent of Documents
     U.S. Government Printing Office
     Washington, D.C. 20402

   - *The Franchise Annual Handbook and Directory*
     Info Press
     Lewiston, N.Y.

   - *Franchising World*
     International Franchising Association
     1015 Connecticut Ave., NW
     Washington, D.C. 20036

5. Another way to enter an existing business as a new venture is to purchase an existing business. The principal sources of these opportunities are the newspapers and business brokers (listed in the Yellow Pages) in your area. These are typically ventures with aging or financially troubled owner/managers. Local bankers may also be able to inform entrepreneurs of such opportunities from time to time.

FIGURE 21-4
Criteria for Attractive
and Unattractive
Venture Opportunities

Criterion	Attractive	Unattractive
Market Issues		
1. Customers	Identified, reachable, and enthusiastic	None yet, unfocused
2. Market size	$100M+	<$10M, unknown, or multibillion $
3. Growth rate	30–50%+	Nil, slow, <10%
4. Gross margins	40–50%+ and durable	<20% and fragile
5. Attainable market share, year 5 (estimated)	Leader, 20%+	Nil, <5%
Economics and Harvest Issues		
1. Profit after tax	>10–15%+ and durable	<5% and fragile
2. Time to break-even point	0–2 years	>2 years
3. Time to positive cash flow	0–2 years	>2 years
4. ROI potential	25%+/year	<10%/year
Competitive Advantages Issues		
1. Degree of control over prices, costs, channels of distribution	Moderate–strong	Weak
2. Cost of production, marketing, and distribution	Lowest	High
3. Response and lead time: technology, product and market innovation, and capacity	Have or can gain an edge	No edge
4. Legal, contractual	Proprietary or exclusive	None
Management Team Issues		
1. Entrepreneurial team	Proven	None, unproven

Source: J. A. Timmons, L. E. Smollen, and A. L. M. Dingee, Jr., *New Venture Creation: A Guide to Small Business Development,* 2nd ed. (Homewood, Ill.: Richard D. Irwin, Inc., 1985), p. 85. © Jeffrey A. Timmons, Leonard E. Smollen, and Alexander L. M. Dingee, Jr., 1977.

Timing to Pursue New Ventures

Once a would-be entrepreneur identifies a business opportunity, a second determinant of its ultimate success is timing. The enterprise must be timed to seize a particular market opportunity, and it must occur at the right time in the entrepreneur's own career. Perhaps the best way to evaluate when "the time is right" for a new venture is to apply the criteria listed in Figure 21-4, which have been applied by venture capitalists to evaluate venture opportunities.

It is important to recognize that these criteria are applied by investors—particularly venture capitalists—interested primarily in high-growth ventures. The criteria for smaller ventures would be less demanding in scope (a minimum $100 million market, for example) but similar in the types of concerns that should be addressed in an effort to determine whether the time for pursuing a small venture is right.[16] Let's look at each criterion individually.

1. *The venture team can clearly identify its customers and the market segments(s) it plans to capture.* Exactly who are the target customers? Who makes the buying

decision? Does the entrepreneur have evidence that these customers are enthusiastic about the product or service and will act favorably (pay in advance, for example) on that enthusiasm? Firm purchase orders or other tangible purchase commitments help confirm the timing is right. If these cannot be done, then the timing is probably not right.

2. *A minimum market as large as $100 million.* A market of this size suggests that the firm can achieve significant sales without having to attain a dominant share of its market. That in turn means the new venture can grow without attracting much competitive reaction. It is important to recognize that this threshold pertains to decisions about high-growth opportunities, not smaller, lifestyle ventures.

3. *A market growing at a rate of 30 to 50 percent.* This is another indicator that the timing is right to act on an opportunity; it means new entrants can enter the fray without evoking defensive reactions from established competitors. On the other hand, if the market is static or growing only marginally, then either the opportunity must offer a realistic chance of revolutionizing the industry—a rare occurrence indeed—or the timing is bad.

4. *High gross margins (selling price less direct, variable costs) that are durable.* When entrepreneurs can sell their product or service at gross margins in the 50+ percent range, there is an attractive cushion built in that covers the mistakes one is likely to make while developing a new enterprise. When gross margins are small, entry into this market may be premature or too late.

5. *There is no dominant competitor in the market segments representing the venture opportunity.* A market share of 40 to 60 percent usually translates into significant power over suppliers, customers, pricing, and costs. The absence of such a competitor means more room for the newcomer to maneuver, without fear of serious retaliation, upon entering the marketplace. When a dominant competitor already exists, the newcomer may be too late.

6. *A significant response time, or lead time, in terms of technologial superiority, proprietary protection, distribution, or capacity.* When a new venture possesses this type of legitimate "unfair advantage," the new firm should be able to create barriers to entry or expansion by others who are aware of the profitable opportunity. When an entrepreneur can take advantage of this sort of proprietary edge, and the edge will last, the timing is right to pursue the opportunity.

7. *An experienced entrepreneur or team capable of enthusiastically and professionally building a company to exploit the profitable opportunity.* Venture capitalists universally identify this as an essential ingredient for the timing to be right to *invest* in a proposed venture. Aspiring entrepreneurs should likewise use it as a criterion for whether it is wise to *pursue* a new-venture opportunity.

A second "timing" concern that any aspiring entrepreneur must address is at what point in his or her career entrepreneurship is an appropriate undertaking. The time for a person to pursue a new venture or an entrepreneurial career is only *after* she or he has experience that is central to the success of the business to be undertaken. Hence most successful entrepreneurs in their early twenties are involved in businesses related to sports, music, hobbies, or family businesses. That is, they spent their early lives developing an intimate appreciation for aspects of the business, its customers, or its technologies. Most other entrepreneurs are in their late twenties or older; they develop experience of a professional or technical nature before initiating a new business venture. For the successful ones, that experience is usually related to the skills required for success in the new business venture.

Successful entrepreneurs bring several characteristics and competencies to their new ventures. The next two sections examine two key competencies and fourteen frequent characteristics.

Competencies of Successful Entrepreneurs

What competencies should an entrepreneur bring to a new venture? Two basic competencies are essential to new business success.

TECHNICAL COMPETENCE

Without question, the new venture's management team should possess the knowledge and skills necessary to create the products or services the new venture will provide. So what is most critical is that the venture be capable of providing the product or service in a manner that is *needed* by the customer, *wanted* by the customer, and for which the customer is *willing to pay* an appropriate price.

A recent example in a major southeastern city serves to illustrate this point. Elmwood Avenue is a six-lane downtown road that receives substantial surburban traffic flow into and out of the city every day. A few years ago, one restauranteur opened a BoJangles fast-food (chicken and biscuits) outlet along this road. It was an instant success; cars were backed up every morning at its drive-in window. It provided a variety of biscuit-style breakfast items that commuters needed, wanted, and were willing to pay for. McDonald's and Krystal outlets soon followed on Elmwood Avenue. Next came a Sister's Chicken 'n Biscuits adjacent to the BoJangles outlet, only even closer to where commuters entered from the interstate. It failed within six months. Yet a full-service, country-style restaurant serving lunch and dinner entered the same location and had immediate success. Why? The Sister's outlet provided what was needed (lunch and dinner fast-food service) at an appropriate price but not what was wanted (full-service, country-style restaurant). The full-service restaurant that took its place provided food service that was needed *and wanted* at a price patrons traveling Elmwood Avenue were willing to pay.

BUSINESS MANAGEMENT SKILLS

The survival and growth of a technically viable new venture depend on the ability of the entrepreneur to understand and manage the economics of the business. Financial and accounting know-how in the areas of cash flow, liquidity, costs and contributions, record keeping, pricing, structuring debt, and asset acquisition are essential skills the venture management team must possess or obtain. "People management" skills, organizational skills, computer literacy, and planning skills are also critical competencies, according to a recent survey of practicing entrepreneurs attending the Harvard Business School's "Small Company" program.[17]

Technical skills and business skills are important ingredients for an entrepreneur to bring to a venture, but they are not enough. The psychological and behavioral characteristics identified in the next section are usually associated with successful entrepreneurs.

Characteristics of Successful Entrepreneurs

What are the characteristics of successful entrepreneurs? This question has long fascinated researchers, investors, and aspiring entrepreneurs. Walt Disney, Mary Kay Ash, Ted Turner, and Ross Perot are but a few entrepreneurs whose success writers in the business and popular press have tried to analyze. Figure 21-5 summarizes efforts dating back to 1848 to identify characteristics unique to entrepreneurs.

Some of the "characteristics" associated with entrepreneurship are learnable, some less so. The ten characteristics that can be learned are as follows:[18]

1. *Endless commitment and determination.* Ask any number of entrepreneurs what is the central ingredient in their success, and they will most often cite this characteristic. Entrepreneurs' level of commitment can usually be gauged by their willingness to jeopardize their personal economic well-being, invest time, tolerate a lower standard of living than they would otherwise have enjoyed, and even sacrifice extended time with their families.

2. *A strong desire to achieve.* One of the most prominent motivators driving entrepreneurs is the need to achieve. They typically are driven by a need to outperform their previous results; money becomes less a motivator and more a way to keep score—to measure their achievement.

FIGURE 21-5
Research Identifying
Key Characteristics of
Entrepreneurs

Date	Author(s)	Characteristics
1848	Mill	Risk bearing
1917	Weber	Source of formal authority
1934	Schumpeter	Innovation; initiative
1954	Sutton	Desire for responsibility
1959	Hartman	Source of formal authority
1961	McClelland	Risk taking; need for achievement
1963	Davids	Ambition; desire for independence, responsibility; self-confidence
1964	Pickle	Drive/mental; human relations; communication ability; technical knowledge
1971	Palmer	Risk measurement
1971	Hornaday and Aboud	Need for achievement; autonomy; aggression; power; recognition; innovative/independent
1973	Winter	Need for power
1974	Borland	Internal locus of control
1974	Liles	Need for achievement
1977	Gasse	Personal value orientation
1978	Timmons	Drive/self-confidence; goal-oriented; moderate risk taker; internal locus of control; creativity/innovation
1980	Sexton	Energetic/ambitious; positive setbacks
1981	Welsh and White	Need to control; responsibility seeker; self-confidence/drive; challenge taker; moderate risk taker
1982	Dunkelberg and Cooper	Growth oriented; independence oriented; craftsman oriented

Source: J. W. Carland, F. Hoy, W. R. Boulton, and J. A. C. Carland, "Differentiating Entrepreneurs from Small Business Owners: A Conceptualization," *Academy of Management Review* 9, no. 2 (1984): 356.

3. *Orientation toward opportunities and goals.* Successful entrepreneurs tend to focus on opportunities that represent unmet needs or problems crying out for solutions. They are strongly goal-oriented in pursuing identified opportunities. Most entrepreneurs can readily respond when asked what their goals are for this week, for this year, and for the next five years.

4. *Internal locus of control.* Successful entrepreneurs are very self-confident. Research has repeatedly shown that they believe *they* are capable of controlling their own destiny and the destiny of their enterprise, rather than feeling that outside forces control them and their fate. Successful entrepreneurs are also coldly realistic about their own and their partners' strengths and weaknesses and about what they can and cannot do.

5. *Tolerance for ambiguity and stress.* Start-up entrepreneurs face the need to meet payrolls with revenue that has yet to be received or even contracted for. Jobs constantly change, customers are ever new, and setbacks and surprises are inevitable. Entrepreneurs accept this as a way of life and thrive on it.

6. *Skill in taking calculated risks.* Entrepreneurs, much like airplane pilots, take calculated risks. They do everything possible to reduce or share the risk. They prepare for and anticipate problems; confirm the opportunity and what is required for success; create ways to share the risk with suppliers, customers, investors, creditors, or partners; and carefully control key roles in the execution of the firm's operations.

7. *Little need for status and power.* It is true that power and status often accrue to the successful entrepreneur, but the successful entrepreneur remains focused on opportunities, customers, the market, and the competition, rather than on any need for status or power over others.

8. *Ability to solve problems.* Successful entrepreneurs seek out problems that may affect their success and methodically go about overcoming them. They are not intimidated by difficult situations. They can be decisive, and they can be patient when a long-term perspective is appropriate.

9. *A high need for feedback.* "How are we doing?" The question is ever-present in the entrepreneur's mind. Entrepreneurs aggressively pursue feedback that will enable them to gauge their progress and effectiveness. They instinctively nurture relationships with people to learn from, which has the secondary effect of expanding their network of useful contacts and influence.

10. *The ability to deal effectively with failure.* J. Paul Getty suffered bankruptcies before building the multibillion-dollar Getty Oil Company. Thomas Monaghan had a similar track record with pizza stores before perfecting the approach that became Domino's Pizza. Entrepreneurs are not afraid of failing. They are intent on succeeding, but they accept failure and use it as a way of learning how better to manage their next undertaking.

Four additional characteristics of entrepreneurs probably are innate.[19]

11. *Boundless energy, good health, and emotional stability.* Entrepreneurs face many challenges that demand tremendous physical and emotional energy. Successful entrepreneurs place a premium on maintaining good physical and emotional health.

12. *Creativity and innovativeness.* The ability to create new ideas, new concepts, and new ways of viewing problems is at the heart of successful entrepreneur-

ship. The ability to see an opportunity instead of a problem and a solution instead of a dilemma is a fundamental skill associated with many entrepreneurs.

13. *High intelligence and conceptual ability.* "Street smarts," a special sense for business, and the ability to see the big picture as it is related to their businesses are common among entrepreneurs. Successful entrepreneurs are good strategic thinkers.

14. *Vision and the capacity to inspire.* The capacity to shape and communicate a vision in a way that inspires others is a valuable skill for the entrepreneur.

These, then, are some of the attributes that aspiring entrepreneurs should develop in themselves and should look for in assembling a new-venture team. Self-Test 21 at the end of this chapter provides an opportunity for you to examine yourself in terms of these and other characteristics associated with entrepreneurs.

One final ingredient that is usually present in successful new ventures is a business plan. The structures of new-venture business plans and their roles in new-venture success are discussed in the next section.

FIGURE 21-6
**Guide to Preparing a
Business Plan**

Table of Contents

Executive Summary

Section 1.0 The Concept

Section 2.0 Objectives

Section 3.0 Market Analysis
    3.1 General description of the entire marketplace for the product or service
    3.2 Precise description of the segment(s) to be pursued
    3.3 Description of intermediate influences on buyers, such as dealers, distributors, sales representatives, associations, etc.
    3.4 Competitive conditions—present and anticipated
    3.5 Pricing conditions—present and anticipated
    3.6 Governmental influences—present and anticipated
    3.7 History of similar products, services, or businesses
    3.8 Break-even point estimates; that is, how many units and/or how much of the market has to be sold to cover costs

Section 4.0 Production
    4.1 Equipment requirements
    4.2 Facility requirements
    4.3 Raw material, labor, and supplies requirements and sources
    4.4 Quality control, packaging, transportation, etc., requirements
    4.5 Program for initial time period
    4.6 Schedule—who is to do what, by when (exhibit)[a]
    4.7 Budget (exhibit)
    4.8 Results expected (exhibit)
    4.9 Contingency plans

Section 5.0 Marketing
    5.1 Method(s) of selling and advertising to be employed
    5.2 Product or service features and benefits to be emphasized
    5.3 Program for initial time period

The New-Venture Business Plan

A **business plan** is a blueprint for building or expanding a business. It is a written document articulating what the business opportunity is; why the opportunity exists; what strategy, actions, and resources are necessary to seize it; and why the new-venture team has what it takes to execute the plan.

Recently a student asked Carol Green, founder of Franchise Services of America and a Colorado-based venture capital fund, "Is it really necessary to prepare a full-blown business plan? They take so much time to prepare." She immediately responded, "There's no question about it. You must prepare a business plan, even—and perhaps especially—when the effort results in an idea abandoned. Every time you prepare a business plan, you become a better entrepreneur. I am certain of that!"[20]

The length of a business plan and the way it is organized vary somewhat with the complexity of the proposed venture. Figure 21-6 provides an outline of the contents of a "typical" business plan. Remember, the business plan should be a blueprint that provides a written picture of how the business will be built. And this blueprint should specify exactly why, how, and when the profitable opportunity will be accomplished.[21]

     5.4 Schedule—who is to do what, by when (exhibit)
     5.5 Budget (exhibit)
     5.6 Results expected (exhibit)
     5.7 Contingency plans

Section 6.0 Organization and People
     6.1 Who is accountable to whom, for what; organization structure (exhibit)
     6.2 Staffing program for initial time period
     6.3 Schedule (exhibit)
     6.4 Budget (exhibit)
     6.5 Results expected (for example, brief position descriptions)
     6.6 Contingency plans

Section 7.0 Funds Flow and Financial Projections
     7.1 Projected cash flows from operations; that is, total funds in and out for the initial time period (exhibit)
     7.2 Pro forma profit and loss statements (exhibit)
     7.3 Pro forma balance sheets
     7.4 Program for monitoring and controlling funds with people and systems included in the organization planning

Section 8.0 Ownership
     8.1 Summary of funding requirements
     8.2 Form of business—partnership, corporation, etc.
     8.3 Program for raising equity and/or debt money required, if any
     8.4 Projected returns to investors

Source: S. Brandt, *Entrepreneuring,* © 1982, Addison-Wesley, Publishing Co., Inc., Reading, Mass. Pages 127–128. Reprinted with permission.

Note: If technology is an important ingredient in the success of the enterprise, a separate section, Technology, should probably be included in the business plan. Such a section would include details on staffing and methods of inquiry and testing as well as schedules, budgets, results expected, and contingency plans. A section on technology would normally be inserted after Section 5.0, Marketing.

ᵃ"Exhibit" means that this part of the plan is best shown as an exhibit or table.

"Why" is normally addressed by identifying who outside the venture is interested in, and qualified to buy, what the venture will sell. This part of the plan should provide compelling evidence of the precise need that the venture's product or service will meet, it should explain why customers with that need will want what the venture has to offer to meet that need, and it should give concrete assurance that these customers will pay a price (proposed by the venture team) that results in substantial profitability for the venture.

"How" is addressed by fully outlining the human, production, organizational, and financial requirements for providing the venture's product or service in a timely manner consistent with the pricing and quality demands of the target market. Particularly important here is evidence of technical expertise and business management skills relevant to the industry in which the venture will compete. Likewise, cost projections consistent with industry norms are important. When international markets are envisioned, several sources are available to help potential exporters answer the "how" question. They are discussed in "Insights for International Managers 21."

"When" is addressed by making sure the plan describes the timing of key events in the process of building the enterprise and the flow of financial resources related to those efforts. Questions pertaining to such issues are usually answered in the section of the plan that presents financial projections over time.

The development of a business plan that effectively answers why, how, and when is neither quick nor easy. Preparing such a plan can take at least 250 hours. And squeezing that amount of time into evenings and weekends—not to mention coordinating the effort across several people—can easily take three to twelve

---

Insights for International Managers 21

HELPING THE SMALL BUSINESS TO SELL ABROAD

Government services that are quite useful to the small business aspiring to sell in foreign markets can be obtained from the United States government and foreign government-supported trade centers.

Many countries have foreign trade offices whose job it is to help importers and exporters. Some publish excellent booklets, such as "How to Approach the German Market," produced by the German Foreign Trade Information Office. The Japan External Trade Organization (JETRO) is the most impressive, providing a complete library of publications and films on Japanese business. JETRO's "Now in Japan" reports are particularly instructive. JETRO and the German FTI office have locations in New York, Los Angeles, Chicago, San Francisco, Houston, and Atlanta.

The U.S. Department of Commerce provides four helpful services. The U.S. and Foreign Commercial Service provides direct and professional counseling by trade specialist in forty-seven district offices throughout the country. They provide information on overseas opportunities, foreign markets, shipping, documentation required, financing, tax advantages, and trade exhibitions as well as advice about finding an international banker, insurance, freight forwarder, and free legal services.

A second service is the International Economic Policy service which provides counselors that specialize in particular countries to provide more specific information. And a third service is their Trade Development program providing industry-specific analysis and assistance for major export sectors. Finally, the Trade Administration office handles export licenses and provides counseling on licensing matters.

Source: From L. Copeland and L. Griggs, *Going International* (New York: Random House, 1985), pp. 260–262.

Guidelines for Management Practice

David Gumpert has helped write several business plans and has long been involved in new-venture development in his role as editor of the *Harvard Business Review*'s "Growing Concerns" section. Stan Rich has founded, funded, operated, and sold seven technology-based businesses over thirty-five years and is a co-founder of the MIT Enterprise forum. The two recently offered the following tips to young entrepreneurs seeking to develop "winning" business plans (ones that attract major investor capital).[22] Investors respond favorably, they believe, when entrepreneurs take this advice:

1. Make sure your plan includes evidence of customer acceptance of the venture's product or service.

2. Be careful to show an appreciation of investors' needs through recognition of their particular financial return goals.

3. Show clear evidence of focus through concentration on only a limited number of products or services.

4. Exploit any proprietary position, particularly those available in the form of patents, copyrights, and trademarks.

And entrepreneurs should also heed the following cautions:

1. Make sure your plan does not convey an infatuation with the product or service rather than familiarity with, and awareness of, marketplace needs.

2. Carefully avoid financial projections that are at odds with accepted industry ranges.

3. Do not use growth projections that are out of touch with reality.

4. Avoid basing the business's success on custom or applications engineering, which make substantial growth difficult.

---

months. Hence development of a document like this serves as a useful test of an aspiring entrepreneur's patience, diligence, and determination.

One of the key ways a business plan is used is to help new-venture entrepreneurs secure financial resources. Different resources essential to a new venture are examined in the next section.

Resources to Support the New Venture

CAPITAL

A vital ingredient for any business venture is the capital necessary to acquire the equipment, facilities, and people to pursue the targeted opportunity. New ventures generate their financial resources in two fundamental ways. **Debt financing** is money provided to the venture that must be repaid in some form. The obligation to repay the money is usually secured by property or equipment bought by the business. **Equity financing** is money provided to the venture that is not expected to be repaid as such. It entitles the source to some form of ownership in the venture, and the source usually expects some future return or gain on that investment.

Debt financing is generally obtained from commercial banks to finance the purchase of property or equipment or to provide working capital. Family members and friends are another common source. Still other sources include leasing companies, suppliers via extended credit terms, the loan guarantee program of the Small Business Administration (SBA), and investors in special debt instruments.

New ventures benefit from debt financing in that owners who raise capital this way (1) retain maximum ownership in their business (remember, debt does not require relinquishing some ownership, whereas equity financing does) and (2) increase the rate of return on their personal investment in the venture. At the same time, debt financing can be disastrous for new ventures because their rapid growth requires steady cash flow (to pay bills, salaries, and interest), which can cause major difficulties if interest rates rise and sales slow down. And as a practical matter, most new ventures find raising substantial debt financing difficult. As a result, gradually building a relationship with a commercial bank and thus gaining increased access to short- and long-term debt financing over time is the best route for the new-venture entrepreneur to take.

Equity financing is usually obtained from one (or more) of three basic sources: friendly sources, informal venture capitalists, and professional venture-capital groups. *Friendly sources* represent a critical source for most ventures; they are mainly personal and professional contacts of the entrepreneurs in the new venture. Such contacts might include

Family and friends

Professional advisers and business acquaintances

Past employers

Potential customers and suppliers

Selected prospective employees

Wealthy individuals who know the entrepreneurs

Informal venture capitalists, usually wealthy individual or family investors, represent a second source of equity financing. They often rely on contacts in commercial banking, trust departments, and other intermediary positions to alert them to investment opportunities.

Professional venture-capital groups are a third source of equity capital that is available primarily to new ventures with high growth potential. Unlike the previous sources, these professional venture-capital groups have very stringent criteria for their investments: They often expect five times their investment in five years!

Public stock offerings represent a fourth source of equity capital for a select group of new ventures. The number of initial public offerings (IPOs) has averaged under three hundred firms per year in the 1980s. Though highly publicized and typically effective in generating substantial capital, IPOs are made by only a very small number of firms in the United States, and they are usually firms that have earlier obtained equity financing from one of the other three sources we have described.

Regardless of the source, equity capital is money that new-venture managers can use without any "pressure" to repay it or to do so on a regular basis, as debt financing requires. So when the business is growing and needs cash faster than it can collect it (via sales revenue), that lack of pressure to repay makes equity more attractive than debt. The unattractive aspect of equity financing for some people is that it constitutes selling part of the ownership of the business and, with it, a say in the decisions directing the venture. The type of debt or equity financing available to a new venture depends on both the growth potential of the business and its stage of development.

Genentech, Inc., a pioneer in the growing field of genetic engineering, used the proceeds from its sale of stock to the public to build several facilities like this state-of-the-art gene splicing laboratory in San Francisco, California. The road from laboratory experimentation to profitable products, however, remains a difficult one at Genentech even today.

MANAGEMENT ASSISTANCE

Another key resource for many new ventures, especially lifestyle or foundation firms started by entrepreneurs with limited experience in business management, is management assistance. **Management assistance** refers to people outside the venture who help owners and managers plan, analyze, and control the present and future activities of the business and its people. Research suggests that the use of outside management assistance may play a critical role in the successful establishment of an ongoing new venture.[23]

Management assistance is available from numerous sources in the private sector. Accounting firms, management consulting firms, and independent consultants are typical sources. Venture-capital firms also serve this role in many of the firms in which they invest. Many lifestyle-oriented new ventures, however, cannot afford their assistance. Fortunately, many sources are now available at little or no cost to provide management assistance to new ventures before and after start-up. Major sources of such assistance are summarized in Figure 21-7.

The four major management assistance programs sponsored by the SBA serve to illustrate the types of assistance available. The *Service Corps of Retired Executives* (SCORE) program provides retired experts to match a particular need. For example, if an aspiring entrepreneur needed help developing a marketing plan, SCORE would pull from its list of volunteers the name of a former marketing executive who could provide counseling assistance. The *Active Corps of Executives* (ACE) provides a similar volunteer matching service, but its volunteers are active executives. The ACE program often helps developing countries. *Small Business Development Centers* (SBDCs) are typically located on college campuses and keep a regular consulting staff available to provide counseling assistance and various research services. The *Small Business Institutes* (SBI) program is likewise operated in conjunction with university business schools and provides student teams to work on planning and analysis with new-venture entrepreneurs under a professor's guidance.

In summary, starting a business is an exciting idea and a personal goal for many people. Successfully developing a new venture requires the vision of a profitable opportunity; the right timing for the opportunity and the entrepreneur; the right skills, capabilities, and characteristics among those on the entrepreneurial team; a well-thought-out business plan; and adequate capital and management resources.

Management Help Offered by	Where Available	FOR SMALL BUSINESSPERSONS			
		BEFORE THEY GO INTO A BUSINESS WHOSE TECHNOLOGY IS		AFTER THEY GO INTO A BUSINESS WHOSE TECHNOLOGY IS	
		High	Low	High	Low
U.S Small Business Administration					
Counseling by:					
Staff	N				✓
Service Corps of Retired Executives	N				✓
Active Corps of Executives	N				✓
Small Business Institutes	N			✓	✓
Small Business Development Centers	S	✓	✓	✓	✓
Prebusiness workshops	N		✓		
Nonaccredited courses and seminars	N				✓
Publications	N		✓		✓
U.S. Department of Commerce					
Seminars and workshops	N			✓	✓
Publications	N	✓	✓	✓	✓
Other federal agencies (example: IRS[a])					
Seminars and workshops	N				✓
Publications	N				✓
State, county, and local governments					
Counseling	S				✓
Seminars and workshops	S				✓
Publications	S				✓
Local development corporations and the like					
Counseling	N				✓
Seminars and workshops	N				✓

FIGURE 21-7
Sources of Help for New-Venture Development

Increasingly, large company managers have looked at the success of entrepreneurial firms and sought to reintroduce an entrepreneurial orientation into their established organizations. Understanding and encouraging entrepreneurship in large companies is a major agenda in thousands of large companies today. The ideas behind these efforts, which have been called *intrapreneurship,* are examined in the next section.

Intrapreneurship: Entrepreneurship in Large Companies

What Is Intrapreneurship?

One interesting consequence of the recent wave of new-venture entrepreneurship in the United States has been a heightened awareness of, and interest in, entre-

Management Help Offered by	Where Available	FOR SMALL BUSINESSPERSONS			
		BEFORE THEY GO INTO A BUSINESS WHOSE TECHNOLOGY IS		AFTER THEY GO INTO A BUSINESS WHOSE TECHNOLOGY IS	
		High	Low	High	Low
Universities					
Accredited courses	S	✓	✓	✓	
Nonaccredited courses and seminars	S				✓
Publications	S	✓	✓	✓	✓
Counseling	S				
Community colleges					
Accredited courses	S				✓
Nonaccredited courses and seminars	N				✓
Counseling	S				✓
Small-business groups (example: NFIB[b])					
Seminars and workshops	S				✓
Counseling	S				✓
Publications	N				✓
Large corporations (example: Bank of America)					
Publications	N		✓		✓
Counseling	S				✓
Trade associations					
Publications	N			✓	✓
Seminars and workshops	N			✓	✓

Source: N. C. Siropolis, *Small Business Management: A Guide to Entrepreneurship,* 3rd ed. Copyright © 1986 by Houghton Mifflin Company, p. 296. Used with permission.

N = Nationally   S = Some parts of nation

[a]U.S. Internal Revenue Service.

[b]National Federation of Independent Business.

preneurship among large companies. American corporations will prosper, according to one expert, only to the extent that they understand the need for, initiate, and carry out innovations at every level of the organization.[24] What is called for is a reemergence of entrepreneurship within large organizations.

Ross Perot built entrepreneurship into EDS as it began to become a large organization. He purposely encouraged experimentation, independence, and freedom of thought and action among EDS employees. He insisted that his top-management team seek out and encourage intrapreneurs, whom Perot called "eagles" to characterize them as self-sufficient, vigilant for opportunity, and endowed with the courage necessary to bring their ideas to fruition. As Gordon Pinchot puts it,

> Individuals do not have to be doing "big things" in order to have their cumulative accomplishments eventually result in big performance for the company. . . . They are only rarely the inventors of the "breakthrough" product or system. They only rarely do something that is totally unique or that no one, in any organization, ever thought of before. Instead, they are often applying ideas that have proved themselves

elsewhere, or they are rearranging parts to create a better result, or they are noting a potential problem before it turns into a catastrophe *and* mobilizing the actions to anticipate and solve it.[25]

This phenomenon has come to be called **intrapreneurship**, a phrase attributed to Gordon Pinchot, the founder of a school for intrapreneurs that serves managers from corporations the world over. Pinchot defines intrapreneurs as "any of the 'dreamers who do.' Those who take hands-on responsibility for creating innovation of any kind within an organization. The intrapreneur may be the creator or inventor but is always the dreamer who figures out how to turn an idea into a profitable reality."

Not everyone is sold on the idea that these intrapreneurs are really entrepreneurs in large corporations. As Harold Geneen, former chairman of ITT Corporation, puts it,

> Where are our corporate entrepreneurs? The answer is: There are none. By definition, an entrepreneur is in business for himself. He organizes, manages, and assumes the risk . . . bets it all, takes a big risk for a big return. . . . A corporate CEO cannot do this [because] he is cast in the role of trustee. . . . Some big companies try to act entrepreneurial in a diluted sort of way, [but] the amount of money at risk is so relatively small that the CEO's "trusteeship" is preserved.[26]

Although Geneen's points about risk and independence are well taken, the renewed interest of larger companies in "corporate entrepreneurship" is primarily a reflection of the success of smaller companies in fostering innovation. Indeed the notion of entrepreneurship in any setting is intertwined with the presence of innovative activity.

Factors Facilitating Intrapreneurship

For intrapreneurship to flourish within a large organization, Pinchot suggests that ten "freedom factors" need to be present.[27]

1. *Self-selection.* Companies should give innovators the opportunity to bring forth their ideas, rather than making the generation of new ideas the designated responsibility of a few individuals or groups.

2. *No hand-offs.* Once ideas surface, managers should allow the person generating the idea to pursue it rather than instructing him or her to turn it over (or "hand it off") to someone else.

3. *The doer decides.* Giving the originator of an idea some freedom to make decisions about its further development and implementation, rather than relying on multiple levels of approval for even the most minor decision, enhances intrapreneurship.

4. *Corporate "slack."* Firms that set aside money and time ("slack") facilitate innovation.

5. *End the "home run" philosophy.* Some company cultures foster an interest in innovative ideas only when they represent major breakthroughs. Intrapreneurship is restricted in that type of culture.

6. *Tolerance of risk, failure, and mistakes.* Where risks and failure are damaging

to their careers, managers carefully avoid them. But innovations inherently involve some risk, so calculated risks and some failures should be tolerated and chalked up to experience.

7. *Patient money.* The pressure for quarterly profits in many U.S. companies stifles innovative behavior. Investment in intrapreneurial activity may take time to bear fruit.

Guidelines for Management Practice

There are at least seven specific ways in which managers in large organizations can reinforce Pinchot's "freedom factors," thereby encouraging intrapreneurship and innovation. Each of the following guidelines is based on the experience of several U.S. companies that have sought to make their company more innovative and their managers better entrepreneurs.[28]

1. *Designate innovation "sponsors."* Formally identify key people with credibility and influence in the company to serve as facilitators of new ideas. These "sponsors" are usually provided with discretionary funds to allocate on the spot to help innovators develop their proposals.

2. *Allow innovation time.* 3M has a "15 percent rule," which means that members of its engineering group can spend 15 percent of their time tinkering with whatever idea they think has market potential. Cheseborough-Pond's allows every person in the company to take a minimum of one-half day per week to work on whatever innovative idea he or she wants to pursue. These are but two examples of efforts to specifically designate or "free up" time to generate innovative ideas.

3. *Accommodate innovation teams.* 3M calls it "tin cupping." American Cement calls it "innovation volunteers." The idea is for companies to give managers some interdepartmental flexibility to let informal idea-development teams (a marketing, engineering, and operations team, for example) interact about promising ideas. Where this is done, companies report that most members pursue idea development on their own time. The motivation comes from the freedom and the opportunity to successfully develop their ideas.

4. *Provide innovation forums.* Owens Corning has what it calls "skunkworks, innovation boards, and innovation fairs." 3M has its "technical forums," annual "technical review fairs," and "sales clubs." These companies and others have set up ongoing forums, conferences, or fair-type shows at which technical people can interact with sales representatives, idea developers can propose their innovations, and action to follow up on the promising ideas can more easily emerge.

5. *Use intrapreneurial controls.* It is often some time before innovations boost corporate profits. Because this is inconsistent with quarterly profit pressures, managers interested in encouraging innovation have started using "milestone reviews" rather than monthly budgets as a basis for reviewing intrapreneurial developments. Basically, this approach asks an innovator to set forth a timetable for idea development and resource requirements. Key milestones in the development process are identified and subsequently used to "control" progress and resource utilization.

6. *Provide intrapreneurial rewards.* Rewards that encourage successful innovation include recognition for the innovation, financial bonuses, and the opportunity to "do it again" with even greater freedom in developing and implementing the next idea.

7. *Articulate specific innovation objectives.* Specifically setting forth organizational objectives that legitimize intrapreneurship and innovation helps encourage the organizational culture to support this activity. For example, 3M has as a corporate objective that "25 percent of annual sales each year will come from products introduced within the last five years." 3M has achieved this goal successfully every year since 1970, providing proof of the value of such a corporationwide priority.

8. *Freedom from turfness.* In any organization, people like to stake out their turf. Intrapreneurship can be inhibited by this phenomenon, because innovative ideas often affect more than one area of the organization.

9. *Cross-functional teams.* Organizations often inhibit cross-functional communication by insisting that communication flow strictly upward. That prevents someone in sales from talking with a knowledgable person in operations, and so on.

10. *Multiple options.* When an individual with an idea has only one person to consult or one channel to inquire into for developing the idea, innovation can be stifled. Intrapreneurship is encouraged when people have many options for discussing or pursuing innovative ideas.

Review of the Learning Objectives

Having studied this chapter, you should be able to respond to the learning objectives with extensions of the following brief answers.

1. **Define the term *entrepreneurship* and explain why entrepreneurship is important in our economy.**

   Entrepreneurship is the process of bringing together creative and innovative ideas and actions with the management and organizational skills necessary to mobilize the appropriate people, money, and operating resources to create wealth. Entrepreneurship is important to our economy because it (1) creates new jobs, (2) fosters innovations, (3) encourages productivity and economic efficiency, (4) decentralizes economic power, and (5) affords self-employment opportunities for women and members of minority groups.

2. **Identify five key elements in the new-venture development process.**

   The first key element is a vision of a profitable *opportunity*, not just an idea. The second key element is whether the *timing* is right, both for the opportunity and for the lead entrepreneur(s). The third element is an entrepreneur or venture team that possesses the necessary *competencies and characteristics* for building and guiding a new business venture. The fourth key element is a written *business plan*. And the fifth key element is the *financial resources* necessary to support the venture.

3. **Cite the special competencies and characteristics that successful entrepreneurs exhibit.**

   The entrepreneur or venture team must possess the technical competence to provide a product or service that meets a need in a way the customer wants that need met and at a price the customer is willing to pay. The venture team must possess the business management skills necessary to oversee management of the marketing, financial, and human resource aspects of the business firm.
   The entrepreneur or venture team should possess as many of the following characteristics as possible: (1) total commitment, determination, and perseverance; (2) need to achieve; (3) orientation toward opportunities and goals; (4)

internal locus of control; (5) tolerance for ambiguity, stress, and uncertainty; (6) propensity to take moderate calculated risks; (7) low need for status; (8) ability to solve problems; (9) skill in seeking and using feedback; (10) ability to deal effectively with failure; (11) high energy, health, and emotional stability; (12) creativity; (13) high intelligence and conceptual ability; and (14) vision and the capacity to inspire.

4. **Explain the key elements of a new-venture business plan.**

Such a business plan should convey "why" target customers are interested in the venture's product or service and why they are willing to pay for it. It should convey "how" the business will be set up and managed to meet this need competitively and profitably. And it should convey "when" key events in the process of building the enterprise will take place and the flow of funds necessary to those efforts. A business plan typically requires 250 or more hours to develop and is provided in written form. Its content is usually organized in accordance with the outline shown in Figure 21-6.

5. **Define the term *intrapreneurship*, and list at least five factors that facilitate it in large organizations.**

An intrapreneur is "any of the 'dreamers who do.' Those who take hands-on responsibility for creating innovation of any kind within an organization. The intrapreneur may be the creator or inventor but is always the dreamer who figures out how to turn an idea into a profitable reality." Ten factors that facilitate intrapreneurship in large organizations are (1) self-selection, (2) no hand-offs, (3) letting the doer decide, (4) corporate slack, (5) ending the "home run" philosophy, (6) tolerance of risk and failure, (7) patient money, (8) freedom from turfness, (9) cross-functional communication, and (10) multiple options in where to take a new idea.

Key Terms and Concepts

After having completed your study of Chapter 21, "Entrepreneurship and Innovation," you will have mastered the following important terms and concepts.

entrepreneurship	debt financing	management	intrapreneurship
business plan	equity financing	assistance	

Questions for Discussion

1. Explain how Ross Perot was both an entrepreneur and an intrapreneur.

2. Explain why entrepreneurship is important to economic development.

3. What distinction should one make between an "opportunity" and an "idea" when considering a new-venture decision?

4. Describe five sources of new-venture opportunities.

5. What types of competencies are important to entrepreneurial success? What implication does this have for ventures headed by a single entrepreneur versus those driven by a team?

6. What key considerations determine the appropriateness of the timing of new business ventures?

7. Explain two types of new-venture financial resources, and indicate where such financing might be obtained.

8. Explain and illustrate three techniques that have been used to successfully encourage and manage intrapreneurship and innovation.

9. How are entrepreneurs and intrapreneurs similar? How are they different?

Notes

1. Excerpted from "Hall of Fame for Business Leadership," *Fortune,* March 14, 1988. *Fortune* © 1988 Time, Inc. All rights reserved.
2. J. A. Timmons, L. E. Smollen, and A. L. M. Dingee, Jr., *New Venture Creation: A Guide to Small Business Development,* 2nd ed. (Homewood, Ill.: Irwin, 1985), p. 143.
3. "Apple Computer's Comeback," *Business Week,* May 5, 1987.
4. J. Naisbitt, *Megatrends* (New York: Bantam, 1984).
5. T. Peters and P. Waterman, *In Search of Excellence* (New York: Harper & Row, 1982); and T. Peters and N. Austin, *A Passion for Excellence* (New York: Random House, 1985).
6. K. H. Vesper, *Entrepreneurship and National Policy* (Chicago: Heller Institute, 1983); and Timmons, Smollen, and Dingee, *New Venture Creation,* p. 4.
7. D. Birch, *Job Creation Process* (Cambridge, Mass.: MIT Press, 1978).
8. Birch, *Job Creation Process,* and Vesper, *Entrepreneurship and National Policy.*
9. *President's Report on the State of Small Business: 1986* (Washington, D.C.: Small Business Administration, 1987).
10. K. H. Vesper, *New Venture Strategies* (Englewood Cliffs, N.J.: 1980).
11. "Entrepreneurs in America," *USA Today,* May 10, 1987.
12. K. H. Vesper, *College & University Programs in Entrepreneurship* (New York: Heller Foundation Press, 1984).
13. "Compaq's Successful Rise to the Top," *Business Week,* August 24, 1986.
14. Vesper, *New Venture Strategies.*
15. Timmons, Smollen, and Dingee, *New Venture Creation,* pp. 88–96.
16. J. Susbauer, "Commentary," in D. Schendel and C. W. Hofer, eds., *Strategic Management* (New York: Little, Brown, 1979).
17. H. H. Stevenson, "A New Paradigm for Entrepreneurial Management" (Boston: Division of Research, Harvard Business School, 1983).
18. This section draws heavily on excellent summaries of research provided by J. Timmons, L. E. Smollen, and A. L. M. Dingee, Jr., *New Venture Creation,* and K. Vesper, *New Venture Strategies.*
19. Timmons, Smollen, and Dingee, *New Venture Creation,* pp. 159–160.
20. From C. Green's presentation to Beta Gamma Sigma, Columbia, South Carolina, April 14, 1987.
21. S. Brandt, *Entrepreneuring* (Reading, Mass.: Addison-Wesley, 1982).
22. S. R. Rich and D. E. Gumpert, *Business Plans That Win $$$* (New York: Harper & Row, 1985).
23. R. Robinson, "The Importance of Outsiders in Small Firm Strategic Planning," *Academy of Management Journal,* September 1982.
24. R. M. Kanter, *The Change Masters* (New York: Simon and Schuster, 1983), pp. 353–355.
25. G. Pinchot, *Intrapreneuring* (New York: Harper & Row, 1985).
26. H. Geneen, with Alvin Moscow, *Managing* (Garden City, N.Y.: Doubleday, 1984), p. 285.
27. This section draws heavily on the pioneering research undertaken and reported by Gordon Pinchot in his book, *Intrapreneuring.*
28. Pinchot, *Intrapreneuring,* p. 31.

Cohesion Incident 21-1

Graniteville Menswear, Ltd.

A few weeks after Charles started working at the Journey's End in Graniteville, Roger invited him to attend a meeting at the local Lion's Club. Roger thought that this would be a good way for Charles to meet people in the area. Charles found the club an excellent way to make new acquaintances, and he particularly enjoyed the company of Bert Truesdale.

Bert was the sole owner of the only store in Graniteville that carried a quality line of menswear, Graniteville Menswear, Ltd. In talking with Bert, Charles learned that until eight months ago, he had been a clerk in the men's department at Belk's, the largest retail operation of its type in Graniteville. While working at Belk's for twelve years, Bert had moved from being a stockroom helper when he graduated from high school to his last job as clerk in the men's department. Although the local Belk's did a lot of business and carried a good line of men's clothing, Bert realized that more and more customers had started driving to the city of Unionville (population 500,000) to shop in menswear stores there.

For the past three years at Belk's, Bert had been in charge of ordering merchandise for the men's department and had thoroughly enjoyed choosing the clothing the store would stock for the coming seasons. Several times, some of his customers had hinted that Bert should leave Belk's and start his own store.

Eight months ago, a store in the local shopping center had become available, and Bert had used most of his savings and a small loan from a local bank to open Graniteville Menswear, Ltd. During the first couple of months, Bert was extremely happy that he had made the switch. He hired one other salesman. His wife did all the alterations. Business was good. Bert was working six days a week, but he did not mind because he finally had his own business and was his own boss. After three months, he had many loyal clients who were also pleased that Bert had made the change from Belk's.

"Charles, I've heard Roger brag about your abilities to some of the men here in the club. Maybe you can help me with some problems I'm having at the store. I thought I knew the men's clothing business inside and out. But I've tried to please most of my customers by carrying the clothing they want, and my inventory has gotten completely out of hand. I probably still have 25 percent of my first order in the stockroom, and now that the summer season is over, I guess I'm stuck with it for the next several months. I just hope styles don't change too drastically over the next year! And even with the back room filled, I still can't keep enough of certain sizes of sportscoats in the wide assortment I know I need. Ellis, my salesman, doesn't want to work more than forty hours a week, which leaves me by myself in the store quite a bit. I don't want to hire someone else whom I hardly know. And this morning, my wife told me she's getting tired of doing alterations and wants me to hire a seamstress. I just don't think I can afford to do that. You know Gerald Caskey, the accountant. He's handling my books, and he tells me I have a 'cash flow problem,' whatever that is. Do you think you could come by some morning, stay a few hours, and give me some pointers on how to improve my management of this place?"

Discussion Questions

1. Is Bert a good entrepreneur? A good manager? Explain.

2. It has been said that all the entrepreneurs are managers but not all managers are entrepreneurs. Discuss that statement in reference to Bert.

3. If you were Charles, what pointers would you give Bert?

4. How would someone like Charles use entrepreneurial skills in his future job as manager of a Journey's End Inn?

Cohesion Incident 21-2
Leslie Contemplates Entrepreneurship

It started over dinner at TGIF's one Friday night when Leslie Phillips, Fred Crowe, and Barbara Holton were talking about their futures. Barbara said that she truly enjoyed her job as a staff attorney for Travis Corporation, but she had always thought that one day she would have her own business. She indicated that this secret ambition had been a major reason why she became a lawyer. Her father had always said that "anybody in business for herself needs to be a lawyer or she might not succeed." Fred, an engineer in the Electronic Controls Division at Travis, and Leslie (in market research) quickly mentioned that they had always wanted to be self-employed, too. The next several Fridays at TGIF found Leslie, Fred, and Barbara talking extensively about starting their own business together.

Soon three ideas began to emerge that held great interest for one or more of them. The first idea was to start a restaurant and bar catering to young professionals. Although none of them had restaurant experience (beyond Fred's experience as a waiter one year while he was in college), they were all regular restaurant patrons and felt that they had a good sense of the atmosphere, food, and format that would attract young professionals like themselves. They envisioned Barbara, who was an excellent cook, running the kitchen; Fred, typically the best organized, overseeing the floor operations; and Leslie, who enjoyed making drinks and was a country music buff, as the bartender and manager of the lounge and entertainment. Each was attracted to the idea of a relaxed lifestyle and the chance to do business and see friends in their own restaurant. The more ambitious Barbara also imagined their enterprise expanding into a chain of similar restaurants catering to young professionals in key cities.

The second idea was the one that Leslie was perhaps most fond of: a small consulting firm. She envisioned the three of them pooling their experience at Travis Corporation—market research, engineering, and legal (contract development) services—into a consulting service that many small businesses would need. Because many small businesses could not afford such talent on a full-time basis but obviously needed help in these areas rather frequently, Leslie speculated that the three could quickly develop a broad base of clients paying regular retainers plus hourly fees for their services. Travis frequently used marketing consultants in this fashion. Fred and Barbara were particularly interested in this idea, because it required little initial capital outlay and because they could start it "after hours" while retaining their Travis positions.

The third idea, proposed by Fred, grew out of a Travis project he had worked on the year before. Fred and a team of engineers in the Electronic Controls Division had developed a special mechanism that attached to the axle of large trucks—those that pull vans and tankers on highways—and precisely measured the number of miles traveled without being easily altered. The product had gained rapid acceptance among national transportation companies that paid drivers by the mile and were required by the U.S. Department of Transportation to maintain meticulous daily logs of where and how many miles each truck traveled.

Fred's idea was to adapt this mileage reading device for use on regular automobiles. For starters, he knew that there were five times as many cars in the fleets of auto rental companies (such as Hertz and Avis) as there were trucks in national transportation fleets. He reasoned that they, like the operators of truck fleets, needed to monitor mileage accurately without fear of tampering by the drivers. Fred felt he could alter the basic design and create a functional prototype in three months. He argued that Leslie could design the marketing program while Barbara developed sales contracts and investor agreements. His estimate was that they would need an initial investment of $500,000 to produce the device.

Having concluded that they could all work together and that they were all very serious about striking out on their own, the three aspiring entrepreneurs decided to meet at Leslie's father's lake house the next weekend to hash out which option they would pursue.

Questions for Discussion

1. Evaluate each of their ideas, and identify the type of business that it would create.

2. Make a list of key questions that must be answered

and issues that must be resolved for each idea.

3. What do you think about this team? What concerns and questions would you have for them?

Management Development Exercise 21
Are You a Potential Entrepreneur?

The Center for Entrepreneurial Management is a more than 2,500-member private organization with a mission of providing educational services to its members and other interested entrepreneurs. The Center has developed an Entrepreneurial Profile based on twenty-six key characteristics found to differentiate its member entrepreneurs.

The Entrepreneurial Profile questions are provided below. Read each of the questions and select the most appropriate answer. After you have scored your responses, your instructor will interpret the results.

1. How were your parents employed?
   a. Both worked and were self-employed for most of their working lives.
   b. Both worked and were self-employed for some part of their working lives.
   c. One parent was self-employed for most of his or her working life.
   d. One parent was self-employed at some point in his or her working life.
   e. Neither parent was ever self-employed.
2. Have you ever been fired from a job?
   a. Yes, more than once.
   b. Yes, once.
   c. No.
3. Are you an immigrant, or were your parents or grandparents immigrants?
   a. I was born outside of the United States.
   b. One or both of my parents were born outside of the United States.
   c. At least one of my grandparents was born outside of the United States.
   d. Does not apply.
4. Your work career has been:
   a. Primarily in small business (under 100 employees).
   b. Primarily in medium-sized business (100 to 500 employees).
   c. Primarily in big business (over 500 employees).

5. Did you operate any businesses before you were twenty?
   a. Many.
   b. A few.
   c. None.
6. What is your present age?
   a. 21–30.
   b. 31–40.
   c. 41–50.
   d. 51 or over.
7. You are the _____ child in the family.
   a. Oldest.
   b. Middle.
   c. Youngest.
   d. Other.
8. You are:
   a. Married.
   b. Divorced.
   c. Single.
9. Your highest level of formal education is:
   a. Some high school.
   b. High school diploma.
   c. Bachelor's degree.
   d. Master's degree.
   e. Doctor's degree.
10. What is your primary motivation in starting a business?
   a. To make money.
   b. I don't like working for someone else.
   c. To be famous.
   d. As an outlet for excess energy.

11. Your relationship to the parent who provided most of the family's income was:
    a. Strained.
    b. Comfortable.
    c. Competitive.
    d. Nonexistent.
12. If you could choose between working hard and working smart, you would:
    a. Work hard.
    b. Work smart.
    c. Both.
13. On whom do you rely for critical management advice?
    a. Internal management teams.
    b. External management professionals.
    c. External financial professionals.
    d. No one except myself.
14. If you were at the racetrack, which of these would you bet on?
    a. The daily double—a chance to make a killing.
    b. A 10-to-1 shot.
    c. A 3-to-1 shot.
    d. The 2-to-1 favorite.
15. The only ingredient that is both necessary and sufficient for starting a business is:
    a. Money.
    b. Customers.
    c. An idea or product.
    d. Motivation and hard work.
16. If you were an advanced tennis player and had a chance to play a top pro like Boris Becker, you would:
    a. Turn it down because he could easily beat you.
    b. Accept the challenge, but not bet any money on it.
    c. Bet a week's pay that you would win.
    d. Get odds, bet a fortune, and try for an upset.
17. You tend to "fall in love" too quickly with:
    a. New product ideas.
    b. New employees.
    c. New manufacturing ideas.
    d. New financial plans.
    e. All of the above.
18. Which of the following personality types is best suited to be your right-hand person?

    a. Bright and energetic.
    b. Bright and lazy.
    c. Dumb and energetic.
19. You accomplish tasks better because:
    a. You are always on time.
    b. You are super-organized.
    c. You keep good records.
20. You hate to discuss:
    a. Problems involving employees.
    b. Signing expense accounts.
    c. New management practices.
    d. The future of the business.
21. Given a choice, you would prefer:
    a. Rolling dice with a 1-in-3 chance of winning.
    b. Working on a problem with a 1-in-3 chance of solving it in the allocated time.
22. If you could choose between the following competitive professions, it would be:
    a. Professional golf.
    b. Sales.
    c. Personnel counseling.
    d. Teaching.
23. If you had to choose between working with a partner who is a close friend and working with a stranger who is an expert in your field, you would choose:
    a. The close friend.
    b. The expert.
24. You enjoy being with people:
    a. When you have something meaningful to do.
    b. When you can do something new and different.
    c. Even when you have nothing planned.
25. In business situations that demand action, clarifying who is in charge will help produce results.
    a. Agree.
    b. Agree, with reservations.
    c. Disagree.
26. In playing a competitive game, you are concerned with:
    a. How well you play.
    b. Winning or losing.
    c. Both of the above.
    d. Neither of the above.

Source: J. R. Mancuso, "The Entrepreneur's Quiz," Joseph Mancuso, The Center for Entrepreneurial Management, Inc., 180 Varick Street, Penthouse, New York City 10014. (212) 633-0060.

22

International Management

Your study of this chapter will enable you to do the following:

1. Describe international management, and explain its importance to the practicing manager in today's world.
2. Cite the two basic types of international business activity and the reasons why each occurs.
3. Identify the general international strategies that a manager may use in developing international business activities.

Learning Objectives

A Book Calling the French Lazy

France, a nation of sunbathers and cafe habitués, has been in an uproar over the question, prompted by a provocative new book, of whether the French work hard enough to compete with the Japanese, the Germans, and the Americans.

The book, *Lazy France,* clearly hit a raw nerve because it challenges the nation's conflicting self-images. On the one hand, how can the nation that had the hard-driving spirit to give the world the supersonic Concorde and high-speed trains be considered lazy? On the other, these are the same people who, with five-week vacations and two-hour, six-course lunches, have long boasted that they know more about the art of good living than anyone else.

The book infuriated many not only because it questions the French way of doing things, but also because it asserts that the French work less than the Spanish and the Italians—the southern neighbors whom the French have often poked fun at for being lazy.

Lazy France grabbed so much attention partly because it appeared just as a deluge of statistics showed that France had been losing out badly in international trade. French newsweeklies devoted cover articles to the 310-page book. The business press showered it with praise. The leftist press excoriated it.

A major finding in the book is that the average French worker spends 1,550 hours a year at the office or factory, compared with 1,850 hours for the average

709

The well-known French penchant for the art of good living is typified by the leisurely meals they enjoy in sidewalk cafés such as this one. (Pascal Maitre/Gamma Liaison)

American worker, 2,000 hours for the average Japanese, and more than 2,700 for the average Korean.

Trade figures show that France is losing jobs to foreign competition. The nation's trade deficit soared to almost $1 billion in May of 1987, the worst monthly result in the nation's history. In addition, its nonmilitary manufacturing balance of payments fell from a $17-billion surplus in 1984 to a break-even level in 1986 and showed a deficit of more than $4 billion in 1987. What is more, France's share of the world market for manufactured goods fell by 2.5 percent in 1986.

"This book definitely hits home," said Jean Loyrette, a senior partner at France's largest law firm. "We're certainly very lazy compared with the Japanese, not to mention the Koreans."

Scherrer, the author, is the forty-four-year-old president of the French subsidiary of Pillsbury. Scherrer, French himself, said that one of the key reasons for France's problems with competitiveness was the high hourly costs of the French work force. His book notes that in 1985 employees at Thomson, one of France's largest electronics companies, worked 1,412 hours a year and that their earnings averaged $15 per hour. By comparison, workers at Thomson's Japanese competitors put in 1,950 hours a year and earned $9 an hour.

To further illustrate this point, IBM Europe compared the work hours of ten of its subsidiaries around the world and found that its Japanese employees worked an average of 1,964 hours apiece in 1985, whereas French employees worked only 1,612 hours, or 82.1 percent as many hours as their Japanese counterparts. Here is the actual breakdown of average hours worked in 1985:

Japan	1,964
U.S.A.	1,873
Canada	1,864
Spain	1,798
Britain	1,758
Italy	1,716
Sweden	1,700
West Germany	1,660
Netherlands	1,628
France	1,612

"I'm not saying we should cut salaries," Scherrer said. "I'm saying we should increase the time at work in order to reduce the cost per hour."

For example, Scherrer said it was excessive for the French to have four holiday weekends in May and early June. There was Friday, May 1, the workers' holiday; Friday, May 8, Victory in Europe Day; Thursday, May 28, Ascension (a holiday that prompted many to take the following day off to get a four-day weekend); and Monday, June 5, Pentecost.

"The Americans have only one holiday during that period, Memorial Day," Scherrer said. "And most Italians have stopped taking time off from work on Ascension and Pentecost, so why can't the French?"

Scherrer urged other companies to adopt his goal of persuading his work force to increase the time worked by thirty hours over the next year. He said he planned to do this by eliminating such common practices as giving workers a day off when they donate blood or half a day off when they take a driver's test.... Seeking to win worker cooperation, he promised to share with them any savings attributable to the increased hours worked. In addition, he said he hoped to motivate his employees "to work more and better" by offering them flexible hours and more extensive training.

Nonetheless, many union officials dismiss the book as part of a management offensive to make labor work harder. Daviel Labbe, head of a union local at Renault, said that reduced hours were important to spread the work around and avoid unemployment. He said that because of automation, unemployment would double if the French worked as many hours today as they did years ago.

Another union official said that the real reason for France's decreasing competitiveness was not the number of hours worked but lack of investment by management. "You can't ask us to work as hard as the Japanese," he said. "We have a completely different culture."[1]

Introduction

What Is International Management?

International management involves the development and control of the flows of capital, labor, raw materials, technology, information, goods, and services across national borders. Ideally, international management extends the activities of the organization into foreign countries in a manner that helps achieve the firm's overall objectives. It differs from domestic management in that it forces managers to deal with an international environment, and managers must contend with additional issues and variables there. These variables include differences in national sovereignties, economic and cultural conditions, societal value systems, nonverbal communication, norms (such as attitudes on what constitutes a fair work week), and institutions, geographic distances, market structures, demographics, and regulatory considerations.[2]

As indicated by the opening case, real differences exist on many of these issues among even the most friendly of nations. Thus, to effectively manage foreign operations, managers need to develop a greater level of awareness of and knowledge about international problems and opportunities and to learn new skills and techniques. For example, managers in foreign locations who are responsible for employees of nationalities different from their own must understand the basic incentives and values that serve to motivate people from each distinct cultural setting. The United States and India serve as a specific example. Research suggests that morale and productivity are higher under authoritarian than under democratic leadership in India, whereas the results are the opposite for the United States.[3] Thus, effective international managers need to evaluate and often adjust the way they use motivation, control, and feedback to manage employees in different cultures.

In this chapter, we will assess the impact of international issues on corporate performance, we will study strategies that can lead to competitive success, and we will explore some of the key factors that result in productive interpersonal relationships for American managers who accept positions overseas.

The Importance of International Business

How important is international business to the United States? To answer this question, we must first define the two fundamental types of international business. The first is international trade, often referred to as importing and exporting. *Importing* is the buying and movement of goods and services from another country. *Exporting* is the selling and movement of goods and services to another country. By these definitions, then, **international trade** is the transfer of products and/or organizational skills and services from one country to another.

The second type of international business is foreign direct investment. **Foreign direct investment** is an investment made by a company in business operations in another country whereby that company retains "effective managerial control" of the foreign operations. The company making the investment is referred to as the **parent company** (it is based in the **home country**), and the country receiving the foreign direct investment is referred to as the **host country**. *Effective managerial control* of a foreign direct investment is defined for U.S. statistical reporting purposes as a minimum of 10 percent ownership. An investment in foreign operations

FIGURE 22-1
U.S. International Transactions: 1974 to 1986 (billions of dollars)

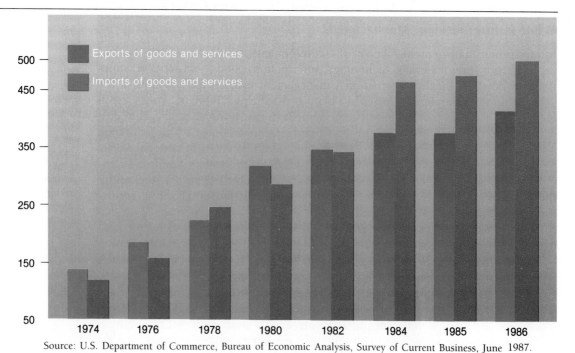

Source: U.S. Department of Commerce, Bureau of Economic Analysis, Survey of Current Business, June 1987.

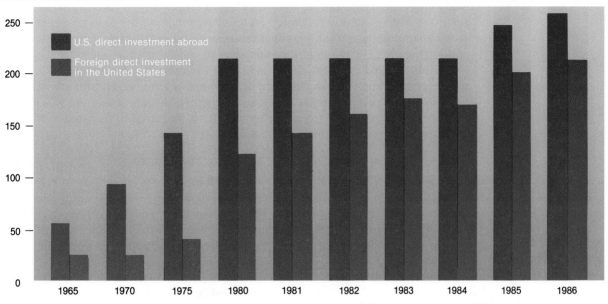

250 —

■ U.S. direct investment abroad

■ Foreign direct investment
  in the United States

200 —

150 —

100 —

50 —

0

1965   1970   1975   1980   1981   1982   1983   1984   1985   1986

Source: U.S. Department of Commerce, Bureau of Economic Analysis, Survey of Current Business, June 1987.

FIGURE 22-2
**U.S. International
Direct Investment
for Selected Years,
1960–1986 (billions
of dollars)**

that does not meet this 10 percent criterion is considered a "portfolio investment" and is typically made for the purpose of merely obtaining investment income or capital gains.[4]

Most countries actively encourage foreign firms to locate operations within their boundaries and local firms to produce products for exporting. Figure 22-1 presents the international trade figures for the United States. Figure 22-2 presents the foreign direct investment of U.S.-based companies and the foreign direct investment that companies from other countries have made in the United States. It is important to note that these investment figures are reported and carried at book value—the actual price of the investment at the time the investment is made. Hence the actual values today of investments made, say, 10 years ago, are grossly understated by these figures when their replacement cost is considered. Nevertheless, it is quite apparent from Figures 22-1 and 22-2 that there has been a massive growth in the last twenty years in U.S. international trade activity, foreign direct investment made by U.S. firms, and foreign direct investment made in the United States. Note too that although exporting remains important to the U.S. economy, the production of goods and services in foreign countries represents a far greater portion of U.S. international business activities.

The majority of foreign direct investment has historically occurred between developed countries. For example, in recent years 75 percent of all the foreign direct investment worldwide has occurred in developed countries. In fact, four countries (the United States, Canada, the United Kingdom, and Germany) have accounted for almost half the total foreign direct investment activity. For the United States, however, foreign direct investment in developing countries has been growing faster than investment in developed countries, although the total investment in developed countries is still three times as large.[5]

Many of the foreign investments made in the United States go unnoticed by the general public but are represented by "household" company names, such as Carnation, Keebler, Food Lion, U.S. Borax and Chemical, Howard Johnson, BI-LO, and Clorox. In fact, in 1985 nearly 130 billion dollars flowed into the United

States from foreign countries. Figure 22-3 lists the ten largest foreign investments that have been made in the United States, determined on the basis of assets.

The importance of international business to individual firms varies widely, of course. Figure 22-4 presents the international involvement of the fifteen largest U.S. multinational corporations. Figure 22-4 indicates that for many U.S. multinational corporations, a large portion of their total revenue and profits are derived from international operations and that a large part of their assets are in foreign countries. It is interesting to note that the fifteen industrial firms listed in Figure 22-4 are also the top fifteen of the *Fortune* 500.

Reasons for Going International

FIGURE 22-3
Largest Foreign
Investments in the U.S.

In view of the growing levels of international trade and investment, it is not surprising that many firms find it highly advantageous to engage in international business. In general, these advantages stem from the firm's ability to benefit from

Rank	Foreign Investor	Country	U.S. Investment	% Owned	Industry	Reverse (millions)	Net Income (millions)	Assets (millions)
1	Seagram Co. Ltd.[a]	Canada	E.I. du Pont de Nemours[a]	23	Chemicals, energy	$27,148	$1,538.0	$26,733
			Joseph E. Seagram & Sons	100	Alcoholic beverages	2,029	337.6	6,301
						29,177		
2	Royal Dutch/Shell Group[a]	Netherlands UK	Shell Oil	100	Energy, chemicals	17,353	883.0	26,214
3	British Petroleum Plc.[a]	UK	Standard Oil Ohio[a]	95	Energy	9,219	−45.0	15,955
			BP North America	100	Energy	4,228	4.0	4,224
						13,447		
4	B.A.T. Industries Plc.[a]	UK	BATUS	100	Multicompany	5,499	393.7	4,242
	Imasco Ltd[a]	Canada	Peoples Drug Stores	100	Drugstores	1,366	NA	NA
			Imasco USA	100	Fast food	1,206	NA	NA
						8,071		
5	Tengelmann Group	Germany	Great A&P Tea[a]	52	Supermarkets	7,835	69.0	2,080
6	Unilever N.V.[a]	Netherlands	Cheseborough-Pond's	100	Personal care	2,731	159.4	NA
			Lever Brothers	100	Consumer goods	2,475	−18.5	837
			Thomas J. Lipton	100	Food and beverages	1,303	91.4	827
			National Starch & Chem	100	Adhesives, starch	1,064	71.8	743
						7,573		
7	Nestlé[a]	Switzerland	Nestlé Enterprises	100	Food, restaurants	3,400E	NA	NA
			Carnation	100	Food	2,500E	NA	NA
			Alcon Laboratories	100	Optical products	400E	NA	NA
						6,300E		
8	Mitsui & Co. Ltd.[a]	Japan	Mitsui & Co. USA	100	Feed additives, plastics	5,561E	44.2E	2,990E
9	Petróleos de Venezuela SA	Venezuela	Citgo Petroleum	50	Refining, marketing	4,103	43.6	1,209
			Champlin Refining (Texas)	50	Refining	1,200	NA	500
						5,303		

Note: Some foreign investors in the list own U.S. companies indirectly through companies in italics.

E = Estimate. NA = Not Available.

Source: "Largest Foreign in the U.S., *Forbes*, July 27, 1987.

[a]Publicly traded in the United States in shares.

1986 Rank	Company	Foreign Revenue (millions)	Total Revenue (millions)	Foreign Revenue as % of Total	Foreign Operating Profit (millions)	Total Operating Profit (millions)	Foreign Operating Profit as % of Total	Foreign Assets (millions)	Total Assets (millions)	Foreign Assets as % of Total
1	Exxon	$50,337	$ 69,888	72.0%	$3,910	$5,219	74.9	$30,740	$ 69,484	44.2
2	Mobil	27,388	46,025	59.5	1,858	1,407	132.1	17,581	37,233	47.2
3	IBM	25,888	51,250	50.5	3,184	4,789	66.5	27,604	57,814	47.7
4	Ford Motor	19,926	62,716	31.8	825	3,285	25.1	18,842	37,933	49.7
5	General Motors	19,837	102,814	19.3	−186	2,945	NA	16,120	72,403	22.3
6	Texaco	15,494	31,613	49.0	1,170	1,187	98.6	10,279	34,940	29.4
7	Citicorp	10,940	23,496	46.6	522	1,058	49.3	86,117	184,013	46.8
8	E.I. duPont de Nemours	9,955	26,907	37.0	644	1,791	36.0	8,035	26,733	30.1
9	Dow Chemical	5,948	11,113	53.5	684	1,285	53.2	6,049	12,242	49.4
10	Chevron	5,605	24,352	23.0	808	1,055	76.6	7,862	34,583	22.7
11	BankAmerica	4,659	12,483	37.3	439	−518	NA	37,263	104,189	35.8
12	Philip Morris	4,573	20,681	22.1	346	3,624	9.5	3,209	17,642	18.2
13	Procter & Gamble	4,490	15,439	29.1	143	709	20.2	3,461	13,055	26.5
14	RJR Nabisco	4,488	15,978	28.1	491	2,617	18.8	3,856	17,019	22.7
15	Chase Manhattan	4,356	9,460	46.0	119	585	20.3	40,940	94,770	43.2

NA = Not Available
Source: "Largest U.S. Multinationals," *Forbes*, July 27, 1987.

foreign market opportunities either through gaining access to a host nation's somewhat less expensive natural resources (labor, raw material, and capital) or through applying its own unique skills or abilities internationally. More specifically, there are five main reasons for going international.

1. *Access to new markets.* Just as local firms may expand regionally and then nationally, many firms find it relatively easy to increase sales by expanding their scope of operations to include international markets. This reason for going international may be particularly important when a firm's domestic market becomes saturated or highly competitive. For example, McDonald's development of restaurants in Europe and Japan has resulted in entirely new markets for its product. Similarly, Lotus Development Corporation recently established operations to market its software in Tokyo, citing the market in Japan as "on the brink of explosive growth." "In Practice 22-1" offers two additional examples of U.S. firms that have found new sources of profit overseas.

2. *Increased profits.* Frequently, foreign markets offer greater profit margins than domestic markets. The firm may incur little or no product development costs if the product has already been developed and the foreign market has given the

---

Guidelines for Management Practice

Both for the United States as a nation and for many individual firms, international business constitutes a significant and growing portion of economic activity. Faced with the increasing importance of international business activity, the practicing manager should keep in mind the following issues.

1. Perhaps the most important implication concerns personal career management. The increasing internationalization of business means that managers must become more knowledgeable about international issues and that this knowledge is becoming more and more vital to managing the modern corporation. International experience may well become a firm prerequisite for top managers. Thus requesting international projects and assignments may facilitate one's advancement within the organization; such assignments are sure to help one develop skills and awareness that will be valuable in a growing sphere of business activity.

2. As business becomes more international, the practicing manager must ensure that the ability to recognize international trends is developed within the firm. When an industry grows increasingly international, both new market opportunities and competitive threats arise. Managers must not only develop their own international expertise but must also take steps to be sure that managers throughout the organization are managing from a perspective that includes the international environment.

---

firm access to lower cost structures. For example, Philip Morris, whose Lark and Parliament brands have 70 percent of Japan's imported cigarette market, originally developed these products for sale in the United States.

3. *Stable supply of raw materials.* Production processes require reliable supplies of raw materials or component parts that are purchased. Firms with operations in several countries have a greater capacity than others for procuring a broad range of raw materials. DeBeers's purchasing of diamond mines throughout the entire world is an example of this advantage of operating internationally.

4. *Host country inducements.* Many countries have become increasingly active in soliciting foreign trade and investments, and they often subsidize local operations through grants, tax holidays, worker training programs, and infrastructure development. For example, the Central Bank of China and the Bank of Communications offer special loans to finance importing machinery in "key" industries, and in Taiwan, no duties are levied on machinery and equipment imported for "sophisticated" industries.

5. *Economies of scale.* Increased economies of scale in production, marketing, financing, and research and development are often achieved through serving additional market segments. Economies of scale in production explain a large part of the competitive advantage that Japanese television manufacturers have over U.S. producers. In the early to mid-1960s, Japanese manufacturers gained market share through cost advantages based largely on low labor rates. By reinvesting the resulting profits in new-process technologies, Japanese TV manufacturers began realizing significant advantages of scale (and quality) over U.S. producers. These advantages reduced the profitability of U.S. producers, and eventually the bulk of U.S. TV production migrated offshore.

Managers have two options in attempting to take advantage of these reasons for going international. The first option is to determine which of the firm's specific strengths can easily be transferred to another environment and yet will be difficult for another firm to copy. For example, Coca-Cola has been able to capitalize on its brand name, producing its product internationally with very few changes required in production process or management expertise.

The second option is to determine which competitive advantages that the firm enjoys can be increased or made more secure through access to production resources existing in other markets. Can access to cheaper labor significantly en-

---

In Practice 22-1

COMPETING IN JAPAN

Water filtration pumps hardly seem like an American product that should sell well in Japan. The technology is mature, and Japanese manufacturers are just as adept as their U.S. counterparts at turning them out. Yet in 1986 alone, Meridien Group, a Los Angeles export management company, supplied Japanese industry with $1 million worth of water filters from half a dozen medium-sized U.S. companies.

Water filters are just one of many industrial products in which "American technology, design, and price are more acceptable to the Japanese than Japan's," says Meridien group president Charles Nevil. "In some instances, I am actually selling U.S. goods in Japan for less than it costs to make them there." Because America has a large enough market to justify high-volume production and Japan does not, "we have the advantage of economies of scale," he says.

The popular notion that "if the Japanese make something themselves, we cannot sell it to them is an unfortunate myth," says Nevil. "The reality is that you do not need to offer a proprietary technology or the lowest price to succeed in Japan."

More than 2,300 U.S. companies are operating in Japan, primarily through subsidiaries or in joint ventures. They sell everything from plastic kitchenware to computer software. But their sales have been neither quick nor easy. Their secret, Nevil says, is willingness to sweat it out in order to create a profitable niche.

One approach is to work directly with a Japanese distributor. To Sandy Kaye, president of Porta-Bote International in Mountain View, California, the key to smooth sailing in Japan has been a distributor "with the wherewithal to market my product."

Kaye knew he had a perfect product for Japan. Storage space is at a premium in Japanese homes, and Kaye reasoned that the Japanese, who love fishing, needed his boat—an $895 motorized or sailing craft that folds to four inches flat and can be carried on top of a car. But as a one-man operation doing about $400,000 in sales a year, Kaye could hardly devote full time to Japan.

Like most imported consumer products, the craft first had to clear government safety tests. Kaye describes the tests as "a veiled attempt to reject the Porta-Bote" and to protect domestic manufacturers. He says the Japanese Coast Guard dropped a boat filled with 600 pounds of concrete twenty feet into the water. The boat was examined for structural damage, and then, to the amazement of the distributor, who was snapping pictures, was subjected to the same test two more times.

The polypropylene boat held together. And—ironically—the distributor used the photos to convince retailers of its strength and durability. By 1981 Kaye was selling more than 500 boats annually to Japanese consumers. Kaye now has annual sales of 2,500 units, which account for 30 percent of Porta-Bote's revenues.

"If your business is very small, your best shot is to work with a skilled distributor who believes in your product and has the capability to move it," advises Kaye. And, despite what many Americans think, the Japanese respect the "Made in U.S.A." label, he says. He was surprised to learn that the distributor was affixing a plastic American flag to each Porta-Bote. "They told me it is a status symbol that will lure customers."

Source: Excerpted from K. Berney, "Competing in Japan," *Nation's Business*, October 1986, pp. 28–30. Reprinted by permission from *Nation's Business*, October 1986. Copyright 1986, U.S. Chamber of Commerce.

hance the firm's ability to lower production costs? Can a new source of raw materials be captured that will provide additional competitive strength? Can increased production volumes enhance a particular product's cost structure? This kind of analysis can help managers pinpoint where unique advantages are attainable for the firm through international operations.

International Business Strategies

International business strategies are typically based on combinations of firm-specific *competitive advantages* and country-specific *comparative advantages,* but there are clear patterns in how these advantages are achieved. ("In Practice 22-2" gives an example of two firms that have successfully exploited these two kinds of advantages to enter the international arena.) This section provides an explanation of how international business strategies are systematically built.

As shown in Figure 22-5, patterns of business strategy can be seen as existing along a continuum from purely domestic to globally integrated.[6] Each of the six major strategies along this continuum deserves some discussion.

International Licensing

International licensing is a contractual agreement that transfers the company's industrial property rights (patents, trademarks, and/or proprietary know-how) to a third party in a foreign country. Generally the transfer is for a specified period of time, and a payment called a *royalty* is received from the third party in exchange for the use of the property rights. An example of licensing occurred when Motorola, Inc., allowed a Japanese firm to use one of Motorola's patents to produce semiconductors in exchange for a fee.

Production abroad through licensing arrangements is generally thought to be especially suitable when competition is particularly intense, as a product matures, when margins are narrow, when the production processes become standardized, and in response to the regulation of foreign direct investment or imports.[7] It is also suitable when managers want to participate in international markets by capitalizing on their skills and technology, not on manufacturing processes. Licensing has been separated from the other elements of the continuum shown in Figure 22-5, because it is frequently an end in itself that requires no formal commitment to foreign markets.

Although licensing arrangements require less of a commitment of management time and corporate funds and are easier to establish than foreign production facilities, there are risks to such arrangements. Witness Intel Corporation's experience. For years Intel had licensed NEC Corporation to manufacture a portion of

FIGURE 22-5
The International
Business Strategy
Continuum

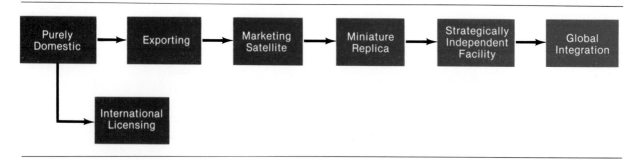

In Practice 22-2

DAEWOO VERSUS HYUNDAI

Two Korean firms, Daewoo and Hyundai, offer an example of firms pursuing comparative and competitive advantages in international markets. Hyundai has a corporate strategy based on the principle of self-sufficiency. The firm's philosophy is to control or internalize as many of the company's operations as possible—from acquiring raw materials to distributing finished products. Inherent in this philosophy is the belief that Hyundai is more efficient than the marketplace. In other words, why buy parts from a supplier when you can make them cheaper yourself? Hyundai's strategy is based on exploiting a variety of competitive advantages in order to penetrate foreign markets. This strategy has proved very successful in international markets.

Daewoo has adopted a considerably different strategy. Daewoo does have certain competitive advantages, but its strategy is largely limited to exploiting Korea's comparative advantage of cheap, trained labor. Daewoo does not believe it has sufficient competitive advantages to single-handedly penetrate foreign markets, so it relies on others to supply parts and distribute finished products. Though eager to seek joint ventures, Daewoo consistently and effectively sells all of its company's goods under U.S. or European brand names, such as Pontiac, Caterpillar, and Carrier.

Increasingly, this difference in strategies is being put to the test in the U.S. computer and automobile markets. In 1987 Hyundai sold 250,000 of its Excels in the United States. Not to be outdone, in April 1987 General Motors began importing Daewoo-produced automobiles under the Pontiac LeMans nameplate. Expected first-year sales: 100,000 cars. In computers, Daewoo's successful Leading Edge computer has come under increasing attack by Hyundai's Blue Chip system, which retails for about $350 less than the base Leading Edge system. Hyundai explains that it is able to offer lower prices because it controls more stages in the manufacturing process.

Source: "Daewoo vs. Hyundai: Battle of the Korean Giants," *Business Week,* December 15, 1986, pp. 72–73.

---

its microprocessor output. Then in 1982, NEC began to manufacture its own microprocessors, introducing in 1984 the V series microprocessors. The V series microprocessors can run software designed for Intel at higher speeds. This higher degree of compatibility is achieved with a microcode that NEC admits is very similar to that used in Intel's microprocessor.[8] Through its licensing agreements, Intel contributed to creating its own competition.

The process of contracting for a licensing agreement or any other multinational business arrangement is one that requires extraordinary care. "Insights for International Managers 22" provides a helpful checklist to aid international managers in drafting a contract.

Exporting

As the firm becomes more aware of the international environment, managers may recognize opportunities to sell their own products abroad. At this early stage in the company's international development, the expertise required for such **exporting** is often not yet fully evolved, and the volume of export activity is small. Consequently, a manager and perhaps a small staff are given the initial responsibility of developing and managing the firm's export activities. Often, independent export middlemen are contracted to operate between the company and the ultimate buyer of the firm's product. These middlemen may have contacts in foreign markets, may serve as commissioned salespeople, or may act as distributors.

Insights for International Managers 22

CHECK LIST FOR CONTRACT DRAFTING

Terms of contracts will vary depending on whether the agreement is a sales contract, technology transfer, joint venture or other transaction. Just a few of the considerations include:

1. State simply the intentions and purposes of both parties.
2. Describe the responsibilities of each party.
3. Specify which codes will apply regarding choice of law and jurisdiction.
4. Define measures of accomplishment (i.e., how you will determine that the job has been done) and methods for evaluation.
5. Agree on what standard principles of accounting will be used.
6. Make provisions (as applicable) for:
   delivery and terms
   discount structures
   payment and credit
   security
   dispute resolution
   taxes (local and foreign)
   force majeure
   controlling language
   notice provisions
   logistics
   expenses of personnel
   work permits for your personnel
   entry visas
   penalties
   exclusivity
   licenses and sublicensing rights
   payment of duties, and other charges
   warrantees and guarantees
   insurance
   installation and start up
   quality control
   disclosure of information and reporting
      requirements
   safeguarding of trade secrets
7. Translate the contract into the foreign language. Again, be careful with interpretation of meaning: use an interpreter who knows the terminology appropriate for your business.

Source: From L. Copeland and L. Griggs, *Going International* (New York: Random House, 1985), p. 96.

The U.S. government offers numerous programs designed to help managers identify and develop overseas markets. Most of these programs are administered by the Office of the U.S. Trade Representative, the Departments of Agriculture and Commerce, the Agency for International Development, the Overseas Private Investment Corporation, the U.S. Trade and Development Program, and the Small Business Administration. For example, the Commerce Department's Market Share Report "Commodity Series" provides export data that can be used to identify overall trends in import markets and the market demand for specific import products.

As export volume increases and expertise within the organization grows, the company often begins to perform the function of the various middlemen internally, exporting directly to importers or buyers located in foreign markets. Frequently, a distinct export department is established.

Marketing Satellite

The establishment of export marketing departments is often followed by investments in foreign sales offices and warehouses called **marketing satellites** that handle the company's affairs overseas. With this growth in international activity, the firm's managers begin to develop an awareness of the opportunities and specific needs of foreign markets. Psychological commitments to markets become substantial. Although marketing satellites handle products that are centrally produced, the local subsidiary may become involved in packaging, bulk breaking, and some final assembly.[9]

A good example of a marketing satellite is Mercedes-Benz of North America, Inc. This subsidiary imports the renowned German automobiles from its parent and distributes them through a system of company-controlled dealerships. The company's U.S. headquarters has little control over the types of products it can sell, but it does oversee an extensive marketing program that is critical in creating an image valued by the U.S. market.

Miniature Replica

A **miniature replica** produces and sells some or all of the parent's products in the local country. An example is General Foods of Canada, which produces and markets in Canada many of the same brands of breakfast cereals, snack foods, and beverages that are found in the United States. Miniature replicas are favored in countries with high tariff walls and in industries with high transportation costs and low economies of scale.

Strategically Independent Facility

Unlike miniature replicas, **strategically independent subsidiaries** have the freedom to develop and market product lines unrelated to those of their parents. A strategy of emphasizing the subsidiary's strategic independence is based on confidence that the subsidiary has the capability (both tangible and intangible) to successfully react to changing environmental opportunities. In most cases of strategic independence, the parent assumes the role of passive investor. For example, according to the United Technologies 1986 Annual Report, a subsidiary of United Technologies called Pratt & Whitney Canada has an effective world mandate for the design, production, and sales of turboprop and turbofan engines used largely in corporate, utility, and commuter aircraft. Pratt & Whitney Canada sales in 1986 totalled $590 million; a large percentage came from sales outside of Canada.

Global Integration

The final international stage depicted in Figure 22-5 is global integration. **Global integration** is exhibited by a company that attempts to maximize the use of all of its foreign investments in a coordinated manner. Decisions are made in such a way as to benefit the entire organization, rather than each business unit operating separately.[10]

A global integration strategy can be achieved only through designing the entire corporate system to be responsive to, and supportive of, this endeavor. For example, intracompany capital and cash flow information must be available in a central location so that decisions can be made in such a way as to maximize total corporate profit; products should be designed to be marketable in as many countries as possible; and manufacturing locations and production schedules should be based on the lowest-cost source throughout the complete system.[11]

Thus global integration recognizes that the primary determinant of worldwide competitiveness is harnessing the *entire* organization's resources to one cart. Managers of the parent company attempt to integrate the activities of the foreign and domestic business units into one multinational system.[12] Firms that are noted for the high degree of coordination of their worldwide activities include Caterpillar, Honda, General Electric, Philips, Pfizer, and Ford.

Sanyo offers an illustration of the radical moves that are sometimes necessary to achieve increased coordination of activities. Sanyo and its affiliate Tokyo Sanyo Electric Company have operated independently for over twenty years. In fact, they have been "friendly" rivals. However, faced with declining profitability, Sanyo recognized that although this rivalry was good for motivation, it was inefficient because of duplication in product designs, engineering efforts, and manufacturing processes. Thus Sanyo merged the two companies, setting up eight divisions structured along product lines and eliminating internal duplication. Beyond increased economies of scale and lower costs, the structure of the new organization also allows for centralization of decisions, which results in better coordination of Sanyo's worldwide competitive efforts.[13]

International Joint Venture

Although it is not part of the strategic continuum depicted in Figure 22-5, one additional international business strategy should be noted—international joint ventures. Local ownership and participation in foreign direct investment are increased concerns of host governments, particularly those of developing countries. This has resulted in an increase in the use of joint ventures as a means of conducting foreign direct investment while meeting government demands.[14] **International joint ventures** typically involve the creation of a third company by two other firms from different countries. The two "parents" then cooperatively manage the "child" for their common benefit. The creation of Nummi by General Motors and Toyota and that of Posco by USX and Pohang are prime examples. Because many countries (such as Mexico and Japan) prohibit wholly owned subsidiaries, international joint ventures have become an essential means for outside firms to expand into these markets.

The flexibility of the joint venture allows it to occur anywhere along the international business strategy continuum. An international joint venture is a distinct entity owned jointly by two or more corporations from different countries; each corporation contributes assets, shares the risks, assumes operational responsibilities, and receives a portion of the earnings.[15] For example, Japan's Nomura Securities Company, Sumitomo Bank, Security Pacific Corporation of the United States, Bank of East Asia Ltd. of Hong Kong, and Beijing's Bank of China have formed the first international financing venture in China, called the China International Financial Company. The bank was capitalized with about $7 million and is equally owned by the five institutions. This is an example of an equity-based joint venture. A joint venture may also be contractual in nature. In this case, the two or more partners contractually agree to a joint undertaking as opposed to creating a separate entity.

A company has several potential partners in joint ventures. For example, a U.S.-based firm could engage in a joint venture with one or more private companies in the host country, with a foreign government, with foreign local investors, or even with a company from yet a third country. Historically, as the size of the joint venture increases, firms in the United States tend to shift from ventures in partnership with local private firms to joint ventures with the local government and third-country private firms.[16]

Partners in joint ventures are generally selected on the basis of complementary skills. This often accelerates a firm's penetration into international markets, because the strengths of the venture partner can compensate for the firm's weaknesses.[17] For example, faced with opposition from India's Parliament to other proposals, PepsiCo proposed a joint venture between the state-owned Punjab Agroindustries and a private company to make and market food and soft drinks in India.

Wholly Owned Subsidiary

The last kind of arrangement associated with foreign direct investment is the wholly owned foreign subsidiary. A **wholly owned subsidiary** is an entity legally incorporated in a foreign country but owned exclusively by the parent organization. Companies in the United States that have been formed in this manner include BI-LO, owned by Ahold N.V. of the Netherlands; Monsanto Oil Company, owned by Broken Hill Proprietary of Australia; AB Dick, owned by General Electric Plc. of the United Kingdom; and Honda of America Manufacturing, owned by Honda Motor Company Ltd. of Japan.

Wholly owned subsidiaries have traditionally been viewed as the ideal method of foreign direct investment in that the corporation is able to maintain complete managerial control over the organization, the subsidiary can be integrated with the resources of the overall corporation, and decisions can be made quickly without having to consider a separate set of interests (such as the objectives of one's partner in a joint venture).[18] Of course, with total ownership, the expanding company assumes all the risks and supplies all the capital for the enterprise.

We have presented the patterns of international business strategy depicted in Figure 22-5 as progressing more or less in sequence. As the organization gains increased international expertise, it evolves from existing purely domestically, to exporting, to participating in some form of foreign facilities, and eventually to operating as a globally integrated firm. It is important for managers to realize that each of these stages requires a different degree of corporate involvement, control, risk, and commitment. As a business goes increasingly international, it also becomes increasingly tied to that course of action because of the correspondingly high level of corporate commitment, the accelerated investment of resources, and the reduced strategic flexibility. These conditions can make the company vulnerable. Many U.S. firms that have expanded extensively overseas have found themselves in troubled relationships, as did Gulf-Chevron when U.S. foreign policy toward Mozambique shifted in favor of anti-government rebel forces.

Although we have characterized the stages of internationalization as a progression, this pattern of development need not occur and often does not. A company may effectively skip certain stages, or it may appropriately choose to remain at a particular stage. For example, the appeal of a product may be based on its being manufactured in a foreign country (French perfume), or unique raw materials may necessitate manufacturing at a particular location (Bordeaux wines).

Planning for International Operations

As a company begins competing in the international marketplace, its strategic decisions become increasingly complex and multidimensional. Managers cannot view managing the firm's international operations as a set of independent decisions. Rather they must make, in the context of the international venture's role in

Coca Cola's international advertising campaigns, although based on a standardized theme, must also be modified to varying degrees to take into account the culture and language of the country in which they appear. (COKE and COCA-COLA are registered trademarks of the Coca-Cola Company. Permission for use granted by the Company.)

the objectives of the overall corporation, decisions considering multiple products, economic environments, supplies of resources, capabilities of the corporation and its subsidiaries, and strategic options.[19]

The diverse nature of a company's operations can be likened to a chain of value-added activities that may be spread across several countries.[20] *Value-added activities* include the typical functional activities of a business, such as purchases of input resources, operations, research and development, marketing and sales, and after-the-sale service. A multinational corporation (MNC) has a wide range of places where each of these activities could be performed and must decide in which locations and in how many locations each set of activities will be carried out. An MNC may want each activity performed at each location, or it may concentrate each activity in one particular location to serve the organization worldwide. For example, research and development may be centralized in one facility to serve the entire organization.

The MNC must also decide on the degree to which these activities are to be coordinated across different countries. Coordination can be extremely low, in which case each location performs each activity autonomously. Or coordination can be extremely high, and the activities in different locations tightly linked together. For example, the Coca-Cola Company closely coordinates research, development, and marketing worldwide to offer a standardized brand name, formula for the concentrated product, market positioning, and advertising theme. However, manufacturing is more tailored to each location, and the sweeteners and packaging differ across countries.[21]

Controlling International Operations

Once a strategy covering location and coordination has been selected, managers must address the key issues of controlling international operations. Control is typically achieved through designing an organizational structure that facilitates the implementation of strategies.

Organizational Structure

The basic structure of the organization should be designed to match the firm's strategy and resources to its environment. This "fit" is so important that global competitive strategies in the late 1980s began to shift from diversification toward corporate restructuring as multinationalization occurred.[22] Because international businesses operate in such divergent environments, finding the best organizational structure is often challenging. Just as competitive strategies change as markets mature, international structures often follow a general evolutionary trend.[23]

The typical pattern begins when firms start to export. Export sales are often handled through the marketing department as shown in Figure 22-6. Licensing is usually supervised through either the production or the research and development department. As sales rise, an independent international division is organized. Within this division, separate functional departments (such as finance, marketing, and production) are established. These divisional departments facilitate each individual country's operations, even though general managers of each international headquarters typically report directly to a corporate vice president, international.

Once the international division compares in competitive strength with the company's largest domestic-product divisions, problems of capital budgeting and transfer pricing become real concerns.[24] In order to accommodate organizational pressures for change, the firm typically adopts either a product or a geographically based global structure.

PRODUCT STRUCTURE

A global *product structure* is ideal when the firm manufactures lines of products that require different technologies and that supply different types of end users.[25] Utilizing a global product structure facilitates economies of scale in production, marketing, distribution, and research and development. Another clear advantage of structuring operations along product lines is that firms that do so are able to select global production sites in such a way as to exploit local comparative advantages with little regard for the nationality of the end user.

GEOGRAPHIC STRUCTURE

Frequently, there are real differences in the demand and taste for products across countries. Industries such as food, beverage, apparel, cosmetics, and construction tend to be driven by unique national or regional demand, so firms in these industries often utilize a global *geographic structure*. Though perhaps less efficient in minimizing production costs, a geographic emphasis facilitates marketing efforts directed at various end users. Area divisions are designed to encompass culturally or geographically similar host marketplaces.

Managing People Abroad

A key factor in the success of businesses competing internationally is the competence of their managers. Consequently, a major challenge that most international

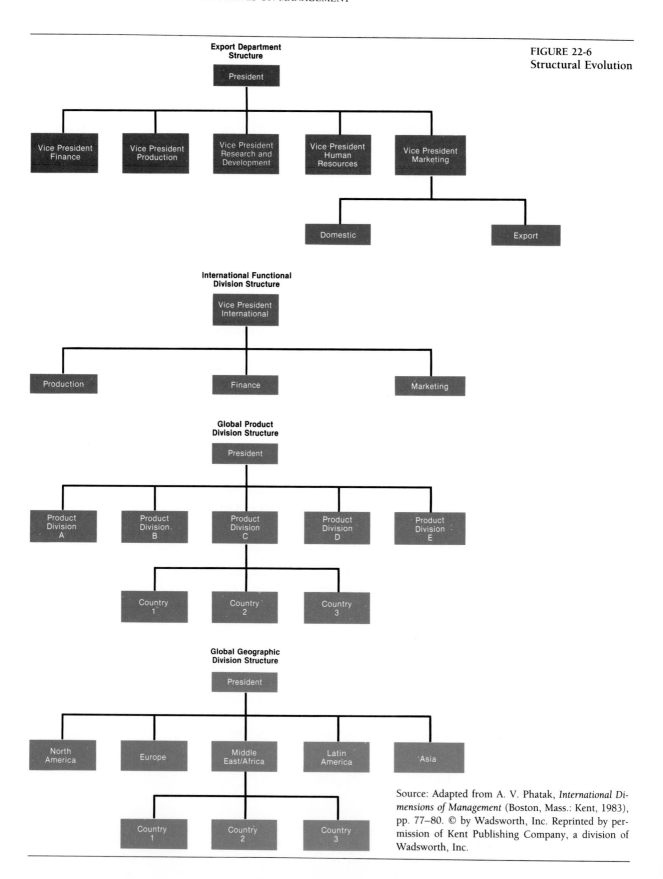

Source: Adapted from A. V. Phatak, *International Dimensions of Management* (Boston, Mass.: Kent, 1983), pp. 77–80. © by Wadsworth, Inc. Reprinted by permission of Kent Publishing Company, a division of Wadsworth, Inc.

FIGURE 22-6
Structural Evolution

firms face is finding the right manager or management team for a given task in a given country. Examining the cultural environment of international business illustrates the difficulty of this challenge.

Culture can be defined as the learned and interrelated set of symbols whose meanings provide a set of shared orientations for individuals in a particular society.[26] Culture influences such concerns as diet selection, family relations, work activities, sexuality, and hygiene. The most significant differences that American managers must be prepared to deal with, when interacting with people in foreign cultures, are language, nonverbal communication, general values, attitudes toward authority, and differences in factors that motivate workers.[27] A striking example of differences between American and Japanese management styles is highlighted in "In Practice 22-3."

Language

With the exception of the Commonwealth nations and (increasingly) Japan, most countries do not have large groups of the population who are fluent in English. Consequently, a very real challenge facing U.S. managers is learning to communicate and to represent themselves favorably in foreign markets. Language is perhaps the purest indication of the cultural diversity facing international managers. And managers must be aware not only of the vocabulary differences between cultures but also of the nuances and subtle shades of meaning that enrich local and regional dialects.

Values

Cultural values underlie the entire communication process. As we noted in the case that opens this chapter, attitudes toward time, work, consumption, achievement, social rank, risk, politics, and religion are all manifest in the values of a particular culture. A country's comparative advantage is much influenced by its cultural values. Cultural values ultimately determine where and how international business is conducted. From a foreign national (expatriate) manager's perspective, two particularly important aspects of cultural values are attitudes toward authority and the kinds of "rewards" that motivate employees to perform effectively in the workplace.

ATTITUDES TOWARD AUTHORITY

From a manager's point of view, one vital element of a culture's value system is its general attitude toward authority. Japanese managers, for example, are frequently found working and sharing offices and facilities with their subordinates. This is usually not the case in the United States, where a major incentive for becoming a manager is to enjoy the "perks" that distinguish the executive from the rank and file.

MOTIVATION

In order to maximize the contributions of foreign workers, managers must find ways to motivate them. Financial rewards are attractive in every culture, but many

■■■■■■■■■■ *In Practice 22-3* ■■■■■■■■■■

MATTER OF HONOR: JAPANESE TOP MANAGERS QUICK TO RESIGN WHEN TROUBLE HITS FIRM

The resignation of Toshiba Corporation's two top executives in June of 1987 said a lot about how Japanese managers differ from their U.S. counterparts. The Toshiba executives said they were taking responsibility for a subsidiary's sale of militarily sensitive technology to the Soviet Union. Most U.S. executives probably would not even *consider* resigning over an issue like that. Although both American and Japanese managers are responsible for the bottom line, the Japanese corporate chief is expected to make symbolic gestures and, at times, personal sacrifices that most U.S. executives are not.

Ritualistic resignations by Japanese chief executives are "almost a feudal way of purging the community of dishonor," said George Lodge, a professor at Harvard University's business school. "This is far different from the Anglo-Saxon legalistic tradition," he said, where an employee is bound by contract rather than as a member of a corporate community.

Toshiba itself noted that the resignations "may be hard to understand in American terms" but called it "the highest form of apology" in the Japanese business world.

The changes at Toshiba have their limits. The two executives, president and CEO Sugiichiro Watari and chairman Shoichi Saba, became consultants to the company—paid roles frequently assigned to past chairmen and presidents of Japanese corporations. As a result, there was "some element of theater" in the resignations, said Herbert Passin, a business consultant and professor emeritus at Columbia University. But he said the resignations were "significant" because the executives surrendered authority.

The incident recalled the resignation in 1985 of the president of Kikkoman Corporation after a scandal over tainted wine. Consider also the resignation that same year of the president of Japan Air Lines, following a jet crash that cost over 500 lives. Then-president Yasumoto Takagi remained in office only long enough to see that arrangements had been made to bury the dead and assist the bereaved—a process that included personal calls on victims' families.

By contrast, it was never seriously suggested in the United States that top executives of Boeing Company step down after the JAL crash, even though the accident was linked to a faulty repair performed years earlier by Boeing mechanics. No executives of Union Carbide Corporation resigned after the 1984 poison gas leak in Bhopal, India. Nor have any top officials resigned from Morton Thiokol over the company's involvement in the space shuttle disaster.

"Within Japanese corporate culture and social ethics, the whole notion is that the leader can delegate the authority to anyone he or she wishes, but *not* the responsibility," said Yoshi Tsurumi, a professor at City University of New York's Baruch Business School. "In the U.S., [leaders] delegate authority *and* responsibility."

The willingness of some Japanese top executives to serve as a kind of scapegoat in extreme circumstances is more than just a curiosity, management experts said. It is one of the many ways in which Japanese companies create a sense of community and employee loyalty in a business culture that demands much of its workers.

other motivators exist. Vacation time, public recognition, foreign travel, company housing and recreation facilities, health and insurance plans, independence from supervision, and size and type of office are a few of the many tools managers employ to motivate employees. The key to choosing which group of incentives to use lies in understanding which benefits are the most highly sought after in the particular host country. But managers should bear in mind that motivation must be designed to achieve specific company goals. In Japan, for example, where land prices are high and adequate housing hard to come by, companies often provide housing for their employees. Not only does this satisfy the worker's desires, but, more important from a management perspective, it fosters company loyalty and augments the company's influence in the lives of its employees.

"Management Development Exercise 22" will help you to gain some additional understanding of how overseas assignments are made. This self-test can also be used to determine what positions you might soon be prepared to fill abroad.

Attitudes of Expatriate Managers

It has been found that managers react in somewhat predictable ways when confronted with diverse cultural environments.[28] Four broad patterns have emerged.

1. Those who take an **ethnocentric attitude** regard management practices in the home country as superior to host country practices.

2. Those who assume a **polycentric attitude** regard local management practices as superior in adapting the firm to its host nation.

Guidelines for Management Practice

Management selection criteria vary widely among firms. How managers view a foreign assignment will depend on the nature of the assignment, its location, the duration of the posting, and the role of the assignment in the career of the employee. But basic to the objectives of the firm, and the manager charged with filling the position, is finding the right "fit" between employee and task. Managers with international responsibilities should take the following factors into account.

1. What is the objective for a particular overseas position? Executives must choose between filling the assignment with a local manager and appointing an expatriate. When the hiring is carried out by a local personnel office, the clear tendency is to hire host nationals. The opposite is often the case when the position is filled by headquarters management.

2. If the position is to be filled by a foreign national, which of the following issues should be central in the selection process:

   • Who is known and available?

   • How competent is the individual?

   • How loyal is the candidate?

   • What sort of management philosophy will the candidate espouse?

   • How much family support is available?

   • Does the candidate speak the language spoken in the home country?

   • How self-reliant is the individual?

   • How loyal is the candidate to the company?

3. What incentives will be necessary to be able to attract the right person? International postings, which often isolate managers from their home cultures, their families, and the inner workings of the corporation itself, are often difficult to fill. To overcome the objections that are frequently raised to overseas postings, many firms have turned to financial inducements. Bonus pay, trips home, maids, luxurious housing, and private schooling for the employee's children are often provided.

4. Is it worth the extra costs of staffing foreign postings with expatriates? Indeed, many firms have found that their international affairs should be managed by citizens of the countries where their foreign facilities are located.

3. Those who assume a **regiocentric attitude** favor managers from a particular regional context (for instance, only managers from countries belonging to the European Economic Community [the Common Market] would be selected to manage European operations).

4. And those who take a **geocentric attitude** favor basing the selection of managers on their qualifications regardless of their cultural background.

Each of these management philosophies can be defended under certain circumstances. For example, it is often beneficial for a company that has built a competitive advantage on its unique management style to foster ethnocentric management attitudes when penetrating new international markets. This was clearly the philosophy behind the late 1980s General Motors–Toyota joint venture to produce automobiles in California. Similarly, in countries that tend to be hostile toward the United States, it often makes good sense to promote polycentric management attitudes. Recent trends, however, have been toward greater overall acceptance of geocentric attitudes.

Review of the Learning Objectives

Having studied the chapter, you should be able to respond to the learning objectives with extensions of the following brief answers.

1. **Describe international business management, and explain its importance to the practicing manager in today's world.**

   International management refers to managing activities that cross national borders. Because the volume of international business is increasing, it is critical for the practicing manager to be aware of and understand the fundamentals of international business.

2. **Cite the two basic types of international business activity and the reasons why each occurs.**

   International trade and foreign direct investment are the basic types of international business. International trade can be accounted for by the concepts of comparative advantage and the international product life cycle. Foreign direct investment is profitable because of the competitive advantages of the multinational corporation or the competitive advantages that the multinational corporation can secure from the host country.

3. **Identify the general international strategies that a manager may use in developing international business activities.**

   Exporting, marketing satellites, miniature replicas, strategically independent facility, and global integration are stages in becoming a multinational corporation.

4. Describe the cultural considerations that affect managing in an international setting.

A foreign language and local values, attitudes toward authority, and factors that motivate all challenge businesses that want to compete in foreign markets. Too, U.S. expatriate managers carry their own attitudes and ethnocentric cultural biases abroad with them. Many managers also adopt polycentric or regiocentric management philosophies, and geocentric attitudes are coming increasingly into favor. Each of these attitudes can be appropriate and beneficial to the parent firm under the right circumstances.

Key Terms and Concepts

Having completed your study of Chapter 22, "International Management," you will have mastered the following important terms and concepts.

international management	home country	miniature replica	international joint ventures	ethnocentric attitude
international trade	host country	strategically independent facility	wholly owned subsidiary	polycentric attitude
foreign direct investment	international licensing	global integration	culture	regiocentric attitude
parent company	exporting marketing satellites			geocentric attitude

Questions for Discussion

1. How does international business management differ from domestic management?

2. If a subordinate of yours expresses the opinion that international business is not important, how will you respond? Is it important for the subordinate to be aware of international business trends?

3. Explain when international trade and when foreign direct investment are each appropriate as a form of international business activity.

4. What competitive advantages that the multinational corporation (MNC) enjoys can be transferred to another country?

5. What competitive advantages cannot be transferred by the MNC but can be secured by establishing operations in another country?

6. If the foreign investment rules in a country are very restrictive, what options does a manager have for promoting the firm's product?

7. Consider the contributions that MNCs make to their host countries. Which host countries stand to gain the most from MNC activities?

8. A firm is contemplating the potential for international sales of its product. What type of international business activity would you recommend that it consider first?

9. Is global integration possible in every industry?

10. Why must even a firm with only domestic operations recognize that it is competing in a global industry?

Notes

1. From S. Greenhouse, "New French *Cause Célèbre:* A Book Calling Nation Lazy," *New York Times,* July 10, 1987. Copyright © 1987 by The New York Times Company. Reprinted by permission.

2. R. D. Robinson, *Internationalization of Business: An Introduction* (Chicago, Ill.: Dryden, 1983).

3. R. D. Meade and J. D. Whittaker, "A Cross-Cultural Study of Authoritarianism," *Journal of Social Psychology* 72, no. 1 (1967): 3–7; and R. D. Meade, "An Experimental Study of Leadership in India," *Journal of Social Psychology* 72, no. 1 (1967): 35–43.

4. S. H. Robock and K. Simmonds, *International Business and Multinational Enterprises* (Homewood, Ill.: Irwin, 1983).

5. S. Roneu, *Comparative and Multinational Management* (New York: Wiley, 1986).

6. R. E. White and T. A. Poynter, "Strategies for Foreign-Owned Subsidiaries in Canada," *Business Quarterly,* Summer 1984; H. Crookell, "Specialization and International Competitiveness," *Business Quarterly,* Fall 1984; and J. Galbraith and R. Kazanjian, *Strategy Implementation: Structure, Systems and Process,* 2nd ed. (St. Paul, Minn.: West, 1986).

7. F. J. Contractor, "The Role of Licensing in International Strategy," *Columbia Journal of World Business* 15, no. 4 (Winter 1980): 73–81.

8. "A Trial with More at Stake than a Copyright," *Business Week,* June 9, 1986.

9. White and Poynter, "Strategies"; Crookell, "Specialization"; and Galbraith and Kazanjian, *Strategy Implementation.*

10. R. Gluck, "Global Competition in the 1980s," *The Journal of Business Strategy* 3, no. 4 (Spring 1983): 67–78.

11. K. Roth and J. A. Pearce, II, "Alterations to Strategy Formulation Required by Multinationalization," *Academy of Management Proceedings* (Atlanta, Ga.: Darby Press, 1986).

12. G. Hamel and C. K. Prahalad, "Managing Strategic Responsibility in the MNC," *Strategic Management Journal* 4 (1983): 341–351.

13. "Sanyo Tries to Stay One Step Ahead of the Year," *Business Week,* June 9, 1986.

14. K. J. Hladik, *International Joint Ventures: An Economic Analysis of U.S.–Foreign Business Partnerships* (Lexington, Mass.: D.C. Heath, 1985).

15. Robinson, *Internationalization of Business.*

16. Hladik, *International Joint Ventures.*

17. F. K. Berlew, "The Joint Venture—A Way into Foreign Markets," *Harvard Business Review* 54, no. 3, (July–August 1984): 48–54.

18. J. Garland and R. N. Farmer, *International Dimensions of Business Policy and Strategy* (Boston: Kent, 1986), pp. 66–67.

19. Y. Wind and S. Douglas, "International Portfolio Analysis and Strategy: The Challenge of the 80's" *Journal of International Business Studies,* Fall 1981, pp. 69–82; and T. H. Naylor, "The International Strategy Matrix," *Columbia Journal of World Business,* Summer 1985, pp. 11–19.

20. M. E. Porter, "Changing Patterns of International Competition," *California Management Review* 28, no. 2 (Winter 1986): 9–40.

21. J. A. Quelch and E. J. Hoff, "Customizing Global Marketing" *Harvard Business Review* 64 (May–June 1986): 59–68.

22. "Europe's Industries Take a Leaner Look," *Wall Street Journal,* March 9, 1987, p. 26.

23. J. Daniels, R. Potts, and M. J. Tretter, "Strategy and Structure of U.S. Multinationals: An Exploratory Study," *Academy of Management Journal* 27, no. 2: 292–307.

24. S. Davis, "Trends in the Organization of Multinational Corporations," *Columbia Journal of World Business* 11, no. 2 (Summer 1976): 60.

25. A. V. Phatak, *International Dimensions of Management* (Boston: Kent, 1983), p. 11.

26. V. Terpstra and K. David, *The Cultural Environment of International Business* (Cincinnati: South-Western, 1988).

27. R. Hawkins, *International Management* 30, no. 9 (September 1983): 49.

28. H. Perlmatter and D. Heenan, "How Multinational Should Your Top Managers Be?" *Harvard Business Review* 53 (1974): 121–132.

Cohesion Incident 22-1
"Parlez-Vous Français?"

During his training at Graniteville, Charles often heard Roger using French words and expressions. In fact, Roger always responded with "merci beaucoup," instead of "thank you." Roger's interest in things French also extended to the kitchen, where he occasionally spent time assisting in the preparation of several French dishes that appeared on the menu from time to time.

One day as he and Roger were talking over a cup of coffee, Charles asked him what explained his interest in French words and cooking. Roger replied that his mother had been born and raised in France. As a child, he had heard as much French in his home as English. And he had made three trips to France to visit his grandparents and once spent an entire summer with them.

"Charles, it's interesting that you have mentioned this to me right now, because Mr. Flynn is in France. In fact, he's probably in Paris at this very moment. The rumor is that he is looking into the possibility of buying a motel outside Paris and expanding our operation there. If it's successful, we'll probably expand to other countries as well. I just hope that he gives it a lot of thought, because there's literally a world of difference between running a business in another country and operating one in the States. But then again, there's a great opportunity right now for us to begin to expand into an international market."

A few months later, Roger showed Charles a press release announcing that Journey's End had purchased a 245-room motel in Paris and hoped to have it renovated before sending one of their managers there to get it started.

Because of Roger's background, Charles was not the least bit surprised when he was told that Roger had been summoned to the corporate headquarters to discuss with Mr. Flynn and the vice president of research and development his possible transfer to the Paris Journey's End.

Discussion Questions

1. Name some personal qualities and managerial skills that are desirable in an international manager. Does Roger have these attributes?

2. What kinds of problems do managers in foreign countries face?

3. In what way do the background cultures of other countries appear to differ from U.S. culture? If you have traveled or lived abroad, give an example of such a difference drawn from your own experience.

Cohesion Incident 22-2
Deciding Whether to Live Overseas

Because Travis Corporation is an international firm with plants in twenty-four countries, Leslie Phillips often came in contact with the marketing problems associated with the foreign distribution of vehicular and industrial equipment. As her knowledge of and experience with these foreign problems grew, so did her interest in the different cultures.

Eileen Thompkins, Leslie's supervisor, noticed and appreciated Leslie's interest and began to give her more responsibility in the planning and conducting of market research in the company's new West German market. Travis Corporation already had offices in Bonn and Frankfurt, but it was seeking to expand into the Stuttgart area because of the heavy concentration of German automobile factories there.

One morning after Leslie had looked over the day's mail, Eileen called her into her office. She told Leslie that Travis Corporation was opening new offices in Stuttgart, West Germany, and needed experienced market researchers from within the Travis organization to run the offices. Eileen had recommended Leslie for one of the positions.

At first Leslie was thrilled and excited at the prospect of living in Europe, traveling, and seeing all the wonderful places she had read about for years. But after the excitement wore off, reality set in—and with it some apprehension.

"But I don't speak German, Eileen. How will I be able to get around, let alone look for an apartment, shop for food, or go out with friends?"

Eileen had already anticipated these concerns and explained to Leslie that Travis Corporation sends employees selected for overseas positions to a six-week language school in Monterey, California. After completing the language school, Leslie would return to Elizabethtown, Travis corporate headquarters, for meetings and seminars in foreign management problems. Eileen assured Leslie that the company would make certain she was prepared professionally as well as emotionally. Besides, the many Travis Corporation employees already living in Germany would gladly lend their support.

Three weeks later, the Elizabethtown general manager, Peter Bostic, called Leslie into his office and offered her the position of assistant market researcher at the new corporate offices in Stuttgart.

Leslie had had three weeks to think about the possibility of a foreign move. Now she was faced with actually making the decision. Moving to a foreign country meant big changes in her life. No, she was not married, nor did she have any children. Yes, she was excited about the challenge and certainly would look forward to the experiences this opportunity would bring.

Discussion Questions

1. In addition to what Travis Corporation will do to prepare Leslie for an overseas position, what could Leslie do on her own to reduce the "culture shock" attendant upon moving to a foreign country and make the transition easier?

2. What are some of the advantages or opportunities Leslie can look forward to during her stay in West Germany? What are some of the disadvantages?

3. In selecting an employee for an overseas position, what professional and personal qualities should a corporation take into consideration?

4. If you were Leslie, would you accept the new position?

Management Development Exercise 22
How Overseas Assignments Are Made

Have you ever wondered what criteria are used to decide who should work overseas?

Think about the following job assignments:

1. Chief executive officer, responsible for overseeing and directing the entire operation.

2. Functional head, responsible for establishing functional departments in a foreign affiliate.

3. Troubleshooter, responsible for analyzing and solving specific operational problems.

4. Operative, rank-and-file employees.

In the following table, you will see a list of eighteen criteria that are considered in making overseas job assignments. Indicate which five criteria you think are most important in selecting employees for each of the four jobs described above. (Each "job title" gets five check marks.) Your instructor can provide you with the correct answers.

Criteria for Overseas Assignment Selection

Criterion	Chief Executive Officer	Functional Head	Trouble-shooter	Operative
Experience in company	———	———	———	———
Technical knowledge of business	———	———	———	———
Knowledge of language of host country	———	———	———	———
Overall experience and education	———	———	———	———
Managerial talent	———	———	———	———
Interest in overseas work	———	———	———	———
Initiative, creativity	———	———	———	———
Independence	———	———	———	———
Previous overseas experience	———	———	———	———
Respect for culture of host country	———	———	———	———
Sex	———	———	———	———
Age	———	———	———	———
Stability of marital relationship	———	———	———	———
Spouse's and family's relationship	———	———	———	———
Adaptability, flexibility in new environment	———	———	———	———
Maturity, emotional stability	———	———	———	———
Communicative ability	———	———	———	———
Same criteria as other comparable jobs at home	———	———	———	———

Source: Based on material from R. L. Tung, "Selection and Training of Personnel for Overseas Assignments," *Columbia Journal of World Business*, Spring 1981.

Glossary

accountability The clear awareness on the subordinate's part that the outcome of the delegated task or activity will be attributed to his or her efforts (p. 320)

achievement-oriented leadership Requires the leader to establish challenging expectations for subordinates, places a high degree of emphasis on constantly improving the quantity and excellence of the subordinates' output, and attempts to provide the supportive and rewarding environment in which exceptional performance can be achieved (p. 502)

action plan Detailed guideline that initiates and controls organizationwide action (p. 239)

administrative management Focuses on the broader aspects of managing large groups of people; grew out of the need to control and shape the behavior of employees in large, complex organizations (p. 36)

administrative skill Manager's ability to execute organizational rules, regulations, policies, and procedures; to operate effectively within budgetary constraints; and to coordinate the flows of information and paperwork within a group and among it and other groups (p. 14)

affirmative philosophy View that managers have a responsibility to promote the mutual best interests of the firm and its various stakeholders, including the general public (p. 136)

aggregate production planning Concerned with matching production levels with the demand for the product over an intermediate range of time (p. 622)

allocation-decision information Information useful for deciding how to assign people, time, equipment, or money to computer projects (p. 648)

alternation ranking Performance appraisal method listing the best and the worst (first and last), then the second best and second worst, the third best and the third worst, and so on until all employees have been ranked (p. 428)

alternative solutions Two or more ways to deal with a particular problem (p. 74)

analogue model Representation of an object or situation by substituting different forms or properties for various real elements (p. 77)

analytical skill Manager's ability to properly use scientific and quantitative approaches, techniques, and tools to solve management problems (p. 14)

assessment center Provides a specialized type of performance appraisal for managers by bringing together groups of managers who participate in simulated decision-making and problem-solving situations (p. 426)

autocratic leadership At one extreme of the leadership continuum; boss-centered leadership (p. 494)

authority The organization's legitimized power that is linked to each position within the organization (pp. 315, 320)

autonomy The extent to which the individual who performs a job has the freedom to plan and schedule the tasks to be carried out (p. 305)

back channel feedback Subtle vocal and visual responses the listener makes without taking over the speaking turn (p. 562)

backward vertical integration Occurs when a business acquires an operation that plays a role earlier in the production and marketing process, such as control of raw materials (p. 217)

barriers to planning Fall into two categories: The first category is the antiplanning bias of individuals toward engaging in planning activity. The second type of barrier is found at the organizational level. Organizational barriers arise out of constraints on resources, the limited information usually available, and the organizational implications of decisions associated with the planning process (pp. 252–58)

BCG matrix Stands for Boston Consulting Group and is one of the earliest frameworks for using the portfolio approach (p. 207)

behaviorally anchored rating scales (BARS) Individual performance appraisal method based on the results of a job analysis that specifies the behaviors that are required to do the job (p. 431)

behavioral school Response to the need to develop a more realistic picture of worker motivation and behavior (p. 39)

737

behavior theory Places emphasis on identifying what behaviors are characteristic of effective leaders (p. 486)

bill of materials (BOM) A structured parts list showing in what different production stages all lower-level components are needed for production (p. 627)

boundaries Points at which an organization meets the outside environment (p. 47)

boundary spanner Person whose job requires him or her to communicate with many different groups, each of which may have its own norms about communication (p. 557)

bounded rationality Limitations of thought, time, and information that restrict a manager's view of problems and situations (p. 70)

break-even point Level of output or sales at which total revenues equal total costs (p. 80)

break-even technique Decision-making model that helps managers determine whether a certain volume of output will result in profit or loss (p. 79)

budgeting A control process that involves expressing the future activities of an organization or subunit in dollar or other quantitative terms (p. 596)

bureaucracy Formulated as a set of rational ideas about the structure of the organization that define the ideal formalized organization (p. 38)

business plan A blueprint for building or expanding a business, articulating what the business opportunity is, why the opportunity exists, what strategy, actions, and resources are necessary to seize it, and how the new venture team has what it takes to execute the plan (p. 693)

business strategy Second level of "game plan" formation that clearly specifies what must be done at that level to support the accomplishment of the organization's objectives; formulated by business managers in such a way as to accomplish the business's long-term objectives (p. 210)

causal modeling Mathematical techniques by which we use independent variables other than time to develop forecasts (p. 275)

centralization The retention of authority at the top of the organization (p. 322)

certainty condition Exists when managers know precisely what the results will be if a certain decision is implemented (p. 82)

change phase Begins when planned changes are made in individuals' behavior or in organizational processes (p. 379)

changing environment Defined by trends that are predictable; thus the organization can be prepared to deal with these changes when they occur (p. 357)

channels The means of conveying the message, including sound, print, and touch (p. 552)

chase strategy Adjusting the number of employees to meet demand (p. 622)

classical school First major systematic approach to management thought; emphasizes finding ways to get the work of each employee done faster (p. 31)

closed system A system that does not interact with its environment (p. 47)

coercive power The ability of managers based on subordinates' fear of the manager (p. 506)

cognitive schema Body of knowledge based on past experience that affects not only our recall of the past (via selective recall) but also our perception and organization of new experiences (via selective perception) (p. 558)

cohesiveness The degree to which group members want to remain in the group and the amount of pressure to remain that the group brings to bear on its members (p. 527)

collective bargaining Negotiation of a contract between the bargaining unit (collection of employees) and the employer (p. 437)

combination strategy Pursuit of a combination of several strategies across the different businesses in which an organization is involved (p. 207)

command group A permanent formal group that consists of managers and their subordinates (p. 521)

communication Process by which one person or group transmits information to another person or group (p. 550)

communication skill Manager's ability to transmit ideas and preferences to others in both oral and written form (p. 15)

company profile Depicts the quantity and quality of a company's principal resources and skills in three broad areas: financial; physical, organizational, and human; and technological (p. 223)

competitive position Comparison of an individual firm to its competitors on such levels as market share, breadth of product line, and effectiveness of sales distribution (pp. 117, 177)

computer-aided design (CAD) A tool that enhances the coordination between the product design engineers and the manufacturing department by simulating the product's appearance and/or performance under various real-life scenarios (p. 616)

computer-aided manufacturing (CAM) Facility layouts in which work stations are located close together as with group technology layout, CAM makes it possible to bring many of the operations under the control of the computer (p. 620)

concentration Continuing to sell the business's present products or services to its existing customer base (p. 216)

conceptual skill Manager's ability to adopt the perspective of the organization as a whole (p. 13)

concern for people Manager's concern for developing mutual trust with subordinates, for promoting two-way communication, and for being sensitive to their feelings and preferences (p. 489)

concern for production Manager's concern for actively directing subordinates in order to get the task done with optimal efficiency (p. 489)

concurrent control Also called screening control and yes/no control; a control process that is in effect while work is being performed (p. 585)

conditional value Worth (usually expressed in dollars) assigned to the predictable occurrence of an event (p. 83)

connection power The ability of a leader based on the leader's relationships with influential persons both inside and outside the organization (p. 507)

consent election Method of decision making to unionize when the company does not contest union representation; if the union receives a majority support vote, then the union is established as the legal representative of the employees (p. 437)

contingency approach Management belief that no approach is universally applicable and that different problems and situations require different approaches (p. 47)

contingency theory Is based on the belief that a manager's success is situationally determined and therefore not attributable to any universally desirable set of leadership qualities (p. 486)

continuous flow The process wherein the work stations are arranged in order of the steps required to produce the product (p. 614)

continuous-process technology Utilizes fewer workers than does mass production, because most of the process is automated; a continuous stream of raw-material input is actually transformed into a continuous flow of output, not into separate definable units (p. 362)

control Process of monitoring and adjusting organizational activities in such a way as to facilitate accomplishment of organizational objectives (p. 580)

control-decision information Information necessary for correcting deviations from the plan when these corrections have not been specified in advance (p. 648)

controlling Guiding, monitoring, and adjusting work activities to help ensure that organizational performance stays in line with the firm's needs and expectations (p. 12)

coordination Integration of the activities of individuals and units into a concerted effort that works toward a common aim (p. 325)

corporate strategy Is concerned with two basic questions: What kind of businesses should the company be engaged in? And how should resources be allocated among those businesses? (p. 205)

culture (organizational) Shared beliefs, attitudes, and opinions about the company and what it stands for (p. 346)

culture (societal) Learned and interrelated set of symbols whose meanings provide a set of shared orientations for individuals in a particular society (p. 727)

customer departmentalization The organization of jobs and resources in such a way that each department can carefully understand and respond to the different needs of specific customer groups (p. 312)

customer profile Geographic, demographic, psychographic, and buyer-behavior information about an industry's or individual firm's customers (pp. 117–18)

data Records of facts and events; they are a source of information. By themselves, data have no meaning (p. 643)

debt financing Money provided to a business venture that must be repaid in some form (p. 695)

decentralization The wide distribution of authority throughout the organization (p. 322)

decertification Process by which employees (bargaining unit) can remove a union as its representative (p. 439)

decision A conscious choice to behave or to think in a particular way in a given set of circumstances (pp. 62–63)

decisional roles Four roles that reflect the top manager's most important responsibility—decision making; roles include entrepreneur, disturbance handler, resource allocator, and negotiator (p. 19)

decision making Process of choosing a course of action from two or more alternatives (p. 62)

decision-making skill Manager's ability to choose an appropriate course of action from two or more alternatives (p. 14)

decision support system (DSS) A computer-based system that helps decision makers deal with ill-structured problems by interacting with data and analysis models (p. 657)

decision tree Graphic model that charts the steps to consider in evaluating each alternative faced in decision making (p. 78)

defensive strategy Emphasized in companies with poorly performing lines of business (p. 207)

degree of change Gauge of the predictability of the environment, which is used to evaluate the extent of stability or dynamism in the environment (p. 108)

degree of complexity Number of "players" that operate and affect competitive operations and the level of sophisticated knowledge required to operate successfully in that environment (p. 108)

delegation Process by which a manager assigns tasks and authority among subordinates and the ongoing distribution of authority to that manager from above (pp. 314, 319)

Delphi technique Involves soliciting opinions or estimates from a panel of "experts" who are knowledgeable about the variable being forecasted; also known as a jury of expert opinion (p. 270)

demand forecast (sales forecast) Gives the expected level of demand for a company's products or services throughout some future period, also referred to as a sales forecast (p. 268)

democratic leadership Employee-centered leadership in which worker participation is encouraged (p. 494)

departmentalization The grouping of jobs, processes, and resources into logical units to perform some organizational task (p. 310)

dependent demand When the level of demand is the production level (p. 626)

descriptive model Representation of an object or situation that shows how it looks (p. 77)

differentiation strategy Requires managers to emphasize competitive methods that ensure that most of the customers in the industry perceive the company's product or service as unique (p. 215)

directing Communicating to others what their responsibilities are in achieving the company plan, as well as providing an organizational environment in which employees can become motivated to perform well (p. 12)

direction-decision information Information used to make decisions about very broad areas of the firm's economic commitments; applied before allocation-decision information, which is applied before control-decision information (p. 648)

directive leadership Requires the leader to set goals, timetables, work methods, and performance standards for the subordinates (p. 501)

discretionary responsibilities Public relations activities, good-citizen, and full corporate responsibilities that are voluntarily assumed by an organization (p. 142)

display rules Determine the situations in which senders find it appropriate to display some nonverbal expressions (p. 554)

diversification Taking on new products and new markets at the same time; **concentric** diversification involves the addition of a business that is related in terms of technology, markets, or products; **conglomerate** diversification requires taking on new businesses unrelated to the core business (p. 218)

divestiture Occurs when managers sell a business or a major component of a business; often occurs when retrenchment fails to accomplish the desired turnaround (p. 219)

divisional structure Organization of the company into distinct divisions that operate with considerable autonomy from other divisions and that usually perform their own marketing and operations activities (p. 349)

division of work Consists of dividing the work of the organization into specialized tasks (p. 301)

downward communication Carries information from people in positions of higher authority to people in positions of lower authority (p. 565)

ecological forces Concern for protecting and preserving the natural environment (p. 99)

econometric model Uses regression techniques at a much broader level in an effort to predict major economic shifts and the potential impact of those shifts on the company (p. 276)

economic forces Pressures on a business that result from the nature and direction of the economy in which the business operates (p. 100)

economic forecast Prediction of the future state of the economy, inflation rates, and interest rates (p. 268)

economic indicators Population statistics or indexes that portray the economic well-being of a specific population (p. 276)

economic responsibilities Basic social responsibilities of business, requiring managers to optimize profits by providing goods and services to society at reasonable cost (p. 141)

effectiveness Successful achievement of organizational goals (p. 20)

efficiency Quantity of inputs that a firm uses to produce one unit of its output (p. 20)

effort-performance expectancy Expresses the concept that the greater the expectancy that one's effort will produce the desired performance, the greater the probability that one will perform a particular task (p. 464)

employee relations and development Expression of management's interest in the workers' welfare that links the welfare of the workforce to the planned pursuits of the company; well-managed companies jointly set specific career development objectives for employees (p. 178)

employee skills inventory Collection of the following types of information about an organization's employees: previous jobs held; length of time in present job; educational and training qualifications; specific knowledge and skills; performance appraisals; past and current compensation and benefits; capacity of the individual, such as test scores and health information; special preferences for the individual, such as location or job preferences (p. 416)

encoding Involves transforming the message into a form (electronic impulses, words, or nonverbal expressions) that is appropriate for the medium and interpretable by the receiver (p. 551)

entrepreneurship The process of bringing together creative and innovative ideas and actions with the management and organizational skills necessary to mobilize the appropriate people, money, and operating resources to meet an identifiable need and create wealth in the process (p. 678)

environmental analysis Systematic assessment of information about the firm's external environment during the strategic planning process to identify strategic opportunities for the company as well as major threats, problems, or other possible impediments (p. 222)

environmental forces External and largely uncontrollable factors that influence managers' decisions and actions and, ultimately, the internal structures and processes of organizations (p. 97)

equal employment opportunity (EEO) The right of all employees and job applicants to be considered for employment, promotion, compensation, termination, and other conditions of work only on the basis of job-related qualifications or performance (p. 410)

equity financing Money provided to a business venture that is not expected to be repaid as such, but instead entitles the source to some form of ownership in the venture. The source usually expects some future return or gain on that investment (p. 695)

equity theory Motivation theory that addresses the issue of whether a person believes that he or she is being fairly treated compared to the treatment of others who are in a similar situation (p. 468)

essay evaluations Written performance appraisals, often in the form of a paragraph or letter of evaluation (p. 430)

esteem needs The need for self-esteem (tied to feelings of achievement, competence, knowledge, and maturity) and the need to be held in esteem by others (centering around personal reputation, recognition, and peer-group status) (p. 455)

ethical responsibilities Obligations for right or proper business behavior that transcend legal requirements (p. 142)

ethics Set of moral principles that governs the actions of an individual or group (p. 148)

ethnocentric attitude Attitude of a person who regards management practices in the home country as superior to host country practices (p. 729)

excellence behavior Reflects the rewards that employees seek which are psychologically intangible; these rewards reflect a broader spectrum of potential need satisfaction than are sought by less motivated co-workers (p. 453)

exception information Similar to trigger information in that it triggers action; however, it triggers a specific type of action, and it is solicited by a general request to be notified when the exception occurs (p. 647)

expectancy theory The theory that subordinates are most productive when they believe there is a high probability that their efforts will lead to high levels of productivity, which will result in desired outcomes that will satisfy their deepest needs (p. 464)

expected value Conditional value of an occurring event multiplied by the probability that it will occur (p. 83)

expert power Power based on the leader's possession of expertise, skill, or knowledge that convinces subordinates that the leader's views should serve as a basis for their action (p. 506)

explicit ("intended") strategy Plan or program that formally states how the organization defines its objectives and how it will achieve them and implement its mission (p. 204)

exporting Selling of a firm's own products abroad (p. 719)

extended expectancy model A model of motivation developed by psychologists Lyman Porter and Edward Lawler that emphasizes the idea that performance leads to satisfaction (p. 466)

external environment Social, political, and economic factors that might affect an organization (p. 48)

extinction The attempt to weaken a particular behavior by failing to provide a desired outcome or even by ignoring the behavior completely (p. 471)

extrinsic rewards Rewards an employee expects management to confer as a direct consequence of the employee's accomplishing the desired level of performance (p. 467)

facility layout Related to the location of machinery, inventory storage areas, customer waiting rooms, and receiving docks within a facility (p. 614)

facility location The process of determining the geographic location of new warehouses and production facilities (p. 614)

feedback (communication) Conveys the receiver's reaction to the sender's message (pp. 305, 552)

feedback (system) Information about various systems used to evaluate their operations and make corrections (p. 47)

feedback control Also called post-action control; the approach to control that focuses on the outputs of organizational activities after the production or operation process has been completed (p. 586)

feedforward control Also called steering control or preliminary control; an approach to control that uses inputs to a system of organizational activities as a means of controlling the accomplishment of organizational objectives (p. 584)

financial audit Mechanism used to control financial resources; includes external audits and internal audits (p. 602)

financial plan Spells out how the firm's resources are to be used and controlled (p. 243)

financial resources Money that the firm has available in the short term and the long term to pay for the materials or services that it seeks from others, including raw materials and labor (p. 20)

first-line manager One who has the lowest level of managerial responsibility, whose title may be supervisor, foreman, project manager, coordinator, operating manager, or office manager (p. 7)

fixed-order-period system Also known as the P-system; keeps the time period between orders constant while the order quantity is allowed to vary (p. 627)

fixed-order-quantity system Also known as the Q-system; the size of the order for items to be placed in inventory is always the same (p. 627)

flow Movement of materials and human energy through a system (p. 47)

focus strategy Attempt to gain a competitive advantage within a narrow market through some combination of cost leadership and differentiation (p. 215)

forced-choice method Performance appraisal method in which each person being evaluated is compared with every other person (p. 429)

forced-distribution method Performance appraisal method in which the evaluator categorizes the employees according to a prescribed determination, such as 10 percent excellent, 20 percent above average, and so forth (p. 428)

force-field analysis (FFA) Technique used to diagram key forces in a situation characterized by conflict or planned change and to plan the change more effectively; first step is to identify the key forces promoting the shift to a new, desired situation (driving forces) and those inhibiting such a change (restraining forces); next step is to estimate the strength or importance of each such force and represent it via the size of its arrow; change, according to the theory, can be achieved only when the driving forces are greater than the restraining forces (p. 393)

forecast Prediction or estimate of future conditions (p. 267)

forecasting Attempting to state beforehand what will happen in the future (p. 267)

foreign direct investment An investment made by a company in business operations in another country whereby that company retains "effective managerial control" of the foreign operations (p. 712)

formal group A group formed at the direction of the organization in order to accomplish organizational goals (p. 521)

forward vertical integration Occurs when a company moves up the distribution chain—through investment or other activity—in order to be closer to the consumers of its products or services (p. 218)

four-fifths rule Relates to EEO requirements; refers to a company's selection rate for any protected group, which must be at least four-fifths, or 80 percent, of the selection rate for a majority group (p. 411)

friendship group A relatively permanent informal group that develops within and across boundaries of formal groups and is often affected by people's attraction for one another and individuals' perceptions that they share common interests or goals (p. 522)

functional authority Assigned to complement line or staff authority in order to accomplish a specific task (p. 319)

functional departmentalization Grouping of jobs and resources within the company in such a way that employees who perform the same or similar activities are in the same department (p. 310)

functional manager One who is responsible for just one type of organizational activity, such as accounting, finance, personnel, production, or marketing (pp. 9–11)

functional plan Describes the specific actions to be taken in the immediate future by people responsible for that particular functional area (p. 242)

functional strategy Third level of "game plan," which also may be a product strategy or geographic strategy; guidance that ensures that such areas as marketing, finance, production, accounting, personnel, and research and development are "doing the right thing" (p. 219)

functional structure Grouping of similar tasks and activities (such as those of production/operations, marketing, finance/accounting, research and development, and personnel) as separate units within the organization (p. 348)

Gantt chart A control chart on which time appears in the horizontal dimension and activities or tasks appear in the vertical dimension. Horizontal bars represent planned schedules and time required for each task, and additional markings on each horizontal bar indicate actual task accomplishment (p. 282)

gap analysis Seeks to determine whether a performance "gap" exists between what the company's existing strategy can realistically be expected to accomplish and the objectives that have been established in these performance areas (p. 225)

general information Information that arises incidentally or in response to nonspecific inquiries or searches (p. 646)

general manager One who is responsible for all of the activities of an organization or one or more of its complex subunits (p. 11)

generic strategies Concept developed by Michael Porter, which states that every business strategy is one of three kinds: overall cost leadership, differentiation, or focus (p. 214)

geocentric attitude Attitude of a person who favors basing the selection of managers on their qualifications regardless of their cultural background (p. 730)

geographical departmentalization Grouping of jobs and resources around particular locations (p. 313)

GE planning grid Tool used by General Electric in which managers sought to improve on the growth-share matrix by incorporating multiple measures of each dimension in their grid and by increasing the number of cells within the grid (pp. 208–9)

global integration Exhibited by a company that attempts to maximize the use of all of its foreign investments in a coordinated manner; decisions are made in such a way as to benefit the entire organization, rather than each business unit operating separately (p. 721)

goal-directed behavior Requires an individual to direct considerable personal energies toward achievement of a specified goal (p. 452)

good An output that can be stored in inventory for use at a later date (p. 612)

graphic scales Probably the most common method of performance appraisal; include techniques for comparing an individual's performance to some predetermined standard of performance (p. 429)

grid OD A comprehensive program for: (a) evaluating the management styles of managers within an organization on the basis of their concern for people and their concern for production, and (b) then using training activities to move them toward a preferred management style (pp. 395–96)

group "Two or more people who interact with one another, are psychologically aware of one another, perceive themselves to be members of the group, and work toward a common goal" (p. 517)

group-dynamics skills Require knowing when to let a group drift and when (and how) to intervene and help it focus its efforts better (p. 391)

group polarization The tendency of groups to make more extreme decisions and judgments than individuals make (p. 534)

group structure The norms the group develops and conforms to in order to reach its goals, the roles that are played by various people within the group, and the group's cohesiveness (its network of communication and interpersonal attraction) (p. 524)

group technology layout Requires the identification of a group of products called a product family, all members of which are similar in shape, size, or material and require similar processing (p. 619)

groupthink A way of thinking that characterizes cohesive group members whose concerns for unanimity take precedence over the needs they feel to objectively evaluate alternative courses of action (p. 535)

growth-share matrix Addresses three questions: What businesses should an organization be in? What basic mission should each business pursue? And how should corporate resources be allocated across the businesses? Growth rate is

the projected increase in share of the primary market, usually over the next few years (p. 207)

growth strategy Appropriate when an organization seeks to expand at a rate greater than the growth in GNP and inflation (p. 206)

halo effect Tendency to assume that a person who performs well in some areas is also good in other areas (p. 427)

Hawthorne effect Phenomenon discovered at the Western Electric Hawthorne plant: Employees work harder when they believe management is concerned about their welfare and when managers pay special attention to them (p. 42)

hierarchy of needs An individual's personal set of priorities to assess the strength of any particular need at any particular time (p. 454)

home country The headquarters country of a parent company (p. 712)

horizontal communication Process of sending information to someone who is at the same level in the formal organizational structure (p. 566)

horizontal integration Growth by acquiring similar businesses that represent the same link in the production and marketing chain—in short, competitors (p. 218)

host country The country receiving foreign direct investment (p. 712)

human constraints Limits imposed by the level of competence of the people employed by an organization (p. 49)

human relations skill Manager's ability to deal effectively with others, both inside and outside the firm, who affect the business's success (p. 15)

human resource development Long-term training designed to increase an employee's job effectiveness and to develop his or her ability to assume greater job responsibilities (p. 425)

human resource forecasting The attempt to predict the demand for labor that an organization will experience if it is to accomplish its objectives in a specified period of time (p. 416)

human resource management Process of ensuring that competent people are available, that they are able to achieve organizational objectives, and that their energy and abilities are used effectively (p. 409)

human resource planning Forecast of the organization's future personnel needs with the number and the skills of its present and anticipated labor supply (p. 413)

human resource ratios Ratios used as means of monitoring and adjusting the use of human resources throughout the organization, including employee turnover, absenteeism, and work force composition ratios (p. 604)

human resources People needed to operate the business and to perform those tasks that require human talent, skills, and abilities (p. 20)

hygiene factors Factors or conditions on the job that, when they are not met, operate to make employees dissatisfied (pp. 456–57)

implementation Process of putting a decision into action (p. 75)

implementation control A concurrent control designed to assess whether the overall strategy should be changed in light of unfolding events and results associated with the sequence of steps and actions involved in implementing the company's strategy (p. 595)

implicit ("realized") strategy "Pattern of the organization's responses to its environment over time" (p. 204)

independent demand Situation in which the source of demand is beyond the control of the company such as with finished goods and distribution inventories (p. 626)

industry Set of businesses that produce products or provide services that are close substitutes for one another (p. 110)

informal group A group created by the choice of its members for the purpose of goals defined by the group (p. 521)

informal organization Unplanned relationships and activities among people in an organization that emerge to expedite the organization's work (p. 298)

information Knowledge of a particular fact, event, or situation (p. 643)

informational roles Activities of top managers whereby they become the informational nerve centers of their group—focal points for receiving and sending (both inside and outside the organization) information that is vital to productivity (p. 18)

information management system (IMS) A system that enables people to use information in support of the organization's operations, control, and planning (p. 652)

information overload Occurs when a person receives more informtion than he or she can deal with (p. 564)

information power The ability of a leader based on the leader's knowledge of or access to information that is believed to be valuable to others (p. 507)

instrumentality A statement of probability based on the notion that the individual's desired outcomes will satisfy his or her deepest desires (p. 465)

intensive technology Involves the application of specific skills, techniques, or services in order to make a change in an input; describes custom work and is consistent with Woodward's unit production technology (p. 362)

interest group Group that exists because of a shared concern of members at any level or area in the firm; develops or becomes active when members believe that their special concerns are receiving insufficient managerial attention (p. 522)

intergroup conflict The mutually perceived incompatibility of goals as well as mutual interference in goal attainment (p. 536)

intermittent flow Also called job shop manufacturing; the product being produced may follow a variety of routes through the shop, unlike the one fixed route found in the line-flow or continuous-flow production process (p. 615)

internal environment The conditions inside an organization (p. 48)

international joint venture Such ventures typically involve the creation of a third company by two other firms from different countries; the two parents then cooperatively manage the "child" for their common benefit (p. 722)

international licensing A contractual agreement that transfers the company's industrial property rights (patents, trademarks, and/or proprietary know-how) to a third party in a foreign country (p. 718)

international management The development and control of the flows of capital, labor, raw materials, technology, information, goods, and services across national borders (p. 711)

international trade The transfer of products and/or organizational skills and services from one country to another (p. 712)

interpersonal roles Activities that top managers perform principally because of their formal position in the firm. Mintzberg identified these roles as figurehead, leader, and liaison (p. 17)

interpersonal skills The ability to facilitate clear communication between people in a situation that is often tense and emotionally charged (p. 390)

intrapreneurship The adoption of entrepreneurial concepts within the existing structures of large organizations (p. 700)

intrinsic rewards Rewards that are inherent in performance of the task itself, such as a sense of pride in one's accomplishment (p. 467)

job analysis Identification of the specific activities performed in a job and the characteristics of the person, the work situation, and the materials or equipment necessary for performing the job effectively (p. 412)

job depth Level of control the worker has over her or his job (p. 302)

job description Specifies the tasks, duties, and responsibilities that a job holder has and describes briefly how, when, and where these activities are to be performed (pp. 412–13)

job enlargement Increase in the number of activities that a worker performs (p. 306)

job enrichment Attempt to increase job depth by allowing more autonomy (p. 307)

job evaluation A systematic process for determining the relative worth of jobs within an organization (p. 413)

job scope Length of time required for the job cycle and the number of operations involved in the job; a job that entails fewer repetitions and more operations has higher scope (pp. 303–4)

job specification Describes the skills, knowledge, and abilities that a person needs in order to perform that job satisfactorily (p. 413)

jury of expert opinion Involves soliciting opinions or estimates from a panel of "experts" who are knowledgeable about the variable being forecasted; also known as Delphi technique (p. 270)

just-in-time system (JIT) An operations technique that was developed in Japan; seeks to eliminate all waste (and the expense it entails) by providing the right part at the right place in the exact quantity and at the exact time it is to be used (pp. 628–29)

knowledge-based system An artificial intelligence program that depends for its performance on knowledge rather than on ingenious computations (p. 659)

labor relations Consist of the ways in which managers relate to employees who are represented by a union (p. 431)

labor union "A formal association of workers that promotes the welfare of its members" by engaging in collective bargaining to determine wages, benefits, and other working conditions (p. 431)

laissez-faire leadership Situation wherein the manager is essentially uninvolved in the functioning of the work group (p. 494)

Laplace criterion States that there is no defensible reason to believe one event is more likely to occur than another (p. 85)

large-batch and mass-production technology An assembly line, where large numbers of the same product are produced (p. 361)

leader-member relations A leader position that when strong allows the leader a full range of personal and organizational bases of influence to use in trying to gain subordinates' support; but when weak, the leader's influence is often reduced to the impersonal power granted by the company (p. 495)

leader position power The extent of formal and informal power granted to the manager by the organization (p. 495)

leadership The process of influencing others to work toward the attainment of specific goals (p. 483)

leadership continuum A full range of options for a manager to consider, from very boss-centered leadership to employee-centered leadership (p. 494)

legal responsibilities A firm's obligation to comply with the law (p. 141)

legitimate power Power based on the perception of the manager's position in the organizational hierarchy (p. 506)

level-work-force strategy Requires the production output to be constant, with the number of employees fairly constant; does not vary when demand changes (p. 622)

linear programming (LP) Mathematical procedure used to determine the best combination of those resources and activities that are necessary to fulfill some objective (p. 277)

line authority The most fundamental type of authority assigned in an organization; concerned with making decisions and giving instructions that have a direct bearing on the accomplishment of organizational goals (p. 318)

line flow Also called repetitive manufacturing, with work centers also arranged in order of the steps required to produce the product; in line flow, products produced can be measured as discrete units (pp. 614–15)

line manager One who is directly responsible for functions or activities central to creating the main product line or service that an organization markets (p. 9)

linking pins Bolts that tie two portions of an object together; objectives are "linking pins" because they are used to coordinate diverse organization activities (p. 168)

liquidation Sale of a business in parts for its tangible assets, not as a going concern (p. 219)

long-linked technology Characterized by a series of sequential tasks that must be performed in a specific order; the assembly line is an example (p. 362)

long-term objectives Clear, simple, measurable statements of the specific outcomes the firm expects to achieve through companywide effort in three to five years (p. 171)

make-to-order system A system in which a firm waits until a customer order is placed before making the product to fill the order (p. 614)

make-to-stock system A system in which a firm produces goods to be stocked in finished goods inventory (p. 614)

management Process of optimizing human, material, and financial contributions for the achievement of organizational goals (p. 4)

management assistance Refers to people outside a business venture who help the owners and managers plan, analyze, and control the present and future activities of the business and its people (p. 697)

management by objectives (MBO) Popular technique that organizations use to integrate objectives into the activities that managers engage in; a formal, or a quasiformal, procedure that begins with objective setting and ends with performance appraisal, usually on an annual cycle (p. 187)

management information system (MIS) An integrated reporting system specifically designed to help managers plan, execute, and control the organization's activities (p. 657)

management science school An approach that stresses an emphasis on decision making, the use of quantitative models, the use of computers, and evaluation of effectiveness (p. 43)

management theories Explanations of why a particular practice is effective or ineffective (p. 30)

Managerial Grid® Enables us to identify a wide range of styles that represent various combinations of concern for people and concern for production (p. 489)

market development Strategy that might focus on geographic expansion: start locally, next expand regionally, then go national (p. 217)

marketing plan Tells sales and marketing personnel who will sell what, where, when, to whom, in what quantity, and how (p. 242)

marketing satellites Investments in foreign sales offices and warehouses that handle a company's affairs overseas (p. 720)

master production schedule (MPS) A schedule that is stated in terms of the actual end product the company produces (p. 623)

materials requirements planning (MRP) A system developed for controlling and planning inventories subject to dependent demand (p. 628)

matrix organization An organization structure that establishes dual channels of authority, performance responsibility, evaluation, and control; job holders are typically assigned to both a basic functional area and a project or product manager (p. 352)

mechanistic system A design that follows Weber's bureaucratic model very closely in that it is characterized by specialized activities, specific rules and procedures, an emphasis on formal communication, and a well-defined chain of command (p. 358)

mediating technology A process that brings together groups that need to be interdependent for the desired action to take place; for example, banking is a mediating technology that facilitates the interaction between depositors and borrowers (p. 362)

message Expressed information that the sender hopes will convey the intended meaning to the receiver (p. 552)

middle-level manager One who is defined in terms of the reporting relationships in the organization; first-line managers report to middle-level managers, and middle-level managers are most often the principal internal managers of a business (p. 7)

milestone review Usually involves the major reassessment of a firm's progress at critical junctures (milestones) in the process of implementing the strategy (p. 596)

miniature replica Company that produces and sells some or all of the "parent"'s products in a local country (p. 721)

model Representation of some real object or situation (p. 77)

monopolistic competition Competition among a relatively large number of companies offering similar products (pp. 111–12)

monopoly A condition in which a single firm serves the entire market (p. 111)

moral rights approach Judgment of whether decisions and actions are in keeping with the maintenance of fundamental personal and group rights and privileges (p. 154)

motivation The outcome of the process by which a manager induces others to work to achieve organizational objectives as a means of satisfying their own personal desires (p. 451)

motivators Job conditions that, when they are met, are associated with high levels of employee motivation and job satisfaction (p. 457)

National Labor Relations Board The federal hearings panel that determines if an employer or union is complying with U.S. laws governing labor relations (p. 433)

need for achievement Reflects the desire of individuals for moderately high levels of risk taking, concrete feedback, and problem-solving responsibility (p. 461)

need for affiliation The desire to have close, cooperative, and friendly relations with others (p. 462)

need for power Expression of an individual's desire to control and influence others (p. 461)

needs Wishes, wants, or desires for certain tangible or intangible outcomes (p. 452)

need satisfaction Positive feelings of relief and well-being that an individual enjoys when he or she has met a need (p. 453)

negative reinforcement The encouragement of a specific behavior via the removal or elimination of an outcome that the individual feels is undesirable (p. 471)

noise Anything that interferes with transmission of the message (p. 552)

nominal group technique A group discussion method in which intermember interaction is carefully controlled and that attempts to get the benefit of the ideas and opinions of people who tend not to speak out during a highly charged group interaction; all group members are asked to write down comments or suggestions and then to respond in writing as the group leader reads the list of suggestions (p. 393)

nonprogrammed decisions Decisions not bound by policy, rules, or procedures (p. 63)

norm A standard of behavior to which group members expect each other to adhere (p. 525)

objective probability Probability based on past experience (p. 87)

objectives Intended or expected end results; recognized by effective managers as essential ingredients contributing to organizational performance (p. 166)

oligopoly Exists when a few sellers control a large percentage of the supply of the product (p. 111)

one-minute managing Developed by Kenneth Blanchard; three basic ideas are objective setting, praising, and reprimanding, each of which should only take one minute (p. 191)

one-time plan Developed to guide the carrying out of activities that are not intended to be repeated (p. 248)

open system A system that interacts with the environment (p. 47)

operating control Managerial control exercised at the operating level, where managers are concerned with using physical, financial, human, and information resources to accomplish organizational objectives (p. 582)

operating environment Forces in a firm's immediate situation that pose many of the challenges it faces when it tries to attract or acquire needed resources or to market its goods and services in a profitable manner (p. 117)

operations management (OM) The designing, planning, controlling, and scheduling of any production system that converts required inputs into desired outputs (p. 612)

optimism criterion Premise that the best outcome will happen (p. 86)

organic system Composed of components in which task activities are loosely defined, with very few rules and procedures; self-control, participative problem solving, and horizontal communication are emphasized (p. 358)

organizational mission The broad objective that sets a business apart from other firms of its type and identifies the scope of its operations in product and market terms (p. 172)

organizational purpose Fundamental reason for an organization's existence (p. 172)

organizational values Philosophical and ethical standards explicitly and implicitly adhered to by company personnel in pursuit of the company's purpose and mission (p. 174)

organization chart Depiction of the formal relationships among people or groups of people in an organization. Usually a simple drawing of lines and boxes that shows how the firm is organized; boxes represent the firm's activities and the people who perform those activities, and lines indicate the relationships among them (pp. 8, 297)

organization design Process of finding the fit between an organization's key elements (structure, people, tasks, decision and reward systems, and informal organization and culture) and its strategy that results in successful performance (p. 341)

organization development (OD) Offers a framework and a perspective that managers can draw on to facilitate planned change; an effort planned, often organizationwide, and managed from the top to increase organization effectiveness and health through planned interventions in the organization's process, using behavioral science knowledge (p. 377)

organization development (OD) process A series of the following six steps: (a) recognizing a problem; (b) diagnosing the situation; (c) identifying the problem and admitting it exists; (d) selecting and "owning" a solution; (e) planning and implementing the change; and (f) evaluating the change (pp. 386–90)

organizing Process of defining the essential relationships among people, tasks, and activities in such a way that all the organization's resources are integrated and coordinated to accomplish its objectives efficiently and effectively (pp. 12, 296)

overall cost leadership strategy Tries to maximize sales by minimizing costs per unit and charging low prices; the idea is to outperform competitors by selling at a lower price and to do so profitably (p. 214)

parent company The company making a foreign investment (p. 712)

participative decision model Argues that managers should adopt whichever of several different leadership styles is most appropriate to the demands of the particular problem at hand (p. 503)

participative leadership Requires the leader to solicit subordinates' recommendations, ideas, and evaluations before making or implementing decisions (p. 502)

parity principle States that responsibility and authority must be equal (p. 320)

path-goal theory Suggests that effective leaders must identify and communicate to subordinates the path that those subordinates should follow in order to achieve personal and organizational goals, must help subordinates make progress along that path; and must clear away any obstacles on the path that might slow or prevent subordinate achievement of goals (p. 500)

payoff approach Technique for estimating the return on an investment under varying degrees of risk (p. 84)

people change Changes in the behaviors, attitudes, skills, and expectations of employees so as to increase organizational performance (p. 385)

performance appraisal Process of determining how well someone is performing his or her job; involves measuring performance and comparing it with an established standard (pp. 425, 603)

performance-outcome expectancy Suggests the higher the subjective probability in the workers' minds that the manager can and will deliver the rewards promised, the greater the likelihood that the workers will pursue the task requested by the manager (p. 464)

peripheral norm Describes what the group expects as desirable behavior (p. 525)

PERT (Program Evaluation Review Technique) A planning technique that enables a manager to create an accurate estimate of the time required to complete a project; developed to help managers schedule and monitor large-scale projects (p. 283)

pessimism criterion Method of basing a decision on the "worst-case situation," or the idea that the least desirable outcome will happen (p. 86)

physical resources The existence, condition, and location of facilities; plants and equipment; machinery; and the raw materials that the business needs to produce goods or deliver services (p. 20)

physiological needs Basic and essentially unlearned primary needs; sometimes called biological needs. In the modern work environment, they include the desire for pay, vacations, pension plans, break periods, comfortable working environments, heating, lighting, and air conditioning (p. 454)

pivotal norm Norm that is closely related to the group's identity and goals; adherence to this type of norm is a requirement of group membership and is typically expected of all members of the group, regardless of their status (p. 525)

placement Process of deciding which of several jobs is best suited to an individual who has been selected and hired (p. 420)

planned change Systematic, deliberate change in the way part or all of an organization functions (p. 378)

planning Determining the direction of a business by establishing objectives and by designing and implementing the strategies necessary to achieve those objectives (p. 12)

policy Statement intended to set parameters for making recurring decisions; offers a general guide to action (p. 249)

political-legal forces Legal and otherwise governing parameters within which the firm must, or may wish to, operate (p. 101)

political skills Require that the OD practitioner learn what to say, what not to say, and how to handle various situations (p. 392)

polycentric attitude Attitude of a person who regards local management practices as superior in adapting the firm to its host nation (p. 729)

POM plan Must guide decisions about the basic nature of firm's production/operations management, which is the core function in any business operation; consists of planning and overseeing the process of converting inputs into value-enhanced output (p. 245)

portfolio approach Views a company as a "portfolio" of business investments that managers must balance by expanding investment in some while reducing investment in others (p. 207)

positive reinforcement The encouragement of a desirable behavior by providing desirable con-

sequences when the employee behaves in a desirable manner (p. 471)

power The ability to act or exert influence, whereas authority is the *right* to do so (p. 315)

premise control A feedforward control designed to check systematically whether the premises underlying the company's plans are still valid (p. 595)

prepotency Assumes individuals progress from motivation by needs at lower levels in the hierarchy of needs to motivation by needs at higher levels (p. 455)

proactive decision making Aimed at creating a future environment that will enable managers to achieve their objectives (p. 116)

problem definition Process of determining the scope and nature of a problem once it has been identified (p. 72)

problem identification Process of establishing that some sort of problem exists (p. 72)

problem-solving skills Include the ability of an OD practitioner to sort out the issues being discussed and to recognize which issues are crucial; the ability to maintain a detached perspective; the ability to express the unspoken concerns of the group members so that others can acknowledge them; and, finally, the ability to maintain composure and control, even when other people do upsetting things (p. 391)

process consultation Requires an OD practitioner to examine some organizational process, develop ideas on how to improve it, and then lead participants in that process through a discussion of those ideas (p. 395)

process layout A layout in which all machines or workers of a similar type or function are grouped together (p. 619)

product departmentalization Grouping of jobs and resources around the products or product lines that a company sells (p. 311)

product development Substantial modification of existing products or the creation of new but related items that can be marketed to current customers through established channels (p. 217)

productivity The level of efficiency organizational members achieve in providing the organization's goods and services; commonly expressed in terms of the number of items produced or sold per unit of input or in terms of the number of services rendered per unit of input (p. 177)

product layout Also called a flow layout; arrangement of machines according to the sequential steps involved in the production of a part (p. 619)

product-market evolution The product life cycle, or the stages that characterize the evolution of a product and market; what business strategy is appropriate depends on what stage of the evolution the business's major product and market have reached (p. 212)

product-market matrix Approach by which managers choose among eight "grand strategy options" at the business-unit level that reflect management decisions about the future product and market focus of the business (pp. 215–16)

product/process design Concerned with designing a product to meet a forecast demand and a process by which to produce the product in the desired quantities (p. 614)

profitability Percent of return on inputs; measured in terms of return on equity (amount owned), return on sales, profit, return on investment, or earnings per share (p. 177)

profit-maximizing management View that business is responsible only to its own direct interests (p. 133)

programmed decision Decision made on the basis of established policies, rules, or procedures (p. 63)

program plan A one-time plan designed to coordinate a diverse set of activities that are necessary to carry out a complex endeavor (p. 248)

project plan Made to guide and control completion of a one-time activity that is typically less involved and complex than a program (p. 248)

public responsibility Objectives that guide company efforts to function as responsible "corporate citizens" in their local, national, and international communities (p. 178)

punishment An attempt to weaken and discourage a specific behavior by providing an undesirable consequence (p. 472)

pure competition Competition among a large number of sellers of the same products (p. 112)

qualitative forecasting technique Often the simplest (but not the least accurate) method; involves only subjective judgment and no mathematical formulas (p. 270)

quality control Ensuring conformity to specifications (p. 633)

quality-of-life management Stems from philosophy that managers and companies should be involved directly in attempting to cure major social ills (p. 133)

quality planning Involves the decisions made about the desired level of quality prior to actual production (p. 629)

quantitative forecasting technique Uses a mathematical expression or model to show the relationship between demand and some independent variable or variables; two major types are time-series analysis and causal models (p. 273)

ratio analysis A mechanism by which managers exercise financial control; Figure 18-7 lists and briefly explains many of the financial ratios that managers use to monitor and adjust the allocation of financial resources (p. 601)

reactive change Change brought about by a sudden or unplanned event (p. 378)

reactive decision making The "wait and see" approach to decision making in which the manager waits for the environment to settle down and become more predictable so that decisions will be less risky (p. 110)

receiver The person who is the destination point for the message (p. 552)

recruitment Process of obtaining qualified applicants for a job (p. 418)

referent power Power of a leader based on the magnetism of the leader's personal traits (p. 506)

refreezing phase The time when changes are accepted as the new status quo; the people most affected by the change accept it as the way they will work or behave in the future (p. 379)

regiocentric attitude Attitude of a person who favors managers from a particular regional culture (p. 730)

regression model A statistical equation designed to estimate some variable (such as sales volume) on the basis of one or more "independent" variables believed to have some association with it (p. 275)

regret criterion Method of choosing an option that minimizes the maximum possible regret (p. 86)

reinforcement theory Argues that a stimulus results in a particular behavior, which results in consequences that result in future behavior (p. 471)

remote environment Set of forces that originate beyond, and usually irrespective of, any single firm's operating situation (p. 97)

representation election Held when, as is usual, the company contests union representation to see if the union is confirmed as the agent of the bargaining unit (p. 437)

resistance to change Arises because of uncertainty, lack of understanding and trust, self-interest, or different opinions about outcomes (p. 380)

resource allocation and risk Concerns the method of distributing the valuable resources of an organization and the level of chance that management is willing to take in that distribution (p. 177)

responsibility The duty, task, activity, or decision that a manager or other organizational member is expected to accomplish (p. 320)

restriction of range Bias that appears when an evaluator uses only a small region of a rating scale to evaluate everyone being rated (p. 427)

retrenchment/turnaround Strategy that seeks to fortify a firm's basic competencies through cost reduction (employee attrition, decreased expense accounts, reduced promotions) or asset reduction (p. 219)

reward power Power of a leader based on the leader's ability to provide rewards for followers (p. 506)

risk condition Situation in which managers have enough information to estimate the probable outcome of an implemented decision (p. 82)

role Describes the way group members expect a person in a particular position within a group to behave (p. 527)

role differentiation Refers to the way a group divides up the behaviors it needs its members to perform (p. 527)

rules and regulations Guidelines stating that specific actions may or may not be taken in a given situation (p. 250)

safety needs Often called security needs; reflect a desire to preserve the rewards already achieved and to protect oneself from danger, harm, threat, injury, loss, or deprivation (p. 454)

sales forecast Gives the expected level of demand for a company's products or services throughout some future period; also referred to as a demand forecast (p. 268)

satisfying behavior Allows workers to do the minimum that will be acceptable to managers (p. 453)

scalar chain States that the line of authority in an organization begins at the top, and authority is scaled down through the organization in an unbroken chain (pp. 326–27)

scientific management The first approach to emerge in the history of management theory; concerned with efficiency—the most productive use of human and material resources (p. 32)

selection Process of choosing which people would best fill specific jobs; an important control mechanism for ensuring the effective use of human resources (pp. 420, 603)

selective perception The tendency to pay attention to only part of a message (p. 558)

self-actualization needs Focus on the need for self-fulfillment by trying to realize one's full potential, to increase one's abilities, to be creative, and to "be the best that one can be" (p. 455)

self-esteem A personality characteristic that can affect one's ability to communicate effectively (p. 557)

self-monitoring The tendency to be aware of the characteristics of the social environment and to adapt one's behavior to the demands of the situation (p. 556)

sender The source, or originator, of the message (p. 551)

service An output that is used as soon as it is produced (p. 612)

short-term objectives Clear, simple, measurable statements of the specific outcomes the firm expects to accomplish this year or in its current endeavors (p. 171)

simple structure Exists in firms that have just one manager and a general group of employees (p. 348)

situational leadership model Developed by Paul Hersey and Kenneth Blanchard; a method to determine the style of leadership that a manager should adopt based upon the maturity level (task-relevant training) of the followers (p. 504)

skill variety Spectrum of talents required on a job (p. 304)

social audit Measurement of the impact of an organization on society; an inventory that identifies, describes, and gathers specific information on the current and prospective plans of an organization (p. 148)

social comparison The inclination to compare oneself to others in order to evaluate and revise one's behavior (p. 520)

socialization The process by which individuals are incorporated into a group, introduced to its norms and role structure, and trained to perform specific task-oriented and/or group-maintenance roles (p. 530)

social justice approach Judgment of how consistent actions are with equity, fairness, and impartiality in the distribution of rewards and costs among individuals and groups (p. 154)

social needs The desire for companionship, love, and belonging; pursued on the job by supporting formal and informal work groups, cooperating with co-workers, and taking part in company-sponsored activities (p. 454)

social power The power of managers over subordinates (p. 506)

social responsibility Organization's obligation to benefit society in ways that transcend the primary business objective of maximizing profits (p. 132)

sociocultural forces Constraints on decision making derived from the beliefs, values, attitudes, norms of behavior, opinions, and lifestyles of the members of the firm's external environment (p. 101)

sociogram Constructed by asking members of the organization to report how frequently they interact with each other, as well as by observing and recording their actual patterns of interaction (p. 522)

span of management Determination of the number of people a manager can supervise (p. 328)

specialization Simplification of tasks so that one person can become expert at efficiently and effectively accomplishing that task (p. 301)

specific information Information that meets particular requirements (p. 646)

stability strategy Adopted when an organization is satisfied with its current courses of action, and management seeks to maintain a steady, profitable growth that is equivalent to the growth in GNP or inflation (p. 206)

stable environment One that experiences little or no unexpected or sudden changes (p. 356)

staff authority Granted to those units that have responsibility for assigning line units; staff units serve an auxiliary role and are located outside the organizational chain of command (p. 318)

staffing Process of obtaining and keeping the number and type of workers necessary to accomplish an organization's objectives (p. 418)

staff manager One who supports the work of line operations (p. 9)

stakeholders Influential persons or groups, including the general public, local communities, stockholders, and unions, who are vitally interested in the actions of a business (p. 120)

stakeholder philosophy One who states that managers are responsible to certain groups that are affected by, or can affect, the company's objectives and interests (p. 135)

standard A desired outcome or expected event with which managers can compare subsequent activities, performance, or change (p. 587)

standard operating procedure (SOP) A standing plan that outlines a series of steps to be followed in accomplishing a specific activity or discharging a specific responsibility (p. 250)

standing plan Serves to increase organizational effectiveness by standardizing many routine decisions (p. 249)

states of nature Conditions under which a decision is being made (p. 83)

stereotypes Schema that contain a set of incoming information that is expected to describe all members of a group (p. 559)

straight ranking Performance appraisal method which lists each employee from the best, who would be ranked first, to the worst, who would be ranked last (p. 428)

strategically independent subsidiary Company that has the freedom to develop and market product lines unrelated to those of the parent company (p. 721)

strategic business unit (SBU) The structure of such groups is usually based on the independent product/market segments served by the firm (p. 351)

strategic choice The process of choosing the firm's future strategy; usually interwoven with the evaluation of alternatives (p. 226)

strategic control Concerned with monitoring and adjusting the direction of overall firm—tracking the strategy that is being implemented, detecting problems or changes in underlying premises, and making necessary adjustments (pp. 227, 583)

strategic planning Process of formulating strategy and guiding its execution by members of the organization (p. 202)

strategic plans Set forth the major actions and investments a firm will make over a five- to ten-year time horizon (p. 170)

strategic surveillance A type of feedforward control designed to monitor a broad range of events inside and outside the company that could make changes in the firm's strategy advisable (p. 595)

strategy Large-scale, future-oriented plans for competing in designated products and markets to achieve organizational objectives (p. 202)

strategy implementation Involves developing short-term plans, covering one year or less, that provide immediate guidelines each area of the company should follow to implement the strategy and the actions of organizational members as they do things called for in the plans (p. 226)

structural change Involves altering organizational design, level of decentralization, lines of communication, and distribution of authority within an organization (p. 382)

subjective probability Probability based on a general assessment of a particular situation (p. 87)

subsystems Individual parts that make up the whole organization (p. 47)

sufficiency Assumes individuals move up the need hierarchy not when a need is totally satisfied, because total satisfaction rarely if ever happens, but when a need is sufficiently satisfied (p. 456)

supportive leadership Requires the leader to stress human relationships by treating subordinates with respect and equality (p. 502)

survey feedback Use of a survey or questionnaire to solicit information about problem areas so that organization members offer their opinions and attitudes anonymously (p. 393)

survival and growth Fundamental concerns of any organization; objectives are set in sales volume, sales growth, and customer base in order to assure ability to compete in the chosen industry of an organization (p. 175)

SWOT analysis Acronym for Strengths and Weaknesses, Opportunities and Threats; intent is to determine what strategic alternatives exist for a company when one evaluates the company's strengths and weaknesses in light of the oppor-

tunities and threats facing it (p. 224)

symbolic model Representation of the various properties or elements of a situation with symbols; mathematical model is one example (p. 77)

synergy Concept that the whole organization is greater than the sum of its parts; emphasizes the interrelationship among all the parts of an organization (p. 47)

system development life cycle (SDLC) Designed to impose some order on the development of computer programs (p. 662)

systems approach Views the organization as a single, integrated system of subsystems (pp. 44–46)

task characteristics Core dimensions of a job (p. 304)

task constraints Limits arising from the actual nature of the jobs performed by workers (p. 49)

task group Relatively impermanent formal group that can be formed for just as long as it is needed to accomplish a specific purpose and can include people who represent several different command groups (p. 521)

task identity The extent to which a job involves the production of a complete product (p. 304)

task significance The extent to which a job affects others; jobs that affect the well-being, safety, or survival of people inside or outside the organization have more task significance than jobs that have no such impact (p. 304)

task structure The degree to which subordinates' jobs are routine (simple and highly defined), as contrasted to nonroutine (complex or unique) (p. 495)

team building A group-oriented OD technique designed to increase the level of trust, openness, and cohesiveness in work groups or management teams (p. 394)

technical skill Specific competence to perform a task (p. 15)

technological change Changes in tools, equipment, processes, actions, materials, and knowledge with which an organization creates and provides its products or services (p. 383)

technological constraints Limits derived from the type and flexibility of an organization's means of producing its goods and/or services (p. 48)

technological development Improvement of and knowledge of the products of the organization; managers must decide whether to lead or follow the improvements in the processes and products they use to serve the markets in which they compete (p. 178)

technological forecast Focuses on the rate of technological progress or the nature of technological developments in area related to a business's core technologies (p. 268)

technology Applications of new knowledge for practical purposes in any aspect of business conduct (p. 106) All of the tools, equipment, processes, actions, materials, and knowledge required to convert an organization's inputs into outputs that can be distributed as useful goods or services (p. 360)

technology innovation Development of new methods, processes, products, and technologies by the basic sciences (p. 107)

technology transfer Conversion of basic science breakthroughs into useful products and applications (p. 107)

Theory X Presumes that subordinates have an inherent dislike for work, little ambition, and require an autocratic management style (p. 484)

Theory Y Assumes that, under the right conditions, people not only accept responsibility but seek it, and that the more the organization is willing to give its people, the harder they will work in pursuing its goals (p. 485)

time-series analysis Analysis of a sequence of data points plotted at constant intervals of time; for example, a chain of daily, weekly, or monthly sales data is a time series (p. 274)

top manager Executive at the highest levels of the organizational pyramid, responsible for the overall coordination of the firm and for directing the major activities of the organization's various divisions or units (p. 8)

traditional philosophy Acceptance that the main concern of business is maximization of profits (p. 135)

training Usually refers to programs designed to teach specific job skills or techniques (p. 425)

trait theory Attempts to identify the characteristics, or traits, of successful leaders in order to help predict the futures of untested managerial candidates (p. 486)

transaction processing systems Those that perform basic data processing (p. 653)

transmitter The sender of a message (p. 551)

trigger information Like specific information in that it too is specific; whereas specific information simply makes the receiver aware of something, trigger information requires action (p. 647)

trusteeship management Requirement that managers maintain a balance among claims other than their own interest in maximizing profits (p. 133)

turbulent environment One that is marked by swift, frequent, and radical changes that occur with little or no warning (p. 357)

uncertainty condition Situation in which managers have no information that can help them predict the outcome of an implemented decision (p. 82)

unfreezing phase Begins when an individual or a group senses the need to do things in a different way; typically, persistent problems signal the need for change, and these problems begin to be discussed in the context of the need to change (p. 379)

unit and small-batch technology Consistent with the notion of a job shop; custom-made items and items only one of which is produced are examples of unit production; small-batch is the production of small quantities of items with each production run (p. 361)

unity of command States that no subordinate should be responsible to more than one superior (p. 326)

upward communication Occurs when someone at a lower level in the organization sends information to someone at a higher level (p. 566)

user-developed systems Systems that managers or users have been involved in developing; as new programming languages that are easier to use come along, it becomes more feasible for users to be involved (p. 665)

utilitarian approach Judgment of the effects of an action on the people directly involved in terms of what provides the greatest good for the greatest number of people (p. 153)

vertical integration Consists of **backward** vertical integration and **forward** vertical integration; used by many businesses as a means both to grow and to secure scarce resources or control distribution channels (pp. 217–18)

wholly owned subsidiary An entity legally incorporated in a foreign country but owned exclusively by the parent organization (p. 723)

Name Index

Organizations Index

Subject Index

Careers in Management

TITLE	JOB DESCRIPTION	REQUIREMENTS	STARTING SALARY*	1990s OUTLOOK	COMMENTS
Two-Year Program					
General Clerk	In small company, writes and types bills, statements, and other documents. Answers inquiries; compiles reports.	High-school diploma minimum. Community college degree desired. General clerical skills required, plus aptitude for office work.	$13,000	Good	Good starting point for learning and growing with a solid organization.
Bookkeeper	Maintains records of financial transactions for organization; computes and mails statements; operates calculating and bookkeeping machines.	Community college training. Some accounting and computer courses a plus. Advancement limited without four-year degree.	$15,000	Good	Excellent training for learning about organization.
Management Trainee	Learns many assigned duties. Usually participates in work assignments under close supervision in sales, finance, personnel, production, and similar departments.	Two-year associate degree. Four-year degree may offer greater growth potential.	$18,000	Very good	Usually involves substantial investment by employer, so candidates with "good potential" usually chosen.
Interviewer (employment agency)	Helps jobseekers find employment and helps employers find qualified staff.	Two-year associate degree. Ability to screen people and match them with jobs. Must know requirements of jobs to be filled.	$16,000 (may be on a commission basis)	Excellent	Good entry-level position for personnel work in business or government.
Blue-Collar Worker Supervisor	Trains other employees and directs their activities. Ensures that equipment and materials are used properly. Recommends wage increases. Where necessary, enforces union requirements.	Community college training a plus. Job knowledge and experience are most important factors, along with ability to work well with others, command respect, and communicate effectively.	$17,600 (usually 10% to 30% higher than subordinates' salaries)	Fair	Most new jobs found in trade and service sectors because of increased foreign competition in manufacturing areas.
Customer-Service Representative	Interacts with clients, researches problems. May do order processing, usually on computer.	Two-year associate degree. Four-year degree preferred. Must have strong communication skills, both oral and written.	$15,000	Very good	Good starting point for learning and for growing with an organization.
Computer Operator	Operates computers that run high-technology machinery. Monitors controls and makes sure operations are running smoothly.	Two-year associate degree. Computer knowledge.	$14,500	Excellent	May be little opportunity for career growth beyond manager of computer operations.
CAM Production Supervisor	In CAM operations, monitors production schedules to maintain appropriate work pace.	Two-year associate degree.	$17,000	Excellent	
Four-Year Program					
Administrative Assistant	Helps coordinate work of administrator, with varied responsibilities.	Four-year degree or two-year associate degree. Aptitude for office work.	$18,000	Very good	Good opportunity for learning administrative function first-hand.